American Encounters

American Encounters

Natives and Newcomers from European Contact to

Indian Removal—1500–1850 · Edited by Peter C.

Mancall and James H. Merrell

Routledge New York · London

PUBLISHED IN 2000 BY

Routledge
29 West 35th Street
New York, NY 10001

Published in Great Britain by
Routledge
11 New Fetter Lane
London EC4P 4EE

Library of Congress Cataloging-in-Publishing Data

American encounters : natives and newcomers from European contact to Indian
    removal / edited by Peter C. Mancall and James H. Merrell.
        p.   cm.
      Includes bibliographical references and index.
      ISBN 0-415-92374-3 (cl : acid-free paper). — ISBN 0-415-92375-1
    (pb : acid-free paper)
        1. Indians of North America—First contact with Europeans. 2. Indians of
North America—History.   3. Indians of North America—Relocation. I. Mancall,
Peter C.   II. Merrell, James Hart, 1953–.
E98.F39A54   2000
970.004'97—dc21   99-28708
                                                                      CIP

For
BERNARD BAILYN AND JACK P. GREENE

Contents

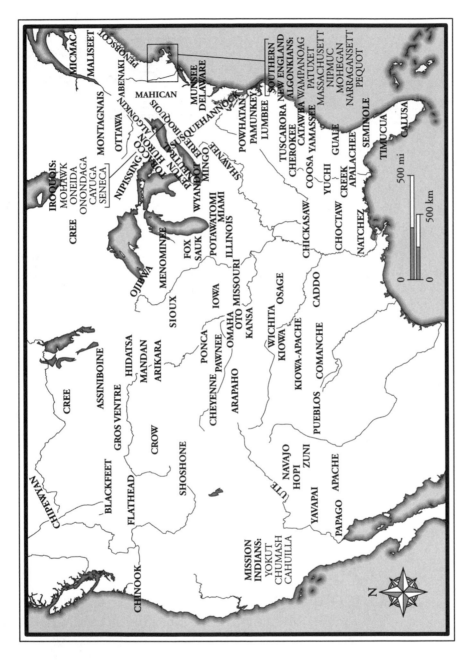

Figure I: Native North America. Adopted from Colin G. Calloway, *New Worlds for All: Indians, Europeans, and the Remaking of Early America* (Baltimore: The Johns Hopkins University Press, 1997).

Introduction

Pocahontas rescuing Captain John Smith, Squanto helping the Pilgrims, Dutchmen buying Manhattan Island—for generations, a handful of colorful tales like these was pretty much all most people knew about Indians in early America. Over the past three decades, however, scholars have begun to piece together a different, more complicated (though no less colorful) story. Inspired by intellectual and political currents calling for fuller attention to the dispossessed and disenfranchised in American life, influenced by greater acceptance of new kinds of evidence—not just written documents but archaeology, folklore, linguistics, and more—historians, anthropologists, and other scholars have transformed our understanding of the Native American experience, and therefore of the American experience.

Nowhere has that transformation been more dramatic than in the long stretch of time from the Columbian landfall to the age of Indian Removal more than three centuries later—fully two-thirds of the period conventionally considered "American History"—an era when most of North America was Indian country. This span, a formative epoch of Native history, largely set the pattern of relations between Indians and other Americans that played out on the Great Plains after 1850 and, indeed, endures to our own day. Looking past the myths and legends, casting their research nets widely and imaginatively in order to retrieve voices long silent, scholars have tried to return native peoples to their proper place in America's past. Instead of making natives bit players in the unfolding American drama who—like Pocahontas, Squanto, and those Indians selling Manhattan—left the stage after the opening act, the recent scholarship insists that Indian peoples were important actors in the drawn-out contest for the continent. Instead of confining the study of Indian America to the Eastern seaboard—to Plymouth, Jamestown, Manhattan, and the vicinity—the revisionists roam widely across the continent. And instead of suggesting that there was *one* Indian story, the new research has many tales to tell about encounters between natives and newcomers.

No single study, however capable its author or ambitious its scope, can encompass so many encounters, can do justice to such a wide chronological and geographical sweep, without sacrificing the specificity, the humanity, that brings the past to life. This collection of articles on Indians and colonists in early America, while making no claim to completeness in its coverage, nonetheless attempts to combine breadth with depth, to offer students, teachers, and other interested readers a sense of the variety and richness of the recent literature as well as something of the flavor, the texture, the feel of native life in many corners of North America during these years.

Choosing a sample of the best work, while a pleasure for us, has been no easy task, given the quality and abundance of the modern scholarship. It would have been harder still had we not been given excellent advice from scholars and teachers in the field. We are grateful to Colin Calloway, Matthew Dennis, Steven Hackel, Jean O'Brien, Ann Marie Plane, and Neal Salisbury for their thoughtful comments on this project, just as we will be grateful to scholars, teachers, students, and other readers who let us know what essays they found most (and least) useful of the ones we have elected to include.

Having selected the articles, we then called upon assistance of a different sort to prepare them for publication. The word processing staff at the University of Kansas—Paula Courtney, Pam LeRow, Lynn Porter, and Jacque West—did much of the work in getting the essays scanned or retyped. At Routledge, our editor, Deirdre Mullane, has been persistent and patient in just the right measure, and Derek Krissoff has labored with impressive diligence and unfailing good cheer on the many tasks needed to turn articles into anthology.

While relying upon help from these quarters, we faced the difficult task of arranging the diverse essays we had chosen. It quickly became apparent that the literature resists easy chronological or geographical categorization. The book, while roughly chronological, does not march steadily forward in time; nor does it travel East to West. Our topical arrangement—with various "Contact Arenas" placed between a brief prologue and a longer section following the story "From Revolution to Removal"—reflects our belief that, across the years and across the continent, different native groups had similar experiences, experiences that can be revealed through such themes as demography and disease, ideology and spirituality, economy and exchange, and diplomacy and warfare.

We hasten to add, however, that these are not hard and fast categories. As readers will discover, the native experience (like native habits of thought) tended to cross boundaries, however drawn. Hence, for example, the terrible new diseases afflicting Indians after 1492 helped shape ideology; production and exchange was often a deeply spiritual enterprise; and gender was paramount in everything from faith and politics to clothing and warfare. It is that very interconnectedness, that seamless fabric in what European newcomers considered discrete strands of life, that perhaps best captures native ways of thinking and being, and helps us to approach, however imperfectly, the transformation of Indian country to 1850.

Chronology

1636–1637	Colonists in New England defeat and nearly destroy the Pequots
1640s	Puritan missionaries begin work among New England native groups
1644	Virginia colonists defeat and nearly destroy the Powhatans
1649	Iroquois destruction of Huron people
1675–1676	King Philip's War in New England
1676	Bacon's Rebellion in Virginia
1680	Pueblo Revolt drives Spanish colonists out of New Mexico; Spaniards return, 1692
c. 1700	Indians on the Great Plains begin to acquire horses
1701	Iroquois Confederacy makes peace with France and England
1702–1704	Raids by South Carolinians and their Indian allies demolish Spanish missions in northern Florida
1711–1713	Tuscarora War with North Carolina; Tuscarora survivors migrate north, become the sixth nation of the Iroquois Confederacy in 1722
1715–1717	Yamasee War against South Carolina nearly destroys that English province
1756–1763	Seven Years' War, also called the French and Indian War
1763	Peace treaty signed in Paris grants Britain all French territories and claims east of the Mississippi River; Indian uprising (often called Pontiac's War) against British rule in the Great Lakes region
1769	Spanish found New California
1775–1783	American War for Independence
1783	In the Treaty of Paris, Britain recognizes American independence and, without consulting its Indian allies, cedes British land claims east of the Mississippi River to the new nation
1787	United States Constitution defines Indians as non-citizens and gives Congress power "to regulate trade with foreign Nations, and among the several States, and with the Indian Tribes"
c. 1800–1815	"Age and Time of Prophecy" among Indians in eastern North America: nativistic, pan-Indian revivals led by Handsome Lake, the Shawnee Prophet, Tecumseh, and others
1803	Louisiana Purchase doubles territory claimed by the United States; President Thomas Jefferson sends Meriwether Lewis and William Clark to explore the West
c. 1810–1830	"Cherokee Renaissance" in response to U.S. government and missionary "civilization" programs
1813	Tecumseh killed by U.S. troops during the War of 1812
1827	Cherokees ratify a national constitution
1828	*Cherokee Phoenix*, the first Native American newspaper, begins publication
1830	U.S. Congress passes Indian Removal Act; subsequent Supreme Court decisions—in *Cherokee Nation v. Georgia* (1831) and *Worcester v. Georgia* (1832)—define Indians' legal status as "domestic dependent nations"
1838	The Cherokee "Trial of Tears"; by the early 1840s, the federal government has also forced most Choctaws, Chickasaws, Creeks, and Seminoles off their traditional lands and into "Indian Country" in modern-day Oklahoma and Kansas
1848	Treaty of Guadalupe Hidalgo ends the United States' war with Mexico and brings new lands, populated mostly by Indians, into the territory claimed by the American nation.

Prologue

THE INDIANS' OLD WORLD: NATIVE AMERICANS AND THE COMING OF EUROPEANS

Neal Salisbury

Precontact, prehistory—the common usage of such terms to describe the Americas before 1492 suggests how deeply rooted are notions of native peoples as static, primitive societies, "people without history" in the words of the anthropologist Eric Wolf, that changed little until Europeans arrived and the progress of "American history" began. Neal Salisbury tells a different story. Rather than a land time forgot, America before Columbus possessed its own particular, rich history stretching back centuries into the remote reaches of the past.

Salisbury is one of a number of scholars who have recognized that understanding these ancient American civilizations—such as those centered at Cahokia (now East St. Louis, Missouri) or in Chaco Canyon (in modern-day New Mexico)—requires employing archaeological techniques to analyze the building sites, pottery fragments, burials, and other material remains that historians have long ignored. Although many Native Americans in recent years have rightly questioned archaeological methods that had too long demonstrated little concern for the spiritual and cultural dimensions of material remains, such evidence, properly collected, gives voice to early peoples who might otherwise remain mute. For example, Salisbury notes that every community engaged in trade of one sort or another with outsiders, a phenomenon most evident in the survival of certain goods among the material artifacts described in archaeologists' reports. Even as the artifacts demonstrate that native peoples were in regular contact with "strangers" or "foreigners" from other native groups, archaeological findings, combined with the earliest written accounts left by Europeans, provide new insight into the ways that newcomers from across the Atlantic were different from any foreigners Indians had known before.

THE INDIANS' OLD WORLD:
NATIVE AMERICANS AND THE
COMING OF EUROPEANS

Neal Salisbury

SCHOLARS IN HISTORY, anthropology, archaeology, and other disciplines have turned increasingly over the past two decades to the study of native peoples during the colonial period of North American history. The new work in Indian history has altered the way we think about the beginning of American history and about the era of European colonization. Historians now recognize that Europeans arrived, not in a virgin land, but in one that was teeming with several million people. Beyond filling in some of the vast blanks left by previous generations' overlooking of Indians, much of this scholarship makes clear that Indians are integral to the history of colonial North America.[1] In short, surveys of recent textbooks and of scholarly titles suggest that Native Americans are well on their way to being "main-streamed" by colonial historians.

Substantive as this reorientation is, it remains limited.[2] Beyond the problems inherent in representing Indian/non-Indian interactions during the colonial era lies the challenge of contextualizing the era itself. Despite opening chapters and lectures that survey the continent's native peoples and cultures, most historians continue to represent American history as having been set in motion by the arrival of European explorers and colonizers.[3] They have yet to recognize the existence of a North American—as opposed to English or European—background for colonial history, much less to consider the implications of such a background for understanding the three centuries following Columbus's landfall. Yet a growing body of scholarship by archaeologists, linguists, and students of Native American expressive traditions recognizes 1492 not as a beginning but as a single moment in a long history utterly detached from that of Europe.[4] These findings call into question historians' synchronic maps and verbal descriptions of precontact Indians—their cultures, their communities, their ethnic and political designations and affiliations, and their relations with one another. Do these really describe enduring entities or do they represent epiphenomena of arbitrary moments in time? If the latter should prove to be the case, how will readings of Indian history in the colonial period be affected?

SOURCE: *William and Mary Quarterly*, 3d Ser. 53 (1996), 435–58.

Far from being definitive, this article is intended as a stimulus to debate on these questions. It begins by drawing on recent work in archaeology, where most of the relevant scholarship has originated, to suggest one way of thinking about pre-Columbian North America in historical terms.[5] The essay then looks at developments in several areas of the continent during the centuries preceding the arrival of Europeans and in the early phases of the colonial period. The purpose is to show how certain patterns and processes originating before the beginnings of contact continued to shape the continent's history thereafter and how an understanding of the colonial period requires an understanding of its American background as well as of its European context.[6]

IN A FORMIDABLE CRITIQUE of European and Euro-American thinking about native North Americans, Robert F. Berkhofer, Jr., demonstrates that the idea of "Indians" as a single, discrete people was an invention of Columbus and his European contemporaries that has been perpetuated into our own time without foundation in historical, cultural, or ethnographic reality. On the contrary, Berkhofer asserts,

> The first residents of the Americas were by modern estimates divided into at least two thousand cultures and more societies, practiced a multiplicity of customs and lifestyles, held an enormous variety of values and beliefs, spoke numerous languages mutually unintelligible to the many speakers, and did not conceive of themselves as a single people—if they knew about each other at all.[7]

While there is literal truth in portions of Berkhofer's statement, his implication that Indians inhabited thousands of tiny, isolated communities in ignorance of one another flies in the face of a substantial body of archaeological and linguistic scholarship on North America and of a wealth of relevant anthropological literature on nonstate polities, nonmarket economies, and noninstitutionalized religions. To be sure, indigenous North Americans exhibited a remarkable range of languages, economies, political systems, beliefs, and material cultures. But this range was less the result of their isolation from one another than of the widely varying natural and social environments with which Indians had interacted over millennia. What recent scholars of precolonial North America have found even more striking, given this diversity, is the extent to which native peoples' histories intersected one another.

At the heart of these intersections was exchange. By exchange is meant not only the trading of material goods but also exchanges across community lines of marriage partners, resources, labor, ideas, techniques, and religious practices. Longer-distance exchanges frequently crossed cultural and linguistic boundaries as well and ranged from casual encounters to widespread alliances and networks that were economic, political, and religious. For both individuals and communities, exchanges sealed social and political relationships. Rather than accumulate material wealth endlessly, those who acquired it gave it away, thereby earning prestige and placing obligations on others to reciprocate appropriately. And as we shall see, many goods were not given away to others in this world but were buried with individuals to accompany them to another.[8]

Archaeologists have found evidence of ongoing exchange relations among even the earliest known Paleo-Indian inhabitants of North America. Ten thousand years before Columbus, in the wake of the last Ice Age, bands of two or three dozen persons regularly traveled hundreds of miles to hunt and trade with one another at favored campsites such as Lindenmeier in northern Colorado, dating to ca. 8800 B.C. At the Lindenmeier site, differences in the flaking and shaping of stone points distinguished regular occupants in two parts of the camp, and the obsidian each used came from about 350 miles north and south of Lindenmeier, respectively.[9] Evidence from a wide range of settlement sites makes clear that, as the postglacial warming trend continued, so-called Archaic peoples in much of the continent developed wider ranges of food sources, more sedentary settlement patterns, and larger populations. They also expanded their exchanges with one another and conducted them over greater distances. Highly valued materials such as Great Lakes copper, Rocky Mountain obsidian, and marine shells from the Gulf and Atlantic coasts have been found in substantial quantities at sites hundreds and even thousands of miles from their points of origin. In many cases, goods fashioned from these materials were buried with human beings, indicating both their religious significance and, by their uneven distribution, their role as markers of social or political rank.[10]

While the Archaic pattern of autonomous bands persisted in most of North America until the arrival of Europeans, the complexity of exchange relationships in some parts of the continent produced the earliest evidence of concentrated political power. This was especially so for peoples who, after the first century A.D., developed food economies that permitted them to inhabit permanent, year-round villages. In California, for example, competition among communities for coveted acorn groves generated sharply defined political territories and elevated the role of chiefs who oversaw trade, diplomacy, and warfare for clusters of villages. Similar competition for prime fishing and trading locations strengthened the authority of certain village chiefs on the Northwest Coast.[11] Exchange rather than competition for resources appears to have driven centralization in the Ohio and Illinois valleys. There the Hopewell peoples imported copper, mica, shell, and other raw materials over vast distances to their village centers, where specialists fashioned them into intricately crafted ornaments, tools, and other objects. They deposited massive quantities of these goods with the dead in large mounds and exported more to communities scattered throughout the Mississippi Valley. Hopewell burials differentiate between commoners and elites by the quantity and quality of grave goods accompanying each.[12] In the Southwest, meanwhile, a culture known as Hohokam emerged in the Gila River and Salt River valleys among some of the first societies based primarily on agriculture. Hohokam peoples lived in permanent villages and maintained elaborate irrigation systems that enabled them to harvest two crops per year.[13]

By the twelfth century, agricultural production had spread over much of the Eastern Woodlands as well as to more of the Southwest. In both regions, even more complex societies were emerging to dominate widespread exchange networks. In the Mississippi Valley and the Southeast, the sudden primacy of maize horticulture is marked archaeologically in a variety of ways—food remains, pollen profiles, studies of human bone (showing that maize accounted for 50 percent of people's diets), and in material culture by a proliferation of chert hoes, shell-tempered pottery for storing and cooking, and pits for storing surplus crops. These developments were accompanied by the rise of what archaeologists term "Mississippian" societies, consisting of fortified political and ceremonial centers and outlying villages. The centers were built around open plazas featuring platform burial mounds, temples, and elaborate residences for elite families. Evidence from burials makes clear the wide social gulf that separated commoners from elites. Whereas the former were buried in simple graves with a few personal possessions, the latter were interred in the temples or plazas along with many more, and more elaborate, goods such as copper ornaments, massive sheets of shell, and ceremonial weapons. Skeletal evidence indicates that elites ate more meat, were taller, performed less strenuous physical activity, and were less prone to illness and accident than commoners.[14] Although most archaeologists' conclusions are informed at least in part by models developed by political anthropologists, they also draw heavily from Spanish and French observations of some of the last Mississippian societies. These observations confirm that political leaders, or chiefs, from elite families mobilized labor, collected tribute, redistributed agricultural surpluses, coordinated trade, diplomacy, and military activity, and were worshipped as deities.[15]

The largest, most complex Mississippian center was Cahokia, located not far from the confluence of the Mississippi and Missouri rivers, near modern East St. Louis, Illinois, in the rich floodplain known as American Bottoms. By the twelfth century, Cahokia probably numbered 20,000 people and contained over 120 mounds within a five-square-mile area (see Figure I). One key to Cahokia's rise was its combination of rich soil and nearby wooded uplands, enabling inhabitants to produce surplus crops while providing an abundance and diversity of wild food sources along with

Figure I: Monks Mound (rear) and two smaller mounds in the central plaza of Cahokia. *Painting by Lloyd K. Townsend, courtesy of Cahokia Mounds State Historic Site.*

ample supplies of wood for fuel and construction. A second key was its location, affording access to the great river systems of the North American interior.[16]

Cahokia had the most elaborate social structure yet seen in North America. Laborers used stone and wooden spades to dig soil from "borrow pits" (at least nineteen have been identified by archaeologists), which they carried in wooden buckets to mounds and palisades often more than half a mile away. The volume and concentration of craft activity in shell, copper, clay, and other materials, both local and imported, suggests that specialized artisans provided the material foundation for Cahokia's exchange ties with other peoples. Although most Cahokians were buried in mass graves outside the palisades, their rulers were given special treatment. At a prominent location in Mound 72, the largest of Cahokia's platform mounds, a man had been buried atop a platform of shell beads. Accompanying him were several group burials: fifty young women, aged 18 to 23, four men, and three men and three women, all encased in uncommonly large amounts of exotic materials. As with the Natchez Indians observed by the French in Louisiana, Cahokians appear to have sacrificed individuals to accompany their leaders in the afterlife. Cahokia was surrounded by nine smaller mound centers and several dozen villages from which it obtained much of its food and through which it conducted its waterborne commerce with other Mississippian centers in the Midwest and Southeast (see Figure II).[17]

At the outset of the twelfth century, the center of production and exchange in the Southwest was in the basin of the San Juan River at Chaco Canyon in New Mexico, where Anasazi culture achieved its most elaborate expression. A twelve-mile stretch of the canyon and its rim held twelve large planned towns on the north

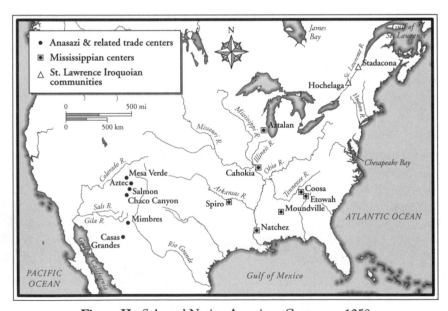

Figure II: Selected Native American Centers, c. 1250.

side and 200 to 350 apparently unplanned villages on the south. The total population was probably about 15,000. The towns consisted of 200 or more contiguous, multistoried rooms, along with numerous kivas (underground ceremonial areas), constructed of veneered masonry walls and log beams imported from upland areas nearly fifty miles distant. The rooms surrounded a central plaza with a great kiva. Villages typically had ten to twenty rooms that were decidedly smaller than those in the towns. Nearly all of Chaco Canyon's turquoise, shell, and other ornaments and virtually everything imported from Mesoamerica are found in the towns rather than the villages. Whether the goods were considered communal property or were the possessions of elites is uncertain, but either way the towns clearly had primacy. Villagers buried their dead near their residences, whereas town burial grounds were apparently located at greater distances, although only a very few of what must have been thousands of town burials have been located by archaeologists. Finally, and of particular importance in the arid environment of the region, the towns were located at the mouths of side canyons where they controlled the collection and distribution of water run-off (see Figures III and IV).[18]

Figure III: Pueblo Bonito, the largest town at Chaco Canyon. This aerial view shows some of the pueblo's more than 800 rooms and dozens of circular kivas (ceremonial centers). *Photo by Paul Logsdon. Reprinted by permission of Marcia L. Logsdon.*

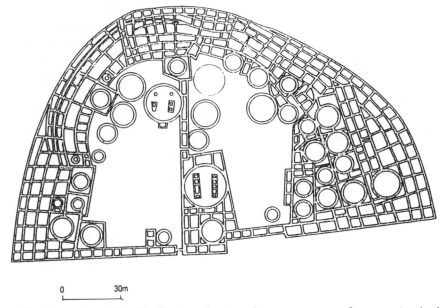

0   30m

Figure IV: Floor plan of Pueblo Bonito, showing the arrangement of rooms, circular kivas, and the divided central plaza. Pueblo Bonito stood four stories high and contained about 800 rooms. From *Ancient North America* by Brian M. Fagan, copyright © 1995 Thames and Hudson. *Reprinted by permission of the publisher.*

The canyon was the core of an extensive network of at least seventy towns or "outliers," as they are termed in the archaeological literature, and 5,300 villages located as far as sixty miles from the canyon. Facilitating the movement of people and goods through this network was a system of roads radiating outward from the canyon in perfectly straight lines, turning into stairways or footholds rather than circumventing cliffs and other obstacles (see Figure V).[19]

What archaeologists call the "Chaco phenomenon" was a multifaceted network. Within the canyon, the towns controlled the distribution of precious water. The abundance of rooms reinforces the supposition that they stored agricultural surpluses for redistribution, not only within the canyon but to the outliers. The architectural uniformity of towns throughout the system, the straight roads that linked them, and the proliferation of great kivas point to a complex of shared beliefs and rituals. Lithic remains indicate that the canyon imported most of the raw materials used for manufacturing utilitarian goods and ornamental objects from elsewhere in the Southwest. Particularly critical in this respect was turquoise, beads of which were traded to Mexico in return for copper bells and macaws and to the Gulf of California for marine shells.[20] The Chaco phenomenon thus entailed the mobilization of labor for public works projects and food production, the control and distribution of water, the distribution of prestige goods of both local and exotic origin, and the control of exchange and redistribution both within and outside the network. In distinct contrast to

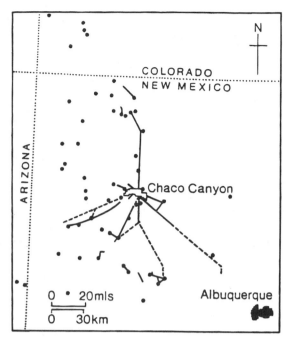

Figure V: Chaco Canyon exchange system. Dots indicate sites of town and village outliers. Solid lines show roads documented by ground surveys; dashed lines are roads documented by aerial surveys. From *Ancient North America* by Brian M. Fagan, copyright © 1995 Thames and Hudson. *Reprinted by permission of the publisher.*

Cahokia and other Mississippian societies, no evidence exists for the primacy of any single canyon town or for the primacy of certain individuals as paramount leaders.[21]

Given the archaeological record, North American "prehistory" can hardly be characterized as a multiplicity of discrete microhistories. Fundamental to the social and economic patterns of even the earliest Paleo-Indian bands were exchanges that linked peoples across geographic, cultural, and linguistic boundaries. The effects of these links are apparent in the spread of raw materials and finished goods, of beliefs and ceremonies, and of techniques for food production and for manufacturing. By the twelfth century, some exchange networks had become highly formalized and centralized. Exchange constitutes an important key to conceptualizing American history before Columbus.

ALTHOUGH IT DEPARTS from our familiar image of North American Indians, the historical pattern sketched so far is recognizable in the way it portrays societies progressing from small, egalitarian, autonomous communities to larger, more hierarchical, and centralized political aggregations with more complex economies. That image is likewise subverted when we examine the three centuries immediately preceding the arrival of Europeans. In both American Bottoms and the San Juan River basin, where twelfth-century populations were most concentrated, agriculture most productive, exchange most varied and voluminous, and political systems most complex and extensive, there were scarcely any inhabitants by the end of the fifteenth century. What happened and why?

Cahokia and other Mississippian societies in the Upper Midwest peaked during the late twelfth and early thirteenth centuries. Data from soil traces indicate that even then laborers were fortifying Cahokia's major earthworks against attack. At the same time, archaeologists surmise, Cahokia was headed toward an ecological crisis: expanded settlement, accompanied by especially hot dry summers, exhausted the soil, depleted the supply of timber for building and fuel, and reduced the habitat of the game that supplemented their diet. By the end of the fourteenth century, Cahokia's inhabitants had dispersed over the surrounding countryside into small farming villages.[22]

Cahokia's abandonment reverberated among other Mississippian societies in the Midwest. Fortified centers on the Mississippi River from the Arkansas River northward and on the Ohio River appear to have been strengthened by influxes of people from nearby villages but then abandoned, and signs from burials indicate a period of chronic, deadly warfare in the Upper Midwest. One archaeologist refers to the middle Mississippi Valley and environs during the fifteenth century as "the vacant quarter." A combination of ecological pressures and upheavals within the alliance that linked them appears to have doomed Cahokia and other midwestern Mississippian centers, leading the inhabitants to transform themselves into the village dwellers of the surrounding prairies and plains observed by French explorers three centuries later.[23]

The upheavals may even have extended beyond the range of direct Mississippian influence to affect Iroquois and Hurons and other Iroquoian speakers of the lower Great Lakes region. These people had been moving from dispersed, riverside settlements to fortified, bluff-top villages over the course of several centuries; the process appears to have intensified in the fourteenth century, when it also led to the formation of the Iroquois and Huron confederacies. The Hurons developed fruitful relations with hunter-gatherers to the north, with whom they exchanged agricultural produce for meat and skins, and Iroquois ties with outsiders appear to have diminished except for small-scale interactions with coastal peoples to the south and east. Across the Northeast, political life was characterized by violence and other manifestations of intense competition. Whether the upheavals in exchange ties occasioned by the collapse of Cahokia were directly linked to the formation of the Iroquois and Huron confederacies, as Dena Dincauze and Robert Hasenstab have suggested for the Iroquois, or were simply part of a larger process generated by the advent of farming and consequent demographic and political changes, the repercussions were still evident when Europeans began to frequent the region during the sixteenth century.[24]

Violence and instability were also apparent across the Southeast. Unlike in the Midwest, where enormous power had been concentrated in a single center, southeastern Mississippian societies were characterized by more frequently shifting alliances and rivalries that prevented any one center from becoming as powerful as Cahokia was from the tenth to thirteenth centuries. A pattern of instability prevailed that archaeologist David Anderson terms "cycling," in which certain centers emerged for a century or two to dominate regional alliances consisting of several chiefdoms and their tributary communities and then declined. Whole communities periodically shifted their locations in response to ecological or political pressures. Thus, for example, the great mound center at Etowah, in northwestern Georgia, lost its preeminence after 1400 and by the time of Hernando de Soto's arrival in 1540 had become a tributary of the nearby upstart chiefdom of Coosa.[25]

From the mid-twelfth century through the fourteenth, the demographic map of the Southwest was also transformed as Chaco Canyon and other Anasazi and Hohokam centers were abandoned. Although southwesterners had made a practice of shifting their settlements when facing shortages of water and arable land and other consequences of climatic or demographic change, they had never done so on such a massive scale. Most archaeologists agree that the abandonments followed changes in the regional cycle of rainfall and drought, so that agricultural surpluses probably proved inadequate. They point to signs that the centralized systems lost their ability to mobilize labor, redistribute goods, and coordinate religious ceremonies and that such loss was followed by outmigration to surrounding and upland areas where people farmed less intensively while increasing their hunting and gathering. Trade between the Southwest and Mesoamerica was disrupted at the same time, though whether as a cause or an effect of the abandonments is unclear.[26]

Most Anasazi peoples dispersed in small groups, joining others to form new communities in locations with sufficient rainfall. These communities are what we know today as the southwestern pueblos, extending from Hopi villages in Arizona to those on the Rio Grande.[27] These dispersals and convergences of peoples reinforced an emerging complex of beliefs, art, and ceremonies relating to kachinas—spirits believed to have influence in both bringing rain and fostering cooperation among villagers. Given their effort to forge new communities under conditions of severe drought, it is not surprising that southwestern farmers placed great emphasis on kachinas.[28] The eastward shift of much of the southwestern population also led to new patterns of trade in which recently arrived Athapaskan speakers (later known as Apaches and Navajos) brought bison meat and hides and other products from the southern Great Plains to semiannual trade fairs at Taos, Pecos, and Picuris pueblos in exchange for maize, cotton blankets, obsidian, turquoise, and ceramics as well as shells from the Gulf of California. By the time of Francisco Vásquez de Coronado's *entrada* in 1540, new ties of exchange and interdependency bound eastern Pueblos, Athapaskans, and Caddoan speakers on the Plains.[29]

When Europeans reached North America, then, the continent's demographic and political map was in a state of profound flux. A major factor was the collapse of the great centers at Cahokia and Chaco Canyon and elsewhere in the Midwest and Southwest. Although there were significant differences between these highly centralized societies, each ran up against the capacity of the land or other resources to sustain it. This is not to argue for a simple ecological determinism for, although environmental fluctuations played a role, the severe strains in each region resulted above all from a series of human choices that had brought about unprecedented concentrations of people and power. Having repudiated those choices and dispersed, midwestern Mississippians and Anasazis formed new communities in which they retained kinship, ceremonial, and other traditions antedating these complex societies. At the same time, these new communities and neighboring ones sought to flourish in their new political and environmental settings by establishing, and in some cases endeavoring to control, new exchange networks.

Such combinations of continuity and change, persistence and adaptability, arose from concrete historical experiences rather than a timeless tradition. The remainder of this article indicates some of the ways that both the deeply rooted imperatives of reciprocity and exchange and the recent legacies of competition and upheaval informed North American history as Europeans began to make their presence felt.

DISCUSSION OF THE TRANSITION from pre- to postcontact times must begin with the sixteenth century, when Indians and Europeans met and interacted in a variety of settings. When not slighting the era altogether, historians have viewed it as one of discovery or exploration, citing the achievements of notable Europeans in either anticipating or failing to anticipate the successful colonial enterprises of the seventeenth century. Recently, however, a number of scholars have been integrating information from European accounts with the findings of archaeologists to produce a much fuller picture of this critical period in North American history.

The Southeast was the scene of the most formidable attempts at colonization during the sixteenth century, primarily by Spain. Yet in spite of several expeditions to the interior and the undertaking of an ambitious colonizing and missionary effort, extending from St. Augustine over much of the Florida peninsula and north to Chesapeake Bay, the Spanish retained no permanent settlements beyond St. Augustine itself at the end of the century. Nevertheless, their explorers and missionaries opened the way for the spread of smallpox and other epidemic diseases over much of the area south of the Chesapeake and east of the Mississippi.[30]

The most concerted and fruitful efforts of the interdisciplinary scholarship entail the linking of southeastern societies that are known archaeologically with societies described in European documents. For example, Charles Hudson, David Hally, and others have demonstrated the connections between a group of archaeological sites in northern Georgia and the Tennessee Valley and what sixteenth-century Spanish observers referred to as Coosa and its subordinate provinces. A Mississippian archaeological site in northwestern Georgia known as Little Egypt consists of the remains of the town of Coosa; the town was the capital of the province ("chiefdom" to the archaeologists) of the same name, containing several nearby towns, and this province/chiefdom in turn dominated a network of at least five others chiefdoms in a "paramount chiefdom." These conclusions would not have been as definitive if based on either documentary or archaeological evidence alone.[31]

Coosa, as previously noted, attained regional supremacy during the fifteenth century, a phase in the apparently typical process whereby paramount chiefdoms rose and fell in the Mississippian Southeast. But Coosa's decline was far more precipitate than others because Spanish diseases ravaged the province, forcing the survivors to abandon the town and move southward. By the end of the sixteenth century, several new provincial centers emerged in what are now Alabama and western Georgia, but without the mounds and paramount chiefs of their predecessors. As with earlier declines of paramount chiefdoms, a center had declined and, out of the resulting power vacuum, a new formation emerged. What differed in this case were the external source of the decline, its devastating effects, and the inability or unwillingness of the survivors to concentrate power and deference in the hands of paramount chiefs. At the same time, the absence of Spanish or other European colonizers from the late sixteenth century to late seventeenth meant that the natives had a sustained period of time in which to recover and regroup. When English traders encountered the descendants of refugees from Coosa and its neighbors late in the seventeenth century, they labeled them "Creek."[32]

Patricia Galloway has established similar connections between Mississippian societies farther west and the Choctaws of the eighteenth century. She argues that the well-known site of Moundville in Alabama and a second site on the Pearl River in Mississippi were the centers of chiefdoms from which most Choctaws were descended. She argues that, unlike Coosa, these centers were probably declining in power before the onset of disease in the 1540s hastened the process. Like the Creeks, the Choctaws were a multilingual, multiethnic society in which individual villages were largely autonomous although precedents for greater coalescence were available if conditions, such as the European presence, seemed to require it.[33]

As in the Southeast, Spanish colonizers in the sixteenth-century Southwest launched several ambitious military and missionary efforts, hoping to extend New Spain's domain northward and to discover additional sources of wealth. The best-documented encounters of Spanish with Pueblos—most notably those of Coronado's expedition (1540–42)—ended in violence and failure for the Spanish who, despite vows to proceed peacefully, violated Pueblo norms of reciprocity by insisting on excessive tribute or outright submission.[34] In addition, the Spanish had acquired notoriety among the Pueblos as purveyors of epidemic diseases, religious missions, and slaving expeditions inflicted on Indians to the south, in what is now northern Mexico.[35]

The Spanish also affected patterns of exchange throughout the Southwest. Indians resisting the spread of Spanish rule to northern Mexico stole horses and other livestock, some of which they traded to neighbors. By the end of the sixteenth century, a few Indians on the periphery of the Southwest were riding horses, anticipating the combination of theft and exchange that would spread horses to native peoples throughout the region and, still later, the Plains and the Southeast.[36] In the meantime, some Navajos and Apaches moved near the Rio Grande Valley, strengthening ties with certain pueblos that were reinforced when inhabitants of those pueblos sought refuge among them in the face or wake of Spanish *entradas*.[37]

Yet another variation on the theme of Indian-European contacts in the sixteenth century was played out in the Northeast, where Iroquoian-speaking villagers on the

Mississippian periphery and Archaic hunter-gatherers still further removed from developments in the interior met Europeans of several nationalities. At the outset of the century, Spanish and Portuguese explorers enslaved several dozen Micmacs and other Indians from the Nova Scotia–Gulf of St. Lawrence area. Three French expeditions to the St. Lawrence itself in the 1530s and 1540s followed the Spanish pattern by alienating most Indians encountered and ending in futility. Even as these hostile contacts were taking place, fishermen, whalers, and other Europeans who visited the area regularly had begun trading with natives. As early as the 1520S, Abenakis on the coast of Maine and Micmacs were trading the furs of beavers and other animals for European goods of metal and glass. By the 1540s, specialized fur traders, mostly French, frequented the coast as far south as the Chesapeake; by the 1550s or soon thereafter, French traders rendezvoused regularly with Indians along the shores of upper New England, the Maritimes, and Quebec and at Tadoussac on the St. Lawrence.[38]

What induced Indians to go out of their way to trap beaver and trade the skins for glass beads, mirrors, copper kettles, and other goods? Throughout North America since Paleo-Indian times, exchange in the Northeast was the means by which people maintained and extended their social, cultural, and spiritual horizons as well as acquired items considered supernaturally powerful. Members of some coastal Indian groups later recalled how the first Europeans they saw, with their facial hair and strange clothes and traveling in their strange boats, seemed like supernatural figures. Although soon disabused of such notions, these Indians and many more inland placed special value on the glass beads and other trinkets offered by the newcomers. Recent scholarship on Indians' motives in this earliest stage of the trade indicates that they regarded such objects as the equivalents of the quartz, mica, shell, and other sacred substances that had formed the heart of long-distance exchange in North America for millennia and that they regarded as sources of physical and spiritual well-being, on earth and in the afterlife. Indians initially altered and wore many of the utilitarian goods they received, such as iron axe heads and copper pots, rather than use them for their intended purposes. Moreover, even though the new objects might pass through many hands, they more often than not ended up in graves, presumably for their possessors to use in the afterlife. Finally, the archaeological findings make clear that shell and native copper predominated over the new objects in sixteenth-century exchanges, indicating that European trade did not suddenly trigger a massive craving for the objects themselves. While northeastern Indians recognized Europeans as different from themselves, they interacted with them and their materials in ways that were consistent with their own customs and beliefs.[39]

By the late sixteenth century, the effects of European trade began to overlap with the effects of earlier upheavals in the northeastern interior. Sometime between Jacques Cartier's final departure in 1543 and Samuel de Champlain's arrival in 1603, the Iroquoian-speaking inhabitants of Hochelaga and Stadacona (modern Montreal and Quebec City) abandoned their communities. The communities were crushed militarily, and the survivors dispersed among both Iroquois and Hurons. Whether the perpetrators of these dispersals were Iroquois or Huron is a point of controversy, but either way the St. Lawrence communities appear to have been casualties of the rivalry, at least a century old, between the two confederations as each sought to position itself vis-à-vis the French. The effect, if not the cause, of the dispersals was the Iroquois practice of attacking antagonists who denied them direct access to trade goods; this is consistent with Iroquois actions during the preceding two centuries and the century that followed.[40]

The sudden availability of many more European goods, the absorption of many refugees from the St. Lawrence, and the heightening of tensions with the Iroquois help to explain the movement of most outlying Huron communities to what is now the Simcoe County area of Ontario during the 1580s. This geographic concentration strengthened their confederacy and gave it the form it had when allied with New France during the first half of the seventeenth century.[41] Having formerly existed at the outer margins of an arena of exchange centered in Cahokia, the Hurons and Iroquois now faced a new source of goods and power to the east.[42]

The diverse native societies encountered by Europeans as they began to settle North America permanently during the seventeenth century were not static isolates lying outside the ebb and flow of human history. Rather, they were products of a complex set of historical forces, both local and wide-ranging, both deeply rooted and of recent origin. Although their lives and worldviews were shaped by long-standing traditions of reciprocity and spiritual power, the people in these communities were also accustomed—contrary to popular myths about inflexible Indians—to economic and political flux and to absorbing new peoples (both allies and antagonists), objects, and ideas, including those originating in Europe. Such combinations of tradition and innovation continued to shape Indians' relations with Europeans, even as the latter's visits became permanent.

THE ESTABLISHMENT OF LASTING European colonies, beginning with New Mexico in 1598, began a phase in the continent's history that eventually resulted in the displacement of Indians to the economic, political, and cultural margins of a new order. But during the interim natives and colonizers entered into numerous relationships in which they exchanged material goods and often supported one another diplomatically or militarily against common enemies. These relations combined native and European modes of exchange. While much of the scholarly literature emphasizes the subordination and dependence of Indians in these circumstances, Indians as much as Europeans dictated the form and content of their early exchanges and alliances. Much of the protocol and ritual surrounding such intercultural contacts was rooted in indigenous kinship obligations and gift exchanges, and Indian consumers exhibited decided preferences for European commodities that satisfied social, spiritual, and aesthetic values. Similarly, Indians' long-range motives and strategies in their alliances with Europeans were frequently rooted in older patterns of alliance and rivalry with regional neighbors.[43] Such continuities can be glimpsed through a brief consideration of the early colonial-era histories of the Five Nations

Iroquois in the Northeast, the Creeks in the Southeast, and the Rio Grande Pueblos in the Southwest.

Post-Mississippian and sixteenth-century patterns of antagonism between the Iroquois and their neighbors to the north and west persisted, albeit under altered circumstances, during the seventeenth century when France established its colony on the St. Lawrence and allied itself with Hurons and other Indians. France aimed to extract maximum profits from the fur trade, and it immediately recognized the Iroquois as the major threat to that goal. In response, the Iroquois turned to the Dutch in New Netherland for guns and other trade goods while raiding New France's Indian allies for the thicker northern pelts that brought higher prices than those in their own country (which they exhausted by midcentury) and for captives to replace those from their own ranks who had died from epidemics or in wars. During the 1640s, the Iroquois replaced raids with full-scale military assaults (the so-called Beaver Wars) on Iroquoian-speaking communities in the lower Great Lakes, absorbing most of the survivors as refugees or captives. All the while, the Iroquois elaborated a vision of their confederation, which had brought harmony within their own ranks, as bringing peace to all peoples of the region. For the remainder of the century, the Five Nations fought a grueling and costly series of wars against the French and their Indian allies in order to gain access to the pelts and French goods circulating in lands to the north and west.[44]

Meanwhile, the Iroquois were also adapting to the growing presence of English colonists along the Atlantic seaboard (see Figure VI). After the English supplanted the Dutch in New York in 1664, Iroquois diplomats established relations with the proprietary governor, Sir Edmund Andros, in a treaty known as the Covenant Chain. The

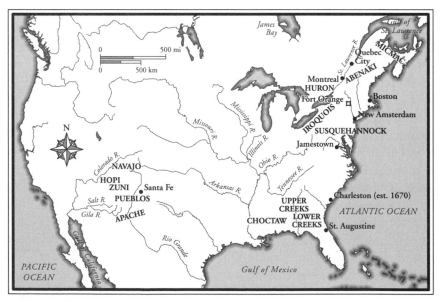

Figure VI: Selected Native American centers, in North America, c. 1645.

Covenant Chain was an elaboration of the Iroquois' earlier treaty arrangements with the Dutch, but, whereas the Iroquois had termed the Dutch relationship a chain of iron, they referred to the one with the English as a chain of silver. The shift in metaphors was appropriate, for what had been strictly an economic connection was now a political one in which the Iroquois acquired power over other New York Indians. After 1677, the Covenant Chain was expanded to include several English colonies, most notably Massachusetts and Maryland, along with those colonies' subject Indians. The upshot of these arrangements was that the Iroquois cooperated with their colonial partners in subduing and removing subject Indians who impeded settler expansion. The Mohawks in particular played a vital role in the New England colonies' suppression of the Indian uprising known as King Philip's War and in moving the Susquehannocks away from the expanding frontier of settlement in the Chesapeake after Bacon's Rebellion.

For the Iroquois, such a policy helped expand their "Tree of Peace" among Indians while providing them with buffers against settler encroachment around their homelands. The major drawback in the arrangement proved to be the weakness of English military assistance against the French. This inadequacy, and the consequent suffering experienced by the Iroquois during two decades of war after 1680, finally drove the Five Nations to make peace with the French and their Indian allies in the Grand Settlement of 1701. Together, the Grand Settlement and Covenant Chain provided the Iroquois with the peace and security, the access to trade goods, and the dominant role among northeastern Indians they had long sought.[45] That these arrangements in the long run served to reinforce rather than deter English encroachment on Iroquois lands and autonomy should not obscure their pre-Euoropean roots and their importance in shaping colonial history in the Northeast.

In the southeastern interior, Vernon Knight argues, descendants of refugees from Coosa and neighboring communities regrouped in clusters of Creek *talwas* (villages), each dominated by a large *talwa* and its "great chief." In the late seventeenth century, these latter-day chiefdom/provinces forged alliances with English traders, first from Virginia and then from Carolina, who sought to trade guns and other manufactured goods for deerskins and Indian slaves. In so doing, the Creeks ensured that they would be regarded by the English as clients rather than as commodities. The deerskin trade proved to be a critical factor in South Carolina's early economic development, and the trade in Indian slaves significantly served England's imperial ambitions vis-à-vis Spain in Florida. After 1715, the several Creek alliances acted in concert as a confederacy—the Creek Nation—on certain occasions. As a result, they achieved a measure of success in playing off these powers and maintaining neutrality in their conflicts with one another. While much differentiates Creek political processes in the colonial period from those of the late Mississippian era, there are strong elements of continuity in the transformation of Mississippian chiefdoms into great Creek talwas.[46]

In the Southwest, the institution of Spanish colonial rule on the Rio Grande after 1598 further affected exchange relations between Pueblo Indians and nearby Apaches and Navajos. By imposing heavy demands for tribute in the form of corn, the Spanish prevented Pueblo peoples from trading surplus produce with their nonfarming neighbors. In order to obtain the produce on which they had come to depend, Apaches and Navajos staged deadly raids on some pueblos, leaving the inhabitants dependent on the Spanish for protection. In retaliation, Spanish soldiers captured Apaches and Navajos whom they sold as slaves to their countrymen to the south. From the beginning, the trading pueblos of Pecos, Picuris, and Taos most resented Spanish control and strongly resisted the proselytizing of Franciscan missionaries. From the late 1660s, drought and disease, intensified Apache and Navajo raids, and the severity of Spanish rule led more and more Indians from all pueblos to question the advantages of Christianity and to renew their ties to their indigenous religious traditions. Spanish persecution of native religious leaders and their backsliding followers precipitated the Pueblo Revolt of 1680, in which the trading Pueblos played a leading role and which was actively supported by some Navajos and Apaches.[47]

When the Spanish reimposed their rule during the 1690s, they tolerated traditional Indian religion rather than trying to extirpate it, and they participated in interregional trade fairs at Taos and other villages. The successful incorporation of Pueblo Indians as loyal subjects proved vital to New Mexico's survival as a colony and, more generally, to Spain's imperial presence in the Southwest during the eighteenth and early nineteenth centuries.[48]

AS SIGNIFICANT AS IS THE divide separating pre- and post-Columbian North American history, it is not the stark gap suggested by the distinction between prehistory and history. For varying periods of time after their arrival in North America, Europeans adapted to the social and political environments they found, including the fluctuating ties of reciprocity and interdependence as well as rivalry, that characterized those environments. They had little choice but to enter in and participate if they wished to sustain their presence. Eventually, one route to success proved to be their ability to insert themselves as regional powers in new networks of exchange and alliance that arose to supplant those of the Mississippians, Anasazis, and others.

To assert such continuities does not minimize the radical transformations entailed in Europeans' colonization of the continent and its indigenous peoples. Arising in Cahokia's wake, new centers at Montreal, Fort Orange/Albany, Charleston, and elsewhere permanently altered the primary patterns of exchange in eastern North America. The riverine system that channeled exchange in the interior of the continent gave way to one in which growing quantities of goods arrived from, and were directed to, coastal peripheries and ultimately Europe.[49] In the Southwest, the Spanish revived Anasazi links with Mesoamerica at some cost to newer ties between the Rio Grande Pueblos and recently arrived, nonfarming Athapaskan speakers. More generally, European colonizers brought a complex of demographic and ecological advantages, most notably epidemic diseases and their own immunity to them, that utterly devastated Indian communities;[50] ideologies and beliefs in their cultural and spiritual superiority to native peoples and their entitlement to natives' lands;[51] and economic, political, and military systems organized for the engrossment of Indian lands and the subordination or suppression of Indian peoples.[52]

Europeans were anything but uniformly successful in realizing their goals, but the combination of demographic and ecological advantages and imperial intentions, along with the Anglo-Iroquois Covenant Chain, enabled land-hungry colonists from New England to the Chesapeake to break entirely free of ties of dependence on Indians before the end of the seventeenth century. Their successes proved to be only the beginning of a new phase of Indian-European relations. By the mid-eighteenth century, the rapid expansion of land-based settlement in the English colonies had sundered older ties of exchange and alliance linking natives and colonizers nearly everywhere east of the Appalachians, driving many Indians west and reducing those who remained to a scattering of politically powerless enclaves in which Indian identities were nurtured in isolation.[53] Meanwhile, the colonizers threatened to extend this new mode of Indian relations across the Appalachians. An old world, rooted in indigenous exchange, was giving way to one in which Native Americans had no certain place.

NOTES

1. See James Axtell, "A North American Perspective for Colonial History," *History Teacher*, 12 (1978–79), 549–62. The beginning of this shift was signaled by Gary B. Nash, *Red, White, and Black* (Englewood Cliffs, N. J., 1973), and Francis Jennings, *The Invasion of America: Indians, Colonialism, and the Cant of Conquest* (Chapel Hill, N.C., 1975).

2. See James H. Merrell, "Some Thoughts on Colonial Historians and American Indians," *William and Mary Quarterly*, 3d Ser., 46 (1989), 108–10, and Daniel K. Richter, "Whose Indian History?" ibid., 50 (1993), 381–82.

3. See Frederick E. Hoxie, *The Indians Versus the Textbooks: Is There Any Way Out?* (Chicago, 1984); Hoxie, "The Problems of Indian History," *Social Science Journal* 25 (1988), 389–99.

4. A volume that draws on all these approaches is Alvin M. Josephy, Jr., ed., *America in 1492: The World of the Indian Peoples Before the Arrival of Columbus* (New York, 1992). The best surveys of North American archaeology are Brian M. Fagan, *Ancient North America: The Archaeology of a Continent* (New York, 1991), and Stuart J. Fiedel, *Prehistory of the Americas*, 2d ed. (Cambridge, 1992). On languages see Harold E. Driver, *Indians of North America*, 2d ed. (Chicago, 1969), and Joseph H. Greenberg, *Language in the Americas* (Stanford, Calif., 1987), esp. chap. 2. Two especially interesting examples of work that utilizes oral traditions as historical sources to supplement "prehistoric" archaeology are Roger C. Echo-Hawk, "Kara Katit Pakutu: Exploring the Origins of Native America in Anthropology and Oral Traditions" (M.A. thesis, University of Colorado, 1994), and Donald Bahr et al., *The Short, Swift Time of Gods on Earth: The Hohokam Chronicles* (Berkeley, Calif., 1994).

5. On archaeology as a foundation for Indian history see Bruce G. Trigger, "Archaeology and the Image of the American Indian," *American Antiquity* 45 (1980), 662–76, and "American Archaeology as Native History: A Review Essay," *WMQ*, 3d Ser. 40 (1983), 413–52. Among works that incorporate archaeology into historical narratives, the most exemplary by anthropologists are Trigger, *The Children of Aataentsic: A History of the Huron People to 1660* (Montreal, 1976), and Kathleen J. Bragdon, *Native People of Southern New England, 1500–1650* (Norman, Okla., 1996), and by historians, Daniel K. Richter, *The Ordeal of the Longhouse: The People of the Iroquois League in the Era of European Colonization* (Chapel Hill, 1992). The most thorough argument for the role of indigenous contexts in shaping post–Columbian American history is Francis Jennings, *The Founders of America: How the Indians Discovered the Land, Pioneered in It, and Created Great Classical Civilizations; How They Were Plunged into a Dark Age by Invasion and Conquest; and How They Are Reviving* (New York, 1993). But Jennings argues for a pervasive "Mexican influence" in North America by the 15th century A.D. and makes several other inferences that are highly speculative at best. Lynda Norene Shaffer, *Native Americans before 1492: The Moundbuilding Centers of the Eastern Woodlands* (Armonk, N.Y., 1992), is a useful overview by a historian whose interest is world, rather than American, history.

6. The need for an understanding of its West African contexts is equally critical but outside the scope of this article and its author's expertise. For a beginning in this direction see John Thornton, *Africa and Africans in*

the Making of the Atlantic World, 1400–1680 (Cambridge, 1992), and the review of that volume by Ira Berlin in *WMQ,* 3d Ser. 51 (1994), 544–47.

7. Robert F. Berkhofer, Jr., *The White Man's Indian: Images of the American Indian from Columbus to the Present* (New York, 1978), 3.

8. The basic contributions to the vast literature on gift exchange economies are Marcel Mauss, *The Gift: Forms and Functions of Exchange in Archaic Societies,* trans. Ian Cunnison (London, 1954); Karl Polanyi, *The Great Transformation* (New York, 1944), chap. 4; Marshall Sahlins, *Stone Age Economics* (Chicago, 1972); and George Dalton, "The Impact of Colonization on Aboriginal Economies in Stateless Societies," in Dalton, ed., *Research in Economic Anthropology: An Annual Compilation of Research* (Greenwich, Conn., 1978), 1:131–84. On North America see William A. Turnbaugh, "Wide-Area Connections in Native North America," *American Indian Culture and Research Journal,* 1:4 (1976), 22–28.

9. Edwin S. Wilmsen, *Lindenmeier: A Pleistocene Hunting Society* (New York, 1974); Turnbaugh, "Wide-Area Connections in Native North America," 23–24.

10. Fiedel, *Prehistory of the Americas,* chap. 4; Turnbaugh, "Wide-Area Connections in Native North America," 24–25; Jesse D. Jennings, "Epilogue," in Jennings, ed., *Ancient Native Americans* (San Francisco, 1978), 651; Barbara Bender, "Emergent Tribal Formations in the American Midcontinent," *American Antiquity,* 50 (1985), 52–62; Lynn Ceci, "Tracing Wampum's Origins: Shell Bead Evidence from Archaeological Sites in Western and Coastal New York," in Charles F. Hayes et al., eds., *Proceedings of the 1986 Shell Bead Conference: Selected Papers,* Rochester Museum and Science Center, Research Records No. 20 (Rochester, N.Y., 1989), 65–67.

11. Fiedel, *Prehistory of the Americas,* 133–43.

12. Joseph R. Caldwell, "Interaction Spheres in Prehistory," in Caldwell and Robert L. Hall, eds., *Hopewellian Studies,* Illinois State Museum, Scientific Papers, 12 (Springfield, 1964), 133–43; David S. Brose and N'omi Greber, eds., *Hopewell Archaeology: The Chillicothe Conference* (Kent, Ohio, 1979); Fiedel, *Prehistory of the Americas,* 240–51.

13. Linda S. Cordell, *Prehistory of the Southwest* (Orlando, Fla., 1984), 207–11; Fiedel, *Prehistory of the Americas,* 209–12.

14. Fiedel, *Prehistory of the Americas,* 251–60; Dan F. Morse and Phyllis A. Morse, *Archaeology of the Central Mississippi Valley* (New York, 1983), chaps. 10–11; Bruce D. Smith, "The Archaeology of the Southeastern United States: From Dalton to de Soto, 10,500–500 B.P.," *Advances in World Archaeology* 5 (1986), 53–63; Vincas P. Steponaitis, "Prehistoric Archaeology in the Southeastern United States, 1970–1985," *Annual Review of Anthropology* 15 (1986), 387–93.

15. The successful integration of archaeology, history, and theory as well as the range of approaches possible with these as foundations can be seen by surveying the relevant essays in Charles Hudson and Carmen Chaves Tesser, eds., *The Forgotten Centuries: Indians and Europeans in the American South, 1521–1704* (Athens, Ga., 1994). See also Chester B. DePratter, "Late Prehistoric and Early Historic Chiefdoms in the Southeastern United States" (Ph.D. diss., University of Georgia, 1983); Charles Hudson et al., "Coosa: A Chiefdom in the Sixteenth-Century Southeastern United States," *American Antiquity* 50 (1985), 723–37; David G. Anderson, *The Savannah River Chiefdoms: Political Change in the Late Prehistoric Southeast* (Tuscaloosa, Ala., 1994). The most recent theoretical discussion is Randolph J. Widmer, "The Structure of Southeastern Chiefdoms," in Hudson and Tesser, eds., *Forgotten Centuries,* 125–55.

16. Melvin L. Fowler, "A Pre-Columbian Urban Center on the Mississippi," *Scientific American* 233 (August 1975), 92–101; William R. Iseminger, "Cahokia: A Mississippian Metropolis," *Historic Illinois* 2:6 (April 1980), 1–4.

17. Archaeologists disagree as to the complexity and power of Cahokia, but see Patricia J. O'Brien, "Urbanism, Cahokia, and Middle Mississippian," *Archaeology* 25 (1972), 188–97; Fowler, "Pre-Columbian Urban Center on the Mississippi"; Iseminger, "Cahokia"; Fowler, *The Cahokia Atlas: A Historical Atlas of Cahokia Archaeology,* Studies in Illinois Archaeology, 6 (Springfield, 1989); George R. Milner, "The Late Prehistoric Cahokia Cultural System of the Mississippi River Valley: Foundations, Florescence, Fragmentation," *Journal of World Prehistory* 4 (1990), 1–43; Thomas E. Emerson and R. Barry Lewis, eds., *Cahokia and the Hinterlands: Middle Mississippian Cultures of the Midwest* (Urbana, 1991). For European accounts of the Natchez and other Mississippians who sacrificed individuals when a paramount chief died see DePratter, "Late Prehistoric and Early Historic Chiefdoms," 64–77.

18. R. Gwinn Vivian, "An Inquiry into Prehistoric Social Organization in Chaco Canyon, New Mexico," in William A. Longacre, ed., *Reconstructing Prehistoric Pueblo Societies* (Albuquerque, 1970), 59–83; Cordell, *Prehistory of the Southwest*, 246–56; Lynne Sebastian, *The Chaco Anasazi: Sociopolitical Evolution in the Prehistoric Southwest* (Cambridge, 1992), 46. For an account of the local archaeological context at Chaco canyon see Sebastian, 21–40.

19. W. James Judge, "The Development of a Complex Cultural Ecosystem in the Chaco Basin, New Mexico," in Robert M. Linn, ed., *Proceedings of the First Conference on Scientific Research in the National Parks* (Washington, D.C., 1979), 2:901–05; Cordell, *Prehistory of the Southwest*, 256–74.

20. David H. Snow, "Prehistoric Southwestern Turquoise Industry," *El Palacio* 79, No. 1 (1973), 33–51, esp. 35, 44, 46; Randall H. McGuire, "The Mesoamerican Connection in the Southwest," *The Kiva*, 46 (1980), 3–38; Cordell, *Prehistory of the Southwest*, 273–74.

21. See Cordell, *Prehistory of the Southwest*, 266–74, for a review of various models of Chacoan development.

22. Fowler, "Pre-Columbian Urban Center," 8–11; Iseminger, "Cahokia"; Milner, "Late Prehistoric Cahokia Cultural System," 30–33.

23. Dena F. Dincauze and Robert J. Hasenstab, "Explaining the Iroquois: Tribalization on a Prehistoric Periphery," in *Comparative Studies in the Development of Complex Societies*, 3 (Southampton, Eng., 1986), 5, 7–8; George R. Milner et al., "Warfare in Late Prehistoric West-Central Illinois," *American Antiquity* 56 (1991), 581–603; Morse and Morse, *Archaeology*, chap. 12; Stephen Williams, "The Vacant Quarter and Other Late Events in the Lower Valley," in David H. Dye and Cheryl Anne Cox, eds., *Towns and Temples along the Mississippi* (Tuscaloosa, 1990), 170–80.

24. James A. Tuck, *Onondaga Iroquois Prehistory: A Study in Settlement Archaeology* (Syracuse, N.Y., 1971), chaps. 2–4; James W. Bradley, *Evolution of the Onondaga Iroquois: Accommodating Change, 1500–1655* (Syracuse, N.Y., 1987), 14–34 passim; Trigger, *Children of Aataentsic*, 1:119–76 passim; Trigger, *Natives and Newcomers: Canada's "Heroic Age" Reconsidered* (Kingston, Ont., 1985), 83–110 passim; Dean R. Snow, *The Archaeology of New England* (New York, 1980), 307–19 passim; Dincauze and Hasenstab, "Explaining the Iroquois." One influential version of the oral account of the Iroquois Confederacy's founding confirms that it occurred against a backdrop of violence among the Five Nations Iroquois and their common enmity with the Hurons; see William N. Fenton, ed., *Parker on the Iroquois* (Syracuse, N.Y., 1968), bk. 3, pp. 14–59.

25. DePratter, "Late Prehistoric and Early Historic Chiefdoms in the Southeastern United States," chaps. 2–3, 9; Smith, "Archaeology of the Southeastern United States," 57–59; Anderson, *Savannah River Chiefdoms*, passim; Hudson et al., "Coosa," 723–37; David J. Hally, "The Archaeological Reality of de Soto's Coosa," in David Hurst Thomas, ed., *Columbian Consequences*, vol. 2: *Archaeological and Historical Perspectives on the Spanish Borderlands East* (Washington, D.C., 1990), 121–38.

26. Judge, "Development of a Complex Cultural Ecosystem in the Chaco Basin," 904; Cordell, *Prehistory of the Southwest*, chap. 9; Cordell, "Why Did They Leave and Where Did They Go?" *Exploration: Annual Bulletin of the School of American Research* (1985), 38; Paul R. Fish, "The Hohokam: 1,000 Years of Prehistory in the Sonoran Desert," in Cordell and George J. Gumerman, eds., *Dynamics of Southwest Prehistory* (Washington, D. C., 1989), 34; Judge, "Chaco Canyon-San Juan Basin," ibid., 248–49.

27. Cordell, *Prehistory of the Southwest*, 330–36; Cordell, "Why Did They Leave?" 38–39; J. Jefferson Reid, "A Grasshopper Perspective on the Mogollon of the Arizona Mountains," in Cordell and Gumerman, eds., *Dynamics of Southwest Prehistory*, 80; Gumerman and Jeffrey S. Dean, "Prehistoric Cooperation and Competition in the Western Anasazi Area," ibid., 127–28; Cordell, "Northern and Central Rio Grande," ibid., 314–24; E. Charles Adams and Kelley Ann Hays, eds., *Homol'ovi II: Archaeology of an Ancestral Hopi Village, Arizona*, Anthropological Papers of the University of Arizona, No. 55 (Tucson, 1991).

28. Cordell, *Prehistory of the Southwest*, 343–46; Adams, *The Origin and Development of the Pueblo Katsina Cult* (Tucson, 1991), esp. 120–21.

29. Cordell, *Prehistory of the Southwest*, chap. 10; David H. Snow, "Protohistoric Rio Grande Pueblo Economics: A Review of Trends," in David R. Wilcox and W. Bruce Masse, eds., *The Protohistoric Period in the North American Southwest, AD 1450–1700*, Arizona State University, Anthropological Research Papers No. 24 (Tempe, 1981), 354–77; Katherine A. Spielmann, "Late Prehistoric Exchange between the Southwest and Southern Plains," *Plains Anthropologist* 28 (1983), 257–72; Wilcox, "Multiethnic Division of Labor in the Protohistoric Southwest," *Papers of the Archaeological Society of New Mexico* 9 (1984), 141–54; Timothy G. Baugh, "Southern Plains Societies and Eastern Pueblo Exchange during the Protohistoric Period," ibid., 157–67;

Spielmann, ed., *Farmers, Hunters, and Colonists: Interaction between the Southwest and the Southern Plains* (Tucson, 1991).

30. David J. Weber, *The Spanish Frontier in North America* (New Haven, 1992), 30–38, 42–45, 49–75, 87–91; Paul E. Hoffman, *A New Andalucia and a Way to the Orient: The American Southeast during the Sixteenth Century* (Baton Rouge, 1990); J. Leitch Wright, Jr., *The Only Land They Knew: The Tragic Story of American Indians in the Old South* (New York, 1981), chap. 2; Marvin T. Smith, *Archaeology of Aboriginal Culture Change in the Interior Southeast: Depopulation during the Early Historic Period* (Gainesville, 1987), chap. 4; Milner, "Epidemic Disease in the Postcontact Southeast: A Reappraisal," *Midcontinental Journal of Archaeology*, 5 (1980), 39–56.

31. Hudson et al., "Coosa"; Hally et al., "Archaeological Reality of de Soto's Coosa"; Robert L. Blakely, ed., *The King Site: Continuity and Contact in Sixteenth-Century Georgia* (Athens, Ga., 1988); Hudson, "A Spanish-Coosa Alliance in Sixteenth-Century Georgia," *Georgia Historical Quarterly* 72 (1988), 599–626; Hudson, *The Juan Pardo Expeditions: Exploration of the Carolinas and Tennessee, 1566–1568* (Washington D.C., 1990), 101–09; Hally, "The Chiefdom of Coosa," in Hudson and Tessier, eds., *Forgotten Centuries*, 227–53.

32. Hally, "Chiefdom of Coosa," 249–50; Marvin T. Smith, "Aboriginal Depopulation in the Postcontact Southeast," in Hudson and Tessier, eds., *Forgotten Centuries*, 265; Vernon James Knight, Jr., "The Formation of the Creeks," ibid., 373–91.

33. Galloway, "Confederacy as a Solution to Chiefdom Dissolution: Historical Evidence in the Choctaw Case," in Hudson and Tessier, eds., *Forgotten Centuries*, 393–420. Historian James H. Merrell notes the role of 16th-century upheavals in shaping the people known to colonial Carolinians as the Catawbas; see *The Indians' New World: Catawbas and Their Neighbors from European Contact through the Era of Removal* (Chapel Hill, 1989), 8–27.

34. Jack D. Forbes, *Apache, Navaho, and Spaniard* (Norman, Okla., 1960), 5–24, 53–54; Elizabeth A. H. John, *Storms Brewed in Other Men's Worlds: The Confrontation of Indians, Spanish, and French in the Southwest, 1540–1795* (College Station, Tex., 1975), 13–37; Daniel T. Reff, *Disease, Depopulation, and Culture Change in Northwestern New Spain, 1518–1764* (Salt Lake City, 1991), 68–84; Ramón A. Gutiérrez, *When Jesus Came, the Corn Mothers Went Away: Marriage, Sexuality, and Power in New Mexico, 1500–1846* (Stanford, Calif., 1991), 39–46; Weber, *Spanish Frontier in North America*, 14–19, 45–49. The major exception to this generalization is the (uncommissioned) journey by Cabeza de Vaca and 3 fellow survivors of an ill-fated Spanish expedition to Florida, who journeyed west from the Gulf of Mexico before turning south in 1535–1536; ibid., 42–45, 56–57; Reff, *Disease, Depopulation, and Culture Change*, 43–68.

35. Forbes, *Apache, Navaho, and Spaniard*, 7–8, 29–34, 38–40, 47–48; Carroll L. Riley, "Sixteenth-Century Trade in the Greater Southwest," *Mesoamerican Studies* 10 (1976), 9–14; Reff, *Disease, Depopulation, and Culture Change*, 17–42, 84–95, 119–32 passim.

36. Forbes, "The Appearance of the Mounted Indian in Northern Mexico and the Southwest, to 1680," *Southwestern Journal of Anthropology* 15 (1959), 189–212; Forbes, *Apache, Navaho, and Spaniard*, 34–38, 43; Preston Holder, *The Hoe and the Horse on the Plains: A Study of Cultural Development among North American Indians* (Lincoln, Neb., 1970), 79, 111–12; Daniel H. Usner, Jr., *Indians, Settlers, and Slaves in a Frontier Exchange Economy: The Lower Mississippi Valley before 1783* (Chapel Hill, 1992), 177–78.

37. Wilcox, "The Entry of Athapaskans into the American Southwest: The Problem Today," in Wilcox and Masse, eds., *Protohistoric Period in the North American Southwest*, 228; David M. Brugge, "Navajo Prehistory and History to 1859," in *Handbook of North American Indians*, ed. William C. Sturtevant, vol. 10: *Southwest*, ed. Alfonso Ortiz (Washington, D.C., 1983), 491; Forbes, *Apache, Navaho, and Spaniard*, 14.

38. Neal Salisbury, *Manitou and Providence: Indians, Europeans, and the Making of New England, 1500–1643* (New York, 1982), 51–56; Trigger, *Natives and Newcomers*, 118–44.

39. Christopher L. Miller and George R. Hammell, "A New Perspective on Indian-White Contact: Cultural Symbols and Colonial Trade," *Journal of American History*, 73 (1986), 311–28, reprinted in this volume; Trigger, *Natives and Newcomers*, 125–27; Bradley, *Evolution*, chap. 2; Calvin Martin, "The Four Lives of a Micmac Copper Pot," *Ethnohistory* 22 (1975), 111–33; James Axtell, "At the Water's Edge: Trading in the Sixteenth Century," in Axtell, *After Columbus: Essays in the Ethnohistory of Colonial North America* (New York, 1988), 144–81; Trigger, "Early Native North American Responses to European Contact: Romantic versus Rationalistic Interpretations," *JAH* 77 (1991), 1195–1215. Compare the barbed Delaware-Mahican tradition of early relations with the Dutch recorded by John Heckewelder in his *An Account of the History, Man-*

ners, and Customs of the Indian Nations, Who Once Inhabited Pennsylvania and the Neighbouring States (Philadelphia, 1819), 71–75.

40. Trigger, *Natives and Newcomers,* 144–48.

41. Ibid., 157–61.

42. See Dincauze and Hasenstab, "Explaining the Iroquois."

43. See, for example, Kenneth E. Kidd, "The Cloth Trade and the Indians of the Northeast during the Seventeenth and Eighteenth Centuries," in Royal Ontario Museum, *Art and Archaeology Annual* (1961), 48–56; Wilcomb E. Washburn, "Symbol, Utility, and Aesthetics in the Indian Fur Trade," *Minnesota History* 40 (1966), 198–202; Donald J. Blakeslee, "The Calumet Ceremony and the Origin of Fur Trade Rituals," *Western Canadian Journal of Anthropology* 7, No. 2 (1977), 78–88; Bruce M. White, "Give Us a Little Milk: The Social and Cultural Meanings of Gift Giving in the Lake Superior Fur Trade," *Minnesota History* 48 (1982), 60–71, and "A Skilled Game of Exchange: Ojibway Fur Trade Protocol," ibid., 50 (1987), 229–40; Francis Jennings et al., eds., *The History and Culture of Iroquois Diplomacy: An Interdisciplinary Guide to the Treaties of the Six Nations and Their League* (Syracuse, N.Y., 1985), chaps. 1, 4–7; Richard White, *The Middle Ground: Indians, Empires, and Republics, 1650–1815* (Cambridge, 1991), chaps. 2–4 passim.

44. Richter, *Ordeal of the Longhouse,* 30–104.

45. Pennsylvania joined the Covenant Chain early in the 18th century; Francis Jennings, *The Ambiguous Iroquois Empire: The Covenant Chain Confederation of Indian Tribes with English Colonies from Its Beginnings to the Lancaster Treaty of 1744* (New York, 1984), chap. 8; Richter, *Ordeal of the Longhouse,* 105–213 passim.

46. Knight, "Formation of the Creeks," 385–90; Joel W. Martin, "Southeastern Indians and the English Trade in Skins and Slaves," ibid., 304–24; Michael D. Green, *The Politics of Indian Removal: Creek Government and Society in Crisis* (Lincoln, Neb., 1982), 17–31.

47. Forbes, *Apache, Navaho, and Spaniard,* chaps. 5–10 passim; John, *Storms Brewed in Other Men's Worlds,* chap. 2; Henry Warner Bowden, "Spanish Missions, Cultural Conflict, and the Pueblo Revolt of 1680," *Church History* 44 (1975), 217–28; John L. Kessell, *Kiva, Cross, and Crown: The Pecos Indians and New Mexico, 1540–1840* (Washington, D.C., 1979), chaps. 3–5; H. Allen Anderson, "The Encomienda in New Mexico, 1598–1680," *New Mexico Historical Review* 60 (1985), 353–77; Thomas D. Hall, *Social Change in the Southwest, 1350–1880* (Lawrence, Kan., 1989), 83–90.

48. Forbes, *Apache, Navaho, and Spaniard,* chaps. 11–12; Weber, *The Taos Trappers: The Fur Trade in the Far Southwest, 1540–1846* (Norman, Okla., 1971), 21–31; John, *Storms Brewed in Other Men's Worlds,* chap. 3; Kessell, *Kiva, Cross, and Crown,* chap. 8.

49. Shaffer, *Native Americans before 1492,* esp. 10–11, 94–96.

50. Alfred W. Crosby, *Ecological Imperialism: The Biological Expansion of Europe, 900–1900* (Cambridge, 1986).

51. Roy Harvey Pearce, *The Savages of America: A Study of the Indian and the Idea of Civilization* (Baltimore, 1953); Richard Slotkin, *Regeneration through Violence: The Mythology of the American Frontier, 1600–1800* (Middleton, Conn., 1973); Berkhofer, *White Man's Indian.*

52. Jennings, *Invasion of America,* pt. 1.

53. For summaries of these developments see Salisbury, "The History of Native Americans from before the Arrival of the Europeans and Africans until the American Civil War," in Stanley L. Engerman and Robert E. Gallman, eds., *The Cambridge Economic History of the United States,* vol. 1: *The Colonial Era* (Cambridge, 1996), chap. 1, and "Native People and European Settlers in Eastern North America, 1600–1783," in *The Cambridge History of the Native Peoples of the Americas,* vol. 1: *North America,* ed. Trigger and Washburn (Cambridge, 1996).

2

James H. Merrell

As Neal Salisbury's essay suggests, America was "new" only to Europeans, not to its indigenous inhabitants. But if colonists did not find a "new world," James Merrell argues, their invasion of America helped create one; European arrival had such profound consequences for native peoples that Indians, too, came to inhabit a "new world."

That new world, Merrell writes, was the creation of new diseases, eager traders, and colonial farmers. To demonstrate how these forces changed Indians' lives, Merrell focuses his attention on the peoples of the Carolina Piedmont who reconstituted themselves as a single cultural entity, the Catawbas, by the beginning of the eighteenth century. The Catawba chronicle suggests at once the power of colonization to disrupt traditional lifeways and the ability of Native Americans from related communities to form new societies in the wake of disease and dispossession. That same process of cultural change and reformation swept through other areas as well. But what makes the Catawba experience significant is that this native group managed to retain some of its aboriginal territory. Unlike many peoples that were pushed out of ancestral lands by the advance of colonial settlements, Catawbas deployed their economic and diplomatic talents to remain in the Piedmont, where they live today as a potent reminder that, contrary to the desires of first English and later American political leaders, the Indians' new world could be enduring as well.

THE INDIANS' NEW WORLD:
THE CATAWBA EXPERIENCE

James H. Merrell

IN AUGUST 1608 John Smith and his band of explorers captured an Indian named Amoroleck during a skirmish along the Rappahannock River. Asked why his men—a hunting party from towns upstream—had attacked the English, Amoroleck replied that they had heard the strangers "were a people come from under the world, to take their world from them."[1] Smith's prisoner grasped a simple yet important truth that students of colonial America have overlooked: after 1492 native Americans lived in a world every bit as new as that confronting transplanted Africans or Europeans.

The failure to explore the Indians' new world helps explain why, despite many excellent studies of the native American past,[2] colonial history often remains "a history of those men and women—English, European, and African—who transformed America from a geographical expression into a new nation."[3] One reason Indians generally are left out may be the apparent inability to fit them into the new world theme, a theme that exerts a powerful hold on our historical imagination and runs throughout our efforts to interpret American development. From Frederick Jackson Turner to David Grayson Allen, from Melville J. Herskovits to Daniel C. Littlefield, scholars have analyzed encounters between peoples from the Old World and conditions in the New, studying the complex interplay between European or African cultural patterns and the American environment.[4] Indians crossed no ocean, peopled no faraway land. It might seem logical to exclude them.

The natives' segregation persists, in no small degree, because historians still tend to think only of the new world as the New World, a geographic entity bounded by the Atlantic Ocean on the one side and the Pacific on the other. Recent research suggests that process was as important as place. Many settlers in New England re-created familiar forms with such success that they did not really face an alien environment until long after their arrival.[5] Africans, on the other hand, were struck by the shock of the new at the moment of their enslavement, well before they stepped on board ship or set foot on American soil.[6] If the Atlantic was not a barrier between one world and another, if what happened to people was more a matter of subtle cultural

SOURCE: *William and Mary Quarterly*, 3d Ser. 41 (1984), 537–65.

processes than mere physical displacements, perhaps we should set aside the maps and think instead of a "world" as the physical and cultural milieu within which people live and a "new world" as a dramatically different milieu demanding basic changes in ways of life.[7] Considered in these terms, the experience of natives was more closely akin to that of immigrants and slaves, and the idea of an encounter between worlds can—indeed, must—include the aboriginal inhabitants of America.

For American Indians a new order arrived in three distinct yet overlapping stages.[8] First, alien microbes killed vast numbers of natives, sometimes before the victims had seen a white or black face. Next came traders who exchanged European technology for Indian products and brought natives into the developing world market. In time traders gave way to settlers eager to develop the land according to their own lights.[9] These three intrusions combined to transform native existence, disrupting established cultural habits and requiring creative responses to drastically altered conditions. Like their new neighbors, then, Indians were forced to blend old and new in ways that would permit them to survive in the present without forsaking their past. By the close of the colonial era, native Americans as well as whites and blacks had created new societies, each similar to, yet very different from, its parent culture.

The range of native societies produced by this mingling of ingredients probably exceeded the variety of social forms Europeans and Africans developed.[10] Rather than survey the broad spectrum of Indian adaptations, this article considers in some depth the response of natives in one area, the southern Piedmont (see Figure I). Avoiding extinction and eschewing retreat, the Indians of the Piedmont have been in continuous contact with the invaders from across the sea almost since the beginning of the colonial period, thus permitting a thorough analysis of cultural intercourse.[11] Moreover, a regional approach embracing groups from South Carolina to Virginia can transcend narrow (and still poorly understood) ethnic or "tribal" boundaries without sacrificing the richness of detail a focused study provides.

Indeed, Piedmont peoples had so much in common that a regional perspective is almost imperative. No formal political ties bound them at the onset of European contact, but a similar environment shaped their lives, and their adjustment to this environment fostered cultural uniformity. Perhaps even more important, these groups shared a single history once Europeans and Africans arrived on the scene. Drawn together by their cultural affinities and their common plight, after 1700 they migrated to the Catawba Nation, a cluster of villages along the border between the Carolinas that became the focus of native life in the region. Tracing the experience of these upland communities both before and after they joined the Catawbas can illustrate the consequences of contact and illuminate the process by which natives learned to survive in their own new world.[12]

FOR CENTURIES, ancestors of the Catawbas had lived astride important aboriginal trade routes and straddled the boundary between two cultural traditions, a position that involved them in a far-flung network of contacts and affected everything from potting techniques to burial practices.[13] Nonetheless, Africans and Europeans were

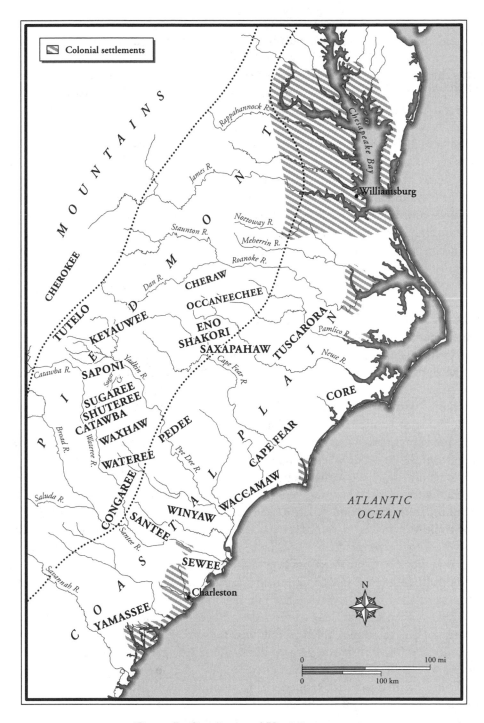

Figure I: Carolinas and Virginia, c. 1700.

utterly unlike any earlier foreign visitors to the Piedmont. Their arrival meant more than merely another encounter with outsiders; it marked an important turning point in Indian history. Once these newcomers disembarked and began to feel their way across the continent, they forever altered the course and pace of native development.

Bacteria brought the most profound disturbances to upcountry villages. When Hernando de Soto led the first Europeans into the area in 1540, he found large towns already "grown up in grass" because "there had been a pest in the land" two years before, a malady probably brought inland by natives who had visited distant Spanish posts.[14] The sources are silent about other "pests" over the next century, but soon after the English began colonizing Carolina in 1670 the disease pattern became all too clear. Major epidemics struck the region at least once every generation—in 1698, 1718, 1738, and 1759—and a variety of less virulent illnesses almost never left native settlements.[15]

Indians were not the only inhabitants of colonial America living—and dying—in a new disease environment. The swamps and lowlands of the Chesapeake were a death-trap for Europeans, and sickness obliged colonists to discard or rearrange many of the social forms brought from England.[16] Among native peoples long isolated from the rest of the world and therefore lacking immunity to pathogens introduced by the intruders, the devastation was even more severe. John Lawson, who visited the Carolina upcountry in 1701, when perhaps ten thousand Indians were still there, estimated that "there is not the sixth Savage living within two hundred Miles of all our Settlements, as there were fifty Years ago." The recent smallpox epidemic "destroy'd whole Towns," he remarked, "without leaving one *Indian* alive in the Village."[17] Resistance to disease developed with painful slowness; colonists reported that the outbreak of smallpox in 1759 wiped out 60 percent of the natives, and, according to one source, "the woods were offensive with the dead bodies of the Indians; and dogs, wolves, and vultures were . . . busy for months in banqueting on them."[18]

Survivors of these horrors were thrust into a situation no less alien than what European immigrants and African slaves found. The collected wisdom of generations could vanish in a matter of days if sickness struck older members of a community who kept sacred traditions and taught special skills. When many of the elders succumbed at once, the deep pools of collective memory grew shallow, and some dried up altogether. In 1710, Indians near Charleston told a settler that "they have forgot most of their traditions since the Establishment of this Colony, they keep their Festivals and can tell but little of the reasons: their Old Men are dead."[19] Impoverishment of a rich cultural heritage followed the spread of disease. Nearly a century later, a South Carolinian exaggerated but captured the general trend when he noted that Catawbas "have forgotten their ancient rites, ceremonies, and manufactures."[20]

The same diseases that robbed a Piedmont town of some of its most precious resources also stripped it of the population necessary to maintain an independent existence. In order to survive, groups were compelled to construct new societies from the splintered remnants of the old. The result was a kaleidoscopic array of migrations from ancient territories and mergers with nearby peoples. While such behavior was not unheard of in aboriginal times, population levels fell so precipitously after contact that survivors endured disruptions unlike anything previously known.

The dislocations of the Saponi Indians illustrate the common course of events. In 1670 they lived on the Staunton River in Virginia and were closely affiliated with a group called Nahyssans. A decade later Saponis moved toward the coast and built a town near the Occaneechees. When John Lawson came upon them along the Yadkin River in 1701, they were on the verge of banding together in a single village with Tutelos and Keyauwees. Soon thereafter Saponis applied to Virginia officials for permission to move to the Meherrin River, where Occaneechees, Tutelos, and others joined them. In 1714, at the urging of Virginia's Lt. Gov. Alexander Spotswood, these groups settled at Fort Christanna farther up the Meherrin. Their friendship with Virginia soured during the 1720s, and most of the "Christanna Indians" moved to the Catawba Nation. For some reason this arrangement did not satisfy them, and many returned to VIrginia in 1732, remaining there for a decade before choosing to migrate north and accept the protection of the Iroquois.[21]

Saponis were unusual only in their decision to leave the Catawbas. Enos, Occaneechees, Waterees, Keyauwees, Cheraws, and others have their own stories to tell, similar in outline if not in detail. With the exception of the towns near the confluence of Sugar Creek and the Catawba River that composed the heart of the Catawba Nation, Piedmont communities decimated by disease lived through a common round of catastrophes, shifting from place to place and group to group in search of a safe haven. Most eventually ended up in the Nation, and during the opening decades of the eighteenth century the villages scattered across the southern upcountry were abandoned as people drifted into the Catawba orbit.

No mere catalog of migrations and mergers can begin to convey how profoundly unsettling this experience was for those swept up in it. While upcountry Indians did not sail away to some distant land, they, too, were among the uprooted, leaving their ancestral homes to try to make a new life elsewhere. The peripatetic existence of Saponis and others proved deeply disruptive. A village and its surrounding territory were important elements of personal and collective identity, physical links in a chain binding a group to its past and making a locality sacred. Colonists, convinced that Indians were by nature "a shifting, wandring People," were oblivious to this, but Lawson offered a glimpse of the reasons for native attachment to a particular locale. "In our way," he wrote on leaving an Eno-Shakori town in 1701, "there stood a great Stone about the Size of a large Oven, and hollow; this the *Indians* took great Notice of, putting some Tobacco into the Concavity, and spitting after it. I ask'd them the Reason of their so doing, but they made me no Answer."[22] Natives throughout the interior honored similar places—graves of ancestors, monuments of stones commemorating important events—that could not be left behind without some cost.[23]

The toll could be physical as well as spiritual, for even the most uneventful of moves interrupted the established cycle of subsistence. Belongings had to be packed and unpacked, dwellings constructed, palisades raised. Once migrants had completed the business of settling in, the still more arduous task of exploiting new terrain awaited them. Living in one place year after year endowed a people with intimate knowledge of the area. The richest soils, the best hunting grounds, the choicest sites for gathering nuts or berries—none could be learned without years of experience, tested by time and passed down from one generation to the next. Small wonder that Carolina Indians worried about being "driven to some unknown Country, to live, hunt, and get our Bread in."[24]

Some displaced groups tried to leave "unknown Country" behind and make their way back home. In 1716 Enos asked Virginia's permission to settle at "Enoe Town" on the North Carolina frontier, their location in Lawson's day.[25] Seventeen years later William Byrd II came upon an abandoned Cheraw village on a tributary of the upper Roanoke River and remarked how "it must have been a great misfortune to them to be obliged to abandon so beautiful a dwelling." The Indians apparently agreed: in 1717 the Virginia Council received "Divers applications" from the Cheraws (now living along the Pee Dee River) "for Liberty to Seat themselves on the head of Roanoke River."[26] Few natives managed to return permanently to their homelands. But their efforts to retrace their steps hint at a profound sense of loss and testify to the powerful hold of ancient sites.

Compounding the trauma of leaving familiar territories was the necessity of abandoning customary relationships. Casting their lot with others traditionally considered foreign compelled Indians to rearrange basic ways of ordering their existence. Despite frequent contacts among peoples, native life had always centered in kin and town. The consequences of this deep-seated localism were evident even to a newcomer like John Lawson, who in 1701 found striking differences in language, dress, and physical appearance among Carolina Indians living only a few miles apart.[27] Rules governing behavior also drew sharp distinctions between outsiders and one's own "Country-Folks." Indians were "very kind, and charitable to one another," Lawson reported, "but more especially to those of their own Nation."[28] A visitor desiring a liaison with a local woman was required to approach her relatives and the village headman. On the other hand, "if it be an *Indian* of their own Town or Neighbourhood, that wants a Mistress, he comes to none but the Girl."[29] Lawson seemed unperturbed by this barrier until he discovered that a "Thief [is] held in Disgrace, that steals from any of his Country-Folks," "but to steal from the *English* [or any other foreigners] they reckon no Harm."[30]

Communities unable to continue on their own had to revise these rules and reweave the social fabric into new designs. What language would be spoken? How would fields be laid out, hunting territories divided, houses built? How would decisions be reached, offenders punished, ceremonies performed? When Lawson remarked that "nowadays" the Indians must seek mates "amongst Strangers," he unwittingly characterized life in native Carolina.[31] Those who managed to withstand the ravages of disease had to redefine the meaning of the term *stranger* and transform outsiders into insiders.

The need to harmonize discordant peoples, an unpleasant fact of life for all native Americans, was no less common among black and white inhabitants of America during these years. Africans from a host of different groups were thrown into slavery together and forced to seek some common cultural ground, to blend or set aside clashing habits and beliefs. Europeans who came to America also met unexpected and unwelcome ethnic, religious, and linguistic diversity. The roots of the problem were quite different; the problem itself was much the same. In each case people from different backgrounds had to forge a common culture and a common future.

Indians in the southern uplands customarily combined with others like themselves in an attempt to solve the dilemma. Following the "principle of least effort," shattered communities cushioned the blows inflicted by disease and depopulation by joining a kindred society known through generations of trade and alliances.[32] Thus Saponis coalesced with Occaneechees and Tutelos—nearby groups "speaking much the same language"[33]—and Catawbas became a sanctuary for culturally related refugees from throughout the region. Even after moving in with friends and neighbors, however, natives tended to cling to ethnic boundaries in order to ease the transition. In 1715 Spotswood noticed that the Saponis and others gathered at Fort Christanna were "confederated together, tho' still preserving their different Rules."[34] Indians entering the Catawba Nation were equally conservative. As late as 1743 a visitor could hear more than twenty different dialects spoken by peoples living there, and some bands continued to reside in separate towns under their own leaders.[35]

Time inevitably sapped the strength of ethnic feeling, allowing a more unified Nation to emerge from the collection of Indian communities that occupied the valleys of the Catawba River and its tributaries. By the mid-eighteenth century, the authority of village headmen was waning and leaders from the host population had begun to take responsibility for the actions of constituent groups.[36] The babel of different tongues fell silent as "*Kàtahba*," the Nation's "standard, or court-dialect," slowly drowned out all others.[37] Eventually, entire peoples followed their languages and their leaders into oblivion, leaving only personal names like Santee Jemmy, Cheraw George, Congaree Jamie, Saponey Johnny, and Eno Jemmy as reminders of the Nation's diverse heritage.[38]

No European observer recorded the means by which nations became mere names and a congeries of groups forged itself into one people. No doubt the colonists' habit of ignoring ethnic distinctions and lumping confederated entities together under the Catawba rubric encouraged amalgamation. But Anglo-American efforts to create a society by proclamation were invariably unsuccessful[39]; consolidation had to come from within. In the absence of evidence, it seem reasonable to conclude that years of contacts paved the way for a closer relationship. Once a group moved to the Nation, intermarriages blurred ancient kinship networks, joint war parties or hunting expeditions brought young men together, and elders met in a council that gave everyone some say by including "all the Indian Chiefs or Head Men of that [Catawba] Nation and the several Tribes amongst them together."[40] The concentration of settlements within a day's walk of one another facilitated contact and communication. From their close proximity, common experience, and shared concerns, people developed ceremonies and myths that compensated for those lost to disease and gave the Nation a stronger collective consciousness.[41] Associations evolved that balanced traditional narrow ethnic allegiance with a new, broader, "national" identity, a balance that tilted steadily toward the latter. Ethnic differences died hard, but the peoples of the Catawba Nation learned to speak with a single voice.

MUSKETS AND KETTLES came to the Piedmont more slowly than smallpox and measles. Spanish explorers distributed a few gifts to local headmen, but inhabitants of the interior did not enjoy their first real taste of the fruits of European technology until Englishmen began venturing inland after 1650. Indians these traders met in upcountry towns were glad to barter for the more efficient tools, more lethal weapons, and more durable clothing that colonists offered. Spurred on by eager natives, men from Virginia and Carolina quickly flooded the region with the material trappings of European culture. In 1701 John Lawson considered the Wateree Chickanees "very poor in *English* Effects" because a few of them lacked muskets.[42]

Slower to arrive, trade goods were also less obvious agents of change. The Indians' ability to absorb foreign artifacts into established modes of existence hid the revolutionary consequences of trade for some time. Natives leaped the technological gulf with ease in part because they were discriminating shoppers. If hoes were too small, beads too large, or cloth the wrong color, Indian traders refused them.[43] Items they did select fit smoothly into existing ways. Waxhaws tied horse bells around their ankles at ceremonial dances, and some of the traditional stone pipes passed among the spectators at these dances had been shaped by metal files.[44] Those who could not afford a European weapon fashioned arrows from broken glass. Those who could went to great lengths to "set [a new musket] streight, sometimes shooting away above 100 Loads of Ammunition, before they bring the Gun to shoot according to their Mind."[45]

Not every piece of merchandise hauled into the upcountry on a trader's packhorse could be "set streight" so easily. Liquor, for example, proved both impossible to resist and extraordinarily destructive. Indians "have no Power to refrain this Enemy," Lawson observed, "though sensible how many of them (are by it) hurry'd into the other World before their Time."[46] And yet even here, natives aware of the risks sought to control alcohol by incorporating it into their ceremonial life as a device for achieving a different level of consciousness. Consumption was usually restricted to men, who "go as solemnly about it, as if it were part of their Religion," preferring to drink only at night and only in quantities sufficient to stupefy them.[47] When ritual could not confine liquor to safe channels, Indians went still further and excused the excesses of overindulgence by refusing to hold an intoxicated person responsible for his actions. "They never call any Man to account for what he did, when he was drunk," wrote Lawson, "but say, it was the Drink that caused his Misbehaviour, therefore he ought to be forgiven."[48]

Working to absorb even the most dangerous commodities acquired from their new neighbors, aboriginal inhabitants of the uplands, like African slaves in the lowlands, made themselves at home in a different technological environment. Indians became convinced that "Guns, and Ammunition, besides a great many other Necessaries, . . . are helpful to Man"[49] and eagerly searched for the key that would unlock the secret of their production. At first many were confident that the "*Quera,* or good Spirit," would teach them to make these commodities "when that good Spirit sees fit."[50] Later they decided to help their deity along by approaching the colonists. In 1757, Catawbas asked Governor Arthur Dobbs of North Carolina "to send us Smiths and other Tradesmen to teach our Children."[51]

It was not the new products themselves but the Indians' failure to learn the mysteries of manufacture from either Dobbs or the *Quera* that marked the real revolution wrought by trade. During the seventeenth and eighteenth centuries, everyone in eastern North America—masters and slaves, farmers near the coast and Indians near the mountains—became producers of raw materials for foreign markets and found themselves caught up in an international economic network.[52] Piedmont natives were part of this larger process, but their adjustment was more difficult because the contrast with previous ways was so pronounced. Before European contact, the localism characteristic of life in the uplands had been sustained by a remarkable degree of self-sufficiency. Trade among peoples, while common, was conducted primarily in commodities such as copper, mica, and shells, items that, exchanged with the appropriate ceremony, initiated or confirmed friendships among groups. Few, if any, villages relied on outsiders for goods essential to daily life.[53]

Intercultural exchange eroded this traditional independence and entangled natives in a web of commercial relations few of them understood and none controlled. In 1670 the explorer John Lederer observed a striking disparity in the trading habits of Indians living near Virginia and those deep in the interior. The "remoter Indians," still operating within a precontact framework, were content with ornamental items such as mirrors, beads, "and all manner of gaudy toys and knacks for children." "Neighbour-Indians," on the other hand, habitually traded with colonists for cloth, metal tools, and weapons.[54] Before long, towns near and far were demanding the entire range of European wares and were growing accustomed—even addicted—to them. "They say we English are fools for . . . not always going with a gun," one Virginia colonist familiar with Piedmont Indians wrote in the early 1690s, "for they think themselves undrest and not fit to walk abroad, unless they have their gun on their shoulder, and their shot-bag by their side."[55] Such an enthusiastic conversion to the new technology eroded ancient craft skills and hastened complete dependence on substitutes only colonists could supply.

By forcing Indians to look beyond their own territories for certain indispensable products, Anglo-American traders inserted new variables into the aboriginal equation of exchange. Colonists sought two commodities from Indians—human beings and deerskins—and both undermined established relationships among native groups. While the demand for slaves encouraged Piedmont peoples to expand their traditional warfare, the demand for peltry may have fostered conflicts over hunting territories.[56] Those who did not fight each other for slaves or deerskins fought each other for the European products these could bring. As firearms, cloth, and other items became increasingly important to native existence, competition replaced comity at the foundation of trade encounters as villages scrambled for the cargoes of merchandise.

Some were in a better position to profit than others. In the early 1670s Occaneechees living on an island in the Roanoke River enjoyed power out of all proportion to their numbers because they controlled an important ford on the trading path from Virginia to the interior, and they resorted to threats, and even to force, to retain their advantage.[57] In Lawson's day Tuscaroras did the same, "hating that any of these Westward *Indians* should have any Commerce with the *English,* which would prove a Hinderance to their Gains."[58]

Competition among native groups was only the beginning of the transformation brought about by new forms of exchange. Inhabitants of the Piedmont might bypass the native middleman, but they could not break free from a perilous dependence on colonial sources of supply. The danger may not have been immediately apparent to Indians caught up in the excitement of acquiring new and wonderful things. For years they managed to dictate the terms of trade, compelling visitors from Carolina and Virginia to abide by aboriginal codes of conduct and playing one colony's traders against the other to ensure an abundance of goods at favorable rates.[59] But the natives' influence over the protocol of exchange combined with their skill at incorporating alien products to mask a loss of control over their own destiny. The mask came off when, in 1715, the traders—and the trade goods—suddenly disappeared during the Yamassee War.

The conflict's origins lay in a growing colonial awareness of the Indians' need for regular supplies of European merchandise. In 1701 Lawson pronounced the Santees "very tractable" because of their close connections with South Carolina. Eight years later he was convinced that the colonial officials in Charleston "are absolute Masters over the *Indians* . . . within the Circle of their Trade."[60] Carolina traders who shared this conviction quite naturally felt less and less constrained to obey native rules governing proper behavior. Abuses against Indians mounted until some men were literally getting away with murder. When repeated appeals to colonial officials failed, natives throughout Carolina began to consider war. Persuaded by Yamassee ambassadors that the conspiracy was widespread and convinced by years of ruthless commercial competition between Virginia and Carolina that an attack on one colony would not affect relations with the other, in the spring of 1715 Catawbas and their neighbors joined the invasion of South Carolina.[61]

The decision to fight was disastrous. Colonists everywhere shut off the flow of goods to the interior, and after some initial successes Carolina's native enemies soon plumbed the depths of their dependence. In a matter of months, refugees holed up in Charleston noticed that "the Indians want ammunition and are not able to mend their Arms."[62] The peace negotiations that ensued revealed a desperate thirst for fresh supplies of European wares. Ambassadors from Piedmont towns invariably spoke in a single breath of restoring "a Peace and a free Trade," and one delegation even admitted that its people "cannot live without the assistance of the English."[63]

Natives unable to live without the English henceforth tried to live with them. No upcountry group mounted a direct challenge to Anglo-America after 1715. Trade quickly resumed, and the Piedmont Indians, now concentrated almost exclusively in the Catawba valley, briefly enjoyed a regular supply of necessary products sold by men willing once again to deal according to the old rules. By mid-century, however, deer were scarce and fresh sources of slaves almost impossible to find. Anglo-American traders took their business elsewhere, leaving inhabitants of the Nation with another material crisis of different but equally dangerous dimensions.[64]

Indians casting about for an alternative means of procuring the commodities they craved looked to imperial officials. During the 1740s and 1750s native dependence shifted from colonial traders to colonial authorities as Catawba leaders repeatedly visited provincial capitals to request goods. These delegations came not to beg but to bargain. Catawbas were still of enormous value to the English as allies and frontier guards, especially at a time when Anglo-America felt threatened by the French and their Indian auxiliaries. The Nation's position within reach of Virginia and both Carolinas enhanced its value by enabling headmen to approach all three colonies and offer their people's services to the highest bidder.

The strategy yielded Indians an arsenal of ammunition and a variety of other merchandise that helped offset the declining trade.[65] Crown officials were especially generous when the Nation managed to play one colony off against another. In 1746 a rumor that the Catawbas were about to move to Virginia was enough to garner them a large shipment of powder and lead from officials in Charleston concerned about losing this "valuable people."[66] A decade later, while the two Carolinas fought for the honor of constructing a fort in the Nation, the Indians encouraged (and received) gifts symbolizing good will from both colonies without reaching an agreement with either. Surveying the tangled thicket of promises and presents, the Crown's superintendent of Indian affairs, Edmond Atkin, ruefully admitted that "the People of both Provinces— . . . have I beleive [*sic*] tampered too much on both sides with those Indians, who seem to understand well how to make their Advantage of it."[67]

By the end of the colonial period delicate negotiations across cultural boundaries were as familiar to Catawbas as the strouds they wore and the muskets they carried. But no matter how shrewdly the headmen loosened provincial purse strings to extract vital merchandise, they could not escape the simple fact that they no longer held the purse containing everything needed for their daily existence. In the space of a century the Indians had become thoroughly embedded in an alien economy, denizens of a new material world. The ancient self-sufficiency was only a dim memory in the minds of the Nation's elders.[68]

THE CATAWBA peoples were veterans of countless campaigns against disease and masters of the arts of trade long before the third major element of their new world, white planters, became an integral part of their life. Settlement of the Carolina uplands did not begin until the 1730s, but once underway it spread with frightening speed. In November 1752, concerned Catawbas reminded South Carolina governor James Glen how they had "complained already . . . that the white People were settled too near us."[69] Two years later five hundred families lived within thirty miles of the Nation and surveyors were running their lines into the middle of native towns.[70] "[T]hose Indians are now in a fair way to be surrounded by White People," one observer concluded.[71]

Settlers' attitudes were as alarming as their numbers. Unlike traders who profited from them or colonial officials who deployed them as allies, ordinary colonists had little use for Indians. Natives made poor servants and worse slaves; they obstructed settlement; they attracted enemy warriors to the area. Even men who respected Indians and earned a living by trading with them admitted that they made unpleasant neighbors. "We may observe of them as of the fire," wrote the South Carolina trader James Adair after considering the Catawbas' situation on the eve of the American Revolution, "'it is safe and useful, cherished at proper distance; but if too near us, it becomes dangerous, and will scorch if not consume us.'"[72]

A common fondness for alcohol increased the likelihood of intercultural hostilities. Catawba leaders acknowledged that the Indians "get very Drunk with [liquor] this is the Very Cause that they oftentimes Commit those Crimes that is offencive to You and us."[73] Colonists were equally prone to bouts of drunkenness. In the 1760s the itinerant Anglican minister Charles Woodmason was shocked to find the citizens of one South Carolina upcountry community "continually drunk." More appalling still, after attending church services "one half of them got drunk before they went home."[74] Indians sometimes suffered at the hands of intoxicated farmers. In 1760 a Catawba woman was murdered when she happened by a tavern shortly after four of its patrons "swore they would kill the first Indian they should meet with."[75]

Even when sober, natives and newcomers found many reasons to quarrel. Catawbas were outraged if colonists built farms on the Indians' doorstep or tramped across ancient burial grounds.[76] Planters, ignorant of (or indifferent to) native rules of hospitality, considered Indians who requested food nothing more than beggars and angrily drove them away.[77] Other disputes arose when the Nation's young men went looking for trouble. As hunting, warfare, and other traditional avenues for achieving status narrowed, Catawba youths transferred older patterns of behavior into a new arena by raiding nearby farms and hunting cattle or horses.[78]

Contrasting images of the Piedmont landscape quite unintentionally generated still more friction. Colonists determined to tame what they considered a wilderness were in fact erasing a native signature on the land and scrawling their own. Bridges, buildings, fences, roads, crops, and other "improvements" made the area comfortable and familiar to colonists but uncomfortable and unfamiliar to Indians. "The Country side wear[s] a New face," proclaimed Woodmason proudly[79]; to the original inhabitants, it was a grim face indeed. "His Land was spoiled," one Catawba headman told British officials in 1763. "They have spoiled him 100 Miles every way."[80] Under these circumstances, even a settler with no wish to fight Indians met opposition to his fences, his outbuildings, his very presence. Similarly, a Catawba on a routine foray into traditional hunting territories had his weapon destroyed, his goods confiscated, his life threatened by men with different notions of the proper use of the land.[81]

To make matters worse, the importance both cultures attached to personal independence hampered efforts by authorities on either side to resolve conflicts. Piedmont settlers along the border between the Carolinas were "people of desperate fortune," a frightened North Carolina official reported after visiting the area. "[N]o officer of Justice from either Province dare meddle with them."[82] Woodmason, who spent even more time in the region, came to the same conclusion. "We are without any Law, or Order," he complained; the inhabitants' "Impudence is so very high, as to be past bearing."[83] Catawba leaders could have sympathized. Headmen informed colonists that the Nation's people "are oftentimes Cautioned from . . . ill Doings altho' to no purpose for we Cannot be present at all times to Look after them." "What they have done I could not prevent," one chief explained.[84]

Unruly, angry, intoxicated—Catawbas and Carolinians were constantly at odds during the middle decades of the eighteenth century. Planters who considered Indians "proud and deveilish" were themselves accused by natives of being "very bad and quarrelsome."[85] Warriors made a habit of "going into the Settlements, robbing and stealing where ever they get an Oppertunity."[86] Complaints generally brought no satisfaction— "they laugh and makes their Game of it, and says it is what they will"—leading some settlers to "whip [Indians] about the head, beat and abuse them."[87] "The white People . . . and the Cuttahbaws, are Continually at variance," a visitor to the Nation fretted in June 1759, "and Dayly New Animositys Doth a rise Between them which In my Humble oppion will be of Bad Consequence In a Short time, Both Partys Being obstinate."[88]

The litany of intercultural crimes committed by each side disguised a fundamental shift in the balance of physical and cultural power. In the early years of colonization of the interior the least disturbance by Indians sent scattered planters into a panic. Soon, however, Catawbas were few, colonists many, and it was the natives who now lived in fear. "[T]he white men [who] Lives Near the Neation is Contenuely asembleing and goes In the [Indian] towns In Bodys . . . ," worried another observer during the tense summer of 1759. "[T]he[y] tretton the[y] will Kill all the Cattabues."[89]

The Indians would have to find some way to get along with these unpleasant neighbors if the Nation was to survive. As Catawba population fell below five hundred after the smallpox epidemic of 1759 and the number of colonists continued to climb, natives gradually came to recognize the futility of violent resistance. During the last decades of the eighteenth century they drew on years of experience in dealing with Europeans at a distance and sought to overturn the common conviction that Indian neighbors were frightening and useless.

This process was not the result of some clever plan; Catawbas had no strategy for survival. A headman could warn them that "the White people were now seated all round them and by that means had them entirely in their power."[90] He could not command them to submit peacefully to the invasion of their homeland. The Nation's continued existence required countless individual decisions, made in a host of diverse circumstances, to complain rather than retaliate, to accept a subordinate place in a land that once was theirs. Few of the choices made survive in the record. But it is clear that, like the response to disease and to technology, the adaptation to white settlement was both painful and prolonged.

Catawbas took one of the first steps along the road to accommodation in the early 1760s, when they used their influence with colonial officials to acquire a reservation encompassing the heart of their ancient territories.[91] This grant gave the Indians a land base, grounded in Anglo-American law, that prevented farmers from shouldering them aside. Equally important, Catawbas now had a commodity to exchange with nearby settlers. These men wanted land, the natives had plenty, and shortly before the Revolution the Nation was renting tracts to planters for cash, livestock, and manufactured goods.[92]

Important as it was, land was not the only item Catawbas began trading to their neighbors. Some Indians put their skills as hunters and woodsmen to a different use, picking up stray horses and escaped slaves for a reward.[93] Others bartered their pottery, baskets, and table mats.[94] Still others traveled through the upcountry, demonstrating their prowess with the bow and arrow before appreciative audiences.[95] The exchange of these goods and services for European merchandise marked an important adjustment to the settlers' arrival. In the past, natives had acquired essential items by trading peltry and slaves or requesting gifts from representatives of the Crown. But Piedmont planters frowned on hunting and warfare, while provincial authorities—finding Catawbas less useful as the Nation's population declined and the French threat disappeared—discouraged formal visits and handed out fewer presents. Hence the Indians had to develop new avenues of exchange that would enable them to obtain goods in ways less objectionable to their neighbors. Pots, baskets, and acres proved harmless substitutes for earlier methods of earning an income.

Quite apart from its economic benefits, trade had a profound impact on the character of Catawba-settler relations. Through countless repetitions of the same simple procedure at homesteads scattered across the Carolinas, a new form of intercourse arose, based not on suspicion and an expectation of conflict but on trust and a measure of friendship. When a farmer looked out his window and saw Indians approaching, his reaction more commonly became to pick up money or a jug of whiskey rather than a musket or an axe. The natives now appeared, the settler knew, not to plunder or kill but to peddle their wares or collect their rents.[96]

The development of new trade forms could not bury all of the differences between Catawba and colonist overnight.[97] But in the latter half of the eighteenth century the beleaguered Indians learned to rely on peaceful means of resolving intercultural conflicts that did arise. Drawing a sharp distinction between "the good men that have rented Lands from us" and "the bad People [who] has frequently imposed upon us," Catawbas called on the former to protect the Nation from the latter.[98] In 1771 they met with the prominent Camden storekeeper Joseph Kershaw to request that he "represent us when [we are] a grieved."[99] After the Revolution the position became more formal. Catawbas informed the South Carolina government that, being "destitute of a man to take care of, and assist us in our affairs," they had chosen one Robert Patten "to take charge of our affairs, and to act and do for us."[100]

Neither Patten nor any other intermediary could have protected the Nation had it not joined the patriot side during the Revolutionary War. Though one scholar has termed the Indians' contribution to the cause "rather negligible,"[101] they fought in battles throughout the southeast and supplied rebel forces with food from time to time.[102]

These actions made the Catawbas heroes and laid a foundation for their popular renown as staunch patriots. In 1781 their old friend Kershaw told Catawba leaders how he welcomed the end of "this Long and Bloody War, in which You have taken so Noble a part and have fought and Bled with your white Brothers of America."[103] Grateful Carolinians would not soon forget the Nation's service. Shortly after the Civil War an elderly settler whose father had served with the Indians in the Revolution echoed Kershaw's sentiments, recalling that "his father never communicated much to him [about the Catawbas], except that all the tribe . . . served the entire war . . . and fought most heroically.[104]

Catawbas rose even higher in their neighbors' esteem when they began calling their chiefs "General" instead of "King" and stressed that these men were elected by the people.[105] The change reflected little if any real shift in the Nation's political forms,[106] but it delighted the victorious Revolutionaries. In 1794 the Charleston *City Gazette* reported that during the war "King" Frow had abdicated and the Indians chose "General" New River in his stead. "What a pity," the paper concluded, "certain people on a certain island have not as good optics as the Catawbas!" In the same year the citizens of Camden celebrated the anniversary of the fall of the Bastille by raising their glasses to toast "King Prow [*sic*]—may all kings who will not follow his example follow that of Louis XVI."[107] Like tales of Indian patriots, the story proved durable. Nearly a century after the Revolution one nearby planter wrote that "the Catawbas, emulating the examples of their white brethren, threw off regal government."[108]

The Indians' new image as republicans and patriots, added to their trade with whites and their willingness to resolve conflicts peacefully, brought settlers to view Catawbas in a different light. By 1800 the natives were no longer violent and dangerous strangers but what one visitor termed an "inoffensive" people and one group of planters called "harmless and friendly" neighbors.[109] They had become traders of pottery but not deerskins, experts with a bow and arrow but not hunters, ferocious warriors against runaway slaves or tories but not against settlers. In these ways Catawbas could be distinctively Indian yet reassuringly harmless at the same time.

The Nation's separate identity rested on such obvious aboriginal traits. But its survival ultimately depended on a more general conformity with the surrounding society. During the nineteenth century both settlers and Indians owned or rented land. Both spoke proudly of their Revolutionary heritage and their republican forms of government. Both drank to excess.[110] Even the fact that Catawbas were not Christians failed to differentiate them sharply from nearby white settlements, where, one visitor noted in 1822, "little attention is paid to the sabbath, or religeon."[111]

In retrospect it is clear that these similarities were as superficial as they were essential. For all the changes generated by contacts with vital Euro-American and Afro-American cultures, the Nation was never torn loose from its cultural moorings. Well after the Revolution, Indians maintained a distinctive way of life rich in tradition and meaningful to those it embraced. Ceremonies conducted by headmen and folk tales told by relatives continued to transmit traditional values and skills from one generation to the next. Catawba children grew up speaking the native language, making bows and arrows or pottery, and otherwise following patterns of belief and behavior derived from the past. The Indians' physical appearance and the meandering paths that set Catawba settlements off from neighboring communities served to reinforce this cultural isolation.[112]

The natives' utter indifference to missionary efforts after 1800 testified to the enduring power of established ways. Several clergymen stopped at the reservation in the first years of the nineteenth century; some stayed a year or two; none enjoyed any success.[113] As one white South Carolinian noted in 1826, Catawbas were "Indians still."[114] Outward conformity made it easier for them to blend into the changed landscape. Beneath the surface lay a more complex story.

Those few outsiders who tried to piece together that story generally found it difficult to learn much from the Indians. A people shrewd enough to discard the title of "King" was shrewd enough to understand that some things were better left unsaid and unseen. Catawbas kept their Indian names, and sometimes their language, a secret from prying visitors.[115] They echoed the racist attitudes of their white neighbors and even owned a few slaves, all the time trading with blacks and hiring them to work in the Nation, where the laborers "enjoyed considerable freedom" among the natives.[116] Like Afro-Americans on the plantation who adopted a happy, childlike demeanor to placate suspicious whites, Indians on the reservation learned that a "harmless and friendly" posture revealing little of life in the Nation was best suited to conditions in post-Revolutionary South Carolina.

Success in clinging to their cultural identity and at least a fraction of their ancient lands cannot obscure the cost Catawba peoples paid. From the time the first European arrived, the deck was stacked against them. They played the hand dealt them well enough to survive, but they could never win. An incident that took place at the end of the eighteenth century helps shed light on the consequences of compromise. When the Catawba headman, General New River, accidentally injured the horse he had borrowed from a nearby planter named Thomas Spratt, Spratt responded by "banging old New River with a pole all over the yard." This episode provided the settler with a colorful tale for his grandchildren; its effect on New River and his descendants can only be imagined.[117] Catawbas did succeed in the sense that they adjusted to a hostile and different world, becoming trusted friends instead of feared enemies. Had they been any less successful they would not have survived the eighteenth century. But poverty and oppression have plagued the Nation from New River's day to our own.[118] For a people who had once been proprietors of the Piedmont, the pain of learning new rules was very great, the price of success very high.

ON THAT AUGUST day in 1608 when Amoroleck feared the loss of his world, John Smith assured him that the English "came to them in peace, and to seeke their loves."[119] Events soon proved Amoroleck right and his captor wrong. Over the course of the next three centuries not only Amoroleck and other Piedmont Indians but natives throughout North America had their world stolen and another put in its place. Though this occurred at different times and in different ways, no Indians escaped the explosive mixture of deadly bacteria, material riches, and alien peoples that was the invasion of America. Those in the southern Piedmont who survived the onslaught were ensconced in their new world by the end of the eighteenth century. Population levels stabilized as the Catawba peoples developed immunities to once-lethal diseases. Rents, sales of pottery, and other economic activities proved adequate to support the Nation at a stable (if low) level of material life. Finally, the Indians' image as "inoffensive" neighbors gave them a place in South Carolina society and continues to sustain them today.

Vast differences separated Catawbas and other natives from their colonial contemporaries. Europeans were the colonizers, Africans the enslaved, Indians the dispossessed: from these distinct positions came distinct histories. Yet once we acknowledge the differences, instructive similarities remain that help to integrate natives more thoroughly into the story of early America. By carving a niche for themselves in response to drastically different conditions, the peoples who composed the Catawba Nation shared in the most fundamental of American experiences. Like Afro-Americans, these Indians were compelled to accept a subordinate position in American life yet did not altogether lose their cultural integrity. Like settlers of the Chesapeake, aboriginal inhabitants of the uplands adjusted to appalling mortality rates and wrestled with the difficult task of "living with death."[120] Like inhabitants of the Middle Colonies, Piedmont groups learned to cope with unprecedented ethnic diversity by balancing the pull of traditional loyalties with the demands of a new social order. Like Puritans in New England, Catawbas found that a new world did not arrive all at once and that localism, self-sufficiency, and the power of old ways were only gradually eroded by conditions in colonial America. More hints of a comparable heritage could be added to this list, but by now it should be clear that Indians belong on the colonial stage as important actors in the unfolding American drama rather than bit players, props, or spectators. For they, too, lived in a new world.

NOTES

1. Edward Arber and A. G. Bradley, eds., *Travels and Works of Captain John Smith.* . . , II (Edinburgh, 1910), 427.

2. Bernard W. Sheehan, "Indian-White Relations in Early America: A Review Essay," *William and Mary Quarterly,* 3d Ser. XXVI (1969), 267–86; James Axtell, "The Ethnohistory of Early America: A Review Essay," ibid., XXXV (1978), 110–44.

3. Benjamin W. Labaree, *America's Nation-Time: 1607–1789* (New York, 1976), cover, see also xi. Two exceptions are Gary B. Nash, *Red White, and Black: The Peoples of Early America* (Englewood Cliffs, N.J., 1974), and Mary Beth Norton et al., *A People and a Nation: A History of the United States* (Boston, 1982), I. For analyses of the scholarly neglect of Indians in colonial America see Thad W. Tate, "The Seventeenth-Century Chesapeake and Its Modern Historians," in Tate and David L. Ammerman, eds., *The Chesapeake in the Seventeenth Century: Essays on Anglo-American Society* (Chapel Hill, N.C., 1979), 30–32; Douglas Greenberg, "The Middle Colonies in Recent American Historiography," *WMQ,* 3d Ser. 35 (1979), 415–16, and Neal Salisbury, *Manitou and Providence: Indians, Europeans, and the Making of New England, 1500–1643* (New York, 1982), 3–7.

4. Turner, "The Significance of the Frontier in American History," American Historical Association, *Annual Report for the Year 1893* (Washington, D.C., 1894), 199–227; Allen, *In English Ways: The Movement of Societies and the Transferal of English Local Law and Custom to Massachusetts Bay in the Seventeenth Century*

(Chapel Hill, N.C., 1981); Herskovits, *The Myth of the Negro Past* (New York, 1941); Littlefield, *Rice and Slaves: Ethnicity and the Slave Trade in Colonial South Carolina* (Baton Rouge, La., 1981).

5. Allen, *In English Ways;* T. H. Breen, "Persistent Localism: English Social Change and the Shaping of New England Institutions," *WMQ,* 3d Ser. 32 (1975), 3–28, and "Transfer of Culture: Chance and Design in Shaping Massachusetts Bay, 1630–1660," *New England Historical and Genealogical Register* CXXII (1978), 3–17.

More generally, others have argued that the European settlement of America marked an expansion of the Old World rather than a separation from it, "an extension of Europe rather than a wholly new world" (G. R. Elton, "Contentment and Discontent on the Eve of Colonization," in David B. Quinn, ed., *Early Maryland in a Wider World* [Detroit, Mich., 1982], 117–18; quotation from Quinn, "Why They Came," ibid., 143).

6. Sidney W. Mintz and Richard Price, *An Anthropological Approach to the Afro-American Past: A Caribbean Perspective* (Philadelphia, 1976), 22; Nathan Irvin Huggins, *Black Odyssey: The Afro-American Ordeal in Slavery* (New York, 1977), 25–34.

7. While never thoroughly examined, the term has often been used this way by students of Indian history and others. For example, see Elizabeth A. H. John, *Storms Brewed in Other Men's Worlds: The Confrontation of Indians, Spanish, and French in the Southwest, 1540–1795* (College Station, Tex., 1975); Carolyn Gilman, *Where Two Worlds Meet: The Great Lakes Fur Trade* (St. Paul, Minn., 1982); Peter Laslett, *The World We Have Lost,* 2d ed. (New York, 1973); Edgar P. Richardson, Brooke Hindle, and Lillian B. Miller, *Charles Willson Peale and His World* (New York, 1982); and Irving Howe, *World of Our Fathers* (New York, 1976).

8. See T. J. C. Brasser, "Group Identification along a Moving Frontier," *Verhandlungen des XXXVIII Internationalen Amerikanistenkongresses* II (Munich, 1970), 261–62.

9. Salisbury divides the course of events into two phases, the first including diseases and trade goods, the second encompassing settlement (*Manitou and Providence,* 12).

10. For the societies created by Europeans and Africans see James A. Henretta, *The Evolution of American Society, 1700–1815: An Interdisciplinary Analysis* (Lexington, Mass., 1973), esp. 112–16; Jack P. Greene, "Society and Economy in the British Caribbean during the Seventeenth and Eighteenth Centuries," *American Historical Review* LXXIX (1974), 1515–17; and Ira Berlin, "Time, Space, and the Evolution of Afro-American Society on British Mainland North America," ibid., LXXXV (1980), 44–78.

11. Among some Indian peoples a fourth stage, missionaries, could be added to the three outlined above. These agents did not, however, play an important part in the Piedmont (or in most other areas of the southeast) during the colonial period. Lack of evidence precludes discussion of native religion among upland communities or the changes in belief and ceremony that occurred after contact. It is clear, however, that Indians there opposed any systematic efforts to convert them to Christianity. See Hugh Jones, *The Present State of Virginia: From Whence Is Inferred a Short View of Maryland and North Carolina,* ed. Richard L. Morton (Chapel Hill, N.C., 1956), 59.

12. Catawbas and their Indian neighbors have been objects of much study and considerable disagreement. Because these peoples lived away from areas of initial European settlement, detailed records are scarce, and archaeologists are only beginning to help fill the gaps in the evidence. Important questions—the linguistic and political affiliations of some groups, their social structures, the degree of influence exerted by powerful societies to the east, west, and south, even their population—remain unanswered. But there are many reasons to argue for a fundamental cultural uniformity in this area beyond a common environment, hints of similar cultural traits, and the shared destiny of the region's inhabitants. Although these scattered villages fought with outsiders from the coast and the mountains, the north and the south, there is a distinct lack of recorded conflict among peoples in the Piedmont itself. Peaceful relations may have been reinforced by a sense of common origin, for some (if not all) of these groups—including Saponis, Tutelos, Occaneechees, Catawbas, and Cheraws—spoke variant forms of the Siouan language and were descended from migrants who entered the area some seven centuries before Columbus arrived in America. Finally, other natives were cognizant of connections among these far-flung towns. The Iroquois, for example, called natives from the Catawbas to the Tutelos by the collective name "Toderichroone." For studies of these peoples see James Mooney, *The Siouan Tribes of the East,* Smithsonian Institution, Bureau of American Ethnology, Bulletin 22 (Washington, D.C., 1894); Joffre Lanning Coe, "The Cultural Sequence of the Carolina Piedmont," in James B. Griffin, ed., *Archeology of Eastern United States* (Chicago, 1952), 301–11; Douglas Summers Brown, *The Catawba Indians: The People of the River* (Columbia, S.C., 1966); Charles M. Hudson, *The Catawba Nation* (Athens,

Ga., 1970), and James H. Merrell, "Natives in a New World: The Catawba Indians of Carolina, 1650–1800" (Ph.D. diss., The Johns Hopkins University, 1982).

13. Coe, "Cultural Sequence," 301–311; Hudson, *Catawba Nation*, 11–17; William E. Myer, "Indian Trails of the Southeast," Bureau of American Ethnology, *Forty-Second Annual Report* (Washington, D.C., 1928), plate 15.

14. "True Relation of the Vicissitudes That Attended the Governor Don Hernando De Soto and Some Nobles of Portugal in the Discovery of the Province of Florida Now Just Given by a Fidalgo of Elvas," in Edward Gaylord Bourne, ed., *Narratives of the Career of Hernando de Soto* . . . (New York, 1904), 66. See also John Grier Varner and Jeannette Johnson Varner, trans. and eds., *The Florida of the Inca* . . . (Austin,Tex., 1951), 298, 315; and Henry E. Dobyns, *Their Number Become Thinned: Native American Population Dynamics in Eastern North America* (Knoxville, Tenn., 1983), 262–64.

15. South Carolina Council to Lords Proprietors, Apr. 23, 1698, in Alexander S. Salley, ed., *Commissions and Instructions from the Lords Proprietors of Carolina to Public Officials of South Carolina, 1685–1715* (Columbia, S.C., 1916), 105; Alexander Spotswood to the Board of Trade, Dec. 22, 1718, C.O. 5/1318, 590, Public Record Office (Library of Congress transcripts, 488); *South Carolina Gazette* (Charleston), May 4, 11, 25, June 29, Oct. 5, 1738. Catawba losses in this epidemic were never tabulated, but fully half of the Cherokees may have died (see John Duffy, *Epidemics in Colonial America* [Baton Rouge, La., 1953], 82–83; Catawbas to the governor of South Carolina, Oct. 1759, William Henry Lyttelton Papers, William L. Clements Library, Ann Arbor, Mich., and *S.C. Gaz.*, Dec. 15, 1759). Dobyns constructs epidemic profiles for the continent and for Florida that offer a sense of the prevalence of disease (*Their Number Become Thinned*, essays, 1, 6).

16. See Edmund S. Morgan, *American Slavery, American Freedom: The Ordeal of Colonial Virginia* (New York, 1975), chaps. 8–9; Darrett B. Rutman and Anita H. Rutman, "Of Agues and Fevers: Malaria in the Early Chesapeake," *WMQ*, 3d Ser. 33 (1976), 31–60; and several of the essays in Tate and Ammerman, eds., *Seventeenth-Century Chesapeake*.

17. Lawson, *A New Voyage to Carolina*, ed. Hugh Talmage Lefler (Chapel Hill, N.C., 1967), 232. See also 17, 34. The population figure given here is a very rough estimate. Lawson reckoned that Saponis, Tutelos, Keyauwees, Occaneechees, and Shakoris numbered 750 and that Catawbas (he called them "Esaws") were "a very large Nation containing many thousand People" (pp. 242, 46). Totals for other groups in the Piedmont are almost nonexistent.

18. Philip E. Pearson, "Memoir of the Catawbas, furnished Gov. Hammond," MS (1842?), Wilberforce Eames Indian Collection, New York Public Library (typescript copy in the York County Public Library, Rock Hill, S.C.). For estimates of population losses see *S.C. Gaz.*, Dec. 15, 1759; Arthur Dobbs to the secretary of the Society for the Propagation of the Gospel in Foreign Parts, Apr. 15, 1760, in William L. Saunders, ed. *The Colonial Records of North Carolina*, 10 vols. (Raleigh, N.C., 1886–90), VI, 235, hereafter cited as *N.C. Col. Recs.*

19. Francis Le Jau to the secretary, June 13 1710, in Frank J. Klingberg, ed., *The Carolina Chronicle of Dr. Francis Le Jau, 1706–1717* (Berkeley, Calif., 1956), 78.

20. John Drayton to Dr. Benjamin Smith Barton, Sept. 9, 1803, Correspondence and Papers of Benjamin S. Barton, Historical Society of Pennsylvania, Philadelphia. I am indebted to Maurice Bric for this reference.

21. Christian E. Feest, "Notes on Saponi Settlements in Virginia Prior to 1714," Archaeological Society of Virginia, *Quarterly Bulletin* XXIII (1974), 152–55; William Byrd, "The History of the Dividing Line betwixt Virginia and North Carolina Run in the Year of Our Lord 1728," in Louis B. Wright, ed., *The Prose Works of William Byrd of Westover: Narratives of a Colonial Virginian* (Cambridge, Mass., 1966), 315; H. R. McIlwaine et al., eds., *Executive Journals of the Council of Colonial Virginia*, 6 vols. (Richmond, Va., 1925–66), IV, 269, hereafter cited as *Va. Council Jours.*; "A List of all the Indian names present at the Treaty held in Lancaster in June 1744," in Samuel Hazard, ed., *Pennsylvania Archives Selected and Arranged from Original Documents* . . . , 1st Ser., I (Philadelphia, 1852), 657.

22. Lawson, *New Voyage*, 173, 63.

23. Edward Bland, "The Discovery of New Brittaine, 1650," in Alexander S. Salley, ed., *Narratives of Early Carolina, 1650–1708* (New York, 1911), 13–14; William P. Cumming, ed., *The Discoveries of John Lederer* . . . (Charlottesville, Va., 1958), 12, 17, 19–20; John Banister, "Of the Natives," in Joseph Ewan and Nesta Ewan, eds., *John Banister and His Natural History of Virginia, 1678–1692* (Urbana, Ill., 1970), 377; William J. Hinke, trans. and ed., "Report of the Journey of Francis Louis Michel from Berne, Switzerland, to Virginia, October 2, 1701–December 1, 1702," *Virginia Magazine of History and Biography*, XXIV (1916), 29; Lawson,

New Voyage, 50; David I. Bushnell, Jr., "'The Indian Grave'—a Monacan Site in Albemarle County, Virginia," *WMQ*, 1st Ser. 33 (1914), 106–112.

24. Lawson, *New Voyage*, 214.

25. Council Journals, Aug. 4, 1716, *N.C. Col. Recs.*, II, 242–43.

26. William Byrd, "Journey to the Land of Eden, Anno 1733," in Wright, ed., *Prose Works*, 398; *Va. Council Jours.*, III, 440.

27. Lawson, *New Voyage*, ed. Lefler, 35, 233.

28. Ibid., 184.

29. Ibid., 190.

30. Ibid., 184, 212, 24.

31. Ibid., 193.

32. Robert A. Levine and Donald T. Campbell, *Ethnocentrism: Theories of Conflict, Ethnic Attitudes, and Group Behavior* (New York, 1972), 108.

33. Spotswood to the bishop of London, Jan. 27, 1715, in R. A. Brock, ed., *The Official Letters of Alexander Spotswood, Lieutenant-Governor of the Colony of Virginia, 1710–1722* (Virginia Historical Society, *Collections*, N.S., II [Richmond, Va., 1885]), 88, hereafter cited as Brock, ed., *Spotswood Letters*. See also Byrd, "History," in Wright, ed., *Prose Works*, 314.

34. Brock, ed., *Spotswood Letters*, 88.

35. Samuel Cole Williams, ed., *Adair's History of the American Indians* (Johnson City, Tenn., 1930), 236; *The Public Accounts of John Hammerton, Esq., Secretary of the Province*, in *Inventories*, LL, 1744–46, 29, 47, 51, South Carolina Department of Archives and History, Columbia, hereafter cited as Hammerton, Public Accounts; "Sketch Map of the Rivers Santee, Congaree, Wateree, Saludee, &c., with the Road to the Cuttauboes [1750?]," Colonial Office Library, Carolina 16, P.R.O. (copy in Brown, *Catawba Indians*, plate 6, between pp. 32–33); "Cuttahbaws Nation, men fit for warr 204 In the year 1756," Dalhousie Muniments, General John Forbes Papers, Document #2/104 (copy in S.C. Dept. Archs. and Hist.).

36. J. H. Easterby, ed., *The Colonial Records of South Carolina: The Journal of the Commons House of Assembly, November 10, 1736–June 7, 1739* (Columbia, S.C., 1951), 481, 482. Compare this to the Catawbas' failure to control Waccamaws living in the Nation a decade before; *Journals of the Upper House of Assembly*, Sept. 13, 1727, C.O. 5/429, 176–77 microfilm, British Manuscripts Project, D 491.

37. Williams, ed., *Adair's History*, 236.

38. Catawba Indians to Gov. Lyttelton, June 16, 1757, Lyttelton Papers (Santee Jemmy); Rev. William Richardson, "An Account of My Proceedings since I accepted the Indian mission in October 2d 1758 . . . ," Wilberforce Eames Indian Collection, entry of Nov. 8, 1758 (Cheraw George). *South Carolina Council Journals* (hereafter cited as *S.C. Council Jours.*), May 5, 1760, in William S. Jenkins, comp., Records of the States of the United States, microfilm ed. (Washington, D.C., 1950) (hereafter cited as Records of States), SC E. 1p, Reel 8, Unit 3, 119 (Congaree Jamie); John Evans to Gov. James Glen, Apr. 18, 1748, in *S.C. Council Jours.*, Apr. 27, 1748, Records of States, SC E.1p, 3/4 233 (Saponey Johnny); Hammerton, Public Accounts, 29, 51 (Eno Jemmy).

39. See, for example, Spotswood's efforts to persuade some tributary groups to join the Piedmont Indians at Fort Christanna. *Va. Council Jours.*, III, 367; Spotswood to bishop of London, Jan. 27, 17 15, in Brock, ed., *Spotswood Letters*, II, 88.

40. Easterby, ed., *Journal of the Commons House, 1736–1739*, 487.

41. See Brasser, "Group Idenufication," *Verhandlungen* II (1970), 261–65.

42. Lawson, *New Voyage*, 38.

43. William Byrd to [Arthur North?], Mar. 8, 1685/6, in Marion Tinling, ed., *The Correspondence of the Three William Byrds of Westover, Virginia, 1684–1776*, I (Charlottesville, Va., 1977), 57; Byrd to Perry and Lane, July 8, 1686, 64; Byrd to [Perry and Lane?], Mar. 20, 1685, 30; Byrd to North, Mar. 29, 1685, 31.

44. Lawson, *New Voyage*, 44–45; George Edwin Stuart, "The Post-Archaic Occupation of Central South Carolina" (Ph.D. diss., University of North Carolina, 1975), 133, fig. 72, B.

45. Lawson, *New Voyage*, 33, 63. Archaeologists have uncovered these arrowheads. See Tommy Charles, "Thoughts and Records from the Survey of Private Collections of Prehistoric Artifacts: A Second Report," Institute of Archeology and Anthropology, University of South Carolina, *Notebook*, XV (1983), 31.

46. Lawson, *New Voyage*, 211, 18.

47. Ibid., 211; Robert Beverley, *The History and Present State of Virginia*, ed. Louis B. Wright (Chapel Hill, N.C., 1947), 182.

48. Lawson, *New Voyage*, 210. See also Craig MacAndrew and Robert B. Edgerton, *Drunken Comportment: A Social Explanation* (New York, 1969), chap. 5.

49. Lawson, *New Voyage*, 220.

50. Ibid., One Santee priest claimed he had already been given this power by "the white Man above, (meaning God Almighty)" (ibid., 26–27).

51. Catawba Nation to Gov. Dobbs, Oct. 5, 1757, encl. in Dobbs to Lyttelton, Oct. 24, 1757, Lyttelton Papers.

52. Immanuel Wallerstein, *The Modern World-System: Capitalist Agriculture and the Origins of the European World-Economy in the Sixteenth Century* (New York, 1974), esp. chap. 6.

53. Harold Hickerson, "Fur Trade Colonialism and the North American Indians," *Journal of Ethnic Studies* I (1973), 18–22; Charles Hudson, *The Southeastern Indians* (Knoxville, Tenn., 1976), 65–66, 316. Salt may have been an exception to this aboriginal self-sufficiency. Even here, however, Indians might have been able to get along without it or find acceptable substitutes. See Gloria J. Wentowski, "Salt as an Ecological Factor in the Prehistory of the Southeastern United States" (M.A. thesis, University of North Carolina, 1970). For substitutes see Lawson, *New Voyage*, 89; Banister, "Of the Natives," in Ewan and Ewan, eds., *Banister and His History*, 376; Beverley, *History*, ed. Wright, 180.

54. Cumming, ed., *Discoveries of Lederer*, 41–42.

55. Banister, "Of the Natives," in Ewan and Ewan, eds., *Banister and His History*, 382.

56. "It is certain the Indians are very cruel to one another," Rev. Francis Le Jau wrote his superiors in England in April 1708, "but is it not to be feared some white men living or trading among them do foment and increase that Bloody Inclination in order to get Slaves?" (Le Jau to the secretary, Apr. 22, 1708, in Klingberg, ed., *Carolina Chronicle*, 39). Over the summer his worst fears were confirmed: "It is reported by some of our Inhabitants lately gone on Indian Trading that [Carolina traders] excite them to make War amongst themselves to get Slaves which they give for our European Goods" (Le Jau to the secretary, Sept. 15, 1708, ibid., 41). For an analysis of the Indian slave trade see J. Leitch Wright, Jr., *The Only Land They Knew: The Tragic Story of the American Indians in the Old South* (New York, 1981), chap. 6. General studies of Indian warfare in the Southeast are John R. Swanton, *The Indians of the Southeastern United States*, Smithsonian Institution, Bureau of American Ethnology, Bulletin 137 (Washington, D.C., 1946), 686–701, and Hudson, *Southeastern Indians*, 239–57.

Evidence of an escalation in competition for hunting territories is sparse. But in 1702, only a year after Lawson noted that deer were scarce among the Tuscaroras, Indians in Virginia complained that Tuscarora hunting parties were crossing into the colony in search of game and ruining the hunting grounds of local groups. See Lawson, *New Voyage*, 65, and *Va. Council Jours.*, II, 275. It seems likely that this became more common as pressure on available supplies of game intensified.

57. "Letter of Abraham Wood to John Richards, August 22, 1674," in Clarence Walworth Alvord and Lee Bidgood [eds.], *First Explorations of the Trans-Allegheny Region by the Virginians, 1650–1674* (Cleveland, Ohio, 1912), 211, 215–17, 223–25; "Virginias Deploured Condition: Or an Impartial Narrative of the Murders committed by the Indians there, and of the Sufferings of his Maties. Loyall Subjects under the Rebellious outrages of Mr. Nathaniell Bacon Junr. to the tenth day of August A. o Dom 1676," Massachusetts Historical Society, *Collections*, 4th Ser., IX (Boston, 1871), 167.

58. Lawson, *New Voyage*, 64.

59. See Cumming, ed., *Discoveries of Lederer*, 41; Lawson, *New Voyage*, 210; and Merrell, "Natives in a New World," 74–77. For the competition between colonies see Verner W. Crane, *The Southern Frontier, 1670–1732* (New York, 1981 [orig. publ. Durham, N.C., 1928]), 153–57, and Merrell, "Natives in a New World," 136–47.

60. Lawson, *New Voyage*, 23, 10.

61. The best studies of this conflict are Crane, *Southern Frontier*, chap. 7, John Phillip Reid, *A Better Kind of Hatchet: Law, Trade, and Diplomacy in the Cherokee Nation during the Early Years of European Contact* (University Park, Pa., 1976), chaps. 5–7, and Richard L. Haan, "The 'Trade Do's Not Flourish as Formerly,' The Ecological Origins of the Yamassee War of 1715," *Ethnohistory*, XXVIII (1981), 341–58. The Catawbas' role in the war is detailed in Merrell, "Natives in a New World," chap. 4.

62. Le Jau to [John Chamberlain?], Aug. 22, 1715, in Klingberg, ed., *Carolina Chronicle*, 162.

63. *Va. Council Jours.*, III, 406, 412, 422.

64. Merrell, "Natives in a New World," 280–300, 358–59.

65. For an example of the gifts received by Catawbas see the list of goods delivered to the Catawba Indians at the Congaree Fort, Feb. 14, 1752, in William L. McDowell, ed., *The Colonial Records of South Carolina: Documents Relating to Indian Affairs, May 21, 1750–August 7, 1754*, Ser. 2, *The Indian Books* (Columbia, S.C., 1958), 217–18, hereafter cited as *Indian Affairs Docs.*

66. J. H. Easterby, ed., *The Colonial Records of South Carolina: Journals of the Commons House of Assembly, September 10, 1745–June 17, 1746* (Columbia, S.C., 1956), 132, 141, 173; George Haig to Gov. James Glen, Mar. 21, 1746, *S.C. Council Jours.*, Mar. 27, 1746. Records of States, SC *E.lp*, 3/2, 74–75.

67. Atkin to Gov. William Henry Lyttelton, Nov. 23, 1757, Lyttelton Papers.

68. Treaty between North Carolina Commissioners and the Catawba Indians, Aug. 29, 1754, *N.C. Col. Recs., V*, 144a.

69. Catawba King and Others to Gov. Glen, Nov. 21, 1752, *Indian Affairs Docs.*, 361.

70. Mathew Rowan to the Board of Trade, June 3, 1754, *N.C. Col. Recs., V*, 124; Samuel Wyly to clerk of Council, Mar. 2, 1754, in *S.C. Council Jours.*, Mar. 13, 1754, Records of States, SC *E.lp*, 6/1, 140.

71. Wilbur R. Jacobs, ed., *Indians of the Southern Colonial Frontier: The Edmond Atkin Report and Plan of 1755* (Columbia, S.C., 1954), 46.

72. Williams, ed., *Adair's History*, 235.

73. Treaty between North Carolina and the Catawbas, Aug. 29, 1754, *N.C. Col. Recs., V*, 143. See also conference held with the Catawbas by Mr. Chief Justice Henley at Salisbury, May 1756, ibid., 581, 583; Matthew Toole to Glen, Oct. 28, 1752, *Indian Affairs Docs.*, 359; Catawbas to Lyttelton, June 16, 1757, Lyttelton Papers; and James Adamson to Lyttelton, June 12, 1759, ibid.

74. Richard J. Hooker, ed., *The Carolina Backcountry on the Eve of the Revolution: The Journal and Other Writings of Charles Woodmason, Anglican Itinerant* (Chapel Hill, N.C., 1953) 7, 12. See also 30, 39, 53, 56, 97–99, 128–29.

75. *S.C. Council Jours.*, May 5, 1760, Records of States, SC *E.lp*, 8/3, 119.

76. Robert Stiell to Gov. Glen, Mar. 11, 1753, *Indian Affairs Docs.*, 371; Gov. Thomas Boone to the Lords Commissioners of Trade and Plantations, Oct. 9, 1762, in W. Noel Sainsbury, comp., Records in the British Public Record Office Relating to South Carolina, 1663–1782, 36 vols., microfilm ed. (Columbia, S.C., 1955), XXIX, 245–46, hereafter cited as Brit. Public Recs., S.C.

77. Treaty between North Carolina and the Catawbas, Aug. 29, 1754, *N.C. Col. Recs., V*, 142–43; Council Journal, Mar. 18, 1756, ibid., 655; Samuel Wyly to Lyttelton, Feb. 9, 1759, Lyttelton Papers.

78. See, for example, Treaty between North Carolina and the Catawbas, Aug. 29, 1754, *N.C. Col. Recs., V*, 142–43, and Catawbas to Lyttelton, June 16, 1757, Lyttelton Papers.

79. Hooker, ed., *Carolina Backcountry*, 63.

80. Augusta Congress, Nov. 1763, in *Brit. Public Recs., S.C.*, XXX, 84.

81. Robert Stiell to Gov. Glen, Mar. 11, 1753, *Indian Affairs Docs.*, 371; Inhabitants of the Waxhaws to Samuel Wyly, Apr. 15, 1759, encl. in Wyly to Lyttelton, Apr. 26, 1759, Lyttelton Papers (colonists attacked). *S.C. Council Jours.*, Feb. 6, 1769, Records of States, SC *E.lp, 10/3*, 9; King Frow to the governor, Mar. 15, 1770, in *S.C. Council Jours.*, Mar. 27, 1770, ibid, SC *E.lp*, 10/4, 56; "At a Meeting Held with the Catabaws," Mar. 26, 1771, Joseph Kershaw Papers, South Carolina Library, University of South Carolina, Columbia (Indians attacked).

82. Information of John Frohock and others, Oct. 10, 1762, *N.C. Col. Recs., VI*, 794–95.

83. Hooker, ed., *Carolina Backcountry*, 45, 52.

84. Treaty between North Carolina and the Catawbas, Aug. 29, 1754, *N.C. Col. Recs., V*, 143, Catawbas to Glen, Nov. 21, 1752, *Indian Affairs Docs.*, 361.

85. Waxhaw inhabitants to Wyly, Apr. 15, 1759, encl. in Wyly to Lyttelton, Apr. 26, 1759, Lyttelton Papers; Meeting between the Catawbas and Henley, May 1756, *N.C. Col. Recs., V*, 581.

86. Toole to Glen, Oct. 28, 1752, *Indian Affairs Docs.*, 358.

87. Ibid., 359; Meeting between the Catawbas and Henley, May 1756, *N.C. Col. Recs., V*, 581.

88. John Evans to Lyttelton, June 20, 1759, Lyttelton Papers.

89. Adamson to Lyttelton, June 12, 1759, ibid.

90. Meeting between the Catawbas and Henley, May 1756, *N.C. Col. Recs., V*, 582.

91. The Indians lobbied for this land beginning in 1757. Crown officials finally reserved it to them in Nov. 1763 and surveyed it in Feb. 1764. See Catawbas to Lyttelton, June 16, 1757, Lyttelton Papers; *S.C. Gaz.*, Aug. 9, 1760; *S.C. Council Jours.*, May 15, 1762, Records of States, SC *E.1p*, 8/6, 497; Augusta Congress, Nov. 1763, *Brit. Public Recs.*, S.C., XXX, 84, 104–106, 112–13; and "A Map of the Catawba Indians Surveyed agreeable to a Treaty Entered into with Them At Augusta in Georgia on the tenth Day of November 1763 . . . Executed, Certified and Signed by me the 22nd Day of February Anno Domini 1764, Sam[ue]l Wyly D[eputy] S[urveyo]r," Miscellaneous Records, H, 460, S.C. Dept. Archs. and Hist.

92. Brown, *Catawba Indians*, 283–84. For contemporary accounts see Thomas Coke, *Extracts of the Journals of the Rev. Dr. Coke's Five Visits to America* (London, 1793), 148–49; "Travel Diary of Marshall and Benzien from Salem to South Carolina, 1790 . . . ," in Adelaide L. Fries et al., eds., *Records of the Moravians in North Carolina,* 11 vols. (Raleigh, N.C., 1922–69), V, 1997; David Hutchison, "The Catawba Indians. By Request," *Palmetto-State Banner* (Columbia), Aug. 30, 1849 (copy in the Draper Manuscript Collection, Ser. U, vol. 10, Doc. #100 [Wisconsin State Historical Society, Madison]), hereafter cited as Hutchison, "Catawba Indians."

This land system broke down in 1840 when the Catawbas ceded their lands to South Carolina in exchange for promises of money and land to be purchased for them in North Carolina. By that time, the Nation's place in South Carolina society was secure enough to survive the economic and social shock of losing its land base. When plans to live in North Carolina fell through and the Indians drifted back to their ancient territory, no one forced them to leave. Instead, the state of South Carolina purchased a small reservation for them, a tract of land that has been the core of Catawba life ever since. See Brown, *Catawba Indians*, chaps. 13–14.

93. Affidavit of John Evans, *S.C. Council Jours.*, Nov. 6, 1755, Records of States, SC *E.1p*, 7/2, 439; Affidavit of Liddy, Jan. 1, 1784, Kershaw Papers (horses). Report of the South Carolina Committee of Council, Apr. 19, 1769, *Brit. Public Recs.*, S.C., XXX, 145–46; Hutchison, "Catawba Indians" (slaves).

94. John F. D. Smyth, *A Tour in the United States of America . . . ,* I (London, 1784), 193–194; Lucius Verus Bierce, "The Piedmont Frontier, 1822–23," in Thomas D. Clark, ed., *South Carolina: The Grand Tour, 1780–1865* (Columbia, S.C., 1973), 64; William Gilmore Simms, "Caloya; Or, The Loves of the Driver," in his *The Wigwam and the Cabin* (New York, 1856), 361–63.

95. Frank G. Speck, *Catawba Hunting, Trapping, and Fishing,* Joint Publications, Museum of The University of Pennsylvania and The Philadelphia Anthropological Society, No. 2 (Philadelphia, 1946), 10; Thomas J. Kirkland and Robert M. Kennedy, *Historic Camden,* I: *Colonial and Revolutionary* (Columbia, S.C., 1905), 58–59.

96. Compare, for example, the bitterness whites expressed to Adair before the Revolution (Williams, ed., *Adair's History,* 234) with the bemused tolerance in Simms's 19th-century fictional account of Catawbas and planters ("Caloya," in his *Wigwam and Cabin,* 361–429).

97. Besides the conflicts over hunting noted above see Hooker, ed., *Carolina Backcountry,* 20; Lark E. Adams, ed., *The State Records of South Carolina: Journals of the House of Representatives, 1785–1786* (Columbia, S.C., 1979), 511–12; Journals of the House of Representatives, Dec. 5, 1792, Records of States, SC A.1b, 23/1, 83.

98. Catawba petition "To the Honourable the Legislature of the State of South Carolina now assembled at Charlestown," Feb. 13, 1784(?), Kershaw Papers. The Indians had made this distinction earlier. See *S.C. Council Jours.*, Oct. 8, 1760, Records of States, SC *E.1p*, 8/5, 36.

99. "At a Meeting Held with the Catabaws," Mar. 26, 1771, Kershaw Papers.

100. Catawba Petition to S.C. Legislature, Feb. 13, 1784(?), ibid.

101. Hudson, *Catawba Nation,* 51.

102. The story of the Indians' service is summarized in Brown, *Catawba Indians,* 260–71.

103. "To the Brave Genl New River and the rest of the Headmen Warrieurs of the Catawba Nation," 1771 (misdated), Kershaw Papers.

104. A. Q. Bradley to Lyman C. Draper, May 31, 1873, Draper MSS, 14VV, 260. For other expressions of this attitude see J. E. White to Draper, n.d., ibid., 15VV, 96; T. D. Spratt to Draper, May 7, 1873, ibid., 107–108; Ezekiel Fewell to Draper, n.d., ibid., 318–19; and David Hutchison, "Catawba Indians."

105. Brown, *Catawba Indians,* 276.

106. The Nation's council "elected" headmen both before and after 1776, and kinship connections to former rulers continued to be important. For elections see *S.C. Council Jours.*, Feb. 20, 1764, Records of States,

SC *E.lp*, 9/2, 40–41; Nov. 9, 1764, ibid, 354; Feb. 12, 1765, ibid., 9/3, 442–443; *S.C. Commons House Jours.*, Jan. 27, 1767, ibid., SC A.lb, 8/1, n.p. For later hereditary links to former chiefs see John Drayton, *A View of South Carolina As Respects Her Natural and Civil Concerns* (Spartanburg, S.C., 1972 [orig. publ., 1802]), 98; Spratt to Draper, Jan. 12, 1871, Draper MSS, 15VV, 99–100.

107. *City Gazette* (Charleston), Aug. 14, 1794, quoted in Kirkland and Kennedy, *Historic Camden*, 320, 319.

108. Spratt to Draper, Jan. 12, 1871, Draper MSS, 15 VV, 99. See also Hutchison, "Catawba Indians."

109. Smyth, *Tour*, I, 192; Report of the Commissioners Appointed to Treat with the Catawba Indians, Apr. 3, 1840, in A. E. Whyte, "Account of the Catawba Indians," Draper MSS, IOU, 112.

110. W. J. Rorabaugh, *The Alcoholic Republic: An American Tradition* (New York, 1979), chap. 1. For reports of excessive drinking by whites along the Catawba River see Records of the General Assembly, Petitions, N.D. (#1916), 1798 (#139), S.C. Dept. Archs. and Hist.; Journals of the Senate, Dec. 11, 1819, Records of States, SC A.1a 57, Journals of the House of Representatives, Nov. 23, 1819, Nov. 21, 1827; Records of States, SC A.lb, 28/1, 8, 29/5, 15, 24.

111. Bierce, "Piedmont Frontier," in Clark, ed., *Grand Tour*, 66.

112. The story of the Catawbas' cultural persistence may be found in Merrell, "Natives in a New World," chap. 9, and "Reading 'an almost erased page': A Reassessment of Frank G. Speck's Catawba Studies," American Philosophical Society, *Proceedings*, CXXVII (1983), 248–62. For an interesting comparison of cultural independence in the slave quarter and the Indian reservation see Thomas L. Webber, *Deep Like the Rivers: Education in the Slave Quarter Community, 1831–1865* (New York, 1978), chap. 18.

113. Hutchison, "Catawba Indians"; Daniel G. Stinson to Draper, July 4, 1873, Draper MSS, 9VV, 274–77.

114. Robert Mills, *Statistics of South Carolina . . .* (Charleston, S.C., 1826), 773. See also the annual reports of the Catawba Agent to the Governor and State Legislature of South Carolina, 1841, 1842, 1848, 1849, 1860–64, in Legislative Papers, Indian Affairs, Governors' Correspondence, S.C. Dept. Archs. and Hist.

115. See Merrell, "Reading 'an almost erased page,'" Am. Phil. Soc., *Procs.*, CXXVII (1983), 256 (names). Smyth, *Tour*, I, 185; Coke, *Extracts*, 149; "Letter from the Country. Landsford, S.C., September 6, 1867," in *Courier* (Charleston), Sept. 12, 1867, 3 (language).

116. Catawba-black relations are analyzed in Merrell, "The Racial Education of the Catawba Indians," *Journal of Southern History*, L (1984), 363–84.

117. Thomas Dryden Spratt, "Recollections of His Family, July 1875," unpubl. MS, South Carolina Lib., 62.

118. See H. Lewis Scaife, *History and Condition of the Catawba Indians of South Carolina* (Philadelphia, 1896), 16–23; and Hudson, *Catawba Nation*, chaps. 4–6.

119. Arber and Bradley, eds., *Works of Smith*, II, 427.

120. Morgan, *American Slavery, American Freedom*, chap. 8.

PART ONE · *Contact Arenas*

3

ECOLOGICAL IMPERIALISM:
THE OVERSEAS MIGRATION OF WESTERN
EUROPEANS AS A BIOLOGICAL PHENOMENON

Alfred W. Crosby

According to a Kiowa legend, smallpox arrived among that people of the southern Plains dressed in the fashion of a missionary. When Saynday, the Kiowas' hero, asked this foreigner what smallpox did, the newcomer replied: "I bring death." The story encapsulates one of Alfred Crosby's central arguments about the force of "Old World" pathogens in the Americas, where they had not existed before Europeans landed; it also reveals how native groups interpreted the arrival of illnesses that devastated their communities.

Epidemic diseases, especially smallpox, were the most lethal ingredient of a process that Crosby has termed the "Columbian Exchange," the transfer of people, plants, animals, and diseases between Europeans and the parts of the world they encountered after 1492. Native American Indians fell victim to a variety of maladies not because they were biologically inferior or (as some European colonizers suggested) because they were not Christian. Instead, pathogens devastated natives across the Americas (and, later, aboriginal populations in Australia) because these peoples lacked the immunities to infectious diseases that Europeans had acquired, typically during childhood when boys and girls were exposed to such scourges.

Before the year 1000, Europeans rarely strayed beyond the boundaries of their continent; but the dawn of their new millennium ushered in an age of wandering for Europeans, who went on crusades to the Mediterranean world to recapture their holy land in the name of their Christian God. In that same epoch, intrepid Norse sailors guided their *knorrir,* those elegant narrow ships, out of their fjordland and into the frigid waters of the North Atlantic, where they established profitable fisheries and, on Iceland, created the first European colony on top of the mid-Atlantic ridge.

But though Crusaders and Norsemen were adventurous, most Europeans chose to remain at home, often in crowded communities where certain pathogens became endemic (ever-present) because there were always fresh hosts to carry them. After news of Columbus's voyages spread through Europe and led men and women to cross the Atlantic to the Western Hemisphere, however, diseases once confined to the Eurasian landmass now had an opportunity to find an endless supply of new hosts as pathogens hitched rides across the ocean. When they did so, these ailments caused perhaps the greatest loss of life in recorded history: from approximately 1500 to 1800, one epidemic after another raced across the Americas, leaving death in its wake.

The migration of microbes was the most tragic element of the "Columbian Exchange," but it was not the only one. As Crosby writes in this essay, diseases were but one of the exports from early modern Europe to the Western Hemisphere. The spread of certain animals and plants that seem, to us, so American—the horse, the honeybee, the plant species known as Kentucky bluegrass, and many others—suggests why Europeans were able to succeed so well in the Americas.

ECOLOGICAL IMPERIALISM: THE OVERSEAS MIGRATION OF WESTERN EUROPEANS AS A BIOLOGICAL PHENOMENON

Alfred W. Crosby

EUROPEANS IN NORTH AMERICA, especially those with an interest in gardening and botany, are often stricken with fits of homesickness at the sight of certain plants which, like themselves, have somehow strayed thousands of miles eastward across the Atlantic. Vladimir Nabokov, the Russian exile. had such an experience on the mountain slopes of Oregon:

> Do you recognize that clover?
> Dandelions, *l'or du pauvre?*
> (Europe, nonetheless, is over.)

A century earlier the success of European weeds in America inspired Charles Darwin to goad the American botanist, Asa Gray: "Does it not hurt your Yankee pride that we thrash you so confoundly? I am sure Mrs. Gray will stick up for your own weeds. Ask her whether they are not more honest, downright good sort of weeds."[1]

The common dandelion, *l'or du pauvre,* despite its ubiquity and its bright yellow flower, is not at all the most visible of the Old World immigrants in North America. Vladimir Nabokov was a prime example of the most visible kind: the *Homo sapiens* of European origin. Europeans and their descendants, who comprise the majority of human beings in North America and in a number of other lands outside of Europe, are among the most spectacularly successful overseas migrants of all time. How strange it is to find Englishmen, Germans, Frenchmen, Italians, and Spaniards comfortably ensconced in places with names like Wollongong (Australia), Rotorua (New Zealand), and Saskatoon (Canada), where obviously other peoples should dominate, as they must have at one time.

None of the major groupings of humankind is as oddly distributed about the world as European, especially Western European, whites. Almost all the peoples we call Mongoloids live in the single contiguous land mass of Asia. Black Africans are

SOURCE: *Germs, Seeds, and Animals: Studies in Ecological History* (1994).

divided among three continents—their homeland and North and South America—but most of them are concentrated in their original latitudes, the tropics, facing each other across one ocean. European whites were all recently concentrated in Europe, but in the last few centuries have burst out, as energetically as if from a burning building, and have created vast settlements of their kind in the South Temperate Zone and North Temperate Zone (excepting Asia, a continent already thoroughly and irreversibly tenanted). In Canada, the United States, Argentina, Uruguay, Australia, and New Zealand they amount to between 75 and nearly 100 percent of the population. The only nations in the temperate zones outside of Asia that do not have enormous majorities of European whites are Chile, with a population of two-thirds mixed Spanish and Indian stock, and South Africa, where blacks outnumber whites six to one. How odd that these two, so many thousands of miles from Europe, should be exceptions in *not* being predominantly pure European.[2]

THE DEMOGRAPHIC TAKEOVER

Europeans have conquered Canada, the United States, Argentina, Uruguay, Australia, and New Zealand not just militarily, economically, and technologically—as they did India, Nigeria, Mexico, Peru, and other tropical lands, whose native peoples have long since expelled or interbred with and even absorbed the invaders. In the temperate zone lands listed above Europeans conquered and triumphed demographically. These, for the sake of convenience, we will call the Lands of the Demographic Takeover.

There is a long tradition of emphasizing the contrasts between Europeans and North American whites—a tradition honored by such people as Henry James and Frederick Jackson Turner—but the vital question is really why Americans are so European. And why Argentinians, Uruguayans, Australians, and New Zealanders are so European in the obvious genetic sense.

The reasons for the relative failure of the European demographic takeover in the tropics are clear. In tropical Africa, until recently, Europeans died in droves of the fevers; in tropical America they died almost as fast of the same diseases, plus a few native American additions. Furthermore, in neither region did European agricultural techniques, crops, and animals prosper. Europeans did try to found colonies for settlement, rather than merely exploitation, but they failed or achieved only partial success in the hot lands. The Scots left their bones as monument to their short-lived colony at Darien at the turn of the eighteenth century. The English Puritans who skipped Massachusetts Bay Colony to go to Providence Island in the Caribbean Sea did not even achieve a permanent settlement, much less a Commonwealth of God. The Portuguese who went to northeastern Brazil created viable settlements, but only by perching themselves on top of first a population of native Indian laborers and then, when these faded away, a population of laborers imported from Africa. They did achieve a demographic takeover, but only by interbreeding with their servants. The Portuguese in Angola, who helped supply those servants, never had a breath of a chance to achieve a demographic takeover.[3] There was much to repel and little to attract the mass of Europeans to the tropics, and so they stayed home or went to the lands where life was healthier, labor more rewarding, and where white immigrants, by their very numbers, encouraged more immigration.

In the cooler lands, the colonies of the Demographic Takeover, Europeans achieved very rapid population growth by means of immigration, by increased life span, and by maintaining very high birth rates. Rarely has population expanded more rapidly than it did in the eighteenth and nineteenth centuries in these lands. It is these lands, especially the United States, that enabled Europeans and their overseas offspring to expand from something like 18 percent of the human species in 1650 to well over 30 percent in 1900. Today 670 million Europeans live in Europe, and 250 million or so other Europeans—genetically as European as any left behind in the Old World—live in the Lands of the Demographic Takeover, an ocean or so from home.[4] What the Europeans have done with unprecedented success in the past few centuries can accurately be described by a term from agriculture: they have swarmed.[5]

They swarmed to lands that were populated at the time of European arrival by peoples as physically capable of rapid increase as the Europeans, and yet who are now small minorities in their homelands and sometimes no more than relict populations. These population explosions among colonial Europeans of the past few centuries coincided with population crashes among the Aborigines. If overseas Europeans have historically been less fatalistic and grim than their relatives in Europe, it is because they have viewed the histories of their nations very selectively.

Explaining the Takeover

Any respectable theory that attempts to explain the Europeans' demographic triumphs has to provide explanations for at least two phenomena. The first is the decimation and demoralization of the aboriginal populations of Canada, the United States, Argentina, and others. The obliterating defeat of these populations was not simply due to European technological superiority. The Europeans who settled in temperate South Africa seemingly had the same advantages as those who settled in Virginia and New South Wales, and yet how different was their fate. The Bantu-speaking peoples, who now overwhelmingly outnumber the whites in South Africa, were superior to their American, Australian, and New Zealand counterparts in that they possessed iron weapons, but how much more inferior to a musket or a rifle is a stone-pointed spear than an iron-pointed one? The Bantu have prospered demographically not because of their numbers at the time of first contact with whites, which were probably not greater per square mile than those of the Indians east of the Mississippi River. Rather, the Bantu have prospered because they survived military conquest, avoided the conquerors, or became their indispensable servants—and in the long run because they reproduced faster than the whites. In contrast, why did so few of the natives of the Lands of the Demographic Takeover survive the initial century of contact with the invaders?

Second, we must explain the stunning, even awesome success of European agriculture, that is, the European way of manipulating the environment in the Lands of the Demographic Takeover. The difficult progress of the European frontier in the Siberian *taiga* or the Brazilian *sertão* the South African *veldt* contrasts sharply with its easy, almost fluid advance in North America. Of course, the pioneers of North America would never have characterized their progress as easy: their lives were filled with danger, deprivation, and unremitting labor; but as a group they always succeeded in taming whatever portion of North America they wanted within a few decades and usually a good deal less time. Many individuals among them failed—they were driven mad by blizzards and dust storms, lost their crops to locusts and their flocks to cougars and wolves, or lost their scalps to understandably inhospitable Indians—but as a group they always succeeded—and in terms of human generations, very quickly.

In attempting to explain these two phenomena, let us examine four categories of organisms deeply involved in European expansion: (1) human beings; (2) animals closely associated with human beings—both the desirable animals like horses and cattle and undesirable varmints like rats and mice; (3) pathogens or microorganisms that cause disease in humans; and (4) weeds. Is there a pattern in the histories of these groups that suggests an overall explanation for the phenomenon of the Demographic Takeover or that at least suggests fresh paths of inquiry?

HUMAN BEINGS

Europe has exported something in excess of 60 million people in the past few hundred years. Great Britain alone exported over 20 million. The great mass of these white emigrants went to the United States, Argentina, Canada, Australia, Uruguay, and New Zealand. (Other areas to absorb comparable quantities of Europeans were Brazil and Russia east of the Urals. These would qualify as Lands of the Demographic Takeover except that large portions of their populations are not European.[6])

In stark contrast, very few Aborigines of the Americas, Australia, or New Zealand ever went to Europe. Those who did often died not long after arrival.[7] The fact that the flow of human migration was almost entirely from Europe to her colonies and not vice versa is not startling, or very enlightening. Europeans controlled overseas migration, and Europe needed to export, not import, labor. But this pattern of one-way migration is significant in that it reappears in other connections.

ANIMALS

The vast expanses of forests, savannahs, and steppes in the Lands of the Demographic Takeover were inundated by animals from the Old World, chiefly Europe. Horses, cattle, sheep, goats, and pigs have for hundreds of years been among the most numerous of the quadrupeds of these lands, which were completely lacking in these species at the time of first contact with the Europeans. By 1600 enormous feral herds of horses and cattle surged over the pampas of the Río de la Plata (today's Argentina, Uruguay, and southern Brazil) and over the plains of northern Mexico. By the beginning of the seventeenth century packs of Old World dogs gone wild were among the predators of these herds.[8]

In the forested country of British North America, population explosions among imported animals were also spectacular, but only by European standards, not by those of Spanish America. By 1700 pigs were everywhere in tidewater Virginia, and young gentlemen were entertaining themselves by hunting wild horses of the inland counties. In Carolina the herds of cattle were "incredible, being from one to two thousand head in one Man's Possession." In the eighteenth and early nineteenth centuries the advancing European frontier from New England to the Gulf of Mexico was preceded into Indian territory by an avant-garde of semiwild herds of hogs and cattle tended, now and again, by semiwild herdsmen, white and black.[9]

The first English settlers landed in Botany Bay, Australia, in January 1788 with livestock, most of it from the Cape of Good Hope. The pigs and poultry thrived; the cattle did well enough; the sheep, the future source of the colony's good fortune, died fast. Within a few months two bulls and four cows had strayed away. By 1804 the wild herds they founded numbered from three to five thousand head and were in possession of much of the best land between the settlements and the Blue Mountains. If they had ever found their way through the mountains to the grasslands beyond, the history of Australia in the first decades of the nineteenth century might have been one dominated by cattle rather than sheep. As it is, the colonial government wanted the land the wild bulls so ferociously defended, and considered the growing practice of convicts running away to live off the herds as a threat to the whole colony; so the adult cattle were shot and salted down and the calves captured and tamed. The English settlers imported woolly sheep from Europe and sought out the interior pastures for them. The animals multiplied rapidly, and when Darwin made his visit to New South Wales in 1836, there were about a million sheep there for him to see.[10]

The arrival of Old World livestock probably affected New Zealand more radically than any other of the Lands of the Demographic Takeover. Cattle, horses, goats, pigs and—in this land of few or no large predators—even the usually timid sheep went wild. In New Zealand herds of feral farm animals were practicing the ways of their remote ancestors as late as the 1940s and no doubt still run free. Most of the sheep, though, stayed under human control, and within a decade of Great Britain's annexation of New Zealand in 1840, her new acquisition was home to a quarter-million sheep. In 1989 New Zealand had over 55 million sheep, about twenty times more sheep than people.[11]

In the Lands of the Demographic Takeover the European pioneers were accompanied and often preceded by their domesticated animals, walking sources of food, leather, fiber, power, and wealth, and these animals often adapted more rapidly to the new surroundings and reproduced much more rapidly than their masters. To a certain extent, the success of Europeans as colonists was automatic as soon as they put their tough, fast, fertile, and intelligent animals ashore. The latter were sources of capital that sought out their own sustenance, improvised their own protection against the weather, fought their own battles against predators and, if their masters were smart enough to allow calves, colts, and lambs to accumulate, could and often did show the world the amazing possibilities of compound interest.

The honeybee is the one insect of worldwide importance that human beings have domesticated, if we may use the word in a broad sense. Many species of bees and other insects produce honey, but the one that does so in greatest quantity and that is easiest to control is a native of the Mediterranean area and the Middle East, the honey bee (*Apis mellifera*). The European may have taken this sweet and short-tempered servant to every colony he ever established, from Arctic to Antarctic Circle, and the honeybee has always been one of the first immigrants to set off on its own. Sometimes the advance of the bee frontier could be very rapid: the first hive in Tasmania swarmed sixteen times in the summer of 1832.[12]

Thomas Jefferson tells us that the Indians of North America called the honey bees "English flies," and St. John de Crèvecoeur, his contemporary, wrote that "the Indians look upon them with an evil eye, and consider their progress into the interior of the continent as an omen of the white man's approach: thus, as they discover the bees, the news of the event, passing from mouth to mouth, spreads sadness and consternation on all sides."[13]

Domesticated creatures that traveled from the Lands of the Demographic Takeover to Europe are few. Australian Aborigines and New Zealand Maoris had a few tame dogs, unimpressive by Old World standards and unwanted by the whites. Europe happily accepted the American Indians' turkeys and guinea pigs, but had no need for their dogs, llamas, and alpacas. Again the explanation is simple: Europeans, who controlled the passage of large animals across the oceans, had no need to reverse the process.

It is interesting and perhaps significant, though, that the exchange was just as one-sided for varmints, the small mammals whose migrations Europeans often tried to stop. The American or Australian or New Zealand equivalents of rats have not become established in Europe, but Old World varmints, especially rats, have colonized right alongside the Europeans in the temperate zones. Rats of assorted sizes, some of them almost surely European immigrants, were tormenting Spanish Americans by at least the end of the sixteenth century. European rats established a beach-head in Jamestown, Virginia, as early as 1609, when they almost starved out the colonists by eating their food stores. In Buenos Aires the increase in rats kept pace with that of cattle, according to an early nineteenth-century witness. European rats proved as aggressive as the Europeans in New Zealand, where they completely replaced the local rats in North Island as early as the 1840s. Those poor creatures are probably completely extinct today or exist only in tiny relict populations.[14]

The European rabbits are not usually thought of as varmints, but where there are neither diseases nor predators to hold down their numbers they can become the worst of pests. In 1859 a few members of the species *Orytolagus cuniculus* (the scientific name for all the Peter Rabbits of literature) were released in southeast Australia. Despite massive efforts to stop them, they reproduced—true to their reputation—and spread rapidly all the way across Australia's southern half to the Indian Ocean. In 1950 the rabbit population of Australia was estimated at 500 million, and they were outcompeting the nation's most important domesticated animals, sheep, for the grasses and herbs. They have been brought under control, but only by means of artificially fomenting an epidemic of myxomatosis, a lethal American rabbit disease. The story of rabbits and myxomatosis in New Zealand is similar.[15]

Europe, in return for her varmints, has received muskrats and gray squirrels and little else from America, and less from Australia or New Zealand, and we might well wonder if muskrats and squirrels really qualify as varmints.[16] As with other classes of organisms, the exchange has been largely a one-way street.

PATHOGENS

None of Europe's emigrants were as immediately and colossally successful as its pathogens, the microorganisms that make human beings ill, cripple them, and kill them. Whenever and wherever Europeans crossed the oceans to settle outside of the Old World, the pathogens they carried created prodigious epidemics of smallpox, measles, influenza, and a number of other diseases. These pathogens, unlike the Europeans themselves or most of their domesticated animals, did at least as well in the tropics as in the temperate Lands of the Demographic Takeover. Epidemics devastated Mexico, Peru, Brazil, Hawaii, and Tahiti soon after the Europeans made the first contact with aboriginal populations. Some of these populations were able to escape demographic defeat because their initial numbers were so large that a small fraction was still sufficient to maintain occupation of, if not title to, the land, and also because the mass of Europeans were never attracted to the tropical lands, even if they were partially vacated. In the Lands of the Demographic Takeover the aboriginal populations were too sparse to rebound from the onslaught of disease or were inundated by European immigrants before they could recover.

The first strike force of the white immigrants to the Lands of the Demographic Takeover were epidemics. A few examples from scores of possible examples follow. Smallpox first arrived in the Río de la Plata region in 1558 or 1560 and killed, according to one chronicler possibly more interested in effect than accuracy, "more than a hundred thousand Indians" of the heavy riverine population there. An epidemic of plague or typhus decimated the Indians of the New England coast immediately before the founding of Plymouth. Smallpox or something similar struck the Aborigines of Australia's Botany Bay in 1789, killed half, and rolled on into the interior. Some unidentified disease or diseases spread through the Maori tribes of the North Island of New Zealand in the 1790s, killing so many in a number of villages that the survivors were not able to bury the dead.[17] After a series of such lethal and rapidly moving epidemics came the slow, unspectacular but thorough cripplers and killers like venereal disease and tuberculosis. In conjunction with the large numbers of white settlers, these diseases were enough to smother aboriginal chances of recovery. First the blitzkrieg, then the mopping up.

The greatest of the killers in these lands was probably smallpox. The exception is New Zealand, the last of these lands to attract permanent European settlers. Europeans came to New Zealand after the spread of vaccination in Europe and so were poor carriers. As of the 1850s, smallpox still had not come ashore, and by that time two-thirds of the Maori had been vaccinated.[18] The tardy arrival of smallpox in these islands may have much to do with the fact that the Maori today comprise a larger percentage (9 percent) of their country's population than that of any other aboriginal people in any European colony or former European colony in either temperate zone, save only South Africa.

American Indians bore the full brunt of smallpox, and its mark is on their history and folklore. The Kiowa of the southern plains of the United States have a legend in which a Kiowa man meets Smallpox on the plain, riding a horse. The man asks, "Where do you come from and what do you do and why are you here?" Smallpox answers, "I am one with the white men—they are my people as the Kiowas are yours. Sometimes I travel ahead of them and sometimes behind. But I am always their companion and you will find me in their camps and their houses." "What can you do?" the Kiowa asks. "I bring death," Smallpox replies. "My breath causes children to wither like young plants in spring snow. I bring destruction. No matter how beautiful a woman is, once she has looked at me she becomes as ugly as death. And to men I bring not death alone, but the destruction of their children and the blighting of their wives. The strongest of warriors go down before me. No people who have looked on me will ever be the same."[19]

Europeans received little in return for the barrage of diseases they directed overseas. Australia and New Zealand provided no new strains of pathogens to Europe—or none that attracted attention. And of America's native diseases, none had any real influence on the Old World—with the possible exception of venereal syphilis, which almost certainly existed in the New World before 1492 and probably did not occur in its present form in the Old World.[20]

WEEDS

Weeds are rarely history makers, for they are not as spectacular in their effects as pathogens. But they, too, influence our lives and migrate over the world despite human wishes. As such, like varmints and germs, they are better indicators of certain realities than human beings or domesticated animals.

The term *weed* in modern botanical usage refers to any type of plant which—because of especially large numbers of seeds produced per plant, or especially effective means of distributing those seeds, or especially tough roots and rhizomes from which new plants can grow, or especially tough seeds that survive the alimentary canals of animals to be planted with their droppings—spreads rapidly and outcompetes others on disturbed, bare soil. Weeds are plants that tempt the botanist to use such anthropomorphic words as "aggressive" and "opportunistic."

Many of the most successful weeds in the well-watered regions of the Lands of the Demographic Takeover are of European or Eurasian origin. French and Dutch and English farmers brought with them to North America their worst enemies, weeds, "to exhaust the land, hinder and damnify the Crop."[21] By the last third of the seventeenth century at least twenty different types were widespread enough in New England to attract the attention of the English visitor, John Josselyn, who identified couch grass, dandelion, nettles, mallowes, knot grass, shepherd's purse, sow thistle, clot burr, and others. One of the most aggressive was plantain, which the Indians called "English-Man's Foot."[22]

European weeds rolled west with the pioneers, in some cases spreading almost explosively. As of 1823, corn chamomile and maywood had spread up to but not across the Muskingum River in Ohio. Eight years later they had crossed the river.[23] The most prodigiously imperialistic of the weeds in the eastern half of the United States and Canada were probably Kentucky bluegrass and white clover. They spread so fast after the entrance of Europeans into a given area that there is some suspicion that they may have been present in pre-Columbian America, although the earliest European accounts do not mention them. Probably brought to the Appalachian area by the French, these two kinds of weeds preceded the English settlers there and kept up with the movement westward until reaching the plains across the Mississippi.[24]

Old World plants set up business on their own on the Pacific coast of North America just as soon as the Spaniards and Russians did. The climate of coastal southern California is much the same as that of the Mediterranean, and the Spaniards who came to California in the eighteenth century brought their own Mediterranean weeds with them via Mexico: wild oats, fennel, wild radishes. These plants, plus those brought in later by the forty-niners, muscled their way to dominance in the coastal grasslands. These immigrant weeds followed Old World horses, cattle, and sheep into California's interior prairies and took over there as well.[25]

The region of Argentina and Uruguay was as radically altered in its flora as in its fauna by the coming of the Europeans. The ancient Indian practice, taken up immediately by the whites, of burning off the old grass of the pampa every year, as well as the trampling and cropping to the ground of indigenous grasses and forbs by the thousands of imported quadrupeds who also changed the nature of the soil with their droppings, opened the whole countryside to European plants. In the 1780s, Félix de Azara observed that the pampa, already radically altered, was changing as he watched. European weeds sprang up around every cabin, grew up along roads, and pressed into the open steppe. Today only a quarter of the plants growing wild in the pampa are native, and in the well-watered eastern portions, the "natural" ground cover consists almost entirely of Old World grasses and clovers.[26]

The invaders were not, of course, always desirable. When Darwin visited Uruguay in 1832, he found large expanses, perhaps as much as hundreds of square miles, monopolized by the immigrant wild artichoke and transformed into a prickly wilderness fit for neither humanity nor its animals.[27]

The onslaught of foreign and specifically European plants on Australia began abruptly in 1778 because the first expedition that sailed from Britain to Botany Bay carried some livestock and considerable quantities of seed. By May 1803 over two hundred foreign plants, most of them European, had been purposely introduced and planted in New South Wales, undoubtedly along with a number of weeds.[28] Even today so-called "clean seed" characteristically contains some weed seeds, and this was much more so two hundred years ago. By and large, Australia's north has been too tropical and her interior too hot and dry for European weeds and grasses, but much of her southern coasts and Tasmania have been hospitable indeed to Europe's willful flora.

Thus, many—often a majority—of the most aggressive plants in the temperate humid regions of North America, South America, Australia, and New Zealand are of European origin. It may be true that in every broad expanse of the world today where there are dense populations, with whites in the majority, there are also dense populations of European weeds. Thirty-five of eighty-nine weeds listed in 1953 as common in the state of New York are European. Approximately 60 percent of Canada's worst weeds are introductions from Europe. Most of New Zealand's weeds are from the same source, as are many, perhaps most, of the weeds of Australia's well-watered southern coasts. Most of the European plants that Josselyn listed as naturalized in New England in the seventeenth century are growing wild today in Argentina and Uruguay, and are among the most widespread and troublesome of all weeds in those countries.[29]

In return for this largesse of pestiferous plants, the Lands of the Demographic Takeover have provided Europe with only a few equivalents. The Canadian waterweed jammed Britain's nineteenth-century waterways, and North America's horseweed and burnweed have spread in Europe's empty lots, and South America's flowered galinsoga has thrived in her gardens. But the migratory flow of a whole group of organisms between Europe and the Lands of the Demographic Takeover has been almost entirely in one direction.[30] Englishman's Foot still marches in seven-league jackboots across every European colony of settlement, but very few American or Australian or New Zealand invaders stride the wastelands and unkempt backyards of Europe.

CONCLUSION

European and Old World human beings, domesticated animals, varmints, pathogens, and weeds all accomplished demographic takeovers of their own in the temperate, well-watered regions of North and South America, Australia, and New Zealand. They crossed oceans and Europeanized vast territories, often in informal cooperation with each other—the farmer and his animals destroying native plant cover, making way for imported grasses and forbs, many of which proved more nourishing to domesticated animals than the native equivalents; Old World pathogens, sometimes carried by Old World varmints, wiping out vast numbers of Aborigines, opening the way for the advance of the European frontier, exposing more and more native peoples to more and more pathogens. The classic example of symbiosis between European colonists, their animals, and plants comes from New Zealand. Red clover, a good forage for sheep, could not seed itself and did not spread without being annually sown until the Europeans imported the bumblebee. Then the plant and insect spread widely, the first providing the second with food, the second carrying pollen from blossom to blossom for the first, and the sheep eating the clover and compensating human beings for their effort with mutton and wool.[31]

There have been few such stories of the success in Europe of organisms from the Lands of the Demographic Takeover, despite the obvious fact that for every ship that went from Europe to those lands, another traveled in the opposite direction.

The demographic triumph of Europeans in the temperate colonies is one part of a biological and ecological takeover that could not have been accomplished by human beings alone, gunpowder notwithstanding. We must at least try to analyze the impact and success of often mutually supportive plants, animals, and microlife, which in their entirety can be accurately described as aggressive and opportunistic, an ecosystem simplified by ocean crossings and honed by thousands of years of competition in the unique environment created by the Old World Neolithic Revolution.

The human invaders and their descendants have consulted their egos, rather than ecologists, for explanations of their triumphs. But the human victims, the Aborigines of the Lands of the Demographic Takeover, knew better, knew they were only one of the many categories being displaced and replaced; they knew they were victims of something more irresistible and awesome than the spread of capitalism or Christianity. One Maori, at the nadir of the history of his race, expressed this when he said, "As the clover killed off the fern, and the European dog the Maori dog—as the Maori rat was destroyed by the Pakeha [European] rat—so our people, also, will be gradually supplanted and exterminated by the Europeans."[32] The future was not so grim as he prophesied, but we must admire his grasp of the complexity and magnitude of the threat looming over his people and over the ecosystem of which they were a part.

NOTES

1. Page Stegner, ed., *The Portable Nabakov* (New York: Viking, 1968), 527; Francis Darwin, ed., *Life and Letters of Charles Darwin* (London: Murray, 1887), 2:391.

2. *The World Almanac and Book of Facts 1993* (New York: Pharos Books, 1992), passim.

3. Philip D. Curtin, "Epidemiology and the Slave Trade," *Political Science Quarterly* 83 (June 1968): 190–216 passim; John Prebble, *The Darien Disaster* (New York: Holt, Rinehart and Winston, 1968), 296, 300; Charles M. Andrews, *The Colonial Period of American History* (New Haven: Yale University Press, 1934), vol. 1, n. 497; Gilberto Freyre, *The Masters and the Slaves*, trans. Samuel Putnam (New York: Knopf, 1946), passim; Donald L. Wiedner, *A History of Africa South of the Sahara* (New York: Vintage Books, 1964), 49–51; Stuart B. Schwartz, "Indian Labor and New World Plantations: European Demands and Indian Responses in Northeastern Brazil," *American Historical Review* 83 (February 1978): 43–79 passim.

4. Marcel R. Reinhard, *Histoire de la population mondiale de 1700 à 1948* (n.p.: Editions Domat-Montchrestien, n.d.), 339–411, 428–31; G. F. McCleary, *Peopling the British Commonwealth* (London: Farber and Farber, n.d.), 83, 94, 109–10; R. R. Palmer and Joel Colton, *A History of the Modern World* (New York: Knopf, 1965), 560; *World Almanac and Book of Facts, 1978* (New York: Newspaper Enterprise Association, 1978), 34, 439, 497, 513, 590.

5. Charles Darwin, *The Voyage of the Beagle* (Garden City, N.Y.: Doubleday Anchor Books, 1962), 433–34.

6. William Woodruff, *Impact of Western Man* (New York: St. Martin's, 1967), 106–8.

7. Carolyn T. Foreman, *Indians Abroad* (Norman: University of Oklahoma Press, 1943), passim.

8. Alfred W. Crosby, *The Columbian Exchange: Biological and Cultural Consequences of 1492* (Westport, Conn.: Greenwood, 1972), 82–88; Alexander Gillespie, *Gleanings and Remarks Collected during Many Months of Residence at Buenos Aires* (Leeds: B. DeWhirst, 1818), 136; Oscar Schmieder, "Alteration of the Argentine Pampa in the Colonial Period," *University of California Publications in Geography* 2 (September 27, 1927): n. 311.

9. Robert Beverley, *History and Present State of Virginia* (Chapel Hill: University of North Carolina Press, 1947), 153, 312, 318; John Lawson, *A New Voyage to Carolina* (Chester, Vt.: Readex Microprint Corp.,

1966), 4; Frank L. Owsley, "The Pattern of Migration and Settlement of the Southern Frontier," *Journal of Southern History* 11 (May 1945): 147–75.

10. Commonwealth of Australia, *Historical Records of Australia* (Sydney: Library Committee of the Commonwealth Parliament, 1914), ser. 1, vol. 1, 550; vol. 7, 379–80, vol. 8, 150–51; vol. 9, 349, 714, 831; vol. 10, 92, 280, 682; vol. 20, 839.

11. Andrew H. Clark, *The Invasion of New Zealand by People, Plants, and Animals* (New Brunswick, N.J.: Rutgers University Press, 1949), 190; *The World Almanac and Book of Facts 1993* (New York: Pharos Books, 1992), 783.

12. Remy Chauvin, *Traité de biologic de l'abeille* (Paris: Masson et Cie, 1968), 1:38–39; James Backhouse, *A Narrative of a Visit to the Australian Colonies* (London: Hamilton, Adams and Co., 1834), 23.

13. Merrill D. Peterson, ed., *The Portable Thomas Jefferson* (New York: Viking, 1975), 111; Michel-Guillaume St. Jean de Crèvecoeur, *Journey into Northern Pennsylvania and the State of New York,* trans. Clarissa S. Bostelmann (Ann Arbor: University of Michigan Press, 1964), 166.

14. Bermabé Cobo, *Obras* (Madrid: Atlas Ediciones, 1964), 1:350–51; Edward Arber, ed., *Travels and Works of Captain John Smith* (New York: Burt Franklin, n.d.), 2:xcv; K. A. Wodzicki, *Introduced Mammals of New Zealand* (Wellington: Department of Scientific and Industrial Research, 1950), 89–92.

15. Frank Fernner and F. N. Ratcliffe, *Myxamatosis* (Cambridge: Cambridge University Press, 1965), 9, 11, 17, 22–23; Frank Fenner, "The Rabbit Plague," *Scientific American* 190 (February 1954): 30–35; Wodzicki, *Introduced Mammals,* 107–41.

16. Charles S. Elton, *The Ecology of Invasions* (Trowbridge and London: English Language Book Society, 1972), 24–25, 28, 73, 123.

17. Juan López de Velasco, *Geografía y descripción universal de las Indias* (Madrid: Establecimiento Topográfico de Fortanet, 1894), 552; Oscar Schmieder, "The Pampa—A Natural and Culturally Induced Grassland?" *University of California Publications in Geography* (September 27, 1927): 266; Sherburne F. Cook, "The Significance of Disease in the Extinction of the New England Indians," *Human Biology* 14 (September 1975): 486–91; J. H. L. Cumpston, *The History of Smallpox in Australia, 1788–1908* (Melbourne: Albert J. Mullet, Government Printer, 1914), 147–49; Harrison M. Wright, *New Zealand, 1769–1840* (Cambridge: Harvard University Press, 1959), 62. For further discussion of this topic, see Crosby, *The Columbian Exchange,* chaps. 1 and 2; Crosby, *Ecological Imperialism: The Biological Expansion of Europe, 900–1900* (Cambridge: Cambridge University Press, 1986); and Henry F. Dobyns, *Native American Demography: A Critical Bibliography* (Bloomington: Indiana University Press/Newberry Library, 1976).

18. Arthur C. Thomson, *The Story of New Zealand* (London: Murray, 1859), 1:212.

19. Alice Marriott and Carol K. Rachlin, *American Indian Mythology* (New York: New American Library, 1968), 174–75.

20. Crosby, *The Columbian Exchange,* 122–64, passim.

21. Jared Eliot, "The Tilling of the Land, 1760," in *Agriculture in the United States: A Documentary History,* ed. Wayne D. Rasmussen (New York: Random House, 1975), 1:192.

22. John Josselyn, *New England's Rarities Discovered* (London: G. Widdowes at the Green Dragon in St. Paul's Church-yard, 1672), 85, 86; Edmund Berkeley and Dorothy S. Berkeley, eds., *The Reverend John Clayton* (Charlottesville: University of Virginia Press, 1965), 24.

23. Lewis D. de Shweinitz, "Remarks on the Plants of Europe Which Have Become Naturalized in a More or Less Degree, in the United States," *Annals Lyceum of Natural History of New York* 3 (1832): 1828–36, 155.

24. Lyman Carrier and Katherine S. Bort, "The History of Kentucky Bluegrass and White Clover in the United States," *Journal of the American Society of Agronomy* 8 (1916): 255–56; Robert W. Schery, "The Migration of a Plant: Kentucky Bluegrass Followed Settlers to the New World," *Natural History* 74 (December 1965): 43–44; G. W. Dunbar, "Henry Clay on Kentucky Bluegrass," *Agricultural History* 51 (July 1977): 522.

25. Edgar Anderson, *Plants, Man, and Life* (Berkeley and Los Angeles: University of California Press, 1967), 12–15; Elna S. Bakker, *An Island Called California* (Berkeley and Los Angeles: University of California Press, 1971), 150–52; R. W. Allard, "Genetic Systems Associated with Colonizing Ability in Predominantly Self-Pollinated Species," in *The Genetics of Colonizing Species,* ed. H. G. Baker and G. Ledyard Stebbins (New York: Academic Press, 1965), 50; M. W. Talbot, H. M. Biswell, and A. L. Hormay, "Fluctuations in the Annual Vegetation of California," *Ecology* 20 (July 1939): 396–97.

26. Félix de Azara, *Descripción e historia del Paraguay y del Río de la Plata* (Madrid: Imprenta de Sánchez, 1847), 1:57–58; Schmieder, "Alteration of the Argentine Pampa," 310–11.

27. Darwin, *Voyage of the Beagle,* 119–20.

28. *Historical Records of Australia,* ser. 1, vol. 4, 234–41.

29. Edward Salisbury, *Weeds and Aliens* (London: Collins, 1961), 87; Angel Julio Cabrera, *Manual de la flora de los alrededores de Buenos Aires* (Buenos Aires: Editorial Acme S.A., 1953), passim.

30. Elton, *The Ecology of Invasions,* 115; Hugo Ilitis, "The Story of Wild Garlic," *Scientific Monthly* 68 (February 1949): 122–24.

31. Otto E. Plath, *Bumblebees and Their Ways* (New York: Macmillan, 1934), 115.

32. James Bonwick, *The Last of the Tasmanians* (New York: Johnson Reprint Co., 1970), 380.

4

AMERINDIAN VIEWS OF FRENCH CULTURE IN THE SEVENTEENTH CENTURY

Cornelius J. Jaenen

Ever since the late fifteenth century, Europeans were eager to read about the native peoples of the Western Hemisphere. When French colonizers arrived in America in the sixteenth century, they followed in the literary path established by Columbus and others, recognizing that they had to let those who remained in Europe know what the Indians were like. As a result, the sources they left behind offer rich testimony about native ways. Rich, too, in these texts, are the insights into European attitudes toward Native Americans.

Those same sources, as Cornelius J. Jaenen shows here, also provide clues to what Indians thought about the newcomers. By reading between the lines, using the colonists' own accounts of Indian beliefs, historians can ferret out a native point of view long thought lost. The result is revealing. Rather than awed by Europeans, many Indians in the St. Lawrence Valley and the Maritime Provinces of modern-day Canada believed that colonists were hopelessly inferior. Natives could not understand why, for example, men and women in New France could go hungry if there was sufficient food to feed everyone; they rejected as well the alleged superiority of monotheism and other facets of colonial culture. It is useful, as well, to compare the views of Canada's First Nations described here to the ideas of Indians in territory colonized by the Spanish and the English.

AMERINDIAN VIEWS OF FRENCH CULTURE
IN THE SEVENTEENTH CENTURY[1]

Cornelius J. Jaenen

OUR HISTORIOGRAPHY has been more concerned with French and Canadian views of the Amerindians than with aboriginal opinions and evaluations of the French culture with which they came into contact during the seventeenth century.[2] Yet, the most elementary canons of historical interpretation require that the values and belief systems of both parties concerned in the contact experience be considered. In general, it has been assumed by historians that not only did Frenchmen consider their civilization superior to the aboriginal cultures of North America but also that the native tribesmen viewed French culture with awe and admiration, that they often attempted to imitate the Europeans, and usually aspired to elevate themselves to the superior level of the white man. This interpretation was firmly established in European and Canadian literature by Charlevoix, Raynal, Chateaubriand, and Bossange.[3]

Not until the mid-nineteenth century was there any notable departure from this accepted approach to French-Amerindian relations. While it is true that a few earlier French writers had been critical of the ideas and ideals of their compatriots in comparison with native behavior, such critical observations were invariably motivated by desires for political and social reforms, by religious toleration, or by skepticism that related to France more than to North America. Clodoré, Abbeville, de Léry, Boyer, Sagard, and Lescarbot made guarded criticisms of French behavior and institutions employing Amerindian examples to strengthen their arguments.[4] Maximilien Bibaud was the first French-Canadian to depict the Amerindians in a consistently favorable light. He was fully conscious, moreover, that the aborigines had resisted francization and, in the majority, had rejected conversion.[5] Napoléon Legendre pleaded eloquently in 1884 for an impartial and just treatment of Amerindian history, but his was still a voice of one crying in the wilderness.[6]

It is therefore only quite recently that the sources for the traditional views of the contact experience have been reexamined more critically and that the accepted interpretations have been challenged. In 1903, Léon Gérin began to study the natives of New France in a new conceptual framework, but his work went largely unnoticed by

SOURCE: *Canadian Historical Review* 55 (1974): 261–91.

his contemporaries. In 1925, F. W. Howay attempted to present the aboriginal case and his pioneer work was followed by Diamond Jenness's *The Indians of Canada* (1932) and A. G. Bailey's *The Conflict of European and Eastern Algonkian Cultures, 1504–1700* (1937). More significant still in setting the state for a thorough-going revision of Amerindian History have been the writings of Jacques Rousseau, Léo-Paul Desrosiers, and André Vachon.[7]

To delineate Amerindian views of French culture and civilization at the time of contact in the seventeenth century is extremely difficult because, first of all, an understanding of both French culture and Amerindian cultures is necessary. More information about French culture in the seventeenth century is available than about Micmac, Montagnais, Algonquian, Huron, and Iroquois cultures, which were described by French travelers, missionaries, and traders as seen through their own understanding of such cultures and interpreted according to their values and beliefs. The missionaries, as France's foremost cultural ambassadors at the time, tended to undervalue tribal customs and practices, but they soon found that the Amerindians were secure, well-adjusted, and self-reliant peoples. As early as 1616 the report back to France was: "For all your arguments, and you can bring a thousand of them if you wish, are annihilated by this single shaft which they always have at hand, *Aoti Chabaya*, (they say) 'That is the Savage way of doing it. You can have your way and we will have ours; every one values his own wares.' "[8] The historian's task is to attempt to understand both cultures in contact.

Secondly, past events must not only be identified but also be interpreted in the manner seen by each of the participants involved. As the archaeologists have contributed much to an understanding of Amerindian cultures, so the ethnohistorians and anthropologists have contributed to an understanding of the moral assumptions and value systems involved. As Wilcomb Washburn has said, "an understanding of conflicting value seems to be a condition of great history, great imaginative writing, and great religious insight."[9] At least one of the missionaries to the Micmacs realized that French and Algonquian value systems and moral assumptions differed greatly. He wrote: "You must know that the are men like us; that intrinsically they reason as all men must think; that they differ only in the manner of rendering their thoughts, and that if something appears strange to us in their way of thinking it is because we have not been educated like them, and we do not find ourselves in a similar situation to theirs, to reach such conclusions."[10] The inability to understand behavior and thought as conceived by the various Amerindian cultures was the greatest barrier to French appreciation of native civilization, and it remains a formidable challenge to the modern historian who attempts to explain and evaluate the contact experience.

The Amerindians, as a nonliterate society, left few documents to assist in reconstructing their views and concepts. The majority of documentary sources are European and, therefore, although designated as primary sources, are interpretations as well as records of events. On the other hand, it can be argued that the recorders were also participants and that this gave them a distinctive advantage over today's social scientists who are deprived of the experience of being eyewitnesses and participants.

It is true that the early observers of native reactions to contact with Frenchmen had commercial, religious, and military interests in the Amerindians and that they studied aboriginal society largely in order to discover vulnerable points that could be exploited to the achievement of their objectives. Nevertheless, in their records, which were sometimes quite comprehensive, they unwittingly related incidents and conversations which enabled one to reconstruct Amerindian reactions motivated by beliefs and objectives which the chroniclers frequently ignored.

Moreover, there are few model studies to guide one through the labyrinth of traditional views, or of narrowly professional views such as the stress placed by the anthropologists on material culture. Acculturation is a two-way process, and important as was the French impact on Amerindian cultures, the aboriginal impact on French culture was continuous and significant. These facts cannot be ignored in the study of Amerindian opinions and evaluations of French culture during the early contact period.

These initial contacts strengthened the Eurocentric view of history. In the seventeenth century Europeans invariably assumed that Europe was the center of the world and of civilization, that its cultures were the oldest, that America was a new continent and that its peoples were necessarily recent immigrants. The literature of the period of exploration was dominated by the theme of a New World populated by peoples of different languages and cultures who conducted European explorers and "discoverers" on tours along well-known and well-traveled water routes and trails to the various centers of aboriginal population. The conceptual frameworks of Europeans—whether Spaniards, French, or English, or whether Catholics or Protestants—were remarkably indistinguishable whenever the circumstances of contact were similar. Explorers were fed, sheltered, offered the other amenities of social life, and provided with multilingual guides. In this context Europeans tended to see themselves and their activities as being at the center of the historical stage.

The French did distinguish, nevertheless, cultural differences among the tribes or "nations" they contacted, although contemporary literature is remarkable for the absence of differentiation on the basis of "race" or pigmentation. On the basis of differences in language and in observable customs and beliefs there was an awareness of the great cultural diversity of the native peoples. It may be postulated, therefore, that the views of Micmacs or Montagnais would differ from the views of the Huron or Iroquois. There are a few indications of different reactions but these can usually be associated with the context of contact rather than with conceptual variations. The nomadic Algonquian cultures were sufficiently different from the Iroquoian groups to elicit varying responses to the French presence, yet the records available to the historian indicate a similarity of response to European intrusion. As there appears now to have been much more of a common European concept of America—rather than markedly different Spanish, French, and English conceptual frameworks—so there appears to have been more of a common Amerindian reaction to the coming of the Europeans than different Micmac, Huron, or Iroquois responses, with the differences in so-called tribal relations with the French better identified in terms of specific and immediate economic and sociopolitical problems. In other words, it is as justifiable to conceive of

Amerindian views of French culture as of European views of the New World, when examining the conceptual frameworks of a generalized culture contact over a period of a century. Such an approach would be less satisfactory if dealing with more specific contact experiences in restricted time periods.

There were a number of features of French life that the Amerindians found admirable and their curiosity was reinforced by a desire to adapt some of the French ways and equipment to their own culture. First of all, they were interested in observing the Europeans in their day-to-day activities. Lescarbot recorded that "the savages from all the country round came to look at the ways of the French, and willingly came among them."[11] Similarly, the Algonquins were amazed at Champlain's men: "The bulk of the savages who were there had never seen a Christian, and could not get over their wonder as they gazed at our customs, our clothing, our arms, our equipment."[12] The Iroquois who held Father Jogues prisoner questioned him at great length about scientific matters and were so impressed by his wisdom and explanations that they regretted the tortures they had inflicted upon him. The greatest appreciation seems to have been for European technology. All tribes showed an appreciation of the knives, hatchets, kettles, beads, cloth, and, eventually, the firearms of the French. Indeed the exchange of the beaver pelt coats worn by the tribesmen of the Atlantic coastal region for European iron goods had been initiated by the Breton, Basque, Norman, and other Western European fishermen at least in the fifteenth century, if not earlier. During the sixteenth century Cartier's accounts, among others, recorded the Amerindian desire to pursue barter. His records of the 1545 voyage in the Gaspé region included the following passage about noisy warriors making signs and "holding up skins on the end of sticks," which they obviously wished to exchange for European goods: ". . . two of our men landed to approach them, and bring them knives and other ironware, with a red hat to give to their captain. Seeing this, they also landed, carrying these skins of theirs, and began to trade with us, showing great and marvellous joy to possess this ironware and other such articles, dancing continually and going through various ceremonies . . ."[13] In 1536 he recorded that each day natives approached his vessel with eels and fish to exchange for European goods: ". . . in return they were given knives, awls, beads, and other such things, wherewith they were much pleased."[14] In time, the coastal tribes became more exacting in their bartering operations. In 1623, for example, the Montagnais objected to the gift of a few figs that the French sea captain had offered them and seized knives and other trade goods saying they would give a fair price for the articles taken. Sagard, who reported the incident, was amazed that the Montagnais not only left furs in payment but did so in quantities that outstripped the value of the goods they had seized.[15]

It should be remarked that originally the fur trade was a noneconomic exchange between fishermen and aborigines, at least in the sense that for the natives noncommercial motives operated. Furs were given to Europeans because they were desired by the visiting fishermen and it was part of Algonquian culture to view exchange in noncommercial terms.[16] They gave their peltries without apparent demand for return, at least at the time of the initial contacts; nevertheless, whatever the fishermen offered in exchange was gratefully accepted. There is reason to believe that the Amerindians valued European trade goods such as beads, mirrors, bells, and caps, for their aesthetic, magical, or purely decorative and fascinating worth, not their economic value.[17] Furthermore, this exchange, for the Amerindians, had a symbolic or diplomatic meaning and was in reality viewed as an exchange of gifts that established rank and prestige. Cartier's journals seem to indicate this to have been the context of the exchanges in the sixteenth century. This difference between European and Amerindian concepts continued into the seventeenth century and was demonstrated in the special meaning the tribesmen attached to the wampum belt, the calumet, or even the hatchet. The French traders and missionaries, both of whom shared the same economic views, regarded wampum in materialistic terms whereas the Amerindians viewed it in symbolic terms. Amerindian admiration of trade goods brought them inevitably into a position of dependence on the French trade. Denys remarked on the changing values among the Micmacs: "They have abandoned all their own utensils, whether because of the trouble they had as well to make as to use them, or because of the facility of obtaining from us, in exchange for skins which cost them almost nothing, the things which seemed to them invaluable, not so much for their novelty as for the convenience derived therefrom. Above everything the kettle has always seemed to them, and seems still, the most valuable article they can obtain from us."[18] He related how a Micmac sent by Governor Razilly to Paris, while passing the street where many coppersmiths were located, asked of his interpreter if they were not "relatives of the king" and if this were not the "trade of the grandest Seignoirs of the Kingdom"!

The Amerindians did not always understand French concepts of personal property, their materialistic outlook as evidenced in their desire to accumulate goods, and their fear of losing personal belongings to covetous colleagues. They expected the French to have a better developed sense of kin-group belongings, of sharing of goods, of using the goods or utensils of others if there was urgent need to do so without the formalities of ownership intervening in such cases, and of showing more respect for articles to which ceremonial or magical qualities were attached. Father Sagard reported at Tadoussac in 1617 that the Montagnais were surprisingly honest compared to Frenchmen and saw no risk in leaving their boats unattended over long periods on the beaches and never stole the boats left by the French.[19] Nevertheless, the Micmacs learned, from their experience over a century with European fishermen and traders, that they could exact more and better quality goods for their furs as the competition grew. Lescarbot said: ". . . so great has been the greed that in their jealousy of one another the merchants have spoiled the trade. Eight years ago, for two biscuits or two knives, one had a beaver, while to-day one must give fifteen or twenty: and in this very year 1610 some have given away to the savages their whole stock in trade, in order to obstruct the holy enterprise of M. de Poutrincourt, so great is human avarice."[20] The Montagnais who had come to trade at Tadoussac in March 1611 were reported as having brought only poor quality furs "and even these few they are fain to employ to the best advantage while awaiting the arrival of a crowd of vessel . . . to have their goods better cheap; wherein they are well skilled now that the avarice of our merchants has made itself known in those parts."[21]

Their developing interest in large-scale trade led them to acquire a taste for brandy and other intoxicants which they soon came to demand and to expect a concomitant of contact. A Dutch version of Denys' history recounted how the aborigines stood along the shores where fishing vessels were known to come and how they made smoke signals to the crews of vessels they sighted inviting them to come to barter for furs: "The skins are bartered for brandy, for which they ever since they have begun to trade with fishermen are very greedy; and they herewith fill themselves up to such an extent that they frequently fall over backwards, for they do not call it drinking unless they overload themselves with this strong drink in a beastly fashion."[22] Whatever the reasons for the low tolerance the Amerindians had for alcohol and their eventual social disorganization as a consequence of its nefarious traffic, it is clear from contemporary sources that they developed an inordinate desire for it. It would appear that, although they never liked its taste and they deplored the violence and disorders they committed under its influence, they coveted it in order to obtain release from their cultural and natural inhibitions, to commit unconventional and illegal acts, to attain a new state of spirit possession, and eventually to reduce the tensions they experienced as a result of the contact with purveyors of an alien civilization which gradually undermined their ancestral way of life, eroded their belief system, and left them alienated from their traditions. Alcohol was a major contributor to the breakdown of Amerindian cultural patterns; nevertheless, it was employed by some tribesmen to create or symbolize in-group solidarity against the French, a rejection of European standards and values, and a defiance of teachings of the Catholic church and of the threatening edicts of the French state.

The Amerindians were very impressed with the French regard for ceremony and for ritual. The French willingness to engage in ceremonial preludes to trading engagements, to military talks, and to parleys brought the two cultures together. There is some indication also that the tribesmen in general were impressed with the ritual and ceremony of the Catholic religion, although on this score there seems to have been considerable concern among the early Catholic missionaries and Governors that the Amerindians also found the congregational singing of the "sons of Marot" and the participatory worship of the Huguenots very attractive.[23] A missionary wrote with obvious satisfaction: "I say nothing of the esteem manifested by this new Church for all The outward signs of our holy Religion. Crosses, medals, and other similar Articles are their most precious jewels. So fondly do they preserve These that they wear them around their necks, even at preaching in New Holland, where The heretics have never been able to tear from Them a single bead of Their Rosaries."[24]

In addition to the beautiful ritual of the mass, the solemn processions and the adoration of the Blessed Sacrament, the secular celebrations of the French impressed the natives. The celebration in 1639 at Quebec upon receipt of the news of the birth of the future Louis XIV was recorded as follows:

> Bon-fires were built with all possible ceremony, rockets were discharged, Roman candles flared, golden rain descended, the night was illuminated with tapers, and the forest resounded with the thunder of guns. On this occasion the Hurons were

present, since they were paying their customary visit to Quebec, which is the market of the whole country. They had never seen the like before and astounded and amazed they put their right hands to their mouths, which is their method of exhibiting joyous emotion.[25]

The French for a long time held to the idea of bringing a few natives from each tribe to France to impress them with France's might and civilization. Lahontan told of six *sagamos* at Versailles at one time, all soliciting aid against the English. But Lahontan inferred that the chieftains were less interested in the beauty and grandeur of Versailles than they were in employing French power and wealth for the achievements of their own ends. Eventually the French Crown concluded that the Amerindians were sufficiently aware of the military might of France and that the bringing of representatives to France was unnecessary. The French did sense the native appreciation of presents, however, and they satisfied them in this matter. LeClercq explained this need of recognition, this need for prestige and security:

> They are fond of ceremony and are anxious to be accorded some when they come to trade at French establishments; and it is consequently in order to satisfy them that sometimes the guns and even the canon are fired on their arrival. The leader himself assembles all the canoes near his own and ranges them in good order before landing, in order to await the salute which is given him, and which all the Indians return to the French by the discharge of their guns. Sometimes the leaders and chiefs are invited for a meal in order to show all the Indians that they are esteemed and honoured. Rather more frequently they are given something like a fine coat, in order to distinguish them from the commonalty. For such things as this they have a particular esteem, especially if the article has been in use by the commander of the French.[26]

Here was a fortunate culture convergence; the French held views of precedence as this related to concepts of rank, estate, dignity, *splendeur*. The Amerindians were very pleased with French commissions, special uniforms, medals, and titles of nobility. The Micmacs regarded medals as "*titres de noblesse*" and it secured their loyalty, according to the missionaries. Dièreville mentioned to the French the loyalty and devotion of a chieftain he met at port Royal whose grandfather hand been "ennobled" by Henry IV.[27]

Another aspect of French life that the Amerindian did not comprehend but in the end came rather to admire was the generous and kindly treatment of the sick by the Sisters Hospitallers who arrived in Quebec in 1639. A dreadful smallpox epidemic, alleged to have come from Virginia—as all accursed events seemed to the colonists to have their origins in the English colonies—took a heavy toll of natives and the nuns themselves were "attacked by the malady." Du Creux recorded of these devout women that: ". . . with scarcely any interruption of their pious labours, they presented such a strange spectacle to the savages, who are quite without the emotion of pity, that they could not restrain their surprise that women could be found eager to encounter so many perils, and to penetrate unknown regions in order to succour those whom the Indians themselves generally abandon or kill."[28] Actually, the Amerindian could not have been astounded by the willingness of women to serve in evangelical labors in a distant land—which was a marvel to Europeans and a most unusual event in Catholic history—but they were astounded by the care the French lavished on the sick and dying. In the native encampments the terminally ill and the very aged were abandoned to their fate. They expected this treatment and there was no lack of pity attached to such action. The moralizing quality attributed to the treatment of the unfortunates is an example of European value judgments being applied to a different culture.

Indeed, on a wide range of points of contact at the military, social, religious, educational, agricultural, medical, and organizational level the Amerindian evaluation of French culture and civilization was often as unflattering as was the low regard of Frenchmen for Amerindian culture. Each group had its own somatic norm image, or "complex of physical characteristics which are accepted by a group as its norm and ideal," by which it evaluated and analysed other societies.[29] Thus, the French considered themselves aesthetically superior to the Amerindians and held views which would be classified as racist today; on the other hand, the Amerindians considered the French inferior to themselves and according to their somatic norm image considered themselves superior aesthetically and otherwise. Pierre d'Avity wrote in 1637 that "although they lack police, power, letters, arts, wealth and other things they despise other nations and esteem themselves highly."[30] He was echoing the sentiments of Father Gabriel Sagard, who had spent the winter of 1623–24 among the Hurons, and who reported that the Hurons esteemed the French "to possess little intelligence in comparison to themselves." Although they respected the knowledge of the Recollet missionaries they "did not have this opinion or belief concerning other Frenchmen in comparison with whom they estimated their own children wiser and more intelligent."[31] The Jesuits were no more highly regarded than the Recollets, the native children sometimes scorning them and ridiculing them "because they do not see in a Frenchman any of the perfections of a Savage and cannot recognize the virtues of a generous Christian."[32] Frenchmen, it would seem, seldom attained the intellectual and moral qualities demanded by the Amerindian somatic norm image.

Furthermore, Frenchmen generally were regarded as physically inferior, as weak and unfitted to stand up to the rigors of arduous canoe journeys, hunting expeditions, and forest warfare. When Champlain proposed to Chief Iroquet of the Algonquins to send young men to live among them there was immediate opposition: ". . . the other savages raised objections, fearing that harm might come to the youth, who was not accustomed to their manner of life, which is all respects hard, and that if any accident befell him the French would be their enemies."[33] Only after Champlain remonstrated angrily, and agreed to accept in exchange an Algonquin youth to be sent to France to be educated, could Iroquet accept the proposal.

If Frenchmen were regarded as "soft" it was because they were raised in a country which reportedly encouraged the development of effeminacy. Two young Algonquins who had spent a year in France, upon their return to Canada, were loud in their praises of the treatment they had been accorded, but one of them did admit that he would find it extremely difficult to readjust to his "former hard life" among his compatriots.[34]

Savignon, one of the youths Champlain had sent to France, "when he saw two men quarrelling without coming to blows or killing one another, would mock at them, saying they were nought but women, and had no courage."[35] Indeed, for an Amerindian to marry a European was not a socially desirable union. When an "honest French surgeon" asked to marry an Amerindian maiden in 1618 the native council refused his request.[36] Le Jeune's *Relation* of 1633 recorded another incident that the natives interpreted as proof of French effeminacy: "Our Savage, seeing Father de Noue carrying wood began to laugh, saying: 'He's really a woman,' meaning that he was doing a woman's work."

The first Frenchmen to inhabit the New World must have appeared singularly ill-equipped to cope with their new environment. It was not long before they stripped off their cumbersome European dress for the hunting shirt and moccasins. The Frenchman learned to travel by canoe and snowshoes, to portage and shoot rapids, to fish through the ice and eat *sagamite* in order to survive. But in the official French view they did this in order to establish good relations with the natives, to advance the economic and cultural objectives of the leaders. This temporary "Indianization" involved a cultural step backward in order to make possible a cultural leap forward later. The Amerindians could only interpret this "going native" by Frenchmen in increasing numbers as a reasonable adjustment to conditions in the New World, as a wise acceptance of folk wisdom, and as an accommodation learned by the *naturels* over centuries of American habitation. Nicolas Perrot maintained that the Hurons, Ottawas, Fox, and Sioux became much aware of this accommodation on the part of the French therefore they became insolent and desired to "dominate us and be our superiors; they even regard us as people who are in some manner dependent on them."[37]

In addition to reproaching Frenchmen for their physical weakness, the Amerindians found them ugly, especially because of their excessive hairiness, and their frequent deformities and infirmities. Sagard related how "one of the ugliest savages in his district" laughed at the bearded Europeans and wondered how any woman could look with favor on such ugly creatures. He added: "They have such a horror of a beard that sometimes when they try to insult us they call us Sascoinronte, that is to say, Bearded, you have a beard; moreover, they think it makes people more ugly and weakens their intelligence."[38] Father Biard sent a similar report from Acadia: "They have often told me that at first we seemed to them very ugly with hair both upon our mouths and heads; but gradually they have become accustomed to it, and now we are beginning to look less deformed."[39] In addition to this common Mongoloid abhorrence of the hairiness of Europeans, the Micmacs showed no compassion for "the one-eyed, and flat-nosed" Frenchmen who they derided. Biard continued:

> For they are droll fellows, and have a word and a nickname very readily at command, if they think they have any occasion to look down upon us. And certainly (judging from what I see) this habit of self-aggrandizement is a contagion from which no one is exempt, except through the grace of God. You will see these poor barbarians, not withstanding their great lack of government, power, letters, art and riches, yet holding their heads so high that they greatly underrate us, regarding themselves as our superiors.[40]

Lahontan, who was generally very sympathetic in his appraisal of aboriginal views, remarked on "their fanatical Opinions of things, which proceeded from their Pre-possession and Bigotry with reference to their own customs and ways of living."[41]

There was much about Catholicism that seemed incongruous and dangerous to the Amerindians. From the first contacts with missionaries, whether seculars or reg-ulars, the zeal for the baptism of dying infants led to a confirmed belief that baptism was the cause of death. The French were responsible for the epidemics of measles, smallpox, influenza, and related bronchial disorders which decimated the encamp-ments and villages, and the natives without being able to understand the precise rela-tionship between contact and infection did realize that there was such a cause-effect relationship. As early as 1616, Biard sent the following observations from Acadia:

> They are astonished and often complain that since the French mingle with and carry on trade with them, they are dying fast, and the population is thinning out. For they assert that, before this association and intercourse, all their countries were very pop-ulous, and they tell how one by one the different coasts, according as they have begun traffic with us have been more reduced by disease; adding, that the reason the Armouchiquois do not diminish in population is because they are not at all careless. Thereupon they often puzzle their brains, and sometimes think that the French poi-son them. . . .[42]

All the tribes contacted by the French in the early seventeenth century—the Mic-macs, Montagnais, Algonquins, Hurons, and Iroquois—charged the French with bringing pestilence and death. The Algonquins went so far as to tell the Hurons infection was a deliberate policy of the French to destroy all the Amerindian nations. By 1647 the Jesuits made the following admission: "The Algonquins and Hurons—and next the Hiroquois, at the solicitation of their captives—have had, and some have still, a hatred and an extreme horror of our doctrine. They say that it causes them to die, and that it contains spells and charms which effect the destruction of their corn, and engender the contagious and general diseases wherewith the Hiroquois now begin to be afflicted."[43] The missionaries taught those who would give them a hear-ing, among other things, the wonder-working power of the sacraments, novenas, and relics. They taught a reverence for the cross, religious images, and pious practices. In the adversities that often accompanied the coming of the missionaries to their villages, the tribesmen concluded that the supernatural invoked for good could also be invoked to produce harmful effects. The missionary report of 1653 from the Huron country included the following observation: "They said the same thing about some images, etc. the prayers that we made, and the masses which we said at an early hour, with closed doors; the litanies; even walking abroad,—a new thing in these countries,—were superstitions which we practiced in order to destroy them."[44] Every unaccustomed, unusual or secretive act became the object of intense suspicion.

Religious symbols were greatly distrusted. In 1635 the Hurons insisted that a cross atop the mission-house be removed as the cause of that summer's drought: "When the Indians gathered from the surrounding villages and insisted that the Fathers should remove the cross; they told them that should the drought wither the crops there was danger that the infuriated Hurons would attack them as sorcerers and poisoners and beat them to death."[45] The following year, the villagers had cause for further alarm, as an epidemic spread rapidly through the lodges taking a heavy toll. The Jesuits had displayed in their chapel two life-size images, one of Jesus and the other of the Virgin Mary, for the edification of their hearers. The rumor spread quickly that the images were the cause of the pestilence:

> This unfounded suspicion, which should have been dismissed with a laugh, spread so rapidly in a few days that throughout the length and breadth of the land it was soon reported that the French priests were the cause of the trouble; and although we may conjecture that those from whom this ridiculous falsehood emanated were not so foolish as to persuade themselves to accept what they wished others to believe, still they told their lie so cunningly that the majority who heard the report had no doubt that the thing was true. For the most part they gradually refused to associate with the Fathers, and the women and children, otherwise of no account but ready to believe anything, execrated them as public male-factors. In all the gatherings and meetings the talk was against the Fathers, who, it was said, had come to the Huron country on an evil day and who were destined to be the ruin of the whole race. The inhabitants of Ihonatiria alone at first zealously defended their cause, but they too, when the conflagration of unpopularity burned more fiercely, whether they were afraid or whether they were tired of the task, ceased to protect them and began to excuse their former conduct with their neighbours as if it had been a serious crime.[46]

The prophets of doom were correct in their predictions, of course, for the French presence in Huronia precipitated their subjugation by the Iroquois.

The Amerindian charge against the missionaries was of engaging in sorcery and witchcraft. Obsessive fear appears to have outweighed hatred as the motive for the "persecution" reported by Mother Marie de l'Incarnation: "They were on the dock as criminals in a council of the savages. The fires were lit closer to each other than usual and they seemed to be so only for them, for they were esteemed convicted of witchcraft, and of having poisoned the air which caused the pestilence throughout the country. What put the Fathers in extreme peril was that the Savages were as it were convinced that these misfortunes would cease with their death."[47] Great assemblies were called throughout Huronia to deliberate on appropriate protective measures. The oldest and most prominent woman of the nation was reported to have harangued the consultative assembly of the four tribes in the following manner:

> It is the Black Robes who make us die by their spells; listen to me, I prove it by the reasons you are going to recognize as true. They lodged in a certain village where everyone was well, as soon as they established themselves there, everyone died except for three or four persons. They changed location and the same thing happened. They went to visit the cabins of the other villages, and only those where they did not enter

were exempted from mortality and sickness. Do you not see that when they move their lips, what they call prayers, those are so many spells that come forth from their mouths? It is the same when they read in their books. Besides, in their cabins they have large pieces of wood (they are guns) with which they make noise and spread their magic everywhere. If they are not promptly put to death, they will complete their ruin of the country, so that there will remain neither small nor great.[48]

The Ursuline correspondent opined that wherever the missionaries traveled in their apostolic labors they carried the epidemic "to purify the faith of those they have converted." News of the alleged French practice of witchcraft and sorcery traveled rapidly to neighboring tribes and forestalled plans Chaumonot and his companion had of carrying the gospel farther afield:

> As for the adults, not only have they not been willing to listen to the good news, but they even prevented us from entering their villages, threatening to kill and eat us, as they do with their most cruel enemies. The reason of this great aversion arose from the calumnies disseminated by some evil inhabitants of the country from which we came. In consequence of these calumnies, they were convinced that we were sorcerers, imposters come to take possession of their country, after having made them perish by our spells, which were shut up in our inkstands, in our books, etc.—inasmuch that we dared not, without hiding ourselves, open a book or write anything.[49]

Association with the new religion meant certain sterility of hunting and fishing. Iroquois captives brought to the Huron villages were forced to kneel before wooden crosses, symbols which filled them with terror. A report of 1647 indicates the extent of the fear Catholicism inspired among the Iroquois: "It is further said that they have seen issuing from the lips of a Christian, whom they were burning, a strange brightness which has terrified them; so, indeed, they have knowledge of our doctrine, but they regard it with horror, as of old the Pagans in the early age of Christianity."[50] This obsessive fear attached itself not only to the external symbols of the new religion and its practices but also to the Eucharist itself. Some of the pagans asked to see the corpse of Christ, which the priests were said to bring to life at mass. Eventually, even purely secular objects such as weather vanes and clocks were shunned as evil spirits associated with the religion of the French.

Although the missionaries, almost without exception, complained of the inadequacies of the Amerindian languages for expressing their religious message and noted the great difficulty in compiling vocabularies of equivalents to common French terms, modern linguistic experts do not find the Amerindian languages deficient for expressing the abstract and symbolic. Nevertheless, the aboriginal tongues did not always have precise equivalents, as Lescarbot emphasized: "For they have no words which can represent the mysteries of our religion, and it would be impossible to translate even the Lord's prayer into their language save by paraphase. For of themselves they do not know what is sanctification, or the kingdom of Heaven, or super-substantial bread (which we call daily), or to lead into temptation. The words glory, virtue, reason, beautitudes, Trinity, Holy Spirit, baptism, faith, hope, charity, and an infinity of others are not in use among them. So that at the beginning there will be no need of great Doctors."[51] The world expressed by the French language was one world and the world expressed by the Huron language, for example, was a distinct world; each were distinct worlds and not merely the same world with different labels attached. LeClercq commended the Micmac language as being "very beautiful and very rich in its expressions," adding that it had a greater range of expression than European languages and that there were distinct styles for solemn and less formal occasions.[52] The Jesuits later asserted on the basis of their experience among both Algonquian and Iroquoian linguistic groups that the languages were definite in meaning, beautiful and regular in expression, "not at all barbarious," and full of force.[53]

The deficiency arose more out of the cultural approach and the implications of evangelization for Amerindian society than from linguistic difficulties. The natives saw some danger in divulging their religious vocabulary to the evangelists of the new religion, therefore they refused to cooperate extensively in the linguistic task of compiling dictionaries and grammars, and of translating religious books.[54] Gravier reported at the close of the century of the Illinois tribes that they were "so secret regarding all the mysteries of their Religion that the Missionary can discover nothing about them."[55] What the pagans refused the neophytes later supplied, although the continued refusal of some coureurs-de-bois to assist in missionary translation suggests that there was pressure in the native encampments to offer no assistance to the missionaries in this aspect of their evangelical labors.

Most natives, seeing the Europeans determined to learn their languages, felt no necessity to learn French; this fact elicited the accusation from one royal official that the Amerindians were too proud to learn French. The Amerindians did not find the Jesuits particularly good linguists, although by any measure that can be applied today to their efforts they appear to have been brilliant. Du Creux recounted that the Hurons "thought it was a joke to ask Le Jeune to speak, and when he made a stammering attempt at their language, laughter and derision greeted his childish efforts."[56]

The religious differences in the French community did not escape Amerindian notice, although the religious chroniclers may have exaggerated this so-called scandal in order to advance their own demands for enforced religious uniformity. Sagard wrote about the intestinal quarrels between Hugenot and Catholic seamen, fishermen, traders, and ministers of religion that tended to confirm the natives in their skepticism.[57] The natives were never slow to point out the weaknesses in the French character, the divergence between the missionaries' ideals and the colonists' practices, and the greater severity with which the clergy sought to repress drunkenness among them than among the French. Governor Montmagny sought to answer one such remonstrance with an unconvincing "don't plead the French as an excuse when they sometimes fall into intemperance themselves; those who do so are stupid fools, and are regarded as trash and a disgrace to the light of day."[58]

Be that as it may, the greatest obstacles to evangelization of the Amerindians remained native religion, the world view of the tribesmen, and (under pressure to convert to Catholicism) the emergence of counter-innovative techniques. Native religion was completely integrated into Amerindian cultures and permeated all aspects of daily living as well as the ideology. Conversion to Catholicism required a rejection of the whole traditional way of life, belief system and tribal ideals of behavior and relationships. When the Jesuits sought to establish a model Catholic "republic" among the Hurons, the medicine-men and elders developed counter-innovative techniques: a version of baptism, for example, was initiated as a part of a healing cult said to be inspired by a deity who revealed himself as "the real Jesus," and anti-Catholic cults spread rapidly throughout Huronia to provide an ideological resistance to the new European religion.[59]

Dreams, both of a symptomatic and visitation variety, played an important role in Amerindian religion and not infrequently turned against the threatening tide of the "French religion." During an epidemic of smallpox among the Hurons in 1640, a young fisherman had a dream in which the spirit appeared to him to advise the tribe in its distress. Jerome Lalemant reported the "demon" as having issued the following warning:

> I am the master of the earth, whom you Hurons honor under the name of Iouskena. I am the one whom the French wrongly called Jesus, but they do not know me. I have pity on your country, which I have taken under my protection; I come to teach you both the reasons and the remedies for your fortune. It is the strangers who alone are the cause of it; they now travel two by two through the country, with the design of spreading the disease everywhere. They will not stop with that, after this smallpox which now depopulates your cabins, there will follow certain colics which in less than three days will carry off all those whom this disease may not have removed. You can prevent this misfortune; drive from your village the two black gowns who are there.[60]

Just as the French tended to fashion God in their own image, so one is assured that Iouskeha spoke as a "true" Huron.

Each culture had its own concept of supernatural intervention in human affairs. On occasion there was a cultural convergence: in such situations the Amerindians held French religious powers, or "good medicine," in high esteem. When in 1673 at Folle Avoine on the Menominee River Louis André replaced sacrifices offered to the sun in order to assure good fishing by a crucifix he invited a contest between the deities. The fact that the following morning a large number of sturgeon entered the river suddenly gave him attentive hearers.[61] The following year, Pierre Millet reported that an Iroquois chieftain exhorted his compatriots to hold prayer in esteem "as Monsieur the governor had recommended them to do at Catarakoui," but far more effective was the fact that the missionary correctly predicted an eclipse of the moon a few days earlier.[62] Paul le Jeune attempted to convince the Huron that neither the French nor any other people could bring rain or fine weather, but that the Creator alone was master of these elements and therefore "recourse must be had only to him." His hearers remained unconvinced and persisted in their belief that the Europeans had influenced the supernatural to bring unfavorable weather. An incident that had occurred when the Recollets had first gone into Huron country probably lived on in their oral history. Sagard recorded that the Recollets had been asked to pray God to stop a long and devastating rain. "And God looked with favour on our prayers, after we had spent the following night in petitioning Him for His promises, and heard us and caused the rain to cease so completely that we had perfectly fine weather; whereat they were so amazed and delighted that they proclaimed it a miracle, and we rendered thanks to God for it."[63]

It was only a short step from belief in beneficial supernatural intervention to belief in malignant and malicious intervention from the spirit world.

The Amerindians soon came to hold a low opinion of French standards of morality. As early as Verrazano's expedition of 1524 it was remarked that contact with European fishing fleets had taught the coastal Algonkian tribes to take appropriate protective measures. Verrazano reported: "Every day the people came to see us at the ship; bringing their women of whom they are very careful; because, entering the ship themselves, remaining a long time, they made their women stay in the barges and however many entreaties we made them, offering to give them various things, it was not possible that they would allow them to enter the ship."[64] Similarly, Biard observed that the Micmac girls and women were "very modest and bashful" and that the men were well behaved and "very much insulted when some foolish Frenchman dares meddle with their women." This Jesuit missionary related an incident to illustrate his judgment: "Once when a certain madcap took some liberties, they came and told our Captain that he should look out for his men, informing him that any one who attempted to do that again could not stand much of a chance, that they would kill him on the spot."[65]

The Jesuit missionaries seem to have expected the tribesmen to respect them for their sacrifices and sufferings in bringing them the Gospel under unattractive conditions, especially when compared to life in the elitist colleges of France where they had taught previously. They also expected to be honored for their vows of poverty and chastity. The natives felt quite otherwise about the missionary mode of life. Sagard observed: "One of the great and most bothersome importunities which they caused us at the beginning of our stay in the country was their continual pursuit of pleas to marry us, or at least that we should join ourselves to them, and they could not understand our manner of Religious life. . . ."[66] The Hurons told the Recollets it was unnatural to remain celibate, that they were abnormal, that conditions could not be as favorable in France as they pretended or they would have remained there, and that they were out of touch with the rhythm of natural provisions the supernatural powers bestowed on mankind. What other conclusions could aborigines, especially the nomadic Algonquian bands, come to in seeking a rational explanation of apostolic poverty, celibacy, and calendar-oriented fasting?

There is sparse documentation dealing with Amerindian reactions to French agriculture, or to life in the towns of Quebec and Montreal. The French diet, as reflected in the kitchen gardens and field crops of the riparian clearings, was a varied one but native palates did not respond well to salted meat and vegetables. Upon being offered a barrel of bread and biscuits, the Hurons examined it, found it tasteless, and threw it into the St. Lawrence: "Our Savages said the Frenchmen drank blood and ate wood, thus naming the wine and biscuits."[67] A chieftain at Isle Percée told Chrestien LeClercq that French contributions in the dietary and culinary realm were not appreciated.

> It is true . . . that we have not always had the use of bread and of wine which your France produces; but, in fact, before the arrival of the French in these parts, did not the Gaspesians live much longer than now? And if we have not any longer among us any of those old men of a hundred and thirty to forty years, it is only because we are gradually adopting your manner of living, for experience is making it very plain that those of us live longest who, despising your bread, your wine, and your brandy, are content with their natural food of beaver, of moose, of waterfowl, and fish, in accord with the custom of our ancestors and of all the Gaspesian nation. Learn now, my brother, once for all, because I must open to thee my heart: there is no Indian who does not consider himself infinitely more happy and more powerful than the French.[68]

The same attitudes prevailed with respect to French clothing, which the natives found inadequate to keep out the winter's cold. Only the decorative aspects held appeal for them.

Although they were impressed by the tall stone buildings erected by the French, and marveled at the layout of their towns, there remained an attachment to the traditional style of building and of life. The Micmac chieftain just cited made the following observations:

> But why now, do men of five of six feet in height need houses which are sixty to eighty? For, in fact, as thou knowest very well thyself, Patriarch—do we not find in our own all the conveniences and advantages that you have with yours, such as reposing, drinking, sleeping, eating, and amusing ourselves with our friends when we wish? This is not all. My brother, hast thou as much ingenuity and cleverness as the Indians, who carry their houses and their wigwams with them so they may lodge wheresoever they please, independently of any seignior whatsoever? Thou art not as bold or as stout as we, because when thou goest on a voyage thou canst not carry upon thy shoulders thy buildings and thy edifices. Therefore it is necessary that thou preparest as many lodgings as thou makest changes of residence, or else thou lodgest in a hired house which does not belong to thee. As for us, we find ourselves secure from all these inconveniences, and we are at home everywhere, because we set up our wigwams with ease wheresoever we go, and without asking permission of anybody.[69]

If they were impressed by French tools and implements there is little record of their adopting any of these in their own house-building or agriculture. One enterprising convert, Manitougache, used a hatchet and some nails salvaged from an old boat to build a board cabin for himself, but he seems to have been exceptional.[70] In point of fact, the fur-covered wigwams of the natives were superior to the later linen tents. The only goods the domiciled reservation natives asked of the Hôtel-Dieu 1643, for example, were blankets and copper kettles—other furnishings apparently had little appeal for them.[71]

In general, the Amerindians do not seem to have retained a favorable impression of the social organization of French life. They were quite unable to understand that in France, where, according to the tales of the Europeans and the few Amerindians who had visited the country and returned to North America, there was apparently an abundance of food, many large towns and many people yet there were also poor people and beggars. Montaigne said that the astonished visitors "thought it strange that these needy halves should endure such an injustice, and did not take the others by the throat, or set fire to their houses."[72] The Recollet missionaries found no beggars in the Huron and Montagnais encampments and whatever food was available was always shared, open hospitality being offered to all travelers. Sagard said: "those of their Nation, who offer reciprocal Hospitality, and help each other so much that they provide for the needs of all so that there is no poor beggar at all in their towns, bourgs and villages, as I said elsewhere, so that they found it very bad hearing that there were in France a great number of needy and beggars, and thought that it was due to a lack of charity, and blamed us greatly, saying that if we had some intelligence we would set some order in the matter, the remedies being simple."[73] To Frenchmen, who thought they had a well-disciplined society, a rational order, and civilized community, it came as quite a shock to be reproved by the aborigines, whom they often regarded as being devoid of "right reason" and "right religion," for their injustice, improvidence, and inequality. LeClercq was told bluntly how the Micmac regarded French notions of superiority:

> Thou reproaches us, very inappropriately, that our country is a little hell in contrast with France, which thou comparest to a terrestrial paradise, inasmuch as it yields thee, so thou sayest, every kind of provision in abundance. Thou sayest of us also that we are most miserable and most unhappy of all men, living without religion, without manners, without honour, without social order, in a word, without any rules, like the beasts in our woods and our forests, lacking bread, wine, and a thousand other comforts which thou hast in superfluity in Europe. Well, my brother, if thou does not yet know the real feelings which our Indians have toward thy country and toward all thy nations, it is proper that I inform thee at once. I beg thee now to believe that all miserable as we seem in thine eyes, we consider ourselves nevertheless much happier than thou in this, that we are content with the little that we have; and believe also, once for all, I pray, that thou deceivest thyself greatly if thou thinkest to persuade us that thy country is better than ours. For if France, as thou sayest, is a little terrestrial paradise, art thou sensible to leave it?[74]

To this rebuke was added the observation that Frenchmen were often inhospitable and parsimonious.

Amerindian hospitality and sharing of goods, on the other hand, were regarded as the most praiseworthy qualities of the aborigines by the fur traders, soldiers, and coureurs-de-bois who were so often the beneficiaries of these traits and whose survival and success depended frequently on the goodwill of the natives. Nicolas Perrot reported that unfortunately the Amerindians soon came to understand and imitate French ways:

This sort of reception is ordinary among the savages; in point of hospitality, it is only the Abenakis, and those who live with the French people, who have become somewhat less liberal, on account of the advice that our people have given them by placing before them the obligations resting on them to preserve what they have. At the present time, it is evident that these savages are fully as selfish and avaricious as formerly they were hospitable. . . . Those of the savages who have not been too much humoured (by the French) are attached to the ancient custom of their ancestors, and among themselves are very compassionate.[75]

Contact with Europeans had resulted in an erosion of both native hospitality and liberality.

There is some indication that the converted Amerindians resented the segregationist practices of the French. Why did the French insist on separate villages, separate churches, separate schools or classes, separate hospital wards, and even separate burial grounds? Sagard reported that the Hurons were not happy when he and his companion came to them and proposed to build their cabin apart from their lodges. The chief and council tried to dissuade them, insisting that it would be preferable if they lodged with Huron families in order to be better cared for than if they remained apart.[76] Had they followed the council's advice, all their food would have been provided by the hunters. However, they preferred privacy to provisions.

Although segregationist practices were not well received, overt attempts to assimilate and dominate the tribesmen were also resented. The decision of the French authorities to provide some tangible encouragement to miscegenation as a means of assimilating the Amerindians met with some resistance in native quarters. When one fur trader had pledged the Ursulines a sizeable donation in order to marry one of their native pupils "it was found that the girl did not want him at all, and preferred a savage and to follow the wishes of her parents."[77] The natives were interested in the provision by the French state of dowries for native women who married Frenchmen and made astute inquires concerning specific terms of the plan: "They would be very glad to know what a husband would give his wife; that among the Hurons the custom was to give a great deal besides,—that is to say—a beaver robe, and perhaps a porcelain collar. Second, whether a wife would have everything at her disposal. Third, if the husband should decide to return to France whether he would take his wife with him; and in case she remained, what would he leave her on his departure. Fourth, if the wife failed in her duty and the husband drove her away, what she could take with her. . . ."[78] The commissioner general of the Company of New France reproached the natives in the vicinity of Trois Rivières for marrying only within their own tribe and for avoiding marriage alliances with Frenchmen.[79] The following year, a chief from Tadoussac replied to French charges that his people "were not yet allied with the French by any marriage" and that their dislike of the French was evident because "they did not care to be one people with us, giving their children here and there to their allied Nations, and not to the French." He told an assembly at Quebec that when young Frenchmen joined with the Montagnais warriors and returned "after the massacre of our enemies" they would find native girls to marry. As for the placement of children in French homes to be raised in the European fashion, he retorted boldly that "one does not see anything but little Savages in the houses of the French." He concluded with a strong argument: "what more do you want? I believe that some of these days you will be asking for our wives. You are continually asking us for our children, and you do not give yours; I do not know any family among us which keeps a Frenchman with it."[80] The Amerindians continued to think of the mutual exchange of children as token of unity and alliance, and had no doubt so accepted Champlain's sending of youths to learn native customs and languages in the early decades of the seventeenth century. The one-way placement of children was interpreted as either a demand for hostages or an attempt to assert dominance over them.

They held French medical practices—bleeding and purges, in particular—in low esteem and preferred their own treatments. Lescarbot told of one Micmac warrior who upon being treated by Poutrincourt's surgeon for a badly cut heel returned two hours later "as jaunty as you please, having tied round his head the bandage in which his heel had been wrapped."[81] In 1640, the annalist of the hospital at Quebec reported that the natives avoided the institution, holding it in horror, and called it "the house of death," and refused to submit to medical treatments there.[82] There is no reason to doubt that the anxious relatives who urged a converted widow to abandon French medical treatments for her ailing son, "and told her that she was more like a cruel beast than a loving mother in deserting her boy at such a time; that his recovery depending upon her allowing the remedies to be employed which all their tribe had always used before the coming of those cursed Europeans," did so in all good faith and out of genuine concern for their fellows.[83]

In the domain of personal hygiene the Amerindians appear to have been more advanced than the French, especially in matters concerning bathing, which the French avoided as both unhealthy and immodest. Some French practices earned open ridicule, such as the use of handkerchiefs: "Politeness and propriety have taught us to carry handkerchiefs. In this matter the Savages charge us with filthiness because, they say, we place what is unclean in a fine white piece of linen, and put it away in our pockets as something very precious, while they throw it upon the ground. Hence it happened that, when a Savage one day saw a Frenchman fold up his handkerchief after wiping his nose, he said to himself laughingly, 'If thou likest that filth, give me thy handkerchief and I will soon fill it.'"[84] There is every indication that the natives were willing to pass on their considerable knowledge and skill in the use of medicinal herbs, ointments, potions, emetics, the practice of quarantining, and the taking of steam baths. Joges had an abscess lanced by the Iroquois, Crépeul was skillfully bled by an Eskimo, and a French captive had shot removed from a deep wound.[85]

One of the difficulties inherent in relying largely on European documentation for an interpretation of Amerindian views is demonstrated in the discussions on child-rearing. The reported reactions of the aborigines were sometimes literary devices of French authors to criticize French customs and conventions. Lescarbot, for example, deplored the French custom of employing "vicious nursemaids" from whom the infants "sucked in with their milk, corruption and bad nature."[86] While there are numerous reports of Amerindian surprise and disdain for French methods of child-rearing, these accounts must be placed in the literary and historical contexts of a period when criticism of government, religion, and social conventions in France was severely circumscribed. Both Lescarbot and Denys extended the idealization of the "noble savage," established in France by such writers as Clodoré d'Abbeville, Montaigne, Du Tertre, Boyer, and de Léry, to an idealization of the New World as a land of opportunity and freedom. The report, therefore, that native women demonstrated more affection to their offspring than French mothers and that they regarded the latter as callous and unfeeling may have been an extension of utopianism in order to criticize metropolitan society. D'Abbeville reported: "They take care not to do like many mothers here, who scarcely can await the birth of their children to put them out to nurse-maids. . . . The Savage women would not want to imitate them in that for anything in the world, desiring their children to be nourished with their own milk."[87] The association between nature and nurture may have been more significant to the authors who reported it than to the Amerindians who purportedly emphasized it.

Certainly all the tribes had a very great love for their children and raised them in what might be termed a permissive manner. As Nicolas Denys noted: "Their children are not obstinate, since they give them everything they ask for, without ever letting them cry for that which they want. The greatest persons give way to the little ones. The father and mother draw the morsel from the mouth if the child asks for it. They love their children greatly."[88] They were quite unable to understand the harder disciplinary methods of the French, the "porcupine-like" affection of French mothers who so readily accepted the separation of their children, and the practice of confining children for months in boarding schools. Marie de l'Incarnation said of the Amerindian children she tried to instruct that "they cannot be restrained and if they are, they become melancholy and their melancholy makes them sick."[89] Education in Amerindian society was part of the everyday life of work and play; unlike French education, it was completely integrated to the rhythm of the adult community. This is the reason for the failure of the early schools to retain their pupils, who, sooner or later, returned home or escaped to the forests.

Marie Arinadsit, a Huron pupil at the Ursuline convent in Quebec, encouraged some Iroquois visitors in 1655 to send their daughters to be educated by the nuns:

> Live, she said to them, with us henceforth as with your brothers, let us be only one people, and as a mark of your affection send some of your daughters to the Seminary; I will be their elder daughter, I will teach them to pray to God, and all the other things our Mothers taught me. And thereupon she started to read before them in Latin, in French and in Huron; then she sang spiritual Hymns in those three languages. Thereat those good people were quite taken aback, asked how long it took to learn so many things and to francize well a Savage girl, promising they would not miss sending their children to such a good school.[90]

Within two decades the Superior of the "seminary" for Amerindian girls had to admit that the response from all the tribes had been most discouraging. She confided to a correspondent in France: "Others are here only as birds of passage and stay with us only until they are sad, something which savage humour cannot suffer; the moment they become sad, the parents take them away for fear they will die. We leave them free on this point, for we are more likely to win them over in this way than by keeping them by force or entreaties. There are others who go off by whim or caprice; they climb our palisades like squirrels, which is as high as a stone wall, and go to run in the woods."[91] French education was designed to assimilate Amerindian youth and therefore was unsuitable to fit them for life and leadership in their tribal community. The French educators came to understand that their classroom techniques, discipline, curriculum, and aims were at complete variance with Amerindian methods and objectives. "The savage life is so charming to them because of its liberty, that it is a miracle to be able to captivate them to the French way of doing things which they esteem unworthy of them, for they glory in not working except at hunting or navigation, or making war."[92] Talon reported in 1670 that on his return to the colony he found the number of native children in the schools established by Bishop Laval and the Jesuits "greatly diminished" but added "they are going to seek new subjects to raise in our ways, our customs, our language and our teaching."[93] These were the very objectives of schooling that so repelled the native children.

Donnacona had offered Cartier three young girls to take to France in 1526 but his people were incensed by this act and managed to free one of the girls from the French vessel. The chieftain intervened and had her returned with the explanation "that they had not advised her to run off, but that she had done so because the ships' boys had beaten her . . . ," whereupon the unfortunate child was returned with her two companions to the tender care of the French crew.[94] Champlain's astonishment in January 1628 at being offered three little native girls to raise came out of his experience that the Amerindians did not readily part with their children, that they did not respect French methods of child-rearing or education; he could only conclude that the offer was motivated by a desire to cement an alliance or to compensate for the murder of two Frenchmen.[95] The case of the three little girls being offered to Marguerite Bourgeoys at Montreal to be educated was virtually an abduction.[96]

The Amerindian distaste for French educational procedures carried over into a general lack of appreciation for French judicial procedures, law, and government. The rigidity, lack of flexibility, authoritarianism, and excessive concentration of power at the top of administrative pyramids contrasted unfavorably with the democratic procedures in Huron and Iroquois cantons. In their leaders the Algonquians looked for such traits as emotional restraint, stoicism, practicality, personal resourcefulness, and bravery. The French seem to have misunderstood the value they placed on deference in interpersonal relationship. Father Le Jeune observed that the Montagnais could not "endure in the least those who seem desirous of assuming superiority over others."[97] It is interesting to recall that the Europeans who came into contact with these democratic native societies were members of a paternalistic monarchy and a hierarchical church, both being authoritarian, highly centralized pyramids of secular and religious power respectively. Paul Boyer wrote enthusiastically of the equality of the people encountered in the New World: "They do not know what are extortions, or subsidies, nor brigandry; no avarice, no cupidity, no lawsuits, no quarrels, no savants, no masters, no unfortunates, no beggars, not so much as an inkling of covetousness, which things should make us blush with shame. No distinctions of estates among them, and they consider men only by the actions they accomplish."[98] The greater measure of liberty and of equality in Amerindian life was a comparison that Frenchmen were more apt to make than were Amerindians because the latter had less experience of both cultural milieux on which to base such conclusions.

French justice did not appeal to the Iroquois because it restricted itself to punishing the wrongdoer, while neglecting to give satisfaction to the wronged. Galinée described the fear that his party had in 1669–70 about passing near a Seneca village because shortly before his party had murdered a Seneca hunter and stolen his furs. The culprits were brought to trial and were executed in public in the presence of several Senecas. Nevertheless, as Galinée said, "although the bulk of the nation was appeased by this execution, the relatives of the deceased did not consider themselves satisfied and wished at all hazards to sacrifice some Frenchmen to their vengeance, and loudly boasted of it. . . ."[99]

During the years of initial contact the Amerindians had every reason to fear kidnapping under the guise of taking "volunteers" to France to be educated as interpreters or trained as a native clergy. From the earliest fishing voyages that made contact through to Cartier and Dupont-Gravé, tribesmen had been taken off to France.[100] In 1622 an Indian who had been taken to Dieppe where he fell ill but showed no desire for baptism, although often encouraged by Huguenots to submit to this rite, returned to Canada in the company of the Recollet Father Irenée Piat. He died shortly after receiving baptism and was buried at sea with full Catholic rites. However, the missionary later regretted not having kept locks of his hair and pieces of his nails to offer relatives proof of his decease because he knew they would suspect foul play and demand compensation: "We did not omit nevertheless to make presents to the closest relatives of the deceased, to remove from them all subject of complaint, and to assure our position in the matter."[101]

Although the French and Amerindians shared a high esteem for qualities considered exclusively masculine—skill in hunting and prowess in war—their cultures were far apart in their concepts of warfare, its objectives, its proper conduct, the treatment of prisoners, and the significance of alliances. The Amerindians never did understand the long-range objectives of European warfare, the sustained campaigns and the highly centralized and authoritarian military organization. They fought their wars for vengeance, for the adoption of prisoners so as to increase their population, and for reasons of prestige. The idea that North Americans were at war with each other because motherlands across the ocean were at war was incomprehensible unless immediate local issues were clearly involved. The humane treatment of prisoners of war by the French was also a mystery to the Amerindian mind: prisoners either should become objects of vengeance or they should be adopted to strengthen or maintain one's manpower. French outrage at scalping, platform torture, and ritual cannibalism was not understood by the natives, especially when French warfare was obviously more destructive than Amerindian action.

On the other hand, Iroquois prisoners brought back to the Christian reservation in 1645 were greeted by Jean-Baptiste Etinechikawat who received his warriors with praise, saying to the war captain: "Thou knowest well that we now proceed in a different fashion than we formerly did. We have overturned all our old customs. That is why we receive you quietly, without harming the prisoners, without striking or injuring them in any way."[102] The startled prisoners, expecting the traditional torture stake and platform and prepared to sing their death-songs, were well treated in spite of the urgent pleadings of two women, sole survivors of families killed by the Iroquois, to be permitted to avenge themselves on the pagans. This incident proved to be the exception for French attitudes were unable to supplant Amerindian motivations, value system, or spiritualist satisfaction in this domain. Even treaties of peace and nonaggression signed with the French or English were interpreted in Amerindian terms of adoption. They spoke of the French monarch as their "father" and themselves as his "adopted children" upon entering what the French considered a military alliance and a political protectorate.[103]

In almost every sphere of activity the Amerindians differed greatly from the French not only in their practices and traditions, but more especially in their conceptualization. Apart from concessions to French material civilization, technology, and military force, they felt equal to, or superior to, the Europeans at the time of contact in the seventeenth century. The fact that the French tended on contact to learn their languages, to adopt to some degree their ways of living, traveling, hunting, and fighting, and to rely heavily on them for their economic and military success confirmed them in their belief that their way of life had advantages over the French lifestyle. In 1685 Governor Denonville wrote to Seignelay, Minister of the Marine responsible for the colonies, that French attempts to assimilate the proud, self-reliant, and dignified Amerindians had had unfortunate consequences: "It was believed for a long time that domiciling the savages near our habitations was a very great means of teaching these peoples to live like us and to become instructed in our religion. I notice, Monseigneur, that the very opposite has taken place because instead of familiarising them with our laws, I assure you that they communicate very much to us all they have that is the very worst, and take on likewise all that is bad and vicious in us. . . ."[104] But already the eroding effects of the new religion, the new economic pressures, the new disease and alcohol addiction, the new military alignments, and the new immigration were beginning to undermine the dignity, self-reliance, and self-assurance of the Amerindians. It was not contact per se, nor the comparisons that Frenchmen and aborigines inevitably made between the two types of civilizations, which proved so destructive to aboriginal belief systems, an integrated social pattern, and self-image, but rather it was the more pervasive long-term concomitants of a permanent and expansionist European presence which undermined the cohesiveness and viability of Amerindian cultures during the ensuing generations and centuries.

While there can be no doubt that the French regarded their own culture as infinitely superior both in material and intellectual aspects to the aboriginal cultures they encountered in North America, it would be a fundamental error to assume that the Amerindians entertained or accepted such a comparative evaluation. Despite the paucity of "Indian sources" there is sufficient primary evidence to indicate that the various tribes

were selective in their adaptation of European technology and cultural patterns, that they rejected outright many behavioral and conceptual innovations, that they developed counter-innovative devices and behavior as a consequence of their contact experience, and that they maintained their own somatic norm image. While there was much in French life and culture that impressed or intrigued the aboriginal tribesmen, it would be inaccurate to assume that they invariably acknowledged the superiority of European culture, much less that they adopted or imitated uncritically French beliefs and behavior. The Amerindian and French folkways and belief systems tended rather to remain parallel and concurrent with a much greater degree of accommodation of French culture to native life and environmental considerations than of Amerindian cultures to French lifestyle. While there is evidence to indicate that French accommodation and adaptation to New World circumstances incorporated a degree of barbarization or "Indianization," on the contrary, assimilationist and adaptive responses on the part of aboriginals usually led to alienation from traditional lifestyle and beliefs, to a rejection of their past and to a close identification of religious conversion with "Frenchification." Few Amerindians crossed the cultural chasm to become identified as domiciled francized converts; on the other hand, new social types, identified as coureurs-de-bois and voyageurs, evolved in New France and the more comprehensive social groups identified as habitants, militiamen, and missionaries all experienced significant adaptation to the aborigines and environment of North America, which distinguished them from their metropolitan French counterparts.

In the past Canadian historiography has taken little account of these primordial facts concerning initial European-Amerindian relations. Our knowledge of both the facts and fantasies of this cultural contact is now sufficiently advanced to make a revision of interpretations both imperative and credible. There is no longer place for the uncritical assumption that the Eurocentric evaluations and comparisons of the French seventeenth-century contemporary sources represented accurately the social realities of the time, much less Amerindian views of events and values. The corrective considerations and the long overdue reappraisal suggested herein can only have the beneficial and stimulating consequence for Canadian historical writing of challenging description, exposition, and evaluation that depict the Amerindians as part of an American environment to be overcome and subdued to European purposes and policies, which relegate the aborigines to the background and stage-setting of national history, or which represent them as awe-stricken inferiors overwhelmed by the impact of a superior civilization that they aspired to acquire but which their own inadequacies denied them as an elusive and unattainable objective.

NOTES

1. This is the revised version of a paper read at the seventh annual Northern Great Plains History Conference, University of Manitoba, 20 Oct. 1972.

2. This orientation is illustrated in the following important writings: Henri Baudt, *Paradise on Earth. Some Thoughts on European Images of Non-European Man* (New Haven 1965); Gilbert Chinard, *L'Amérique et le rêve exotique dans la littérature française au XVIIe et au XVIIIe siècle* (Paris 1913); René Gonnard, *La légende du*

bon sauvage (Paris 1946); George R. Healy, "The French Jesuits and the Idea of the Noble Savage," *William and Mary Quarterly* xv, no. 2, April 1958, 143–67; Douglas Leechman, "The Indian in Literature," *Queen's Quarterly* 1, no. 2, summer 1943, 156–63; Roy Harvey Pearce, *The Savages of America. A Study of the Indian and the Idea of Civilization* (Baltimore 1953); Donald Boyd Smith, *French Canadian Historians' Images of the Indian in the 'Heroic Period' of New France, 1534–1663* (unpublished Master's thesis, Université Laval 1969).

3. D. Danville, pseudonym (Adolphe Bossange), *Beautés de l'histoire du Canada ou époques remark-quables, traits intéressans, moeurs, usages, coutumes des habitans du Canada, tant indigènes que colons, depuis sa découverte jusqu'à ce jour* (Paris 1821); F.-X. Charlevois, *Histoire et description générale de la Nouvelle-France avec le journal historique d'un Voyage fait par ordre du Roi dans l'amérique septentrionale*, 3 vols. (Paris 1744); F. R. Chateaubriand, *Le Génie du Christianisme* (Paris 1802); J. F. X. Lafitau, *Moeurs des Sauvages amériquians comparés aud moeurs des premiers temps* (Paris 1724); G.-T. Raynale, *Histoire philosophique et politique des éstab-lissements et du commerce dans les deux Indes* (Genève 1780).

4. Claude d'Abbeville, *Histoire de la Mission des Pères Capucins en l'Isle de Maragnan et terres circon-voisines* (Paris 1614); Paul Boyer, *Véritable Relation de tout ce quis s'est fait de passé ou voyage que Monsieur Bretigny fit à l'Amérique Occidentale* (Paris 1654); J. de Clodoré, *Relation de ce qui s'est passé dans les Isles et Terre ferme de l'Amérique* (Paris 1671); Jean de Léry, *Histoire d'un Voyage fait en le Terre du Brésil autrement dite Amérique* (La Rochelle 1578); Marc Lescarbot, *Histoire de la Nouvelle France* (Paris 1609); Gabriel Sagard-Théodat, *Le Grand Voyage du Pays des Hurons* (Paris 1632).

5. Maximilien Bibaud, *Biographie des Sagamos Illustres de l'Amérique septentrionale* (Montréal 1848).

6. Napoléon Legendre, "Les races indigènes de l'Amérique devant l'histoire," *Mémoires de la Société Royale du Canada*, II, 1884, sec. 1, 25–30.

7. Léo-Pual Desrosiers, *Iroquoisie, 1534–1646* (Montréal 1947); Jacques Rousseau, *L'Indien at notre milieu* (mimeographed Laval university televised course, 1966); André Vachon, "L'Eau-de-vie dans la société indienne," *Canadian Historical Association Annual Reports*, 1960, 22–32. The author has been much encouraged in this line of research by Wilcomb E. Washburn. The debt to the writings of Clark Wissler, Harold Driver, Edward Spicer, Anthony F. C. Wallace, Bruce Trigger, and William Fenton is also acknowledged.

8. R. G. Thwaites, ed., *The Jesuit Relations and Allied Documents* (Cleveland 1896–1901), III, 123.

9. Wilcomb E. Washburn, "A Moral History of Indian-White Relations: Needs and Opportunities for Study," *Ethnohistory*, IV, no. 1, winter 1957, 48.

10. P. A. S. Maillard, "Lettre sur les missions de l'Acadie et particulièrement sur les missions Mic-maques," *Les Soirs Canadiennes*, III, 1863, 299.

11. W. L. Grant, ed., *The History of New France by Marc Lescarbot* (Toronto, 1911), II, 247.

12. Ibid., III, 21.

13. Ibid., II, 45–46.

14. Ibid., II, 146.

15. Gabriel Sagard-Théodat, *Histoire du Canada et Voyages que les Frères Mineurs Recollects y ont faicts pour la Conuersion des Infidelles* (Paris 1636), 154.

16. E. E. Rich, "Trade Habits and Economic Motivation among the Indians of North America," *Canadian Journal of Economics and Political Science*, XXVI, Feb. 1960, 35–53.

17. Wilcomb E. Washburn, "Symbol, Utility, and Aesthetics in the Indian Fur Trade," *Aspects of the Fur Trade, Selected Papers of the 1965 North American Fur Trade Conference* (St. Paul 1967), 50–54.

18. William F. Ganong, ed., *The Description and Natural History of the Coasts of North America (Acadia) by Nicholas Denys* (Toronto 1908), 442–43.

19. Sagard, *Histoire du Canada*, 36.

20. Grant, *History of New France*, III, 3.

21. Ibid., 25.

22. Nicolas Denys, *Geographische en Historische Beschrijving den Kusten van Noord America. Met de Naturirlijke Historie des Lendts* (Amsterdam 1688), 67.

23. William F. Ganong, ed., *New Relations of Gaspesia with the Customs and Religion of the Gaspesian Indians by Father Chrestien LeClercq* (Toronto 1910), 101–2; also Thwaites, *Jesuit Relations*, III, 81.

24. Thwaites, *Jesuit Relations*, LVII, 95–97.

25. James B. Conacher, ed., *The History of Canada or New France by Father François du Creux, S.J.* (Toronto 1951), 267–68.

26. Ganong, *New Relation by LeClercq*, 246.

27. J. C. Webster, ed., *Sieur de Dièreville, Relation of the Voyage to Port Royal in Acadia or New France* (Toronto 1933), 150.

28. Conacher, *History of Canada*, 274.

29. Harry Hoetink, *The Two Variants in Caribbean Race Relations* (New York 1967), 120–59.

30. Pierre d'Avity, *Description générale de l'Amérique troisième partie du Monde* (Paris 1637), 30.

31. Sagard, *Le Grand Voyage du Pays des Hurons*, 176–77.

32. Thwaites, *Jesuit Relations* XXVII, 215.

33. Grant, *History of New France*, III, 22.

34. Ibid., 27.

35. Ibid., 22.

36. Conacher, *History of Canada*, I, 36.

37. Nicolas Perrot, "Memoir on the Manners, Customs, and Religion of the Savages of North America," in E. H. Blair, ed., *The Indian Tribes of the Upper Mississippi Valley and Region of the Great Lakes* (Cleveland 1911), I, 145.

38. George M. Wrong, ed., *The Long Journey to the Country of the Hurons by Father Gabriel Sagard* (Toronto 1939), 137.

39. Thwaites, *Jesuit Relations*, III, 22.

40. Ibid., 75.

41. R. G. Thwaites, ed., *New Voyages to North America by Baron de Lahontan* (Chicago 1905), II, 471.

42. Thwaites, *Jesuit Relations*, III, 105. This is the work cited in ensuing references, not Lahontan's *New Voyages*, also edited by Thwaites.

43. Ibid., XXXI, 121.

44. Ibid., XXXIX, 129–31.

45. Conacher, *History of Canada*, I, 194.

46. Ibid., 227.

47. Dom Guy Oury, *Marie de l'Incarnation, Ursuline (1599–1672). Corrèspondence* (Solesmes 1971), 67–68.

48. Thwaites, *Jesuit Relations*, I, 117–18.

49. Ibid., XVIII, 41.

50. Ibid., XXXI, 123.

51. Grant, *History of New France*, 179–80.

52. Ganong, *New Relation by LeClercq*, 140–41.

53. Thwaites, *Jesuit Relations*, VI, 289; X, 119; XV, 155; XXIX, 119; LXVII, 145.

54. Ibid., LXIII, 299.

55. Ibid., LXV, 131.

56. Conacher, *History of Canada*, I, 160.

57. Sagard, *Histoire du Canada*, 9.

58. Conacher, *History of Canada*, I, 313–14.

59. Thwaites, *Jesuit Relations*, XX, 27–31; XXX, 27, 29–31.

60. Ibid., XX, 27–29.

61. Ibid., LVIII, 275.

62. Ibid., LVIII, 201.

63. Wrong, *Long Journey*, 78.

64. Alessandro Bacchiani, "Giovanni da Verrazzano and His Discoveries in North America, 1524, according to the Unpublished Contemporaneous Cellère Codex of Rome, Italy," *Fifteenth Annual Report, 1910, of the American Scenic and Historic Preservation Society* (Albany 1910), Appendix A, 192.

65. Thwaites, *Jesuit Relations*, III, 103–5.

66. Sagard, *Histoire du Canada*, 165.

67. Thwaites, *Jesuit Relations*, V, 119–21.

68. Ganong, *New Relation by LeClercq*, 106.

69. Ibid., 103–4.

70. Thwaites, *Jesuit Relations*, V, 121.

71. Dom Albert Jamet, ed., *Les Annales de l'Hôtel-Dieu de Québec, 1636–1716* (Québec 1939), 47.

72. Donald H. Frame, ed., *Montaigne's Essays and Selected Writings* (New York 1963), 117. The account is given in much more detail in an unlikely source: Michel Baudier, *Histoire de la Religion des Turcs* (Paris 1625), 122.

73. *Histoire du Canada*, 241–42.

74. Ganong, *New Relation by LeClercq*, 104.

75. Perrot, "Memoir," 134–35.

76. Sagard, *Histoire du Canada*, 219.

77. C. H. Laverdière and H.-R. Casgrain, eds., *Le Journal des Jésuites* (Québec 1871), 77–78.

78. Thwaites, *Jesuit Relations*, XIV, 19–21.

79. Ibid., 216–18.

80. Ibid., 233.

81. Grant, *History of New France*, II, 326.

82. Jamet, *Annales*, 25.

83. Conacher, *History of Canada*, II, 651.

84. Thwaites, *Jesuit Relations*, XLIV, 297.

85. Ibid., V, 143; XVII, 213; XXXIX, 73; XLIX, 121; LXI, 85; LXVII, 61. F. Speiser, K. R. Andrae, and W. Krickberg, "Les Peaux-Rouges et leur médecine," *Revue Ciba*, no. 10, April 1940, 291–318.

86. Marc Lescarbot, *Histoire de la Nouvelle-France* (Paris 1609), 667.

87. d'Abbeville, *Histoire de la Mission*, 281.

88. Ganong, *Description by Denys*, 404.

89. Joyce Marshall, ed., *Word from New France. The Selected Letters of Marie de l'Incarnation* (Toronto 1967), 341.

90. Oury, *Marie de l'incarnation*, 995.

91. Ibid., 801–2.

92. Ibid., 828.

93. Pierre Margry, ed., *Découvertes et Etablissements des Français dans l'Ouest et dans le Sud de l'Amérique septentrionale* (Paris 1879), I, Talon to Colbert, 10 Nov. 1670, 92.

94. Conacher, *History of Canada*, 35–36.

95. Grant, *History of New France*, II, 146–48.

96. PAC, MG17/A,7-1, St. Sulpice, Mélanges carton B, no 28(h), 199–200.

97. Thwaites, *Jesuit Relations*, VI, 165.

98. Paul Boyer, *Véritable Relation de tout ce qui s'est fait et passé au voyage que Monsieur de Bretigny fit à l'Amérique Occidentale* (Paris 1654), 227.

99. James H. Coyne, "Dollier de Casson & De Bréhaut de Gallinée: Exploration of the Great Lakes, 1669–1670," *Ontario Historical Society Papers and Records*, IV, 1903, 19.

100. PAC, MG2, Archives de la Marine, Series B³, IX, Sieur de Narne to Minister of the Marine, 3 Sept. 1671, fol. 374.

101. Sagard, *Histoire du Canada*, 95.

102. Thwaites, *Jesuit Relations*, XXVII, 235.

103. Ibid., XLII, 121–23; G. Snyderman, "Behind the Tree of Peace: A Sociological Analysis of Iroquois Warfare," *Pennsylvania Archaeologist*, XVIII, nos. 3 and 4, 1948, 30–37.

104. PAC, MG I, *Archives des Colonies, Series* C¹¹A, VII, Denonville to Seignelay, 13 Nov. 1685, 45–46.

5

IROQUOIS WOMEN, EUROPEAN WOMEN

Natalie Zemon Davis

Of all the challenges that natives and newcomers faced in the American encounter, perhaps none was more perplexing than fathoming the other's notions of proper gender roles. The issue confounded people precisely because these roles differed so dramatically, and were so deeply rooted as to be thought the "natural" result of biological differences rather than cultural constructions. To be sure, there were similarities: in both European and Indian societies, men took the lead in hunting, warfare, diplomacy, and politics. But the differences were profound. Europeans were shocked to discover that among natives, premarital sex was common and accepted, as was divorce. No less surprising was that many native societies were matrilocal and matrilinear; that is, a man, upon marrying, went to live with his new wife's kin group in her household, and children were considered part of that family, and not part of their father's family. Those natives, meanwhile, were appalled by European men who farmed, believing that such labor was "women's work"; "only squaws and hedgehogs are made to scratch the ground," scoffed one Indian man who contemplated the prospect of hoeing a field.

Other differences could be found in the spiritual realm. Paul's Biblical dictum—"Let your women be silent in church"—might have been questioned by Europeans in the generations following the Protestant Reformation initiated by Martin Luther in 1517, but the central notion remained intact: in neither Catholic nor Protestant Europe did women (other than nuns) have a special sacred role; nor, with rare exceptions, did they play a leading part in religious movements. By contrast, native women's participation in religious affairs suggested an equality between men and women unknown in Europe. That participation, many natives believed, commenced at the very beginning of time: in Iroquois and Cherokee origin stories, for example, women played a prominent role in the creation of the world.

During the seventeenth and eighteenth centuries, gender conflicts often became the subject of heated debate. Yet there were accommodations as well, especially among Indian women who converted to Christianity. As Natalie Davis demonstrates here, comparing the lives of women on each side of the cultural divide provides new insight into the meeting of peoples in North America.

IROQUOIS WOMEN, EUROPEAN WOMEN

Natalie Zemon Davis

IN THE OPENING YEARS of the seventeenth century in the Montagnais country, Pierre Pastedechouan's grandmother loved to tell him how astonished she had been at the first sight of a French ship. With its large sails and many people gathered on the deck, she had thought the wooden boat a floating island. She and the other women in her band immediately set up cabins to welcome the guests.[1] The people on a floating island appeared also to a young Micmac woman of the Saint Lawrence Gulf in a dream that she recounted to the shaman and elders of her community and which came true a few days later when a European ship arrived.[2]

Across the Atlantic, Mother Marie Guyart de l'Incarnation also first saw the Amerindian lands in a dream-vision, a vast space of mountains, valleys, and fog to which the Virgin Mary and Jesus beckoned her and which her spiritual director then identified as Canada. By the time she had boarded the boat in 1639, she hoped to "taste the delights of Paradise in the beautiful and large crosses of New France." Once at Quebec, she and her sister Ursulines kissed the soil, Marie finding the landscape just like her dream except not so foggy. The Christianized Algonquin, Montagnais, and Huron girls, "freshly washed in the blood of the lamb, seem[ed] to carry Paradise with them."[3]

The similarities and differences in the situation and views of these women in the sixteenth and first half of the seventeenth centuries is my subject in this essay. I want to look at the Amerindian women of the eastern woodlands in terms of historical change—and not just change generated by contact with Europeans, but by processes central to their own societies. I want to insist on the absolute simultaneity of the Amerindian and European worlds, rather than viewing the former as an earlier version of the latter, and make comparisons less polarized than the differences between "simple" and "complex" societies. I want to suggest interactions to look for in the colonial encounter other than the necessary but overpolarized twosome of "domination" and "resistance," and attribute the capacity for choice to Indians as to Europeans. The Amerindian case may also be a source of alternative examples

SOURCE: Margo Hendricks and Patricia Parker, eds., *Women, "Race," and Writing in the Early Modern Period* (New York: Routledge, 1994), 243–58.

and metaphors to illumine the European case. Indeed, an ideal sequel to this essay would be an inquiry about the history of European women that made use of Iroquois tropes and frames.

The term "Iroquois women" in my title is a shorthand for both the Hurons and the Iroquois among the nations speaking the Iroquoian languages, from whom many of my examples will be drawn, and in some instances for women of the groups speaking Algonquian languages, peoples from primarily hunting, fishing, and gathering communities such as the Montagnais, Algonquins, Abenakis, and Micmacs. On the whole, I will stay within the region penetrated by the French, though the woodlands Indians themselves ranged well beyond its reach. My sources are the classic travel accounts and the Jesuit and other religious relations from the eastern woodlands (including the writings of Marie de l'Incarnation and the women Hospitalers of Quebec); ethnographic studies, including those based on archeological research and material culture; and collections of Amerindian tales and legends and customs made over the last 150 years and more.[4]

The Hurons and Iroquois alike lived from a digging-stick agriculture, gathering, fishing, and hunting.[5] The men opened the fields for cultivation, but the women were the farmers, growing maize, beans, squash, and in some places tobacco. The women also were the gatherers, picking fruits and other edible food and bringing in all the firewood. When villages changed their base, as they did every several years, it was sometimes in fear of their enemies, but ordinarily because the women declared the fields infertile and the suitable wood exhausted for miles around. The men were in charge of hunting, fishing, and intertribal trading, but the active women might well accompany their husbands or fathers on these expeditions when not held back by farming or cabin tasks. Along the way the women were expected to do much of the carrying, although if there were male prisoners with the band, their masters would have them help the women.[6] Warfare was in the hands of the men.

Responsibility for the crafts and arts was similarly divided. Men made weapons and tools of stone, wood, and sometimes bits of copper, carved the pipes, built the cabins, and constructed frames for canoes and snowshoes. Women were in charge of anything that had to do with sewing, stringing and weaving, preparing thread and laces by hand-spinning and winding, stringing snowshoes, and making baskets, birchbark kettles, nets, and rush mats. Once the men had made a kill at the hunt, the animal was the women's domain, from skinning and preparing the hide, softening and greasing the furs, to making garments and moccasins. The women were the potters, and also made all the decorative objects of porcupine quills, shells (including wampum necklaces and belts), beads, and birchbark. They painted the faces and bodies of their husbands and sons so that they would look impressive when they went visiting, and decorated each other for dances and feasts. As for the meals, the women took care of them all, pounding the corn into flour and cooking much of the food in a single kettle. (Similar work patterns were found among the Algonquian-speaking peoples, where horticulture was only occasionally practiced and where the women were thus on the move much of the time with the men.)

This division of labor looked very lopsided to the French men who first reported it, presumably contrasting it with European agriculture, where men did the ploughing, where women did the weeding and gardening, and where both did wooding and carrying, and with European crafts like leather and pottery, where men had a predominant role. "The women work without comparison more than the men," said Jacques Cartier of the Iroquois whom he had met along the Saint Lawrence in 1536; "the women do all the servile tasks, working ordinarily harder than the men, though they are neither forced or constrained to do it," said the Recollet Gabriel Sagard of the Huron women in 1623. "Real pack-mules," a Jesuit echoed a few years later.[7] Marie de l'Incarnation, in contrast, took the women's heavy work for granted, perhaps because she heard about it from the Huron and Algonquin women in a matter-of-fact way in the convent yard rather than seeing it, perhaps because she herself had spent her young womanhood in a wagoner's household, doing everything from grooming horses and cleaning slops to keeping the accounts.[8] In any case, Sagard noted that the Huron women still had time for gaming, dancing, and feasts, and "to chat and pass the time together."[9]

The differences that even Marie de l'Incarnation could not fail to recognize between her life in France and that of Huron and Iroquois women concerned property, kinship structures, marriage, and sexual practice. Whereas in France private or at least family property was increasingly freeing itself from the competing claims of distant kin and feudal lords, among both the Iroquois and the Hurons collective property arrangements—village, clan, band, or tribal—prevailed in regard to hunting and gathering areas and to farming plots. Matrilineality and matrilocality seem to have been more consistently practiced among the Iroquois than among the Hurons,[10] but for both societies the living unit was a longhouse of several related families, in which the senior women had a major say about what went on. (The Algonquian-speaking peoples counted descent patrilineally and dwelt in smaller wigwams and summer lodges.)

Parents often suggested potential marriage partners to their children (among the Iroquois, it was the mothers who took the initiative), but then the younger generation had to act. A Huron youth would ask the permission of the parents of a young woman and give her a substantial present of a wampum collar or beaver robe; if, after a sexual encounter for a few nights, she gave her consent, the wedding feast took place.[11] As there was no dowry and dower but only a bride gift, so there was no property in the way of inheritance: the deceased took some of his or her mats and furs and other goods away to the other world, while the bereaved kin were given extensive gifts "to dry their tears" by the other members of their village and clan.[12]

Without property inheritance and without firm notions about the father's qualities being carried through sexual intercourse or the blood,[13] sexual relations between men and women were conducted without concern about "illegitimate" offspring. There could be several trial encounters and temporary unions before a marriage was decided on, and openly acknowledged intercourse with other partners was possible for both husband and wife. When a Huron father was questioned one day by a Jesuit about how, with such practices, a man could know who his son was, the man answered, "You French love only your own children; we love all the children of our people." When Hurons and Algonquins first saw the Quebec Hospital nuns in 1639—three women all in their twenties—they were astonished (so one of the sisters reported) "when they were told that we had no men at all and that we were virgins."[14]

Clearly there was room in the Iroquoian longhouse and Algonquian wigwam for many quarrels: among wives at their different longhouse fires, among daughters and parents about consent to a suitor,[15] among husbands and wives about competing lovers.[16] One Jesuit even claimed in 1657 that some married women revenged themselves on their husbands for "bad treatment" by eating a poisonous root and leaving the men with "the reproach of their death."[17] Much more often, an unsatisfactory marriage simply ended in divorce, with both man and woman free to remarry and the woman usually having custody of the children.[18]

In such a situation the debate about authority had a different content from that in Renaissance and early seventeenth-century Europe, where a hierarchical model of the father-dominated family was at best moderated by the image of companionate marriage or reversed by the husband-beating virago. Among the Amerindians, physical coercion was not supposed to be used against anyone within the family, and decisions about crops, food consumption, and many of the crafts were rightfully the women's. If a man wanted a courteous excuse not to do something, he could say without fear of embarrassment "that his wife did not wish it."[19]

When we leave the longhouse fire and kettle for the religious feast or dance and council meeting, we have a different picture again. Religious belief among both the Algonquian- and Iroquoian-speaking peoples was diverse and wide-ranging, their high divinities, sacred manitous, and omnipresent lesser spirits remembered, pondered over, and argued about through decentralized storytelling. Recollets and Jesuits, hearing such accounts, would challenge the speakers: "How can the creator Yoscaha have a grandmother Aataentsic if Yoscaha is the first god?" they would ask a Huron. "And how could Aataentsic's daughter get pregnant with Yoscaha and his evil twin Tawiscaron if men had not yet been created?" "Was Atahocan definitely the first creator?" they would ask a Montagnais. Huron or Montagnais would then reply that he did not know for sure: "Perhaps it was Atahocan; one speaks of Atahocan as one speaks of a thing so far distant that nothing sure can be known about it." Or that he had the account from someone who had visited Yoscaha and Aataentsic or had seen it in a dream. Or, politely, that the French beliefs about "God" were fine for Europe but not for the woodlands. Or, defiantly, that he would believe in the Jesuits' God when he saw him with his own eyes.[20]

The Recollets and Jesuits reported such exchanges only with men, Father Le Jeune even adding, "there are among them mysteries so hidden that only the old men, who can speak with credit and authority about them, are believed."[21] Marie de l'Incarnation, always attentive to women's roles and pleased that Abenaki belief included the virgin birth of the world-saver Messou, said only that traditional accounts of the "Sauvages" were passed on "from fathers to children, from the old to the young."[22] Women were certainly among the listeners to Amerindian creation accounts, for the "ancient tales" were told, for instance, at gatherings after funerals,[23] but were they among the tellers of sacred narratives? Speculation from the existing evidence suggests the following picture: during the sixteenth and early seventeenth centuries, men, especially older men, were the tellers of creation stories at male assemblies (as for the election of a chief)[24] and at mixed gatherings, but women recounted Aataentsic's doings along with many other kinds of narrative to each other and to their children.[25] If this be the case, then the situation of women in the eastern woodlands was rather like that of their Catholic contemporaries in Europe. There, for the most part, Catholic belief systems were formally taught by doctors of theology and male preachers and catechizers, and women reflected on such doctrine among themselves in convents and told Christian stories to their children.

To the all-important realm of dreams, however, Amerindian women and men had equal access. Huron and Iroquois notions of "the soul" and "the self" were more inflected, articulated, or pluralistic than Christian notions of the living person, where a single soul animated the body and where reason, will, and appetite were functions warring or collaborating within. Huron and Iroquois saw "the soul" as "divisible" (to use Father Brébeuf's term about the Huron), giving different names and some independence to different soul-actions: animation, reason, deliberation, and desire. The desiring soul especially spoke to one in dreams—"this is what my heart tells me, this is what my appetite desires" (*ondayee ikaton onennoncwat*); sometimes the desiring soul was counseled by a familiar *oki* or spirit who appeared in a dream in some form and told it what it needed or wanted, its *ondinoc*, its secret desire.[26] In France, dreams and the time between sleeping and waking were the occasion for extraordinary visits from Christ, the saints, the devil, or the ghosts of one's dead kin. In the American woodlands, dreams were a visit from part of oneself and one's *oki*, and their prescriptions had wider effect, forestalling or curing illness and predicting, sanctioning, or warning against future events of all kinds.

Amerindian women and men thus took their dreams very seriously, describing, evaluating, and interpreting them to each other, and then acting on them with intensity and determination. For a person of some standing, the village council might decide to mobilize every cabin to help fulfill a dream. So a woman of Angoutenc in the Huron country went outside one night with her little daughter and was greeted by the Moon deity, swooping down from the sky as a beautiful tall woman with a little daughter of her own. The Moon ordered that the woman be given many presents of garments and tobacco from surrounding peoples and that henceforth she dress herself in red, like the fiery moon. Back in her longhouse, the woman immediately fell ill with dizziness and weak muscles, and learned from her dreams that only a curing feast and certain presents would restore her. The council of her birth-village of Ossassané agreed to provide all she needed. Three days of ritual action followed, with the many prescribed gifts assembled, the woman in her red garments walking through fires that did not burn her limbs, and everyone discussing their dream desires through riddles.[27] She was cured in an episode that illustrates to us how an individual woman could set in motion a whole sequence of collective religious action.[28]

Women also had important roles in dances intended to placate the *oki* spirits or to drive out evil spirits from the sick. Among the Hurons, a few women who had received a dream sign might be initiated along with men into a society whose curative dance was considered "very powerful against the demons"; among the Iroquois, women were received in several healing and propitiary societies.[29] To be sure, women were accused of witchcraft—that is, of causing someone's death by poisoning or charms—but no more than Huron and Iroquois men, and *okis* or *manitous* in mischievous action were not gendered female more than male.[30]

The major asymmetry in religious life in the sixteenth and seventeenth centuries concerned the shamans. The Arendiwane, as the Hurons called them ("sorcerers" or "jugglers" in the language of the Jesuits), comprised the master shamans, who diagnosed and cured illness by dealing with the spirit world, and the lesser religious leaders, who commanded winds and rains, predicted the future, or found lost objects. The Jesuits scarcely ever described women in these roles among either the Algonquian-speaking or Iroquoian-speaking peoples, and Marie de l'Incarnation mentioned none at all. An Algonquin woman was known "to be involved in sorcery, succeeding at it better than the men"; a woman "famous" among the Hurons for her "sorcery" sought messages from the *Manitou* about what kinds of feasts or gifts would cure an illness; a Montagnais woman entered the cabin where the male shamans consulted the spirits of the air and through shaking the tent-posts and loud singing was able to diagnose an illness and foresee an Iroquois attack.[31] Indeed, soothsaying seems to have been the one shamanic function in which women were welcome, as with the old woman of Teanaostaiaë village in the Huron country, who saw events in distant battles with the Iroquois by looking into fires, and the Abenaki "Pythonesses" who could see absent things and foretell the future.[32]

Most of the time, however, a woman was simply an aide, marking on a "triangular stick" the songs for the dead being sung by a Montagnais medicine man so their order would be remembered; walking around the shaman and his male performers at a prescribed moment in a ritual to kill a far-away witch.[33] Surely the herbal remedies known to be used by later Amerindian women must have had their antecedents in the female lore of the sixteenth and early seventeenth centuries,[34] and it is hard to imagine that there were no religious specialists associated with the menstrual cabins of the Iroquoian communities and the Montagnais. It may have been precisely the beliefs about defilement that barred women from handling the sacred shamanic objects and rattle used in spirit cures. Across the Atlantic, the powers and dangers of menstruation kept European *religieuses* from touching altars and chalices too directly and kept Catholic laywomen away from the mass during their periods. Among the Hurons, the presence of a pregnant woman made a sick person worse, but was required for the extraction of an arrow; among the French Catholics, the glance of a postpartum woman brought trouble to people in streets and roadways. Among the Amerindians, medicine men were to abstain from sexual intercourse before their ceremonies; among the Europeans, Catholic priests were to abstain from sexual intercourse all the time.[35]

The most important asymmetry among Indian men and women was political. In the female world of crops, cooking, and crafts, women made the decisions; in lodge and long-house, their voice often carried the day. Village and tribal governance, however, was in the hands of male chiefs and councils, and, apart from the Iroquois, women's influence on it was informal. (Only among the Algonquian peoples of southern New England and the mid-Atlantic coast do we hear of women sometimes holding authority as sunksquaws along with the more numerous male sachems.)[36] Huron villages and Algonquian and Montagnais settlements often had two or more chiefs, their access to this honor partly hereditary but even more based on assessments of their eloquence, wisdom, generosity, or past prowess. The chiefs presided over frequent local council meetings, where women and young warriors were rarely present and where pipe-smoking men gave their views, the eldest among them being accorded particular respect. At larger assemblies of several clans and villages, the young men were invited as well, and sometimes the women.[37] When council or assembly decisions required embassies to other villages or nations—to seek support in war or to resolve disputes—the envoys were chiefs and other men.

In Iroquois communities, women had more formal roles in political decisions than elsewhere. Here, to women's advantage, succession to chieftaincies was more strictly hereditary, passing matrilineally to a sister's son or another male relative named by the woman. Here among the Onondagas—so we learn from the pen of Marie de l'Incarnation—there were "women of quality" or "Capitainesses" who could affect decisions at local council meetings and select ambassadors for peace initiatives.[38] At least by the eighteenth century important women could attend treaty councils of the Iroquois nations, and perhaps they did so earlier.[39]

Now it is precisely in regard to this political life that major historical changes had occurred in the American/Canadian woodlands and villages from the fourteenth through sixteenth centuries. The evidence for these changes comes in part from archaeologists: tobacco-pipes become more elaborate, pottery and sea shells are found further from their place of origin, and human bones in ossuaries show signs of being "cut, cooked and split open to extract the marrow."[40] The evidence comes also from the collective memory of Hurons and Iroquois after European contact and from Indian stories and legends.

A double picture emerges. First, warfare became more prevalent and intense, with the seizure of women as wives[41] and the adoption of some male captives and the torture and cannibalization of others. European contact then added to the complicated history of enmity and exchange between Iroquois and Hurons. As a Huron chief recalled to some Onondagas in 1652,

> Have you forgotten the mutual promises our Ancestors made when they first took up arms against each other, that if a simple woman should take it on herself to uncover the Sweat-house and pull up the stakes that support it, that the victors would put down their arms and show mercy to the vanquished?"[42]

The two roles assigned to women by intensified warfare—the woman-adoptor of an enemy and the woman-enemy incorporated as wife—must have had important consequences for consciousness. Let us consider here only the enemy wife, a position in which women living in Europe rarely found themselves (even though the foreign queens of Spain and France might have felt divided loyalties when their husbands went to war in 1635, the marriages had been made as peaceful alliance).[43] In the eastern American woodlands, Algonquin and Huron captives became Iroquois wives; Iroquois captives became Huron wives. Nor was their origin forgotten: Pierre Esprit Radisson among the Mohawks in 1652 discovered that his adoptive mother had been taken from the Huron country in her youth; Father Le Moyne among the Onondagas the next year was approached by a Huron wife who "wanted to pour out her heart to him."[44] This suggests that to the Amerindian habit of self-discovery through dream analysis was added for the enemy wife another source for self-definition: the experience of being forcibly transplanted, alone or with only a few of her kin, to a people who had a different language and burial ground from her ancestors. When the enemy wife was also a Christian in a non-Christian village, the impulse toward self-definition might be all the stronger, but the process predated conversion.

This setting for self-consciousness is rather different from those in which Renaissance historians usually locate the discovery of "the individual" or of a renewed sense of self among European Christians. There we stress how persons set themselves off against those whom they resembled, against their own kind and kin: some of Montaigne's best self-discovery occurred when he played himself off against his friend La Boétie and against his own father. The Amerindian enemy wife (and the adopted male enemy as well) represent a contrasting historical trajectory. Still, they should make us more attentive to European situations where the experience of "foreignness" and "strangeness" could prompt consciousness of self as well as of group. The emergence of Jewish autobiography by the early seventeenth century is a case in point.[45]

Along with intensified warfare, a second associated change took place in the eastern American woodlands in the fifteenth, sixteenth, and early seventeenth centuries: intertribal political federations appeared along with a new peacemaking diplomacy. The Huron League, or League of the Ouendats as they called themselves, was made up of four nations or tribes, two of them establishing themselves as "brother" and "sister" with a grand council in the fifteenth century, the other two being adopted, one in the last decades of the sixteenth century and the other in the early seventeenth century.[46] The Iroquois League of the Five Nations, the Houdénosaunee—three Elder Brothers and two Younger Brothers—was probably founded around 1500.[47] Its origin was memorialized in the Deganawidah Epic about a divine Iroquois seer, Deganawidah, who preached peace, converted a Mohawk chief Hiawatha away from cannibalism, and then together with him transformed the wicked and obstructive Onondaga chief Thadodaho into a willing collaborator. (Women enter the epic through Deganawidah's grandmother, who foresaw his peace-bringing role in a dream; his mother, who received divine guidance in hidden seclusion and then gave birth to Deganawidah as a virgin; and the daughter of Hiawatha, who died sacrificially in the encounter with Thadodaho.)[48]

Among the many fruits of the League formation was the development of a language of politics and diplomacy: a set of rules and styles of communication that operated around the local council fire, on embassies to rouse for war or make amends for a murder, at large assemblies, and at general councils of the federation. At council meetings, where many opinions were given, matters opened with the leader's appreciative words about the men's safe arrival, no one lost in the woods or fallen in the stream or slain by an enemy. A special tone of voice was used for all the comments and opinions—the Hurons called it *acouentonch*—"a raising and lowering of the voice like the tone of a Predicant à l'antique, an old style Preacher," said a Jesuit in 1636.[49] Always the men spoke slowly, calmly, and distinctly, each person reviewing the issues before giving his opinion. No one ever interrupted anyone else, the rhythm of taking turns aided by the smoking of pipes. No matter how bitter the disagreement—as when some Huron villages wanted to rebury their ancestors' bones in a separate grave—courteous and gentle language was sought. The Hurons said of a good council, *Endionraondaoné*, "even and easy, like level and reaped fields."[50]

In more elaborate public speeches, for example, as an envoy or at a large assembly or to make a treaty, still another tone of voice was used—"a Captain's tone," said a Jesuit, who tried to imitate it among the Iroquois in 1654. Mnemonic devices were used "to prop up the mind," such as marked sticks and, for a major event, the ordered shells on a wampum necklace or belt. Arm gestures and dramatic movements accompanied the argument, and the speaker walked back and forth, seeming "marvelous" to Jacques Cartier in 1535, and to the later Jesuits "like an actor on a stage."[51] At the 1645 treaty between the Iroquois, the French, the Algonquins, and the Montagnais, the tall Mohawk chief Kiotseaeton arose, looked at the sun and then at all the company and said (as taken from a rough French translation):

> "Onotonio [the French governor], lend me ear. I am the whole of my country; thou listenest to all the Iroquois in hearing my words. There is no evil in my heart; I have only good songs in my mouth. We have a multitude of war songs in our country; we have cast them all on the ground; we have no longer anything but songs of rejoicing." Thereupon he began to sing; his countrymen responded; he walked about that great space as if on the stage of a theatre; he made a thousand gestures; he looked up to Heaven; he gazed at the Sun; he rubbed his arms as if he wished to draw from them the strength that moved them in war.[52]

Throughout, in all political speech, many metaphors and circumlocutions were used, which made it difficult to follow for anyone who had not learned the system. "Kettle" could denote hospitality ("to hang the kettle"), hostility or killing ("to break the kettle," "to put into the kettle"), and ritual reburial of ancestors ("Master of the Kettle," the officer for the Feast of the Dead).[53]

Meanwhile, the persons who were literally in charge of the kettle and who literally reaped the cornfields so that they were easy and even were not deliverers of this oratory. Women strung the shells for the wampum necklaces and belts used in all diplomacy, but they did not provide the public interpretations of their meaning. (Even the

Algonquian sunksquaws of the central Atlantic coast are not known for their speeches, and it is significant that Mary Rowlandson, captive of the sunksquaw Weetamoo in 1676, said of her mistress only that "when she had dressed herself, her work was to make Girdles of Wampom and Beads.)"[54] To be sure, councils had to accede to the request of any woman to adopt a prisoner who would replace her slain or dead male relative, but this desire could be discovered by a word or gesture. Only one occasion has come down to us where a Huron woman gave a speech at an assembly: during the smallpox epidemic of 1640 at a large and tumultuous gathering of Ataronchronons, an older woman denounced the Jesuit Black Robes as devils spreading disease.[55] Even in the most favored case of the Iroquois, where the chiefs had been enjoined by Hiawatha to seek the advice of their wisest women about resolving disputes and where captains' wives might accompany an embassy, women never orated as ambassadors—the Five Nations never "spoke through their mouths"—and their opinion at treaty councils was given by a male Speaker for the Women.[56]

Indian men trained their sons in oratory: "I know enough to instruct my son," said an Algonquin captain in refusing to give his son to the Jesuits. "I'll teach him to give speeches." Huron men teased each other if they made a slip of the tongue or mistake, and accorded the eloquent speaker praise and honor. When the Mohawk chief Kiot-seaeton wanted to persuade the Hurons to take part in a peace treaty with the Iroquois, he presented a wampum necklace "to urge the Hurons to hasten forth to speak. Let them not be bashful [*honteux*] like women." The Hurons "call us Frenchmen women," said the Recollet Sagard, "because too impulsive and carried away [*trop précipités et bouillants*] in our actions, [we] talk all at the same time and interrupt each other."[57]

It seems to me that connections between political change, eloquence, and gender can be similarly constructed in the North American villages and woodlands and in Western Europe in the fifteenth, sixteenth, and early seventeenth centuries. Renaissance political oratory, emerging in both republics and monarchies, and the art of formal diplomacy were part of a masculine political culture. As Leonardo Bruni said, "Rhetoric in all its forms—public discussion, forensic argument, logical fencing and the like—lies absolutely outside the province of women." The privileged few with a right to public pronouncement -the queens or queen regents and a rare learned woman—required exceptional strategies if their voice were to have an authoritative ring.[58]

Some European women sought the chance to speak publicly (or semipublicly) in religion instead: members of radical and prophetic sects from the first Anabaptists to the Quakers; Protestants in the early days of the new religion, before Paul's dictum that women should not speak in church was strictly enforced; Catholics in the new religious orders, like Marie de l'Incarnation's Ursulines and the Visitation of Jeanne de Chantal, where women preached to and taught each other.[59]

Can we find evidence for a similar process in the eastern American woodlands, that is, did Amerindian women try to expand their voice in religious culture while Amerindian men were expanding political oratory? Conceivably, the role of women in dream analysis (which, as we have seen, involved describing one's dreams publicly and playing riddle games about them at festive fires) may have increased in the course of the sixteenth century. In 1656 an Onondaga woman used her dreamswoon to unmask the Christian Paradise to her fellow Iroquois: she had visited "Heaven," she announced to them, and had seen the French burning Iroquois.[60] Conceivably, the women soothsayers whom the Jesuits met were not simply filling a timeless function open to women, but were recent shamanic innovators. Conceivably, the Iroquois Ogiweoano society of Chanters for the Dead, described in nineteenth-century sources as composed of all or predominantly women, was not a timeless institution, but a development of the sixteenth and seventeenth centuries.[61]

The evidence we do have concerns Amerindian women who converted to Christianity. Some of them used the new religion to find a voice beyond that of a shaman's silent assistant, even while Jesuits were teaching them that wives were supposed to obey their husbands. Khionrea the Huron was one such woman, her portrait drawn for seventeenth-century readers by Marie de l'Incarnation. Brought to the Ursuline convent by her parents in 1640, when she was about twelve, Khionrea had been given the name Thérèse, Marie de l'Incarnation's favorite saint, and had learned to speak both French and Algonquin and to read and write. Two Huron men from her village came to the convent two years later and she preached to them through the grill:

> They listened to this young woman with unrivalled attention, and one day, when they were on the point of being baptized, one of them pretended no longer to believe in God and so she need no longer speak to him of faith or baptism. Our fervent Thérèse . . . became disturbed and said, "What are you talking about? I see the Devil has overturned all your thoughts so that you will be lost. Know you well that if you died today, you would go to Hell where you would burn with Devils, who would make you suffer terrible torments!" The good man laughed at everything she said, which made her think that he spoke with a spirit of contempt. She redoubled her exhortations to combat him, but failing, she came to us in tears. "Ah," she said, "he is lost; he's left the faith; he will not be baptized. It hurt me so to see him speak against God that if there had not been a grill between us, I would have thrown myself on him to beat him." We went to find out the truth . . . and the man affirmed that he had done this only to test her faith and zeal.[62]

Several months afterward Khionrea's parents came to take her back to her village to marry, expecting her to be "the example of their Nation and the Teacher (Maîtresse) of the Huron girls and women." Instead her party was captured by Iroquois, a number were slain, and Thérèse was married to a Mohawk. A decade later, in 1653, she was the mistress of the several families of her Iroquois longhouse, still praying to her Christian God and leading others publicly in prayer.[63] Khionrea may have been placating *oki* spirits as well—though Marie de l'Incarnation would have hated to think so—and inspired non-Christian women in her village to experimental religious action. One thinks especially of how Christian forms and phrases could have been appropriated to elaborate and lengthen Indian propitiary prayer.

Cécile Gannendaris is another example of a Huron woman who found an authoritative voice through a new religious mix. Her biography was left by the Sisters of the

Quebec Hospital where she died at an advanced age in 1669, her Christian "virtue" being demonstrated not only by her fighting off "seducers" in her youth with smoldering logs and spanking her children "when they deserved it," but by giving spiritual guidance to her first and second husbands. Especially she taught and preached, "converting numerous Savages and encouraging them to live more perfectly."

> She was so solidly instructed in our mysteries and so eloquent in explaining them that she was sent new arrivals among the Savages who were asking to embrace the faith. In a few days she had them ready for baptism, and had reduced the opinionated ones beyond defense by her good reasoning.

The French were impressed with her as well, the Jesuits learning the Huron language from her lips, the newly established Bishop of Québec coming to visit her in her cabin, and the Frenchwomen sending her gifts of food. The Hospital Sisters thought that Gannendaris's clarity of expression and discernment were a break with her Huron past, or, as they put it, "had nothing of the savage [*rien de sauvage*] about them." We would interpret these talents differently, as drawing on a Huron tradition of lucid male discussion around the council fire and on a longhouse practice of women's teaching, here transformed by Christian learning and opportunity into a new realm of speech.[64]

When Iroquois women became interested in Christianity, the oratorical force of young converts struck them right away. In the fall of 1655, an Onondaga embassy came to Québec to confirm peace with the Hurons and their French allies and to invite the Black Robes to their villages. A chief's wife ("*une Capitainesse,*" in the words of Marie de l'Incarnation) visited the Ursulines with other Onondagas several times and listened to the Huron Marie Aouentohons, not yet fifteen and able to read and write in French, Latin, and Huron. Aouentohons catechized her sister seminarians before the company and made a speech (*une harangue*) both to the chief and his wife:

> Send me as many of my Iroquois sisters as you can. I will be their older sister. I will teach them. I will show them how to pray and to worship the Supreme Parent of All. I will pass on to them what my teachers have taught me.

She then sang hymns in Huron, French, and Latin. The Capitainesse asked the Ursulines how long it would take their daughters to acquire such accomplishments.[65]

Religious eloquence was not, of course, the only kind of expressiveness that attracted some Indian women to Christianity.[66] The spirituality of the "Servant of God" Katherine Tekakwitha, daughter of a Mohawk chief and an enemy-wife Algonquin, was marked by heroic asceticism, intense female companionship, and absorption in mental prayer. Her holy death in 1680 at age 24 was followed by shining apparitions of her and by miracles at her tomb near Caughnawaga. But even Tekakwitha's life involved teaching, as she spoke to the women while they did their cabin tasks of the lives of the saints and other sacred themes and as, toward to the end of her life, she instructed those drawn by her reputation on the virtues of virginity and chastity. As her confessor reported it, "At these times her tongue spoke from the depths of her heart."[67]

In one striking way, then, Iroquois and Huron women faced what European historians could call a "Renaissance" challenge in regard to voice and some of them made use of religious tools and the "Catholic Reformation" to meet it. But neither rebirth nor a return to a privileged past would be an image of change that came readily to them. In the thought of the Algonquian- and Iroquoian-speaking peoples of Marie de l'Incarnation's day, sacred time turned around on itself, but there was no historical golden age from which humankind had declined and to which it might hope to return. When people died, their souls divided into two, one part gradually moving toward the setting sun to the Village of the Dead, the other part remaining with the body "unless someone bears it again as a child."[68] There was no fully developed theory of reincarnation among the Hurons, however. Gaps were filled not so much by rebirth as by adoption: the adoption of the dead person's name, which otherwise could not be mentioned; the adoption of a captured enemy to replace a slain son. Things could be created anew, like wampum, which came from the feathers of a fierce and huge wampum bird, slain to win the hand of an Iroquois chief's daughter and then put to the new uses of peacemaking.[69] Institutions could be created anew by joint divine and human enterprise, as with Deganawidah and Hiawatha and the confederating of the Five Iroquois Nations.

Models for abrupt change were also available. One was metamorphosis, the sudden and repeatable change from bear to man to bear, from trickster to benefactor to trickster—changes emerging from the double possibilities in life, the ever-present destabilizing potentiality for twinning[70] (a potentiality that makes interesting comparison with the sixteenth-century fascination with Ovidian metamorphosis). A second model was the sudden fall to a totally different world. The first fall was at creation, when the pregnant woman Aataentsic plunged from the sky through the hole under the roots of a great tree (according to one version recounted to the Jesuit Brébeuf), landed on the back of a great turtle in the waters of this world, and after dry land had been created, gave birth to the deity Yoscaha and his twin brother. Falls through holes, especially holes under trees, are the birth canals to experiences in alternative worlds in many an Indian narrative.[71] A seventeenth-century Huron woman, describing Marie de l'Incarnation's life, might say that she tried to fulfill the promptings of a dream, as a person must always do, but what she thought would only be a boat trip turned out to be a fall down a hole. What that alternative world would become remained to be seen.

I hope that one of the Amerindian women in Marie's convent yard told her a seventeenth-century version of the Seneca tale of the origin of stories. We know it from the version told by the Seneca Henry Jacob to Jeremiah Curtin in 1883, where a hunting boy is its protagonist;[72] perhaps a woman's version 230 years before would have used a wooding girl instead. Set in the forest, the tale called to my mind Marguerite de Navarre's rather different storytelling field in the Pyrenees—a conjoining of alternative worlds. An Orphan Boy was sent each day into the woods by his adoptive mother to hunt for birds. One day he came upon a flat round stone in the midst of a clearing. When he sat upon it he heard a voice asking, "Shall I tell you stories?" "What does it mean—to tell stories?" the boy asked. "It is telling what happened a long time ago. If you will give me your birds, I'll tell you stories."

So each day the Orphan sat on the stone, heard stories, and left birds, bringing home to his mother only what he could catch on the way back. His mother sent other boys from the longhouse and even men to follow him to find out why his catch had diminished, but they too were captivated by the stories and would say "haa, haa" with approval now and again. Finally, the stone told the Orphan Boy that he should clear a larger space and bring everyone in the village to it, each of them with something to eat. The boy told the chief, and for two days at sunrise all the men and women of the village came, put food on the stone, and listened to stories till the sun was almost down. At the end of the second day the stone said,

> I have finished! You must keep these stories as long as the world lasts. Tell them to your children and your grandchildren. One person will remember them better than another. When you go to a man or a woman to ask for one of these stories, bring a gift of game or fish or whatever you have. I know all that happened in the world before this; I have told it to you. When you visit one another, you must tell these things. You must remember them always. I have finished.

NOTES

1. Paul Le Jeune, *Relation de ce qui s'est passé en la Nouvelle France en l'année 1633* (Paris, 1634) in Reuben Gold Thwaites, *The Jesuit Relations and Allied Documents* (henceforth *JR*), 73 vols. (Cleveland, Ohio: Burrows Brothers, 1896–1901), 5: 118–21, 283 n. 33. Pierre Pastedechouan was born about 1605 and taken to France around 1618 by the Recollet brothers, then returned to Canada in 1625, living sometimes with the Jesuits and much of the time with the Montagnais. See also Gabriel Sagard, *Le Grand Voyage du pays des Hurons* (1632), ed. Réal Ouellet (Québec: Bibliothèque québécoise, 1990), 58.

2. "The Dream of the White Robe and the floating island/Micmac," in Ella Elizabeth Clark, *Indian Legends of Canada* (Toronto: McClelland & Stewart, 1991), 151–52; also Silas Rand, *Legends of the Micmac* (New York: Longmans Green, 1894). For another Amerindian telling of the floating island and the coming of Europeans, see the excerpt from William Wood (1634) in William S. Simmons, *Spirit of the New England Tribes. Indian History and Folklore* (Hanover, NH: University Press of New England, 1986),66. For a use of the floating island to describe origins of the Amerindians from a race of white giants, see "The Beginning and the End of the World (Okanogan of the Salishan Languages)," in Paula Gunn Allen, ed., *Spider Woman's Granddaughters. Traditional Tales and Contemporary Writing by Native American Women* (Boston: Beacon Press, 1989), 106–7. For references to the motif-type "Island canoe," see Stith Thompson, ed., *Tales of North American Indians* (Cambridge, Mass.: Harvard University Press, 1929), 275 n. 14.

3. Marie de l'Incarnation and Claude Martin, *La Vie de la vénérable Mère Marie de l'Incarnation première supérieure des Ursulines de la Nouvelle France* (Paris: Louis Billaine, 1677; facsimile ed. Solesmes: Abbaye Saint-Pierre, 1971), 228–30, 400, 408. Marie de l'Incarnation, *Correspondance,* ed. Dom Guy Oury (Solesmes: Abbaye Saint-Pierre, 1971), no. 28, 64–65, no. 41, 91.

4. General bibliographical orientation can be found in Dean R. Snow, *Native American Prehistory. A Critical Bibliography* (Bloomington: Indiana University Press for the Newberry Library, 1979); Neal Salisbury, *The Indians of New England. A Critical Bibliography* (Bloomington: Indiana University Press for the Newberry Library, 1982); James P. Ronda and James Axtell, *Indian Missions. A Critical Bibliography* (Bloomington: Indiana University Press for the Newberry Library, 1978). The writings of James Axtell have been pioneering in the study of the American Indians in their encounter with Europeans: *The European and the Indian: Essays in the Ethnohistory of Colonial North America* (New York and Oxford: Oxford University Press, 1981); *The Invasion Within.*

The Contest of Cultures in Colonial North America (New York and Oxford: Oxford University Press, 1985); *After Columbus. Essays in the Ethnohistory of Colonial North America* (New York and Oxford: Oxford University Press, 1988); *Beyond 1492. Encounters in Colonial North America* (New York and Oxford: Oxford University Press, 1992). A general historical and ethnographical orientation to the Amerindian peoples of Canada is R. Bruce Morrison and C. Roderick Wilson, eds., *Native Peoples. The Canadian Experience* (Toronto: McClelland & Stewart, 1986). Bruce G. Trigger's *Natives and Newcomers. Canada's "Heroic Age" Reconsidered* (Kingston and Montréal: McGill-Queen's University Press, 1985) is an excellent presentation of both archeological and historical evidence. Important studies of Iroquoian-speaking peoples include Elisabeth Tooker, *An Ethnography of the Huron Indians, 1615–1649* (Washington, DC: Smithsonian Institution for the Huronia Historical Development Council, 1964); Conrad Heidenreich, *Huronia. A History and Geography of the Huron Indians* (Toronto: McClelland & Stewart, 1971); Bruce G. Trigger, *The Children of Aataentsic. A History of the Huron People to 1660*, new edn (Kingston and Montréal: McGill-Queen's University Press, 1987) [with much archaeological material from before the seventeenth century]; Lucien Campeau, *La mission des Jésuites chez les Hurons, 1634–1650* (Montreal: editions Bellarmin, 1987), especially 1–113 on the pre-contact Hurons; Francis Jennings, *The Ambiguous Iroquois Empire. The Covenant Chain Confederation of Indian Tribes with English Colonies from its Beginnings to the Lancaster Treaty of 1744* (New York: W. W. Norton, 1984); Francis Jennings, William Fenton, Mary Druke, and David R. Miller, eds., *The History and Culture of Iroquois Diplomacy. An Interdisciplinary Guide to the Treaties of the Six Nations and Their League* (Syracuse: Syracuse University Press, 1985); and Daniel K. Richter, *The Ordeal of the Longhouse. The Peoples of the Iroquois League in the Era of European Colonization* (Chapel Hill: University of North Carolina Press for the Institute of Early American History and Culture, 1992). Important studies of Algonquian-speaking peoples include Alfred Goldsworthy Bailey, *The Conflict of European and Eastern Algonkian Cultures, 1504–1700*, 2nd edn (Toronto: University of Toronto Press, 1969); Simmons, *Spirit of the New England Tribes;* Colin G. Calloway, ed., *Dawnland Encounters. Indians and Europeans in Northern New England* (Hanover, NH, and London: University Press of New England, 1991); W. Vernon Kinietz, *The Indians of the Western Great Lakes, 1615–1760* (Ann Arbor: University of Michigan Press, 1965); Richard White, *The Middle Ground: Indians, Empires, and Republics in the Great Lakes Region, 1650–1815* (Cambridge: Cambridge University Press, 1991). Penny Petrone provides an introduction to Amerindian literary genres in *Native Literature in Canada. From the Oral Tradition to the Present* (Toronto: Oxford University Press, 1990). A major study of the art and material culture of Amerindian peoples, with much early historical evidence, is *The Spirit Sings. Artistic Traditions of Canada's First Peoples. A Catalogue of the Exhibition* (Toronto: McClelland & Stewart for the Glenbow-Alberta Institute, 1988). Special studies of Iroquois women have a long history behind them: a collection of essays from 1884 to 1989 is W. G. Spittal, ed., *Iroquois Women. An Anthology* (Ohsweken: Iroqrafts, 1990). Marxist and feminist approaches opened a new chapter in the study of Indian women of northeastern America in the work of Judith K. Brown, "Economic Organization and the Position of Women among the Iroquois," initially published in *Ethnohistory*, 17 (1970) and reprinted in *Iroquois Women*, 182–98, and Eleanor Leacock, "Montagnais Women and the Jesuit Program for Colonization," in Mona Etienne and Eleanor Leacock, eds., *Women and Colonization. Anthropological Perspectives* (New York: Praeger, 1980), 25–42. Karen Anderson's recent *Chain Her by One Foot. The Subjugation of Women in Seventeenth-Century New France* (London and New York: Routledge, 1991) does not carry the conceptual argument beyond Leacock's pioneering essay. A new historical and ethnographical study of Iroquois women is under way by Carol Karlsen. An introduction to the history of Amerindian women of many regions is Carolyn Niethammer, *Daughters of the Earth. The Lives and Legends of American Indian Woman* (New York: Macmillan, 1977). Paul Gunn Allen has published several works that draw on a mix of historical examples, legends, and women's values and lore in her own Lakota family in order (as she says in the subtitle to *The Sacred Hoop*) "to recover the feminine in American Indian traditions": *The Sacred Hoop: Recovering the Feminine in American Indian Traditions*, 2nd edn (Boston: Beacon Press, 1992); *Spider Woman's Granddaughters;* and *Grandmothers of the Light. A Medicine Woman's Sourcebook* (Boston: Beacon Press, 1991).

5. Among many primary sources for this information on the division of labor is Sagard, *Grand Voyage*, Part 1, ch. 7 and passim, and *JR*, 5: 132–33.

6. On women being assisted in carrying tasks by male prisoners, see Marc Lescarbot, *The History of New France*, trans. W. L. Grant, 3 vols. (Toronto: Champlain Society, 1907–1914), Book 6, ch. 17, 3: 200, 412.

7. Jacques Cartier, "Deuxième voyage de Jacques Cartier (1535–1536)," ed. Théodore Beauchesne in Charles A. Julien, ed., *Les Français en Amérique pendant la première moitié du 16e siècle* (Paris: Press Universitaires de France 1946), 159. Sagard, *Grand Voyage, 172*. Sagard applied to the Huron women what Lescarbot

had said in his *Histoire de la Nouvelle France* (1609), about women of the Micmacs and other Algonquian-speaking groups:

> J'ay dit au chapitre de la Tabagie [on banquets] qu'entre les Sauvages les femmes ne vent point en si bonne condition qu'anciennement entre les Gaullois et Allemans. Car (au rapport même de Iacques Quartier) "elles travaillent plus que les hommes," dit-il, "soit en la pecherie, soit au labour, ou autre chose." Et neantmoins elles ne sont point forcées, ne tourmentées, mais elles ne sont ni en leurs Tabagies [at their banquets], ni en leurs conseils, et font les ouevres serviles, à faute de serviteurs.

Lescarbot, *New France* 3: 411. *JR*, 4: 204–5 ("ces pauvres femmes sont de vrais mulets de charge").

    8. Marie de l'Incarnation, *Correspondance*, no. 97, 286; no. 244, 828–49. Marie de l'Incarnation and Claude Martin, *Vie*, 41–53, 54–55.

    9. Sagard, *Grand Voyage*, Part 1, ch. 7, 172.

    10. Heidenreich (*Huronia*, 77) gives two sources for Huron matrilineality. First, a single sentence from Samuel Champlain where, after noting that Hurons are not always sure of the father of a child because of permitted sexual promiscuity in marriage, he goes on,

> in view of this danger, they have a custom which is this, namely that the children never succeed to the property and honors of their fathers, being in doubt, as I said, of their begetter, but indeed they make their successors and heirs the children of their sisters, from whom these are certain to be sprung and issued (*The Works of Samuel Champlain*, trans. H. P. Biggar, 6 vols. [Toronto: Champlain Society, 1922–1936], 3: 140). Second, an unclear description of cross-cousin marriage by Sagard (*Grand Voyage*, Part 1, ch. 11, 199) that could apply to either a patrilineal or matrilineal situation. Elsewhere Sagard said that after divorce Huron children usually stayed with their father (201). Heidenreich concluded that matrilocality was sometimes practiced, sometimes not (77). In *Children of Aataentsic*, Trigger talks of a "matrilineal" preference among the Iroquoians more generally, but adds that their "kinship terminology and incest prohibitions seem to reflect a bilateral ideal of social organization." He suggests that Huron boys in the lineages of chiefs lived with their mother's brother, and that when they married their wives came to live with them rather than following the matrilocal principle (55, 100–2). See also Trigger's *Natives and Newcomers*, 117, 208, and Richter, *Ordeal of the Longhouse*, 20. Lucien Campeau shows from evidence about specific Huron families described in the *Jesuit Relations* that the Hurons were not consistent in matrilocal living arrangements nor in the matrilineal passing of chiefly honors (*Mission des Jésuites*, 54–58). Karen Anderson takes Huron matrilineality and matrilocality for granted, but does not review the Jesuit evidence or mention Campeau's book (*Chain Her by One Foot*, 107, 193). A mixed practice in regard to lineage and dwellings creates an interesting and variegated situation for Huron women.

    11. Sagard, *Grand Voyage*, Part 1, ch. 11, 198–99; *JR*, 14: 18–19, 27: 30–31, 30: 36–37; Claude Chauchetière, *The Life of the Good Katherine Tegakoüita, Now Known as the Holy Savage* (1695) in Catholic Church, Sacred Congregation of Rites, *Position . . . on the Introduction of the Cause for Beatification and Canonization and on the Virtues of the Servant of God Katharine Tekakwitha, the Lily of the Mohawks* (New York: Fordham University Press, 1940), 123–25; Pierre Cholenec, *The Life of Katharine Tegakoüita*, (1696) in Catholic Church Sacred Congregation of Rites, *Cause for Beatification*, 273–75. Tooker, *Ethnography*, 126–27; Trigger, *Children of Aataentsic*, 49.

    12. Sagard, *Grand Voyage*, Part 1, ch. 1, 291–92. *JR*, 10: 264–71. The remaining goods of the deceased were not given to his or her family, but after the burial were given to "recognize the liberality of those who had made the most gifts of consolation" at the funeral (*JR*, 43: 270–71).

    13. Intercourse itself as the sole source of conception was problematized in folktales in which females get pregnant from passing near male urination or scratching themselves with an object used by a male (Claude Lévi-Strauss, *Histoire de lynx* [Paris: Plon, 1991], 21–22). Among some Amerindian peoples today, pregnancy is believed to occur only through many occasions of intercourse (Niethammer, *Daughters of the Earth*, 2). Among the Hurons in the seventeenth century, it was believed that the body-soul of a deceased person might sometimes enter the womb of a woman and be born again as her child (*JR*, 10: 285–77). When an adult male died, and especially an important male, such as a chief, his name was given to another person, not necessarily kin to the bereaved, and he then took up the deceased person's role and attributes (*JR:* 10: 274–77, 23: 164–69; Alexander von Gernet, "Saving the Souls: Reincarnation Beliefs of the Seventeenth-Century Huron," in

Antonia Mills and Richard Slobodin, *Amerindian Rebirth: Reincarnation Belief among North American Indians and Inuit* [Toronto: University of Toronto Press, 1993]). These adoptive practices carry with them a very different sense of the succession of qualities from that current in sixteenth- and seventeenth-century Europe, where lineage and stock were so important.

14. *JR*, 6: 254–55. Jeanne-Françoise Juchereau de St. Ignace and Marie Andrée Duplessis de Ste. Hélène, *Les Annales de l'Hôtel-Dieu de Québec,* ed. Albert Jamet (Québec: Hôtel-Dieu, 1939), 20.

15. Sagard reported a "grande querelle" between a daughter and a father who refused to give his consent to the suitor she desired, so the latter seized her (*Grand Voyage,* Part 1, ch. 11, 199–201; this story was already recounted by Lescarbot, ibid., 203 n. 4). Marie de l'Incarnation, *Correspondance,* no. 65, p. 163.

16. In addition to occasional reports in the *Jesuit Relations* of jealousy among spouses are the legends about a wife who goes off with a bear lover and the husband's efforts at retrieval or revenge. Lévi-Strauss, *Histoire de lynx,* 146; "The Bear Walker (Mohawk)," in Herbert T. Schwarz, ed., *Tales from the Smokehouse* (Edmonton, Al.: Hurtig Publishers, 1974), 31–35, 101. A similar theme with a buffalo lover in "Apache Chief Punishes His Wife (Tiwa)," in Richard Erdoes and Alfonso Ortiz, eds., *American Indian Myths and Legends* (New York: Pantheon Books, 1984), 291–4.

17. *JR*, 43:270–71.

18. *JR*, 8: 151–52; 23: 186–87; 28: 50–53 ("en leurs mariages les plus fermes, et qu'ils estiment les plus conformes à la raison, la foy qu'ils se donnent n'a rien de plus qu'une promesse conditionelle de demeurer ensemble, tandis qu'un chacun continuera à rendre les services qu'ils attendent mutuellement les uns des autres, et n'offensera point l'amitié qu'ils se doivent; cela manquant on iuge le divorce estre raisonnable du costé de celuy qui se voit offensé, quoy qu'on blasme l'autre party qui y a donné occasion"). On women ordinarily having custody of the children, *JR*, 5: 136–39; Marie de l'Incarnation, *Correspondance,* no. 52, 123 ("c'est la coûtume du païs que quand les personnes mariées se séparent, la femme emmène les enfans").

19. *JR*, 5: 172–73, 180–81. For an example of a wife using the need for her husband's assent to allow her infant to be baptized (possibly an excuse to cover her own reluctance), see *JR*, 5:226–29.

20. Sagard, *Grand Voyage,* Part 1, ch. 18, 25–27; *JR*, 5: 152–57, 6: 156–63, 7: 100–3, 8: 118–21, 10: 128–39, 144–48. Marie de l'Incarnation, *Correspondance,* no. 270, 916–17. Tooker, *Ethnography,* 145–48 and Appendix 2; Elisabeth Tooker, ed., *Native North American Spirituality of the Eastern Woodlands. Sacred Myths, Dreams, Visions, Speeches, Healing Formulas, Rituals and Ceremonies* (New York: Paulist Press, 1979); Campeau, *Mission des Jésuites,* ch. 7; Axtell, *Invasion Within,* 13–19.

21. *JR*, 8: 117–19. *JR*, 30: 60–61, for an evidently all-male gathering to elect a new captain among the Hurons:

> Ils ont coustume en semblables rencontres de raconter les histoires qu'ils ont appris de leurs ancestres et les plus éloignées, afin que les ieunes gens qui vent presens et les entendent, en puissent conserver la memoire et les raconter à leur tour, lors qu'ils seront devenus vieux.

Creation accounts were among the tales told at the gathering.

22. Marie de l'Incarnation, *Correspondance,* no. 270, 917–18. Also, Jean de Brébeuf on the Hurons: "Or cette fausse creance qu'ils ont des ames s'entretient parmy-eux, par le moyen de certaines histoires que les peres racontent à leurs enfans" (*JR*, 10: 148–49).

23. *JR*, 43: 286–87.

24. *JR*, 30: 58–61: Paul Ragueneau describes the telling of creation stories by men at meeting for the election of a chief, where "les anciens du païs" were assembled.

25. Women storytellers are documented among the Amerindians in the early nineteenth century (Clark, *Indian Legends of Canada,* x–xi; Jeremiah Curtin, ed., *Seneca Indian Myths* (New York: E. P. Dutton, 1922), 243, 351; Marius Barbeau, ed., *Huron-Wyandot Traditional Narratives in Translations and Native Texts* [Ottawa: National Museum of Canada, 1960], 2–3), and individual women can be traced back to the eighteenth century (e.g., the Seneca grandmother of Johnny John, who told her grandson "A Man Pursued by his Uncle and by His Wife" and whom John described in 1883 as having lived "to be one hundred and thirty years old" [Curtin, *Seneca Indian Myths,* 307]; the Huron-Wyandot Nendusha, who lived to a hundred and told the traditional tales to her grandson, an elderly man in 1911 [Barbeau, *Huron-Wyandot Narratives,* 2]). According to Penny Petrone, herself an honorary chief of the Gull Lake Ojibway and specialist on Amerindian tales, some oral narratives were "the private property" of certain tribes, societies within tribes, or of particular persons

(*Native Literature in Canada,* 11). Petrone does not mention gender as a factor in these exclusions and has herself collected sacred tales from Tlingit women; but the cultural habit of restricting the pool of tellers for certain narratives might account for the fact that formal recitals of creation accounts were attributed by the Jesuits and even by Marie de l'Incarnation to men. On the other hand, these sacred stories could not have been successfully passed on if the women with good memories and narrative skills had not also told them on many occasions. (For a woman with evident storytelling skills, see *JR,* 22: 292–95: the blind woman's story about how her grandfather got a new eye.) Petrone thinks my speculation about different settings in which men and women told the sacred stories in the early period is plausible (phone conversation of January 18, 1993). Paula Gunn Allen maintains that Amerindian stories about "women's matters" were for the most part told by women to other women (Allen, ed., *Spider Woman's Granddaughters,* 16–17).

26. *JR,* 8: 22–23; 10: 140–41, 168–73; 17: 152–55; 33: 188–91. Tooker, *Ethnography,* 86–91, and Iroquois evidence, 86, n. 62, 87, n. 63. Dreams could also involve the departure of the rational soul from the body to observe distant events or places.

27. *JR,* 17: 164–87.

28. *JR,* 43: 272–73 for an Iroquois woman who came to Québec to get a French dog of which her nephew had dreamed, and discovering the dog had been taken elsewhere, took a voyage of over four hundred miles through snow, ice, and difficult roads to find the animal.

29. *JR,* 30: 22–23. On the Huron "confraternities," Campeau, *Mission des Jésuites,* 105. Brébeuf's description of a special dance group for curing a man of madness had 80 persons in it, 6 of whom were women (*JR,* 10: 206–7). Games of lacrosse were also ordered for healing purposes (10: 184–87), but this would be only for men. Shafer, "The Status of Iroquois Women" (1941), in Spittal, ed., *Iroquois Women,* 88–89. For an early eighteenth-century picture of Iroquois women and men doing a curing dance together, see the illustration to *Aventures du Sr. C. Le Beau* reproduced by Ruth Phillips, "Art in Woodlands Life: the Early Pioneer Period," in *The Spirit Sings,* 66.

30. *JR,* 10: 222–23, for the Amerindian definition of *sorciers:* "ceux qui se meslent d'empoisonner et faire mourir par sort," who, once declared as such, can have their skulls smashed by anyone who comes upon them without the usual amends for a murder (compensatory gifts to the bereaved kin). For old men accused and punished as sorcerers: *JR,* 13: 154–57, 15: 52–53. Tooker, *Ethnography,* 117–20. The Jesuits also use the word "sorcerer" as one of several pejorative terms for all the various medicine men and shamans among the Amerindians, though there was some uncertainty among the fathers about whether they were actually assisted by Satan (*JR,* 6: 198–201; 10: 194–95, Brébeuf: "Il y a donc quelque apparence que le Diable leur tient la main par fois").

31. *JR,* 14: 182–83; 8: 26–61; 9: 112–15. A Montagnais *sorcière* received messages from the Manitou (*JR,* 31: 242–43). Huron women were prepared to blow on a sick person when no medicine man was around to do it (*JR,* 24: 30–8:1).

32. *JR,* vol. 8: 124–27; 38: 36–37. The Huron soothsayer is the only reference given to women shamans in Tooker, *Huron Indians,* 91–101. Leacock's statement that "Seventeenth-century accounts . . . referred to female shamans who might become powerful" ("Montagnais Women," 41) gives as supporting *JR,* 6: 61, which includes no reference whatsoever to this topic, and 14:183, the woman "involved in sorcery," mentioned in my text. Robert Steven Grumet gives seventeenth-century evidence for women "powwows" or "pawwaws" among the central coast Algonquians of southern New England ("Sunksquaws, Shamans, and Tradeswomen: Middle Atlantic Coastal Algonkian Women during the 17th and 18th Centuries," in Etienne and Leacock, eds., *Women and Colonization,* 53).

33. *JR,* 6: 204–7. On sticks as mnemonic devices, see William N. Fenton, "Structure, Continuity, and Change in the Process of Iroquois Treaty Making," in Jennings, ed., *Iroquois Diplomacy,* 17. *JR,* 6: 194–79: at this ceremony, intended to make a distant enemy die, all the women were sent from the cabin but one who sat next to the shaman and moved around the backs of all the men once during a specified point in the ceremonies. A similar ceremonial role in the sacrifice of the corpse of a person dead by drowning or freezing (*JR,* 10: 162–65). To appease the sky's anger, the body is cut up by young men and thrown into the fire. Women walk around the men several times and encourage them by putting wampum beads in their mouths. Among the Hurons, if a pregnant woman entered the cabin of a sick person, he or she would grow sicker (*JR,* 15: 180–81). By the presence of a pregnant woman and the application of a certain root, an arrow could be extracted from a man's body. In all of these examples, it is the female body, pregnant or not-pregnant, which is the source of power or danger.

34. Niethammer, *Daughters of the Earth*, 146–63 on herbal medicine and medicine women. Her examples of women shamans come from a later period and, except for the Menominee story about Hunting Medicine (collected 1913), are all from regions other than those of the Algonquian- and Iroquoian-speaking peoples. In *Grandmothers of the Light* and *The Sacred Hoop*, Paula Gunn Allen develops a modern medicine woman's culture based on Amerindian values and tales of goddesses. Her examples of women shamans are all from the late nineteenth and twentieth centuries (*Sacred Hoop*, 203–8). On the earlier period: "Pre-contact American Indian women valued their role as vitalizers because they understood that bearing, like bleeding, was a transformative ritual act" (ibid., 28).

35. Champlain, *Works*, 3: 97–98; Sagard, *Grand Voyage*, Part 1, ch. 4, 132–33. The critical issue may be the menstrual taboos, which would allow women to deal with certain matters, but, as Niethammer points out, would prevent women from handling "the sacred bundle" of the shaman (*Daughters of the Earth*, xii). Pregnant women: *JR*, 15: 180–81; 17: 212–13. Sexual restraint for men before shamanic ceremonial: *JR*, 15: 180–81. Menstrual separation and the power of the glance of the menstruating woman: *JR*, 29: 208–9; 9: 122–23. Separation of postpartum women among Algonquian peoples: Nicholas Perrot, *Memoir on the Manners, Customs, and Religion of the Savages of North America* (c. 1680), in Emma Helen Blair, ed. and trans., *The Indian Tribes of the Upper Mississippi Valley and Region of the Great Lakes*, 2 vols. (Cleveland, Ohio: Arthur Clark, 1911; New York: Klaus Reprint, 1969), 1:48.

36. The best study is Grumet, "Sunksquaws, Shamans, and Tradeswomen," 46–53. See also Niethammer, *Daughters of the Earth*, 139–41; Carolyn Thomas Foreman, *Indian Women Chiefs* (Muskogee: Hoffman Printing Co., 1966); Samuel G. Drake, *The Aboriginal Races of North America*, 15th edn. (Philadelphia: Charles Desilver, 1860), Book III, ch. 1, 4 on the Wampanoag sunksquaws Weetamoo and Awashonks.

37. Descriptions of government and councils from Champlain, *Works*, 3:157–59; Sagard, *Grand Voyage*, Part 1, ch. 17, 229–32; Brébeaf in *JR*, 10:229–63; Bailey, *Algonkian Cultures*, 91–92; Heidenreich, *Huronia*, 79–81; Campeau, *Mission des Jésuites*, ch. 5; Fenton, "Iroquois Treaty Making," 12–14. Evidence in regard to women: Champlain on men's conduct on council meetings: "ils usent bien souvent de ceste façon de faire parmy leurs harangues au conseil, où il n'y a que les plus principaux, qui sont les antiens: Les femmes et enfans n'y assistent point" (1:110); Sagard, 230–31, talking about local council meetings: "Les femmes, filles et jeunes hommes n'y assistent point, si ce n'est en un conseil général, où les jeunes hommes de vingt-cinq à trente ans peuvent assister, ce qu'il connaissent par un cri particulier qui en est fait," 230–31); Brebeuf, on the council chamber:

> la Chambre de Conseil est quelque fois la Cabane du Capitaine, parée de nattes, ou ionchées de branches de Sapin, avec divers feux, suivant la saison de l'année. Autrefois chacun y apportoit sa busche pour mettre au feu; maintenant cela ne se pratique plus, les femmes de la Cabane supportent cette dépense, elles font les feux, et ne s'y chauffent pas, sortant dehors pour ceder la place à Messieurs le Conseillers. Quelquefois l'assemblée se fait au milieu du Village, si c'est en Este [this may have been the time when women could most easily attend and listen, NZD], et quelquefois aussi en l'obscurité des forests à l'ecart, quand les affaires demandent le secret. (*JR*, 10: 250)

Paul Le Jeune on the Huron community of both "pagans" and Christians at Saint Joseph (Sillery): The Christian elders decided

> d'assembler les femmes pour les presser de se faire instruire et de recevoir le sainct Baptesme. On les fit donc venir, et les ieunes yens aussi. Le bon fut qu'on les prescha si bien que le iour suivant une partie de ces pauvres femmes, rencontrant le Pere de Quen, luy dirent, "Où est un tel Pere, nous le venons prier de nous baptiser, *hier les hommes nous appellerent en Conseil, c'est la premiere fois que iamais les femmes y sont entrées.* (italics mine; *JR*, 18: 104)

Drawing from a general description of Huron civility, in which Brebeuf talks of marriages, feasting, and other kinds of sociability and comments

> Ce qui les forme encor dans le discours sont les conseils qui se tiennent quasi tous les iours dans les Villages en toutes occurrences: et quoy que les anciens y tiennent le haut bout, et que ce soit de leur iugement qui dépende la decision des affaires; neantmoins s'y trouve qui veut et chacun a droit d'y dire son advis. (*JR*, 10: 212)

Karen Anderson assumes that women could be present at any Huron council meeting and speak whenever they wanted (*Chain Her by One Foot*, 124). But this is in contradiction to other evidence, including more specific evidence given some pages later by Brébeuf himself. Brébeuf was following the usual practice in men's writing in the sixteenth and seventeenth centuries and using "chacun" (and other general nouns and pronouns) to refer to men; the paragraph in question is describing male civility.

38. Marie de l'Incarnation, *Correspondance*, no. 161, 546, September 24, 1654 ("Ces capitainesses sont des femmes de qualité parmi les Sauvages qui ont voix deliberative dans les Conseils, et qui en tirent des conclusions comme les hommes, et même ce furent elles qui déléguèrent les premiers Ambassadeurs pour traiter de la paix"); no. 191, 671. In 1671, Father Claude Dablon said of Iroquois women of high rank that they are much respected; they hold councils, and the Elders decide no important affair without their advice. It was one of these women of quality who, some time ago, took the lead in persuading the Iroquois of Onnontague, and afterward the other nations, to make peace with the French. (*JR*, 54: 280–81)
This is surely the same Onondaga "capitainesse" who visited the Ursuline convent during the embassy of 1654. In contrast, in the early eighteenth century Pierre-François-Xavier de Charlevoix claimed of the Iroquois that "the men never tell the women anything they would have to be kept secret, and rarely any affair of consequence is communicated to them, though all is done in their name" (quoted in W. M. Beauchamp, "Iroquois Women," *Journal of American Folklore*, 13 [1900], reprinted in Spittal, ed., *Iroquois Women*, 42–43). Carol Karlsen, currently engaged in a study of Iroquois women, says she has found considerable variation from period to period and nation to nation: in some instances, women attend council, in some they have meetings of their own and their views are communicated to the council (Lecture at Princeton University, March 25, 1993). Daniel Richter, in his important recent study *The Ordeal of the Longhouse*, describes women's roles in naming which man in a hereditary chiefly family would assume the role of leadership, and concludes that there "appears to have been a form of gender division of political labor corresponding to the economic and social categories that made women dominant within the village and its surrounding fields while men dealt with the outside world (43)."

39. Jennings, ed., *Iroquois Diplomacy*, 124.

40. Trigger, *Natives and Newcomers*, 94–108. An example of the archeological work that allows one to historicize the Amerindian past is James F. Pendergast and Bruce G. Trigger, *Cartier's Hochelaga and the Dawson Site* (Montreal and London: McGill University Press, 1972), see especially 155–56, 158–61.

41. Sagard mentions women and girls kept by Hurons from war as wives or to be used as gifts, *Grand Voyage*, Part 1, ch. 17, 239. *JR*, 9: 254–55: Le Jeune, talking of some Iroquois prisoners seized by Algonquins, comments more generally: "Il est vray que les Barbares ne font point ordinairement de mal aux femmes, non plus qu'aux enfans, sinon dans leurs surprises, voire mesme quelque ieune homme ne fera point de difficulté d'épouser une prisonniere, si elle travaille bien, et par apres elle passe pour une femme du pays."

42. *JR*, 40: 180–81.

43. Elizabeth of France, sister of Louis XIII, was the wife of Philip IV of Spain; Anne of Austria, sister of Philip IV, was the wife of Louis XIII. John Elliott, *Richelieu and Olivares* (Cambridge: Cambridge University Press, 1984), 12, 113.

44. Pierre Esprit Radisson, *The Explorations of Pierre Esprit Radisson*, ed. Arthur T. Adams (Minneapolis: Ross & Haines, 1961), 26. *JR*, 41: 102–3.

45. I treat and give further bibliography on the issues in this paragraph in "Boundaries and the Sense of Self in Sixteenth-Century France," in Thomas Heller, Morton Sosna, and David Wellbery, eds., *Reconstructing Individualism. Autonomy, Individuality, and the Self in Western Thought* (Stanford: Stanford University Press, 1986), 53–63, 332–35, and "Fame and Secrecy: Leon Modena's *Life* as an Early Modern Autobiography," in Mark Cohen, trans., *The Autobiography of a Seventeenth-Century Venetian Rabbi: Leon Modena's "Life of Judah"* (Princeton: Princeton University Press, 1988), 50–70.

46. *JR*, 16: 226–29; Trigger, *Children of Aataentsic*, 58–59, *Natives and Newcomers*, 104; Campeau, *Mission des Jésuites*, 22–6.

47. Fenton, "Structure, Continuity, and Change," in Jennings, ed., *Iroquois Diplomacy*, 16; Jennings, *Iroquois Empire*, 34–40; Trigger, *Children of Aataentsic*, 162–63, and Richter, *Ordeal of the Longhouse*, ch. 2. Grumet talks of "Coastal Algonkian confederacies" in the "early historic contact period" ("Sunksquaws," 47), but he may be referring to alliances rather than federations. White, *The Middle Ground* does not give evidence for Algonquin confederations in the Great Lakes region until the late eighteenth century. Of course, these alliances must also have stimulated diplomatic and oratorical skills.

48. Horatio Hale, ed., *The Iroquois Book of Rites* (Philadelphia: D. C. Brinton, 1883), ch. 2: a historical telling of the founding work of Deganiwidah and Hiawatha, collected during Hale's visits to the Reserve of the Iroquois nations in the 1870s; 180–83: the stories he collected about the death of Hiawatha's daughter. J. N. B. Hewitt, "Legend of the Founding of the Iroquois League," *American Anthropologist* 5 (April 1892): 131–48 (the legend of Deganiwidah, Hiawatha, and Thadodaho, collected by Hewitt in 1888). Clark, *Indian Legends*, 138–45; Erdoes and Ortiz, *American Indian Myths and Legends*, 193–99. Fenton, "Structure, Continuity, and Change," 14–15; J. N. B. Hewitt, "The Status of Woman in Iroquois Polity before 1784," in *Iroquois Women*, 61–63.

49. Brébeuf in *JR*, 10: 256–57. "Ils haussent et flechissent la voix comme d'un ton de Predicateur à l'antique." "Raise and lower the voice" would seem a better translation than "raise and quiver the voice," the translation given on 257.

50. Champlain, *Works*, 1: 110; Sagard, *Grand Voyage*, Part 1, ch. 15, 220; and especially Brébeuf in *JR*, 10: 254–63. Le Jeune on the Montagnais, *JR*, 5: 24–25: "They do not all talk at once, but one after the other, listening patiently."

51. On mnemonic devices and wampum belts strung by women, see Fenton, "Structure, Continuity, and Change," 17–18, and Michael K. Foster, "Another Look at the Function of Wampum in Iroquois-White Councils," in Jennings, ed., *Iroquois Diplomacy*, 99–114. Captain's tone and walking back and forth: *JR*, 41: 112–13. Cartier, "Deuxième voyage," 132: "Et commença ledict agouhanna . . . à faire une prédication et preschement à leur modde, en démenant son corps et membres d'une merveilleuse sorte, qui est une sérmonye de joye et asseurance."

52. Barthélemy Vimont in *JR*, 27: 252–53. Vimont himself was depending on an interpreter for the words, and admitted that he was getting only "some disconnected fragments" (264–65).

53. Brébruf in *JR*, 10: 256–59, 278–79. Fenton, "Structure, Continuity, and Change," 16, and "Glossary of Figures of Speech in Iroquois Political Rhetoric," in Jennings, ed., *Iroquois Diplomacy*, 115–24; Petrone, *Native Literature*, 27–28.

54. "Narrative of the Captivity of Mrs. Mary Rowlandson, 1682," in Charles H. Lincoln, ed., *Narratives of the Indian Wars, 1675–1699* (New York: Charles Scribner's Sons, 1913), 150. It would be interesting to know what speech strategies Weetamoo used when she negotiated her support for King Philip in his war against the English in the 1670s. When a Wyattanon woman spoke to President Washington together with other delegates from Prairie Indian communities in 1793, she did so only because her uncle, Great Joseph, had died and she was representing him. In the transcription made by Thomas Jefferson, she said, "He who was to have spoken to you is dead, Great Joseph. If he had lived you would have heard a good man, and good words flowing from his mouth. He was my uncle, and it has fallen to me to speak for him. But I am ignorant. Excuse, then, these words, it is but a woman who speaks." Thomas Jefferson, *The Writings of Thomas Jefferson*, ed. Andrew A. Lipscomb, 20 vols. (Washington, DC: Thomas Jefferson Memorial Association, 1903), 16: 586–87.

55. Marie de l'Incarnation to Mother Ursule de Ste Catherine, September 13, 1640, *Correspondance*, no. 50, 117–18. This is the only account we have of the woman's speech; Marie must have heard about it from one of the Jesuits on the Huron mission, and with her characteristic sensitivity to women's words and actions, included it in her letter to the Mother Superior at her former convent at Tours. In the *Relation* of 1640, the Jesuit Superior Jerome Lallemant talks about the conflict about the Jesuits at this same "conseil general," but does not mention a woman speaker (*JR*, 19: 176–79).

56. "Hiawatha the Unifier," in Erdoes and Ortiz, *American Indian Myths*, 198; Marie de l'Incarnation, *Correspondance*, no. 168, 565. Jennings, ed., *Iroquois Diplomacy*, 13, 124, 249. "Speaking through my mouth" is the phrase used by envoys and ambassadors: "Escoute, Ondessonk, Cinq Nations entieres te parlent par ma bouche" (*JR*, 41: 116).

57. *JR*, 5: 180–81; 10: 258–59; 27: 262–63; Sagard, *Grand Voyage*, Part 1, ch. 15, 220. Le Jeune also comments on Montagnais reaction to the French talking all at the same time: "A Sagamore, or Captain, dining in our room one day, wished to say something; and not finding an opportunity, because [we] were all talking at the same time, at last prayed the company to give him a little time to talk in his turn, and all alone, as he did" (*JR*, 5:24–25).

58. Leonardo Bruni, "Concerning the Study of Literature, A Letter to . . . Baptista Malalesta," in W. H. Woodward, *Vittorino da Feltre and other Humanist Educators* (Cambridge: Cambridge University Press, 1897; reprinted New York: Teachers College of Columbia University, 1963), 126. Margaret L. King, *Women of the Renaissance* (Chicago: University of Chicago Press, 1991), 194. For a few well-born Italian women with training in good letters who managed to give orations, see Margaret L. King and Albert Rabil, Jr. *Her Immaculate Hand. Selected Works by and about the Women Humanists of Quattrocento Italy* (Binghamton: Medieval & Renaissance

Texts & Studies, 1983), nos. 2, 4, 6, 7. For an overview of queenly strategies, see N. Z. Davis, "Women in Politics," in Natalie Zemon Davis and Arlette Farge, eds. *A History of Women in the West, 3: Renaissance and Enlightenment Paradoxes,* (Cambridge, Mass: Harvard University Press, 1993), ch. 6.

59. Phylis Mack, *Visionary Women: Ecstatic Prophecy in Seventeenth-Century England* (Berkeley: University of California Press, 1992). [Margaret Fell Fox], *Womens Speaking Justified, Proved and Allowed of by the Scriptures* (London, 1666 and 1667). Natalie Zemon Davis, "City Women and Religious Change," *Society and Culture in Early Modern France* (Stanford: Stanford University Press, 1975), ch. 5. Elizabeth Rapley, *The Dévotes. Women and Church in Seventeenth-Century France* (Montréal and Kingston: McGill-Queen's University Press, 1990). Linda Lierheimer, "Female Eloquence and Maternal Ministry: The Apostolate of Ursuline Nuns in Seventeenth-Century France" (Ph.D. diss., Princeton Univeristy, 1994).

60. *JR*, 43: 288–91.

61. Ann Eastlack Shafter, "The Status of Iroquois Women," in Spittal, ed., *Iroquois Women,* 108; Tooker, *Ethnography,* 91, n. 75. It has been suggested that the False Face society was created among the Iroquois during the 1630s (Trigger, *Natives and Newcomers,* 177) and that the Midewiwin society of shamans developed in the central Great Lakes region in the course of the eighteenth century (Phillips, "Art in Woodlands Life," 64–65). Could one find archeological, visual, or other evidence that would allow one to historicize the relation of Amerindian women to religious action in the healing and other shamanic societies?

62. Marie de l'Incarnation, *Correspondance,* no. 65, 165–66.

63. Marie de l'Incarnation, *Correspondance,* no. 65, 165–69; no. 73, 201; no. 97, 281; Appendix, no. 9, 975; no. 11, 977 (letter from Thérèse), no. 18, 988, (letter from an Ursuline, almost certainly Marie, to Paul Le Jeune, 1653: "Nous avons appris que nostre Séminariste Huronne, qui fut prise il y a environ dix ans par les Iroquois, estoit mariée en leur pays; qu'elle estoit la maistresse dans sa cabane, composée de plusieurs families; qu'elle priot Dieu tous les jours et qu'elle le faisoit prier par d'autres." Campeau provides the name Khionrea (*La Mission des Jésuites,* 86).

64. Juchereau and Duplessis, *Hôtel-Dieu de Quebec,* 161–63.

65. Marie de l'Incarnation to Claude Martin, 12 October 1655, in *Correspondance,* no. 168, 565–66. François du Creux, *The History of Canada or New France,* trans. Percy J. Robinson, 2 vols. (Toronto: The Champlain Society, 1951–52), 2:698–700. Du Creux's report was based on the letters sent to him by Marie de l'Incarnation (referred to in her *Correspondance,* 642, 719), which he simply incorporated into his *Historia canadensis* (Paris: Sebastien Cramoisy, 1664).

66. See the fine discussion of Jacqueline Peterson in her essay "Women Dreaming: The Religiopsychology of Indian White Marriages and the Rise of Metis Culture," in Lillian Schlissel, Vicki Ruiz, and Janice Monk, eds., *Western Women. Their Land, Their Lives* (Albuquerque: University of New Mexico Press, 1988), 49–68. I treat the relation of Amerindian women to Christianity from other points of view in my chapter on Marie de l'Incarnation in *Women on the Margins: Three Seventeenth-Century Lives* (Cambridge, Mass.: Harvard University Press , 1995).

67. Cholenec, *Life of Katharine Tegakoüita* in *The Cause for Beatificiation and Canonization . . . of the Servant of God Katharine Tekakwitha,* 257, 299.

68. *JR,* 10: 286–87. Alexander von Cernet analyzes the evidence for Huron beliefs regarding souls after death and the various ways in which the qualities of the dead could be saved for the living in a remarkable essay, "Saving the Souls," in Mills and Slobodin, eds., *Amerindian Rebirth.*

69. "The first wampum (Iroquois and Huron-Wyandot)," in Clark, *Indian Legends,* 55–56, from a story collected by Erminnie A. Smith, in 1883 (170, 176). Another Iroquois version of the origin of wampum, which also connects it indirectly with feathers and directly with treaty use, in "Hiawatha and the Wizard (Onondaga)," ibid., 138–41, from a story collected by J. N. B. Hewitt in 1892 (172, 174). See Hewitt, "Legend of the Iroquois," 134–35.

70. The twin motif is widely discussed in regard to Indian stories (for example, Erdoes and Ortiz, eds., *American Indian Myth and Legend,* 73ff.) and is the central theme of Lévi-Strauss, *Histoire de lynx.*

71. Brébeuf, *JR,* 19: 121–29. Erdoes and Ortiz discuss the "fall through a hole" as a motif in *American Indian Myths and Legends,* 75, and there are several examples analyzed in Lévi-Strauss, *Histoire de lynx.*

72. Curtin, ed., *Seneca Indian Myths,* 70–75. Curtin collected myths in the Seneca reservation in Versailles, NY, in 1883 as an agent of the Bureau of Ethnology of the Smithsonian Institute (v). Curtin's version given in Clark, ed., *Indian Legends,* 37–40, and in Susan Feldmann, ed., *The Story-Telling Stone. Traditional Native American Myths and Tales* (New York: Dell, 1991), 161–66.

THE *BERDACHE* AND THE ILLINOIS INDIAN TRIBE
DURING THE LAST HALF OF THE
SEVENTEENTH CENTURY

Raymond Hauser

In the seventeenth century, a number of Indian nations—including the Cahokia, Kaskaskia, Peoria, and Michigamea—together constituted a cultural entity known as the "Illinois." Among those people, as among all peoples, accepted gender roles prescribed different lifeways for men and women. For the Illinois, as for many native North American groups discussed in these essays, everything from work to warfare, from politics to religion, followed clearly differentiated gender lines.

But among these natives during the late seventeenth century, as Raymond Hauser notes, there was another group, defined in gender terms as well: the people the Illinois termed *Ikoneta* and the French called *berdache*, individuals who were biologically male yet lived and dressed as females. The *Ikoneta* were not necessarily homosexuals or transvestites; they inhabited a third gender, at times having sexual relations with men, at times with women. They became berdache as a result of certain attitudes, often displayed during childhood, that suggested a fascination with traditionally female gender roles; when they grew up, they were unable to perform certain customary male roles, but natives regarded the berdache as individuals who possessed some supernatural power.

Hauser's essay strives to understand the nature of the berdache in Illinois society and to explain why the phenomenon was so evident only during a fifty-year span. In the process, he uncovers evidence not only about certain social practices among a centrally located Algonquian people, but also the ability of European observers to describe individuals whose behavior represented a startling contrast to the ways that men and women acted in early modern Europe. Like Natalie Zemon Davis's essay, his work reminds us that, among the many sorts of frontiers in early America, there was also what the historian Kathleen Brown has termed a "gender frontier," in which people's notions of what was "natural" came into question when confronted with new, "unnatural" social arrangements.

THE *BERDACHE* AND THE ILLINOIS INDIAN TRIBE DURING THE LAST HALF OF THE SEVENTEENTH CENTURY

Raymond Hauser

FROM THEIR EARLIEST RECORDED encounters with the Illinois Indians, French observers described with amazement and disapproval males who "glory in demeaning themselves to do everything that the women do" (Marquette 1959: 129; cf. Deliette 1934: 329). The Illinois referred to these individuals as *Ikoneta* but the French employed the term *Bardache* or *berdache* (La Salle 1966 [1880]: 368; Deliette 1934: 343).[1] The Illinois berdache dressed in female clothing, assumed the female role, and pursued sexual relationships with both males and females. "The transformation of a berdache was not a complete shift from his . . . biological gender to the opposite one," concluded anthropologists Charles Callender and Lee M. Kochems (1983: 453), "but rather an approximation of the latter in some of its social aspects, effecting an intermediate gender status that cut across the boundaries between gender categories."

Anthropologists have advanced four hypotheses to explain the emergence of the berdache. One hypothesis, now largely discounted, is that the institution evolved to accommodate homosexuality; another, equally suspect, is that the men who became berdaches were unable to fulfill demanding male roles, especially that of the warrior. A third hypothesis, advanced by European anthropologists, focuses on the religious nature of the phenomenon; according to Callender and Kochems (ibid.: 455), it is explained "as part of a much more widespread pattern of institutionalized transvestism that [the Europeans] examine as a primarily religious phenomenon." The last interpretation, offered by Harriet Whitehead (1981), concentrates on occupational prestige and holds that North American Indian men were superior to women (Callender and Kochems 1983: 454–55). Individually, each of these hypotheses generates scholarly controversy; a more satisfactory evaluation of the berdache in a particular tribe may involve two or more of them. For the Illinois, the homosexuality thesis does not appear applicable. The rejection of the male role argument might be successfully applied, although one of the more reliable French sources concluded

SOURCE: *Ethnohistory* 37:1 (winter 1990), 45–65.

that potential Illinois berdaches were attracted by the female role rather than repelled by the male role (Deliette 1934: 329; Raudot 1940: 388–89). However, the supernatural thesis, together with some useful inferences from the male superiority thesis, offers the most insight.

Twentieth-century anthropological investigations of the berdache, especially that of Callender and Kochems (1983), make it possible to interpret brief French observations that refer to this phenomenon as it existed in the Illinois Indian tribe during the last half of the seventeenth century.[2] The portrait of the Illinois berdache that emerges is reasonably clear but not complete, because, like that for other societies, the evidence is so meager (ibid.: 443).[3] The berdache varied by tribe, and an examination of the Illinois example should partially satisfy the call made by various scholars for further research on the subject (ibid.: 465; Holmberg 1983: 459; Brown 1983: 457; Jacobs 1983: 460) and clarify certain questions of the function and social position of the phenomenon among North American Indians. Finally, the eighteenth- and nineteenth-century sources contain no references to berdaches, and the disappearance of the institution offers scholars an intriguing mystery.

CONJECTURED ORIGINS OF THE BERDACHE

The Illinois subtribes, including the Cahokia, Kaskaskia, Moingwena, Michigamea, Peoria, and Tamaroa, occupied much of Illinois, southern Wisconsin, eastern Iowa, eastern Missouri, and northeastern Arkansas during the protohistoric and early historic periods. The Jolliet and Marquette expedition opened the historic period in the Illinois country in 1673 when the Europeans encountered various subtribes along the Mississippi and Illinois rivers. Speaking a central Algonquian language, the Illinois were closely related to other Prairie culture populations, such as the Miami, Sauk, and Fox. The institution of the berdache was so well established among the Illinois in 1673 that it must have existed for at least the previous generation, or since about 1650 (Hauser 1973: 411–12).

Anthropologists have proposed two basic views of how individuals became berdaches. The secular one holds that children did so when they demonstrated an interest in the occupations of the opposite sex, began to associate with them, and were accepted in their new lives by their society. The religious view contends that adolescents were confirmed as berdaches in a vision-quest validation, which permitted the society to recognize the transformation formally (Callender and Kochems 1983: 451). Both views are valid for an examination of the Illinois berdache phenomenon.

Those Illinois destined to live as berdaches began this way of life during childhood. Pierre Deliette, nephew of La Salle's chief lieutenant, Henri de Tonti, noticed that when young boys "were seen frequently picking up the spade, the spindle, the axe, but making no use of the bow and arrows, as all the other small boys do," the Illinois raised them as females. These boys wore skirts, made of "a piece of leather or cloth which envelops them from the belt to the knees," just like the women; covered their upper torso with "a little skin like a shoulder strap passing under the arm on one side and tied over the shoulder on the other"; and grew their hair long and "fastened [it] behind the head." Deliette completed his portrait of the berdache by noting that they were "tattooed on their cheeks like the women and also on the breast and the arms." Berdaches even spoke the Illinois language in the accent reserved for females (Deliette 1934: 329; cf. Raudot 1940: 388–89).

Deliette said nothing about a supernatural role in berdache recruitment or assignment, but Father Jacques Marquette alluded to one (Callender and Kochems 1983: 451). Although he did not "know . . . through what superstition" berdaches began their careers, Marquette was probably referring to the dream-fast or vision-quest experience. He certainly did imply a supernatural connection for Illinois berdaches when he observed that "they pass for Manitous,—That is to say, for Spirits" (Marquette 1959: 129). Deliette (1934: 353) noted that girls engaged in a dream-fast at the onset of puberty. It is possible, therefore, that boys entered a transitional stage to berdachehood while rather young and then were confirmed or formalized in it through the dream-fast during adolescence. The fact that other populations, such as the Miami and the Sauk, who were culturally related and geographically close to the Illinois, employed the dream-fast suggests that the Illinois did also (Callender and Kochems 1983: 452).

GENDER ROLES AMONG THE ILLINOIS

When berdaches accepted female occupations in Illinois society, they found themselves engaged in arduous toil.[4] Women worked at least as hard as men to maintain the Illinois standard of living. The sources, reflecting a European bias, portray them as exceptionally active. They worked "from morning till night," declared Deliette (1934: 351), and were "very industrious, being rarely idle, especially when they are married" (ibid.: 339; cf. Raudot 1940: 390). Although "their first care . . . [was] to supply the cabin with everything that is necessary," women did much more than perform routine housework tasks. They were responsible for agricultural fieldwork, carried the reed mats used to construct cabins from one location to another when villages were relocated, hauled meat from the kill site to the preparation site, and even portaged the baggage of Frenchmen (Hauser 1973: 217). Callender and Kochems (1983: 447) noticed that berdaches in other societies often developed a reputation for proficiency in women's tasks. Except for the spurious account attributed to Tonti (1814 [1698]), the sources are silent on this issue. Illinois women achieved some reputation for working "with porcupine quills, with which they trim their gala moccasins" (Deliette 1934: 339), and it is likely that berdaches also attained celebrity by becoming skilled in this and similar pursuits.

The tribe defined different social roles for men and women, and this prevented berdaches from participating in raids or the hunt. Careful interpretation of the sources, even though they appear to disagree, supports this conclusion. Father Zénobe Membré (1881, 2: 135), who accompanied La Salle on his expedition to the mouth of the Mississippi in 1682, wrote that berdaches did not take "part in the chase or war" (see also Hennepin 1903 [1698], 1: 168).[5] While correct in regard to traditional hunting and warfare, this statement is not completely accurate. According to Marquette (1959), for example, who made his observations just eight years before Membré, the berdaches did go to war, but with the same restrictions that governed the participation of women. Marquette (ibid.: 129), acknowledging the role differences that separated men and women, wrote that berdaches could "use only clubs, and not bows and arrows, which are the weapons proper to men."

If interpreted as a reference to general marches or village army operations rather than raids, however, Marquette's comment agrees with Membré's. The Illinois reserved traditional warfare for males, for groups of six to twenty combatants, and for tactics employing stealth, secrecy, and caution, such as capturing enemy males. On general marches or when the village army acted, on the other hand, entire villages went to war, moved boldly toward their objective, and brought back women and children as captives (Hauser 1984–85: 368–69, 380–81). Women did accompany these village armies, and therefore the Illinois must have also included berdaches on the expeditions. Since under tribal convention berdaches, like women, could use only clubs as weapons, they could not participate in raids, but they did engage in village army warfare.[6] Both Marquette and Membré reported accurately but failed to explain completely the role of the berdache in war.

The observation that berdaches did not participate in the hunt, although largely correct, also requires some explanation. Women accompanied communal bison hunts; berdaches, therefore, were also likely to be present. Neither women nor berdaches, however, could hunt large game because sex role distinctions prohibited them from using bows and arrows; perhaps they pursued smaller targets, such as rabbits, because they could use clubs. Women, and therefore berdaches, were confined to preparing and transporting the meat procured by men. Even in traditional or small-scale hunting, women and berdaches were often responsible for locating field kills, skinning and butchering them, and hauling the meat back to the village, where they then worked to preserve it (Hauser 1973: 82–88, 109–10).

If one accepts the idea that the Illinois allowed berdaches to engage in activities open to women, the references in the French sources become more understandable. For example, when Deliette (1934: 341) described the ceremonial game of lacrosse, which the tribe sponsored before setting off on the summer communal bison hunt, he observed that "a few women" mingled with the men players. After considering the way the Illinois played the game, Deliette (ibid.: 343) described "a Bardache who was standing aside like the women [ready] to send back the ball to his party, in case it came his way." The berdache's participation in the game drew Deliette's attention because the Indian was hit in the head by the ball so hard that he lost an eye. The participation of berdaches and women in communal hunting and warfare may have been sanctioned for the female role by the Illinois during the late protohistoric period. They began to engage in communal warfare, for example, no later than the mid-1660s and continued through the 1680s (Hauser 1984–85: 371–79).

SEXUALITY AND THE BERDACHE

Transvestism and Hermaphroditism

Three circumstances that bear some similarity to the berdache phenomenon may be the source of the confusion in both French colonial observation and modern scholarship: cross-dressing as a punishment for cowardice, hermaphroditism, and homosexuality (Callender and Kochems 1983: 443). Cowards dressed in female clothing were not recognized as berdaches, but they could have confused European reporters. The French at times also erroneously identified berdaches as hermaphrodites, or intersexuals (Parkman 1916: 207n.1; Whitehead 1981: 85). A hermaphrodite might dress and live as a woman, but, because of sexual ambiguity, he by definition could not qualify as a berdache (Angelino and Shedd 1955: 124–25; Forgey 1975: 12). More than this, however, even those early sources that mention hermaphrodites are open to challenge. Father Louis Hennepin (1903 [1698], I: 168), a Recollet missionary associated with the La Salle venture, thought that hermaphrodites were "very common amongst [the Illinois], which is so much the more surprizing, because I have not observ'd any such thing amongst the other Nations of the Northern *America*" (see also Membré 1881, 2: 135; Lahontan 1905 [1703], 2: 462). This statement appears incorrect, because hermaphrodites are rare, especially when the identification is based upon external genitalia alone (Baber 1970 [1944]: 141; Karlen 1971: 348; Whitehead 1981: 86; cf. Williams 1986: 77). Hennepin, however, did not employ the term *berdaches,* and his remark may not have been intended as a reference to them; the hermaphrodite comment is distinguished from a more easily recognized description of berdaches as homosexuals by several sentences about Illinois marriage practices. The Illinois may have been one of those societies in which berdache and intersexual merged and then were relegated to different subclasses; nevertheless, intersexuals do not meet the anatomical or cultural requirements of the berdache (Callender and Kochems 1983: 444).

Homosexuality

Any description of the berdache must deal with the question of sexual orientation, insofar as this is possible, even though social standing is more important. Most of the French references to the Illinois institution link it to male homosexuality. It is probably true that not all berdaches were homosexual (Williams 1986: 93), and certainly not all Illinois homosexuals were berdaches (Deliette 1934: 329). Male homosexuality, however, was common among seventeenth-century Illinois. "The sin of sodomy," declared Deliette (ibid.), "prevails more among them than in any other nation" (see also Hennepin 1903 [1698], I: 167; Raudot 1940: 388). Many potential Illinois berdaches began to engage in homosexual practices during childhood (Marquette 1959: 129; La Salle 1901: 145; St. Cosme 1967: 360). Although not all sources are as clear on this point as Deliette, Frenchmen commenting on male homosexuality appear to have made most of the references while describing the berdache. La Salle

(1901: 145), for example, wrote that "they are accused of being addicted to the sin against nature, having men set apart from childhood for this detestable purpose." It is possible, of course, that observers merely assumed that the Illinois transvestites they saw were homosexual.

Homosexuality alone could not assign an Illinois to life as a berdache. In other societies, erotic focus followed, rather than preceded, confirmation in the role (Callender and Kochems 1983: 454). Homosexuality was merely a secondary characteristic often associated with the phenomenon. It is instructive to note that in other societies berdaches always selected sex partners who were not berdaches (ibid.: 444; Whitehead 1981: 96; Williams 1986: 93). While Deliette (1934: 329–30) describes Illinois berdaches as bisexual, they could in fact also have been asexual, heterosexual, or homosexual.

In looking for an explanation for Illinois homosexuality, Deliette (ibid.: 329) decided that men sought homosexual liaisons because "the women, although debauched, retain some moderation, which prevents the young men from satisfying their passions as much as they would like." The scholarly explanations of homosexuality, which generate much disagreement, include chastity concepts, customs restricting social contact with the opposite sex, the advanced age traditionally required for marriage, and polygyny (Bullough 1976: 27; Whitehead 1981: 80). The Illinois did place a certain premium on chastity, even though some reporters lamented the profligacy of unmarried women (at the very least, young people must have been frustrated by mores which held it unseemly for young women to converse with any males), and the traditional age for marriage for men was about thirty, while that for women was about twenty-five; the delay allowed individuals the time to develop the skills required for success as heads of their own families. However, Deliette also identified a factor which he thought should have frustrated the development of male homosexuality: a sex ratio of four women for every man, which would have lessened the contribution of polygyny to it. Finally, after contact with the Europeans, the acceptable age for marriage sometimes declined to less than twenty for men and less than eighteen for women (Deliette 1934: 330; Raudot 1940: 388).[7]

Residency

The sources also do not clearly establish a residency pattern for Illinois berdaches. The different, but complementary, economic roles reserved for men and women should have required a place for the berdache in patrilocal polygynous families, but the exact nature of this place is difficult to determine. A berdache could have lived alone, as an unmarried member of a parent's or sibling's extended family, or even as a secondary wife in a polygynous family. When Marquette (1959: 129) noted that the berdaches did not marry, he may have intended to refer to the absence of the usual family relationships between them and women.

A heterosexual or bisexual berdache created serious problems for his female partners. Deliette (1934: 329–30) drew attention to this fact when he wrote that "the women and girls who prostitute themselves to these wretches are dissolute creatures" (see also Raudot 1940: 389).[8] The dilemma was compounded for married partners, because a cuckolded husband might attempt the revenge characteristic of the double standard maintained by Illinois men: he might drive his wife from his home; have her scalped, murdered, or gang-raped; or cut off her ears and nose (Hauser 1973: 307).

RELIGION AND THE BERDACHE

The role of the berdache among the Illinois was closely associated with their religious traditions. While the sources do not clearly identify any berdaches as shamans, they do imply that some were spiritual and healing specialists. Sauk and Fox berdaches fulfilled the shaman role (Jacobs 1968: 35), and it is therefore probable that Illinois berdaches also did. Illinois men and women both practiced the shamanistic arts and participated in the public demonstrations that the association of shamans, the Midewiwin or Grand Medicine Society, sponsored several times each year (Deliette 1934: 369); Marquette (1959: 129) wrote that berdaches were "present at all the juggleries." It is true that other references to these performances do not specifically mention the berdaches, or describe a role reserved for them, but this very circumstance suggests that berdaches were in attendance in the same capacity as other shamans.

Young men did not ordinarily choose to become shamans, because the Illinois considered such individuals cowards; "unless he excel in the profession," observed Deliette (1934: 375), "he is despised." A fear of being thought unmanly, of course, would not have deterred a berdache from becoming a shaman; moreover, the general tribal population ordinarily treated shamans and berdaches with deference because they both were thought to possess—or to be—*manitous*, the "generalized essence of spiritual power" (Miller 1955: 279, 283). The shaman based his or her position in the tribe on fear: he or she possessed the power of life or death over others (Deliette 1934: 374; see also Thayer 1980: 290; Williams 1986: 41, 193).

The Illinois defined the ceremonial religious role of the berdaches rather clearly, apparently because of their acceptance as manitous. At other public rituals, however, the berdache may have played a more limited role. For example, they attended "the solemn dances in honor of the Calumet" (Marquette 1959: 129). While they did sing on these occasions, Illinois convention did not permit berdaches to dance.[9] Tribal councils also called upon the berdaches when they met, "and nothing . . . [could] be decided without their advice" (ibid.).

SOCIAL POSITION OF THE BERDACHE

The attitude of the Illinois toward berdaches is difficult to determine with any confidence, and scholars therefore have not agreed with one another on the issue of their social position. Perhaps basing his comments on documentary references to "wretches," Francis Parkman (1916: 207n.1) determined that berdaches "were held in great contempt"; Reuben Gold Thwaites, editor of *The Jesuit Relations* and other works, agreed (see Hennepin 1903 [1698], 1: 168n.1). In a contradictory evaluation, probably influenced by the berdache's ceremonial function, Ralph Linton (c. 1915: 46) concluded that the tribe honored true berdaches: "The statement frequently made by early writers that they were held in utmost contempt . . . probably [represents a] confusion . . . between true berdaches and men who had been 'dressed in skirts.'" Modern scholars who have examined the status of the berdache in other societies have concluded that primary sources claiming low status reflect a change from earlier Native American attitudes, which ranged from neutrality to esteem (Callender and Kochems 1983: 453; Forgey 1975: 3). The disagreement over the Illinois attitude toward berdaches may be the result of a misapprehension of the special position which they maintained in the tribe, as well as a misunderstanding of the roles of those transvestites who were not berdaches.

A review of the activities that brought social standing to Illinois men and women will permit us to evaluate the social position of the berdache more precisely. Men established their reputations while hunting and taking part in raids. "Among the Illinois," explained Father Sebastien Rasles (1959: 171), who lived among the Illinois from 1692 until 1694, "the only way of acquiring public esteem and regard is . . . to gain the reputation of a skillful hunter, and, still further, of a good warrior; it is chiefly in this latter that they make their merit consist, and it is this which they call being truly a man." While Rasles placed weight on acquiring a warrior's reputation, Father Jean Francois Buisson de St. Cosme (1967: 353) emphasized hunting capabilities, noting that a related act, giving banquets, was "the way to acquire the esteem of the savages and of all their nations in a short time." Men appear to have been the ceremonial, economic, military, and political leaders in seventeenth-century Illinois society.

Status of Illinois Women

The French sources offer an incomplete account of the role played by women in Illinois society. This is understandable in view of the more visible role played by men, and because men—European men—prepared the documents upon which any sketch must be based. Those Frenchmen who referred to Illinois women as "slaves" of the men reached this erroneous conclusion because they were unable to cross the cultural and gender barriers which separated them from the Indians (Binneteau 1959: 67). Women attained social standing in the system reserved for them by industriously nurturing children, constructing and tending cabins, gathering wood, procuring and preparing food, dressing skins, and tilling fields.[10] Evidence of their achieving proficiency in and esteem through these tasks may be found in the practice of tattooing women (Deliette 1934: 329); men wore tattoos as signs of accomplishment, and it is reasonable to assume that the tattoos worn by women also represented significant performance.[11] Nevertheless, it is important to note that the prevailing role restrictions for women did not permit them to attain social positions that were reserved for men.

Women did exercise limited power within the female sphere of activity. For example, women led age groups of females that pursued female responsibilities such as mortuary customs for deceased women (ibid.: 360; Gravier 1959: 199). They did not ordinarily wield power in arenas that also included males. The sources, for example, contain just one reference to a female village or civil chief (St. Cosme 1967: 353); this single instance suggests that women enjoyed some status but little power. It "is implausible to argue that women may have less visible prestige but an equal claim on dominance," Nancy Datan (1983: 458) argues, "as it must also be posited that women are content with power so subtle that its effects are difficult to detect. It is far more parsimonious, though less pleasing, to concede that women have unequal access to power."

The status and power of Illinois women may be evaluated according to four criteria: division of labor, polygyny, marriage gift exchange, and control over sexuality (Weiss 1983: 41). In the sexually segregated, complementary task system of the Illinois, the male contribution, meat, outranked that of the females (Deliette 1934: 309, 313–14; St. Cosme 1967: 353). The status of women would still appear substantial in view of the fact that the survival of the group depended on them when meat was unavailable (Klein 1983: 149, 165; Brown 1979: 240). Sororal polygyny must not have contributed to the status of women, because a girl's brother played a prominent role in her accepting a husband, but polygyny did provide the first wife with a position superior to that of second and successive wives. A gift exchange was an important part of the marriage arrangements, and this circumstance testifies to a high status for Illinois women (Hauser 1973: 228–30).[12] Finally, these women did not control their own sexuality, because their brothers could force them into extramarital liaisons (Deliette 1934: 328).

Illinois women earned status in their own prestige system through their labor and through marriage gift exchanges. Evidence that men enjoyed greater status, however, is found in their more prestigious labor, their control of the sexuality of women, and their domination in polygynous practices. Socially, Illinois women occupied an important arena separate from the one filled by men; any young man who attempted to involve himself in these activities would probably have brought scorn and ridicule upon himself (Klein 1983: 239).[13] Illinois women did attain status in their system, and men must have appreciated those women who successfully filled the female role.

Sanctioned male and female activities were not entirely distinct, however. Both men and women transported heavy loads of meat from the site of communal bison kills back to the village; they played lacrosse together, although women and berdaches filled less active roles than men; and they both functioned as shamans. The role of men also changed as they aged. Individual prestige increased with age, and so old men ate first, served as officials during games of lacrosse, and helped to decide the disposition of war prisoners. Paradoxically, they also worked with women in the fields (Deliette 1934: 312, 341, 369, 309, 342, 384; Dablon 1959: 99), and this again testifies to the prominent status of women.

While men and women acquired prestige in different systems, men did enjoy certain power advantages over women; this power difference appears to establish a male orientation, if not domination. Fathers and brothers offered their daughters and sisters as prostitutes, and brothers used their sisters to cover wagers "after having lost all they had of personal property" (Deliette 1934: 352; cf. 337, 328). Cuckolded husbands also exercised their power when they physically abused their wives (Hauser 1973: 302).

The attitudes of Illinois men toward women were based at least partially on fear. Husbands, for example, did not permit their wives to remain in the cabin during childbirth or menstruation because they were afraid of the blood (Deliette 1934: 352, 354; Raudot 1940: 391–92). The position of the men became more clear in remarks dating from the mid-eighteenth century, but which may also apply to the late seventeenth century. An unidentified Frenchman wrote that "perhaps no nation in the world scorns women more than these savages usually do" (Stevens, Kent, and Woods 1941: 140). This statement is only partially accurate; men did not scorn women so much as they disdained the female role for themselves. "The bitterest insult that can be offered a savage is to call him a woman" (ibid.).

Another eighteenth-century Frenchman further clarified the position of Illinois men when he discovered the contempt of the warriors for those Frenchmen whom they saw displaying effeminate manners at the court of the king of France. An Illinois informant who said that he had been one of several Illinois Indians to visit Paris in 1720 reported "that he had noticed at the Tuileries and in other public places men who were half women, with curled hair, earrings, and corsages on their chests. He suspected that they wore rouge, and he said that they smelled like alligators" (Bossu 1962: 84).[14] According to the Frenchman, "This American spoke with the great scorn of these people, whom we call *petite maîtres*. They are born with the natural weakness and coquetry of women. Nature seems to have started to make them women and then forgot and gave them the wrong sex" (ibid.).

Interesting though this remark identifying French transsexuals is, the final comment of the Illinois informant constitutes more important and conclusive evidence of the social place reserved for the berdache: "Such effeminate manners [as he had witnessed] dishonor a respectable nation" (Bossu 1962: 84). The attitudes of this mid-eighteenth-century warrior toward an early-eighteenth-century experience may reflect the influence of European values and may have been different from those of his late seventeenth-century relatives, even though they do tend to confirm the opinions of the latter toward women and the female role. However, if the testimony of this warrior does reflect new values, then it could explain why eighteenth-century French reporters did not mention seeing berdaches among the Illinois.

Status of the Berdache

The Illinois Indians did not hold berdaches in contempt. Berdaches could not attain the social goals reserved for males, but they could reach the status positions available to women (Whitehead 1981: 107). Even if they were not actually inferior, women occupied a radically different status from men, and it was this difference that made it unacceptable for a male to assume the female role. Ironically, although berdaches could not claim the honors that were possible for men, the tribe deferred to them because of the difference between their lives and those of men. The only explanation acceptable to the Illinois that might account for the behavior of the berdache identifies him as a manitou: the berdache's voluntary rejection of the privileged male role involved divine intervention (see Forgey 1975: 4, 5). For this reason, those young berdaches who became shamans were not despised even though shamanism was considered unacceptable for young men (Deliette 1934: 375).

Although the Illinois did not hold berdaches in contempt, they did not honor or respect them, either. Marquette (1959: 129) alluded to a supernatural validation for them when he reported that "through their profession of leading an Extraordinary life," they were accepted as manitous. The Illinois, especially the younger people, considered successful shamans to be manitous, to possess supernatural power; the tribespeople thought that shamans could cause death through their use of magic (Deliette 1934: 369; Raudot 1940: 400). The Illinois feared shamans; they did not respect or admire them. The berdaches' commitment to living as women and to functioning as shamans, and their acceptance as manitous, must have contributed to the fearful attitude that the Illinois maintained toward them (Bowers 1965: 167–68, 259–60; Thayer 1980: 292–93; Williams 1986: 41, 193).

The intermediate nature of the berdache status was less well defined for the Illinois than for other societies. Berdaches obviously engaged in gender mixing rather than gender crossing. Illinois berdaches crossed genders when they assumed women's dress, occupations, and warfare restrictions. They mixed gender roles when they engaged in certain ritual ceremonies, because their participation was "associated with the vision-based power," and "also depended on their definition as nonwomen" (Callender and Kochems 1983: 454). They also mixed gender roles when they engaged in sex both with men, in the female role, and with women (ibid.).

PREVALENCE AND DECLINE OF THE BERDACHE

There is no indication in the sources of how many Illinois lived as berdaches during the last quarter of the seventeenth century. When Marquette (1959: 129) first visited these Indians in 1673, for example, he merely reported that "some" of them were berdaches. St. Cosme (1967: 360) noticed that these individuals were "quite common" among the Illinois in 1698, the date of the last recorded encounter. There is no way to determine precisely the frequency or incidence of the berdache phenomenon among the Illinois, since the attitude of the French was that any berdaches was far too many. Berdaches were rare in other North American Indian societies, ranging from none to four or five (Callender and Kochems 1983: 448; Forgey 1975: 1).

There are several reasons why eighteenth-century sources do not make reference either to Illinois berdaches or to homosexuality.[15] Anthropological research into the institution in other North American Indian societies has discovered that, for a variety of causes, berdaches usually faded from view shortly after contact (Callender and Kochems 1983: 443; Bowers 1965: 168; Broch 1983: 457). For the Illinois, their disappearance was certainly related to an actual reduction. First, the tribal effort to accommodate the Europeans (Deliette 1934: 328, 330; Brown 1979: 225) presumably resulted in a decline in the number of berdaches:[16] the Illionois may have discouraged potential berdaches from becoming fulfilled because of European hostility toward the institution, and they may have become increasingly reluctant to acknowledge those who attempted to continue to live as berdaches (Lurie 1953: 708; Hill 1935: 274).[17] Second, the absolute number of berdaches must have also decreased when the population of the tribe diminished by more than 40 percent between 1680 and 1700 (Blasingham 1956: 365).

The most significant question concerning the disappearance of the institution is, at "what point . . . do berdaches go underground but persist, and at what later point does their behavior become vestigial?" (Callender and Kochems 1983: 465). The berdache phenomenon could have gone underground after 1698, with berdaches abandoning cross-dressing and other habits, and then died out within a generation because new "recruits" were no longer added to their ranks. The absence of documentary references to Illinois berdaches by the eighteenth-century French, who saw nearly everything else, however, suggests that the institution actually disappeared (ibid.: 444). This conclusion is supported by reports of berdaches living in closely related tribes, such as the Miami, Sauk, and Fox, long after they disappeared from the Illinois (Trowbridge 1938: 68; Keating 1825: 216; Catlin 1926, 2: 243–44; Michelson 1925: 257). The French attitude toward berdaches must have placed the institution under attack from the very beginning of the contact period. This pressure probably put the institution into decline by the 1680s, and by 1698 either the number of berdaches had fallen to zero or the beleaguered survivors had moved to other tribes where the institution still thrived. It is noteworthy that St. Cosme (1967: 360) encountered what seems to have been the last berdache in a distant Quapaw village rather than in an Illinois village.

The Illinois did change their cultural institutions in response to the French presence, but the changes did not please the Indians. For example, French priests employed religious instruction to attack what they saw as licentiousness. They induced young women to "mock at the superstitions of their nation. . . .This often greatly incenses the old men and daily exposes these fathers to ill-treatment, and even to being killed" (Deliette 1934: 361). Also, the ages at which young people married declined markedly. Before contact young men had waited to marry until about the age of thirty because of the tribal conviction that men could not "possess resolution," or hunt or raid their enemies, until then (ibid.: 330). Contact with the French apparently made it possible for young people to marry earlier, perhaps because possession of various trade goods made it possible for them to set up their own households earlier. The Illinois resented these profound changes that contact with Europeans worked upon their social institutions. "The old men," declared Deliette (ibid.), "say that the French have corrupted them" (see also Raudot 1940: 388).

Cross-dressing continued after 1698, even if the berdache phenomenon did not. In the only description of its kind for the Illinois, Jean-Bernard Bossu (1962: 82), a French naval officer who visited the Illinois country several times during the 1750s, identified a transvestite as a disgraced warrior: "They are called old ladies, and even the women scorn them." The degraded man was able to restore himself to a position of public honor only after successfully performing an especially brave martial feat. This is the first reference in the sources to transvestism in more than half a century, and the attitude of these Illinois may have changed considerably after the seventeenth century, reflecting their adoption of European prejudices. The status of the dishonored eighteenth-century warrior was not that of a berdache: cross-dressing was forced upon him by secular authorities and therefore did not result from any supernatural endorsement; it carried a stigma; and it was at least potentially reversible (Callender and Kochems 1983: 444).

CONCLUSION

Illinois berdaches were bisexual male transvestites who played a female role in their seventeenth-century society. They began their special lives when attracted to this female role as children and were confirmed as berdaches through a dream-fast religious experience. Gender role restrictions kept them from engaging in the traditional warfare or hunting activities reserved for men, but they did accompany the communal warfare and hunting expeditions open to women. Functioning as shamans and accepted as manitous, berdaches enjoyed a special position in Illinois society, a place based upon fear and different from that of men or women. The Illinois did not honor berdaches, because they saw them as males who had voluntarily abjured the male route to esteem or status by electing to live as women; yet the tribespeople did not hold berdaches in contempt, because their "Extraordinary life" identified their special relationship to a supernatural power. As a consequence of their fear, the Illinois reserved a place in their society for berdaches which honored supernatural power. Because they were accepted as manitous, berdaches attended important political, religious, and social functions, such as council meetings, Midewiwin ceremonies, and calumet dances.

NOTES

1. For the etymology of the term *berdache*, see Thwaites 1959 [1896–1901], 59: 310n.26; Angelino and Shedd 1955: 121; Bullough 1976: 32; Forgey 1975: 2; and Jacobs 1983: 459.

2. Pierre Deliette wrote the most important account of seventeenth-century Illinois life about 1704, several years after he left the Illinois country (Jablow 1974: 115; cf. Kinietz 1940: 332). The De Gannes who signed the only extant copy of the Deliette manuscript on October 20, 1721, may have been a secretary (Pease and Werner 1934: ix). Several scholars agree that Deliette's comments refer to seventeenth-century observations (ibid.: iv; Hickerson 1962: 406; Jablow 1974: 115). Antoine Denis Raudot, who served as an *intendant* of New France from 1705 until 1710, apparently took his account of the Illinois from the same Deliette manuscript used by De Gannes (Kinietz 1940: 336).

3. For the Illinois berdache, the problem of fragmentary sources is compounded by the existence of questionable or fraudulent sources. Louis-Armand de Lom d'Arce, Baron de Lahontan, a French army officer who began his career in New France in 1683, may not have even visited the Illinois country (Thwaites 1905: xl–xli); information about the berdache in his account is available in other sources (see Lahontan 1905 [1703], 2: 462). Tonti (1814 [1698]: 237–38), La Salle's lieutenant, denied writing a source attributed to him which does contain interesting information. The spurious source claims that berdaches were "forbidden to wear the . . .

name of man," that women reacted more negatively toward them than men did, and that they "work[ed] fine mats for hanging their cottages." Although these comments are plausible, they must be considered unreliable because Tonti denied his authorship and because the document has long been regarded as replete with error (Parkman 1916: 129n.1; Kellogg 1967 [1917]: 285; Hamilton 1970: xi).

4. "That Indian women worked hard goes without question," observes Weist (1983: 39), who challenges the concept of Indian women as "beasts of burden and menial slaves." The French sources, which reflect the reporters' European and sexual attitudes toward "the value of household labor" (Albers 1983: 4), do not accurately reflect the status of Illinois women.

5. Membré, a Recollet missionary, recorded the progress of La Salle's expedition; his cousin, Father Christian Le Clercq, also a Recollet, published the Membré material as his own work in 1691. Father Louis Hennepin, another Recollet missionary on the La Salle expedition, embellished his role in the venture with his second publication, and his reputation suffered as a result. Although Hennepin also copied from Membré in this suspect volume, published in 1697, it must be remembered that he did serve as a witness for Membré and therefore corroborated his account of the Illinois berdache.

6. Nineteenth-century Miami berdaches occasionally did go to war, "on which occasion the habiliments of the women were exchanged after leaving the village for the warriors [sic] dress, and a re-exchange made upon returning to it" (Trowbridge 1938: 68).

7. None of the French reporters ever mention female homosexuality among the Illinois, even though the sex ratio and polygyny might have encouraged it (female members of the tribe may have engaged in homosexual acts unnoticed, of course; see Bullough 1976: 27). The French records do not contain any descriptions of female berdaches, either, but this is hardly surprising for a society that institutionalized the role of the berdache for males (Schaeffer 1965: 193; Callender and Kochems 1983: 446). For an explanation of the relative scarcity of female berdaches in other societies, see Whitehead 1981: 91–93. Callender and Kochems (1983: 446) conclude that "female berdaches tended to be more prevalent in less complex societies and those in which agriculture was absent or less important." Schlegel (1983: 462) concludes that "female berdaches are tolerated, but probably not encouraged, in societies where (1) females make a lesser contribution to production than men and (2) male labor is in actual or potential short supply."

8. Nineteenth-century Miami berdaches "sometimes . . . [took] advantage of the liberty which is afforded them in their intercourse with the females and carnal connection . . . [was] not rare" (Trowbridge 1938: 68).

9. In the 1830s, George Catlin rendered a painting, entitled *Dance to the Berdashe,* of a Fox ceremony sponsored once a year; it was followed by a feast (see Catlin 1926, 2: 243–44; cf. Williams 1986: 107–8).

10. According to Weist (1983: 41), "Cross-cultural studies of women's status indicate that labor by itself need not be associated with a relatively low status, however lack of control over the products of one's labor is." While the items in the cabin may have been considered the property of the wives, the manufacturers, the cabin itself may have belonged to the husband even though the women also constructed it (Deliette 1934: 361, 355). It is possible that ownership confusion "may be explained if we view women as subsumed by men so that their [female] ownership is superseded by" male ownership (Klein 1983: 157).

11. "Perhaps men of the Plains and western Prairie cultures . . . promote[d] the male berdache status to assert their superiority over women in an occupational sphere defined [as] female and associated with prestige" (Callender and Kochems 1983: 456; cf. Whitehead 1981: 108). An intriguing anthropological alternative is that "women encouraged and promoted the status of male berdache, while 'defending' their side of the occupational boundary, by insisting that men who crossed it had to go through a transformation" (Callender and Kochems 1983: 456; cf. Tonti 1814 [1698]: 238).

12. This exchange of gifts among the Illinois, as on the Plains, "served to cement ties between kin groups. . . . Cross-culturally, this type of exchange tends to be associated with an equality between the two kin groups rather than a ranked relationship of giver and receiver" (Weiss 1983: 44).

13. An argument for high status for Illinois, as for Hidatsa, women is that "men were excluded from participation in female activities, particularly resource procurement and processing, or the construction of structures, facilities, and material goods all centrally important to the lives of the women and to the survival of the group" (Spector 1983: 94–95).

14. The date and the number of Illinois in this party of Indian travelers are at variance with the 1725 visit to Paris made by the group which included Agapit Chicago, a Michigamea-Illinois village chief (Ellis and Steen 1974: 391).

15. Father Joseph Francois Lafitau (1724, 1: 48–49) and Charlevoix (1966, 2: 80) made references to berdaches that at first glance place them among the Illinois after 1701. However, both mention the Illinois by name just once, and their comments appear to have been based on information obtained from informants or documents, not on observation. Their objective was to make a general reference to berdaches among North American Indians. Charlevoix did travel through Illinois country, but the passage in question, which focuses on the Iroquois, occurs in his *Journal* before the passages describing his experiences in the Illinois country (see also Kinietz 1940: x; Callender and Kochems 1983: 464).

16. The desire of the Illinois to cooperate with the French is reviewed in Hauser 1976: 135; 1984–85: 379–81.

17. The evidence that the French disapproved of the berdaches is found in Marquette's (1959: 129) comment that they "glor[ied] in demeaning themselves," in La Salle's (1901: 145) and Deliette's (1934: 329) describing berdache homosexual activity as "the sin," and in references to berdaches as "wretches" by Deliette (1934: 329) and St. Cosme (1967: 360). When Callender and Kochems (1983: 443) evaluated the bias of French observers toward Illinois berdaches they found Marquette neutral but not Deliette.

REFERENCES

Albers, Patricia. "Introduction: New Perspectives on Plains Indian Women." In *The Hidden Half: Studies of Plains Indian Women*. Patricia Albers and Beatrice Medicine, eds. Lanham, Md.: University Press of America, 1983, pp. 1–26.

Angelino, Henry, and Charles L. Shedd. "A Note on Berdache." *Plains Anthropologist* 57 (1955): 121–26.

Baber, Ray E. "Hermaphrodite." In *Dictionary of Sociology and Related Sciences*. Henry Pratt-Fairchild et al., comps. Totowa, N.J.: Littlefield, Adams, 1970 [1944], p. 141.

Binneteau, Julien. Letter to a Jesuit Friend, [January] 1699. In *The Jesuit Relations and Allied Documents*. Reuben Gold Thwaites, ed. vol. 65, New York: Pageant, 1959, pp. 65–77.

Blasingham, Emily J. "The Depopulation of the Illinois Indians." *Ethnohistory* 3 (1956): 193–224, 361–412..

Bossu, Jean-Bernard. *Travels in the Interior of North America, 1751–1762*. Seymour Feller, ed. Norman: University of Oklahoma Press, 1962.

Bowers, Alfred W. "Hidatsa Social and Ceremonial Organization." *Bureau of American Ethnology Bulletin*, no. 194 (1965). Washington: Smithsonian Institution.

Broch, Harald Beyer. "Comments." *Current Anthropology* 24 (1983): 457.

Brown, Judith K. "Comments." *Current Anthropology* 24 (1983): 457–58.

Brown, Margaret Kimball. *Cultural Transformations among the Illinois: An Application of a Systems Model*. Publications of the Michigan State University Museum. East Lansing: Michigan State University, 1979.

Bullough, Vern L. *Sexual Variance in Society and History*. New York: John Wiley, 1976.

Callender, Charles, and Lee M. Kochems. "The North American Berdache." *Current Anthropology* 24 (1983): 443–70.

Catlin, George. *North American Indians, Being Letters and Notes on Their Manners, Customs, and Conditions, Written during Eight Years' Travel amongst the Wildest Tribes of Indians in North America, 1832–1839*. 2 vols. Edinburgh: John Grant, 1926.

Charlevoix, Pierre F. X. de. *Journal of a Voyage to North America*. 2 vols. Ann Arbor, Mich.: University Microfilms, 1966.

Dablon, Claude. "Letter to a Superior in France, August 1, 1674." In *The Jesuit Relations and Allied Documents*. Reuben Gold Thwaites, ed. vol. 58, New York: Pageant, 1959, pp. 93–109.

Datan, Nancy. "Comments." *Current Anthropology* 24 (1983): 458.

Deliette, Pierre. "Memoir of De Gannes Concerning the Illinois Country [1704]." In *The French Foundations, 1680–1693*. Theodore Calvin Pease and Raymond C. Werner, eds. Collections of the Illinois State Historical Library, vol. 23. Springfield: Illinois State Historical Library, 1934, pp. 302–95.

Ellis, Richard N., and Charlie R. Steen, eds. "An Indian Delegation in France, 1725." *Journal of the Illinois State Historical Society* 67: (1974) 385–405.

Forgey, Donald G. "The Institution of Berdache among the North American Plains Indians." *Journal of Sex Research* II (1975): 1–15.

Gravier, Jacques. "Letter to Jacques Bruyas, February 25, 1694." In *The Jesuit Relations and Allied Documents.* Reuben Gold Thwaites, ed. vol. 64. New York: Pageant, 1959, pp. 159–237.

Hamilton, Raphael N. *Marquette's Explorations: The Narratives Reexamined.* Madison: University of Wisconsin Press, 1978.

Hauser, Raymond E. "An Ethnohistory of the Illinois Indian Tribe, 1673–1832." Ph.D. diss., Northern Illinois University, 1973.

———. "The Illinois Indian Tribe: From Autonomy and Self-Sufficiency to Dependency and Depopulation." *Journal of the Illinois State Historical Society* 69 (1976): 127–38.

———. "Warfare and the Illinois Indian Tribe during the Seventeenth Century: An Exercise in Ethnohistory." *Old Northwest* 10 (1984–85): 367–87.

Hennepin, Louis. *A New Discovery of a Vast Country in America.* Reuben Gold Thwaites, ed. 2 vols. Chicago: A. C. McClurg, 1903 [1698].

Hickerson, Harold. "Notes on the Post-Contact Origin of the Midewiwin." *Ethnohistory* 9 (1962): 404–23.

Hill, Willard W. "The Status of the Hermaphrodite and Transvestite in Navaho Culture." *American Anthropologist* 37 (1935): 273–79.

Holmberg, David. "Comments." *Current Anthropology* 24 (1983): 458–59.

Jablow, Joseph. *Indians of Illinois and Indiana: Illinois, Kickapoo, and Potawatomi Indians.* New York: Garland Publishing, 1974.

Jacobs, Sue-Ellen. "Berdache: A Brief Review of the Literature." *Colorado Anthropologist* 1 (1968): 25–40.

———. "Comments." *Current Anthropology* 24 (1983): 459–60.

Karlen, Arno. *Sexuality and Homosexuality: A New View.* New York: W. W. Norton, 1971.

Keating, William H. *Narrative of an Expedition to the Source of St. Peter's River.* vol. I. Philadelphia: H. C. Carey and I. Lea, 1825.

Kellogg, Louise Phelps, ed. *Early Narratives of the Northwest, 1634–1699.* New York: Barnes and Noble, 1967 [1917].

Kinietz, W. Vernon, trans. and ed. *Indians of the Western Great Lakes, 1615–1760.* Ann Arbor: University of Michigan Press, 1940.

Klein, Alan M. "The Political-Economy of Gender: A Nineteenth Century Plains Indian Case Study." In *The Hidden Half: Studies of Plains Indian Women.* Patricia Albers and Beatrice Medicine, eds. Lanham, Md.: University Press of America, 1983, pp. 143–73.

Lafitau, Joseph Francois. *Moeurs des sauvages ameriquains, comparées aux moeurs des premiers temps.* 4 vols. Paris: Saugrain and Hochereau, 1724.

Lahontan, Louis-Armand de Lom d'Arce, Baron de. *New Voyages to North-America.* Reuben Gold Thwaites, ed. 2 vols. Chicago: A. C. McClurg, 1905 [1703].

La Salle, Robert Cavelier, Sieur de. *Relation of the Discoveries and Voyages of Cavelier de La Salle from 1679 to 1681: The Official Narrative.* Melville B. Anderson, ed. Chicago: Caxton Club, 1901.

———. "Account of Hennepin's Exploration in La Salle's Letter of August 22, 1682." In Louis Hennepin. *A Description of Louisiana.* John D. G. Shea, ed. March of America Facsimile Series, no. 30. Ann Arbor, Mich.: University Microfilms, 1966 [1880] pp. 361–71.

Linton, Ralph. "The Indians of Illinois." Unpublished paper, Illinois Historical Survey, University of Illinois at Urbana-Champaign, c. 1915.

Lurie, Nancy Oestreich. "Winnebago Berdache." *American Anthropologist* 55 (1953): 708–12.

Marquette, Jacques. "Of the First Voyage Made by Father Marquette toward New Mexico, and How the Idea Thereof Was Conceived [1674], by Claude Dablon." In *The Jesuit Relations and Allied Documents.* Reuben Gold Thwaites, ed. vol. 59, New York: Pageant, 1959, pp. 86–183

Membré, Zénobe. In Christian Le Clercq. *First Establishment of the Faith in New France.* John D. G. Shea, trans. 2 vols. New York: Shea, 1881 [Relation 1691.].

Michelson, Truman. "The Mythical Origin of the White Buffalo Dance of the Fox Indians." Bureau of American Ethnology, *Annual Report,* no. 40, Washington: U.S. Government Printing Office, 1925, pp. 23–289.

Miller, Walter B. "Two Concepts of Authority." *American Anthropologist* 57 (1955): 271–89.

Parkman, Francis. *La Salle and the Discovery of the Great West.* Boston: Little, Brown, 1916.

Pease, Theodore Calvin, and Raymond C. Werner, eds. *The French Foundations, 1680–1693.* Collections of the Illinois State Historical Library, vol. 23. Springfield: Illinois State Historical Library, 1934.

Rasles, Sebastien. "Letter to His Brother, Narantsouak, October 12, 1723." In *The Jesuit Relations and Allied Documents*. Reuben Gold Thwaites, ed. vol. 62 New York: Pageant, 1959, pp. 133–229.

Raudot, Antoine Denis. "Memoir Concerning the Different Indian Nations of North America [1710]." In *The Indians of the Western Great Lakes, 1615–1760*. W. Vernon Kinietz, trans. and ed. Ann Arbor: University of Michigan Press, 1940, pp. 341–410.

St. Cosme, Jean François Buisson de. "Letter to Bishop Laval in Quebec, January 2, 1699." In *Early Narratives of the Northwest, 1634–1699*. Louise Phelps Kellogg, ed. New York: Barnes and Noble, 1967, pp. 342–61.

Schaeffer, Claude E. "The Kutenai Female Berdache: Courier, Guide, Prophetess, and Warrior." *Ethnohistory* 23 (1965): 193–236.

Schlegel, Alice. "Comments." *Current Anthropology* 24 (1983): 462.

Spector, Janet D. "Male/Female Task Differentiation among the Hidatsa: Toward the Development of an Archeological Approach to the Study of Gender." In *The Hidden Half: Studies of Plains Indian Women*. Patricia Albers and Beatrice Medicine, eds. Lanham, Md.: University Press of America, 1983, pp. 77–99.

Stevens, Sylvester K., Donald H. Kent, and Emma Edith Woods, eds. *Travels in New France, by J. C. B. [1750s–1760s]*. Harrisburg: Pennsylvania Historical Commission, 1941.

Thayer, James Steel. "The Berdache of the Northern Plains: A Socioreligious Perspective." *Journal of Anthropological Research* 36 (1980): 287–93.

Thwaites, Reuben Gold. "Introduction." In *New Voyages to North-America, by Louis-Armand de Lom d'Arce, Baron de Lahontan*. Reuben Gold Thwaites, ed. vol. I, Chicago: A. C. McClurg, 1905, pp. ix–xlix.

Thwaites, Reuben Gold, ed. *The Jesuit Relations and Allied Documents*. 73 vols. New York: Pageant, 1959 [1896–1901].

Tonti, Henri de. *An Account of Monsieur de La Salle's Last Expedition and Discoveries in North America*. New York Historical Collections, 1st ser., 2 (1814) [1698]: 217–341.

Trowbridge, Charles Christopher. *Meearmeear Traditions*. W. Vernon Kinietz, ed. Occasional Contributions from the Museum of Anthropology, no. 7. Ann Arbor: University of Michigan, 1938.

Weist, Katherine M. "Beasts of Burden and Menial Slaves: Nineteenth Century Observations of Northern Plains Indian Women." In *The Hidden Half: Studies of Plains Indian Women*. Patricia Albers and Beatrice Medicine, eds. Lanham, Md.: University Press of America, 1983, pp. 29–52.

Whitehead, Harriet. "The Bow and the Burden Strap: A New Look at Institutionalized Homosexuality in Native North America." In *Sexual Meanings: The Cultural Construction of Gender and Sexuality*. Sherry B. Ortner and Harriet Whitehead, eds. New York: Cambridge University Press, 1981, pp. 80–115.

Williams, Walter L. *The Spirit and the Flesh: Sexual Diversity in American Indian Culture*. Boston: Beacon, 1986.

James P. Ronda

Were Christian missionaries gods or devils? Indians—who stood amazed as these men performed strange rites and told strange stories, predicted eclipses and spread disease, "made paper speak," and ordered others to change their ways—could not agree on an answer to this question. Neither can modern scholars. Some, following the missionaries' own accounts, depict these men as selfless souls braving hardship, torture, even death, to bring the light of the gospel to the pagan darkness of America. Others, recoiling at the arrogance of such a vision and insisting that natives possessed rich, sophisticated, satisfying spiritual beliefs and rituals of their own, tend to see missionaries as agents of empire bent on the coercion, even the destruction, of Indian Country.

As Cornelius Jaenen's essay on Indian attitudes toward the French suggests, many natives in colonial times were indeed skeptics about these men and their message. Firm in their own beliefs, dubious about the wisdom or efficacy of monotheism and the divinity of Jesus Christ, Indians often had little use for Christianity and its trappings. Some simply walked away; others listened politely enough, but rejected such notions for themselves; others still argued with the missionaries, and a few even killed these intruders.

But some natives did decide to convert to Christianity. By doing so, James P. Ronda argues in this essay on the Wampanoags of Martha's Vineyard, they did not cease to be Indians. Rather, they, like the Catawbas James Merrell describes, found ways to blend old and new in order to adjust to rapidly changing circumstances. What was the secret to the missionary success on Martha's Vineyard? Was there a gender frontier in this community akin to the one in the Illinois country and the St. Lawrence Valley? How much did native converts change Christianity, and how much did it change them?

GENERATIONS OF FAITH:
THE CHRISTIAN INDIANS OF
MARTHA'S VINEYARD

James P. Ronda

IN NEW ENGLAND there was an Indian king that said he saw that there were many of their people of the Indians turned to the New England professors. He said they were worse since than they were before they left their own religion. And an Indian said, before the English came, that a white people should come in a great thing of the sea, and their people should be loving to them and receive them, but if they did hurt or wrong the white people, they would be destroyed. And this hath been seen and fulfilled, that when they did wrong the English they never prospered and have been destroyed. So that Indian was a prophet and prophesied truly.[1]

These lines from the 1672 travel journal of George Fox remain the standard gloss on the complex relationship between Indians and Christianity in colonial New England. As Fox's informants testified, those who accepted the Christian god and became "praying Indians" declined in numbers and lost their tribal identity. The cultural demise of the converts was paralleled by the physical extinction of those who openly resisted the Puritan gospel and were swept away by the servants of an angry English Jehovah. The Indians who spoke with Fox scarcely considered the possibility of self-sustaining communities where native people might live as both Christians and Indians.

Modern scholarship has generally concurred. Studies of New England missions have emphasized either the culturally destructive effects of conversion or native resistance to the gospel.[2] While many Puritan missionaries demanded what amounted to cultural suicide from their converts, we must not overlook the possibility of genuine conversion on the part of Indians searching for spiritual meaning in an increasingly hostile world. So long as the mission did not demand immediate and radical cultural change, there was a fair chance that Indians would accept substantial portions of the Christian message. The vital, self-sufficient Christian Indian communities and churches of Martha's Vineyard testify to the actuality of becoming a faithful Christian while remaining no less an Indian.

SOURCE: *William and Mary Quarterly*, 3d Ser. 38 (1981), 369–94.

In numbers of Indians and English, and in relations between the peoples, Martha's Vineyard was substantially different from the mainland. When Thomas Mayhew, Jr., began missionary work among Indian islanders in the 1640s, the Wampanoag population was at least fifteen hundred and may have been as high as three thousand. At the same time, the English numbered about sixty-five, all living at the east end of the island. Although reduced by disease, natives clearly outnumbered English folk throughout the seventeenth century. On the eve of King Philip's War there were only 180 English settlers while the Wampanoag population was well over one thousand. Fragmentary census records show that whites did not become the majority on the island until 1720.[3] On the mainland, the mission was part of a wider attack on Indian land and leadership mounted by a large and well-armed English population, but Thomas Mayhew's preaching had no such resources or ambitions. His efforts had little success until 1645, when an epidemic swept the island and the failure of the powwows to cure the sick touched off a rapid series of conversions.[4] Most important, the mission did not insist upon sudden cultural change. Mayhew and the very small English population could not compel Indians to follow John Eliot's demand that natives must "have visible civility before they can rightly enjoy visible sanctities in ecclesiastical communion."[5] No codes required Vineyard Indians to cut their hair, wear English clothing, give up customary mourning ceremonies, or attend church meetings. It was in this more permissive environment, as Indian congregations and praying towns rose and flourished, that political power and cultural leadership remained in Wampanoag hands. Study of the Martha's Vineyard faithful reveals Christianity Indianized as well as Indians Christianized. William Simmons has aptly characterized Indian Christianity on the island as "the most profound social conversion to occur anywhere in New England."[6]

Only on Martha's Vineyard can the process by which Indian converts transformed Christianity to suit native cultural needs be traced through four generations. That tracing is possible because a substantial body of biographies of Martha's Vineyard converts exists for the period 1642–1722. This evidence is unlike any other compendium of convert stories in mission literature. The narratives in the Jesuit Relations, the confessions of faith in the Eliot tracts, and the testimonies of converts in the Moravian records all suffer from stereotyped language and missionary ghostwriting. Though some of those narratives contain such vivid phrases as "I am as a dead man in my soul, and desire to live," and "God broke my head," they only rarely and dimly exhibit Indians as active shapers of their own lives and thoughts.[7] Only for Martha's Vineyard do we have multigenerational records that allow us to view the dynamics of conversion and community over a long period.

These records are contained in Experience Mayhew's *Indian Converts*, the product of a lifetime of direct contact with Martha's Vineyard Indian Christians.[8] Grandson of Thomas Mayhew, Jr., Experience was born on the island in 1673, spoke Wampanoag, and knew most of the people whose stories he wrote. In the early 1720s he began to collect material for capsule biographies of Christian Indians.[9] *Indian Converts* is a kind of oral history assembled by an informed observer with a sharp eye for detail and a keen ear for arresting tales. Mayhew composed 126 biographies, touching 208 Indians in at least sixteen family lineages. Although primarily concerned with the lives of the godly and the good, he did not fail to note their frailties. The struggles of Jacob Sockakonnit with alcoholism, the unruliness of the children of Deacon Abel Wauwompuhque, Jr., and the touchy temper of Abiah Paaonit were all faithfully set down. While it is possible to claim too much for this evidence, the greater danger is to claim too little. *Indian Converts* was written neither to raise funds for the mission nor to perpetuate the Mayhew family's reputation. Rather, Mayhew intended to demonstrate the validity of Indian Christianity by showing that not all the gospel seeds sown among the natives had fallen on stony ground. Supplemented by other mission records, the *Indian Converts* provides a rare look into the lives of New England's Indian Christians.

CONVERSION ON MARTHA'S Vineyard most often followed family lines. *Indian Converts* shows that as early as the 1650s Christian Indian families were perpetuating the faith within their lineages. Mayhew took pains to trace the gospel pedigree in many such families. To illustrate the generations of faith on the island, two Wampanoag lines are offered here for detailed discussion. The families reveal the generational conversion links, the emergence of Indian Christianity, and the persistence of native identity after conversion.

One of the most prominent lineages at Gay Head was the Mittark-Panu connection. In 1663, the sachem Mittark became embroiled with his people in a controversy over conversion, left for the east end of the island and remained there among the English in semi-exile for three years. In 1666, he returned to Gay Head, where he founded the Indian Congregational Church.[10] As Mittark made the transition from sachem to preacher he worked to convert members of his family and to ensure the perpetuation of the gospel within his lineage. In his own generation, Mittark's most important convert was his brother, Abel Wauwompuhque, Sr. As a Gay Head magistrate, Wauwompuhque was in a unique position to influence both converts and those who had not accepted the new belief. Mayhew characterized him as "a zealous reprover of the sins of the times in which he lived." But for all his reproving, Wauwompuhque did not abandon the traditional Indian style of resolving disputes. Rejecting coercion and seeking consensus, he "earnestly endeavored to promote peace and unity."[11] Mittark the sachem-turned-preacher and Wauwompuhque the magistrate were signs in the first generation that Christianity did not necessarily mean cultural and political disruption.

The test came in subsequent generations. Would Christianity grow to become an integral part of Indian life, or would it require constant infusions of English missionary support and direction? The second generation of the Mittark-Panu lineage demonstrated the vitality of Christian families on the island. When Akoochuk married one of Mittark's daughters, he soon felt family pressure to convert. Abandoning his habit of heavy drinking, he became a mainstay of the Gay Head Christian community and one of Mittark's *antoskouaog*, or counselors. He was called a magistrate by the English but functioned as a traditional counselor, whose duties included giving advice to neighbors, meting out justice as "a terror to evil doers," and dispensing charity. It was for his charity, long a counsellor's responsibility, that Akoochuk was best known. Mayhew recorded that he ministered to the poor, "not only feeding them, . . . but also giving them what was convenient to carry home with them."[12]

Mittark's nephew Annampanu was also an important second-generation convert. Annampanu did not accept the faith until late in life, having in his younger days a "loving and following after strong drink."[13] The record does not show why he changed his ways to become a full member of the Gay Head congregation, but it is clear that he became very much a part of the Christian family tradition founded by Mittark. In old age, when he had no home of his own, Annampanu lived with other Christian Indian families. "He was," wrote Mayhew, "a blessing to them by his many good prayers in them, and good councils given to them. He then also used to go about doing good, as in visiting the sick and afflicted, and counselling and comforting of them."[14]

The most important figure in the second generation of the Mittark-Panu lineage was Abel Wanwompuhque, Jr., a genuine product of Christian family nurture. Though raised in a household dominated by his convert father and uncle, he did not experience conversion as a child. A good deal of drinking and an inclination "to the same youthful vanities as unconverted young men generally are" marked his young manhood. After his marriage to a Christian Indian, Wauwompuhque abandoned his "youthful vanities," made a public profession of faith, and joined the Gay Head church. He soon found that the Christian example of his own family, like that of his father's, did not automatically produce faithful children. Some of his children "were persons of no good character."[15] Nevertheless, he was regarded as an exemplary magistrate and a possible future preacher for the Gay Head congregation. However, events in 1690 changed island history as well as the future of the Mittark-Panu line.

In 1690, parts of Martha's Vineyard were struck by a devastating epidemic.[16] Abel Wauwompohque, Jr., was "very sorely visited by the disease and lost his hearing." As illness had caused Indian traditionalists to question ancient ways in the 1640s, so this sickness led Wauwompuhque to become a serious inquirer into matters of faith and doctrine, and a voracious reader of religious books in both English and Algonquian. He quickly learned lip reading and sign language. "He would also," reported Experience Mayhew, "ask many necessary questions and not be satisfied till either by writing, or some other means, he had obtained an answer to them."[17] In 1712, when Gay Head Indian preacher Japheth Hannit died, Wauwompuhque became spiritual leader of the Indian faithful. Mayhew commended his sermons as a stout assault on "their drunkenness, whoredom, thieving, lying, sabbath-breaking, and letting them know, that those who do such things should not inherit the kingdom of God."[18] Until his death in 1722, Abel Wauwompuhque, Jr., remained a potent force among Indian Christians. As deacon, magistrate, and preacher, he exemplified the maturity of Indian Christianity on Martha's Vineyard.

The third generation of the Mittark-Panu lineage continued to produce Christian leaders for the Gay Head Indian community. Joash Panu, son of Annampanu and one of Mittark's daughters, was taught his early lessons by his mother. Mayhew noted with approval that after Panu married, he established proper family worship with his wife Naomi and their children. Although Gay Head believers felt that he was worthy of full membership in the Indian church, he was reluctant to seek it. He confessed that he was waiting for a clear sign from God, a call to the ministry. That call evidently came in 1716, the year in which Panu was formally ordained as preacher at Gay Head. He soon gained a reputation for effective, forceful preaching. "The longer he continued in the work of the ministry, the more zealous and earnest his discourses appeared to be." Mayhew, who heard Panu preach, observed that his sermons were not "impertinent, unstudied discourses, but had many very good things in them, and these delivered in something of order and method."[19]

Joash and Naomi Panu were earnest Christian parents. Yet they, like both Abel Wauwompuhques, discovered that piety and Christian commitment were not necessarily passed intact from one generation to the next. Their son Laban was hardly the perfect Christian child. Until age nine, he was "rude and disorderly, apt to profane the sabbath day, and could scarcely be restrained from playing at meeting." Mayhew lamented that "the many good instructions and exhortations given him by his parents" failed to change Laban's behavior. Accepting the more rigorous methods of English nurture, the Panus decided "to deal more sharply with him," and this discipline produced "a remarkable change in the carriage and behavior of their child." Unfortunately, however, the boy fell sick and soon died. During his illness young Laban spoke often of "his own frailty and mortality" and the mercy of God preparing him for joy in heaven. Those sentiments surely pleased his parents, but his death in 1715 robbed the Mittark-Panu connection and the Gay Head community of a future leader.[20]

The Mittark-Panu lineage illustrates the continuity of political and cultural leadership on the Gay Head end of the island. From Mittark to Joash Panu, political power remained in native hands. The family successfully negotiated the conversion passage and made the Christian practices of prayer, Bible reading, family devotions, and public worship essential parts of their lives. If the Mittark-Panu line demonstrates the persistence of one family, the rise of the Coomes-Amos lineage suggests ways in which hitherto unimportant Wampanoags gained considerable influence as members of God's tribe.

One of the largest Christian Indian families on Martha's Vineyard, the Coomes-Amos lineage contributed twenty-seven persons to Mayhew's compilation, for sixteen of whom he was able to construct detailed biographies. The Christian line was founded by Hiacoomes of Great Harbor, Taphaus and Amos of Chappaquiddick, and Myoxeo, a minor sachem at Nunpang. This large connection showed considerable diversity in Christian commitment. At least eight lineage members never formally professed the faith, yet each of these held important positions of leadership on the island. Because the line was so large, it is neither possible nor desirable to discuss here all individuals in every generation. The following analysis offers a representative sample from each generation to illustrate the growth of a powerful Christian Indian family.

Thomas Mayhew, Jr.'s first Indian convert on Martha's Vineyard was Hiacoomes, a Great Harbor Wampanoag. In 1642, when Mayhew was preaching to the

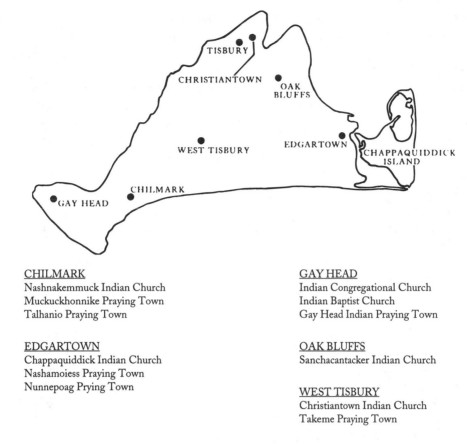

CHILMARK
Nashnakemmuck Indian Church
Muckuckhonnike Praying Town
Talhanio Praying Town

GAY HEAD
Indian Congregational Church
Indian Baptist Church
Gay Head Indian Praying Town

EDGARTOWN
Chappaquiddick Indian Church
Nashamoiess Praying Town
Nunnepoag Prying Town

OAK BLUFFS
Sanchacantacker Indian Church

WEST TISBURY
Christiantown Indian Church
Takeme Praying Town

Figure I: Martha's Vineyard Indian Towns and Churches, c. 1680–1720.

handful of English settlers around Edgartown, Hiacoomes was attracted to the ways of his new neighbors. No sachem but a man of "mean descent," he also seems to have captured English attention. Edgartown Puritans were pleased when Hiacoomes attended several Sunday meetings, something no other Indian had done. What began as social visits by pastor Mayhew and other English folk to Hiacoomes's wigwam became opportunities for the Puritan divine to undertake missionary teaching, which he improved by inviting Hiacoomes to come regularly to the Mayhew house. Under Mayhew's direction, the Indian exchanged the supernatural order and symbols of the powwows and traditional healing rites for equally supernatural Christian explanations. Those explanations stressed the wiles of Satan, the strength of sin, and the transforming power of Christian belief. Hiacoomes accepted this new set of symbols and became a Christian. He enjoyed increased standing in the eyes of the English, but his study of Christian doctrine and ties to the English earned him the derisive label, "the English man," from other Wampanoags. The new convert's influence increased in 1643 and 1644 when disease killed many Indian islanders but left Hiacoomes's family untouched. Hiacoomes became established as a powerful Christian preacher when, during the epidemic crisis of 1645–46, he helped convert several prominent sachems and faced down a group of angry powwows. By the 1650s, he was a respected magistrate and spiritual leader. Ordination as a minister in 1670 capped a life in which faith brought rewards of power and esteem.[21]

One of Hiacoomes's first converts was the sachem Myoxeo. When disease struck the island in 1643, many Wampanoags saw the illness as a sign of divine displeasure and responded with renewed zeal for the ancient rituals. But when epidemic illness returned in 1645 and again left Hiacoomes's family unscathed, the reaction was quite different. Clearly worried about the impotence of his powwows in the face of strange ailments, Myoxeo invited Hiacoomes to make what amounted to a pastoral call at the sachem's wigwam, where he gathered a considerable number of Indians, among them the influential east end sachem Tawanquatuck. The exchange between Hiacoomes and Myoxeo at first focused on Hiacoomes's declaration that his one god was far more powerful than Myoxeo's thirty-seven. When the sachem was brought to accept monotheism as a sovereign remedy, Hiacoomes went on to discourse on sin, punishment, and salvation. Revealing their expectation that Christianity would give them special power and protection from present dangers, Myoxeo and Tawanquatuck agreed "that true believers did live above the world, and did keep worldly things always under their feet." Myoxeo eventually assumed the post of magistrate at Edgartown.[22]

The conversion experiences of the two Chappaquiddick founders of the Coomes-Amos line are less well documented. Experience Mayhew noted that he had "heard nothing remarkable" about Taphaus.[23] Something more is known of Amos, one of the first Indian Christians at Chappaquiddick. Converted by Hiacoomes, he established a convert family, and his children married into the Coomes line.[24]

Conversion efforts by Hiacoomes and Thomas Mayhew, Jr., bore fruit in the second generation. Once again, family and kinship meant more than any other factor in propagating the faith. Hiacoomes struggled to convert his several children, but only the story of one of his younger sons, Samuel, survived for Mayhew to record. The sometimes troubled life of Samuel Coomes suggests the tensions in many Christian Indian families and the special dilemma of a dutiful son living in the shadow of a newly important father. When Samuel was very young, Hiacoomes sent him to live with Thomas Mayhew, Sr. There the boy learned the essentials of the Christian faith as well as reading and writing. "Notwithstanding all these advantages," Experience Mayhew wrote, "he was in his youthful days a carnal man." Samuel's excessive drinking and his sexual adventures with an English woman must have given Hiacoomes cause to wonder if Christian nurture, even at the hands of a Mayhew, was effective.[25]

After Samuel's marriage to an Indian Christian woman, his behavior began to change, but drinking remained a serious problem as long as his father lived in Samuel's household. When Hiacoomes died in 1690, his son's habits were transformed. Though Samuel never formally joined an Indian church, he became an active layman in the Chilmark congregation. "If a meeting house was to be repaired, or any thing else was to be done for the promoting of religion," Experience Mayhew recorded, "none would contribute more liberally to it than he. And when there was a day of public Thanksgiving, and provision to be made for it, which among our Indians is brought into common stock, (which the poor as well as the rich may come to and be filled) this our Samuel was one of the principal providers for that feast."[26] Hiacoomes was "of mean descent," but his son Samuel's family and active faith made him a respected member of the Indian Christian community and a powerful magistrate.

One of Myoxeo's children, his daughter Rachel, also became prominent in Christian Indian society. Like Samuel Coomes, Rachel was sent as a child to live in the Mayhew household but proved resistant to Christianity. Her early years were punctuated by drinking and wild behavior. These ended with her marriage to Jonathan Amos. Soon after their wedding, the couple moved to Dartmouth in the Bay Colony, but, disturbed by the "low ebb" of religion on the mainland, eventually returned to Chilmark to "enjoy God in all His ordinances here, where they both thought church discipline was better managed than there." Experience Mayhew portrayed Rachel Amos as the model Christian Indian woman. She carefully instructed each of her eight daughters in gospel fundamentals and conducted family worship when her husband was absent. As the wife of a deacon, she assisted Jonathan in his charitable duties. And, as a practicing Christian, she was "very constant and serious in her attendance on, and improvement of the privileges to which she was admitted."[27]

Her husband was the son of Amos of Chappaquiddick. As with so many other second-generation Christian Indians, his family heritage propelled him into active public service in the convert community. Beyond the fact that he was raised in a Christian family and was literate, little is known of Jonathan Amos's early life. In the Chilmark Indian church he earned respect as a pious believer and a faithful supporter of the congregation. That respect became more evident in 1698 when David Wuttinomanomin, long-time Chilmark deacon, died. The office of deacon was especially important in Martha's Vineyard Indian churches because it perpetuated and gave Christian meaning to ancient patterns of charity, feasting, and care for the poor. Amos undertook those responsibilities and executed them with considerable skill. He often spoke fervently at meeting about charity as an essential Christian duty. When the Chappaquiddick Indian pulpit fell vacant in 1703, the congregation called Amos as their preacher. Much of the worship in Indian churches consisted of lengthy prayers, bringing the needs and failings of the believers to the attention of both God and the community. Experience Mayhew heard Jonathan Amos deliver such petitions and declared, "I think I have scarcely ever heard any man in prayer plead with God with greater importunity than he used to do; and these his fervent prayers availed much."[28] For all his spirited rhetoric, however, Amos experienced personal temptations, and "it pleased God to permit him to fall very shamefully." After one spectacular drinking bout, he made public confession of his sins, and Mayhew insisted that the preacher never fell again.[29] Whatever Jonathan Amos's private failings, his role as deacon and minister suggests the ways Christianity permeated the lives of so many Martha's Vineyard Indians.

In its third and fourth generations, the Coomes-Amos family grew in size if not in influence. Yet the early deaths of several Coomes-Amos children from the infectious diseases that frequently swept the island weakened the family. An increasing number of family members "felt unworthy" of full church membership, a state common among mainland Puritans. Experience Mayhew seems to have sensed the dilemma of the children of pious parents when he wrote about later Coomes-Amos offspring. Typical of the third generation, Abigail Amos, a daughter of Rachel and Jonathan, was literate, well catechized, and "not . . . given to keep evil company." She was an obedient child who grew to be a diligent worker alongside her seven sisters. But she never married, died young, and at the end of her life was overwhelmed by a sense of all-pervasive sin and spiritual insufficiency.[30]

ON MARTHA'S VINEYARD, Christian Indian families faithfully propagated the gospel from generation to generation. Those Indians, like their Puritan counterparts, maintained that Christian family life was essential to prepare the heart for an infusion of grace. But the converts on the island were more than clusters of praying Indian families. They were members of genuine communities and churches with Wampanoag clerical and lay leadership. The presence of that native leadership over a long period illustrates the strength of Christian Indian culture, a culture secure and confident enough to sustain its own corporate life without depending on English sources. Cotton Mather and other preachers made occasional forays to the island, but the day-to-day spiritual lives of Indian Christians were fully in the hands of native pastors, ruling elders, home-devotion leaders, discoursers, catechists, and musicians.

As the influence of the powwows declined in the 1640s and 1650s, a leadership vacuum developed on the island, and Indian pastors, beginning with Hiacoomes and John Tackanash, began to fill that void. The formal ordination of these two men in 1670 by John Eliot and John Cotton, Jr., put the stamp of approval on an indigenous ministerial elite. The traditional shamanistic functions were now subsumed under the larger preacher-pastor role. Indian ministers became the new holy men, the special repositories of wisdom, healing, and power. Communicants looked to them for advice, support, encouragement, and ethical guidance, and they acted as intermediaries in English-Indian disputes. A close look at the ministers reveals the workings of Christian Indian life on the island and some of the reasons for its vitality.

John Tackanash has long stood in the shadow of his fellow preacher, Hiacoomes. The two were ordained at the same time, but because Hiacoomes was the first Mayhew convert he has captured the larger measure of historical attention. While Hiacoomes was an effective evangelist, Tackanash deserves to be recalled as a leader who steadily built Indian churches throughout the island and strengthened Indian Christian life at its beginnings. Nothing is known of his early life. Experience Mayhew observed that Tackanash and Hiacoomes were long-time friends; Hiacoomes may have been responsible for Tackanash's conversion. After his ordination, Tackanash promptly took up duties as pastor and teacher at several locations—in Chilmark at Talhano praying town and Nashnakemmuck Indian church; in Edgartown at Nashamoiess praying town and Sanchacantacket Indian church; and in West Tisbury at Takeme praying town. He evidently made a lasting impression on all who knew him and heard him preach. Experience Mayhew wrote that "he was reckoned to exceed the said Hiacoomes, both in his natural and acquired abilities, and being accounted a person of a very exemplary conversation."³¹

Tackanash's conception of the ministerial role represented a synthesis of traditional powwow functions and English clerical practices. A bearer of the new wisdom and an interpreter of that knowledge to believers, Tackanash served not only as preacher and pastor but also as a healer who applied medical as well as spiritual remedies. Priding himself on his theological scholarship, he "followed his study and reading closely, allowing himself . . . but little time for such diversions as many ministers and other persons use." This Indian pastor's desire to fully understand Christian doctrine often led him to consult with English divines for information and direction. English islanders frequently attended his services, recognizing his ordination as valid for both peoples. When Tackanash died in January 1684, he left behind flourishing, well-disciplined Indian congregations.³²

Toward the end of the seventeenth century, the first generation of Indian convert leadership passed from the scene. If the Christian Indians of Martha's Vineyard were to remain a functioning community of worship, they would have to produce from among themselves a second generation of pastors. This need was even more acute by the end of the century as Experience Mayhew devoted an increasing share of his time to mainland preaching and no fulltime English missionary planned to live on the island. If Indian Christianity were to survive, it would have to do so by its own power. Wampanoag preachers such as Japheth Hannit, William Lay, Joash Panu, and Isaac Ompany exemplified the response to that challenge.

Indian Converts provides an exceptionally detailed account of the life and ministry of Japheth Hannit. Born at Chilmark in 1638, he was the son of a minor sachem. Both his parents were converts; they sent Japheth, at age thirteen, to the Indian school established by Thomas Mayhew, Jr. From schoolmaster Peter Folger, young Japheth learned to read and write both English and Algonquian. Though the pious son of believing parents, the young man did not promptly join any established Indian church. In fact, when John Tackanash formally organized the Chilmark congregation in 1670, Hannit found himself "in a most distressed condition." He "feared to offer himself to the society of God's people, lest he should be unqualified for the privileges to which they were admitted."³³ He eventually made a public profession of faith but still declined for a time to take communion.

Although his Christian family background and education prepared him for an active role in the Indian church, Hannit at first accepted only civil and military posts. During King Philip's War he was "employed by the English to observe and report how things went among the Indians," and Mayhew thought him instrumental in keeping the island at peace 'when the people on the Main were all in war and blood." Sometime in 1680, and for reasons now unclear, Hannit resolved those questions that had kept him from full participation in the Indian church. He undertook a preaching apprenticeship with his uncle Janawanit and John Tackanash. When Tackanash died, Hannit assumed the Chilmark pulpit. Like Tackanash, he saw himself as both a Puritan preacher and a traditional powwow healer and holy man. "He was faithful and diligent in the work of God, unto which he was called, preaching the Word in season and out of season, with all long-suffering and doctrine, and used frequently to catechise the children of his flock in public."[34] Although Hannit steadily worked at improving his preaching, Mayhew noted that his "sermons were not very accurate, . . . and he seemed to me to do his best when he did not try to oblige himself to any strict method in them."[35] Hannit was more effective in maintaining church discipline and in resolving quarrels within his congregation. Always working to avoid open conflict that might weaken the church, "he would not side with any party of them, but would in such case make most winning and obliging speeches to them all, tending to accommodate the matter about which they were ready to fall out; and so wonderful an ability had he this way, that he seldom failed of the end he aimed at."[36] He was equally diligent in such ministerial duties as regular visiting of the sick, a traditional Indian practice. In this and other ways, pastors like Hannit were the new powwows.

Japheth Hannit's fellow ministers functioned much as he did, engaging in regular preaching, catechizing, and family visitation. Clergymen like William Lay and Joash Panu of Chilmark, and Isaac Ompany of Christiantown developed ministerial styles that reflected their own abilities and temperaments as well as the need to keep believers strong in the faith. As both preacher and magistrate, Lay used pulpit and court to further the Christian cause by direct application of fear and punishment. If as preacher he could not convert an errant Indian, as magistrate he would order the maximum number of lashes allowed for a particular misdeed. When some English islanders complained of such harshness, Lay offered an arresting comment on English-Indian cultural differences and his recognition of them. "When an Englishman was whipped, the shame of it was commonly at least one half of the punishment, but the case being not so with the Indians, they ought to have the more in smart, for that they had no more shame in them."[37]

Joash Panu and Isaac Ompany substituted sharp tongues for stinging whips. Panu was an ardent student of homiletics who carefully wrote out the heads of all his sermons and collected outlines from other clergymen. As Chilmark pastor between 1716 and 1720, he was known as "a most zealous preacher against the sins of his own countrymen, crying aloud and not sparing to show the people their transgressions."[38] Mayhew often heard Panu's sermons and admired both their force and thoughtful order. Zealous reproving, so much a part of Puritan and Indian preaching styles, was bound to elicit some anger from even the most pious believers. Isaac Ompany, preacher at Christiantown, was the target of considerable verbal abuse from his congregation. "In his preaching," wrote Mayhew, "he was not very popular, and with many he was the less so, because he was a sharp and serious reprover of the sins to which he could not but see his countrymen were much addicted."[39]

The pastoral care provided by Tackanash, Lay, Panu, Ompany, and the other Indian ministers was essential for the survival of Wampanoag Christian life on Martha's Vineyard. But in most ways the day-to-day leadership was in the hands of laymen. Within Indian churches there was a vigorous tradition of lay direction, a tradition that pervaded Indian Christian life both in worship and in the wider community. Indian men and women served as ruling elders, deacons, discoursers, catechists, festival managers, counsellors, and musicians. These native initiatives reveal both the strength of Christianity on the island and the Indianization of the gospel.

For men like Joshua Momatchegin, ruling elder at Chappaquiddick, and Thomas Sockakonnit, deacon at Edgartown, Christianity was not an alien ideology. Rather, it gave shape and meaning to their lives. Momatchegin, who had been ordained by Eliot and Cotton in 1670, was especially concerned with the mounting problem of alcoholism at Chappaquiddick. Admitting that he lived in "dark and declining times," he struggled to bind the faithful together and witness against the "flood of strong drink."[40] Every Indian church had at least one deacon, and Thomas Sockakonnit was typical of those who filled the office. Sockakonnit organized the charitable activities of the Edgartown church, and when no preacher was available he led the congregation in prayer, scripture reading, and psalm singing.

While Indian laymen filled the English offices of ruling elder and deacon, the special needs of converts for regular religious instruction required a new lay post, that of discourser. Discoursers were lay preachers who served in family worship and also filled pulpits when regular preachers were unavailable. Two of the most prominent were Noquittompany, discourser at Christiantown and father of the preacher Isaac Ompany, and Abiah Paaonit, wife of Chilmark pastor Elisha Paaonit. Noquittompany long resisted conversion, preferring to "lie at home, or go a fishing or hunting on the Lord's day, to the great grief of such as were better disposed." When his conversion finally came, he spoke of himself as "a praying man" and "a new creature." In old age he became a discourser. Mayhew's vivid portrait of "the character and carriage of this good man" accents "his ability and willingness to entertain with good discourses, all those with whom he conversed. His God and Savior, and those things which have a relation to another life after this is ended, were the subjects about which he continually delighted to confer; and he used earnestly to invite and excite his neighbors and friends to the great duties which ought to be attended by all such as fear God, and would be happy in the enjoyment of him."[41] Abiah Paaonit was an especially effective discourser among Indian women. Women concerned about faith and practice often visited her, and she would "lay her work aside that she might sit and discourse with them." Assuring his readers that these were not occasions for idle gossip, Mayhew insisted that Paaonit's talks "were not vain and frothy, but such as were good for the use of edifying, and might administer grace to the hearers."[42]

The persistence of traditional religious practices in the corporate life of Martha's Vineyard Indian Christians was manifested in such activities as group singing and observance of a steady round of festival days. The island's Wampanoags filled the year with rituals celebrating planting and harvest. Those events, as well as powwow healing rites, featured group singing and chanting. Indian churches, in turn, held communal feasts for worship, charity, and fellowship, in the organization of which laypersons took the initiative. Thus on such occasions Yonohhumuh of Gay Head, a successful farmer and one of Mittark's counselors, purchased or donated much of the food, arranged for its preparation, invited poor families to attend, and secured a preacher to deliver a sermon and administer communion.[43] The singing of metrical psalms was a central part of Indian Christian worship. Since the singing was done in antiphonal fashion, every congregation had at least one tune-setter, yet another lay office.[44]

While men served as ruling elders and deacons, the lay tradition also provided important roles for women. Abiah Paaonit was by no means unique as an active lay leader. Margaret Osooit of Gay Head, for example, often met with Indian women troubled by personal wrong-doing or family difficulty, and "she would not willingly leave them till she brought them to a confession of their faults, sometimes with tears, and to engage to endeavor to reform what was amiss in them."[45] Momchquannum of Edgartown was one of many literate converts who regularly catechized young Indians. She sought out boys and girls and "frequently admonished [them] for their faults, and excited [them] to their duty."[46]

The activities of Sarah Cowkeeper are worthy of special note because this woman made a substantial contribution to the life of the Indian Christian community. She was a longtime member of the Edgartown Indian church and was known for her industry and piety. Because she lived on a main road into Edgartown, travelers often spent the night in her home. Taking her Christianity seriously, Cowkeeper regularly visited and fed the sick, though she herself was poor. The rituals of charity were very much a part of her faith, despite the fact that she had to clothe and feed her own large family. In addition, Mayhew made special mention of "the care she took of poor fatherless and motherless children; when she heard of any such under suffering circumstances, she used to fetch them to her own house, and . . . keep them till they could in some other way be provided for." When her family complained, she replied that God would provide food and care for all. Sarah Cowkeeper's Christian commitment gave added dimension to her Indian name, Assannooshque, "woman that is a giver of victuals."[47]

ASSANNOOSHQUE AND HER spiritual sisters were part of a sizable group of Indian Christian women on Martha's Vineyard. Indeed, so many Wampanoag women were active Christians that Experience Mayhew found "a greater number of women appearing pious than of the men among them."[48] In *Indian Converts* he offered the biographies of thirty-seven "good women," most of whom were second- or third-generation Christians. Mayhew was able to glean information about the ages at conversion of thirty-three women, finding that fourteen waited until they were adults to join churches, while nineteen had a childhood conversion experience of some kind. Mayhew reported that seventeen of the thirty-seven women were literate. Most important for the future of the Christian Indian communities, twenty-four of these "good women" were instrumental in converting their children. Though Mayhew was either unwilling or unable to suggest reasons why so many Indian women were attracted to the gospel, that attraction appears to have had four main sources.

The Christianity preached by Thomas Mayhew, Jr., and his Indian successors tended to elevate and honor the roles and tasks of Indian women. The wife-mother-housekeeper functions were given special value in a public way unknown in precontact Wampanoag life. Experience Mayhew's glowing description of Hepzibah Assaquanhut expresses an ideal that emphasized the self-worth and importance of women in families. Assaquanhut "was a good wife . . . , being a discreet and chaste keeper at home, and one that loved her husband and children, being also very obedient to him; and was one that labored diligently with her hands, to provide necessaries for the family."[49] This description of the ideal Christian Indian woman is more complex than it appears. The gospel, as preached to and by Indian women, held that what women did in their lives was an act of virtue and worship as well as duty. Thus Abigail Ahhunnut, who outlived three husbands, found favor with the body of Indian believers because "she was such a wife to them all, as whoso finds, finds a good thing, and obtains favor of the Lord."[50] Like Ahhunnut, Mary Coshomon's patient relationship with her husband won esteem among Indian Christians. "She was remarkable," reported Mayhew, "for her dutiful carriage towards her husband, even showing him great reverence and respect; and when he was guilty of any miscarriage, she would bring no railing accusations against him, but would in a very submissive manner advise and entreat him."[51]

An Indian Christian woman's faithful performance of household tasks was also noted and praised. Industry in the wigwam became not simply a domestic duty but a service to God. Clean and orderly homes were pointed to as marks of a godly and sober woman. Mayhew's catalogue of the interior of Sarah Hannit's wigwam has more than passing ethnographic interest. "The fair and large *wigwam* wherein she with her husband lived was a great part of it her own work; the mats, or platted straw, flags and rushes with which it was covered, being wrought by her own hands; and those of them that appeared within side the house were neatly embroidered with the inner barks of walnut trees artificially softened, and dyed several colors for that end."[52]

If Christianity had attracted Indian women by valuing their traditional roles, it had even stronger appeal for women with special abilities. Articulate and literate women like Abiah Paaonit and Margaret Osooit found the Indian church and community a supportive arena for their ready minds and quick wits. When male powwows were discredited during the epidemics of the 1640s, the way was opened for Christian women healers. Most prominent of these was Hannah Nohnosoo, a herb doctor with a large practice among both Indian and English islanders. Like her powwow predecessors, Nohnosoo believed that the efficacy of her medicine depended on a proper relationship with supernatural forces. When asked if she could cure a certain disease, she replied, "I do not know but I may, if it please God to bless means for that end." Her patients included both Wampanoag and English women who were "divers years after marriage without the blessing of children, having barren wombs and dry breasts, which persons in a married state are scarce ever pleased with." Mayhew claimed that after Hannah Nohnosoo's ministrations, these women became "joyful mothers of children, for which comfort, under God, they have been obliged to her."[53]

Nohnosoo's Chilmark neighbor Hannah Ahhunnut also possessed abilities that combined Christian faith and medical skill. Ahhunnut regularly visited the sick, bringing them food and herbal medications. Like Hannah Nohnosoo, she believed that prayer was essential to healing; her sickroom visits combined applications medicinal and spiritual. One of Hannah Ahhunnut's most valued skills was her experience as a midwife. She was sent for whenever a birth was expected to be especially dangerous. By methods as much religious as medical, she brought Christian comfort and encouragement while aiding in the delivery.[54]

From the time of Thomas Mayhew, Jr., Christianity on the island was closely linked to formal schooling for converts. Educational opportunities extended to Indian women proved a powerful incentive for both conversion and continued Christian affiliation. The Indian churches promoted literacy among women and gave educated women a place to use their learning. Of the thirty-seven women in *Indian Converts,* seventeen were literate. Indian women clearly prized learning. Rebecca Sissetom, who was taught to read as a child, "appeared to delight in her book."[55] Sarah Hannit struggled to read her favorite book, an Algonquian translation of William Perkins's *Six Principles of Religion.*[56] Women who knew how to read wanted to pass on the skill to their children. Abigail Kesoehtaut "loved to read in good books and after she was married, and had some children, (not being nigh any school) she did herself teach them to read, and did otherwise carefully instruct them."[57] Few could match the zeal for learning displayed by Jerusha Ompan. An unmarried daughter in a large family, she labored under a heavy burden of household duties. Denied time to read during the day, "she would not ordinarily fail of reading in the night, and for that end always used to be provided with something to make a light withal."[58]

Christianity attracted Indian women by honoring their traditional tasks, rewarding their special abilities, and offering them educational opportunities. Indian churches also provided certain women with special support and solace in the face of a steadily worsening social problem. By the 1680s, alcoholism and the violence bred of excessive drinking had become epidemic among island Indian males. Native preachers lashed out at the abuse of alcohol, describing alcoholics as members of "the drinking tribe."[59] Mayhew called heavy drinking "the National Sin of our Indians."[60] Alcoholism was a serious problem even among Christian Indian men. Some eleven of the thirty-seven males in Mayhew's section on "good men" either had had or were continuing to have difficulties with alcohol. Immoderate drinking caused tension and violence within many Indian families.

The experiences of two women, Hannah Tiler and Hannah Sissetom, suggest ways by which Indian Christianity prepared women to deal with alcoholic and often abusive husbands. Hannah Tiler of Edgartown was the child of Christian parents. But in her case such nurture did not produce the desired results; Experience Mayhew found that young Hannah "was as bad by nature as any other." Her marriage to a vicious drunkard further threatened her wavering faith. According to Mayhew, her husband "would frequently have his drunken fits, and was often very contentious in them." Husband and wife became caught in a ceaseless round of drinking sprees and fierce arguments. Finally convinced that the cycle had to be broken, Hannah Tiler turned to Christian friends in the Edgartown Indian congregation for support and advice. At first she sharply criticized her husband for his drinking but soon discovered that "this was an occasion of sore contentions betwixt them." Counseled by fellow Christians to use gentler means, she tried "mild entreaties and a good carriage." Although this approach proved equally ineffective, "she found peace in it, and God helped her, in this way of well-doing, to cast all her care on him."[61]

Experience Mayhew recorded the tempestuous marriage of Hannah and Haukkings Sissetom with an almost clinical fascination. Hannah was raised by an English family on the island; Haukkings was part of the Christian Sissetom lineage. The placid first years of their marriage were marked by regular family worship and steady attendance at the Edgartown Indian church. However, Haukkings developed "such an excessive lust after strong drink that he was frequently overcome by it," spent his wages on hot liquors, and thus reduced his family to poverty. Confronted with his failings by both his wife and members of the congregation, "he sometimes appeared to be under great convictions" and seemed prepared to reform. But these resolutions were short-lived; "the temptation prevailed too much against him, and sometimes overcame him." Urged by her English neighbors to employ stiff words and strong measures, Hannah replied that she had tried but found that such efforts only angered her husband. With children to feed and instruct, she turned to the Indian church and the Christian Sissetoms. The solution suggested by the Sissetom family and approved by the church was to have Haukkings's mother live with the family. Mayhew reported that the older Sissetom woman was "very kind and obliging" to Hannah, "endeavoring to comfort her under all her trials."[62]

THE LEAST SATISFYING evidence presented by Experience Mayhew deals with convert children. Unlike his accounts of ministers and lay adults, Mayhew's descriptions of "pious children" are thin and often stereotyped. If some children displayed less than godly behavior before their conversion, Mayhew would have us believe that all became sober, obedient, faithful, and industrious after accepting the gospel. Despite the deficiencies in the evidence, the twenty-two narratives of boys and girls who died in the faith between the ages of four and twenty reveal several salient characteristics of Indian Christianity as it grew on Martha's Vineyard.

These biographies show how seriously Christian Indian parents took their educational and religious responsibilities. Nurture in the principles of the faith was an essential part of Christian Indian family life. Most parents began that teaching when their children were very young. Bethia Tuphaus's parents began to instruct her "in the things of God, as soon as she was in any measure capable of understanding them."[63] Lydia and Jerusha Ohquanhut were taught at an equally early age.[64] In only a handful of cases does the evidence show how children responded to this guidance. Mayhew insisted that early instruction produced "good impressions on the young heart" of many an Indian child.[65] Only rarely, as when Jane Pomit wept and was "much affected when spoken to about the things of God," is there any hint that children were bewildered and frightened by a heavy dose of Christian teaching.[66] What is clear is that Indian parents fully incorporated Christian ideas about sin, salvation, punishment, and death into their family lives.

There is only meager evidence to illustrate the ways in which children demonstrated their Christian faith. They were expected to be obedient to parents and energetic at their work, but did they display any special patterns of piety that might manifest the Indianization of Christianity? In the precontact Northeast it was common for young men to undertake solitary vision quests searching for personal identity, special powers, and a guardian spirit.[67] By Mayhew's account, solitary prayer in isolated places was common among young Indians, and it is possible that this practice represented a kind of Christian vision quest. Since Christian Indian children were taught that the act of prayer put the believer into contact with God and his awesome power, boys and girls like Eleazar Ohhumuh, Jeremiah Wesachippau, and Elizabeth Pattompan may have been behaving in ways that originated deep in the traditional past of Martha's Vineyard.[68]

BEGINNING SLOWLY IN the 1640s and gathering momentum by the 1670s, Christianity became an integral part of the lives of many Martha's Vineyard Wampanoags.[69] Indians worshiping at native churches and living in praying towns were no less Indian for their Christian beliefs. Tobit Potter, Martha Coomes, and James Nashcompait all claimed Christianity as their faith and Wampanoag as their tribe. What needs to be thoughtfully analyzed are the attractions of the new gospel and the reasons why it flourished from generation to generation.

Precontact religion of the island offered a set of explanations, interpreted through the powwows, of the world and the supernatural forces alive in it. Those explanations and the rituals of healing, thanksgiving, and charity satisfied Indian spiritual needs and gave a sense of order and meaning to the routines of daily life. In the 1640s, those explanations and the powwow interpreters encountered diseases that resisted traditional cures. Since healing rites were at the heart of Wampanoag religion, the failure of the ceremonies appeared more than a simple lapse of medical skill. That the rites had lost their power seemed a sign of deep disorder in the traditional relationship between the human and spirit worlds. At the same time, the Mayhew mission introduced a rival set of explanations, explainers, and ritual techniques. That Hiacoomes, the first convert, was not stricken in the wave of epidemics had a powerful impact on Indian islanders. The Christianity propounded first by Mayhew and later by native preachers claimed to be more than a reliable cure-all for new diseases. It offered a cluster of creedal statements about God, man, and the world that proved believable to a people who had always lived in a spirit-filled world. Thus the sachem Tawanquatuck spoke in 1646 about the decline of the old wisdom and the rise of the new: "A long time ago the *Indians* had wise men among them, that did in a grave manner teach the people knowledge; but they . . . are dead, and their wisdom is buried with them and now men live a giddy life in ignorance till they are white-headed, and tho ripe in years, yet they go without wisdom to their graves."[70] The sachem left no doubt that he wanted the gospel—a gospel that would explain a confused world and help set it in order.

An essential part of the Christian gospel for Indian islanders was a new identity, one that did not deny all aspects of native culture but offered membership in God's tribe. Worship in Indian churches and life among believing neighbors powerfully strengthened the sense of Christian commitment and solidarity. The fragments of sermons included in Mayhew's collection show native preachers struggling to encourage God's Indians by zealous reproving of sin.[71] Such preaching served to remind Wampanoag believers of their Christian identity by holding up unregenerate Indians as examples of faithlessness, violence, and wrongdoing. John Shohkow, ruling elder at Christiantown, offered this direction for native pilgrims. Indian Christians were to "follow hard after God, . . . that they should not be weary or faint in their minds, but go on sincerely and diligently to seek the Lord, and then they might expect to receive all needful good from him."[72] What emerged from preaching, worship, and corporate rituals was an image of the ideal Christian Indian. Shaped as much by Indian cultural needs as by English Puritan requirements, the ideal called for charity, prudence, industry, temperance, family worship, and attendance at public meeting, as well as belief in the gospel message. This Christian identity did not represent a radical break with the traditional past. Communal ceremonies for healing and charity were rooted in Wampanoag culture. Being part of God's tribe at once preserved and extended those ancient values, while giving them a fresh rationale.[73]

The rise of Christian family lineages gave an added dimension to conversion and new identity. Some Indians in Eliot's mainland mission rejected Christianity because they did not want to renounce family and kinship ties.[74] Such renunciations were not necessary on Martha's Vineyard. An Indian child or adult could convert or profess the faith within a supportive Christian family. The presence of many Christian lines offered Indian believers emotional shelter and a sense of belonging. Because identity had always been linked to kinship, it was possible to know who one was as a Christian Indian without stepping outside family relationships.

That sense of identity and community was strengthened by the names used by native Christians. Some mainland missionaries attempted to persuade Indians to abandon traditional names in favor of English ones as a sign of conversion. This was not the case on Martha's Vineyard. What did happen illustrates yet another blending of Indian and English ways. First- and second-generation native Christians generally assumed English names while still using and being known by their Indian ones. Paul, a deacon in the Edgartown church, was also known by his Wampanoag name, Mashquattuhkooit. John Shohkow, a Christiantown ruling elder, kept his traditional name, Assaquanhut. Sometime in the second generation, Indian Christian families began to make use of the dual European given name/patronym style. But this was done with an important and interesting difference. The surname was based on the last part of the traditional Indian name. Hence, Noquittompany's children used Ompany as a last name, and Hiacoomes's descendants used Coomes. Isaac Ompany's name showed both his Christian faith and his native heritage. Mayhew noted that this process was "a thing very common among our Indians."[75]

Being an Indian Christian on Martha's Vineyard also meant some measure of acceptance by the English. This was especially so for convert sachems like Myoxeo and Tawanquatuck who became magistrates. Preachers Japheth Hannit and John

Tackanash were addressed as Master. Experience Mayhew found that Indian Christians like Joseph Pompmahchohoo and Hannah Nohnosoo were persons of good report among their English neighbors. There was some tension, however, between Indian Christians and English settlers. Matthew Mayhew, writing in 1694, admitted that English islanders who were not church members resented Indian piety and thought "it no small disparagement to themselves that Indians should be accounted worthy of what themselves cannot be admitted to."[76] English cultural arrogance was surely present, but Wampanoag Christians had family and church resources to buffer that prejudice. As hostility toward natives increased throughout New England in the years before King Philip's War, Christianity served Indian islanders as a lifeboat to weather the storm. That lifeboat might be more aptly termed a survival ideology—a set of beliefs and behaviors that allowed Indians to meet English expectations while maintaining native identity.

A fundamental part of that ideology and a potent attraction to the gospel was the offer of literacy. James Axtell has written that among Puritans "literacy was a universal prerequisite to spiritual preparedness."[77] Eliot's early converts who could not read and had no access to Algonquian Bibles and catechisms made professions of faith correctly characterized by Neal Salisbury as owing "a great deal to the missionaries' suggestions."[78] Martha's Vineyard Indians who wanted to partake of the gospel had to learn to read. Thomas Mayhew, Jr., recognized this when he obtained the services of Peter Folger as schoolmaster at Great Harbor. By the end of the first convert generation, several Indians were sufficiently literate to read both English and Indian books.[79]

Often considerable effort was put forth to become literate. Janawannit and Akoochuk struggled as adults to read English.[80] Indian parents who were poorly educated frequently made substantial sacrifices to ensure the schooling of their children. David Paul, believing that Christian learning would bless both the minds and the souls of his children, went to great lengths to secure a good education for them. Because his farm was far from the nearest school, Paul paid a Christian family to board his children. When the school closed, he hired a young Indian ministerial candidate to tutor them.[81] Perhaps no two people portray better how much books and reading meant to Christian Indians than Job Somannan and Tobit Potter. Somannan was known throughout the island as the lame weaver of Christiantown. After a long day at the loom he would turn to his Algonquian and English books for comfort and strength. "He was," said Experience Mayhew, "a great lover of good books."[82] So was the orphan Tobit Potter, illegitimate son of Elizabeth Uhquat. Potter lived and worked with an English family in Tisbury. When asked by Mayhew about his diligent reading after long hours of work, he replied that he would not take twenty shillings for any of his books.[83]

Because so many were literate, the Martha's Vineyard Indian faithful displayed a genuine understanding of Christian fundamentals. The conversion experiences of Eliot's praying Indians have been criticized for "their lack of intellectual content," there being "no indication that the converts understood the Word, except as applied to themselves, or the most basic tenets of Puritan theology."[84] Such was not the case among the Wampanoag converts. Exposed to sermons by Indian preachers, taught in Christian homes, and conversant with books in both English and Algonquian, native Christians demonstrated a sure grasp of ideas such as sin, grace, redemption, and reward or punishment after death. They knew these ideas as realities in their own lives and as subjects for communal discussion. Concerned lest his English readers doubt the authenticity of Indian religious expressions, Experience Mayhew made a special point of closely questioning natives on matters of faith and doctrine. From the scores of interviews he conducted emerges a consistent picture of Indians clearly comprehending and using Christian theological language.[85] Thus Mary Coshomon spoke about "the wisdom, goodness, and sovereignty of God"; Japheth Skuhwhannan "discoursed frequently of Jesus Christ, and the way of life and salvation;" and James Nashcompait witnessed to "the mercy of God in sending his Son to redeem mankind from sin and damnation." When Indian pastor Peter Ohquonhut questioned Yonohhmuh on his faith, the native believer talked knowingly about God, sin, and salvation through Christ.[86]

To become embedded in the Indian universe, Christianity had to do more than serve as an intellectually acceptable set of spiritual explanations. Wampanoags did not divide life into separate sacred and secular categories. For them, the ritual and the explanation were part of a single experience. Christianity had to kill the void left by the decline of traditional communal rites. Ancient beliefs had their public celebrations, and Christianity had to provide equally public acts of faith, solidarity, and reassurance. A recent survey of North American Indian mission literature concludes that Catholic Christianity, with its ceremonies, images, processions, and symbols, was far more effective in this replacement process than was Protestantism.[87] On Martha's Vineyard, Indians shaped Christian forms to serve native public and familial needs. The communal functions once undertaken at powwow ceremonies were now carried on in worship services, thanksgiving feasts, and home devotions. Each Sunday, Indian Christians gathered for a full day of preaching, worship, and fellowship. The typical order of worship consisted of an opening prayer, the singing of a metrical psalm, a sermon in Algonquian, and further prayers and psalms. This service was performed twice each Sunday. Communion was usually celebrated seven or eight times a year. It was customary for members of a congregation to meet on the Thursday or Friday before communion Sunday to examine persons who had been suspended from participation in the sacrament. Those found to have repented were then permitted to take the eucharist.[88] Public worship and private family devotions, with sermons, exhortations, prayers, and sung psalms, filled the spiritual space left by the decay of traditional beliefs. Indian Christianity became its own tradition, nourishing the lives of native believers.

Lawrence W. Levine has written that "culture is not a fixed condition but a process: the product of interaction between the past and the present. Its toughness and resiliency are determined not by a culture's ability to withstand change, which indeed may be a sign of stagnation not life, but its ability to react creatively and responsively to the realities of a new situation."[89] The Indian Christians of Martha's Vineyard demonstrated just that sort of toughness and resiliency. Many Indian islanders used Christianity to revitalize their lives in a world growing more and more unfriendly. That one could be a Christian and still live in a wigwam and bear a traditional name was not doubted by the Martha's Vineyard faithful. One of those faithful was Old Katherine, a basket maker at Edgartown. She exemplifies that blending of Indian tradition and Christian commitment. Old Katherine was devoted to public worship services, which "she attended with very great constancy and seriousness." She was equally devoted to charity. Whenever she heard that a neighbor needed extra money for food, she would spend long hours making additional baskets for sale to English villagers. Even when she grew old and "was but meanly clothed," she continued to travel long distances for sabbath observances. In the coldest storms of winter she made her way to meeting with a dedication that astounded her friends.[90] Old Katherine, like many other Martha's Vineyard Indian Christians, found that the rituals of her faith gave shape and meaning to her life. She remains a witness to the vitality of a culture that was simultaneously Christian and Indian.

NOTES

1. George Fox, *The Journal of George Fox,* ed. John L. Nickalls (Cambridge, 1952), 624.

2. Francis Jennings, *The Invasion of America: Indians, Colonialism, and the Cant of Conquest* (Chapel Hill, N.C., 1975), 228–53; James P. Ronda, "'We Are Well As We Are': An Indian Critique of Seventeenth-Century Christian Missions," *William and Mary Quarterly,* 3d Ser., XXXIV (1977), 66–82; Neal Salisbury, "Red Puritans: The 'Praying Indians' of Massachusetts Bay and John Eliot," ibid., XXXI (1974), 27–54; David C. Stineback, "The Status of Puritan-Indian Scholarship," *New England Quarterly,* LI (1978), 80–90.

3. Charles Edward Banks, *The History of Martha's Vineyard, Dukes County, Massachusetts,* 1 (Boston, 1911), 28–29; S. F. Cook, *The Indian Population of New England in the Seventeenth Century* (Berkeley and Los Angeles, 1976), 42–43; Experience Mayhew, *A Discourse Showing that God Dealeth with Men as with Reasonable Creatures in a Sermon . . . with a Brief Account of the State of the Indians on Martha's Vineyard . . .* (Boston, 1720), [App.], 2; Matthew Mayhew, *A Brief Narrative of the Success which the Gospel hath had, among the Indians, of Martha's Vineyard . . .* (Boston, 1694), 28.

4. Banks, *History of Martha's Vineyard,* 1, 127–30; Lloyd C. M. Hare, *Thomas Mayhew, Patriarch to the Indians (1593–1682)* (New York, 1932), 189–203, 209–17; Neal Salisbury, "Conquest of the 'Savage': Puritans, Puritan Missionaries, and Indians, 1620–1680" (Ph.D. diss., University of California, Los Angeles, 1972), chap. 5. Important for Indian history and culture on Martha's Vineyard are Cook, *Indian Population of New England,* 35–45; Regina Flannery, *An Analysis of Coastal Algonquian Culture* (Washington, D.C., 1939); William A. Ritchie, *The Archaeology of Martha's Vineyard* (New York, 1969); Bert Salwen, "Indians of Southern New England and Long Island: Early Period," in William C. Sturtevant, ed., *Handbook of North American Indians. XV: Northeast* (Washington, D.C., 1978), 160–76; and William S. Simmons, "Southern New England Shamanism: An Ethnographic Reconstruction," in William Cowan, ed., *Papers of the Seventh Algonquian Conference, 1975* (Ottawa, 1976), 217–56.

5. John Eliot to Jonathan Hanmer, May 19, 1652, in Rendel Harris, ed., "Three Letters of John Eliot and a Bill of Lading of the 'Mayflower,'" *Bulletin of the John Rylands Library,* V (1918–20), 104. Capitalization, spelling, and punctuation in quotations are modernized throughout this article. The Mayhew mission reports are in Edward Winslow, *The Glorious Progress of the Gospel, amongst the Indians in New England . . .* (London, 1649), in Massachusetts Historical Society, *Collections,* 3d Ser., IV (1834), 77–79; Henry Whitfeld, *The Light Appearing more and more toward the perfect Day. Or, A farther Discovery of the Present State of the Indians in New-England . . .* (London, 1651), ibid., 107–18; Henry Whitfield, *Strength out of Weaknesse; Or a Glorious Manifestation of the further Progresse of the Gospel among the Indians in New England . . .* (London, 1652), ibid., 185–89, [John] Eliot and Thomas Mayhew [Jr.], *Tears of Repentance: Or, A further Narrative of the Progress of the Gospel Amongst the Indians in New-England . . .* (London, 1653), ibid., 201–11.

6. William S. Simmons, "Cultural Bias in the New England Puritans' Perception of Indians," *WMQ,* 3d Ser., XXXVIII (1981), 69.

7. Eliot and Mayhew, *Tears of Repentance*, Mass. Hist. Soc., *Colls.*, 3d Ser., IV, 237, 239, 251, 257. The expressions of self-loathing end feelings of worthlessness in these mainland confessions are very rare in the Martha's Vineyard records.

8. Experience Mayhew, *Indian Converts: Or, Some Account of the Lives and Dying Speeches of a Considerable Number of the Christianized Indians of Martha's Vineyard* . . . (London, 1727), hereafter cited as *Indian Converts*. No edition was published in the colonies.

9. The idea for *Indian Converts* may have come from Cotton Mather, who had long maintained an interest in Martha's Vineyard Indian Christians and occasionally preached at Indian churches on the island. As early as March 1713, Mather proposed "a convenient collection of them [convert biographies] to be anon employed for many valuable purposes." *Diary of Cotton Mather, 1709–24* (Mass. Hist. Soc., *Colls.*, 7th Ser., VIII [1912]), 190.

10. *Indian Converts*, 21–22.

11. Ibid., 98–99.

12. Ibid., 101–2.

13. Ibid., 109.

14. Ibid., 110.

15. Ibid., 67.

16. Matthew Mayhew reported that the epidemic killed about a hundred Indians, of whom three-fourths were Christians (*Brief Narrative*, 28).

17. *Indian Converts*, 68.

18. Ibid., 69.

19. Ibid., 63–67, quotation on p. 66.

20. Ibid., 247–49.

21. Ibid., 1–7. An incisive analysis of Hiacoomes's conversion, as well as other first-generation conversions, is William S. Simmons, "Conversion from Indian to Puritan," *NEQ*, LII (1979), 197–218.

22. *Indian Converts*, 78–79; Thomas Mayhew, Jr., in Whitfeld, *Light Appearing*, Mass. Hist. Soc., *Colls.*, 3d Ser., IV, 111–12; Simmons, "Conversion from Indian to Puritan," *NEQ*, LII (1979), 207.

23. *Indian Converts*, 95.

24. Ibid., 37.

25. Ibid., 91.

26. Ibid., 92–93.

27. Ibid., 152–53.

28. Ibid., 39.

29. Ibid., 41.

30. Ibid., 154–55.

31. Ibid., 14–15.

32. Ibid., 15–16.

33. Ibid., 44–46, quotation on p. 46.

34. Ibid., 46–48.

35. Ibid., 49.

36. Ibid., 49.

37. Ibid., 26.

38. Ibid., 65.

39. Ibid., 60.

40. Ibid., 34–35.

41. Ibid., 84–86.

42. Ibid., 159.

43. Ibid., 89.

44. Ibid., 107.

45. Ibid., 200.

46. Ibid., 161.

47. Ibid., 142–43.

48. Ibid., 135.

49. Ibid., 202.

50. Ibid., 163.

51. Ibid., 181.

52. Ibid., 167. While many Martha's Vineyard Wampanoags wore English-style clothing and used English farming techniques, most continued to live in wigwams. Cotton Mather, *India Christiana. A Discourse, Delivered unto the Commissioners, for the Propagation of the Gospel Among the American Indians* . . . (Boston, 1721), App., "The Present Condition of the Indians on Martha's Vineyard . . . ," 94.

53. *Indian Converts*, 165.

54. Ibid., 141.

55. Ibid., 151.

56. Ibid., 168.

57. Ibid., 145.

58. Ibid., 176.

59. Ibid., 225.

60. Ibid., 15.

61. Ibid., 190–91.

62. Ibid., 184–85.

63. Ibid., 230.

64. Ibid., 246.

65. Ibid., 230.

66. Ibid., 251.

67. Flannery, *Analysis of Coastal Algonquian Culture*, 94–96.

68. *Indian Converts*, 225, 235, 238.

69. Grindal Rawson and Samuel Danforth, "Account of an Indian Visitation, A.D. 1698 . . . ," Mass. Hist. Soc., *Colls.*, 1st Ser., X (1809), 131–32, indicates seven active Indian churches with 932 persons attending. How many were in full communion is not known.

70. *Indian Converts*, 80; Thomas Mayhew, Jr., in Whitfield, *Light Appearing*, Mass. Hist. Soc., *Colls.*, 3d Ser., IV, 112.

71. *Indian Converts*, 21, 61, 112.

72. Ibid., 30.

73. Ibid., 83, 120–21, 126, 203.

74. Henry W. Bowden and James P. Ronda, eds., *John Eliot's Indian Dialogues: A Study in Cultural Interaction* (Westport, Conn., 1980), 89.

75. *Indian Converts*, 44.

76. M. Mayhew, *Brief Narrative*, 27–28.

77. James Axtell, *The School upon a Hill: Education and Society in Colonial New England* (New Haven, Conn., 1974), 13. See also Kenneth A. Lockridge, *Literacy in Colonial New England: An Equity into the Social Context of Literacy in the Early Modern West* (New York, 1974), 45.

78. Salisbury, "Red Puritans," *WMQ*, 3d Ser., XXXI (1974), 49.

79. Of the 126 persons whose biographies appear in *Indian Converts*, 54 were literate. All second- and third-generation Indian Christians over the age of six in *Indian Converts* were literate.

80. *Indian Converts*, 20, 101.

81. Ibid., 115.

82. Ibid., 111.

83. Ibid., 259.

84. Salisbury, "Red Puritans," *WMQ*, 3d Ser., XXXI (1974), 49–50.

85. *Indian Converts*, 86, 94, 118, 122, 128, 172, 186.

86. Ibid., 182, 105, 100, 90.

87. James P. Ronda and James Axtell, *Indian Missions: A Critical Bibliography* (Bloomington, Ind., 1978), 8–9, 13–18.

88. Mather, *India Christiana*, App., 90; *Indian Converts*, 16, 61; M. Mayhew, *Brief Narrative*, 26.

89. Lawrence W. Levine, *Black Culture and Black Conciousness: Afro-American Folk Thought from Slavery to Freedom* (New York, 1977), 5.

90. *Indian Converts*, 171.

8

OF MISSIONARIES AND THEIR CATTLE: OJIBWA PERCEPTIONS OF A MISSIONARY AS EVIL SHAMAN

Rebecca Kugel

Before colonists arrived in North America, native peoples possessed few domesticated animals; Europeans, by contrast, had tamed cattle, sheep, swine, and horses. When they crossed the Atlantic, colonists brought animals with them, and most of these creatures thrived in North America. Norse sagas tell of cattle in Greenland and Vinland becoming more plentiful, at least during the earliest years of their colonial enterprise, and many travelers' accounts from the seventeenth and eighteenth centuries testify to the success of European livestock; Anglo-Carolinians, for example, made African slaves (the first "cowboys" in North America) tend free-ranging cattle that foraged in the forests. Over time, many native groups adopted European livestock. Court cases from seventeenth-century New England reveal conflicts between natives and newcomers over ownership of particular cattle; such hostilities contributed to the estrangement of English colonists and many Algonquian-speaking peoples in the years leading to the wars of the mid-1670s.

But if some native groups adopted cattle, swine, or horses, livestock remained troubling to many other Indian peoples. In one remarkable instance described by Rebecca Kugel, a group of Ojibwas of Fond du Lac (near modern-day Duluth, Minnesota) had grown wary of Protestant missionaries stationed among them. Friction between missionaries and the Indians they believed were their charges was nothing new; as Cornelius Jaenen's essay on French colonists shows, natives had long expressed concern, even outrage, about the missionaries' presence, believing—correctly—that these men were intent on destroying Indian religious belief and practice. After 1800, when Native Americans in the heart of the continent came into more sustained contact with Protestant missionaries, their suspicions about these potential spirit stealers at times led to accusations that the visitors were themselves malevolent forces. It is perhaps not surprising that an incident involving a missionary's cow became the focus for the Ojibwa critique of the Christian outsiders. In the drama that Kugel describes, the natives considered the cow an agent of the missionary, a new twist on the notion of a bestial "familiar" that, Europeans had once believed, accompanied the witches who tormented their world. In this case, the Ojibwa focus on the cow revealed both the persistence of ancient ideas about the proper relationship between animals and humans as well as the ongoing attempt to weigh the benefits and costs of the goods (in this case, livestock) that Europeans brought to Indian Country. In reading about this contest, it is useful to consider how different the Ojibwas' response was from the Christian Indians James P. Ronda describes on Martha's Vineyard.

OF MISSIONARIES AND THEIR CATTLE: OJIBWA PERCEPTIONS OF A MISSIONARY AS EVIL SHAMAN

Rebecca Kugel

IN FEBRUARY 1839, the Reverend Edmund Franklin Ely of the American Board of Commissioners for Foreign Missions (ABCFM), stationed at the Ojibwa village of Fond du Lac near present-day Duluth, Minnesota, recorded in his diary the rather unspecific illness of a youthful villager named Makwawaian, or Bear Skin.[1] The young man lay ill for several days after being charged by one of Ely's cattle. Amid the diary's prosaic entries noting the activities of the fur-trade post's personnel, and the far more pressing issue of relocating the mission station to a village more promising than Fond du Lac, Makwawaian's illness seems unremarkable. However, a more detailed examination of the diary, coupled with ethnohistoric insight into Ojibwa culture, reveals a far more complex story.[2]

Makwawaian and the Fond du Lac Ojibwa did not view the illness as a simple, if regrettable, accident. The Ojibwa understood Ely to have assaulted Makwawaian with spiritual power, using one of Ely's cattle as the means of inflicting illness on a young man who, as it turned out, had a history of confrontations with the missionary. The incident provides an example of the well-developed Ojibwa concern with witchcraft, but it also raises several other important and interrelated issues. The circumstances surrounding Ely's perceived sorcerous attack significantly shaped Ojibwa attitudes toward the missionaries themselves. Closely linked to emerging Ojibwa perceptions of the missionaries were Ojibwa views of the United States, that new and, in the 1830s, not well-known political power, whose representatives the missionaries were understood to be. The attack also illuminates Ojibwa attitudes toward an Old World domesticated animal, the cow, and provides a compelling example of a native people's efforts to appropriate that animal into their own contexts.

Although Ely and his fellow missionaries self-consciously viewed themselves as "pioneers," the first representatives of "civilization" and Christianity in the western Great Lakes region, they did not, in fact, introduce cattle to the Ojibwa. Intent on

SOURCE: *Ethnohistory* 41:2 (*Spring* 1994), 227–44.

bringing their variant of Euro-American culture to "the unlimited wilderness," they overlooked ample evidence of the thriving French and British presences that had preceded them. These earlier traders had first introduced cattle at Fond du Lac. By 1806, if not earlier, the North West Company's trader at Fond du Lac had maintained livestock including "a Cow [and] a Bull" at his establishment. Thus, the Ojibwa had had several decades in which to observe domestic cattle by the time the American Board missionaries appeared. A thoughtful and lively community debate concerning cattle still existed by the time of Ely's arrival in 1834.[3]

In conversations with the curious young missionary, the Ojibwa shared their insights and observations on the attributes of cattle. Clearly, cattle resembled the wild ruminants the Ojibwa hunted, a resemblance made even more striking by the traders' common practice of letting their cattle run loose in the summers to forage in the woods. Indeed, the Ojibwa called cattle by the word meaning "buffalo," *pijiki.* But the Ojibwa, who were keen observers of the habits of the animals they relied on for food, noticed that domesticated cattle ate plants no buffalo or deer or moose ever did. This suggested that cattle possessed special spiritually-derived powers. They must, the Ojibwa reasoned, "be endowed with extraordinary virtue, because they eat all manner of herbs, and is [*sic*] yet unharmed."[4]

Ely was a minute and careful observer of Ojibwa behavior. More than any of his American Board colleagues, he sought detailed knowledge of Ojibwa religious beliefs and described with accuracy Ojibwa religious practice. From his journal entries, it seems evident that the Ojibwa at Fond du Lac were ascribing spiritual power to cattle, and that shamans sought to channel this spiritually charged power in healing ceremonies. Puzzled when he observed that "drawings of Cows and Cattle are sometimes put up before the sick," Ely sought explanations from Ojibwa religious leaders. A shaman named Inini informed him that "the sick dream of [cattle] . . . by having the image before them." In what was clear proof to the Ojibwa of the spiritual power of cattle, Inini added that after such dreams, the sick "then recover." In another telling instance, Ely attended an elaborate Midewiwin curing ceremonial, sponsored for an ailing elderly woman by her family. Prominently featured in the healing ceremony was "a large picture of a Cow, on Bark."[5]

Although Ely sought knowledge of Ojibwa religion, he was no cultural relativist; he interpreted what he saw in terms of his own culturally constituted belief system. To his mind, his New England-derived Calvinist Protestantism exclusively represented spiritual truth. All Ojibwa religious expression was degraded heathenism that needed to be rooted out and replaced with Christianity. Yet Ojibwa salvation, in Ely's mind, would include not simply conversion to Protestant Christianity. It also would entail the acceptance of the agriculturally based, market-oriented Euro-American society and culture. Militantly religious, intolerant of Ojibwa culture as well as much of the life he found at the fur-trading posts, the missionary proved a troublesome and disruptive presence at Fond du Lac. His fractious behavior carried over into nearly all aspects of life.[6]

Ely continually violated Ojibwa values, norms, and deeply held beliefs. The Ojibwa stressed harmony in interpersonal relations; Ely delighted in confronting people and rebuking them loudly and publicly for transgressions against an alien and, from the Ojibwa view, incomprehensible moral code. His strictures against work or travel on Sundays, for instance, struck the Ojibwa as ludicrous, and, in such cases as refusing to help procure food during a long, difficult, winter journey in "intensely cold" January weather, as downright dangerous.[7]

Possibly the Ojibwa would have tolerated Ely's idiosyncratic demands for selected cultural changes had he participated willingly in the ongoing reciprocal exchanges that marked village life. These exchanges of food, clothing, tools, and services had enormous significance: they not only formed the base of the Ojibwa economy, but also carried an even more important ideological implication. On the level of metaphor, reciprocity defined human society. The Ojibwa esteemed the generous individual and accorded great respect to the man or woman who had plenty and gave from their possessions to the poor and less fortunate. Ely tried constantly both to demonstrate and to impose his own cultural norms of thrift, hard-bargaining, and individual accumulation of surplus wealth. Obviously a rich man by Ojibwa standards (the ABCFM had a line of credit with the American Fur Company, and Ely could purchase supplies when he chose), he scolded people for improvidence and shared his abundant supplies only with reluctance. In the rare instances when he did agree to share food or clothing, he haggled over the amounts.[8]

Besides his assaults on fundamental aspects of Ojibwa culture and society, Ely had become embroiled in a festering political dispute within the Fond du Lac village in 1836. He had insisted on conducting negotiations for building his mission with a particular leader named Mang'osid, whom the American government officials considered the village chief. The majority of the Fond du Lac populace, troubled by Mang'osid's friendliness with these American officials and worried he would agree to a land cession, supported Nindindibens, the son of a recently deceased tribal leader, who took a much tougher line with the American officials regarding land sales. Many months of unsettling argument had been necessary to convince Ely to deal with the village's recognized authorities.[9]

In the contentious environment that marked Ely's stay at Fond du Lac, the missionary noted no specific Ojibwa reactions to his own acquisitions of cattle. In fact, since he "purchased a Bull, cow, [and] calf" from the Fond du Lac trader, Pierre Cotte, in 1836, the Ojibwa likely saw little of note in the transaction. By the 1830s, most traders evidently owned a few head of cattle, and the simple fact of ownership seems to have occasioned no Ojibwa comment. Ely's own acquisitions were not unique among the missionaries; his American Board colleagues also stocked their missions with cattle. If ownership by traders and missionaries was a common occurrence, however, the Ojibwa still found cattle deeply fascinating, and continued to make efforts to observe them and learn more about them. Indeed, close firsthand observation of a particularly interesting facet of animal life, namely gestation and birth, seems to have motivated Makwawaian's curious attention to Ely's cow in the first place, thus bringing about the accident that caused his illness.[10]

Throughout the winter of 1838–39 Makwawaian had observed the progress of the pregnancy of Ely's cow. In late February 1839, Makwawaian had remarked with concern on the cow's condition; he thought that "she would die, because her belly was so big." When the cow gave birth to "a fine heifer calf" in the afternoon of 22 February 1839, Makwawaian was "surprized to hear that the Calf was already on his [*sic*] feet" within several hours of birth. Visiting Ely's house that evening with two friends, Makwawaian went with Ely to see the calf. Ely had placed the cow in a corner of his barn and had hammered together some boards to create a rough partition separating the new mother and her calf from the remainder of the livestock and any curious human visitors. As Ely and Makwawaian were looking at the new calf, the cow was nosing about in the straw, cleaning up stray bits of the afterbirth, when suddenly she turned and charged Makwawaian. In Ely's words, the cow "suddenly . . . bounded forward" breaking through the boards Ely had thrown up, and striking the young Ojibwa who, "slipping fell [a]gainst a Heifer near us." Makwawaian was badly shaken by the incident. Ely "asked him if She struck him?" and Makwawaian "did not answer, but stared at [Ely]." The missionary repeated his question, and this time the young man replied yes, adding "perhaps I shall be sick." Ely took him back to the house and rubbed opodeldoc, a camphorated liniment, on his side "just below the shoulder blade" where the cow had struck him. Later that night, Ely observed that "there was no external wound."[11]

About nine o'clock that same evening, however, a man the missionary identified as Wabeno came to Ely's house and announced that "Bear Skin is killed—by [your] Cow." Ely hurried to Makwawaian's home and "found him in a Swoon." Family and friends were wiping "blood and frothy mucus" from his mouth. Ely rubbed opodeldoc on Makwawaian's face, which revived him, and fixed a poultice that he applied to Makwawaian's side where the cow had struck him. For the next two days Makwawaian languished, too ill to get out of bed. Ely, visiting daily, described Makwawaian as "a sick man," and added, "I fear for his life."[12]

Then, on the fourth day after the attack, Makwawaian came to Ely's house. He visited with the "astonished" missionary, who further commented on the tremendous physical exertion the event was clearly costing Makwawaian. Ely described the young Ojibwa as "exhausted," still spitting up blood, and in "great pain." After spending much of the day with Ely, Makwawaian turned to Kaiashkibas, a shaman who had accompanied him, remarking "I wish to say something." Makwawaian then "made an effort to rise—got upon his knees and commenced singing—to the Spirit, for strength to throw off the burden from his lungs." Makwawaian "finished his song . . . and made an effort to rise first on his hands and knees—with difficulty he gained his feet." Turning to Kaiashkibas once more, Makwawaian asked the shaman to accompany him to the barn, as he now "must go to see the Cow." Ely recorded that "they went out, Bear Skin leading the way—singing—with feeble voice [and] step—K[aiashkibas] next and followed by two young women bearing some food." Ely's passing mention of the two young women, without any explanation of their presence, is suggestive of the very different understandings the missionary and the Ojibwa were assigning to the unfolding events.[13]

As the Ojibwa party left the missionary's house, Ely and his wife feared that Makwawaian "had gone to *stab* the Cow." Catharine Ely, a métis who spoke better, though apparently not flawless, Ojibwa, pursued Makwawaian's party to the barn. Makwawaian "went directly to the stable and approached the Cow and sung some time." As Catharine Ely explained it, this "act is considered equivalent to asking favor of [the cow]." Makwawaian specifically asked for "strength," as he had done with Edmund Ely himself. Evidently he felt his prayer was granted, for "as he came out of the yard," Makwawaian said that "he felt better and should be able to reach home." The next day, the young man again visited the Elys, looking, in Edmund's words, "unusually cheerful." He felt better, the young Ojibwa reported, "[Ely] had shown him great mercy." Nine days after the cow's attack, Makwawaian was sufficiently recovered to travel, and made plans to go to his brother's maple sugar-making camp some distance from the main Fond du Lac village. Makwawaian's attitude toward Ely had also changed; the missionary remarked that the young Ojibwa "grows very insolent." Ely had been providing Makwawaian's family with a "suitable diet" during his illness. As his strength returned, Makwawaian pressed Ely to act generously; in the missionary's words, to give "more of an article I was giving him, than I saw fit to give." Ely "promptly told him No!" and complained that Makwawaian, rather than suitably acknowledging the missionary's assistance during his illness, instead "calls for food." Makwawaian further offended the missionary by remarking that one of his brothers was now ill, and that his family was growing angry about it. Ely interpreted this as a further effort to extort more corn and dismissed Makwawaian's remarks as "a common artifice with the Indians." To Ely's mind, Makwawaian's words were not merely ungrateful, they were "insolent." When Makwawaian departed for the sugar camps, the missionary was only too ready to put the whole incident behind him.[14]

Not surprisingly, Ely interpreted the entire sequence of events within the framework of his own religious and cultural traditions. When Makwawaian came to his house to challenge the illness, Ely drew from the event the sort of pious moral lesson he frequently drew from the large and small occurrences in the Fond du Lac community. Witnessing Makwawaian's struggle to overcome the illness, Ely described him as a "poor heathen able only to get upon his knees . . . resorting to his pagan worship for help." Limited by the constraints of his own culture, there was no other interpretation open to Ely. As had happened throughout his years at Fond du Lac, Ely recorded the unfolding series of events with no comprehension of Ojibwa perceptions of the situation.[15]

Taken from an Ojibwa perspective, however, the events of Makwawaian's story are open to another interpretation, one with tremendous meaning to Makwawaian and the rest of the Ojibwa villagers. Edmund Ely was central to their interpretation, but decidedly not in the way he expected to be. Makwawaian believed that Ely had used spiritual power to injure him: Makwawaian believed that he had been bewitched. Through the agency of the cow, acting in the capacity of what might be considered a "familiar," Ely had inflicted the sickness upon Makwawaian. The Ojibwa had a healthy respect for the abilities of the spiritually powerful to turn that power to evil ends, and they were certain that people who abused spiritual power relied on certain animals to help injure other people. Bears, for instance, were suspect, as were owls.[16]

Certainly Makwawaian's behavior suggests strongly that he believed himself assaulted by spiritual power. The cow's attack, seemingly unprovoked, literally scared him speechless. When finally able to talk, his first words were that he expected to be sick, and, on the very night of the attack, he in fact became seriously ill. The power of suggestion probably played a role in Makwawaian's sickness, as indeed it was a significant component in most cases of Ojibwa witchcraft. Nevertheless, it also seems probable that the young man suffered from internal injuries likely to produce pain and the expectoration of blood. He had, after all, been struck by a large animal so forcibly that he was knocked off his feet. To whatever degree physical and psychosomatic injuries intermingled, the real issue remains the interpretation that Makwawaian, his family, and friends attached to his illness. They did not see a simple accident; they saw human malevolence at work. The cow that charged Makwawaian had not acted disinterestedly to their minds; it had acted out of the conscious design of another person.

Makwawaian must have suspected this the night of the attack when he stared speechlessly at Ely. His behavior in consulting a shaman confirms that he was thinking along these lines. Indeed, Wabeno, the man who first notified Ely that Makwawaian was ill, was probably not known by this name, although Ely's identification implied this was a given name. More likely, the name referred to the man's shamanistic abilities as a *wabeno;* in Ojibwa society, a particularly powerful type of spiritual practitioner. Wabenos were known for their abilities to perform spiritual assaults of the very sort to which Makwawaian apparently had been subjected. Although it was Kaiashkibas, also a shaman of repute and member of the Midewiwin curing society, who accompanied Makwawaian on his visit to Ely and who probably served as spiritual adviser in the struggle against the cow's power, it is possible the young man had consulted another shaman already, shortly after the attack. If Makwawaian believed Ely had used spiritual power to injure him, conferring with a powerful shaman whose specialization, as it were, spoke to his situation, made eminent sense.[17]

Makwawaian's subsequent actions offer further support for the interpretation that he believed himself bewitched. Reflecting Ojibwa conceptions of the sacredness of the number four, Makwawaian visited Ely on the fourth day after the attack, accompanied by a ritual party totaling four persons, composed for ceremonial purposes and bringing an offering of food. Thus fortified, Makwawaian confronted his tormentor and appealed to the spiritual power he believed Ely had used to inflict the illness. He appealed to the cow as well, as a being also possessed of power and, perhaps, volition of her own. His recovery must have persuaded him that he had correctly diagnosed the problem as a spiritual attack.

On a second, more complex level, Makwawaian must have felt both renewed confidence in himself and a new degree of caution regarding the missionary. His appeal *had* succeeded; he began to feel better. He must have felt his own abilities to control and manipulate spirit power, combined with those of his ally, the shaman

Kaiashkibas, were stronger than Ely's. At the same time, he had also learned a valuable, if hard, lesson about circumspection in dealings with spiritually powerful persons. His acknowledgment of Ely's "mercy" in helping counteract the spell speaks to
this. Furthermore, Makwawaian did not court further demonstrations of Ely's considerable abilities by openly bragging of his victory. He chose instead more subtle
demonstrations of his own power: pressing the missionary to share food, warning Ely
not to try to injure his kinfolk—behavior Ely could only understand as "insolent."

Ely's relations with the Fond du Lac community had deteriorated by 1839 to the
point where Makwawaian could easily conceive of the missionary as a witch. This
was not simply because Ely was an outsider; the Ojibwa were familiar with many outsiders by the 1830s—fur traders, American government bureaucrats, the métis population of the trading post. They did not dismiss all outsiders as witches. Certain
characteristics marked one, whether Ojibwa or not, as likely to abuse spiritual power,
to turn it against others, and Ely typified almost all these characteristics. His bump-
tious insensitivity to Ojibwa norms and values, in particular his refusal to share generously with other members of the community, suggested a fundamental hostility to
organized human social life.

To the Ojibwa, their own religious traditions, rituals, and practices represented
proper spiritual expression. Any person who rejected conventional spirituality must,
by definition, be engaging spiritual forces for malevolent purposes. Spiritual power
suffused the universe and could be contacted by nearly all persons; whether they
directed it toward socially desirable or malevolent ends depended upon the person.
Ely's attacks on Ojibwa religion were deeply disturbing and were seen by the Ojibwa
as assaults on their entire social and cosmic order. Ely's efforts at Christianizing
the Ojibwa provided further evidence of his basic hostility to the principles that
guided Ojibwa life. Although the missionary met with little success in his proscly-
tizing efforts, his attempts to isolate the few Ojibwa who showed an interest in his
religious message again violated basic Ojibwa norms. The Ojibwa strove for societal
unity, while Ely's emphasis on Christian exclusivity, on the social and physical segregation of the Christianized population, created a social division of the sort the
Ojibwa expended great effort to prevent. Social or political divisions were to be
avoided, not deliberately encouraged. Ely's behavior once again underscored his antisocial and disruptive nature. He was obviously a person who gloried in chaos and
disharmony, and thus, was one who might easily abuse spiritual power.[18]

If Ely's antisocial behavior alone was not enough to condemn him in Ojibwa
opinion, it was also obvious that he "worked medicine"; that is, he engaged spiritual
forces in efforts to heal illnesses. Ely paid close attention to sick and injured Ojibwa,
for many reasons. In large measure, he was simply performing a customary duty of
the Christian clergy to care for the sick. To this traditional concern was coupled an
ABCFM policy objective: it was hoped that if missionaries treated and cured sick
Native Americans, it would impress upon native peoples the power of the Christian
God and pave the way for conversions. Yet Ely was also sincerely concerned with the
human suffering he saw around him. Life in Ojibwa country was hard. Seasonal food

shortages were common; the weather was frequently dangerous; accidents were many and the consequences often severe. "A little Knowledge of medicine [would be] very desirable in this region" he wrote in 1833, "great suffering might be relieved." Although not a doctor, Ely did minister to sicknesses and injuries as best he could. In one representative month, March 1835, he treated a "Blister" for an elderly woman, and applied "a Musilage Poultice" to the swollen foot of a child. Such efforts only reinforced in Ojibwa minds that he was a healer, and his use of medicines they had never seen or heard of before—such as opodeldoc—affirmed that he was a man of great spiritual power. At the same time, his combative and alienating behavior hinted strongly that he was also a deeply evil man.[19]

Apart from these general Ojibwa perceptions of Ely, Makwawaian had specific reason to think the missionary might bear him a personal grudge. Eighteen months earlier, he had had an angry confrontation with Ely that only the intervention of one of the Euro-American fur traders and his bicultural interpreter had kept from escalating to blows. Ely had caught Makwawaian's grade-school-aged nephew, Madjigindas, pulling turnips in his field shortly after Ely had refused, characteristically, to give any turnips to the uncle and nephew. Hiding in the ditch surrounding his field, Ely "rose up" just as Madjigindas was slipping out between the fence rails. In the missionary's words, the child "stood aghast with surprize and terror—burst into a cry—begged I would not hurt him—and roared out 'Nimishome! Nimishome!' [my father's brother]." Ely gripped Madjigindas "by the collar" and marched the child to his house for a stern talk. When the alarmed Makwawaian, hearing Madjigindas's cries, entered the mission house, he saw his nephew sitting on a bench, still crying, with one knee bloodied. Ely dismissed the scraped knee as a "scratch," and claimed Madjigindas "probably received [it] in creeping in to or out of the garden." At this point, Makwawaian lost his temper. He upbraided the missionary for frightening a child, and added stinging Ojibwa epithets, accusing the missionary of greed and stinginess. "In a biting tone," Makwawaian asked "if [Ely] loved his turnips?" Ely replied sharply, "Yes! and corn too!" Furthermore, Ely asserted, he "would *scare* every child . . . whom [he] should take in [his] garden stealing." When Makwawaian retorted that he would take turnips from Ely's garden whenever he wanted, with or without permission, Ely implied Makwawaian was too cowardly to do anything in broad daylight and would only come to pilfer produce "if at night." At this Makwawaian stalked off, only to return immediately, dressed, in Ely's words, "as for war," in breech cloth, leggings, and moccasins, "with his gun in his hand" and "War-Club, and Scalper at his back."[20]

While the two men exchanged more threats and heated words, Hester Crooks Boutwell, the mixed-blooded wife of another of the missionaries, "took her children and started for the fort."[21] She returned with one of the fur traders, James Scott, and an interpreter, named, appropriately, Wemitigoshe, or Frenchman. These two men dissuaded Makwawaian from violence: "They asked him why he came here [and] in such an equipment?" It was he, Makwawaian, who had committed the greater breach of social conduct by losing his temper, Wemitigoshe and Scott stressed. This was not an argument lost on Makwawaian. "He appeared ashamed," Ely observed, "and said he should be very sad." Chastened, Makwawaian then apologized to Ely for "com[ing] into [his] house . . . angry" and "enquired if [Ely] was willing to forgive him?" Ely's reply was not as gracious or straightforward as it might have been. The missionary "repeated part of the Lord's Prayer and told [Makwawaian] that God required me to forgive him." Angry himself, and no doubt also frightened, the missionary must have had a difficult time controlling his emotions and behaving in accordance with his own religious principles. From Makwawaian's perspective, however, this rather indirect acknowledgment of forgiveness must have allowed a lingering doubt about Ely's sincerity to remain, which resurfaced at a later time, when Makwawaian was charged by Ely's cow.[22]

In Ojibwa thinking, Makwawaian *had* committed an unpardonable social breach. He had lost his temper in public; he had said and done very offensive and aggressive things; he had threatened Ely. As a result, he had aroused the anger of a dangerous man. In Ojibwa thinking, Makwawaian had made himself a probable target for a witch's revenge. Just when and how Ely might choose to retaliate remained to be seen. That Ely might wait months to avenge himself was not surprising: witches were known to nurse grudges for long periods of time, long after their victims had forgotten the original incident.[23]

This initial clash was certainly enough from the Ojibwa's perspective to kindle Ely's wrath. Relations between the two men continued to deteriorate, which only increased the likelihood of a spiritual retaliation. In the following summer, that of 1838, a party of warriors, incensed by Ely's continual stinginess, killed one of his cattle and butchered the animal in plain sight of the missionary. Makwawaian's father, Eninabondo, and Akiwenzi, one of his brothers, were conspicuous participants. Indeed, Makwawaian himself may have been among the unnamed "others" Ely mentioned as being present. In a final incident, Ely once again refused a request to share food. Makwawaian asked Ely to help provide for the ritual graveside feast at the funeral of one of his nephews, and Ely balked, saying he "could give nothing for pagan feasting."[24]

Apart from intense personal confrontations between the two men, Makwawaian also had a political reason for assuming Ely's hostility toward him. By the late 1830s, the people of Fond du Lac were greatly concerned over Euro-American encroachment into Ojibwa country, as Ely's earlier troubles with the village leadership underscore. Living at the western end of Lake Superior, the Fond du Lac villagers had watched their Wisconsin congeners sign land cession treaties, and they were suspicious of the motives of the American government. A village elder explained that the Ojibwa "hated what they had heard of the treatment of the Americans towards other Indian Nations." The missionaries, with their requests to buy land for their mission sites, aroused grave suspicions. Ely was especially suspect, for, as Makwawaian's older brother Manitons pointed out, Ely had "never called the band together" to inform them of "the object of [Ely's] residence among them." The Ojibwa believed the missionaries "to be a fore-runner of the Americans," with designs on Ojibwa lands. Makwawaian's family was particularly outspoken in their opposition to missionaries and to land sales. This same brother, Manitons, consistently and publicly questioned the missionary's intentions, and his father, Eninabondo, in spite of a kinship tie to Edmund's métis wife, Catharine, stoutly resisted any accommodation with the Americans, be it missionaries at Fond du Lac, a land sale, or recognizing the complaisant Mang'osid as village leader. From Makwawaian's perspective, then, Ely had a compelling additional motive in attacking him, one related to American government policy goals. This, in combination with the considerable irritant of personal confrontations, made him a particularly likely target.[25]

If Makwawaian had numerous reasons, both personal and public, to assume Ely might mark him for retaliatory witchcraft, he likewise had reason to consider the cow a likely participant in Ely's spiritual abuses. As previously mentioned, domestic cattle fascinated the Ojibwa. They looked for clues in how they ought to approach cattle in the behavior of the EuroAmericans. They were struck by the obvious high regard in which the missionaries and the traders held their domestic cattle, an observation that suggests why angry warriors would injure only cattle out of all a missionary's possessions. The level of control the missionaries exerted over the cattle was truly amazing to the Ojibwa. With no traditions of plow agriculture or domestic cattle themselves, the Ojibwa had never considered utilizing cattle as draft animals. Awed Ojibwa marveled at the way the missionaries yoked and harnessed these spiritually powerful beings, whipped them, and used them to break a field or to draw a wagon. Obviously the missionaries had much more control over cattle than even the most powerful Ojibwa shaman. A shaman might channel the cow's power in a healing ritual; he could not hitch it to a wagon. Ely further demonstrated his personal power over cattle when he occasionally milked the cows of the fur trader William Aitkin.[26]

Observing the Elys' domestic life, the Ojibwa found further proof of the singularity of the missionaries' relationship to their cattle. Innocently attempting to set an example of civilized Christian living in the wilderness, the missionaries hung bucolic prints on their cabin walls featuring scenes of farms with cattle grazing. To Ojibwa eyes, there was little difference between a drawing of a cow hung up before an ailing villager and the agrarian prints on the Elys' cabin walls. The devout French fur trader Pierre Cotte, who clashed often with Ely in matters of religion, also inadvertently affirmed this Ojibwa perception, though for reasons of his own. He claimed the Protestant missionaries "worshipped the pictures of Cows" that hung on their walls. This seemed eminently reasonable to many Ojibwa; cattle had spiritual power. The missionaries, they felt, also knew this: when a hotheaded youth from a family outspoken in their opposition to the missionaries' presence visited Ely's barn, the missionary seized the opportunity and directed the cow's attack.[27]

In sum, although the missionaries seemed unaware of it, they had entered into communities that had been evaluating items of Old World origin for some time. With respect to at least one of these items, domesticated cattle, the evaluation was far from complete. Cattle were possessed of numerous attributes, and Ojibwa perceptions of cattle were necessarily complex. The Ojibwa continuously sought clues from the Euro-Americans in their midst as to the nature of cattle. When new groups of Euro-Americans appeared, the Ojibwa added to their store of knowledge by observing the newcomers' relations with cattle.

Alongside their ongoing evaluation of cattle, the Ojibwa in the 1830s also commenced an assessment of the missionaries. With protestations that they had "come here to do good and teach [the] children," and in possession of new and seemingly potent medications, the missionaries ought to have been positive forces within Ojibwa communities. Instead, they quarreled with the people, refused to share food, made incomprehensible demands about work and travel, and in numerous other ways seemed bent on community destruction. In ways the missionaries only dimly understood, the Ojibwa viewed them as political representatives of the American government, whose land hunger and treatment of other Native Americans were already giving the Ojibwa pause. The American Board missionaries' ambivalent behavior only fueled Ojibwa concerns of Euro-American intentions. From the Ojibwa's perspective, the missionaries seemed akin to the American government, whose words and deeds were so often contradictory.[28]

Ironically, the Ojibwa may have felt they had a firmer grasp of the attributes of cattle than of missionaries during the 1830s. Certainly, as they searched for clues to the missionaries' essential character, the Ojibwa scrutinized the clergy's relations with cattle. During the years of the American Board's presence in their villages, the Ojibwa came to the conclusion that the missionaries were spiritually powerful and decidedly malevolent. This decision was based on the empirical evidence of the missionaries' combative and antisocial behavior. The missionaries' treatment of domestic cattle formed an important strand of this evidence. Not only did the missionaries recognize the power of cattle by placing their pictures on their cabin walls, they also physically controlled cattle in numerous ways, from milking them to harnessing them to wagons and ploughs. Missionary control of cattle extended into the realm of spirit power, too, when Edmund Ely compelled his cow to attack his enemy, Makwawaian. In a final irony, Ely's use of his cow to inflict spiritual damage also reinforced Ojibwa perceptions of cattle as spiritually powerful.

This discussion of missionaries and their cattle, although in many respects incomplete, nonetheless provides an important glimpse into the processes of culture contact. It reminds the twentieth-century scholar that Native Americans did not necessarily encounter all of the Old World's cultural and material baggage at the same moment in time. Although Edmund Ely and his colleagues believed themselves to be "pioneers" introducing a radically different way of life into a "boundless wilderness," they were, in fact, only the latest in a long line of Europeans and Euro-Americans to reside for considerable periods of time in Ojibwa country. By the time Ely and his fellows were self-consciously "planting a tender shoot in the desert," the Ojibwa had been involved in processes of cultural exchange for generations.[29]

Within this context, it is equally important to remember that Native Americans sought continually to comprehend and integrate objects of Old World origin, including domesticated animals, into their existing belief systems. They did not simply accept European-derived interpretations of Old World animals or items of material culture. Furthermore, native perceptions of Old World animals or items of material culture were not static, they changed to renect additional knowledge or altered circumstances. Even minor events such as an attack by a missionary's cow contributed to the pool of knowledge available for understanding an introduced animal or material item, and thus even small incidents had far-reaching repercussions in the larger unfolding process of cultural exchange. The mundane encounter of a Native American community with an Old World domesticated animal underscores the subtlety and complexity of the process of cultural exchange.

NOTES

1. Previous versions of this paper were read at the American Society for Ethnohistory Conference in Tulsa, Oklahoma, November 1991, and the Organization of American Historians Conference in Chicago, April 1992. The author would like to thank the Research Committee of the Academic Senate of the University of California, Riverside, for their support of this research.

2. Accounts of the travels of trade personnel include 18, 28 February and 20 March 1839; the decision to retrench mission operations is found in entries for 19 January, 28 February, and 2 March 1839; Edmund F. Ely Diaries (hereafter cited as Ely Diaries), Box I, Edmund Franklin Ely and Family Papers, Minnesota Historical Society. Originals at the St. Louis County Historical Society, Duluth, MN.

3. "Extracts from the Instructions of the Prudential Committee to the Reverend Sherman Hall and Reverend William T. Boutwell, Missionaries to the Ojibways of the North West Territory of the United States," 10 June 1832, American Board of Commissioners for Foreign Missions Papers (hereafter cited as ABCFM Papers), Box I, Minnesota Historical Society (actual date of publication is 1831). Originals at the Houghton Library, Harvard University, Cambridge, MA. George Henry Monk, "Some Account of the Department of Fond du Lac or Mississippi," *Minnesota History Bulletin* 5 (1923–24: 28-39, 34. Instances of Ely's own perception of his role as pioneering missionary can be found in his diary entries for 17, 25 August 1833; 26 September and 16 November 1834, Ely Diaries. For previous French and British contact, see Harold Hickerson, *The Chippewa and Their Neighbors: A Study in Ethnohistory* (New York, 1970) and *The Southwestern Chippewa: An Ethnohistorical Study*, American Anthropological Association Memoir 92 (Menasha, WI, 1962). For important insights into Ojibwa perceptions of the French, British, and Americans, see William Whipple Warren, "History of the Ojibways, Based Upon Traditions and Oral Statements," *Collections* (Minnesota Historical Society) 5 (1885): 23–394. Jean Baptiste Perrault, "Narrative of the Travels and Adventures of a Merchant Voyageur in the Savage Territories of Northern America," *Collections* (Michigan Pioneer and Historical Society) 37 (1909–10): 574, mentions a trading post located at Fond du Lac in 1789. William Watts Folwell, *A History of Minnesota*, 4 vols. (St. Paul, MN, 1921), 1: 66—72, discusses North West Company activity at Fond du Lac. See also Helen Hornbeck Tanner, *Atlas of Creat Lakes Indian History* (Norman, OK, 1987), 143, 146.

4. 17 August 1833, Ely Diaries. For the word *pijiki*, see Bishop Frederic Baraga, *A Dictionary of the Ojibway Language* (St. Paul, MN, 1992 [1878]), pt. 2, 354. For the traders' habit of allowing cattle to forage, see Sherman Hall to David Greene, 17 September 1831, ABCFM Papers.

5. August 1836 and 3 June 1835, Ely Diaries. References to Inini's shamanistic practice are found in 7 March 1835, 14 December 1836, 21 October 1837, and 7 January 1838.

6. 3 June 1835, Ely Diaries. Ely's contentious relations with the Fond du Lac community can be seen repeatedly throughout his diaries. For representative instances, see 14 February 1833; 26 September, 15, 18, 21 December 1834; 6 January 1835; 4, 21 February, 9, 20 March, 22, 24 May, 2, 11 June, and 8 September 1836; June 1837; and 7 August 1838.

7. 25 January 1836, Ely Diaries. See the entry for the previous day, Sunday, 24 January 1836, for Ely's lecture to two Ojibwa members of his traveling party who spent the day spearfishing. For his repeated strictures against work on Sundays, see 6 June 1834; 18 January, 26 May, and 13 December 1835; 31 January, 22 February, and 22 May 1836 and passim.

8. For representative instances, see 16, 25 October 1837; 6 June, 11, 13 September 1838; and 27, 29 July 1839, Ely Diaries. For Ojibwa conceptions of the reciprocal process, see A. Irving Hallowell, "Ojibwa Ontology, Behavior and World View," in *Teachings from the American Earth: Indian Religion and Philosophy*, Dennis Tedlock and Barbara Tedlock, editors (New York, 1975), 141–78, and "Property as a Social Institution," in *Culture and Experience*, A. Irving Hallowell (Philadelphia, 1955), 236–49.

9. For an extended discussion of the dispute, see Rebecca Kugel, "Religion Mixed with Politics: The 1836 Conversion of Mang'osid of Fond du Lac," *Ethnohistory* 37 (1990): 126–57.

10. Selected references to the cattle owned by various traders are from 17, 23 August 1833 and 26 March 1837, Ely Diaries. Also of interest is the fact that Ely purchased a bull from a trader named Fairbanks the year following his purchases from Cotte, thus apparently obtaining his entire original stock from the fur traders. See 27 March 1837. References to cattle obtained by Ely's fellow American Board missionaries include Sherman Hall to David Greene, 14 June 1832 and 17 October 1834, and William T. Boutwell to David Greene, 16 December 1835, ABCFM Papers.

11. All quotes from 22 February 1839, Ely Diaries. Original in italics.

12. Ibid., 22, 24 February 1839.

13. Ibid., 25 February 1839.

14. Ibid., 25, 26 February and 2 March 1839. Emphasis in original. For evidence of Catharine Ely's level of fluency in Ojibwa, see Edmund F. Ely to David Greene, 31 December 1835, ABCFM Papers.

15. 25 February 1839, Ely Diaries.

16. The literature contains considerable information on Ojibwa witchcraft beliefs. See Hallowell, *Culture and Experience*, especially 17–110, 125–50, 172–82 277–90, for the most detailed and insightful understanding of the role of witchcraft in Ojibwa society. Other works including substantive discussion are Ruth Landes, *The Ojibwa Woman* (New York, 1971 [1938]) and *Ojibway Religion and the Midewimin* (Madison, WI, 1968); Victor Barnouw, *Acculturation and Personality among the Wisconsin Chippewa*, American Anthropological Association Memoir 72 (Menasha, WI, 1950) and *Wisconsin Chippewa Myths and Tales* (Madison, WI, 1997); and Edward S. Rogers, *Natural Environment, Social Organization, Witchcraft: Cree vs. Ojibwa, A Test Case*, National Museums of Canada Bulletin 230 (Ottawa, ON, 1969), 24–39.

17. The author is indebted to Professor David Edmunds, commentator on the draft of this paper read at the Organization of American Historians Conference in Chicago, April 1992, for his observations on wabenos. A copy of Professor Edmunds's comments are in the author's possession. Kaiashkibas's Midewiwin affiliation and practice is described in 24 May 1836, 6 May 1837, and 23 October 1838, Ely Diaries. It seems likely that Kaiashkibas was not himself a wabeno. Ely's descriptions of his curing activities do not describe him as practicing rituals associated with wabenos, and wabenos tended not to join the Midewiwin society. The literature on Ojibwa religiously oriented healing practices is rich. See, for instance, Diamond Jenness, *The Ojibwa Indians of Parry Island: Their Social and Religious Life*, National Museums of Canada Bulletin 78 (Ottawa, ON, 1935) for a discussion of wabenos; Walter J. Hoffman, "The Midewiwin or 'Grand Medicine Society' of the Ojibwa," *Annual Report of the Bureau of American Ethnology*, no. 7 (Washington, DC, 1886), 143–300; Ruth Landes, *Ojibway Religion and the Midewimin* (Madison, WI, 1968); A. Irving Hallowell, *The Role of Conjuring in Saulteaux Society* (Philadelphia, 1942).

18. For Ojibwa conceptions of spiritual power, see Jenness, *The Ojibwa Indians of Parry Island*; Hallowell, *The Role of Conjuring in Saulteaux Society*; also Hallowell, "Some Empirical Aspects of Northern Saulteaux Religion," *American Anthropologist* 36 (1934): 389–404; *Culture and Experience*, 151–82. For Ely's exclusionary expectations of his converts, see 13, 14 February 1836 and passim, Ely Diaries.

19. 16 October 1833 and 6, 7 March 1835, Ely Diaries. For additional references to Ely's doctoring activities, see 16, 17, 22 October 1833; 2 September and 1 November 1834; 2 March 1835; 23 January and 12, 14, 20, 24 April 1836, and passim, Ely Diaries. For ABCFM policy, see Sherman Hall and William T. Boutwell to the Prudential Committee of the ABCFM, May 1833, "Journal of Reverend S. Hall," 27 December 1831; and "Journal of G. T. Sproat," 14, 21, 27 April 1837, ABCFM Papers.

20. All quotes from 21 September 1837, Ely Diaries.

21. Ibid. The daughter of American Fur Company official Ramsey Crooks and an Ojibwa woman Hester Boutwell had been educated at the Mackinaw Mission school in the late 1820s and early 1830s. She did not speak fluent Ojibwa and seemingly had no cultural connections to the predominantly French/Indian métis community. As such, she would appear to merit a description as "mixed-blooded" rather than as métis.

Catharine Ely, on the other hand, although also educated at Mackinaw, retained ties to the métis population. Her elderly father, Joseph Goulais, upon retiring from the trade, lived briefly with the Elys in 1841. His Catholicism and French Canadian culture caused conflicts with his Protestant American son-in-law, who considered Goulais "unfit as a companion for my children," Edmund F. Ely to David Greene, 26 August 1841, ABCFM Papers. For brief biographical sketches of Hester Boutwell and Catharine Ely, see "Complete List of Dakota and Ojibwa Missionaries," [1867?], ABCFM Papers.

22. All quotes from 21 September 1837, Ely Diaries.

23. "The Ojibwa World View and Disease," in A. Irving Hallowell, *Contributions to Anthropology: Selected Papers of A. Irving Hallowell,* (Chicago, 1976 [1963]), 391–448, makes explicit Ojibwa thinking on the connection between socially inappropriate behavior and resultant illness induced by retaliatory witchcraft. An additional incident that occurred shortly after the confrontation over the turnips may have kept alive Makwawaian's concerns regarding Ely's intentions. Ely attempted to heal one of Makwawaian's kinswomen, who died anyway. Although she was apparently in critical condition before Ely made any attempts to assist her, Makwawaian and his family might well have seen her death as an instance of Ely refusing to help someone whose family he actively disliked. See 12 (the actual date is 14), 15, 17, 18, 20 October 1837, Ely Diaries.

24. Ibid., 7 August and 23 October 1838. Ely identifies Akiwenzi as a son of Eninabondo in the entry for 7 August 1838. In the entry for 21 September 1837, Ely identified Madjigindas, the child who took the turnips, as a son of Akiwenzi. Madiigindas referred to Makwawaian as "Nimishome," the Ojibwa word translating as "my father's brother," thus indicating that Akiwenzi and Makwawaian were brothers, and, indirectly, sons of the same father. Baraga, *A Dictionary of the Ojibway Language,* pt. 2, 293. For a discussion of the Ojibwa kinship system, see Ruth Landes, *Ojibwa Sociology,* Columbia University Contributions to Anthropology, vol. 29 (New York, 1937).

25. 31 June, 20, 22 May, and 22 June 1836, Ely Diaries. For Manitons's challenges, see 19, 20 August 1836. Eninabondo's sentiments are recorded in the entries for 12, 16 May 1836; his kinship tie to Catharine Ely in 2 September 1838. Manitons is identified as "another older brother" of Makwawaian in 2 March 1839.

26. Ibid., 19 September 1834 and 4 January 1838 provide examples of the missionaries' control of their cattle. Ely discusses his liberal use of "the *Lash* well laid on" in bringing home his bull in 29 March 1837. Emphasis in original. The missionaries' use of whips on any animal, let alone one with the obvious power of cattle, must have struck the Ojibwa very forcibly, given the powerful sanctions in Ojibwa culture against the mistreatment of animals. See Hallowell, "Ojibwa World View," 391–448, especially 419, 433.

27. 11 April 1836, Ely Diaries. See also 21 September and 14 October 1833; 28 October 1834; 28 January and 13 December 1835; 15 May 1836; and 30 June 1837, for mention of colored prints, often with scriptural themes, that Ely utilized in his school teaching efforts. The Ojibwa regarded these prints, many containing pastoral scenes and livestock, as further proof of the power of the animals depicted. Ely's conflicts with the Catholic métis community were numerous; for a representative sampling, see 8, 13 June, 27 September, 15 October, 23 November, and 6, 15, 18 December 1834, Ely Diaries.

28. Ibid., 4 March 1836.

29. "Extracts," ABCFM Papers; 17 August 1833, Ely Diaries.

9

A NEW PERSPECTIVE ON INDIAN-WHITE CONTACT:
CULTURAL SYMBOLS AND COLONIAL TRADE

Christopher L. Miller and George R. Hamell

Few American myths are more enduring than the legend that Dutch colonists purchased the island they named Manhattan for a chest full of worthless trinkets. That story has survived in part because it provides white Americans with the reassuring notion that, while colonists might have been duplicitous, at least they were more clever than the Native Americans they encountered. It also endures because colonists often did exchange goods that had little value to them (such as glass beads) for goods, they believed, that had enormous value (such as land).

But the story of the purchase of Manhattan Island and other transactions between Europeans and Native Americans, needs to be set into a larger context. It is impossible to understand exchange in North America if we view it only through colonial eyes; trade, after all, is by definition always a two-way process. Rather than considering the Indians dupes, we must try to explain why items such as glass beads had such an appeal in native communities. In many instances, as Christopher Miller and George Hamell note here, that appeal lay in the cultural value Indians gave to particular objects: an item of little use to a colonist might be precious to a Native American.

Just as beauty is in the eye of the beholder, just as one person's superstition is another person's religion, so one trader's "trinket" might be another's most prized possession. While the analysis that follows delineates the value of certain goods to Indians, readers should remember that Europeans also had desires that struck their Indian commercial partners as rather bizarre. Native Americans, for example, could not at first understand the European belief that land itself was a commodity that could be bought and sold and, once purchased, used only by its owner; Indians, who thought that all people had a legitimate claim to what the land produced (firewood that they gathered, crops that they had planted, game that they hunted) considered a claim to owning land itself ridiculous, even inconceivable. Other goods that were trash to an Indian made a European trader's eyes light up. As James Axtell has noted, colonists were eager to buy old beaver coats—begrimed by years of smoke and sweat—that Native Americans were ready to discard, because it was easier to transform these coats than raw pelts into felt hats, the primary use of beaver fur in early modern Europe. Indians were often incredulous at what they viewed as the stupidity of Europeans, who were happy to offer durable goods such as knives for old clothes. Who, here, was the dupe and who the shrewd trader?

A NEW PERSPECTIVE ON INDIAN-WHITE CONTACT: CULTURAL SYMBOLS AND COLONIAL TRADE

Christopher L. Miller and George R. Hamell

> Metaphor is largely in use among these Peoples; unless you accustom
> yourself to it, you will understand nothing.
> —PAUL LE JEUNE, New France, 1636

IN A 1982 *NEWSWEEK* ARTICLE, a Nicaraguan, commenting on the caliber of Soviet military and economic support, complained that "the Russians treat us like Indians . . . they give us a few mirrors and trinkets."[1] This former Sandinista's complaint illustrates both Western culture's low estimation of "mirrors and trinkets" and its assumption of Indian naiveté. The result of both has been a literarily satisfying but wholly inaccurate view of the role of "baubles, bangles, and beads" in Indian-white contact relations.

Of course, the historical record is full of references to the Indians' attraction to "trinkets." At Narragansett Bay in 1524, Florentine navigator Giovanni de Verrazzano noted the high value that the Indians placed on wrought copper because of its red color and observed that they cared not for, nor valued, implements of steel and iron. Verrazzano also stated that of "those things which we gave them, they prized most highly the bells, azure crystals, and other toys to hang in their ears and about their necks." Nor was that enthusiastic response to European glass beads, copper bells, and other such goods an isolated incident. In Virginia, John Smith noted that the Indians were "generally covetous of copper, beads, & such like trash." Elsewhere we are told of bargaining between Smith and Powhatan, "who fixed his humor upon a few blew beads," and that "for a pound or two of blew beads he [Smith] brought over my king for 2 or 300 bushels of corne, yet parted good friends."[2]

The cultural assumptions reflected in those observations continue to inform American popular culture and lie at the base of many persisting stereotypes concerning Indian rationality and motivation. For example, it is difficult to think about colonial-era

SOURCE: *Journal of American History* 73:2 (1986), 311–28.

Indian-white contact without envisioning Peter Minuit's buying Manhattan Island for twenty-four dollars' worth of costume jewelry. That this sort of imagery predominates in the "popular mind" is merely unfortunate; what is tragic is that the same misimpressions (albeit in a less cartoon like form) seem to be held by those whose profession it is to educate the public.

In a recent essay concerning the treatment of Indians in American history textbooks, Frederick E. Hoxie pointed out that in all those books the authors "either ignore Indian motives completely, or Native Americans appear in the narrative as irrational primitives clinging tenaciously to a doomed way of life." Not discussed in his essay is the fact that this is an accurate reflection of the way in which Indians are treated in most historical literature. It would be difficult, for example, to go much further in ignoring Indian motivation than did Frederick Jackson Turner when he reduced their role to that of a "consolidating agent in *our* history," a perspective adopted by subsequent generations of American-frontier historians.[3] When motivation is addressed at all, Indians appear to be psychotic: either the violent paranoid savages who skulk through Francis Parkman's and similar works or the sweetly schizophrenic innocents arrested in permanent infancy who occupy Helen Hunt Jackson's and others' pages.[4] (It is difficult to decide which is worse, denying Indians volition or endowing them with irrationality.)

To make matters worse, the broad acceptance of Indian (and other aboriginal) insanity spawned a vast literature ranging from Sigmund Freud's *Totem and Taboo* through Lucien Lévy-Bruhl's various writings up to Carlos Castaneda's psychedelic "insights," in which "primitivism" is characterized as a category of thinking universal among nonwestern (tribal or traditional) peoples.[5] Thus not only are Indians irrational, but also their irrationality is directly related to their "primitiveness," which can be traced either to their geographical remoteness from "civilization," to some cultural impediment, or to racial inferiority.[6] This perspective has fed back into literature, leading to ever greater heights of absurdity, an extreme example of which might be Ruth Beebe Hill's *Hanta Yo.*[7] Understandably, many historians and anthropologists have rebelled against the image of Indians either as psychotically hostile savages or as gullible children, and much of the current literature on the subject of early Indian-white contact either denies the significance (and occasionally the very existence) of an exchange of "nonutilitarian" items or is simply silent on the subject—emphasizing, instead, the practicality of Indian economic behavior and showing that, far from being gullible, Indians were demanding and sophisticated consumers.[8] Thus Indians have been casuistically lifted out of "primitivism" and firmly established as "rational" economic beings in the European sense. Perhaps the best illustration of this sort of casuistry is the work of Francis Jennings, who stresses repeatedly the utilitarian motives of Indians in "intersocietal commerce" and consistently denies the significance of nonutilitarian items in the trade.[9] In his most recent offering, Jennings accuses those who have tried to come to grips with the ideological aspects of Indian trade relations of reviving "savagery mythology." In fact, Jennings refuses to acknowledge such "savages," contemptuously calling the Indians in these works "hantayoyos."[10]

While such analysis may be ideologically satisfying (and has, perhaps, served as a necessary corrective), it simply does not hold up under close scrutiny. Both the historical and the archaeological records indicate that the impact of early European utilitarian trade goods on practical subsistence was negligible.[11] Summarizing the archaeological literature, John Witthoft concluded that utilitarian items played almost no role in the Indian trade during the sixteenth century; that "steel table knives and steel axes are present but not abundant, and brass was known, but kettles were still cut up rather than used as cooking utensils." Similar findings forced Bruce G. Trigger to concede that the real catalyst for the extensive changes in Huron social, political, and exchange relationships during the protohistoric period was apparently "a few scraps of metal," primarily ornaments crafted from pieces of broken copper kettles.[12] Hence Indians were not acquiring European goods during the early stages of intercultural contact primarily for what Europeans would have considered practical reasons. From the early stages through the seventeenth century, utilitarian items were increasingly being acquired and were being used in European fashion, but such nonutilitarian commodities as glass beads continued to be traded in huge volume.[13]

This pushes us toward the conclusion that despite Jennings's and others' protestations to the contrary, pre- and protohistoric American Indians did not think of the trade in the same way that Europeans did. As Wilcomb E. Washburn has said, "When Europeans first met Indians, the exchange of goods that took place bore almost no relation to the economic process with which we are familiar." More recently Calvin Martin observed that "their ideals and mode of action, phenomenology, ontology, and epistemology differed radically from that of Europeans then and Westerners now. We know this from ethnohistorical inquiry." Emphatically, we are not attempting to resurrect Lévy-Bruhl's timeless "primitives." We are, instead, in complete agreement with Claude Lévi-Strauss's statement:

> Of course, so-called primitive societies belong in history; their past is as old as ours, since it goes back to the origin of the species. Over thousands of years, they have undergone all sorts of transformations, gone through periods of crisis and prosperity; they have known wars, migrations, adventure. But they have specialized in ways different from those we have chosen. They may have remained, in some respects, close to very ancient conditions of life. This is not to deny that, in other respects, they are farther from them than we are.[14]

This being the case, we must be wary of casting Indian cultural processes in European cultural terms.[15]

Thus to deny or to underplay the role of what Jennings calls "gimcracks and baubles" in Indian-white trade relations is both theoretically inappropriate and historically inaccurate. If we are going to address Indian motivation (as we believe we must), it becomes necessary to explain the Indians' desire for those "baubles, bangles, and beads" of Western civilization. The explanation must satisfy the demand of being "rational" within the cultural milieu of American Indian societies and at the same time must avoid the all too common tautological device of simply defining such items as "luxury," "prestige," and "status" goods, thus inherently valuable and desirable. Moreover, we must be equally wary of the pitfall of which Jennings warns us—that of reviving the image of Indians as savages, noble or otherwise.[16]

Our analysis of historical, archaeological, ethnographic, and psychological materials has led us to what we believe is a valid hypothesis. It would appear that during the sixteenth and early seventeenth centuries, Indians did not perceive European copper or glass as something new. Rather, imported copper goods and glasswares were assimilated into traditional native ideological systems alongside native copper, exotic siliceous stones, and shells as material components of great ritual significance.[17] It was that conventional but highly charged ideological value, not some Indian psychosis, that made European trade goods so enormously attractive.

The formation of this hypothesis came as a direct result of observing archaeological artifacts from the Woodland region of the proto- and early historic periods.[18] Here we find trade goods directly alongside spiritually charged native items in ceremonial contexts. This incorporation of novel materials is readily apparent in protohistoric Iroquois mortuary practices, in which glass beads appear to have been preferentially disposed along with shell beads. In protohistoric and early historic Seneca burials, glass beads are sometimes found with quartzite pebbles in box turtle rattles. Playing pieces for the Plumstone Bowl or dice game made from the "raspberry" prunts of a glass drinking vessel and from white-glazed majolica and delft fragments have been found at seventeenth-century Seneca sites, and a Seneca child wore the foot of another glass drinking vessel suspended on a brass chain. Additionally, majolica and delft fragments have been found reworked into small circular gorgets and pendants, analogues of more traditional shell fragments. In all of these cases, the new materials were incorporated with similar traditional materials into a shared ceremonial context.[19]

In the historical record for eastern North America, we find evidence that "glass" entered native thought and behavior as "crystal." In 1699 a "bottle and the foot of a glass which they guarded as very precious" were observed in a Taënsa temple, which also had preserved within it some pieces of native crystal. Among the furnishings of a Bayogoula temple was "a double glass bottle . . . which Tonti had given these people." Glasswares and glazed European ceramics were among the Tunica's "treasures" placed with the dead during the early eighteenth century, and Reo F. Fortune noted that in this century a clear glass marble is used in the "shooting" rituals of the Omaha Siouans' Water Monster Society, perhaps replacing quartz crystals.[20]

Further archaeological and linguistic information confirms that glass was also incorporated into the native thought-world as a replacement for traditional divining implements. Traditionally, water and crystal were widely used for such purposes, as were polished free-state metals, metallic-ore mosaics, muscovite mica, and perhaps water- or grease-slicked polished stone surfaces, in which a spirit or soul was reflected.[21] In 1643 Roger Williams noted that the Narragansett Algonquians' word for soul had an affinity "with a word signifying a looking glasse, a cleare resemblance." Nearly three hundred years later, in his study of the Naskapi Algonquians, Frank G. Speck observed that the same linguistic and conceptual linkage between "soul" and "mirror" was found over much of the Algonquian-speaking area of North America.[22] Clearly in both cases, European-manufactured mirrors were incorporated into an already existing category, one highly charged with ceremonial significance.

Any number of further examples could be given to illustrate the transubstantiation of European-manufactuted items into Native American artifacts, all of which point to the fact that the key to understanding early trade relations between whites and Indians is the realization that to the Indians nonutilitarian trade goods were valuable, not for their uniqueness, but for their similarity to native substances. These materials were incorporated with native shells, crystals, and metals into ceremonial objects possessing great ideological and symbolic meaning.

As interesting as that may be, more significant is the implication that the perceived similarity between novel items and familiar ones permitted the Woodland Indians to incorporate, not just the trade goods, but also the people who bore them. Through that process of conventionalization, Indians were able to understand colonial cultural contact, a process that otherwise would have been exceedingly disturbing, perhaps incomprehensible. This implication opens a door to a new and, we believe, much more constructive way of analyzing the acculturation of European goods and European people into the native American world.

In both the Old World and the New, crystals and shells were highly valued aesthetically. In the Old World the manufacture of glass and porcelain was developed to produce substances imitative of rock or quartz crystal and other precious stones and of shell. In western Europe during the sixteenth through the eighteenth centuries, glasswares imitated "cristallo," and the shell-like whiteness and luster of Oriental porcelains were imitated in white, or "milk," glass. Similarly, European potters produced ersatz porcelain with its shell-like color and luster in white-glazed majolica, faience, and delft.[23]

North American Indians also valued the luster and reflective quality of crystal and shell, but they did not reproduce those items synthetically. In fact, the idea would have been unthinkable to Indians since those things were believed to be "other-worldly" in origin. In the Woodland Indian mythic world, crystal, shell, and reflective metals were obtained by real human man-beings through reciprocal exchanges with extremely powerful Other World Grandfathers, man-beings of horned or antlered serpent, panther, and dragon forms. The Other World Grandfathers were related to humans as personal guardian spirits or as patrons of animal-medicine societies, and their gifts often assured long life, physical and spiritual well-being, and success, especially in the conceptually related activities of hunting, fishing, warfare, and courtship. Consequently, those substances were prominent in myths and in rituals of creation and re-creation, resuscitation, and the continuity of life. On the other hand, as other-worldly items, those substances were charged with great power and were also potentially very dangerous to the real human man-beings who came to possess them. Thus Indians developed an ingenious and highly ritualized technology for incorporating real shell, crystal, and native copper into ceremonially significant artifacts and surrounded it with a rich mythic tradition.[24]

It is not too surprising, then, that when delft, glass, and other European items that were deliberately imitative of natural lustrous minerals were introduced into North

America, they were received into native semantic categories as "crystal" and "shell" and were used as such. To the Indians, however, the similarity of appearance was greatly reinforced by a putative similarity in origin. Like the traditional ceremonial items, European wares initially also appeared other-worldly. Thus the objects and their bearers were entirely consistent with familiar aspects of the aboriginal world.

Indian accounts of initial contact give evidence for the way in which European artifacts and people were received by Woodland Indians. In the early seventeenth century, William Wood recorded a New England Indian version according to which the natives

> tooke the first Ship they saw for a walking Iland, the Mast to be a Tree, the Saile white Clouds, and the discharging of Ordinance for Lightning and Thunder, which did much trouble them, but this thunder being over, and this moving Iland stedied with an Anchor, they manned out their cannowes and goe and picke strawberries there, but being saluted by the way with a broad side, they cried out, what much hoggery, so bigge walke, and so bigge speak, and by and by kill; which caused them to turne back, not daring to approach till they were sent for.[25]

One year earlier, in 1633, Jesuit pioneer Paul le Jeune recorded a similar tradition among the Montagnais Algonquians. Le Jeune's informant told him that his grandmother used to relate how they thought that the first French ship they had seen was a floating island and knew not what to say about the great sails that made it go. Their

Figure I: Human head effigy from a clay smoking pipe with red glass-bead eye inlays. Seneca Iroquois, c. A.D. 1655–75. Excavation, Dann site, Monroe County, New York. Drawing by Gene Mackay; photograph by Jack Williams. *Courtesy Rochester Museum and Science Center, Rochester, New York.*

astonishment was redoubled when they saw men on deck. The women began to prepare houses for their guests, and the men ventured out in canoes to board the vessel
and to invite the French to the houses. In general, the Indians were much astonished,
saying that "the Frenchmen drank blood and ate wood, thus naming the wine and
the biscuits."[26]

About 1761 the Rev. John Heckewelder, a Moravian missionary to the Indians of
Pennsylvania, was given an account by "aged and respected Delawares, Momeys and
Mahicanni" of the first Europeans' arrival at Manhattan Island. Their ancestors had
originally mistaken the Europeans' approaching ship as a large fish, but as it got closer
they concluded "it to be a large canoe or house, in which the great Mannitto (great or
Supreme being) *himself* was, and that he probably was coming to visit them." Sacrifices,
food, and entertainment were prepared for him. The tradition also recorded that their
ancestors admired the white skins of the men who landed on shore in a small boat, particularly that of the man in "red clothes which shone" who gave them presents, "to wit,
beads, axes, hoes, stockings &c." The Europeans then departed, promising to return the
following year. Meanwhile, not knowing their utilitarian functions, the Indians suspended the axes and hoes on their breasts as ornaments and used the stockings as tobacco
pouches. It was not until the following year, when the ship returned, that the Indians
were taught the practical functions of these objects by the greatly amused Europeans.[27]

In 1869 Silas Tertius Rand recorded a Micmac Algonquian tradition of their initial contact with Europeans, which firmly ties this event to the supernatural bearers of
other-worldly ceremonial gifts. According to Rand's informant, at a time when only
the Indians lived in North America, a young woman had had a singular dream "that a
small island came floating in towards the land, with tall trees on it, and living beings—
among whom was a man dressed in rabbit-skin garments." Within two days the event
had occurred; the island had drifted toward the shore and then become stationary.
There were trees on it, branches on the trees, and bears crawling about the branches.
At first the Indians seized their bows and arrows and spears and ran down to the shore,
intending to shoot the bears. But then they recognized that the "bears" were really men,
and that among them was a man "dressed in white,—a priest with his white stole on."
The girl was later questioned by the tribal magicians and affirmed that the ship was the
island of her dream and that the priest was, indeed, the man in rabbit skins. This tale
and others collected among the Micmac during the last half of the nineteenth century
indicate that Europeans, especially priests, had become associated with the Woodland
Algonquians' culture hero, Mahtigwess, the White Rabbit Man-being.[28]

Similarly, Verrazzano described how one of his sailors in a small boat, which was
unable to beach because of the high surf, attempted to swim ashore in order to convey to the Indians there "some knick-knacks, as little bells, looking-glasses, and other
like trifles; when he came near three or four of them he tossed the things to them,
and turned about to get back to the boat, but he was thrown over by the waves, and
so dashed by them that he lay as if he were dead upon the beach." To the sailor's great
distress, the Indians picked him up and carried him from the surf, showing him that
he had nothing to fear. "Afterwards they laid him down at the foot of a little hill,

when they took off his shirt and trowsers, and examined him, expressing the greatest astonishment at the whiteness of his skin."[29]

We do not wish to imply here that the stories are "true" in an objective sense. Rather, they are a reflection of how those societies chose to incorporate novel historical events into their cognitive world. In this sense, these traditions, like those told concerning Capt. James Cook's arrival on the Sandwich Islands, are instances of what Marshall D. Sahlins describes as a "received category"—a conjunction of historical metaphors and mythical realities.[30] Through that process the nonrational becomes rational—the unknown is made known. Hence a totally unknown creature—a priest— was conceptually transformed into a supernatural, but very familiar, white rabbit man-being; and an incomprehensible beast—a sailor—was perceived as a marvelous, but entirely understandable, white-skinned monster man-being from the sea. Similarly, when confronted with magical "walking islands," the Indians interviewed by Wood naturally assumed that they could venture out and "pick strawberries" and were, no doubt, rewarded with metaphorical ones.

A linguistic and conceptual correlation between beads and berries added greatly to the conventionalization of European trade items and their identification as otherworldly, in that berries were frequently associated with a supernatural mythic and ritual motif.[31] According to Seneca legend, strawberries were not native to the earth but had been brought from the Sky World by Sky Woman and were still to be found along the road to the afterworld. Similarly, the Chippewa-Ojibwa Algonquians believed that strawberries were among the most prominent features along the road to the spirit world. In fact, berries were widely recognized as a proper food for spirits.[32] Thus, like crystal, shell, and native copper, berries were associated with the other world and with the supernatural beings who dwelt there.

As other-worldly things, berries shared shell, crystal, and native copper's efficacy in promoting physical and spiritual well-being. According to the Huron genesis myth, the Master of the Sky World caused the celestial tree of light and life to be cut down so that he could eat of the fruit and thereby cure a sickness afflicting his soul. Evidence of fruit as a curative among the Huron was apparent in 1637, when a fasting Huron sorcerer was reportedly taught to cure the sick by "demons" who advised him to live as they did on a diet of clear strawberry soup.[33] Such beliefs were also widespread among the Northern Iroquois, who credited berries with the power to cure the seriously ill, both in myth and in practice.[34] Given such power, it is not surprising that berries are specifically mentioned in the Iroquois Thanksgiving Address that opens most ceremonies and in which thanks are offered to the life-supporting beings on earth and above. Here they are called "hanging fruits," signifying the liminal position they occupy between earth and sky and reflecting their symbolic liminality in Woodland ceremonial life.[35] Since beads were linguistically and conceptually associated with berries, when shell, crystal, and native copper were rendered into beads, these substances became metaphorical berries. Hence the items became exponentially more powerful in that they were berries but were also shell, crystal, and native copper.

In addition even to those qualities, all such other-worldly gifts had a specific symbolic association that was conveyed by the objects' color. Extensive cross-cultural research on color coding has led linguists Brent Berlin and Paul Kay to three conclusions concerning that cognitive process:

> First, there exist universally for humans eleven basic perceptual color categories, which serve as the psychophysical referents of the eleven or fewer basic color terms in any language. Second, in the history of a given language, encoding of perceptual categories into basic color terms follows a fixed partial order. . . . Third, the overall temporal order is properly considered an evolutionary one; color lexicons with few terms tend to occur in association with complex cultures and complex technologies (to the extent that complexity of culture and technology can be assessed objectively).

This evolutionary pattern follows the order:

1. All languages contain terms for white and black.
2. If a language contains three terms, then it contains a term for red.
3. If a language contains four terms, then it contains a term for either green or yellow (but not both).
4. If a language contains five terms, then it contains terms for both green and yellow.
5. If a language contains six terms, then it contains a term for blue.
6. If a language contains seven terms, then it contains a term for brown.
7. If a language contains eight or more terms, then it contains a term for purple, pink, orange, grey, or some combination of these.[36]

This may seem a throwback to Lévy-Bruhl's and others' social Darwinism, but it is not necessary to agree with Berlin and Kay's evolutionary scheme. Instead, Sahlins's suggestion that the basic color "stage" is a reflection of the conceptual relationships within a perceptual system, that it is a function of cultural choice, not of linguistic or cultural retardation, seems more likely. One might also follow Marc H. Bornstein in asserting that these categories are dependent on biological differences in iris pigmentation.[37] Whatever the case, in the Woodland Indian ceremonial perceptual system, conceptual relationships were tripartite; therefore, the ritual language of Woodland Indian groups falls into category two, or Stage II, dividing basic color conceptions and their symbolic associations into three essential categories: white, black, and red.[38]

As in many cultures, Northeastern Woodland Indians associated light with concepts of greatest cultural and social value.[39] Light was life, light was mind, light was knowledge, and light was greatest being; and semantically related concepts such as brightness, transparency, visibleness, and whiteness were also life, mind, knowledge, and greatest being. Thus other-worldly objects displaying those qualities—some shells and crystals as well as the hair of grandfathers—were associated with the cognitive and social aspects of life, that is, the well-being, harmony, and purposefulness of mind, knowledge, and greatest being. The positive symbolic quality of light colors found ritual expression in many realms, but most obviously in the presentation of a white wampum belt, which conveyed a semantic context of peace, desire for understanding, and sociability for the oral message that accompanied it.[40]

As is commonly the case in Stage I and Stage II language systems, white was also associated with other light colors. Thus as white was life, mind, knowledge, and greatest being, so hues ranging from sky blue (the color of the bright, clear daytime sky) to green (the color of crystal-clear reflecting waters and of growing grasses and leaves) were also life, mind, knowledge, and greatest being and appear to have been interchangeable in most mythic and ritual contexts.[41]

Also common in Stage I and Stage II language systems, the absence of light—darkness—conveys the complement to light and everything it stands for.[42] For traditional Northeastern Indians, darkness, conveyed by black, indigo, or any dark color, stood in contrast to life, mind, knowledge, and greatest being. Thus other-worldly objects displaying that quality—charcoal, some crystals and shells, as well as some berries and fruits, the masked faces of rattlesnakes, Canadian jays, some falcons, and the night itself—were associated with the noncognitive and asocial aspects of life: a stark contrast to well-being, harmony, and purposiveness of mind, knowledge, and greatest being, as in death, mourning, and confinement of the womb. As with white, the symbolic quality of blackness found ritual expression in many realms, but again most obvious was the presentation of a "black" (actually dark blue) wampum belt, which conveyed a semantic context of death, mourning, and asociability.[43]

It is the presence of a third axis in the division of the cognitive world, symbolized by the color red, that makes Northeastern Woodland Indian ceremonial language a Stage II system. Perceptually, red is a very special color. An effect known as "chromatic aberration" causes red surfaces to seem nearer to an observer than do surfaces of other colors at an equal objective distance. Most important, red maintains its chromatic perceptibility over a range of light conditions broader than that for any other color; red appears brighter than other colors at the same level of saturation and is perceived as purer or more saturated than are other colors of the same brightness. Thus red remains red in the light and in the dark.[44]

Consistent with its chromatic nature, red mediates between light and dark, as the red flames of the fire mediate between day's brightness and night's darkness. Consistent with its intensity, red is associated with animation, emotion, intense experience—with fire, heat, and blood.[45] Among the Woodland Indians other-worldly objects displaying that quality—some crystals, mineral pigments, and native copper—as well as some berries and fruits, red willows, red cedars, and blood were associated with the animation that mediates between light-life and dark-death and with the emotion that mediates between light-cognition and dark-autism. As with both white and black, the symbolic quality of redness found ritual expression in many realms, but again most obvious was the presentation of a red wampum belt, which conveyed a semantic context of high emotion and excitement and the ultimate expression of antisociability: war.[46]

To summarize, whiteness connoted the cognitive aspects of life, redness connoted the emotional aspect of life, and blackness connoted the absence of either cognition or animacy, or both, that is, death, mourning, and other inferior and asocial states of being. Depending on the ritual context, redness could be contrasted with either whiteness or darkness or could serve as a mediator between the two.[47] Thus white, red, and black shell, crystal, and metals had contrasting and complementary functions, values, and meanings in ritual. That color code was pervasively expressed in Northeastern Woodland Indian material culture and was the context into which European trade beads and other "decorative" items were received. Like native items, European beads and metal objects displayed the all-important aesthetic attributes that qualified them for a significant place in the Indian metaphysical world.

Thus the glass beads and other items offered to Indians by early European voyagers were seen as being the other-worldly ceremonial materials traditionally given by creatures different from themselves in appearance, yet related to them in a metaphorical and ceremonial sense. Is it any wonder then that the Indians Verrazzano met treasured gifts of copper and azure crystals or that Powhatan believed that he got a fair bargain in trading 200–300 bushels of corn for "a pound or two of blew beads"? In both their color and form, these items resembled those that had always been received from supernatural beings through reciprocal exchange. The new simply slipped in beside the old. Furthermore, because trade items were overwhelmingly either white, blue, or red in color, the items and the people who bore them were received into familiar social contexts.[48]

It therefore appears to us that Father le Jeune was quite correct; that in the initial phases of intercultural trade relations, the Indians in the Woodland region were trading in metaphors and that the value of trade goods was predominantly ceremonial and ideological. The value, in turn, was a function of the similarity, both in form and in putative origin, between the novel items and familiar ones. By fitting the objects and the people who bore them into familiar categories, the Woodland Indians transformed what ought to have been an incomprehensible series of events into something understandable and desirable. Only after that ideological world was shattered and the true nature of the newcomers became known did the situation become baffling; only then did the magical crystals turn into cheap glass beads.

The process of disenchantment began fairly quickly and was predominantly the result of the fur trade.[49] The destruction of traditional Indian perceptions was not an event but a protracted process that varied enormously in its pace from Indian society to Indian society. In coastal areas the destruction of the ritual context we have been discussing came fairly quickly, whereas in the interior it survived for some time. In any case, the process was essentially the same: growing dependency, at first mutual and then inclining consistently toward white dominance, which increasingly pushed intercultural exchange out of the symbolic ceremonial realm and into the realm of the white marketplace. Discussing the influence of that process on cultural change among Indian societies in contact situations, Richard White observed, "A . . . fundamental cause which emerges from an analysis of the histories of these peoples is the attempt, not always successful or consistent, by whites to bring Indian resources, land, and labor into the market," and the fur trade was eminently successful at doing just that. Not only did the trade in animal skins involve Woodland Indians in the white marketplace, but the conjunction of that economic factor with the concomitant depletion of the native habitat had far-reaching social and cultural effects. Add the dislocating influences of white population pressure, European and native imperial warfare, climatic change, disease, and major dietary changes, including the introduction of alcohol, and what emerges is a dynamic pressure against which traditional Indian societies rooted in mutual dependence and reciprocity could not stand. As White concluded, "Understanding change involves, not finding the invisible hand of economic interests, but rather finding the reciprocal influences of culture, politics, economics, and the environment."[50]

The late seventeenth century was a particularly critical time in the transition from ceremonial exchange to economic transaction among most Woodland groups. The years between 1689 and 1763 were marked by constant diplomatic and military jockeying for imperial control over the New World, and the Woodland Indians were a major factor in that process.[51] These developments are significant for several reasons. First, the military and diplomatic necessity of involving the Indians in European war efforts brought the natives even more firmly into the world of the marketplace. In addition, European efforts at diplomacy pushed enormous amounts of trade goods into Indian hands. Furthermore, regardless of their color and substance, the European gifts were almost universally presented in contexts of war and other antisocial activities. These factors no doubt combined to facilitate the erosion of their metaphorical identity and ceremonial value.[52]

Once the erosion began, Indian people were quick to put aside the once magical, now commonplace items. Annemarie Anrod Shimony has noted that Northern Iroquoian groups eventually prohibited the inclusion of glass beads in burials, possibly marking a nativistic shift of attitude toward the "white man's" goods. Not surprisingly, as the perception of the exchange process changed, so did the type of commodities that were exchanged. Arthur J. Ray has noted for the Hudson's Bay District that although the trade in utilitarian items (metal knives, hatchets, kettles, and European cloth) fluctuated enormously, it was generally on the rise during the latter seventeenth and early eighteenth centuries, while trade in beads declined precipitously. Despite that decline, traditional color symbolism continued to play a role in intercultural exchange. Wilbur R. Jacobs has noted that as late as the 1770s, European traders were forced to dye fabrics "red, blue, and aurora [a shade of light orange]" in order to attract customers among the Iroquois and other Eastern tribes, and even Francis Jennings points out that the Indian demand for "scarlet and blue cloth" was so significant that the pattern of economics in England was tilted toward Bristol, the shipping source of such dyed materials.[53]

It is not a coincidence that European governments were taking increasing official interest in Indians during the same period. That they were is important because their interest resulted in volumes of documents concerning Indian societies, the interior trade, and Indian-white relations. Because those documents are the products of European observers who were absorbed in their own life-and-death struggles and because they were recorded at precisely the time during which the traditional nature of Indian-white trade relations was undergoing its most precipitous erosion, it is only natural that the subtlety of reciprocal ceremonial exchange goes largely unnoticed in their pages and, since traditional histories have been based largely on those documents, it has continued to go unnoticed. As William N. Fenton noted, "The fault lies partly in the sources themselves. Virtually all that we know of Indians at the time comes to us through the eyes and pens of white men whose interests and values differed from those of the Indians," but historians' slavish dependence on those documents and their continuing adherence to the "interests and values" of the documents' authors have played at least an equal role.[54] Thus we have perpetuated the stereotype of the irrational (or nonvolitional) primitive, and the cartoon image of Minuit and his costume jewelry continues to pop into mind when the subject of Indian-white trade is mentioned. As le Jeune warned, we have neglected the trade in metaphors and as a result have "understood nothing."

In concluding his masterful analysis of the Indian in the American imagination, Robert F. Berkhofer, Jr., observed rather fatalistically that "so long as the modern understanding of human actions assumes some sort of cultural influence between stimulus and response, then the future of the Indian as image must be determined by the preconceptions of White cultural premises." "The great question," he continued, "then becomes: To what extent can new meanings be infused into the old term to cancel old prejudices and invent a new evaluative image?"[55] In coming to understand that what were "toys" to Verrazzano and "trash" to John Smith were to the Woodland Indians powerful cultural metaphors that helped them to incorporate novel items and their bearers into their cognitive world, we believe that we have taken a step forward in forging such a new "evaluative image." In form, color, and putative origin, those objects and the people associated with them were like objects and creatures that were well known to have great mythic and ceremonial significance and were accepted accordingly.[56]

Given this understanding, Indians need no longer be considered mad nor have their minds colonized by white motivations. Instead, they and we are liberated from the old stereotypes and can get on with the business of evaluating the historical and continuing cultural relationship between comparably complex, rational, and real human man-beings.

NOTES

1. James LeMoyne with John Walcott, "An End to the Covert War?" *Newsweek,* Nov. 29, 1982, p. 65.

2. Henry C. Murphy, *The Voyage of Verrazzano: A Chapter in the Early History of Maritime Discovery in America* (New York, 1875), 178; John Smith, *A Map of Virginia, With a Description of the Countrey, the Commodities, People, Government, and Religion* (Oxford, Eng., 1612), 20; W. S., *The Proceedings of the English Colonie in Virginia Since Their First Beginning From England in Yeare of Our Lord 1606, Till This Present 1612, With All Their Accidents That Befell Them on Their Journies and Discoveries* (Oxford, Eng., 1612), 42, 20.

3. Frederick E. Hoxie, "The Indians versus the Textbooks: Is There Any Way Out?" *Perspectives* 23 (April 1985), 20; Frederick Jackson Turner, "The Significance of the Frontier in American History," in *The Turner Thesis concerning the Role of the Frontier in American History,* ed. George Rogers Taylor (Lexington, Mass., 1972), 12 [emphasis added].

4. Francis Parkman, *The Conspiracy of Pontiac and The Indian War after the Conquest of Canada* (rev. ed., 2 vols., Boston, 1870); Helen Hunt Jackson, *A Century of Dishonor: A Sketch of the United States Government's*

Dealings with Some of the Indian Tribes (New York, 1881). For assessments of Francis Parkman's work, see, for example, Francis P. Jennings, "Francis Parkman: A Brahmin among the Untouchables," *William and Mary Quarterly* 42 (July 1985), 305–28; Wilbur R. Jacobs, *Dispossessing the American Indian: Indians and Whites on the Colonial Frontier* (New York, 1972), 83–93; and Robert Shulman, "Parkman's Indians and American Violence," *Massachusetts Review* 12 (Spring 1971), 221–39. On Helen Hunt Jackson's work, see, for example, John R. Byers and Elizabeth S. Byers, "Helen Hunt Jackson (1830–1885): A Critical Bibliography of Secondary Comment," *American Literary Realism 1870–1910* 6 (Summer 1973), 197–241; and Allan Nevins, "Helen Hunt Jackson, Sentimentalist vs. Realist," *American Scholar* 10 (Summer 1941), 269–85. For an overview of the "good Indian–bad Indian" mythic structure, see Robert F. Berkhofer, Jr., *The White Man's Indian: Images of the American Indian from Columbus to the Present* (New York, 1978), 27–29, 95–96, 106–107.

5. Sigmund Freud, *Totem and Taboo: Resemblances between the Psychic Lives of Savages and Neurotics,* trans. A. A. Brill (1918; reprint, New York, 1960); Lucien Lévy-Bruhl, *Primitive Mentality,* trans. Lilian A. Clare (London, 1923); Lucien Lévy-Bruhl, *How Natives Think,* trans. Lilian A. Clare (London, 1923); Lucien Lévy-Bruhl, *The "Soul" of the Primitive,* trans. Lilian A. Clare (1928; reprint, New York, 1966); Carlos Castaneda, *The Teachings of Don Juan: A Yaqui Way of Knowledge* (Berkeley, 1968).

6. Berkhofer, *White Man's Indian,* 33–71. Carlos Castaneda is rather different from either Sigmund Freud or Lucien Lévy-Bruhl in that he celebrates rather than degenerates Indian "primitveness." As Robert F. Berkhofer, Jr., points out, "White views of Indians are inextricably bound up with the evaluation of their own society and culture," so that while Castaneda may be different in his perspective, he is participating in the same general process. Ibid., 27.

7. Ruth Beebe Hill, *Hanta Yo: An American Saga* (Garden City, 1979).

8. Arthur J. Ray's work is perhaps most representative. See Arthur J. Ray, "Indians as Consumers in the Eighteenth Century," in *Old Trails and New Directions: Papers of the Third North American Fur Trade Conference,* ed. Carol M. Judd and Arthur J. Ray (Toronto, 1980), 255–71; and Arthur J. Ray, *Indians in the Fur Trade: Their Role as Trappers, Hunters, and Middlemen in the Lands Southwest of Hudson Bay, 1660–1870* (Toronto, 1974). See also John C. McManus, "An Economic Analysis of Indian Behavior in the North American Fur Trade," *Journal of Economic History* 32 (March 1972), 36–53.

9. The best overall summary of the problems inherent in Francis P. Jennings's writing is Calvin Martin, "The Covenant Chain of Friendship, Inc.: America's First Great Real Estate Agency," *Reviews in American History* 13 (March 1985), 14–20.

10. Francis P. Jennings, *The Ambiguous Iroquois Empire: The Covenant Chain Confederation of Indian Tribes with English Colonies from Its Beginnings to the Lancaster Treaty of 1744* (New York, 1984), 81, xix. See also Francis P. Jennings, *The Invasion of Amenca: Indians, Colonialism, and the Cant of Conquest* (New York, 1975).

11. Bruce G. Trigger, *The Children of Aataentsic: A History of the Huron People to 1660* (2 vols., Montreal, 1976), 1, 243–45; John Witthoft, "Archaeology as a Key to the Colonial Fur Trade," *Minnesota History* 40 (Winter 1966), 205. See also James E. Fitting, "Patterns of Acculturation at the Straits of Mackinac," in *Cultural Change and Continuity: Essays in Honor of James Bennett Griffin,* ed. Charles E. Cleland (New York, 1976), 331; and William A. Ritchi, *Dutch Hollow, an Early Historic Period Seneca Site in Livingston County, New York* (Rochester, N.Y, 1954), 2.

12. Witthoft, "Archaeology as a Key to the Colonial Fur Trade," 205; Trigger, *Children of Aataentsic,* 1, 245.

13. Witthoft, "Archaeology as a Key to the Colonial Fur Trade," 205–207; Wilbur R. Jacobs, *Wilderness Politics and Indian Gifts: The Northern Colonial Frontier, 1748–1763* (Lincoln, 1966); Ray, *Indians in the Fur Trade,* 79–85.

14. Wilcomb E. Washburn, "Symbol, Utility, and Aesthetics in the Indian Fur Trade," *Minnesota History* 40 (Winter 1966), 198; Martin, "Covenant Chain of Friendship, Inc.," 20; Claude Lévi-Strauss, *Structural Anthropology: Volume 11,* trans. Monique Layton (Chicago, 1976), 28.

15. For a clear statement of this problem in a comprehensive and insightful study, see Alfred Goldsworthy Bailey, *The Conflict of European and Eastern Algonkian Cultures, 1504–1700: A Study in Canadian Civilization* (rev. ed., Toronto, 1969), 47. More recently, both Calvin Martin and Bruce G. Trigger have again called to our attention the problems of attempting to understand native acculturative processes solely from a Western cultural perspective. Calvin Martin, "The Metaphysics of Writing Indian-White History," *Ethnohistory* 26 (Spring 1979), 153–59; Bruce G. Trigger, "Archaeology and the Image of the American Indian," *American Antiquity* 45 (Oct. 1980), 662–76.

16. Jennings, *Invasion of America,* 99; Jennings, *Ambiguous Iroquois Empire,* 81.

17. In this discussion the term "shell" includes both freshwater and marine univalves and bivalves and pearls. The term "crystal" includes quartz crystal and other siliceous minerals, especially light-colored transparent and translucent varieties. For the sake of brevity, we are subsuming all metals found in a free state (for example, silver and meteoric iron) or as reflective metallic ores (for example, pyrite and galena) under the term "native copper."

18. The following discussion is confined to the Woodland Algonquians, Siouans, and Iroquois and their trade contact with whites during the colonial era. We believe, however, that similar symbolic interpretations were made of European trade items by all Indian (and, perhaps by all traditional) groups and that without an analysis of the symbolic categories into which European goods (and people) were received, the history of contact must suffer from the sort of distortion discussed above.

19. Witthoft, "Archaeology as a Key to the Colonial Fur Trade," 205–208; Charles F. Wray and Harry L. Schoff, "A Preliminary Report on the Seneca Sequence in Western New York, 1550–1687," *Pennsylvania Archaeologist* 23 (July 1953), 53–63; Robert Graham and Charles F. Wray, "The Percentage of Recovery in Salvaging Beads from Disturbed Burials," *Bulletin of the New York State Archaeological Association* 23 (Nov. 1961), 15. See also George R. Hamell, "Trading in Metaphors: The Magic of Beads: Another Perspective upon Indian-European Contact in Northeastern North America," in *Proceedings of the 1982 Glass Trade Bead Conference,* ed. Charles F. Hayes III et al. (Rochester, N.Y., 1983), 48–49.

20. John R. Swanton, *Indian Tribes of the Lower Mississippi Valley and Adjacent Coast of the Gulf of Mexico* (Washington, 1911), 164, 269, 275; John R. Swanton, *The Indians of the Southeastern United States* (Washington, 1946), 618; Jeffrey P. Brain et al., *Tunica Treasure* (Cambridge, Mass., 1979), passim; Reo F. Fortune, *Omaha Secret Societies* (New York, 1932), 90.

21. John Bartram, *Travels in Pensilvania and Canada* (1751; reprint Ann Arbor, 1966), 33; Charles G. Leland, *The Algonquian Legends of New England; or, Myths and Folklore of the Micmac, Passamaquoddy, and Penobscot Tribes* (Boston, 1884), 284; Silas Tertius Rand, *Legends of the Micmac* (New York, 1894), 3; Erminnie A. Smith, "Myths of the Iroquois," in *Second Annual Report of the Bureau of Ethnology to the Secretary of the Smithsonian Institution, 1880–'81* (Washington, 1883), 68–69; Frank G. Speck, *Naskapi: The Savage Hunters of the Labrador Peninsula* (1935; reprint, Norman, 1977), 164–65; Reuben Gold Thwaites, ed., *The Jesuit Relations and Allied Documents: Travels and Explorations of the Jesuit Missionaries in New France, 1610–1791* (73 vols., Cleveland, 1896–1901), VIII, 123; Arthur C. Parker, *Seneca Myths and Folk Tales* (Buffalo, 1923), 267–68; Alanson B. Skinner, "Mascoutens or Prairie Potawatomi Indians: Part III—Mythology and Folklore," *Bulletin of the Public Museum of the City of Milwaukee* 6 (Jan. 1927), 343.

22. Hammond Trumbull, ed., "A Key into the Language of America," in *The Complete Writings of Roger Williams* (7 vols., New York, 1963), I, 154; Speck, *Naskapi,* 33, 250.

23. Corning Museum of Glass, *Glass from the Corning Museum of Glass: A Guide to the Collections* (Corning, 1974). See also Joseph François Lafitau, *Customs of the American Indians Compared with the Customs of Primitive Times,* trans. and ed. William N. Fenton and Elizabeth L. Moore (2 vols., Toronto, 1974–77), I, 309; and Thwaites, ed., *Jesuit Relations and Allied Documents,* VIII, 312.

24. On the origin, use, and significance of other-worldly charms, especially sacred shells, crystals ("white flint," "white stone," and so on), and native copper, see C. Marius Barbeau, *Huron and Wyandot Mythology, with an Appendix Containing Earlier Published Records* (Ottawa, 1915), 102–103, 108–109, 140–41; Jeremiah Curtin and J. N. B. Hewitt, "Seneca Fiction, Legends, and Myths," in *Thirty-second Annual Report of the Bureau of American Ethnology to the Secretary of the Smithsonian Institution, 1910–1911* (Washington, 1918), 336–37; Walter Pilkington, ed., *The Journals of Samuel Kirkland: 18th Century Missionary to the Iroquois, Government Agent, Father of Hamilton College* (Clinton, N.Y., 1980), 141; Thwaites, ed., *Jesuit Relations and Allied Documents,* LI, 183; Victor Barnouw, *Wisconsin Chippewa Myths & Tales and Their Relations to Chippewa Life: Based on Folktales Collected by Victor Barnouw, Joseph B. Casagrande, Ernestine Friedl, and Robert E. Ritzenthaler* (Madison, 1977), 133; Henry R. Schoolcraft, *Archives of Aboriginal Knowledge. Containing All the Original Papers Laid Before Congress Respecting the History, Antiquities, Language, Ethnology, Pictography, Rites, Superstitions, and Mythology, of the Indian Tribes of the United States* (6 vols., Philadelphia, 1860), I, 352, 418; Paul Radin and A. B. Reagan, "Ojibwa Myths and Tales," *Journal of American Folk-lore* 41 (Jan.–Feb. 1928), 145–46; and J. G. Kohl, *Kitchi-Gami: Wanderings Round Lake Superior* (1860; reprint, Minneapolis, 1956), 208.

25. William Wood, *New England prospect. A true, lively and experimental description of that part of America, commonly called New England* (1634; reprint, New York, 1967), 87.

26. Thwaites, ed., *Jesuit Relations and Allied Documents,* V, 119–21.

27. John Heckewelder, "Indian Tradition of the First Arrival of the Dutch at Manhattan Island, Now New York," in *Collections of the New-York Historical Society* (2d ser., 4 vols., New York, 1841), I, 71–74.

28. Rand, *Legends of the Micmacs,* 225–26; Bailey, *Conflict of European and Eastern Algonkian Cultures,* 174–75.

29. Murphy, *Voyage of Verrazzano,* 173–74.

30. Marshall D. Sahlins, *Historical Metaphors and Mythical Realities: Structure in the Early History of the Sandwich Islands Kingdom* (Ann Arbor, Mich. 1981), 7.

31. References to the linguistic or conceptual identity of berries and beads have been reported for the Abnaki, Chippewa-Ojibwa, Montagnais-Naskapi, Menominee, Proto-Algonquian, and Cherokee. Frank G. Speck, *The Functions of Wampum among the Eastern Algonkian* (Lancaster, Pa., 1919), 54; Frances Densmore, *Chippewa Customs* (Washington, 1929), 15, 22, 35, 191; Speck, *Naskapi,* 28, 199–200, 247–48; Alanson B. Skinner, *Medicine Ceremony of the Menomini, Iowa, and Wahpeton Dakota, with Notes on the Ceremony among the Ponca, Bungi Ojibwa, and Potawatomi* (New York, 1920), 45, 179; George E. Aubin, *A Proto-Algonquian Dictionary* (Ottawa, 1975), 154; James Mooney, "The Sacred Formulas of the Cherokee," in *Seventh Annual Report of the Bureau of Ethnology to the Secretary of the Smithsonian Institution, 1885–'86* (Washington, 1891), 393; James A. Mooney, *The Swimmer Manuscript: Cherokee Sacred Formulas and Medicinal Prescriptions,* ed. Frans M. Olbrechts (Washington, 1932), II, 393; Frans M. Olbrechts, "Some Cherokee Methods of Divination," in *Proceedings of the Twenty-Third International Congress of Americanists, Held at New York, September 17–22, 1928* (New York, 1930), 548.

32. Jesse J. Cornplanter, *Legends of the Longhouse* (Philadelphia, 1938), 7; Arthur C. Parker, *The Code of Handsome Lake: The Seneca Prophet* (Albany, 1913), 25; Peter Jones, *History of the Ojebway Indians; With Especial Reference to Their Conversion to Christianity* (1861; reprint, New York, 1970), 103; William W. Warren, *History of the Ojibways, Based Upon Traditions and Oral Statements* (1885; reprint, Minneapolis, 1970), 73; Kohl, *Kitchi-Gami,* 223; William Jones and Truman Michelson, *Ojibwa Texts* (New York, 1919), 311; W. J. Hoffman, "The Midě'wiwin or 'Grand Medicine Society' of the Ojibwa," in *Seventh Annual Report of the Bureau of Ethnology to the Secretary of the Smithsonian Institution,* 280; Densmore, *Chippewa Customs,* 75; Curtin and Hewitt, "Seneca Fiction, Legends and Myths," 571; Parker, *Code of Handsome Lake,* 25.

33. Thwaites, ed., *Jesuit Relations and Allied Documents,* X, 129, XIII, 227–331.

34. Parker, *Seneca Myths and Folk Tales,* 203, 326; Parker, *Code of Handsome Lake,* 24–25; David Boyle, *Archeological Report [for] 1898. Being Part of an Appendix to the Report of the Minister of Education, Ontario* (Toronto, 1898), 139–40; Harold Blau, "Notes on the Onondaga Bowl Game," in *Iroquois Culture, History, and Prehistory,* ed. Elisabeth Tooker (Albany, 1967), 35–49.

35. See Michael K. Foster, *From the Earth to Beyond the Sky: An Ethnographic Approach to Four Longhouse Iroquois Speech Events* (Ottawa, 1974), 60–62, 120–27, 142. For a definition and discussion of "liminality," see Victor Turner, *The Ritual Process: Structure and Anti-Structure* (1969; reprint, Ithaca, 1977), 95–96.

36. Brent Berlin and Paul Kay, *Basic Color Terms: Their Universality and Evolution* (Berkeley, 1969), 104, 2–3.

37. Marshall D. Sahlins, "Colors and Cultures," *Semiotica* 16 (Sommaire 1976), 13; Marc H. Bornstein, "The Influence of Visual Perception on Culture," *American Anthropologist* 77 (Dec. 1975), 774–98.

38. George S. Snyderman, "The Functions of Wampum," *Proceedings of the American Philosophical Society* 98 (Dec. 1954), 475–77.

39. Snyderman, "Functions of Wampum," 475; Sahlins, "Colors and Cultures," 14. See also A. R. Radcliffe Brown, *The Andaman Islanders* (Glencoe, Ill., 1948), 316.

40. Snyderman, "Functions of Wampum," 469–94; George S. Snyderman, "The Function of Wampum in Iroquois Religion," *Proceedings of the American Philosophical Society* 105 (Dec. 1961), 571–608; Speck, *Functions of Wampum among the Eastern Algonkian,* 3–71; Frank G. Speck, "The Eastern Algonkian Wabanaki Confederacy," *American Anthropologist* 17 (July–Sept. 1915), 492–508.

41. Berlin and Kay, *Basic Color Terms,* 17, 25–28, 52–63; Bornstein, "Influence of Visual Perception on Culture," 774–98. See also Hoffman, "Midě'wiwin," 298; and Kohl, *Kitchi-Gami,* 16, 158.

42. Snyderman, "Functions of Wampum," 475; Betlin and Kay, *Basic Color Terms,* 17, 25–28, 52–63; Sahlins, "Colors and Cultures," 14.

43. Snyderman, "Functions of Wampum," 469–94; Snyderman, "Function of Wampum in Iroquois Religion," 571–608; Speck, *Functions of Wampum among the Eastern Algonkian,* 3–71; Speck, "Eastern Algonkian Wabanaki Confederacy," 492–508.

44. Snyderman, "Functions of Wampum," 477; Sahlins, "Colors and Cultures," 4–5.

45. Sahlins, "Colors and Cultures," 14; Victor Turner, *The Forest of Symbols: Aspects of Ndembu Ritual* (Ithaca, 1967), 70–71.

46. Snyderman, "Functions of Wampum," 469–94; Synderman, "Function of Wampum in Iroquois Religion," 571–608; Speck, *Function of Wampum among the Eastern Algonkian,* 3–71; Speck, "Eastern Algonkian Wabanaki Confederacy," 492–508.

47. Sahlins, "Colors and Cultures," 14.

48. Witthoft, "Archaeology as a Key to the Colonial Fur Trade," 205–208; Wray and Schoff, "Preliminary Report on thc Seneca Sequence in Western New York," 53–63.

49. The correlation between the fur trade and Indian cultural change is accepted fairly universally, but controversy rages over the specific nature of the relationship. Some sense of this conflict may be derived from Calvin Martin, *Keepers of the Game: Indian-Animal Relationships and the Fur Trade* (Berkeley, 1978); Shepard Krech III, ed., *Indians, Animals, and the Fur Trade: A Critique of* Keepers of the Game (Athens, Ga., 1981); and Ray, *Indians in the Fur Trade,* 80–81.

50. James Axtell, "The English Colonial Impact on Indian Culture," in James Axtell, *The European and the Indian: Essays in the Ethnohistory of Colonial North America* (New York, 1981), 253–54; Richard White, *The Roots of Dependency: Subsistence, Environment, and Social Change among the Choctaws, Pawnees, and Navajos* (Lincoln, 1983), xv.

51. Axtell, "English Colonial Impact on Indian Culture,"261. See also Jacobs, *Wilderness Politics and Indian Gifts;* Howard H. Peckham, *The Colonial Wars, 1689–1762* (Chicago, 1964); and Georgiana Nammack, *Fraud, Politics, and the Dispossession of the Indian: The Iroquois Land Frontier in the Colonial Period* (Norman, 1969).

52. Jacobs, *Wilderness Politics and Indian Gifts,* 5.

53. Shimony, *Conservatism among the Iroquois,* 235; Ray, *Indians in the Fur Trade,* 79–85; Jacobs, *Wilderness Politics and Indian Gifts,* 50; Jennings, *Invasion of America,* 99.

54. William N. Fenton, *American Indian and White Relations to 1830: Needs & Opportunities for Study: An Essay* (Chapel Hill, 1957), 17.

55. Berkhofer, *White Man's Indian,* 196–97.

56. It must also be pointed out here that what seemed enormously valuable to Europeans was often considered trash by American Indians. For example, "coat beaver," so treasured by early European fur traders, were merely cast-off clothes to the Indians. As James Axtell points out, "Each group considered its own donations 'worthless trifles' or common 'baubles' and those it received valuable prizes. From their own perspectives, of course, they were not wrong." E. E. Rich, *The History of the Hudson's Bay Company, 1670–1870* (2 vols., London, 1958–59), 1, 43; Axtell, "English Colonial Impact on Indian Culture," 253.

10

"THE BEWITCHING TYRANNY OF CUSTOM": THE SOCIAL COSTS OF INDIAN DRINKING IN COLONIAL AMERICA

Peter C. Mancall

Of all the goods that Europeans brought to North America, perhaps none had the devastating effect of alcohol. Though some indigenous peoples of the Western Hemisphere possessed alcoholic beverages before 1492 (most notably the Indians of the present-day Southwest of the United States as well as Mexico and Latin America), the peoples who lived in eastern North America possessed neither fermented nor distilled alcohol before Europeans brought it with them. What a contrast to Europe, where the consumption of beer, wine, brandy, rum, and other liquor had long been an accepted part of daily life.

Anthropologists, historians, and native leaders continue to debate the reasons why alcohol has caused such devastation in Indian communities. Some observers (including many Native Americans, according to surveys) argue that the persistent problems that some Indians have with alcohol are genetic in origin: Indians, so some suggest, possess some innate inclination to abuse alcohol. But there is, at this point, no solid evidence of such a genetic predisposition. As a result, many observers tend to look for social causes of alcohol abuse.

Whatever an individual's views on why a person chooses to drink destructively, the historical record contains overwhelming evidence that alcohol, notably rum in territory controlled by the English and brandy in the French-controlled St. Lawrence Valley, had a devastating impact in Indian Country during the colonial era. Indian leaders and colonial officials alike recognized the destructive consequences that alcohol use had in many native communities. And though actual alcohol abuse was widespread among colonists themselves, who invariably drank more liquor than Indians, attention often focused on the use of alcohol in Indian communities. For it was in those settlements, Peter C. Mancall argues, that alcohol became what the Delaware Prophet Neolin called a "deadly medicine," often destroying those who drank it as well as the native social fabric.

"THE BEWITCHING TYRANNY OF CUSTOM": THE SOCIAL COSTS OF INDIAN DRINKING IN COLONIAL AMERICA

Peter C. Mancall

ALCOHOL ABUSE HAS BEEN the most significant ongoing health problem American Indians have experienced since the mid-seventeenth century. The social costs of Indian drinking in modern society are staggering: Deaths related to alcoholism (including cirrhosis) remain four times higher for Indians than for the general population; alcohol plays a role in perhaps 90 percent of all homicides involving Indians; inebriated Indians die while walking along roads, either hit by cars or succumbing to hypothermia; 70 percent of all treatment provided by Indian Health Service physicians is for alcohol-related disease or trauma.[1] Alcohol abuse at times appears among Indian children by age thirteen; most seek complete intoxication. There is even one reported case of delirium tremens in a nine-year-old boy in northern New Mexico, himself the son of an alcoholic father. Maternal drinking has contributed to the growing incidence of fetal alcohol syndrome and has led also to an increased rate of other neonatal problems.[2] So intense is the desire to become intoxicated among some Indians today, especially on reservations in the West, that they mix cleaning solvents with other fluids in order to produce what is now known as "Montana Gin," a concoction that can cause profound somatic disorders, including aspiration pneumonia and organic brain syndrome, which can lead to death.[3] These social and clinical problems have occurred in spite of the fact that North American Indians, so far as clinicians and medical researchers can tell, are no more susceptible physiologically to abusing alcohol than other Americans.[4]

Yet in spite of the myriad problems associated with drinking, Indians' early use and abuse of alcohol have not been described in much depth. Some researchers, notably Nancy O. Lurie, Craig MacAndrew, and Roger Edgerton, have attempted to demonstrate the ways in which Indians have structured their drinking practices, but they have not focused on the social costs of the alcohol trade for Indians in early America.[5] Historians, often following the documentary evidence, have recognized

SOURCE: *American Indian Culture and Research Journal* 17:2 (1993), 15–42.

the catastrophic consequences of drinking; most today accept the fact that alcohol contributed to problems, particularly violence, in early Indian communities. Russell Thornton has even suggested that alcohol abuse contributed directly to mortality and thus to the depopulation of many groups.[6] Historians have made these assertions because colonial sources make one indisputable point: From Canada to West Florida and from the Atlantic to the western margins of British America in the Mississippi Valley, alcohol reached diverse groups of Indians during the seventeenth and eighteenth centuries, and most of the Indians who became involved in the liquor trade ultimately suffered as a result.[7]

But, although historians have recognized the outlines of the problem, virtually no substantial studies exist of alcohol use among the Indians who inhabited colonial British America. Such an absence is particularly noticeable given the existing work on Indians and alcohol in other parts of the Western Hemisphere, notably New France (Canada) and New Spain (Mexico). This work draws on the extensive documentation available for drinking practices in these Catholic colonies, much of it left by missionaries or church officials. Together, these studies describe, in more than general terms, the precise uses and costs of drinking in Indian communities in the colonies created by Europeans in the early modern period.[8]

This essay attempts to fill the gap by describing the ways that alcohol destabilized Indian communities in British America, the territory between the Atlantic and the Mississippi Valley from the mid-seventeenth century to the late eighteenth century. The sources for such study are vast; evidence of Indian drinking and the problems it created appear in colonial statutes, travelers' accounts, traders' ledgers, missionaries' diaries, and treaty negotiations, to name only the most prominent locations. Though abundant, the surviving accounts are not, in themselves, necessarily the surest evidence of abusive drinking among Indians. Most important, colonial descriptions of Indian drinking appear to conform to certain formulae; the dominant image of the drunken Indian often seems more a projection of ubiquitous colonial anxieties than an accurate assessment of Indian drinking practices. Further, colonial sources emphasize the consumption of alcohol by hunters, typically young men, but reports of children drinking, women selling liquor as well as consuming it, and older men imbibing along with others suggest that drinking was not limited to trading sessions where hunters met with liquor purveyors. Finally, colonists who wrote about Indian drinking often ignored the many Indians who abstained, thus giving the mistaken impression that all Indians drank. Still, the surviving evidence, however flawed, points unambiguously toward one conclusion: In the opinion of many colonists, Indians suffered from the alcohol trade.

Significantly, Indians agreed with colonists that liquor brought problems, but they drew their own conclusions about how alcohol changed their lives and who was responsible for liquor-related troubles. There are, to be sure, problems in interpreting Indian testimony, too. It has survived in documents written primarily by colonists and thus no doubt was constructed through certain culturally defined parameters. Further, colonists were not always aware that many Indians believed in the benefits of alcohol;

in eastern North America, alcohol helped some to achieve highly valued dream-like states of mind, and many Indians also incorporated alcohol into hospitality and mourning rites, marriages, and ceremonial dances.[9]

But although Indians throughout eastern North America often organized their drinking in culturally approved ways, many came to believe that liquor created tension and animosity in their villages, dangerously reoriented the economies of their communities, led to domestic violence, and further facilitated the conquest of eastern North America by colonists. Most important, while some Indians blamed other Indians for the ill effects of drinking, many placed the responsibility for their problems with colonists who either participated in the trade directly or allowed it to continue in spite of mounting evidence of its enormous costs. In the end, as many Indians discovered, the alcohol trade became perhaps the most insidious aspect of European colonialism in North America.

"A Peculiar Kind of Insobriety"

Europeans first provided liquor to Indians in the sixteenth century, and, over time, alcohol became increasingly prominent in intercultural trade in British America. Hundreds of references to Indian drinking appear in the extant documents from the colonial period. Colonial accounts provide unambiguous evidence that spirits, particularly rum, threatened groups of Indians and thus made their survival, already at risk because of the spread of Old World pathogens, ever more precarious. Given the apparent impact of alcohol on Indians and the persistent colonial fears about the threats represented by disorderly Indians, it is not surprising that colonists often wrote about the destructive impact of liquor on Indians. These observations contain more than information about the consumption of alcohol. Taken together, they represent what colonists intended to be a devastating critique of Indian society. Yet, in spite of their cultural blinders, colonists left ample testimony about the social costs of alcohol for Indians, especially the way that drinking led to violence, accidents, community disruptions, poverty, and, on occasion, death. The diffusion of such information throughout the colonies had little impact on the trade. Colonists were so eager to trade with the indigenous peoples of America that they maintained the commerce in spite of its devastating impact on Indian communities.

The liquor trade developed and grew over time, because traders believed they could always sell liquor to Indians; unlike durable manufactured goods, it was depleted when used. Unfortunately, the paucity of exact information about the population history of Indians in eastern North America and the even less accessible information regarding the numbers of Indians who actually consumed alcohol when it was available make estimates of per capita consumption exceedingly vague and limited; the best that exist relate to local areas only and pertain to episodic drinking bouts.[10]

Still, it is possible to estimate the extent of the trade, at least for the eighteenth century. In the northern reaches of European colonization, Hudson's Bay Company traders made brandy a staple of their fur trade. Although they sold only seventy gallons to Indians in 1700 from their post at Fort Albany-Eastmain, the volume increased to just over two thousand gallons of brandy sold each year from the four posts they operated in the late 1750s, and the trade continued well beyond the colonial period.[11] Further south, the trade was far more extensive, at least by the 1760s and 1770s, when the best evidence is available. In spite of problems associated with overland and water carriage of liquor from the coast across the Appalachian Mountains, George Morgan, a partner in the prominent Philadelphia trading firm of Baynton, Wharton, and Morgan, had almost eight thousand gallons of alcohol, most of it distilled spirits from the West Indies, at his trading post at Kaskaskia in the Illinois country in December 1767; he intended to sell most (if not all) of it to Indians.[12] Traders brought at least sixty-five hundred gallons of rum to Fort Pitt in 1767, and Alexander McKee, the local commissary of Indian affairs at the post, believed that "double that Quantity is brought here by them exclusive of large Quantities brought up by Sutlers and others." According to Jehu Hay, the Detroit commissary of Indian affairs, traders brought over twenty-four thousand gallons of rum to that post in 1767. As both McKee and Hay informed Sir William Johnson, the fur trade prospered at both posts, with traders receiving more than 300,000 skins that year.[13] Johnson was already well aware of the extent of the rum trade: In 1764, he estimated that traders sold fifty thousand gallons of rum to Indians in the territory under the auspices of the northern department of the superintendent of Indian affairs.[14]

Although it seems unlikely that there was sufficient liquor to allow any Indian who wanted alcohol to be constantly inebriated if he or she so chose, the available rum did allow for fairly regular drinking bouts. Colonial observers often attended Indian drinking sessions, although they did not quite know what to make of the Indians' drinking practices. Missionaries and colonial officials generally believed that drinking led to the decay of Indian communities and that sexual excess, violent death, domestic strife, and poverty all followed in the wake of drinking. Some colonists particularly lamented the impact of alcohol on their efforts to convert Indians to Christianity.

Colonial descriptions of Indian drinking sprees began with the premise that intoxicated Indians followed a predictable pattern. François Vachon de Belmont, who became a missionary in the Sulpician Order in the early 1680s and traveled from France to New France to convert Indians to Christianity, observed drinking practices among Indians who inhabited the Northeast and wrote the most extensive critique of Indian drinking patterns. Liquor, he argued, caused three basic changes in Indians: First, he wrote, it "enlivens their natural sluggishness, dispels their timidity, their sense of shame and inferiority, which their dull nature gives them." Second, liquor prompted Indians "to undertake with vigor and bravado almost any evil action such as anger, vengeance, or impurity." Third, drunkenness provided Indians with "a valid excuse for any evil which they might commit in such a condition." These changes were unique to Indians, or so he thought when he wrote that "this is a peculiar kind of insobriety."[15]

Indians "imbibe only to become drunk," Belmont declared. This was most evident when there was a limited amount of alcohol available to a particular group. Rather than share the liquor equally, presumably as Europeans would do in such circumstances, the Indians chose one of their number to consume all of the liquor and thereby become inebriated, while the others remained completely sober. There was, he wrote, "only one degree of drunkenness worthwhile, the sort which they call 'Gannontiouaratonseri,' complete insobriety. And when they begin to feel the effects of the brandy they rejoice shouting, 'Good, good, my head is reeling.'" Most of those who drank in this fashion were young men "who are professedly given to bravado, whose pride urges them to seek notoriety whereby they may receive attention for some deed or other."[16] The Reverend John Clayton, rector of the parish at James City, Virginia, during the mid-1680s offered a similar view of the reasons Indians drank as they did. "[T]hey will allways drink to excess if they can possibly get [spirits]," he wrote in 1697, "but do not much care for them unless they can have enough to make them drunk. I have heard it said that they wonder much of the English for purchasing wine at so dear a rate when Rum is much cheaper & will make them sooner drunk."[17]

Along with the other horrors, Indian drinking proved particularly frustrating to clerics because drunkenness impeded conversion to Christianity. Inebriated Indians could not, they believed, make the rational choice to convert; made senseless by liquor, Indians were unable to realize the full import of the missionaries' teachings. Such views were common among Catholic missionaries in Canada,[18] and British colonists had similar thoughts. At times, missionaries themselves came under fire for allegedly taking liquor to Indians and thus compromising the effort to spread Christianity. In a sermon published in Boston in 1704, Cotton Mather attacked an "Indian-Preacher" who possessed both scripture and liquor. "But he minded his Bottel more than his *Bible*," Mather declared, and thus weakened his ability to convert Indians to Christian ways.[19]

The colonists' critique of Indian drinking also included a great interest in the role liquor played in releasing Indians from their sexual inhibitions. Inebriated Indians' sexual behavior particularly fascinated natural historians. Nicholas Denys, during his travels in Acadia, and Bernard Romans, during his sojourn in East and West Florida, noted that consumption of alcohol had an immediate impact on Indians' sexual mores.[20] So did William Bartram, who, while touring the Southeast in the early 1770s, found a rapid change in a group of Creeks near Mount Royal, in Georgia, after they had returned from St. Augustine with "a very liberal supply of spirituous liquors, about twenty kegs, each containing five gallons." Once they began to drink, they continued for ten days. "In a few days this festival exhibited one of the most ludicrous bacchanalian scenes that is possible to be conceived," Bartram wrote. "White and red men and women without distinction, passed the day merrily with these jovial, amorous topers, and the nights in convivial songs, dances, and sacrifices to Venus, as long as they could stand or move; for in these frolics both sexes take such liberties with each other, and act, without constraint or shame, such scenes as they would abhor when sober or in their senses; and would endanger their ears and even their lives." Soon, however, the liquor ran out. Most of the Creeks, Bartram noted, were "sick through intoxication," and, when they became more sober, "the dejected lifeless sots would pawn every thing they were in possession of, for a mouthful of spirits to settle their stomachs, as they termed it."[21]

While some colonists came to lament the way that liquor led to sexual license and thus interfered with the civilizing of Indians, most had more mundane concerns, especially related to the violent consequences of Indian drinking for both colonists and Indians. For this reason, colonists had feared Indian drunkenness from the start. On the eve of settlement, the governor and deputy of the New England Company forbade colonists going to Massachusetts Bay from selling liquor to Indians. "Wee pray you endeavor," they wrote, "though there be much strong water sent for sale, yett so to order it as that the salvages may not for lucre sake bee induced to the excessive use, or rather abuse of it, and of any hand take care or people give noe ill example."[22] William Bradford, ever wary of disorder that could threaten Plymouth, acted swiftly to limit what he believed were the dangerous excesses of Thomas Morton's antics at Merrymount. Among Morton's sins, along with providing the Indians with firearms and scrawling salacious verse on a maypole, was his apparent provision of liquor to Indians.[23]

Over the course of the seventeenth century, New England colonists repeatedly tried to limit the sale of alcohol to Indians. As early as July 1633, provincial officials in Massachusetts Bay ordered that "noe man shall sell or (being in a course of trading) give any stronge water to any Indean." Although the colony relaxed its statutes when it allowed Indians who brought in the head of a wolf to receive three quarts of wine for their reward and even allowed some traders to sell wine to Indians, problems of Indian intemperance prompted provincial officials in the late 1650s to stop the trade. Since the General Court lamented its failure to limit "excessive drinkinge & drunkenes among the Indians" and noted that "the fruits whereof are murther & other outrages," the elimination of the liquor trade was not surprising. Fearing the disorder that accompanied Indian drinking, provincial officials detailed severe fines and corporal punishment for Indians found inebriated and for colonists who provided them with liquor.[24]

Nonetheless, over time the use of liquor spread throughout British America and led to violence, at least in the opinion of colonial witnesses who were quick to describe what they believed were the savage aspects of Indians' lives. Explorer and author John Lawson wrote in his widely reprinted account of early eighteenth-century Carolina that Indians "will part with the dearest Thing they have" to buy rum, "and when they have got a little in their Heads, are the impatients Creatures living, 'till they have enough to make 'em quite drunk; and the most miserable Spectacles when they are so, some falling into the Fires, burn their Legs or Arms, contracting the Sinews, and become Cripples all their Life-time; others from Precipices break their Bones and Joints, with abundance of Instance, yet none are so great to deter them from that accurs'd Practice of Drunkenness, though sensible how many of them (are by it) hurry'd into the other World before their Time, as themselves oftentimes confess." Lawson noted that "[m]ost of the Savages are addicted to Drunkenness," and that it contributed directly to the decline of southern Indians; combined with smallpox, rum "made such a Destruction amongst them, that, on good grounds, I do believe, there is not the sixth Savage living within two hundred Miles of all our Settlements, as there were fifty Years ago."[25]

The violence attending Indian drinking sessions troubled colonists throughout British America. "Drunkenness hath occasioned some *Indians* to be burnt to Death in their little Houses," declared Samuel Danforth, preaching at Bristol, Rhode Island, in October 1709 at the execution of two Indians who had committed murder while intoxicated. "Other *Indians* by their being drowned first in Drink, have been exposed to a second drowning in Water. Nor are these the first (who now stand in the midst of this great Assembly) who have committed Murder, when overcome with Drink, and have been Executed for it."[26] Charles Stuart, brother of the southern superintendent of Indian affairs John Stuart and an agent to the Choctaw, believed that liquor constituted four-fifths of the trade goods purchased by those Indians in 1770. Traveling among their settlements a few years later, he wrote that he "saw nothing but rum Drinking and Women Crying over the Dead bodies of their relations who have died by Rum." Liquor, he believed, fundamentally disrupted the social order because of the violence it seemingly released; it was "the cause of their killing each other daily" and the "[c]ause of every disturbance in the nation."[27] Stuart was not the only one in the southern Indian administration concerned with the violence committed by drunken Indians; the emissary to the Creek in 1771, David Taitt, often encountered intoxicated Indians seemingly always on the verge of attacking him or someone nearby. Taitt, like agents throughout the South, knew well that rum had become a staple of the skin trade in the Southeast in spite of the troubles it brought.[28]

According to colonial observers, drinking often led Indians to injure or kill each other. Some colonists speculated that Indians feigned drunkenness in order to attack other Indians and not suffer any consequences.[29] Others described less deliberate assaults. The sale of rum by unlicensed traders throughout the South endangered "the general Peace and Tranquility" of southern Indians, agent Thomas Bosworth wrote in December 1752; a "general Peace and Quietness reigns among them," another agent wrote to South Carolina Governor Glen in August 1754, "excepting what Disturbance is occasioned by immoderate Quantities of Rum brought among them, which if a Stop put to, would very much contribute towards a good Harmoney among the Indians."[30] Trader and historian James Adair, writing on the eve of the Revolution, also noted decidedly self-destructive behavior. "By some fatality," he wrote in a description of the Catawba, "they are much addicted to excessive drinking, and spirituous liquors distract them so exceedingly, that they will even eat live coals of fire."[31] William Byrd joined the chorus as well. "The trade [the Indians] have had the misfortune to drive with the English," he wrote in his *History of the Dividing Line betwixt Virginia and North Carolina,* "has furnished them constantly with rum, which they have used so immoderately that, what with the distempers and what with the quarrels it begat amongst them, it has proved a double destruction."[32]

The violence brought on by alcohol, combined with an apparent decline in the health of drinkers, led some observers to make direct links between the trade and Indian mortality. Drinking, familiar to the Powhatan Indians of the Chesapeake region by the 1680s, prompted the governor of Maryland to speculate that "the Indians of these parts decrease very much, partly owing to smallpox, but the great cause of all is their being so devilishly given to drink."[33] Almost a century later, Guy Johnson, who briefly served as superintendent of Indian affairs in the northern colonies after the death in 1774 of his uncle, Sir William Johnson, also believed that alcohol contri-buted to Indian population decline. "The State of Population is greatest where there is the least Intercourse with the Europeans," he wrote, in part because alcohol was "peculiarly fatal to their Constitutions, & to their Increase," especially when combined with small-pox.[34] Benjamin Franklin agreed. "[I]f it be the Design of Providence to extirpate these Savages in order to make room for Cultivators of the Earth," he wrote in his autobi-ography, "it seems not improbable that Rum may be the appointed Means. It has already annihilated all the Tribes who formerly inhabited the Sea-Coast."[35]

Though such statements demonstrated concern on the part of colonists for the apparent plight of Indians, other colonists had more mundane concerns: They feared Indian drinking because of the potential for violence by inebriated Indians against colonists. Concerns about Indian assaults led numerous colonial officials to pass laws banning the sale of alcohol to Indians in virtually every British North American colony, although some of these statutes were short-lived.[36]

But, even when these laws were in force, traders quickly discovered ways to cir-cumvent them, and some inebriated Indians acted exactly as colonists feared.[37] At times, colonists caused the trouble,[38] but more often, in the opinion of colonial lead-ers, Indians were to blame. Indians in Maine, purportedly inebriated, traveled to a colonial settlement and threatened to attack colonists and their livestock; other colonists apprehended them before they had done much damage, and the colonist who had provided them with rum subsequently found himself facing a magistrate in Boston, charged with violating laws prohibiting the sale of liquor to Indians.[39] John Toby, a Nanticoke in Pennsylvania, purportedly sexually assaulted an eight-year-old colonial girl. According to the complaint of the girl's father, recorded in a deposition, Toby responded to the allegation by saying "that he had been drunk and did not Remember what he did with the girl." Three colonists then took him off to jail to await a trial.[40] Readers of the first edition of *The American Magazine, or a Monthly View of the Political State of the British Colonies,* published in Philadelphia in January 1741, could read about a murder committed by a drunken Indian. "The *Indians* who live nearer the *English,* and, by Reason of that Vicinity, have more frequent Oppor-tunities of intoxicating themselves with strong Liquors," the magazine reported, "are indeed more dangerous: so that it happen'd once in about fifty Years, that one of them, in a drunken Fit slew an *Englishman.*" The murderer was, the readers were reassured, subsequently hanged, and "[h]is Country-men, instead of murmuring at, highly approved of that Act of Justice."[41] For missionaries living among Indians, the risks seemed even more immediate, as the Protestant missionary Gideon Hawley dis-covered during a 1753 trip to Oquaga, a community of Indians from various tribes located alongside the Susquehanna River; there he encountered a number of inebri-ated Indians, one of whom, apparently by accident, nearly shot his head off. After his experiences with Indian drinking, it was no wonder that he refused to establish a mis-sion in any community where Indians allowed alcohol.[42]

Violence, however, proved only the most obvious risk of Indian drinking; the long-term economic consequences of the liquor trade appeared, to numerous colonial observers, just as devastating to Indians and, ultimately, to colonists also. In spite of a 1711 law in South Carolina forbidding the sale of rum by unlicensed traders, Indians there continued to fall into debt to liquor purveyors. The problem so exasperated southern colonial officials that they periodically forgave the debt of the Indians.[43] Yet the problems remained. Thomas Bosomworth, an agent to the Creek, noted in his journal that liquor continued to impoverish Indians. "Nothing worthy of Notice during our Stay here," he wrote in October 1752 in a discussion of a meeting of provincial agents with the lower Creek, "though I could not help remarking the extream Poverty and Nakedness of those Indians that are contiguous to the French Fort [where] they are supplied with Liquor for those Goods they purchase from our Traders. The fatal Effects of which the Indians themselves are sencible off."[44] Northern commentators agreed. New England Indians "will part with all they have to their bare skins" to purchase rum, naturalist John Josselyn wrote in the mid-1670s, "being perpetually drunk with it, as long as it is to be had, it hath killed many of them, especially old women who have dyed when dead drunk."[45]

By the mid-eighteenth century, the problems associated with the illegal rum trade, especially the economic plight of Indians apparently defrauded by liquor dealers, greatly troubled some colonists involved in the transatlantic skin trades. Charleston merchant Edmund Atkin, who became the southern superintendent of Indian affairs in 1755, believed that alcohol undermined the trade network and had disastrous consequences for the English. Rum traders working out of Augusta were particularly troublesome. These nefarious dealers placed "themselves near the Towns, in the way of the Hunters returning home with their deer Skins," he wrote. "The poor Indians in a manner fascinated, are unable to resist the Bait; and when Drunk are easily cheated. After parting with the fruit of three or four Months Toil, they find themselves at home, without the means of buying the necessary Clothing for themselves or their Families." In such a state, they were "dispose[d] for Mischief"; a "licentiousness hath crept in among [the young] men, beyond the Power of the Head Men to Remedy." Even the quality of the deerskins declined in such circumstances, since the rum peddlers needed to deal quickly and then leave with their wares, and Indians accustomed to trading lower quality skins for liquor proved to be less cooperative commercial partners: "[T]he Indians require the other Traders in their Towns to take [deerskins] in the same Condition." Drunken Indians, Atkin warned, became embittered when liquor was used to purchase their land, as he claimed it was among the Chickasaw on the Savannah River, and inebriated Indians proved easy prey to colonists who wished to murder Indians.[46] Northern officials also believed that colonists threatened the entire system of intercultural trade when they deceived Indians with alcohol.[47]

Faced with a growing body of evidence that drunken Indians threatened colonists, as well as other Indians, in a number of ways, some observers looked for the source of the problem. Many blamed selfish traders for undermining efforts to convert Indians and for supplying Indians with liquor. "While the present ill adapted measures are continued," Adair wrote in a plea for better organization of the Indian trade, "nothing less than the miraculous power of deity can possibly effect the Indians' reformation; many of the present traders are abandoned, reprobate white savages. Instead of showing good examples of moral conduct, besides their other part of life, they instruct the unknowing and imitating savages in many diabolical lessons of obscenity and blasphemy." It would have been impossible for colonial commentators to imagine a worse group of people to be in constant contact with Indians.[48]

Many colonists believed that Indians were ultimately accountable for their own behavior. Although high-ranking colonial officials periodically sought to limit the trade by passing laws making it illegal, they also repeatedly excoriated Indians for their drinking; their efforts to stop Indian drinking often seem little more than criticism of particular Indians' ways of life, especially their inability to control their appetites. Governor George Johnstone of West Florida, addressing a group of Chickasaw and Choctaw at a treaty in Mobile in March 1765, feared that liquor-bearing traders created animosity among the Indians. To prevent trouble, he urged Indians not to drink, stressing the economic and social plight that resulted from drinking. But, although the governor cast blame on the traders (those "Guilty of carrying that Liquor amongst you ought to be Considered as your real Enemies much more than if they lifted the Hatchet against you," he stated) he tried to shame Indians into avoiding liquor. "He who dies in War, his Time shall be remembered," he declared, "but he who is destroyed by Drunkenness shall be forgott like the Hog who has perished in the swamp."[49]

Few expressed criticism of Indian life as effectively as Sir William Johnson, perhaps the best-informed colonial official in regards to the rum trade because of his many years living in the New York hinterland, where he was first a trader and then superintendent of Indian affairs for the northern colonies. Although he, like others, blamed traders for carrying rum into the backcountry, he ultimately believed it was the Indians' inability to resist liquor that caused their problems. "The Indians in general are so devoted to & so debauched by Rum," he wrote to James Abercromby in May 1758, "that all Business with them is thrown into confusion by it & my transactions with them unspeakably impeded. The Mohock Castles in particular are become scenes of perpetual riot, and the Indians selling the necessaries they receive from the Crown thro me for Rum, to the infinite detriment of His Majestys service & the increase of Indian Expences." But what, he wondered, could he do about the problem. "Provincial penal Laws have been made, but to no purpose," he averred. "I have done all in my power against this universal Enemy, to indeed His Majestys service in general, but it is too subtle & too powerful a one for me to reduce within proper bounds as to the Indians."[50]

Nine years later, after he had defended the economic utility of the liquor trade in a report to the Lords of Trade,[51] Johnson clarified his views further when he told a group of Indians who claimed they had been unable to control their desire for liquor that "[t]he best Medicine I can think of to prevent your falling into your former Vice of drinking is to embrace Christianity" and that they should follow the example of other sober Indians.[52] Johnson, it should be noted, was at the same time sending his own trading agents into the woods, often supplying them with little else but rum for trade with the Indians.[53]

The reports of colonial observers, despite their biases, reveal certain similarities. Young men drank more often than other members of most communities, no doubt because they had the most frequent interactions with traders, especially liquor purveyors who worked beyond the bounds of legal trading posts. Further, in all likelihood, the costs of drinking, whether borne by the young hunters or the entire community, differed somewhat by season; mortality rates due to accidents were higher in winter when inebriated Indians ran a greater risk of exposure, especially in northern climates. In addition, regardless of the gender or age of the person who died as a result of an alcohol-related accident, Indian families suffered profoundly; the loss of family members disrupted the domestic economy and had a shattering impact on those who remained after the tragedy.[54]

In the end, many colonial descriptions of Indian drinking reveal that liquor played a key role in the effort to colonize British America. In the seventeenth and eighteenth centuries, missionaries, traders, and government officials were engaged in a campaign, not always successful, to convert Indians to European ways.[55] Indians needed to trade, colonizers argued, to become civilized. And even though the liquor trade was destructive, it had to be maintained. Without it, Johnson informed the Lords of Trade in October 1764, in a moment of remarkable frankness, "the Indians can purchase their cloathing with half the quantity of Skins, which will make them indolent, and lessen the fur trade."[56] Legislators who tried to ban the liquor trade because they believed that Indians were unable to control their thirst for alcohol took a different approach, to be sure. But their inability to stop the commerce revealed that many other colonists believed the trade should continue, and these commercial interests prevailed. However diverse the existing views on the liquor trade, colonial observers shared one belief: Indians needed colonists to guide them in a world seemingly awash in liquor. Many Indians saw the situation quite differently.

"The Accursed Use We Make of Rum"

Despite some colonists' fears, Indians suffered more than colonists did from drinking and from the alcohol trade. The survival of their testimony on the subject leaves little doubt that the social problems observed by colonists—including poverty, domestic violence, and even fatalities—were far more desperate than colonists could understand. But, although Indians who have left records of their beliefs about alcohol did not always agree with one another, they also did not necessarily agree with colonial commentators. While many acknowledged that they could not control alcohol consumption and thus needed assistance in their battle against liquor, they also believed that colonists bore ultimate responsibility for the havoc alcohol brought to their communities. Colonists, not Indians, had initiated what an anonymous author, purported to be a Creek Indian, termed "the bewitching Tyranny of Custom."[57] Such logic led many Indians to condemn the alcohol trade and those colonists who let it continue.

To be sure, some Indians, perhaps following the lead of colonial leaders, blamed themselves for the ill effects of drinking. "[W]hen we drink it, it makes us mad," declared several leaders of Delaware Valley Indians in the late seventeenth century. "[W]e do not know what we do, we then abuse one another; we throw each other into the Fire, Seven Score of our People have been killed, by reason of the drinking of it, since the time it was first sold us."[58] Alcohol, some Indians believed, eroded the ties needed to maintain communities. A group of Chickasaw informed a colonial official in 1725 that they were unable to keep members of their village under control because "if the Young Men were drunk and Mad," they "could not help it," but they would do their best to minimize the problems.[59]

In what became the most famous printed assault of any Indian on the liquor trade, Samson Occom, a Mohegan who became a missionary and who himself purportedly had problems with liquor, exhorted his "Indian Brethren" to stop drinking. Occom's attack on Indian intemperance clearly shows the influence of his Christian teachings. Writing in response to the execution of Moses Paul, a Christian Indian who, when drunk, had murdered Moses Cook, Occom wrote a broadside in 1772 warning of the dangers of alcohol. "My kindred Indians, pray attend and hear," he wrote in verse form, "With great attention and with godly fear; / This day I warn you of that cursed sin, That poor, despised Indians wallow in." The sin was drunkenness, and it led to a host of social problems in addition to this particular murder.

> Mean are our houses, and we are kept low,
> And almost naked, shivering we go;
> Pinch'd for food and almost starv'd we are,
> And many times put up with stinking fare. . . .
> Our little children hovering round us weep,
> Most starv'd to death we've nought for them to eat;
> All this distress is justly on us come,
> For the accursed use we make of rum.

Occom continued his attack on liquor in sixteen verses, most often noting the social costs of drinking: Drunken Indians, he wrote, were unable to "go, stand, speak, or sit"; they risked increased chances for being defrauded and scorned; children and women also became inebriated; Indians who drank descended to a lower order of existence, "On level with the beasts and far below / Are we when with strong drink we reeling go." Not surprisingly, Occom concluded his remarks with an appeal that Indians convert to Christianity and thus presumably shed the barbarous traits that had led to drunkenness in the first place.[60] His sermon on the subject covered these points in greater depth, often echoing the tone of Puritan assaults on excessive drinking; it proved so popular that it was published in a ninth edition by 1774.[61] As Occom no doubt knew well, however, even Indians who converted to Christianity occasionally stumbled into intemperance.[62]

Indians living in communities with missionaries also blamed themselves for alcohol-related maladies. They thought that members of their towns who were thirsty for rum threatened the economies of backcountry villages by concentrating their efforts on hunting instead of agriculture, since pelts, not corn, purchased liquor. Not coincidentally, Indians in these communities also overhunted indigenous furbearing animals, thereby endangering the fur trade. Some men, village residents complained, spent so much time hunting that they neglected their crops, with devastating implications for the survival of their communities. "It is quite evident that there are now so few Indians, when they had been so numerous formerly," several Nanticokes told two Moravian missionaries visiting Onondaga, the meeting place of the Iroquois tribes in central New York, in July 1754. "The cause of this falling off is their use of too much rum. Let the Indians try to do without rum for but four years even, and they will be astonished at the increase of the population, and at the decrease of diseases and early death. All this is the result of rum drinking, which is also the primary cause of famine among them, caused by their not planting their crops at the proper time."[63]

Although some Indians accepted responsibility for the troubles brought by drinking, others looked outward for the source of their distress. They decided to act on their beliefs by demanding that colonial officials end the liquor trade because of its disastrous effects on the economies of their villages. Time and again, Indians claimed that colonists had repudiated earlier agreements to stop the flow of alcohol into the hinterland. Charles Thomson recounted numerous Indian complaints about the alcohol trade, and he publicized his views in *An Enquiry into the Causes of the Alienation of the Delaware and Shawnee Indians from the British Interest,* printed in London in 1759. At a treaty council between leaders of the Mingo, Shawnee, and Conoy at Conestoga in 1722, the Indians, according to Thomson, urged Governor Keith of Pennsylvania to stop the trade. "At this Treaty the *Indians* complain of the Damage they receive by strong Liquor being brought among them," he wrote. "They say, 'The *Indians* could live contentedly and grow rich, if it were not for the Quantities of Rum that is suffered to come amongst them, contrary to what *William Penn* promised.'" At other sessions, Indians in Pennsylvania complained that traders brought little else but rum with them to trading sessions, instead of the goods, such as shot and powder, that the Indians needed. Many Indians sold their clothing for liquor, the Conestoga chief Tawenna noted at a meeting in Philadelphia in 1729, "'and are much impoverished thereby.'"[64]

Indians throughout the hinterland joined the effort to stop the liquor trade. In August 1731, two Indian leaders, the Delaware sachem Sassoonan and the Iroquois Shickellamy, pleaded with Pennsylvania officials to stop rum sellers traveling to Indian villages because, as Sassoonan declared, "'tis to be feared by means of Rum Quarrels may happen between them & Murther ensue, which may tend to dissolve that Union & loosen the Tye" between British colonists and Indians; to prevent problems, these Indians wanted rum to be available for sale only in colonial settlements.[65] Later, Indians became more strident in their requests. In the late 1760s and early 1770s, Sir William Johnson received reports or heard complaints from groups of Miami, Shawnee, Delaware, and Oneida who wanted the alcohol trade stopped.[66] "[I]t is You that Make the liquor," a Shawnee spokesman informed a colonial official at Fort Pitt in 1771, "and to you we must look to Stop it." The Indians wanted help immediately. "[I]f no Method can be fallen upon to prevent their bringing Rum into the Country, the Consequences must be dreadful; All the Western Nations fear it as well as us, and we all know well that it is in your great Men's Power to Stop it, and make us happy, if they thought it worth the Trouble."[67]

Indians battled the liquor trade because the commerce could, on occasion, lead to profoundly destructive tensions within their communities; on occasion, it created trouble between men and women in backcountry villages. A group of Delaware Indians told Charles Beatty, who was traveling through the Ohio country in 1766 on an exploratory venture for the Presbyterian church, that they wanted to complain about the participation of Indian women in the trade. "[T]here are some that do at times hire some of our Squaws to goe to Bed with them & give them rum for it," they declared; "this thing is very Bad, & the Squaws again selling the Rum to our People make them Drunk." Although intercultural sexual relations were not new in the region, these Indians found the inclusion of rum in the relationship wholly inappropriate. "[W]e Beseech you," they concluded, "to advise our Brothers against this thing & do what you can to have it stopped."[68]

More devastating still was the alcohol-related poverty that led some Indians to contemplate putting an end to the fur trade. When Pennsylvania trader and provincial negotiator Conrad Weiser traveled through the backcountry of the middle colonies in March 1737, he found Indians at Otsiningo battling the alcohol trade. He had been to the town of the Onondaga and Shawnee along the Susquehanna River twelve years earlier and now discovered that this village was experiencing hard times. In his journal, he noted that the Indians were "short of provisions" and that "their children looked like dead persons and suffered much from hunger." Local Indians then presented what must have been a devastating omen. They told Weiser that they had difficulty finding game and that "the Lord and Creator of the world was resolved to destroy the Indians." They explained that one of their seers had "seen a vision of God," who declared that Indians killed game "for the sake of the skins, which you give for strong liquor and drown your senses, and kill one another, and carry on a dreadful debauchery. Therefore have I driven the wild animals out of the country, for they are mine. If you will do good and cease from your sins, I will bring them back; if not, I will destroy you from off the earth." The Indians, according to Weiser, believed the seer's story. "Time will show, said they, what is to happen to us," he wrote. "[R]um will kill us and leave the land clear for the Europeans without strife or purchase."[69] Contained within the vision was an unambiguous message. If Indians halted the fur trade, they would no longer suffer from the liquor trade; the hunters' sins could be erased and the community purged of its debauchery.

To many Indians, the social costs of the liquor trade were ubiquitous, especially the violence drinking caused. Colonists mistreated Indians when they were drunk, declared a group of Maine Indians in 1677. "[W]e love yo," their petition declared, "but when we are dronk you will take away our cot & throw us out of dore." Further, meanspirited colonists sometimes gave Indians liquor "& wen we were drunk killed us."[70] Dutch traveler Jaspar Danckaerts, journeying through New York near the end of the seventeenth century, encountered an Indian who explained, quite clearly, that although drinking weakened Indian communities, the fault lay entirely with those who sold alcohol to the Indians. The Indian, named Jasper, noted that divine spirits governed life on earth and punished those "'who do evil and drink themselves drunk,'" yet he also freely admitted that he drank to excess and did not have to fear retribution. Asked by colonists why he drank, Jasper replied, "'I had rather not, but my heart is so inclined that it causes me to do it, although I know it is wrong. The Christians taught it to us, and give us or sell us the drink, and drink themselves drunk.'" Apparently annoyed at his answer, the colonists responded that if they lived near the Indians, the Indians would never see them inebriated nor would they provide liquor to the Indians. "'That,'" he replied, according to Danckaerts, "'would be good.'"[71]

In some important ways, Indian beliefs differed markedly from those of colonists. Indians did not share the view that drinking led to bacchanalian orgies, although some felt that drinking threatened relations between men and women in Indian communities. Most Indians did not believe that liquor impeded their religious lives but some certainly thought that the trade did threaten their customary relations with the animals they hunted. Indians in eastern North America had many reasons to consume alcohol, and they did not believe their drunken comportment indicated, as some colonists apparently believed, that they were culturally inferior to colonists.

ALCOHOL AND COLONIALISM

For all their differences, the testimony of Indians and colonists agrees on one point: The alcohol that came from trade with colonists destabilized many Indian communities. Although it was not clear to early Americans, it now seems evident that the liquor trade promoted British imperial expansion in North America. While some colonists and Indians might have exaggerated the role played by alcohol in the decline of Indian populations, abundant evidence confirms that the liquor trade impoverished Indians and threatened their families. Since Indians throughout most of the colonial period had to cope with the continuing inroads of epidemic disease as well as colonists' seemingly insatiable hunger for land, alcohol apparently played a key role in the social decline and eventual disappearance of many villages. The desire to become intoxicated did not, in itself, force Indians into desperate circumstances, but the poverty caused by the liquor trade could have contributed to the decision of many Indians to sell their lands to colonists and migrate westward in search of greater opportunity.

Further, the liquor trade and Indian responses to it reinforced the cultural chasm separating the peoples of North America. To colonists, Indians' inability to control their drinking—to drink, that is, as colonists did—seemed a sign that Indians remained a people apart, perhaps forever inferior and savage. Although colonists often recognized the problems brought by liquor—as early as September 1673, the General Assembly of Rhode Island condemned the "abominable filthynes" of selling alcohol to Indians[72]— colonial officials proved either unable or unwilling to halt the trade. Economic logic dictated that the trade continue lest the English receive fewer skins, a prospect even those intimately familiar with the costs of Indian drinking chose to avoid. Stopping this commerce, even if it was possible, would also have meant repudiating a long-standing effort, dating to the sixteenth century, to turn Indians into trade partners.[73]

Although alcohol contributed to the spread of the empire by weakening the social structure and economic basis of Indian communities, it simultaneously created resentment among Indians that gave them added determination to battle the expansion of colonial settlements. It is thus not surprising that Indian prophets who led revitalization movements in the late colonial period made temperance one of their primary goals.[74] It is also quite likely that whatever success these prophets enjoyed stemmed, at least in part, from earlier Indian efforts to resist the tide of colonization by battling the liquor trade.

Whatever the social costs of the alcohol trade, liquor remained a staple of Indian-colonist trade in the American hinterland. The commerce survived because it apparently was profitable to colonists involved in the business, and because it represented a valuable enterprise in the mercantile empire. Few, if any, colonists celebrated the troubles Indians experienced because of the liquor trade. But even when Indians made the social costs known, colonists too easily ascribed the Indians' sufferings to faults of the Indians themselves. In an age when many other Americans were working relentlessly to overthrow the imperial tyrant who, they believed, threatened their freedom, many Indians found the liquor trade, and the empire it represented, another kind of tyranny that threatened to destroy their world.

NOTES

1. Roland J. Lamarine, "Alcohol Abuse among Native Americans," *Journal of Community Health* 13 (1988), 143–55; Ronet Bachman, "The Social Causes of American Indian Homicide as Revealed by the Life Experiences of Thirty Offenders," *American Indian Quarterly* 15 (1991), 471, 484–87; Margaret M. Gallaher et al., "Pedestrian and Hypothermia Deaths among Native Americans in New Mexico," *JAMA* 267 (1992), 1345–48. See also Patricia Silk-Walker et al., "Alcoholism, Alcohol Abuse, and Health in American Indians and Alaska Natives," *American Indian and Alaska Native Mental Health Research,* monograph no. 1 (1988), 65–67.

2. David Swanson et al., "Alcohol Abuse in a Population of Indian Children," *Diseases of the Nervous System* 32 (1971), 835–42; Duane Sherwin and Beverly Mead, "Delirium Tremens in a Nine Year Old Child," *American Journal of Psychiatry* 132 (1975), 1210–12; L. P. Peterson et al., "Pregnancy Complications in Sioux Children," *Obstetrics and Gynecology* 64 (1984), 519–23; Albert DiNicola, "Might Excessive Maternal Alcohol Ingestion During Pregnancy Be a Risk Factor Associated with an Increased Likelihood of SIDS?" (letter) *Clinical Pediatrics* 24 (1985), 659. The most moving account of FAS is Michael Dorris's *The Broken Cord* (New York: Harper & Row, 1989).

3. Larry Burd et al., "'Montana Gin': Ingestion of Commercial Products Containing Denatured Alcohol among Native Americans," *Journal of Studies on Alcohol* 48 (1987), 388–89.

4. Lynn J. Bennion and Ting-Kai Li, "Alcohol Metabolism in American Indians and Whites: Lack of Racial Differences in Metabolic Rate and Liver Alcohol Dehydrogenase," *New England Journal of Medicine* 294 (1976), 9–13; Carol Lujan, "Alcohol-Related Deaths of American Indians," *JAMA* 267 (1992), 1384; and Arthur W. K. Chan, "Racial Differences in Alcohol Sensitivity," *Alcohol and Alcoholism* 21 (1986), 93–104. These studies replace earlier ones that suggested racial differences did exist; for one of these studies, see D. Fenna et al., "Ethanol Metabolism in Various Racial Groups" *Canadian Medical Association Journal* 105 (1971), 472–75.

5. Nancy O. Lurie, "The World's Oldest Ongoing Protest Demonstration: North American Indian Drinking Patterns," *Pacific Historical Review* 40 (1971), 311–22, and Craig MacAndrew and Robert B. Edgerton, *Drunken Comportment: A Social Explanation* (Chicago: Aldine, 1969), esp. 100–64.

6. Russell Thornton, *American Indian Holocaust and Survival: A Population History Since 1492* (Norman, OK: University of Oklahoma Press, 1987), 44–45, 54, 65–66, 83, 87–88.

7. For historians' views on Indian drinking and its consequences among particular groups of Indians, see, for example, Colin Calloway, *The Western Abenakis of Vermont, 1600–1800: War, Migration, and the Survival of an Indian People* (Norman, OK: University of Oklahoma Press, 1990), 87; James H. Merrell, *The Indians' New World: Catawbas and Their Neighbors from European Contact through the Era of Removal* (Chapel Hill, NC: University of North Carolina Press, 1989), 39–40, 98; Timothy Silver, *A New Face on the Countryside: Indians, Colonists, and Slaves in South Atlantic Forests, 1500–1800* (New York: Cambridge University Press, 1990), 87–88; Calvin Martin, *Keepers of the Game: Indian-Animal Relationships and the Fur Trade* (Berkeley, CA: University of California Press, 1978), 63–64; Peter C. Mancall, *Valley of Opportunity: Economic Culture along the Upper Susquehanna, 1700–1800* (Ithaca, NY: Cornell University Press, 1991), 60–64; Richard White, *The Roots of Dependency: Subsistence, Environment, and Social Change among the Choctaws, Pawnees, and Navajos* (Lincoln, NE: University of Nebraska Press, 1983), esp. 8286; idem, *The Middle Ground: Indians, Empires, and Republics in the Great Lakes Region, 1650–1815* (New York: Cambridge University Press, 1991), 115, 127–28, 131, 205, 207, 247, 264, 322–23, 333–35, 342; Eric Hinderaker, "The Creation of the American Frontier: Europeans and Indians in the Ohio River Valley, 1673–1800," (Ph.D. diss., Harvard University, 1991), 141–45, 324; Daniel H. Usner, Jr., *Indians, Settlers, and Slaves in a Frontier Exchange Economy: The Lower Mississippi Valley Before 1783* (Chapel Hill, NC: University of North Carolina Press, 1992), 97–98, 126–29, 135, 274. For one historian's view of the impact of alcohol on a number of Indian groups, see James Axtell, "The English Colonial Impact on Indian Culture," in Axtell, *The European and the Indian: Essays in the Ethnohistory of Colonial North America* (New York: Oxford University Press, 1981), 257–59.

8. For New Spain, see William Taylor, *Drinking, Homicide and Rebellion in Colonial Mexican Villages* (Stanford, CA: Stanford University Press, 1979); and Michael C. Scardaville, "Alcohol Abuse and Tavern Reform in Late Colonial Mexico City," *Hispanic American Historical Review* 60 (1980), 643–71. For New France, see William B. Munro, "The Brandy Parliament of 1678," *Canadian Historical Review* 2 (1921), 172–89; George F. G. Stanley, "The Indians and the Brandy Trade During the Ancien Regime," *Revue Historique de L'Amérique Française* 6 (1952–53), 489–505; André Vachon, "L'Eau-De-Vie Dans La Société Indienne," Canadian Historical Association *Report* (1960), 22–32; R. C. Dailey, "The Role of Alcohol among North American Indian Tribes as Reported in the Jesuit Relations," *Anthropologica* 10 (1968), 45–59; Alfred G. Bailey, *The Conflict of European and Eastern Algonkian Cultures, 1504–1700: A Study in Canadian Civilization* (Toronto, ON: University of Toronto Press, 1969), 66–71; Cornelius Jaenen, *Friend and Foe: Aspects of French-Amerindian Cultural Contact in the Sixteenth and Seventeenth Centuries* (New York: Columbia University Press, 1976), esp. 110–15. Even an analysis based on modern alcohol studies drew on the experiences of Indians in eastern Canada to make its points; see Jill R. Schumann, "The Diffusion of Alcohol: Through Membrane into Culture," in *Papers of the Thirteenth Algonquian Conference,* ed. William Cowan (Ottawa, ON: Carleton University, 1982), 37–45.

9. Dailey, "The Role of Alcohol among North American Indian Tribes," 49–50; Edmund S. Carpenter, "Alcohol in the Iroquois Dream Quest," *American Journal of Psychiatry* 116 (1959), 148–51; "The Narrative of Peter Pond," in *Five Fur Traders of the Northwest,* ed. Charles M. Gates (St. Paul [?], 1933), 35–36, 41; David Pietersz de Vries, "Short Historical and Journal Notes of Several Voyages Made in the Four Parts of the World, Namely Europe, Africa, Asia, and America" [1655] in *Historical Chronicles of New Amsterdam, Colonial New York and Early Long Island,* ed. Cornell Jaray, Empire State Historical Publications Series no. 35 (Port Washington, NY: Empire State Historical Publications, n.d.), 55–56; Thomas Butler to Sir William Johnson, 6 January 1757, in James Sullivan et al., eds., *The Papers of Sir William Johnson,* 14 vols. (Albany, NY: The University of the State of New York, 1921–65), 2: 664; J. R. Bartlett, ed., *Records of the Colony of Rhode Island and Providence Plantations,* 10 vols. (Providence, RI: A. C. Greene and Brothers, 1856–65), 4:425–26.

10. For one estimate, see Jack O. Waddell, "Malhiot's Journal: An Ethnohistoric Assessment of Chippewa Alcohol Behavior in the Early Nineteenth Century," *Ethnohistory* 32 (1985), esp. 251–64.

11. Arthur J. Ray and Donald B. Freeman, *"Give Us Good Measure": An Economic Analysis of Relations between the Indians and the Hudson's Bay Company before 1763* (Toronto, ON: University of Toronto Press, 1978), 132–34. For early nineteenth century estimates, see J. C. Yerbury, *The Subarctic Indians and the Fur Trade, 1680–1860* (Vancouver, BC: University of British Columbia Press, 1986), 69.

12. George Morgan Letterbook, 1767–68, p. 35, Historical Society of Pennsylvania. See also Account of Baynton, Wharton and Morgan, September 25, 1766: Goods sent to Edward Cole, Commissary for Indian Affairs of the Illinois &c., *Johnson Papers* 13, 400–404; and Baynton, Wharton & Morgan against the Crown, June 12, 1766, *Johnson Papers* 5: 248, 256.

13. Report of Indian Trade, *Johnson Papers* 12: 396–400.

14. A Scheme for Meeting Expenses of Trade, October 8, 1774, *Johnson Papers* 4: 559. For a lower estimate (of 30,000 gallons per year in 1770), see John J. McCusker, Jr., "The Rum Trade and the Balance of Payments of the Thirteen Continental Colonies, 1650–1775" (Ph.D. diss., University of Pittsburgh, 1970), 502–504. The trade existed well beyond the borders of British America and French settlements in the St. Lawrence Valley; traders took liquor to the Sioux by the late seventeenth century and to the Wichita in the eighteenth century, and Indians in the Canadian West participated actively in the trade by the eighteenth century. See Gerald Mohatt, "The Sacred Water: The Quest for Personal Power through Drinking among the Teton Sioux" in *The Drinking Man*, ed. David C. McClelland et al. (New York: Free Press, 1972), 264; Wayne Morris, "The Wichita Exchange: Trade on Oklahoma's Fur Frontier, 1719–1812," *Great Plains Journal* 9 (1970), 80; Thomas F. Schlitz, "Brandy and Beaver Pelts: Assiniboine-European Trading Patterns, 1695–1805," *Saskatchewan History* 37 (1984), 95–102; and Lawrence J. Burpee, ed., "The Journal of Anthony Hendry, 1754–55," Royal Society of Canada *Proceedings and Transactions*, 3d. ser., 1 (1907), 352, 354.

15. [François Vachon de Belmont] "Belmont's History of Brandy," ed. Joseph Donnelly, *Mid-America* 34 (1952), 45.

16. [Belmont], "History of Brandy," 47–49; elsewhere, Belmont noted that virtually every member of an Indian community became inebriated on occasion; see 53–57. Other missionaries shared Belmont's belief that Indians drank only to get drunk; see, for example, Reuben G. Thwaites, ed., *The Jesuit Relations and Allied Documents, 1610–1791*, 73 vols. (Cleveland, OH: Burrows Bros. Co., 1896–1901), 52: 193.

17. [John Clayton], "The Aborigines of the Country," in *The Reverend John Clayton, A Parson with a Scientific Mind: His Scientific Writings and Other Related Papers*, ed. Edmund Berkeley and Dorothy Smith Berkeley (Charlottesville, VA: University Press of Virginia, 1965), 37–38; see also "Another 'Account of Virginia' by the Reverend John Clayton," ed. Edmund Berkeley and Dorothy Smith Berkeley, *Virginia Magazine of History and Biography* 76 (1968), 436.

18. See, for example, Thwaites, *The Jesuit Relations* 22: 243 and 46: 105; and James Axtell, *The Invasion Within: The Contest of Cultures in Colonial North America* (New York: Oxford University Press, 1985), 65–67.

19. [Cotton Mather], *Sober Considerations, on a Growing Flood of Iniquity* (Boston: Nicholas Boone, 1708), 16.

20. Nicholas Denys, *The Description and Natural History of the Coasts of North America*, ed. William F. Ganong (Toronto, ON: The Champlain Society, 1908), 448–50; Bernard Romans, *A Concise Natural History of East and West Florida* (1775; Gainesville, FL: University of Florida Press, 1962), 55.

21. William Bartram, *Travels through North and South Carolina, Georgia, East and West Florida, The Cherokee Country, the Extensive Territories of the Muscogulges, or Creek Confederacy, and the Country of the Chactaws* (1791; New Orleans, LA: Pelican Publishing Company, 1961), 214–15.

22. Nathaniel B. Shurtleff, ed., *Records of the Governor and Company of the Massachusetts Bay in New England*, 5 vols. (1855–61), 1:406–407.

23. William Bradford, *Of Plymouth Plantation*, ed. Samuel Eliot Morison (1952; New York: Knopf, 1967), 205–206. On the threat Morton posed to the settlers of Plymouth and Massachusetts Bay, see Michael Zuckerman, "Pilgrims in the Wilderness: Community, Modernity, and the Maypole at Merry Mount," *New England Quarterly* 50 (1977), 255–77.

24. Shurtleff, *Records of Massachusetts Bay* 1: 106; 2: 84–85, 258; 3: 425–26; vol.4, pt. 1, 201–202, and part 2, 297.

25. John Lawson, *A New Voyage to Carolina*, ed. Hugh T. Lefler (Chapel Hill, NC: University of North Carolina Press, 1967), 18, 211–12, 232.

26. Samuel Danforth, *The Woful Effects of Drunkenness* (Boston: Samuel Gerrish, 1710), 10–11.

27. As quoted in White, *The Roots of Dependency*, 75, 85–86 (quotations at 85–86).

28. "Journal of David Taitt's Travels from Pensacola, West Florida, to and through the Country of the Upper and the Lower Creeks, 1772," in *Travels in the American Colonies*, ed. Newton D. Mereness (New York: The Macmillan Co., 1916), 513–15, 525n., 553n., 555–56, 560; John Stewart to John Pownall, 24 August 1765, in *Colonial Records of North Carolina*, 10 vols, ed. William Saunders (Raleigh, NC: 1886–90), 7: 110.

29. See Denys, *Description and Natural History,* 450, and Merrell, *The Indians' New World,* 39.

30. Thomas Bosworth to Mr. Elsinor, 23 December 1752, and Lachland McGillivray to Glen, 14 April 1754, in *Colonial Records of South Carolina: Documents Relating to Indian Affairs, May 21, 1750–August 7, 1754* [hereafter *CRSC: Indian Affairs, 1750–1754*], ed. William L. McDowell, Jr. (Columbia, SC: South Carolina Archives Department, 1958), 325, 502.

31. James Adair, *The History of the American Indians* (London: E. and C. Dilly, 1775), 224.

32. Louis B. Wright, ed., *The Prose Works of William Byrd of Westover* (Cambridge, MA: Harvard University Press, 1966), 302–303.

33. As quoted in Helen C. Rountree, *Pocahontas's People: The Powhatan Indians of Virginia through Four Centuries* (Norman, OK: University of Oklahoma Press, 1990), 151, 127 (quotation at 127).

34. Milton W. Hamilton, ed., "Guy Johnson's Opinions of the American Indian," *Pennsylvania Magazine of History and Biography* [hereafter *PMHB*] 77 (1953), 325–26.

35. *The Autobiography of Benjamin Franklin,* ed. Leonard W. Labaree (New Haven, CT: Yale University Press, 1964), 199.

36. For New Hampshire, see *Laws of New Hampshire . . . Volume One: Province Period* (Manchester, NH: The John B. Clarke Co., 1904), 117, 739–40, and *Acts and Laws of His Majesty's Province of New Hampshire, in New England* (Portsmouth, NH: D. Fowle, 1761), 220. For Rhode Island, see Bartlett, *Records of the Colony of Rhode Island and Providence Plantation* 1: 274, 279, 307–308, 338, 413–14; 2: 487–88, 500–503; 4:233, 425–26. For Connecticut, see J. H. Trumbull and C. J. Hoadly, eds., *Public Records of the Colony of Connecticut,* 15 vols. (Hartford, CT: Press of the Case, Lockwood & Brainard Co., 1850–90), 1: 254–55, 263, 338, 354; 2: 119; 3: 94; 6: 31–32; 7: 472–73. For New York, see *Colonial Laws of New York from the Year 1664 to the Revolution,* 5 vols. (Albany, NY: J. B. Lyon, 1894–96), 1: 657–58, 685–86, 740–41, 751, 755; 3: 1096–98; 4: 93. For New Jersey, see H. Clay Reed and George J. Miller, eds., *The Burlington Court Book: A Record of Quaker Jurisprudence in West New Jersey, 1680–1709* (Washington, DC: American Historical Association, 1944), 2, 3. For Pennsylvania, see J. T. Mitchell and Henry Flanders, eds., *Statutes at Large of Pennsylvania from 1682 to 1801* (Harrisburg, PA: C. M. Busch, 1896–1908), 2: 168–70; 3: 250, 310–13; 5: 320–30; 6: 283–93. For Maryland, see William Hand et al., eds., *Archives of Maryland* (Baltimore, MD: Maryland Historical Society, 1833–), 15: 260; 22: 511; 38: 15–16, 69–70, 78–80, 84–86. For Virginia, see W. W. Hening, ed., *The Statutes at Large; Being a Collection of All the Laws of Virginia,* 13 vols. (Richmond, VA: Samuel Pleasants, Jr., 1809–23), 3: 468; 5: 273; 7: 117; 8: 116. For South Carolina, see Thomas Cooper and D. J. McCord, eds., *Statutes at Large of South Carolina,* 10 vols. (Columbia, SC: A. S. Johnston: 1836–41), 2: 64–68, 309–16. For Georgia, see A. D. Candler, ed., *Colonial Records of the State of Georgia,* 26 vols. (Atlanta, GA: Franklin Printing and Publ. Co., 1904–1916), 18: 223. For West Florida, see Robert R. Rea and Milo B. Howard, Jr., eds., *The Minutes, Journals and Acts of the General Assembly of British West Florida* (Tuscaloosa: University of Alabama Press, 1979), 347 (disallowed), 381, 390. For Massachusetts, see note 25, above.

37. See, for example, Matthew Toole to Glen, 28 October 1752; Ludwock Grant to Glen, 8 February 1753; and Glen to Lt. Gov. Dinwiddie, 1 June 1754, in *CRSC: Indian Affairs, 1750–1754,* 359, 367, 526.

38. See the depositions relating to the death of Thomas Wright in a fight with drunken Indians initiated by the trader John Burt *in Pennsylvania Colonial Records,* 16 vols. (Harrisburg, PA: T. Fenn, 1838–53), 3: 285–87.

39. The Indians' actions and the subsequent charges against the liquor seller, who claimed the Indians had stolen rum from him, are documented in James P. Baxter, ed., *Documentary History of the State of Maine* (Portland, ME: Collections of the Maine Historical Society, 1900), second series, 6: 413–20. Indians in Massachusetts, it should be noted, received harsh punishments if they were found inebriated; see Edwin Powers, *Crime and Punishment in Early Massachusetts, 1620–1692* (Boston: Beacon Press, 1966), 379–80.

40. The story is documented in a series of complaints in the Conrad Weiser papers, dated 15 February 1750, Correspondence 1: 25, Historical Society of Pennsylvania.

41. *The American Magazine,* January 1740–41, p. 7, facsimile reprint (New York: Columbia University Press, 1937); for drunkenness and the murder of a colonist in New Hampshire in 1688, see Colin Calloway, ed., *Dawnland Encounters* (Hanover, NH: University Press of New England, 1990), 185–86.

42. "Rev. Gideon Hawley's Journey to Oghquago (Broome Co.) 1753," in *Documentary History of the State of New York,* 4 vols., ed. E. B. O'Callaghan (Albany, NY: Weed, Parsons & Co., 1849–51), 3: 1043–46.

43. See the instructions of the commissioners of the Indian trade to traders for 27 July 1711, 2 August 1711, and 3 August 1711, in *Colonial Records of South Carolina: Journals of the Commissioners of the Indian Trade,*

September 20, 1710–August 29, 1718, ed. W. L. McDowell (Columbia, SC: South Carolina Archives Department, 1955), II, 13–15.

44. Journal of Thomas Bosomworth, in *CRSC: Indian Affairs, 1750–1754,* 298.

45. Paul J. Lindholdt, ed., *John Josselyn, Colonial Traveler: A Critical Edition of Two Voyages to New-England* (Hanover, NH: University Press of New England, 1988), 99.

46. Wilbur R. Jacobs, ed., *The Appalachian Indian Frontier: The Edmund Atkin Report and Plan of 1755* (1954; Lincoln, NE: University of Nebraska Press, 1967), 35–36, 45, 59.

47. See "The Opinions of George Croghan on the American Indian," *PMHB* 71 (1947), 159; Hamilton, "Guy Johnson's Opinions on the American Indian," 325. Colonial officials also tried to prevent any colonists from getting Indians drunk in order to purchase land from them; for one notorious case, see the response of Sir William Johnson to the attempt by George (Ury) Klock to purchase land from some Indians after getting them drunk in *Johnson Papers* 3: 312–14, 338–41, 619–20; 4: 53–56, 112–115.

48. Adair, *History of the American Indians,* 286; see also "Journal of David Taitt," 544.

49. Dunbar Rowland, ed., *Mississippi Provincial Archives, 1763–1766: English Dominion* (Nashville, TN: Press of Brandon Printing Co., 1911), 1: 219–20.

50. Johnson to Abercromby, 17 May 1758, *Johnson Papers* 9: 905–906.

51. Johnson to the Lords of Trade, October 1764, in *Documents Relative to the Colonial History of the State of New York,* 15 vols., ed. E. B. O'Callaghan and Berthold Fernow (Albany, NY: Weed, Parsons, & Co., 1856–87), 7:665.

52. *Journal of Indian Affairs,* 25 February 1767, *Johnson Papers* 12: 273–75.

53. See White, *The Middle Ground,* 335.

54. For a single report detailing some of these problems, though with some exaggeration, see Daniel Claus to Sir William Johnson, 8 July 1772, *Johnson Papers* 12: 971–72. Consumption of alcohol increased the risk of hypothermia; see Gallaher et al., "Pedestrian and Hypothermia Deaths," 1346–47.

55. See Axtell, "The Invasion Within: The Contest of Cultures in Colonial North America," in *The European and the Indian,* 39–86.

56. Johnson to the Lords of Trade, October 1764, 7: 665.

57. *The Speech of a Creek-Indian, against the Immoderate Use of Spirituous Liquors* (London: Printed for R. Griffiths, 1754), 11.

58. Thomas Budd, *Good Order Established in Pennsilvania & New-Jersey in America* (Philadelphia: 1685), 29.

59. "Colonel Chicken's Journal to the Cherokees," in *Travels in the American Colonies,* 171.

60. "Mr. Occom's Address to His Indian Brethren," (n.p., 1772 [Evans 4236a]); Occom's broadside is reprinted in William Sturtevant, ed., *Handbook of North American Indians,* vol. 4, *History of Indian-White Relations,* vol. ed. Wilcomb Washburn (Washington, DC: Smithsonian Institution, 1988), 434. For Occom's own drinking history, see the obviously outdated, but still somewhat useful in its presentation of documentary evidence, W. DeLoss Love, *Samson Occom and the Christian Indians of New England* (Boston: The Pilgrim Press, 1899), 162–68. Occom's sensitivity to his own drinking, and to gossip about it, indicated the stigma he associated with drunkenness; see David Murray, *Forked Tongues: Speech, Writing and Representation in North American Indian Texts* (London: Pinter, 1991), 53–54.

61. Occom, *A Sermon Preached at the Execution of Moses Paul,* 3d. ed. (New London, CT: T. Green, 1772), esp. 21–23. The ninth edition was published in Boston in 1774.

62. See James D. McCallum, ed., *The Letters of Eleazar Wheelock's Indians* (Hanover, NH: Dartmouth College Publications, 1932), 45–46, 61–62, 259–60.

63. William Beauchamp, ed., *Moravian Journals Relating to Central New York, 1745–1766* (Syracuse, NY: Dehler Press, 1916), 199–200.

64. [Charles Thomson], *An Enquiry into the Causes of the Alienation of the Delawares and Shawanese Indians from the British Interest, and the Measures Taken for Recovering Their Friendship* (1759; St. Clair Shores, MI: Scholarly Press, 1970), 11, 13, 24, 31–32, 74–76. For Tawenna's speech, see *Pennsylvania Col. Recs.,* 3: 363.

65. Colonists agreed with the Indians and on 20 August issued a proclamation banning the sale of liquor to Indians "in the Woods"; see *Pennsylvania Col. Recs.,* 3: 404–12.

66. *Johnson Papers* 4: 557–58; 7: 348–49; 10: 69, 73; 12: 635.

67. Speech of the Shawnees, July 1771, *Johnson Papers* 12: 914–15.

68. "Journal of Beatty's Trip to the Ohio Country in 1766," in *Journals of Charles Beatty, 1762–1769,* ed. Guy S. Egett (University Park, PA: Pennsylvania State University Press, 1962), 67. On this and other sexual relations in the region, see White, *The Middle Ground,* 60–75, 214–15, 334.

69. "Narrative of a Journey, Made in the Year 1737, by Conrad Weiser, Indian Agent and Provincial Interpreter, from Tulpehocken in the Province of Pennsylvania to Onondaga," trans. H. H. Muhlenberg, Pennsylvania Historical Society *Collections* 1 (Philadelphia, PA: Pennsylvania Historical Society, 1853), 17.

70. Moses & Indians W. H. & G. recd by Mrs Hamond, July 1, [16]77, in Baxter, ed., *Documentary History of Maine,* 2d ser., 6: 178–79.

71. Jaspar Danckaerts, *Journal of a Voyage to New York in 1679–1680,* in *Memoirs of the Long Island Historical Society* 1 (Upper Saddle River, NJ: Gregg Press, 1867), 149–50.

72. Bartlett, *Records of the Colony of Rhode Island,* 2: 500.

73. The English were not alone in their early desire to establish trade with Indians; see Axtell, "At the Water's Edge: Trading in the Sixteenth Century," in Axtell, *After Columbus: Essays in the Ethnohistory of Colonial North America* (New York: Oxford University Press, 1988), 144–81.

74. John Heckewelder, *History, Manners, and Customs of the Indian Nattions who once Inhabited Pennsylvania and the Neighbouring States,* ed. William C. Reichel (Philadelphia: Historical Society of Pennsylvania, 1881), 293–94; Anthony F. C. Wallace, *The Death and Rebirth of the Seneca* (1969; New York: Knopf, 1972), 278; Gregory Dowd, *A Spirited Resistance: The North American Indian Struggle for Unity, 1745–1815* (Baltimore, MD: Johns Hopkins University Press, 1992), 31–33, 126.

11

THE FRONTIER EXCHANGE ECONOMY
OF THE LOWER MISSISSIPPI VALLEY
IN THE EIGHTEENTH CENTURY

Daniel H. Usner, Jr.

Since long before Columbus, peoples have used the Mississippi River and its tributaries, a natural highway system through the vast interior of the continent, to travel and trade. As Daniel H. Usner, Jr., reveals here, during the eighteenth century the lower reaches of the Mississippi Valley became an international trading complex, bringing together hunters, farmers, merchants, and mariners. New Orleans, the most important French settlement south of the St. Lawrence River, became the focal point for exchange, but intercultural commerce took place well into its hinterland. The nature of the business that took place in this region was perhaps as sophisticated as the types of trade taking place elsewhere in the Atlantic world; by the 1720s, for example, the area boasted well-established exchange rates, revealing that Indians and colonists alike had learned to appreciate the value both of what they had to offer as well as what they wanted to obtain.

The success of this economy (which also involved transported African slaves) and the extent of relations between the French and their American neighbors reminds us that Britain's eventual control of the Mississippi Valley could not have been predicted before the Seven Years' War. Compare Usner's story with Miller and Hamell's account of colonial trade and Merrell's Catawba experience; how can we account for the similarities and differences as these Indians confronted their "new world"?

THE FRONTIER EXCHANGE ECONOMY
OF THE LOWER MISSISSIPPI VALLEY
IN THE EIGHTEENTH CENTURY

Daniel H. Usner, Jr.

IT IS AN OLD FACT AND FAR from a new observation that the lower Mississippi Valley has been generally relegated to the margins of early American historiography. The region has been borderland territory for historians as it once was for the English colonies of the Atlantic coast, and its people have been largely ignored or casually dismissed as mere bit-players in the drama of American development—colorful, no doubt, but peripheral and unimportant. The historical point of view has been determinatively eastern: our impression of the great West, during the years before it fell under the expanding sovereignty of the United States, is still dominated by images of white explorers, trappers, and traders, and of Indian warriors fighting European imperial wars. The lands along the Mississippi River have remained an amorphous area "dimly realizing westward" (in Robert Frost's phrase) and waiting to be occupied by Anglo-Americans and their Afro-American slaves. This West, in a word, has been only dimly realized by historians as a place with a history of its own and a people whose tale is worth telling in its own right.

This is not to imply that the vast region known in colonial times as Louisiana has been wholly neglected. Such nineteenth-century historians as Francis Parkman and Justin Winsor depicted it as an arena of international contests for empire. But this grand stage upon which great men acted long overshadowed the people who actually shaped society and economy within the region.[1] Historians based in the Mississippi Valley, beginning with Charles Gayarré in the 1850s, have vigorously studied French and Spanish Louisiana, and a growing cadre of scholars now excavates important details about government, immigration, slavery, and Indian affairs in the colony. But what is conveniently categorized as French colonial and Spanish borderlands history still goes slightly noticed by students of British North America.[2]

Even the most devoted historians of Louisiana are quick to point out that the colony in the Mississippi Valley constitutes "a study in failure" or "a holding action"

SOURCE: *William and Mary Quarterly*, 3d Ser. 44 (1987), 165–92.

in comparison with the English colonies along the Atlantic seaboard. Louisiana suffered from a low priority in the mercantile designs of both France and Spain. Immigration and population growth proceeded slowly, exportation of staple products to Europe fluctuated, and subsistence agriculture predominated over production of cash crops.[3] But Louisiana's sparse populace and tentative transatlantic commerce can actually be used to the historian's advantage, allowing one to turn more attentively to dimensions of economic life that have been neglected in the lower Mississippi Valley as well as in other colonial regions of North America. Studies of economic change in North American colonies concentrated for a long time on linkages with home countries and with each other through the exportation of staple commodities. Historians are now turning to economic relationships that developed within regions, with greater attention to activities not totally dependent upon production for the Atlantic market.[4]

Here I will examine the formation of a regional economy that connected Indian villagers across the lower Mississippi Valley with European settlers and African slaves along the Gulf Coast and lower banks of the Mississippi. The term *frontier exchange* is meant to capture the form and content of economic interactions among these groups, with a view to replacing the notion of frontier as an interracial boundary with that of a cross-cultural network. For this conceptualization of an interethnic web of economic relations I am indebted to anthropologists and historians who give as much emphasis to the prosaic features of livelihood as to the institutional structures of commerce. Small-scale, face-to-face marketing must be taken seriously, especially for understanding how peoples of different cultures related to and influenced each other in daily life.[5]

In order to underscore this sphere of exchange, the lower Mississippi Valley is here defined as an economic region that was shaped by common means of production and by regular forms of trade among its diverse inhabitants. Upper Louisiana, the area known as Illinois country, is not examined, therefore, because economic connections between the upper Mississippi Valley and lower Louisiana were more impersonal and less predictable before the last quarter of the eighteenth century. The inhabitants of the Illinois settlements, numbering 768 French settlers, 445 black slaves, and 147 Indian slaves at mid-century, belonged to Louisiana politically but were more closely integrated economically into the Great Lakes region. The standard image of Louisiana as a vast territory spread along a thousand miles of the meandering Mississippi and sparsely occupied by Frenchmen and their Indian allies not only exaggerates the boundlessness of life in the valley but distracts attention from the substantial intraregional connections that differentiated lower Louisiana from upper Louisiana.[6] In 1762–63 the lower Mississippi Valley was partitioned into the Spanish province of Louisiana and the English province of West Florida. The latter colony, therefore, must be included in any study of the region's economy. The persistence of frontier exchange across the political boundary can too easily be overlooked when Louisiana and West Florida are treated separately.

Regional analysis of frontier exchange can also highlight the diverse and dynamic participation of Indians, settlers, and slaves in a way that may prove useful to historians of other colonial regions. For colonies examined more thoroughly than are Louisiana and West Florida, racial categories dictate selection and organization of data by historians. Afro-Americans and American Indians are finally receiving scholarly attention commensurate with their presence in colonial America, and the old tendency to read nineteenth-century race relations and racism back into earlier periods is being corrected. Nonetheless, analyses of colonial society and economy still tend to compartmentalize ethnic and cultural groups by socioeconomic status and geographical location. In the 1980s Indians and Africans are at last sharing the forestage of colonial scholarship with Europeans, but mostly under separate—even if equally bright—spotlights.[7]

The focus of this study falls not directly on familiar economic settings—the fur trade for Indians and plantation agriculture for blacks—but rather on the interstices in which people exchanged small quantities of goods in pursuit of their livelihood. A brief summary of how the formal network of towns and outposts took shape is accompanied by an outline of population changes in the lower Mississippi Valley. Then the reader is asked to follow more closely the multiple directions of interaction through which deerskins and foods circulated from group to group. Over most of the eighteenth century, exchanges of these two kinds of products contributed strongly to the notable fluidity of social relations among lower Mississippi Valley inhabitants. It must be emphasized, however, that exchanges occurred under, and often despite, very unequal social conditions because a colonial elite worked steadily to enforce bondage upon black Louisianians and West Floridians, dependency upon Indians, and subordination upon a mixed lot of white settlers.

I

Sent by France late in 1698 to establish a military post near the mouth of the Mississippi River and to forestall Spanish and English advances in the region, naval captain Pierre Le Moyne d'Iberville encountered dismal prospects for what he hoped would become a colony. Already overextended imperially and facing shortages of food at home, France was not prepared to deliver supplies with any regularity to the Gulf Coast. Like many other nascent colonial ventures before it, Iberville's isolated outpost therefore depended heavily upon trade with neighboring Indian villages for its survival. Soldiers and sailors either purchased food directly from Indians or acquired peltry from them to exchange for imported grains and meats.[8] During the second decade of the eighteenth century, this trade expanded from localized exchange with villages near the Gulf into an extensive network of interior posts that not only facilitated the movement of deerskins to the coast but functioned as marketplaces for the exchange of food. In 1714 the French built a storehouse at Natchez in order to acquire deerskins from the up-country villages and to counteract English intrigue and commerce. Joining the Yamassees in war against South Carolina, the Alibamons, Tallapoosas, and Abehkas—who eventually became known as the Upper Creeks—ousted English traders from their villages. In 1715 they began to carry deerskins to Mobile and in 1717 allowed Jean-Baptiste Le Moyne de Bienville, Iberville's brother, to build Fort Toulouse near the junction of the Coosa and Tallapoosa rivers. Fort Rosalie was built among the Natchez

Indians in 1716, following execution of some hostile chiefs at Bienville's order. In 1719 a garrison was established at Fort St. Pierre on the Yazoo River.[9]

To advance trade up the Red River, a French garrison occupied a post near the Caddo village of Natchitoches in 1716, and a subsidiary trade station was established at an upriver Indian town called Upper Nasoni in 1719. Only twenty miles southwest of Natchitoches, the Spanish, who had been gradually edging toward the Red River, constructed a military post at Los Adaes in 1721. Louis Juchereau de St. Denis, who became commandant of French Natchitoches in 1719, had already been trading in this area for several years—with both Spaniards and Indians. In 1721 a small detachment of soldiers from the Yazoo River garrison joined a group of about one hundred settlers at the lower Arkansas River, where, in 1686, the Quapaws had allowed Henri de Tonti to situate a short-lived trade house.[10]

A decade of immigration and slave trading to Louisiana, attended by death for hundreds of Europeans and Africans, resulted by 1732 in a population of only about 2,000 settlers and soldiers with some 3,800 slaves, at a time when the number of Indians of the lower Mississippi Valley, though rapidly declining from disease and war, was still in the range of 50,000.[11] Large-scale immigration from Europe stopped by the mid-1720s, and only about 400 black slaves reached the colony between 1732 and the 1760s. This slow growth of population—to approximately 5,000 slaves, 4,000 settlers, and 100 free people of color—meant minimal encroachment on Indian lands:

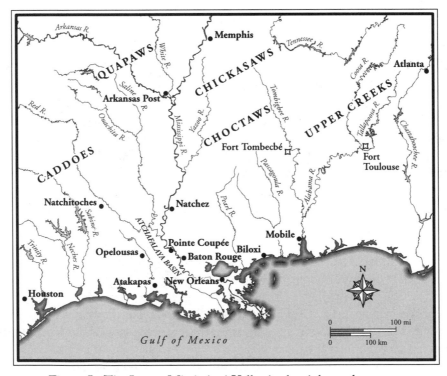

Figure I: The Lower Mississippi Valley in the eighteenth century.

most settlers and slaves lived along the Gulf Coast and the Mississippi River below its junction with the Red River. Trade relations with the Indians developed more freely because, for a time at least, the region's tribes were not markedly agitated by French pressure on their territory.[12]

At first, given the scanty and erratic supply of trade goods from France, Louisiana officials relied on distribution of merchandise among Indian leaders in the form of annual gifts. In doing so, they accommodated by necessity to Indian protocols of trade and diplomacy. For the Indians, exchanges of material goods represented political reciprocity between autonomous groups, while absence of trade was synonymous with a state of war. Because commerce could not operate independently from ritual expressions of allegiance, such formal ceremonies as gift giving and smoking the calumet had to accompany economic transactions between Indians and Europeans. Conformity to these conventions recognized the leverage of such large tribes as the Choctaws and Caddoes on Louisiana's commerce and defense. They were essential to the initiation of the network of trade for deerskins and food—both items important to the success of Louisiana—against the threat of English competition from South Carolina and Georgia.[13]

Even so, the formation of this network did not occur without costly conflict. Only after a long war against the Chitimachas, which provided Louisiana with many of its first slaves, did the French secure the alliance of all Indian tribes in the Mississippi delta. While small tribes like the Chitimachas confronted French power directly, conflict between larger Indian nations was fueled by intercolonial competition. In the 1720s Choctaw and Upper Creek villagers helped the French thwart British expansion to the Mississippi River, while the Chickasaws and Lower Creeks fought against them to protect English traders still operating within the Louisiana hinterland. The most explosive crisis came in 1729 when, after a decade of deteriorating relations with encroaching settlers, the Natchez Indians waged a desperate war against the French. Meanwhile, a push by Louisiana officials and planters for the production of tobacco and indigo provoked resistance within: as the volume of these exports rose during the late 1720s, so did the level of slave rebelliousness. A Negro plot was discovered in New Orleans shortly after the Indians destroyed the French plantations at Natchez, and many of the slaves taken captive there assisted the Natchez in their ensuing, but losing, defense against the Louisiana army. Dealing with a black majority within the colonial settlements, and living in the midst of an even larger Indian population, officials employed greater vigilance and harsher coercion as time went on.[14]

Toward mid-century, chronic shortages of merchandise and English intervention nearly turned the Choctaw nation, a bulwark of Louisiana's security, against the French. The benign policy of gift giving could go only so far in mitigating the effects of unreliable imports upon the deerskin trade with Indians. Unable to divert the powerful Chickasaw nation from the English because of inadequate quantities of trade goods, French officials resorted to a strategy of intimidation and debilitation, employing Choctaw warriors on major campaigns and in continuous guerrilla raids against Chickasaw villages. Participation in this conflict through the 1740s, which was motivated by the need to avenge enemy hostilities as well as to fulfill obligations to the

French, took its toll on the Choctaws. Rebellion by a pro-English party within the nation broke out in 1746, costing the Choctaw people much suffering and death in what became a violent civil war waged to preserve their alliance with French Louisiana.[15]

Louisiana's frontier exchange economy survived the Choctaw revolt, with the exportation of deerskins steadily increasing alongside that of tobacco and indigo. Demographic and geopolitical changes that began in the 1760s, however, portended greater challenges to the trade-alliance network. Immigration into the lower Mississippi Valley resumed after Great Britain drove French settlers from Nova Scotia in 1755. By 1767, seven years after Spain obtained Louisiana from France, more than a thousand of these Acadian refugees reached the colony, forming new settlements along the Mississippi about seventy miles above New Orleans and at Atakapas and Opelousas on Bayou Teche. From 1778 to 1780, two thousand "Islenos" migrated from the Canary Islands and established their own communities, along the Mississippi and Bayou Lafourche below New Orleans. In 1785 seven ships carried another 1,600 Acadians from France to Louisiana. Meanwhile Great Britain was accelerating colonization on the eastern side of the river, having acquired West Florida by the Treaty of Paris in 1763. Settlers from the Atlantic seaboard, many with slaves, increased the colonial population of West Florida to nearly 4,000 whites and 1,500 blacks by 1774. An even larger influx occurred after the outbreak of the American Revolution as loyalist refugees sought asylum in the Florida colony and settled mainly in the Natchez area. By 1783, when Spain gained sovereignty over West Florida and control over both sides of the Mississippi, the colonial population of the lower Mississippi Valley approached 16,000 Negro slaves, 13,000 whites, and over 1,000 free people of color.[16]

By the 1780s, the Indian population in the region was, for the first time, becoming outnumbered by colonial inhabitants, while the colonial economy shifted toward greater dependence upon expanding commercial agriculture. Consequently, Louisiana officials exerted tighter political control over interethnic exchange in order to concentrate slave labor on cash crops and to reduce the mobility of Indian villagers. The frontier exchange economy did not fade from the lower Mississippi Valley, however, for efforts continued to be made into the nineteenth century by many old and new inhabitants to perpetuate small-scale trade across heightening racial divides.

II

Before 1783 the deerskin trade had encouraged widespread participation in a network of diffuse exchange from Indian villages to colonial port towns. Indian customs and French commercial weaknesses, as already seen, required a formal sphere of trade-alliance relations, but many people across the region also relied upon informal and intimate forms of cross-cultural trade. For historians, the less systematic trade in deerskins that evolved in Louisiana has long been overshadowed by a sequence of frustrated French efforts to create a commercial empire in the Mississippi River Valley, beginning with the ventures of René-Robert Cavelier, Sieur de La Salle. During the 1680s La Salle had attempted, but failed, to expand commerce in bison robes and beaver pelts.

At the threshold of the eighteenth century, while his men were barely surviving the rigors of building an outpost on the Gulf Coast, Iberville promoted a grand scheme to entrench French power in North America through a system of trading posts and tanneries around which well-armed Indian allies in the Mississippi Valley would concentrate. Antoine Crozat's plans for Louisiana commerce in 1712 included hopes of profitably controlling the fur trade throughout the region. Paling beside these mercantile designs, the Indian trade in lower Louisiana was shaped by a complex of more pedestrian circumstances. A small number of colonial troops with minimal support from the crown had to be dispersed among a few select posts. Intertribal conflicts and English trade with Indians in the region determined when and where French stations were constructed and, furthermore, continued to be destabilizing influences on Louisiana's trade. The irrepressible eastward flow of beaver skins from the upper Mississippi Valley to Canada also affected the trade network in Louisiana, making the lower valley a separate, predominantly deerskin-producing, trade region.[17]

The economic and political importance of the Indian trade to Louisiana is evidenced by the close attention that officials paid to the details of its operation. The overall interest of colonial administrators centered upon the interference and competition of English traders, but particular measures were required for regulation of the region's internal commerce as well. In order to maintain stable relations between traders and villagers, governments in all North American colonies administered tariffs or rates of exchange. In 1721 the Choctaws and the French agreed to trade at the following prices: a quarter of an ell (one meter) of woolen cloth called *limbourg* or one axe for four dressed deerskins; one blanket or tomahawk for two dressed deerskins; and two-thirds of a pound of gunpowder or twenty gun flints for one dressed deerskin.[18] As the cost of European manufactures rose and additional goods entered the regional economy, new tariffs were negotiated from time to time by colonial and tribal leaders. Although much of the trading occurred at varying rates, depending upon local conditions and individual circumstances, official tariffs represented colonial accommodation to Indian insistence that trade be contained within the political sphere of relations. Once it established rates of exchange, the Superior Council of Louisiana had to contend with complaints from traders and Indians alike about inadequate supplies or inappropriate prices. Operating between a fixed ceiling of rates set between tribal and colonial governments and a rising floor of costs charged by import merchants, the traders tended to have, as noted in the minutes of a meeting in December 1728, "a greater share in the complaints that have been made about the high price of the goods than the Indians themselves."[19] For their part, Indian representatives bargained for better exchange rates by repeatedly comparing the expense and quality of French and English merchandise.[20]

Despite attempts by groups of merchants and officials to monopolize Indian commerce, the deerskin trade involved many colonial inhabitants as well as Indians. Even during the demographic and agricultural expansion of Louisiana in the 1720s, settlers relied upon deerskins, acquired directly or indirectly from Indian villagers, as a means of buying imported goods. "In order to support by this new accommodation the trade with the Indians," the Company of the Indies decided in 1729 to make its warehouse in the colony the exclusive exporter of deerskins. After 1732, officials of the king further advanced this commerce "by entrusting in small lots the merchandise that he sends to settlers who will trade it to the Indians and who will settle their accounts with his Majesty with the skins that they have taken in trade."[21] As the difficulty of finding among the traders "people of sufficiently well known integrity" continued to make it "almost impossible to avoid bad debts," the deerskin trade fell into the hands of "solvent inhabitants who have given security for the merchandise."[22] Consequently, the many anonymous individuals who traded in the Indian villages became middlemen between the Indians who hunted and processed the skins and the colonial merchants who were able to acquire and forward imported trade goods. "On their return from the Indians," as one observer described the traders, "they disperse in the city their peltries or produce, which they bring in payment to those from whom they have borrowed in order to carry on their trade."[23]

Many settlers and even slaves exchanged something for deerskins once in a while, and innumerable colonists passed in and out of the deerskin trade as a temporary means of livelihood. Others made a lifetime occupation from seasonally trading imported merchandise for peltry and other native products. The identities of some professional traders among the Choctaws offer informative glimpses into the business. Marc Antoine Huché grew up among the Choctaws, was hired in 1721 as interpreter for the company at "five hundred livres per year with two rations for himself and his wife," and traded for Mobile commandant-entrepreneur Bernard Diron d'Artaguette. As reported by general commissioner Edmé Gatien Salmon in 1732, the Great Chief of the Choctaw nation considered Huché to be "brave, firm and faithful."[24] Another employee of Diron d'Artaguette and later an independent trader, Joseph Poupart *dit* Lafleur, sent 581 skins to the Mobile commandant in July 1729, along with a letter describing the activities of English traders among the Chickasaws. A decade later his widow, Marie Roy, ran a warehouse among the Alibamons, which had to be withdrawn in 1740 because of trouble with English traders in the area.[25] Individuals known as Gaspard, Dupumeaux, and Antoine Chauvin Des Islets traded in Choctaw country at mid-century, the last described by general commissioner Honoré Michel de la Rouvillière in 1751 as "a famous trader who is set forth as an oracle" by the Choctaws.[26]

After 1762 the number of traders operating in Indian villages increased with the growth of the colonial population, and their ethnic composition became more English. By the mid-1780s, Spanish officials estimated that five hundred traders, employees, and transients were living in and around Choctaw and Chickasaw towns, while nearly three hundred more operated in Creek towns. Considered "vagabonds and villains" by colonial administrators interested in orderly commerce, many of these men married Indian women and became affiliated with specific villages. A "List of Choctaw Towns and Traders" compiled by Juan de la Villebeuvre in 1787 reveals the names of an array of persons involved in the deerskin trade. Frenchmen identified as Favre, Louis, Chastany, and Petit Baptiste lived respectively in the eastern district towns of Yanabé, Ouatonloula, Yazoo, Loukfata, and Bitabogoula. In three other villages of the same district "there are many whites, both Traders and Vagabonds." Among the people trading with particular towns in the western district of the Choctaw nation were Englishman Alexander Fraizer and three employees at West Yazoo; Louis Mulatto, evidently employed at Cushtusha by Simon Favre; Frenchman Louis Leflore at Caffetalaya; the Pitchlynn brothers, English traders at Tchanké; and an American, Moise Forstar, at Mongoulacha. A similar mixture of traders and employees occupied villages in the Sixtown district.[27] The children born to this generation of traders and their Indian wives belonged to the clans of their mothers, and some became important tribal leaders by the beginning of the nineteenth century.[28]

Most deerskin traders learned to speak the language of the tribe with whom they dealt. As emphasized by an anonymous chronicler of the Choctaws' trade with Louisiana, who may have been a trader sometime before the mid-1730s, "it is necessary to know their language well." Many traders probably spoke Mobilian, a trade language or lingua franca, instead of or in addition to distinct tribal languages: "when one knows it," noted Lt. Jean François Benjamin Dumont de Montigny, "one can travel through all this province without needing an interpreter."[29] Antecedents of Mobilian may have existed in the region before European contact, but economic relations with the colonial populace of Louisiana undoubtedly accelerated and expanded its usage—resembling the evolution of Delaware, Occaneechee, and Catawba into trade languages along the Atlantic coast. Based upon the western Muskhogean grammar of the Choctaw, Chickasaw, and Alibamon languages—all mutually unintelligible—Mobilian served as a second language, mixing with wide variation lexicon and phonology derived from both Indian and European speech. Well before the mid-eighteenth century, Mobilian became familiar to colonists and Indians west of the Mississippi River. All Caddo villages, as reported by Antoine Le Page du Pratz, contained someone who could speak this "Langue vulgaire." Mobilian was a convenient second language for many settlers and slaves as well as traders to use among Indians, and through the nineteenth century it continued to be spoken by Indians, Negroes, and whites in southern Louisiana and eastern Texas.[30]

Among the goods exchanged for deerskins, liquor was the most volatile item. As in other colonial regions, alcoholic beverages in Louisiana functioned both as a lubricant for expanding Indian commerce and as a stimulant for satisfying military and other colonial personnel. Louisiana and West Florida governments tried to control this commerce, but the very frequency of ordinances regulating trade in liquor reveals its ever-widening use among Indians, settlers, and slaves. In 1725 the Louisiana Superior Council attempted to remedy abuses caused by the "many persons here who have no other trade than that of selling brandy and other drinks at exorbitant prices and even grant credit to all the soldiers, workmen, and sailors." Beginning in 1717, innumerable orders were issued prohibiting the unauthorized sale of liquor to Indians and slaves whose consumption of it, officials feared, would increase chances of violent rebellion.[31] By mid-century a cheap rum called *tafia* became the region's most popular drink and a convenient medium of exchange. The English government in Pensacola attempted to restrict Indian traders to fifteen gallons every three months, which was considered a necessary amount for their purchase of food from Indian villagers. But in 1772 several Choctaw chiefs bitterly complained about the quantity of rum that "pours in upon our nation like a great Sea from Mobille and from all the Plantations and Settlements round about." Traders sometimes watered their rum, four kegs of which could buy a Choctaw pony during the 1770s, and encouraged excessive consumption among Indians in order to make more profitable bargains for their deerskins. Peddlers and tavern-keepers persistently violated their licenses by selling *tafia* and eau de vie to soldiers and slaves as well as to Indians.[32]

Deerskin traders and other peddlers played a dynamic role in the frontier exchange economy. While immediately helping distribute the produce of Indians, slaves, and settlers, they performed a long-term economic function. Indian hunters required an advance in goods before they pursued the winter season's thickly furred animals, forcing traders to wait until spring for their pay. In response to this seasonal pattern, traders acquired goods on credit from town merchants and obliged themselves to pay with interest within a year.[33] By extending larger amounts of credit to more inhabitants of the area and by dealing more frequently in dry goods and export commodities, itinerant traders contributed to the commercialization of marketing in the lower Mississippi Valley. By the mid-eighteenth century the average value of trade goods carried by individual peddlers ranged from 1,000 to 2,500 livres (200–500 pesos or 40–110 pounds sterling). A bill owed by Charles Labau of Opelousas to a New Orleans merchant for goods received in 1768 reveals both the composition and the value of merchandise that was becoming characteristic of peddling in the increasingly commercial economy of Louisiana: 2 barrels of rum worth 250 livres, 2 barrels of wine for 200 livres, 450 pounds of sugar for 168 livres, 134 pounds of coffee worth 167 livres and 15 sous, 22 ells of cottonade for 96 livres and 15 sous, 22 ells of ticking for 56 livres and 9 sous, 1 barrel of flour for 40 livres, 8 ells of hair cloth for 20 livres, and 1 roll of tobacco for 1 livre—all amounting to 1,000 livres to be paid in piastres "or in pelts at current prices."[34]

The deerskin trade operated to a large degree on credit—credit extended to traders by merchants who supplied goods and by traders to Indians to be made good in skins at some future date. Such arrangements were essential to the trade yet made all parties vulnerable to mischance or misdoing: a poor hunting season, loss of or damage to goods in transit, death by accident, or simple evasion. Indians often postponed payment of debts because hunting conditions were unfavorable or in order to stretch their trade among peddlers; they refused to pay interest on goods advanced; they resisted paying back debts: "Nothing so much offends an Indian," observed Amos Stoddard early in the nineteenth century, "as to be requested to pay his old debts. 'If, says he, I deliver you my peltries to pay for the goods I received last season, my family must suffer, and perhaps starve'."[35] Traders, for their part, could find themselves unable to make good their debts to merchants. Thus, on December 26, 1773, John Fitzpatrick, merchant at Manchac, lent goods worth 233 pesos to a Monsieur Valliere for trade to the Atakapas, payable the following April, but Valliere failed to pay his debt on time.[36] In another instance, Joseph Montard proposed to pay thirteen packs of skins to Juan Macarty, but the merchant refused them because the delivery came a year and a half late and during the summer, when the market value of pelts was at its annual nadir.[37] Under such circumstances, it is not surprising that traders often inflated the price of merchandise to meet their debts and interest costs.

III

The frontier exchange economy also involved trade in foodstuffs. Colonists in Louisiana, though ill supplied from home, were at first reluctant to labor to feed themselves by growing crops; fortunately for them, Indians were able to produce more than they needed for their own use. Thus there developed a lively trade, though one less visible to historians even than the diffuse trade in deerskins. While sailors and soldiers from France, with some Canadian coureurs de bois, were constructing the colony's first fort at Biloxi Bay, the Pascagoulas, Mobilians, and other coastal Indians eagerly swapped surpluses of corn, beans, and meat for axes, beads, and other useful items of European manufacture. During the first decade of the eighteenth century, colonial officials regularly sent parties up the Mobile and Mississippi rivers to purchase maize from Indians. In order to facilitate their trade with the French, some villages relocated closer to the coast and planted larger volumes of grain. The Houmas, for example, abandoned their town several miles east of the Mississippi and settled downriver along the west bank near Bayou Lafourche, where they became reliable suppliers of food to both travelers and settlers.[38] In 1708, when the colony consisted of 122 military men, 80 Indian slaves, and only 77 settlers (24 men, 28 women, and 25 children), "everybody," according to special commissioner Martin d'Artaguette, was asking for gunpowder "to trade with the Indians for the things we need." Through sales of venison to these people, Indians who hunted around Fort St. Louis were acquiring guns, each musket worth ten deer by 1710.[39]

The availability of Indian produce tempted some officials and colonists to profiteer in the sale of food. Louisiana's first political conflict, in fact, centered upon accusations—not entirely false—that the Le Moyne brothers engrossed "the meat and other produce that the Indians have brought to Mobile," trading with the king's merchandise and marking up the price of food for their own profit. Far away from France, where local governments and traditional constraints still protected buyers of food from profiteering middlemen, colonial merchants and administrators tried to intercept corn and game from Indian suppliers and resell the food to consumers at exorbitant prices.[40] The Superior Council assumed responsibility for fixing the price of basic food items beginning in 1722, when buffalo beef was set at eight sous per pound, cattle beef at ten sous per pound, a quarter of a deer at four livres, poultry at three livres apiece, and eggs at fifty sous per dozen. Such regulations, however, never stopped commandants of military posts from attempting to monopolize food supplies and other goods delivered by neighboring Indian villagers.[41]

Many *habitants* of Louisiana preferred direct exchange with Indians for their subsistence, which proved easier than learning how to produce their own food from the soil and wildlife of an unfamiliar land. Trade with Indians for food also allowed a degree of freedom from the pressures inherent in colonial agriculture, causing alarm among colonial officials and merchants who hoped to build a colony that would export some profitable staple. Although general commissioner Marc-Antoine Hubert found the soil along the rivers and bayous to be "of surprising fertility," he lamented in 1716 that "the colonists of the present time will never be satisfied with this infallible resource, accustomed as they are to the trade with the Indians the easy profit from which supports them, giving them what they need day by day like the Indians who find their happiness in an idle and lazy life." Another observer found in France's feeble commitment to colonizing the lower Mississippi Valley the reason why inhabitants had for two decades "done nothing else than try to get a little trading merchandise to obtain from the savages their sustenance, consisting of Indian corn, beans, pumpkins, or small round pumpkins, game and bear grease."[42] The Indian trade, by deflecting colonists from agriculture, thus helped frustrate early efforts to integrate the region into the world market for the benefit of both the colony and the mother country. What looked to officials like laziness was really a testimony to the vitality of the exchange economy.

When the Company of the Indies sent a flood of immigrants to Louisiana between 1717 and 1721, dependence on Indian supplies of food actually expanded. A food crisis was created as seven thousand settlers and two thousand slaves disembarked on the Gulf Coast without adequate provisions. Malarial fevers, dysentery, and scurvy combined with hunger to kill hundreds of French and German immigrants and Bambara and Wolof captives. Soldiers and workers employed by the company were sent to live in nearby Indian villages, and shipments of corn were sought from interior tribes.[43]

Like the deerskin trade, food marketing followed a more open and diffuse pattern than colonial administrators desired. Although France treated Louisiana as an importer of flour, alcohol, and a few more luxurious foodstuffs, supply lines were too tenuous and shipments always too small or spoiled for *habitants* to rely upon external sources for grain and meat. Colonists accused merchants who exported flour from France of shipping inedible and short-measured supplies. The Illinois country also proved to be an unreliable source of wheat for the colonists downriver.[44] Therefore, Indian villages and colonial settlements within the lower valley came to depend upon a regional network of exchange, in which food surpluses were periodically traded in bulk to areas in short supply, and smaller-scale transactions regularly occurred among Indians, settlers, and slaves.

The generous system of distributing land to settlers in Louisiana helped stimulate a domestic market in corn, rice, and other produce. In order to keep colonists in the colony and to encourage agriculture, France offered settlers moderately sized tracts of free land, usually with five arpents of river frontage and forty arpents deep from the bank (200 square arpents or 170 acres). "A man with his wife or his partner," wrote Father Paul du Poisson in 1727, "clears a little ground, builds himself a house on four piles, covers it with sheets of bark, and plants corn and rice for his provisions; the next year he raises a little more for food, and has also a field of tobacco; if at last he succeed[s] in having three or four Negroes, then he is out of his difficulties. This is what is called a *habitation*, a *habitant*; but how many of them are as nearly beggars as when they began!"[45] Settlers who failed to make their *habitations* productive depended upon food shared by kin or distributed through the market, while those who succeeded in farming maintained a diversity of crops that helped minimize their dependency upon the export-import economy.

The presence of numerous military personnel in the region and the fact that about 25 percent of Louisiana's colonial populace lived in New Orleans by mid-century especially stimulated cross-cultural food marketing. Corn, game, and other provisions consumed at interior posts like Natchitoches and Tombecbé came from neighboring Indian villagers who bartered for such trade goods as metalware, brandy, and cloth either directly with the soldiers or more formally through their officers. The government also purchased large quantities of grain for its troops from settlers along the Mississippi River.[46] The Choctaws not only sold foodstuffs to the garrison stationed at Fort Tombecbé, beginning in 1736, but also carried corn, vegetables, and poultry to the Mobile market.[47]

New Orleans and Mobile benefited from food crops and meats and even from such prepared items as persimmon bread, cornmeal, and bear oil that were sold by Indian communities in their vicinity. During the 1720s those Acolapissas, Chitimachas, and Houmas who had resettled closer to New Orleans continued to produce corn, fish, and game for city dwellers and travelers. On the Pearl River, between New Orleans and Biloxi, the Pensacolas, Biloxis, Pascagoulas, and Capinas furnished "an abundance of meat to all the French who are near enough to trade for it." Of a group of Chaouachas who migrated from the lower Mississippi to the Mobile River outside the town of Mobile, Bienville declared that "their sole occupation is to produce corn by means of which they obtain from the French what they need."[48] Other *petites nations*—the Alibamons, Biloxis, Pascagoulas, and Chahtas—migrated during the 1760s to the lower Mississippi, where they participated in riverside trade and the New Orleans market. In 1776 there were ten Indian villages, over 1,000 people altogether, interspersed among plantations along the Mississippi upriver between New Orleans and the mouth of the Red River.[49]

Many of the several thousand African slaves shipped to Louisiana during the 1720s to expand commercial agriculture turned to small-scale cultivating and marketing of foodstuffs. As in other plantation colonies, the autonomous production and distribution of foodstuffs by slaves resulted from more than the economic interests of slaveowners. In addition to producing such export staples as tobacco, indigo, and timber, black Louisianians on both small and large grants of land, called *concessions,* grew food crops for their own consumption and occasionally for their owners to sell to other colonists. On their own time slaves attended to their personal subsistence needs and eating tastes. As director of a large plantation at Chapitoulas owned by the Company of the Indies (its population in 1731 included 230 slaves), Antoine Le Page du Pratz recognized this inclination and recommended that owners give "a small piece of waste ground" to their slaves, "engage them to cultivate it for their own profit," and purchase their produce "upon fair and just terms." He also prescribed this arrangement as an alternative to the dances and assemblies held by slaves on Sundays, where he suspected they traded stolen goods and plotted rebellion.[50]

Afro-Americans became aggressive traders in the food market of Louisiana. Many slaves were sent from plantations to the towns of Mobile, New Orleans, Natchez, and Natchitoches to sell poultry, meats, vegetables, and milk on their owners' behalf. They also sold foodstuffs and other items independently of their owners whenever and wherever possible. Although the colonial government intermittently enforced regulations upon slave peddlers, requiring them by 1751 to carry written permits from their owners, the open marketing of goods by slaves benefited too many people to be forcibly prohibited during the first half of the eighteenth century. The limited self-determination for slaves that stemmed from the production and trading of food had several advantages. It helped owners to maintain their slaves at a level of subsistence minimizing hardship, death, and rebellion; it provided consumers with a larger quantity and wider array of foods than would otherwise have been available; and it gained for slaves some means of autonomy from their masters. From these circumstances in the marketplace, not to mention those in colonial kitchens, came the heavy African influence upon Louisiana's famous creole cuisine.[51]

Many slaves moved food in and out of the market with great resourcefulness. Pilferage became a means of protest against slaveowners, of supplemental nutrition within the slave community, and even of escape from bondage. In 1729 a group of young runaway slaves from *concessions* between New Orleans and Chapitoulas stole a heifer, bacon, corn, and some hens. Changereau, a Bambara from the Senegal region of West Africa, admitted to eating some of the meat but denied stealing it. Another captured member of this group, François, said he did not kill any cattle but confessed that he "stole some bacon and sold it to another negro for tobacco." A third black, Sabany, while claiming not to have joined these maroons, told the prosecutor that they had given him fresh meat in one of the Bienville cabins.[52] Throughout the eighteenth century, small fugitive camps fed themselves from plantation herds and storehouses, traded leftovers with other slaves, and even channeled goods into the open market. The fifteen or more inhabitants of one camp, discovered behind the Bienvenu estate in 1781, survived by killing stray cattle, by growing patches of corn and vegetables, and by making "baskets, sifters and other articles made of willow," which slaves on a nearby plantation sold for them in New Orleans.[53]

Most day-to-day pilferage on plantations and in towns occurred without much official notice, but cases in which theft led to arrest and prosecution reveal the variety of ways that slaves illicitly exchanged food with other Louisianians. After Alexandre Boré discovered one hundred chickens and five quarters of rice missing from his plantation at Cannes Bruslées in 1753, one of his many slaves was flogged into admitting that he had traded them away for *tafia*. The settler who bartered with him, one Faussier of Chapitoulas, was sentenced to pay fifty livres indemnity to Boré as well as a fine of one hundred livres. Meanwhile, the pilferer managed to break his chains, steal a gun, and flee into the forest. On June 3, 1782, a twenty-six-year-old slave named Juan was arrested in New Orleans; his interrogation disclosed an ambitious flight financed by theft. He crossed Lake Pontchartrain to the city after taking from his owner a pirogue, a gun and ammunition, a shirt, and some sweet potatoes. On the way he stole turkeys and hens from the De La Chaise plantation and, after selling them in New Orleans, stole five more hens from a courtyard in town. Juan sold the hens to a Frenchman named La Rochelle for cash, with which he had intended to buy gunpowder.[54]

Farmers as well as slaves from the surrounding countryside brought grains, vegetables, fruits, and poultry to the multiethnic market at New Orleans. German immigrants who settled above the city during the 1720s, numbering about fifty families in 1726, became a notable group of food provisioners. "They bring every day to the market," observed one contemporary, "all kinds of produce to the city." When raids by Choctaw rebels caused them to flee from the "German Coast" to the city in 1748, New Orleans became, as Gov. Philippe de Rigaud de Vaudreuil reported, "deprived of the comforts that those settlers provided for it by their industry and their thrift."[55] These very independent farmers, who eventually returned to their settlement, were later joined by Acadian refugees who settled just north of them and proved especially active in growing corn and rice for the colonial market. Many French, free Negro, and Canary Island families also provisioned the New Orleans vicinity from their gardens and fields. While individual transactions were usually small, collectively they amounted to a substantial volume of provisions. In August 1770, Spanish officials complained that New Orleans was suffering corn and rice shortages because upriver farmers found it more profitable to sell their produce to the English in West Florida.[56] The marketing of both food and deerskins defied trade barriers that were being raised by officials along new political boundaries.

Venison, wild fowl, and other products of hunting, fishing, and gathering made up another set of widely marketed foods. Slaves hunted, fished, and collected edible plants both for their own use and for their owners' kitchens. The Houma, Chitimacha, and other Indian communities dispersed among the plantations, as noticed by Bernard Romans in the 1770s, "serve as hunters, and for some other laborious uses, something similar to subdued tribes in New England." Within the colonial towns lived professional hunters and fishermen who like Aougust Savan, a free mulatto of New Orleans, supported their families by selling food on the levees and streets. In 1770 a traveler observed that along Lake Pontchartrain behind New Orleans, at the mouth of Bayou St. John, there were "Fishermen and Fowlers and when unemploy'd in that Business they gather Wood & burn it into Charcoal."[57] During the winter months Indian villagers dispersed into small hunting camps of ten or so families. These mobile groups were such a regular feature of the eighteenth-century landscape that they rarely drew special attention—except from visitors like Bernard Romans, who was hospitably welcomed in the winter of 1771–72 by more than one Choctaw hunting party and who observed that "there only they will entertain a stranger at free cost." These Indian camps, spread along the Alabama, Mississippi, and Red river drainages, were principally occupied with producing for the deerskin trade, but they rarely neglected to exchange venison, bear meat, and tallow for ammunition, cloth, and drink with settlers and travelers whom they encountered during the hunting season.[58]

For a long time domestic beef was scarce and expensive in Louisiana; early attempts to build herds from imported livestock proved fruitless. But a regional network of cattle trading gradually developed and, like other kinds of food exchange and the deerskin trade, involved extensive interethnic participation. In the 1720s French traders and Indian villagers around Natchitoches began moving horses and cattle eastward, down the Red River. The Caddoes, experienced horsemen since the mid-seventeenth century, when Spanish livestock herded by other Indians began to reach their villages, exchanged cattle and horses with the French and other Indians.[59] The Tunicas and Avoyelles, situated near the junction of the Red and Mississippi rivers, became important middlemen in the livestock trade; Le Page du Pratz praised the latter group "for the services they have done the colony by the horses, oxen, and cows they have brought from New Mexico."[60] The amount of beef available to Louisianians was increasing by the mid-eighteenth century, and some settlers were operating meat and dairy farms at Pointe Coupée, Barataria, and other places near New Orleans. By 1766 the average number of cattle on each farm along the lower Mississippi River was approaching fourteen head.[61] Meanwhile the settlement of Bayou Teche by Acadian farmers also expanded the livestock trade. Along with Atakapa and Opelousa Indians in southwest Louisiana, Acadians acquired cattle from the Trinity River area and started raising their own herds on open grazing lands.[62]

Slaves participated in this livestock network as drovers, herders, and dairy producers. When Joseph LeKintrek and Daniel Bopfé formed a livestock-raising partnership at the German settlements in 1741, seven of LeKintrek's slaves—three men, two women, and two children—accompanied his cattle to the new *vacherie*, where they also tended sheep, hogs, and poultry. In 1783, when New Orleans merchant Jean Baptiste Macarty purchased 180 head of oxen from the settlement of Atakapas, he employed a crew of one Indian, one Negro slave, and a few whites to drive and ferry the animals over the tricky drainage of the Atchafalaya Basin.[63] As in the case of hunting and peddling foodstuffs, bringing beef to the colonial market provided slaves with greater freedom of movement and closer contact with colonists and Indians than existed in plantation labor.

IV

The participation of Indian villagers, black slaves, and white colonists in fur and food marketing discloses closer interaction and greater cultural exchange among them than historians of colonial regions have generally portrayed. In this respect, trade in the lower Mississippi Valley generated economic roles and ethnic relations similar in flexibility and fluidity to those recently discovered for blacks in early South Carolina and Virginia.[64] Clearly, Indians did not just hunt, blacks did not just grow crops for export, and whites did not merely choose to become either subsistence farmers or staple planters. However, a complex of forces circumscribed economic and ethnic relations and minimized the leveling potential of frontier exchange. The institution of slavery, European class divisions, racism, colonial policy, and violent conflict all contributed to the building of racial barriers in Louisiana and West Florida, especially after the demographic scale tipped unfavorably for Indians. The transformation of the lower

Mississippi Valley into an agricultural export economy, which accelerated during the last quarter of the eighteenth century, further intensified the hierarchical stratification of both race and class.

Changes in the deerskin trade implemented by Spain after 1783 signaled that the network of frontier exchange stitched by inhabitants over the previous decades was beginning to ravel. Indians of the large interior nations, who had close ties to many traders, entered this period wirh high expectations of further commerce. Following the withdrawal of Great Britain from West Florida, the Choctaws, Chickasaws, and Upper Creeks negotiated new trade tariffs with the Spanish government in June 1784.[65] The deerskin trade, however, rapidly slipped under the control of a few merchant houses. The English firm of Panton, Leslie and Company, with Spanish authorization, began to monopolize trade with Indian villages east of the Mississippi. On the other side of the river, Natchitoches traders and settlers likewise gave way to better-financed and more-organized merchants.[66] Accelerated commercialization of the frontier exchange economy inexorably upset its traditional customs and patterns. Most notably, traders carried ever-larger quantities of rum into Indian villages, the distribution of gifts occurred less often, and the tribes fell into chronic debt to merchant houses and thereby became more vulnerable to pressure against their land.[67]

Sheer demographic force explains the gradual marginalization of Indians in the regional food market. As settlers increased in number and grew their own crops, the volume and variety of foodstuffs provided by Indian communities declined. Scattered bands of Louisiana Indians concentrated on bartering venison and bear oil with travelers and settlers mostly during winter months. The declining political power and economic importance of Indians also manifested itself in the formal sphere of relations, where gifts of food had customarily bound parties into a reciprocal relationship. A reduction in the level of intercolonial rivalry for Indian allegiance after 1783 diminished the willingness of Louisiana officials to share food with visiting Indians. Food thus became more strictly a market commodity just as the role of Indians in the marketplace was diminishing. Indians responded to this breakdown in food-giving protocol by committing acts of banditry against the livestock and crops of settlers.[68]

The role of slaves in food exchange was threatened by general changes in the region's economy. By the 1780s a large number of people in New Orleans had become professional peddlers or *marchands* who bought foodstuffs from producers and resold them to consumers. Increasing commercialization and the growing volume of trade made traditional price tariffs issued by the government less effective. "The peddlers are moving around in different parts of the City," reported the cabildo, "and their wares cannot be inspected by the officials and for this reason they sell the good as well as the spoiled commodities at an arbitrary price so they will not lose anything in their business." Accordingly, in September 1784 the government established a marketplace and required food *marchands,* both free and slave, to rent stalls. Slaves sent daily to sell "vegetables, milk, wild fowl, quartered venison and mutton" for their owners continued "to enjoy the liberty to sell their commodities in the City as they did before." Farmers bringing their own produce to town were allowed to sell directly to the public for three hours, after which their goods had to be sold at wholesale to the licensed traders.[69] The formation of an institutionalized marketplace in New Orleans, with fees to be paid and goods closely watched, contributed to the gradual relegation of black producers and peddlers to a subordinate status in the food market. Without either an owner's permit or an official license, slaves found it more difficult to trade openly. One visitor to New Orleans in 1797 observed that blacks vended "to raise a scanty pittance" from small stalls located between the levee and the first row of houses. But he found that most "were obliged to account to the master for the profits of the day."[70]

By the end of the eighteenth century, the frontier exchange network was rapidly being superseded by the commercial production of cotton and sugar. Even so, people living in the region did not wholly relinquish older forms of economic exchange. Even after the large tribes of the deep South were removed, Indians continued to peddle foodstuffs and other goods along the Mississippi and in Mobile, Natchez, and New Orleans. Hundreds of Louisiana Indians—Choctaws, Houmas, Chitimachas, Tunicas, and others—camped on the outskirts of New Orleans, usually during the late winter, and peddled in the city an array of foods and food-related items: venison, water fowl, and other game; such manufactures as baskets, sieves, and cane blowguns; and kindling wood, wild fruits, medicinal herbs, and such culinary spices as filé, a powder ground from sassafras leaves and used by Louisianians to make filé gumbo. Indian families also seasonally traveled Louisiana's waterways during the nineteenth century trading the same kinds of goods with both planters and slaves.[71]

Afro-Americans resorted to surreptitious forms of exchange to compensate for their deteriorating trade opportunities. In violation of ordinances adopted in the early nineteenth century by the Orleans and Mississippi territories, many residents continued to exchange goods with slaves as well as Indians. Some of the very middlemen whose appearance marked the marginalization of slaves in the food market were willing to buy items from them. Peddlers called *caboteurs,* who traveled the waterways in pirogues and bought all kinds of produce for the New Orleans market, became infamous for their illicit trade with slaves. They were frequently accused of encouraging Negroes to steal from their owners, but pilferage by slaves had long been part of their resistance and survival under bondage. Observing the plight of the marketer who was also treated as marketable property, Charles Robin aptly explained why slaves bartered with *caboteurs:* "True, the Negroes do have chickens and pigs of their own, but they can sell nothing without the permission of their masters. It is better for both the buyer and seller to do without permission."[72]

Economic life in the lower Mississippi Valley during the eighteenth century, in which many later subsistence activities and adaptive strategies were rooted, evades historians who seek only strong commercial institutions and growing export values for their evidence. Within an extensive network of coastal towns and interior posts stretching from the Alabama River to the Red River, the region's inhabitants participated in a cross-cultural web of economic relations. When one follows the movement of deerskins and foodstuffs through this network, the importance of small-scale trade among diverse groups of people comes into focus. Louisiana was indeed an extraordinary North American colony, imposing even less demographic and commercial pressure upon the continent than did French Canada. But the backcountry of England's Atlantic seaboard provinces, as well as Canada and New Mexico, also passed through a long period of frontier exchange. The form and content of interethnic relations discussed here, and made more visible by Louisiana's history, can be profitably explored at the obscure crossroads and marketplaces of other colonial regions.

NOTES

1. The most influential 19th-century studies of the imperial significance of the Mississippi Valley are Parkman, *La Salle and the Discovery of the Great West* (Boston, 1869), and Winsor, *The Mississippi Basin: The Struggle in America between England and France, 1697–1763* (Boston, 1895). The skewed emphasis in Louisiana colonial historiography on explorers and other "great men" is noted in Carl A. Brasseaux, "French Louisiana," in Light Townsend Cummins and Glen Jeansonne, eds., *A Guide to the History of Louisiana* (Westport, Conn., 1982), 4, and Patricia K. Galloway, ed., *La Salle and His Legacy: Frenchmen and Indians in the Lower Mississippi Valley* (Jackson, Miss., 1982), xii–xiii.

2. For recent historiographical assessments of Louisiana colonial scholarship see Brasseaux, "French Louisiana," and Light Townsend Cummins, "Spanish Louisiana," in Cummins and Jeansonne, eds., *Guide to the History of Louisiana,* 3–25. The most comprehensive bibliographical guide is Glenn R. Conrad and Carl A. Brasseaux, *A Selected Bibliography of Scholarly Literature on Colonial Louisiana and New France* (Lafayette, La., 1982).

3. Joe Gray Taylor's chapters on the 18th century in *Louisiana: A Bicentennial History* (New York, 1976) are entitled "Colonial Louisiana: Study in Failure" and "A Holding Action: Louisiana as a Spanish Colony." The peripheral position of Louisiana in the Atlantic economy is cogently explained in Donald J. Lemieux, "The Mississippi Valley, New France, and French Colonial Policy," *Southern Studies,* XVII (1978), 39–56.

4. For discussions of colonial economic historiography see Jacob M. Price, "The Transatlantic Economy," Richard B. Sheridan, "The Domestic Economy," and James T. Lemon, "Spatial Order: Households in Local Communities and Regions," in Jack P. Greene and J. R. Pole, eds., *Colonial British America: Essays in the New History of the Early Modern Era* (Baltimore, 1984), 18–42, 43–85, 86–122, and John J. McCusker and Russell R. Menard, *The Economy of British America, 1607–1789* (Chapel Hill, N.C., 1985), 17–34.

5. Pertinent samples of anthropological work on marketing are available in Carol A. Smith, ed., *Regional Analysis,* 2 vols. (New York, 1976), and Stuart Plattner, ed., *Markets and Marketing: Proceedings of the 1984 Meeting of the Society for Economic Development,* Monographs in Economic Anthropology, IV (Washington, D.C., 1985). The redefinition of frontier from a linear to a regional perspective has been advanced in Robin F. Wells, "Frontier Systems as a Sociocultural Type," *Papers in Anthropology,* XIV (1973), 6–15; D. W. Meinig, "The Continuous Shaping of America: A Prospectus for Geographers and Historians," *American Historical Review,* LXXXIII (1978), 1186–1217; Robert F. Berkhofer, Jr., "The North American Frontier as Process and Context," in Howard Lamar and Leonard Thompson, eds., *The Frontier in History: North America and Southern Africa Compared* (New Haven, Conn., 1981), 43–75; Kenneth E. Lewis, *The American Frontier: An Archaeological Study of Settlement Pattern and Process* (Orlando, Fla., 1984); and Francis Jennings, *The Ambiguous Iroquois Empire: The Covenant Chain Confederation of Indian Tribes with English Colonies from Its Beginnings to the Lancaster Treaty of 1744* (New York, 1984), esp. 58–83.

6. The tenuous economic connection between upper and lower Louisiana before the American Revolution is affirmed in W. J. Eccles, *France in America* (New York, 1972), 167, and John G. Clark, *New Orleans, 1718–1812: An Economic History* (Baton Rouge, La., 1970), 30. See also Carl J. Ekberg, *Colonial Ste. Genevieve: An Adventure on the Mississippi Frontier* (Gerald, Mo., 1985), 201.

7. For evaluations of the colonial historiography on Indians and blacks, respectively, see James Axtell, "The Ethnohistory of Early America: A Review Essay," *William and Mary Quarterly,* 3d Ser., XXXV (1978), 110–44, and Peter H. Wood, "'I Did the Best I Could for My Day': The Study of Early Black History during the Second Reconstruction, 1960 to 1976," ibid., 185–225. An update is available in T. H. Breen, "Creative Adaptations: Peoples and Cultures," in Greene and Pole, eds., *Colonial British America,* 195–232.

8. Dunbar Rowland and Albert Sanders, trans. and eds., *Mississippi Provincial Archives: French Dominion*, 3 vols. (Jackson, Miss., 1929–32), II, 81–89, 129–32, 232, III, 177–78, hereafter cited as *Miss. Provincial Archs.* The early dependence on trade with Indians is vividly described in Marcel Giraud, *A History of French Louisiana. 1: The Reign of Louis XIV, 1698–1715*, trans. Joseph C. Lambert (Baton Rouge, La., 1974), and Jay Higginbotham, *Old Mobile: Fort Louis de la Louisiane, 1702–1711* (Mobile, Ala., 1977). For an overview of France's colonial and domestic commitments at the time of Louisiana's beginnings see Charles Woolsey Cole, *French Mercantilism, 1683–1700* (New York, 1943), 60–111, 195–228.

9. *Miss. Provincial Archs.*, III, 183, 187–88, 193–94, 198, 213; Jean-Baptiste Bernard de La Harpe, *The Historical Journal of the Establishment of the French in Louisiana*, trans. Joan Cain and Virginia Koenig and ed. Glenn R. Conrad (Lafayette, La., 1971), 91–98, hereafter cited as La Harpe, *Historical Journal*. For overviews of the pan-Indian war against English Carolina and the shift toward the French in Louisiana see Verner W. Crane, *The Southern Frontier, 1670–1732* (Durham, N.C., 1928), 162–86, and Patricia Dillon Woods, *French-Indian Relations on the Sonthern Frontier, 1699–1762* (Ann Arbor, Mich., 1980), 33–63.

10. *Miss. Provincial Archs.*, III, 314–15, 515; La Harpe, *Historical Journal*, 130–42. See also Mildred Mott Wedel, *La Harpe's 1719 Post on Red River and Nearby Caddo Settlements* (Austin, Tex., 1978), and Stanley Faye, "The Arkansas Post of Louisiana: French Domination," *Louisiana Historical Quarterly*, XXVI (1943), 665–66.

11. This approximation of Louisiana's colonial population in 1732 is compiled from a census of inhabitants along the Mississippi River dated 1731 and a census of inhabitants and property owners of New Orleans of Jan. 1732 (Charles R. Maduell, Jr., comp. and trans., *The Census Tables for the French Colony of Louisiana from 1699 through 1732* [Baltimore, 1972], 113, 123) and from Salmon to Maurepas, May 12, 1732, Archives des Colonies, Series C13A, Correspondance Generale Louisiane, XV, 105, microfilm in Loyola University of New Orleans Library, hereafter cited as Archives des Colonies, C13A. The calculation of changes in Indian population is made in Daniel Henry Usner, Jr., "Frontier Exchange in the Lower Mississippi Valley: Race Relations and Economic Life in Colonial Louisiana, 1699–1783" (Ph.D. diss., Duke University, 1981), 66–103.

12. "General Census Taken in New Orleans and in All Districts below the City of New Orleans to Pointe Coupée in the Year 1763," in Jacqueline K. Voorhies, trans. and comp., *Some Late Eighteenth-Century Louisianians: Census Records, 1758–1796* (Lafayette, La., 1973), 103–105; Katherine Bridges and Winston DeVille [trans.], "Natchitoches in 1766," *Louisiana History*, IV (1963), 156–59.

13. *Miss. Provincial Archs.*, II, 23–24, 128, III, 52, 575–76. For theoretical discussions of the function of gift giving and other exchange rituals see the seminal works of Marcel Mauss, *The Gift: Form and Function of Exchange in Archaic Societies*, trans. Ian Cunnison (London, 1954), and Marshall Sahlins, *Stone Age Economics* (Chicago, 1972), 149–314. One of the outstanding features of Neal Salisbury's *Manitour and Providence: Indians, Europeans, and the Making of New England, 1500–1643* (New York, 1982) is his analysis of how reciprocity in Indian exchange customs operated and changed through the colonial trade.

14. Woods, *French-Indian Relations*, 13–109; Daniel H. Usner, Jr., "From African Captivity to American Slavery: The Introduction of Black Laborers to Colonial Louisiana," *La. Hist.*, XX (1979), 25–48.

15. One of the most important conflicts in the Indian and colonial history of the South, the Choctaw War had gone largely unnoticed until the recent work of Patricia Kay Galloway and Richard White. In addition to her "Choctaw Factionalism and Civil War, 1746–1750," *Journal of Mississippi History*, XLIV (1982), 289–327, Galloway has made an abundance of pertinent documents available with highly informative annotation in Dunbar Rowland and A. G. Sanders, trans. and eds., *Mississippi Provincial Archives: French Dominion, 1729–1763*, rev. and ed. Patricia Kay Galloway, 2 vols. (Baton Rouge, La., 1984). For White's provocative interpretation of French-Choctaw relations see his *The Roots of Dependency: Subsistence, Environment, and Social Change among the Choctaws, Pawnees, and Navajos* (Lincoln, Neb., 1983), 34–68.

16. Census of Louisiana in the year 1785, *American State Papers: Miscellaneous*, 2 vols. (Washington, D.C., 1834), I, 381. For information about migration into the region during the 1760s and 1770s see Gilbert C. Din, "Early Spanish Colonization Efforts in Louisiana," *Louisiana Studies*, XI (1972), 31–49, and "Spain's Immigration Policy and Efforts during the American Revolution," ibid., XIV (1975), 241–57; and J. Barton Starr, *Tories, Dons, and Rebels: The American Revolation in British West Florida* (Gainesville, Fla., 1976), 230–40.

17. For the most informative survey of the deerskin trade in Louisiana, which also exemplifies the emphasis on plans and policies, see Paul Chrisler Phillips, *The Fur Trade*, with concluding chapters by J. W. Smurr, 2 vols. (Norman, Okla., 1961), I, 220–45, 361–76, 448–83, 536–40, 569–73.

18. *Miss. Provincial Archs.*, III, 303.

19. Ibid., II, 613–14.

20. Ibid., I, 261–63, III, 497, IV, 39, 208–209.

21. Ibid., II, 647–48, III, 565.

22. Ibid., III, 596, 651–52.

23. Relation de la Louisiane [c. 1735], MS, 158–59, Edward E. Ayer Collection, Newberry Library, Chicago.

24. *Miss. Provincial Archs.*, I, 21, 86, 95, 103, III, 303–304, IV, 13–16.

25. Ibid., IV, 17–19, 170–71.

26. Ibid., 196, 198, 285, V, 89–93, 97–104.

27. Lawrence Kinnaird, trans. and ed., *Spain in the Mississippi Valley, 1765–1794*, 3 vols. (Washington, D.C., 1946–49), II, 137, 143–47, hereafter cited as *Spain in the Mississippi Valley*; Juan de la Villebeuvre, List of the Choctaw Towns and Traders, Nov. 24, 1787, Legajo 200, Papeles Procedentes de Cuba, Archivo General de Indias, Seville, Spain.

28. H. B. Cushman, *History of Choctaw, Chickasaw and Natchez Indians* (Greenville, Tex., 1899), 386–403; Alexander Spoehr, "Changing Kinship Systems: A Study in the Acculturation of the Creeks, Cherokee, and Choctaw," Field Museum of Natural History, *Anthropological Series*, XXXIII (1947), 153–235.

29. Relation de la Louisiane [c. 1735], 125; Dumont de Montigny, *Memoires Historiques Sur la Louisiane . . .*, 2 vols. (Paris, 1753), I, 181–82.

30. [Antoine] Le Page du Pratz, *Historie de la Louisiane . . .*, 3 vols. (Paris, 1758), II, 242. For major contributions to our understanding of Mobilian see James M. Crawford, *The Mobilian Trade Language* (Knoxville, Tenn., 1978); Emanuel Johannes Drechsel, "Mobilian Jargon: Linguistic, Sociocultural, and Historical Aspects of an American Indian Lingua Franca" (Ph.D. diss., University of Wisconsin, Madison, 1979), and "Towards an Ethnohistory of Speaking: The Case of Mobilian Jargon, an American Indian Pidgin of the Lower Mississippi Valley," *Ethnohistory*, XXX (1983), 165–76.

31. Le Page du Pratz, *Histoire*, I, 347; "Records of the Superior Council," *La. Hist. Qtly.*, III (1920), 74. For summaries of alcohol-related policies during the French period see N. M. Miller Surrey, *The Commerce of Louisiana during the French Regime, 1699–1763* (New York, 1916), 273–74, and Henry P. Dart, "Cabarets of New Orleans in the French Colonial Period," *La. Hist. Qtly.*, XIX (1936), 578–83.

32. Talk of Captain Ouma of Seneacha, Mobile, Jan. 2, 1772, Mississippi Historical Society, *Publications*, Centenary Ser., V (Jackson, Miss., 1925), 150–51; Bernard Romans, *A Concise Natural History of East and West Florida . . .* (New York, 1775), 56; *Spain in the Mississippi Valley*, II, 150–51.

33. "Superior Council Recs.," *La. Hist. Qtly.*, XVIII (1935), 705, 708; Juan de la Villebeuvre and Pedro Chabert vs. Simon Favre, late interprerer for the Indians, Oct. 20, 1783, Spanish Judicial Records, Louisiana Historical Center, New Orleans.

34. "Spanish Judicial Records," *La. Hist. Qtly.*, VIII (1925), 244. The symbiotic relationship between such traditional forms of exchange as itinerant peddling and more modern channels of commerce during a transitional period is illuminated in Clifford Geertz, *Peddlers and Princes: Social Change and Economic Modernization in Two Indonesian Towns* (Chicago, 1963), and Brian S. Osborne, "Trading on a Frontier: The Function of Peddlers, Markets, and Fairs in Nineteenth-Century Ontario," *Canadian Papers in Rural History: Volume II*, ed. Donald H. Akenson (Gananoque, Ont., 1980), 59–81. The adaptability and resilience of peddling are asserted in Fernand Braudel, *The Wheels of Commerce*, trans. Siân Reynolds (New York, 1982), 75–80.

35. Amos Sroddard, *Sketches, Historical and Descriptive, of Louisiana* (Philadelphia, 1812), 445.

36. Margaret Eisher Dalrymple, ed., *The Merchant of Manchac: The Letterbooks of John Fitzpatrick, 1768–1798* (Baton Rouge, La., 1978), 287–88.

37. "Spanish Judicial Recs.," *La. Hist. Qtly.*, XIV (1931), 608–10.

38. Richebourg Gaillard McWilliams, trans. and ed., *Iberville's Gulf Journals* (Tuscaloosa, Ala., 1981), 78, 170; *Miss. Provincial Archs.*, II, 13; Richebourg Gaillard McWilliams, ed. and trans., *Fleur de Lys and Calumet: Being the Pénicaut Narrative of French Adventure in Louisiana* (Baton Rouge, La., 1953), 98–103.

39. *Miss. Provincial Archs.*, II, 32–34, 52–53.

40. Ibid., III, 64. The conflict between the pro–Le Moyne and anti–Le Moyne factions, much of which centered on distribution of food supplies, is thoroughly explored in Charles Edwards O'Neill, *Church and State in French Colonial Louisiana: Policy and Politics to 1732* (New Haven, Conn., 1966), 44–47. For the regulation of food marketing in the ancien regime see Steven L. Kaplan, *Bread, Politics and Political Economy in the Reign of Louis XV*, 2 vols. (The Hague, 1976), I, 65–68.

41. *Miss. Provincial Archs.*, III, 326. For examples of profiteering by post commandants see Archives des Colonies, C13A, XI, 174–76, XIX, 142, XLIV, 21–22.

42. *Miss. Provincial Archs.*, II, 232; William M. Carroll, *Beranger's Discovery of Aransas Pass. A Translation of Jean Beranger's French Manuscript* (Corpus Christi, Tex., 1983), 33.

43. Dumont de Montigny, *Memoires Historiques*, II, 41–42; Glenn R. Conrad, trans. and ed., *Immigration and War. Louisiana, 1718–1721. From the Memoir of Charles Le Gac* (Lafayette, La., 1970), 1–8, 30–35; La Harpe, *Historical Journal*, 113, 154, 167–73.

44. *Miss. Provincial Archs.*, II, 347; Surrey, *Commerce of Louisiana*, 265–66, 291–99; Clark, *New Orleans, 1718–1812*, 30, 59–60.

45. Reuben Gold Thwaites, ed., *The Jesuit Relations and Allied Documents: Travels and Explorations of the Jesuit Missionaries in New France, 1610–1791*, 73 vols. (Cleveland, Ohio, 1896–1901), LXVII, 283. The influence of French land policy upon the development of mixed farming in Louisiana is examined in Lewis Cecil Gray, *History of Agriculture in the Southern United States to 1860*, 2 vols. (Washington, D.C., 1933), I, 337–40, and Clark, *New Orleans, 1718–1812*, 52, 183–86.

46. *Miss. Provincial Archs.*, III, 423, 535–36; Heloise H. Cruzat, trans., "Louisiana in 1724: Banet's Report to the Company of the Indies, Dated Paris, December 20, 1724," *La. Hist. Qtly.*, XII (1929), 126. Examples of military contracts with colonists for food supplies include "Superior Council Recs.," ibid., V (1922), 377–78, VI (1923), 287, VIII (1925), 275–89, XIII (1930), 157, 309. The influence of urbanization at New Orleans upon Louisiana's marketing system is suggested in J. Zitomersky, "Urbanization in French Colonial Louisiana (1706–1766)," *Annales de demographic historique 1974: Etudes, comptes, rendus, documents, bibliographie* (Paris, 1974), 263–78.

47. Romans, *Concise Natural History*, 57; Bernard Romans, "An Attempt towards a Short Description of West Florida," in P. Lee Phillips, ed., *Notes on the Life and Works of Bernard Romans* (Deland, Fla., 1924), 120.

48. *Miss. Provincial Archs.*, III, 535–36; Antoine Le Page du Pratz, *The History of Louisiana*, ed. Joseph G. Tregle, Jr. (Baton Rouge, La., 1975), 202, 233, 262–63.

49. English Provincial Records, 1763–83, III, 94–95, IV, 20–21, transcripts from the Colonial Office Records, British Public Record Office, in the Mississippi Department of Archives and History, Jackson; Philip Pittman, *The Present State of the European Settlements on the Mississippi*, ed. Robert Rea (Gainesville, Fla., 1973), 22–35.

50. Le Page du Pratz, *History of Louisiana*, ed. Tregle, 387.

51. Dumont de Montigny, *Memoires Historiques*, 242–43; Archives des Colonies C13A, XXV, 39–52; Records and Deliberations of the New Orleans Cabildo, Jan. 10, 1772, Louisiana Division, New Orleans Public Library.

52. "Superior Council Recs.," *La. Hist. Qtly.*, IV (1921), 348.

53. "Spanish Judicial Recs.," ibid., XVI (1933), 516–20, quotation on p. 520.

54. "Superior Council Recs.," ibid., XX (1937), 229–30; "Spanish Judicial Recs.," ibid., XVIII (1935), 1004–1011. Illicit marketing in another slave colony is examined as a means of autonomy and resistance in Peter H. Wood, *Black Majority: Negroes in Colonial South Carolina from 1670 through the Stono Rebellion* (New York, 1974), esp. 211–17.

55. Relation de la Louisiane [c. 1735], 19; *Miss. Provincial Archs.*, V, 30.

56. Carl A. Brasseaux, trans. and ed., "Official Correspondence of Spanish Louisiana, 1770–1803," *Revue de Louisiane/Louisiana Review*, VII (1978), 172–73; Charles Cesar Robin, *Voyage to Louisiana, 1803–1805*, trans. Stuart O. Landry, Jr. (New Orleans, La., 1966), 114–15; Thomas Ashe, *Travels in America Performed in 1806, for the Purpose of Exploring the Rivers Alleghany, Monongahela, Ohio, and Mississippi, and Ascertaining the Produce and Condition of Their Banks and Vicinity* (London, 1808), 316–27.

57. Romans, *Concise Natural History*, 71; Edward Mease, "Narrative of a Journey through Several Parts of the Province of West Florida in the Years 1770 and 1771," Miss. Hist. Soc., *Pubs.*, Centenary Ser., V, 63. For examples of plantation slaves who served as hunters see "Superior Council Recs.," *La. Hist. Qtly.*, V (1922), 385, VII (1924), 334–36, XIX (1936), 211–28. The census of June 1778 listed twelve hunters living in New Orleans (Albert J. Robichaux, Jr., comp., trans., and ed., *Louisiana Census and Militia Lists, 1770–1789* [Harvey, La., 1973], 23–68).

58. Relation de la Louisiane [c. 1735], 198; Seymour Feiler, trans. and ed., *Jean-Bernard Bossu's Travels in the Interior of North America, 1751–1762* (Norman, Okla., 1962), 146; Romans, *Concise Natural History*, 56, 202–219.

59. *Miss. Provincial Archs.*, II, 594; Surrey, *Commerce of Louisiana*, 251–54; Gray, *History of Agriculture*, I, 78–80; Elizabeth A. H. John, *Storms Brewed in Other Men's Worlds: The Confrontation of Indians, Spanish, and*

French in the Southwest, 1540–1795 (College Station, Tex., 1975), 165–95, 338–44. In their proficient participation in the formative livestock trade of the lower Mississippi valley, these Indians resembled indigenous peoples in other frontier regions. See S. Daniel Neumark, *Economic Influences on the South African Frontier, 1652–1836* (Stanford, Calif., 1957), 94–107, and Silvio R. Duncan Baretta and John Markoff, "Civilization and Barbarism: Cattle Frontiers in Latin America," *Comparative Studies in Society and History,* XX (1978), 587–620.

60. Pierre de Charlevoix, *Journal of a Voyage to North-America . . . ,* 2 vols. (London, 1761), II, 280; Le Page du Pratz, *Histoire,* I, 297–98, II, 241–42. The recent work of geographer Terry G. Jordan has revived debate over the primacy of Spanish or English influence upon cattle ranching in Texas. In *Trails to Texas: Southern Roots of Western Cattle Ranching* (Lincoln, Neb., 1981) Jordan traces the Anglo-Saxon influence to the Carolinas and follows its diffusion through the Gulf Coastal Plain. Jordan misses the cross-cultural dimension of livestock trade because the 18th-century trails *from* Texas are not examined. For a study of Texas ranching that does describe the eastward movement of cattle and horses into Louisiana see Sandra L. Myres, *The Ranch in Spanish Texas, 1691–1800* (El Paso, Tex., 1969).

61. My calculation of the average number of cattle per farm is derived from the census of the militias and inhabitants of Louisiana in 1766, in *Some Late Eighteenth Century Louisianians,* 163–214. These livestock holdings in Louisiana resemble those in some English colonial regions of North America for which figures are available. See James T. Lemon, *The Best Poor Man's Country; A Geographical Study of Early Southeastern Pennsylvania* (Baltimore, 1972), 162; Carville V. Earle, *The Evolution of a Tidewater Settlement System: All Hallow's Parish, Maryland, 1650–1783* (Chicago, 1975), 124; and Robert D. Mitchell, *Commercialism and Frontier: Perspectives on the Early Shenandoah Valley* (Charlottesville, Va., 1977), 185.

62. Herbert Eugene Bolton, trans. and ed., *Athanase de Me'zières and the LouisianaTexas Frontier, 1768–1780,* 2 vols. (Cleveland, Ohio, 1914), I, 179, II, 105–106, 242; Lauren C. Post, "The Old Cattle Industry of Southwest Louisiana," *McNeese Review,* IX (1957), 43–55, and "Some Notes on the Attakapas Indians of Southwest Louisiana," *La. Hist.,* III (1962), 221–42.

63. Elizabeth Becker Gianelloni, comp., *Calendar of Louisiana Colonial Documents. St. Charles Parish* (Baton Rouge, La., 1965), 2; "Spanish Judicial Recs.," *La. Hist. Qtly.,* XXI (1938), 1257–60. For examples of black *vacheres* or cowherds see "Superior Council Recs.," ibid., V (1922), VI (1923), 661, IX (1926), 454, XXVI (1943), 205–206. See Wood, *Black Majority,* 31, 105–106, 212–13, for the role of blacks in South Carolina herding.

64. Wood, *Black Majority;* T. H. Breen and Stephen Innes, *"Myne Owne Ground": Race and Freedom on Virginia's Eastern Shore, 1640–1676* (New York, 1980).

65. Tariff for Trade with the Chickasaw, Choctaw, and Alibamon Nations Established at a Congress in Mobile, June 22–23, 1784, Papers of Panton, Leslie and Company, University of West Florida Library, Pensacola.

66. *Spain in the Mississippi Valley,* II, 232–233; Gayoso to Morales, Feb. 7, 1799, trans. D. C. Corbitt, *Georgia Historical Quarterly,* XXV (1941), 164–69; Phillips, *Fur Trade,* II, 184–222.

67. The decline of the deerskin trade among the Upper Creeks, Choctaws, and Chickasaws is examined in Daniel H. Usner, Jr., "American Indians on the Cotton Frontier: Changing Economic Relations with Citizens and Slaves in the Mississippi Territory," *Journal of American History,* LXXII (1985), 297–317.

68. *Spain in the Mississippi Valley,* II, 59; Villebouvre to Carondelet, Mar. 30, 1793, East Tennessee Historical Society, *Publications,* XXX (1958), 101–102. The deteriorating economic position of the Choctaws during these years has been closely examined in its environmental context and in regard to its political impact in White, *Roots of Dependency,* 97–146.

69. *Spain in the Mississippi Valley,* I, 239–241; Records and Deliberations of the New Orleans Cabildo, Sept. 10, 1784.

70. Francis Baily, *Journal of a Tour in Unsettled Parts of North America in 1796 and 1797,* ed. Jack D. L. Holmes (Carbondale, Ill., 1969), 165.

71. For descriptions of Indian peddlers in the 19th century see Paul Alliot "Historical and Political Reflections on Louisiana," in James Alexander Robertson, trans. and ed., *Louisiana under the Rule of Spain, France, and the United States, 1785–1807,* 2 vols. (Cleveland, Ohio, 1911), II, 81–83; Christian Schultz, Jr., *Travels on an Inland Voyage . . . ,* 2 vols. (New York, 1810), II, 198; John Francis McDermott, ed., and Albert J. Salvan, trans., *Tixier's Travels on the Osage Prairies* (Norman, Okla., 1940), 55–59, 81–82; and Meloncy C. Soniat, "The Tchoupitoulas Plantation," *La. Hist. Qtly.,* VII (1924), 309–310.

72. Robin, *Voyage to Louisiana, 1803–1815,* trans. Landry, 36–37, 118–19.

12

THE THREE LIVES OF KEOWEE: LOSS
AND RECOVERY IN THE EIGHTEENTH-CENTURY
CHEROKEE VILLAGES

M. Thomas Hatley

In its various guises—through European settlement, military conquest, and the spread of disease—colonization devastated countless Indian villages. But as M. Thomas Hatley shows here, sometimes those communities could rise from the ashes to take on new life. While many Indians abandoned their homeland to establish new communities farther from land-hungry colonists, many others chose to remain as close as possible to territory they cherished. The Cherokees, like many Indians who stayed in the east during the eighteenth century, had to find ways to adjust to the presence of colonists, their microbes, and their livestock without abandoning traditional cultural forms. That meant participation in a market economy, increased attention to the deerskin trade or the trade in medicinal plants, and integrating colonists' livestock into their lives. While Hatley offers another example of how Indians across the east accommodated themselves to what James Merrell has called a "new world" for Native Americans, he deepens and broadens that story with his treatment of how trade had different meaning to men and women, and of how environmental change had a subtle yet profound impact on native life. Further, his account helps us understand "the process of disenchantment" of the Indian trade mentioned by Christopher L. Miller and George R. Hamell; it also contrasts with Rebecca Kugel's depiction of Ojibwa resistance to livestock Europeans introduced to Indian country.

THE THREE LIVES OF KEOWEE: LOSS AND RECOVERY IN THE EIGHTEENTH-CENTURY CHEROKEE VILLAGES

M. Thomas Hatley

THE CHEROKEE FARMING TOWN OF KEOWEE was abandoned three times in the thirty years between 1750 and 1780. The earliest Keowee was emptied in the late 1740s at the climax of war between the Cherokees and the Creeks.[1] Soon again a thriving place, Keowee was abandoned a second time amid smallpox outbreaks, famine, and warfare with the colonies.[2] After the peace, the houses were rebuilt and fields replanted with borrowed seed corn.[3] The third reformation of the town was to be the last on the old site. Its inhabitants, fatigued and pressured by the rapidly moving white farmers' frontier to the east, slowly moved away.

On the eve of the Revolutionary War William Bartram turned away from the slow, muddy Savannah and rode north along the clearer river that shared the town's name. But upon arriving at Keowee he was disappointed to find only "several dwellings inhabited by white people concerned in the Indian trade." In the surrounding valley bottom the naturalist observed an emptiness made more disturbing by evidence of recent abandonment, a vacant mountain valley where "the vestiges of the ancient Indian dwellings are yet visible on the feet of the hills bordering and fronting on the vale, such as the posts or pillars of their habitations."[4]

The short history of Keowee tells more than the story of a single unlucky place. The residents of Keowee were not alone in either their suffering or in their determined will to survive the hardships of the eighteenth century. Other Cherokee towns also faced destruction and accomplished reconstructions of their own, and though some towns resisted final abandonment more successfully than Keowee, no Cherokee hamlet could offer its people sanctuary against hard times. Towns like Keowee survived through most of the eighteenth century as the homeplaces of Cherokee life, but by the middle years of the century village economies, settlement patterns, and demography were all undergoing rapid change. The experience of

SOURCE: Peter H. Wood et al., eds., *Powhatan's Mantle: Indians in the Colonial Southeast* (Lincoln, Neb.: University of Nebraska Press, 1989), 223–48.

collective change, and the vital tribal resistance that shaped its course, was not confined to the villagers of Keowee, or even to the Cherokees as a whole, but was a historical experience to which indigenous folk across the southeastern region could also lay claim (see Figure I).

"THEY ARE NOT NOW HALF": VILLAGE POPULATION DECLINE

The central influence on the eighteenth-century Cherokee villages was a painful and prolonged population decline. The histories of towns such as Keowee encapsulate this demographic and economic theme. The places families walked away from in the depression of the 1930s—the Piedmont of Georgia, the Texas panhandle, or the sandhills of Nebraska—offered no scenes of rural decay more striking than Cherokee settlements hard hit by warfare or famine. William Bartram recognized the characteristic landscape of depression and out-migration around the Keowee ghost town. Other white contemporaries of the tribespeople were even better positioned than Bartram to understand the demographic riptide that had caught Keowee. Four traders, forty-year veterans of the mountain villages, testified in 1751 to the population disaster they had witnessed during their long residence in the towns. "The nation," they reported, "in our time has been greater than at present. We remember since there were six thousand stout men in it. They are not now half."[5]

The "true and exact account" of the Cherokee population submitted by missionary Francis Varnod to his English home office provides an early and exceptionally valuable corroboration of this impression.[6] Varnod's "account" reveals a damaged tribal population in 1721, with at least two significant symptoms of ill health. First, the Cherokee sex ratio was slightly skewed, with women outnumbering men in the towns by a small margin.[7]

Another, much more significant population feature was indicated by the Varnod figures: the proportion of children in the villages was much lower than would be expected in a normal population. If Varnod's Cherokee data are compared with contemporary figures for other major tribes of the same period and region, the mountain towns rank at the bottom in percentage of children.[8] The youthful population cohort of the 1720s matured into a proportionally small adult generation by the middle years of the century. Thus the diminished number of children lowered the resilience of the Cherokee population, and whatever upward rebound may have occurred from time to time was all too easily erased by war and disease. For this reason the Cherokee population showed few intervals of recovery and either declined or simply failed to grow through most of the century.[9]

Slow population recovery from seventeenth-century losses, compounded by mortality suffered during invasion by eighteenth-century colonial armies and pathogens, further undermined the Cherokee towns from within. Epidemics are remembered almost as clearly as war in the historical record. The smallpox epidemic among the tribe in 1738 may have killed half of the tribespeople; the disease recurred a generation

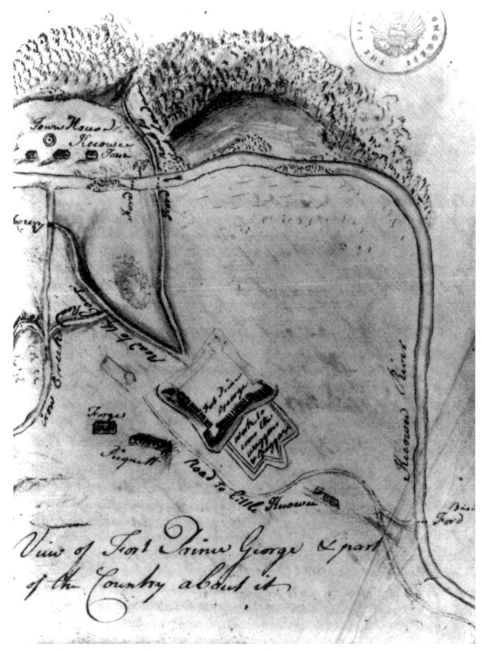

Figure I: Keowee and Fort Prince George, from Christoph French's journal, 1761. *Courtesy of the Library of Congress.*

later in 1759–60 during the so-called Cherokee War with the English colonists, and again in the early 1780s.[10] These outbreaks drew some of their intensity from a background of chronic sickness in the towns, which set the stage for damaging synergies of "infection with infection."[11] Precisely this kind of epidemiologic double-threat occurred in 1760 when a handful of western towns already suffering from smallpox were hard hit by "a violent disorder in their stomach and a flux." This outbreak changed the map of the western Cherokee settlements at one stroke; an informant reported "that in Eyoree they had lost about sixty men, women and children, and in Settiquoh, thirty-five, and Nottehh was almost depopulated by it, most that escaped the disorder there having removed from thence."[12]

The well-being of towns' economies was inseparable from the health of their residents. For example, malnutrition (prompted by warfare or crop failure) would have increased the severity and duration of cases of measles, a disease that did killing work among southeastern tribespeople.[13] Warfare affected many villages and in its wake left survivors and noncombatants weakened and susceptible to disease. The scorched-earth campaigns waged by the colonial whites during the Cherokee and Revolutionary wars killed far more people by creating starvation in the towns than by battlefield combat. A colonial officer remembered the scene near the Keowee garrison in 1761: "These creatures had been reduced to live for a considerable time upon old-Acorns, a food that we know will barely keep Hogs alive and their hunger was so pinching that some of them were detected in grabbling up the grains of Corn and beans after they were planted around the Fort."[14]

Though natural causes—drought or insect pests—are readily identifiable and have traditionally been blamed for famine, hunger, and sickness, has not only an environmental but also a social pathology. Damage to community safety nets, whether stored food supplies or medical care, could trigger starvation in the villages.[15] During the war with the colonies in 1759–61, basic town-based social services were taxed far beyond their limits. Dwellings and storehouses were burned. Even the promise of new crops in the field was destroyed without much effort. "It may not be amiss to observe," as a colonial military campaigner noted, "that ten acres of Indian corn are much sooner and easier pulled up and effectually destroyed than one of wheat or any British grain; as 'tis supposed, there are at least 1000 stalks of wheat for one of Indian corn in an acre of ground, and a stalke of this may be pulled up with very little trouble or stooping."[16]

The late-colonial military campaigns against the Cherokees cost much more than a "little trouble" for the colonists. Yet the overwhelming hardships were suffered by the tribespeople. Invasions, famine, and disease outbreaks, especially when they occurred in combination to create "crisis times" of short but immensely damaging duration (and of which the three years of the Cherokee War are the best example), disrupted the older round of village activities and crippled the effectiveness of the basic life support provided in the towns. By the end of the century, the obstacles of the time were remembered in the stories of town elders, but they were also revealed in a silent, but just as compelling, record of economic change.

"Little Farms": Depopulation and Mountain Farming

Farming constituted the fundamental underpinning of the "social services" on which the health of the villagers depended. In threatened villages such as Keowee, tribespeople improved their odds of survival not only by rebuilding houses but also by replanting fields in new ways. Cherokee towns, like farm communities the world over, were not only habitations but also designs for agricultural production. This double-sidedness meant that changes in the appearance or geography of the towns themselves also reflected underlying economic adjustments. The traditional shape of the Cherokee town was linear, snaking alongside rivers where moist and nitrogen-rich alluvial soils could be found. In 1761 the 120 houses of Nukassee were, to the appraising eye of an English captain, "straggling" in a thin line as they followed the bends of the Little Tennessee River, the houses themselves placed far enough apart that they could not be "commanded by a single musket shott."[17]

When towns with a diffuse and extensive settlement pattern like that of Nukassee lost population, the cultivation of faraway fields became more difficult. Effective communal work in land clearing and tending (which was originally carried out mostly on larger fields away from the towns) required time, which was growing scarcer in the towns. Distant outfields were easy targets during war, and military engagements with colonial forces encouraged the abandonment of outfields as temporary measures. And this shift often became permanent. James Adair observed the change in planting locations, writing that "planting a great many fields of beans and pease, in distant places after the summer crops were over" had "contracted since the general peace."[18] As a result of these factors, the microgeography of Cherokee farming changed; fields moved nearer the villages and, consequently, closer to the household domains of Cherokee women.[19]

Nearly all of the new crops acquired by the Cherokees during the colonial period fit into the gardens tended by women. William Bartram labeled these gardens "little plantations" and only with great effort avoided trampling the "lots" as he rode into Cowee town in 1775.[20] James Adair stressed the household tie of "small farms" by noting that "every dwelling-house has a small field pretty close to it."[21] Annual crops new to the Appalachians, such as the sweet potato, were planted in these spots by the middle decades of the century. Domestic animals accepted by the Cherokees, notably hogs and chickens, were fed from garden sites. While confined to "convenient penns" during the growing season, hogs were fattened on the surplus of culled wild garden plants such as "long pursly and other wholesome weeds" gathered in the course of tending.[22] Thus selective crop and animal introductions, along with parallel changes in cultivation style, increased the productivity of indigenous Appalachian farming at a time of great need. The recasting of agroecology and field patterns partially bridged the farm labor gap and allowed the villages to better resist famine, disease, and warfare.

The progressive impact of population stress within the Cherokee farming economy could also be seen in the decline in the actual number of Cherokee towns. The

Varnod list contained the names of fifty-two towns, but forty years later the number had dwindled to fewer than thirty-five.[23] However, the pace of this decline, 10 percent per decade over this interval, may well have been slower than the overall drop in Cherokee population. If this was in fact the case, not only did the number of towns fall, but the average size of the villages also decreased. Furthermore, because villages were the productive center of tribal agriculture, the diminished number of towns can be understood as a proxy agricultural statistic—and a negative one. The loss of each town entailed the loss of the prior investment made over many years in clearing fields and building storehouses. Less concrete but just as important was the alienation of environmental information, hard won on some sites through generations of experiment, of individual fields, microclimates, and soils, knowledge crucial to farming success.

The Cherokees had an affection for individual places and townsites that cannot be evoked by statistics and that was based on just such close observation. The repeated recolonization of the Keowee townsite reflected this continuing identification and understanding of local landscapes. The meanings of many Cherokee town names recall landscape familiarity that was threatened in the eighteenth century. Kunstutsiyi meant "sassafras place," Kulsetsiyi identified "honey-locust place," and Itseyi meant "new green place."[24] Rebuilding towns like Keowee or the neighboring village of Seneca after forced abandonment seems in retrospect to have been a poor piece of strategy, since other pullbacks often followed.[25] However, there was an economic wisdom in returning to the favorable locations and easily reopened fields of the old towns. For towns suffering severe casualties, the labor saved by not creating a new town from scratch was a persuasive reason to risk staying with old sites.

While the option of rebuilding was favored at certain towns, it was clearly not always possible. Although there seems to have been an abundance of room in a depopulated countryside, the dynamics of mid-eighteenth century settlement patterns sometimes meant that just the opposite was true. For example, during the 1760s some towns had begun to occupy distinctly unproductive sites, not accommodating to farming, along higher-elevation river valleys. For instance, a soldier-diarist of the Cherokee War judged one such settlement, the town of Allijoy, "but a poor place standing upon a narrow strip of Land under high hills" where fields were restricted to "deep narrow bottom, surrounded by very high mountains."[26] Towns such as Allijoy may have offered refuge from the brunt of conflict in more exposed parts of Cherokee territory, but such safety was bought at an economic cost.

The dark shading of the picture presented of Allijoy and other eighteenth-century Cherokee townscapes foreshadowed hard times to come. The occupation of marginal village sites was a first step toward the eventual breakup of tribal towns late in the century and the transformation of the Cherokee territory into a land of more or less isolated farmsteads, somewhat like those of white farmers.[27] Yet until the 1780s the Cherokees seem to have determinedly remained villagers. Against the corrosive population stress that taxed Cherokee farming in various ways and the recurrent persecution by the colonists that took a toll in the lives of Keowee and Allijoy, the

Cherokees survived by adapting their farming to the hard circumstances of the century. However, the Cherokee economy was too complex for a complete solution to be found solely in the reform of farming.

"BUYING AS WE DO":
CROPS AS COMMODITIES IN TWO MARKETPLACES

During the late colonial period, village subsistence crops were at times also commodities for exchange. Commerce between the Cherokees and the colonists involved far more than buying and selling such "consumer goods" as cloth. The most basic elements of village nutrition, such as corn, also emerged as trade items. The role of crops as both village foods and commodities revealed some of the stresses affecting production and exchange in the villages, as well as an accommodation made by villagers to their changing subsistence situation.

During the worst years for the Cherokees, entire regions failed to achieve a proper harvest, and these oscillations were made more erratic by the tribe's decline in population—and hence in available labor. Natural enemies of crops—insect outbreaks and frosts—worked along with social disruptions to exaggerate the normal swing of corn supplies between plenty and scarcity.[28] On the one hand, abundance was liberally documented by colonial invaders in the villages, who paused with torch in hand to comment on the sophistication of the tribe's farming: "The neatness of these towns and their knowledge of agriculture would surprize you," wrote one correspondent, "they abounded in every comfort of life, and may curse the day we came among them."[29]

Further causes of stress lay outside the village boundaries and were related to regional trends affecting other tribal economies in the Southeast. The declining circulation of tribal foods in a damaged network of intertribal trade also affected the subsistence base of the tribe. Corn, along with other commodities, had been an element in a precontact, intertribal trading system that had helped compensate for local insufficiencies.[30] The breakdown of this trade owing to the political disruptions of the period progressively heightened the problems the villages faced in continuing to achieve a reliable food supply.

The mid-century scarcity of salt—another vital element of nutrition and one for which the tribespeople had been largely dependent upon trade—suggests the former importance of indigenous commerce and the consequences of its disruption, already in full swing at the beginning of the eighteenth century. Highly valued by the tribe and unavailable in the Cherokee mountains, salt had been acquired by the tribe through indigenous supply lines stretching from the limestone country to the west and north.[31] The widespread use by the middle of the eighteenth century of an ersatz salt, made from the ashes of plants and consequently poor in sodium, suggests the disruption of the salt trade. As a consequence of the virtual interdiction of salt trading, the health of the villagers was unavoidably affected for the worse.[32] And the villages became more and more tied to bargaining with colonists for salt.

The changing pattern of corn exchange is better documented than the trade involving salt and is no less suggestive of basic changes in subsistence possibilities for the tribe. With good harvests the Cherokees supplied corn to their neighbors, whether Native American or white. The reply of Connecortee of Chota, a principal Overhill liaison with the English, to a request for corn to feed South Carolina's military construction crews in 1756 throws light on the traditional conduct of transactions for a critical food:

> 'Tis true it is very hungry times here but what little we have we will share it with them and when there is a Want we will all want together, 'tis true it is very hungry Times and believe we shall be all very poor but in the Fall of the Year we shall recover our Flesh and grow fatt again. We get nothing here but what we buy from one another and what Cloaths we buy from Mr. Elliott. It is as if it was lent us for we are obliged to give it away again for corn. We have but little amongst us and your people may also have a part of what there is for buying as we do, one from another.[33]

Connecortee's message contains the phrases of reciprocity—"we will all want together"—that were essential to the traditional conduct of Cherokee trade. This obligation, stated several times in the passage, translates roughly into the following: because we share corn as a matter of courtesy and necessity among ourselves, we shall do the same for you. The willingness to participate in formalized sharing, perhaps derived from past scarcities of vital foods, provided an ethical motivation for the cycling and redistribution of corn and other elements essential to the stability of traditional Cherokee subsistence. However, hard and even hostile bargaining over price had, at least by the middle of the century, become part of Cherokee negotiations concerning the sale of corn. In a letter to Charlestown, the commander of the English garrison at Fort Loudoun apologized for the high price he was forced to pay to the Cherokees for "ten Cannoes" of corn and laid the blame squarely on the villagers: "I perceive that they begin to grow very saving of their corn on account of the great Famine that was amongst them last year. Indeed I must say that there was a very wrong method to purchase their corn, too much salt was given to the Indians for it, by which means they were soon supplied with salt and immediately ceased to bring any more corn."[34] During the siege of the Overhills fort, the Cherokees were still selling corn to their near-hostages, but for a price so high that the garrison managed to meet the asking price only by "almost stripping themselves (both men and women), to make one joint public stock."[35]

"THE WENCHES, AS USUAL, BROUGHT CORN": CULTURAL RESTRAINTS IN TRADING

Women played a dominant role not only in growing corn but also in selling it. The role of indigenous women in supplying colonial military garrisons was well documented because it was a cause of unease on the colonial Cherokee War home front,

since sexual and commercial traffic were presumed to go together as partners in sub-
version. "The wenches, as usual, brought corn," and other sentences to the same
effect regularly inspired alarm among readers of the Charlestown newspaper.[36]
However, Cherokee women, in spite of their often ambiguous role in political crises,
clearly managed to avoid the market dependency into which "settlement tribes" and
other crossroad-peoples were falling at mid-century. Among the Catawbas, the
marketplace had usurped traditional tribal farming in providing food for the villages.
"King Haigler," the tribe's spokesman to South Carolina, acknowledged this
reliance on white farmstead-produced foods and accepted it as a benefit of peace
with Charlestown: "So long shall we live in peace with all the Indians and Brothers
with the white People, we can go where we will to purchase corn or hunt for there
is nothing to hurt us but sickness."[37]

Traditional village products such as herbs for medicines and dyes were collected
mainly by Cherokee women and traded even more extensively than corn. Sales of
medicinal herbs, like corn trading, must be understood in the context of trading and
gift giving within the village as well as colonial marketplace economies. Gathering
plants remained largely women's (and perhaps children's) work, as it traditionally had
been, but Cherokee women also embraced the economic opportunities extended by
an enthusiastic colonial demand for *materia medica*.

By the 1760s the Cherokees were major southeastern suppliers of three plants,
each adapted to Appalachian hill habitats: Indian pink, ginseng, and Virginia snakeroot.[38] The dried roots of these plants had become high-value commodities in part
because of the changing disease environment of the colonies. Parasites newly imported
to the Southeast created a new demand for Indian pinkroot in ports like Charlestown,
where during the 1760s the "worm fevers" remedied by the herb were rife among children.[39] Not only was the herb consumption of the "low country" of South Carolina
and Georgia substantial, but merchants shipped a large volume of the dried plants
from Charlestown to England. Fourteen barrels of dried Virginia snakeroot left the
dock in 1764 alone.[40]

Such a large quantity of herb export provides a crude index to the considerable
time required in the mountain villages of the Cherokees to gather and dry the plants.
Collecting had to take place at many kinds of sites, and at only certain seasons. As a
result, some villagers may have been tempted to neglect the farming tasks that overlapped with the collection seasons of the herbs. This situation had occurred earlier
around Montreal, where the local tribespeople were "so taken up with the trade that
they could not be engaged for any other business."[41] However, the Cherokees seem
to have managed to avoid this problem, even while they fully participated in the new
enterprise.

The limits enforced by the villagers themselves to avoid labor conflict were reinforced by the biological response of the plants themselves. As John Drayton reported
from South Carolina late in the century: "Ginseng has been so much sought after by
the Cherokee Indians that it is by no means so plentiful as it used to be in this state."[42]
Though the villagers could scarcely be blamed for the declining statewide ginseng

population late in the century, local scarcities obviously did occur and limited profitable collection. Such scarcity may partially explain the high prices (at least relative to the colonial market price) paid for ginseng by neighboring tribal trade partners of the Cherokees. For instance, one ginseng root was bringing three buckskins (20 or 30 percent of the price of a gun in the colonial trade) in the Lower Creek towns by 1770.[43]

However, the commercial logic of intercolonial or intertribal trade did not completely govern the exchange of corn or herb stocks. In both cases, cultural restraints implicit in Cherokee patterns of governance and gender relationships also dampened the scale of participation. For instance, a certain degree of control over gathering ginseng was exercised by priestly authorities and through the less formal almanac wisdom of the townspeople. By collecting for commercial purposes herbs that had ritual uses among the tribe, village women likely found themselves in conflict with the priestly elders, with whom they also clashed in other domains (for instance, in farming activities when male "rainmakers" accused the female farmers of conspiring to rob them of their "fee" for a good summer's rainfall). However much the village women may have chafed at restrictions and admonitions from the "old cunning prophets" about herb collecting, they listened with at least some measure of respect.[44] Perhaps a kind of village compromise was made, as was often the case in consensual Cherokee politics.

Whatever the exact terms of this compromise, the collection of ginseng for sale to white merchants continued long after the colonial period and coexisted with a noncommercial, ritual collection practiced by Cherokee shamans. Working in the 1880s, James Mooney recorded the persistence of sacred formulas employed in digging the "little man" (as ginseng was called). The ceremony began with the shaman asking forgiveness from the mountainside where he was about to dig the root of the plant. Only after this invocation could the shaman put his hoe into the "flesh" of the mountain, the "great man."[45] Market collectors, if they bothered with this formality at all, must have dramatically shortened it in order to quickly fill the barrels on the Charlestown docks; however, at least a few and perhaps many Cherokees long preserved a degree of restraint in the commercial pursuit of the "little man."

The Deerskin Trade as a Damaging Village Cottage Industry

Another trading endeavor affected the village economy in a more extensive and less controlled fashion. Killing deer and preparing deerskins for trade are usually depicted as activities carried out on the hunting grounds and, consequently, the nearly exclusive handiwork of Native American men helped by female companions. While this may have been accurate in the earlier years of the trade, by the middle years of the century, many skin-preparation tasks—scraping, tanning or smoking the hides, and transporting the finished leather—had grown into cottage industries operating out of the villages. Both the diminished resident labor pool of the towns and the contraction (forced by competition with settlers for white-tailed deer) of hunting territories toward settled areas contributed to the intensification of trade-connected work in the towns. The large volume of deerskin leather shipped from Charlestown and other ports, of which a large fraction was of Cherokee origin, suggests the scale of village work required in producing the skins.[46]

Each of the tens of thousands of tanned skins sent to Charlestown represented an accumulation of village labor. The traditional brain-tanning process could take a week or more, and this, as well as many other tasks, was undertaken by "poor hunters and women."[47] The early years of the trade, when human "burdening" was still the rule, may have been the harshest for villagers, with women carrying more of the load even than "poor hunters." In his trip up the Savannah River, Mark Catesby witnessed the manner in which tribal "women serve instead of packhorses carrying the skins of deer which they kill, which by much practice they perform with incredible labor and patience. I have often travelled with them fifteen or twenty miles a day for many days successively, each woman carrying at least sixty and sometimes eighty weight at their back."[48] Horses offered a way of transforming this hard task, so they were quickly adopted by the tribe. Leather rapidly moved from human to horseback, and the Cherokees even became providers of packhorses to white traders for a time.

Cherokees continued to participate heavily in the deerskin trade up until the Revolutionary War. But as early as the 1760s there were periodic problems in this commerce that reflected the diminished labor resources of the villages. Maintaining a proper quality of skins shipped from the mountains had by then become a chronic concern for colonial merchants. The Directors of the Indian Trade, empowered in the wake of the Cherokee War to oversee the operation of the newly regulated trade, complained in 1763 of "the enormous foul Dressing of Deer Skins by the Indians, and their still leaving the same incumbered with Hoofs and Snouts, so detrimental to the Leather."[49]

Processing large quantities of skins grew increasingly difficult with fewer persons, and tribal control of the carrying trade had ended before mid-century. Given these facts and the escalating strain of processing skins, it was not surprising that the Cherokees, especially village women, never (as far as records show) protested the proposal of a former trader who had planned in the late 1750s to build a "lanyard and shoe and harness factory" near one of their towns.[50] What became of this trader and his entrepreneurial ambitions apparently went unreported. However, within two decades the demand for deerskins had started to decline, along with the incentive of tribespeople and white merchants alike to trade. Many Cherokees, especially the female farmers of the diminished towns, must have welcomed the slipping away of the deerskin trade and the intensive labor obligations it had created for them.

RUM, RED STROUDWATER, GUNS, AND EAGLES: THE IMPACT OF GENDER-RELATED TRADING

The deerskin trade absorbed the efforts of many Cherokee men and overshadowed the effects of other commercial entanglements with the colonies. However, there was also a less well-known form of deerskin trading within the villages, where deerskins and leather were used as a kind of currency. The purchases made in the villages were different from the items bought at trading houses. Five hundred dressed skins, paid to the family of a murder victim, was the prevailing cost of absolution from the crime; two pounds of leather in one case excused the killer of a village dog.[51] James Adair remembered a village's pooling contributions amounting to two hundred pounds of leather to pay for killing a "large eagle" to be used in village rituals.[52] Headmen quoted Josiah Wedgwood's agent a very steep price of "five-hundred weight of leather for every ton" of "ayoree white earth" from a pit near Cowee.[53] John Stuart described the way such prices were reckoned. "If one man kills another's horse, breaks his gun, or destroys anything belonging to him, by accident or intentionally when in liquor; the value in deerskins is ascertained before the Beloved Man; and if the aggressor has not the quantity of leather ready he either collects it amongst his relations or goes into the woods to hunt for it."[54]

The cost of village-purchased goods and of services such as crime-related compensation set by headmen was high relative to the usual cost of items in the colonial trade. For instance, a gun listed for only fourteen pounds of leather just after the Cherokee War.[55] The cost of the trade gun (though often presumed to be ultimate in high-technology trade items most valuable to the tribe) seems modest and even undervalued next to prices paid for eagles, ginseng roots, or buying off revenge in the villages.

In the village-centered commerce, as well as in the better-known trade with whites, men were the primary sellers and purchasers of goods. Consequently the various goods and services obtained in these transactions for the most part reflected the values and preferences of Cherokee men. For Cherokee warriors, rifles, eagle wings, horses, red cloth, and eventually even rum were essential to the proper conduct of Cherokee manhood. Of course women also benefitted from the colonial trade by acquiring iron hoes, fabric scraps for dying, dresses, and even sidesaddles. But it is arguable that the male-to-male conduct of most transactions made it impossible for indigenous women to benefit as much as did Cherokee and white men.[56]

While women did not share equally from the acquisition of trade goods, they also paid a disproportionate price by laboring to produce the finished deer leather, and in this way they subsidized a male-dominated commerce. Because deerskin work absorbed the efforts of towns already taxed by depopulation, the volume of the trade represented a direct and increasing expenditure of the village labor and a distraction from basic subsistence tasks. Another, less direct cost was also entailed in the long absences of men from the villages while hunting. The work of women was therefore increased in several ways by both intra- and extra-village trading by men.

The tension between the economic activities of Cherokee men and women is highlighted in the different trading modes utilized by Cherokee women selling corn and by Cherokee men selling deerskins. Whether sold inside or outside the village boundaries, deerskins were less raw trade material than, in a sense, indigenous commercial paper freely traded at whatever price the market would bear. On the other hand, corn was bought and sold much more conservatively. In fact, corn was often given away in the villages in accordance with traditional subsistence ways. When corn was traded to whites, however, the price asked was often very high. High prices for Cherokee corn sold to village outsiders and respect for reciprocal trading inside the towns were consistent elements of domestic economic adaptation. Corn prices were used defensively, to shield essential foods from being drawn into the colonial market-place. In this way important routines of cooperation in the distribution of these essential commodities within the village agricultural economy were preserved.

The apparent distinction in trading strategy between the Cherokee sexes may also reflect lessons women learned from their firsthand observations of the problems in the villages induced by the deerskin trade. Even though there were more limited trading opportunities for corn than for deerskins outside the villages, Cherokee women seem to have also been more reticent than men about selling their harvest. As the principal sellers (or givers) of corn, Cherokee women played a significant role in avoiding the close and damaging market link forged by Cherokee men in their involvement with the colonial deerskin trade. When they chose to do so they traded corn, but on their own terms and in accordance with their own interest in maintaining the female dominance of the Cherokee domestic subsistence economy. Significantly, Cherokee women were willing to become active participants in colonial commerce in other arenas than core farming activities, for example, in collecting and selling herbs. But the trading conducted by Cherokee men was more overtly commercial, much more extensive, and more closely attuned to the pattern of personal political leadership that increasingly marked the public arena of intercultural relations. An unmistakably Cherokee and distinctly male pattern of consumption, funded by deerskin production and trade, increasingly became a route to personal prestige and power for some Cherokee men. In this light the existence of two gender-related trading patterns among the tribe seems to reflect both the distinctive experiences and the collective ambitions of the Cherokee sexes.

"ACROSS THE OPEN PLAIN": BRITTLENESS IN THE VILLAGE FOREST ECONOMY

Other economic conflicts developed as a result of the separate evolution of apparently unconnected village-based economic pursuits. The advent of the horse in the mountain towns early in the century, for example, immediately conflicted with the farming activities of women. Those who had acquired European animals, mainly men but sometimes women, were forced to "tether the horses with tough young bark-ropes, and confine the swine to a convenient penn, from the time the provisions are planted, till they are gathered in." Owners who balked at these restraints were likely to find the women "as good as their word, by striking a tomohawk into the horse."[57] Yet men seem to have won out, and horses became a fixture of villages. By the 1760s, James Adair could write that "almost everyone hath horses, from two to a dozen."[58]

Other land-based activities combined with widespread horse husbandry to profoundly change the outlying village landscape. For example, conflict with white settlers

over access to good land and village labor scarcity had by the 1760s caused the Cherokee hunters to pull back their hunting activities into the hills of the tribal heartland.
Since fire was the traditional tool the Cherokees used to enhance hunting success, the
pullback translated into more frequent low-intensity burning by deer hunters. As a
result of the effects of increased fire and grazing, which overrode the natural tendency
of the Appalachians toward forest, the Cherokee country progressively took on a more
open and pastoral look.[59]

The changed landscape surrounding the Cherokee villages presented a problem
for continuing ancient and important subsistence activities of female villagers. The
progressive disappearance of easily accessible forests near villages meant new difficulties in collecting the nuts, fruits, and herbs that were a familiar part of Cherokee
subsistence. The quality and reliability of forest gathering, in many respects a kind of
quasi-agriculture, had been enhanced over generations by selecting and protecting
valuable shrubs and trees.[60] During the early eighteenth century, collecting nuts and
processing them into oil still complemented village diets of corn, beans, and sweet
potatoes. William Bartram was impressed during his visit to the tribe by the "incredible amount" of hickory nuts he saw gathered and converted to oil by village women.[61]

Over centuries village gathering had evolved a flexible and opportunistic style
designed to take advantage of temperate-forest phenomena even less predictable than
annual nut crops. For example, passenger-pigeon flocks arrived in the Tennessee
River Valley at irregular intervals. Returning to habitual roosts, the flocks hovered
like a "biological storm" in the forest while taking advantage of the same surplus nut-
fall the tribespeople sought.[62] The sudden advent of the flocks caused the Cherokees
to switch quickly from nut to pigeon collection, after which the birds themselves were
processed into storable fat. "The pigeons," Mark Catesby wrote, "afford them some
years great plenty of oyl which they preserve for winter use . . . with it they also supply the want of fat in wild Turkeys; which in some Winters become very lean of being
deprived of their food by the numerous flights of the migratory pigeons devouring
the acorns and other mast."[63]

Though gathering was not as labor-intensive as farming, its success was also
affected by population decline. The ability to be in the right place at the right time to
take advantage of a fleeting appearance of nuts, pigeons, or herbs depended upon a latitude of time for work. Maintaining this flexibility—whether in fields or in forests—
was increasingly difficult as both labor and time became scarcer in the villages. With
the transformation of the semi-cultivated Cherokee countryside into a quite different
land in the last quarter of the eighteenth century, the villages found themselves to a
degree cut off from an old and formerly dependable source of sustenance.[64]

The new appearance of the "Cherokee country" was due largely to tensions stemming from activities—hunting and horse keeping—dominated by Cherokee men.
William Bartram observed that while men were hunting away from the villages, "the
whole care of the house falls on the women, who are then obliged to undergo a good
deal of labor, such as cutting and bringing home the winter's wood, which they toat
on their back or head a great distance, especially those of the ancient large towns,

where the commons or old fields extend some miles to the woodland."[65] For the farmer/villager (who was in all likelihood a woman) changes in the heartland often meant longer and less profitable workdays.

One legacy of the intercultural conflicts of the previous century and a half was the vegetational instability of the grassy parklands, where European plants, assisted by fire and other disturbances, had colonized the habitats of native species. This botanical invasion mirrored the social realities in the villages; young forests and "old fields" no longer effectively concealed approaches to the towns. Revolutionary-era militia, mimicking the invasion of the plants, seized upon the new open surroundings of some Cherokee villages as easy avenues for horseback attack. South Carolinian Andrew Pickens led such a raid in 1781; armed with specially smithed short swords, his men hacked to death the unarmed occupants of a village as they fled defenseless and on foot "across the open plain" newly fringing their town.[66]

Bittersweet Survival: "Greatest Prosperity in Their Way"

The name of the persistently resettled town of Keowee meant "mulberry grove place." Like many other Cherokee town names, the meaning of Keowee evoked more than local scenery; it concealed an oblique economic reference. Mulberry trees had been one of the forest species encouraged near the villages by the tribespeople as a source of food and fiber. In 1724 Mark Catesby returned to Charlestown from his trip up the Savannah River with "an Indian apron made of the bark of wild mulberry," quite possibly made by Cherokee women.[67] Their mastery of this traditional material and others was so admired by Edmond Atkin that he described the Cherokees as "the most ingenious Indians."[68] The Cherokee women of one town were themselves confident enough of their craft, and of the political and economic status it implied, to ask an early Carolina colonist to send to "that good Woman," Queen Anne, "a present from them viz a large carpet made of mulberry bark for herself to sit on and twelve small ones for her Counsellours."[69]

The possibility of profitably rechanneling the products of the useful mulberry tree did not escape diligent colonial development experts. The earl of Egmont, searching for a livelihood for the settlers in newly established Georgia, jotted this bit of intelligence in his journal: "The Chickasaws report they have a multitude of mulberry trees in their country, and if instructed to make silk, will bring great quantities."[70] In spite of the ambitions of the colonists, however, neither the Chickasaws nor their neighbors to the east, the Cherokees, proved to be easily "instructed." The inhabitants of "mulberry grove place" and other villages continued to carry on with adaptations of the old ways, making baskets of bark instead of silk cloth.

A kind of cultural self-instruction took place in the survival of this and other elements of village work. The most successful and visible economic adaptation to population loss, the "little farms," appeared in the villages themselves. Based on garden cultivation and the acquisition of crops and domestic animals new to the Appalachians, the improved manner of village farming added a crucial measure of crop productivity while overcoming the labor problems that stemmed from depopulation. In this way the Cherokees removed themselves from the breakdown encountered in the farming of neighboring groups such as the Catawbas. Even after the crisis time of the Cherokee War, the tribe was reported to have soon rebounded and to have temporarily seized the "greatest prosperity in their way" before the fighting of the Revolution took it away again. The "fowl houses," hog pens, potato storage pits, and corn houses destroyed during the Revolution were reconstructed and continued to contribute in large measure to the survival of the towns.[71]

In contrast to farming evolution, Cherokee hunting underwent an unprofitable involution. The tools of the hunter—especially fire—were forced back on the villages by diminished numbers of hunters, land cessions, and other factors. By the last quarter of the century, the Cherokee country and the opportunities it offered had been altered. Older subsistence pathways, particularly those related to the gathering carried out by women, were foreshortened. Even the mulberries probably disappeared with frequent burning, so that the village residents either walked farther to find them or did without. The herb and skin trade also added to the work of the increasingly short-handed villages. These pressures were added to by the gender-based split in the conduct of trade inside and outside the towns. The skins of deer initially hunted by men were sold less cautiously than were the corn crops cultivated by women. By late in the century, the underlying distinction between successful agriculture and a troubled hunting economy had grown more definite; a deeper wedge had been driven into the gender-related economic pursuits of the villagers.

But villagers, male or female, remained Cherokees first of all. The casualties of this struggle in places like Keowee were not forgotten, and the history of this and other more successful Cherokee towns suggests the hardship overcome throughout the century. The Cherokees continued to rebuild their towns in the face of the military aggression and economic power of colonial society. Equally impressive was the way the Cherokees resisted threats from the outside while addressing critical problems within their towns. However, these conflicts did not subdue the voice of village consensus among the Cherokees. During the long eighteenth-century struggle, the Cherokees fought to avoid either political or economic colonization, an intention reflected in the famous words of Utsidsata, Corn Tassel, "We are a separate people!"[72]

NOTES

1. Wilbur R. Jacobs, *Indians of the Southern Colonial Frontier: The Edmond Atkin Report and Plan of 1755* (Columbia: University of South Carolina Press, 1954), 53; James Mooney, "Myths of the Cherokees," in *Nineteenth Annual Report of the Bureau of American Ethnology for the Years 1897–98*, part 1 (Washington, D.C.: Government Printing Office, 1900), 525.

2. Lud. Grant to James Glen, August 20, 1755, in *Documents Relating to Indian Affairs, Colonial Records of South Carolina, 1754–1765*, ed. William L. McDowell, Jr., ser. 2, vol. 3 (Columbia: University of South Carolina Press, 1958), 74; Alex Miln to Governor Lyttelton, February 24, 1760, in *Documents Relating to Indian Affairs*, 3: 498.

3. As the winter of 1761 came on, the Keowee town leader Tistoe returned with "200 Indians to resettle there"; *South Carolina Gazette,* June 20–27, November 7–14, 1761. In 1767 the settlement on the west side of the Keowee River was already called "Old Keowee." After the Revolution the former town residents may have regrouped north of the former Fort Prince George. See Betty A. Smith, "Distribution of Eighteenth-Cherokee Settlements," in *The Cherokee Indian Nation: A Troubled History,* ed. Duane H. King (Knoxville: University of Tennessee Press, 1979), 46–60.

4. William Bartram, *Travels of William Bartram,* ed. Mark Van Doren (1791; reprint, New York: Dover Publications, 1955), 270–71.

5. Memorial of Robert Bunning and Others, November 22, 1751, *Documents Relating to Indian Affairs,* May 21, 1750–August 7, 1754, ed. William L. McDowell, Jr., ser. 2, vol. 2 (Columbia: University of South Carolina Press, 1970), 148.

6. The original population estimate was included in a letter from Francis Varnod to the secretary, Society for the Propagation of the Gospel in Foreign Parts, 1 April 1723, Letters from the Carolinas, Letter Book 18, doc. 173 (microfilm copy in Western Carolina University Library). This document was reprinted in Berthold Fernow, *The Ohio Valley in Colonial Days* (Albany: J. Munsell's Sons, 1890), 273–74.

7. The sex ratio for the Varnod figures is 97 men per 100 women; compare with modern Amerindian populations, which are reported to have an average sex ratio of 108 men to 100 women among all censused groups of Panama and the United States. F. Salzano writes further that the "excess of males is expected in populations with a low average age"; this observation suggests that the sex ratio reported by Varnod, dominated by women, may have been consistent with a relatively "old" early eighteenth-century Cherokee population. See Francisco M. Salzano, "Genetic Aspects of the Demography of American Indians and Eskimos," in *The Structure of Human Populations,* ed. G. A. Harrison and A. J. Boyce (Oxford: Clarendon Press, 1972), 238–39; Ludwik Krzywicki, *Primitive Society and Its Vital Statistics* (London: Macmillan, 1934), 232–34. Eighteenth-century observers commented on the longevity of Cherokee women as opposed to tribal men. See Samuel Cole Williams, ed., *Adair's History of the American Indians* (1930; reprint, New York: Promontory Press, 1974), 241; Samuel Cole Williams, ed., *Lieut. Henry Timberlake's Memoirs* (Johnson City, Tenn.: Watauga Press, 1927), 81.

8. Compare Krzywicki, *Primitive Society,* 253; Salzano, "Genetic Aspects," 238.

9. John Stuart to Board of Trade, April 19, 1764, in Great Britain, Public Record Office, Colonial Office Papers (hereafter cited as PRO, CO) 323/17/170 (microfilm copy in the Western Carolina University Library).

10. Peter H. Wood, "The Impact of Smallpox on the Native Population of the Eighteenth-Century South," *New York State Journal of Medicine* 87 (January 1987): 30–36; Williams, *Adair's History,* 244; Alex. Miln to Governor Lyttelton, 24 February 1760, in *Documents Relating to Indian Affairs,* 3: 498.

11. Ann G. Carmichael, "Infection and Hidden Hunger," in *Hunger and History: The Impact of Changing Food Production and Consumption Patterns on Society,* ed. R. I. Rotberg and T. K. Rabb (Cambridge: Cambridge University Press. 1983), 59.

12. *South Carolina Gazette,* September 6–13, October 18–26, 1760.

13. Carmichael, "Infection," 59.

14. Henry Laurens, "A Letter Signed Philolethes," March 2, 1763, in *The Papers of Henry Laurens,* vol. 3, ed. Philip M. Hamer and George C. Rogers, Jr. (Columbia: University of South Carolina Press, 1972), 286.

15. The connection between famine and disease has been reported by Western historians since Thucydides but is still highly controversial. See Carmichael, "Infection," 50–66; Carl E. Taylor, "Synergy among Mass Infections, Famines and Poverty," in Rotberg and Rabb, *Hunger and History,* 285–303; Roland Mousnier, *Peasant Uprisings in Seventeenth-Century France, Russia and China* (New York: Harper and Row, 1970), 305–19; Amartya K. Sen, *Poverty and Famines: An Essay on Entitlement and Deprivation* (New York: Oxford University Press 1981), 1–217.

16. Christopher Gadsden, *Some Observations of the Two Campaigns against the Cherokee Indians in 1760 and 1761 in a Second Letter from Philopatrios* (Charlestown: Peter Timothy, 1761), 53 (Readex microprint edition in the Vanderbilt University Library).

17. Captain Christopher French, "An Account of the Towns in the Cherokee Country with Their Strengths and Distance," *Journal of Cherokee Studies* 2 (Summer 1977): 297.

18. Williams, *Adair's History,* 94. Adair's explanation hinged more on village politics than on economics, though both factors were related.

19. Thomas Hatley, "Holding Their Ground: Cherokee Women and Their Agriculture" (paper delivered at Conference on the Appalachian Frontier, George Mason University, Harrisonburg, Virginia, March 1985); Diane Rothenberg, "Mothers of the Nation: Seneca Resistance to Quaker Intervention," in *Women and Colonization: Anthropological Perspectives,* ed. Mona Etienne and Eleanor Leacock (New York: Praeger, 1980), 78.

20. Bartram, *Travels,* 284.

21. Williams, *Adair's History,* 435.

22. Ibid., 242.

23. Varnod, "True and Exact Account"; Ensign John Boggs, "A List of Towns in the Cherokee Nation," February 21,1757, in *Documents Relating to Indian Affairs,* 3: 412–13; French, "Account," 297–99. French lists twenty-five towns, Boggs thirty-four.

24. Mooney, "Myths," 517, 525.

25. Bartram, *Travels,* 269.

26. French, "Account," 297–98. The distinction made by traders between rich and poor towns may have related to agricultural production and population as well as to political or commercial standing. Anthony Dean to Governor Glen, April 13, 1752, in *Documents Relating to Indian Affairs,* 2:259–60.

27. Compare Richard Pillsbury, "The Europeanization of the Cherokee Settlement Landscape prior to Removal: A Georgia Case Study," *Geoscience and Man* 22 (1983): 56–69.

28. During his visit Henry Timberlake was told of the recent "badness of crops." Williams, *Timberlake's Memoirs,* 67; also see Raven of Hiawassie to Glen, June 5, 1748, South Carolina Council Journal, book 15, 364 (microfilm in South Carolina Department of Archives and History); Reply of James Beamer to Governor Glen in "Proceedings of the Council concerning Indian Affairs," July 6, 1753, in *Documents Relating to Indian Affairs,* 1: 447; Raymond Demere to Governor Lyttelton, July 28, 1756, in *Documents Relating to Indian Affairs,* 3: 150; John Chevillette to Governor Lyttelton, March 1,1757, in *Documents Relating to Indian Affairs,* 3: 344; Captain Rayd. Demere to Governor Lyttelton, January 12, 1757, in *Documents Relating to Indian Affairs,* 3: 313.

29. *South Carolina Gazette,* October 26, 1760.

30. Compare Neal Salisbury, *Manitou and Providence* (New York: Oxford University Press, 1982),30, 145; William Cronon, *Changes in the Land* (New York: Hill and Wang, 1983), 92–97.

31. Isham Clayton to Captain Rayd. Demere, 7 July 1756, in *Documents Relating to Indian Affairs,* 3: 140. Saline and sodic soil licks as well as mineral springs are widely distributed through areas underlain by sedimentary rock and are largely missing from the Appalachian and Piedmont geologic provinces. Robert L. Jones and Harold L. Hanson, *Mineral Licks, Geophagy and the Biogeochemistry of North American Ungulates* (Ames: Iowa State University Press, 1985), 134–35. For a superb account of precontact salt manufacture and trade, see Ian W. Brown, *Salt and the Eastern North American Indian* (Cambridge: Peabody Museum, Harvard University, 1980).

32. Williams, *Adair's History,* 122. The physiology of higher plants works to exclude rather than to accumulate sodium, and except for certain salt-marsh grasses and herbs, these plants would have been poor sources of this particular human nutrient.

33. Connecortee to Governor Glen, March 20,1756, in *Documents Relating to Indian Affairs,* 3: 108–9.

34. Captain Rayd. Demere to Governor Lyttelton, October 28,1756, in *Documents Relating to Indian Affairs,* 3: 232; John Chevillette to Governor Lyttelton, March 1, 1757, 3: 344.

35. *South Carolina Gazette,* August 9–13, 1760.

36. Ibid., September 6–13, 1760.

37. The Catawba King to Governor Glen, March 11, 1753, in *Documents Relating to Indian Affairs,* 1: 370–71; Williams, *Adair's History,* 234.

38. In the colonial *materia medica* Virginia snakeroot (*Aristolochia serpentaria* L.) was a diaphoretic (and was tried as a plague cure in London), ginseng (*Panox quinquefolium* L.) was a tonic, and Indian pink (*Spigelia marlandica* L.) was a vermifuge. See Benjamin Barton, *Collections for an Essay towards a Materia Medica of the United States* (Philadelphia: Edward Earle, 1810), 1: 51–52; and Jacob Bigelow, *American Medical Botany* (Boston: Cummings and Hilliard, 1818), 1: 6–7. The Cherokees used ginseng in their villages on "religious occasions." Williams, *Adair's History,* 388–89. For plague reference, see *London Magazine* 14 (1745) : 568.

39. Early Carolina physician John Milligan speculated on the origin of these parasite infections: "Worm fevers are very frequent and common to all ages, though children of all ages suffer most . . . the sweet potato,

Indian corn or maize and pompion, all much used in diet, seem to have a larger share of the eggs of these mischievous insects than the rest of the farinaceous or leguminous kind." John Milligan, "Description of South Carolina," in *Historical Collections of South Carolina,* ed. B. R. Carroll (New York: Harper, 1838), 2: 498.

40. Joseph Gayle, "The Nature and Volume of Exports from Charlestown, 1724–1774," *Proceedings of the South Carolina Historical Association* 4 (1937): 32.

41. Quoted in Bigelow, *American Medical Botany,* 2: 89–90.

42. John Drayton, *The Carolinian Florist of Governor John Drayton,* ed. Margaret B. Meriwether (manuscript, 1807; Columbia: South Caroliniana Library, 1943), 109.

43. William Bartram, "Observations on the Creek and Cherokee Indians," *Transactions of the American Ethnological Society* 3 (1853): 47; Williams, *Adair's History,* 388.

44. Williams, *Adair's History,* 89–91; Alexander Longue, "A Small Postscript on the Ways and Manners of the Indians Called Cherokees," ed. David H. Corkran, *Southern Indian Studies* 21 (October 1969): 1–16.

45. Mooney, "Myths," 339; Jack F. Kilpatrick and Anna G. Kilpatrick, "Cherokee Rituals Pertaining to Medicinal Roots," *Southern Indian Studies* 16 (October 1964): 24–25.

46. When the Cherokee War closed the trade paths to the Cherokees, deerskin export volumes also fell substantially. See John Stuart to Board of Trade, April 19, 1764, PRO, CO 323/17/240 (microfilm copy in the Western Carolina University Library); Verner Crane, *The Southern Frontier, 1670–1732* (1928; reprint New York: Norton, 1981), 327–31; R. Nicholas Olsberg and Helen Craig Canon, *Duties on Trade at Charleston, 1784–89,* South Carolina Microcopy 6 (Columbia: South Carolina Department of Archives and History, 1972). For an approximation of intravillage demand for shoes and other items, see Richard M. Gramley, "Deerskins and Hunting Territories: Competition for a Scarce Resource of the Northeastern Woodlands," *American Antiquity* 42 (1977): 601–5.

47. Mark Catesby, *The Natural History of Carolina, Florida and the Bahama Islands* (London: Printed at the expense of the author, 1731–43), 1: ix.

48. Mark Catesby, "Of the Indians of Carolina and Florida," Royal Society, Decade I (n.d., cat. 1730), no. 186 (microfilm copy in the Library of Congress).

49. The Directors to Edward Wilkinson, June 21, 1763, in *Documents Relating to Indian Affairs,* 3: 586–87.

50. Fort Loudoun Association, "Contemporary Newspaper Accounts of the Massacre of the Fort Loudoun Garrison and the Plight of the Captive Survivors" (microfilm copy in Tennessee State Library and Archives), 16 (10) 58.

51. Stuart to Board of Trade, April 19, 1764, 257–58.

52. Williams, *Adair's History,* 32.

53. William L. Anderson, ed., "Cherokee Clay, from Duche to Wedgwood: The Journal of Thomas Grifffiths, 1767–1768," *North Carolina Historical Review* 63 (October 1986): 503–507.

54. Stuart to Board of Trade, April 19, 1764, 257.

55. For example, "Table of Goods and Prices," July 9, 1762, in *Documents Relating to Indian Affairs,* 3: 567.

56. Theda Perdue, "Southern Indians and the Cult of True Womanhood," in *Web of Southern Social Relations: Woman, Family and Education,* ed. Walter J. Fraser, Jr., R. Frank Saunders, Jr., and Jon L. Wakelyn (Athens: University of Georgia Press, 1985), 35–52.

57. Williams, *Adair's History* 436.

58. Ibid., 242.

59. See the discussion of fire in various southeastern habitats in E. V. Komarek, "Effects of Fire on Temperate Forests and Related Ecosystems," in *Fire and Ecosystems,* ed. T. T. Kozlowski and Nelson Ahlgren (New York: Academic Press, 1974), 261–65; John G. W. DeBrahm, *Report of the General Survey in the Southern District of North America,* ed. Louis DeVorsey, Jr. (Columbia: University of South Carolina Press, 1971), 181. Compare Emily W. B. Russell, "Indian-Set Fires in the Forests of the Northeastern United States," *Ecology* 64 (January 1983): 78–88.

60. Hatley, "Holding Their Ground."

61. Bartram, "Observations," 32.

62. "Biological storm" was Aldo Leopold's phrase for the passage of pigeon flocks through deciduous forest.

63. Mark Catesby, "Of the Aborigines of North America," Royal Society, Decade I (n.d., cat. 1730), no. 19, 8 (microfilm copy in the Library of Congress).

64. "Report of Brethren Steiner and von Schweinitz," in *Early Travels in the Tennessee Country: 1540–1800*, ed. Samuel Cole Williams (Johnson City, Tenn,: Watauga Press, 1928), 477–78, 490–91; French, "Account," 83, 98.

65. William Bartram, "Observations," 31.

66. Andrew Pickens to Lyman Draper, Draper Collection, 3XX, 141–49; F. W. Pickens to Charles H. Allen, 26 March 1848, in "Transcripts of Dr. John H. Logan," *Historical Collections of the Joseph Habersham Chapter of the Daughters of the American Revolution* 3 (1910): 94–97.

67. Mark Catesby to Sir Hans Sloane, November 27, 1724, British Museum, Sloane Manuscripts 4047/290 (microfilm in Western Carolina University Library).

68. Jacobs, *Indians of the Southern Colonial Frontier*, 49.

69. Price Hughes to Duchess of Ormonde, October 13, 1715, quoted in Crane, *Southern Frontier*, 103 n. 101.

70. "Journal of the Earl of Egmont," in *Colonial Records of Georgia*, ed. Allen D. Candler (Atlanta: Franklin Printing and Publishing, 1904–16), 5: 10.

71. Martin Schneider, "Report of His Journey to the Upper Cherokee Towns," in Williams, *Early Travels*, 257; Williams, *Adair's History*, 443.

72. Corn Tassel, "Cherokee Reply to the Commissioners of North Carolina and Virginia, 1777," trans. William Tatum, *Journal of Cherokee Studies* 1 (Fall 1976): 129.

13

Daniel Vickers

Most of the attention on exchange between natives and Europeans is focused, not surprisingly, on the colonists' trade in furs with Indian nations living beyond the frontier. But contrary to popular belief, many native peoples lived amid colonial settlements, as islands in an alien sea, and these groups, too, had to find some way to earn a livelihood when the fur-bearing animals, and much of the native land base, were gone. Long over-looked and forgotten, invisible to colonists and historians alike, these groups, like the Catawbas of Carolina and the Narragansetts of Rhode Island described in this volume, managed to eke out a precarious existence.

For natives on Nantucket, an island off the coast of Cape Cod, one strategy of survival was to become involved in the whaling trade, a busi-ness crucial to fledgling coastal English settlements. As Daniel Vickers demonstrates, the Native Americans of Nantucket chose to work in the trade for certain reasons, all of them associated with their attempt to maintain their communities in the wake of the destabilizing forces (such as epidemic diseases) unleashed by European colonists. Yet the decision to work for whalers, either in seaside whaling stations or on deep-sea vessels, often had disastrous consequences for any Native American Indian who had hoped that such employment would sustain indepen-dence. Many fell into debt peonage, a form of labor exploitation in which English colonists used the court system and native demand for alcohol to control local Indians.

Vickers's story is, then, both idiosyncratic and typical: whaling never became an occupation for the vast majority of Native American Indians, but it represented yet another way that the arrival of Europeans transformed indigenous communities and made their survival ever more precarious. Compare the Nantucket experience with Merrell's account of Catawba sur-vival, with Herndon and Sekatau's chronicle of the Narragansetts, and with Ronda's essay on Christian Indians on Martha's Vineyard.

THE FIRST WHALEMEN OF NANTUCKET

Daniel Vickers

IN THE YEAR 1690, so a Nantucket story goes, several townspeople were standing on a hill watching the whales sporting with one another off the south coast of the island. "There," observed one of them, gesturing toward the ocean, "is a green pasture where our children's grandchildren will go for bread."[1] If the sea was to be their garden, however, these islanders, like other American colonists, were only interested in cultivating it as their own. The thought of purchasing and managing vessels may have ignited their imaginations, but few of them entertained any wish to toil on the deep in the service of other men.

Finding help was therefore no easy task. Free men on Nantucket as in most corners of early America had seized upon the easy availability of land to establish themselves as independent producers. Accordingly, those who launched the whale fishery at the end of the seventeenth century, like all colonists who wanted to expand production beyond the limits of the household, found labor hard to procure at any price, let alone one that ensured what they felt was a reasonable rate of return. It was not the gathering of capital that troubled the first whaling merchants, for in the early years the costs of entering the industry were moderate. The demand for whale oil and whalebone was well established and markets were easy to locate, while the sources of supply were clearly visible as they swam along Nantucket's coastline. The real challenge to these early entrepreneurs was to find a few men who understood the techniques of whaling, and above all to recruit a larger group to man the oars. In most parts of the New World the scarcity of obedient and reliable workmen pushed employers to consider the institution of bound labor. Historians of tropical production generally invoke this proposition in their explanations of slavery. But should not the same principle have held true in the thinly populated northern colonies, wherever men were producing for the market? This article investigates how capitalist development in one corner of the New England economy took place without wholesale recourse to slavery or indentured servitude.

Nantucket is a low sandy island of forty-six square miles, half a day's journey by sail off the south coast of Cape Cod. The earliest Europeans to call there at the beginning

SOURCE: *William and Mary Quarterly,* 3d Ser. 40 (1983), 560–83.

of the seventeenth century found it an attractive if not especially fertile place, inhabited by 2,500 Wampanoag and Nauset Indians, who supported their numbers, enormous for an island that size, by hunting and farming, and especially by fishing.[2] Although they must have profited by the occasional drift whale that washed up on shore, they never pursued these great creatures on the open sea.

The first white settlers arrived in 1660 and purchased from the Indians both permission to settle at the west end of the island and rights to gather hay, graze cattle after the harvest, and cut timber on the rest of the land.[3] In the decade that followed, over twenty families—Coffins, Colemans, Barnards, Bunkers, Husseys, Starbucks, Swains, Worths, Macys, and Folgers being the most prominent—purchased shares in the propriety and moved to the island. By virtue of their control over the land, reinforced by a tight policy of intermarriage, these few families maintained near-total domination over the Nantucket economy through the next hundred years.

Most of the settlers came to farm, but it was soon evident that the island contained too little room to support the generations to come. Some of the early arrivals were craftsmen whose skills must have enabled the newly planted settlement to provide some goods for itself, but certain items would always have to come from the mainland. To pay for these, the settlers began to cast about for commodities that could find markets in Boston.

Most of the colonists of coastal New England were familiar with the whales that the sea washed up and stranded on their beaches, and with the economic value of blubber and baleen. During the seventeenth century, towns from Plymouth to Long Island passed orders governing the ownership of the great creatures, the organization to cut them up, and the manner in which the first casks of oil were to be shared out.[4] On Nantucket, where most of the beaches and beachcombing privileges remained in Indian hands, these problems were normally settled outside the white community, although in fights over the ownership of the animals the Indians sometimes turned for arbitration to the English courts. As their attention was drawn to the abundance of whales around the island, the settlers began to consider the possibilities of commercial exploitation themselves.[5]

Nantucketers knew that elsewhere in the colonies whales were pursued in boats from the shore. The Englishmen who settled on Cape Cod and the eastern end of Long Island had been hunting these beasts and selling their oil and bone to merchants in Boston and New York since the early 1650s.[6] Naturally enough, the men of Nantucket came to envision these products as commodities that could right their balance of trade with the mainland. The problem was that nobody on the island really knew how whaling was carried on.

In 1672, therefore, the settlers invited a Long Island whaleman named James Loper to practice his trade on Nantucket. If he would "Ingage to carry on a Design of Whale Catching," the town would bear two-thirds of the cost, guarantee Loper a near-monopoly in the fishery, and throw in a house lot and commonage to boot. Financing the venture was clearly not a problem for the islanders, who were chiefly interested in the whaleman not for his capital but for his mastery of technique. Unfortunately, although Loper accepted the offer, he must have changed his mind, for he continued to follow the fishery from Long Island and never moved to Nantucket. Not until 1690, when one Ichabod Paddock arrived from Yarmouth on Cape Cod, did the island manage to attract a competent whaleman.[7] Once the expertise had been acquired, however, whaling from the shore developed rapidly. Almost at once the settlers began to organize their own companies, and we have evidence that, by the turn of the century, Indians were purchasing goods from Nantucket merchants out of their earnings in the hunt. The shore fishery continued to expand into the mid-1720s, when close to thirty boats were engaged in the chase.[8]

The object of their pursuit was the right whale. Every autumn these animals returned along the American coast from a summer of feeding in the far reaches of the North Atlantic. From early November to March or April they wintered between Cape Cod and the Carolinas, usually within thirty miles of the shore. At any time during these months, whales could be spotted from the land. Nantucket was especially favored because of its position off the headland of Cape Cod, around which all whales had to swim. During the months of migration, vast numbers of them passed within a few miles of the island.[9] The oil refined from the blubber of the right whale was of a poor grade, suitable only for outdoor lamps and lubrication. In the animal's head, however, hung hundreds of strips of baleen or whalebone, a hard yet flexible material, which the whale used for straining food from the sea; for Europeans of the time this substance served some of the functions that plastics do today. Both oil and bone found steady markets in England.

Over the course of their lives, right whales varied enormously in size. Paul Dudley, a resident of Massachusetts and America's first cetologist, described their development in these words:

> This fish, when first brought forth, is about twenty Feet long, and of little Worth, but then the Dam is very fat. At a Year old, when they are called Short-heads, they are very fat, and yield to fifty Barrels of Oil, but by that Time the Dam is very poor, and term'd a Dry-skin, and won't yield more than thirty Barrels of Oil, tho' of large Bulk. At two Years old, they are called Stunts, being stunted after weaning, and will then yield generally from twenty four to twenty eight Barrels. After this, they are term'd Scull-fish, their Age not being known, but only guess'd at by the Length of the Bone in their Mouths.[10]

Full-grown adults commonly produced up to 90 barrels of oil, and occasionally as much as 120 or 130, but the average produce of all right whales caught ranged around 60 barrels of oil and 750 pounds of bone.[11]

The pursuit of these creatures from the shores of Nantucket had become a regular seasonal activity by the end of the seventeenth century. The fishery was carried on by companies of six men stationed at various points on the south and east coasts of the island. Crèvecoeur, an early visitor, related that each company "erected a mast, provided with a sufficient number of rounds, and near it they built a temporary hut, where five of the associates lived, whilst the sixth from his high station carefully looked toward the sea, in order to observe the spouting of the whales. As soon as any were discovered, the sentinel descended, the whale-boat was launched, and the company went forth in quest of their game."[12] In these slim, double-ended boats, built of cedar clapboards to a length of twenty feet, the company might row after whales the entire day among the Nantucket shoals. The method of the hunt they borrowed from the British Greenland fishery. If a company managed to draw even with its prey—not too difficult a task since right whales were lazy swimmers—the harpooner, perched in the bow, attempted to "fasten on" by sinking his harpoon, or iron, into its flesh. If the iron, connected by hundreds of feet of line to the whaleboat, stuck fast, the whale usually sounded in terror and attempted to flee, with the vessel and crew in tow. As the boat sped across the waves in the wake of the stricken animal, the company drew near to it at every opportunity, hurling lances and harpoons tied to heavy wooden drogues into the enraged beast, trying to bring its life to a speedy conclusion. The outcome of the chase could vary, as Dudley noted: "The Whale is sometimes killed with a single Stroke, and yet at other Times she will hold the Whale-men in Play, near half a Day together, with their Lances, and sometimes they will get away after they have been lanced and spouted blood, with Irons in them, and Drugs fastened to them."[13]

The skills required in whaling from the shore varied from post to post. The harpooner directed the chase from the bow; he gave the orders, paid out the towline when the whale sounded, and handled the actual harpooning and lancing. He needed both an understanding of whale behavior and the capacity to make rapid, correct judgments, two things that came only with years of experience. Since the success of the hunt hung largely on his ability to make his harpoons stick and to wreak damage with his lance on the poor beast's innards, he also needed strength, agility, and a rudimentary knowledge of cetacean anatomy. The steersman took his place in the stern and managed the large steering oar. Although subordinate to the harpooner under normal circumstances, he too had to make quick independent decisions, once the heat of the chase and the thrashing of the whale had begun to interrupt the regular chain of command. As accurately as they could, both of these endsmen had to follow the movements of the whale; their judgment on where the creature was headed—not an easy matter since it spent most of its time below the surface—often decided the contest. The three or four oarsmen, by comparison, were relatively unskilled, the chief requirements in this post being a strong back and the ability to row. Since handling an oar was as easy to learn as it was backbreaking to execute, the position attracted, as we shall see, a different class of men.[14]

On occasion, companies entered the chase alone, but more frequently they hunted in groups. Alone they stood the chance, if the whale were captured, of claiming the entire prize for themselves; with a sixty-barrel whale at stake, this could mean the equivalent on land of over half a year's wages for each man.[15] In pairs or threesomes, however, though the animal would have to be shared, companies were far less likely to run into danger or to lose their prey completely. The parties might wrangle over their portions of oil and bone, but in the course of time whalemen worked out equitable methods of sharing the produce.[16]

If the chase succeeded, the whalemen towed the dead leviathan back to shore, where pieces of blubber were cut and stripped from its body with the help of a capstan. The blubber was wheeled off in carts to the tryhouses, where the oil was boiled out, cooled down, and poured into wooden casks. The oil, along with the bundles of scrubbed whalebone, was then hauled over the island and stored in warehouses in preparation for shipment to market.[17]

The whaling industry of Nantucket was blessed throughout most of the later colonial period with extraordinarily healthy markets. Owing in part to the collapse of the Dutch North Atlantic fishery and in part to rising demand in Britain and America, oil prices moved upward from about £8 sterling per barrel in 1725 to £10 in 1730, to £13–14 in the 1750s and 1760s, to almost £30 on the eve of the Revolution.[18] The incentive to carry the chase out onto the deep and exceed the limited range of the shore fishery was therefore enormous. Accordingly, about 1715, when Nantucketers first discovered that another species of whale, the spermaceti, frequented the ocean waters beyond sight of land, they began sending out small sloops and schooners with crews of twelve or thirteen on regular short voyages in pursuit. Hunting from the two whaleboats carried on board and cutting up the creatures at sea, they packed the blubber into casks and brought it home every two or three weeks to be boiled out in the tryhouses that stood near the town wharf.[19]

The spermaceti was smaller than the right whale; it was also swifter, hence more difficult to catch; and it lacked the strips of whalebone that in its counterpart made up to half the value of the carcass. The oil rendered from its body, however, was of a higher grade than that of other cetaceans, and the pure "headmatter" culled from the case in its skull commanded between double and triple the price of common whale oil. It was "parmecitys" that excited the islanders' acquisitive instincts and drew them out farther and farther from their native shores. By 1730, Nantucket whalers were carrying copper pots with them and establishing temporary tryworks anywhere on the coast from Newfoundland to the Carolinas that they found convenient. Finally, after 1750, merchants who wished to cut their vessels free from the coastline entirely and thus engage them in voyages of several months' duration, began to have the trypots installed in brick housings right on the ship's deck. Such technological advances caused the annual product of each deep-sea whaleman to climb from 8.3 barrels in 1715 to 16.7 barrels by the 1770s. Under this impetus, the total output of Nantucket's ocean-going vessels soared from 600 barrels in 1715, to 3,700 in 1730, to 11,250 in 1748, and finally to 30,000 by 1775.[20]

The radical lengthening of voyages that made such growth possible transformed the character of whaling as an occupation. The shore fishery of course involved brutal and dangerous work. Storms, shoals, and angry whales could pound a whaleboat to pieces in a moment, leaving its crew at the mercy of the deep. Flying loops of towline, paid out from the craft to reduce tension while being hauled along by the fleeing beast, could wrap around a hand or an arm and snap it from the body like a brittle twig. Up the coast in Boston harbor, one extraordinarily trusting young seaman named Jonathan Webb was killed when "in coiling up the line unadvisedly he did it about his middle thinking the whale to be dead, but suddenly she gave a Spring and drew him out of the boat, he being in the midst of the line."[21] Even a safely concluded chase was not necessarily a successful one; more often than not, all that a whaleman gained from his hours of straining at the oars was an aching back. In small doses, however, all of this could be borne easily enough, especially when balanced against the spacious living quarters, the fresh food and water, and the proximity to one's family and friends that the shore fishery allowed.

Whaling at sea, by comparison, admitted none of these possibilities. After three or four months of cruising the Atlantic, the tedious spells of inactivity, the rancid meat and stinking water, the cramped quarters, and, above all, the restrictions on one's freedom wore heavily on most whalemen's nerves. "No whales to be seen," complained young Peleg Folger off the Carolina coast in 1751: "Much toil and Labour Mortal man is forcd to endure & Little profit to be Got by it."[22] And as the ordinary hardships increased, so did the physical danger. Zaccheus Macy, an eighteenth-century islander, speaking for the English if not the Indians, claimed that in all the years of shore whaling there, not a single man was lost. The annals of the deep-sea fishery, by comparison, record dozens of fatal accidents. On a voyage to the eastward of the Grand Banks, some crewmates of the same Peleg Folger were in pursuit of a large spermaceti when suddenly "she gave a flank & went down & coming up again, She bolted her head out of the Water almost if not quite down to her fins: And then pitchd the whole weight of her head on the Boat & Stove the Boat & ruin[d] her & kill[d] their midshipman, an Indian Named Sam Samson Outwright." A "sad and awful Providence," Folger termed it, but not an uncommon one, at least in the experience of a seasoned deep-sea whaleman.[23] Such a life demanded levels of commitment quite foreign to the shore fishery.

Every hand was paid a share or "lay," expressed as a fraction of the whales his company caught. In the shore fishery, once the owner of the boat had taken one-quarter of the bone and oil to cover his investment, the remainder was divided among the crew; each of the six whalemen, therefore, received a one-eighth lay. On deep-sea voyages, the share of labor was further trimmed by half to defray the cost of keeping the oceangoing vessel afloat.[24] What all this meant in absolute amounts is difficult to tell. Different companies met with varying levels of success: some might kill several whales in a space of a few weeks, while others could pass the entire season without a single capture. The few financial records that pertain to the shore fishery, however, suggest that lays were generally unimpressive. None of the surviving account books that report "oyl & bone got along shore" mention any instances of annual earnings greater than £5 sterling.[25] Ocean voyages paid better over the course of the year because they could be extended through a longer season; but recast on a monthly basis, the lays of Nantucket oarsmen usually ranged no higher than £1–2 sterling per month, about what a common Boston mariner could expect to earn.[26] One might be able to support a household on an income of this size, but not in much comfort. Would the sons of freeborn Englishmen consent to work in the lower ranks of this demanding trade on such terms?

Apparently not, for throughout its first fifty years, the Nantucket whaling industry recruited most of its hands from the Indian community. This was particularly true of the shore fishery. "Nearly every boat," wrote Obed Macy in 1830, "was manned in part, many almost entirely, by natives: some of the most active of them were made steersmen, and some were allowed even to head the boats." My research reveals not a single reference to white men credited with earnings from shore whaling, save occasionally as steersmen.[27] Likewise, the oceangoing fishery depended in its early years mostly upon Indian hands. More than half of the fifty-five oarsmen and steersmen who shipped with Silvanus Hussey, one of the island's wealthiest merchant outfitters, between 1725 and 1733 possessed identifiably Indian names. By mid-century, the balance in recruitment had tipped toward whalemen of English origin drawn mostly from the mainland; but in its early years the fishery relied to an extraordinary extent upon Indian labor.[28]

The ownership of capital, on the other hand, was concentrated entirely in the hands of the English. That Indians could not purchase oceangoing vessels is hardly a surprise, but even the whaleboats and appurtenances of the shore fishery appear to have lain beyond their reach. A list of boat owners compiled in 1726 contains mostly the names of well-established island families. Of the twenty-seven owners mentioned, eighteen were descendants of the first proprietors, the Gardners and the Coffins alone accounting for eleven; four more came from the more prominent families among the later arrivals; only the remaining five had been born off-island. The list contains not a single Indian. On one occasion, in 1758, a native islander named Peter Micah received slightly under £1 sterling for his "1/2 of boats part" from Zaccheus Macy, a whaling merchant with whom he apparently shared its ownership. Otherwise, in neither the probate records nor the account books of outfitters were Indians ever credited with whaling investments.[29] In the early years of the Nantucket whale fishery, therefore, class and ethnicity were contiguous. The English were masters; the Indians were servants; and between the two groups there was no mobility at all.

Can we explain this in strictly economic terms? Were the Indians simply too poor to buy whaleboats and equipment? Judged from probate records of the 1720s, Nantucket men who participated financially in the shore fishery normally had about £4 sterling invested in their establishments. Each company required living quarters and a whaleboat with all its accessories: oars, rigging, harpoons, lances, and hundreds of feet of high-quality line. Tryhouses had to be supplied with large trying pots, knives, spades, barrels, wheelbarrows, and a capstan. Horses, carts, warehousing, and wharfage were also necessary if the oil and bone were to be shipped to markets on the mainland. No single investor owned all of these. George Coffin, a prosperous cooper who died in 1727, owned a "tryhouse and furniture" worth £10.5 sterling and a well-equipped but ancient whaleboat appraised at £3.4. His uncle, Joseph Coffin, whose estate was probated in 1725, owned a newer boat valued with its gear at £5. A mariner named Nathan Skiffe, a newcomer to the island, held shares in two boats at his death in 1725, worth together £1.3. Outfitting a complete whaling station from scratch would probably cost over £20, but, by purchasing equipment secondhand, by sharing it, and by paying others to perform a part of the work (especially trying and carting), Nantucketers succeeded in reducing expenses to a level where most of the propertied white community could participate. In no case did shore whaling capital exceed 4 percent of the inventoried personal estate of any white islander.[30]

Expenses such as these would have placed a far greater strain on an Indian's resources. The natives who made their way into the probate records in the eighteenth century usually owned no more than a small shack, a horse or cow, a few tools, some furniture, and their clothing—an average of only £16.6 in personal wealth. These estates were not impressive by comparison to those of their shore fishery employers, which averaged £170; few Indians could muster the funds for even a modest investment of £4 or £5.[31]

This purely economic explanation, however, tells only part of the story, for in maritime New England capital equipment of this nature was normally bought not with ready funds but on credit. In Essex County, fishermen who were no wealthier than the Nantucket Indians could secure advances in supplies well over £100 if their creditors were in the market for fish.[32] Moreover, the whale fishery was profitable: the returns on a single capture could recompense the boat owner for his entire investment and more. Even a moderately successful season would have freed the Indian investor of the debts incurred in the initial outlay. Why, then, did native Nantucketers never purchase whaleboats? Were they uninterested, or did their English neighbors consider them poor risks? Perhaps allowing Indians to control their own labor did not fit into the white men's plans. But what were their plans? To resolve these problems adequately, we must retrace our steps and examine the history of economic relations between the two groups from their earliest encounters.

NANTUCKET IS SUCH a treeless and barren place today that it is difficult to imagine how it once could have supported 2,500 Indians. Before contact with the Europeans, almost fifty five natives were squeezed onto every square mile of soil, a density many times that of mainland New England and the equal of most parts of western Europe.[33] The truth is that at the beginning of the seventeenth century, Nantucket, for all its infertility, possessed in some abundance most of what Indians required for their subsistence. Not only was the island stocked with deer and other game, but its freshwater ponds held great flocks of waterfowl, and the surrounding ocean teemed with fish and shellfish.[34] The Indians sustained themselves by exploiting these resources in a seasonal pattern. Like all coastal Algonquians, they lived in semipermanent villages surrounded by partially cleared fields and large tracts of forest, which they maintained by slash-and-burn techniques as hunting parks. John Brereton, who visited the islands south of Cape Cod in 1602, reported that the woods were so clear of undergrowth that "in the thickest parts . . . you can see a furlong or more round about."[35] Every spring, the Indians planted corn, beans, and squash among the stumps in the fields near their villages, then departed for temporary camps near the ocean. Although they came back periodically to tend their crops, most of the summer was spent along the shore, fishing from canoes, gathering shellfish, and drying both for winter consumption. That Nantucket and all of seaboard New England could support a population so much greater than the interior, testifies to the importance of marine creatures in the diet. The Indians returned from the shore in September for the harvest and spent the remainder of the year based in their villages, venturing out only to hunt.[36]

The English settlers wrought many changes in Indian society, most of them catastrophic. Their agriculture eventually destroyed the fertility of the island, denuding it of trees and exposing its soil to the relentless action of the wind. Their fecundity and their appetite for property crowded the original inhabitants into an ever-shrinking portion of the land. Most important, their diseases eventually wiped out the entire native population. In the beginning, however, the Indians entertained the idea of admitting the English as neighbors with few misgivings. Because their own numbers had been declining since the first European contacts at the beginning of the century, they were willing enough by 1660 to sell the rights to settle on what they saw as functionally surplus land. The newcomers were few in number and seemed prepared to recognize all native rights not specifically restricted by the deed of sale.[37] Best of all, the settlers could provide the Indians with European goods.

Both parties were eager to trade, the Indians because they recognized the low cost and technological superiority of English manufactures, and the settlers because they needed commodities to send to Boston for goods that the island could not produce. The survival of an account book, kept by the Starbuck family between 1683 and 1757, allows us to examine the nature of this trade. Until the end of the seventeenth century, almost 90 percent of the goods that Indians bought from the Starbucks consisted of cloth, apparel, and equipment for farming, fishing, and hunting (see Table I). Shoes, coats, woolen cloth, fishhooks, lines, powder and shot, horses, and ploughshares were the most sought-after items; foodstuffs were almost never purchased. In return, they brought in feathers, grain, and fish, each of which the Starbucks probably sent to the mainland. In essence, the natives were employing English technology partly in order to produce a surplus that could be exchanged for manufactured goods and probably also to save labor.[38]

In the seventeenth century, the Indians bargained from a position of strength. Because they provided most of their own food, shelter, and fuel, they rarely had to trade from real desperation. Furthermore, as the native population succumbed to diseases,

TABLE I: PURCHASES OF SELECTED INDIANS FROM STARBUCK FAMILY, 1680–1750

	Cloth and Clothing	Food	Productive Equipment	Services, Cash, and Misc.
1680–1700 (n = 12)	60	7	30	3
1701–1720 (n = 13)	35	9	38	19
1721–1750 (n = 9)	38	12	9	41

Indians were selected for the legibility and completeness of their accounts. The figures represent a percentage of the value of total purchases.

the supply of Indian goods began a parallel decline, leaving whatever the lucky survivors could produce in considerable demand. Now they could take their business to any of a growing number of white families that kept a stock of goods, playing one off against another, taking advantage of the scarcity of their own labor. Every white trader had to confront this dilemma: how could one maintain the volume of one's trade and keep the costs of native produce down in the face of a decline in supply and an increase in demand? Under the pressures of competition, these traders resorted to a potent commercial weapon: the extension of credit.

Too easily, historians make connections between credit and wealth, debt and poverty. While it is obvious that those who lend money must have wealth to lend, it is less clear that those who borrow are necessarily needy. The decision to extend credit is ultimately the creditor's; the amount of goods and cash he is willing to advance depends on the advantage he sees in the action. Earned interest could be one attraction, but in colonial New England, where interest rates were rarely attached to retail accounts, the primary function of credit was to enable the lender to gain control over the labor and property of the borrower. In Europe, where labor was plentiful and inexpensive, it was land, the scarcest element in the process of production, that the serious moneylender hoped most to acquire. In the New World, as the native population collapsed, land lay increasingly vacant and labor became the dearest factor. Colonial merchants advanced goods in order to assure themselves in the coming year the fruits of their customers' toil.

To virtually every Indian with whom they dealt, the Starbucks advanced enough cloth and other supplies (although never more than £10 worth) to oblige him to continue bringing in his produce. We can follow this process in detail for the Starbuck family; we know that the same techniques were also used by other settlers. Hardly a session passed in the Nantucket courts during the seventeenth century without a Swain, Hussey, or Gardner launching an action against some native debtor who was refusing to continue this exchange.[39]

The courts were essential to the working of the system. Only if defaulting debtors could be apprehended could white traders be assured that Indians would honor their obligations. Under similar conditions in the Canadian west at the end of the eighteenth century, the Hudson's Bay Company attempted to use credit in the fur trade to build up a dependable clientele of native trading partners. The system functioned well enough in the wilderness as long as the company could monopolize trade through a small number of posts, but with the rise in competition from Montreal traders after 1763, the credit system became unmanageable. The Indian to whom goods had been advanced could disappear into the forest and carry his furs in the ensuing year to another trader at a different post. Where there was no legal guarantee that debts could be collected, the extension of credit was impracticable.[40] On Nantucket the collection of debts was, by the standard of the times, remarkably easy. The local courts were close at hand and dominated by magistrates, often traders themselves, who understood the need for strictly enforcing native obligations. More important, the limited and featureless confines of the island left few places to hide;

unless the debtor could escape to the mainland (leaving behind his kin, his property, and his rights as a member of the tribe), he could not evade the arm of the law.

The extension of credit soon found a useful adjunct in the liquor trade. Alcohol as an item of exchange had risks: as often as not, drinking encouraged in the Indians precisely the stubborn, unpredictable, and even violent behavior that Englishmen feared most. In strictly economic terms, however, liquor possessed one enormous advantage: the elasticity of its demand. The native economy could absorb only so many blankets and knives, whereas a pot of wine or rum could be consumed in a moment and refilled. In the Canadian west, the trade in strong drink reached its peak in the period 1760–1820, when rivalry between the Hudson's Bay and North West companies was most intense.[41] Likewise, on Nantucket a crowd of aggressive English traders, locked in sharp competition among themselves, employed alcohol as a means of gaining control over Indian labor. "Many of the inhabitants," noted Thomas Macy in 1676, "do frequently purchase it p[re]tending for their own use and sel it to the Indians."[42] The chief offender in this regard was John Gardner, a settler from Salem with merchant connections, who carried on a fishing operation with the help of Indian hands. According to Macy, these merchants "have some Yeares past sent Goods to trade with the Indians upon the accompt of Fishing and otherwise and great quantities of strong Liquor have bin sent. . . . The agent here [Gardner] that carried on the Trade for the Gentlemen hath bargained with the Indians to give each Man a dram before they go out fishing in the Morning; but under that p[re]tence much Abuse hath bin."[43] Recently Gardner had delivered a shipment of sixteen gallons to the Indians, but as it was, in the words of Macy, a trader himself, merely "a small quantity," we can assume that the trade was normally quite vigorous. To the end of the colonial period, in fact, drink remained an important source of native indebtedness.[44]

The practice of advancing credit took hold on the island because the Indians appreciated the *short-term* advantages it afforded and because each English trader wished to build up a dependable circle of customers who would be obliged to supply him with trade goods on a continual basis. As the entire body of traders turned to this system, it became a type of communal labor control, an informal brand of debt peonage. Its purpose was not to force the Indian to trade, for he was anxious to do that on his own accord, but to limit the competition over the fruits of his labor and thereby to control their price.

THE WHITE NANTUCKETERS who launched the shore fishery in the 1690s were certain about two things. First, though they participated in the chase as steersmen or harpooners, they refused the menial labor of manning the oars. Partly, they knew that rowing after whales was exhausting and dangerous toil; partly, they thought it demeaning to work for others. After all, they had hardly moved to the island to become servants. Since Nantucket was out of the way and shore whaling was a seasonal occupation, recruiting hands from the mainland was unlikely to meet with success. Under these circumstances, the only viable source of labor was the local Indian population.

Second, the English insisted on retaining complete control of the industry themselves. In Indian-white relations on Nantucket, this was a significant departure. Until the 1690s the settlers had always advanced such capital equipment as fishing lines, powder, and shot to the Indians interest-free, on the promise of being repaid in local produce. The natives remained independent operators, following traditional pursuits with European technology and selling their surpluses to the English to finance their purchases. Some Indians were accustomed to work on occasion in the white community—ploughing, carting, or harvesting—but almost no one worked for his English neighbors on a regular basis.[45] Now, in the shore fishery, Indians were being asked for the first time to participate not as self-employed men working with their own tools and equipment, but as servants.

Some might argue that the Indians were not interested in investing in capital equipment on this scale.[46] Profits and accumulated wealth, it is true, were utterly foreign to the native ethos, but the privilege of working on one's own terms was not. Indifferent to legal ownership though they were, they alternative of toiling at the oars under the command of white steersmen while relinquishing one-quarter of each whale to their employers "for the Boat & Craft" was new and unwelcome. The same point—that ownership equaled control—was driven home even more forcefully when, about 1715, the launching of the more capital-intensive deep-sea fishery resulted in whalemen's lays being slashed in half. Indignantly, the Indians petitioned the General Court and complained of their white neighbors' policy of allowing them "but half Price for their Whaling." When called upon to answer, the Nantucket representative to the court, Joseph Coffin, obviously perplexed that anyone would challenge the right of an employer to determine the terms of employment, replied that the Indians had "no reason to Complain, they being allowed according to the Custom of the Island, one Half . . . which is a proportion as is allowed to white Men." The court, too, was a bit mystified by the petition and the matter was dropped.[47] It is difficult to imagine that, in the light of this incident, the Indians remained oblivious to the advantages of capital ownership.

The real barrier to investment in the shore fishery by natives was their reputation for unreliability. Although the English were willing, even anxious, to entrust the Indians with debts, they were highly skeptical of the latter's capacity for regular daily work. In the first decades of interracial trade, the Starbucks' native clients delivered their produce at irregular intervals, often only two or three times a year, and the annual volume of business swung up and down erratically. If white Nantucketers were to spend time and money building boats, forging harpoons, and purchasing cordage from the mainland, they wanted men ready to join the chase every day throughout the whaling season. As long as the natives were allowed to own the boats they worked in, they would only hang around the beach watching for whales (the English were perhaps correctly convinced), if it suited their wider economic interests; once these were satisfied, they might well head back to their villages. Such routines of work as these were inconsistent with the levels of return that the English demanded.

Whites perceived this sort of behavior as typical of a people who had "little Regard to their own wellfare."[48] In reality, what they saw as irresponsibility was more often simple independence. For those who preferred to stay on shore and work on their own, there were still ways of supporting themselves within the native economy. The supply of fish and shellfish, always the major source of nutrition for the Nantucket tribe, was almost limitless. Waterfowl were still abundant, and the herds of deer did not diminish for many decades.[49] Of an island that in 1700 was "much commended for goodness of soil," Indians still owned over half in 1690 and about a quarter in 1720.[50]

While the traditional Indian economy remained intact, perhaps in the short run enhanced by the application of European technology, the human demands on their portion of the island diminished. The native population of Nantucket had been declining ever since the initial contact with white men at the beginning of the seventeenth century (see Table II)—so rapidly, indeed, that until well into the eighteenth century, the quantity of land owned by individual survivors probably rose. And since the Indians continued to enjoy free access to the sea, as well as hunting and gathering rights on many parts of the island that they had already sold, the mere fact of ownership underestimates the resources within a native's reach. The admittedly substantial estate of Jeremy Netowa, an Indian whaleman who died at sea in 1728, contained not only the earnings from his voyage but also spinning wheels, livestock, and the produce of his fields.[51] Even Isaac Cododah, whose estate (valued at £5.7 sterling) was the poorest of any recorded on the island in the colonial period, owned at his death in 1721, besides his personal effects, a hog and twenty bushels of grain.[52] As Table I demonstrates, the natives did grow dependent on their English neighbors for a number of items, above all cloth and clothing; and after 1720, when they began to spend more and more of the spring and summer months in the deep-sea fishery, they had to pay white islanders to look after their fields.[53] Through the first quarter of the eighteenth century, however, they remained remarkably self-sufficient and could afford to be choosy about the terms on which they worked.

TABLE II: INDIAN POPULATION OF NANTUCKET, 1600–1792

Year	Population
1600	2,500
1640	2,000
1670	1,250
1698	830
1700	800
1763	358
1764	136
1792	22

Sources: Cook, *Indian Population of New England*, 42–43; Z. Macy, "Journal of Nantucket," 158–59; O'Callaghan et al., eds., *N.-Y. Col. Docs.*, IV, 787.

The white boat owners were therefore in a quandary: Indian whalemen, because of their shrinking numbers and natural independence, were growing difficult to recruit. As the competition over their labor increased, and the need for discipline became evident, so too did the temptation to draw them into indebtedness and servitude.

The links between indebtedness and the shore fishery in the early eighteenth century can be viewed through the records of probate. Of the eight islanders, all white, who died in possession of whaling gear, whaleboats, or tryhouses between 1700 and 1730, six were credited with Indian debts that ranged from £8.5 to £45.1 sterling. Among the eight (five whites, two Indians, and one free Negro) with no whaling appurtenances to their name, money was owed by natives to only one, Nathaniel Barnard, and he owned a fishing operation.[54] Those who dictated the division of their estates on their deathbeds always grouped the two together. Jonathan Bunker, a farmer who died in 1721, bequeathed to his four sons "all my whaling and fishing Craft with all my Indian debts."[55] In 1725, Stephen Coffin, Jr., left to his sons, Shubael and Zephaniah, "the one half of all my fishing and whaling craft with the half of all my Indian debts," and to his wife, Experience, the other half of these debts and half of "Everything used or improved in the Carrying on and Managing the fishing and whaling voyages . . . and all my Shipping Imploy'd in fishing and whaling on Nantucket shoals."[56]

Indebtedness had been important in Indian-white relations since the very beginning, but to the shore fishery it was indispensable. A series of exchanges between native islanders, the English inhabitants, and the General Court in Boston makes this plain. In November 1716, an Indian named John Punker petitioned the General Court on behalf of his tribe, "Complaining of great Injustice and Oppression they suffer from some of their *English* Neighbours," and requesting that Nantucket be annexed to some other county so that, in legal contests with the settlers, they might obtain justice before impartial courts. Why was this becoming an issue in 1716? The petition has been lost, but its content is revealed by the resulting order that a committee of three be sent to Nantucket to "enquire into the Matters of Grievance Complained of; and more especially their Whaling: And Assist the Indians in making a proper Representation thereof to [the] Court."[57] The committee visited the island that winter, spent twelve days in investigation, and presented their report the following June. The report too has disappeared, but it must have testified to the truth of Punker's claims, for the General Court decided to act. Although for reasons of physical convenience it denied the annexation request, the court in effect conceded the Indians' difficulty in obtaining justice from the white islanders when it ordered that two magistrates from the mainland be appointed as "Justices . . . of the Peace, to Hear & Determine, all Causes and Matters of Difference, between the English & Indians, and Indian & Indians on the said Island. And that a Bill be prepared accordingly."[58] In June 1718, this bill, entitled "An Act in Addition to the Act for Preventing Abuses to the Indians," was passed and made law. Its preamble, describing these abuses, was drawn from the experience of Nantucket and its whale fishery: "notwithstanding the care taken and provided by said act, a great wrong and injury happens to said Indians, natives of this country, by reason of their being drawn in by small gifts, or for small debts, when they are in drink, and out of capacity for trade, to sign unreasonable bills or bonds for debts, which are soon sued, and great charge brought upon them, when they have no way to pay the same but by servitude."[59] The act went on to declare that no bond or labor contract could be made with an Indian without the approbation of two local justices of the peace, who would ensure (so the legislators hoped) that the Indian had entered into the agreement out of choice. It was the possibility of coercion in the drawing up of indentures that concerned them; to the idea of servitude they had no objection. Indeed, the purpose of the act was to establish a formal indenting procedure.

With the rise of the deep-sea fishery after 1716, the competition over available hands grew even more acute. Each new voyage required eight to ten oarsmen and steersmen to perform work that was both more tedious and more disruptive to the Indians' domestic economy than the shore fishery had ever been. Coercion became so routine in the recruitment process that by the early 1720s the General Court was flooded with Indian complaints of indebtedness and ill-treatment.[60] In 1725, therefore, it supplemented the 1718 legislation with still another act, the general intent of which was to reinforce the earlier laws against fraudulent indentures and to prohibit the binding of Indian householders. Recognizing the necessity, however, "as well for the English as the Indians . . . that the Indians be employed in the whaling and other fishing voyages," the court agreed to grant an exemption for the whaling towns of Cape Cod, Martha's Vineyard, and Nantucket. Native whalemen might henceforth be bound for up to two years at a time, and their employers could contract to "assist the said Indians in building houses for them on their own lands, and furnish them and their families as well with fuel, as necessary subsistence, during such time."[61] An indebted Indian who entered into such an indenture would be required not only to work for his master but to procure supplies from him as well. The cycle of dependence was thus complete: whaling employers could bind their native seamen to as long a series of two-year stints as they pleased, provided that they took responsibility for their upkeep. Fraud had been prohibited, but servitude was now institutionalized.

By 1730, few Indian whalemen were working on their own account. Of those hired in both the shore and deep-sea fisheries between 1725 and 1733 by Silvanus Hussey, probably the greatest whaling merchant of the period, at least three-quarters were the indebted clients of white islanders. Listed anonymously as "Indians" or "hands," these men were under obligation to deliver their earnings to their white masters after every voyage.[62]

Some of these agreements were formal indentures. Jonas Cooper, an Indian mariner from Martha's Vineyard, who was living on Nantucket in the early 1720s, fell into debt to a cooper and whaleboat owner named John Clark. Clark eventually forced Cooper to "seal, bind and oblige himself to go a whaling for him both winter for the space of three years." Cooper, who was unusual in this period for being an off-islander, fled with his belongings after a year's service, and Clark learned a lesson in the advantages of hiring local help.[63] A more detailed indenture survives from Cape Cod, where in 1737 an Indian named Robin Mesrick, in order to repay a debt of £9 to his creditor,

Gideon Holway, agreed to "worke On Shoar and Whale for him Three years." In return, Holway was to pay Mesrick 11s a month for his labor on land and

> when he Goes on the Spring [deep-sea] Whaleing to find him a suitable Berth to Pro-
> ceed in voiages In and to allow him half an Eighteenth of what is Obtained On Each
> of Spring voiages after the vessels Parte is first deducted and to finde him his Diat &
> Liquor on s'd Spring voiage into the Bargaine, and on the Bay [shore] voiages the s'd
> Robin may find himself Diat house room & wood and have a whole Eighth Clear
> according to Custom and if s'd Holway finds him Diat half his house room & wood
> then s'd Robin to Draw but Half an Eighth as according to custom.

The whole of Mesrick's earnings was to go toward repaying the debt after deductions were made for clothing and other current necessities. If he succeeded in amassing the sum before the three years were out, he was to be freed from all further obligations.[64]

The rarity of surviving indentures suggests that many, perhaps most, of these agreements were informal. Certain of the terms were customary and understood; others were probably in a constant state of renegotiation. Insults, threats, sulking, and brute force were all part of a bargaining idiom in which both parties tried to obtain the best terms possible. Indians were anxious to avoid the heavy hand of the island's courts, and as long as the threat of prosecution was present, merchants could usually get what they wanted without recourse to law. Naturally, records of the thrusts and parries of this subtle interchange were never kept, but an account of recruiting practices on Martha's Vineyard in 1806 may help to give an idea of how it operated:

> This business of inviting the Indians is a sort of crimping, in which liquor, goods
> and fair words are plied, till the Indian gets into debt, and gives his consent. Taking
> the history from the mouths of white people only, it appears that there is often much
> to be complained of in the business of the voyage, both in the Indian and in those
> with whom he connects himself. On the one hand great advantage is taken of his
> folly, his credulity and his ignorance. On the other, he torments the ship or share
> owner with his indecision and demands, till the moment of the sailing of the ship.
> First, he agrees to go, and accordingly receives some stipulated part of his outfit; then
> he "thinks he won't go;" and then he is to be coaxed and made drunk. Again he
> "thinks" he "won't go" unless such and such articles are supplied; and these articles
> he often names at random for the sake of inducing a refusal. One Indian was men-
> tioned to me that he thought he would not go unless five pounds of soap were given
> him; and another thought the same unless he received seven hats.[65]

If bargaining along these lines came to nothing, merchants could resort to force. In 1747, Paul Quaab from Sakedan Indian Town at the east end of the island com-plained to the General Court that a man named James Gase (Chase), with the assis-tance of the constable and two other men, had forcibly carried him away from his home on the back of a horse and sent him out whaling, although, in his words, "I was no ways obliged to him by any account or bromes [*sic*] to go whaling so long time [f]or I never bromesth."[66] The Nantucket selectmen denied the truth of Quaab's assertions but did concede the existence of "some Evil minded persons among us that makes a trade of supplying the Indians with Rum and have had the produce of their Land and Labour for little or no value."[67] Another group of Indians objected to being dragged off to whale on the Sabbath. As they argued,

> how can we be any ways be like christians when we should be praying to God on the Sabbath day morning then we must be Rowing after whal or killing whal or cutting up whal on Sabbath day when we should be at rest on that day and do no worly labour only to do sum holy duties to draw near to God and when on land then we have no time to go to the meeting and then we are call to go away again to sea whaling. how can we serve God or to worship him on the Sabbath days or at any time when our masters lead us to darkness and not In light[?][68]

Clearly, the need to spend every hour on the lookout was more obvious to the white men than to their Indian servants. Force was sometimes the only insurance that hands would be in ready supply.

COERCION WAS INDEED THE KEY. In the early years of the whale fishery on Nantucket, capitalism and free labor could never coexist. The continued vitality of the native economy, the declining supply of local whalemen, and the burgeoning demands of the fishery all combined to strengthen the natural bargaining position of the Indian and to leave the labor-hungry whaling merchants no alternative but the use of force. In itself, this does not explain the special importance of Indian labor. If the native islanders were hesitant to ship themselves as oarsmen on the white men's terms, surely the English boat owners could have sent their own sons to sea or procured indentured servants from the mainland.[69] That they chose not to do so suggests that free market forces alone cannot account for the entire story, but that native labor attracted English employers precisely because coercion was necessary and the natives could be coerced.

White Nantucketers, writing at the end of the eighteenth century when the aboriginal population had nearly disappeared, retained a sentimental fondness for their Indian neighbors of earlier years. Zaccheus Macy remembered them as kind and hospitable, always ready, "if the English entered their houses, whilst they were eating . . . to offer them such as they had, which sometimes would be very good."[70] In 1807 an anonymous member of the Massachusetts Historical Society described them in a similar way, adding that the natives were "religiously punctual" in their payments to the English, and that "they made excellent oarsmen, and some of them were good endsmen."[71] Nevertheless, this adulation was bought at a price. Our anonymous contributor concluded, "So useful have men of this class been found in the whale fishery, that the Indians having disappeared, negroes are now substituted in their place. Seamen of colour are more submissive than the whites."[72] The implication was clear: Indians, like blacks, merited praise, but only as long as they bent to the white man's rule. An anecdote related by Macy, a onetime employer of Indian whalemen himself, reveals this attitude in a particularly compelling manner:

But it happened once, when there were about thirty boats about six miles from the shore, that the wind came round to the northward, and blew with great violence, attended with snow. The men all rowed hard, bur made but little head way. In one of the boats there were four Indians and two white men. An old Indian in the head of the boat, perceiving that the crew began to be disheartened, spake out loud in his own tongue and said, *Momadichchator auqua sarshkee sarnkee pinchee eyoo sememoochkee chaquanks wihehee pinchee eyoo:* which in English is, "Pull a head with courage: do not be disheartened: we shall not be lost now: there are too many Englishmen to be lost now." His speaking in this manner gave the crew new courage. They soon perceived that they made head way; and after long rowing, they all got safe on shore.[73]

In Macy's conviction of the esteem in which Indian whalemen held the English, so that only the threat of a lost white man could rally them, even in the face of death, the story is almost touching. Men so apparently devoted to their masters were fond memories indeed.

What white Nantucketers perceived as natural submissiveness, however, was rather the product of a long and lively struggle. Macy came of age only in 1734, by which time the years of native independence had passed. The Indians he knew in the 1730s and 1740s, vastly outnumbered, riddled by disease, barred by their ethnicity from the avenues of social mobility, and trapped in the southeast corner of the island, were a defeated people. In truth, only the forcible deprivation of their independence had made the success of the whale fishery possible.

Neither labor scarcity nor coercion in recruitment was unique to Nantucket. The Spanish mines and haciendas of Mexico and Peru, the Portuguese sugar plantations of Brazil, and the British sugar and tobacco colonies of the West Indies and the Chesapeake all demanded a level of work commitment and submission to discipline that free Europeans were reluctant to provide, and all turned in time to the institution of bondage. Indeed, in the New World of the seventeenth and eighteenth centuries, New England was an anomaly, for it flourished without resorting to widespread formal servitude. Nevertheless, where conditions were appropriate, as the case of the whale fishery illustrates, colonists in Massachusetts felt the same need to restrict labor's freedom as did their southern counterparts. Granted, by comparison to the forms of servitude that prevailed in the plantation colonies, debt peonage as practiced on Nantucket was both a gentler solution and easier to scuttle when it no longer made economic sense. The principle involved, however, was little different. As long as land in the New World remained sufficiently abundant that an ordinary European could entertain real possibilities of obtaining a plot of his own, market-oriented production and free labor would seldom keep company.

Notes

1. Obed Macy, *The History of Nantucket; Being a Compendious Account of the First Settlement of the Island by the English, Together with the Rise and Progress of the Whale Fishery* . . . (Boston, 1835), 33.

2. Sherburne Cook, *The Indian Population of New England in the Seventeenth Century* (Berkeley, Calif., 1976), 41–45.

3. Alexander Starbuck, *The History of Nantucket: County, Island and Town* . . . (Rutand, Vt., 1969 [orig. publ. Boston, 1924]), 20–22. On the nature of Indian deeds see Francis Jennings, *The Invasion of America: Indians, Colonialism, and the Cant of Conquest* (Chapel Hill, N.C., 1975), 128–45.

4. Glover M. Allen, "The Whalebone Whales of New England," Boston Society of Natural History, *Memoires*, VIII (1916), 146–58, hereafter cited as Allen, "Whalebone Whales"; Alexander Starbuck, *History of the American Whale Fishery: From Its Earliest Inception to the Year 1876*, 2 vols. (New York, 1964 [orig. publ. Washington, D.C., 1878]), 1, 7, 9, 10; William B. Weeden, *Economic and Social History of New England, 1620–1789*, 2 vols. (New York, 1963 [orig. publ. 1890]), I, 432.

5. Starbuck, *Nantucket*, 128–30, 172.

6. Starbuck, *Whale Fishery*, I, 9–13; Allen, "Whalebone Whales," 148; William R. Palmer, "The Whaling Port of Sag Harbor" (Ph.D. diss., Columbia University, 1959), chap. 1.

7. Starbuck, *Nantucket*, 32–33, 33n.

8. Starbuck, *Whale Fishery*, I, 22.

9. Allen, "Whalebone Whales," 141–43.

10. Paul Dudley, "An Essay upon the Natural History of Whales, with a Particular Account of the Ambergris Found in the *Sperma Ceti* Whale," Royal Society of London, *Philosophical Transactions*, XXXIII (1725), 257.

11. Allen, "Whalebone Whales," 170–71; William Scoresby, *An Account of the Arctic Regions, with a History and Description of the Northern Whale-Fishery*, 2 vols. (New York, 1969 [orig. publ. Edinburgh, 1820]), II, 156–57. One barrel of oil equaled 31.5 gallons.

12. J. Hector St. John de Crèvecoeur, *Letters from an American Farmer* (New York, 1957 [orig. publ. London, 1782]), 110.

13. Dudley, "Natural History of Whales," Royal Soc. London, *Phil. Trans.*, XXXIII (1725), 263.

14. Ibid.; Crèvecoeur, *Letters*, 110–11; O. Macy, *Nantucket*, 30–31; Felix Christian Spörri, *Americanische Reiss-beschreibung nach den Caribes Insslen und Neu-Engelland* (Zurich, 1677), 44–45, quoted in Carl Bridenbaugh, *Fat Mutton and Liberty of Conscience: Society in Rhode Island, 1636–1690* (Providence, R.I., 1974), 144–45; *Griffin & Co. v. Thomas*, 2 Mass. Vice-Admiralty Court, 27–28 (1718); *Davis v. Sturges*, 2 MVAC 68 (1720); *Cowing v. Cushing*, 2 MVAC 166 (1723).

15. One man's share of a 60-barrel whale was worth £10–15 sterling, oil and bone included, in the 1720s. For wages on land see Gary B. Nash, *The Urban Crucible: Social Change, Political Consciousness, and the Origins of the American Revolution* (Cambridge, Mass., 1979), 114–15, and Jackson Turner Main, *The Social Structure of Revolutionary America* (Princeton, N.J., 1965), 70. All prices and values in this paper have been converted from Massachusetts currency to British sterling using Table 12: Value of Massachusetts Paper Currency, 1685–1775, in Nash, *Urban Crucible*, 405–406.

16. See, for example, *Davis v. Sturges*, 2 MVAC 68 (1720).

17. O. Macy, *Nantucket*, 31.

18. Zaccheus Macy, "A Short Journal of the First Settlement of the Island of Nantucket . . . ," Massachusetts Historical Society, *Collections*, 1st Ser., III (1794), 161, hereafter cited as Z. Macy, "Journal of Nantucket"; Silvanus Hussey Account Book, 1725–34, Peter Foulger Museum Library, Nantucket, Mass.; William Rotch Journal B, 2 vols., 1769–76, Old Dartmouth Historical Society, New Bedford, Mass.

19. O. Macy, *Nantucket*, 37; Z. Macy, "Journal of Nantucket," 157; Starbuck, *Nantucket*, 355–356; Silvanus Hussey Account Book, 1724–34.

20. Starbuck, *Nantucket*, 356–58; O. Macy, *Nantucket*, 37–38, 54, 71; O. Macy, "Journal of Nantucket," 161; Richard C. Kugler, "The Whale Oil Trade, 1750–1775," *Old Dartmouth Historical Sketch Number 79* (New Bedford, Mass., 1980), 3–9; Silvanus Hussey Account Book, 1724–34; Mary and Nathaniel Starbuck Account Book, 1662–1757, Foulger Museum Lib.

21. Samuel Bradstreet, Diary, quoted in Allen, "Whalebone Whales," 154.

22. Sloop *Grampus* (1751), July 8, 1751, Peleg Folger Journal, 1751–57, Nantucket Atheneum, Nantucket, Mass.

23. Z. Macy, "Journal of Nantucket," 157; Starbuck, *Nantucket*, 356, 356n–357n; Sloop, *Phebe* (1754), Aug. 9, 1754, Peleg Folger Journal, 1751–57.

24. Jo. Micah's Account, 1758, Miscellaneous MSS, Nantucket, Mass., American Antiquarian Society, Worcester, Mass.; Indenture of Robin Mesrick, July 6, 1737, Miscellaneous Bound Papers, Mass. Hist. Soc.,

Boston, Mass.; *Clark v. Cooper,* I Nantucket Inferior Court of Common Pleas 35 (1726); William Rotch Journal B, 1769–76.

25. Mary and Nathaniel Starbuck Account Book, 1662–1757; Silvanus Hussey Account Book, 1724–1734.

26. Daniel Frederick Vickers, "Maritime Labor in Colonial Massachusetts: A Case Study of the Essex County Cod Fishery and the Whaling Industry of Nantucket, 1630–1775" (Ph.D. diss., Princeton University, 1981), 295–96; Nash, *Urban Crucible,* 414.

27. O. Macy, *Nantucket,* 30; Mary and Nathaniel Starbuck Account Book, 1662–1757; Silvanus Hussey Account Book, 1724–34. This pattern is confirmed by evidence on the composition of crews from the mainland. Of 34 whalemen from Barnstable and Eastham on Cape Cod, named in a list dated Jan. 20, 1700/1, 26 were Indians. On the assumption that the 8 Englishmen served mostly as steersmen and harpooners, we can infer that almost all the oarsmen were Indians. Attachment of Goods, Jan. 20, 1700/1, Miscellaneous Bound Papers, Mass. Hist. Soc. See also James Truslow Adams, *History of the Town of Southampton (East of Canoe Place)* (Bridgehampton, N.Y., 1918), 231, 231n; E. B. O'Callaghan et al., eds., *Documents Relative to the Colonial History of the State of New-York . . .* , 15 vols. (Albany, N.Y., 1856–87), XIV, 648, 664, 675, 708–709.

28. Silvanus Hussey Account Book, 1724–34. In calculating the ethnic composition of Hussey's crews, each whaleman was counted once for every voyage in which he participated. See also Vickers, "Maritime Labor," 283–94.

29. Starbuck, *Nantucket,* 356n; Jo. Micah's Account, 1758; Mary and Nathaniel Starbuck Account Book, 1662–1757; Silvanus Hussey Account Book, 1724–34; John Barnard Account Book, 1699–1738, Foulger Museum Lib.; Probate Records of Nantucket County, vols. 1–3 (1706–1789), Probate Court Office, Town Hall, Nantucket, Mass., hereafter cited as Nantucket Probates.

30. Nantucket Probates, I, 59–62, 70–71, 92–94, 103, 139–41, 146–47, 157, 162. It should be noted at this point that the quantifiable documentation relating to the shore fishery on Nantucket is often slim. The probate records, for example, record the estate inventories of only eight Indians and eight more shore whaling investors for the entire colonial period. I have tried to be explicit about the size of my samples and to avoid drawing distinctions too fine for the data to support.

31. Nantucket Probates, vols. 1–3 (1706–1789).

32. Vickers, "Maritime Labor," 76–77, 110–16.

33. Cook, *Indian Population of New England,* 44–45, T. J. C. Brasser, "The Coastal Algonkians: People of the First Frontiers," in Eleanor Burke Leacock and Nancy Oestreich Lurie, eds., *North American Indian in Historical Perspective* (New York, 1971), 65; Jennings, *Invasion of America,* 28; Geoffrey Barraclough, ed., *The Times Atlas of World History* (London, 1978), 180–81.

34. John Brereton, *A Briefe and True Relation of the Discoverie of the North Part of Virginia . . .* (London, 1602), 5–7; O. Macy, *Nantucket,* 16–17.

35. Brereton, *Discoverie,* 7.

36. Brasser, "Coastal Algonkians," in Leacock and Lurie, eds., *North American Indians,* 64; Dean R. Snow, *The Archaeology of New England* (New York, 1980), 76–79; William A. Ritchie, *The Archaeology of Martha's Vineyard: A Framework for the Prehistory of Southern New England* (Garden City, N.J., 1969), 81–89; "Notes on Nantucket, August 1, 1807," Mass. Hist. Soc., *Colls.,* 2d Ser., III (1815), 34–35; O. Macy, *Nantucket,* 17.

37. For several instances of the English courts confirming Indian rights within the tract which the English had purchased see Starbuck, *Nantucket,* 124–29.

38. Mary and Nathaniel Starbuck Account Book, 1662–1757.

39. Ibid.; Nantucket Court of Sessions of the Peace, 1672–1705, in County Records (1661–), vol. 2 (1672–1705), Registry of Deeds, Town Hall. Nantucket, Mass.

40. Arthur J. Ray, *Indians in the Fur Trade: Their Role as Trappers, Hunters, and Middlemen in the Lands Southwest of Hudson Bay, 1660–1870* (Toronto, 1974), 137–38, 196.

41. Ibid., 85, 198.

42. Thomas Macy to Gov. Andros, May 9, 1676, quoted in Starbuck, *Nantucket,* 59.

43. Ibid.

44. Petition of Richard Coffin and Abishai Folger to the General Court, 1752, quoted ibid., 161; Petition of Nantucket Proprietors to the General Court, Apr. 2, 1752, quoted ibid., 164; O. Macy, *Nantucket,* 44: Z. Macy, "Journal of Nantucket," 158; Notes on Nantucket," Mass. Hist. Soc., *Colls.,* 2d Ser., III (1815), 36.

45. Mary and Nathaniel Starbuck Account Book, 1662–1757.

46. Jennings, *Invasion of America*, 102–104.

47. Records of the General Court, Nov. 17, 1718, quoted in Starbuck, *Nantucket*, 143; Silvanus Hussey Account Book, 1724–1734.

48. Quotation from the Petition of Richard Coffin and Abishai Folger to the General Court, 1752, quoted in Starbuck, *Nantucket*, 161.

49. O. Macy, *Nantucket*, 17; "Notes on Nantucket," Mass. Hist. Soc., *Colls.*, 2d Ser., III (1815), 36.

50. Earl of Bellomont to the Lords of Trade, Nov. 28, 1700, O'Callaghan et al., eds., *N.-Y. Col. Docs.*, IV, 787.

51. O. Macy, *Nantucket*, 20, 42; Nantucket Probates, I, 129. Netowa's estate was valued at £23.4 sterling.

52. Nantucket Probates, I, 75.

53. See Table 1 and O. Macy, *Nantucket*, 42.

54. Nantucket Probates, I.

55. Ibid., 89.

56. Ibid., 121, II, 214.

57. *Journals of the House of Representatives of Massachusetts*, 51 vols. (Boston, 1919–), I, 137–38.

58. Ibid., 245–46.

59. Ibid., II, 27; *The Acts and Resolves, Public and Private, of the Province of the Massachusetts-Bay*, 21 vols. (Boston, 1869–1922), II, 104.

60. *Acts and Resolves*, II, 159, 289, 438, 583, 668, 705.

61. Ibid., 363–65.

62. Silvanus Hussey Account Book, 1724–34.

63. *Clark v. Cooper*, I Nantucket Inferior Court of Common Pleas 35 (1726).

64. Indenture of Robin Mesrick, July 6, 1737, Indenture of Simon Portage, Apr. 10, 1738, Miscellaneous Bound Papers, Mass. Hist. Soc.

65. Edward Augustus Kendall, *Travels through the Northern Part of the United States . . .* (New York, 1809), II, 196, quoted in Charles E. Banks, *The History of Martha's Vineyard, Dukes County, Massachusetts*, 3 vols. (Edgartown, Mass., 1911–25), I, 440–41.

66. Petition of Paul Quaab to the General Court, May 6, 1747, quoted in Starbuck, *Nantucket*, 150–51.

67. Petition of Nantucket Selectmen to the General Court, May 27, 1747, quoted ibid., 152.

68. Petition of Nantucket Indians to the General Court, July 14, 1747, quoted ibid., 153–54.

69. The boat owners of Long Island manned their craft with their own sons when Indian whalemen grew scarce in the 1670s. See Palmer, "Sag Harbor," 9.

70. Z. Macy, "Journal of Nantucket," 158.

71. "Notes on Nantucket," Mass. Hist. Soc., *Colls.*, 2d Ser., III (1815), 36.

72. Ibid.

73. Z. Macy, "Journal of Nantucket," 157.

D CULTURE:

)QUOIS EXPERIENCE

. *Richter*

RACTER OF ALL THESE [Iroquois] Nations is warlike and
.it missionary Paul le Jeune in 1657. "The chief virtue of these poor
.elty, just as mildness is that of Christians, they teach it to their chil-
very cradles, and accustom them to the most atrocious carnage and
us spectacles."¹ Like most Europeans of his day, Le Jeune ignored
men's capacity for bloodlust and attributed the supposedly unique
Iroquois to their irreligion and uncivilized condition. Still, his obser-
a kernel of truth often overlooked by our more sympathetic eyes: in
niliar and largely unfathomable to Europeans, warfare was vitally
cultures of the seventeenth-century Iroquois and their neighbors.
of Euro-Americans, the significance that Indians attached to war-
abstantiate images of bloodthirsty savages who waged war for mere
cent decades have ethnohistorians discarded such shibboleths and
ndian wars in the same economic and diplomatic frameworks long
of European conflicts. Almost necessarily, given the weight of past
work has stressed similarities between Indian and European warfare.²
nmonplace stereotypes nor scholarly efforts to combat them have left
erious consideration of the possibility that the nonstate societies of
a America may have waged war for different—but no less rational
age—purposes than did the nation-states of Europe.³ This article
ssibility through an analysis of the changing role of warfare in Iro-
ing the first century after European contact.
s Confederacy (composed, from west to east, of the Five Nations of
ıga, Onondaga, Oneida, and Mohawk) frequently went to war for
much in internal social demands as in external disputes with their
ame observation could be made about countless European states, but
ernal motives that often propelled the Iroquois and other northeast-
ake war have few parallels in Euro-American experience. In many
pattern known as the "mourning-war" was one means of restoring
ensuring social continuity, and dealing with death.⁴ A grasp of the

SOURCE: *William and Mary Quarterly*, 3d Ser. 40 (1983), 528–59.

Ambushes, scalping, torture of prisoners, end
Indian ways of war were one of the main rea
sidered Native Americans uncivilized. Unabl
causes of Indian conflict or the rationale fc
impressed and terrified by natives' martial pro
colonists concluded that Indians were blood
"For them to live in Peace," wrote the Carol
1709, "is to live out of their Element, War, C
what they delight in."

Lawson was talking here of "the *Iroquois,*
ans that we know of." Indeed, no native peopl
the Five Nations Iroquois, a confederacy in
York, which in the seventeenth century in
Onondagas, Cayugas, and Mohawks. Yet as
Iroquois and other Indians were not engaged
bloodlust; their conceptions of the purpose of
different from Europeans', made perfect sense
one of the principal reasons for fighting was to
of a community with captives who would be t
the heartache of the bereaved. As Richter reve
flict, known as a "mourning war," did not invol
selected members of a community avenged t
townsfolk by going on raiding parties to captur

But the traditional practice of the "mournir
as the pace of death accelerated in native comm
quois men went to war evolved over the course
tury, in direct response to changes in the Confe
its territory. New stresses brought on by coloniza
and conflicts with other Indians over the dwir
essential for trade—led to a rise in violence and
increase in the need for warfare to satisfy cultura
cious Iroquois John Lawson wrote about in 1709
to cope with the forces unleashed by Europeans.

"THE C
cruel," wrote
Pagans being
dren from th
the most bai
his own cou
bellicosity o
vations cont
ways quite
important i
For genera
fare seemed
sport. Only
begun to st
used by stu
prejudice,
Thus neith
much roo
aboriginal
and no m
explores t
quois cult

The I
the Senec
reasons r
neighbor
the partic
ern India
Indian c
lost pop

changing role of this pattern in Iroquois culture is essential if the seventeenth- and early eighteenth-century campaigns of the Five Nations—and a vital aspect of the contact situation—are to be understood. "War is a necessary exercise for the Iroquois," explained missionary and ethnologist Joseph François Lafitau, "for, besides the usual motives which people have in declaring it against troublesome neighbours . . . , it is indispensable to them also because of one of their fundamental laws of being."[5]

I

Euro-Americans often noted that martial skills were highly valued in Indian societies and that, for young men, exploits on the warpath were important determinants of personal prestige. This was, some hyperbolized, particularly true of the Iroquois. "It is not for the Sake of Tribute . . . that they make War," Cadwallader Colden observed of the Five Nations, "but from the Notions of Glory, which they have ever most strongly imprinted on their Minds."[6] Participation in a war party was a benchmark episode in an Iroquois youth's development, and later success in battle increased the young man's stature in his clan and village. His prospects for an advantageous marriage, his chances for recognition as a village leader, and his hopes for eventual selection to a sachemship depended largely—though by no means entirely—on his skill on the warpath, his munificence in giving war feasts, and his ability to attract followers when organizing a raid.[7] Missionary-explorer Louis Hennepin exaggerated when he claimed that "those amongst the *Iroquoise* who are not given to War, are had in great Contempt, and pass for Lazy and Effeminate People," but warriors did in fact reap great social rewards.[8]

The plaudits offered to successful warriors suggest a deep cultural significance; societies usually reward warlike behavior not for its own sake but for the useful functions it performs.[9] Among the functions postulated in recent studies of nonstate warfare is the maintenance of stable population levels. Usually this involves—in more or less obvious ways—a check on excessive population growth, but in some instances warfare can be, for the victors, a means to increase the group's numbers.[10] The traditional wars of the Five Nations served the latter purpose. The Iroquois conceptualized the process of population maintenance in terms of individual and collective spiritual power. When a person died, the power of his or her lineage, clan, and nation was diminished in proportion to his or her individual spiritual strength.[11] To replenish the depleted power the Iroquois conducted "requickening" ceremonies at which the deceased's name—and with it the social role and duties it represented—was transferred to a successor. Vacant positions in Iroquois families and villages were thus both literally and symbolically filled, and the continuity of Iroquois society was confirmed, while survivors were assured that the social role and spiritual strength embodied in the departed's name had not been lost.[12] Warfare was crucial to these customs, for when the deceased was a person of ordinary status and little authority the beneficiary of the requickening was often a war captive, who would be adopted "to help strengthen the familye in lew of their deceased Freind."[13] "A father who has lost his son adopts a young prisoner in his place," explained an eighteenth-century commentator on Indian customs. "An orphan takes a father or mother; a widow a husband; one man takes a sister and another a brother."[14]

On a societal level, then, warfare helped the Iroquois to deal with deaths in their ranks. On a personal, emotional level it performed similar functions. The Iroquois believed that the grief inspired by a relative's death could, if uncontrolled, plunge survivors into depths of despair that robbed them of their reason and disposed them to fits of rage potentially harmful to themselves and the community. Accordingly, Iroquois culture directed mourners' emotions into ritualized channels. Members of the deceased's household, "after having the hair cut, smearing the face with earth or charcoal and gotten themselves up in the most frightful negligence," embarked on ten days of "deep mourning," during which "they remain at the back of their bunk, their face against the ground or turned towards the back of the platform, their head enveloped in their blanket which is the dirtiest and least clean rag that they have. They do not look at or speak to anyone except through necessity and in a low voice. They hold themselves excused from every duty of civility and courtesy."[15] For the next year the survivors engaged in less intense formalized grieving, beginning to resume their daily habits but continuing to disregard their personal appearance and many social amenities. While mourners thus channeled their emotions, others hastened to "cover up" the grief of the bereaved with condolence rituals, feasts, and presents (including the special variety of condolence gift often somewhat misleadingly described as *wergild*). These were designed to cleanse sorrowing hearts and to ease the return to normal life. Social and personal needs converged at the culmination of these ceremonies, the "requickening" of the deceased.[16]

But if the mourners' grief remained unassuaged, the ultimate socially sanctioned channel for their violent impulses was a raid to seek captives who, it was hoped, would ease their pain. The target of the mourning-war was usually a people traditionally defined as enemies; neither they nor anyone else need necessarily be held directly responsible for the death that provoked the attack, though most often the foe could be made to bear the blame.[17] Raids for captives could be either large-scale efforts organized on village, nation, or confederacy levels or, more often, attacks by small parties raised at the behest of female kin of the deceased. Members of the dead person's household—presumably lost in grief—did not usually participate directly. Instead, young men who were related by marriage to the bereaved women but who lived in other longhouses were obliged to form a raiding party or face the matrons' accusations of cowardice.[18] When the warriors returned with captured men, women, and children, mourners could select a prisoner for adoption in the place of the deceased or they could vent their rage in rituals of torture and execution.[19]

The rituals began with the return of the war party, which had sent word ahead of the number of captives seized. Most of the villagers holding clubs, sticks, and other weapons, stood in two rows outside the village entrance to meet the prisoners. Men— but usually not women or young children—received heavy blows designed to inflict pain without serious injury. Then they were stripped and led to a raised platform in an open space inside the village, where old women led the community in further physical abuse, tearing out fingernails and poking sensitive body parts with sticks and firebrands.[20] After several hours, prisoners were allowed to rest and eat, and later they were made to dance for their captors while their fate was decided. Headmen apportioned them to grieving families, whose matrons then chose either to adopt or to execute them.[21] If those who were adopted made a sincere effort to please their new relatives and to assimilate into village society, they could expect a long life; if they displeased, they were quietly and unceremoniously killed.

A captive slated for ritual execution was usually also adopted and subsequently addressed appropriately as "uncle" or "nephew," but his status was marked by a distinctive red and black pattern of facial paint. During the next few days the doomed man gave his death feast, where his executioners saluted him and allowed him to recite his war honors. On the appointed day he was tied with a short rope to a stake, and villagers of both sexes and all ages took turns wielding firebrands and various red-hot objects to burn him systematically from the feet up. The tormentors behaved with religious solemnity and spoke in symbolic language of "caressing" their adopted relative with their firebrands. The victim was expected to endure his sufferings stoically and even to encourage his torturers, but this seems to have been ideal rather than typical behavior. If he too quickly began to swoon, his ordeal briefly ceased and he received food and drink and time to recover somewhat before the burning resumed. At length, before he expired, someone scalped him, another threw hot sand on his exposed skull, and finally a warrior dispatched him with a knife to the chest or a hatchet to the neck. Then the victim's flesh was stripped from his bones and thrown into cooking kettles, and the whole village feasted on his remains. This feast carried great religious significance for the Iroquois, but its full meaning is irretrievable; most European observers were too shocked to probe its implications.[22]

Mourners were not the only ones to benefit from the ceremonial torture and execution of captives. While grieving relatives vented their emotions, all of the villagers, by partaking in the humiliation of every prisoner and the torture of some, were able to participate directly in the defeat of their foes. Warfare thus dramatically promoted group cohesion and demonstrated to the Iroquois their superiority over their enemies. At the same time, youths learned valuable lessons in the behavior expected of warriors and in the way to die bravely should they ever be captured. Le Jeune's "barbarous spectacles" were a vital element in the ceremonial life of Iroquois communities.[23]

The social demands of the mourning-war shaped strategy and tactics in at least two ways. First, the essential measure of a war party's success was its ability to seize prisoners and bring them home alive. Capturing of enemies was preferred to killing them on the spot and taking their scalps, while none of the benefits European combatants derived from war—territorial expansion, economic gain, plunder of the defeated—outranked the seizure of prisoners.[24] When missionary Jerome Lalemant disparaged Iroquoian warfare as "consisting of a few broken heads along the highways, or of some captives brought into the country to be burned and eaten there," he was more accurate than he knew.[25] The overriding importance of captive taking set Iroquois warfare dramatically apart from the Euro-American military experience.

"We are not like you CHRISTIANS for when you have taken Prisoners of one another you send them home, by such means you can never rout one another," explained the Onondaga orator Teganissorens to Gov. Robert Hunter of New York in 1711.[26]

The centrality of captives to the business of war was clear in precombat rituals: imagery centered on a boiling war kettle; the war feast presaged the future cannibalistic rite; mourning women urged warriors to bring them prisoners to assuage their grief; and, if more than one village participated in the campaign, leaders agreed in advance on the share of captives that each town would receive.[27] As Iroquois warriors saw it, to forget the importance of captive taking or to ignore the rituals associated with it was to invite defeat. In 1642 missionary Isaac Jogues observed a ceremony he believed to be a sacrifice to Areskoui, the deity who presided over Iroquois wars. "At a solemn feast which they had made of two Bears, which they had offered to their demon, they had used this form of words: 'Aireskoi, thou dost right to punish us, and to give us no more captives' (they were speaking of the Algonquins, of whom that year they had not taken one . . .) 'because we have sinned by not eating the bodies of those whom thou last gavest us; but we promise thee to eat the first ones whom thou shalt give us, as we now do with these two Bears.'"[28]

A second tactical reflection of the social functions of warfare was a strong sanction against the loss of Iroquois lives in battle. A war party that, by European standards, seemed on the brink of triumph could be expected to retreat sorrowfully homeward if it suffered a few fatalities. For the Indians, such a campaign was no victory; casualties would subvert the purpose of warfare as a means of restocking the population.[29] In contrast to European beliefs that to perish in combat was acceptable and even honorable, Iroquois beliefs made death in battle a frightful prospect, though one that must be faced bravely if necessary. Slain warriors, like all who died violent deaths, were said to be excluded from the villages of the dead, doomed to spend a roving eternity seeking vengeance. As a result, their bodies were not interred in village cemeteries, lest their angry souls disturb the repose of others. Both in burial and in the afterlife, a warrior who fell in combat faced separation from his family and friends.[30]

Efforts to minimize fatalities accordingly underlay several tactics that contemporary Euro-Americans considered cowardly: fondness for ambushes and surprise attacks; unwillingness to fight when outnumbered; and avoidance of frontal assaults on fortified places. Defensive tactics showed a similar emphasis on precluding loss of life. Spies in enemy villages and an extensive network of scouts warned of invading war parties before they could harm Iroquois villagers. If intruders did enter Iroquoia, defenders attacked from ambush, but only if they felt confident of repulsing the enemy without too many losses of their own. The people retreated behind palisades or, if the enemy appeared too strong to resist, burned their own villages and fled— warriors included—into the woods or to neighboring villages. Houses and corn supplies thus might temporarily be lost, but unless the invaders achieved complete surprise, the lives and spiritual power of the people remained intact. In general, when the Iroquois were at a disadvantage, they preferred flight or an insincerely negotiated truce to the costly last stands that earned glory for European warriors.[31]

That kind of glory, and the warlike way of life it reflected, were not Iroquois ideals. Warfare was a specific response to the death of specific individuals at specific times, a sporadic affair characterized by seizing from traditional enemies a few captives who would replace the dead, literally or symbolically, and ease the pain of those who mourned. While war was not to be undertaken gladly or lightly, it was still "a necessary exercise for the Iroquois,"[32] for it was an integral part of individual and social mourning practices. When the Iroquois envisioned a day of no more wars, with their Great League of Peace extended to all peoples, they also envisioned an alternative to the mourning functions of warfare. That alternative was embodied in the proceedings of league councils and Iroquois peace negotiations with other peoples, which began with—and frequently consisted entirely of—condolence ceremonies and exchanges of presents designed to dry the tears, unstop the mouths, and cleanse the hearts of bereaved participants.[33] Only when grief was forgotten could war end and peace begin. In the century following the arrival of Europeans, grief could seldom be forgotten.

II

After the 1620s, when the Five Nations first made sustained contact with Europeans, the role of warfare in Iroquois culture changed dramatically. By 1675, European diseases, firearms, and trade had produced dangerous new patterns of conflict that threatened to derange the traditional functions of the mourning-war.

Before most Iroquois had ever seen a Dutchman or a Frenchman, they had felt the impact of the maladies the invaders inadvertently brought with them.[34] By the 1640s the number of Iroquois (and of their Indian neighbors) had probably already been halved by epidemics of smallpox, measles, and other European "childhood diseases," to which Indian populations had no immunity.[35] The devastation continued through the century. A partial list of plagues that struck the Five Nations includes "a general malady" among the Mohawk in 1647; "a great mortality" among the Onondaga in 1656–57; a smallpox epidemic among the Oneida, Onondaga, Cayuga, and Seneca in 1661–63; "a kind of contagion" among the Seneca in 1668; "a fever of . . . malignant character" among the Mohawk in 1673; and "a general Influenza" among the Seneca in 1676.[36] As thousands died, ever-growing numbers of captive adoptees would be necessary if the Iroquois were even to begin to replace their losses; mourning-wars of unprecedented scale loomed ahead. Warfare would cease to be a sporadic and specific response to individual deaths and would become instead a constant and increasingly undifferentiated symptom of societies in demographic crisis.

At the same time, European firearms would make warfare unprecedentedly dangerous for both the Iroquois and their foes, and would undermine traditional Indian sanctions against battle fatalities. The introduction of guns, together with the replacement of flint arrowheads by more efficient iron, copper, and brass ones that could pierce traditional Indian wooden armor, greatly increased the chances of death in combat and led to major changes in Iroquois tactics. In the early seventeenth century Champlain had observed mostly ceremonial and relatively bloodless confrontations between large Indian armies, but with the advent of muskets—which Europeans had designed to be fired in volleys during just such battles—massed confrontations became, from the Indian perspective, suicidal folly. They were quickly abandoned in favor of a redoubled emphasis on small-scale raids and ambushes, in which Indians learned far sooner than Euro-Americans how to aim cumbersome muskets accurately at individual targets.[37] By the early 1640s the Mohawk were honing such skills with approximately three hundred guns acquired from the Dutch of Albany and from English sources. Soon the rest of the Five Nations followed the Mohawk example.[38]

Temporarily, the Iroquois' plentiful supply and skillful use of firearms gave them a considerable advantage over their Indian enemies: during the 1640s and 1650s the less well armed Huron and the poorly armed Neutral and Khionontateronon (Petun or Tobacco Nation) succumbed to Iroquois firepower. That advantage had largely disappeared by the 1660s and 1670s, however, as the Five Nations learned in their battles with such heavily armed foes as the Susquehannock. Once muskets came into general use in Indian warfare, several drawbacks became apparent: they were more sluggish than arrows to fire and much slower to reload; their noise lessened the capacity for surprise; and reliance on them left Indians dependent on Euro-Americans for ammunition, repairs, and replacements. But there could be no return to the days of bows and arrows and wooden armor. Few Iroquois war parties could now expect to escape mortal casualties.[39]

While European diseases and firearms intensified Indian conflicts and stretched the mourning-war tradition beyond previous limits, a third major aspect of European contact pushed Iroquois warfare in novel directions. Trade with Europeans made economic motives central to American Indian conflicts for the first time. Because iron tools, firearms, and other trade goods so quickly became essential to Indian economies, struggles for those items and for furs to barter for them lay behind numerous seventeenth-century wars. Between 1624 and 1628 the Iroquois gained unimpeded access to European commodities when Mohawk warriors drove the Mahican to the east of the Hudson River and secured an open route to the Dutch traders of Albany.[40] But obtaining the furs to exchange for the goods of Albany was a problem not so easily solved. By about 1640 the Five Nations perhaps had exhausted the beaver stock of their home hunting territories; more important, they could not find in relatively temperate Iroquoia the thick northern pelts prized by Euro-American traders.[41] A long, far-flung series of "beaver wars" ensued, in which the Five Nations battled the Algonquian nations of the St. Lawrence River region, the Huron, the Khionontateronon, the Neutral, the Erie, and other western and northern peoples in a constant struggle over fur supplies. In those wars the Iroquois more frequently sought dead beavers than live ones: most of their raids were not part of a strategic plan to seize new hunting grounds but piratical attacks on enemy canoes carrying pelts to Montreal and Trois-Rivières.[42]

The beaver wars inexorably embroiled the Iroquois in conflict with the French of Canada. Franco-Iroquois hostilities dated from the era of Champlain, who consistently based his relations with Canada's natives upon promises to aid them in their traditional raids against the Five Nations. "I came to the conclusion," wrote Champlain in 1619, "that it was very necessary to assist them, both to engage them the more to love us, and also to provide the means of furthering my enterprises and explorations which apparently could only be carried out with their help."[43] The French commander and a few of his men participated in Indian campaigns against the Five Nations in 1609, 1610, and 1615, and encouraged countless other raids.[44] From the 1630s to the 1660s, conflict between the Five Nations and Canadian Indians intensified, and Iroquois war parties armed with guns frequently blockaded the St. Lawrence and stopped the flow of furs to the French settlements. A state of open war, punctuated by short truces, consequently prevailed between New France and various members of the Five Nations, particularly the Mohawk. The battles were almost exclusively economic and geopolitical—the Iroquois were not much interested in French captives—and in general the French suffered more than the Iroquois from the fighting.[45] Finally, in 1666, a French army invaded Iroquoia and burned the Mohawks' fortified villages, from which all had fled to safety except a few old men who chose to stay and die. In 1667, the Five Nations and the French made a peace that lasted for over a decade.[46]

While the fur trade introduced new economic goals, additional foes, and wider scope to Iroquois warfare, it did not crowd out older cultural motives. Instead, the mourning-war tradition, deaths from disease, dependence on firearms, and the trade in furs combined to produce a dangerous spiral: epidemics led to deadlier mourning-wars fought with firearms; the need for guns increased the demand for pelts to trade for them; the quest for furs provoked wars with other nations; and deaths in those conflicts began the mourning-war cycle anew. At each turn, fresh economic and demographic motives fed the spiral.

Accordingly, in the mid-seventeenth-century Iroquois wars, the quest for captives was at least as important as the quest for furs. Even in the archetypal beaver war, the Five Nations–Huron conflict, only an overriding—even desperate—demand for prisoners can explain much of Iroquois behavior. For nearly a decade after the dispersal of the Huron Confederacy in 1649, Iroquois war parties killed or took captive every starving (and certainly peltry-less) group of Huron refugees they could find. Meanwhile, Iroquois ambassadors and warriors alternately negotiated with, cajoled, and threatened the Huron remnants living at Quebec to make them join their captive relatives in Iroquoia. Through all this, Mohawks, Senecas, and Onondagas occasionally shed each other's blood in arguments over the human spoils. Ultimately, in 1657, with French acquiescence, most of the Huron refugees filed away from Quebec—the Arendaronon nation to the Onondaga country and the Attignawantan nation to the Mohawk country.[47]

Judging by the number of prisoners taken during the Five Nations' wars from the 1640s to the 1670s with their other Iroquoian neighbors—the Neutral, Khionontateronon, Erie, and Susquehannock—these conflicts stemmed from a similar mingling of captive-taking and fur trade motives. Like the Huron, each of those peoples shared with the Iroquois mixed horticultural and hunting and fishing economies, related languages, and similar beliefs, making them ideal candidates for adoption. But they could not satisfy the spiraling Iroquois demand for furs and captives; war parties from the Five Nations had to range ever farther in their quest. In a not atypical series of raids in 1661–62, they struck the Abenaki of the New England region, the Algonquians of the subarctic, the Siouans of the Upper Mississippi area, and various Indians near Virginia, while continuing the struggle with enemies closer to home.[48] The results of the mid-century campaigns are recorded in the *Jesuit Relations,* whose pages are filled with descriptions of Iroquois torture and execution of captives and note enormous numbers of adoptions. The Five Nations had absorbed so many prisoners that in 1657 le Jeune believed that "more Foreigners than natives of the country" resided in Iroquoia.[49] By the mid-1660s several missionaries estimated that two-thirds or more of the people in many Iroquois villages were adoptees.[50]

By 1675 a half-century of constantly escalating warfare had at best enabled the Iroquois to hold their own. Despite the beaver wars, the Five Nations still had few dependable sources of furs. In the early 1670s they hunted primarily on lands north of Lake Ontario, where armed clashes with Algonquian foes were likely, opportunities to steal peltries from them were abundant, and conflict with the French who claimed the territory was always possible.[51] Ironically, even the Franco-Iroquois peace of 1667 proved a mixed blessing for the Five Nations. Under the provisions of the treaty, Jesuit priests, who had hitherto labored in Iroquois villages only sporadically and at the risk of their lives, established missions in each of the Five Nations.[52] The Jesuits not only created Catholic converts but also generated strong Christian and traditionalist factions that brought unprecedented disquiet to Iroquois communities. Among the Onondaga, for example, the Christian sachem Garakontié's refusal to perform his duties in the traditional manner disrupted such important ceremonies as dream-guessings, the roll call of the chiefs, and healing rituals.[53] And in 1671, traditionalist Mohawk women excluded at least one Catholic convert from her rightful seat on the council of matrons because of her faith.[54] Moreover, beginning in the late 1660s, missionaries encouraged increasing numbers of Catholic Iroquois—particularly Mohawks and Oneidas—to desert their homes for the mission villages of Canada; by the mid-1670s well over two hundred had departed.[55] A large proportion of those who left, however, were members of the Five Nations in name only. Many—perhaps most—were recently adopted Huron and other prisoners, an indication that the Iroquois were unable to assimilate effectively the mass of newcomers their mid-century wars had brought them.[56]

Problems in incorporating adoptees reflected a broader dilemma: by the late 1670s the mourning-war complex was crumbling. Warfare was failing to maintain a stable population; despite torrents of prisoners, gains from adoption were exceeded by losses from disease, combat, and migrations to Canada. Among the Mohawk—for whom more frequent contemporary population estimates exist than for the other nations of the confederacy—the number of warriors declined from 700 or 800 in the 1640s to approximately 300 in the late 1670s. Those figures imply that, even with a constant infusion of captive adoptees, Mohawk population fell by half during that period.[57] The Five Nations as a whole fared only slightly better. In the 1640s the confederacy, already drastically reduced in numbers, had counted over 10,000 people. By the 1670s there were perhaps only 8,600.[58] The mourning-war, then, was not discharging one of its primary functions.

Meanwhile, ancient customs regarding the treatment of prisoners were decaying as rituals degenerated into chaotic violence and sheer murderous rage displaced the orderly adoption of captives that the logic of the mourning-war demanded. In 1602 missionary Jean de Lamberville asserted that Iroquois warriors "killed and ate . . . on the spot" over six hundred enemies in a campaign in the Illinois country; if he was even half right, it is clear that something had gone horribly wrong in the practice of the mourning-war. The decay of important customs associated with traditional warfare is further indicated by Lamberville's account of the return of that war party with its surviving prisoners. A gauntlet ceremony at the main Onondaga village turned into a deadly attack, forcing headmen to struggle to protect the lives of the captives. A few hours later, drunken young men, "who observe[d] no usages or customs," broke into longhouses and tried to kill the prisoners whom the headmen had rescued. In vain, leaders pleaded with their people to remember "that it was contrary to custom to ill-treat prisoners on their arrival, when They had not yet been given in the place of any person . . . and when their fate had been left Undecided by the victors."[59]

Nevertheless, despite the weakening of traditional restraints, in the 1670s Iroquois warfare still performed useful functions. It maintained a tenuous supply of furs to trade for essential European goods; it provided frequent campaigns to allow young men to show their valor; and it secured numerous captives to participate in the continual mourning rituals that the many Iroquois deaths demanded (though there could never be enough to restock the population absolutely). In the quarter-century after 1675, however, the scales would tip: by 1700 the Anglo—French struggle for control of the continent would make warfare as the Five Nations were practicing it dangerously dysfunctional for their societies.

III

During the mid-1670s the Five Nations' relations with their Indian and European neighbors were shifting. In 1675 the Mohawk and the Mahican made peace under pressure from Albany and ended—except for a few subsequent skirmishes—over a decade of conflict that had cost each side heavily.[60] In the same year the long and destructive war of the Oneida, Onondaga, Cayuga, and Seneca against the Susquehannock concluded as the latter withdrew from Pennsylvania to Maryland. The end of hostilities with the Mahican and Susquehannock allowed the Iroquois to refocus westward their quest for furs and captives. In the late 1670s and early 1680s conflicts with the Illinois, Miami, and other western peoples intensified, while relations with the Wyandot (composed of remnants of the Huron and other Iroquoian groups forced to the west in earlier wars with the Five Nations) and with various elements of the Ottawa alternated between skirmishes and efforts to cement military alliances against other enemies of the Iroquois.[61] As the Onondaga orator Otreouti (whom the French called *La Grande Gueule*, "Big Mouth") explained in 1684, the Five Nations "fell upon the *Illinese* and the *Oumamies* [Miami], because they cut down the trees of Peace that serv'd for limits or boundaries to our Frontiers. They came to hunt

Beavers upon our Lands; and contrary to the custom of all the Savages, have carried off whole Stocks, both Male and Female."[62] Whether those hunting grounds actually belonged to the Five Nations is questionable, but the importance of furs as an Iroquois war aim is not. And captives were also a lucrative prize, as the arrival in 1682 of several hundred Illinois prisoners demonstrated.[63] But this last of the beaver wars—which would melt into the American phase of the War of the League of Augsburg (King William's War)—was to differ devastatingly from earlier Iroquois conflicts. At the same time that the Five Nations began their fresh series of western campaigns the English and French empires were also beginning to compete seriously for the furs and lands of that region. The Iroquois would inevitably be caught in the Europeans' conflicts.[64]

Until the mid-1670s the Five Nations had only to deal, for all practical purposes, with the imperial policies of one European Power, France. The vital Iroquois connection with the Dutch of New Netherland and, after the 1664 conquest, with the English of New York had rested almost solely on trade. But when the English took possession of the province for the second time in 1674, the new governor, Sir Edmund Andros, had more grandiose designs for the Iroquois in the British American empire. He saw the Five Nations as the linchpin in his plans to pacify the other Indian neighbors of the English colonies; he hoped to make the Five Nations a tool in his dealings with the Calverts of Maryland; and he sought an opportunity to annex land to New York from Connecticut by encouraging the Iroquois to fight alongside New England in its 1675–76 war on the Wampanoag Metacom ("King Philip") and his allies.[65] After Andros, New York–Iroquois relations would never be the same, as successors in the governor's chair attempted to use the Five Nations for imperial purposes. Thomas Dongan, who assumed the governorship in 1683, tried to strengthen New York's tenuous claims to suzerainty over the Five Nations—in 1684 he ceremoniously distributed the duke of York's coat of arms to be hung in their villages—and he directly challenged French claims in the west by sending trading parties into the region.[66]

Meanwhile the French had begun their own new westward thrust. In 1676 Canadian governor Louis de Buade de Frontenac established a post at Niagara and a few years later René-Robert Cavelier de La Salle began to construct a series of forts in the Illinois country. The French had long trodden a fine line in western policy. On the one hand, Iroquois raids in the west could not be allowed to destroy Indian allies of New France or to disrupt the fur trade, but, on the other hand, some hostility between the Iroquois and the western Indians helped prevent the latter from taking their furs to Albany markets. In the late 1670s and the 1680s Frontenac and especially the governors during the interval between his two tenures, Joseph-Antoine Le Febvre de La Barre and Jacques-René de Brisay de Denonville, watched that policy unravel as they noted with alarm New York trading expeditions in the west, Iroquois raids on Indian hunters and coureurs de bois, Iroquois negotiations with the Wyandot and Ottawa, and the continual flow of firearms from Albany to the Five Nations.[67] As Iroquois spokesmen concisely explained to Dongan in 1684, "The French will have all the Bevers, and are angry with us for bringing any to you."[68]

French officials, faced with the potential ruin of their western fur trade, determined to humble the Five Nations. For over a decade, Canadian armies repeatedly invaded Iroquoia to burn villages, fields, and corn supplies. Although the first French attempt, led by La Barre against the Seneca in 1684, ended in ignoble failure for the French and diplomatic triumph for the Iroquois, later invasions sent the Five Nations to the brink of disaster. In 1687 La Barre's successor, Denonville, marched against Iroquoia with an army of over 2,000 French regulars, Canadian militia, and Indian warriors. Near Fort Frontenac his troops kidnapped an Iroquois peace delegation and captured the residents of two small villages of Iroquois who had lived on the north shore of Lake Ontario for nearly two decades. Denonville sent over thirty of the prisoners to France as slaves for the royal galleys, and then proceeded toward the Seneca country. After a brief but costly skirmish with Seneca defenders who hid in ambush, the invaders destroyed what was left of the Seneca villages, most of which the inhabitants had burned before fleeing to safety. Six years later, after war had been declared between France and England, the Canadians struck again. In January 1693, 625 regulars, militia, and Indians surprised the four Mohawk villages, captured their residents, and burned longhouses and stores of food as they retreated. Then, in 1696, the aged Frontenac—again governor and now carried into the field on a chair by his retainers—led at least 2,000 men to Onondaga, which he found destroyed by the retreating villagers. While his troops razed the ripening Onondaga corn, he received a plea for negotiation from the nearby Oneida village. The governor despatched Philippe de Rigaud de Vaudreuil and a detachment of 600 men, who extracted from the few Oneida who remained at home a promise that their people would soon move to a Canadian mission. Vaudreuil burned the village anyway.[69]

The repeated French invasions of Iroquoia took few lives directly—only in the campaign against the Mohawk in 1693 did the invaders attack fully occupied villages—but their cumulative effect was severe. One village or nation left homeless and deprived of food supplies could not depend on aid from the others, who faced similar plights. And as the Five Nations struggled to avoid starvation and to rebuild their villages, frequent raids by the Indian allies of the French levied a heavy toll in lives. In December 1691 a Mohawk-Oneida war party sustained fifteen deaths in an encounter on Lake George—losses significant beyond their numbers because they included all of the two nations' war chiefs and contributed to a total of 90 Mohawk and Oneida warriors killed since 1689. The Mohawk, who in the late 1670s had fielded approximately 300 warriors, in 1691 could muster only 130.[70] Combat fatalities, the continued exodus of Catholic converts to Canada, and the invasion of 1693 had, lamented a Mohawk orator, left his nation "a mean poor people," who had "lost all by the Enemy."[71] Fighting in the early 1690s had considerably weakened the three western Iroquois nations as well. In February 1692, for example, 50 Iroquois encountered a much larger French and Indian force above Montreal, and 40 suffered death or capture; a month later, 200 met disaster farther up the St. Lawrence, when many were "captured, killed and defeated with loss of their principal chiefs."[72] Through the mid-1690s sporadic raids in and around Iroquoia by Canada's Indian allies kept the Five Nations on the defensive.[73]

The Five Nations did not meekly succumb. In 1687, soon after Denonville's capture of the Iroquois settled near Fort Frontenac and his invasion of the Seneca country, a Mohawk orator declared to Governor Dongan his people's intention to strike back at the French in the tradition of the mourning-war. "The Governor of Canada," he proclaimed, "has started an unjust war against all the [Five] nations. The Maquase [Mohawk] doe not yet have any prisoners, but that Governor has taken a hundred prisoners from all the nations to the West. . . . Therefore the nations have desired to revenge the unjust attacks."[74] Iroquois raids for captives kept New France in an uproar through the early 1690s.[75] The warriors' greatest successes occurred during the summer of 1689. That June a Mohawk orator, speaking for all Five Nations, vowed "that the Place where the French Stole their Indians two years ago should soon be cut off (meaning Fort Frontenac) for to steal people in a time of Peace is an Inconsiderate work."[76] Within two months the Iroquois had forced the temporary abandonment of Frontenac and other French western posts, and, in an assault at Lachine on Montreal Island, had killed twenty-four French and taken seventy to ninety prisoners.[77]

Later in the 1690s, however, as the Five Nations' losses mounted, their capacity to resist steadily diminished. They repeatedly sought military support from governors of New York, but little was forthcoming. "Since you are a Great People & we but a small, you *will protect us from the French,*" an Iroquois orator told Dongan in 1684. "We have put *all our Lands & ourselves,* under the Protection of the Great Duke of york."[78] Yet as long as the crowns of England and France remained at peace, the duke's governors largely ignored their end of the bargain. England's subsequent declaration of war against France coincided with the Glorious Revolution of 1688, which unleashed in New York the period of political chaos known as Leisler's Rebellion. In 1689 Mohawks visiting Albany witnessed firsthand the turmoil between Leislerians and anti-Leislerians, and soon the Iroquois observed the resulting English military impotence. In February 1690, a few miles from the easternmost Mohawk village, a party of French and their Indian allies destroyed the sleeping town of Schenectady, whose Leislerian inhabitants had ignored warnings from anti-Leislerian authorities at Albany to be on guard.[79] Soon after the attack, the Mohawk headmen visited Albany to perform a condolence ceremony for their neighbors' losses at Schenectady. When they finished, they urged prompt New York action against the French. But neither then nor during the rest of the war did the Iroquois receive a satisfactory response. New York's offensive war consisted of two ill-fated and poorly supported invasions of Canada: the first, in 1690, was a dismal failure, and the second, in 1691, cost nearly as many English casualties as it inflicted on the enemy.[80] After 1691 New York factional strife, lack of aid from England, and the preoccupation of other colonies with their own defense prevented further commitments of English manpower to support the Iroquois struggle with the French. The Five Nations received arms and ammunition from Albany—never as much or as cheap as they desired—and little else.[81]

What to the Five Nations must have seemed the most typical of English responses to their plight followed the French invasion of the Mohawk country in 1693. Though local officials at Albany and Schenectady learned in advance of the Canadian army's approach and provided for their own defense, they neglected to inform the Mohawk. In the wake of the attack, as approximately 300 Mohawk prisoners trooped toward Canada, Peter Schuyler assembled at Schenectady a force of 250 New Yorkers and some Mohawks who had escaped capture, but he was restrained from immediate pursuit by his vacillating commander, Richard Ingoldsby. At length Schuyler moved on his own initiative and, reinforced by war parties from the western Iroquois nations, overtook the French army and inflicted enough damage to force the release of most of the captive Mohawk. Meanwhile, when word of the invasion reached Manhattan, Gov. Benjamin Fletcher mustered 150 militia and sailed to Albany in the unprecedented time of fewer than three days; nevertheless, the fighting was already over. At a conference with Iroquois headmen a few days later, Fletcher's rush upriver earned him the title by which he would henceforth be known to the Five Nations: Cayenquiragoe, or "Great Swift Arrow." Fletcher took the name—chosen when the Iroquois learned that the word *fletcher* meant arrow-maker—as a supreme compliment. But, in view of the Mohawk's recent experience with the English—receiving no warning of the impending invasion, having to cool their heels at Schenectady while the enemy got away and Schuyler waited for marching orders, and listening to Fletcher rebuke them for their lax scouting and defense—the governor's political opponent Peter De La Noy may have been right to claim that Cayenquiragoe was a "sarcasticall pun" on Fletcher's name, bestowed for a showy effort that yielded no practical results.[82]

Yet if the English had been unable—or, as the Iroquois undoubtedly saw it, unwilling—to give meaningful military aid to the Five Nations, they were able to keep the Indians from negotiating a separate peace with the French that might leave New York exposed alone to attack. Although after 1688 ambassadors from several Iroquois nations periodically treated with the Canadians, New Yorkers maintained enough influence with factions among the Five Nations to sabotage all negotiations.[83] New York authorities repeatedly reminded their friends among the Iroquois of past French treacheries. At Albany in 1692, for example, Commander-in-Chief Ingoldsby warned the ambassadors of the Five Nations "that the Enemy has not forgot their old tricks." The French hoped "to lull the Brethren asleep and to wine and distroy them at once, when they have peace in their mouths they have warr in their hearts."[84] Many Iroquois heeded the message. Lamberville complained in 1694 that "the english of those quarters have so intrigued that they have ruined all the hopes for peace that we had entertained."[85] The repeated failure of negotiations reinforced Canadian mistrust of the Iroquois and led French authorities to prosecute the war with more vigor. By the mid-1690s, with talks stymied, all the Five Nations could do was to accept English arms and ammunition and continue minor raids on their enemies while awaiting a general peace.[86]

For the Iroquois that peace did not come with the Treaty of Ryswick in 1697. At Ryswick, the European powers settled none of the issues that had provoked the conflict, yet they gained a respite that allowed each side to regroup. Paradoxically, however, a truce between the empires precluded an end to conflict between the French and the Five Nations; jurisdiction over the Iroquois and their territory was one of the sticking points left unsettled. Accordingly, Frontenac and his successor, Louis-Hector de

Callière, refused to consider the Iroquois—whom they called unruly French subjects—to be included in the treaty with England and insisted that they make a separate peace with New France. Fletcher and his successor, Richard Coote, earl of Bellomont, argued equally strenuously that the Iroquois were comprehended in the treaty as English subjects. Thus they tried to forbid direct Franco-Iroquois negotiations and continued to pressure their friends among the Five Nations to prevent serious talks from occurring.[87] While Iroquois leaders struggled to escape the diplomatic bind, the Indian allies of New France continued their war against their ancient Iroquois enemies. In the late 1690s the Ojibwa led a major western Indian offensive that, according to Ojibwa tradition, killed enormous numbers of Seneca and other Iroquois. Euro-American sources document more moderate, yet still devastating, fatalities: the Onondaga lost over ninety men within a year of the signing of the Treaty of Ryswick, and the Seneca perhaps as many. Such defeats continued into 1700, when the Seneca suffered over fifty deaths in battles with the Ottawa and Illinois. All along at Albany, authorities counseled the Five Nations not to strike back, but to allow Bellomont time to negotiate with Callière on their behalf.[88]

IV

By 1700 Iroquois warfare and culture had reached a turning point. Up to about 1675, despite the impact of disease, firearms, and the fur trade, warfare still performed functions that outweighed its costs. But thereafter the Anglo-French struggle for control of North America made war disastrous for the Five Nations. Conflict in the west, instead of securing fur supplies, was cutting them off, while lack of pelts to trade and wartime shortages of goods at Albany created serious economic hardship in Iroquoia.[89] Those problems paled, however, in comparison with the physical toll. All of the Iroquois nations except the Cayuga had seen their villages and crops destroyed by invading armies, and all five nations were greatly weakened by loss of members to captivity, to death in combat, or to famine and disease. By some estimates, between 1689 and 1698 the Iroquois lost half of their fighting strength. That figure is probably an exaggeration, but by 1700 perhaps 500 of the 2,000 warriors the Five Nations fielded in 1689 had been killed or captured or had deserted to the French missions and had not been replaced by younger warriors. A loss of well over 1,600 from a total population of approximately 8,600 seems a conservative estimate.[90]

At the turn of the century, therefore, the mourning-war was no longer even symbolically restocking the population. And, far from being socially integrative, the Five Nations' current war was splitting their communities asunder. The heavy death toll of previous decades had robbed them of many respected headmen and clan matrons to whom the people had looked for guidance and arbitration of disputes. As a group of young Mohawk warriors lamented in 1691 when they came to parley with the Catholic Iroquois settled near Montreal, "all those . . . who had sense are dead."[91] The power vacuum, war weariness, and the pressures of the imperial struggle combined to place at each other's throats those who believed that the Iroquois' best chance lay in a separate peace with the French and those who continued to rely on the English alliance. "The

[Five] Nations are full of faction, the French having got a great interest among them," reported the Albany Commissioners for Indian Affairs in July 1700. At Onondaga, where, according to Governor Bellomont, the French had "full as many friends" as the English, the situation was particularly severe. Some sachems found themselves excluded from councils, and factions charged one another with using poison to remove adversaries from the scene. One pro-English Onondaga headman, Aquendero, had to take refuge near Albany, leaving his son near death and supposedly bewitched by opponents.[92] Their politics being ordered by an interlocking structure of lineages, clans, and moieties, the Iroquois found such factions, which cut across kinship lines, difficult if not impossible to handle. In the 1630s the Huron, whose political structure was similar, never could manage the novel factional alignments that resulted from the introduction of Christianity. That failure perhaps contributed to their demise at the hands of the Five Nations.[93] Now the Iroquois found themselves at a similar pass.

As the new century opened, however, Iroquois headmen were beginning to construct solutions to some of the problems facing their people. From 1699 to 1701 Iroquois ambassadors—in particular the influential Onondaga Teganissorens—threaded the thickets of domestic factionalism and shuttled between their country and the Euro-American colonies to negotiate what one scholar has termed "The Grand Settlement of 1701."[94] On August 4, 1701, at an immense gathering at Montreal, representatives of the Seneca, Cayuga, Onondaga, and Oneida, also speaking for the Mohawk, met Governor Callière and headmen of the Wyandot, Algonquin, Abenaki, Nipissing, Ottawa, Ojibwa, Sauk, Fox, Miami, Potawatomi, and other French allies. The participants ratified arrangements made during the previous year that provided for a general peace, established vague boundaries for western hunting territories (the Iroquois basically consented to remain east of Detroit), and eschewed armed conflict in favor of arbitration by the governor of New France. A few days later, the Iroquois and Callière reached more specific understandings concerning Iroquois access to Detroit and other French western trading posts. Most important from the French standpoint, the Iroquois promised neutrality in future Anglo-French wars.[95]

A delegation of Mohawks arrived late at the Montreal conference; they, along with ambassadors from the western Iroquois, had been at Albany negotiating with Lt. Gov. John Nanfan, who had replaced the deceased Bellomont. The Five Nations' spokesmen had first assured Nanfan of their fidelity and told him that the simultaneous negotiations at Montreal were of no significance. Then they had agreed equivocally to perpetuate their military alliance with the English, reiterated that trade lay at the heart of Iroquois-New York relations, consented to the passage through Iroquoia of western Indians going to trade at Albany, and granted the English crown a "deed" to the same western hunting territories assured to the Five Nations in the Montreal treaty. In return, Nanfan promised English defense of Iroquois hunting rights in those lands. Meanwhile, at Philadelphia, yet a third series of negotiations had begun, which, while not usually considered part of the Grand Settlement, reflected the same Iroquois diplomatic thrust; by 1704 those talks would produce an informal trade agreement between the Five Nations and Pennsylvania.[96]

On one level, this series of treaties represented an Iroquois defeat. The Five Nations had lost the war and, in agreeing to peace on terms largely dictated by Callière, had acknowledged their inability to prevail militarily over their French, and especially their Indian, enemies.[97] Nevertheless, the Grand Settlement did secure for the Iroquois five important ends: escape from the devastating warfare of the 1690s; rights to hunting in the west; potentially profitable trade with western Indians passing through Iroquoia to sell furs at Albany; access to markets in New France and Pennsylvania as well as in New York; and the promise of noninvolvement in future imperial wars. The Grand Settlement thus brought to the Five Nations not only peace on their northern and western flanks but also a more stable economy based on guaranteed western hunting territories and access to multiple Euro-American markets. Henceforth, self-destructive warfare need no longer be the only means of ensuring Iroquois economic survival, and neither need inter-Indian beaver wars necessarily entrap the Five Nations in struggles between Euro-Americans.[98] In 1724, nearly a generation after the negotiation of the Grand Settlement, an Iroquois spokesman explained to a delegation from Massachusetts how the treaties, while limiting Iroquois diplomatic and military options, nevertheless proved beneficial. "Tho' the Hatchett lays by our side yet the way is open between this Place and Canada, and trade is free both going and coming," he answered when the New Englanders urged the Iroquois to attack New France, "if a War should break out and we should use the Hatchett that lays by our Side, those Paths which are now open wo[u]ld be stopped, and if we should make war it would not end in a few days as yours doth but it must last till one nation[.] or the other is destroyed as it has been heretofore with us[.] . . . [W]e know what whipping and scourging is from the Governor of Canada."[99]

After the Grand Settlement, then, Iroquois leaders tried to abandon warfare as a means of dealing with the diplomatic problems generated by the Anglo-French imperial rivalry and the economic dilemmas of the fur trade. Through most of the first half of the eighteenth century the headmen pursued a policy of neutrality between the empires with a dexterity that the English almost never, and the French only seldom, comprehended. At the same time the Iroquois began to cement peaceful trading relationships with the western nations. Sporadic fighting continued in the western hunting grounds through the first decade and a half of the eighteenth century, as the parties to the 1701 Montreal treaty sorted out the boundaries of their territories and engaged in reciprocal raids for captives that were provoked by contact between Iroquois and western Indian hunters near French posts. Iroquois headmen quickly took advantage of Canadian arbitration when such quarrels arose, however, and they struggled to restrain young warriors from campaigning in the west.[100] As peace took hold, Alexander Montour, the son of a French man and an Iroquois woman, worked to build for the Iroquois a thriving trade between the western nations and Albany.[101]

The new diplomatic direction was tested between 1702 and 1713, when the imperial conflict resumed in the War of the Spanish Succession (Queen Anne's War). Through crafty Iroquois diplomacy, and thanks to the only halfhearted effort each European side devoted to the western theater, the Five Nations were able to maintain their neutrality and avoid heavy combat losses. Only between 1709 and 1711 did the imperial struggle again threaten to engulf the Five Nations. In 1709 Vaudreuil, now governor of New France, ordered the murder of Montour to prevent further diversion of French western trade to the Iroquois and the English. As a result, many formerly pro-French Iroquois turned against the Canadians, and most Mohawk and Oneida warriors, with many Onondagas and Cayugas, joined in the plans of Samuel Vetch and Francis Nicholson for an intercolonial invasion of Canada. Only the Senecas, who were most exposed to attack by Indian allies of the French, refused to participate.[102] The army of colonists and Iroquois, however, never set foot in Canada because Whitehall reneged on its promise of a fleet that would simultaneously attack Canada from the east. After the 1709 fiasco, Iroquois-French relations continued to deteriorate. The Seneca determined on war with the French in 1710, when they were attacked by western Indians apparently instigated by the Canadians. Then, in the spring of 1711, a party of French came to Onondaga and, spouting threats about the consequences of further Iroquois hostility, attempted to build a blockhouse in the village. When Vetch and Nicholson planned a second assault on Canada in the summer of 1711, large war parties from all Five Nations eagerly enlisted. Once more, however, the seaborne wing of the expedition failed, and the land army returned home without seeing the enemy.[103] The debacles of 1709 and 1711 confirmed the Iroquois in their opinion of English military impotence and contributed to a chill in Anglo-Iroquois relations that lasted for the rest of the decade.[104] Iroquois leaders once again steered a course of neutrality between the empires, and after the peace of Utrecht trade once again flourished with the western Indians.[105]

In addition to its diplomatic benefits, the Grand Settlement of 1701 provided a partial solution to Iroquois factionalism. Iroquoian nonstate political structures could not suppress factional cleavages entirely, and in the years after 1701 differences over relations with the French and the English still divided Iroquois communities, as each European power continued to encourage its friends. Interpreters such as the Canadian Louis-Thomas Chabert de Joncaire and the New Yorker Lawrence Claeson (or Claes) struggled to win the hearts of Iroquois villagers; each side gave presents to its supporters; and on several occasions English officials interfered with the selection of sachems in order to strengthen pro-English factions. As a result, fratricidal disputes still occasionally threatened to tear villages apart.[106] Still, in general, avoidance of exclusive alliances or major military conflict with either European power allowed Iroquois councils to keep factional strife within bounds. A new generation of headmen learned to maintain a rough equilibrium between pro-French and pro-English factions at home, as well as peaceful relations with French and English abroad. Central to that strategy was an intricate policy that tried to balance French against English fortified trading posts, Canadian against New York blacksmiths, and Jesuit against Anglican missionaries. Each supplied the Iroquois with coveted aspects of Euro-American culture—trade goods, technology, and spiritual power, respectively—but each also could be a focus of factional leadership and a tool of Euro-American domination. The Grand Settlement provided a way to lessen, though hardly eliminate, those dangers.[107]

The Iroquois balancing act was severely tested beginning in 1719, when Joncaire persuaded pro-French elements of the Seneca to let him build a French trading house at Niagara. Neither confederacy leaders nor Senecas opposed to the French encroachment attempted to dislodge the intruders forcibly, as they had done in the previous century at Fort Frontenac. Instead, Iroquois headmen unsuccessfully urged New York authorities to send troops to destroy the post, thus hoping to place the onus on the British while avoiding an open breach between pro-French and pro-English Iroquois. But New York Gov. William Burnet had other plans. In 1724 he announced his intention to build an English counterpart to Niagara at Oswego. With the French beginning to fortify Niagara, league headmen reluctantly agreed to the English proposals. In acquiescing to both forts, the Iroquois yielded a measure of sovereignty as Europeans defined the term; yet they dampened internal strife, avoided exclusive dependence on either European power, and maintained both factional and diplomatic balance.[108]

The years following the Grand Settlement also witnessed the stabilization of Iroquois population. Though the numbers of the Iroquois continued to decline gradually, the forces that had so dramatically reduced them in the seventeenth century abated markedly after 1701. The first two decades of the seventeenth century brought only one major epidemic—smallpox in 1716[109]—while the flow of Catholic converts to Canadian missions also slowed. The missions near Montreal had lost much of the utopian character that had previously attracted so many Iroquois converts. By the early eighteenth century, drunkenness, crushing debts to traders, and insults from Euro-American neighbors were no less characteristic of Iroquois life in Canada than in Iroquoia, and the Jesuit priests serving the Canadian missions had become old, worn-out men who had long since abandoned dreams of turning Indians into Frenchmen.[110]

As the population drain from warfare, disease, and migration to mission villages moderated, peaceful assimilation of refugees from neighboring nations helped to replace those Iroquois who were lost. One French source even claimed, in 1716, that "the five Iroquois nations . . . are becoming more and more formidable through their great numbers."[111] Most notable among the newcomers were some 1,500 Tuscaroras who, after their defeat by the English and allied Indians of the Carolinas in 1713, migrated north to settle on lands located between the Onondaga and Oneida villages. They were adopted as the sixth nation of the Iroquois Confederacy about 1722. There are indications that the Tuscarora—who, according to William Andrews, Anglican missionary to the Mohawk, possessed "an Implacable hatred against Christians at Carolina"—contributed greatly to the spirit of independence and distrust of Europeans that guided the Six Nations on their middle course between the imperial powers. The Tuscarora, concluded Andrews, were "a great Occasion of Our Indians becoming so bad as they are, they now take all Occasions to find fault and quarrel, wanting to revolt."[112]

V

The first two decades of the eighteenth century brought a shift away from those aspects of Iroquois warfare that had been most socially disruptive. As the Iroquois freed themselves of many, though by no means all, of the demographic, economic, and diplomatic pressures that had made seventeenth-century warfare so devastating, the mourning-war began to resume some of its traditional functions in Iroquois culture.

As the Five Nations made peace with their old western and northern foes, Iroquois mourning-war raids came to focus on enemies the Iroquois called "Flatheads"— a vague epithet for the Catawba and other tribes on the frontiers of Virginia and the Carolinas.[113] Iroquois and Flathead war parties had traded blows during the 1670s and 1680s, conflict had resumed about 1707, and after the arrival of the Tuscarora in the 1710s Iroquois raiding parties attacked the Flatheads regularly and almost exclusively.[114] The Catawba and other southeastern Indians sided with the Carolinians in the Tuscarora War of 1711–13, bringing them into further conflict with warriors from the Five Nations, who fought alongside the Tuscarora.[115] After the Tuscarora moved north, Iroquois-Flathead warfare increased in intensity and lasted—despite several peace treaties—until the era of the American Revolution. This series of mourning-wars exasperated English officials from New York to the Carolinas, who could conceive no rational explanation for the conflicts except the intrigues of French envoys who delighted in stirring up trouble on English frontiers.[116]

Canadian authorities did indeed encourage Iroquois warriors with arms and presents. The French were happy for the chance to harass British settlements and to strike blows against Indians who troubled French inhabitants of New Orleans and the Mississippi Valley.[117] Yet the impetus for raiding the Flatheads lay with the Iroquois, not the French. At Onondaga in 1710, when emissaries from New York blamed French influence for the campaigns and presented a wampum belt calling for a halt to hostilities, a Seneca orator dismissed their arguments: "When I think of the Brave Warriours that hav[e] been slain by the Flatheads I can Govern my self no longer. . . . I reject your Belt for the Hatred I bear to the Flatheads can never be forgotten."[118] The Flatheads were an ideal target for the mourning-wars demanded by Iroquois women and warriors, for with conflict channeled southwards, warfare with northern and western nations that, in the past, had brought disaster could be avoided. In addition, war with the Flatheads placated both Canadian authorities and pro-French Iroquois factions, since the raids countered a pro-English trade policy with a military policy useful to the French. And, from the perspective of Iroquois-English relations, the southern campaigns posed few risks. New York officials alternately forbade and countenanced raids against southern Indians as the fortunes of frontier war in the Carolinas and the intrigues of intercolonial politics shifted. But even when the governors of the Carolinas, Virginia, Pennsylvania, and New York did agree on schemes to impose peace, experience with English military impotence had taught the Iroquois that the governors could do little to stop the conflict.[119]

While the diplomatic advantages were many, perhaps the most important aspect of the Iroquois-Flathead conflicts was the partial return they allowed to the traditional ways of the mourning-war. By the 1720s the Five Nations had not undone the ravages of the preceding century, yet they had largely extricated themselves from the socially disastrous wars of the fur trade and of the European empires. And though prisoners no longer flowed into Iroquois villages in the floods of the seventeenth century, the southern raids provided enough captives for occasional mourning and condolence rituals that dried Iroquois tears and reminded the Five Nations of their superiority over their enemies. In the same letter of 1716 in which missionary Andrews noted the growing independence of the Iroquois since the Tuscarora had settled among them and the southern wars had intensified, he also vividly described the reaction recently given to captives of the Onondaga and Oneida.[120] Iroquois warfare was again binding Iroquois families and villages together.

NOTES

1. Reuben Gold Thwaites, ed., *The Jesuit Relations and Allied Documents: Travels and Explorations of the Jesuit Missionaries in New France, 1610–1791* (Cleveland, Ohio, 1896–1901), XLIII, 263, hereafter cited as *Jesuit Relations.* ·

2. See, for example, George T. Hunt, *The Wars of the Iroquois: A Study in Intertribal Trade Relations* (Madison, Wis., 1940); W. W. Newcomb, Jr., "A Re-Examination of the Causes of Plains Warfare," *American Anthropologist*, N.S., LII (1950), 317–30; and Francis Jennings, *The Invasion of America: Indians, Colonialism, and the Cant of Conquest* (Chapel Hill, N.C., 1975), 146–70.

3. While anthropologists disagree about the precise distinctions between the wars of state-organized and nonstate societies, they generally agree that battles for territorial conquest, economic monopoly, and subjugation or enslavement of conquered peoples are the product of the technological and organizational capacities of the state. For overviews of the literature see C. R. Hallpike, "Functionalist Interpretations of Primitive Warfare," *Man*, N.S., VIII (1973), 451–70, and Andrew Vayda, "Warfare in Ecological Perspective," *Annual Review of Ecology and Systematics*, V (1974), 183–93.

4. My use of the term *mourning-war* differs from that of Marian W. Smith in "American Indian Warfare," New York Academy of Sciences, *Transactions*, 2d Ser., XIII (1951), 348–65, which stresses the psychological and emotional functions of the mourning-war. As the following paragraphs seek to show, the psychology of the mourning-war was deeply rooted in Iroquois demography and social structure; my use of the term accordingly reflects a more holistic view of the cultural role of the mourning-war than does Smith's. On the dangers of an excessively psychological explanation of Indian warfare see Jennings, *Invasion of America*, 159; but see also the convincing defense of Smith in Richard Drinnon, "Ravished Land," *Indian Historian*, IX (Fall 1976), 24–26.

5. Joseph François Lafitau, *Customs of the American Indians Compared with the Customs of Primitive Times*, ed. and trans. William N. Fenton and Elizabeth L. Moore (Toronto, 1974, 1977 [orig. publ. Paris, 1724]), II, 98–99.

6. Cadwallader Colden, *The History of the Five Indian Nations of Canada, Which Are Dependent on the Province of New-York in America, and Are the Barrier between the English and French in That Part of the World* (London, 1747), 4, hereafter cited as Colden, *History* (1747).

7. Gabriel Sagard, *The Long Journey to the Country of the Hurons*, ed. George M. Wrong and trans. H. H. Langton (Toronto, 1939 [orig. publ. Paris, 1632]), 151–52; *Jesuit Relations*, XLII, 139, William N. Fenton, ed., "The Hyde Manuscript: Captain William Hyde's Observations of the 5 Nations of Indians at New York, 1698," *American Scene Magazine*, VI (1965), [9]; Bruce G. Irigger, *The Children of Aataentsic: A History of the Huron People to 1660* (Montreal, 1976), I, 68–69, 145–47.

8. Hennepin, *A New Discovery of a Vast Country in America . . .* , 1st English ed. (London, 1698), II, 88.

9. Newcomb, "Re-Examination of Plains Warfare," *Am. Anthro.*, N.S., LII (1950), 320.

10. Andrew R Vayda, "Expansion and Warfare among Swidden Agriculturalists," *Am. Anthro.*, N.S., LXIII (1961), 346–58; Anthony Leeds, "The Functions of War," in Jules Masserman, ed., *Violence and War, with Clinical Studies* (New York, 1963), 69–82; William Tulio Divale and Marvin Harris, "Population, Warfare, and the Male Supremacist Complex," *Am. Anthro.*, N.S., LXXVIII (1976), 521–38.

11. J. N. B. Hewitt, "Orenda and a Definition of Religion," *Am. Anthro.*, N.S., IV (1902), 33 46; Morris Wolf, *Iroquois Religion and Its Relation to Their Morals* (New York 1919), 25–26; Alvin M. Josephy, Jr.,

The Indian Heritage of America (New York, 1968), 94; Åke Hultbrantz, *The Religions of the American Indians,* trans. Monica Setterwall (Berkeley, Calif., 1979), 12.

12. *Jesuit Relations,* XXIII, 165–69; Lafitau, *Customs of Amencan Indians,* ed. and trans. Fenton and Moore, I, 71; B. H. Quain, "The Iroquois," in Margaret Mead, ed., *Cooperation and Competition among Primitive Peoples* (New York, 1937), 276–77.

13. Fenton, ed., "Hyde Manuscript," *Am. Scene Mag.,* VI (1965), [16].

14. Philip Mazzei, *Researches on the United States,* ed. and trans. Constance B. Sherman (Charlottesville, Va., 1976 [orig. publ. Paris, 1788]), 349. See also P[ierre] de Charlevoix, *Journal of a Voyage to North-America . . .* (London, 1761 [orig. publ. Paris, 1744]), I, 370–73, II, 33–34, and George S. Snyderrnan, "Behind the Tree of Peace: A Sociological Analysis of Iroquois Warfare," *Pennsylvania Archaeologist,* XVIII, nos. 3–4 (1948), 13–15.

15. Lafitau, *Customs of American Indians,* ed. and trans. Fenton and Moore, II, 241–45, quotation on p. 242.

16. *Jesuit Relations,* X, 273–75, XIX, 91, XLIII, 267–71, LX, 35–41. On *wergild* see Lewis H. Morgan, *League of the Ho-de-no-sau-nee, or Iroquois* (Rochester, N.Y., 1851), 331–33, and Jennings, *Invasion of America,* 148–49. The parallel between Iroquois practice and the Germanic tradition of blood payments should not be stretched too far; Iroquois condolence presents were an integral part of the broader condolence process.

17. Smith, "American Indian Warfare," *N.Y. Acad. Sci., Trans.,* 2d Ser., XIII (1951), 352–54; Anthony F. C. Wallace, *The Death and Rebirth of the Seneca* (New York, 1970), 101. It is within the context of the mourning-war that what are usually described as Indian wars for revenge or blood feuds should be understood. The revenge motive—no doubt strong in Iroquois warfare—was only part of the larger complex of behavior and belief comprehended in the mourning-war. It should also be noted that raids might be inspired by *any* death, not just those attributable to murder or warfare and for which revenge or other atonement, such as the giving of condolence presents, was necessary. Among Euro-American observers, only the perceptive Lafitau seems to have been aware of this possibility (*Customs of American Indians,* ed. and trans. Fenton and Moore, II, 98–102, 154). I have found no other explicit contemporary discussion of this phenomenon, but several accounts indicate the formanon of war parties in response to deaths from disease or other nonviolent causes. See H. R. Biggar et al., eds. and trans., *The Works of Samuel de Champlain* (Toronto, 1922–36), II, 206–208, hereafier cited as *Works of Champlain; Jesuit Relations,* LXIV, 91; Jasper Dankers [Danckaerts] and Peter-Sluyter, *Journal of a Voyage to New York and a Tour in Several of the American Colonies in 1679–80,* trans. and ed. Henry C. Murphy (Long Island Historical Society, *Memoirs,* I [Brooklyn, N.Y., 1867]), 277; and William M. Beauchamp, ed., *Moravian Jurnals Relating to Central New York, 1745–66* (Syracuse, N.Y., 1916), 125–26, 183–86.

18. *Jesuit Relations,* X, 225–27; E. B. O'Callaghan et al., eds., *Documents Relative to the Colonial History of the State of New-York . . .* (Albany, N.Y., 1856–87), IV, 22, hereafter cited as *N.-Y. Col. Docs.,* Lafitau, *Customs of American Indians,* ed. and trans. Fenton and Moore, II, 99–103; Snyderman, "Behind the Tree of Peace," *Pa. Archaeol.,* XVIII, nos. 3–4 (1948), 15–20.

19. The following composite account is based on numerous contemporaneous reports of Iroquois treatment of captives. Among the more complete are *Jesuit Relations,* XXII, 251–67, XXXIX, 57–77, L, 59–63, LIV, 23–35; Gideon D. Scull, ed., *Voyages of Peter Esprit Radisson: Being an Account of His Travels and Experiences among the North American Indians, from 1652 to 1684* (Boston, 1885), 28–60; and James H. Coyne, ed. and trans., "Exploration of the Great Lakes, 1660–1670, by Dollier de Casson and de Brehant de Galinee," Ontario Historical Society, *Papers and Records,* IV (1903), 31–35. See also the many other portrayals in *Jesuit Relations;* the discussions in Lafitau, *Customs of American Indians,* ed. and trans. Fenton and Moore, II, 148–72; Nathaniel Knowles, "The Torture of Captives by the Indians of Eastern North America," American Philosophical Society, *Proceedings,* LXXXII (1940), 181–90; and Wallace, *Death and Rebirth of the Seneca,* 103–107.

20. The gauntlet and the public humiliation and physical abuse of captives also served as initiation rites for prospective adoptees; see John Heckewelder, "An Account of the History, Manners, and Customs of the Indian Nations Who Once Inhabited Pennsvlvania and the Neighbouring States," Am. Phil. Soc., *Transactions of the Historical and Literary Committee,* I (1819), 211–13. For a fuller discussion of Indian methods of indoctrinating adoptees see James Axtell, "The White Indians of Colonial America," *William and Mary Qvarterly,* 3d Ser., XXXII (1975), 55–88.

21. Usually only adult male captives were executed, and most women and children seem to have escaped physical abuse. Occasionally, however, the Iroquois did torture and execute women and children. See

Scull, ed., *Voyages of Radisson,* 56, and *Jesuit Relations,* XXXIX, 219–21, XLII, 97–99, LI, 213, 231–33, LII, 79, 157–59, LIII, 253, LXII, 59, LXIV, 127–29, LXV, 33–39.

22. Several authors—from James Adair and Philip Mazzei in the 18th century to W. Arens in 1979—have denied that the Iroquois engaged in cannibalism (Adair, *The History of the American Indians . . .* [London, 1775], 209; Mazzei, *Researches,* ed. and trans. Sherman, 359; Arens, *The Man-Eating Myth: Anthropology & Anthropophagy* [New York, 1979] 127–29). Arens is simply wrong, as Thomas S. Abler has shown in "Iroquois Cannibalism: Fact Not Fiction," *Ethnohistory,* XXVII (1980), 309–316. Adair and Mazzei, from the perspective of the late 18th century, were on firmer ground; by then the Five Nations apparently had abandoned anthropophagy. See Adolph B. Benson, ed., *Peter Kalm's Travels in North America* (New York, 1937), 694.

23. Robert L. Rands and Carroll L. Riley, "Diffusion and Discontinuous Distribution," *Am. Anthro.,* N.S., LX (1958), 284–89; Maurice R. Dane, *The Evolution of War: Study of Its Role in Early Societies* (New Haven, Conn., 1929), 36–38; Hennepin, *New Discovery,* II, 92.

24. *Jesuit Relations,* LXII, 85–87, LXVII, 173; Knowles, "Torture of Captives," Am. Phil. Soc., *Procs.* LXXXII (1940), 210–11.

25. *Jesuit Relations,* XIX, 81.

26. *N.-Y. Col. Docs.,* V, 274.

27. *Works of Champlain,* IV, 330; Charlevoix, *Voyage to North-America,* I, 316–33.

28. *Jesuit Relations,* XXXIX, 221.

29. *Works of Champlain,* III, 73–74; *Jesuit Relations,* XXXII, 159.

30. *Jesuit Relations,* X, 145, XXXIX, 29–31; J. N. B. Hewitt, "The Iroquoian Concept of the Soul," *Journal of American Folk-Lore,* VIII (1895), 107–116.

31. Sagard, *Long Journey,* ed. Wrong and trans. Langton, 152–56; *Jesuit Relations,* XXII, 309–311, XXXII, 173–75, XXXIV, 197, LV, 79, LXVI, 273; Hennepin, *New Discovery,* II, 86–94; Patrick Mitchell Malone, "Indian and English Military Systems in New England in the Seventeenth Century" (Ph.D. diss., Brown University, 1971), 33–38.

32. Lafitau, *Customs of American Indians,* ed. and trans. Fenton and Moore, II, 98.

33. Paul A. W. Wallace, *The White Roots of Peace* (Philadelphia, 1946); A. F. C. Wallace, *Death and Rebirth of the Seneca,* 39–48, 93–98; William M. Beauchamp, *Civil, Religious and Mourning Council and Ceremonies of Adoption of the New York Indians,* New York State Museum Bulletin 113 (Albany, N.Y., 1907). For a suggestive discussion of Indian definitions of peace see John Phillip Reid, *A Better Kind of Hatchet: Law, Trade, and Diplomacy in the Cherokee Nation during the Early Years of European Contact* (University Park, Pa., 1976), 9–17.

34. On the devastating impact of European diseases—some Indian populations may have declined by a factor of 20 to 1 within a century or so of contact—see the works surveyed in Russell Thornton, "American Indian Historical Demography: A Review Essay with Suggestions for Future Research," *American Indian Culture and Research Journal,* III, no. 1 (1979), 69–74.

35. Trigger, *Children of Aataentsic,* II, 602; Cornelius J. Jaenen, *Friend and Foe: Aspects of French Amerindian Cultural Contact in the Sixteenth and Seventeenth Centuries* (New York, 1976), 100. Most of the early Iroquois epidemics went unrecorded by Europeans, but major smallpox epidemics are documented for the Mohawk in 1634 and the Seneca in 1640–41, see [Harmen Meyndertsz van den Bogaert], "Narrative of a Journey into the Mohawk and Oneida Country, 1634–35," in J. Franklin Jameson, ed., *Narratives of New Netherland, 1609–1664* (New York, 1909), 140–41, and *Jesuit Relations,* XXI, 211.

36. *Jesuit Relations,* XXX, 273, XLIV, 43, XLVII, 193, 205, XLVIII, 79–83, L, 63, LIV, 79–81, LVII, 231–53, LX, 175.

37. *Works of Champlain,* II, 95–100; Malone, "Indian and English Military Systems," 179–200; Jennings, *Invasion of America,* 165–66. After the introduction of firearms the Iroquois continued to raise armies of several hundred to a thousand men, but they almost never engaged them in set battles. Large armies ensured safe travel to distant battlegrounds and occasionally intimidated outnumbered opponents, but when they neared their objective they usually broke into small raiding parties. See Daniel Gookin, "Historical Collections of the Indians in New England" (1674), Massachusetts Historical Society, *Collections,* I (1792), 162, and Cadwallader Colden, *The History of the Five Indian Nations Depending on the Province of New-York in America* (New York, 1727), 8–10, hereafter cited as Colden, *History* (1727).

38. *N.-Y. Col. Docs.*, I, 150; "Journal of New Netherland, 1647," in Jameson, ed., *Narratives of New Netherland*, 274; *Jesuit Relations*, XXIV, 295; Carl R. Russell, *Guns on the Early Frontiers: A History of Firearms from Colonial Times through the Years of the Western Fur Trade* (Berkeley, Calif., 1957), 11–15, 62–66.

39. *Jesuit Relations*, XXVII, 71, XLV, 205–207; Elisabeth Tooker, "The Iroquois Defeat of the Huron: A Review of Causes," *Pa. Archaeol.*, XXXIII (1963), 115–23; Keith F. Otterbein, "Why the Iroquois Won: An Analysis of Iroquois Military Tactics," *Ethnohistory*, XI (1964), 56–63; John K. Mahon, "Anglo-American Methods of Indian Warfare, 1676–1794," *Mississippi Valley Historical Review*, XLV (1958), 255.

40. Bruce G. Trigger, "The Mohawk-Mahican War (1624–28): The Establishment of a Pattern," *Canadian Historical Review*, LII (1971), 276–86.

41. Harold A. Innis, *The Fur Trade in Canada: An Introduction to Canadian Economic History* (New Haven, Conn., 1930), 1–4, 32–33; Hunt, *Wars of the Iroquois*, 33–37; John Witthoft, "Ancestry of the Susquehannocks," in John Witthoft and W. Fred Kinsey III, eds., *Susquehannock Miscellany* (Harrisburg, Pa., 1959), 34–35; Thomas Elliot Norton, *The Fur Trade in Colonial New York, 1686–1776* (Madison, Wis., 1974), 9–15.

42. The classic account of the beaver wars is Hunt, *Wars of the Iroquois*, but three decades of subsequent scholarship have overturned many of that work's interpretations. See Allen W. Trelease, "The Iroquois and the Western Fur Trade: A Problem in Interpretation," *MVHR*, XLIX (1962), 32–51; Raoul Naroll, "The Causes of the Fourth Iroquois War," *Ethnohistory*, XVI (1969), 51–81; Allan Forbes, Jr., "Two and a Half Centuries of Conflict: The Iroquois and the Laurentian Wars," *Pa. Archaeol.*, XL, nos. 3–4 (1970), 1–20; William N. Fenton, "The Iroquois in History," in Eleanor Burke Leacock and Nancy Oestreich Lurie, eds., *North American Indians in Historical Perspective* (New York, 1971), 139–45; Karl H. Schlesier, "Epidemics and Indian Middlemen: Rethinking the Wars of the Iroquois, 1609–1653," *Ethnohistory*, XXIII (1976), 129–45; and Trigger, *Children of Aataentsic*, esp. II, 617–64.

43. *Works of Champlain*, III, 31–32; see also II, 118–19, 186–91, 246–85, III, 207–28.

44. Ibid., II, 65–107, 120–38, III, 48–81.

45. *Jesuit Relations*, XXI–L, *passim;* Robert A. Goldstein, *French-Iroquois Diplomatic and Military Relations, 1609–1701* (The Hague, 1969), 62–99. The actual Canadian death toll in wars with the Iroquois before 1666 has recently been shown to have been quite low. Only 153 French were killed in raids while 143 were taken prisoner (perhaps 38 of those died in captivity); John A. Dickison, "La guerre iroquoise et la mortalité en Nouvelle-France, 1608–1666," *Revue d'histoire de l'amérique française*, XXXVI (1982), 31–54. On 17th-century French captives of the Iroquois see Daniel K. Richter, "The Iroquois Melting Pot: Seventeenth-Century War Captives of the Five Nations" (paper presented at the Shelby Cullom Davis Center Conference on War and Society in Early America, Princeton University, March 11–12, 1983), 18–19.

46. *Jesuit Relations*, L, 127–47, 239; *N.-Y. Col. Docs.*, III, 121–27; A. J. F. van Laer, trans. and ed., *Correspondence of Jeremias van Rensselaer, 1651–1674* (Albany, N.Y., 1932), 388.

47. *Jesuit Relations*, XXXV, 183–205, XXXVI, 177–91, XLI, 43–65, XLIII, 115–25, 187–207, XLIV, 69–77, 165–67, 187–91; A. J. F. van Laer, trans. and ed., *Minutes of the Court of Fort Orange and Beverwyck, 1677–1660*, II (Albany, N.Y., 1923), 45–48; Scull, ed., *Voyages of Radisson*, 93–119; Nicholas Perrot, "Memoir on the Manners, Customs and Religion of the Savages of North America" (c. 1680–1718), in Emma Helen Blair, ed. and trans., *The Indian Tribes of the Upper Mississippi Valley and Region of the Great Lakes . . .* (Cleveland, Ohio, 1911), I, 148–93.

48. *Jesuit Relations*, XLVII, 139–53.

49. Ibid., XLIII, 265.

50. Ibid., XLV, 207, LI, 123, 187.

51. *N.-Y. Col. Docs.*, IX, 80; Victor Konrad, "An Iroquois Frontier: The North Shore of Lake Ontario during the Late Seventeenth Century," *Journal of Historical Geography*, VII (1981), 129–44.

52. *Jesuit Relations*, LI, 81–85, 167–257, LII, 53–55.

53. Ibid., LV, 61–63, LVII, 133–41, LVIII, 211, LX, 187–95.

54. Ibid., LIV, 281–83.

55. Ibid., LVI, 29, LVIII, 247–53, LX, 145–47, LXI, 195–99, LXIII, 141–89.

56. Ibid., LV, 33–37, LVIII, 75–77.

57. E. B. O'Callaghan, ed., *The Documentary History of the State of New York*, octavo ed. (Albany, N.Y., 1849–51), I, 12–14; *Jesuit Relations*, XXIV, 295. Reflecting the purposes of most Euro-Americans who made estimates of Indian population, figures are usually given in terms of the number of available fighting men. The limited data available for direct comparisons of estimates of Iroquois fighting strength with estimates of total

population indicate that the ratio of one warrior for every four people proposed in Sherburne E. Cook, "Interracial Warfare and Population Decline among the New England Indians," *Ethnohistory*, XX (1973), 13, applies to the Five Nations. Compare the estimates of a total Mohawk population of 560–580 in William Andrews to the Secretary of the Society for the Propagation of the Gospel in Foreign Parts, Sept. 7, 1713, Oct. 17, 1715, Records of the Society for the Propagation of the Gospel, Letterbooks, Ser. A, VIII, 186, XI, 268–69, S.P.G. Archives, London (microfilm ed.), with the concurrent estimates of approximately 150 Mohawk warriors in Bernardus Freeman to the Secretary of S.P.G., May 28, 1712, ibid., VII, 203; Peter Wraxall, *An Abidgement of the Indian Affairs . . . Transacted in the Colony of New York, from the Year 1678 to the Year 1715*, ed. Charles Howard McIlwain (Cambridge, Mass., 1915), 69; *N.-Y. Col. Docs.*, V, 272; and Lawrence H. Leder, ed., *The Livingston Indian Records, 1666–1723* (Gettysburg, Pa., 1956), 220.

58. The estimate of 10,000 for the 1640s is from Trigger, *Children of Aatuentsic*, I, 98; the figure of 8,600 for the 1670s is calculated from Wentworth Greenhalgh's 1677 estimate of 2,150 Iroquois warriors, in O'Callaghan, ed., *Documentary History*, I, 12–14. Compare the late 1670s estimate in Hennepin, *New Discovery*, II, 92–93, and see the tables of 17th- and 18th-century Iroquois warrior population in Snyderman, "Behind the Tree of Peace," *Pa. Archaeol.*, XVIII, nos. 3–4 (1948), 42; Bruce G. Trigger, ed., *Northeast*, in William C. Sturtevant, ed., *Handbook of North American Indians*, XV (Washington, D.C., 1978), 421; and Gunther Michelson, "Iroquois Population Statistics," *Man in the Northeast*, no. 14 (1977), 3–17. William Starna has recently suggested that all previous estimates for 1635 and earlier of Mohawk—and by implication Five Nations—population are drastically understated ("Mohawk Iroquois Populations: A Revision," *Ethnohistory*, XXVII [1980], 371–82).

59. *Jesuit Relations*, LXII, 71–95, quotation on p. 83.

60. Leder, ed., *Livingston Indian Records*, 35–38; Allen W. Trelease, *Indian Affairs in Colonial New York: The Seventeenth Century* (Ithaca, N.Y., 1960), 229–30; Francis Jennings, "Glory, Death, and Transfiguration: The Susquehannock Indians in the Seventeenth Century," Am. Phil. Soc., *Procs.*, CXII (1968), 15–53.

61. *Jesuit Relations*, LVI, 43–45, LIX, 251, LX, 211, LXII, 185; Hennepin, *New Discovery*, I, 100–295. Although the western nations had been included in the Franco-Iroquois peace of 1667, skirmishing in the west had never totally ceased; see *Jesuit Relations*, LIII, 39–51, LIV, 219–27, and *N.-Y. Col. Docs.*, IX, 79–80.

62. Baron [de] Lahontan, *New Voyages to North-America . . .* (London, 1703), I, 41.

63. *Jesuit Relations*, LXII, 71.

64. For fuller accounts of the complex diplomacy, intrigue, trade wars, and military conflicts concerning the west between 1675 and 1689 touched on in the following paragraphs see, from a Canadian perspective, W. J. Eccles, *Frontenac: The Courtier Governor* (Toronto, 1959), 99–229, and, from a New York perspective, Trelease, *Indian Affairs in Colonial New York*, 204–301. A brief discussion of the Iroquois role is Richard Aquila, "The Iroquois Restoration: A Study of Iroquois Power, Politics, and Relations with Indians and Whites, 1700–1744" (Ph.D. diss., Ohio State University, 1977), 16–29.

65. *N.-Y. Col. Docs.*, III, 254–59; Francis Paul Jennings, "Miquon's Passing: Indian-European Relations in Colonial Pennsylvania, 1674 to 1755" (Ph.D. diss., University of Pennsylvania, 1965), 10–50, Douglas Edward Leach, *Flintlock and Tomahawk: New England in King Philip's War* (New York, 1958), 59–60, 176–77.

66. O'Callaghan, ed., *Documentary History*, I, 391–420; Wraxall, *Abridgement of Indian Affairs*, ed. McIlwain, 10; Helen Broshar, "The First Push Westward of the Albany Traders," *MVHR*, VII (1920), 228–41; Henry Allain St. Paul, "Governor Thomas Dongan's Expansion Policy," *Mid-America*, XVII (1935), 172–84, 236–72; Gary B. Nash, "The Quest for the Susquehanna Valley: New York, Pennsylvania, and the Seventeenth-Century Fur Trade," *New York History*, XLVIII (1967), 3–27; Daniel K. Richter, "Rediscovered Links in the Covenant Chain: Previously Unpublished Transcripts of New York Indian Treaty Minutes, 1677–1691," American Antiquarian Society, *Proceedings*, XCII (1982), 63–66.

67. Hennepin, *New Discovery*, I, 20–144; Lahontan, *New Voyages*, I, 269–74; *Jesuit Relations*, LXII, 151–165; *N.-Y. Col. Docs.*, IX, 296–303.

68. *N.-Y. Col. Docs.*, III, 417.

69. *N.-Y. Col. Docs, JX*, 234–248, 358–369, 550–561, 639–656; *Jesuit Relations*, LXIII, 269–281, LXIV, 239–59, LXV, 25–29, Lahontan, *New Voyages*, I, 29–45, 68–80; Francis Parkman, *Count Frontenac and New France under Louis* XIV (Boston, 1877), 89–115, 139–57, 309–16, 410–17.

70. *N.-Y. Col. Docs.*, III, 814–16.

71. Ibid., IV, 38–39.

72. Ibid., IX, 531–35, quotation on p. 531.

73. Leder, ed., *Livingston Indian Records*, 172–74; *N.-Y. Col. Docs.*, IX, 599–632; Colden, *History* (1747), 180–81.

74. Leder, ed., *Livingston Indian Records*, 136–37.

75. Ibid., 139–40; *Jesuit Relations*, LXIII, 279, 287–89, LXIV, 249–59, LXV, 29; *N.-Y. Col. Docs.*, IX, 503–504, 538, 554–55.

76. Treaty Minutes, June 17, 1689, untitled notebook, Indians of North America, Miscellaneous Papers, 1620–1895, Manuscript Collections, American Antiquarian Society, Worcester, Mass.

77. Richard A. Preston, trans., and Leopold Lamontagne, ed., *Royal Fort Frontenac* (Toronto, 1958), 175–80; Lahontan, *New Voyages*, I, 98–102, 147–51; *N.-Y. Col. Docs.*, IX, 434–38; Eccles, *Frontenac*, 186–97. English sources claimed 200 French deaths and 120 captures at Lachine (Trelease, *Indian Affairs in Colonial New York*, 297–98).

78. Treaty Minutes, Aug. 2, 1684, untitled notebook, Indians of North America, Miscellaneous Papers, 1620–1895, Manuscript Collections, AAS.

79. O'Callaghan, ed., *Documentary History*, I, 284–319, II, 130–32; Leder, ed., *Livingston Indian Records*, 158–60.

80. O'Callaghan, ed., *Documentary History*, II, 164–290, *N.-Y. Col. Docs.*, III, 800–805, IV, 193–96, IX, 513–15, 520–24.

81. *N.-Y. Col. Docs.*, III, 836–44; Leder, ed., *Livingston Indian Records*, 165–66; O'Callaghan, ed., *Documentary History*, I, 323–25, 341–45; Herbert L. Osgood, *The American Colonies in the Eighteenth Century*, I (New York, 1924), 228–65.

82. *N.-Y. Col. Docs.*, IV, 6–7, 14–24, 222; Colden, *History* (1747), 142–50.

83. *N.-Y. Col. Docs.*, IX, 384–93, 515–17, 565–72, 596–99; *Jesuit Relations*, LXIV, 143–45.

84. *N.-Y. Col. Docs.*, III, 841–44; see also ibid., IV, 77–98, 279–82.

85. *Jesuit Relations*, LXIV, 259.

86. *N.-Y. Col. Docs.*, IX, 601–671.

87. Trelease, *Indian Affairs in Colonial New York*, 323–42; *N.-Y. Col. Docs.*, IV, 367–74, 402–409.

88. Leroy V. Eid, "The Ojibwa-Iroquois War: The War the Five Nations Did Not Win," *Ethnohistory*, XXVI (1979), 297–324; Wraxall, *Abridgement of Indian Affairs*, ed. McIlwain, 29–30; *N.-Y. Col. Docs.*, IX, 681–88, 708–709.

89. Aquila, "Iroquois Restoration," 71–79.

90. A 1698 report on New York's suffering during the War of the League of Augsburg states that there were 2,550 Iroquois warriors in 1689 and only 1,230 in 1698. The report probably contains some polemical overstatement: the first figure seems too high and the second too low. By comparison, 2,050 Iroquois warriors were estimated by Denonville in 1685, 1,400 by Bellomont in 1691, 1,750 by Bernardus Freeman in 1700, and 1,200 by a French cabinet paper in 1701 (*N.-Y. Col. Docs.*, [V, 337, 768, IX, 281, 725; Freeman to the Secretary, May 28, 1712, Records of S.PG., Letterbooks, Ser. A, VII, 203). If the figure of 1,750 warriors cited by Freeman—a minister who worked with the Mohawk—is correct, the total Iroquois population in 1700 was approximately 7,000, calculated by the ratio in note 57.

91. *Jesuit Relations*, LXIV, 59–61.

92. *N.-Y. Col. Docs.*, IV, 648–661, 689–690.

93. Trigger, *Children of Aataentsic*, II, 709–724. See also the discussions of Indian factionalism in Robert E. Berkhofer, Jr., "The Political Context of a New Indian History," *Pacific Historical Review*, XL (1971), 373–80, and Edward H. Spicer, *Cycles of Conquest: The Impact of Spain, Mexico, and the United States on the Indians of the Southwest, 1533–1960* (Tucson, Ariz., 1962), 491–501.

94. Anthony F. C. Wallace, "Origins of Iroquois Neutrality: The Grand Settlement of 1701," *Pennsylvania History*, XXIV (1957), 223–35. The best reconstruction of the Iroquois diplomacy that led to the Grand Settlement is Richard L. Haan, "The Covenant Chain: Iroquois Diplomacy on the Niagara Frontier, 1697–1730" (Ph.D. diss., University of California, Santa Barbara, 1976), 64–147.

95. Bacqueville de La Potherie, *Histoire de l'Amérique Septentrionale*, IV (Paris, 1722), passim; *N.-Y. Col. Docs.*, IX, 715–25.

96. *N.-Y. Col. Docs.*, IV, 889–911; *Minutes of the Provincial Council of Pennsylvania*, II (Harrisburg, Pa., 1838), 142–43; William M. Beauchamp, *A History of the New York Iroquois, Now Commonly Called the Six Nations*, New York State Museum Bulletin 78 (Albany, N.Y., 1905), 256; Jennings, "Miquon's Passing," 118–21.

97. Eid, "Ojibwa-Iroquois War," *Ethnohistory*, XXVI (1979), 297–324.

98. Aquila, "Iroquois Restoration," 109–171; Richard Haan, "The Problem of Iroquois Neutrality: Suggestions for Revision," *Ethnohistory*, XXVII (1980), 317–30.

99. *N.-Y. Col. Docs.*, V, 724–25.

100. Leder, ed., *Livingston Indian Records*, 192–200, *N.-Y. Col. Docs.*, IX, 759–65, 848–49, 876–78; Yves E. Zoltvany, "New France and the West, 1701–1713," *Can. Hist Rev.*, XLVI (1965), 315–21.

101. Wraxall, *Abridgement of Indian Affairs*, ed. McIlwain, 44–67; "Continuation of Colden's History of the Five Indian Nations, for the Years 1707 through 1770," New Historical Society, *Collections*, LXVIII (1935), 360–67, hereafter cited as Colden, "Continuation," Hann, "Covenant Chain," 152–53.

102. Wraxall, *Abridgement of Indian Affairs*, ed. McIlwain, 64–69; *N.-Y. Col. Docs.*, IX, 902; Leder, ed., *Livingston Indian Records*, 207–210; Colden, "Continuation"; 370–80.

103. Colden, "Continuation," 398–409; *N.-Y. Col. Docs.*, V, 242–49, 267–77; G. M. Waller, "New York's Role in Queen Anne's War, 1702–1713," *New York History*, XXXIII (1952), 40–53; Bruce T. McCully, "Catastrophe in the Wilderness: New Light on the Canada Expedition of 1709," *WMQ*, 3d Ser., XI (1954), 441–56; Haan, "Covenant Chain," 148–98.

104. *N.-Y. Col. Docs.*, V, 372–76, 382–88, 437, 484–87, Wraxall, *Abridgement of Indian Affairs*, ed. McIlwain, 98–105.

105. *N.-Y. Col. Docs.*, V, 445–46, 584; Colden, "Continuation," 414–32; Haan, "Problem of Iroquois Neutrality," *Ethnohistory*, XXVII (1980), 324.

106. *N.-Y. Col. Docs.*, V, 545, 569, 632, IX, 816; Thomas Barclay to Robert Hunter, Jan. 26, 1713 (extract), Records of S.R.G., Letterbooks, Ser. A, VIII, 251–52. For examples of Claeson's and Joncaire's activities see Colden, "Continuation," 360–63, 432–34, and *N.-Y. Col. Docs.*, V, 538, 562–69, IX, 759–65, 814, 876–903.

107. *N.-Y. Col. Docs.*, V, 217–27; Colden, "Continuation," 408–409; Wraxall, *Abridgement of Indian Affairs*, ed. McIlwain, 79n–80n.

108. The evolution of Iroquois, French, and English policies concerning Niagara and Oswego may be followed in *N.-Y. Col. Docs.*, V, passim, IX, 897–1016, Jennings. "Miquon's Passing," 256–74; and Haan, "Covenant Chain," 199–237.

109. Andrews to the Secretary, Oct. 11, 1716, Records of S.P.G., Letterbooks, Ser. A. XI, 241; *N.-Y. Col. Docs.*, V, 484–87, IX, 878.

110. *Jesuit Relations*, LXVI, 203–207, LXVII, 39–41; *N.-Y. Col. Docs.*, IX, 882–84; George F. G. Stanley, "The Policy of 'Francisation' as Applied to the Indians during the Ancien Regime," *Revue d'histoire de l'amérique française*, III (1949–50), 333–48; Cornelius J. Jaenen, "The Frenchification and Evangelization of the Amerindians in the Seventeenth Century New France" *(sic)*, Canadian Catholic Historical Association, *Study Sessions*, XXXV (1969), 57–71.

111. *Jesuit Relations*, LXVII, 27.

112. Andrews to the Secretary, Apr. 20, 1716, Apr. 23, 1717, Records of S.R.G., Letterbooks, Ser. A, XI, 319–20, XII, 310–12.

113. Henry R. Schoolcraft, *Notes on the Iroquois: Or, Contributions to the Statistics, Aboriginal History, Antiquities and General Ethnology of Western New York* (New York, 1846), 148–49; Fenton, "Iroquois in History," in Leacock and Lurie, eds., *North American Indians*, 147–48: Beauchamp, *History of New York Iroquois*, 139.

114. On Iroquois-Flathead conflicts before 1710 see Colden, *History* (1727), 30–71, and "Continuation," 361–63, and Wraxall, *Abridgment of Indian Affairs*, ed. McIlwain, 50–61. References to raids after 1710 in Colden, *N.-Y. Col. Docs.*, and other sources are too numerous to cite here; a useful discussion is Aquila, "Iroquois Restoration," 294–346.

115. Wraxall, *Abrdgement of Indian Affairs*,, ed. McIlwain, 94–86; *N.-Y. Col. Docs.*, V, 372–76, 382–88, 484–93; Verner W. Crane, *The Southern Frontier, 1670–1732* (Durham, N.C., 1928), 158–61.

116. *N.-Y. Col. Docs.*, V, 542–45, 562–69, 635–40.

117. Ibid., IX, 876–78, 884–85, 1085, 1097–98.

118. Colden, "Continuation," 382–83, brackets in original.

119. For examples of shifting New York policies regarding the Iroquois southern campaigns see *N.-Y. Col. Docs.*, V, 446–64, 542–45, and Wraxall, *Abridgment of Indian Affairs*, ed. McIlwain, 123.

120. Andrews to the Secretary, Apr. 20, 1716, Records of S.P.G., Letterbooks, Ser. A., XI, 320.

RULING "THE REPUBLIC OF INDIANS" IN SEVENTEENTH-CENTURY FLORIDA

15

Amy Turner Bushnell

Long before Englishmen landed at the North American sites they called Roanoke, Jamestown, and Plymouth, their Spanish counterparts were busy exploring and occupying southeastern North America, a vast territory the newcomers called "la Florida." There, as Amy Turner Bushnell argues, Spanish adventurers took a very different course than elsewhere in the Western Hemisphere. Peripheral to Spanish imperial interests, Florida always remained something of a backwater compared to the Caribbean basin, Mexico, central America, and northern South America. Once Spanish leaders recognized that they lacked the military might to conquer the indigenous peoples in Florida as Spanish forces had elsewhere (most notably in Moctezuma's Aztec empire), they tried to create a system in which a "republic" of Indians would rule natives while maintaining cordial, and subordinate, relations with the newcomers.

The Florida arrangement had its difficulties, to be sure. But at first, at least, natives and newcomers tried to coexist. Their efforts to get along can be compared to the account of James Ronda's Christian Indians on Martha's Vineyard above, as well as the essays by Timothy Shannon, Helen Tanner, and Steven Hackel that follow, providing a complex portrait of different paths of accommodation.

RULING "THE REPUBLIC OF INDIANS" IN SEVENTEENTH-CENTURY FLORIDA

Amy Turner Bushnell

IN THE LITERATURE ON COLONIAL North America, scholars commonly contrast the English colonists, who courted the Indians through trade goods while holding them at a distance, with the French, who converted the Indians to Christianity and themselves to native life. Historians and anthropologists alike tend to discount Spanish and Indian interaction, regarding it as marginal to the central story—that of the French and English.[1] Yet the Spanish presence in eastern North America lasted more than three centuries, irrevocably altering the lives of thousands of Spanish-speaking colonists and many thousands of American Indians.

An examination of the ways Spanish and native cultures adapted to each other in the New World can provide a third model to lay against the better-known French and English ones. In the Spanish model, Indians accepted vassalage along with Christianity and were turned, through the agency of their own leaders, into a labor reserve. It was a system the Spanish applied with success throughout Central and South America wherever they encountered natives who were agricultural, sedentary, and with leaders they could co-opt. In due course they brought the system to North America to use in the self-contained polity of the provinces of Florida. This chapter introduces the native leadership of those provinces and examines the means by which Indians and Spaniards shared authority, as well as the reasons why authority could be seen as something to share.

Spaniards arrived in the Southeast with a sober respect for the formalities of conquest, developed over centuries of reconquering Spain from the Moors and generations of experience in the New World. The sweatiest of *entradas* into unknown territory was a matter of order and record, with banners flying and notaries at the ready. If the entrada resulted in the extension of the king's domains, the royal coat of arms was left as evidence in every town, mounted on the council house.[2] Religious entradas were equally formal, and more than a little military looking when the friars

SOURCE: Peter H. Wood et al., eds., *Powhatan's Mantle: Indians, in the Colonial Southeast (Lincoln: University of Nebraska Press, 1989)*, 134–50.

had an armed escort and carried the cross painted on a banner.[3] Anywhere the friars gained access they erected a cross, added a saint to the town's name, and gave directions for building a church.[4] To raise a cross was to found a *visita,* or a stop on the missionary circuit, which in the course of time could develop into a *doctrina* complete with resident friars.[5] Indians, recognizing the symbols of occupation, often signaled a rebellion by pulling down coats of arms and crosses and burning them.[6]

Besides the secular and church officials, a third power existed in the provinces of Spanish Florida, that of the region's chiefs, who survived the foreign invasion to become integral to the governmental system that developed out of it. Their underlying, continuing authority could well have been symbolized by the ball poles of their towns. Raising a ball pole in the Southeast was tantamount to founding a town, which was not so much a place as a corporate entity. Although the townsite had to be relocated periodically as the fertility of surrounding soil became exhausted and firewood gave out, the town's playing field and ball pole remained in place as a sign of ownership and continuity.[7] Aware that the Indian ball game had non-Christian significance, some of the friars would have had the natives take down their ball poles and raise crosses, but other Spaniards said that the playing leagues and the gatherings for games were necessary to the functioning of native government.[8]

As always, what the chiefs had to say on the subject remains open to question. Although some of them became literate in their own languages, they did not often resort to writing.[9] Officers and friars occasionally wrote for a chief's signature, and interpreters were used to translate their statements for recording by notaries, yet one can seldom be sure of what a native ruler really said, much less what he or she had in mind.[10] Nevertheless, we cannot allow the difficulty of the sources to make us underestimate the importance of these rulers or omit them from the provincial picture.

It had not been easy to bring them into line. In the sixteenth century the Spanish tried an array of tactics: wholesale enslavement, wars, trade alliances, conversion with and without force, and intermarriage. The first official expedition to touch Florida, that of Juan Ponce de León in 1513, was little more than a legalized slave raid. Explorers Pánfilo de Narváez and Hernando de Soto in subsequent decades, seeking other Mexicos and other Perus, took slaves to serve their large armies as they penetrated the southern interior. The natives retaliated in kind. The Dominicans who came to Tampa Bay in 1547 were martyred on the beach, while the castaways from ship-wrecks along the Florida coast, if not slaughtered, became slaves. The mutual ransoming of captives, called *rescate,* evolved into a wary sort of barter similar to that between Caribbean colonists and the French and English corsairs who ventured into their ports.[11]

In 1557 Philip II decided that Florida had strategic importance for the return route of the treasure fleet and must be occupied. After an unsuccessful attempt by the viceroy of New Spain to plant a colony at Pensacola, Pedro Menéndez de Avilés sailed directly from Spain in 1565 to surprise French Fort Caroline and establish a colony on the west coast.[12] The king of Spain might want Spaniards in Florida, but the Indians did not. Although Menéndez founded three settlements and put a Jesuit and a fort at nearly every deepwater harbor, the price in Spanish lives was high. He finally declared that one could do nothing with the "treacherous" Indians of Florida except wage a "just war" on them, transport them to the islands, and sell them.[13]

This drastic a solution the Crown forbade. Menéndez and his successors had to pull in the borders, withdrawing isolated garrisons and unprotected missionaries. The three original settlements contracted to two, then one: St. Augustine. From that single outpost the Spanish slowly "pacified" the Indians of Florida as they had the Chichimecos of northern New Spain, by a combination of "wars of fire and blood" on the one hand and presents on the other.[14] One after another, as the Spanish conquered the various tribes or maneuvered them into treaties of alliance, the rulers were forced to agree to a monopoly of their trade, to cooperation in time of war, to the levying of tribute upon their vassals, and not least, to the presence in their towns of Franciscans, who had replaced Jesuits as the indoctrinating agents in Florida.

In return, the new allies received access to the royal largesse. Every year, when the chiefs came to kiss the governor's hands, he distributed lengths of cloth, axes, felt hats, and other gifts among them in the name of the king, while the king's coffer outfitted their churches with altar furnishings and bells.[15] The expense of the gifts to the chiefs rose from 1,500 ducats in 1615 to four times as much in 1650. They accepted this bounty as no more than their due, and when presents were delayed, loyalty faltered.[16]

Franciscans urged their converts to live year-round in towns "like rational beings," within reach of the sacraments. In Florida this met with varying success. The wandering Ais and Tequesta Indians of the coast south of St. Augustine, "possessionless as deer," were never Hispanicized, nor were the nonagricultural Calusas of the southwestern coast.[17] The Guales and eastern Timucuans, hunters and gatherers as well as corn growers, took to the woods seasonally, abandoning both friars and "reductions"— the new towns formed at Spanish instance through a process of aggregation. One anticlerical governor said that if he were an Indian, he would run away too.[18] Only those natives who were both agricultural and sedentary, the Apalaches and western Timucuans, were what a friar could call "Indians of sense and satisfaction."[19]

In the sixteenth century the Spanish, thinking it possible to absorb sensible Indians into their own society through Christian association, encouraged close ties. Priests performed marriages between soldiers and high-ranking native women, and Menéndez himself accepted an Indian consort. Concubinage was common—the traditional Spanish form of union with a woman of lesser rank.[20] Governors served as godfathers to chiefs, bestowing their surnames with their baptismal gifts, so that the frontier of conversions might be traced by matching names of chiefs to names of governors. Native nobles sent their children to be raised in St. Augustine; painted warriors fought side by side with soldiers in padded cotton doublets, and at least one chief was favored with a military pension.[21] Expectations for trade were idyllic, and priests foresaw a time when happy natives would paddle downriver to the towns of Spaniards, bringing canoeloads of chickens and taking back civilization.[22]

Efforts toward an integrated polity ended at the close of the sixteenth century with the Guale Rebellion, which showed how far from idyllic Indians could be. One governor pronounced the conversion of the natives a chimera.[23] The seventeenth century saw the development of the far different system of social order known as the two republics.[24] The Republic of Spaniards and the separate Republic of Indians were to be united in allegiance to the Crown and obedience to the "law of God"; otherwise they were intended to stay strictly apart.

The two republics occupied different territories of the same country. Until the refounding of Pensacola in 1698, St. Augustine remained Florida's one authorized Spanish municipality, whereas there were up to forty towns of Christian Indians, divided by language group into the provinces of Guale (on the Georgia coast), Timucua (in central Florida), and Apalache (around present Tallahassee).[25] Indians were not to come to St. Augustine without a pass.[26] Spaniards, blacks, mestizos, and mulattoes traveling on the king's business could stay no more than three days in an Indian town and must sleep in the council house.[27]

The Franciscans would willingly have quarantined the converts they instructed in doctrine and provided with the consolations and discipline of their religion[28]—and discipline it was, for the natives of the "lower sort" attended mass with regularity out of fear of a whipping.[29] The missionaries asked only to live peaceably in their convents, meeting in chapter at St. Augustine every three years to elect a *padre provincial* as administrator and spokesman. But the king did not intend the friars to create theocracies. Through a series of papal concessions known as the *patronato real,* the Crown had long since gained control of the Spanish church and clergy in all but matters of doctrine, and the governor represented royal authority to the friars, as he often reminded them.[30]

To show the flag and keep track of the friars, the governor stationed in every province a detachment of troops under a *teniente,* or deputy governor. Because married soldiers imposed less of a burden on the Indians, many of the soldiers brought along dependents, some of them mixed-bloods. In the garrison town of San Luis de Apalache a rough frontier settlement emerged, far to the west of the Spanish center of order and government in St. Augustine.[31] The soldiers and Florida-born creoles, called *floridanos,* tried the patience of missionaries with their incorrigible swearing, womanizing, mass skipping, and gambling at the ball games. Yet the system itself was clearly stable, for in the seventeenth century there were never more than two or three hundred able-bodied, armed Spaniards in all Florida to hold in check up to 26,000 Christian Indians.[32]

The Republic of Indians remained less centralized than the Spanish republic. Each town had its government of chief (*cacique*) and headmen (*principales* or *mandadores*), whom the Spanish interpreted as a town council (*cabildo*).[33] Sometimes a larger town would have subsidiary or satellite towns with subchiefs or tolerate a settlement of refugees from another tribe within its jurisdiction. The chiefs of the principal towns in a province met as needed to deal with defense and other intertown problems. The Spanish governor addressed them familiarly as "my sons and cousins."[34]

The formal means of communication was the yearly *visita,* a tour of inspection by the governor or his representative. As the *visitador* traveled from place to place the chiefs spoke to him one at a time, then gathered at an appointed location in the province to address him in council. The visita notary recorded their complaints about soldiers in debt to their vassals, floridanos running cattle across their fields, friars interfering with their games and dances, deputies treating them with disrespect, and other offenses to the Republic of Indians of which they were the acknowledged rulers. In the hundreds of pages of testimony one fact becomes clear. The chiefs were a force to reckon with in the provinces; they could have deputies withdrawn and friars reassigned.[35]

They had this power because to Spaniards it was unthinkable for them not to have it. According to medieval rationale, the right way to govern a country was to obtain the allegiance of its natural lords and through them the loyalty of their vassals. In Florida those Indian nobles who accepted Christianity and paid homage to the king of Spain could not reasonably be set aside, for that would have destroyed legitimacy in government. Instead they were drawn into alliances, favored, and supported in their rights as the natural lords (*señores naturales*) of the land. The rights of such leaders before contact varied from tribe to tribe. But during the Spanish hegemony their rights, as seen through Spanish eyes, were seigneurial. Equally with a Spanish *señor*, an Indian noble had the right to inherit title and position, the right to the preeminences of rank, the right to enjoy lands and rule vassals, and the right to combine with other lords and make war.

Like most Europeans, Spaniards traced descent patrilineally, from father to son. Southeastern natives, in contrast, were matrilineal. This meant that a chief's successor would be not his son but his nephew, son of his eldest sister. At first the Spanish found this system unnatural and lent their support to the "rightful heirs," particularly when the chief was a *cacica* married to a Spanish soldier.[36] In time, however, they came to understand that the imposition of Spanish inheritance patterns would undermine chiefs and disrupt clans, and so they accepted matriliny as the norm for the Republic of Indians.[37]

Because of the impermanent nature of townsites in Florida, a native title of nobility based itself upon a body of vassals rather than a tract of land. Don Patricio de Hinachuba, for instance, held the title chief of Ivitachuco, a town in Apalache province. He retained the appellation after leading an exodus of his vassals and their cattle to a place called Abosaya, far into Timucua province.[38] Such a title could be valid even without the vassals. Owing to the fortunes of war, disease, and famine, doña María, cacica of San Francisco, no longer had vassals of her own. She and her Cuban husband entered the historical record in the 1670s by trying unsuccessfully to persuade the subjects of another cacica to join her and form a new town.[39]

From a European standpoint, chiefs and headmen formed the equivalent of a Second State. They did not pay head tax or tribute; they were not subject to corporal punishmen; they lived off the labor of commoners. Like their Spanish counterparts, the hidalgos, they were entitled to wear swords and ride horses.[40] Some chiefs of Apalache traded horses to the chiefs of Apalachicola, who in turn traded them to the English for guns. Determinedly heathen, the chiefs of told the Spanish governor that if God ever wanted them to accept Christianity they would let the Spanish know.[41]

Government in the Republic of Indians was financed by what might be called the "*sabana* system." Once or twice a year the common people of a town cleared, dug, and planted a sabana, or field, for their chief and each of their headmen, as well as the medicine man or woman, the best ballplayers, and the interpreter. There was one large communal field to provide for widows, orphans, and travelers and to put away a reserve.[42]

Church expenses were met by another sabana, although friars were not impressed by the Indians as husbandmen and said that for the things of this world they were not ones to kill themselves.[43]

Chiefs and headmen did no manual labor, and neither did their families. Common women were expected to shuck and smoke oysters, parch cassina leaves for tea, shell and grind corn, and extract hickory oil, but an outraged chief of Guale threatened in writing to abandon his post on the frontier and bring all his people to be fed in St. Augustine if his daughter was called to such tasks at the convent.[44]

A chief convicted of rebellion or another crime could forfeit his or her position but not the preeminences of rank, which were a birthright. A ruler was sentenced to a term of exile rather than to hard labor.[45] Hence Governor Rebolledo made a serious mistake in 1655 when he ordered up the Timucuan militia to reinforce St. Augustine—for who knew where the piratical English would attack after capturing Jamaica—and peremptorily told them all, including the headmen, to bring three arrobas of corn, a backpack load of seventy-five pounds. The Franciscans tried to enlighten him on social stratification. In the provinces, they explained, chiefs were the same as lords, sometimes absolute lords, and principales were the same as hidalgos; they were not of the "vile" (in other words "common") people who carried burdens on their backs. Rebolledo ignored this wise counsel, whereupon the rulers rose in rebellion. Rebolledo executed eleven of them, and the Council of the Indies had him arrested for provoking the lords of the land to revolt and then cruelly hanging them.[46]

Spaniards tended to confuse the communal lands or properties of a town with its chief's patrimony. (Perhaps a better word would be "matrimony," with both title and property coming by way of the mother.) They referred, for instance, to the old fields of the *chief* of Asile when they meant of the *town*. This was because a chief frequently did speak for his or her town in matters of land use, whether to grant hunting rights within its jurisdiction or grazing rights to its fallow fields.[47] The Laws of the Indies stipulated that no cattle ranches were to be situated nearer than three leagues from any native settlement, but in both republics there were ways to get around a law. The Crown objected to chiefs who leased their lands for money, not because the land was being alienated but because rents were a form of tribute, and tribute remained a royal prerogative.[48] In time, the depopulation of the provinces left more and more vacant lands where there had once been people,[49] but these lands did not revert to the royal domain as long as there was an heir of the chief's line.

Land was plentiful; without improvements it had little value. A town had other properties that were worth more, such as the herd of individually owned cattle (not to be confused with the cattle belonging to the chief)[50] and the food reserve in the town's several public granaries. In a good year the combined contents of all the granaries of all the towns could amount to a sizable surplus for the province and might become the subject of bitter dispute among Spaniards. The governors expected to purchase the corn and beans at low prices to feed St. Augustine. They instructed their deputies to enforce extra plantings to that end. The Franciscans, believing they were the ones who had taught double-cropping to the Indians, wanted to sell the same surplus in Havana to reduce their chapter's debts and beautify the native sanctuaries.[51] A large amount of money went into the competitive adorning of churches; the value of chrismatories, diadems, and other religious treasure in Apalache province once amounted to 2,500 pesos per town, more than a single Indian could earn in a lifetime of work at the king's wages.[52]

A town granary was double-locked, with Spanish locks and keys. Whoever might be fighting over the second of the locks, the key to the first remained in the hands of the chief, who upon the advice of his headmen might choose not to sell the town's surplus at all.[53] Officers and friars quarreled similarly over who held jurisdiction over the church confines. For the Indians this too was a moot point. The church structure they had built; the contents they had either purchased or been given by the Crown.[54] One friar who had to close down a mission was sued by his erstwhile parishioners for carrying off their church ornaments and bell. To represent them the governor appointed a "defender of the Indians," as was required when natives appeared in a Spanish court, and the decision was in their favor.[55]

Just as in Spain each kingdom preserved its ancient *fueros,* or privileges, the Republic of Indians governed itself according to established law and custom which the Crown saw no need to alter.[56] Only the practices contrary to the "law of God," such as magical cures and multiple wives, could be forbidden. (In their innocence the Indians had imagined that sororate polygyny, in which one's wives were close relatives of each other, was no worse than Spanish concubinage.)[57] A chief retained considerable power over his or her vassals,[58] and if they obeyed poorly, the governor could be called upon to help subdue them even if heathen mercenaries had to be brought in to do it. It was one of the ways the Spanish made themselves indispensable in the provinces.[59]

The relationship between chiefs and governor was symbiotic. He guaranteed their authority; they provided him with labor, and as far as the Spanish were concerned this was their principal function. Communities in the Republic of Indians were liable to a head tax based on the number of married males in the census the friars made every Lenten season. Soon this tribute was commuted to a labor levy, the *repartimiento.*[60] The Spaniards made themselves the cobeneficiaries of the sabana system described earlier by having workers sent to the city in relays to clear, dig, and plant the "king's" sabana, do the first, second, and third hoeings, and guard the ripening corn for the harvest.[61] These field hands, called *indios de cava,* were given rations only. The chiefs who sent them to St. Augustine received tools and other items needed by the town.[62]

From time to time authorities asked the chiefs to send additional workers for the king's service to unload ships, paddle canoes, cut firewood, carry messages, and be servants to important people. These *indios de servicio* got their rations plus a daily wage in trade goods originally figured to be worth one real per day, an eighth of a peso. The choices ran to beads, knives, and half-blankets.[63] One subset of the indios de servicio was the *indios de fábricas* assigned to public works projects, usually building fortifications such as the stone Castillo de San Marcos. When the public works were in their own province the chiefs sometimes donated their vassals' labor and paid for materials out of provincial tithes, which were apparently theirs to administer.

A second subset of the indios de servicio was the *indios de carga,* who carried heavy loads of supplies or trade goods on their backs for long distances. The Crown repeatedly prohibited this use of Indians without addressing the cause, which was the lack of mules and packhorses in Florida. The use of indios de carga became another heated issue between the friars and the governors, each side—with justification—accusing the other of abuses. Still, Spaniards believed that the Indians of Florida were not ill treated compared with the natives in the rest of the Indies. As a contemporary compiler pointed out, in Florida there were no *encomiendas* or factories or mines in which the natives could be occupied, and they did not pay tribute.[64]

The labor quota of a town was adjusted if its inhabitants had soldiers quartered on them, operated a ferry, or moved to a new place on the frontier or along the king's highway to accommodate the Spanish.[65] The quota was not adjusted to account for the Indians who had left the town to become craftsmen or apprentices or to work for private persons (at a better wage than the Crown paid), whether by the day, by the job, or on yearly contract. This is why Spanish and Indian authorities united to oppose peonage. A peon on a ranch was likely to be a man evading his turn on the labor levy and letting his neighbors support his family.[66]

If the Spanish took advantage of the sabana system, they also profited by the native inclination to war. Again, the chiefs were the agency. The vassals they supplied were used at first for couriers and indios de carga. Later, as the Spanish learned respect for Indian archers, their allies were enjoined to keep fifty arrows in their quivers. By the middle of the seventeenth century the Christian Indians were organized into companies of militia under their chiefs. When called to service they received rations and sometimes firearms. If after King Philip's War in 1675 and the Pueblo Revolt of 1680 the Crown had reservations about putting guns in the hands of Indians,[67] the Florida governors usually felt this was justified. The Indians fought more bravely than the Spanish did, they said, and with greater readiness.[68] Prowess in battle allowed an Indian warrior to advance through the ranks to *noroco* or *tascaya,* dancing in the council house with a fine string of scalps and exempt from the labor levy.[69]

Chiefs and Spanish officers might have joint command, as on the expeditions sent northward in the 1620s to locate de Soto's lagoon of pearls.[70] Or the chiefs might go out on their own. In 1680 the chief of Santa Fé took warriors out the Suwanee River in canoes and down the west coast to Charlotte Harbor to rescue Spaniards held captive by the powerful Calusas; two years later Timucuan chiefs rescued a floridano rancher and his people being held for ransom by French buccaneers.[71] The chiefs legalized their campaigns in the Spanish manner, meeting in junta and listing the provocations that called for retaliation and entitled them to take booty. Sometimes a few soldiers went with the Indians; more and more often toward the end of the century they were not invited because of what was called "*la mala unión.*"[72]

Relations between the Republic of Spaniards and the Republic of Indians were becoming strained, and the cause was Carolina, founded in 1670. True to the English model, the initial colonists of Charlestown wanted only to trade with the natives. Governor James Colleton ingenuously expressed their policy in these words to his counterpart, Florida governor Diego de Quiroga y Losada: "As for the Yamassees, . . . they have nothing to do with our government nor do we trouble ourselves about them . . . showing no profit but of a few deerskins for which we sell them powder, guns and shot as we do to all Indians indifferently."[73]

In the 1680s, Indians equipped with English firearms and ammunition began to raid Florida towns to take slaves for the markets of Charlestown. This onslaught intensified during Queen Anne's War, when Colonel James Moore twice led armies of Creeks and Carolinians into Florida to destroy the provinces. Martyrologist accounts of the invasion of Apalache relate how Christians were burned on their own crosses, coats of arms defaced, and ball poles uprooted.[74]

The Spanish in the provinces recognized that in addition to invasion they and the chiefs faced a vassals' rebellion. Provincial and town government broke down. Mixed-bloods turned to brigandage. Native warriors demanded that soldiers dismount and fight beside them with ammunition equally divided, while officials became reluctant to issue firearms to Indians who were probably going to defect.[75] Among the several thousand Florida natives who accompanied Moore back to Carolina many went voluntarily, unaware that they would all be sold into servitude. Others headed for the new Spanish fort at Pensacola, for French territory, or for parts unknown, saying they would not stay to die with Spaniards.

Faced with wholesale desertion, the teniente at San Luis spiked the cannons, packed up the salvaged church treasure, and carted it to St. Augustine. In the end only one chief of importance, don Patricio de Hinachuba of the town of Ivitachuco, remained an ally. Having compounded with Moore to spare his town at the expense of its sacred treasure, he settled his vassals and their livestock on the empty savannas of Timucua, far from the Spanish capital.[76]

In the eighteenth century little was left in the provinces to remind one of the time of the two republics or of the rulers who had shared sovereignty with Spaniards. It was the English system that survived. With sadness the Spanish acknowledged that the southeastern Indians had become interested only in guns and gewgaws and that they gave their vassalage to no one. Baptism they might consent to for the sake of the presents, but once out of sight they made a mockery of it, striking their foreheads and calling, "Water, begone! I am no Christian!"[77]

NOTES

1. James Axtell, who treats both French and English cultural interaction in *The Invasion Within: The Contest of Cultures in Colonial North America* (New York: Oxford University Press, 1985), x, pleads the demands of stylistic economy for leaving out the Spanish.

2. Alonso de las Alas and Juan Menéndez Marquez to the Crown, St. Augustine, 12–13–1595, *Archivo General de Indias, ramo Gobierno: Santo Domingo, legajo 229, número 18.* (Hereafter cited as SD; unless otherwise noted, origin is St. Augustine and addressee the Crown.)

3. Fr. Francisco Pareja, 1-17-1617, SD 235.

4. Friars in chapter, 10-16-1612, SD 232/61.

5. Fr. Alonso del Moral, [summary seen in Council 9-18-1676], SD 235/102.

6. Francisco Menéndez Marquez and Pedro Benedit Horruytiner, 7-27-1647, SD 235.

7. John R. Swanton, *Modern Square Grounds of the Creek Indians*, Smithsonian Miscellaneous Collections 85, no. 8 (Washington, D.C.: Government Printing Office, 1931), 38.

8. Amy Bushnell, "'That Demonic Game': The Campaign to Stop Indian *Pelota* Playing in Spanish Florida, 1675–1684," *The Americas* 35 (July 1978): 1–19.

9. Father Luis Gerónimo de Oré, a contemporary observer, said that the Indians, men and women, learned to read easily and wrote letters to one another in their own languages. *The Martyrs of Florida, 1513–1616*, ed. and trans. Maynard Geiger, O.F.M., Franciscan Studies 18 (New York: Joseph F. Wagner, 1936), 103.

10. On the reliability of interested parties see Gov. Alonso de Aranguíz y Cotes, 11-14-1661, SD 225.

11. Irene Wright, "*Rescates:* With Special Reference to Cuba, 1599–1610," *Hispanic American Historical Review* 3 (August 1920): 336–61; Paul E. Hoffman, *The Spanish Crown and the Defense of the Caribbean, 1535–1585: Precedent, Patrimonialism and Royal Parsimony* (Baton Rouge: Louisiana State University Press, 1980), 112–22.

12. Eugene Lyon, *The Enterprise of Florida: Pedro Menéndez de Avilés and the Spanish Conquest of 1565–1568* (Gainesville: University Presses of Florida, 1976), is definitive on this expedition and the first years of conquest.

13. The contemporary arguments for and against Menéndez's plan can be found in Jeannette Thurber Connor, trans. and ed., *Colonial Records of Spanish Florida*, 2 vols. (DeLand: Florida Historical Society, 1925, 1930), 1: 31–37, 77–81; Cédula to Gerónimo de Montalva, Governor of Cuba, 8-10-1574, in "Registros: Reales órdenes y nombramientos dirigidos a autoridades y particulares de la Florida. Años 1570 a 1604," typescript, [1907], P. K. Yonge Library of Florida History, 70–74.

14. Juan Menéndez Marquez, 3-14-1608, SD 229/58; Gov. Juan Fernández de Olivera, 10-13-1612, SD 229/74.

15. Domingo de Leturiondo, in *Auto* on Mayaca and Enacape, 3-15-1682 to 9-7-1682, SD 226/95.

16. For a discussion of the fund for the "expense of Indians" (*gasto de indios*) see Amy Bushnell, *The King's Coffer: Proprietors of the Spanish Florida Treasury, 1565–1702* (Gainesville: University Presses of Florida, 1981), 66.

17. Friars in chapter, 12-5-1693, SD 235/134, and 10-16-1612, SD 232/61; Gov. Laureano de Torres y Ayala, 9-19-1699, SD 228/155.

18. Francisco Menéndez Marquez and Pedro Benedit Horruytiner, 3-18-1647, SD 229; Informe against Gov. Juan Marques Cabrera, Havana, 8-4-1688, SD 864/8.

19. Fr. Juan de Paiva, Pelota Manuscript, San Luis de Talimali, 9-23-1676, in the Domingo de Leturiondo Visita of Apalache and Timucua, 1677–78, Residencia of Gov. Pablo de Hita Salazar, ramo Escribanía de Cámara 156-A, fols. 568–83 (hereafter cited as EC).

20. Stephen Edward Reilly, "A Marriage of Expedience: The Calusa Indians and Their Relations with Pedro Menéndez de Avilés in Southwest Florida, 1566–1569," *Florida Historical Quarterly* 59(April 1981): 395–421; Kathleen A. Deagan, "*Mestizaje* in Colonial St. Augustine," *Ethnohistory* 20, no. 1 (Winter 1973): 55–65.

21. Don Gáspar Marquez, Chief of San Sebastian and Tocoy, 6-23-1606, SD 232/47; Catalina de Valdés, 1606, SD 19; idem, [1616], SD 232/76; Gov. Melchor de Navarrete, 11-15-1749, SD 2541/101.

22. In Informe on St. Augustine, 9-16-1602, SD 235/10.

23. Fr. Francisco Pareja, 1-17-1617, SD 235.

24. The ordering of the two republics is described by Lyle N. McAlister in *Spain and Portugal in the New World, 1492–1700* (Minneapolis: University of Minnesota Press, 1984), 391–95.

25. Mark F. Boyd, "Enumeration of Florida Spanish Missions in 1675," *Florida Historical Quarterly* 27 (October 1948): 181–88. A *provincia* in Florida was the same as a *partido* in Honduras, according to Gov. Juan Marques Cabrera, 6-14-1681, SD 226.

26. Junta of Guale chiefs, Santa María, 2-7-1701, and Orders for Guale and Mocama, San Juan del Puerto, 2-11-1701, Residencia of Gov. Joseph de Zúñiga y Cerda, SD 858/ 4, fols. 179–85; Juan de Pueyo Visita of Guale and Mocama in 1695, Residencia of Gov. Laureano de Torres y Ayala, EC 157-A.

27. Orders for Timucua, San Francisco de Potano, 12-24-1694, in the Joachin de Florencia Visita of Apalache and Timucua, 1694–95, Residencia of Gov. Laureano de Torres y Ayala, EC 157-A.

28. Fr. Juan de Pareja, 1-17-1617, SD 235; Friars in chapter to Gov. Diego de Rebolledo, 5-10-1657, in idem, 9-10-1657, SD 235; Junta de Guerra, [Spain], 7-15-1660, SD 839; Gov. Juan Marques Cabrera, 5-10-1681 to 5-30-1681, SD 226.

29. The mission beadle, a native known as a *fiscal*, administered the punishment. See friars in chapter vs. Gov. Juan Marques Cabrera, 5-10-1681 to 5-30-1681, SD 226.

30. Gov. Pedro de Ybarra to Fr. Pedro Bermejo, 12-13-1605, SD 232; Gov. Juan Marques Cabrera, 12-8-1680, SD 226/68.

31. For discussions of Spanish settlers in the provinces see Amy Bushnell, "The Menéndez Marquez Cattle Barony at La Chua and the Determinants of Economic Expansion in Seventeenth-Century Florida," *Florida Historical Quarterly* 56 (April 1978): 407–31; idem, "Patricio de Hinachuba: Defender of the Word of God, the Crown of the King, and the Little Children of Ivitachuco," *American Indian Culture and Research Journal* 3 (July 1979): 1–21; idem, *King's Coffer,* 14.

32. In 1655 the Franciscans reported 70 friars, 38 doctrinas, and 26,000 Christian Indians in Florida. See Michael V. Gannon, *The Cross in the Sand: The Early Catholic Church in Florida, 1513–1870* (Gainesville: University of Florida Press, 1967), 57.

33. These are terms the Spanish brought with them. In the Indian languages, words for chiefs were *mico, inija, usinjulo,* and *alayguita.*

34. Gov. Joseph de Zúñiga y Cerda to the chiefs and principales of Vitachuco and San Luis, 4-24-1704, SD 858/B.

35. For accounts of visitas see Fred Lamar Pearson, Jr., "The Florencia Investigation of Spanish Timucua," *Florida Historical Quarterly* 51 (October 1972): 166–76; idem, "Spanish-Indian Relations in Florida, 1602–1675: Some Aspects of Selected *Visitas,*" *Florida Historical Quarterly* 52 (January 1974): 261–73; Bushnell, "That Demonic Game"; idem, "Patricio de Hinachuba," 4–5.

Ecclesiastical visitas were also made, usually by the padre provincial. See Gov. Francisco de la Guerra y de la Vega, 2-28-1668, SD 233/68; Gov. Juan Marques Cabrera, 12-8-1680, SD 226/68.

36. Kathleen A. Deagan, "Cultures in Transition: Fusion and Assimilation among the Eastern Timucua," in *Tacachale: Essays on the Indians of Florida and Southeastern Georgia during the Historic Period,* ed. Jerald T. Milanich and Samuel Proctor (Gainesville: University Presses of Florida, 1978), 103–4; don Gaspar Marques, Chief of San Sebastian and Tocoy, 6-23-1606, SD 232/47.

37. Leturiondo Visita of 1677–78, EC 156-A; Florencia Visita of 1694–95, EC 157-A; Patricio, Chief of Ybitachuco [at Abosaya], to Gov. Joseph de Zúñiga y Cerda, 5-291705, SD 858/4.

38. Bushnell, "Patricio de Hinachuba."

39. Reported petition of María de Jesús, Cacica of San Francisco de Potano, 1-25-1678, acted upon at Salamototo, 1-30-1678, in the Leturiondo Visita of 1677–78, EC 156-A.

40. Florencia Visita of 1694–95, EC 157-A.

41. Gov. Joseph de Zúñiga y Cerda, 9-30-1702, SD 840/58; Gov. Juan Marques Cabrera, 9-20-1681, SD 226/95.

42. Gov. Juan Marques Cabrera, 6-14-1681, SD 226; Florencia Visita of 1694–95, EC 157-A; Orders for Guale and Mocama, San Juan del Puerto, 2-11-1701, SD 858/4, fol. 179; Teniente Antonio Mateos to Gov. Juan Marques Cabrera, [San Luis de Talimali], 3-14-1686, SD 839/82.

43. "Por las cosas deste mundo no se matan mucho" (Friars in chapter vs. Gov. Juan Marques Cabrera, 5-10-1681 to 5-30-1681, SD 226).

44. Chief of Guale to Gov. Juan Marques Cabrera, Sapala, 5-5-1681, SD 226.

45. Gov. Pablo de Hita Salazar, 7-5-1677, EC 158.

46. Fr. Juan Gómez de Engraba to Fr. Francisco Martínez, Havana, 3-13-1657 and 4-41657, SD 225; Investigation of Gov. Diego de Rebolledo by the Council of the Indies, 7-7-1657, included with Anon., Informe against Gov. Diego de Rebolledo, 6-15-1657, SD 6/17; Friars in chapter, 9-10-1657, SD 235.

47. Friars in chapter, 9-10-1657, SD 235; Pedro Benedit Horruytiner, 11-10-1657, SD 233/55.

48. For discussions of land grants and use in Florida see Bushnell, *King's Coffer,* 80–82, 113, and idem, "Menéndez Marquez Cattle Barony."

49. Henry F. Dobyns examines Timucuan depopulation as a representative case in *Their Number Become Thinned: Native American Population Dynamics in Eastern North America* (Knoxville: University of Tennessee Press, 1983), but his conclusions on total figures should be used with care. David Henige, in "Primary Source by Primary Source? On the Role of Epidemics in New World Depopulation," *Ethnohistory* 33 (Summer 1986): 293–312, shows Dobyns to be incautious in his handling of the sources.

50. Florencia Visita of 1694–95, EC 157-A. Owners identified their stock by ear notching.

51. Bushnell, *King's Coffer,* 11–12, 24, 70, 99; Gov. Pablo de Hita Salazar, 9-6-1677, SD 839/46; Gov. Juan Marques Cabrera to Teniente Juan Fernandez de Florencia, 1-20-1681, SD 226/76; Friars in chapter vs. Gov. Juan Marques Cabrera, 5-10-1681 to 5-30-1681, SD 226.

52. See Bushnell, "Patricio de Hinachuba," 12.

53. Orders for Guale and Mocama, San Juan del Puerto, 2-11-1701, SD 858/4, fol. 179; Florencia Visita of 1694–95, EC 157-A.

54. Gov. Juan Marques Cabrera to Fr. Blas de Robles, 5-10-1681, SD 226/76.

55. Domingo de Leturiondo, n.d., in Auto on Mayaca and Enacape, 3-15-1682 to 9-7-1682, SD 226/95; idem, 8-26-1682, with Gov. Juan Marques Cabrera, 10-7-1682, SD 226/95. On the defender of the Indians in Florida see Bushnell, *King's Coffer*, 40, 111. Cf. Charles R. Cutter, *The Protector de Indios in Colonial New Mexico, 1659–1821* (Albuquerque: University of New Mexico Press, 1986).

56. Captain Antonio de Arguelles, 2-24-1688, SD 234/87; Fiscal of the Council of the Indies, 7-23-1700, with Gov. Laureano de Torres y Ayala, 9-16-1699, SD 228/151.

57. Florencia Visita of 1694–95, EC 157-A; Lewis H. Larson, Jr., "Historic Guale Indians of the Georgia Coast and the Impact of the Spanish Mission Effort," in Milanich and Proctor, *Tacachale*, 120–40; Bushnell, "That Demonic Game," 8.

58. Jerald T. Milanich and William C. Sturtevant, eds., *Francisco Pareja's 1613 "Confessionario": A Documentary Source for Timucuan Ethnography,* trans. Emilio Moran (Tallahassee: Florida Department of State, 1972), 34–35.

59. Friars, Informe on St. Augustine, 9-16-1602, SD 235/10; Gov. Juan Fernández de Olivera, 10-13-1612, SD 229/74; Florencia Visita of 1694–95, EC 157-A.

60. On the tribute and repartimiento see Bushnell, *King's Coffer*, 11–13, 16–25, 37–46, 97–99, 106, 110–11, and idem, "Patricio de Hinachuba," 8; Florencia Visita of 1694–95, EC 157-A; Francisco Menéndez Marquez and Pedro Benedit Horruytiner, 727–1647. SD 235.

61. Friars to Gov. Diego de Rebolledo, 5-10-1657, with Friars in chapter, 9-10-1657, SD 235.

62. Bartolome de Arguelles, 10-31-1598, SD 229/25; Fr. Antonio de Somoza, Commissary General of the Indies, [Spain], 5-2-1673, SD 235/97: Teniente Antonio Mateos to Gov. Juan Marques Cabrera, 2-8-1686, SD 839/82.

63. Apparently the blanket fabric was woven on a narrow backstrap loom, and a full blanket had a seam down the middle.

64. Juan Diez de la Calle, *Memorial y noticias sacras y reales del imperio de las Indias occidentales* (Madrid, 1646).

65. Friars in chapter to Gov. Diego de Rebolledo, 5-10-1657, in idem, 9-10-1657, SD 235; Florencia Visita of 1694–95, EC 157-A. For examples of town relocation to serve the communications network, see Leturiondo Visita of 1677–78, EC 156-A, fols. 56883, and Bushnell, "Menéndez Marquez Cattle Barony," 420.

66. Fr. Alonso del Moral, [summary seen in Council 11-5-1676], SD 235/104; Auto on the abuses of the friars, 6-28-1683, SD 226/105; Florencia Visita of 1694–95, EC 157-A.

67. Francisco Menéndez Marquez and Pedro Benedit Horruytiner, 7-27-1647, SD 235; Fr. Miguel de Valverde and Fr. Rodrigo de la Barrera, San Nicolas de Tolentino, 9-10-1674, SD 234; Gov. Pablo de Hita Salazar, 5-14-1680, SD 839/63; Cedula, 3-22-1685, SD 852/34; Florencia Visita of 1694–95, EC 157-A.

68. Gov. Juan Marques Cabrera, 3-30-1686, SD 852.

69. Gov. Joseph de Zúñiga y Cerda, Orders on scalp taking, 3-14-1701, SD 858/B-252; Bushnell, "That Demonic Game," 11–12, 16; idem, *King's Coffer*, 96–97.

70. Bushnell, *King's Coffer*, 92.

71. Gov. Pablo de Hita Salazar, 3-6-1680, SD 226; Bushnell, "Menéndez Marquez Cattle Barony," 428.

72. Juntas de Guerra, St. Augustine, 11-3-1694, and San Luis de Talimali, 10-22-1702, SD 858/B-14.

73. Gov. James Colleton of Carolina, Charlestown, n.d., to Gov. Diego de Quiroga y Losada, translation sent to the Crown on 4-1-1688, SD 839.

74. See Charles W. Arnade, *The Siege of St. Augustine in 1702* (Gainesville: University of Florida Press, 1959); Mark E. Boyd, Hale G. Smith, and John W. Griffin, eds., *Here They Once Stood: The Tragic End of the Apalachee Missions* (Gainesville: University of Florida Press, 1951).

75. Bushnell, "Patricio de Hinachuba," 10; Captain Francisco Romo de Uriza, San Luis de Talimali, 10-22-1702. SD 858/B-14.

76. Bushnell, "Patricio de Hinachuba," 7–14.

77. Gov. Francisco del Moral Sanchez, 6-8-1734, SD 844/28; "Florida in the Late First Spanish Period: The 1756 Grihan Report," ed. Michael C. Scardaville and trans. Jesus Maria Belmonte, *El Escribano* 16(1979): 16; Francisco de Buenaventura, Bishop of Tricale, 4-29-1736, SD 863/119.

16

THE WHITE INDIANS OF COLONIAL AMERICA

James Axtell

When the English planned their colonies in North America, they almost invariably claimed that their chief goal was to spread Christianity to Native American Indians. As early as 1585, Richard Hakluyt the Elder, among the most influential promoters of English colonization, asserted that the first reason to engage in such an effort was "to plant Christian religion." Englishmen were concerned not only with gathering souls for Christ, of course; they also believed that the only way to stem the spread of Catholicism in North America (and its French or Spanish sponsors) was to convert Indians to Protestant Christianity. Behind this imperative was the assumption that European culture, and particularly English culture, was superior to Native American ways. Thus the English believed that Indians would logically reject their own cultures once colonists arrived to show them how to live "properly."

But this notion proved more than offensive to natives in the colonial era; as Cornelius Jaenen's essay on Indian attitudes toward the French suggests, it also proved wrong. As James Axtell notes here, it was always difficult, if not impossible, for the English to convince many Indians to embrace European culture and religion. Instead, time and again, English colonists captured by Indians in eastern North America decided to live like their captors. Rather than finding native life depraved, those who spent time in an Indian community often found it more rewarding than the world they had come from and decided to stay there, even when they had the chance to be "redeemed" and returned to the colonial world. An entire literally genre, of literature, known as the "captivity narrative," emerged to detail the progress of those who returned and to describe how Indians transformed a colonist who decided to stay into one of their own. While many colonists could never understand why any "civilized" person would make such a decision, that decision both frightened and fascinated them. For us, too, captivity narratives have become among the most valuable of sources depicting relations between natives and newcomers in North America.

THE WHITE INDIANS OF COLONIAL AMERICA

James Axtell

THE ENGLISH, like their French rivals, began their colonizing ventures in North America with a sincere interest in converting the Indians to Christianity and civilization. Nearly all the colonial charters granted by the English monarchs in the seventeenth century assigned the wish to extend the Christian Church and to redeem savage souls as a principal, if not *the* principal, motive for colonization.[1] This desire was grounded in a set of complementary beliefs about "savagism" and "civilization." First, the English held that the Indians, however benighted, were capable of conversion. "It is not the nature of men," they believed, "but the education of men, which make them barbarous and uncivill."[2] Moreover, the English were confident that the Indians would want to be converted once they were exposed to the superior quality of English life. The strength of these beliefs was reflected in Cotton Mather's astonishment as late as 1721 that

> Tho' they saw a People Arrive among them, who were Clothed in *Habits* of much more Comfort and Splendour, than what there was to be seen in the *Rough Skins* with which they hardly covered themselves; and who had *Houses full of Good Things,* vastly out-shining their squalid and dark *Wigwams;* And they saw this People Replenishing their *Fields,* with *Trees* and with *Grains,* and useful *Animals,* which until now they had been wholly Strangers to; yet they did not seem touch'd in the least, with any *Ambition* to come at such Desirable Circumstances, or with any *Curiosity* to enquire after the *Religion* that was attended with them.[3]

The second article of the English faith followed from their fundamental belief in the superiority of civilization, namely, that no civilized person in possession of his faculties or free from undue restraint would choose to become an Indian. "For, easy and unconstrained as the savage life is," wrote the Reverend William Smith of Philadelphia, "certainly it could never be put in competition with the blessings of improved life and the light of religion, by any persons who have had the happiness of enjoying, and the capacity of discerning, them."[4]

SOURCE: *William and Mary Quarterly,* 3d Ser. 32 (1975), 55–88.

And yet, by the close of the colonial period, very few if any Indians had been transformed into civilized Englishmen. Most of the Indians who were educated by the English—some contemporaries thought *all* of them—returned to Indian society at the first opportunity to resume their Indian identities. On the other hand, large numbers of Englishmen had chosen to become Indians—by running away from colonial society to join Indian society, by not trying to escape after being captured, or by electing to remain with their Indian captors when treaties of peace periodically afforded them the opportunity to return home.[5]

Perhaps the first colonist to recognize the disparity between the English dream and the American reality was Cadwallader Colden, surveyor-general and member of the king's council of New York. In his *History of the Five Indian Nations of Canada,* published in London in 1747, Colden described the Albany peace treaty between the French and the Iroquois in 1699, when "few of [the French captives] could be persuaded to return" to Canada. Lest his readers attribute this unusual behavior to "the Hardships they had endured in their own Country, under a tyrannical Government and a barren Soil," he quickly added that "the *English* had as much Difficulty to persuade the People, that had been taken Prisoners by the *French Indians,* to leave the *Indian* Manner of living, though no People enjoy more Liberty, and live in greater Plenty, than the common Inhabitants of *New-York* do." Colden, clearly amazed, elaborated:

> No Arguments, no Intreaties, nor Tears of their Friends and Relations, could persuade many of them to leave their new *Indian* Friends and Acquaintance[s]; several of them that were by the Caressings of their Relations persuaded to come Home, in a little Time grew tired of our Manner of living, and run away again to the *Indians,* and ended their Days with them. On the other Hand, *Indian* Children have been carefully educated among the *English,* cloathed and taught, yet, I think, there is not one Instance, that any of these, after they had Liberty to go among their own People, and were come to Age, would remain with the *English,* but returned to their own Nations, and became as fond of the *Indian* Manner of Life as those that knew nothing of a civilized Manner of living. What I now tell of Christian Prisoners among *Indians* [he concluded his history], relates not only to what happened at the Conclusion of this War, but has been found true on many other Occasions.[6]

Colden was not alone. Six years later Benjamin Franklin wondered how it was that

> When an Indian Child has been brought up among us, taught our language and habituated to our Customs, yet if he goes to see his relations and makes one Indian Ramble with them, there is no perswading him ever to return. [But] when white persons of either sex have been taken prisoners young by the Indians, and lived a while among them, tho' ransomed by their Friends, and treated with all imaginable tenderness to prevail with them to stay among the English, yet in a Short time they become disgusted with our manner of life, and the care and pains that are necessary to support it, and take the first good Opportunity of escaping again into the Woods, from whence there is no reclaiming them.[7]

In short, "thousands of Europeans are Indians," as Hector de Crèvecoeur put it, "and we have no examples of even one of those Aborigines having from choice become Europeans!"[8]

THE ENGLISH CAPTIVES who foiled their countrymen's civilized assumptions by becoming Indians differed little from the general colonial population when they were captured. They were ordinary men, women, and children of yeoman stock, Protestants by faith, a variety of nationalities by birth, English by law, different from their countrymen only in their willingness to risk personal insecurity for the economic opportunities of the frontier.[9] There was no discernible characteristic or pattern of characteristics that differentiated them from their captive neighbors who eventually rejected Indian life—with one exception. Most of the colonists captured by the Indians and adopted into Indian families were children of both sexes and young women, often the mothers of the captive children. They were, as one captivity narrative observed, the "weak and defenceless."[10]

The pattern of taking women and children for adoption was consistent throughout the colonial period, but during the first century and one-half of Indian-white conflict, primarily in New England, it coexisted with a larger pattern of captivity that included all white colonists, men as well as women and children. The Canadian Indians who raided New England tended to take captives more for their ransom value than for adoption. When Mrs. James Johnson gave birth to a daughter on the trail to Canada, for example, her captor looked into her makeshift lean-to and "clapped his hands with joy, crying two monies for me, two monies for me." Although the New England legislatures occasionally tried to forbid the use of public moneys for "the Ransoming of Captives," thereby prolonging the Indians' "diabolical kidnapping mode of warfare," ransoms were constantly paid from both public and private funds. These payments became larger as inflation and the Indians' savvy increased. Thus when John and Tamsen Tibbetts redeemed two of their children from the Canadian Indians in 1729, it cost them £105 10s. (1,270 livres). "Being verry Poore," many families in similar situations could ill afford to pay such high premiums even "if they should sell all they have in the world."[11]

When the long peace in the Middle Atlantic colonies collapsed in 1753, the Indians of Pennsylvania, southern New York, and the Ohio country had no Quebec or Montreal in which to sell their human chattels to compassionate French families or anxious English relatives.[12] For this and other reasons they captured English settlers largely to replace members of their own families who had died, often from English musketballs or imported diseases.[13] Consequently, women and children—the "weak and defenceless"—were the prime targets of Indian raids.

According to the pattern of warfare in the Pennsylvania theater, the Indians usually stopped at a French fort with their prisoners before proceeding to their own villages. A young French soldier captured by the English reported that at Fort Duquesne there were "a great number of English Prisoners," the older of whom "they are constantly sending . . . away to Montreal" as prisoners of war, "but that the Indians keep many of the Prisoners amongst them, chiefly young People whom they adopt and bring up in their own way." His intelligence was corroborated by Barbara Leininger and Marie LeRoy, who had been members of a party of two adults and eight children captured in 1755 and taken to Fort Duquesne. There they saw "many other Women and Children, they think an hundred who were carried away from the several provinces of P[ennsylvania] M[aryland] and V[irginia]." When the girls escaped from captivity three years later, they wrote a narrative in German chiefly to acquaint "the inhabitants of this country . . . with the names and circumstances of those prisoners whom we met, at the various places where we were, in the course of our captivity." Of the fifty-two prisoners they had seen, thirty-four were children and fourteen were women, including six mothers with children of their own.[14]

The close of hostilities in Pennsylvania came in 1764 after Col. Henry Bouquet defeated the Indians near Bushy Run and imposed peace. By the articles of agreement reached in October, the Delawares, Shawnees, and Senecas were to deliver up "all the Prisoners in [their] Possession, without any Exception, Englishmen, Frenchmen, Women, and Children, whether adopted in your Tribes, married, or living amongst you, under any Denomination, or Pretence whatever." In the weeks that followed, Bouquet's troops, including "the Relations of [some of] the People [the Indians] have Massacred, or taken Prisoners," encamped on the Muskingum in the heart of the Ohio country to collect the captives. After as many as nine years with the Indians, during which time many children had grown up, 81 "men" and 126 "women and children" were returned. At the same time, a list was prepared of 88 prisoners who still remained in Shawnee towns to the west: 70 were classified as "women and children." Six months later, 44 of these prisoners were delivered up to Fort Pitt. When they were captured, all but 4 had been less than sixteen years old, while 37 had been less than eleven years old.[15]

The Indians obviously chose their captives carefully so as to maximize the chances of acculturating them to Indian life. To judge by the results, their methods were hard to fault. Even when the English held the upper hand militarily, they were often embarrassed by the Indians' educational power. On November 12, 1764, at his camp on the Muskingum, Bouquet lectured the Shawnees who had not delivered all their captives: "As you are now going to Collect all our *Flesh*, and *Blood*, . . . I desire that you will use them with Tenderness, and look upon them as Brothers, and no longer as Captives." The utter gratuitousness of his remark was reflected—no doubt purposely—in the Shawnee speech when the Indians delivered their captives the following spring at Fort Pitt. "Father—Here is your *Flesh*, and *Blood* . . . they have been all tied to us by Adoption, although we now deliver them up to you. We will always look upon them as Relations, whenever the *Great Spirit* is pleased that we may visit them. . . . Father—we have taken as much Care of these Prisoners, as if they were [our] own Flesh, and blood; they are become unacquainted with your Customs, and manners, and therefore, Father we request you will use them tender, and kindly, which will be a means of inducing them to live contentedly with you."[16]

The Indians spoke the truth and the English knew it. Three days after his speech to the Shawnees, Bouquet had advised Lt.-Gov. Francis Fauquier of Virginia that the returning captives "ought to be treated by their Relations with Tenderness and Humanity, till Time and Reason make them forget their unnatural Attachments, but unless they are closely watch'd," he admitted, "they will certainly return to the Barbarians."[17] And indeed they would have, for during a half-century of conflict captives had been returned who, like many of the Ohio prisoners, responded only to Indian names, spoke only Indian dialects, felt comfortable only in Indian clothes, and in general regarded their white saviors as barbarians and their deliverance as captivity. Had they not been compelled to return to English society by militarily enforced peace treaties, the ranks of the white Indians would have been greatly enlarged.

From the moment the Indians surrendered their English prisoners, the colonists faced a series of difficult problems. The first was the problem of getting the prisoners to remain with the English. When Bouquet sent the first group of restored captives to Fort Pitt, he ordered his officers there that "they are to be closely watched and well Secured" because "most of them, particularly those who have been a long time among the Indians, will take the first Opportunity to run away." The young children especially were "so completely savage that they were brought to the camp tied hand and foot." Fourteen-year-old John McCullough, who had lived with the Indians for "eight years, four months, and sixteen days" (by his parents' reckoning), had his legs tied "under the horses belly" and his arms tied behind his back with his father's garters, but to no avail. He escaped under the cover of night and returned to his Indian family for a year before he was finally carried to Fort Pitt under "strong guard." "Having been accustomed to look upon the Indians as the only connexions they had, having been tenderly treated by them, and speaking their language," explained the Reverend William Smith, the historian of Bouquet's expedition, "it is no wonder that [the children] considered their new state in the light of a captivity, and parted from the savages with tears."[18]

Children were not the only reluctant freedmen. "Several women eloped in the night, and ran off to join their Indian friends." Among them undoubtedly were some of the English women who had married Indian men and borne them children, and then had been forced by the English victory either to return with their mixed-blood children to a country of strangers, full of prejudice against Indians, or to risk escaping under English guns to their husbands and adopted culture. For Bouquet had "reduced the Shawanese and Delawares etc. to the most Humiliating Terms of Peace," boasted Gen. Thomas Gage. "He has Obliged them to deliver up even their Own Children born of white women." But even the victorious soldier could understand the dilemma into which these women had been pushed. When Bouquet was informed that the English wife of an Indian chief had eloped in the night with her husband and children, he "requested that no pursuit should be made, as she was happier with her Chief than she would be if restored to her home."[19]

Although most of the returned captives did not try to escape, the emotional torment caused by the separation from their adopted families deeply impressed the colonists. The Indians "delivered up their beloved captives with the utmost reluctance; shed torrents of tears over them, recommending them to the care and protection of the commanding officer." One young woman "cryed and roared when asked to come and begged to Stay a little longer." "Some, who could not make their escape, clung to their savage acquaintance at parting, and continued many days in bitter lamentations, even refusing sustenance." Children "cried as if they should die when they were presented to us." With only small exaggeration an observer on the Muskingum could report that "every captive left the Indians with regret."[20]

Another problem encountered by the English was the difficulty of communicating with the returned captives, a great many of whom had replaced their knowledge of English with an Algonquian or Iroquoian dialect and their baptismal names with Indian or hybrid ones.[21] This immediately raised another problem—that of restoring the captives to their relatives. Sir William Johnson, the superintendent of Indian affairs, "thought it best to advertise them [in the newspapers] immediately, but I believe it will be verry difficult to find the Freinds of some of them, as they are ignorant of their own Names, or former places of abode, nay cant speak a word of any language but Indian." The only recourse the English had in such instances was to describe them "more particularly . . . as to their features, Complexion etc. That by the Publication of Such descriptions their Relations, parents or friends may hereafter know and Claim them."[22]

But if several colonial observers were right, a description of the captives' physiognomy was of little help after they had been with the Indians for any length of time. Peter Kalm's foreign eye found it difficult to distinguish European captives from their captors, "except by their color, which is somewhat whiter than that of the Indians," but many colonists could see little or no difference. To his Maine neighbors twelve-year-old John Durell "ever after [his two-year captivity] appeared more like an Indian than a white man." So did John Tarbell. After thirty years among the Indians in Canada, he made a visit to his relatives in Groton "in his Indian dress and with his Indian complexion (for by means of grease and paints but little difference could be discerned)." When O. M. Spencer returned after only eight months with the Shawnees, he was greeted with a newspaper allusion "to [his] looks and manners, as slightly resembling the Indians" and by a gaggle of visitors who exclaimed "in an under tone, 'How much he looks like an Indian!'" Such evidence reinforced the environmentalism of the time, which held that white men "who have incorporated themselves with any of [the Indian] tribes" soon acquire "a great resemblance to the savages, not only in their manners, but in their colour and the expression of the countenance."[23]

The final English problem was perhaps the most embarrassing in its manifestations, and certainly was so in its implications. For many Indians who had adopted white captives, the return of their "own Flesh, and Blood" to the English was unendurable. At the earliest opportunity, after bitter memories of the wars had faded on both sides, they journeyed through the English settlements to visit their estranged children, just as the Shawnee speaker had promised Bouquet they would. Jonathan Hoyt's Indian father visited him so often in Deerfield, sometimes bringing his captive sister, that Hoyt had to petition the Massachusetts General Court for reimbursement for their support. In 1760 Sir William Johnson reported that a Canadian Indian "has been since down to Schenectady to visit one Newkirk of that place, who was some years a Prisoner in his House, and sent home about a year ago with this Indians Sister, who came with her Brother now purely to see Said Newkirk whom she calls her Son and is verry fond of."[24]

Obviously the feelings were mutual. Elizabeth Gilbert, adopted at the age of twelve, "always retained an affection toward John Huston, her Indian father (as she called him), for she remembered his kindness to her when in captivity." Even an adult who had spent less than six months with the Indians honored the chief who had adopted him. In 1799, eleven years after Thomas Ridout's release, his friend and father, Kakinathucca, "accompanied by three more Shawanese chiefs, came to pay me a visit at my house in York town (Toronto). He regarded myself and family with peculiar pleasure, and my wife and children contemplated with great satisfaction the noble and good qualities of this worthy Indian." The bond of affection that had grown in the Indian villages was clearly not an attachment that the English could dismiss as "unnatural."[25]

Children who had been raised by Indian parents from infancy could be excused perhaps for their unwillingness to return, but the adults who displayed a similar reluctance, especially the women who had married Indian men and borne them children, drew another reaction. "For the honour of humanity," wrote William Smith, "we would suppose those persons to have been of the lowest rank, either bred up in ignorance and distressing penury, or who had lived so long with the Indians as to forget all their former connections. For, easy and unconstrained as the savage life is, certainly it could never be put in competition with the blessings of improved life and the light of religion, by any persons who have had the happiness of enjoying, and the capacity of discerning, them." If Smith was struck by the contrast between the visible impact of Indian education and his own cultural assumptions, he never said so.[26]

TO FIND A SATISFACTORY explanation for the extraordinary drawing power of Indian culture, we should begin where the colonists themselves first came under its sway—on the trail to Indian country. For although the Indians were known for their patience, they wasted no time in beginning the educational process that would transform their hostile or fearful white captives into affectionate Indian relatives.

Perhaps the first transaction after the Indians had selected their prisoners and hurried them into cover was to replace their hard-heeled shoes with the footwear of the forest—moccasins. These were universally approved by the prisoners, who admitted that they traveled with "abundant more ease" than before. And on more than one occasion the knee-deep snows of northern New England forced the Indians to make snowshoes for their prisoners in order to maintain their pace of twenty-five to thirty miles a day. Such an introduction to the superbly adapted technology of the Indians alone would not convert the English, but it was a beginning.[27]

The lack of substantial food supplies forced the captives to accommodate their stomachs as best they could to Indian trail fare, which ranged from nuts, berries, roots, and parched corn to beaver guts, horseflank, and semi-raw venison and moose, eaten without the customary English accompaniments of bread or salt. When there was nothing to eat, the Indians would "gird up their loins with a string," a technique that at least one captive found "very useful" when applied to himself. Although their food was often "unsavory" and in short supply, the Indians always shared it equally with the captives, who, being hungry, "relished [it] very well."[28]

Sometimes the lessons learned from the Indians were unexpectedly vital. When Stephen Williams, an eleven-year-old captive from Deerfield, found himself separated from his party on the way to Canada, he "Hellowed" for his Indian master. When the boy was found, the Indian threatened to kill him because, as Williams remembered five years later, "the Indians will never allow anybody to Hollow in the woods. Their manner is to make a noise like wolves or any other wild creatures, when they call to one another." The reason, of course, was that they did not wish to be discovered by their enemies. To the young neophyte Indian this was a lesson in survival not soon forgotten.[29]

Two other lessons were equally unexpected but instrumental in preparing the captives for even greater surprises when they reached the Indian settlements. Both served to undermine the English horror of the Indians as bloodthirsty fiends who defile "any Woman they take alive" before "putting her to Death." Many redeemed prisoners made a point of insisting that, although they had been completely powerless in captivity, the Indians had never affronted them sexually. Thomas Ridout testified that "during the whole of the time I was with the Indians I never once witnessed an indecent or improper action amongst any of the Indians, whether young or old." Even William Smith admitted that "from every enquiry that has been made, it appears—that no woman thus saved is preserved from base motives, or need fear the violation of her honour." If there had been the least exception, we can be sure that this champion of civilization would have made the most of it.[30]

One reason for the Indians' lack of sexual interest in their female captives was perhaps aesthetic, for the New England Indians, at least, esteemed black the color of beauty.[31] A more fundamental reason derived from the main purpose of taking captives, which was to secure new members for their families and clans. Under the Indians' strong incest taboos, no warrior would attempt to violate his future sister or cousin. "Were he to indulge himself with a captive taken in war, and much more were he to offer violence in order to gratify his lust, he would incur indelible disgrace." Indeed, the taboo seems to have extended to the whole tribe. As George Croghan testified after long acquaintance with the Indians, "they have No [J]uri[s]diction or Laws butt that of Nature yett I have known more than onest thire Councils, order men to be putt to Death for Committing Rapes, wh[ich] is a Crime they Despise." Since murder was a crime to be revenged by the victim's family in its own way and time, rape was the only capital offense punished by the tribe as a whole.[32]

Captive testimony also chipped away at the stereotype of the Indians' cruelty. When Mrs. Isabella M'Coy was taken from Epsom, New Hampshire, in 1747, her neighbors later remembered that "she did indeed find the journey [to Canada] fatiguing, and her fare scanty and precarious. But in her treatment from the Indians, she experienced a very agreeable disappointment. The kindness she received from them was far greater than she had expected from those who were so often distinguished for their cruelties." More frequent still was recognition of the Indians' kindness to children. Thomas Hutchinson told a common story of how "some of the children who were taken at Deerfield, they drew upon slays; at other times they have been known to carry them in their arms or upon their backs to Canada. This tenderness," he noted, "has occasioned the beginning of an affection, which in a few years has been so rivetted, that the parents of the children, who have gone to Canada to seek them, could by no means prevail upon them to leave the Indians and return home." The affections of a four-year-old Pennsylvania boy, who became Old White Chief among the Iroquois, seem to have taken even less time to become "rivetted." "The last I remember of my mother," he recalled in 1836, "she was running, carrying me in her arms. Suddenly she fell to the ground on her face, and I was taken from her. Overwhelmed with fright, I knew nothing more until I opened my eyes to find myself in the lap of an Indian woman. Looking kindly down into my face she smiled on me, and gave me some dried deer's meat and maple sugar. From that hour I believe she loved me as a mother. I am sure I returned to her the affection of a son."[33]

When the returning war parties approached the first Indian village, the educational process took on a new complexion. As one captive explained, "whenever the warriors return from an excursion against an enemy, their return to the tribe or village must be designated by war-like ceremonial; the captives or spoils, which may happen to crown their valor, must be conducted in a triumphant form, and decorated to every possible advantage." Accordingly, the cheek, chin, and forehead of every captive were painted with traditional dashes of vermillion mixed with bear's grease. Belts of wampum were hung around their necks, Indian clothes were substituted for English, and the men and boys had their hair plucked or shaved in Indian fashion. The physical transformation was so effective, said a twenty-six-year-old soldier, "that I began to think I was an Indian." Younger captives were less aware of the small distance between role-playing and real acceptance of the Indian life-style. When her captor dressed Frances Slocum, not yet five years old, in "beautiful wampum beads," she remembered at the end of a long and happy life as an Indian that he "made me look, as I thought, very fine. I was much pleased with the beautiful wampum."[34]

The prisoners were then introduced to a "new school" of song and dance. "Little did we expect," remarked an English woman, "that the accomplishment of dancing would ever be taught us, by the savages. But the war dance must now be held; and every prisoner that could move must take its awkward steps. The figure consisted of circular motion round the fire; each sang his own music, and the best dancer was the one most violent in motion." To prepare for the event each captive had rehearsed a short Indian song on the trail. Mrs. Johnson recalled many years later that her song was "danna witchee natchepung; my son's was nar wiscumpton." Nehemiah How could not master the Indian pronunciation, so he was allowed to sing in English "I don't know where I go." In view of the Indians' strong sense of ceremonial propriety, it is small wonder that one captive thought that they "Seem[e]d to be Very much a mind I Should git it perfect."[35]

Upon entering the village the Indians let forth with some distinctive music of their own. "When we came near the main Body of the Enemy," wrote Thomas Brown, a captive soldier from Fort William Henry, "the *Indians* made a Live-Shout, as they call it when they bring in a Prisoner alive (different from the Shout they make when they bring in Scalps, which they call a Dead-Shout)." According to another soldier, "their Voices are so sharp, shrill, loud and deep, that when they join together after one has made his Cry, it makes a most dreadful and horrible Noise, that stupifies the very Senses," a noise that naturally frightened many captives until they learned that it was not their death knell.[36]

They had good reason to think that their end was near when the whole village turned out to form a gauntlet from the entrance to the center of the village and their captors ordered them to run through it. With ax handles, tomahawks, hoop poles, clubs, and switches the Indians flogged the racing captives as if to beat the whiteness out of them. In most villages, significantly, "it was only the more elderly People both Male and Female wh[ic]h rece[iv]ed this Useage—the young prisoners of Both Sexes Escaped without it" or were rescued from any serious harm by one or more villagers, perhaps indicating the Indian perception of the captives' various educability. When ten-year-old John Brickell was knocked down by the blows of his Seneca captors, "a very big Indian came up, and threw the company off me, and took me by the arm, and led me along through the lines with such rapidity that I scarcely touched the ground, and was not once struck after he took me."[37]

The purpose of the gauntlet was the subject of some difference of opinion. A French soldier who had spent several years among the northeastern Indians believed that a prisoner "so unfortunate as to fall in the course of the bastonnade must get up quickly and keep on, or he will be beaten to death on the spot." On the other hand, Pierre de Charlevoix, the learned traveler and historian of Canada, wrote that "even when they seem to strike at random, and to be actuated only by fury, they take care never to touch any part where a blow might prove mortal." Both Frenchmen were primarily describing the Indians' treatment of other Indians and white men. Barbara Leininger and Marie LeRoy drew a somewhat different conclusion from their own treatment. Their welcome at the Indian village of Kittanning, they said, "consisted of three blows each, on the back. They were, however, administered with great mercy. Indeed, we concluded that we were beaten merely in order to keep up an ancient usage, and not with the intention of injuring us."[38]

William Walton came closest to revealing the Indians' intentions in his account of the Gilbert family's captivity. The Indians usually beat the captives with "great Severity," he said, "by way of Revenge for their Relations who have been slain." Since the object of taking captives was to satisfy the Indian families who had lost relatives, the gauntlet served as the first of three initiation rites into Indian society, a purgative ceremony by which the bereaved Indians could exorcise their anger and anguish, and the captives could begin their cultural transformation.[39]

If the first rite tried to beat the whiteness out of the captives, the second tried to wash it out. James Smith's experience was typical.

The old chief, holding me by the hand, made a long speech, very loud, and when he had done he handed me to three squaws, who led me by the hand down the bank into the river until the water was up to our middle. The squaws then made signs to me to plunge myself into the water, but I did not understand them. I thought that the result of the council was that I should be drowned, and that these young ladies were to be the executioners. They all laid violent hold of me, and I for some time opposed them with all my might, which occasioned loud laughter by the multitude that were on the bank of the river. At length one of the squaws made out to speak a little English (for I believe they began to be afraid of me) and said, "No hurt you." On this I gave myself up to their ladyships, who were as good as their word; for though they plunged me under water and washed and rubbed me severely, yet I could not say they hurt me much.[40]

More than one captive had to receive similar assurance, but their worst fears were being laid to rest.

Symbolically purged of their whiteness by their Indian baptism, the initiates were dressed in new Indian clothes and decorated with feathers, jewelry, and paint. Then, with great solemnity, the village gathered around the council fire, where after a "profound silence" one of the chiefs spoke. Even a hostile captive, Zadock Steele, had to admit that although he could not understand the language spoken, he could "plainly discover a great share of native eloquence." The chief's speech, he said, was "of considerable length, and its effect obviously manifested weight of argument, solemnity of thought, and at least human sensibility." But even this the twenty-two-year-old New Englander could not appreciate on its own terms, for in the next breath he denigrated the ceremony as "an assemblage of barbarism, assuming the appearance of civilization."[41]

A more charitable account was given by James Smith, who through an interpreter was addressed in the following words:

My son, you are now flesh of our flesh and bone of our bone. By the ceremony that was performed this day, every drop of white blood was washed out of your veins. You are taken into the Caughnewaga nation and initiated into a war-like tribe. You are adopted into a great family and now received with great seriousness and solemnity in the room and place of a great man. After what has passed this day you are now one of us by an old strong law and custom. My son, you have now nothing to fear. We are now under the same obligations to love, support and defend you that we are to love and to defend one another. Therefore you are to consider yourself as one of our people.[42]

"At this time," admitted the eighteen-year-old Smith, "I did not believe this fine speech, especially that of the white blood being washed out of me; but since that time I have found that there was much sincerity in said speech; for from that day I never knew them to make any distinction between me and themselves in any respect whatever until I left them . . . we all shared one fate." It is a chord that sounds through nearly every captivity narrative: "They treated me . . . in every way as one of themselves."[43]

When the adoption ceremony had ended, the captive was taken to the wigwam of his new family, who greeted him with a "most dismal howling, crying bitterly, and wringing their hands in all agonies of grief for a deceased relative." "The higher in favour the adopted Prisoners [were] to be placed, the greater Lamentation [was] made over them." After a threnodic memorial to the lost member, which may have "added to the Terror of the Captives," who "imagined it to be no other than a Prelude to inevitable Destruction," the mood suddenly shifted. "I never saw . . . such hug[g]ing and kissing from the women and crying for joy," exclaimed one young recipient. Then an interpreter introduced each member of the new family—in one case "from brother to seventh cousins"—and "they came to me one after another," said another captive, "and shook me by the hand, in token that they considered me to stand in the same relationship to them as the one in whose stead I was placed."[44]

Most young captives assumed the places of Indian sons and daughters, but occasionally the match was not exact. Mary Jemison replaced a brother who had been killed in "Washington's war," while twenty-six-year-old Titus King assumed the unlikely role of a grandfather. Although their sex and age may not always have corresponded, the adopted captives succeeded to all the deceased's rights and obligations—the same dignities, honors, and often the same names. "But the one adopted," reported a French soldier, "must be prudent and wise in his conduct, if he wants to make himself as well liked as the man he is replacing. This seldom fails to occur, because he is continually reminded of the dead man's conduct and good deeds."[45]

So literal could the replacement become at times that no amount of exemplary conduct could alter the captive's reception. Thomas Peart, a twenty-three-year-old Pennsylvanian, was adopted as an uncle in an Iroquois family, but "the old Man, whose Place [he] was to fill, had never been considered by his Family as possessed of any Merit." Accordingly, Peart's dress, although in the Indian style, was "in a meaner Manner, as they did not hold him high in Esteem after his Adoption." Since his heart was not in becoming an Indian anyway, and "observing that they treated him just as they had done the old worthless Indian . . . he therefore concluded he would only fill his Predecessor's Station, and used no Endeavours to please them."[46]

When the prisoners had been introduced to all their new relatives and neighbors, the Indians proceeded to shower them with gifts. Luke Swetland, taken from Pennsylvania during the Revolution, was unusually feted with "three hats, five blankets, near twenty pipes, six razors, six knives, several spoons, gun and ammunition, fireworks, several Indian pockets [pouches], one Indian razor, awls, needles, goose quills, paper and many other things of small value"—enough to make him the complete Indian warrior. Most captives, however, settled for a new shirt or dress, a pair of decorated moccasins, and abundant promises of future kindness, which later prompted the captives to acknowledge once again that the Indians were "a[s] good as their word." "All the family was as kind to me," related Thomas Gist, "as if I had realy been the nearest of relation they had in the world." The two women who adopted Mary Jemison were no less loving. "I was ever considered and treated by them as a real sister," she said near the end of a long life with them, "the same as though I had been born of their mother."[47]

Treatment such as this—and it was almost universal—left an indelible mark on every captive, whether or not they eventually returned to English society. Although captives like Mrs. Johnson found their adoption an "unnatural situation," they had to defend the humanity of the practice. "Those who have profited by refinement and education," she argued, "ought to abate part of the prejudice, which prompts them to look with an eye of censure on this untutored race. . . . Do they ever adopt an enemy," she asked, "and salute him by the tender name of brother?" It is not difficult to imagine what effect such feelings must have had in -younger people less habituated to English culture, especially those who had lost their own parents.[48]

The formalities, purgations, and initiations were now completed. Only one thing remained for the Indians: by their daily example and instruction to "make an Indian of you," as the Delawares told Brickell. This required a steady union of two things: the willingness and gratitude of the captives, and the consistent love and trust of the Indians. By the extraordinary ceremonies through which they had passed, most captives had had their worst fears allayed. From a state of apprehension or even terror they had suddenly emerged with their persons intact and a solemn invitation to begin a new life, as full of love, challenge, and satisfaction as any they had known. For "when [the Indians] once determine to give life, they give every thing with it, which, in their apprehension, belongs to it." The sudden release from anxiety into a realm of affirmative possibility must have disposed many captives to accept the Indian way of life.[49]

According to the adopted colonists who recounted the stories of their new lives, Indian life was more than capable of claiming their respect and allegiance, even if they eventually returned to English society. The first indication that the Indians were serious in their professions of equality came when the adopted captives were given freedom of movement within and without the Indian villages. Naturally the degree of freedom and its timing depended on the captive's willingness to enter into the spirit of Indian life.

Despite his adult years, Ridout had earned his captor's trust by the third night of their march to the Shawnee villages. Having tied his prisoner with a rope to himself the first two nights, the Indian "never afterwards used this precaution, leaving me at perfect liberty, and frequently during the nights that were frosty and cold," Ridout recalled, "I found his hand over me to examine whether or not I was covered." As soon as seventeen-year-old John Leeth, an Indian trader's clerk, reached his new family's village, "my father gave me and his two [Indian] sons our freedom, with a rifle, two pounds of powder, four pounds of lead, a blanket, shirt, match-coat, pair of leggings, etc. to each, as our freedom dues; and told us to shift for ourselves." Eleven-year-old Benjamin Gilbert, "considered as the [Indian] King's Successor," was of course "entirely freed from Restraint, so that he even began to be delighted with his Manner of Life." Even Steele, a somewhat reluctant Indian at twenty-two, was "allowed the privilege of visiting any part of the village, in the day time, and was received with marks of fraternal affection, and treated with all the civility an Indian is capable to bestow."[50]

The presence of other white prisoners complicated the trust relationship somewhat. Captives who were previously known to each other, especially from the same family, were not always allowed to converse "much together, as [the Indians] imagined they would remember their former Situation, and become less contented with their present Manner of Life." Benjamin Peart, for example, was allowed the frequent company of "Two white Men who had been taken Prisoners, the one from Susquehanna, the other from Minisinks, both in Pennsylvania," even though he was a Pennsylvanian himself. But when he met his captive wife and infant son by chance at Fort Niagara, the Indians "separated them again the same Day, and took [his] Wife about Four Miles Distance."[51]

Captives who were strangers were permitted not only to visit frequently but occasionally to live together. When Gist suddenly moved from his adopted aunt's house back to her brother's, she "imajined I was affronted," he wrote, and "came and asked me the reason why I had left her, or what injury she or any of the family had done me that I should leave her without so much as leting her know of it. I told her it was the company of my fellow prisoners that drew me to the town. She said that it was not so far but I mite have walked to see them every two or three days, and ask some of them to come and see me those days that I did not chuse to go abroad, and that all such persons as I thought proper to bring to the house should be as welcom[e] as one of the family, and made many promises how kind she would be if I would return. However," boasted the twenty-four-year-old Gist, "I was obstinate and would not." It is not surprising that captives who enjoyed such autonomy were also trusted under the same roof. John Brickell remarked that three white prisoners, "Patton, Johnston, and Mrs. Baker [of Kentucky] had all lived with me in the same house among the Indians, and we were as intimate as brothers and sisters."[52]

Once the captives had earned the basic trust of their Indian families, nothing in Indian life was denied them. When they reached the appropriate age, the Indians offered to find them suitable marriage partners. Understandably, some of the older captives balked at this, sensing that it was calculated to bind them with marital ties to a culture they were otherwise hesitant to accept. When Joseph Gilbert, a forty-one-year-old father and husband, was adopted into a leading family, his new relatives informed him that "if he would marry amongst them, he should enjoy the Privileges which they enjoyed; but this Proposal he was not disposed to comply with, . . . as he was not over anxious to conceal his Dislike to them." Elizabeth Peart, his twenty-year-old married sister, was equally reluctant. During her adoption ceremony "they obliged her to sit down with a young Man an Indian, and the eldest Chieftain of the Family repeating a Jargon of Words to her unintelligible, but which she considered as some form amongst them of Marriage," she was visited with "the most violent agitations, as she was determined, at all events, to oppose any step of this Nature." Marie LeRoy's honor was even more dearly bought. When "it was at length determined by the [Indians] that [she] should marry one of the natives, who had been selected for her," she told a fellow captive that "she would sooner be shot than have him for her husband." Whether her revulsion was directed toward the act itself or toward the particular suitor was not said.[53]

The distinction is pertinent because the weight of evidence suggests that marriage was not compulsory for the captives, and common sense tells us that any form of compulsion would have defeated the Indians' purpose in trying to persuade the captives to adopt their way of life. Mary Jemison, at the time a captive for two years, was unusual in implying that she was forced to marry an Indian. "Not long after the Delawares came to live with us, at Wiishto," she recalled, "my sisters told me that I must go and live with one of them, whose name was She-nin-jee. Not daring to cross them, or disobey their commands, with a great degree of reluctance I went; and Sheninjee and I were married according to Indian custom." Considering the tenderness and kindness with which most captives reported they were treated, it is likely that she was less compelled in reality than in her perception and memory of it.⁵⁴

For even hostile witnesses could not bring themselves to charge that force was ever used to promote marriages. The Puritan minister John Williams said only that "great *essays* [were] made to get [captives] married" among the Canadian Indians by whom he was captured. Elizabeth Hanson and her husband "could by no means obtain from their hands" their sixteen-year-old daughter, "for the squaw, to whom she was given, had a son whom she intended my daughter should in time *be prevailed with to marry.*" Mrs. Hanson was probably less concerned that her daughter would be forced to marry an Indian than that she might "in time" want to, for as she acknowledged from her personal experience, "the Indians are very civil towards their captive women, not offering any incivility by any indecent carriage." An observer of the return of the white prisoners to Bouquet spoke for his contemporaries when he reported—with an almost audible sigh of relief—that "there had not been a solitary instance among them of any woman having her delicacy injured by being compelled to marry. They had been left liberty of choice, and those who chose to remain single were not sufferers on that account."⁵⁵

Not only were younger captives and consenting adults under no compulsion, either actual or perceived, to marry, but they enjoyed as wide a latitude of choice as any Indian. When Gist returned to his Indian aunt's lodge, she was so happy that she "dress'd me as fine as she could, and . . . told me if I wanted a wife she would get a pretty young girl for me." It was in the same spirit of exuberant generosity that Spencer's adopted mother rewarded his first hunting exploit. "She heard all the particulars of the affair with great satisfaction," he remembered, "and frequently saying, 'Enee, wessah' (this is right, that is good), said I would one day become a great hunter, and placing her forefingers together (by which sign the Indians represent marriage) and then pointing to Sotonegoo" (a thirteen-year-old girl whom Spencer described as "rather homely, but cheerful and good natured, with bright, laughing eyes") "told me that when I should become a man I should have her for a wife." Sotonegoo cannot have been averse to the idea, for when Spencer was redeemed shortly afterward she "sobbed loudly as [he] took her hand, and for the moment deeply affected, bade her farewell."⁵⁶

So free from compulsion were the captives that several married fellow white prisoners. In 1715 the priest of the Jesuit mission at Sault-au-Recollet "married Ignace shoetak8anni [Joseph Rising, aged twenty-one] and Elizabeth T8atog8ach [Abigail Nims, aged fifteen], both English, who wish to remain with the Christian Indians, not only renouncing their nation, but even wishing to live *en sauvages.*" But from the

Indians' standpoint, and perhaps from their own, captives such as John Leeth and Thomas Armstrong may have had the best of all possible marriages. After some years with the Indians, Leeth "was married to a young woman, seventeen or eighteen years of age; also a prisoner to the Indians; who had been taken by them when about twenty months old." Armstrong, an adopted Seneca, also married a "full blooded white woman, who like himself had been a captive among the Indians, from infancy, but who unlike him, had not acquired a knowledge of one word of the English language, being essentially Indian in all save blood."[57] Their commitment to each other deepened their commitment to the Indian culture of which they had become equal members.

The captives' social equality was also demonstrated by their being asked to share in the affairs of war and peace, matters of supreme importance to Indian society. When the Senecas who had adopted Thomas Peart decided to "make a War Excursion," they asked him to go with them. But since he was in no mood—and no physical condition—to play the Indian, "he determinately refused them, and was therefore left at Home with the Family." The young Englishman who became Old White Chief was far more eager to defend his new culture, but his origins somewhat limited his military activity. "When I grew to manhood," he recalled, "I went with them [his Iroquois kinsmen] on the warpath against the neighboring tribes, but never against the white settlers, lest by some unlucky accident I might be recognized and claimed by former friends." Other captives—many of them famous renegades—were less cautious. Charlevoix noticed in his travels in Canada that adopted captives "frequently enter into the spirit of the nation, of which they are become members, in such a manner, that they make no difficulty of going to war against their own countrymen." It was behavior such as this that prompted Sir William Johnson to praise Bouquet after his expedition to the Ohio for compelling the Indians to give up every white person, even the "Children born of White Women. That mixed Race," he wrote, referring to first-generation captives as well, "forgetting their Ancestry on one side are found to be the most Inveterate of any, and would greatly Augment their numbers."[58]

It is ironic that the most famous renegade of all should have introduced ten-year-old Spencer to the ultimate opportunity for an adopted captive. When he had been a captive for less than three weeks, Spencer met Simon Girty, "the very picture of a villain," at a Shawnee village below his own. After various boasts and enquiries, wrote Spencer, "he ended by telling me that I would never see home; but if I should 'turn out to be a good hunter and a brave warrior I might one day be a chief.'" Girty's prediction may not have been meant to tease a small boy with impossible delusions of grandeur, for the Indians of the Northeast readily admitted white captives to their highest councils and offices.[59]

Just after Ridout was captured on the Ohio, he was surprised to meet an English-speaking "white man, about twenty-two years of age, who had been taken prisoner when a lad and had been adopted, and now was a chief among the Shawanese." He need not have been surprised, for there were many more like him. John Tarbell, the man who visited his Groton relatives in Indian dress, was not only "one of the wealthiest" of the Caughnawagas but "the eldest chief and chief speaker of the tribe."

Timothy Rice, formerly of Westborough, Massachusetts, was also made one of the clan chiefs at Caughnawaga, partly by inheritance from his Indian father but largely for "his own Super[io]r Talents" and "war-like Spirit for which he was much celebrated."[60]

Perhaps the most telling evidence of the Indians' receptivity to adopted white leadership comes from Old White Chief, an adopted Iroquois.

> I was made a chief at an early age [he recalled in 1836] and as my sons grew to manhood they also were made chiefs. . . . After my youngest son was made chief I could see, as I thought, that some of the Indians were jealous of the distinction I enjoyed and it gave me uneasiness. This was the first time I ever entertained the thought of leaving my Indian friends. I felt sure that it was displeasing to the Indians to have three of my sons, as well as myself, promoted to the office of chief. My wife was well pleased to leave with me, and my sons said, "Father, we will go wherever you will lead us."
>
> I then broke the subject to some of my Indian relatives, who were very much disturbed at my decision. They immediately called the chiefs and warriors together and laid the plan before them. They gravely deliberated upon the subject for some hours, and then a large majority decided that they would not consent to our leaving. They said, "We cannot give up our son and brother" (meaning myself) "nor our nephews" (meaning my children). "They have lived on our game and grown strong and powerful among us. They are good and true men. We cannot do without them. We cannot give them to the pale faces. We shall grow weak if they leave us. We will give them the best we have left. Let them choose where they will live. No one shall disturb them. We need their wisdom and their strength to help us. If they are in high places, let them be there. We know they will honor us."[61]

"We yielded to their importunity," said the old chief, and "I have never had any reason to regret my decision." In public office as in every sphere of Indian life, the English captives found that the color of their skin was unimportant; only their talent and their inclination of heart mattered.

Understandably, neither their skill nor their loyalty was left to chance. From the moment the captives, especially the young ones, came under their charge, the Indians made a concerted effort to inculcate in them Indian habits of mind and body. If the captives could be taught to think, act, and react like Indians, they would effectively cease to be English and would assume an Indian identity.[62] This was the Indians' goal, toward which they bent every effort in the weeks and months that followed their formal adoption of the white captives.

The educational character of Indian society was recognized by even the most inveterately English captives. Titus King, a twenty-six-year-old New England soldier, spent a year with the Canadian Indians at St. Francis trying—unsuccessfully—to undo their education of "Eight or ten young [English] Children." What "an awfull School this [is] for Children," he wrote. "When We See how Quick they will Fall in with the Indians ways, nothing Seems to be more takeing in Six months time they Forsake Father and mother Forgit thir own Land Refuess to Speak there own toungue and Seemin[g]ly be Holley Swollowed up with the Indians." The older the person, of course, the longer it took to become fully Indianized. Mary Jemison, captured at the age of twelve, took three or four years to forget her natural parents and the home she had once loved. "If I had been taken in infancy," she said, "I should have been contented in my situation." Some captives, commonly those over fifteen or sixteen years old, never made the transition from English to Indian. Twenty-four-year-old Gist, soldier and son of a famous scout and Indian agent, accommodated himself to his adoption and Indian life for just one year and then made plans to escape. "All curiosity with regard to acting the part of an Indian," he related, "which I could do very well, being th[o]rougherly satisfied, I was determined to be what I really was."[63]

Children, however, took little time to "fall in with the Indians ways." Titus King mentioned six months. The Reverend John Williams witnessed the effects of eight or nine months when he stopped at St. Francis in February 1704. There, he said, "we found several poor children, who had been taken from the eastward [Maine] the summer before; a sight very affecting, they being in habit very much like Indians, and in manners very much symbolizing with them." When young Joseph Noble visited his captive sister in Montreal, "he still belonged to the St. François tribe of Indians, and was dressed remarkably fine, having forty or fifty broaches in his shirt, clasps on his arm, and a great variety of knots and bells about his clothing. He brought his little sister . . . a young fawn, a basket of cranberries, and a lump of sap sugar." Sometime later he was purchased from the Indians by a French gentleman who promptly "dressed him in the French style; but he never appeared so bold and majestic, so spirited and vivacious, as when arrayed in his Indian habit and associating with his Indian friends."[64]

The key to any culture is its language, and the young captives were quick to learn the Indian dialects of their new families. Their retentive memories and flair for imitation made them ready students, while the Indian languages, at once oral, concrete, and mythopoeic, lightened the task. In less than six months ten-year-old Spencer had "acquired a sufficient knowledge of the Shawnee tongue to understand all ordinary conversation and, indeed, the greater part of all that I heard (accompanied, as their conversation and speeches were, with the most significant gestures)," which enabled him to listen "with much pleasure and sometimes with deep interest" to his Indian mother tell of battles, heroes, and history in the long winter evenings. When Jemima Howe was allowed to visit her four-year-old son at a neighboring Indian village in Canada, he greeted her "in the Indian tongue" with "Mother, are you come?" He too had been a captive for only six months.[65]

The early weeks of captivity could be disquieting if there were no English-speaking Indians or prisoners in the village to lend the comfort of a familiar language while the captives struggled to acquire a strange one. If a captive's family left for their winter hunting camp before he could learn their language, he might find himself, like Gist, "without any com[p]any that could unders[t]and one word that I spake." "Thus I continued, near five months," he wrote, "sometimes reading, other times singing, never melancholy but when alone. . . . About the first of April (1759) I prevailed on the family to return to town, and by the last of the month all the Indians and prisoners returned, when I once more had the pleasure to talk to people that understood what I said."[66]

Younger captives probably missed the familiarity of English less than the adult Gist. Certainly they never lacked eager teachers. Mary Jemison recalled that her Seneca sisters were "diligent in teaching me their language; and to their great satisfaction I soon learned so that I could understand it readily, and speak it fluently." Even Gist was the recipient of enthusiastic, if informal, instruction from a native speaker. One of his adopted cousins, who was about five or six years old and his "favorite in the family," was always "chattering some thing" with him. "From him," said Gist affectionately, "I learn'd more than from all the rest, and he learn'd English as fast as [I] did Indian."[67]

As in any school, language was only one of many subjects of instruction. Since the Indians generally assumed that whites were physically inferior to themselves, captive boys were often prepared for the hardy life of hunters and warriors by a rigorous program of physical training. John McCullough, aged eight, was put through the traditional Indian course by his adoptive uncle. "In the beginning of winter," McCullough recalled, "he used to raise me by day light every morning, and make me sit down in the creek up to my chin in the cold water, in order to make me hardy as he said, whilst he would sit on the bank smoking his pipe until he thought I had been long enough in the water, he would then bid me to dive. After I came out of the water he would order me not to go near the fire until I would be dry. I was kept at that till the water was frozen over, he would then break the ice for me and send me in as before." As shocking as it may have been to his system, such treatment did nothing to turn him against Indian life. Indeed, he was transparently proud that he had borne up under the strenuous regimen "with the firmness of an Indian." Becoming an Indian was as much a challenge and an adventure for the young colonists as it was a "sore trial," and many of them responded to it with alacrity and zest. Of children their age we should not expect any less.[68]

The captives were taught not only to speak and to endure as Indians but to act as Indians in the daily social and economic life of the community. Naturally, boys were taught the part of men and girls the part of women, and according to most colonial sources—written, it should be noted, predominantly by men—the boys enjoyed the better fate. An Ohio pioneer remembered that the prisoners from his party were "put into different families, the women to hard drudging and the boys to run wild with the young Indians, to amuse themselves with bow and arrow, dabble in the water, or obey any other notion their wild natures might dictate." William Walton, the author of the Gilbert family captivity narrative, also felt that the "Labour and Drudgery" in an Indian family fell to "the Share of the Women." He described fourteen-year-old Abner Gilbert as living a "dronish Indian life, idle and poor, having no other Employ than the gathering of Hickory-Nuts; and although young," Walton insisted, "his Situation was very irksome." Just how irksome the boy found his freedom from colonial farm chores was revealed when the ingenuous Walton related that "Abner, having no useful Employ, amused himself with catching fish in the Lake. . . . Not being of an impatient Disposition," said Walton soberly, "he bore his Captivity without repining."[69]

While most captive boys had "nothing to do, but cut a little wood for the fire," draw water for cooking and drinking, and "shoot Blackbirds that came to eat up the corn," they enjoyed "some leisure" for "hunting and other innocent devertions in the woods." Women and girls, on the other hand, shared the burdens—onerous ones in English eyes—of their Indian counterparts. But Mary Jemison, who had been taught English ways for fifteen years before becoming an Indian, felt that the Indian women's labor "was not severe," their tasks "probably not harder than that [*sic*] of white wamen," and their cares "certainly . . . not half as numerous, nor as great." The work of one year was "exactly similar, in almost every respect, to that of the others, without that endless variety that is to be observed in the common labor of the white people. . . . In the summer season, we planted, tended and harvested our corn, and generally had all our children with us; but had no master to oversee or drive us, so that we could work as leisurely as we pleased. . . . In the season of hunting, it was our business, in addition to our cooking, to bring home the game that was taken by the [men], dress it, and carefully preserve the eatable meat, and prepare or dress the skins." "Spinning, weaving, sewing, stocking knitting," and like domestic tasks of colonial women were generally unknown. Unless Jemison was correct, it would be virtually impossible to understand why so many women and girls chose to become Indians. A life of unremitting drudgery, as the English saw it, could certainly hold no attraction for civilized women fresh from frontier farms and villages.[70]

The final and most difficult step in the captives' transition from English to Indian was to acquire the ability to think as Indians, to share unconsciously the values, beliefs, and standards of Indian culture. From an English perspective, this should have been nearly an impossible task for civilized people because they perceived Indian culture as immoral and irreligious and totally antithetical to the civilized life they had known, however briefly. "Certainly," William Smith assumed, "it could never be put in competition with the blessings of improved life and the light of religion."[71] But many captives soon discovered that the English had no monopoly on virtue and that in many ways the Indians were morally superior to the English, more Christian than the Christians.

As early as 1643 Roger Williams had written a book to suggest such a thing, but he could be dismissed as a misguided visionary who let the Narragansetts go to his head. It was more difficult to dismiss someone like Brickell, who had lived with the Indians for four and one-half years and had no ax to grind with established religion. "The Delawares are the best people to train up children I ever was with," he wrote. "Their leisure hours are, in a great measure, spent in training up their children to observe what they believe to be right. . . . [A]s a nation they may be considered fit examples for many of us Christians to follow. They certainly follow what they are taught to believe right more closely, and I might say more honestly, in general, than we Christians do the divine precepts of our Redeemer. . . . I know I am influenced to good, even at this day," he concluded, "more from what I learned among them, than what I learned among people of my own color." After many decades with them, Jemison insisted that "the moral character of the Indians was . . . uncontaminated. Their fidelity was perfect, and became proverbial; they were strictly honest; they despised deception and falsehood; and chastity was held in high veneration." Even the tory historian Peter Oliver, who was no friend to the Indians, admitted that "they have a Religion of their own, which, to the eternal Disgrace of many Nations who boast of Politeness, is more influential on their Conduct than that of those who hold them in so great Contempt." To the acute discomfort of the colonists, more than one captive maintained that the Indians were a "far more moral race than the whites."[72]

In the principled school of Indian life the captives experienced a decisive shift in their cultural and personal identities, a shift that often fostered a considerable degree of what might be called "conversion zeal." A French officer reported that "those Prisoners whom the Indians keep with them . . . are often more brutish, boisterous in their Behaviour and loose in their Manners than the Indians," and thought that "they affect that kind of Behaviour thro' Fear of and to recommend themselves to the Indians." Matthew Bunn, a nineteen-year-old soldier, was the object of such behavior when he was enslaved—not adopted—by the Maumee in 1791. "After I had eaten," he related, "they brought me a little prisoner boy, that had been taken about two years before, on the river called Monongahela, though he delighted more in the ways of the savages than in the ways of Christians; he used me worse than any of the Indians, for he would tell me to do this, that, and the other, and if I did not do it, or made any resistance, the Indians would threaten to kill me, and he would kick and cuff me about in such a manner, that I hardly dared to say my soul was my own." What Bunn experienced was the attempt of the new converts to pattern their behavior after their young Indian counterparts, who, a Puritan minister observed, "are as much to be dreaded by captives as those of maturer years, and in many cases much more so; for, unlike cultivated people, they have no restraints upon their mischievous and savage propensities, which they indulge in cruelties."[73]

Although fear undoubtedly accounted for some of the converts' initial behavior, desire to win the approval of their new relatives also played a part. "I had lived in my new habitation about a week," recalled Spencer, "and having given up all hope of escaping . . . began to regard it as my future home. . . . I strove to be cheerful, and by my ready obedience to ingratiate myself with Cooh-coo-cheeh [his Indian mistress], for whose kindness I felt grateful." A year after James Smith had been adopted, a number of prisoners were brought in by his new kinsmen and a gauntlet formed to welcome them. Smith "went and told them how they were to act" and then "fell into one of the ranks with the Indians, shouting and yelling like them." One middle-aged man's turn came, and "as they were not very severe on him," confessed the new Indian, "as he passed me I hit him with a piece of pumpkin—which pleased the Indians much." If their zeal to emulate the Indians sometimes exceeded their mercy, the captives had nonetheless fulfilled their new families' expectations: they had begun to act as Indians in spirit as well as body. Only time would be necessary to transform their conscious efforts into unconscious habits and complete their cultural conversion.[74]

"BY WHAT POWER does it come to pass," asked Crèvecoeur, "that children who have been adopted when young among these people, . . . and even grown persons . . .

can never be prevailed on to re-adopt European manners?"[75] Given the malleability of youth, we should not be surprised that children underwent a rather sudden and permanent transition from English to Indian—although we might be pressed to explain why so few Indian children made the transition in the opposite direction. But the adult colonists who became Indians cannot be explained as easily, for the simple reason that they, unlike many of the children, were fully conscious of their cultural identities while they were being subjected to the Indians' assiduous attempts to convert them. Consequently, their cultural metamorphosis involved a large degree of personal choice.

The great majority of white Indians left no explanations for their choice. Forgetting their original language and their past, they simply disappeared into their adopted society. But those captives who returned to write narratives of their experiences left several clues to the motives of those who chose to stay behind. They stayed because they found Indian life to possess a strong sense of community, abundant love, and uncommon integrity—values that the English colonists also honored, if less successfully. But Indian life was attractive for other values—for social equality, mobility, adventure, and, as two adult converts acknowledged, "the most perfect freedom, the ease of living, [and] the absence of those cares and corroding solicitudes which so often prevail with us." As we have learned recently, these were values that were not being realized in the older, increasingly crowded, fragmented, and contentious communities of the Atlantic seaboard, or even in the newer frontier settlements.[76] By contrast, as Crèvecoeur said, there must have been in the Indians' "social bond something singularly captivating."[77] Whatever it was, its power had no better measure than the large number of English colonists who became, contrary to the civilized assumptions of their countrymen, white Indians.

NOTES

1. See, for example, Samuel Purchas, *Hakluytus Posthumus or Purchas His Pilgrimes,* XIX (Glasgow, 1906 [orig. publ. London, 1625]), 19:406–409, and Merrill Jensen, ed., *American Colonial Documents to 1776,* in David C. Douglas, ed., *English Historical Documents,* IX (New York, 1964), 65, 82, 85, 93.

2. Robert Gray, A *Good Speed to Virginia* (London, 1609), sigs. [Clv]-C2r. See also Michael Wigglesworth, *God's Controversy with New-England* (1662), Massachussetts Historical Society, *Proceedings,* XII (1873), 57–68, 169; H. H. Brackenridge in Archibald Loudon, ed., *A Selection, of Some of the Most Interesting Narratives, of Outrages, Committed by the Indians, in Their Wars, with the White People,* I (Carlisle, Pa., 1808), 5; and [William Smith, D.D.], *Historical Account of Colonel Bouquet's Expedition Against the Ohio Indians, in 1764* (Cincinnati, 1868 [orig. publ. Philadelphia, 1765]), 77–78 (hereafter cited as *Bouquet's Expedition*).

3. Cotton Mather, *India Christiana* (Boston, 1721), 28–29. See also Solomon Stoddard, *Question, Whether God is not Angry with the Country for doing so little towards the Conversion of the Indians?* (Boston, 1723), 10.

4. *Bouquet's Expedition,* 80–81.

5. See my *The Invasion Within: The Contest of Cultures in Colonial North America* (New York, 1985), which explores both the Europeans who ran away to join Indian societies and the many reasons for the English and French failure to convert the Indians to civilization and Christianity. Consequently, and for reasons of length, both subjects are omitted from the present essay.

6. Cadwallader Colden, *The History of the Five Indian Nations of Canada* (London, 1747), 203–204 (1st pagination).

7. Benjamin Franklin to Peter Collinson, May 9, 1753, in Leonard W. Labaree et al., eds., *The Papers of Benjamin Franklin,* IV (New Haven, 1961), 481–82.

8. J. Hector St. John de Crèvecoeur, *Letters from an American Farmer* (London, 1912 [orig. publ. 1782]), 215. Other contemporaries who recognized the disparity between Indian and European conversion results were Pierre de Charlevoix, *Journal of a Voyage to North-America,* II (London, 1761), 108; Joseph Doddridge, *Notes on the Settlement and Indian Wars of the Western Parts of Virginia and Pennsylvania, from 1763 to 1783, Inclusive,* ed. Alfred Williams (Albany, 1876 [orig. publ. 1824]), 218; Adolph B. Benson, ed., *Peter Kalm's Travels in North America: The English Version of 1770,* II (New York, 1937), 456–57; Johann David Schoepf, *Travels in the Confederation [1783–1784],* trans. and ed. Alfred J. Morrison, I (Philadelphia, 1911), 283; J. P. Brissot de Warville, *New Travels in the United States of America, 1788,* trans. Mara Soceanu Vamos and Durand Echeverria, ed. Durand Echeverria (Cambridge, Mass., 1964), 420; John F. Meginness, *Biography of Frances Slocum, the Lost Sister of Wyoming* (Williamsport, Pa., 1891), 196; and Felix Renick, "A Trip to the West," *American Pioneer,* 1 (1842), 79.

Later students of the "white Indians" are John R. Swanton, "Notes on the mental assimilation of races," *Journal of the Washington Academy of Sciences,* XVI (1926), 493–502; Erwin H. Ackerknecht, "'White Indians': Psychological and Physiological Peculiarities of White Children Abducted and Reared by North American Indians," *Bulletin of the History of Medicine,* XV (1944), 15–36; A. Irving Hallowell, "American Indians, White and Black: The Phenomenon of Transculturalization," *Current Anthropology,* IV (1963), 519–31; and J. Norman Heard, *White into Red: A Study of the Assimilation of White Persons Captured by Indians* (Metuchen, N.J., 1973). All four draw upon western captives as well as colonial in a search for ethnological generalizations. See also Richard Drinnon's sensitive *White Savage: The Case of John Dunn Hunter* (New York, 1972).

9. This generalization is based on a reading of over 100 captivity narratives and accounts.

10. [William Walton], *The Captivity and Sufferings of Benjamin Gilbert and His Family, 1780–83,* ed. Frank H. Severance (Cleveland, 1904 [orig. publ. 1784]), 27 (hereafter cited as *Captivity of Benjamin Gilbert*).

11. [Susannah] Johnson, *A Narrative of the Captivity of Mrs. Johnson* [Walpole, N.H., 1796], reprint of 3d rev. ed. [1814] (Springfield, Mass., 1907), 36; Emma Lewis Coleman, *New England Captives Carried to Canada . . .* (Portland, Me., 1925), I:120–21, 132, II:159–60, 261; Samuel G. Drake, ed., *Tragedies of the Wilderness . . .* (Boston, 1846), 100, 168, 280.

12. This is not to say that no expense was involved for the English in securing the release of captive colonists, but it was in the nature of modest presents rather than exorbitant ransoms. Sylvester K. Stevens and Donald H. Kent, eds., *The Papers of Col. Henry Bouquet* (Harrisburg, Pa., 1941–43), XVII:28, 169, XVIII:182–84 (hereafter cited as *Bouquet Papers*).

13. In the 1770s Guy Johnson and George Croghan, both authorities on the Indians of the Middle Atlantic colonies, thought that the English prisoners had been "generally adopted" rather than put to death. "The Opinions of George Croghan on the American Indian," *Pennsylvania Magazine of History and Biography,* LXXI (1947), 157; "Guy Johnson's Opinions on the American Indians," ibid., LXXVII (1953) 322. See also Mary Jemison's remarks in James E. Seaver, *A Narrative of the Life of Mrs. Mary Jemison* [Canandaigua, N.Y., 1824], ed. Allen W. Trelease (New York, 1961), 46–47 (hereafter cited as *Life of Mary Jemison*). While older men and women could be ransomed from the Middle Atlantic tribes, most Indians who had adopted English children could not be persuaded to "sell [their] own Flesh and Blood," not even for "one thousand Dollars," as the Indian father of twelve-year-old Elizabeth Gilbert put it. *Captivity of Benjamin Gilbert,* 103, 107.

14. "Further Examination of Michael La Chauvignerie, Jun'r, 1757," in Samuel Hazard et al., eds., *Pennsylvania Archives,* III (1853), 306; "Examination of Barbara Liningaree and Mary Roy, 1759," ibid., 634; "Narrative of Marie Le Roy and Barbara Leininger, for Three Years Captives Among the Indians," *PMHB,* XXIX (1905), 417–20.

15. James Sullivan et al., eds., *The Papers of Sir William Johnson* (Albany, N.Y., 1921–62), XI:446, 484–91, 720–21, hereafter cited as *Johnson Papers*; *Bouquet Papers,* XVIII:253; William S. Ewing, "Indian Captives Released by Colonel Bouquet," *Western Pennsylvania Historical Magazine,* XXXIX (1956), 187–203. On his two-month journey to a conference with the western Indians in 1760, John Hays saw 23 English prisoners; at least 14 were children. Their average age was 10 years. Two other prisoners were women, one aged 22 and the other "A[l]most A Woman." *Pennsylvania Archaeologist,* XXIV (1954), 63–83.

16. *Johnson Papers,* XI:466, 728.

17. *Bouquet Papers,* XVII:51.

18. Ibid., 38; "Provincial Correspondence: 1750 to 1765," in Samuel Hazard et al., eds., *Register of Pennsylvania*, IV (1829), 390, hereafter cited as *Pa. Reg.; A Narrative of the Captivity of John McCullough, Esq.*, in Loudon, ed., *Selection of Some of the Most Interesting Narratives*, I:326–27; *Bouquet's Expedition*, 80.

19. "Provincial Correspondence," *Pa. Reg.*, IV (1829), 390–91; *Johnson Papers*, XI:496–98.

20. *Bouquet's Expedition*, 76, 80; *Johnson Papers*, XI:496–98; "Provincial Correspondence," 390; "Relation by Frederick Post of Conversation with Indians, 1760," *Pa. Archives*, III (1853), 742. I have translated Post's phonetic German spelling.

21. "Prisoners Delivered to Gov., by the Six Nations, 176," *Pa. Archives*, IV (1853), 100–101; *Johnson Papers*, XI:720–21; Coleman, *New England Captives*, I:323, II:58. In a "List of Prisoners deliv[ere]d up by the Shawanese Nations of Indians at *Fort Pit, 10th May 1765*," the following names were among those given for 14 captives who had been with the Indians from 2 to 10 years: Wechquessinah ("cant speak Eng[li]sh. knows not from whence taken"), Joseph or Pechyloothume, Jenny or Ketakatwitch, Wapatenaqua, and Nalupeia, sister to Molly Bird. *Johnson Papers*, XI:720–21. In an earlier list were Sour Mouth, Crooked Legs, Pouter or Wynima, David Bighead, Sore Knee, Sour Plumbs (*Bouquet Papers*, XVIII:248). It would be important to know if these names were given in derision to resistant, older captives, or in good humor to accepting, younger ones.

22. *Johnson Papers*, XI:812; *Bouquet Papers*, XVII:39–41.

23. Benson, ed., *Peter Kalm's Travels*, II:457; Coleman, *New England Captives*, I:296, II:11; O. M. Spencer, *The Indian Captivity of O. M. Spencer*, ed. Milo Milton Quaife, reprint of 1917 ed. (New York, 1968 [orig. publ. New York, 1835]), 168–69; Samuel Stanhope Smith, *An Essay on the Causes of the Variety of Complexion and Figure in the Human Species*, 2d ed. (New Brunswick, N.J., 1810 [orig. publ. Philadelphia, 1787]), 70n–71n. Seel also Bernard W. Sheehan, *Seeds of Extinction: Jeffersonian Philanthropy and the American Indian* (Chapel Hill, 1973), ch. 1, esp. 40–42; and Doddridge, *Notes on the Settlement and Indian Wars*, 91.

24. Coleman, *New England Captives*, II:91, 117–18; *Johnson Papers*, X:160, XI:728. O. M. Spencer's Indian father for "several years" paid him an annual visit. *Indian Captivity of O. M. Spencer*, 171.

25. *Captivity of Benjamin Gilbert*, 181; Thomas Ridout, "An Account of My Capture By the Shawanese Indians . . . [1788]," *Blackwood's Magazine*, CCXIII (1928), 313.

26. *Bouquet's Expedition*, 80–81.

27. Drake, ed., *Tragedies of the Wilderness*, 128; Stephen Williams, *What Befell Stephen Williams in his Captivity*, ed. George Sheldon (Deerfield, Mass., 1889 [orig. publ. Greenfield, Mass., 1837]), 5; John Williams, *The Redeemed Captive Returning to Zion* (Springfield, Mass., 1908 [orig. publ. Boston, 1707]), 14, 30.

28. Captivity narrative of Joseph Bartlett in Joshua Coffin, *A Shetch of the History of Newbury . . .* (Boston, 1845), 332; *An Account of the Remarkable Occurrences in the Life and Travels of Col. James Smith* [1799], in Howard Peckham, ed., *Narratives of Colonial America, 1704–1765* (Chicago, 1971), 82; Samuel Lee to Nehemiah Grew, 1690, *Publications of the Colonial Society of Massachusetts*, XIV (1911–13), 148.

29. *What Befell Stephen Williams*, 6; Drake, ed., *Tragedies of the Wilderness*, 61.

30. Charles H. Lincoln, ed., *Narratives of the Indian Wars, 1675–1699*, Original Narratives of Early American History (New York, 1913), 30; Drake, *Tragedies of the Wilderness*, 125, 145; Ridout, "Account of My Capture," 303; *Bouquet's Expedition*, 78; "Provincial Correspondence," *Pa. Reg.*, IV (1829) 390–91.

31. J. Franklin Jameson, ed., *Johnson's Wonder-Working Providence, 1628–1651*, Original Narratives of Early American History (New York, 1910), 150, 263; "Morrell's Poem on New England," *Collections of the Massachusetts Historical Society*, 1st ser., 1 (1792), 135.

32. Charles Thomson in Thomas Jefferson, *Notes on the State of Virginia*, ed. William Peden (Chapel Hill, 1955), 200; "Opinions of George Croghan," *PMHB*, LXXI (1947), 157. See also *Life of Mary Jemison*, 73, and Sylvester K. Stevens et al., eds., *Travels in New France by J. C. B.* (Harrisburg, Pa., 1941), 69.

33. Drake, ed., *Tragedies of the Wilderness*, 61, 115–16, 145, 158; Thomas Hutchinson, *The History of the Colony and Province of Massachusetts-Bay*, ed. Lawrence Shaw Mayo, II (Cambridge, Mass., 1936), 104n; Mrs. Harriet S. Caswell, *Our Life Among the Iroquois* (Boston, 1892), 53. See also *Life of Mary Jemison*, 47, 57, and Timothy Alden, ed., "An Account of the Captivity of Hugh Gibson . . . ," *Mass. His. Soc., Coll.*, 3d Ser. VI (1837), 153. The source of Hutchinson's information was Williams, *Redeemed Captive*. Jacob Lunenburg was bound so tightly on his captor's back that he was somewhat crippled for life. Coleman, *New England Captives*, II:215.

34. Johnson, *Narrative of the Captivity of Mrs. Johnson*, 62; [Titus King], *Narrative of Titus King . . .* (Hartford, 1938), 10; Meginness, *Biography of Frances Slocum*, 65. See also Peckham, ed., *Narratives of Colonial*

America, 89; Howard H. Peckham, ed., "Thomas Gist's Indian Captivity, 1758–1759," *PMHB,* LXXX (1956), 297; [Zadock Steele], *The Indian Captive; or a Narrative of the Captivity and Sufferings of Zadock Steele . . .* (Springfield, Mass., 1908 [orig. publ. Montpelier, Vt., 1818]), 68; Loudon, ed., *Selection of Some of the Most Interesting Narratives,* I:303–304.

35. Johnson, *Narrative of the Captivity of Mrs. Johnson,* 57–58; Drake, ed., *Tragedies of the Wilderness,* 129; King, *Narrative of Titus King,* 8.

36. *A Plain Narrative of the Uncommon Sufferings and Remarkable Deliverance of Thomas Brown, of Charlestown, in New-England,* 2d ed. (Boston, 1760), in *Magazine of History with Notes and Queries,* Extra Number No. 4 (1908), 8, 12; *The History of the Life and Sufferings of Henry Grace, of Basingstoke in the County of Southampton,* 2d ed. (London, 1765 [orig. publ. Reading, Eng., 1764]), 12. See also Peckham, ed., *Narratives of Colonial America,* 81; Peckham, ed., "Thomas Gist's Indian Captivity," *PMHB,* LXXX (1956) 298; Drake, ed., *Tragedies of the Wilderness,* 269, 272; and *Captivity of Benjamin Gilbert,* 56, 121.

37. Beverley W. Bond, Jr., ed., "The Captivity of Charles Stuart, 1755–57," *Mississippi Valley Historical Review,* XIII (1926–27), 66; "Narrative of John Brickell's Captivity Among the Delaware Indians," *Am. Pioneer,* 1 (1842), 46.

38. Stevens et al., eds., *Travels in New France by J C. B.,* 68; Charlevoix, *Journal of a Voyage,* I: 369–70; "Narrative of Marie Le Roy and Barbara Leininger," In *PMHB,* XXIX (1905) 409.

39. *Captivity of Benjamin Gilbert,* 56.

40. Peckham, ed., *Narratives of Colonial America,* 81. See also Alden, ed., "Captivity of Hugh Gibson," Mass. Hist. Soc., *Colls.,* VI (1837), 143; Loudon, ed., *Selection of Some of the Most Interesting Narratives,* 1:306; and *Life of Mary Jemison,* 44.

41. Steele, *Indian Captive,* 70–71; Johnson, *Narrative of the Captivity of Mrs. Johnson,* 66.

42. Peckham, ed., *Narratives of Colonial America,* 91–92.

43. Ibid.; "John Brickell's Captivity," *Am. Pioneer,* I (1842), 46; Johnson, *Narrative of the Captivity of Mrs. Johnson,* 68.

44. *Life of Mary Jemison,* 44–47; *Captivity of Benjamin Gilbert,* 107, 123; Loudon, ed., *Selection of Some of the Most Interesting Narratives,* 307; Peckham, ed., "Thomas Gist's Indian Captivity," *PMHB,* LXXX (1956), 299; Luke Swetland, *A Very Remarkable Narrative of Luke Swetland . . . Written by Himself* (Hartford, n.d.), 7–8.

45. *Life of Mary Jemison,* 46; King, *Narrative of Titus King,* 14; Stevens et al., *Travels in New France by J. C. B.,* 73. See also *Johnson Papers,* XIII:191, and Charlevoix, *Journal of a Voyage,* I:373.

46. *Captivity of Benjamin Gilbert,* 126–27, 135.

47. Swetland, *Remarkable Narrative,* 5; Peckham, ed., "Thomas Gist's Indian Captivity," *PMHB,* LXXX (1956), 299; *Life of Mary Jemison,* 47.

48. Johnson, *Narrative of the Captivity of Mrs. Johnson,* 67–68, 71, 76–77.

49. "John Brickell's Captivity," *Am. Pioneer,* I (1842) 44; *Bouquet's Expedition,* 78. The Canadian captors of Titus King told him that "I Should never go hum [home] that I was an Indian now and must be and Do as they Did." King, *Narrative of Titus King,* 14.

50. Ridout, "Account of My Capture," *Blackwood's Mag.,* CXXIII (1928); John Leeth, *A Short Biography of John Leeth* [Lancaster, Ohio, 1831], ed. Reuben Gold Thwaites (Cleveland, 1904), 28, hereafter cited as *Biography of Leeth; Captivity of Benjamin Gilbert,* 109; Steele, *Indian Captive,* 72.

51. *Captivity of Benjamin Gilbert,* 81, 83.

52. Peckham, ed., "Thomas Gist's Indian Captivity," *PMHB,* LXXX (1956), 301; "John Brickell's Captivity," *Am. Pioneer,* I (1842), 54. Joseph Bartlett also lived with other white captives while a prisoner in Canada (Coffin, *Sketch of the History of Newbury,* 332–33).

53. *Captivity of Benjamin Gilbert,* 74, 87, 124; Alden, ed., "Captivity of Hugh Gibson," Mass. Hist. Soc., *Colls.,* 3d Ser., VI (1837), 149. Women were not the only captives alarmed by the specter of forced marriage. When Thomas Gist was first brought to the Huron village where he was to be adopted, he was made to stand naked at a post for an hour "while the Indian Ladies was satisfied as to their sight. For my part," he recalled, "I expected they was going to chuse some of the likeliest of us for husbands, by their standing and looking so long at us in this condition" (Peckham, ed., "Thomas Gist's Indian Captivity," *PMHB,* LXXX (1956), 298).

54. *Life of Mary Jemison,* 52–53.

55. Williams, *Redeemed Captive,* 131 (my emphasis); Drake, ed., *Tragedies of the Wilderness,* 125, emphasis mine; "Provincial Correspondence," *Pa. Reg.,* IV (1879), 390–91.

56. Peckham, ed., "Thomas Gist's Indian Captivity," *PMHB*, LXXX (1956), 301; *Indian Captivity of O. M. Spencer*, 82, 120, 129.

57. Coleman, *New England Captives*, II:107; *Biography of Leeth*, 39–40; Orlando Allen, "Incidents in the Life of an Indian Captive," *American Historical Record*, 1 (1872), 409. The "8" used by the French in Indian words signifies "w," which did not exist in French.

58. *Captivity of Benjamin Gilbert*, 135; Caswell, *Our Life Among the Iroquois*, 54; Charlevoix, *Journal of a Voyage*, I:371; *Johnson Papers*, IV:620.

59. *Indian Captivity of O. M. Spencer*, 92–93.

60. Ridout, "Account of My Captivity," *Blackwood's Mag.*, CCXXIII (1928), 295; Coleman, *New England Captives*, I:21, 296, 325–26, II:190–91.

61. Caswell, *Our Life Among the Iroquois*, 54–55.

62. A. Irving Hallowell has coined the unwieldy term "transculturalization" to denote the process whereby individuals, rather than groups, are detached from one society, enter another, and come under the influence of its customs and values. "American Indians, White and Black," *Current Anthropology*, IV (1963), 519–31.

63. King, *Narrative of Titus King*, 17; *Life of Mary Jemison*, 57; Peckham, ed., "Thomas Gist's Indian Captivity," *PMHB*, LXXX (1956), 302.

64. Williams, *Redeemed Captive*, 37; Drake, ed., *Tragedies of the Wilderness*, 169–70.

65. *Indian Captivity of O. M. Spencer*, 129–91; Drake, ed., *Tragedies of the Wilderness*, 161.

66. Peckham, ed., "Thomas Gist's Indian Captivity," *PMHB*, LXXX (1956), 300–301.

67. *Life of Mary Jemison*, 48; Peckham, ed., "Thomas Gist's Indian Captivity," *PMHB*, LXXX (1956), 301.

68. Loudon, ed., *Selection of Some of the Most Interesting Narratives*, 1:307; *Indian Captivity of O. M. Spencer*, 65.

69. Renick, "A Trip to the West," *Am. Pioneer*, I (1842), 78; *Captivity of Benjamin Gilbert*, 98–100.

70. "Narrative of the Capture of Abel Janney by the Indians in 1782," *Ohio Archaeological and Historical Quarterly*, VIII (1900), 472; *Indian Captivity of O. M. Spencer*, 113, 117–18; Peckham, ed., "Thomas Gist's Indian Captivity," *PMHB*, LXXX (1956), 300; *Life of Mary Jemison*, 55–56.

71. *Bouquet's Expedition*, 81.

72. Roger Williams, *A Key into the Language of America* (London, 1643); "John Brickell's Captivity," *Am. Pioneer*, I (1842), 47–49; *Life of Mary Jemison*, 72–73; Douglass Adair and John A. Schutz, ed., *Peter Oliver's Origin & Progress of the American Rebellion: A Tory View* (San Marino, Calif., 1961), 5; Coleman, *New England Captives*, II:312. In 1758 four pro-English Delaware chiefs accused the English of treaty-breaking and hypocrisy. "We Love you more than you Love us, for when we take any Prisoners from you we treat them as our own children; we are Poor and we cloath them as well as we can, you see our own children are as naked as the first, by this you may see our hearts are better then your heart." "Journal of Frederick Post," *Pa. Archi.*, III (1853), 534.

73. "Further Examination of Michael La Chauvignerie," *Pa. Arch.*, III (1853), 306; *Narrative of the Life and Adventures of Matthew Bunn . . . 7th rev. ed.*, (Batavia, N.Y. [orig. publ. Providence, *ca.* 1796]), 11; Loudon, ed., *Selection of Some of the Most Interesting Narratives*, I:311; *Captivity of Benjamin Gilbert*, 112.

74. *Indian Captivity of O. M. Spencer*, 86; Peckham, ed., *Narratives of Colonial America*, 108.

75. Crèvecoeur, *Letters*, 214.

76. Ibid., 215; Charles S. Grant, *Democracy in the Connecticut Frontier Town of Kent* (New York, 1961); Richard L. Bushman. *From Puritan to Yankee: Character and the Social Order in Connecticut, 1690–1765* (Cambridge, Mass., 1967); Kenneth Lockridge, "Land, Population and the Evolution of New England Society 1630–1790," *Past and Present*, XXXIX (1968), 62–80; Gary B. Nash, *Quakers and Politics: Pennsylvania, 1681–7726* (Princeton, 1968); Kenneth A. Lockridge, *A New England Town, The First Hundred Years: Dedham, Massachusetts, 1636–1736* (New York, 1970); Edward M. Cook, Jr., "Social Behavior and Changing Values in Dedham, Massachusetts, 1700 to 1775," *William and Mary Quarterly*, 3d Ser. XXVII (1970), 546–80; Patricia U. Bonomi, *A Factious People: Politics and Society in Colonial New York* (New York, 1971); James A. Henretta, *The Evolution of American Society, 1700–1815: An Interdisciplinary Analysis* (Lexington, Mass., 1973); Kenneth Lockridge, "Social Change and the Meaning of the American Revolution," *Journal of Social History*, VI (1973), 403–439. Indeed, it may well be that the adults who chose to become Indians did so for some of the reasons that many of their countrymen turned to revolution.

77. Crèvecoeur, *Letters*, 215.

17

DRESSING FOR SUCCESS ON THE MOHAWK FRONTIER: HENDRICK, WILLIAM JOHNSON, AND THE INDIAN FASHION

Timothy J. Shannon

In the late seventeenth century, the Iroquois developed a complex set of diplomatic links with various British colonial governments that, together, were known as "the covenant chain." Though some scholars have questioned the true extent of Iroquois power—Daniel Richter's essay suggests why there are doubts—in fact throughout the colonial period savvy provincial authorities recognized that peace in the northern part of British America required friendship with the Iroquois.

Chief among those eager to cement close ties with these Indians was William Johnson, a trader, diplomat, and ambassador on the New York-Iroquois frontier who would eventually serve as the Crown's Superintendent of Indian Affairs for the northern colonies from the mid-1750s until his death in 1774. Johnson, well-versed in Indian ways, knew that he could not broker peace agreements on his own, and therefore worked closely with the Mohawk headman, Hendrick. The two men were masters of the diplomatic arts, with the linguistic and cultural skills to bridge the very real cultural divide between Iroquois and colonist.

Not least of those skills, as Timothy Shannon reveals here, was knowledge of dress, appearance, and deportment. In an eye-centered age, an age when Indian and European alike had elaborate "dress codes" by which to read another person, Johnson and Hendrick learned what people on the far side of the frontier wore, what that garb signified, and each man came to adopt at least some elements of the other's costume to demonstrate cultural breadth, flexibility, and understanding. Clothing thus became, as Shannon puts it, "an important means of cultural mediation." It signaled that the wearer wanted to find what the historian Richard White has termed "the middle ground," a place where alien peoples could meet, talk, and solve problems, where each party could express its desires and try to achieve its goals.

Over time, visual depictions of Johnson, Hendrick, and others involved in the cross-cultural conversation circulated in the Anglo-American world. Not only do these images introduce yet another rich source of evidence on the American encounter; they also, in Shannon's view, have much to say about the changing nature of colonial attitudes toward Indians, attitudes that, in time, would fail to show that any middle ground had ever existed.

DRESSING FOR SUCCESS ON THE MOHAWK FRONTIER: HENDRICK, WILLIAM JOHNSON, AND THE INDIAN FASHION

Timothy J. Shannon

IN THE MID-EIGHTEENTH CENTURY, colonist William Johnson and Mohawk leader Hendrick forged a partnership that dominated European-Indian relations in the Mohawk Valley of New York. Johnson, an Irish fur trader and merchant who settled in the region in 1738, served as New York's Indian agent from 1746 to 1751 and in 1755 became the British crown's first Superintendent of Indian Affairs. Hendrick, a Mohawk from the village of Canajoharie, had been active in European-Indian diplomacy since the late 1690s; by the 1740s he was the most widely recognized Indian leader in the northern colonies. Together, Johnson and Hendrick exerted a tremendous influence on the Covenant Chain, an alliance governing economic and diplomatic relations between the Iroquois confederacy and Great Britain's North American colonies.[1]

Visual images of Johnson and Hendrick provide insight into the roles they played within the Covenant Chain. In an early portrait, Johnson appears in a fine scarlet coat, green vest, and cravat—dress that declared his status as a colonial merchant and militia officer (see Figure I).[2] This portrait contrasts with another recorded by Cadwallader Colden, a New York councillor and contemporary of Johnson's. Colden attended a Covenant Chain treaty conference in Albany in August 1746, where he saw Johnson enter the city gates, "riding at the head of the *Mohawks*, dressed and painted after the manner of an *Indian* War Captain," followed by Indians "likewise dressed and painted, as is usual when they set out in War."[3] Such a dramatic scene offers a striking juxtaposition to the portrait of a staid, well-dressed colonial gentleman.

An impressive portrait of Hendrick dates to a visit he made to London in 1740, when he was about sixty years old (see Figure II). Hendrick appears in costume appropriate for the royal court: blue suit and cocked hat trimmed in lace, a ruffled shirt with long cuffs, and cravat. Tradition has it that King George II presented this outfit to him.[4] Hendrick holds a tomahawk in one hand and a string of wampum in the other,

SOURCE: *William and Mary Quarterly*, 3d Ser. 53 (1996), 13–42.

Figure I: Sir William Johnson (1715–1774) by John Wollaston, c. 1750, oil on canvas. *Collection of the Albany Institute of History and Art. Gift of Laura Munsell Tremaine.*

combining the attire of eighteenth-century English gentry with symbolic props of North American Indian diplomacy. Four years later, Dr. Alexander Hamilton, an Annapolis physician touring the northern colonies, provided a verbal description of Hendrick to complement this visual one. In Boston, Hamilton observed a procession of Indians attending a treaty conference. He noted that Hendrick and the other Indian leaders "had all laced hats, and some of them laced matchcoats and ruffled shirts."[5]

Scholars of material culture have long noted the importance of clothing in self-presentation. Costume and fashion provide what one cultural anthropologist has called "an expressive medium" through which individuals communicate with others.[6] Such factors as the color, fabric, and fit of the clothing, along with posture and manners, tell us about the wearer's social position, occupation, and elements of personal identity from religious beliefs to sexual preferences. In addition to keeping the body warm and dry, clothing may denote status, signify a rite of passage, or even convey spiritual powers. The importance of clothing to material culture therefore extends far beyond its utility to include a variety of expressive properties that may be manipulated by its wearer.[7]

Historians of the British-Atlantic world have applied these insights in studying the eighteenth-century consumer revolution. In England, the expansion of markets and consumer choices profoundly affected clothing fashion and the public's buying

Figure II: "The brave old Hendrick," anonymous engraving, 1755. *Courtesy of the John Carter Brown Library at Brown University.*

habits.[8] In North America, consumption of British manufactures increased dramatically after 1740, altering colonists' everyday activities and reshaping their notions of taste and refinement. Through goods and styles imported from England, provincial Americans imitated British consumers and cultivated new standards of gentility based on self-presentation.[9]

For the Indians of northeastern America, this consumer revolution had been under way since European contact. They too encountered expanding markets and new choices as they became increasingly dependent on European weapons, tools, and clothing. Indians adopted these goods when they found them technologically advantageous but valued then also for aesthetic properties, such as color and shape, and for ceremonial uses, such as mourning the dead, that Europeans were slow to comprehend. Indian consumers were selective and demanding, often haggling over prices and refusing inferior goods. In short, they engaged wholeheartedly in the consumer revolution, but on their own terms and in ways shaped by their cultural values and practices.[10]

Within this consumer revolution, both Europeans and Indians found uses for the expressive properties of clothing. As the portraits of Johnson and Hendrick indicate, costume played an important role in intercultural contact and exchange. The Mohawk Valley in which Johnson and Hendrick lived was a jumble of differing ethnicities and languages. Clothing helped the valley's inhabitants communicate in ways other than the written or spoken word. Apparel had been a popular trade good in the Mohawk Valley since the early seventeenth century. Under the Covenant Chain alliance, it acquired considerable importance as a tool of diplomacy. Indians and colonists gathered periodically in Albany to make speeches and renew the alliance that preserved peace and trade between them. Treaty participants exchanged presents, usually bundles of furs from the Indians and manufactured items from the colonists. Over the course of the eighteenth century, the Indians' presents remained small and symbolic, but the colonists' grew into substantial donations of material goods. Clothing included in such grants ranged from cheap woolens to fine linens, from such necessaries as shirts and blankets to ornamental ribbons, earrings, and beads. Europeans also presented Indians with weapons, liquor, tools, food, and even cash, but none of these items had the universal appeal and diversity of choice that clothing offered to Indian men, women, and children.[11]

Clothing helped the Mohawk Valley's inhabitants establish what Richard White calls a "middle ground" of cultural mediation. In White's study, middle ground both refers to a geographic region between the Mississippi River and the Appalachian Mountains and describes a culturally constructed space shaped by the rituals and customs that governed the fur trade and European-Indian diplomacy.[12] Clothing helped establish such a space in the Mohawk Valley. Through their participation in the consumer revolution, Indians and colonists there did more than simply imitate the fashions of English gentlefolk. They used trade goods to invent new appearances, new ceremonies, and a new, visual language by which they communicated in a diverse and contentious world.

Clothing provided an important means of cultural mediation in the Mohawk Valley because it endowed its possessor with a capacity for self-fashioning. Other assets, such as multilingual fluency and political connections, certainly helped overcome cultural differences, but the careers of Johnson and Hendrick prove the importance of looking the part as well. Costume, when used correctly, increased the cultural mobility of its wearer. Clothing was acquired more easily than a foreign language and changed more readily than a native accent. It provided people with constant opportunity to reinvent themselves from one audience to the next, to create new appearances, and to gain influence through participation in trade.[13] In the Mohawk Valley, no one manipulated these opportunities more skillfully than Hendrick and Johnson.

FROM THE PERSPECTIVE of London or Paris in the mid-eighteenth century, the Mohawk Valley divided North America into three distinct units: British to the east, Indian to the west, French to the north. In actuality, colonial and native populations did not neatly arrange themselves *in partes tres*. Albany, its population still predominantly Dutch, served as an eastern gateway to the region from the Hudson River. It was also a trading center for Indians who carried furs and goods between Canada and New York by way of Lake Champlain. The Mohawks inhabited two villages west of Albany: Tiononderoge, which Europeans called the "lower castle," and Canajoharie, the "upper castle." German, Irish, and Scots-Irish colonists lived near Tiononderoge, where the Schoharie River met the Mohawk; many of them were tenants of William Johnson and his uncle Peter Warren. Mount Johnson, Johnson's diplomatic and mercantile head-quarters, stood north of the Mohawk between the two Indian villages. Moving farther upstream, a traveler entered German Flats, settled by German Palatines in the 1720s. More Germans and Scots-Irish lived south of this region in Cherry Valley, near the headwaters of the Susquehanna River. Farther west, on the southeastern shore of Lake Ontario, a handful of British soldiers garrisoned Oswego, a post that attracted Indian and colonial traders throughout the Great Lakes region to its summer markets.[14]

Although far inland from major seaports, the Mohawk Valley's inhabitants actively engaged in the British-Atlantic economy. Indians and colonists ferried goods along the Mohawk River between Albany and Oswego.[15] Johnson lived in the mid-dle of this trade. To agents in New York City and London, he sent furs, along with wheat and peas grown by local farmers and ginseng gathered by Indians. He imported clothing, tools, weapons, and liquor for his storehouse, which he located to intercept Indians and colonists headed downstream to Albany.[16]

The goods that flowed into the Mohawk Valley had a pervasive effect on cultural identities there, allowing inhabitants to engage in behaviors and habits not normally associated with colonial frontier life. Johnson himself is an excellent example. By 1749, he had amassed a fortune large enough to live in the style of an English gentleman. On the Mohawk River, forty miles removed from the nearest colonial population cen-ter, he built a home "60 foot long, by 32 Wide two Story High, all Stone."[17] He pur-chased household slaves and servants and imported the luxuries that defined colonial gentility: books and newspapers, the *Gentleman's Magazine* from London, fine writ-ing paper and sealing wax, musical instruments, and prints.[18] In 1763, Johnson built his own Georgian-style mansion, Johnson Hall, to complement the baronetcy the crown awarded him during the Seven Years' War.[19]

Johnson was not the only Mohawk Valley inhabitant to indulge in imported goods. Traveling in the region in 1748–49, Swedish naturalist Peter Kalm encountered a world shaped by consumerism. While he found Albany overwhelmingly Dutch in character— its citizens spoke Dutch, had Dutch manners, and practiced Dutch religion—he qual-ified this observation with one telling remark: "Their dress is however like that of the English."[20] English clothing had managed to penetrate the insular world of Dutch Albany well in advance of English language or politics. Even more noteworthy are Kalm's observations on tea drinking, a practice he found almost universal among colonists. In the Mohawk Valley, he saw Indian women enjoying this new luxury as well. Johnson, recorded Kalm, said that "several of the Indians who lived close to the European settlements had learned to drink tea." Kalm, who criticized colonial women for drinking tea as hot as possible, added that "Indian women in imitation of them, swallowed the tea in the same manner." Johnson included tea, sugar, and teapots for "Chief Familys" among his Indian presents.[21] Tea drinking, a consumer activity by which colonial Americans commonly expressed their gentility, became an agent of cultural assimilation between Europeans and Indians in the Mohawk Valley.[22]

Clothing exchanged in the Mohawk Valley trade also challenged traditional cultural differences. Indians wore European clothing, but they did so in a distinctive way that contemporaries recognized as the "Indian Fashion."[23] Indian consumers rarely adopted European costume from head to foot, and they expressed strong distaste for tight-fitting clothing such as breeches and shoes. Instead, they traded for European cloth cut from the bolt, which they put to any number of uses. The coarse woolen blankets, strouds, duffels, and half-thicks that made up the bulk of this trade they arranged around their bodies as shirts, skirts, robes, and coats. Indian men also favored long linen hunting shirts, which they wore draped over the waist. On the lower body, Indians used European cloth as loincloths, leggings, and moccasins that left more skin exposed than Europeans considered proper. The Indian fashion favored certain colors and fabrics, and European traders adjusted their stock accordingly.[24] Johnson provided woolens in shades of blue, red, and black as well as flowered serge and striped calicoes in "lively Colours."[25]

The Indian fashion also adopted European goods for bodily decoration. Indians painted and tattooed their bodies with such traditional materials as bear's grease and natural dyes; they added to this mix with imported verdigris, which has a green pigment, and vermillion, which has a red. Objects of European origin became jewelry for the hair, nose, ears, and arms. Johnson listed glass beads, silver armbands, brass wire, and medals embossed with the British arms among his trade goods as well as buttons, buckles, lace, and brightly colored ribbons. Indians could incorporate these items into their dress with cloth-working tools provided by European traders: scissors, needles, thread, pen knives, and awl blades. Items for personal grooming included buckling combs and looking glasses.[26]

Indians of both sexes valued these European goods, but contemporaries noted gender differences in their tastes and habits. Kalm observed that women were not as quick to "clothe themselves according to the new styles," although he occasionally saw some wearing caps of homespun or "coarse blue broad-cloth" in imitation of colonial women.[27] Men frequently examined their decorations in mirrors and "upon the whole, [were] more fond of dressing than the women." Another indication of male immersion in fashion is Johnson's inclusion of ribbons, combs, razors, and looking glasses among the presents he made to warriors.[28] Johnson gave women and children blankets, shirts, and stockings earmarked in special sizes for them, and women adopted European items as jewelry. Richard Smith, a land speculator visiting the Mohawk Valley in 1769, recalled that some women wore "Silver Broaches each of which passes for a Shilling and are as current among the Indians as Money," while "the younger sort" of both sexes used "Bobs and Trinkets in their Ears and Noses, Bracelets on their Arms and Rings on their Fingers."[29]

A further distinction within the Indian fashion arose between the costumes of sachems and warriors. Johnson's account for presents he distributed during King George's War gives detailed portraits of the well-dressed sachem and the well-dressed warrior.[30] For example, on May 11, 1747, ten Senecas appeared at Johnson's home with news about Indian affairs. To nine of them Johnson gave a shirt, paint, and knives. To the tenth, whom he identified as "the Capt[ain]," he also gave paint and knives, along with "A Shirt very fine with Ruffles & ribon" and "A fine lac'd Hatt . . . with a Cockade."[31] The same account shows that Johnson distributed shirts, blankets, stockings, laps, ribbons, paint, combs, scissors, razors, and looking glasses to warriors, along with weapons and provisions. Sachems received many of these goods, but their presents always included a ruffled shirt, laced hat, silver medal, or fine coat. Presents for warriors—paint, razors, combs, ribbons, mirrors—emphasized bodily decoration for battle. Presents for sachems featured clothing—fine shirts, hats, and coats—appropriate for diplomacy (see Figures III and IV).

Judging from contemporary reports, Indians attending treaty conferences with Europeans observed this fashion distinction between sachems and warriors. Visitors in the Mohawk Valley recognized a visual difference between "the common sort" of Indians, who generally wore clothing limited to "a Shirt or Shift with a Blanket or Coat," and their leaders, who were more likely to "imitate the English Mode" and appear in hats, coats, and ruffled shirts.[32] Europeans viewed Indian costume in the same way that they looked at their own—as an indication of the wearer's place within a hierarchical social order. Coming from a culture that regulated colors and fabrics

Figure III: "Guerrier Iroquois," hand-colored etching, by J. Laroque, from Jacques Grasset de Saint-Sauveur, *Encyclopédie des voyages. . . .*, vol. 2: *Amérique* (Paris, 1796). *Photograph courtesy National Archives of Canada, C-003163.*

Grand Chef de Guerriers Iroquois

Figure IV: "Grand Chef de Guerriers Iroquois," hand-colored etching, by J. Laroque, from Jacques Grasset de Saint-Sauveur, *Encyclopédie des voyages...*, vol. 2: *Amérique* (Paris, 1796). *Photograph courtesy National Archives of Canada, C-003161.*

worn by different classes, Europeans interpreted the Indian fashion as a similar means of establishing social distinctions. A sachem who appeared at a public treaty meeting wearing a ruffled shirt, fine coat, and laced hat became the visual counterpart of the colonial gentlemen across the council fire. Even such novices to Indian affairs as Dr. Hamilton could readily distinguish sachems from "a multitude of the plebs of their own complexion" by analyzing their dress.[33]

Indians attached their own meaning to the European clothing they wore. Ethnohistorians and anthropologists have argued that Indians invested presents they received from Europeans with ideological value that often outweighed their utilitarian value. Beads and cloth of a certain color or shape, for example, represented physical or emotional well-being and gave spiritual wealth to their possessor. Presents received at a treaty council symbolized friendship between the giver and recipient, and Indians perceived them as material evidence of peace and goodwill.[34] The context in which Indians acquired European clothing thus shaped the way they used it: they might invest clothing presented to them at a treaty conference with a ceremonial significance that would merit saving and wearing it again on similar occasions. Such ideological value helps explain why Indian men were more likely than Indian women to dress in a distinctive fashion when among Europeans. Johnson's accounts reveal that he distributed clothing to sachems and warriors personally—often in one-to-one encounters—when going to war, honoring the dead, or entertaining friends. When he gave clothing to Indian women and children, he distributed it in much greater quantities and for more utilitarian reasons: on May 24, 1747, for example, he entered a debit in his accounts of £49.17.0 for "Cloathing for their [Indian warriors'] Women and Children being naked."[35] Under such circumstances, men were more likely than women or children to attach ideological value to their presents; warriors and sachems more often received clothing as a result of diplomatic ceremony than of simple need.[36]

Europeans and Indians recognized the peculiar type of costume known as the Indian fashion, but for entirely different reasons. Europeans distributed clothing in ways that allowed them to construct a visual sense of social difference and hierarchy among Indians. Indians incorporated this clothing into their dress for the decorative, ideological, and utilitarian value they attached to it. This blending of European goods with Indian custom enabled each side to interpret the clothing from its own perspective yet still use it as an agent of cultural exchange and mediation. The Indian fashion became part of the middle ground between Europeans and Indians in the Mohawk Valley. Because this fashion relied on the acquisition and distribution of material goods, individuals involved in European-Indian trade and diplomacy could manipulate it to their advantage. Johnson's and Hendrick's attention to self-presentation thus contributed to their power. Realizing that an impressive outfit, a well-orchestrated entrance, or a ceremonial presentation of a gift could speak volumes, Johnson and Hendrick used the nonverbal language of appearance to negotiate cultural borders.

HENDRICK'S LIFE BLENDED European and Indian experiences on the Mohawk Valley's middle ground. Born a Mahican sometime around 1680, he was adopted by the Mohawks as a child and converted to Christianity as a young man. The various names he used throughout his life attest to his cultural mobility. At an Albany conference in 1701, Hendrick signed his mark to the proceedings, and the colonial secretary penned "Teoniahigarawe alias Hendrik" alongside it.[37] When he visited the court of Queen Anne nine years later, Englishmen rendered his Indian name as "Tee Yee Neen Ho Ga Row" and attached to it the title, "Emperour of the Six Nations."[38] British records also identify him as King Hendrick and Hendrick Peters. Pennsylvania Indian interpreter Conrad Weiser knew him as "Henery Dyionoagon."[39] Each of these names reveals a different facet of Hendrick's reputation. "Tee Yee Neen Ho Ga Row" and "Dyionoagon" obviously had Indian origins. "Hendrick Peters," a name he most likely acquired at the time of his baptism, reflected his interaction with the local Dutch. "King Hendrick" carried the authority of an ambassador to royal courts and colonial governments.[40]

Englishmen often called Hendrick "king" or "emperour," but his interests and concerns were rooted in a much smaller world than such a title would indicate. He was one of the headmen of Canajoharie, the "upper castle" of Mohawks, located about sixty miles west of Albany. As a representative of Canajoharie at treaty conferences, he conducted land sales, presented grievances against trade and land frauds, and negotiated terms of war, alliance, and peace with European neighbors. Although his reputation reached throughout the northern colonies and across the Atlantic, Hendrick's perspective on European-Indian relations remained local, and his constituency rarely stretched beyond the perimeter of his village.[41]

Hendrick had a reputation for pride and stubborn independence that often frustrated colonial officials. European contemporaries called him a "politician," a term that implied opportunism, intrigue, and deceit in the eighteenth century, as it often does today. Johnson referred to him as "the Politician Hendrick." Peter Wraxall, Johnson's secretary, noted "the great Hendricks Political Talents." Thomas Pownall called Hendrick "a bold artfull intriguing fellow [who] has learnt no small share of European politics." Weiser, who grew up in Mohawk country, expressed a similar sentiment. He lamented that the Indians had become "apostates as to their Old Natural Principle of Honesty" and in the same sentence vented his distaste for "that Proud and Impudent Henery Dyionoagon." Even Dr. Hamilton, the touring physician from Annapolis, knew enough of Hendrick's reputation to call him "a bold, intrepid fellow."[42]

Hendrick's appearance blended European and Indian identities in a way that created a special category of Indian: the intercultural diplomat who learned European politics but remained independent of European control. Consider the earliest portrait of Hendrick, painted in 1710 when he and three other Indians visited Queen Anne's court. Two leading New Yorkers, Peter Schuyler and Francis Nicholson, sponsored this trip in an effort to win royal support for an expedition against Canada. Styling their native ambassadors "the Four Indian Kings," they introduced Hendrick as Tee Yee Neen Ho Ga Row, "the Emperour of the Six Nations." So that the Indians would make an appearance befitting their titles, Schuyler and Nicholson provided them with new clothing, including scarlet mantles trimmed in gold. At court, the Indians made a speech, most likely spoken by Hendrick, and the queen responded with presents including cottons, woolens, necklaces, combs, scissors, mirrors, tobacco boxes, and a sword and pair of pistols for each king. She also commissioned John Verelst to paint their full-length likenesses.[43]

Comparison of two of these portraits (see Figures V and VI) reveals Hendrick's emerging role as an intercultural diplomat. Both Indians appear in standard poses, wearing scarlet mantles. Each stands before a wooded background that includes an animal denoting his clanship (wolf, bear, or turtle). Several important differences set Hendrick, or Tee Yee Neen Ho Ga Row, apart from the others. Each king holds a weapon—gun, club, or bow—except Hendrick, who displays a wampum belt, a tool of diplomacy. Hendrick is the only king wearing the genteel costume of breeches and buckled shoes; the others wear hunting shirts draped over bare legs and moccasined feet. The portraits indicate that Hendrick's power is derived from his political skills rather than his martial talents.[44] These paintings were reproduced as prints and widely circulated in England and the colonies, making Hendrick's visage one of the most common images of an Indian in the British empire.[45]

Figure V: "Tee Yee Neen Ho Ga Row Emperour of the Six Nations," engraving by J. Simon after John Verelst, 1710. *Courtesy of the John Carter Brown Library at Brown University.*

The elements of an Indian diplomat's appearance are confirmed in the portrait done when Hendrick returned to London in 1740 (see Figure II). In this work Hendrick is the well-dressed sachem described in Johnson's accounts, wearing a laced hat, fine coat, and ruffled shirt. The influence of native custom on the Indian fashion is apparent in the tattooing on Hendrick's face. The wampum belt so prominently displayed in the 1710 portrait has been reduced to a single string held at the waist, and he now flourishes an impressive tomahawk in his right hand. While this portrait is more militant than the previous one, the most important element remains consistent: Hendrick's fine court dress.

Hendrick's costume added to his prestige and influence among Indians as well. Much of his power as a sachem rested on his ability to funnel goods from his European counterparts to his fellow villagers. In this capacity, the people of Canajoharie could not have asked for a more productive emissary. From 1701, when his name first appears in English records, until his death in 1755, Hendrick regularly attended treaty conferences and received presents from colonial and royal officials. His diplomacy played an important role in his village's livelihood. By the 1730s, Canajoharie faced a precarious existence: the fur trade had bypassed the village in the late 1720s with the construction of Oswego. At about the same time, the Albany magistrates who administered New York's Indian affairs turned their attention from the Mohawks to the

Figure VI: "Sa Ga Yeath Qua Pieth Tow King of the Maquas," engraving by J. Simon after John Verelst, 1710. *Courtesy of the John Carter Brown Library at Brown University.*

Canadian Indians who carried furs south from Montreal.[46] Missionaries in the region reported that Canajoharie's population declined as families "have gone over to the french Interest & settled in their Territories."[47] In this context of shrinking population and eroding economic independence, Hendrick's diplomacy helped sustain the village.

Hendrick's influence peaked between 1744 and 1755, precisely at the time when Canajoharie—because of a decreasing land base, warfare, and disrupted trade—was losing other means of support. In his own brand of shuttle diplomacy, Hendrick traveled beyond the Mohawk Valley to attend European-Indian councils in Montreal, Boston, New York City, and Philadelphia. These missions enabled him to tap into the flow of goods in the British-Atlantic economy and divert a larger share of them to his village. Before European audiences, he followed the Indian fashion. Costume enabled Hendrick to gain further access to European presents, which, when redistributed at Canajoharie, increased his standing among the villagers.[48] Dress, in short, helped preserve Hendrick's reputation abroad and at home, among Indians and Europeans.

Europeans who observed Hendrick's activities in the 1740s and 1750s often accused him of greed and extortion. Pownall, reporting on New York Indian affairs in 1753, believed Hendrick made himself rich through presents, taking "at different times above six hundred dollars of [New York governor] Mr. Clinton."[49] In 1745, New

York Indian interpreter Arent Stevens warned that Hendrick would not do business without "a promise of a handsom present" and advised his superiors always to provide the Mohawk sachem with more "than you gave him hopes of."[50] Weiser, conducting diplomacy in the Mohawk Valley in 1750, claimed that Hendrick offered assistance if Weiser would make him "a handsome Present."[51] The New York Assembly, aware of Hendrick's reputation for avarice, recommended that Governor Clinton privately present him with twenty Spanish dollars before ending an Indian conference in 1753.[52]

Hendrick, it seems, had become almost too European. When Weiser and Pownall complained of his familiarity with "European politics," they lamented the loss of honesty they associated with Indians they met in public councils. William Smith, the eighteenth-century New York historian, referred to sachems as blanket-clad republicans gathered in outdoor assemblies, like "the ancient orators of Greece and Rome."[53] Hendrick's willingness, and that of other sachems, to dress in genteel finery called to mind instead images associated with European courtiers. Such sachems might say one thing and mean another; they might deceive to further private ambition. These Indians wore clothing that reflected power rather than humility, intrigue rather than honesty. The Indian diplomat enjoyed greater mobility because his costume helped him move beyond his village into colonial council chambers and royal courts. Hendrick, like any other participant in the eighteenth-century consumer revolution, adapted himself to a changing world by taking part in it, and the goods he acquired expanded rather than limited his choices in presenting himself to others.

Hendrick's wide-ranging influence in the 1740s and 1750s represented a moment in European-Indian affairs in the Mohawk Valley when British goods had penetrated the region, but colonists and soldiers did not yet control it. During this time of mediation, the well-dressed sachem emerged as a model of Indian leadership. His dress incorporated European elements but did not symbolize submission to European authority. Once this period of accommodation passed, however, so too did this image of intercultural diplomacy.

The transition is evident in portraits of Hendrick published after his death. In them, he has lost his genteel costume and donned clothing and accoutrements that European artists more commonly attributed to Indians. A print published in London in 1756 presents him as one of the blanket-clad sachems William Smith likened to the orators of antiquity (see Figure VII). The transformation is complete in an 1847 lithograph entitled "Soi-En-Ga-Rah-Ta, or King Hendrick" (see Figure VIII). Here the facial scarring and tattoos visible in the 1740 portrait (see Figure II) have been grafted onto a much younger Indian warrior draped in an animal robe and bareheaded except for a scalplock decorated with feathers. Gone are the wampum, scarlet mantle, breeches, buckled shoes, cocked hat, ruffled shirt, and fine coat that Hendrick wore or carried in portraits completed during his lifetime. Gone, in short, is Hendrick the well-dressed intercultural diplomat, replaced by a nineteenth-century artist's stereotypical depiction of the nearly naked, noble savage.[54]

Hendrick the Sachem, or Chief of the Mohawks.
Etched from an Original Drawing.
Publish'd according to the Act March 8, 1756. by T. Jeffrys at Charing Cross.

Figure VII: "Hendrick the Sachem, or Chief of the Mohawks," etching published by T. Jeffrys, 1756. *Collection of The New-York Historical Society.*

HENDRICK'S COOPERATION WITH William Johnson in European-Indian diplomacy began during King George's War (1744–48). In 1746, Governor George Clinton appointed Johnson New York's Indian agent. By distributing presents and supplies, Johnson sponsored Mohawk raids on French colonists and their Indian allies. In his expense account between December 1746 and November 1747 he identified by name more than thirty Indians with whom he conducted this business. Hendrick's name appears in thirteen entries, eight more than any other. He received from Johnson a pair of boots, a laced coat, medicine, cash, and an unspecified "private present" as well as provisions, transportation, and entertainments for his friends, warriors, and dependents.[55]

After the war ended, Johnson and Hendrick continued their diplomatic partnership. In this Irish trader Hendrick found a supplier of goods for his village to replace the Albany Dutch, who now curried the favor of Canadian Indians. Johnson's mercantile business and political reputation profited from the relationship. As a merchant supplying the western fur trade at Oswego, he needed to preserve friendly relations with his Indian neighbors, and his success in this regard made him a favorite of Clinton and other royal officials. Indian diplomacy also provided Johnson with constant demand for his goods. The presents he distributed among Indians came from his own stock, and he charged the expense to the colonial treasury.

By the early 1750s, Johnson and Hendrick had become indispensable to New York's Indian relations. Johnson provided the Mohawks with goods, and they refused

Figure VIII: "Soi-En-Ga-Rah-Ta, or King Hendrick," colored lithograph by Sarony and Major, from Henry R. Schoolcraft, *Notes on the Iroquois* (Albany, 1847), frontispiece. *Photograph courtesy of Special Collections, Bird Library, Syracuse University.*

to treat with any New York official except him. His influence was obvious at a treaty conference convened in 1751. Johnson, who had recently resigned as the colony's Indian agent because the assembly refused to pay his expenses, declined the governor's invitation to the meeting. In Albany, Hendrick told Clinton "one half of Collo. Johnson belonged to his Excellency [Clinton], and the other to them [the Mohawks]." He then asked permission to send a messenger to Johnson, who attended after receiving the Indians' request.[56] At another conference three years later, Johnson and Hendrick reversed these roles. This time the Mohawks failed to show for an Albany conference called to address their grievances. They finally arrived after the governor prevailed on Johnson to secure their attendance.[57] In December 1754, Pennsylvania's colonial secretary Richard Peters enlisted Johnson's help in convincing the Mohawks to confirm a land deed in Philadelphia. Hendrick was reluctant to go at first, but he agreed after Johnson promised to "join, & back him here among the Six Nations."[58] Cooperation between Hendrick and Johnson enabled both to extend their reputations and cement their hold over Covenant Chain proceedings.

Through his involvement with Indian trade and diplomacy Johnson became interested in the Indians' material culture. Like many eighteenth-century gentlemen, he collected and displayed within his home "curiosities," objects he valued for beauty, craftsmanship, or rarity. These included wampum, bows and arrows, calumets, and Indian clothing. Other gentleman-collectors requested Johnson's assistance in procuring such items of Indian dress as beaver coats, moccasins, and belts.[59] A Continental army officer visiting Johnson Hall in 1776 noted many such artifacts, including "Trappings of Indian Finery" and "good old King Hendrick's Picture."[60]

Johnson's curiosities attested to his acquaintance with and influence among the Indians. Colden believed Johnson owed this influence to his "compliance with their humours in his dress & conversation." Johnson's secretary, Wraxall, noted that the Indians looked on his boss "as their Chief, their Patron & their Brother." Johnson himself wrote of his relationship with the Indians, "I am no Stranger to their Customs & Manners."[61] Red Head, an Onondaga sachem, thanked Johnson at a 1753 conference for speaking to the Indians "in our own way, which is more Intelligable to us, because more conformable to the Customs and Manners of our Fore Fathers."[62]

Johnson spoke to the Indians in their own way in actions and appearances as well as words. He made a constant effort to transact his business in the Indians' cultural context. No colonial agent was more successful in presenting himself in a pleasing and impressive manner. This ability extended far beyond Johnson's willingness to don Indian dress and war paint: he cultivated the art of self-presentation in various forms adapted to Covenant Chain treaty making. In staging entrances, conducting negotiations, and distributing presents, Johnson used material goods to create appearances that advanced his reputation among Indians and Europeans.

Johnson's success as an Indian agent began with his work as a merchant. Johnson, the primary supplier of manufactured goods between Albany and Oswego, commanded considerable business and dominated the Mohawk Valley trade.[63] Two lists of presents he distributed among the Indians illustrate the types of goods that flowed along this route.[64] They fall into six broad categories. The first is weapons and ammunition—rifles, pistols, hatchets, knives, swords, powder, shot, and flints—to assist the Indians in hunting and warfare. Second, the Indians received tools and wares for everyday tasks: kettles, frying pans, scissors, needles, awls, pen knives, fire tongs. Toys and novelties such as jews harps, hawks bells, looking glasses, liquor, tobacco, pipes, tea, and sugar make up a third category. In times of war and famine, Johnson provided a fourth category: grants of food, including cows, corn, bread, and peas. Fifth, he made occasional cash grants for influential sachems. Clothing, the sixth category, is the most diverse, comprising the manufactured items that shaped the Indian fashion, from such staple products as blankets and strouds to such finery as laced hats, ribbons, buttons, and beads.

Table I offers a closer look at some goods Johnson purchased for a treaty conference at his home in June 1755. All of the categories described above are represented except food, which Johnson distributed along with numerous other incidental gifts once the meeting convened.[65] As the table indicates, clothing made up by far the largest part of the purchase. It accounted for fifteen kinds of items and approximately 66.5 percent of the total value of the presents.

TABLE I: GOOD DISTRIBUTED BY WILLIAM JOHNSON AT A TREATY CONFERENCE, JUNE 1755

Item	Quantity	Value
Weapons and Ammunition:		
Long Knives, Sheathed	10 dozen	£ 6.0.0
Large Pistols	10 dozen	5.0.0
Gun Flints	3,000	5.5.0
Holland Gun Powder	9 kegs	8.0.0
Lead in Small Bars	2,000 lb.	45.0.0
Subtotal:		69.5.0
Tools and Wares:		
Brass Kettles	400	60.0.0
Frying Pans	50	12.10.0
Razors	10 dozen	7.10.0
Awl Blades	4 gross	2.0.0
Cups: 1 Gill	1 dozen	
1/2 Gill	2 dozen	8.10.0
Brass Wire	20 lb.	4.10.0
Subtotal:		95.0.0
Toys and Novelties:		
Looking Glasses	8 dozen	12.0.0
Jews Harps	24 dozen	3.0.0
Fine Wrought Pens	30 dozen	12.0.0
Hawks Bells	38 dozen	4.15.0
Buckling Combs	20 dozen	5.0.0
Pipes	1 case	
Tobacco	1,000 lb.	21.12.4
Subtotal:		58.7.4
Cash:		
Private Grants to Sachems		107.4.0
Subtotal:		107.4.0
Clothing and Bodily Decoration:		
Strouds	16 pieces	144.0.0
Blankets	8 pieces	72.0.0
Penniston	3 pieces	39.17.4
Garlix	6 pieces	40.0.0
Calico	8 pieces	26.0.0
Callamancoe	16 pieces	24.0.0
French Blankets	40	32.0.0
French Blankets, second size	40	20.0.0
French Blankets, third size	40	16.0.0
Flowered Serge	4 pieces	20.0.0
Gartering	20 rolls	7.0.0
Gimps	40 pieces	12.0.0
Vermillion	40 lb.	28.0.0
Worsted Clocked Hose	8 dozen	11.4.0
Worsted Clocked Hose, small	10 dozen	9.10.0
Private Presents—Stroud, Shirt, and Lap to Each Sachem	97	155.4.0
Subtotal:		656.18.4
Total:		£986.11.8

Source: *Johnson Papers,* 2:570–71

The sheer amount of goods supplied by Johnson could be misleading: quantity was not the only factor that contributed to his success. Indeed, any agent with resources from a colonial or royal treasury could dump goods in Indian laps. Critics of Albany's Commissioners of Indian Affairs often complained of just that: colonial officials saddled visiting Indians with wagon loads of goods, caring little for how the goods were presented or how the Indians got them home. Local merchants then traded rum to the Indians for their presents as they left the city, only to sell the goods back to them at "a dear rate" later.[66] Such conduct on the part of colonial officials indicated either stubborn ignorance or callous disregard for the ceremonial nature of gift giving.

Johnson, by contrast, exhibited a keen appreciation for the cultural dynamics of this practice. An account he kept during King George's War illustrates how he went about distributing presents. In Table II, all the presents of clothing Johnson made between December 1746 and November 1747 are classified by recipient. Warriors received items necessary to outfit war parties: paint, shirts, ribbon, gimps, caps, laps, hides, and snowshoes. Sachems received finery associated with the Indian fashion: laced hats, fine coats, ruffled shirts, and silver medals. Johnson gave strouds, hose, shirts, and other necessaries to the women and children of Indian men who went to war. Lastly, he clothed the dead by presenting black burial strouds to their relatives.

Women and children received most of the clothing Johnson distributed: they accounted for almost 69 percent of his total expenditure on clothing during this period. Outfitting warriors and sachems accounted for 16.3 percent and 12.5 percent

---

TABLE II: CLOTHING DISTRIBUTED BY WILLIAM JOHNSON AS INDIAN
PRESENTS, DECEMBER 1746–NOVEMBER 1747

	Number of Account Entries	Value	Number of Entries Greater Than £10	Percent of Total Expense
Clothing for Warriors (shirts, paint, ribbon, caps, laps, snowshoes, hides)	25	£149.8.7	3	16.3
Clothing for Sachems (laced hats, fine coats, ruffled shirts, silver medals)	15	114.11.0	2	12.5
Clothing for Families (blankets, strouds, hose, caps, laps, shirts, deerskins)	24	629.5.2	14	68.6
Clothing for the Dead (black burial strouds)	5	24.8.0	0	2.6
Total:	69	£917.12.9	19	100.0

Source: *Johnson Papers*, 9:15–31.

respectively and outfitting the dead only 2.6 percent. Johnson distributed presents to warriors and sachems in small quantities, usually valued at no more than £1 or £2 at a time, when they visited his home to share news or hold councils. The presents he gave to women and children involved much larger donations. Of the twenty-four entries for presents of this type, fourteen were for disbursements valued at £10 or more, and two top £100. By comparison, only three entries for warriors' presents and two for sachems' presents top £10. Presents made for outfitting the dead seem to have involved the most personal contact between Johnson and the recipient. Of five entries, none exceeded £10, and in two of them Johnson mentions the living recipient by name.[67]

Johnson selected his gifts according to the intended recipient, and he often presented these goods in person. In this sense, he owed his influence to his role as a distributor of Indian goods rather than as a mere supplier of them. Indians treated presents as tangible symbols of reciprocity and friendship; to them, peace and alliance could not be purchased by large, one-time donations of goods. Rather, they needed to be continually renewed and strengthened by the periodic exchange of presents. As Johnson explained it, in addition to large presents made at treaty conferences, the Indians "expect to be indulged with constant little Presents, this from the Nature of the Indians cannot be avoided & must be complied with."[68]

A large proportion of the goods Johnson distributed fell into the category of "constant little Presents."[69] The expense was staggering. By his own account, Johnson spent £7,177 on Indian presents during King George's War. Between March 1755 and October 1756, early in the Seven Years' War, he expended a total of £17,446.[70] His liberality caused friction with the New York assembly, which refused to reimburse him fully for outlays during King George's War. Johnson blasted the assembly for failing to help "defray from time to time the expences I am dayly obliged to be at in treating with all sorts of Indians—The well ordering of whom is of much more importance to the Welfare of His Ma[jes]tys Government than the whole act of governing the unruly Inhabitants [of New York]." On the eve of renewed Anglo-French hostilities in 1754, Johnson predicted disaster for New York because of the assembly's parsimony, noting that it had appropriated only "the miserable pittance of £170 [New] York Curr[en]cy P[er] Annum" for Indian presents.[71]

Johnson knew that the practice of gift giving required more than deep pockets. His greatest asset as an Indian agent was his penchant for ceremonial presentations of both himself and the goods he distributed. He had a flair for the theatrical that suited the pageantry of treaty making, as evidenced in his taste for spectacular entrances. His arrival at Albany in 1746 dressed as a Mohawk war captain is one example. Two years later, he staged another grand entrance, this time at Onondaga, the seat of the Iroquois confederacy. Johnson arrived at this treaty conference with a party of Indian and European attendants. On entering Onondaga, he found "all the Sachims & Warriours . . . stood in order with rested arms and fired a Volley, after which my Party returned the Compliment." That evening, he provided two feasts, one for the village's sachems and one for "the Warriours & dancers who I hope will be merry which is my greatest pleasure to make & see them so."[72]

In such instances, Johnson imitated, not Albany's Indian commissioners, but French Indian agents, whom he praised for always putting on a good show. Unlike the Albany Dutch, Johnson explained to Clinton in 1749, the French "observe a quite different conduct, much to their own advantage. . . . They never employ a Trader to negotiate any matters with the Indians but a Kings officer, who in whatever Rank or capacity is attended by a Retinue of Soldiers accordingly to denote his consequence[.] If he be but a Lieutenant or Ensign it is sufficient to command Respect from the Savages, who tho' somewhat warlike are actuated by their Fears at *a small appearance of Power.*"[73] Johnson cultivated this small appearance of power in his Indian negotiations not only through his dress but also through warriors and sachems who accompanied him and served as visual testimony of his influence. Such a retinue could not be secured or maintained without the liberal distribution of personal presents detailed in Johnson's accounts.

Johnson paid attention to the ceremonial nature of gift giving and particularly honored the Indians' condolence rituals. When a treaty conference began, Europeans and Indians usually exchanged condolence speeches to honor each side's recent dead. The Indians also expected and customarily received a present of black burial strouds. When colonial agents omitted these presents, Indians might delay negotiations or express anger than the proper ceremony had not been observed.[74] Johnson regularly complained that the Albany magistrates ignored this custom in treating with the Indians. "This ceremony is also attended with a great deal of form," he explained to Clinton in 1749. "It was always neglected in the late [Albany Indian] Commiss[ione]rs time, which gave the French an opportunity of doing it." To Weiser, Johnson wrote that the condolence ceremony was "always expected by the five Nations to be performed by Us, and [is] what th[e]y look much upon." As the evidence in Table II indicates, Johnson also made private condolence presents to Indians when requested.[75]

In distributing goods, Johnson never lost the opportunity to enhance his appearance as the Indians' friend and benefactor. At a conference in June 1755, Indians from several nations approached Johnson with three young men they claimed worthy to be sachems and asked him to "distinginish them with the usual cloathing." Johnson readily complied. His accounts show an entry from the same day for "3 Ruffled Shirts for 3 young Sachems."[76] Through such presentations, Johnson moved beyond merely supplying the Indians with goods to inserting himself into their rituals and identities. The Indians' consumer revolution redefined how a sachem was supposed to dress, and Johnson, through the manipulation of material goods, made himself a pivotal figure in those changing definitions.

Just as Hendrick appreciated the importance his European contemporaries attached to clothing, so Johnson understood the Indians' interpretation of presents. When Europeans bestowed presents, they believed the goods symbolized the recipients' submission to and dependence on a crown or colonial government. The Indians, on their part, perceived these presents as evidence of mutual regard between treaty participants. By making "constant little Presents" and observing ceremonial detail, Johnson recognized the important role goods played in the Indians' view of the Covenant

Chain. The Indians acknowledged his incorporation of their values by accepting him into their councils and naming him "Warraghiyagey," doer of great business.[77]

BETWEEN 1744 AND 1755, Hendrick and Johnson became the two most influential figures in the Covenant Chain. Their participation in treaty conferences was essential for preserving peace between New Yorkers and Indians. Each one, however, continued to operate independently of the other and for different reasons. Johnson pursued political influence and royal favor. Hendrick's perspective remained local, as he employed his diplomatic skills to acquire presents and restore Canajoharie's prominence in New York's Indian relations.[78] Both men made masterly use of the material culture of the other, manipulating goods associated with the Indian fashion to extend and preserve their influence on the Mohawk frontier.

Close examination of the careers of Johnson and Hendrick suggests the great potential of material culture methods to enlighten us about European-Indian relations. The Indian trade was not simply a matter of economics, of European supply versus Indian demand. Participants attached meaning to these goods beyond the utilitarian value of a new gun, a shirt, or a knife. The goods that passed between Europeans and Indians, like the rituals involved in their exchange, created a language of speech, deportment, and appearance that crossed cultural barriers. Today, Iroquois nations in western New York continue to receive bolts of cloth from the United States according to eighteenth-century treaty obligations. The federal government has offered to convert these grants into monetary payments, but the Iroquois have declined, explaining that the cloth's value as a symbol of their territorial and political sovereignty cannot be rendered in a cash equivalent.[79] Johnson's and Hendrick's use of clothing illustrated the ideological element in the material culture of European-Indian relations, which allowed both sides to express themselves in ways not typically recorded in treaty minutes.

NOTES

1. On the early life of William Johnson see Milton W. Hamilton, *Sir William Johnson: Colonial American, 1715–1763* (Port Washington, N.Y., 1976), 3–14, and James Thomas Flexner, *Lord of the Mohawks: A Biography of Sir William Johnson*, rev. ed. (Boston, 1979; orig. pub. 1959), 13–27. On Hendrick's early life see Hamilton, "Theyanoguin," in George Brown, ed., *Dictionary of Canadian Biography*, vol. 3: *1741 to 1770* (Toronto, 1974), 622–23. The best introductions to the Covenant Chain alliance are Francis Jennings, *The Ambiguous Iroquois Empire: The Covenant Chain Confederation of Indian Tribes with the English Colonies from Its Beginnings to the Lancaster Treaty of 1744* (New York, 1984), and Daniel K. Richter and James H. Merrell, eds., *Beyond the Covenant Chain: The Iroquois and Their Neighbors in Indian North America, 1600–1800* (Syracuse, N.Y., 1987). William Johnson's and Hendrick's careers in the 1740s and 1750s are examined in Jennings, *Empire of Fortune: Crowns, Colonies, and Tribes in the Seven Years War in America* (New York, 1988), 71–108, and Richard Aquila, *The Iroquois Restoration: Iroquois Diplomacy on the Colonial Frontier, 1701–1754* (Detroit, 1983), 85–112. I would also like to thank Dan Murphy of Hanover College for allowing me to read his unpublished paper on Johnson's and Hendrick's diplomatic partnership. For a recent study of the Iroquois confederacy during the 17th and early 18th centuries see Richter, *The Ordeal of the Longhouse: The Peoples of the Iroquois League in the Era of European Colonization* (Chapel Hill, 1992).

2. In a letter to his father, Johnson complained about his appearance in this portrait. He wrote, "The Drapery I would have altered . . . the greatest fault in it is, the narrow hanging Shoulders, w[hic]h I beg you

may get altered as Mine are verry broad and square." These comments are indicative of the careful attention he paid to dress and appearance whenever presenting himself to an audience. See Johnson to Christopher Johnson, Oct. 31, 1754, in *The Papers of Sir William Johnson*, 14 vols., ed. James Sullivan, Alexander C. Flick, Milton W. Hamilton, and Albert B. Corey (Albany, 1921–1962), 1: 931. On the costume of an 18th-century English gentleman see James Laver, *The Concise History of Costume and Fashion* (New York, 1969), 134–38.

3. [New York], *A Treaty between his Excellency . . . George Clinton . . . And the Six . . . Nations* (New York, 1746), 8. Alice Mapelsden Keys attributed the authorship of this pamphlet to Colden in *Cadwallader Colden: A Representative Eighteenth Century Official* (New York, 1906), 155–57.

4. This anonymous portrait, in all likelihood completed during Hendrick's last trip to London in 1740, was published as a print after his death in 1755. His clothes match a description Anne Grant made of clothing worn by Henrick's son when she encountered him in 1760; Grant, *Memoirs of an American Lady, with Sketches of Manners and Scenes in America as They Existed Previous to the Revolution* (1808), 2 vols. (New York, 1901), 1: 62, 2: 57–58. Also see R. W. G. Vail, "Portraits of 'The Four Indian Kings of Canada,' A Bibliographical Footnote," in *To Doctor R.: Essays Here Collected and Published in Honor of the Seventieth Birthday of Dr. A. S. W. Rosenbach, July 22, 1946,* comp. Percy E. Lawler et al. (Philadelphia, 1946), 218–26.

5. Carl Bridenbaugh, ed., *Gentleman's Progress: The Itinerarium of Dr. Alexander Hamilton, 1744* (Chapel Hill, 1948), 112.

6. Grant McCracken, *Culture and Consumption: New Approaches to the Symbolic Character of Consumer Goods and Activities* (Bloomington, Ind., 1988), 57–58.

7. See Fred Davis, *Fashion, Culture, and Identity* (Chicago, 1992), Joanne Finkelstein, *The Fashioned Self* (Philadelphia, 1991), and Alison Lurie, *The Language of Clothes* (New York, 1981).

8. See Neil McKendrick, "The Commercialization of Fashion," in McKendrick, John Brewer, and J. H. Plumb, eds., *The Birth of a Consumer Society: The Commercialization of Eighteenth-Century England* (Bloomington, Ind., 1982), 34–99, and McCracken, *Culture and Consumption*, 16–22.

9. The literature on the 18th-century consumer revolution in the British-Atlantic empire has been growing in recent years. See especially Richard L. Bushman, *The Refinement of America: Persons, Houses, Cities* (New York, 1992), Carole Shammas, *The Pre-industrial Consumer in England and America* (Oxford, 1990), and T. H. Breen, "'Baubles of Britain': The American and Consumer Revolutions of the Eighteenth Century," *Past and Present,* no. 119 (1988), 73–104, and "An Empire of Goods: The Anglicization of Colonial America, 1690–1776," *Journal of British Studies,* 25 (1986), 467–99.

10. James Axtell looked at the consumer revolution from the Indians' perspective in "The First Consumer Revolution," in *Beyond 1492: Encounters in Colonial America* (Oxford, 1992), 125–51. For the Indians' adaptive response to European goods see Richter, *Ordeal of the Longhouse,* 75–104, and James H. Merrell, *The Indians' New World: Catawbas and Their Neighbors from European Contact through the Era of Removal* (Chapel Hill, 1989), 32–34. On the Indians' role as consumers see Arthur J. Ray, "Indians as Consumers in the Eighteenth Century," in Carol M. Judd and Ray, eds., *Old Trails and New Directions: Papers of the Third North American Fur Trade Conference* (Toronto, 1980), 255–71. For analysis of the ideological meanings that Indians invested in European trade goods see Christopher L. Miller and George R. Hamell, "A New Perspective on Indian-White Contact: Cultural Symbols and Colonial Trade," *Journal of American History,* 73 (1986), 311–28.

11. A classic study of the role of presents in 18th-century European-Indian diplomacy is Wilbur R. Jacobs, *Diplomacy and Indian Gifts: Anglo-French Rivalry along the Ohio and Northwest Frontiers, 1748–1763* (Stanford, Calif., 1950). For more recent discussions of the cultural context of gift giving see Richard White, *The Middle Ground: Indians, Empires, and Republics in the Great Lakes Region, 1650–1815* (Cambridge, 1991), 94–119, Richter, *Ordeal of the Longhouse,* 47–48, and Merrell, *Indians' New World,* 149–50.

12. White, *Middle Ground,* 50–93.

13. Jonathan Prude has noted that in the commercial culture of 18th-century America contemporaries worried that people would use new consumer goods to create "masks" for themselves—purposely deceptive appearances that enabled them to project status or attributes they did not possess. See Prude, "To Look Upon the 'Lower Sort': Runaway Ads and the Appearance of Unfree Laborers in America, 1750–1800," *JAH,* 78 (1991), 127. A similar theme was apparent in the colonists' concern over impressions they left on British army officers who witnessed colonial consumption of British goods during the Seven Years' War. See Breen, "Narrative of Commercial Life: Consumption, Ideology, and Community on the Eve of the American Revolution," *William and Mary Quarterly,* 3d Ser., 50 (1993), 471–501.

14. For descriptions of the 18th-century Mohawk Valley see William Smith, *The History of the Late Province of New-York* . . . , 2 vols., in New-York Historical Society, *Collections*, 4–5 (1829–30), I: 264–66, and T[homas] Pownall, *A Topographical Description of the Dominions of the United States of America* . . . (1776), ed. Lois Mulkearn (Pittsburgh, 1949), 33–38. For a good introduction to this region during the colonial era see Thomas E. Burke, Jr., *Mohawk Frontier: The Dutch Community of Schenectady, New York, 1661–1710* (Ithaca, 1991).

15. An excellent brief description of the Mohawk Valley trade may be found in Lewis Evans, *An Analysis of a General Map of the Middle British Colonies in America* . . . (Philadelphia, 1755), 20, reprinted in Lawrence Henry Gipson, *Lewis Evans* (Philadelphia, 1939), 41–76.

16. See Johnson to Peter Warren, May 20, 1739; Johnson to Capt. Ross, May 30, 1749; Samuel and William Baker to Johnson, Jan. 22, 1749/50; and Johnson to the Bakers, Sept. 12, 1751, *Johnson Papers*, 1: 4–7, 229–30, 259–60, 346–47.

17. Johnson to Samuel and William Baker, Dec. 31, 1748, ibid., 198.

18. Johnson to Capt. Ross, May 30, 1749, and Johnson to Samuel and William Baker, Feb. 19, 1749/50, ibid., 229–30, 264–65.

19. On Johnson Hall see Hamilton, *William Johnson*, 311–19. On the symbolic import of the Georgian mansion to 18th-century notions of gentility see Bushman, *Refinement of America*, 3–25.

20. See Adolph B. Benson, ed., *Peter Kalm's Travels in North America: The English Translation of 1770*, 2 vols. (New York, 1937), 1: 343. On the insular quality of colonial Albany see Patricia U. Bonomi, *A Factious People: Politics and Society in Colonial New York* (New York, 1971), 39–48, and Stefan Bielinski, "The People of Colonial Albany, 1650–1800: The Profile of a Community," in William Pencak and Conrad Edick Wright, eds., *Authority and Resistance in Early New York* (New York, 1988), 1–26.

21. Benson, ed., *Peter Kalm's Travel in North America*, 1: 190–91. On Johnson's use of tea and related items in Indian presents see *Johnson Papers*, 2: 576, 587, 618.

22. Archaeological evidence from the site of the Indians' chapel at Fort Hunter includes teapots, teacups, and saucers, indicating that "the tea ceremony was a ritual adopted by members of the eighteenth century community at this site"; Keith Moody and Charles L. Fisher, "Archaeological Evidence of the Colonial Occupation at Schoharie Crossing State Historic Site, Montgomery County, New York," *The Bulletin: Journal of the New York State Archaeological Association*, no. 99 (1989), 8.

23. For descriptions of the "Indian Fashion" by Mohawk Valley visitors see Mark E. Lender and James Kirby Martin, eds., *Citizen Soldier: The Revolutionary War Journal of Joseph Bloomfield* (Newark, N. J., 1982), 91; Richard Smith, *A Tour of Four Great Rivers: The Hudson, the Mohawk, the Susquehanna, and the Delaware in 1769*, ed. Francis W. Halsey (Fleischmanns, N.Y., 1989; orig. pub. 1906), 149–50; Grant, *Memoirs of an American Lady*, 2: 58; "Journal of Tench Tilghman," in Samuel A. Harrison, ed., *Memoir of Lieut. Col. Tench Tilghman, Secretary and Aid to Washington* . . . (Albany, 1876), 87.

24. For the Indians' use of European cloth see Axtell, *The European and the Indian: Essays in the Ethnohistory of Colonial North America* (New York, 1981), 57–59, 254–55, and Richter, *Ordeal of the Longhouse*, 79–84.

25. See *Johnson Papers*, 2: 898–900.

26. Ibid.

27. Benson, ed., *Peter Kalm's Travels in North America*, 2: 560, 520–21.

28. See Johnson's account for presents distributed during King George's War, in *Johnson Papers*, 9: 15–31.

29. See Richard Smith, *Tour of Four Great Rivers*, 134–35, 149–50.

30. See *Johnson Papers*, 9: 15–31. This account covers Johnson's expenditures as New York's Indian agent from Dec. 13, 1746, to Nov. 7, 1747.

31. Ibid., 23.

32. Richard Smith, *Tour of Four Great Rivers*, 149–50.

33. Bridenbaugh, ed., *Gentleman's Progress*, 112.

34. See Miller and Hamell, "New Perspective on Indian-White Contact," 316–18, White, *Middle Ground*, 99–112, and George R. Hamell, "Strawberries, Floating Islands, and Rabbit Captains: Mythical Realities and European Contact in the Northeast during the Sixteenth and Seventeenth Centuries," *Journal of Canadian Studies/Revue d'études canadiennes*, 21, no. 4 (1987), 79–90.

35. See *Johnson Papers*, 9: 24. Johnson's accounts from King George's War indicated that he often granted presents to Indian women and children to provide for their subsistence while the men were away fighting. See ibid., 15–31.

36. One notable exception to this trend is Johnson's practice of presenting gifts to Indian women whose sons or husbands died in battle. Such presents included black burial strouds for the deceased as well as food and clothing for the family. See ibid., 24, 28.

37. Deed from the Five Nations to the King of their Beaver Hunting Ground, July 19, 1701, in E. B. O'Callaghan, ed., *Documents Relative to the Colonial History of the State of New-York,* 15 vols. (Albany, 1853–1887), 4: 911 (hereafter cited as *NYCol. Docs.*).

38. See Richmond P. Bond, *Queen Anne's American Kings* (Oxford, 1952).

39. Weiser to Richard Peters, Mar. 15, 1754, in *The Susquehannah Company Papers,* vol. 1, ed. Julian P. Boyd (Ithaca, 1962; orig. pub. 1930), 66.

40. For a full listing of Hendrick's aliases see Brown, ed., *Dictionary of Canadian Biography,* 3: 622. Of these names, I use "Hendrick" for two reasons: it is most commonly used in the documents that are my source, and it appears to have been the one most widely recognized by his neighbors in the Mohawk Valley.

41. Hendrick's representation of Canajoharie's interests in European-Indian councils is well documented in the treaty records of this period. In particular, see the proceedings from treaty councils held in 1745, 1746, 1748, 1751, 1753, 1754, and 1755 in O'Callaghan, ed., *NYCol. Docs.,* 6: 289–305, 317–26, 441–52, 717–25, 781–88, 853–92, 964–89.

42. Johnson to Richard Peters, Dec. 9, 1754, *Minutes of the Provincial Council of Pennsylvania,* vol. 6 (Harrisburg, Pa., 1851), 269; Wraxall, "Some Thoughts upon the British Indian Interest in North America . . . ," in O'Callaghan, ed., *NYCol. Docs.,* 7: 22; Weiser to Richard Peters, Mar. 15, 1754, in Boyd, ed., *Susquehannah Papers,* 1: 66; Pownall, "[Notes on] Indian Affairs" (1753–1754), Loudoun Papers—Americana, 10, 460: 8–9, Huntington Library, San Marino, Calif.; Bridenbaugh, ed., *Gentleman's Progress,* 112.

43. For the 4 Indian kings' trip see Bond, *Queen Anne's American Kings,* and John G. Garratt with the assistance of Bruce Robertson, *The Four Indian Kings* (Ottawa, 1985). The kings' speech to Queen Anne is reproduced in Bond, *Queen Anne's American Kings,* 94–95.

44. See Robertson, "The Portraits: An Iconographical Study," in Garratt and Robertson, *Four Indian Kings,* 143–44.

45. Nicholson brought back several sets of the portraits on the 4 Indian kings' return to New York. In 1712, a Society for the Propagation of the Gospel in Foreign Parts (SPG) missionary brought over many more for distribution to each of the Five Nations and the colonial governments of New York, New Jersey, Massachusetts, New Hampshire, Rhode Island, Pennsylvania, Maryland, and Virginia; ibid., 10–14.

46. On the changing nature of New York's fur trade and Indian relations see Thomas Elliot Norton, *The Fur Trade in Colonial New York, 1686–1776* (Madison, Wis., 1974), 43–197.

47. See John Ogilvie to Philip Bearcroft, July 27, 1750, in Records of the Society for the Propagation of the Gospel in Foreign Parts, Letterbooks (microfilm) (London, 1964), series B, 18: 102–03.

48. Richter, *Ordeal of the Longhouse,* 21–22, discusses the redistributive economics involved in village leadership.

49. Pownall, "Notes on Indian Affairs," 9.

50. Arent Stevens, Oct. 5, 1745, in Francis Jennings et al., eds., *Iroquois Indians: A Documentary History of the Diplomacy of the Six Nations and Their League* (microfilm) (Woodbridge, Conn., 1985), reel 12.

51. Entry for Aug. 27, 1750, "A Journal of the Proceedings of Conrad Weiser in his Journey to Onondago," *Minutes of the Provincial Council of Pennsylvania* (Harrisburg, Pa., 1851), 5: 471.

52. June 15, 1753, New York Council Minutes, 23: 78, New York Stare Archives, Albany.

53. William Smith, *History of New York,* 1: 54.

54. For further information on these portraits see Vail, "Portraits of 'The Four Indian Kings of Canada,' " 223–25, Garrat and Robertson, *Four Indian Kings,* 148–49.

55. *Johnson Papers,* 9: 15–31. Other Indians named multiple times in this account include Hendrick's brother Abraham (4 times), his son Young Hendrick (2 times), and Mohawks David (5 times), Brant (4 times), Nickus (3 times), and Seth (3 times).

56. Ibid., 1: 341–42

57. See New York Council Minutes, June 26, 1754, 23: 191; [William Livingston and William Smith, Jr.], *A Review of Military Operations in North-America* (New York, 1757), 76, and John Penn and Richard Peters to James Hamilton, [Aug. 5, 1754], *Pennsylvania Archives,* 4th ser., vol. 2: *Papers of the Governors, 1747–1759* (Philadelphia, 1900), 699.

58. Johnson to Peters, Dec. 9, 1754, *Johnson Papers,* 9: 150.

59. Wanda Burch provided an excellent description of Johnson's collection in "Sir William Johnson's Cabinet of Curiosities," *New York History,* 71 (1990), 261–82.

60. Lender and Martin, *Citizen Soldier,* 49.

61. Colden, "The present state of the Indian affairs with the British & French Colonies in North America," Aug. 8, 1751, in Cadwallader Colden Papers, N.-Y. Hist. Soc., *Colls.,* 53 (1920), 272; Wraxall, *An Abridgment of the Indian Affairs Contained in Four Folio Volumes, Transacted in the Colony of New York, From the Year 1678 to the Year 1751,* ed. Charles Howard McIlwain (Cambridge, Mass., 1915) 248 n.1; Johnson to William Shirley, Dec. 17, 1754, *Johnson Papers,* 1: 433.

62. Minutes of Johnson's Conference at Onondaga, Sept. 8–10, 1753, in New York Council Minutes, 23: 114.

63. Colden referred to Johnson as "the most considerable trader with the Western Indians & sends more goods to Oswego than any other person does," in "Present State of the Indian Affairs," 273.

64. For these two lists see Johnson's account, Mar. 1755 to Oct. 1756, and a list of goods requested for the Northern Indian Department, in *Johnson Papers,* 2: 566–646, 898–900.

65. For a list of these items, which Johnson distributed between June 21 and July 5, see ibid., 575–79.

66. See the complaints levied against the Albany Indian Commissioners by New York councillor Archibald Kennedy, in *The Importance of Gaining and Preserving the Friendship of the Indians to the British Interest, Considered* (New York, 1751), 23. See also Thomas Pownall to Lord Halifax[?], July 23, 1754, in Beverly McAnear, ed., "Personal Accounts of the Albany Congress of 1754," *Mississippi Valley Historical Review,* 39 (1953), 743. New York governors attending Albany treaty conferences often issued proclamations that forbade trading with the Indians for their presents, but as Pownall observed, local merchants ignored such prohibitions. For one such proclamation, issued by Gov. James DeLancey on July 5, 1754, see New York Colonial Manuscripts, 103 vols., New York State Archives, Albany, 78: 146.

67. See *Johnson Papers,* 9: 15–31.

68. Johnson to William Shirley, May 16, 1755, ibid., 1: 505.

69. See, for example, the detailed listing of items that Johnson distributed between Mar. 1755 and Oct. 1756, ibid., 2: 566–646.

70. Ibid., 1: 343, 2: 646

71. See Johnson to George Clinton, Nov. 22, 1749, in O'Callaghan, ed., *NYCol. Docs.,* 6: 541, and Johnson to Clinton, Mar. 12, 1754, *Johnson Papers,* 9: 126–27.

72. Journal entry, Apr. 24, 1748, *Johnson Papers,* 1: 155, 157.

73. Johnson to Clinton, Nov. 22, 1749, in O'Callaghan, ed., *NYCol. Docs.,* 6: 540–41 (emphasis added). Johnson expressed a similar sentiment to William Shirley, Dec. 17, 1754, *Johnson Papers,* 1: 479–34.

74. For a typical example of a condolence exchange see the minutes to a council held in Albany, July 3, 1751, *Johnson Papers,* 1: 340–42. At a treaty conference in Carlisle, Pa., in 1753, the Indians refused to begin negotiations until the proper condolence presents arrived. See *A Treaty Held with the Ohio Indians at Carlisle in October, 1753* (Philadelphia, 1753), 3. Also of note is Hendrick's angry speech to Pennsylvania governor Robert Hunter Morris, Jan. 17, 1754/5, in which he complained that after King George's War, "No Presents were given—No Notice of Peace—No Satisfaction for Blood spilled," a reference to the New York government's failure to acknowledge properly the Mohawks' losses. See *Minutes of the Provincial Council of Pennsylvania,* 6: 283.

75. Johnson to Clinton, May 26, 1749, in O'Callaghan, ed., *NYCol. Docs.,* 6: 512–13; Johnson to Weiser, Apr. 2, 1751, *Johnson Papers,* 1: 326.

76. For the exchange between Johnson and the Indians see O'Callaghan, ed., *NYCol. Docs.,* 6: 977. For the account entry see *Johnson Papers,* 2: 577.

77. On Johnson's Indian name and acceptance among the Indians see Hamilton, *William Johnson,* 45, and Wraxall, *Abridgment of Indian Affairs,* 248 n.1.

78. See Timothy J. Shannon, "The Crossroads of Empire: The Albany Congress of 1754 and the British-Atlantic Community" (Ph.D. diss., Northwestern University, 1993), 94–125, 274–328.

79. See Francis X. Clines, "Peace Prevails in an Offering of Simple Cloth," *New York Times,* Sept. 25, 1994, p. 39.

PART TWO · *From Revolution to Removal, and Beyond*

THINKING AND BELIEVING:
NATIVISM AND UNITY IN THE
AGES OF PONTIAC AND TECUMSEH

18

Gregory Evans Dowd

European colonists were not the only people in eastern North America declaring—and, ultimately, fighting for—their independence in the late eighteenth century. As Gregory Evans Dowd suggests here, many Native Americans were involved in their own quests for liberation during those years. Like American patriots, Indians in the Ohio country articulated their grievances in speeches and writings, sought to unify disparate peoples under a single banner of resistance, launched boycotts and nonimportation movements, and finally went to war in defense, they said, of their liberties, their sovereignty, their very way of life.

Two of these native movements for cultural and political survival, one in the early 1760s and the other some four decades later, framed the event we conventionally call "the American Revolution." Each movement featured dynamic leaders who were, so generations of historians have asserted, either political pragmatists or religious visionaries. But as Dowd's analysis here reveals, Indians were less likely than their European American counterparts to separate the worlds of politics and religion. In the nativist contests of this epoch, spiritual concerns were political concerns, and political movements by necessity had spiritual dimensions.

What was it about these resistance movements that made white Americans so anxious? Did the fusion of political dissent with a spiritual quest represent a new danger in Indian country? The patterns of resistance Dowd chronicles here can usefully be compared with those depicted by Helen Tanner in Ohio and James A. Sandos in California. Taken together, can these essays help to explain why pan-Indian movements were so difficult to sustain?

THINKING AND BELIEVING: NATIVISM AND UNITY IN THE AGES OF PONTIAC AND TECUMSEH

Gregory Evans Dowd

IF WE THINK SERIOUSLY ABOUT BELIEF, if we take Indian religion seriously, we will have to revise a stock interpretation of two early movements for pan-Indian unity. The first movement, dated roughly from 1760 to 1765, we associate with the Ottawa warrior Pontiac and the Delaware Prophet Neolin. The second movement, dated roughly from 1805 to 1813, we associate with the Shawnee diplomat and warrior Tecumseh and his brother, the Shawnee Prophet, Tenskwatawa.[1]

Histories of the two movements for intertribal unity resonate with a distinction between the sacred and the profane. Each of the two movements has been keenly subdivided in our book-length histories into its religious and its secular dimensions. Each dimension is, in turn, personified in our histories by a leader. The two Prophets—separated by a half century—dream, traverse the heavens, and stir souls as atavistic, charismatic leaders. The two warriors—Pontiac and Tecumseh—stand, negotiate, and fight as great, even pragmatic, Americans. Several works from the age of Francis Parkman to our own day have explicitly placed the Prophets in one camp and the war leaders in another, claiming that the Delaware Prophet "may serve as a counterpart to the famous Shawnee Prophet," that Tecumseh "took Pontiac for his model."[2]

The distinction between the sacred and the secular, between the believer and the thinker, a distinction that goes far beyond that between the priest and the soldier, cannot be maintained. Perhaps this distinction results from the paradoxical product of Christian hostility toward native belief and of secular hostility toward belief in general. If so, then this interpretive framework should be dismantled. In this paper I will argue that the prophets and the military leaders drew inspiration from the same sources. My hypothesis implies that figures at opposite corners of the standard interpretation, for instance the Shawnee Prophet of the 1800s and the Ottawa Pontiac of the 1760s, shared visions and strategies, and shared them with their compatriots. This implication, I should add, does not originate with me. It was first suggested by the

SOURCE: *American Indian Quarterly* 16 (1992), 309–35.

Shawnee Prophet himself who in 1810 "boasted that he would follow in the footsteps of the Great Pontiac."[3] Declaring himself an heir to a figure that scholars have mistakenly isolated with Tecumseh as a pragmatist, even as a nonbeliever, the Prophet was creating good history.

MILITANT FOUNDATIONS

Let us first briefly investigate the relationship between Pontiac and Neolin. It is worth noting that our most extensive report of the Delaware Prophet's visions comes to us through Pontiac's voice. According to most analyses of the relationship between the two leaders, the pragmatic Pontiac found Neolin's spiritual message useful, altering it for his political ends.[4] A fresh look at the record strongly suggests that Pontiac got Neolin's message right after all, and got it in the heart.

The interpretation that isolates Pontiac from Neolin hinges upon their differing perceptions of the French. Versions of Neolin's message recorded in the Delawares' and Shawnees' Upper Ohio Country reveal no concern for the French, yet Pontiac's version of the Delaware prophecy has the Master of Life proclaiming of the French that "I love them," while for the Master the English "are my enemies, and the enemies of your [French] brothers."[5] Scholars have understandably, though unconvincingly, concluded that Pontiac, out of a desire to win over Detroit's *habitants,* revised Neolin's message to suit his own ends.

Neolin may, however, have spoken as favorably of the French as did Pontiac. A party of Ohioan Delawares and Shawnees, visiting Pontiac when his siege was already six weeks old, insisted, in the Great Spirit's name, that care be taken of Detroit's French inhabitants. Denouncing Pontiac's seizure of the local French people's arms and ammunition, a spokesman for the Delawares chided, presumably with Neolin in mind, that "the Master of Life . . . forbade us to attack our brothers the French."[6] Pontiac, it appears, did not twist Delaware worlds, but reported what he believed he had heard reported, to put it simply, what he believed.

He behaved like a believer. Visiting Fort Chartres, Illinois, in an abortive effort to secure French aid, he attempted to persuade French officers to take the messianic movement seriously. It was, he argued in 1764, the Master of Life who "put Arms in our hands, and it is he who has ordered us to fight against this bad meat that would come and infest our lands. . . . Think then my Father that thou goest against the Master of life and that all the red Men conform to his will."[7] It is difficult to read a cynic into these lines, spoken to Christians who would not find them automatically persuasive. It is, of course, possible that Pontiac sought to impress his Indian listeners, but such speculation only underscores the hypothetical nature of the standard assessment of Pontiac's spirituality.

Pontiac, in short, belongs among his people. While he did indeed seek to wage what Howard Peckham and Wilbur Jacobs have called an "Indian war of Independence," he sought to do it in Indian ways; he did not have to depart from, or worse, to rise above his people's way of thinking to come up with the notion. The idea of

Indian unity, fostered by a long history of native interaction, most recently by wide-spread intertribal cooperation during the Seven Years' War, had been circulating among the peoples since the withdrawal of the French from the Lakes. Pontiac did not develop the notion single-handedly, nor did he develop it devoid of its spiritual content. He could both think and believe. In the same spirit, let us turn to Tecumseh and his brother, the Shawnee Prophet Tenskwatawa, and because their movement drew heavily upon the earlier movement's thought, we will not leave Pontiac and Neolin behind.

INTERPRETING THE SHAWNEE BROTHERS

Histories of Tecumseh and Tenskwatawa, far more than of Pontiac and Neolin, place a barrier between religion and realpolitik. The dramatic effect is to raise tensions, for not only does religion confront reason, but brother battles brother. In creating this distinction, the histories portray Tecumseh not only as a great man, but also as an exceptional Indian, thinking beyond the traditions of his people.[8] Tecumseh did *not*, however, differ from his followers in culture or in vision any more than did Pontiac, nor was it a lack of traditional tribal identity that blocked his success. His most recent biographer credits Tecumseh with having "conceived of a plan for uniting the red people," but Tecumseh did not conceive of the plan from scratch. Indeed, he drew upon traditions of nativism and well-established networks of intertribal relations that had long been vibrant throughout the trans-Appalachian borderlands, reaching back into the past far beyond the time of Pontiac. With Tecumseh, also drawing from this legacy, stood the Shawnee Prophet.[9]

Tenskwatawa, like the Delaware Prophet before him, did not possess a strictly "tribal" identity. In fact, his first visions occurred while living among Delawares, not Shawnees. The Delaware Prophet, forty years earlier, had similarly displayed his trans-tribal identity, by dwelling among the Shawnees in the final months of Delaware involvement in Pontiac's War.[10] Such mingling among Indians was hardly exceptional in the turbulent late eighteenth-century Old Northwest. More striking was Tenskwatawa's invitation in 1806 to all Indian peoples to join him in settling a new, deliberately polyglot town at Greenville, Ohio. The Shawnee Prophet made the move in clear symbolic defiance of the 1795 Treaty of Greenville, which had imposed a massive land cession upon the Indians and had firmly established the annuity system in the Old Northwest. He repeated the gesture by establishing his town at Tippecanoe (1808–12), in outright defiance of the Miami Little Turtle, who claimed tribal authority over that land, and who had negotiated several recent treaties with the United States.[11] Plans for the Tippecanoe settlement, Tenskwatawa declared, had been "layed by all the Indians in America." He informed the Miami leader that Indian unity alone would end Indian poverty and defend Indian land.[12] Before Tecumseh entered the historical record, then, the Prophet had demonstrated that he could think beyond the boundaries of tribe.

That Indians were conscious of Tenskwatawa's participation in a tradition of pan-Indian militancy is indicated by the actions of a band of Wyandots. Joining the

Shawnee Prophet in 1810, they bound the movement to earlier decades by bringing with them "the Great Belt which was the Symbol of Union between the Tribes in their late war with the United States." Consciously reviving the pan-Indianism of their recent past, these Wyandots, in the Shawnee Prophet's words, could not "sit still and see the property of all the Indians usurped."[13]

THE SEPARATE CREATION AND INDIAN UNITY

To support his intertribal call, the Shawnee Prophet had at his disposal a concept of Indian identity that had been developing since at least the middle of the eighteenth century, a concept embodied in the notion of the separate creation of Anglo-Americans and Indians. As early as 1751 a Presbyterian encountered the notion among Delawares on the Susquehanna River in Pennsylvania, and in the 1760s Neolin employed separation theology in forming his movement.[14] The idea was taken up by other lesser-known Delawares and Shawnees in the late 1760s and early 1770s, the years of Tenskwatawa's youth.[15] The notion, however, did not lead directly to nativism; it was so widespread that even such federally recognized chiefs as Black Hoof and the Wyandot Tahre expressed the view at the turn of the nineteenth century.[16] But leaders seeking accommodation with the United States could never turn the notion of separate creation to their advantage with the dexterity of their nativistic opponents, for in its logical conclusion, the doctrine meant an Indian rejection of American domination. The Great Spirit warned the Shawnee Prophet to be wary, for the "white man was not made by himself but by but by another spirit who made and governed the whites and over whom he had no control."[17]

The separate, even evil, nature of American citizens emerged also in Indian interpretations of Christianity. The line here also derives from at least as far back as Neolin's mid-eighteenth century, when some Indians turned Christianity against Christians to demonstrate the depth of the missionaries' abomination. One Delaware contemporary of Neolin's claimed that he had read the Bible cover to cover, but nowhere in it could he find it written that Indians "should live like the white people."[18] A Mingo in the same period listened to a sermon about the crucifixion of Jesus, then quipped, "If it is true, the Indians are not to blame for his death, but the white man."[19] At the crucifixion, he argued, Europeans had killed their own God. In the early militant phase of the Seneca movement under Handsome Lake (1798–1802), his half-brother Cornplanter, who "liked some ways of the white people," told the Quaker missionary Henry Simmons, "It was the white people who kill'd our Saviour." Simmons countered, "It was the Jews," and then tried to drive the point home by dragging out the already hackneyed argument that Indians were members of the lost tribes of Israel: "Indians were their descendants, for many of their habits were similar to the Jews, in former days." We don't know what Cornplanter made of that contention—perhaps he was simply at a loss for words—but twentieth-century practitioners of the Handsome Lake Religion make no mention of it and still consider the crucifixion a deed performed by whites. They learn that the Seneca Prophet, in his early visions, met Jesus, who described himself as "a man upon the earth who was slain by his own people." Furthermore, Jesus had ordered Handsome Lake to "tell your people that they will become lost when they follow the ways of the white people." Among the literally surrounded Senecas the notion did not lead to a complete break with the United States, nor did it prevent their exploration of Anglo-American culture. But the more militant, and still more autonomous, Old Northwestern peoples leaned more heavily on the argument.

Responding to a Moravian missionary in 1806, one of Tenskwatawa's followers said of the crucifixion, "Granted that what you say is true, He did not die in Indian land but among the white people."[20] In 1810, Tecumseh himself revealed his own concerns for spiritual things, asking Indiana Territory's governor William Henry Harrison in pointed terms, "How can we have confidence in the white people [?] when Jesus Christ came upon the earth you kill'd and nail'd him on a cross."[21] Given the Shawnee warrior's nativistic assumptions, his participation in a way of thinking common among his people, it was a logical question.

If, as the Shawnee Prophet said, Americans were inimical to Indians, if "the Great Spirit did not mean that the white and red people should live near each other [because the newcomers] poison'd the land,"[22] and if all Indians came from a common creation different from others, then it made sense that only Indians should unite against the American threat. It seems likely that, as in Pontiac's day, the threat was not felt from Canada (however British it was now), but from the Americans alone. Room for the British is explicitly written into at least one report of militant nativism during the age of Tecumseh: in the midst of the War of 1812, Potowatomis received news from the Lake Erie theatre that "a Prophet had arisen in England, [who told the King that] the Great Spirit was much displeased with the Americans." The Great Spirit ordered the King to "assist all the Indians to drive the Americans out."[23] Leaving room, perhaps, for cooperation from British Canada, Indian militants emphasized their spiritual separation from the Americans, giving sacred sanction to Native American unity.

Overhunting

Neolin and Tenskwatawa shared a material concern over changes in the environment that also meshed with their spiritual concerns. According to Pontiac, the Great Spirit explained to Neolin that "I led the wild animals into the depths of the forests so that ye had to depend on your brothers to feed and shelter you. Ye have only to become good again and do what I wish, and I will send back the animals for your food." Forty-five years later Tenskwatawa knew that the Indians' gross overhunting of game for the peltry trade had led to a decline in deer stocks. Moravian missionaries reported that the Great Spirit "had shown him the deer were half a trees' length under the ground and that these would soon appear again on the earth if the Indians did what he told them to do, and then there would be an abundance of deer once more."[24] Tenskwatawa would allow trade with Anglo-Americans, as long as it was on terms that the Indians deemed just. He proposed that a one-for-one trade be instituted: one shirt for one raccoon skin and one blanket for one deerskin.[25] The call for such a trade, albeit impossible given the Indians' complete lack of influence on an overseas market upset by the Napoleonic Wars, stood as an open challenge to Anglo-American economic authority. Tenskwatawa sought isolation far less than he sought to free Indians from the outside control that in his view was ensnaring the Indians of the borderlands.

Both Neolin in the wake of the Seven Years' War and Tenskwatawa on the eve of the War of 1812 addressed economic and political issues. And though proceeding from a theological base, they played the politics of Indian autonomy and unity. The standard assessment of Pontiac, that he "possessed the ability to channel red resentment toward meaningful goals," as if the Delaware Prophet and his believing disciples lacked worthy objectives, is in need of revision.[26] An even stronger case for revision should be made regarding the history surrounding Tenskwatawa and Tecumseh. With these two leaders the historians' division of the sacred from the profane has been given not only a pair of names but a pair of dates: 1809, the year of the Treaty of Fort Wayne, and 1811, the year of the scrap at Tippecanoe. To understand fully both these events and the origins of the conventional wisdom, we must investigate, as Daniel Richter suggests, the issue of factionalism.

FACTIONS

By the winter of 1805–1806, when the Shawnee Prophet began to prophesy, several men had secured recognition by the United States as the leaders of their "tribes" in areas now known as Ohio and Indiana.[27] Most of these men had built distinguished military careers in the wars against the Anglo-Americans; each of them had ended those wars by signing the Treaty of Greenville. Their military reputations gave them widespread support among their peoples; their cooperation with the United States following the wars gave them the confidence of American officialdom. By 1804 they had fashioned themselves into the chief conduits for the passage of the United States' annuities to Indians. Of them, Little Turtle of the Miamis and Black Hoof of the Shawnees became useful foils for the nativist movement. In fact, "annuity chiefs," leaders with both a native base and federal support, provided the anvil upon which the prophets forged this early nineteenth-century phase of the struggle for Indian unity.

During the first decade of the nineteenth century, Little Turtle gathered a great deal of power in the Old Northwest. His influence was so strong that the Secretary of War, Dearborn, informed Harrison that "the neighboring Indians are . . . extremely jealous of the Little Turtle."[28] His influence may be partially attributed to his success in winning an unusually large annuity for the Miamis at the Treaty of Greenville. He accomplished this feat by insisting that the Eel River Indians were a separate tribe, confederated under his authority. Partly too, he basked in the former glory of his reportedly brilliant leadership in the victories over Harmar and St. Clair (1790 and 1791, respectively). In general, however, he retained power through his effective management of the Miami annuity: his refusal to indulge in luxuries, his generosity toward his Miami people, and his hospitality to whites.[29] Once in power, he handled himself with such skill that animosities toward him often worked in his favor. For example, the federal agents opposed "those jealousies" with "all the fair means in [their] power."[30] "All the fair means" tended to translate, into "all means fair or foul." This was demonstrated in the Miami leader's partnership with William Wells, the federal government's agent at Fort Wayne.

Wells, who knew several Indian languages as a result of his childhood captivity among the Northwesterners, worked closely with Little Turtle in attempting to manage Indian-American relations in his quarter—so closely, in fact, that by 1809 charges of misconduct led to his demotion from agent to translator. This demotion, despite his impressive skills and connections, makes little sense when viewed in the light of accusations, leveled in 1807, that he had mistranslated speeches to advance his own and Little Turtle's interests.[31] Whatever the logic of his demotion, he was suspected in 1809 of both deliberately exaggerating the Prophet's friendship for the British, and, more seriously as far as the federal government was concerned, of embezzling Delaware annuities.[32]

Wells and Little Turtle had also interfered with the federal and Quaker effort to "civilize" the Shawnees. They intended to prevent rival Old Northwestern leaders, including Black Hoof, from rising to prominence in relations with the federal government. Throughout the first decade of the nineteenth century, Little Turtle had managed to secure annuities for his Miamis at almost every cession of land, often by challenging the claims made by other peoples. He wanted no contenders to threaten his hold on the disposition of what he came to view as the Miamis' most precious commodity.

But in Little Turtle's efforts against the Shawnee annuity chief, he misspent energies better devoted toward those who would become more serious opponents: those who hoped to prevent land from ever being traded as a commodity again. For the true threat to Little Turtle came not from his accommodating rivals, but from the resurgence of militant pan-Indian nativism under the direction of the prophets. Not until the Shawnee Prophet threw down the gauntlet by settling among the Miamis in 1808 did Little Turtle and Wells move strongly against him, and even then, it was Wells, not Little Turtle, who dealt the telling blows. So hostile was Wells to Tenskwatawa that in 1809, when groups of starving nativists appeared at Vincennes, Harrison reported to the Secretary of War that the Indian agent "was for having me starve all."[33] And in the months following the Battle of Tippecanoe (1811), Wells boasted: "Yes sir I would of [sic] destroyed this scoundrel 4 years ago had I not of [sic] been prevented by my superiors."[34] By 1809, Wells and Little Turtle sought to combat the resurgence of militant nativism and all challenges from other accommodating leaders (their earlier efforts were directed mainly against the latter). Little Turtle played the part of tribal Chief, and put his Miamis's interests before those of other peoples.

Black Hoof, Little Tuttle's rival among the faction of Shawnees eager to accommodate the United States, also dispensed government annuities.[35] Like the Miami, Black Hoof carried a good record as a warrior and defender of his people. As an elderly though still active man in the early nineteenth century, he was reported to be among those who surprised Braddock in 1755; it is certain that he had fought valorously in the wars of the 1780s and 1790s.[36] Balancing his youthful show of military zeal was his more mature posture of warmth for the Americans. The moment when youth and age balanced was in 1795, after devastating Northwestern defeats, when Black Hoof put his mark on the Greenville cession. For the next two decades he cooperated with the federal government.

Little Turtle and Black Hoof did not simply cede land, accept annuities, and redistribute the proceeds among their people. They too had designs for the future. To carry them out, they actively cooperated with the Quaker bearers of the civilizing mission. These missionaries of religion and culture sought to establish "demonstration farms" to be used to persuade Indian men to replace hunting with agriculture and Indian women to abandon agriculture for domestic pursuits.[37] The Friends received federal support and cooperation.

In 1804—in accordance with an agreement among Quaker delegates, Little Turtle, and the Potawatomi Five Medals—Quaker Philip Dennis planted his twenty-acre farm about forty miles southwest of Fort Wayne, on rich soil beside the Wabash. There, argued Little Turtle, both the Potawatomis and the Miamis could benefit by observing Dennis's progress, but Dennis was clearly in the heartland of the Miamis.[38]

In 1807, Black Hoof likewise allowed the Quaker William Kirk to set up a demonstration farm near the Shawnee town of Wapakoneta,[39] within reach of the Wyandots at Sandusky. Black Hoof's support enabled Kirk to enclose one hundred acres of land and to plant a full two hundred acres in corn. By April 1808, Kirk reported progress: several of the Shawnees operated private farms; the people as a whole possessed "a good stock of Cattle and Hogs." The Wyandots' "improvements," he claimed, were similar. A year later Indian agent John Johnson noted that Black Hoofs people had both a saw mill and a grist mill under construction; many lived in log houses with chimneys; their village, overall, bore "the marks of industry."[40] However, despite these developments and petitions on Kirk's behalf the war department (apparently because of Kirk's poor record keeping) withdrew its support from the mission in late 1808.[41] It is worth noting that Little Turtle and Wells, seeking to prevent potential rivals, had stood against Kirk's arrangement with the Shawnees and Wyandots. The brief history of Kirk's agency demonstrated, and this is the critical point, that the Quakers, the federal government, the Indian agents, and the government chiefs—all the main advocates of accommodation in the Old Northwest—were seriously divided, often for the most petty of reasons. This division gave rise to a strong nativist movement that challenged these scattered projects.

The Quaker missionaries faced obstacles more difficult to negotiate than factionalism among the forces of accommodation. For one thing, they had underestimated the difficulties of their mission. For example, they clearly intended to alter the gender division of labor among the Indians they observed. Philip Dennis actively attempted to dissuade the young Indian women who "wished to work in preparing the ground and in tending the corn," by hiring a white woman to teach them spinning and knitting. The Quakers, arguing against Indian tradition, claimed that women "are less then Men, they are not as strong as Men, they are not as able to endure fatigue and toil as men." Rather, women should "be employed in our houses, to keep them clean, to sew, knit, and weave; to dress food for themselves and [their] families."⁴² Such an arrangement practically reversed the contemporary production arrangements among Indians, for the men obtained clothing through hunting and trade, while women raised the crops and vegetables. Quite apart from the cosmological consequences Indians would fear in such a transformation, the material demands of the Friends' proposal were enormous: among the Indians, women alone possessed the knowledge of field work. If carried out, then, the proposed gender reversal might have resulted in a dangerous drain of horticultural skills.

Therefore, even proponents of accommodation could support the role reversal with little more than words. When the Quakers arrived, Little Turtle claimed that he "and some others of my brother Chiefs have been endeavouring to turn the minds of our People [men] towards the Cultivation of the Earth," but he admitted no success.⁴³ The Quakers would not do much better. For the moment then, this aspect of the mission proved a failure in the Northwest.

The Shawnee Prophet, who emerged as the chief opponent of the civilizing mission, clearly preferred traditional gender roles to those sponsored by the Quakers. According to William Wells, the Prophet declared Kirk to be a "Master" imposed over the Indians by the President, "from which circumstance it was evident that the President intended making women of the Indians—but when the Indians was [sic] all united they would be respected by the President as men."⁴⁴

The Prophet's concern with the civilizing mission, and the gender revolution it would have entailed, grew out of both the very earthly grounds that it robbed from the Indians, their political independence, and the cosmological proposition that robbed the Indians of their sacred powers. He and other opponents of the mission directed their most searing attacks at its Indian sponsors, whom they believed were undermining the strength of the Indian peoples.

In 1805, shortly after his first visions, the Shawnee Prophet directly challenged the authority of the annuity chiefs. The Prophet spoke openly against those "chiefs who were very wicked, would not believe, and tried to keep the people from believing, and encouraged them on in their former wicked ways." Black Hoof, the Prophet's strong Shawnee opponent, maintained the loyalties of many Shawnees, despite the Prophet's vigorous denunciations. In order for the Prophet to gain independence from Black Hoof and his followers, as well as to challenge the Greenville Treaty upon which Black Hoof's authority partially rested, "the Great Spirit told" Tenskwatawa "to separate from these wicked chiefs and their people and showed him particularly where to come, towards the big ford where the peace was concluded with the Americans; and there [to] make provision to receive and instruct all from the different tribes that were willing to be good."⁴⁵

A realignment of Indian loyalties resulted. While Black Hoof and Little Turtle each worked against the other, lobbying with their particular American allies to secure their influence within the federal government, Tenskwatawa sought intertribal support for both a rebellion against these government chiefs and a posture of defiance toward American expansion. Thus, Tenskwatawa's effort was against both domestic and foreign authority. The moment for domestic success, moreover, was opportune. His Indian opponents, as we have seen, were divided among themselves.

The struggle for the control of Indian councils manifested itself most violently in the Shawnee Prophet's witch hunt, a hunt for witches who bore little resemblance to those of earlier Anglo-colonial society: the first accused were often powerful men. Opposition to witchcraft, a long-standing feature of nativism, lay at the center, not the periphery, of the Prophet's code. Tenskwatawa began preaching, one source has it, on the death of Pengahshega (Change of Feathers), a powerful Shawnee opponent of witches.[46] What's more, witch hunts had bedeviled Indian communities during the nativistic upheavals of the 1750s, 1760s, and early 1770s.[47]

Tenskwatawa claimed that the Great Spirit had given him the power to discover witches, even among powerful leaders of the community. To find the guilty parties, the Prophet stood the villagers in a circle about him, and "after a great many ceremonies," he pointed to the evil beings.[48] Tenskwatawa's witch hunt initially hit the Delawares with the greatest severity. The Prophet had been living among the Delawares when he experienced his first visions. By the late winter of 1805–1806, strong parties of Delawares sought "to destroy all the reputed witches, . . . as well as those who had poison among them. They resolved to use fire to bring about the confessions of those whom the Schawano would accuse."[49] All of the known condemned Delawares had close ties with the Americans and with the civilizing mission. Two of the condemned, Tedapachsit and Hackingpomska, were chiefs, and they had both signed the Greenville Treaty of 1795 and had ceded land to the United States at the Delaware Treaty of 1804, agreeing that the new annuities would be "exclusively appropriated to the purpose of ameliorating their condition and promoting their civilization." Tedapachsit, killed by the Prophet's followers, had openly supported the activities of Christian missionaries. Hackingpomska, though taken prisoner, was not executed, perhaps because he yielded momentarily to the growing opposition to the white missions, by joining a Delaware Council in favoring native prophets over American ministers.[50] An old woman, baptized by the Moravians, fell victim to the charge; so did the Indian "Brother Joshua," who not only had converted to Christianity, but who had been, as the militants suspected, an active spy for the United States during the American Revolution. Tenskwatawa's Delaware targets accepted and cultivated direct American intervention in Indian government, religion, and society. For the nativists, such cultivation was tantamount to sorcery.

By mid-summer, internal Delaware opposition to the killings led many to recoil from the witch hunt and to turn their suspicions against the hunters, leaving the Delawares deeply divided over killings that had so clearly reflected political and cultural conflict. As one Moravian missionary put it while he fled Delaware country, "The Indians hate each other with a bitter hatred, which may flame forth at the slightest provocation."[51] (Note that this hatred was not tribal.) Here, Delaware followers of a Shawnee attacked one another.

Among the Shawnees, two of Black Hoof's followers, accused of using "bad Medisin [sic]," lost their lives to the Prophet's assassins in the spring of 1807. Not surprisingly, in light of the nativists' hostility toward leaders who cooperated with the Americans, Tenskwatawa had even discovered Black Hoof to be a witch, along with chiefs Black Snake and Butler. None of them was killed, but it is worth noting that the three accused supported the federally sponsored Quaker mission.[52]

Recriminations between Black Hoof's and the Prophet's parties flew so furiously that the federal government temporarily treated the nativist movement as a strictly internal Shawnee affair. In early August 1807, while anti-British passions over the *Chesapeake-Leopard* naval affair boiled in the United States, President Thomas Jefferson declined to relate Indian matters to British maritime policy. With "respect to the Prophet," he informed his Secretary of War, "if [the chiefs] who are in clanger from him would settle it their own way, it would be their affair. But we should do nothing towards it." Nothing, in Jefferson's curious usage, meant a little judicious peddling of influence: "The best conduct we can pursue to countervail these movements among the Indians is to confirm our friends by redoubled acts of justice and favor."[53]

Throughout 1807, beating against the winds of continued federal favor for annuity chiefs, the nativists' notions slipped deeper into the Upper Great Lakes region. In the spring, when Michigan Territorial Governor William Hull advertised the intent of the federal government to purchase some lands from the Ottawas. As a result, Tenskwatawa's messianic Ottawa ally, the Trout, launched a more stringent brand of nativism, though he did so in the Shawnee's name.[54] By September, Michigan's traders felt the first force of the Ottawa revival. One merchant wrote, "All the Ottawas from L'arbe au Croche adhere strictly to the Shawney Prophets advice they do not wear Hats, Drink, or Conjure." These Ottawas planned on spending the autumn at the Prophet's Town and refused liquor even when offered it free of charge. The traders lamented, "Rum is a Drug [on the market]. . . . Indians do not purchase One Galln [*sic*] per month."[55]

By the spring of 1808, when the Prophet gathered his followers for a move to the Wabash River, near Tippecanoe Creek, on lands claimed by the Miamis, the Miami chief Little Turtle finally took serious notice of the Prophet. With the Potawatomi Five Medals, Little Turtle threatened to kill Tenskwatawa if he made the proposed move. In response, Tenskwatawa loudly condemned all government chiefs who had "sold all the Indian land to the United States" and who had asked the President to "appoint masters over them to make them work."[56]

If the nativists opposed the accommodating chiefs for their advocacy of the civilizing mission and for their role in land sales, it was the latter role they most vocally condemned. Between 1804 and the end of 1808 the governors of the Indiana and Michigan Territories had negotiated a half dozen treaties with the annuity chiefs. According to these treaties, the United States had obtained a large chunk of southeastern Michigan, large cessions in southern Indiana and Illinois, and most of the land that had been left to the Indians in Ohio. The United States had also gained the right to build and use a road running through a portion of what remained of Indian territory. Washington paid for these grants with increased annuities, to be distributed through the leaders it recognized. To opponents of the annuity chiefs, the payments reeked of bribery.[57]

THE TREATY OF FORT WAYNE

In 1809, the annuity chiefs unwittingly, even negligently, galvanized the nativists with another land cession, embodied in the Treaty of Fort Wayne. The treaty has long been recognized as a milestone on the road to the battle of Tippecanoe, a transforming event that took a religious movement and made it political. The treaty, concluded between the United States and the federally recognized leaders of the Delaware, "Eel River," Miami, and Potawatomi Indians, gained for the states "upwards of two milions [*sic*] and a half of acres" at the cost of "less than two cents per acre."[58] From the Treaty forward, according to several histories on the eve of the War of 1812, Tenskwatawa's brother, Tecumseh, fashioned and led the pan-Indian movement, while the Prophet himself receded.[59] The Prophet, however, lost no authority following the treaty. More power to Tecumseh did not, by some law of finite volume, mean less power for the Prophet: the two were brothers, allies, and believers. It is a mistake to assign them relative weights with reference to their peoples' affairs; they were too closely intertwined in the struggle for autonomy and power, albeit playing different roles, to be separated without doing both men injury.

Tenskwatawa's preaching continued to exhibit both the political overtones and material concerns that political and social historians find worth in understanding. Like Tecumseh, Tenskwatawa spoke out vigorously against both the Fort Wayne cession and the Indians who had agreed to it. In the spring and summer of 1810, half a year after the signing of the treaty, the Prophet informed an uncovered American spy that his people were "much exasperated at the cession of Lands made last winter" and that they had "agreed that the Tract on the N. west side of the Wabash should not be surveyed."[60] His disciples followed up this declaration by successfully opposing a surveying party in September.[61]

TIPPECANOE (AND TOTO TOO?): A REVISION

The second date assigned to the demise of the Prophet's authority is November 7, 1811, at the battle of Tippecanoe. Tenskwatawa's career, already eclipsed by Tecumseh's meteoric rise in the traditional account, here described a pitiful coda. According to conventional knowledge, the Shawnee Prophet had promised his followers a marvelous victory on the battle's eve. After his defeat and the abandonment of his village, the Prophet met massive dissent among his erstwhile disciples, and was placed under Winnebago bondage, blamed for Indian losses, and finally threatened with death. Tecumseh, the tale continues, upon his return to the North from his southern mission sometime in the middle of January 1812, exploded in rage before his brother, taking him by the hair and chastising him for having precipitously attacked the Americans. The historians who so argue have not done so without evidence.[62] Even if we screen out the memoirs written by those who had always been hostile to the Prophet and stick mainly to the contemporary documents, we find some evidence to support the standard narrative. But we also see serious, overwhelming, reason for doubt.

Two arguments will be challenged here. First, that Tenskwatawa was abandoned by his followers following the Battle of Tippecanoe. There is sufficient evidence in the record to contradict the standard description, which has Harrison play the part of Dorothy's dog Toto, exposing the Shawnee as just another "very bad Wizard," an ordinary man behind the curtain, no longer worthy of attention. The most extravagant contemporary rumors that spread among Americans had the Shawnees surrender the Prophet to the jailkeepers of Vincennes, but such vapors dissipated quickly, and fortunately did not infect our histories.[63] Other stories, however, found a host in the full body of writing on the subject. They were passed into the histories through the medium of a storm of euphoric correspondence brewed in the confusion that followed William Henry Harrison's victory. This correspondence, however, proves to be deeply flawed as evidence, for its very writers would soon revise their precipitous claims about the Prophet's fall, as they came to recognize his continuing power.

In one early and influential passage, for instance, Captain Josiah Snelling, commanding Fort Harrison, notified Harrison that the Indians were "reproaching the Prophet in bitter terms for the defeat he had brought on them." The Winnebagos, Snelling had heard charged the Prophet with fraud, "bound him with cords, and it was the opinion of Little Eyes [Snelling's Miami informant] they would sacrifice him." Snelling concluded that "all the confederated tribes had abandoned their faith in the Prophet except about forty Shawanoes who still adhered to him."[64] The letter, written in late November, was supplemented by others that described widespread distrust of the Prophet, the refusal of villages to allow him to join them, and the general abandonment of his movement. From this letter springs the standard interpretation that the Prophet fell after Tippecanoe. Missing, however, are the letters' notes of caution: "I cannot say sir how much of the above may be depended on," or, "It is however pretty certain that the Winnebagos have not returned home as the Kickapoos asserted."[65]

Correction soon supplemented caution. Within seven weeks of Snelling's first letter, Americans found reason to revise their information. Snelling told Harrison that

> he was informed confidentially by a Wea Indian that the Disposition of the Kickapoos and Winnebagos was by no means such as they wished us to believe. That many of them still retained their confidence in the Prophet, who had assured them that his want of success in the late action was caused by an accident of an uncommon kind. . . . That many of them believed that they would all die as soon as the Prophet was put to death.[66]

Harrison soon came to doubt the sincerity of Snelling's original informant, Little Eyes, who, Harrison decided, had "long been in the interest of the Prophet."[67] Snelling himself had noted that Little Eyes committed robberies against American settlers, supporting Harrison's suspicions and casting into question any word this militant Miami gave to his American enemies. In another two weeks Snelling learned that "it was the determination of all the Indians to go to War with the United States."[68]

In the months after Tippecanoe, evidence continued to accumulate suggesting that the Prophet still commanded a following, and that the militants among the Indians, as the *National Intelligencer* put it in February, "will generally attach themselves to the Prophet and his measures."[69] Thomas Forsyth at Peoria summed up the results of the Battle of Tippecanoe as the following: "the Prophet's party was dispersed only for a moment."[70] Such evidence finds occasional contradiction, even including the renewal of open warfare in the summer of 1812. It is worth noting that by May, possibly as early as January, the Prophet's village of Tippecanoe, the scene of his supposed demise, had repopulated with "about 300 winebagoes [*sic*] and about 200 of other tribes and that he [that is, the Prophet] was daily gaining strength." By June Harrison noted that the militants' force at Tippecanoe was "equal to that which they commanded last summer."[71] When the Prophet's village was again destroyed by American troops in the fall of 1812, it and the adjoining and allied Kickapoo village supported some 200 cabins and huts, a considerable settlement by the region's standards.[72] The Indians, dejected according to the standard interpretation, had rebounded after the first attack on Tippecanoe, and had prepared to resist the continued expansion of the United States. As Governor Ninian Edwards of the Illinois Territory had worried with the approach of the post-Tippecanoe spring, "the Prophet is regaining his influence."[73] So much was this the case that Harrison had sought to have "the Prophet or Tecumseh or both" visit the President of the United States. Still conceiving of the Prophet as worthy of special attention, Harrison, by the late winter of 1812, shaped a policy around the equal consideration of the brothers.[74] Tenskwatawa remained indispensable.

The second argument of the standard interpretation, that Tecumseh rejected his brother after Tippecanoe, is more difficult to assess, for it involves the personal beliefs of an individual who left us no writings. A violent scene—which includes Tecumseh's shock at the defeat at Tippecanoe, his furious manhandling of the Prophet, charging him with a premature assault on the Americans—has repeatedly been reconstituted to suggest that Tecumseh's involvement in the movement was largely secular; that Tecumseh was at heart indifferent to prophecy, and went along with it only as long as it met his higher purpose: the formation of his confederacy. The interpretation originates with Anthony Shane, a Shawnee-metis employee of the federal government, a man long hostile to the Prophet, interviewed by historian Benjamin Drake ten years after the fact. Shane claimed that Tecumseh, always silently cognizant of his brother's fraud, was twice on the verge of killing Tenskwatawa, the second time after the Tippecanoe fiasco. Shane's Tecumseh had opposed Tenskwatawa's religion at its very beginning, but had later realized that "as a matter of policy" he might wield it "to further his own designs."[75] Others who knew the two men recalled events differently, but there is some evidence from the period itself to support Shane's story.[76] Strikingly similar to tales of Pontiac's manipulation of Neolin's message, the story of Tecumseh's falling out with his brother bears examination.

The best piece of evidence to support the Shane thesis comes from the pen of William Claus, British commander at Amherstburg, who received it from Isidor Chaine, a Wyandot culture broker. Claus wrote that "Teekumthie was much dissatisfied with his Brother [*sic*] for engaging Governor Harrison, last fall, as their plans were not sufficiently matured."[77] A less direct but good piece of evidence describes

Tecumseh "much exasperated against his brother."[78] Still, these letters and similar rumors in American soldiers' journals and memoirs cannot support the weight they now bear, the hefty loads not merely of Tecumseh's disappointment at the results of the confrontation at Tippecanoe, a limited point that is quite plausible, but, far less plausibly, of his final overthrow of his brother. The contemporary documents simply do not address Tecumseh's devotion, nor do they suggest, as Shane's memoir and subsequent histories have, that Tecumseh either defrocked his brother or was on the verge of putting the Prophet to death. What they do tell us is that Tecumseh was "much dissatisfied," even "exasperated," at the Prophet for his failure to prevent the battle. These words cannot be stretched to suggest that Tecumseh contemplated even apostasy, much less his brother's assassination.

Three interrelated questions must be addressed: Did Tecumseh blame his brother for the Indians' losses at Tippecanoe? Did he think the losses were significant? And did he abandon his brother's convictions? The traditional interpretation's affirmative answer to each question, supported by the Shane memoir and the letters, finds contradiction elsewhere in more direct records.

On May 15, 1812, for example, Tecumseh spoke to a council of Indians from a dozen peoples, militant and nonmilitant alike. Tecumseh claimed, as the traditional interpretation would have it, that the battle would not have occurred had he been at Tippecanoe to prevent it. But nowhere did Tecumseh blame his brother. Among Indians, he blamed only "a few of our younger men," a description, that could not, in terms of either age or occupation, apply to Tenskwatawa. Indeed, the quotation throws into question Tenskwatawa's role at Tippecanoe. Was it the Prophet who ordered the fight? We have no uncontradicted contemporary evidence. British agent Matthew Elliot's mid-January battle report to Major Brock removed the blame from Tenskwatawa; Elliot described the incidents leading to the battle as haphazard and unpredictable. The Indians wisely placed pickets around Harrison's camp, but "Two young Winibiegoes, no doubt out of curiosity," went too near the American sentinels and were fired on, precipitating an unintended battle." In a later report by Elliot, Tecumseh himself, though calling the Prophet's village in his absence "a poor set of people," again absolves his brother, declaring at the battle of Tippecanoe that "You cannot blame Your Younger Brothers the Shawanoes." Instead he charged Potawatomis with precipitating the crisis.[79]

But Tecumseh placed the bulk of the blame, during the Indian Council of May 15, 1812, on the Americans. He said, "Governor Harrison made war on my people in my absence." The traditional interpretation, by emphasizing Tecumseh's anger at his brother, implies that he charged Tenskwatawa with attempting to defend the village against Americans who, in Tecumseh's words, came "to our village with the intention of destroying us."[80] Nor was the Prophet's brother alone in charging the Americans with aggression. The Kickapoo Permoratome explained that the widespread Indian disaffection with the Americans in the spring of 1812 was due to "the army that went last fall against the Shawanoe Prophet," a victim of aggression for whom Permoratome had no harsh words.[81] The standard depiction, in other words, displays

Tecumseh as a man who, while devoting his life to his peoples' defense, rose in anger at his brother's attempt to defend his people. This is not plausible.

On the significance of the battle, there is also room for doubting the validity of the traditional story. First, as early as January 1812, the early expectation that peace would reside along the borderlands had evaporated. Doubts as to the decisiveness of Tippecanoe had, as we have seen, already emerged among its very celebrants in the United States. Second, the British and the Indians did not see the battle as decisive. Indeed, Elliot wrote only two months after the battle that "The Prophet and his people do not appear as a vanquished enemy; they re-occupy their former ground."[82] Then in June 1812, Tecumseh referred to the battle as simply "a struggle between little children who only scratch each others faces." That description, though contrary to the standard narrative, may in fact describe the general attitude at Tippecanoe as the village repopulated with Winnehagoes, Kickapoos, and other militants. Again, Tecumseh's image removes Tenskwatawa, neither a child nor a young man, from the picture.[83]

Finally, there is the vexing question of Tecumseh's belief in his brother's religion. While we cannot enter his soul, we do see him defend his brother against Potawatomi government chiefs at the Indian council of May 15, 1812. These Potawatomis, chastising the militants whom they had long opposed, twice refer to Tenskwatawa as a *"pretended* prophet." In his rejoinder, Tecumseh attacks the *"pretended* chiefs of the Potawatomis and others, who have been in the habit of selling land to the white people that did not belong to them." It is a cutting response, turning about the charge of fraud. As to a second charge levied by the government chiefs that the Prophet and Tecumseh had been giving evil counsel to young men of the different tribes, Tecumseh, speaking for both himself and his brother, admits only that "it is true, we have endeavored to give all our brothers *good advice;* and if they have not listened to it, we are sorry for it. We defy any living creature to say we ever advised any one, directly or indirectly, to make war on our white brothers."[84] Tecumseh and his brother continued, in short, to speak in one voice, to act in union, and to command support. As William Wells reported when Tecumseh had only just returned from his southern journey, the two men had together pledged their lives against further encroachments by the United States: "they both say they will consent to be put to Death if Governor Harrison will pledge himself to the Indians that the United States will neither buy nor take any more land from the Indians."[85]

Tenskwatawa's loss of power following the battle of Tippecanoe has been, at best, exaggerated and selectively extracted from contradictory evidence. We do not know that Tenskwatawa was responsible for the Indians' defeat in 1811, and we do not know that Tecumseh or other militant Indians held him responsible, nor is it clear that militants saw the battle as critical. An alternative is both plausible and supported by much of the contemporary evidence: Tenskwatawa remained an important spiritual leader of a movement that continued to animate its participants, Tecumseh included, with a quest for power, sacred and profane. Indeed, for over a year following the Battle of Tippecanoe, a year that saw the outbreak of full-scale war and the consequent rise to military fame of Tecumseh, references abound in the documents to the "Prophet's Party," the

"Prophet's town," the "followers of the Prophet," the "Prophet's interest," the "Prophet's Army," and even the "Prophet's confederacy," denominations which, along with others, render Tenskwatawa as a commander of persistent, militant loyalties. Tecumseh is often cited as the true military Iecader, but never, before his death, is the movement given his name.[86] The standard interpretation, however correct in assigning different attributes to each brother, is in error in driving a wedge between them. In rendering one a falling priest and the other a rising statesman, it overexposes the differences between the two, underestimating the strength, resilience, and credibility of their shared beliefs.

DIPLOMATIC MISSIONARY

It might be argued that Tecumseh's southern journey in the late summer and fall of 1811 demonstrates a vision grander than all others, but even here, Tecumseh traveled with others and in others' footsteps.[87] There is tantalizing evidence that Shawnees and other northernwestern Indians carried the Shawnee Prophet's message to the Creeks *before* Tecumseh's famous southward journey. As early as July 1807, when Tecumseh had not yet entered the historical record, Harrison informed his superiors that, on the basis of "information which cannot be doubted," he knew "that war belts have been passing through all the Tribes from the Gulf of Florida to the lakes. The Shawnees are the bearers of these belts and they have never been our friends." In June 1810, a Potawatomi government chief informed Harrison that the Shawnee Prophet "will now endeavor to raise the southern Indians, the Choctaws and the Creeks particularly (the Prophet's mother was a Creek)."[88] One year later, Tecumseh fulfilled the Potawatomi's predictions.[89]

Visits in the other direction, from the south to the north, also prepared Tecumseh's way. In 1807, while the Secretary of War, Henry Dearborn, worried about Tenskwatawa's movement, he recommended that a "banditti of Creeks" should "be driven out of" Indiana Territory.[90] In 1810, twenty to thirty Creeks were reportedly visiting the Prophet at Tippecanoe.[91] Dissident Cherokees also maintained their presence in the Northwest. In July 1805, a Cherokee family that maintained contact with its southeastern kin annoyed the Moravian mission to the Delawares at White River, Indiana, preparing "a heathen sacrificial feast . . . and [inviting] to it a large number."[92] This event may have had no direct connection with the Prophet's similar activities toward the end of the year, but it does indicate an anti-Christian Cherokee presence in his very neighborhood. Five years later a Cherokee at Black Hoof's Shawnee town informed John Norton, a Mohawk who was at the time returning from a visit with the Cherokee Nation, that "many" Cherokees "were at the Village of the Prophet."[93] Cherokees, then, may have joined the militant followers of the Shawnee Prophet before Tecumseh's renowned tour; both Cherokees and Creeks were certainly acquainted with the Northern movement.

Tecumseh was as much one of his people as was his brother. This was true in diplomacy as in other endeavors. Scholars wishing to distinguish between the pragmatic Tecumseh and his religious brother have dwelt on the "statesman's" diplomacy. Tecumseh's journey, however, had another, inextricably related object: he sought to spread religion, to spread the call for a restoration of sacred power. To that end, he traveled with another Shawnee prophet, a religious leader who remained among the Southerners and fought with the Red Sticks in the Creek War.[94]

None of the versions of Tecumseh's speeches to Southern Indians are very trustworthy, but the American reports of his address to the Creeks are nonetheless packed with revealing assumptions. Creeks and Americans in the Southeast describe Tecumseh as a religious extremist, a holy warrior; indeed both Benjamin Hawkins, who knew the Creeks better than any government official of his day, and Alexander Cornells, one of Hawkins's Creek allies, thought Tecumseh *was* the Shawnee Prophet.[95] The Creeks' identification of Tecumseh with religion long survived him. In the late nineteenth century Creeks continued to remember Tecumseh as a mystic. Similarly, among emigrant peoples from Tecumseh's homeland, miraculous tales surrounded the story of his death, and modern Shawnees have called him a "saint." So it has also been said of Pontiac. An Ojibwa Indian in the mid-nineteenth century informed Francis Parkman that Pontiac had been the member of a religious society, a memory that renders a sacred aura to his calls for war against the English.[96]

Historians might pay more attention to such memories, for they bear a closer relation to the four nativists' understandings of power than do the popular biographies of the brothers and the professional histories of their movements. The four men did not divide themselves neatly into the charismatic and the pragmatic, for none believed that power could be gained without attention to spirits and to ceremony. As their peoples remembered them, attending to the teachings and achievements of their fellow militants, both were participants in what amounted to a half-century of struggle for Indian unity, autonomy, and sacred power.

NOTES

1. A portion of this paper was presented in October, 1989, at the Shelby Cullum Davis Center for Historical Studies, Princeton University.

2. Parkman arranged the figures in what has since become the conventional scheme. Francis Parkman, *The Conspiracy of Pontiac and the Indian Uprising of 1763* (Boston, 1898) 1: 186, 191. See also Helen Hornbeck Tanner, ed., *Atlas of Great Lakes Indian History* (Norman, 1986), 103.

3. Harrison to Secretary of War, June 14, 1810, Logan Esarey, ed., *Governor's Messages and Letters of William Henry Harrison, 1800–1811,* 2 vols. (Indianapolis, 1922) 1: 425, hereafter cited as *Harrison's Letters and Messages.* Both Mooney, *The Ghost Dance Religion,* Annual Report of the Bureau of American Ethnology, vol. 2, part 2 (1986), and Melvin Delano Thurman, in Chapter Seven, "The Algonquian Prophetic Tradition," of his "The Delaware Indians: A Study in Ethnohistory (Ph.D. diss.; University of California, Santa Barbara, 1977); suggest that there were continuities between the Delaware prophets of the 1760s and the Shawnee Prophet's movement in the 1800s. They maintain the traditional division, however, between the sacred and the pragmatic.

4. For the thesis that Pontiac deployed the Prophet's message to further his already established plans see Howard Peckham, *Pontiac and the Indian Uprising* (Princeton, 1947), 116; Charles E. Hunter, "The Delaware Nativist Revival of the Mid-Eighteenth Century," *Ethnohistory* 18 (1971), 46; Wilbur Jacobs, "Pontiac's War—a Conspiracy," in Jacobs, ed., *Dispossessing the American Indian* (New York, 1972), 89; Parkman, 1: 187–191. Anthony Wallace similarly reports in an early work that Pontiac employed the Prophet's message to "rationalize his assault on Detroit." Later, and I think more accurately, he sees Pontiac as a convert, but even here the Ottawa uses "Neolin's

doctrine as supernatural sanction for his conspiracy," much as Peckham's Pontiac had deployed the Prophet's message as an "ingenious trick, by which he gained divine sanction for his own scheme." Anthony F.C. Wallace, "New Religions Among the Delaware Indians, 1600–1900," *Southwestern Journal of Anthropology* 12 (1956): 9; Wallace, *The Death and Rebirth of the Seneca* (New York, 1969), 121.

5. [Robert Navarre], *Journal of Pontiac's Conspiracy*, ed. C. M. Burton, trans., R. Clyde Ford (Detroit, 1912), 28–30. Hereafter, Navarre, *Journal.*

6. Navarre, *Journal,* 174–76. For a fuller rendition of this argument see my article, "The French King Wakes Up in Detroit: 'Pontiac's War' in Rumor and History," *Ethnohistory*, forthcoming.

7. "A council in Illinois, Pontiac addresses Mons., Neyon de Villiers, April 15, 17, 1764," Gage Papers, William Clements Library, microfilm of Great Lakes materials at Glen Black Archaeological Laboratory, Bloomington, Indiana.

8. Glenn Tucker's biography credits Tecumseh with devising the Prophet's religion as a means of achieving unity. R. David Edmunds rightly rejects that particular interpretation; yet even this best biographer of the brothers sees something quintessentially un-Indian about Tecumseh's endeavor, which "seemed logical to whites because it was what *they* would have done. His plans reflect a white solution of the Indians' problems. Unfortunately, they were much less appealing to the Indians. . . . Tecumseh may have dreamed of a pan-Indian union, but most of his followers remained a tribal people." See Glenn Tucker, *Tecumseh: Vision of Glory* (Indianapolis, 1956), 93. R. David Edmonds, *The Shawnee Prophet* (Lincoln, 1983), 189. Richard Drinnon, more specifically than Tucker, chooses aspects of Tenskwatawa's preaching as the product of Tecumseh's thought: "Their insistence upon racial solidarity and their angry refusal to consider land cessions were no doubt largely Tecumseh's contribution to the Code." Richard Drinnon, *Facing West: The Metaphysics of Indian Hating and Empire-Building* (New York, 1980), 92. The notion of racial solidarity is explained to a greater degree in the most recent work on Tecumseh, Bill Gilbert's *God Gave us this Country: Tekamthi and the First American Civil War* (New York, 1989), 208. The term "racial," however, is misleading; while nativists saw Indians as having spiritual differences with American citizens, their relationship with British and French Canadians is less clear, and they never moved against adopted "white Indians."

9. Gilbert, *God Gave us this Country,* 3.

10. Bouquet to Lieut. Francis and Col. Clayton, Fort Pitt, September 23, 1764, in Sylvester K. Stevens and Donald H. Kent, eds., *The Papers of Colonel Henry Bouquet* (Harrisburg, 1943), vol. 13, pt. 2: 142 (British Museum Add. Mss. 21650, f., 511, A.L.S.).

11. At Greenville, Tenskwatawa hosted Chippewas, Ottawas, Potawatomis, Delawares, Shawnees and Wyndots. See, for example, Edmunds, *The Shawnee Prophet,* 59–60; Harrison to Secretary of War, September 5, 1807, *Harrison's Messages and Letters,* 1: 247; Wells to Dearborn, Fort Wayne, January 23, 1808, Nat. Arch Micro. M221, roll 15: W-457 (3); Lawrence Henry Gipson, ed., *The Moravian Mission on White River: Diaries and Letters,* Harry E. Stocker, Herma T. Frueauff, and Samuel C. Zeller, trans. (Indianapolis, 1938), 392. At Tippecanoe, the list grew to include members of all the above-mentioned tribes, with members of the Kickapoos, Winnebagos, Miamis, Sacs, and Foxes. See, for example, Wells to Dearborn, Fort Wayne, March 6, 1808, Nat. Arch. Micro. M221, roll 15: W-520 (3); Harrison to Secretary of War, April 25, 1810, June 14, 1810, July 18, 1810, and July 25, 1810, in *Harrison's Messages and Letters* 1: 417–18, 424, 446–47, 449.

12. Wells to Dearborn, Fort Wayne, April 22, 1808, Clarence Edwin Carter, ed., *The Territorial Papers of the United States* (Washington, D.C., 1934–37), 7: 558 (cited hereafter as *TPUS*). I differ here with the dominant interpretation, claiming that Tenskwatawa acts "the holy man . . . , while Tecumseh promoted a multitribal confederacy to resist Indian cessions of land to the United States and to forge a more nationalist Indian identity." John Sugden, "Early Pan-Indianism, Tecumseh's tour of the Indian Country, 1811–1812," *American Indian Quarterly*, 10 (1986): 273–304.

13. Harrison to Secretary of War, June 14, 1810, *Harrison's Messages and Letters,* 1: 423.

14. John Brainerd to Israel Pemberton, 1751, in Thomas Brainerd, ed., *Life of John Brainerd* (Philadelphia, 165), 234; James Kenny, "Journal of James Kenny," John W. Jordan, ed., *Pennsylvania Magazine of History and Biography,* 37 (1913), 171.

15. David Zeisberger, "1767 Diary," 610a, and Zeisberger, "1769 Diary," 91, both translated typescripts in Miscellaneous File, Glenn A. Black Archaeological Laboratory, Indiana University, Bloomington; David Zeisberger, Diary, 1772–1773, *Records of the Moravian Mission among the Indians of North America,* microfilm of records of the Moravian Archives, Bethlehem, Pennsylvania, Reel 8 file 141, 13: 7–8, located at the American Philosophical Society, Philadelphia; David Jones, *Journal of Two Visits Made to Some Nations on the West Side of the River Ohio in the Years 1772 and 1773* (Burlington, NJ, 1774), 63.

16. Benjamin Drake, *Life of Tecumseh and of his Brother the Prophet* (Cincinnati, 1841), 21–22; James Smith to Charlotte Ludlow, Bourbon County, December 21, 1801, Historical and Philosophical Society of Ohio, microfilm at the Glenn Black Archaeological Laboratory, Bloomington, Indiana.

17. C.C. Trowbridge, "Shawnese Tradilions," edited by Vernon Kinietz and Ermine W. Voegelin, *Occasional Contributions from the Museum of Anthropology at the University of Michigan,* 9 (1939), 3. For similar views expressed in the first decade of the nineteenth century see Gipson, ed., *Moravian Mission on White River,* 406, 419, 562; and Harrison to Secretary of War, June 26, 1810, *Harrison's Messages and Letters,* 1: 434. This last report says it clearly: the Prophet "was commissioned by the Great Spirit of the Indians (who was himself an Indian and different from the Great Spirit of the Whites)."

18. Zeisberger, "1769 Diary," 150.

19. Ibid., 601–602.

20. Gipson, ed., *Moravian Mission on White River,* 438. See Wallace, *Death and Rebirth,* 244, 247; "Henry Simmons' Version of the Visions," in Halliday Jackson, "Halliday Jackson's Journal to the Seneca Indians, 1798–1800," Anthony F.C. Wallace, ed., *Pennsylvania History,* 19 (1952), 349; and Arthur C. Parker, "The Code of Handsome Lake, the Seneca Prophet," in William N. Fenton, ed., *Parker on the Iroquois* (Syracuse, 1968), Book Two, 67–68, for the notion among the Senecas.

21. Tecumseh's reply to Harrison, August 10, 1810, *Harrison's Messages and Letters,* 1: 467. Late in the nineteenth century the son of Stephen Ruddell—a Baptist missionary to and former captive of the Shawnees—recalled his father's story of similar religious questioning on Tecumseh's part. Stephen Ruddell had tried to convince Tecumseh that he should pay no attention to the Prophet, for the age of "revelations from The Great Spirit had closed—Tecumseh's answer would be that it may be closed to the white man but not to the Indian and so Tecumseh believed all the extravagant sayings of the Prophet." J. M. Ruddell to Draper, Marcelline, Ill., Nov. 15, 1884, Tecumseh Papers Lyman Draper MSS, State Historical Society of Wisconsin, 8yy 42–43, cited hereafter as Draper MSS.

22. Harrison to Secretary of War, June 26, 1810, *Harrison's Messages and Letters,* 1: 435.

23. Thomas Forsyth to Benjamin Howard, St. Louis, May 7, 1813, Richard C. Knopf, ed., *Document Transcriptions of the War of 1812 in the Northwest,* 10 vols. (Columbus, Ohio, 1959–62), *Letters to the Secretary of War, 1813,* v.7: pt.2: 87. The full collection will be cited hereafter as Knopf, ed., *Documents 1812,* the series as *LSW.* Forsyth took such notions seriously. He would later recall, as if against the bulk ol scholarship, that "Tecumseh always stood up for his brother." See "Sketch of Tecumseh by Thomas Forsyth . . . ," Draper MSS, 8yy54.

24. Entry for December 3, 1805, Gipson, ed., *Moravian Mission on White River,* 392; Navarre, *Journal,* 30.

25. William Wells to Henry Dearborn, Fort Wayne, April 22, 1808, *TPUS,* 7:58.

26. R. David Edmunds, *The Potawatomis: Keepers of the Fire* (Norman, Oklahoma 1978), 79; Peckham, *Pontiac;* 116, Hunter, "Delaware Nativist Revival," 46; Wallace "New Religions among the Delaware Indians, 1600–1900," 9.

27. Raymond Fogelson has recently argued against the existence of "tribes" in North America until the intervention of colonial powers, particularly the federal government. Raymond D. Fogelson, "The Context of American Indian Political History: An Overview and Critique," in *The Struggle for Political Autonomy: The Second Newberry Library Conference on Themes in American Indian History,* Occasional Papers in Curriculum Series, 11 (Chicago, 1989): 8–21.

28. Secretary of War Dearborn to Governor Harrison, War Dept, February 23, 1802, *TPUS,* 7: 50. My assessments of Little Turtle and William Wells differ markedly from those of Paul Hutton,

400 • From Revolution to Removal, and Beyond

"William Wells: Frontier Scout and Indian Agent," *Indian Magazine of History* 74 (1978): 183–222; and Harvey Lewis Carter, *The Life and Times of Little Turtle: First Sagamore of the Wabash* (Chicago, 1987), 197–208. But whether one accepts my assessment or theirs, the fact remains that these advocates of accommodation had embroiled themselves in self-destructive bickering with like-minded members of other peoples, while the forces of nativism rose again to offer an intertribal alternative.

29. C.F. Volney, *A View of the Soil and Climate of the United States of America: with Supplemental Remarks.* C.B. Brown, trans. (Philadelphia, 1804), 378.

30. Secretary of War Dearborn to Governor Harrison, War Dept, February 23, 1802, *TPUS*, 7: 48–50.

31. William Kirk to Dearborn, Black Hoof's Town, July 20, 1807, National Archives Microfilm M221 roll 9: K-46 (3); Dearborn to Wells, August 5, 1807, *TPUS*, 7: 467.

32. John Johnson to Secretary of War William Eustice, Fort Wayne, July 1, 1809, National Archives Microfilm, M221, roll 24: J-263 (4); Hutton, 210–13.

33. Harrison to Dearborn, Vincennes, February 14, 1809, National Archives Microfilm, M221 roll 23: H-347 (4).

34. Wells to Eustice, Fort Wayne, December 20, 1811, National Archives, Microfilm M221 roll 49.

35. Harrison to Secretary of War, Vincennes, November 9, 1808, *Harrison's Letters and Messages*, 1: 322.

36. Drake, *Life of Tecumseh*, 41–45; William Albert Galloway, *Old Chillicothe: Shawnee and Pioneer History* (Xenia, Ohio, 1934), 71–75.

37. George Ellicott and Gerard T. Hopkins, "A Visit to the Delaware, Miami and Eel River Indians [September 23, 1802–May 27, 1803], Reported to the Baltimore Yearly Meeting, 1803," 3–5, 12–13, Ayer Manuscripts, Newberry Library, Chicago; Philip Thomas "Brief Account: Friends Committee for the Improvement and Civilization of the Indians," *The Massachusetts Missionary Magazine*, 5 (1807): 267–70.

38. Ellicott and Hopkins, "A Visit," 13; Philip Thomas, "Brief Account," 267–70.

39. Edmunds, *Shawnee Prophet*, 18–19.

40. Kirk to Dearborn, Black Hoof's Town, July 20, 1807, National Archives Microfilm, M221 roll 9: K-46 (3); Kirk to Dearborn, Kirk's Settlement, April 12, 1808, ibid., M221 roll 25: K-16 (4); John Johnson to Dearborn, Fort Wayne, April 15, 1809, *TPUS*, 7:648.

41. Ibid., 647; F. Duchoquet to Sec. of War, Kirk's Settlement, Dec. 4, 1808, National Archives Microfilm, M221, roll 25: K-54 (4); Shawnee Chiefs to President and Secretary of War, December 1, 1808, ibid.

42. Thomas, "Brief Account," 267–70.

43. Ellicott and Hopkins, "A Visit," 8–9.

44. Wells to Dearborn, Fort Wayne, April 23, 1808, *TPUS*, 7: 560.

45. Richard McNemar, *The Kentucky Revival* (New York, 1846, reprinted 1974), 126–27.

46. Anthony Shane, Draper MSS, 12 YY 8–10.

47. David Zeisberger, "1769 Diary," translated typescript in Glenn A. Black Archaeological Laboratory, University of Indiana, Bloomington, Indiana, 62–63, 74, 125, 172; John Heckewelder, *Narrative of the Mission of the United Brethren among the United Brethren among the Delaware and Mohegan Indians* (Philadelphia, 1820), 108, 135–36. See also Handsome Lake's accusations against Red Jacket, in Wallace, *Death and Rebirth*, 254–62; Parker, 68.

48. Gipson, ed., *Moravian Mission on White River*, 413–15, 556–65; MacLean, 224; Shane, Draper MSS, 12 YY 13–14.

49. Gipson, ed., *Moravian Mission on White River*, 556.

50. Gipson, ed., *Moravian Mission on White River*, 414 416, 624; Edmunds, *The Shawnee Prophet*, 43–46; Charles J. Kappler, ed., *Indian Affairs, Laws and Treaties* (Washington, 1904) 2: 44–45, 70–71. The names read "Tetabokshke" and "Hawkinpumiska" on the 1795 treaty and "Jeta Buxika" and "Hoking Pomskann" on the 1804 treaty. "Hocking Pomskan" also signed a treaty with the U.S. in 1805, ibid., 81. "Topethteboxie," supported the Quaker's proposed reforms in 1804; see Thomas, "Brief Account," 268.

51. Gipson, ed., *Moravian Mission on White River*, 414–16, 565.

52. Kirk to Dearborn, Fort Wayne, May 28, 1807, Nat. Arch. Micro. M229 roll 9: K-36 (3); Shawnee Chiefs to the President and the Secretary of War, December 1, 1808, National Archives Microfilm, M221 roll 25: K-54.

53. Thomas Jefferson to Dearborn, August 12, 1807, Monticello, Daniel Parker Papers, Historical Society of Pennsylvania, Philadelphia.

54. "Substance of a Talk . . . ," Nat. Arch. Micro. M222 roll 2: L-1807. For the Trout's alliance with Tenskwatawa see Edmunds, *Shawnee Prophet*, 51–52.

55. John Askin, Jr., to John Askin, St. Josephs, September 1, 1807, Milo Milton Quaife, ed., *The John Askin Papers*, 2 vols. (Detroit, 1931) 2: 568–69.

56. Wells to Dearborn, April 23, 1808, *TPUS*, 7: 560; Wells to Dearborn, April 2, 1808, ibid., 7: 541; Edmunds, *The Shawnee Prophet*, 69.

57. Reginald Horsman, *Expansion and American Indian Policy, 1783–1812* (East Lansing, Mich., 1967): 146–55; Kappler, 2: 70, 72, 77, 80, 89, 93, 99.

58. Harrison to Secretary of War, Fort Wayne, 10 October, 1809, *Harrison's Messages and Letters*, 1: 358.

59. R. David Edmunds powerfully demonstrates Tenskwatawa's earlier leadership, and I must emphasize that achievement, but both Edmunds and Reginald Horsman agree that following the treaty of Fort Wayne, it was Tecumseh who, in Horsman's words, "transformed a religious revival into an attempt at Indian unity"; it was Tecumseh, who, in Edmunds' words, "used his brother's religious movement as a base for his ill-fated, political-military confederacy." Horsman, *Expansion*, 152–53, 166–67; Edmunds, "National Expansion from the Indian Perspective," in Frederick Hoxie, ed., *Indians in American History: an Introduction* (Arlington Heights, Ill., 1988) 162. James H. Merrell agrees that Tecumseh "translated" the Prophet's plan "from the spiritual to the political realm," in "Declarations of Independence: Indian-White Relations in the New Nation," in Jack Greene, ed., *The American Revolution: Its Character and Limits* (New York, 1987), 212. See also Tanner, *Atlas of Great Lakes Indian History*, 104.

60. Michel Brouille to Harrison, June 30, 1810, *Harrison's Messages and Letters* 1: 436–37. See also Harrison to Secretary of War, June 14, 1810, in ibid., 1: 425.

61. Jared Mansfield to Gallatin, September 18, September 28, and Gallatin to Mansfield, October 12, 1810, *TPUS*, 8: 47, 49, 52–53.

62. In chronological order, the exponents of the standard narrative, as here described, include Drake, *Life of Tecumseh*, 156; Edward Eggleston, *Tecumseh and the Shawnee Prophet* (New York, 1878), 231; Tucker, *Tecumseh: Vision of Glory*, 230–31; Edmunds, *The Shawnee Prophet*, 115–16, 119; R. David Edmunds, *Tecumseh and the Quest for Indian Leadership* (Boston, 1984), 159–62; Bill Gilbert, *God Gave us this Country*, 271–72.

63. Jesup A. Couch to Thomas Worthington, Chillicothe, Ohio, January 3, 1812 in Knopf, ed., *Documents 1812, Thomas Worthington and the War of 1812*, v.3: 32.

64. Snelling to Harrison, Fort Harrison, Nov. 20, 1811, in *Harrison's Messages and Letters*, 1: 643–44.

65. Harrison to Secretary of War, Vincennes, December 4, 1811, and same to same, December 24, 1811, in *Harrison's Messages and Letters*, 1: 657, 685.

66. Harrison to Secretary of War, January 7, 1812, Vincennes, in *Harrison's Messages and Letters*, 2: 5–6.

67. Harrison to Eustis, Vincennes, April 15, 1812, Knopf, ed., *Documents 1812, LSW*, v.6: pt. 1: 133.

68. Snelling to Harrison, Fort Harrison, January 18, 1812; Harrison to Secretary of War, January 29, 1812, Vincennes; Snelling to Harrison, Fort Harrison, April 16, 1812, all in *Harrison's Messages and Letters*, 2: 15, 21.

69. Knopf, ed., *Documents 1812, The National Intelligencer Reports the War of 1812 in the Northwest*, v. 5: pt. 1: 54.

70. Forsyth to Benjamin Howard, Peorias, Feb. 18, 1812, and Extract of letter, Feb. 10, 1812, in Knopf, ed., *Documents 1812, LSW*, v.6: pt. 1: 57.

71. Harrison to Secretary of War, Vincennes, May 13, 1812, and same to same, June 3, 1812, in Harrison's *Messages and Letters*, 2: 49–58; Reuben Atwater to Secretary of War, Detroit, January 21, 1812, Knopf, ed., *Documents 1812, LSW,* v.6: pt. 1:22.

72. Major General Samuel Hopkins to Governor Shelby, Wabash, November 27, 1812, Knopf, ed., *Documents 1812, The National Intelligencer,* v.5: pt. 1: 292.

73. Edwards to Eustis, Elvirade, March 3, 1812, Knopf, ed., *Documents 1812, LSW,* v.6: pt. 1: 68.

74. Harrison to Shaw, Vincennes, 6 March 1812, Knopf, ed., *Documents 1812, LSW,* v.6: pt. 1: 76.

75. Draper MSS, 12 yy, 46–47.

76. Both Stephen Ruddell, on his death bed in 1884, and his son provided Lyman Draper with stories of Tecumseh's conviction in his brother's religion. See Draper MSS, 8 yy, 40, 42–43, 54.

77. William Claus to Major-General Brock, Amherstburg, June 16, 1812, E.A. Cruikshank, ed., *Documents Relating to the Invasion of Canada and the Surrender of Detroit, 1812,* Publications of the Canadian Archives—No. 7 (Ottawa, 1912), 33; hereafter *DRIC.*

78. Harrison to Eustis, Vincennes, March 4, 1812, Knopf, ed., *Documents 1812, William Henry Harrison and the War of 1812,* v.1: 9.

79. Colonel Matthew Elliot to Major-General Brock, Amberstburg, January 12, 1812, and Speech of the Indians on the Wabash in Reply to Message of Colonel M. Elliott, S.I.A., Amherstburg, June 8, 1812, both in Cruikshank, ed., *Documents Relating to the Invasion of the Canada,* 6–8, 33–35.

80. Indian Council, May 15, 1812, *Harrison's Messages and Letters,* 2: 49–51.

81. Permoratome to Edwards, Peorias, June 8, 1812, in Knopf, ed., *Document Transcriptions of the War of 1812 in the Northwest, Letters to the Secretary of War, 1812,* v.6: pt. 2: 23.

82. Elliot to Brock, January 12, 1812, in Cruikshank, ed., *DRIC,* 7.

83. Speech of Indians. . . . June 8, 1812, Amherstburg, in Cruikshank, ed., *DRIC,* 34.

84. Indian Council, May 15, 1812, *Harrison's Messages and Letters,* 2: 49–51, emphasis added.

85. Wells to Eustis, Fort Wayne, 10 Feb. 1812, Knopf, ed., *Documents 1812, LSW,* v.6: pt. 1: 44.

86. See, for example, William Henry Harrison to William Eustis, Vincennes, 28 July 1812; Brigr. Genl. Edmund munder to Return Jonathan Meigs, Montgomery County, Ohio, May 14, 1812; B.F. Stickney to John Johnson, Fort Wayne, July 20, 1812; Zachary Taylor to Gen. Harrison, Fort Harrison, September 10, 1812; Enos Terry to Meigs, Greenville, January 14, 1812; Reuben Atwater to Secretary of War, Detroit, January 21, 1812; Reuben Atwater to James Monroe, Detroit, Feb. 11, 1812; Jno. Shaw to James Rea, Fort Wayne, March 1, 1812; Shaw to Eustis, Fort Wayne, March 10, 1812; Indian Council-[Ninian] Edwards, April 25, 1812; Harrison to Eustis, Vincennes, April 29, 1812; Johnson to Eustis, Piqua, May 1, 1812; Edwards to Eustis, Elvirade, May 6, 1812; same to same, Elvirade, June 2, 1812; Thomas Forsyth to Benjamin Howard, Peorias, June 9, 1812; Stickney to Eustis, Fort Wayne, July 19, 1812; Edwards to Eustis, Elvirade, August 8, 1812; Taylor to Harrison, Fort Harrison, August 9, 1812; Forsyth to Howard, Peorias, Sept. 7, 1812; Taylor to Harrison, Fort Harrison, September 10 1812; Report of August LeRoche and Louis Chevalier, St. Louis, 4 April 1812, Edward to John Armstrong Elvirade April 12, 1813; Harrison to Armstrong, Headquarters, Camp Meigs, 21 April 1813; all the foregoing from Knopf, ed., *Documents 1812,* 10 vols., as follows: *Harrison and the War of 1812* (material from the Library of Congress), v.1: 15; *Return Jonathan Meigs, Jr. and the War of 1812* (material from the Ohio State Library and the Ohio State Museum Library), v.2: 176; *The National Intelligencer* (material from the Library of Congress) v.5: pt.1: 132, 236–38; *LSW* (material from the National Archives) v.6: pt.1: 12, 22, 18, 66, 89, 161, 166, 170 180; v.6: pt. 2: 7, 25, 113–114; v.6: pt. 3: 14, 21, 119, 135–37; *LSW,* v.7: pt. 2: 13, 28, 50. See also Elliot to Brock, Amherstburg, 12 January 1812, in *DRIC,* 7.

87. Seventeenth- and eighteenth-century Shawnees had previously established relations with the Cherokees and Creeks. At least one of Tecumseh's parents must have been widely traveled, for Tecumseh's mother was a Creek. Harrison to Secretary of War, June 26, 1810, *Harrison's Letters and Messages,* 1: 434.

88. Harrison to Dearborn, Vincennes, July 11, 1807, *Harrison's Messages and Letters,* 1: 224; Harrison to Secretary of War, Vincennes, July 26, 1810, ibid., 1: 434, the parenthetical remark is Harrison's.

89. Historian John Sugden has recently argued that Tecumseh probably made "preliminary overtures to the various tribes" as he prepared to journey southward. These findings confirm Sugden's suspicion, although they give credit to the Prophet as well as to his brother. Sugden, "Early Pan-Indianism," 278–79.

90. Secretary of War to Harrison, War Dept., June 20, 1807. *TPUS,* 7: 462.

91. Harrison to Secretary of War, Vincennes, May 15, 1810, *Harrison's Letters and Messages,* 1: 420–21. One of these may have been the Creek warrior Tuskenea, who, according to a memoir written much later, had journeyed briefly to the Wabash "some few years before the war [of 1812]." Thomas Simpson Woodward, *Woodward's Reminiscences of the Creek, or Muskogee Indians* (Montgomery, Alabama, 1859), 94–95.

92. Gipson, ed., *Moravian Mission on White River,* 297–98, 371, 521, 539.

93. Carl F. Klink and James J. Talman, eds., *The Journal of Major John Norton, 1816: Publications of the Champlain Society,* 46 (Toronto, 1970), 175.

94. Little is known of this man, known in the record as Seekaboo. Thomas S. Woodward, an American officer in the Creek War, much later recalled that Seekaboo was a "Warpicanata chief and prophet." This probably identifies the visionary as a Mequashake Shawnee, a dissident from Black Hoof's town of Wapakoneta. Woodward further recounted both that Seekaboo remained with the Creeks when Tecumseh returned north and that Seekaboo shortly thereafter took up arms with the Creek nativists. Early historians of the Creek War (1813–14) describe him as about forty years of age in 1811, with skills as an interpreter and orator. Woodward also recalled that other Shawnee prophets, either from the northwest or from the Southern Shawnee confederates of the Creeks, joined Seekaboo in raising militant Creek spirits. Woooward, *Reminiscences,* 36, 99; H. S. Halbert and T. H. Ball, *The Creek War of 1813 and 1814,* ed., Frank Lawrence Owsley, Jr. (University of Alabama, 1969, first pub. Chicago, 1895), 40.

95. Cornells to Hawkins, June 22, 1813, and Hawkins to Gen. Armstrong, June 28, 1813, Walter Lowrie and Mathew St. Clair, eds., *American State Papers. Documents, Legislative and Executive of the Congress of the United States (1789–1815) Class 11, Indian Affairs,* 1: 845–47.

96. John Howard, *Shawnee! The Ceremonialism of a Native Indian Tribe and its Cultural Background* (Athens, Ohio, 1981), 198; Galloway, *Old Chillicothe,* 162–63; W. [Anon.], "From the Baltimore American: Black Hawk-Tecumseh," *Army and Navy Chronicle,* 7 (1838): 296; Colin G. Ironside to L.C. Draper, Vinita, Indian Territory, May 4, 1885, Draper MSS, 7yy, 76: "From Joseph N. Bournassa, born March 19, 1810, near Bertraud, Michigan, resides near Topeka, Kansas," in Draper MSS, 23S, 185; Statement of Tustenokochee, August 22, 1883, enclosed in I. G. Vore to L. C. Draper, Sasakwa, Seminole Nation, Indian Territory, Jan. 11, 1882, Draper MSS, 4yy, 2–3, 16; George Stiggins, "A Historical Narration of the Geneology, Traditions and Downfall of the Ispocaga or Creek Tribe of Indians," Theron A. Nunez, ed., *Ethnohistory,* 5 (1958), 42, 146–48, 151, 152, 167. On Pontiac: Parkman, *The Conspiracy of Pontiac,* 191 n.

19

THE GLAIZE IN 1792:
A COMPOSITE INDIAN COMMUNITY

Helen Hornbeck Tanner

The years following the American Revolution were hard times for Indians. In New England, as Ruth Wallis Herndon and Ella Wilcox Sekatau discuss below, state officials were trying to define the Narragansett people out of existence. In the South, William L. McLoughlin points out later in this volume, Cherokees also seemed on the verge of extinction. The Ohio country was at that time, Gregory Dowd suggests, between nativist revivals; nonetheless, hatred between Indians and the people now calling themselves "Americans" ran deep. Those Americans, pressing deeper into the heart of the continent, met fierce native resistance to this invasion of Indian country. The result was terrible bloodshed. "One of the first sights that Vermont native Asa Farrar witnessed upon his arrival" in 1788, the historian Elizabeth A. Perkins has written, "was another boat landing with 'a dead woman, two wounded children, and a dead horse, on board.' An infant still suckled the dead woman's breast." According to Perkins another white settler in the region, Daniel Drake, recalled that at bedtime he and his siblings were told to "lie still and go to sleep, or the Shawnees will catch you." The warning sank so deep, Drake said, that "nearly all my troubled . . . dreams included either Indians or snakes—the copper-colored man, and the copper-colored snake." Indians, meanwhile, had their own bad dreams, their own horror stories to tell of white men. Frontier folk, reported one federal official, "consider the murdering of the Indians in the highest degree meritorious."

Helen Hornbeck Tanner's careful reconstruction of the Glaize, on the Maumee River in present-day Ohio, suggests a more complicated story. In 1792 the place was, if not a melting pot, then certainly a colorful mosaic of different peoples. Miamis lived there, as did Shawnees and Delawares; nearby was a white trader's village. Hence the site suggests that, for all the hatred and hostility, for all the mistrust and bloodshed, it was possible—at some times and in some places—for Indians and whites to coexist, to construct a sort of middle ground. What conditions and circumstances made this particular social configuration possible here and elsewhere in North America? Which is more remarkable: that the Glaize looked like this in 1792, or that, just two years later, hostilities engineered by United States troops destroyed it?

THE GLAIZE IN 1792:
A COMPOSITE INDIAN COMMUNITY

Helen Hornbeck Tanner

THE GLAIZE, AN old buffalo wallow on the Maumee River at the mouth of the Auglaize (present Defiance, Ohio fifty miles southwest of Toledo) is the geographical focus for this description of a multicultural frontier society in 1792. The appearance, surroundings, and activities of this late eighteenth century community can be at least partially reconstructed from contemporary literature. At this particular place, the year 1792 has a special significance because in the fall of 1792, the Glaize became the headquarters for the militant Indian confederacy protesting American advance northwest of the Ohio River. The distinctive place name, assigned by the French, referred to the clay banks most conspicuous on the southwest side of the confluence of the two streams (Sabrevois 1902:375). The northflowing river entering the Maumee at that point became known as the river "at the *glaize*" or Auglaize River.[1]

The vicinity of The Glaize was already well-known to hunters and traders as a rich hunting ground by the middle of the eighteenth century (Le Porc Epic 1940:168), but was not used as a place for longer residence until about the period of the American Revolution when Ottawa lived at the river juncture (Hamilton 1951:113). Traffic up and down the Maumee and Auglaize rivers increased as intertribal war parties gathered at The Glaize for attacks on settlers in southern Ohio and Kentucky. The principal war path for Indians from Detroit and the upper Great Lakes led up the Maumee River from Lake Erie, crossing to the west bank of the Auglaize River right at the Glaize, and continued southward along the courses of the Auglaize and Miami rivers to the Ohio River near modern Cincinnati (see Figure I).

The complete pattern of Indian towns gathered around the Glaize in 1792 was a recent development, a regrouping formed in response to American expeditions launched from Cincinnati in 1790, and from both Vincennes and Cincinnati in 1791 (McKee 1895:366; Mesquakenoe 1923:228). The military objective of these expeditions had been the population of Shawnee, Delaware, and Miami then living at "the Miami towns" on the headwaters of the Maumee River, present Fort Wayne. In 1790, the seven "Miami Towns" comprised two Miami, two Shawnee, and three

SOURCE: *Ethnohistory* 25:1 (Winter 1978), 15–39.

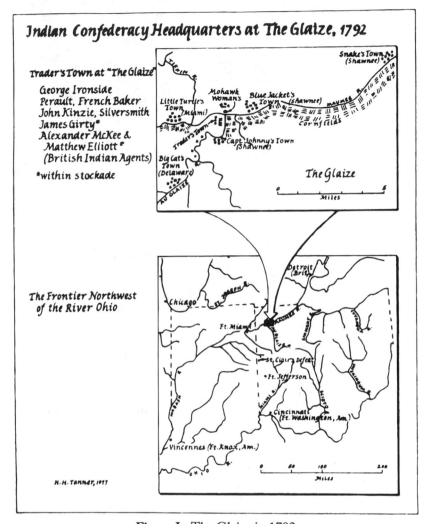

Figure I: The Glaize in 1792.

Delaware villages, along with Fort Miami whose inhabitants were principally French and British traders (Butterfield 1890:246; Hay 1915:255; Harmar 1790). General Josiah Harmar's expedition in October 1790 burned 300 houses and 20,000 bushels of corn at the temporarily abandoned villages. After he withdrew, an intertribal Indian force attacked and killed about 200 of his troops (Hammer to Knox 1832:104; Horsman 1964:60–63). The Indians rebuilt their homes, but soon began to transfer to safer locations. The nucleus for the new town formation down river at the Glaize was Captain Johnny's Shawnee town in existence near the mouth of the Auglaize River probably since 1789 (Hay 1915; Tanner 1956:7; Voegelin 1794b:417–19). As it developed by 1792, the total community at the Glaize encompassed seven main towns all within ten miles of the river mouth: three Shawnee, two Delaware, one

Miami, and a European trading town, as well as outlying dwellings, gardens, pastures, and cornfields (Aupaumut 1827:97–98). Combined population for these towns is estimated at about 2,000 persons.

Children and adults of European heritage, as well as warriors and families from eastern and southern Indian tribes, formed an integral part of this Ohio frontier society. One noticeable population component was the white captives, some adopted in childhood and raised as members of Indian families; and other more recent arrivals, mainly white but a few black, taken in the periodic raids on river boats and pioneer settlements along the Ohio River. Among the residents of the trading town were French settlers, and British traders who had Indian wives and families. The interesting diversity of this composite community coupled with the prevading sense of common interest, is revealed by a closer examination of life in the individual towns. The description will begin with the Shawnee towns, since they represented the dominant population element.

THE INDIAN TOWNS

Shawnee military headquarters on the Maumee River in 1792 was the town of the Shawnee leader Blue Jacket's, located a mile below The Glaize on the north bank of the river.[2] The town was composed of perhaps thirty or forty bark cabins housing a population estimated very roughly at 300 people. Vegetable gardens and pasture lands for horses and cattle lay behind the town, while the extensive acreage of unfenced cornfields were across the river separated from potentially marauding livestock (Spencer 1968:79, 96).

Blue Jacket himself was an impressive figure, dignified in appearance. His wife was half-French, daughter of a Shawnee woman and Colonel Duperon Baby, prominent Detroit resident and former Indian agent (Draper 1863:Mss S17, 176).[3] A young visitor at Blue Jacket's home on an important social occasion in July of 1792 wrote the following description of this Shawnee leader and his family:

> His person, about six feet high was finely proportioned, stout, and muscular; his eyes large, bright, and piercing; his forehead high and broad; his nose aquiline; his mouth rather wide, and his countenance open and intelligent, expressive of firmness and decision . . . . He was dressed in a scarlet frock coat, richly laced with gold and confined around his waist with a part-colored sash, and in red leggings and moccasins ornamented in the highest style of Indian fashion. On his shoulders he wore a pair of gold epaulets, and on his arms broad silver bracelets; while from his neck hung a massive silver gorget and a large medallion of His Majesty, George III. Around his lodge were hugh rifles, war clubs, bows and arrows, and other implements of war; while the skins of deer, bear, panther, and otter, the spoils of the chase, furnished pouches for tobacco, or mats for seats and beds. His wife was a remarkably fine looking woman; his daughters, much fairer than the generality of Indian women, were quite handsome; and his two sons, about eighteen and twenty years old, educated by the British, were very intelligent (Spencer 1968:89–92).

Blue Jacket maintained a broad range of contacts among the regional French inhabitants, the British governmental administration, and occasionally even American agents sent from Vincennes or Cincinnati. In the complex affairs of the northwest Indian confederacy formed in 1786, Blue Jacket often served as representative to the British officials in Detroit and Montreal, speaking in behalf of the Delaware and Miami as well as the Shawnee (Blue Jacket 1895:135). In 1790, when his home was near the Miami towns at the head of the Maumee, he had provided lodging for Isaac Freeman, messenger from John Cleves Symmes, promoter of the American settlement at Cincinnati (Symmes 1926:104). The same spring he had entertained at his residence the American emissary, Antoine Gamelin, sent from Fort Knox, the military post at Vincennes (Gamelin 1882:157).

A second Shawnee village, Snake's Town, was situated about eight miles down the Maumee River from Blue Jacket (Voegelin 1974:200). A noted warrior, but less striking than his neighboring tribal leader, the Great Snake was described in 1788 as an "elderly, robust and rather corpulent" individual, whose wife remained a "pretty, well-looking woman" of stately carriage (Ridout 1890:366–67). Four years later, the Snake seemed to be "a plain, grave chief of sage appearance" (Spencer 1968:92). Snake's Town occupied the most easterly position of the group of Indian towns around the Glaize.

The third and oldest Shawnee town in the area lay on the east bank of the Auglaize more than a mile south of the Maumee River. The intervening land between the village and the mouth of the Auglaize River comprised part of a vast tract of Indian cornfields extending several miles along the south bank of the Maumee River (Spencer 1968:85, 96). This central town site is associated with Captain Johnny, in 1791 identified as "chief of the River Glaize" (Anonymous 1895:223). In the immediate vicinity were small settlements of Nanticokes originally from the Potomac Bay region, and Chicamaugua Cherokee warriors from Tennessee. The Cherokee's long connection with the Shawnee in Ohio is indicated by their frequent participation in intertribal councils and war parties north of the Ohio River, beginning in 1750 (Trent 1911: 294, 297). Living within the Shawnee towns were families of Mohawk, Cayuga, and Seneca who were sometimes classified together as "Mingoes of the Glaize." The term *Mingo*, of Algonquian language origin, was commonly used during the eighteenth century to identify independent splinter groups of Six Nations Iroquois living in Ohio and western Pennsylvania (Hodge 1911:1:867–68). A separate Delaware group, not mapped, also formed part of the Auglaize Indian community, and may have been located adjacent to Captain Johnny's town.

Across the Auglaize from the third Shawnee town, occasional dwellings spread southward about four miles along the west bank of the river. The south end of this Indian metropolitan district, about eight miles upriver on the Auglaize, was marked by a prominent Delaware village headed by Buckongahelas, principal warrior, and Big Cat, civil leader. A small village of Conoys, another eastern refugee group from Potomac Bay, formed part of the Delaware community (Aupaumut 1827:97–99). Big Cat himself lived in a bark-roofed log cabin lacking a floor, but possessing a fine door of hewed puncheons and a fireplace with a chimney constructed in the French fashion of reeds and clay. The principle interior furnishings were the beds made by supports of forked sticks driven into the earth with cross pieces inserted in holes in the log walls. On these frames were laid large slips of bark covered over with skins. Big Cat acquired a second dwelling, a fine military marker, as part of his booty from St. Clair's defeat on November 4, 1791. This engagement, which took place at the later site of Fort Recovery, has been recognized as the most humiliating defeat ever suffered by the American army, with the loss of 630 lives out of a force of 1,400 (St. Clair 1812:69, 71; Horsman 1964:68–69).[4]

Big Cat's family in 1792 included an adopted son, John Brickell, a Pennsylvania lad captured by a Delaware warrior in May of 1791. Throughout his later life, Brickell retained a feeling of warmth and admiration for this exceptionally kindly Indian leader. Recounting his four years' experience living with Big Cat, Brickell observed:

> The Delawares are the best people to train up children I ever was with. They never whip, and scarce ever scold them. I was once struck one stroke, and but once while a member of the family, and then but just touched. They are remarkably quiet in the domestic circle. A dozen may be in one cabin, of all ages, and often scarcely noise enough to prevent the hearing of a pin fall on a hard place. Their leisure hours are, in a great measure, spent in training up their children to observe what they believe to be right. They often point out bad examples to them and say, "See that bad man; he is despised by everybody. He is older than you; if you do as he does, everybody will despise you by the time you are as old as he is." They often point good as worthy of imitation such as brave and honest men. l know I am influenced to good, even at this day (1842) more from what I learned among them, than what I learned among my own color . . . (Brickell 1842:47–48).

The final town to be covered in this description of a pan-Indian settlement complex is Little Turtle's Miami village located that year on the north bank of the Maumee River near the Tiffin River about five miles west of Blue Jacket's Town (Spencer 1968:111). His customary residence was Eel River town twenty miles northwest of the Miami Towns (Hodge 1907:771). In 1792, Little Turtle, son of a Miami chief and a Mahican woman, was recognized as leading warrior of the Northwest Indian confederacy, his reputation based in large measure on his role in the stunning victory of the Indian forces over St. Clair's army in 1791. Similar in composition to the neighboring Indian towns, this Miami village also had a representation from the pioneer White settlements. Little Turtle's own family is a good example. The military hero of the Miamis took as his second wife a white captive, Polly Ford, previously married to a Frenchman living at Vincennes (Graves 1937:ms.).

His adopted son, later his son-in-law, was William Wells, member of a prominent Kentucky family, captured in 1784 at the age of thirteen. Although he had fought in 1791 with the Indian contingent, in 1792, Wells was employed by the American army staff at Vincennes to carry pacifically phrased messages to the "hostile tribes" on the Maumee River (Putnam 1791a, b:ms.; Putnam 1903:371–74). Consequently, he often passed back and forth from Little Turtle's town at the Glaize within British territory to the American occupied town on the lower Wabash River (Spencer 1968:114).

THE MOHAWK WOMAN'S CABIN

On the north bank of the Maumee between the towns of Little Turtle and Blue Jacket, stood a solitary cabin of considerable importance in local society. This lone dwelling belonged to Coo-coo-chee, an independent and influential Mohawk woman frequently consulted by Indian leaders because of her highly valued spiritual power and knowledge of herbal medicine. Before the outbreak of the American Revolution, Coo-coo-chee and her husband, with three sons and a daughter, left their homeland on the Richelieu River in the St. Lawrence Valley near Montreal and came to live with the Shawnee in Ohio. The husband and father of this Mohawk family, a distinguished leader of the Bear clan, was mortally wounded in hand-to-hand combat with an American soldier during Harmar's 1790 attack on the Miami towns at present Fort Wayne. Since his death, Coo-coo-chee had moved out of Blue Jacket's town, selecting as a site for her widow's cabin a sloping hillside opposite the mouth of the Auglaize River. Behind the cabin, she cultivated a large vegetable garden and five acres of corn. Her food resources also included a maple grove for spring sugar-making located a few miles away near a creek on the south side of the Maumee (Spencer 1968:77–78, 125).

In 1792, the four children no longer lived with the Mohawk woman. Two grown sons, Black Loon and White Loon, were leading warriors in Blue Jacket's town, while the third brother had his home on the Auglaize River about five or six miles upstream (Spencer 1968:74). The daughter was the wife of George Ironside, a British merchant living in the trading village established on the point of land on the west side of the Auglaize River entrance, directly across the Maumee River from her bark cabin.

Yet Coo-coo-chee did not lead a solitary existence. Her household in which Shawnee served as the common language, included two grandchildren, a thirteen-year-old girl and a younger boy, as well as the "faithful dog" ever-present in an Indian family. The boy, whom his grandmother called "Simon" was rumored to be a son of Simon Girty, British partisan leader of many Indian expeditions and probably the man most hated by frontier Americans of that period. For seven months beginning in July 1792, the Mohawk woman also had charge of an eleven-year-old boy, Oliver Spencer, captured by a Shawnee and her son, White Loon. The Shawnee warrior had come across the boy on the Ohio River returning to his new home in Columbia from a Fourth of July celebration in Cincinnati (Spencer 1968: 41–47, 82, 120).

Spencer's captivity narrative provides an illuminating inside view of Coo-coo-chee's establishment and the events in which she participated, the details contributing to a general understanding of the contemporary Indian society. Her cabin in its construction was typical of homes in the surrounding villages, but somewhat above average in size (fourteen by twenty-five feet) and more elaborate in its furnishings. As Spencer described the building:

> Its frame was constructed of small poles, of which some, planted upright in the ground, served as posts and studs, supporting the ridge poles and eave bearers, while others firmly tied to these by thongs of hickory bark formed girders, braces, laths and rafters. This frame was covered with large pieces of elm bark seven or eight feet long and three or four feet wide; which being pressed flat and well dried to prevent their curling, fastened to the poles by thongs of bark, formed the weather boarding and roof of the cabin. At its western end was a narrow doorway about six feet high, closed when necessary by a single piece of bark placed beside it, and fastened by a brace, set either within or on the outside as occasion required (Spencer 1968:83).

Spencer also noted that neither locks nor bolts were used in Indian villages:

> a log placed against its door affords ample protection to its contents and abundant evidence of the right of possession in its owner; a right seldom violated even by the most worthless among them. The same respect is paid, even in the wilderness, to property known or believed to belong to Indians of the same tribe or to those of other tribes at peace with them (Spencer 1968:68–69).

The unusual feature of Coo-coo-chee's home was its two-room interior, for Indian cabins seldom had more than a single living space. The main room of her cabin had on the outside walls a low frame covered with bark and deerskins, serving as seats and bedsteads. Fires for cooking and warmth were laid in the center of the room, directly under the opening in the roof for smoke, while from the ridgepole was suspended a wooden trammel used to support a cooking kettle. The inner room, separated by a bark partition, was her private religious sanctuary, though the area also served as a pantry for food storage and spare bedroom. The addition to Coo-coo-chee's home had been built by William Moore, a fellow townsman of young Spencer from Columbia, captured earlier in 1792 by her sons, White Loon and Black Loon. Moore became a great favorite of the Mohawk woman and was often at her home that summer (Spencer 1968:97–98, 101).

Coo-coo-chee's personal possessions included all the implements and containers that were considered basic necessities in frontier living, and probably differed little from the household articles used in American pioneer homes at the same time. As Oliver Spencer observed:

> Her household furniture consisted of a large brass kettle for washing and sugar making; a deep, close-covered copper hominy kettle; a few knives, tin cups, pewter and horn spoons, sieves, wooden bowls, and baskets of various sizes; a hominy block, and four beds and bedding comprising each a few deerskins and two blankets . . . (Spencer 1968:86–87).

The Mohawk woman resembled other older women of the Shawnee village in which she had been living for many years. She wore a long calico shirt fastened in front with a silver brooch, a skirt of blue cloth with white edging belted at the waist with a striped sash, matching blue cloth leggings and deerskin moccasins. Younger belles of the town fancied more elaborate attire displaying their own handiwork, such as beaded designs and quillwork on moccasins, and more beading and ribbon borders around the bottom of skirts. Young women were also extremely fond of silver jewelry, covering skirt bodices with rows of silver buttons and brooches, lining their arms with bracelets one to four inches wide, and attaching tinkling silver bells to leggings. Yet they were seldom as ostentatious as the warriors who suspended as many as five sets of heavy ornaments from the rims of their ears (Spencer 1968:87–88). The importance of silver jewelry is illustrated by the fact that General Rufus Putnam, sent from Philadelphia in 1792 to make a peace treaty with the Northwest Indians, took along with him twenty sets of silver jewelry and additional ear and nose ornaments. The jewelry was intended to serve as presents at the treaty signing (Knox 1903:265).

During the course of the spring and summer of 1792, Coo-coo-chee presided over two important Indian ceremonies at her home, the annual Feast of the Dead and the Green Corn Festival. In observance of the Feast of the Dead, her husband's bones were reverently removed from their original burial site and placed in a grave a few rods from her cabin, in view of the warrior's path crossing the Maumee River. The Mohawk leader was buried in a sitting posture facing westward; and by his side were placed all the items necessary for a successful warrior and hunter, his rifle, tomahawk, knife, blanket, and moccasins. Friends attending the ceremony dropped additional gifts into the open grave. When the reburial was completed, a four-foot post was placed at the head of the grave. This marker, painted bright red, had near the top a rudely carved image of a face, below which was recorded the number of scalps he had taken in battle. On important occasions thereafter, as many as nineteen scalps attached to a long, slender pole, swayed in the wind over his gravesite (Spencer 1968:80–82).

The next important ceremony at Coo-coo-chee's cabin, the Green Corn Festival, took place in mid-August. The Shawnee were among the more northern groups to share this harvest tradition, annually observed by agriculturally skilled Indian people from East Texas to Florida. At Coo-coo-chee's home in 1792, the festival was an all-day celebration with sombre, sportive, joyous and dangerously rowdy phases. Her guests included her three sons and their wives, her daughter and George Ironside, William Moore, and a number of other Shawnee families. The program opened with the ritual of passing a pipe several times around the circle of participants seated on the grass. Next, a venerable leader delivered a solemn speech first extolling the bountiful gifts provided for Indian people by the Great Spirit, then denouncing the murderous oppression of the encroaching "pale faces." At the conclusion of his oration, the speaker exhorted the warriors to drive the Americans from the land, or at least force them back to the other side of the Ohio River. This rousing finale drew the listeners to their feet with whoops of approval for the commencement of the sports contests (Spencer 1968:102–104).

In preparation for this next section of the festivities, William Moore had built a viewing stand behind Coo-coo-chee's cabin. This structure consisted of a raised platform with a rear wall and roof to shield the older guests from the sun as they watched the athletic events. Footraces were first on the schedule, followed by a series of wrestling matches and a special test of warrior strength in retaining a grip on a slippery length of greased leather thong. Moore was permitted to join in the wrestling competition and managed to throw one of the principal Shawnee contestants. This imprudent victory he managed to explain as a lucky accident rather than superior skill, for he knew that it was scarcely safe to demean the physical prowess of his captors (Spencer 1968:105, 111).

At mid-day, everyone joined in the feast provided by Coo-coo-chee. The menu consisted of boiled jerky, fish, stewed squirrels, venison, squashes, roast pumpkins, and corn in several forms. Tender ears of corn on the cob were prepared, along with a mixture of cut corn and beans called succotash, regular corn bread, and a special pounded corn batter poured into a corn leaf mold and baked in ashes. All the food was served in wooden bowls, and eaten with wooden, horn, or tin spoons. Most of the guests carried their own knives to cut the meat (Spencer 1968:106–107).

Following a short interval of after-dinner smoking, a small keg of rum was brought out and passed around. At this point, the men turned all their knives and tomahawks over to Coo-coo-chee for safekeeping before continuing with the sports. Among the Shawnee, this safeguard was observed before indulging in any "frolic." Later in the afternoon, the recreation turned to social dancing led by an experienced singer who also beat a small drum, adjusting the tempo to suit each number. Men and women formed separate dance circles, rotating in opposite directions.

By nightfall, when the Green Corn Festival reached the final stage of an intoxicated revel, George Ironsides, William Moore and young Oliver Spencer had all left the scene. Unfortunately, White Lion challenged a fellow-warrior to a final wrestling match and was badly burned when he was thrown into the fire, a circumstance that brought the day's activities to a hasty close (Spencer 1968:112–13).

THE TRADERS' TOWN

When George Ironside and Coo-coo-chee's daughter retired from the Green Corn celebration, they crossed the Maumee to their home in the British and French trading village at the point of land most precisely defining the *grand glaize*. The high ground southwest of the juncture of the Maumee and Auglaize rivers had long been a seasonal trading site, but the local population increased markedly early in 1792 when the last European inhabitants of Fort Miami at "The Miami Towns" followed their Indian clientele downriver to new sites at the Glaize (McKee 1895:366; Vigo 1792:ms.). Here they settled in a clearing 200 yards wide and a quarter of a mile long, bordered on the west and south by tall oak trees and hazel underbrush. At the north end of the clearing, half a dozen buildings had been erected for traders and for the British Indian agency. Further upstream on the Auglaize River lived several more French and English families as well as an American couple who had been taken prisoner at St. Clair's defeat in November, 1791. The Americans were working to repay their ransom fee, the woman by washing and sewing, and the man by serving as oarsman on the boats plying between the Glaize and the British supply base at the Rapids, sixty miles further downriver on the Maumee (Spencer 1968:95–96). This small trading settlement adjacent to six sizeable Indian towns probably numbered no more than fifty individuals.

The traders living on the Point in 1792 were all men prominent in the history of the Old Northwest. George Ironsides, the most wealthy and influential of the small group, had attended King's College, Aberdeen, before coming to North America and entering the Indian trade (Quaife 1928:332 n.77). His establishment, most northerly in the row of traders, was a three-room hewed log cabin with a loft, used as a dwelling, store and warehouse. Next to him lived the French baker named Perault, who supplied bread for the entire European settlement, and occasionally to Indians (Spencer 1968:95).

The other side of the bakery stood the building belonging to John Kinzie, a silversmith and trader whose father had been a British surgeon during the Seven Years' War. John Kinzie was born in Quebec in 1763 shortly before his father's death. After his mother remarried and took him to New York, he ran away to Quebec where he became a silversmith's apprentice. He subsequently moved to Detroit and began making jewelry for Indians in the Maumee River Valley. The mother of his two children was a Shawnee captive taken from her father's home in West Virginia in 1774, when she was ten years old, and ransomed in Detroit in 1784 (Andreas 1884:100–102).

Between George Ironside's establishment and the banks of the Auglaize River, a small stockade enclosed two buildings belonging to men who had been living and trading with the Shawnee for almost thirty years by 1792. One building served as a supply depot intermittently used by Alexander McKee, British Indian agent in Detroit, and his assistant, Matthew Elliott (Horsman 1964:59). The second building was occupied by the trader James Girty, who shared his home for considerable periods of time during the summer and fall of 1792 with his older brother, Simon Girty. These men to varying degrees had been integrated into Indian society through family and trading connections, yet they also had played significant roles in American and British diplomacy and warfare in the Ohio Valley. A sketch of their interwoven personal histories indicates their long connection with the Shawnee and allied tribes, and their place in the composite community at the Glaize in 1792.

The Indian life of the Girtys, Simon, James, and a younger brother, George, began in the summer of 1756 when their ages were thirteen, eleven, and nine. With the rest of their family they were captured by a Delaware-Shawnee war party on the Pennsylvania frontier, but were repatriated in 1759. For three years, Simon lived with the Seneca, James with the Shawnee, and George with the Delaware. The social experience and knowledge of Indian language gained during the period of captivity actually determined the subsequent course of their lives. The trio first became official interpreters for the British Indian agency at Pittsburgh (Butterfield 1890:8, 13–15).

Before the outbreak of the American Revolution, James Girty along with the deputy Indian agent at Pittsburgh, Alexander McKee, and Matthew Elliott were all traders in the Shawnee villages clustered around Chillicothe, Ohio, on the Scioto River and its tributaries. Elliott, an Irishman who had come to Pennsylvania in 1761, entered the Shawnee trade after serving in Colonel Henry Bouquet's expedition against the Delaware towns on the Muskingum River near present Coshocton, Ohio in 1764 (Cruikshank 1923:157 n.). In Dunmore's War, 1774, the first military action directed against the Shawnee in Ohio, Simon Girty scouted for Lord Dunmore; while Matthew Elliott carried the peace message to Dunmore from the Shawnee (Gibson 1842:1:18).

The political sympathies of the Indian agency staff at Pittsburgh were open to question throughout the early years of the American Revolution. The year 1778 was a watershed year marking the divide between the American and British association of the McKee, Elliott, and Girty faction. Early in 1778, all three Girtys were involved in American projects organized in Pittsburgh. Their changing personal loyalties became evident on the night of March 28, however, when McKee, Elliott, and Simon Girty precipitously left American-occupied Pittsburgh, picked up James Girty in the Ohio Shawnee country, and enlisted in the British Indian service at Detroit. For the balance of the Revolutionary War, and throughout the battles of mutual retaliation between Kentuckians and the Northwest Indian Confederacy beginning in 1786, all these men were active partisans in Indian warfare, although McKee as top officer was seldom involved in actual combat (Butterfield 1890:47–51, 75ff).

Living within the stockaded section of the trading town at the Glaize with a Shawnee wife, James Girty in 1792 evinced a wariness of strangers and overt hostility toward captured Americans (Spencer 1968:132). His brother, Simon, joined him at intervals while performing the duties of mobile trouble-shooter for the British Indian service. By this time, Simon Girty at the age of fifty-three had become an awesome veteran of Ohio frontier warfare, his sunken grey eyes shaded by heavy brows meeting above a flat nose, and a forbidding facial expression. Dressed in Indian attire but without the usual silver ornaments and decorations worn by tribal leaders, he customarily wore a silk handkerchief knotted about his shaggy head and pulled low over one eyebrow to conceal an ugly scar. Simon had received a serious tomahawk wound not from an enemy, but from an ally, the Mohawk leader Joseph Brant, about whom he had made allegedly disparaging remarks following a joint expedition across southeastern Ohio in 1781 (Spencer 1968:92). Socially as well as spatially, James Girty existed on the periphery of the predominantly British-French trading town at the Glaize. He had little in common with the French inhabitants whose homes were further from the Point; his ties were much closer to his Shawnee relatives and associates.

Very little detailed information about the social life of the trading community at the Glaize in 1792 has survived, but a vivid account of the manners and customs of the same group at Fort Miami (modern Fort Wayne) has been preserved in the journal entries of a Detroit visitor who lived in the town from late December 1789 until April 1790 (Hay 1915:208–261). Fort Miami, an old French settlement, had a closely knit population of about a dozen families, some of whom had been there thirty to fifty years by 1790. Social leader of the community, Madame Adahmer, wife of one of the older French traders, ran a household largely dependent upon the labor of a "ponnie wench," a term identifying a Pawnee or any other western Indian captured by eastern tribes and sold into slavery. The ladies of the traders' town served tea and coffee at afternoon gatherings, supplying ample quantities of port, madeira, and sometimes grog at dinners and evening parties. Menus were European in character, including such items as roast turkey, corned pork, loin of veal, cucumber pickles and cheese (Hay 1915:220, 225, 227–29).

Card playing, singing, and dancing were the regular pastimes in the predominantly French atmosphere. Frequently music was provided by two violinists, John Kinzie, the silversmith, and a trader named LaChambre, and by the Detroit visitor who brought along his flute. The same trio played for morning mass and vespers on Christmas Day. On Sundays, the settlers were called to prayers held at the home of an elderly inhabitant, by three small boys who circulated through the village ringing cow bells (Hay 1915:221, 224–25, 255).

A gallant young man at Fort Miami began the New Year by kissing all the ladies and in the following weeks joined the impromptu serenades further honoring the female contingent in the small town. On the evening preceding special saints' days, everyone joined in presenting a bouquet to the person bearing the name of that particular saint, then carrying the bouquet from house to house, stopping each time for a round of dancing. When the creeks and marshes froze, ice skating became a popular outdoor activity (Hay 1915:239, 242).

British traders promoted a full day's celebration of Her Majesty's Birthday on January 18, 1790. In the morning, the sergeant of the small contingent of Canadian volunteers was persuaded to fire off three vollies, a noise that brought the Snake and other Shawnee leaders into town to inquire the cause of the disturbance. The grand ball held that evening, opening with a formal minuet, marked the third consecutive night of dancing in Miamitown. In honor of this patriotic occasion, two of the leading French traders appeared in "very fine fur caps on their heads adorned with a great quantity of black ostrich feathers," also sporting "amazingly large cockades" of white tinsel ribbon (Hay 1915:240–41). Small hats with large feathers were in vogue among the Indians at that time, but the cockades were a European embellishment (Ridout 1890:358). At the ball, singing followed dancing, and one trader's wife toward the end of the evening contributed a lively ballad with verses filled undeniably with double-entendres. On the holiday calendar for Fort Miami, Mardi Gras, and St. Patrick's Day also called for special observance (Hay 1915:250, 258).

Early in 1790, the most prominent traders including John Kinzie and George Ironsides, formed a fraternal organization called "The Friars of St. Andrews" with rules written in English and translated into French. It is interesting to note that although they were trading in the area at the time, James Girty with the Shawnee and George Girty with the Delaware, neither became a member of this exclusive club. On the other hand, the list of members did include the acting Miami chief, J. B. Richardville, son of a deceased Quebec trader and an enterprising Miami woman known as Maria Louisa, who was busy at her trading post that winter improving the substantial family fortune (Hay 1915:223, 246–47).

Day to day activities in the neighboring Miami, Shawnee, and Delaware towns were always of interest to residents of Fort Miami. The casual comments in the 1790 journal reveal the deferent but sympathetic personal relations that had developed between the tribal leaders, traders and settlers. For example, Blue Jacket, the Snake, and other Indians were commonly entertained by the traders at breakfast time. Indian families frequently sent gifts of turkey or venison, receiving in return tobacco and rum or brandy. George Ironsides, accompanied James Girty back to the Shawnee camp to help collect furs. Later, George Girty brought his Delaware wife and her sister from their hunting lodge for a recreational trip to town. Blue Jacket in company with the French trader Antoine Lascelle, whose more distinguished relatives were members of the Friars of St. Andrew, arrived from a brief excursion to the Ouiatenon village lower on the Wabash, present Lafayette, Indiana (Hay 1915:229, 235–36, 244, 250).

More unusual, perhaps, as an example of intercultural relations is the billeting of Indian warriors at the homes of the European residents of Fort Miami. When LeGris, the Miami chief, returned from a military expedition, he divided his war party according to the accommodations available at each French or British household, assigning as many as six Indians to a single home. In March 1790, when the Shawnee had decided to build an additional town for families scattered by the recent period of hostilities, they convoked a town meeting of the European traders and settlers to announce their intentions, requesting presents of vermillion and tobacco. After the assembled Fort Miami residents had signified their unanimous assent, the leading Indian handed to the leading trader the string of wampum signifying this decision. Such incidents point out the way in which Europeans became involved in the life of their Indian neighbors on the frontier (Hay 1915:221, 222, 255, 257).

The convivial spirit of Fort Miami and the easy association of the settlers and traders with Indian people in the adjoining towns, demonstrated so clearly in the 1790 journal, were social qualities undoubtedly carried along to their new location in 1792. At the Glaize, even the pattern of town sites virtually duplicated the previous formation at the headwaters of the Maumee (Voegelin 1974:159–61; Tanner and Hast 1976:21). In addition to their personal ties, the trading group also maintained strong economic links to the Indian community through the fur trade. At this time, traders operating out of Detroit, backed by firms in Montreal, were struggling to preserve British control over an Indian hunting territory southwest of Lake Erie valued at £30,000 annually. Although this sum represented only about 20 percent of the income from the Mackinac hinterland, it was still far from negligible in an era of generally declining fur trade returns (Henry et al. 1895:163).

While life on the local scene at the Glaize followed a traditional round of economic and ceremonial events, in the broader sphere of Indian affairs, the region became prominent as the headquarters for the intertribal front line of hostilities along the Ohio River. The geographical location of the Glaize, equidistant from the nearest British and American forts, points up the intermediate frontier position of the confederate towns in the Maumee River Valley in 1792. Detroit, about 110 miles northeast of the Glaize by water routes, functioned as a rear supply base for the Northwest Indian Confederacy centered at the juncture of the Maumee and Auglaize rivers. Directly to the south, about 110 miles of open country intervened between the clustered Indian towns and the nearest American outpost, Fort Jefferson. Seventy miles further, the principal American base, Fort Washington at present Cincinnati, had been constructed as recently as 1790.

The military strength of the Northwest Indian Confederacy attained impressive concentration by 1792. A thousand warriors and their families gathered at the Glaize in May for a spring council with Matthew Elliott, deputy Indian agent for the British government (Western Indian Nations 1923:157). Allied with the community at the mouth of the Auglaize River were Ottawa, Wyandot, and Delaware located near McKee's supply base at the rapids of the Maumee River. The Ottawa village at Roche de Bout had been established by Pontiac's followers in 1764, but Snipe's Wyandot town and Capt. Pipe's Delaware and Munsee followers had moved from the Upper Sandusky River in 1791 concurrent with the movement of villages from the Miami Towns to the Glaize (Peckham 1947:250; Knox 1960:23). Many well-known tribal leaders, particularly of the Shawnee, were not in evidence at the Maumee in 1792 because they were living in secret camps or patrolling the Ohio River banks. For example, Tecumseh, by 1812 a renowned pan-Indian leader, made his first notable appearance as a warrior in 1792 during an engagement with Kentuckians on the lower course of the Little Miami River (Draper ms.:5 BB:83, 101; 9 BB:47).

On the other hand, the Indians assembled at the Glaize represented only a part of the total tribal manpower. In 1791, a number of Shawnee and Delaware had emigrated from the Miami Towns to Missouri, occupying land near Cape Girardeau granted by the Spanish governor of Upper Louisiana (Vigo 1792:ms.; Trudeau 1909:51). Other Shawnee were living with the Creeks and a few of the most militant were with the "outcast Cherokee" in Tennessee, at Running Water Town, present Chattanooga, Tennessee (Draper ms.:1 yy 14; Finnelson 1832:390; Leonard 1832:308). The dispersed Delaware included two communities in the Chippewa country on the Thames River, Canada (Tanner and Hast 1976:21). Most of the Miami remained within the area of present-day Indiana.

In assessing the overall capability of the allied Indians, the role of the British in Detroit was a critical factor. The British Indian agency, scarcely distinguishable from the trading interests, provided the arms and ammunition vital to continuation of the Indian protest against American encroachment. Moreover, in the spring of 1792, Agent Alexander McKee distributed 500 bushels of seed corn to families at the Glaize who had exhausted their reserves in order to feed allies during the previous two years of strenuous but successful warfare (McKee 1895a:366).

The question of peace or continued war was debated at length among the leaders of the Confederacy as well as among their potential military allies as soon as invitations to a general meeting were sent out early in the year. The future course of the Northwest Confederacy became a matter of concern to Indian people from Quebec to Missouri, and in the Cherokee and Creek country of the South. In addition, British, American, and Spanish administrations sought to influence the outcome of deliberations by sending messages or emissaries to the confederated Indians in 1792. The intensity and complexity of diplomatic affairs increased during the summer as runners came and went from all four directions, delegations arrived, and news and rumor circulated through the villages and camps. Activity reached a climax at the grand council held at the Glaize from September 30 to October 9, an occasion requiring considerable linguistic skill and management of intertribal protocol (Aupaumut 1827:76–125; McKee 1895b:483–98).

Preparations for the general Indian council were well under way by May 1792, even in the distant St. Lawrence River Valley, upper New York, and the city of Philadelphia. By 1793, the Iroquois tribes comprising the Six Nations, the Mohawk, Oneida, Onondaga, Cayuga, Seneca, and Tuscarora, were living on both sides of the Great Lakes in territory now divided between the United States and Canada. The Seven Nations of Canada included Catholic groups organized by French missionaries in the vicinity of Montreal: Hurons of Lorette, Caughnawaga Mohawk, St. Regis Mohawk, St. Francis Abenaki, Lake of the Two Mountains or Oka Mohawk, Oka Algonkin, and Oka Nipissing.

In the spring of 1791, three eastern Indian leaders, representing the Seven Nations of Lower Canada, the Six Nations Iroquois, and the Stockbridge (Mahigan), conferred with American Secretary of War, Henry Knox, before their parties left for the Maumee River meeting ground. Most pro-American of the three was Col. Louis, Indian-Negro chief of the Caughnawaga Mohawks and a man of influence among the Seven Nations of Canada, who had received his military title after serving as an American spy during the Revolutionary War. Joseph Brant, representing a pro-British faction among the Six Nations, cautiously sent a messenger to the Maumee to secure approval for going alone to Philadelphia, an action at variance with the Confederacy's agreed procedure to talk with Americans only in authorized group delegations. The third man, Capt. Hendrick Aupaumut of the Mahigan Indians, ultimately undertook the difficult task of bearing the peace message of the United States to the hostile tribes' central headquarters (Knox 1903:59 fn., 257–67; Knox 1792a:ms.; Aupaumut 1827:113).

In performing this service, Capt. Hendrick conscientiously carried on a two-hundred-year-old responsibility of the Mahigan people for taking news of the white people on the Atlantic coast to the western Indians. From Oneida, he fetched his own bag of peace containing ancient wampum, and took along written messages as well as messages in the form of specially prepared belts and strings of wampum. On his way from Philadelphia, he conferred with the Six Nations at Buffalo Creek, New York, the Delaware on the Thames River, and Capt. Pipe at the Maumee Rapids. Before settling with a fellow Mahican living at Big Cat's Delaware town, he bought bread and salt at the traders' town at the Glaize. The news he brought received varying reactions: indifference to the wars among European nations, audible enthusiasm for the report that slaves were killing their masters in the Caribbean, and long pondering over the import of the "peace" message from the United States (Aupaumut 1827:76, 79, 89, 98).

Capt. Pipe had advised Capt. Hendrick to circulate the peace message through the Delaware, Wyandot, and Chippewa, accumulating a block of support before the message was formally presented to the Shawnee. Hendrick was never able to carry out his instructions from Knox, to arrange for a delegation from the tribes assembled at the Glaize to meet General Rufus Putnum at Fort Jefferson. After receiving a series of excuses, Hendrick realized that since a war party had killed haymakers at Fort Jefferson, the ground was "bloody" and no peace meeting could take place there. Ultimately, the reports that General Wayne was organizing a new army at Pittsburgh and Fort Jefferson was being reinforced and additional posts erected became knowledge more persuasive than the beautiful four foot wampum belt with the fifteen squares representing the fifteen United States displayed by Capt. Hendrick (Aupaumut 1827:95, 121, 126–30). The Mahigan visitor frankly criticized the obviously superior position of the Shawnee war leaders whom he observed sitting in front of civil leaders at councils, contrary to traditionally accepted seating arrangements (Aupaumut 1827:118).

In the meantime, delegations arrived and set up their camps. Among the earliest were Shawnee and Delaware from the Spanish side of the Mississippi River (Johnson 1895:422). The Seven Nations of Lower Canada arrived at the Glaize, complained of the primitive facilities to which they were not accustomed, and soon departed leaving behind a few representatives. Most of the Chippewa and Ottawa, weary of waiting and anxious about the arrival of fall storms, left for the upper lakes before the council officially commenced. The large sixty-five member Six Nations delegation crossed Lake Erie on the same vessel bringing William Johnson, British Indian interpreter, and members of the British army staff from Niagara (W. Johnson 1895:468–70; Aupaumut 1827:114). Neither these men nor Alexander McKee attended the sessions, for the council at the Glaize was a pan-Indian conclave. Delegates from west of Lake Michigan were the last to arrive. Early in the year, Blue Jacket had toured the western nations and brought back a calumet presented at the council. In response to his messages and counter-propaganda from Col. Hamtramck at Vincennes, eleven western nations had held a preliminary conference in June at the confluence of the Kankakee and Desplaines rivers, predictably resulting in divided opinions (McKee 1895b:485; Hamtramck 1792:ms.).

After a series of private conferences among the various factions represented, the Grand Council at the Glaize finally opened on September 30, 1792. Indians who participated in the meeting represented the following tribes: Shawnee, Wyandot, Delaware, Munsee, Miami, Connoy, Nanticoke, Mahigan, Ottawa, Chippewa, Potawatomi, Cherokee, Creek, Sauk, Fox, Ouiatenon, Six Nations, and the Seven Nations of Lower Canada. All these Indian people knew absolutely that the Ohio River had been set as the permanent boundary between Indian and white settlements by the Treaty of Fort Stanwix in 1768 with the British, and had been agreed to by American authorities in Pittsburgh at the beginning of the American Revolution. Yet the problem of illegal American settlements in the Indian country, the basis for eighteen years of hostilities, remained unresolved. On October 7, the council decided to demand recognition of the border stipulated in the 1768 treaty, i.e., the Ohio River, "a fine natural boundary" in the opinion of a Six Nations speaker. Joseph Brant, detained in New York by illness, did not arrive at the Glaize until after this decision had been made. Brant himself favored a compromise line along the

Muskingum River that would cede to Americans an area of Ohio from which it would be difficult to evict settlers (McKee 1895b:482, 496; Aupaumet 1827:117; W. Johnson 1895:470).

The outcome of the decision made by the Grand Council in 1792 is part of the standard history of the Northwest Territory. The Indian towns at the Glaize became General Anthony Wayne's military target. Though the buildings were razed in August 1794, the residents were warned by an American deserter, and escaped down the Maumee River to regroup near the rapids. At the traders' town, Wayne established his military headquarters, Fort Defiance. The ripe corn along the south bank of the Maumee, visible from the high ground at that site, was the beginning of the impressive fifty miles of cornfields that Wayne boasted of destroying. Final defeat of the Northwest Indian Confederacy came at the Battle of Fallen Timbers, August 20, 1794, not far from McKee's post and a hastily constructed British fort at the foot of the Maumee rapids (Wayne 1960:351–55). This event usually marks the end of a chapter in Northwestern frontier history, except to add that the Indian tribes agreed to give up the southern two-thirds of Ohio at the Treaty of Greenville in 1795. On the other hand, the Indian community from the region of the Glaize did not come to an end with the destruction of the townsite on the Maumee River. After relying on the British for food distribution for two years, most of the tribal groups filtered back to familiar territory in Ohio and Indiana.

But there is a more important epilogue to this brief account of the life and death of the multicultural society at the Glaize. The Europeans who formed an unobtrusive part of the local community advanced to more spectacular careers. From this milieu emerged the men with a dual cultural heritage who became the principal intermediaries in Indian-white relations, particularly treaty negotiations, in Canada and the United States for more than a quarter of a century. A glance at the subsequent life of the traders and Indian agents at the Glaize indicates that they, as well as their Indian associates, readjusted their lives following the double loss represented by the Greenville treaty with the Indians and the concessions made by the British in the Jay Treaty of 1794. Although the British army had to give up Detroit in 1796, the British Indian department continued the direction of Indian affairs on both sides of the American-Canadian border well into the nineteenth century from their new base at Fort Malden at Amherstberg on the east bank of the Detroit River. Furthermore, several members of a second generation carried on as intermediaries in Indian relations.

Alexander McKee was succeeded as British Indian agent by his Shawnee son Thomas, who unfortunately became an alcoholic. Old Matthew Elliott, at nearly seventy years of age then had to undertake responsibility for managing Indian military support of the British during the War of 1812 (Horsman 1964:177ff.). His clerk and storekeeper, George Ironsides, next served as British Indian agent until 1831 and was succeeded by his son George Ironsides, Jr., who in all probability was the grandson of the Mohawk woman, Coo-coo-chee, although George himself thought his mother was Shawnee. Young George became involved in Wyandot affairs and

Reserve problems at Manatoulin Island. A second son, Robert Ironsides, at times served as physician to the Indians in Ontario (G. Ironside, Sr. 1831; G. Ironside, Jr. 1831; and R. Ironside 1845:mss.).

On the American side of the border, William Wells became Indian Agent at Fort Wayne at the request of the Miami, though they knew he had served with General Wayne. He died at the Chicago massacre in 1812, sacrificing life in trying to evacuate the residents and the Fort Dearborn garrison. Indian assailants, who admired his personal courage and bravery, paid him the tribute of eating his heart (Quaife 1913: 224–28).

John Kinzie, in later years more trader than silversmith, apparently also gave up violin playing. The aftermath of the Battle of Fallen Timbers dislocated his personal life more than the lives of other men who transacted business at the Glaize. The father of his Indian captive wife came from Virginia and took back from Detroit all Kinzie's family. Kinzie later married a woman widowed by the Battle of Fallen Timbers, who had been a captive among the Seneca as a child. He took up trading among the Potawatomi and in 1804 moved to a more advanced frontier location at Chicago. Treated as a neutral, he and his family survived the Fort Dearborn massacre. The children of his first family came from Virginia to become part of the new pioneer community on the southwest side of Lake Michigan. The oldest child of his second family, John H. Kinzie, served as Indian agent at Fort Winnebago at the portage between the Fox and Wisconsin rivers. By 1830, his network of relatives were involved in Indian affairs as traders and government agents from Mackinac Island to Peoria, Illinois (Quaife 1913:246, 269, 280, 347, 361–64).

Billy Caldwell, who became prominent in Potawatomi affairs at Chicago in 1829, also stems from the tight knit circle of people concerned with developments at the Glaize and along the Maumee River. In 1792, at age twelve, Billy had recently transferred from his Mohawk mother's home near Niagara to the Amherstberg residence of his father, Captain William Caldwell of the British Rangers. His father had been a trading partner of Matthew Elliott at Cuyahoga in 1785, and in 1794 brought belated military support to the Indian contingent at the Battle of Fallen Timbers. His stepmother, Susan Baby, was a half-sister of Blue Jacket's wife, both being daughters of Col. Duperon Baby (Quaife 1928:1:292 n11). The old Shawnee leader, Blue Jacket, established his postwar town on the American side of the Detroit River near Brownstown, the Wyandot village at present Gibraltar, Michigan. His daughters married into the local French population (Quaife 1928:1:561). In 1843, Blue Jacket's descendants and other Shawnee were still in the Detroit area living on the Wyandot reservation established in 1818 at Flat Rock on the Huron River.

CONCLUSION

This local history vignette has been created for multiple purposes: (1) to call attention to the diverse cultural components of a complex eighteenth-century community and demonstrate the long-standing ties that developed between Indian people and

Europeans in a frontier setting; (2) to indicate the geographic range of the communications network radiating from a single Indian nerve center; (3) to reconstruct the events of a critical year; and finally, (4) to point out that the community at the Glaize—active in 1792 and struck off the map in 1794—left a recognizable legacy in the history of Indian-white relations on the Great Lakes Frontier.

Notes

1. The author wishes to thank Gordon Day for information on the Seven Nations of Canada, Jacqueline Peterson for notes on the Caldwell and Baby families, James A. Clifton for information on George Ironsides and Billy Caldwell, and Robert Karrow and Emily Rosenthal for preparation of the map. Research was supported by a grant from the Research Tools Program of the National Endowment for the Humanities.

2. In the 18th century, the Maumee River was usually called *Miami-of-the-Lakes* to distinguish it from the Great Miami and Little Miami rivers flowing into the Ohio River near Cincinnati. The transition to Maumee began with the French *Au Miami* for "at the Miami," abbreviated to *Au Mi*, and phonemically into English as *Omee*. This term was used in American correspondence beginning about 1790 (Harmar 1790:ms.). Americans also called the river the *Tawa*, an abbreviation of *wa*. The name *Maumee* as a development from *Au Mi* and *Omee* took place in the early 19th century.

3. The erroneous notion that Blue Jacket was actually a white captive named Marmaduke Van Swearingen has received wide acceptance since the 1967 publication of Allen W. Eckert's novel *The Frontiersman*. The identity is based on a family tradition originating in Kansas in 1877. After a thorough examination of available evidence, it is apparent that one crucial inconsistency is the matter of age. Blue Jacket was a recognized chief of the Mequachake division of the Shawnee in 1772 while Marmaduke was reportedly but a youth at the time of his capture tentatively dated at 1778.

4. Indians publicized this victory by painting the trees near their homeward encampment: ". . . the general colour was red and all the small samplings were stripped and painted with hieroglyphicks quite to their top branches. You know, sir, this is their general custom after signal victories. . . ." (Winthrop Sargent to Arthur St. Clair Feb. 8, 1792). Winthrop Sargent Papers, Massachusetts Historical Society, Transcript in Ohio Valley-Great Lakes Ethnohistorical Archives, Indiana University.

References

American State Papers (1832) Indian Affairs, 2 vols. Vol. 1. Washington: Gales and Seaton.

Andreas, A. T. (1884–86) *History of Chicago*, 3 vols. Chicago: A. T. Andreas.

Anonymous. Journal, Detroit, 1st of May 1191. In *Collections and Researches made by the Michigan Pioneer and Historical Society* 24 (1895):220–23.

Aupaumut, Hendrick. "A Narrative of an Embassy to the Western Indians from the Original Manuscript of Hendrick Aupaumut." B. H. Coates, ed., *Memoirs, Historical Society of Pennsylvania* 2:1 (1827):63–131.

Blue Jacket. "Information of Blue Jacket, Blue Jacket's Speech and Answer No. 1, 1790." In *Collections and Researches made by the Michigan Pioneer and Historical Society* 29 (1895):135–38.

Brickell, John. "John Brickell's Narrative." *American Pioneer*, 2 vols. Cincinnati: R. Clarke and Company, (1842) 1:4346.

Butterfield, Consul W. *History of the Girty's.* Cincinnati: R. Clarke and Company (1890).

Cruikshank, Ernest A. *The Correspondence of Lieut. Govenor John Graves Simcoe*, 5 vols. Vol. 1, 1789–1793. Toronto: The Ontario Historical Society (1923) .

Draper, Lyman. "Interview with Nanette Caldwell." Draper mss. S17, 176. Wisconsin Historical Society, n.d. ms. 1 yy 14, 9 BB:47, and 5 BB:83–101. Wisconsin Historical Society. Transcripts in Ohio Valley Great Lakes-Ethnohistorical Archives. Indiana University (1863) .

Finnelson, Richard. Information of Richard Finnelson, enclosed in Blount to Knox, Sept. 26, 1972. *American State Papers, Indian Affairs* 1: 287–290. Washington: Gales and Seaton.

Gamelin, Antonine. "Journal of Antonine Gamelin," in W. H. Smith, *The St. Clair Papers*, 2: 155–60. Cincinnati: R. Clarke and Company, 1882.

Graves, William J. ms. William Wells' Genealogy. Collections: Wells, William. 1770–1812. Chicago Historical Society, 1937.

Hamilton, Henry. "The Journal of Henry Hamilton, 1778–1779." In *Henry Hamilton and George Rogers Clark in the American Revolution,* edited by John D. Barnhart. Crawfordsville, Indiana: R. E. Banta, 1951, pp. 101–205.

Hamtramck, John Francis. ms. Hamtramck to St. Clair, June 17, 1792. Copy, Wayne Papers, vol. 20. Historical Society of Pennsylvania. Transcript in Ohio Valley-Great Lakes Ethnohistorical Archives. Indiana University, 1792.

Harmar, Josiah. Report of Harmar to Knox, Nov. 23, 1790. ms. Harmar Papers, 11:16–28, Letter 8. Clements Library. The University of Michigan, 1790.

———. Harmar to Knox, Nov. 4, 1790. *American State Papers, Indian Affairs* 1. Washington: Cales and Seaton, 1832.

Hay, Henry. "Journal of Henry Hay, a Narrative of Life on the Old Frontier." Milo M. Quaife, ed., Wisconsin Historical Society, *Proceedings* 1914:208–261, 1915.

Henry, Alexander et al. Memorial and Petition of the Merchants of Montreal Trading to the Indian or Upper Country, December 28, 1790. In *Collections and Researches made by the Michigan Pioneer and Historical Society* 24 (1895): 162–64.

Hodge, Frederick W. *Handbook of American Indians North of Mexico,* 2 vols. Bureau of American Ethnology Bulletin 30. Washington: Smithsonian Institution, 1907–1910.

Horsman, Reginald. *Matthew Elliott, British Indian Agent.* Detroit: Wayne State University Press, 1964.

Ironsides George, Jr. ms. Letter to Jas. Given, June 6, 1831. Record Group 10. Indian Affairs V. 569. Ottawa: Public Archives of Canada, 1831.

Ironsides, George, Sr. ms. Letter to Mudge, April 11, 1831. Record Group 10. Indian Affairs V. 569. Ottawa: Public Archives of Canada, 1831.

Ironsides, Robert. ms. Memorial of Robert Ironside, MD. Dec. 26, 1845. Record Group 10. Indian Affairs V. 122:5722. Ottawa: Public Archives of Canada, 1845.

Johnson, John. Journal of William Johnson's proceedings from Niagara to the Westward. In *Collections and Researches made by the Michigan Pioneer and Historical Society* 24 (1895): 468–72.

Knox, Henry. Instructions to Brigadier General Rufus Putnam, May 22, 1792. Rowena Buell, comp. *The Memoirs of Rufus Putnam.* Boston & New York. Houghton Mifflin and Company, 1913, pp. 257–267.

———. Knox to Wayne, June 22, 1792. Richard C. Knopf, ed., *Anthony Wayne, A Name in Arms.* Pittsburgh: University of Pittsburgh Press, 1960.

Leonard, James. Information of James Leonard to James Seagrove, July 24, 1792. *American State Papers Indian Affairs* 1: 307–308. Washington: Gales and Seaton.

Le Porc Epic. Report of Le Porc Epic, March 15, 1750. Theodore C. Pease and Ernestine Jenison, eds. *Illinois on the Eve of the Seven Years' War. Collections of the Illinois State Historical Library* 29:166–68. Springfield: Illinois State Historical Library, 1940.

McKee, Alexander. Alexander McKee to John Johnson, Jan. 28, 1792. *Collections and Researches made by the Michigan Pioneer and Historical Society* 24, 1895a.

———. Proceedings of a General Council of Indian Nations. *Collections and Researches made by the Michigan Pioneer and Historical Society* 24, 1895b: 483–98.

Messquakenoe. "Speech of Messquakenoe at the Indian Council at the Glaize, 1792," in Ernest A. Cruikshank, ed. *The Correspondence of Lieut. Governor John Graves Simcoe.* 5 vols. Vol. 1, 1789–1793: 228. Toronto: Ontario Historical Society, 1923.

Peckham, Howard H. *Pontiac and the Indian Uprising.* Princeton, N.J., Princeton University Press, 1947.

Putnam, Rufus, ms. Letter of Rufus Putnam, July 14, 1792. Copy, Wayne Papers, Reel 6, Historical Society of Pennsylvania. Transcript in Ohio Valley-Great Lakes Ethnohistorical Archives. Indiana University, 1792a.

———. ms. Putnam to Wells, Sept. 7, 1792. Putnam Papers, vol. 3, no. 52. Marietta College Library. Transcript in Ohio Valley-Great Lakes Ethohistorical Archives. Indiana University, 1792b.

———. Putnam to Knox, Dec. 20, 1792. Rowena Buell, comp., *The Memoirs of Rufus Putnam.* Boston & New York: Houghton, Mifflin and Company, 1903.

Quaife, Milo M. *Chicago and the Old Northwest, 1673–1835.* Chicago: University of Chicago Press, 1913.

————. *The John Askin Papers.* 2 vols. Vol 1. Detroit: Detroit Library Commission, 1928.

Ridout, Thomas. Narrative of the Captivity among the Shawanese Indians, in 1788, of Thomas Ridout, Afterwards Surveyor-General of Upper Canada. In *Ten Years of Upper Canada in Peace and War, 1805–1815,* Appendix:339–71. Toronto: William Briggs, 1890.

Sabrevois de Blury, Jacques. "Memoir on the Savages of Canada as Far as the Mississippi River, Describing Their Customs and Trade." *Collections of the State Historical Society of Wisconsin* 16 (1902): 363–76.

St. Clair, Arthur. *A Narrative of the Manner in Which the Campaign against the Indians in the Year One Thousand Seven Hundred and Ninety-One Was Conducted.* . . . Philadelphia: Jane Aitken, 1812.

Spencer, Oliver M. *The Indian Captivity of O. M. Spencer.* Milo M. Quaife, ed. New York: The Citadel Press, 1968.

Symmes, John Cleves. Symmes to Jonathan Dayton, July 17, 1789. In *The Correspondence of John Cleves Symmes.* Beverly Bond, ed. New York: MacMillan, 1926.

Tanner, Helen, and Adele Hast. Southern Indian Villages 1760–1794, and Indian Villages, Ohio, Pennsylvania, New York, 1760–1794, in *Atlas of Early American History.* Lester Cappon, ed. Princeton: Princeton University Press, 1976.

Tanner, John. *A Narrative of the Captivity and Adventures of John Tanner.* Edwin James, ed.; introduction and notes by Milo M. Quaife. Minneapolis: Ross and Haines, 1956.

Trent, William. "Trent's Journal." In *The Wilderness Trail.* Charles A. Hanna, 2 vols. 2: 291–98. New York & London: G. P. Putnam's Sons, 1911.

Treudeau, Zenon. Treudeau to Louis Lorimer May 1, 1793. In *The Spanish Regime In Missouri.* Louis Houck, ed., 2 vols. Chicago: R. R. Donnelly and Sons Company, 1909.

Vigo, Francois. ms. Vigo to Sargent, April 12, 1792. Winthrop Sargent Papers, Massachusetts Historical Society. Transcript in Ohio Valley-Great Lakes Ethnohistorical Archives. Indiana University, 1792.

Voegelin, Erminie W. *Indians of Northwest Ohio.* New York: Garland Publishing Inc., 1974a.

————. *Indians of Ohio and Indiana Prior to 1795.* 2 vols. New York: Garland Publishing Inc., 1974b.

Wayne, Anthony. Wayne to Knox, August 28, 1794. In *Anthony Wayne, A Name in Arms.* Richard C. Knopf, ed. Pittsburgh: The University of Pittsburgh Press, 1960 pp. 351–55.

Wentworth, John. *Fort Dearborn.* Appendix. Chicago: The Fergus Publishing Company, 1881.

Western Indian Nations. Speech of The Western Indian Nations to Captain Matthew Elliott, May 16, 1792. In *The Correspondence of Lieut. Governor John Graves Simcoe.* Ernest A. Cruikshank, ed., 5 vols. Vol. 1, 1789–1793, p. 157. Toronto: Ontario Historical Society, 1931.

20

THE RIGHT TO A NAME: THE NARRAGANSETT PEOPLE AND RHODE ISLAND OFFICIALS IN THE REVOLUTIONARY ERA

Ruth Wallis Herndon and Ella Wilcox Sekatau

As the essays by Daniel Vickers, James Ronda, and James Merrell make clear, many native groups during the colonial era found ways to live as conquered people on or near their ancestral lands, surrendering a share of that territory and of their political independence yet struggling to retain their cultural integrity and tribal identity. In Rhode Island for much of the seventeenth and eighteenth centuries, colonists' relations with the local natives, the Narragansetts, were relatively peaceful, in part because those who governed the province held, at least at times, the notion that the Indians needed to be converted to English ways rather than eliminated.

During the Revolutionary era the situation changed. Using a combination of written and oral sources, Ruth Wallis Herndon, an academic historian, and Ella Wilcox Sekatau, a Narragansett tribal historian, have discovered that Rhode Island authorities in the late eighteenth century tried to redefine the Narragansetts in a way that would consign them to oblivion. Local town records reveal an effort to see these natives as "Negro" or "black," peoples who were free of bondage in Rhode Island after the Revolution but who also lacked the land rights Narragansetts had customarily enjoyed. Oral tradition, however, reveals that this attempted redefinition did not alter the Narragansetts' understanding of their own cultural identity; they remained, to themselves, undeniably Narragansett.

The argument made by Herndon and Sekatau needs to be understood on two levels. On the one hand, it is a fascinating account of the ways that non-Indians chose, for political reasons, to alter the legal definition of the Narragansetts in order to deprive them of the limited privileges they would have received if they had remained, in the official reckoning of the age, "Indians." On the other hand, the essay is also an exploration in the collaborative possibilities made evident when students of written documents and experts in oral texts combine their efforts to explore native history.

THE RIGHT TO A NAME:
THE NARRAGANSETT PEOPLE AND
RHODE ISLAND OFFICIALS IN THE
REVOLUTIONARY ERA

Ruth Wallis Herndon and Ella Wilcox Sekatau

IN 1675, IN THE HEAT of a regional war with native peoples, New England colonists killed hundreds of the Narragansett, uninvolved in the war at that point, in an unprovoked attack on one of their winter camps located in the Great Swamp in South Kingstown, Rhode Island. Two hundred years later, in 1880, the Rhode Island state legislature, without federal approval, declared the Narragansett people "extinct" and illegally took away the tribal status of people who still called themselves by that name.[1]

In the centuries between these notorious events, generations of the Narragansett faced the choice of staying on their native land, surrounded by non-Indians, or migrating to western land less settled by Europeans. Many of these native people, deeply alienated by the religious beliefs and cultural practices of the Europeans, left, mainly for Massachusetts, New York, and Wisconsin. Others stayed on ancestral lands; oral history tells us that they continued their tribal affairs and government, held frequent meetings, kept track of their heritage and lineage, and kept alive the religion, language, and customs of the people.

Preserving Narragansett culture on Narragansett land was an arduous task initially. Within the first decades of English colonization, Narragansett leaders realized what were the goals of these newly arrived people. The colonists' attitudes toward land clashed radically with the practices of native people. Traditional ways of gardening and hunting proved impossible for the Narragansett after English settlers had altered the ecosystem by dividing the land into private tracts for individual use; by prosecuting trespassers; by cutting down forests, constructing fences, and otherwise helping to extinguish game; and by introducing free-ranging livestock.[2] The Rhode Island government's protective act to set apart sixty-four square miles of land as a

SOURCE: *Ethnohistory* 44:4 (Fall 1997), 433–62.

Narragansett reservation in 1709 signaled that native people could no longer move freely over their ancestral territory and observe the cultural practice of having summer and permanent residences in different places. During the eighteenth century, moreover, the reserved area shrank as non-Narragansett people acquired tracts through sale, theft, and gifts.[3]

The Narragansett living on the reservation could not always avoid contact with Rhode Island colonists; some were pulled into the European American world by the economic necessity of working as day laborers in nearby towns.[4] Others left the reservation and drifted away, physically and spiritually, from the paths of the elders. Some converted to Christianity. Some married non-Indians and merged into the cultures of European and African Americans.[5] Some, prisoners at the end of the 1675–76 conflict or trapped in debt to Rhode Islanders, became bound servants to and thus members of English households.[6] Oral tradition tells us that many native family and clan names disappeared as local officials attached English names to Narragansett people who were indebted or bound to colonists.

So things seemed to outsiders. But tribal history passed down orally from generation to generation informs us that hardship and oppression strengthened the resolve of many Narragansett to maintain traditional ways. The majority of the Narragansett on or around the reservation did not convert to Christianity, and those who did usually moved away from Rhode Island. Many native people whom outsiders counted as converts were actually struggling to coexist with the English. These Narragansett presented themselves in ways that won the approval of outside observers and authorities, but in their own confines they continued to practice the cultural ways of the ancients. Not until the illegal detribalization of 1880 did true conversions begin in some Narragansett families.[7]

Historians have studied the general outline of Narragansett history, although not often from the native point of view, from 1675 to 1880,[8] but little has been written about the details of relationships between native people and Rhode Islanders during those two centuries. This essay analyzes interactions between the Narragansett people and local Rhode Island officials in the latter half of the eighteenth century, a fifty-year period midway between the Great Swamp massacre and illegal detribalization. We investigate how the officials viewed the Narragansett and how the Narragansett viewed the officials.

By "Narragansett" we mean native people who lived on ancestral Narragansett land in what is now called Rhode Island. In the view of some tribal members, Narragansett tribal boundaries encompassed all of what is now Rhode Island and much more land inhabited by all the subtribal divisions and tribute tribes dwelling in what became parts of Massachusetts, Connecticut, New Hampshire, Vermont, and a small area of southeastern Maine. Since the written records rarely refer to the "Narragansett"—only to "Indians" or "mustees"—it is impossible to be sure that every native person in the record was indeed of the Narragansett except where the name coincides with tribal genealogies. Some native people in the documents may have been members of neighboring tribes.[9] But since fourteen of the towns under study were established directly on Narragansett land and the fifteenth (Warren) bordered it, we assume that the majority of native people in the record were of Narragansett heritage.

We also include in this study people described in the record as "mustees."[10] Rhode Island town records provide ample evidence that local officials used this term to refer to people of native ancestry. For example, town clerks described as "mustee" the children of "Indian" women Elizabeth Broadfoot, Moll Pero, Deborah Anthony, and Lydia Rodman.[11] Contemporaries recognized "mustee" people as native, at least in part; so do we.

Native people lived among colonists in every Rhode Island town in the eighteenth century, when local officials thought of themselves as "fathers of the towns." Just as they ruled over their own households, so these leaders headed a civic "family" as well. Theoretically, all of a town's inhabitants came under their patriarchal authority, and thus Narragansett people living away from the reservation had to deal with them from time to time.[12]

Even the Narragansett living on the reservation and under tribal government could not avoid contact with town magistrates. Colonial officials had long tried to have a say in how the Narragansett governed themselves, a habit that local officials also adopted. During the late 1700s, when the sachemship was replaced by the Indian council that formerly had governed the Narragansett people under the sachem's leadership since time immemorial, officials from Charlestown, which completely surrounded the shrinking Narragansett reservation (see Figure I), sometimes attempted to influence tribal affairs.[13] Town records show that tribal council members and town councilmen met and talked on a number of occasions, but always at the convenience of the latter.[14]

How did Narragansett people and local officials view each other? Town leaders dealt with the Narragansett most often as "the poor," in need of official oversight, and thus reinforced the dispossessed and demeaned status of Indians. Further, and just as hurtful to native people in the long run, town officials stopped identifying native people as "Indian" in the written record and began designating them as "Negro" or "black," thus committing a form of documentary genocide against them. Yet Narragansett people often maintained a sense of their own identity, understood that the English system of government sometimes conflicted with their interests, and at times manipulated that system to their advantage.

Our argument rests upon two kinds of sources: the oral history of the Narragansett people and the written records of fifteen Rhode Island towns. Ella Sekatau is the source of Narragansett oral history. She has been learning Narragansett history, language, religion, and medicine from her parents, grandparents, and tribal elders since her birth, when she was charged with the responsibility of ensuring her people's continuity. Further, she has acted in official capacities for the Narragansett people since the 1970s, when the tribal governing body appointed her as an ethnohistorian and the tribe approved her as a medicine woman (a responsibility inherited through her father's line). Like the majority of present-day Narragansett, she traces her genealogy to the sachems of the sixteenth and early seventeenth centuries. During

Figure I: Narragansett Reservation in the Late 1700s. John Hutchins Cady, *Rhode Island Boundaries 1636–1936* (Providence, 1936), 18. *Adapted by Ruth Wallis Herndon.* Note: There is no map that we know of which shows the boundaries of the tribal territory as they existed during the Revolutionary era. The land set apart for the tribe's exclusive use in 1709 had considerably diminished by 1770. In 1767, two Narragansett men mourned that "all the land joining to the sea is already sold, that we can't in no one place go to the salt water without passing through land now in possession of the English." (Letter from Samuel Niles and Tobias Shattock to Matthew Robinson, cited in Simmons and Simmons, *Old Light on Separate Ways,* 39.)

the intervening centuries Narragansett elders have trained young people to maintain the tribe's unwritten history through oral tradition.[15] Now in her late sixties, Sekatau trains young people of the tribe and educates outsiders about Narragansett history through presentations in classrooms and other public forums. In this essay, we use the terms *oral history* and *oral tradition* to refer to the knowledge that she embodies, passed down to her and through her to others.

Ruth Herndon has investigated the archival sources: town meeting minutes, town council minutes, vital statistics, and probate documents for Charlestown, Cumberland, East Greenwich, Exeter, Glocester, Hopkinton, Jamestown, Middletown, New Shoreham, Providence, Richmond, South Kingstown, Tiverton, Warren, and Warwick. The population of these towns, which constituted about half of Rhode Island's population in 1770, fairly represents the wealth, age, economic orientation, and geographic location of the colony's thirty late-eighteenth-century towns.

Both oral and archival sources have their problems. Narrators have probably introduced some changes in the oral history entrusted from one Narragansett memory to another over two hundred years, but the documentary sources also reflect mediation, since town clerks served as gatekeepers who decided what material should be included in the historical record and in what form. Internal evidence from rough drafts and final copies of town records reveals that clerks edited out of the official version any matters and any people they considered "unimportant."[16]

We need both sources to reconstruct the relations between Narragansett people and Rhode Island leaders in the eighteenth century, and we find the oral history of the Narragansett people particularly important as a corrective to the archival sources. Narragansett oral traditional and unwritten laws and lore challenge the records of the official gatekeepers in many respects, and they challenge us to hear voices long ignored and suppressed. Since native people were half of the equation in interactions between Indians and English colonists, we had better take the word of the former as seriously as we have taken that of the latter.

Narragansett People as "the Poor of the Town"

Narragansett people who lived away from the reserved lands and among colonists were legal inhabitants of the towns where they were born. As such, they had certain obligations (e.g., paying taxes) and certain rights (e.g., access to poor relief). But tax revenues were rare, and no native people appear in the probate records as owners of lavish estates. Most Narragansett existed on the economic margins of colonial society. Stripped of their ancestral lands, they were seen as people without property in a society that measured worth by ownership of real estate.

Narragansett people seldom participated in English-style private land ownership in the eighteenth century. A few wrote wills that disposed of their property in accordance with colonial probate law. In 1781, for example, Narragansett man James Niles left a will that satisfied the Charlestown council acting as a court of probate on his estate.[17] In 1788 Joseph Cozens, also of Charlestown, left his "Lands" to his daughters

Sarah and Mary, stipulating that the property "be Equally Divided between them in Quantity & Quality." But Cozens combined English and Narragansett customs: he appointed a non-Indian as his sole executor, but in his will he appealed to "my indian Brethren" to see that his daughters "have [the Land] & Enjoy it according to our Indian custom."[18]

If wills were rare, guardianships were nonexistent. In eighteenth-century Rhode Island, local officials routinely placed minor children under guardianship when their fathers died, ensuring that adults experienced in such matters would manage the property until the children reached adulthood. But of 1,504 guardianships enacted by local Rhode Island officials between 1750 and 1800, none was on behalf of a child identified as an Indian.[19] Apparently, local officials did not extend the protection of guardianship to Narragansett people with property.

From the official point of view, this was only logical. Most native people accumulated only meager estates. When Thomas Bartlet of Hopkinton died in 1759, his outstanding debts totaled almost £174; not surprisingly, the officials who inventoried his estate valued his possessions at little more than £174, leaving a mere 8s. 5d. for his heirs.[20] When Betty Sawnos died of smallpox in Exeter in 1760, an inventory of her property revealed only some clothing and a pair of shoes.[21] When Tent Anthony was rendered helpless by a stroke in 1767, the Jamestown town leaders inventoried her goods before taking control of her estate; they valued her possessions at less than £24—about $3.00 in silver.[22]

What officials saw as a lack of property may simply have been evidence of a traditional native life unencumbered by material objects. Oral tradition tells us that ownership and accumulation of goods, in personal property and also in real estate, were foreign concepts to the Narragansett. To this day, members of the tribe have "give-away celebrations" to avoid building up large amounts of material things. Narragansett people who wrote wills very likely did not attach the same significance to them that Rhode Island officials did; instead they intended that their children should enjoy and use an area as long as they treated it with respect and honor, in accordance with traditional Narragansett belief (still adhered to by the tribe). Human beings do not own the Earth Mother; she owns them.

From the viewpoint of Rhode Island officials, however, a lack of property meant vulnerability to debt and bondage. A number of native people appear in the records as someone else's "property" by virtue of bound service. In 1764, when Capt. Benjamin Sheffield of Jamestown died, he left behind, among his chattels, "an Indian Woman Slave called Philis."[23] Five years later Jamestown officials inventoried Robert Hull's estate, which included "1 Mustee boy named Tavin," a slave valued at £23.[24] In a not untypical labor contract, Alice Arnold bound herself to Dr. Jabez Bowen of Providence for five years to work off a debt of £150; she had no property at all to offer in payment.[25]

People without property and separated from the native community of support needed public assistance in times of crisis, when town leaders most frequently interacted with them. In New England, poor relief was administered locally; town officials arranged for the support of aged, ill, or helpless inhabitants, including native people. When Hannah Broadfoot of East Greenwich became too old and blind to care for herself, her town provided "all Nessarys [*sic*] of Life at the Cheapest Lay."[26] Rose Davids, "a blind squaw," was supported by Tiverton.[27] When Eunice Yocake was "badly hurt" and "in a helpless Condition," South Kingstown councilmen ordered the overseer to "go imediately & take proper Care of sd. Indian in order that She may not suffer."[28]

For native people, poor relief often came too late. Jamestown did not see to Sarah Fitten's needs prior to her death in 1751, although it did pay for her coffin and burial.[29] In the winter of 1767–68 the Tiverton councilmen reimbursed the inhabitants who had cared for two native women during their final illnesses—and then buried them.[30] When Dorcas Fry died in East Greenwich in 1780, the town underwrote the cost of burying her "in a Decent Manner."[31]

As these examples suggest, women dominate the records of poor relief granted to native people, in part because local officials encountered more native women than native men.[32] Oral tradition relates that women lived among colonists more often than men did; they moved more easily between the two worlds. Narragansett men, in contrast, were reluctant to be identified by officials; they adopted aliases and took to the woods, unwilling to risk servitude. Anecdotal evidence in the archival sources suggests that Indian men suffered higher mortality because of their involvement in military and maritime occupations, and Narragansett oral history tells us that women always outnumbered men; until recently, female babies survived more often than male babies.[33] It is not surprising, then, that native women appear in the records more often than native men, especially as they approach old age.

There may be more behind the poor relief figures. The overrepresentation of women suggests also that native women were more likely than native men to draw official attention. Local leaders, steeped in traditions of male responsibility, probably were more disposed to "see" needy women than needy men. Conversely, women familiar with the conventions of patriarchal hierarchies probably were more apt than men to seek assistance from authorities. In any case, local officials opened the town treasury to native women far more often than to native men.

Native children seldom appear as recipients of poor relief, for a very good reason: most needy children were bound out as indentured servants to colonial masters. This was a common practice in eighteenth-century New England; town "fathers," acting in the stead of natural parents, placed poor and/or orphaned children of all races in more prosperous households under contracts that obligated the children to live with and work for their masters until adulthood. Town officials did not hesitate to remove a child from birth parents and thus break up a family; they considered it better to take the child from an "improper" situation than to support its family with poor relief. This practice saved the town the cost of raising the child on welfare, and some "respectable" family gained the labor of another household member.

If the master fulfilled the contract, the servant child received more than "suitable" food, clothing, and shelter; at the end of the term of indenture the young adult was equipped with a rudimentary education (reading and writing) and training in some marketable skill.[34] Job Smith contracted to teach Peter Norton, "a Poor Mustee Boy," the cooper's trade, but he also promised that Norton would learn to read, write, and "keep common Book Accounts."[35] Town leaders expected indentured servitude to prepare poor children for independent adulthood. Whether or not masters always fulfilled their obligations to the children is another question. Oral history tells us that many native people emerged from indenture without literacy skills.

From the child's point of view, indentured servitude was only as good as the master or mistress. Bonds of real affection and support formed between the servant and the master's family in some cases. In other cases, servitude was only slightly disguised slavery; the town records document servants "absconding" from their masters and masters being charged with abusing their servants.[36]

Native children appear frequently in the public indentures of the towns under review for the latter half of the eighteenth century: ninety-eight contracts name a child identified as "Indian" or "mustee" (see Table I). Boys were indentured twice as often as girls, but both boys and girls could expect a dozen or more years of servitude. The children averaged eight years old at the beginning of the contracts, but some were considerably younger. One Indian boy named John entered bound service when he was "4 years 4 months & 6 days old"; another, also named John, was only twenty-one months old.[37] Both youngsters were obligated until they were twenty-four years old, but the average "freedom" age for native children was about twenty-two years for boys and nineteen years for girls, higher than for white children.[38]

By placing poor children as bound servants and supplying care for helpless adults, local officials met their obligation to the needy members of their town family. But public charity did not cover everyone; towns were required to support only their own legal inhabitants.[39] Local officials invested considerable time in determining the legal settlement of "transient" residents; if transients ever needed public assistance, town leaders would compel them, by means of "warn-out order" or "removal order," to return to their hometowns, where they were entitled to poor relief. Since transient people often had lived within a town for years, being warned out meant the loss of homes, jobs, and neighbors and the total disruption of their lives. Sarah Greene had

TABLE I: PUBLIC INDENTURES OF CHILDREN IN RHODE ISLAND, 1750–1800				
	Native		*All*	
Total indentures	98		712	
Indentures of girls	30	(30.6%)	227	(31.9%)
Indentures of boys	64	(65.3%)	461	(64.7%)
Child's sex unknown	4	(4.1%)	24	(3.4%)
Average age at contract	8.0		7.6	
Average age at freedom, male	21.7		21.0 (whites)	
Average age at freedom, female	19.1		18.0 (whites)	

lived in Providence "for 24 Years past" and Deborah Church for "near Twenty-five Years" when the councilmen ordered these two native women back to the towns where they had been indentured servants in their youth.[40]

For warned-out transients, the trip back to a "hometown" emphasized their powerlessness. Those who were too ill or weak to leave on their own were "removed" by the town sergeant or his constables. At the end of this unwelcome journey, other town officials took over the management of their lives. The Providence town sergeant was ordered to take transient Isabel Hope to South Kingstown "by the most direct way" and to put her in the care of the overseers of the poor there.[41] Primus Thompson, a sailor crippled by a wharf accident in Jamestown, was carried by horse and sled across the frozen Rhode Island countryside to Westerly, where the overseer of the poor boarded him out.[42] When Warwick and Jamestown councilmen squabbled over which town had responsibility for Mary Pisquish, the poor woman was transported several times between the homes of the overseers in the two towns.[43]

Women were the targets of most of the warnout orders issued to native people.[44] Town leaders throughout Rhode Island kept a close eye on transient women unrepresented by men. Women who did not live in patriarchal households as daughters, wives, and mothers seemed "out of place" to the town fathers, for they did not have male heads present to govern them.[45] Narragansett women especially fell into this trap, since native traditions of household formation did not emphasize the nuclear unit that the English expected. Oral history tells us that native women often migrated between two worlds: they lived for a time in the woods with their mates and other native people; then they moved into Rhode Island towns for another space of time. Such independent women stirred fears of disorder in town officials wedded to their own customs and prompted their close attention.

Indian men contributed to this "problem" (as town leaders saw it) by supporting their families through work as sailors and soldiers, which meant being absent for long periods of time.[46] Such jobs accommodated traditional male roles more easily than others.[47] Unlike most European men, native men were not farmers; archival sources and oral tradition tell us that many Narragansett men provided for their families by hunting and fishing, which required travel and separations. Although Narragansett families had flourished under this way of life for centuries, Rhode Island town leaders believed that absent husbands and fathers left their families vulnerable. Consequently, councilmen stayed alert to what they considered poverty or trouble in these households and were quick to warn out native women to their hometowns. The Jamestown councilmen had become anxious to move Mary Pisquish because she was "lame & uncapable of supporting herself."[48] Mary Carder, with two small children but no husband present, stirred the Providence councilmen to order this small family removed to Warwick "as soon as may be."[49]

Charlestown councilmen presented a sharp contrast to most local Rhode Island leaders, who stayed busy ordering transient families out of towns where they had settled, placing grieving children as servants among strangers, and supporting elderly people in their last days as boarders in households they did not choose. Charlestown leaders kept their distance from needy Narragansett people, whom they considered the responsibility of tribal members. Only once did these officials act on behalf of a suffering native person—"a Cripple and unable to support himself"—and their action was limited to identifying this man as "one of the Tribe of Indians called Ninegretts Tribe" and notifying the Indian council to take care of him.[50] One other time the councilmen complained that the Narragansett tribe "doth neglect to Support their Poor," suggesting that these leaders were aware of need among native people but were determined to avoid this obligation.[51]

This curious lack of official oversight in Charlestown extended to public indentures of native children; there are none in the town records. This leaves the impression that Charlestown had no Indian inhabitants, that all native people in its vicinity belonged to the reservation tribe on adjoining land. But not so. At one council meeting, Charlestown leaders referred to the Narragansett as the "Tribe of Indians belonging to this Town," and during the 1777 census of men for military fitness, Charlestown officials counted sixty-six "Indians" among the town's adult male inhabitants.[52] Charlestown leaders did not hesitate to claim native men willing to enlist as soldiers, and their possessiveness became pronounced when recruits were hard to find in the last years of the Revolutionary War.[53] Then, Charlestown officials took offense because surrounding towns enlisted "several Indians that were Inhabitants of this Town" and complained that the other towns "had no right to inlist them until this Town had inlisted their full Quota."[54] In times of crisis, it seems, local leaders viewed native men as a labor pool for jobs that colonists would not undertake.

Charlestown leaders ignored or recognized native people as official convenience dictated. When native people needed aid, the authorities were blind to their presence, but when townspeople needed bodies to perform dangerous or tedious manual labor, official vision was miraculously restored. In each case, town leaders solved their problems to their own advantage and to the disadvantage of the Narragansett, thus sending a clear message that Indians were disposable people.

WRITING THE NARRAGANSETT OFF THE RECORD

In October 1793 a Rhode Island physician named John Aldrich brought suit against Narragansett man John Hammer before the Hopkinton justices of the peace. Aldrich wanted payment from Hammer (a matter of three and one-half shillings) for medical care provided the year before. The official warrant for Hammer's arrest described him as a "Black Man" and a "Husbandman," but neither description was accurate. When Hammer appeared before Justice Abram Coon, he asked for a reduction of the charge because of the error in racial designation: "[Hammer] pleads that he is Not [a black man] But that he is an Indian man." When the judge overruled this objection, Hammer pleaded instead that the charge should be reduced because "Husbandman" was an incorrect description of his livelihood. The judge overruled this second objection as well, and all subsequent paperwork for the case referred to Hammer as both "Black man" and "Husbandman."[55]

John Hammer's remarkable objections reveal that he understood the judicial system sufficiently well to counter the original suit with complaints about the mechanics of his case. Equally remarkable is the struggle revealed in the court papers between a Narragansett man and a European-American man over the right to determine a person's racial designation in official documents. The magistrate did not dispute Hammer's identity as an Indian; Aldrich's book account, presented to the court as evidence, detailed his professional services to "John Hammer Indian." But in the magistrate's eyes, Hammer's identity as an Indian did not clash with his official designation as a "Black Man." Coon, who heard Hammer's protests, persisted in retaining the original description of Hammer in the arrest warrant drawn up by Justice David Nichols. To Coon and Nichols, Hammer had been described adequately by a term that signified non-European skin in a general way.

By registering his protest before a magistrate, Hammer forced the recordkeepers to document a new weapon that local leaders wielded against the Narragansett a century after the Great Swamp massacre. The native people in southern New England had been drastically reduced by war, disease, and outmigration; now those who remained struggled to exist on paper and to retain the rights of freedom, land ownership, and state revenues that paper documents alone secured in the European-American system.

The Hopkinton justices' decision to describe Hammer as a "Black Man" was no fluke; it was part of a pattern traceable throughout the official documents of Rhode Island's towns. Between 1750 and 1800 "Indians" disappeared from these records. Individual native people were still named in the pages, of course; officials simply called them something besides "Indian."

Early on Rhode Island leaders exhibited their reluctance to acknowledge the name of the people who had welcomed Europeans to this part of North America: the town records contain only rare references to "Narragansett." After the war of 1675–76 colonists found even more reason to rely on general terms such as *Indian* and *natives,* since Narragansett people sometimes intermarried with neighboring tribes.[56] But in the late 1700s official recordkeepers made an even greater leap in racial designations. By 1800 the town records contain only scattered references to "Indians"; instead, "Negroes" and "blacks" fill the pages.

This redesignation of subjugated people had antecedents on the other side of the Atlantic. The first European slave dealers to the west coast of Africa often erased the heritage of the native people they purchased there and sold elsewhere. Seldom did the European sellers or buyers know what kingdoms, states, tribes, or villages these men, women, and children left behind.[57] The Europeans lumped them all together under the umbrella designation *Negro* which means "black" in Portuguese and Spanish. In eighteenth-century Rhode Island, local leaders stretched this designation to cover not only the people among them who had been torn from their African homeland but also the Narragansett among them who had been pushed off their native land.

New England officials made liberal use of the term *mustee* as a first step in transforming "Indians" into "Negroes." In the latter half of the eighteenth century town clerks used *mustee* most frequently to describe children bound out in indentures. Where clerks record the parentage of these children, it is always the mother who is identified as Indian.[58] But what of the father? The use of *mustee* indicates that officials considered the child to have a non-Indian father, even though no details about the father are provided. The implications of this designation are enormous. In the tribes of southern New England a child was a member of the mother's clan and tribe, regardless of who the father was. But in the colonial world, inheritance came through the father. By denying "mustee" children an "Indian" father, officials prepared the ground for denying these children any rights they might later claim as descendants of Narragansett or other native fathers.[59]

Thus officials transformed Indians into "mustees" and then into "Negroes" and "blacks." The labels are applied so haphazardly in the record that the changes are easy to overlook. They would have passed undetected if we had assumed that a clerk used the same racial designation each time he referred to a particular individual. But he did not. The East Greenwich town clerk described Benjamin Austin as an "Indian" in 1767 but as "a Malatoo Fellow" in 1768.[60] Sarah Hill was an "Indian or Mustee Woman" to the Providence clerk in 1784, but he recast her as a "Negro" in 1791.[61] Harriet (given no last name) was first described as "an Indian" by the Jamestown clerk in 1788 and five months later as "a Molato girl."[62] Mary Carder appears as an "Indian" in the Warwick town records in 1775 but as a "Negro" in 1784.[63] From 1780 on a certain ambiguity appears in the record as clerks replace their previously clear descriptions of native people with unclear ones. In Providence, Susannah Tripp was "a Molatto or Indian Woman," Eber Hopkins "a Mustee or Mulatto Man," and an unnamed stranger "a Negro, Indian or Molatto Woman."[64] In East Greenwich, Dorcas Fry was "an Indian or Negro Woman," and in Warwick three-year-old Lucy Spywood was "a molatto, or Mustee Child."[65]

Although specific examples provide the clearest evidence of the shift in racial designations, there are other ways to document it. One is to trace the racial designations of people warned out of Rhode Island towns between 1750 and 1800. People identified as "Indian" constituted 2.5 percent of this group; however, over two-thirds of these warn-outs occurred before 1776. Thereafter the number of "Indians" dropped off sharply, and only two persons warned out after 1787 were described as "Indian" or "mustee." Warnout statistics for "Negro," "mulatto," and "black" people show the opposite trend. Those so identified accounted for about 10 percent of all warn-out orders, the great majority of them after 1775 (see Table II).

TABLE II: WARNOUTS OF NON-EUROPEAN PEOPLE FROM RHODE ISLAND TOWNS, 1750–1800

	Native		*African American*	
Warnouts	48		184	
1750–75	33	(68.8%)	22	(12.0%)
1776–1800	15	(31.2%)	162	(88.0%)

Note: Between 1750 and 1800, 1,913 people were warned out. Of that total, 48 (2.5 percent) were designated Indian and 184 (9.6 percent) were designated African American.

The same trend occurs in public indentures. Of all indentures binding out minors, 14 percent were for children identified as "Indian" or "mustee."[66] But the great majority, 78 percent, were arranged between 1750 and 1775. The number of contracts affecting native children dwindled after the mid-1770s, and none were recorded after 1795. The opposite is true for children identified as "Negro," "mulatto," or "black." Only a handful of contracts for them were recorded before 1776; then the number surged, reaching a peak in the 1790s (see Table III).

That "Indians" pepper the town records before the Revolution and "Negroes" and "blacks" afterward strikes us as suspect. Of course, unusual forces were at work during the Revolutionary era. The increase in African American transients may be due in part to an increase in mobility, thanks to manumission fervor during the war and gradual emancipation laws of the 1780s. The increase in African American indentures may reflect a change in European American tactics of controlling black labor by indentured servitude rather than by slavery.[67] But those dynamics cannot explain the *disappearance* of native people from the ranks of transients and indentured children. The evidence points to the deliberate redesignation of native people as Negro or black as officials replaced cultural description with physical description.

NARRAGANSETT IDENTITY

The Narragansett were keenly aware of the pressure to lose their Indianness. Then, and for generations afterward, oral history tells us, they expressed hatred for the terms *mulatto* and *mustee,* which implied the loss of tribal distinctiveness. Some grew to hate white people for grouping Indians and Africans together without regard for their heritage, and some grew to hate the latter as well, for being the group that the Narragansett were conflated with. That hatred surfaced at "crying rocks" and unmarked graves, where some native mothers abandoned babies fathered by non-Indians. Traditionally, the Narragansett had used these sites to abandon babies born with physical disabilities. After contact with Europeans and Africans, some Narragansett considered children fathered by non-Indians imperfect and rejected them instead of incorporating them into the tribe. Other women found a less grim alternative by abandoning children in the care of non-Indians. Now and then colonial householders complained that native women had "left" them little children and disappeared. Ironically, the complainers were willing to take care of the children as long as officials enacted indentures that bound the youngsters until adulthood.[68] The children that Narragansett mothers grieved over thus became a labor supply for the colonists.

TABLE III: PUBLIC INDENTURES OF NON-EUROPEAN CHILDREN IN RHODE ISLAND, 1750–1800

	Native		African American	
Total contracts	98		74	
1750–75	76	(77.6%)	15	(20.3%)
1776–1800	22	(22.4%)	59	(79.7%)

A strong Narragansett identity sometimes surfaced in the town records, occasionally in phrases that the Narragansett used to describe their native heritage. Delight Robbins informed the Providence councilmen that her father was "one of the Native Inhabitants of the said Charlestown."[69] Mary Fowler told the South Kingstown officials that "her Mother was one of the Tribe of the Indians in Charlestown." She also followed native customs: she had lived with James Fowler "for about thirty Years & had Ten Children by him," but she had not married him "in the Manner white People are married in these parts." Similarly, her daughter Mary Champlin had lived with John Champlin for eleven years and had six children by him "but never was Married to him according to the form Used by the White People in these Parts."[70] (These women had very likely married their spouses in traditional native ceremonies. Such weddings were and still are accepted as valid under federal law.)

Native people not only identified themselves and each other but sought each other's company. Some families stayed together well after their children reached maturity. Mary Fowler and Mary Champlin (and their children) were living together in South Kingstown when they were questioned by the councilmen. Sarah Gardner, a mother of twelve, kept her family together against formidable odds. In 1763 the South Kingstown council ordered her to bind out her children to various masters when it seemed to them that she could not support them all. Later Gardner managed to gather together her scattered offspring; when she left South Kingstown for Providence in 1767, she had six of her children with her. In 1780, when she was warned out of Providence, four of her adult daughters were still living with her; in 1787, when she was warned out again, her household included three adult daughters and a grandson.[71]

The Narragansett also took in and cared for other native people in distress. Jack Marsh, an elderly Narragansett man living in Jamestown, housed and tended "an Indian Squaw" until she died; he then arranged the details of her burial.[72] In another case, an Indian woman named only Freelove received payment from the town of Warren for supplying room and board to Phebe Wood, a native woman who was one of the town's poor.[73] The Jamestown council acknowledged the cohesiveness of native people when they decided that the best way to care for Mary Mew, an elderly and lame Indian woman, was "to put her into some Indian Family."[74]

The records also suggest that native people sought each other out for times of relaxation and celebration. Homes whose householders had liquor licenses often served as gathering places. In 1753 Christopher Fowler was accused of "Entertaining Indeons, Negros &c" in his tavern.[75] In 1760 Joshua Gardner obtained a tavern license on the condition "that he Entertain no Indian or Black people on ye day Calld Fair day at his House on any presence whatever."[76] The Rhode Island General Assembly had long been distressed at the tendency of native and black servants to patronize taverns and had passed legislation in 1704 and again in 1750 to restrict their activities. This legislation made it an offense to sell liquor "to any Indian, Mulatto or Negro Servant or Slave" or to entertain such a person in one's home without the master's consent; it also forbade any Indian or black servant to be out and about after 9 P.M. without the master's consent.[77] Colony and town records suggest that the Narragansett, both bound and free, knew where they might enjoy each other's company and often did.

As evidence of their cultural heritage, some Narragansett living among non-Indians chose traditional dwellings. South Kingstown's local leaders were aware of "ye wigwam [of] Jo Robinson in Point Judeth"; others caught the attention of town leaders, who feared that they would be unable to survive winter weather unless they moved into English-style houses.[78]

Given these links to their people and their past, it is not surprising that the Narragansett living among non-Indians rarely thought of themselves as "belonging" to a particular Rhode Island town. Oral tradition tells us that the Narragansett customarily moved from winter residence to summer residence and back again, in accordance with the seasons. In addition, they often traveled to home clans and familiar places for celebrations and long-term visits. They moved and lived where they wished; there is little evidence that they felt rooted in the settled, ordered communities that English people valued.

Narragansett habits of travel and long-term visiting clashed with European concepts of "belonging" to a particular place. Local Rhode Island officials, alert to the presence of "strangers" within their jurisdictions and uneasy about the large numbers who congregated for native celebrations, sometimes tried to break up gatherings by warning out the participants who were not legal inhabitants. When confronted by the town sergeant with order in hand, oral tradition tells us, many Narragansett quietly melted into the woods; several days later they returned and resumed the visit or celebration. Local officials, for their part, complained about transients who returned persistently, despite repeated warnouts. Native people appear regularly in warnout orders, but these orders probably netted only a fraction of the native people actually moving around the region.[79]

Because European regulations interfered with their traditional customs, native people seldom obtained settlement certificates as they traveled from one place to another. The settlement certificate was the "passport" that poor people needed to reside for more than a week in a town where they did not have a legal settlement by virtue of birth or bound service; that certificate promised that the bearer's hometown would pay the costs of support and transportation if the need arose. Of the 919 settlement certificates granted by town councils between 1750 and 1800, only 10 (1.1 percent) were issued to people identified as Indians. To judge from the warn-out orders, native people moved about in greater numbers than the settlement certificates indicate, but they ignored the regulations associated with legal settlement, a concept that had little resonance for native people adrift on occupied ancestral lands.

Occasionally, town leaders made the Narragansett people aware of those regulations in a way that could not be ignored. Cato Gardner moved from South Kingstown to Jamestown without a certificate, and in time the Jamestown council demanded that he leave or get a certificate. Gardner disregarded this first warning, but a second citation some months later was delivered so forcefully that he made the trip back to South Kingstown to get a certificate from the council.[80] Martha Bristol dodged the Jamestown town council for five years, but after receiving her fourth warn-out, she obtained a settlement certificate from the New Shoreham council to avoid further harassment in Jamestown.[81] Bristol, Gardner, and other native people complied with regulations only when they could not avoid them. By doing so, they signaled their unconcern about pleasing the non-Indian "fathers" of the town family; they had another agenda, derived from their own and their families' needs.

NARRAGANSETT PEOPLE MANEUVERING THROUGH THE SYSTEM

Just as Bristol and Gardner learned to keep local authorities at bay over the issue of certificates, some Narragansett learned to maneuver through a system heavy with regulations. The record is rich with instances of Indians beating officials at their own game. It is tempting to think of native people relating such "trickster tales" to delighted audiences at home and in taverns, encouraging those who labored daily to make European-Americans even more prosperous.

Old Toby Smith, Young Toby Smith, and Moses (no last name) figured out how to avoid paying taxes. As inhabitants of Rhode Island towns, native people who owned real estate were subject to paying taxes, just as the colonists were. In Middletown the assessors included these three men on the rate list for a town tax due in March 1757. But the men failed to pay the six pounds they owed, even after repeated visits from the tax collector and a two-month extension. The collector finally reported to the councilmen "that he Cannot get the Rates" from the Indians, and the council covered the sum out of the town treasury.[82] It was not unusual for towns to write off uncollected taxes as "bad rates" from time to time, when the collector advised that certain cases were not worth pursuing.[83] Moses and the Smiths somehow convinced the collector that theirs was such a case; perhaps by pleading, spinning a tale, or temporarily moving away, they beat the system.

Simeon Matthews got out of both a tax assessment and a guardianship. The Charlestown town council had put him under guardianship "on account of his being a common Drunkard." The idea was to keep him from purchasing liquor by assigning a guardian who would control his ward's money and property. At the same time, perhaps to underscore the town's authority, the tax assessors levied a tax on him. Matthews promptly petitioned the General Assembly, arguing that he was a member of the Narragansett tribe and therefore not under Charlestown's jurisdiction. The General Assembly agreed. The tax was canceled, and the Charlestown officials dismissed Matthews's guardian, noting that "it is not the Duty of this Council to appoint Guardians to the Indian Tribe."[84]

Marcy Scooner used persistence and skill in hiding to beat the warnout system. In 1759 the Jamestown councilmen warned her out to North Kingstown, the hometown where she did not wish to live. She soon returned to Jamestown and continued to live there until the council caught wind of her presence and warned her out again in 1763. And again in 1766. Each time, the councilmen ordered the town sergeant to whip Scooner publicly to deter her from returning. But she was so adept at hiding that the councilmen had to extend the usual time granted the sergeant to find and whip a miscreant. For seven years Scooner dodged the council and the sergeant, coming and going as she pleased. After 1766, she disappears from the record. Perhaps she died. Perhaps she changed her name. Perhaps she found a more congenial place to live and moved on. In any case, she provided a fine example of how to frustrate authority.[85]

One young Indian boy (unnamed in the record) figured out how to escape indentured servitude without flight and the dangers of capture and prosecution. In 1780, this young servant of Capt. Samuel Babcock enlisted in the Continental Army as part of Hopkinton's quota in the most recent draft. Upset about this defection, Babcock disputed the validity of his enlistment, claiming that his "apprentice" was under sixteen, the lawful age of enlistment, and that he had "a Right to detain him." The town's voters, who met to break this impasse, overruled Babcock's objection and accepted the enlistment of the young man, choosing to believe that he was of legal age. Three weeks later, Babcock produced the indenture papers, which "proved" that the Indian apprentice was underage, but it was too late; Hopkinton's latest soldier had already gone to muster. The record contains no explanation of where the servitude contract had been when Babcock so vigorously objected to the boy's enlistment.[86]

Narragansett people living among European-Americans were not helpless against local officials and the systems they constructed to keep order in their towns. Native people understood these systems and could maneuver around them. The evidence is there in the very records kept by the officials who tried to govern their lives. Assuredly, some Indians lived and died among non-Indians without fighting back, but people like John Hammer, Simeon Matthews, and Marcy Scooner dot the record in sufficient numbers to remind us that the war did not end in the Great Swamp.

CONCLUSION

At the heart of our study of Indian-European relations in Rhode Island is the phenomenon of local leaders erasing native people from the written record by redesignating them as "Negro." By 1793, when John Hammer vainly argued his case before a local justice, authorities clearly considered "Indians" to be "black." A major shift had occurred in official thought about native people in the latter part of the 1700s. Those leaders certainly knew the difference between Indian and African peoples; in earlier days they had not hesitated to make the distinction. But as European-Americans drew lines between themselves and persons of color, they lumped all non-Europeans together as the other.[87]

What prompted this particular expression of racism during the Revolutionary era? Social upheaval, economic depression, and political nation making are all possible answers. Most obvious, perhaps, is the tension in race relations occasioned by the end of slavery in New England. In their revolutionary fervor, many masters voluntarily freed their slaves during or soon after the war. Then, in 1784, gradual emancipation became a legal reality in Rhode Island; it signaled the eventual freeing of young adult slaves beginning in the early 1800s.[88] During and after the Revolution a growing number of former slaves from the farms and plantations of southern Rhode Island swelled the ranks of free African Americans seeking employment on the docks and in domestic service in the commercial centers of the state. Joanne Melish has shown that emancipation upset the carefully ordered world of European-Americans in Rhode Island. No longer did all (or even most) people of color fit neatly into the category of "slave," with all the subservience and control that implied. Faced with free black people in growing numbers, European-Americans directed at "blacks" the attitudes they had had toward "slaves." They replaced old regulations designed to control slaves with new ones designed to control free blacks; racism bloomed in a political environment that encouraged emancipation.[89]

European-Americans swept up the Narragansett in their effort to control people of color. Indians had already been associated with people of African descent by their shared status as others in a world governed by Europeans, by their bondage in European households, and by their unions that produced children who were both Indian and African. In the racially charged atmosphere of the late 1700s European American bigotry affected the Narragansett just as it did Africans and others of a darker color.[90]

Narragansett land provided another catalyst. The Narragansett had been stripped of most of their land by the 1780s, but even the remnants looked appealing to European-American farmers who were faced with economic depression, exhausted soil, and unprofitable harvests, and whose restless sons were ready to migrate westward. But there was a more fundamental problem. Some European Americans must have considered the possibility that the Narragansett would seek to regain what had been tribal territory. The way to forestall them was to deny the existence of people with any claim to the land. New Shoreham voters tolled that bell in 1780. Noting that "the native Indians [are] extinct in [this] Town," they passed a law taking over the reserved Indian lands, which were to be sold to augment the town treasury.[91] By writing Indians out of the record, local leaders helped ensure that native people would not regain land in their towns.

European-American leaders were right to be concerned. When the United States was born, native peoples on tribal land came under the authority of Congress, not the state legislatures. Article 9 of the Articles of Confederation, ratified in 1781, gave Congress "the sole and exclusive right and power of . . . regulating the trade and managing all affairs with the Indians, not members of any of the States." The federal Constitution, ratified by the required nine states in 1788 (Rhode Island, the last of the original thirteen states to ratify it, did so, reluctantly, in 1790), granted Congress the right to "regulate Commerce" with all the Indian tribes. Since state and local leaders could not be sure how the federal government would treat native people, it made sense to them to prevent unwelcome interference by making those people disappear.

We can never know exactly why Rhode Island officials wiped native people from the written record in the late eighteenth century. The full answer, including a burgeoning racial ideology that would divide the nation into white and nonwhite peoples, is probably as complicated as the explanation for the Rhode Island state government's resistance to Narragansett economic development in the late twentieth century. Nevertheless, the Narragansett survived in the flesh, keeping their identity and tribal history intact.

NOTES

PTP = Providence Town Papers (located in the Rhode Island Historical Society Library, Providence)
TCM = Town Council Meeting
TCR = Town Council Records (located in the respective town clerks' offices)
TM = Town Meeting
TMR = Town Meeting Records (located in the respective town clerks' offices)

1. No federal law ever took away the tribal status of the Narragansett people. To detribalize the Narragansett and sell all but a two-acre parcel of their reserved land, the Rhode Island state legislature violated the provisions of the federal Trade and Intercourse Act of 1790. This was the basis of the Narragansett claim that eventually won the return of eighteen hundred acres in 1978 and tribal recognition from the federal government in 1983. See Paul A. Robinson, "The Impact of Federal Recognition on the Narragansett Indian Tribe" (paper presented to the Second Mashantucket Pequot History Conference, Mystic, CT, 21–23 October 1993). See also Glenn W. LaFantasie and Paul R. Campbell, "Land Controversies and the Narragansett Indians, 1880–1938" (report lodged in the Office of the Attorney General, State of Rhode Island, Providence, February 1978).

2. On the differing attitudes of native and English people in New England toward landownership and land use see William Cronon, *Changes in the Land: Indians, Colonists, and the Ecology of New England* (New York, 1983), 54–156; Carolyn Merchant, *Ecological Revolutions: Nature, Gender, and Science in New England* (Chapel Hill, NC, 1989), 69–111; and James Warren Springer, "American Indians and the Law of Real Property in Colonial New England," *American Journal of Legal History* 30 (1986): 25–58. Carl Bridenbaugh, in *Fat Mutton and Liberty of Conscience: Society in Rhode Island, 1636–1690* (Providence, RI, 1974), argues that the first English settlers of Rhode Island intended to establish large, private estates (like those of the aristocracy in England) where they could grow grains and raise livestock on a grand scale.

3. In 1709 Rhode Island leaders negotiated a land deal with the sachem Ninigret II, who deeded all "vacant" lands (that is, lands not yet possessed by colonists) to Rhode Island except for the reservation in the southwestern part of the colony. Ninigret I, the father of Ninigret II, had received the sachemship as a reward for assisting the English settlers in Connecticut during their 1675–76 conflict with Pequot, Mohegan, and Niantic peoples. (This conflict had spilled over into Narragansett territory and resulted in the massacre in the Great Swamp.) The land that Ninigret II retained for the Narragansett people soon began to shrink, as sachems sold off tracts to pay their creditors, despite the vigorous objections and legal maneuvers of members of the tribe.

4. John A. Sainsbury believes that "the overwhelming majority" of native people in Rhode Island did day labor with, or were bound servants living with, colonists ("Indian Labor in Early Rhode Island," *New England Quarterly* 48 [1975]: 379–80). The practice of living on a reservation but going out to do day labor among whites was common also among Indians in Massachusetts during the 1700s. See Yasu Kawashima, "Legal Origins of the Indian Reservation in Colonial Massachusetts," *American Journal of Legal History* 13 (1969): 54. We believe that Sainsbury overstates the case. Many Narragansett prospered without ever experiencing such bondage; they knew how to survive on the land and continued to do so out of sight and off the record of colonial officials.

5. Intermarriage led to increasing racial complexity among people who still considered themselves Narragansett. See Rhett S. Jones, "Miscegenation and Acculturation in the Narragansett Country of Rhode Island, 1710–1790," *Trotter Institute Review* 3 (1989): 8–16.

6. Although the Rhode Island General Assembly banned perpetual slavery of Narragansett people in 1676, Rhode Island colonists continued to put some Narragansett in bondage well into the 1700s by means of

indentured servitude of children and debt peonage of adults. In 1730, pressured by citizens outraged at this latter practice, the legislature passed an act "to prevent Indians from being abused by designing and ill-minded Persons, in making them Servants." The act condemned the business of whites "draw[ing] Indians into their Debt, by selling them Goods, at extravagant Rates" and then forcing them into bondage to pay off the debt. But this legislation came too late for the considerable number of Narragansett people already trapped in servitude; the act did not free them (*Acts and Laws of the English Colony of Rhode-Island and Providence Plantations, in New-England, in America* [Newport, RI, 1767], 150; see also Sainsbury, "Indian Labor," 378–93). Exploitation of native people continued, however, and in 1783 the General Assembly passed "an Act to prevent Impositions upon Indians of the Narragansett Tribe," once again citing the problem of their being trapped in enormous and spurious debts (*The Public Laws of the State of Rhode-Island and Providence Plantations* [Providence, RI, 1798], 615–16).

7. On illegal detribalization see note 1.

8. The most thorough discussion of this period is Paul R. Campbell and Glenn W. LaFantasie, "Scattered to the Winds of Heaven—Narragansett Indians, 1676–1880," *Rhode Island History* 37, no. 3 (1978): 67–83. See also Ethel Boissevain, *The Narragansett People* (Phoenix, AZ, 1975); Laura E. Conkey, Ethel Boissevain, and Ives Goddard, "Indians of Southern New England and Long Island: Late Period," in *Handbook of North American Indians*, vol. 15, *Northeast*, ed. Bruce G. Trigger (Washington, DC, 1978), 177–89; Sainsbury, "Indian Labor"; and William S. Simmons and Cheryl L. Simmons, eds., *Old Light on Separate Ways: The Narragansett Diary of Joseph Fish, 1765–1776* (Hanover, NH, 1982).

9. Campbell and LaFantasie argue that by 1700 the native population in Rhode Island was "an aggregate of peoples" and that the postcontact Narragansett tribe was considerably reduced and diluted ("Scattered to the Winds," 70). Sainsbury cites evidence that native people from *outside* New England were imported as slaves during the early 1700s by Rhode Islanders frustrated by the ban on enslaving Narragansett people ("Indian Labor," 379, 386–88). Campbell and LaFantasie assume that non-Indian assessments of tribal identity are correct, but Narragansett oral history tells us that some tribal members have maintained a solely Narragansett lineage since well before the arrival of Europeans.

10. Samuel Johnson's dictionary contains no definition of the term *mustee*. In fact, it contains none of the terms used by New England officials to describe native people. See Johnson, *A Dictionary of the English Language*, 2 vols. (London, 1755). This dictionary's importance to town leaders is attested to by its appearance in their probate inventories. See, for example, the estate inventories of Providence town clerks James Angell (14 February 1785, Providence *Wills* 6:460–61) and Daniel Cooke (9 January 1794, Providence *Wills* 6:557–60). Since *Indian, squaw,* and *mustee,* which appear frequently in the local records, do not have official definitions, we infer their meaning from the text of the colonial records. This approach is recommended by Jack D. Forbes, whose study of the changing meanings of such terms as *mustee* and *mulatto* between the 1500s and the 1900s emphasizes the necessity of "engag[ing] the primary data" (*Africans and Native Americans: The Language of Race and the Evolution of Red-Black Peoples,* 2d ed. [Urbana, IL, 1993], 3). Providing specific geographic and chronological context demonstrates that such terms had different meanings in different times and places. After studying the use of *mustee* in various eighteenth-century documents, Forbes concludes that in its most general sense it denoted "part-American [Indian] persons (usually slaves) who were mixed with either European or African or both" (227).

11. TCM 29 August 1761, East Greenwich TCR 3:76; TCM 27 March 1762, Jamestown TCR 1:143–44; TCM 14 March 1764, Warwick TCR 2:241–42; TCM 11 May 1769, South Kingstown TCR 5:215.

12. Sainsbury figures that 35.5 percent of all native people in Rhode Island lived with white families in 1774 ("Indian Labor," 379). If so, over one-third of the Indians in the colony were legal inhabitants of Rhode Island towns.

13. See Simmons and Simmons, *Old Light on Separate Ways,* xxx–xxxvii. John Wood Sweet has studied the archival material relating to Narragansett leadership in this period and has produced a thorough analysis from that perspective in "Bodies Politic: Colonialism, Race, and the Emergence of the American North: Rhode Island, 1730–1830" (Ph.D. diss., Princeton University, 1995), chap. 1.

14. For example, on 1 October 1772 the Charlestown councilmen sent the town sergeant to the "Indian Council" with an order for its members to appear at the next town council meeting "to Render an accompt of what Blacks their [*sic*] is now amongst them & on their Land, that does Not Belong to their Tribe" (Charlestown TCR 2:210). A few years later the tribal council had to bring its complaint about a Charlestown

inhabitant to a regularly convened Charlestown council meeting (TCM 6 February 1775, Charlestown TCR 2:256–57).

15. Narragansett young people are trained by watching and repeating verbatim the history, language, unwritten laws, and ceremonies spoken and enacted by their parents and elders, who guide them through repeated enactments and tellings. Thus, for example, Ella Sekatau learned from her parents the Narragansett morning ceremony. She was taught to begin the day by going outside, speaking the words *wunnegan nippaus* (Welcome, sun), and giving verbal thanks to the creator for the sun, the Earth Mother, and the four directions whence all things come.

16. Ruth Wallis Herndon, "On and Off the Record: Town Clerks as Interpreters of Rhode Island History," *Rhode Island History* 50, no. 4 (1992): 103–115.

17. TCM 18 June 1781, Charlestown TCR 3:66.

18. Will of Joseph Cozens, 7 January 1788, Charlestown TCR 3:219.

19. The Charlestown town councilmen did try to appoint a guardian over an adult Narragansett named Simeon Matthews, whom they considered a drunkard and thus incapable of managing his own affairs, but they had to cancel the guardianship when the General Assembly ruled that Charlestown had no authority to place a member of the Narragansett tribe under guardianship.

20. Inventory of Thomas Bartlet, 25 June 1759, Hopkinton TCR 1:33–35. The monetary amounts were expressed in Rhode Island Old Tenor currency. In 1759, £6 in this currency was worth $1.00 in silver, so Bartlet's estate (and debts) totaled about $29.00 in silver. See "Rhode Island Currency Conversion Ratios, 1751–1800," in Ruth Wallis Herndon, "Governing the Affairs of the Town: Continuity and Change in Rhode Island, 1750–1800" (Ph.D. diss., American University, 1992), 364–70.

21. Inventory of Betty Sawnos, 21 March 1760, Exeter TCR 2:112.

22. Tent Anthony's "Numb Palsey fit" left her "Bad" on one side, and one of the overseers of the poor supported her at the town's cost (TCM 19 May, 23 May, and 1 August 1767, Jamestown TCR 2:2, 5). In 1767, £8 was worth $1.00 in silver. See Herndon, "Governing the Affairs of the Town," 364.

23. Inventory of Benjamin Sheffield, 5 January 1764, Jamestown TCR 1:170–72. Philis was not mentioned in this inventory, but she was identified as part of Sheffield's estate when she needed assistance some seven years later. See TM 16 July 1771, Jamestown TMR 1:171; TCM 12 November 1772, Jamestown TCR 2:73.

24. Inventory of Robert Hull, 11 March 1769, Jamestown TCR 2:43–45.

25. Indenture contract of "Indian Woman" Alce [*sic*] Arnold, 2 April 1759, PTP 1:149. In 1759, £150 was worth $25.00 in silver. See Herndon, "Governing the Affairs of the Town," 364.

26. TCM 7 October 1758, East Greenwich TCR 3:45a.

27. TCM 5 June 1781, Tiverton TCR vol. 1.

28. TCM 11 May 1767, South Kingstown TCR 5:181–82.

29. TCM 16 July 1751, Jamestown TCR 1:44.

30. TCM 5 October 1767 and 1 February 1768, Tiverton TCR 2:227, 231.

31. TCM 14 July 1780, East Greenwich TCR 3:204. "A Decent Manner" suggests Christian burial but may refer to native rituals.

32. The records of the towns under study include thirty-five instances of native people receiving direct financial assistance: thirty involved women, and only five involved men.

33. On Indian males in dangerous occupations see note 46. The census records fail to offer a European perspective on the sex ratio of native peoples. The 1755 census is the only early count that distinguishes non-white men from nonwhite women, but Indians were counted as "Blacks," so we have no reference point for the sex ratio of native people at midcentury. According to the 1755 census, the numbers of "black" men and women were nearly equal overall, but nonwhite men outnumbered nonwhite women in Newport (400 to 341) and South Kingstown (137 to 109).

34. In a typical contract, the widow Esther Tefft promised to provide Amos Ookus "meet Drink Clothing Lodging and washing Suitible for an apprntice [*sic*]" (TCM 26 October 1778, Richmond TCR 2:256–57). The word *suitable* or *fit* appears in most contracts, indicating that the clothing they wore, the food they ate, and the beds they slept on all marked bound servants off from the rest of the household. Although both boys and girls were taught to read, writing was usually taught only to the boys. Hetty Sharp's contract, for example, specified only that her master teach this native girl "to Read Well in the Bible" (TCM 6 January 1777, Warren TCR 1:455).

35. Indenture of Peter Norton, 16 March 1780, Providence TCR 5:163–64 and PTP 5:38.

36. See Ruth Wallis Herndon, "'To live after the manner of an apprentice': Public Indenture and Social Control in Rhode Island, 1750–1800" (paper presented to the American Studies Association, Boston, 7 November 1993).

37. TCM 13 July 1767 and 16 April 1760, South Kingstown TCR 5:184, 90.

38. Longer servitude for natives was acknowledged explicitly by the South Kingstown councilmen after they had mistakenly arranged a contract for "Peter a mustee boy" that would have freed him at age twenty. Since the councilmen's intent was "that he Should be bound until he was Twenty four years oald [sic]," they amended the agreement (TCM 20 August 1753, South Kingstown TCR 4:237).

39. In eighteenth-century New England, people were usually legal inhabitants of the towns where they were born. Indentured servants could claim their masters' towns when their service was completed. At marriage women automatically gained settlement in their husbands' hometowns (and lost their own birth settlement). The only other way to change one's legal settlement was to purchase substantial real estate—a "freehold" in another town. Because poor people could not do so, they lived as transients wherever they moved and were constantly vulnerable to being warned out to their hometowns. See Josiah Henry Benton, *Warning Out in New England, 1656–1817* (1911; rpt. Freeport, NY, 1970); and Ruth Wallis Herndon, *Poverty, Perversity, and Public Policy in Early America: Records of Warning Out in Rhode Island, 1750–1800* (forthcoming).

40. TCM 7 August and 5 October 1786 (Sarah Greene); TCM 13 August 1787 (Deborah Church), Providence TCR 5:393, 5:401, 6:16. On average, transient people lived about five years in a town before being warned out, but ten or twenty years was not unusual, especially for nonwhite females. See Ruth Wallis Herndon, "Women of 'No Particular Home': Town Leaders and Female Transients in Rhode Island, 1750–1800," in *Women and Freedom in Early America*, ed. Larry D. Eldridge (New York, 1997), 269–89.

41. Examination of Isabel Hope, 7 January 1756, and town council judgment of 14 January 1756, PTP 1:129.

42. TCM 20 January 1775, Jamestown TCR 2:117–18; TCM 30 January 1775, Westerly TCR 4:250.

43. TCM 4 July 1759, 4 February 1760, and 16 June 1760, Jamestown TCR 1:99, 105, 113.

44. The records of the towns under study show forty-eight warn-outs of people identified as native: thirty-six were women and only twelve were men.

45. See Carole Shammas, "Anglo-American Household Government in Comparative Perspective," *William and Mary Quarterly*, 3d ser., 52 (1995): 104–44, esp. 109–115.

46. See, for example, the story of Aaron Stephenson, who became gravely ill during one of his many sea voyages under Capt. William Read (TCM 21 April 1752 Jamestown TCR 1:53). A highly disproportionate number of native men were seamen. See Ruth Wallis Herndon, "The Domestic Cost of Seafaring: Town Leaders and Seamen's Families in Eighteenth-Century Rhode Island," in *Iron Men, Wooden Women: Gender and Seafaring in the Atlantic World, 1700–1920*, ed. Margaret S. Creighton and Lisa Norling (Baltimore, MD, 1996), 55–69. The record is also peppered with evidence of native men enlisting as soldiers. Jack Sawnos, for example, served as a soldier during the Seven Years' War, leaving his wife Betty to manage a household and children without him. Because he unwittingly brought smallpox back from New York and began a small epidemic in Exeter, his story is documented in the town records. Sawnos and his entire family were killed by the infection (TCM 26 December 1759 to 13 May 1760, Exeter TCR 2:66–87).

47. See Shammas, "Anglo-American Household Government," 109–111.

48. TCM 4 July 1759, Jamestown TCR 1:99.

49. Examination of Mary Carder, 14 February 1775, Providence TCR 5:18 and PTP 2:127.

50. TCM 7 October 1782, Charlestown TCR 3:115.

51. TCM 7 April 1783, Charlestown TCR 3:132.

52. TCM 6 February 1775, Charlestown TCR 2:256; *The Rhode Island 1777 Military Census* (Baltimore, MD, 1985), 12–13.

53. See, for example, the payments made to Thomas Sachem and Samuel Niles for their "Six Month's service" in 1781 (TCM 1 January 1781, Charlestown TCR 3:18a). Most Indian men who had been classified by the 1777 military census as able to serve appear in military papers, evidence that they did in fact serve (Revolutionary War card index, Rhode Island State Archives, Providence).

54. TCM 25 March 1782, Charlestown TCR 3:27.

55. *John Aldrich v. John Hammer*, 8 October 1793, Justice of the Peace Documents [1793], Hopkinton Town Clerk's Office. Hammer eventually stopped battling the judicial system in Rhode Island. In 1799 he

petitioned the Smithfield Friends Meeting to assist him and a number of other Narragansett people who wished to relocate in Oneida, New York. At that point Hammer was "a prisoner for Debt which arose from his purchasing a horse which he lost by Death"—a matter of eleven dollars. The meeting voted to raise two hundred dollars to pay off the debts of Hammer and the other Narragansett and to fund their move (Records of the New England Yearly Meeting of Friends, Box 158, 1790 Meeting for Sufferings, Rhode Island Historical Society, Providence). I am indebted to Carla Cesario of the University of Wyoming for sharing with me her discovery of Hammer's petition to the Friends Meeting.

56. See Conkey et al., "Indians of Southern New England," 177–78.

57. The Rhode Island town records occasionally refer to Africans whose names connected them to their previous lives or places of birth. See, for example, the examinations of Solomon Salters of the Mine (TCM 17 December 1795, Providence TCR 7:67) and Titus Guinea (TCM 15 March 1788, Providence TCR 6: 39–40).

58. See note 10.

59. In 1880 a committee appointed by the state reported that no pure-blooded Indians remained in Rhode Island: "We learn that there is not a person of pure Indian blood in the tribe, and that characteristic features varying through all the shades of color, from the Caucasian to the Black race, were made manifest at the several meetings of the Committee. Their extinction as a tribe has been accomplished as effectually by nature as an *Act* of the General Assembly will put an end to the name" (State of Rhode Island and Providence Plantations, *Narragansett Tribe of Indians, Report of the Committee of Investigation Made to the House of Representatives at Its January Session, A.D.* 1880 [Providence, RI, 1880], 6). The state used this report to justify official action to "detribalize" the Narragansett people and appropriate their land. As early as 1852 Rhode Island officials had claimed that there were "no Indians of whole blood remaining" among the people of the tribe (State of Rhode Island and Providence Plantations, *Report of the Committee on the Indian Tribe* [Providence, RI, 1852], 4–5; cited in LaFantasie and Campbell, "Land Controversies," 11).

60. TCM 29 August 1767 and 26 November 1768, East Greenwich TCR vol. 3. We have included *mulatto* along with *Negro* for the same reason that we included *mustee* along with *Indian*. Town officials made it clear in the record that for them *mulatto* described a person with African ancestry. Further, Johnson's dictionary defines *mulatto* as "one begot between a white and a black" (see note 10).

61. TCM 3 and 6 February 1784 and 30 May 1791, Providence TCR 5:256–58, 6:163.

62. TCM 11 March 1788, Jamestown TCR 2:2022; TM 26 August 1788, Jamestown TMR 1:325.

63. TCM 13 March 1775 and 14 June 1784, Warwick TCR 3:39, 161.

64. TCM 16 February 1780, 17 September 1787, and 9 August 1784, Providence TCR 5:162, 6:20, and PTP 7:159.

65. TCM 14 July 1780, East Greenwich TCR 3:204; TCM 9 February 1784, Warwick TCR 3:152. Usually town officials could observe the person involved, since they were on opposite sides of the council table. The indecisiveness of certain descriptions suggests that when white officials were unable to distinguish one race from the other, they were unwilling or unable to obtain the information from the person before them. Occasionally, officials made decisions about a person who was not present, relying on the opinions of others about his or her race.

66. Between 1750 and 1800 the leaders of the towns under study contracted 712 indentures of poor and orphaned children. Of these, 98, or 13.8 percent, were for Indian children. This percentage far exceeds the share of the state population designated native: 3.8 percent in 1749; 1.0 percent in 1783 (Evarts B. Greene and Virginia D. Harrington, *American Population before the Federal Census of 1790* [Gloucester, MA, 1966], 66, 69–70). It suggests either that the proportion of poor and orphaned Indian children in the towns was unusually large or that they were more likely to be indentured than white children.

67. Another factor worth considering is that, officially, the "Negro" population was falling in Rhode Island, from 6.3 percent of the population in 1790 to 5.3 percent in 1800 (U.S. Bureau of the Census, *Negro Population, 1790–1915* [Washington, DC, 1918], 51).

68. See, for example, the complaint lodged by Joseph Clarke about "Indian Woman," Mary's abandonment of her "mustee" son Jem (TCM 27 March 1762, Jamestown TCR 1:143) and the complaint lodged by Jonathan Hazard about "Indian Squaw" Lydia Rodman's "mustee" son London (TCM 11 May 1769, South Kingstown TCR 5:215).

69. TCM 6 March 1798, Providence TCR 7:226–27.

70. TCM 14 May 1796, South Kingstown TCR 6:230. We assume that the clerk used the words of Mary Fowler and Mary Champlin, and not his own, when he included the term *white* in these examinations.

The local records only rarely use the term, and then only at the very end of the eighteenth century. For most of the eighteenth-century clerks identified by color only those who were not European-American.

71. TCM 13 December 1762 and 14 June 1773, Warwick TCR 2:221–22, 3:25; TCM 5 March 1770, 17 February 1772, 20 March and 4 April 1780, and 1 October 1787, Providence TCR 4:299, 4:322, 5:168–69, 5:172, 6:23; warrant for removal of Sarah Gardner, 1 October 1787, PTP 10:148.

72. TCM 16 July 1751, Jamestown TCR 1:44.

73. TCM 10 December 1764, Warren TMR 1:87.

74. TCM 1 November 1758, Jamestown TCR 1:95.

75. The council eventually dismissed the complaint against Fowler (TCM 12 February and 12 March 1753, South Kingstown TCR 4:224, 227).

76. TCM 8 September 1760, South Kingstown TCR 5:96.

77. Specifically, the General Assembly adopted "an Act to prevent all Persons, within this Colony, from entertaining Indian, Negro or Mulatto Servants or Slaves" (*Acts and Laws of Rhode Island,* 151–52).

78. Robinson's wigwam is mentioned in TCM 10 October 1768, South Kingstown TCR 5:204. White leaders' concerns are evident, for example, in the South Kingstown council's decision to rent a house so that Sarah Gardner, a native mother with three young children, would have a place "to live in this Winter" (TCM 19 November 1762, Warwick TCR 2:218). The Jamestown council made similar arrangements for Jack Marsh, who was so "very decrepit" that it was feared that he would "perish in the Winter Season" (TCM 27 August 1754, Jamestown TCR 1:76).

79. Of 1,913 warn-out orders, 47, or 2.5 percent, named a person described as Indian. There were probably many more native people named, but not described as native, in the record. Reuben Suckmug, for example, bears a name with a decidedly Indian ring, but the town clerk who wrote down his transient examination made no mention of his race (TCM 13 October 1797, Providence TCR 7:200).

80. TCM 28 August 1759 and 24 May 1760, Jamestown TCR 1:100–102; TCM 3 June 1760, South Kingstown TCR 5:91. The South Kingstown clerk identified Gardner as "Cato a Mustee Late a Bound Servant to Mr. John Gardner," thus emphasizing his former servitude and diluting his Indian heritage. In contrast, the Jamestown clerk identified him as "Cato Gardner" and described him as an "Indian." It is likely that the Jamestown records reflect how Gardner described himself—fully Indian, with a full name—to the councilmen who questioned him.

81. TCM 24 May 1763, 15 May 1764, 23 March 1767, and 30 April 1768, Jamestown TCR, vol. 1; TCM 18 July 1768, New Shoreham TCR 4:174.

82. TM 5 January and 20 April 1757, Middletown TMR 1:60–61; TCM 16 May 1757, Middletown TCR I:332.

83. Herndon, "Governing the Affairs of the Town," 149–54.

84. TCM 15 January 1781, Charlestown TCR 3:49–50.

85. TCM 4 July 1759, 18 October 1763, and 27 January 1766, Jamestown TCR 1:99, 154, 211.

86. TM 16 July and 3 August 1780, Hopkinton TMR 1:291–93. Babcock was the second wealthiest man assessed in Hopkinton in 1779 and 1780. (See the state tax lists of 23 March, 6 April, 16 July, and 10 September 1779 and the town tax list of 26 January 1780, Hopkinton Town Clerk's Office.) Because of his strong objections to his servant's enlistment, the townspeople promised him that if the boy turned out to be underage, Babcock could claim him as his own substitute in the next draft. If Babcock had been unable to find the indenture among his own records, he would have had to obtain a copy from the town clerk or from the boy's parents or guardians in his hometown, which could easily have taken three weeks.

87. A number of scholars have argued persuasively that racial ideology developed in the United States during the Revolutionary era when European-Americans tried to explain away the unfree status of slaves in the newly free republic. See especially Barbara Jean Fields, "Slavery, Race, and Ideology in the United States of America," *New Left Review,* no. 282 (1990): 95–118. For the emergence of racial ideology in New England during the Revolutionary era see Sweet, "Bodies Politic," and Joanne Pope Melish, "Disowning Slavery: Gradual Emancipation and the Cultural Construction of 'Race' in New England, 1780–1860" (Ph.D. diss., Brown University, 1996).

88. Gradual emancipation provided that all children born to slave mothers after 1 March 1784 would be freed when they reached eighteen (for girls) or twenty-one (for boys). Masters were under no obligation to free anyone born before that date; it took an act of the state legislature in 1842 to free all remaining slaves.

89. See Melish, "Disowning Slavery."

90. Yasu Kawashima has suggested that government officials in colonial Massachusetts expected "the eventual assimilation of the Indians into the whites' society" ("Legal Origins of the Indian Reservation," 56). We find it more likely that white leaders expected native people to assimilate into the nonwhite society that existed on the economic, political, and social margins of white society. Kawashima has discovered that the Indian reservation system in Massachusetts "began to deteriorate rapidly during the Revolutionary period" as whites purchased tracts within the reservations and took up positions as reservation officials (66). The timing of this white takeover, about which Kawashima does not speculate, was probably due to the same forces that drove Rhode Island officials to write native people off the record: the growing population of free blacks provided an opportunity to advance Indian-African "assimilation."

91. TM 22 April 1780, New Shoreham TMR 5:8.

21

CHEROKEE ANOMIE, 1794–1810: NEW ROLES FOR
RED MEN, RED WOMEN, AND BLACK SLAVES

William G. McLoughlin

As M. Thomas Hatley's essay on the town of Keowee has shown, during the late colonial era Cherokee life underwent dramatic, far-reaching change. But that change seemed minor compared to the whirlwind of death and destruction that visited the Cherokee Nation during and after the American Revolution. In that conflict many Cherokees, like most Indians in eastern North America, allied themselves with Britain against her rebellious colonists. The alliance seemed to make sense: Indian nations had long-standing ties to "the good King over the Great Water" in England; the King's Indian agents, men known and trusted in Indian country, were influential in native councils; and the current monarch, George III, had even issued a proclamation in 1763 designed to protect Indian lands from further encroachment by colonial farmers—farmers who now, in 1776, were usually on the rebels' side.

However logical supporting King George seemed, the decision was disastrous for Cherokees and other Indian Loyalists. As William G. McLoughlin explains, years of warfare against the United States—for many Cherokees, the conflict lasted until 1794—would kill untold numbers of natives. Many more were driven from their ancestral lands by white settlers, while others still found the new nation's system of justice anything but just. The result of all this, McLoughlin argues, left Cherokees reeling. Old rituals lost their meaning and withered away; old men no longer had the answers to the current questions bedeviling the Cherokee people; young men, with customary avenues to status and glory such as hunting and warfare closed off, took to horse stealing in order to avoid the "women's work" in the fields that Christian missionaries pressed upon them. In addition, new and volatile elements were added to the mix of Cherokee life, including African-American slaves and "mixed bloods."

Even as he charts the depths of this "anomie," McLoughlin also finds in the Cherokee Nation an abiding confidence, even arrogance, that would help these natives withstand the latest threats to their existence. Ironically, he shows how that confidence was in part the product of a Cherokee brand of racism that posited native superiority over whites or blacks. However we might feel about Indians adopting racial attitudes from Europeans, it is yet another example of how native peoples borrowed from the far side of the cultural divide, then fashioned that foreign import into something they found useful and meaningful.

CHEROKEE ANOMIE, 1794–1810: NEW ROLES FOR RED MEN, RED WOMEN, AND BLACK SLAVES

William G. McLoughlin

> Anomie—a dissociation between culturally prescribed aspirations and socially structured avenues for realizing these aspirations.
> —ROBERT K. MERTON

THE RISE OF THE CHEROKEE REPUBLIC in the eastern part of the United States between 1794 and 1828 has generally been written as a success story with an unhappy ending: the Cherokees lifted themselves by their own bootstraps after their defeat in the American Revolution to become "the most civilized tribe" in America, only to be forcibly ejected from their homeland in 1838. Standard histories of the Cherokees explain their rapid acculturation in terms of the benevolence of the federal government's civilization program, the dedicated zeal of evangelical missionaries, the able leadership of chiefs like Charles Renatus Hicks and John Ross, the brilliant invention by Sequoyah of a written Cherokee language, and the high percentage of Cherokees of mixed Indian-white ancestry who led the march to success.[1] A closer look at the record, however, indicates that their rise was not so simple an upward-curving arc. In fact, the true measure of Cherokee accomplishment can be appreciated only if we understand how totally disoriented their culture became between 1794 and 1810. They had to sink even lower than military defeat. Before their revitalization process began, they had first to drink the dregs of anomie.

They had taken a more fatal step than they realized by remaining loyal to the British in 1776. Joining hands with Southern Tories in the summer of 1776, they initiated a concerted series of destructive raids upon the white settlements from the Ohio River to the Carolinas. But the king and the Tories were unable to give them sufficient supplies or military assistance to sustain the attack. White frontiersmen quickly mobilized a massive counterattack which, by August 1777, so devastated the

SOURCE: Richard Bushman and Stephan Thernstrom, eds., *Uprooted Americans: Essays in Honor of Oscar Handlin* (Boston: Little, Brown Publishers, 1979).

Cherokee villages and overwhelmed their warriors that the chiefs sued for peace. To gain that peace the tribe was forced to yield more than half of its 100,000 square miles of territory, forcing thousands of Cherokees to resettle within the shrunken nation. In addition, this defeat divided the tribe against itself.

Many younger chiefs, angry at the price the victors exacted, withdrew to the westernmost edge of their territory and took their families with them. Aligning themselves with the Creeks, on whose borders they settled, these dissidents founded a series of new towns along the lower Tennessee River Valley from Chickamauga to Muscle Shoals. Known as "the Lower Towns" or "Chickamaugans," this Cherokee faction continued to raid the white settlements in a guerrilla war that flared sporadically from 1780 to 1794. Refusing to honor treaties made with the new American government by the Upper Town chiefs in 1785, 1791, and 1792, the Lower Towns continued fighting long after the British had made peace. Time after time the white frontiersmen send invading armies to burn the Lower Towns, destroy their crops, slaughter their livestock, burn their granaries. But the Chickamaugans always melted into the forest before them, returning later to rebuild the towns, reconstruct their homes and farms, continue their raiding parties. Enraged frontier settlers refused to distinguish between the friendly Upper Towns and the guerrillas in the Lower Towns. Invading peaceful Cherokee villages, they provoked many of them to join the guerrillas. Eventually almost every Cherokee village, of which there were close to sixty, was ravaged, often more than once. The population of the tribe was cut from an estimated 22,000 in 1770 to perhaps 14,000 in 1794. In 1809 there were only 12,395. Almost one thousand Cherokees left the East in these years to find peace in Spanish Territory across the Mississippi.

This devastating war back and forth across their land was only the military culmination of the gradual destruction of the Cherokee way of life. The Cherokees had first seen the white European in 1540 and since 1640 had been in continual contact with the English colonists. This contact slowly destroyed the old patterns of life and rapidly disrupted the equilibrium that had existed among the various tribes in the Southeast. The original Cherokee economic system was only marginally subsistent, based upon a combination of hunting, fishing, food gathering, and agriculture.[2] Except for overpopulation (usually kept in environmental balance by famine, war, disease, and infanticide), they had managed, like most Indians, to live off the land without depleting its resources and without excessive effort. The soil was rich, the climate generally mild, the fish and game plentiful. The territorial imperatives necessitated by a similar economic system among the neighboring tribes made for constant warfare, but at the beginning of the eighteenth century a generally harmonious relationship among the Indians existed throughout the South. In that era tribal war served primarily socioeconomic purposes; it was a highly traditionalized system for maintaining vague hunting boundaries and a cultural process by which young braves established their status. But the European method of massive warfare, the political competition of empires to control the New World, and the economic restructuring brought by the fur trade radically altered Indian life. Moreover, the rapid influx of British settlers after 1640 and their expanding settlements forced the Indians into bitter wars in which the Europeans frequently manipulated the Cherokees to assist in the extermination of smaller Eastern tribes.

The European concepts of permanent alliances, trade treaties, total war, and enforced land cessions compelled the Cherokees to create "kings" or "emperors" who were, at least in European logic, held responsible for the behavior of the whole tribe. This began a long process of limiting the local self-government of individual towns, the power of local chiefs, and the general concept of noncoercive, consensus government, which had formerly constituted what little governance there was. In addition, the trade alliances made the Cherokees partners in exploiting the game that had formerly been hunted only for food or clothing. It also made them increasingly dependent upon the manufactured goods of the Europeans—guns, traps, powder, lead, knives, axes, kettles, cloth, and blankets. Their own native skills in pottery and weaving deteriorated and, for some, spirituous liquor became a major necessity. As exploited employees of European trading companies, the Indians destroyed their own supply of game and found themselves thrown into the vagaries of European market fluctuations over which they had no control. Gradually new lifestyles were introduced among them by English and Scottish traders who settled in their villages, married Cherokee wives, introduced European agricultural methods (including the use of black slaves), and taught them the uses of horses, cattle, pigs, and chickens. Prior to 1776 the acculturation process was essentially voluntary. The Cherokees took from the Europeans what seemed useful to them, while the major aspects of their daily life and culture remained the same. Despite periodic epidemics of European diseases, the Cherokees managed to grow and thrive as a people. It was the warfare between 1776 and 1794 that destroyed them.

By 1800 their hunting grounds in Kentucky and Tennessee were wholly occupied by white Americans, and their role in the fur-trade economy was gone. Even by extended hunting expeditions across the Mississippi, it was impossible to obtain enough furs and hides to pay for the manufactured goods that had now become necessities. The only way to avoid starvation was to accept the white man's way of cultivation and animal husbandry. But the problems of such a social reorientation were almost overwhelming. Daily contact with white settlers who now surrounded them on three sides (leaving only their southwestern borders contiguous to other Indians) made the transition even more difficult. Charles Royce, writing of the Cherokees in these years, said that "they were, as a nation, being slowly but surely compressed within the contracting coils of the giant anaconda of civilization; yet they held to the vain hope that a spirit of justice and mercy would finally prevail in their favor. Their traditions furnished them no guide by which to judge the results certain to follow. . . ."[3]

The surrounding settlers, bristling with greed, contempt, and animosity, darted in and out of the tribal area, carrying on illicit trade, cheating, robbing, frequently assaulting the now-defenseless Cherokees.[4] Ostensibly the treaties had left the political infrastructure of the tribe intact. Their chiefs and councils were still free to govern internal affairs. However, with white men continually in their midst and encroaching upon their borders, with the critical control over crimes between whites and Indians fixed by treaty in the hands of white troops and courts, it was almost impossible for the local town chiefs to retain order under the old, unwritten patterns of noncoercive authority and clan revenge. The efforts of tribal chiefs with broader authority to sustain order were thwarted by continuing animosity between the Upper Towns and the Lower.[5] They were harried from without and divided within.

Furthermore, the frequent cessions of land forced upon the Cherokees after 1777 (in the treaties of 1798, 1804, 1805, and 1807) cut the heart out of the original Cherokee homeland along the western borders of South Carolina, the eastern valleys of the Great Smokies, the upper valleys of the Tennessee River and its tributaries in northeastern Tennessee.[6] In these years their oldest settlements fell into white hands and thousands of Cherokees made homeless by these cessions had to reestablish themselves in what remained of their land to the west and south. By 1800 more than forty of their towns had disappeared in the advancing white tide. More than two-thirds of their families were uprooted and forced to move—some two or three times. Resettling into already overcrowded and disorganized towns, they placed a severe strain upon limited resources, depleting precious supplies of grain and livestock. Before they could start new fields and harvest a crop, these displaced families often reduced whole communities to virtual starvation.[7] To this great demographic disruption must be added the psychological and spiritual shock of leaving behind so many of their graves and sacred places; in an animistic or zootheistic religious culture, every spring, waterfall, mountain, cave, or lake had special supernatural significance. When villages were forced to abandon these sacred sites to white desecration, they lost basic spiritual landmarks as well as the territory itself. In addition, much of the Cherokee medicine, as well as many religious potions, was based upon the gathering and concocting of certain kinds of herbs and flowers not always or so easily available in their new homes.

Cutting even deeper than economic hardships into cultural vitality was the breakdown of traditional patterns of enculturation such as child rearing. It struck the Southern Indians with particular pain to learn that they were no longer allowed to raise their sons and nephews to be warriors. In 1802 a Creek chief, speaking to the resident federal agent, informed him that he hoped the government would not see fit to prevent the customary small-scale warfare between the Cherokees, Creeks, Choctaws, and Chickasaws. How else, he asked, were their young men to learn the skills to attain manhood and respect? "Brother, if we red men fall out, dispute and quarrel, you must look upon it as two children quarreling and you, our white friends and brothers, must remain neutral. There is among us four Nations old customs, one of which is war. If the young, having grown to manhood, wish to practice the ways of the old people, let them try themselves at war, and when they have tried, let the chiefs interpose and stop it. We want you to let us alone."[8] There was in Cherokee culture an achievement orientation, which encouraged young and old warriors to measure their status by exploits of daring in war and hunting—through the number of their scalps or captives, the quality of their furs and hides. These exploits were then celebrated in songs and dances for the edification and glory of all. More than self-achievement, they were measures of a man's importance to his family, clan, and tribe, and signs of his harmony with the spirits that controlled life.

What for the Cherokee was basic training, education, and testing was to the American government, after 1794, merely a source of troublesome "savagery." According to the treaties, the Indians were to give up hunting and war for farming and book learning. The Cherokee treaty of 1791 stipulated that in order for "the Cherokee nation [to] be led to a greater degree of civilization and to become herdsmen and cultivators, instead of remaining in a state of hunters, the United States will, from time to time, furnish, gratuitously, the said nation with useful implements of husbandry."[9] Henceforth Cherokee boys were to prove their mettle by the sweat of their brows. Plowing a straight furrow, not shooting a straight arrow, was to be the test of a man. But this was not a skill their fathers, uncles, and chiefs could teach them.

What role, then, were the old to play and what respect could they sustain? Not only had they nothing worth teaching the young, but they were held responsible for the failure of the old system. Power, skill, prestige, and hence legitimate social authority now rested with "the white fathers" who found the warfare of the old chiefs merely a childish game. With the breakdown of the tribal elders, authority, the disintegration of self-regulating custom, the imposition of external force (the soldiers patrolling the borders, the government factor regulating trade, the federal agent enforcing their treaty obligations, the state constables and courts arresting and trying criminals), the internal political structure of the nation fell apart. It had no function to perform. Before the Cherokees could reestablish legitimate authority over their people, the chiefs and councils had to learn new roles, deal with new political and economic realities, accept the responsibility for inculcating new social values and sustaining new behavior patterns.

Even religious rituals and festive ceremonies had to be reconstructed. The old songs, rites, and dances associated with war (like the Eagle Dance) fell into disuse. The decline of hunting made the Bear and Buffalo dances obsolete. The communal ceremonies of the new year and the relighting of the clan fires lost their meaning. The spiritual leaders of the community—priests or shamans—lost their authority as well. Cleansing and purification rites made sense only if one knew what values were being reaffirmed and what was pure and what impure. Of all the Cherokee ceremonies, only the Green Corn Dance and the Ball Plays retained any vitality in these years. But even these became increasingly secularized. The Green Corn Dance, originally a harvest ritual, became a plaything of the federal agents, who worked with the chiefs to have it scheduled at times and places convenient to the government, either when annuities were to be distributed or when a treaty was about to be made. The government contributed provisions and whiskey for these occasions on the grounds that they put the Indians in a good mood for bargaining.

The Ball Plays, instead of communal festivals with religious overtones, became spectacles for white visitors and scenes of wild orgies of gambling, drunkenness, and brawling. Instead of replacing hunting and war as they might have done to enable young men to exhibit skill, strength, endurance, and daring, they became a kind of professionalized gambling, a quick way to make money (or to lose it)—a symptom of despair, not of vitality. In better days, and in the more conservative parts of the nation, the Ball Plays were hallowed by sacred prayers, dances, and rituals; players abstained from sexual intercourse prior to playing in order to retain their strength; to be chosen as a player marked one as a person of high integrity and honor. But during the Cherokee nadir, all this was forgotten. In 1792 Governor William Blount reported two Ball Plays on two successive days in the Lower Towns where Chief Eskaqua (or Bloody Fellow) "was on the losing side and having staked much bore it not quite well" the first day. "His getting drunk on Monday night was supposed to be a maneuver to get some of the best players of the adverse party in the same situation, which he effected. He did not play himself and none of his players drank to excess," so the next day Eskaqua's team recouped his losses because of the hangovers of the opposing team.[10] Bloody Fellow had previously been a mighty war leader; now he seemed concerned only to enrich himself.

The distribution of the federal annuity itself became a great national holiday, though it had no religious significance to the Cherokees. Its only purpose was the selfish one of getting all the liquor and booty one could for oneself. These occasions attracted hordes of disreputable white men—traders, gamblers, whiskey dealers—eager to extort some of these treaty funds from the Cherokees. The secretary of war instructed the agent to discourage the whole business in 1802, but it did not come to an end until the council regained its authority and asserted tribal control over the annuities in the form of a national treasury in 1817.

Recognizing the importance of national holidays in establishing national pride, the Cherokee agent appointed by the government in 1801, Colonel Return J. Meigs, tried to encourage new ones more in keeping with the new status of the Indians as wards of the Republic. A native of Connecticut and a loyal Jeffersonian, Meigs sought like a true *philosophe* to construct a new civil religion for his charges. Why not have "festival days [on] 4th July and New Year's Day, dividing the year equally," he wrote. "On those occasions political and moral sentiment will be diffused while the mind is alive and awakened by agreeable impressions made on such occasions not easily effaced."[11] No doubt he expected orations on the rising glory of America and the role of the Indian in that destiny, but nothing appears to have come of his suggestion. The Cherokees were not exactly moving in that direction.

For reasons not necessarily associated with Christianization, the Cherokees and other Southern tribes appear to have adopted the festival of the Twelve Days of Christmas. The first New England missionaries noted this with surprise in 1818: "Christmas is a great day among the whites and half breeds in this country. It has been kept in such a manner that the Cherokees have given it the name which signifies shooting-day. Almost all the slaves have their time from Christmas to the end of the year and generally spend it in frolicking and drinking."[12] Few Cherokees were Christians at this time, however, and as the description implies, it was more a secular than a holy day. Trying to capitalize on the day's popularity, some of the missionaries held a religious service on Christmas, but only the blacks attended. The obvious inference is that the more prosperous Cherokees adopted it from their slaves and not out of any respect for the founder of Christianity. Christmas had long been a slave holiday in the white South. It was probably brought into the tribe by white traders and Tory refugees, if not by the slaves themselves.

The first missionaries to ask to establish a mission station and school among the Cherokees were Moravians from North Carolina. Their first request to do this in 1799 was rejected, but approval came in 1801 when the Cherokees were convinced that it would be useful for their children to learn to read and write English. The Moravians did not accept their first pupils in Spring Place, Georgia, until 1804, and taught only a handful of children prior to 1810. A more successful missionary school was started near the federal agency in eastern Tennessee in 1804 by the Presbyterians, but it collapsed in 1810 for want of denominational support. By and large the missionaries provided little help to the Cherokees in these trying times; but by the same token, neither can they be blamed as a major source of the Cherokees' cultural disorientations.[13]

In 1800 the possibility that the Cherokees would ever recover their old tribal integrity and self-respect as a people must have seemed nonexistent. Nor did the alternative way of total assimilation offered by the American government appear feasible. Quite apart from the fact that few Cherokees possessed at that time the skill, the tools, or the capital to become successful farmers, almost everything about this new system ran counter to their traditions and beliefs. "Exclusive property"—the idea of private ownership of the land—ran counter to the staunch belief in tribal ownership of the land; private profit ran counter to communal sharing and the hospitality ethnic; aggressive personal ambition ran counter to the high value placed upon self-effacement and affability. To leave the village, stake out a clearing in the woods, and start farming for oneself and family alone meant to repudiate neighborliness. Perhaps most important of all, it meant the establishment of a nuclear family system, patrilineal inheritance, the end of the clan relationships, and a reversal of roles for both men and women. Anomie at bottom meant for the Cherokees not only a loss of sovereignty and land, but with the breakdown of the cultural order, it also meant a loss of identity. What exactly did it mean after 1794 to be a Cherokee?

THE CHANGING ROLE of Indian women in the years 1794 to 1810 was directly related, not only to the changing role of Indian men, but to the changing status of black men in the Cherokee Nation and in the white South. Where there were only whites and blacks in a community, the role of each was clearly defined. But among the Cherokees, there were red, white, and black men (not to mention mixed bloods). Since the red was told that his future lay in adapting himself to white beliefs and behavior, the status of the black became even more problematic. In the eighteenth century the first blacks to enter the Indian nations, usually as runaways, were treated with lenience and familiarity. They provided useful skills and manpower and served as interpreters. There is evidence of black intermarriage and adoption; moreover, a number of freed slaves had an independent status. In the Revolutionary fervor for natural rights, the Indian was considered by philosophers like Jefferson to be virtually equal to the white, even if there were doubts about the black man. But as this fervor faded, as the white South moved toward the cotton kingdom, and as the Indian was forced to defend his own status as a "man of color" in the face of white frontier prejudice, the multiracial aspect of Cherokee society posed bitter problems for black and red.

Similarly, the new role of yeoman farmer or planter compelled a new relationship between Indian men and women. The Indian male, though he had in former days labored occasionally in the field with the women, never had his dignity as a warrior or hunter questioned for this any more than did the poor white who sometimes labored beside his slave. The respective status lines in both cases were established beyond doubt. But as the Cherokee woman went into the farmhouse to spin, sew, cook, after 1794 she lost some of her former dignity and decision-making power in the tribal councils. At the same time, the Cherokee man, shorn of his primary status as a hunter-warrior and told to work steadily with ax and hoe, had to worry about how he could henceforth distinguish himself from black field hands.

Working in the fields was as hot and burdensome to the Cherokee as to the white Southerner. He did not share Jefferson's view of the nobility of that occupation. At first the Cherokee man considered it ignoble to be only and always working in the fields. Many years later, after the Cherokees had completed their transformation and could look back with less embarrassment on this problem, the editor of the *Cherokee Phoenix* wrote of the Cherokees at the turn of the century, "From the soil they derived a scanty supply of corn, barely enough to furnish them with gah-no-ha-nah [a corn dish] and this was obtained by the labor of women and grey headed men, for custom would have it that it was disgraceful for a young man to be seen with a hoe in his hand except on particular occasions."[14] Like his white Southern counterpart, an acculturated Cherokee farmer hoped someday to own slaves to do his work. His model of American farming and capitalism was inevitably that of the Southern cotton plantation, not the Northern diversified subsistence farm that the federal government and Eastern philanthropists held up to him. Hence to sustain his new role as a Cherokee man, and his wife's as a Cherokee woman, he would have to reduce the blacks to a servile laboring caste and transform his women into genteel mistresses of the hearth and home.

Eighteenth-century observations regarding the status of Cherokee women varied widely. James Adair argued in 1762 that their status was virtually equal to that of Cherokee men. Jefferson in 1783 believed they were little more than slaves: "The women were submitted to unjust drudgery. This, I believe, is the case with every barbarous people. With such, force is law. The stronger sex imposes on the weaker. It is civilization alone which teaches us to subdue the selfish passions and to respect those rights in others which we value in ourselves. Were we in equal barbarism, our females would be equal drudges."[15] A Tennessee historian of the Cherokees, drawing upon a wide variety of early sources, came closer to Adair's conclusion:

> The Cherokees [in 1760] were just emerging, as were all Iroquoian people, from the matriarchal stage. "They have been a considerable while under petticoat government," Adair comments. Extraordinary respect was paid to womankind. When a Cherokee married, he took residence with the clan of his wife. His children were the property of the mother, and were classed as members of her clan. The wigwam and its contents belong to the woman. She had a voice in the daily council and the deciding vote for chieftainships.

The women of each clan selected a leader. These leaders constituted the Women's Councils, which did not hesitate to override the authority of the chiefs when it was thought that the welfare of the tribe demanded it. The head of the Women's Council was the Beloved Woman of the tribe, whose voice was considered that of the Great Spirit speaking though her. . . . The white pioneer mother, with her large family, was far more of a drudge than her red sister.[16]

While the evidence is scanty and contradictory on details, there seems general agreement that prior to 1794 Cherokee women did have a participatory role of some kind in tribal decisions, a major interest in household property and care of the children, and the largest share of work in cultivating the fields. Thereafter, their role in tribal affairs became almost negligible. Part of the difficulty in "civilizing" the Indian was that it bothered nineteenth-century white Americans intensely to see women working in the fields. The government considered it a primary object of its civilization program to get the Indian women out of the field and into the kitchen. It was considered a marked step forward when Indian women began to take up spinning and weaving while the men grudgingly and of necessity took to the plow. In August 1802 the federal agent to the Cherokees reported the following items of husbandry and domestic manufacture, which he had so far distributed among the Cherokees as part of the government's economic aid program: 58 plows, 13 mattocks, 44 hoes, 215 spinning wheels, 4 looms, 204 pairs of cotton cards, 53 sheep, 28 reels. He reported with mixed feelings that "the raising and manufacturing of Cotton is all done by the Indian Women; they find their condition so much bettered by this improvement that they apply for wheels, cards, etc, with great earnestness" and were disappointed that the government could not give them more. "The Indian men," however, "attend to the raising of Cattle and Swine—this costs them no labour, a thing they will avoid as long as possible."[17]

In 1805 Colonel Meigs reported that what seemed like progress to most white Americans was not so viewed by most Cherokee males. "Raising cotton, spinning and weaving is carried on the domestic way in almost every part of the nation, but this is totally done by the females who are not held in any degree of reputable estimation by the real Indian and therefore neither them [women] nor their occupation have any charms to tame the savage."[18] To the Cherokee man, whether the women made clothes by preparing skins and furs or by spinning cotton, it was all the same. The great difficulty now was that she, not he, was providing the clothing for the family while he could contribute almost nothing. Only by growing a good crop could he sustain his prestige as a provider. Being unable to maintain his old role as hunter-provider was frustrating in the extreme.

By 1802 Cherokee hunters who did not make the long trek across the Mississippi to hunt were bringing to the trading posts only the skins of small animals—"raccoons, foxes, and wild cats"—for which they received twenty-five cents each.[19] American Indian agents, observing the reluctance of the Indian men to undertake the onerous task of farming, concluded that they were inveterately lazy and shiftless: "Labour is painfull and the idea to the most of them dishonorable; the love of ease is their predominant passion," wrote the Cherokee agent, Return J. Meigs, in 1808.[20] It never occurred to him that the Cherokee did not oppose all labor, but only that degrading to his status and lacking in the sort of self-respect that came from the exercise of traditional skills.

Since working all day behind a plow, hoeing a cornfield, or feeding hogs was considered honorable and rewarding by a Connecticut Yankee, Return J. Meigs could not see why it had so little appeal to the Cherokees. What he saw as feckless Cherokee "roaming" in worn-out hunting grounds week after week was not a desire to avoid work but in part an urge to cling to an older way of life and in part a need to hide an ignorance of husbandry. It also was necessitated by lack of capital and tools to become a farmer. Despite its good intentions the government seldom provided more than a few hundred dollars' worth of agricultural tools per year; a Congress interested in keeping taxes low found it easy to cut the budget for nonvoting Indians. Consequently the Cherokees did not have in these years enough plows, hoes, or mattocks, and the few the government did supply were not evenly distributed.[21] Nor could the Indians keep the implements they did get in repair without a blacksmith, and these were always in short supply. Cherokees in mountainous regions or among the sandhills had little chance of making a living from farming. Even white frontiersmen who had grown up on farms in the East, who had some experience and capital and were able to pay for the services of blacksmiths, wheelwrights, or coopers, often had a difficult time starting out in the wilderness. Yet the Protestant ethic of hard work, self-discipline, and delayed gratification was assumed to be the divinely ordained system of values for all men. God had ordered Adam to support himself by the sweat of his brow and to cultivate the fields, and the sooner the Indian adopted this way of life the happier and more prosperous he would presumably be. The economic whip was there, but not the religious, social, or cultural incentive.

Those Cherokees, however, who were the sons and grandsons of white traders, Tory refugees, army deserters, and those white men who had married into the nation and cast in their lot with it made the most of the government's economic aid and got the lion's share of it. They also used their superior experience to take up the best farming land in the Cherokee Nation. And, most important, they had the capital to invest in slaves. By 1809 there were 583 black slaves in the Cherokee Nation, but they were owned by comparatively few of the 2,000 families. Not only did some have ten, fifteen, or twenty of them, but geographically the great bulk of them were in northern Georgia and Alabama where the rich black soil was fit for cotton plantations. Among that third of the Cherokees who lived in "the Valley Towns" of the Unicoi and Great Smoky mountains where there was the least intermixture of white ancestry and intermarriage, there were only five black slaves.[22] The Valley Towns long remained a center of traditionalist friction within the nation.

Eventually there were those who argued that the progress the Cherokees made toward civilization was primarily "owing to the prevalence of slavery" among them.[23] Others argued that their progress resulted from the high proportion of white blood in their veins: "When every effort to introduce among them the ideal of separate property as well in things real as personal shall fail, let intermarriages between them and the whites be encouraged by the Government. This cannot fail to preserve the race, with the modifications necessary to the enjoyment of civil liberty and social happiness."[24] The problems of mingling red, white, and black in the Southeastern United States led the Indians logically to wonder whether the white man was sincere in suggesting, as Jefferson and others did, the hope that the Indian could ultimately attain full and equal citizenship within white America.

Seeking to discover their new role within the American system now that they had agreed to give up the right of arms to sustain their sovereignty, the Cherokees received three conflicting answers. In official documents of the federal governments, they were "wards" or "younger brothers" with a potential for full citizenship when they became fully "civilized" and "Christianized." To many American scientists they were "a dying race" more to be pitied than censured, but nevertheless incapable of meeting the challenge required to become part of that Anglo-Saxon people who stood at the forefront of human progress. To the neighboring frontiersmen, they were irredeemable "savages," defeated enemies who had lost all right to their land and whose existence, on mere sufferance, was an irritating impediment to the westward march of white civilization. The only reason most frontier people tolerated them was that they wished the federal government would bear the expense of removing them. The federal government took pains to treat the tribes as quasi-independent states partly because it wanted them as a buffer zone or potential allies should France, Spain, or England press their claims to the Mississippi Valley and partly because it could not decide whether to "civilize" them where they were or remove them westward. (Prior to the Louisiana Purchase in 1803, there was no place to which they could be removed, but one of Jefferson's reasons for acquiring the Louisiana Territory was to facilitate such a relocation.)

The ambivalence of the white American attitude toward the Native American is clearly revealed in an early missionary letter. The missionary who wrote it was a New England Federalist and philanthropist. Arriving in Tennessee, he was shocked to find that "the sentiment very generally prevails among the white people near the southern tribes (and perhaps with some farther to the north) that the Indian is by nature radically different from all other men and that this difference presents an insurmountable barrier to his civilization."[25] The missionary, however, believed that "Indians are men and their children, education alone excepted, [are] like the children of other men." This same ambivalence prevailed among the Cherokees in different form. Colonel Meigs reported in 1805 that most Cherokees were not ready to accept white men as their equals: "Many of the Cherokees think that they are not derived from the same stock as the whites, that they are favorites of the great spirit and that he never intended they should live the laborious lives of the whites; these ideas, if allowed to have a practical effect, would finally operate [to] their destruction."[26]

Despite this theory of racial polygenesis—the belief that God had, in effect, created the races biologically different—there were Cherokees ready to take up the white man's ways and work toward the goal of ultimate citizenship. These civilizationists were generally Cherokees of mixed white and Cherokee ancestry, the so-called mixed bloods, but not always. The chief whom James Mooney considered the leader of the "progressive" faction among the Cherokees after 1794 was a full blood called Double-head. Colonel Meigs commented upon this theme in 1805: ". . . where the blood [of the Cherokees] is mixed with the whites, in every grade of it, there is an apparent disposition leaning toward civilization and this disposition is in proportion to its distance from the original stock. But it is evident at the same time that this does not arise from any augmentation of their intellectual power, for it is a fact that in this nation several of the Chiefs who are from unadulterated Indian [stock] have strong minds and more acute discernment than any of the Half Breeds."[27]

Meigs fully sympathized with the federal government's plan to civilize and ultimately "incorporate" the Indians into the nation as citizens, but he recognized that it would take time. It might appear, he wrote to his subagent, Major William S. Lovely, in 1802, that "the civilization of a whole people of Savages seems sometimes a hopeless piece of business, but patience and perseverance will overcome great difficulties." It was the job of the federal agents to push this effort with vigor. The method, however, was ruthless in its disregard for their traditional way of life. "If it was within my power," said Meigs, "I would do away [with] every [Cherokee] custom inconsistent with civilized life." He noted with regret that "the Cherokees are extremely jealous of their Customs, Customs which have descended down to them from their Ancestors from time immemorial, many of which it is to be wished were done away [with]. . . ."[28]

Meigs viewed his tasks as that of a latter-day, enlightened Pygmalion, hewing away with vigor at the marble block of savagism within which the civilized man was held captive by the encrusted prejudices and superstitions of his forefathers. Government agents, he said, were to hammer away at the stone of culture until every vestige of the old ways was chipped away: "They, like that Statuary [sculptor], believe that the Statue is in the Block and that by the repeated strokes of the means, the desired effect will be produced."[29]

However, an irresistible urge to attribute white supremacy to hereditary or biological superiority provided Meigs with a convenient explanation for the apparent reluctance of many of the full bloods—"the real Indians"—to adapt to the white man's ways: "The number of the real Indians and those of Mixed Blood are nearly equal.[30] The last are almost without exception in favor of improvements and have very much thrown off the savage manner and habits: But those of the real Indians still hug the manners and habits of their ancestors [sic] and are unwilling to give [up] the pleasures of the shade and idleness. . . ."[31]

Almost all the attention focused by historians on families of intermarried whites and Cherokees has been given to that small but usually respectable element of resident traders and government officials (and later a few missionaries) who established themselves for life, married with serious intentions (and increasingly in Christian ceremonies), and accepted a certain responsibility to act for the best interests of the nation that had adopted them and bestowed full tribal rights upon them. It is the names of these families that have come down through the years as mixed-blood chiefs and influentials: Adair, McDonald, Ross, Lowery, McIntosh, Chisholm, Rogers, Riley, Baldridge, Vann, Foreman, Walker, McCoy, Pettit, Brown, Martin, Hicks.

In later years, when the Cherokees became very conscious of their ancestry, it was fashionable to trace it back to the first respectable white trader or agent to intermarry, and for many of these families we can ascertain precise dates and places of entry into the nation. The children of such marriages tended to intermarry among the same group, creating what some considered a mixed-blood elite. Despite animosities between this group and the full bloods, their contributions to Cherokee life were considerable. They provided skills in trade, farming, domestic manufactures, technology, recordkeeping, and diplomacy, which they put at the disposal of the Cherokees. They helped not only by their activities but by their example. More indirectly, but not less important, they inculcated historical perspective and memory; they stressed the importance of long-range planning, the need to see Cherokee affairs in the broader perspective of the wider world around them.

These contributions, however, were sometimes offset by their disdain for those Cherokees who did not zealously push toward acculturation and progress. They made few concessions to tribal custom, and insisted upon raising their children by white standards. These families caused serious internal problems after the 1790s by their disruption of clan kinship patterns and their desire to alter customs regarding private property and inheritance. Furthermore, because of their obvious advantages in dealing with whites, they began to assume important positions of leadership. Their children—normally called "half-breeds" by whites—grew up in the most difficult position of all, between two worlds. Their white fathers wanted them to live, act, and think like white men; their peers and Indian relatives wanted them to assert their Indian loyalty. The most popular, and yet typical, story illustrating this dilemma is the one told by Chief John Ross of his own childhood. His father, Daniel Ross, a Scottish trader from Baltimore, entered the Cherokee Nation in the 1780s on a trading trip, married the daughter of "Tory" John McDonald, who was then living at Chickamauga, and settled down to raise his family among the Cherokees. In 1797 young John Ross, then about seven years old, attended the festival of the Green Corn Dance. His mother

> on this occasion had dressed him in his first suit of nankeen, brand new, made after the white man's style, and he sauntered out to meet his playmates with all the self-consciousness of one wearing, for the first time, his new spring suit. . . . Shouts of derision and taunts of "Unaka" [white boy] greeted him on all sides; even his most intimate friends held aloof. . . . While being dressed by his [Cherokee] grandmother the next morning, he burst into tears and after much coaxing told her of his humiliation the day before. She comforted him as grandmothers are wont to do . . . the nankeen suit came off, the hunting shirt, leggings, and moccasins went on, and the small boy ran shouting to his play, happy and "at home" again, as he termed it.[32]

Ross's father, however, took care to hire white tutors to teach his son English and arithmetic so that he could learn his father's business, and Ross grew up to be a wealthy trader. His first marriage was to a Cherokee full blood; his second, after he had become principal chief, was to a well-to-do white Quaker who lived in Baltimore. Ross never overcame his "twoness." From the profits of trade, he bought a large number of slaves to till his plantation fields and lived according to the style of a Southern gentleman, while defending to the last ditch the right of the Cherokees to remain on their homeland in the East. He was so unsure of his command of Cherokee language that as a chief he always spoke and wrote in English.

In regard to racial equality as well as in regard to adopting the white man's ways, the Cherokee was left with an impossible dilemma: either he adopted a theory of polygenesis and racial separatism (that God had created the different races and they must not be mixed)—thereby throwing his weight on the side of reactionary bigots along the frontier—or he accepted the "enlightened" view of liberal philanthropists and accepted amalgamation, assimilation, and disappearance. Either route led to his extinction. I have found only one explicit statement by a Cherokee of what may have been a more general view, a faith that heredity and complexion were not the real issues. This occurred during a conversation that Meigs had early in the century with the Lower Town chief named Eskaqua, or Bloody Fellow. Meigs had tried to persuade him that it might be best if he led his people to the West since he appeared reluctant to adopt total acculturation. "Bloody Fellow replied that he had no inclination to leave the country of his birth. Even should the habits & customs of the Cherokees give place to the habits & customs of the whites, or even should they themselves become white by intermarriage, not a drop of Indian blood would be lost; it would be spread more widely, but not lost. He was for preserving them together as a people regardless of complexion."[33] It was this fundamental racial pride and confidence attached, let it be noted, to the critical notion of roots in their homeland, which sustained the Cherokees in their struggle for survival as a distinct people in the years ahead.

Although the Cherokees probably learned of the importance whites attached to racial differences primarily from daily experience with them, they also experienced their legal implications in various courtroom situations. Sometimes they found that there were advantages to be gained, as in the case of the Cherokee who was placed on trial for murdering, in a fit of drunken anger, a black slave owned by a white man. A white jury in Tennessee found him guilty of manslaughter, a crime punishable by branding. But when the judge examined the statute, he discovered that it applied only to the killing of white men. Nevertheless, the attorney for the state demanded that the Indian be branded. The judge refused and the Cherokee was released. He had, however, learned an important lesson about the nice legal distinctions involved in interracial criminal justice. Meigs wrote that the Cherokees were pleased at the fairness of the trial and its outcome; but it was a fairness they seldom found in trials involving Indians charged with crimes against white men.[34]

WHILE SOUTHERN STATE COURTS may have shown partiality toward Indians who murdered black slaves, they were not prepared to deal in the same way with Indians accused of crimes against whites. Meigs discussed this matter with the secretary of war in 1812 when Governor Tatnall of Georgia demanded the arrest of two Cherokees accused of murdering two white Georgians. He said the Cherokees were "afraid of a trial" by a white jury. They had reminded Meigs that in a recent trial involving a white man accused of murdering a Cherokee, the case was dismissed for want of evidence because only Cherokees had witnessed the murder. The Cherokees, Meigs told Tatnall, had also informed him that there were at least eight recent cases where state courts refused to bring charges against white murderers. "This I have no doubt is true," Meigs told the governor. The reason the white murderers had not been tried was that there was "no proof but that of Indians" available as evidence. In such cases, he said, "the murderers could not be convicted and never will." He went on to remind the governor that "the state of Indians is a deplorable one in this respect. We arraign them as moral agents, charge them with crimes that cannot be committed without including an idea that they are more like ourselves, at the same time we exclude them from all the advantages of being capable of moral or religious conceptions; their testimony on oath is not admissible."[35]

Meigs fought consistently against this double standard of American justice. Like a true Jeffersonian, he deplored the effort to read the Christian religion into the common law. Indians were denied the right to give legal testimony on the ground that they were heathens. Heathens did not believe in a God who administered rewards and punishments after death. Presumably, therefore, they would have no compunction about lying. Meigs was always eager to demonstrate that the Indians did indeed believe in a God and an afterlife. "I have been informed," he wrote to a lawyer in Tennessee who was trying to help an Indian named Stone (or Stone Carrier) on trial for horse stealing, "that the Moors have been admitted to give Evidence at Gibraltar in Capital cases. The religion of the Cherokees is a good as that of Mahomet." Though not Christians, "the Indians believe in the being of a God and in the immortality of the soul; it is an instinctive idea with them."[36] He and Silas Dinsmoor, agent to the Choctaws, searched through Blackstone's *Commentaries* until they found support for their position. Dinsmoor wrote to Meigs about it in 1803: "In 3d Blackstone, Lib. 3, cap. 23, p. 369, it is said, 'All witnesses of whatever religion or country that have the use of their reason are to be examined except such as are infamous or such as are interested in the event of the cause. All others are competent witnesses though the jury from other circumstances will judge of their credibility.' This being the law, the Indians are and of right ought to be admissible as witnesses."[37]

Dinsmoor argued that it was not "absolutely necessary that an Indian should take an oath to make his testimony valid" because, as in the case of Quakers, "an affirmation might be sufficient." But even admitting that an oath was necessary and that an Indian had no idea of the being of a God nor of future existence, "should these considerations bar an Indian from being admitted to oath and testimony? Which would be the most dubious testimony, the honest Indian who has never heard of or known a God or the Atheist or Deist who has convinced *himself* that there is none, or if there be, that he suffers the actions of men to pass unheeded and unnoted? Yet no one pretends to bar a white man on account of his religious opinions."[38] Despite Dinsmoor's arguments, he could not make the courts of the Mississippi Territory admit Indian witnesses any more than Meigs could in Tennessee or Georgia.[39] Even where Indians' cases were taken to court, Meigs frankly acknowledged, "It is a fact that they cannot have justice done to them in the courts of law." The judges, he said, were "just and liberal in their Sentiments and look on the human race with equal eye as far as related to distributive justice," but "a jury impaneled in the frontier Counties dare not bring in a Verdict to take the life of a Citizen for killing an Indian." The result was that Indians were regularly "accused, tried, and condemned and executed on the testimony of any white citizen of common character and understanding when at the same time a white man can kill an Indian in the presence of 100 Indians and the testimony of these hundred Indians to the fact amounts to nothing and the man will be acquitted."[40] The impact of this upon the dignity and self-respect of the Indian was devastating. Richard Brown, one of the leading Cherokee chiefs, wrote to Meigs in 1811 about the feelings aroused in the Indians by their not being allowed to testify against white horse thieves: "We have found a horse belonging to an Indian near Dittoes landing or near Huntsville [in Mississippi Territory, now part of Alabama]. We cannot recover him without aid. The oath of the Indians is not known by your laws. Decide in some way to give us our right. Are we considered as negroes who cannot support our claims?"[41]

The Indians were always described as a proud people. They considered themselves the equal not only of white men but of the upper class of white men in the South. In 1760 Henry Timberlake noted that the Cherokees "are extremely proud, despising the lower class of Europeans; and in some athletick diversions I once was present at, they refused to match or hold conference with any but officers."[42] But after 1794 frontier whites became contemptuous of the rights of Indians, knowing that no white jury would ever convict them for anything they did to an Indian. In 1813 Meigs described four separate cases of Indian murders in which "prosecutions were instituted and all failed of producing punishment." It seriously undermined Meigs's faith in the Republic: "Let us not advocate a system of Ethics that only subjects the weak and simple honest man to become the prey of the bold villain who laughs at the restraints which bind the multitude."[43] The only means by which Meigs and the secretary of war could make a pretense of justice was to offer the family of a murdered Indian a cash compensation. In 1802 Secretary of War Henry Dearborn wrote to Silas Dinsmoor, the Choctaw agent: "you will endeavor to settle the disputes and if necessary engage to satisfy the Chickasaws for the loss of their friend by a pecuniary compensation not exceeding two or three hundred dollars to the family or friends of the deceased."[44] In this case the Chickasaw appears to have been murdered by a Delaware Indian, but the same "satisfaction" was offered for murders attributed to whites. In 1803 Dearborn authorized Meigs to provide "such pecuniary satisfaction as in your Judgement may be acceptable and proper" to the families of murdered Cherokees. He suggested a figure of "from one hundred to two hundred dollars for each man or woman actually murdered by white citizens since our last Treaty." Of course, the Cherokees were to be told that "the compensation is not intended to operate [sic] as an acquittal of the murderers."[45] In effect, though, such payments ended the agent's and the government's concern with the case.

The use of murder-compensation payments continued until 1820 when John C. Calhoun, as secretary of war, decided to put a stop to it. "I have received your letter of the 14th November last," he wrote to Meigs, "submitting the claim of the Headmen of the Cherokees for the Indians killed by Americans." Grudgingly he acknowledged the precedents for the practice and said "you will accordingly pay the sum of $100 to the widow of the deceased." But he added, "You will inform the chiefs that the practice will not be continued in future as it is repugnant to those principles by which we govern ourselves in such case."[46] Calhoun either had forgotten or did not realize that the practice had arisen in the first place because the principles by which the "Americans" governed themselves did not seem to be available to the Indians. Nor did he take notice that the cost of an Indian's life had declined in twenty years from three hundred to one hundred dollars.

The failure of American jurisprudence in regard to white murderers was equally glaring in the much more frequent cases of fraud and theft perpetrated by white men upon the Indians: their horses, their furs, their traps, their guns—virtually anything they owned of any value was fair game for marauding whites. The federal agent, faced with trying to evaluate and adjudicate these claims, was compelled to establish his own investigatory and judicial system: "The nature of these kinds of claims cannot be equitably determined by strictly adhering to the law of evidence. The Indians cannot give legal testimony and by means of this disability the whites have an advantage; but by attending carefully to all the circumstances and to the character of the parties, justice can be done to the claimant, for altho' the claims may be just, the parties, especially the Indians, cannot support their rights and some characters of each party cannot be credited; but by care here we can, with few exceptions, make equitable decisions."[47] In short, Meigs heard the evidence and made the decisions himself; they were forwarded to the Department of War, and the Department more or less had to accept his word in compensating the Indian or the white involved. Consequently, much depended upon the honesty and ability of the agent; and not a little on how much money the War Department felt it could afford for this sort of thing.

Meigs was an honest and conscientious agent; many agents were neither. Trying to explain to a friend why, after all the Americans had tried to do for them, the Cherokees still had certain "prejudices" against the white man, Meigs said, "It does not arise from pride, as ours does; it arises in the Indian from his humble conception of himself and of his race from the discovery he makes that we look down on him as an inferior being [which] has a tendency to make him despise himself as the offspring of an inferior race of beings."[48] Lack of respect by others led to loss of respect for himself. This self-rejecting rage, frustration, and despair often led Indians to drink themselves into oblivion, but at other times they found more objective vents for their anger. There were other ways to avenge themselves on their persecutors. Although some took vengeance into their own hands, as traditional tribal custom formerly prescribed, this was usually self-defeating. A more subtle and satisfying way to get even with the white man was to steal his horses. For several reasons horse stealing became a way of life for many Cherokees in these years of anomie.

According to all early accounts of the Cherokee people, they were notable for their honesty. Not only had they no locks on their own houses, barns, and stables, but a visitor might leave his horse, gun, or goods with any of them for months at a time and find it unharmed when he called for it. In a culture committed to sharing even the last piece of food with strangers as well as neighbors, neither avarice nor acquisitiveness was a virtue. Not placing a high value on personal property and seldom needing much, the Cherokees had no written laws governing theft, only social disdain for the thief. Robbery was not a crime included in clan revenge, no matter what the object stolen. Not even the extensive use of western manufactures (guns, axes, kettles, and blankets) after 1700 seems to have produced any problem in this regard. So long as the cultural values were intact and healthy, the Cherokees maintained their standards of honesty. But as the cultural system broke down, so did its values. By the last decade of the eighteenth century, the problem of horse stealing and its allied vices had risen to monumental proportions.

In times of war, horse stealing had always been an understandable and acceptable source of plunder. In times of peace it became a source of revenge, of excitement, of courageous achievement for those denied other means of self-esteem and success. Horse stealing had become a major problem during the guerrilla warfare of 1780–94, and the treaty ending that war prescribed that "in the future, to prevent the practice of stealing horses, attended with the most pernicious consequences to the lives and peace of both parties," the Cherokees were to "agree that for every horse which shall be stolen from the white inhabitants by any Cherokee Indians and not returned within three months, that the sum of fifty dollars shall be deducted" from the annuity the government paid to the tribe annually for the land the Cherokees had sold to the government.[49] In addition, the congressional acts regulating trade and intercourse with the Indians passed in 1796, 1799, and 1802 all contained clauses designed to prevent this illicit traffic.

Horse stealing, of course, was not merely a symptom of the breakdown of Indian culture; it was so endemic upon the American frontier that it obviously represents also the breakdown of European culture on its outer fringes. Horse stealing provided one of the few areas of frontier life in which Indians and whites worked harmoniously together (sometimes in trying to catch the thieves who stole from both groups with equal disregard, sometimes in belonging to the "pony clubs" constituted to do the stealing). Slave stealing, while closely allied, was more dangerous as well as more profitable.[50] Cattle rustling was less profitable in the eastern woodlands because cattle were slow-moving, noisy, and difficult to conceal. When out to steal, thieves might take whatever came first and most easily to hand, but only in regard to horse stealing was the traffic so common as to become a profession. The members of the pony clubs were thieves by vocation.

Horse stealing was directly related to the depletion of game in the old hunting grounds and the loss of status faced by Indian men who could not use their old skills to provide for their families. Return J. Meigs explained this (from the white man's viewpoint) in a letter to Benjamin Hawkins, the Creek agent, in 1805. He was justifying the government's effort to persuade the Indians to cede "the mountainous land lying between East and West Tennessee. . . . That land is of no use to them; there is not a single family [living] on it, and the hunting is very poor. Yet those of an idle disposition spend much time in ramblin' there and often return with a stolen horse which they have afterwards to pay for [from the annuity]. In fact, it is only a nursery of savage habits and operates [*sic*] against civilization which is much impeded by their holding such immense tracts of wilderness."[51] The "savage habit" of stealing horses from an enemy was an old one, but too many otherwise honest Indians felt justified in resorting to it when their best efforts to support their families by hunting failed—largely because the whites had killed or chased away the game. How could a man return empty-handed from an extended hunting trip without feeling disgraced? While horse stealing had its roots in tribal warfare, in which booty taken from an enemy was always a sign of prowess and bravery, it also stemmed from the fact that Cherokees owned their land in common. Since no man could buy or sell land as a means of enriching himself, this prime source of frontier enterprise was closed to them. (The fact that Indians had to measure private wealth in terms of personal property—horses or slaves—and not, as whites did, in terms of real estate, was of course part of the argument used by those who demanded that the Cherokees adopt the practice of owning their land "in severalty.") Hence moveable or personal property became more important to them than to a white man as a means of investment or growing wealth once they were told to become capitalists. Moreover, horse stealing utilized many of the old-fashioned skills of the warrior and hunter: it was exciting; it tested a man's daring; it required quick wits and courage for, make no mistake about it, human life was at stake in these encounters. The respectable among the older generation frowned upon this practice and did not find it a valid substitute for war and hunting; but the elders had lost their right to command. Many young Indians preferred the risk of sudden death to the plodding routine of grubbing and hoeing in the fields day after day. Moreover, the profits from horse stealing were not only quicker but much larger than any Cherokee farmer could earn. Some less respectable chiefs managed to profit by it, if not to justify it.

Horse stealing, like slave stealing, was more than simply a way to vent one's anger at the white men or prove oneself a hell of a daring fellow. It also fulfilled an economic need on the frontier. The slave dealer had provided cheap labor for a system desperately in need of it. The horse dealer provided a substitute for specie in an economy desperately short of cash. The dishonest vendors in stolen goods were simply providing more cheaply in the black market what there was a high demand for from the public. In this sense it was not strictly a white-Indian problem but a source of economic livelihood for those willing to take chances—the poor, the desperate, the angry, the alienated.[52]

Meigs readily recognized this aspect of the profession: "A considerable part of the land purchased in this country is paid for in horses; they serve as a kind of currency for this purpose all over this western country and hence arises the facility with which they are stolen by Indians and others."[53] Governor William Blount of Tennessee (the superintendent of Indian affairs for the Southern District of the United States—south of the Ohio) noted this same bartering aspect when he asked James Carey, the official Cherokee interpreter, in 1793, "In what manner do the Indians dispose of stolen horses?" Carey answered, "Generally they sell them to the traders for a trifle, who run them out of the nation in a different direction to that from whence they came and barter them off for negroes or articles of merchandise."[54]

A detailed study of horse stealing on the frontier would reveal a great deal about its economic development and difficulties. For example, it seems evident that in the 1790s the Cherokees stole horses in the West and bartered them for goods in the East where the market was better, while in the early nineteenth century the need for specie on the frontier made it more profitable to steal horses in the East and trade them in the West. "This business is carried on by white people and Indians in combination," wrote Blount in 1792, "and as soon as a horse is stolen he is conveyed through the Indian nation to North or South Carolina or Georgia and in a short time to the principal towns on the seaboard for sale so as to effectually prevent recovery."[55] But fifteen years later Meigs reported, "The number of horses carried thro' and into this [Cherokee] country is almost incredible—from Georgia, both the Carolinas and Kentucky."[56]

The Indian nations were ideally situated for the business. Being centrally located between East and West, among various settlements scattered throughout the frontier, and being largely wilderness without roads, the various Indian territories became common channels for shuttling stolen horses. "Considerable numbers of horses are stolen by citizens and by Indians," wrote Meigs, "that never will or can be detected on account of the Wilderness country, so that detection is easily avoided."[57] Not only was it difficult for victims to interrogate friendly Indians who might have been willing to help them trace the thieves, but the Indians themselves possessed no system of internal police to keep track of their own people and recapture their own horses. Since the traffic was interstate and through federal territory, the policing of it was the job of the federal government.

With only one agent or two in the thousands of square miles of wilderness that constituted each Indian nation, it was impossible for the federal government to provide adequate policing. Even the licensing system under the trade and intercourse acts produced no convictions. "Horse stealing is a subject of complaint (almost continual) to me," wrote Governor Blount in 1792, "without my being able to give any redress. The only thing I can do is to give passports to the sufferers to go into the nation in search of their horses and letters to the chiefs, which, as yet, has never been attended with recovery."[58] The chiefs, even if they knew who the thieves were, were hardly likely to turn them over to frontier justice. Consequently, horse stealing became one of the most constant causes of friction between Indians and whites on the frontier—each tending to lay the blame primarily on the other. "Horse stealing," Blount continued in this letter, "is the grand source of hostility between the white and red people in this district, and I fear will actually produce it if not desisted from. It is a subject on which the whites are very sore and with difficulty restrain themselves from taking what they call satisfaction, that is from killing some of the Indians."

While the Indians usually acted as the employees of white traders, who paid them a trifle for the dangerous work and then shuttled the horses off to profitable sales in distant communities, more than once Indians bought stolen horses from each other—sometimes knowingly, sometimes not. On one occasion a white man forcibly took from a Cherokee a mare he said had been stolen from him by the Creeks. The Cherokee complained that the white man should pay him what he had paid the Creek for it. The white man refused, and the case was taken to Blount by a Cherokee chief. Blount told the chief that the white settler who "took possession of her brought her to me and proved her before a justice of the peace, by the oath of several disinterested evidences, to be his property; and by the law of the white people, he is entitled to keep her without paying anything. The [Cherokee] man when he bought her from a Creek must have known that she had been raised by the white people [white people's horses were said to be rounder in the belly] and was stolen. Does not all your nation agree in informing me that the Creeks are daily stealing horses from the white people? Then why do they purchase horses from them?"[59]

There was, of course, no honor among thieves. They stole from each other and sold to each other, and when questioned by white authorities, blamed each other. Since there was no effective way to enforce the laws, both sides took the law into their own hands. Vigilantism prevailed and real or suspected horse thieves were frequently whipped, beaten, or shot by angry owners not too concerned about trying to differentiate one Indian from another. It was generally the Indians who suffered the most from vigilantes since they dared not assault any white man openly; yet because their oath was unacceptable before a justice of the peace, it was impossible for them to "prove" legal ownership without written evidence or white witnesses. Even when Meigs accepted Indian evidence in his extrajudicial proceedings regarding depredation claims, they had no assurance of success. Meigs might trust their word, but the government auditors frequently demanded more concrete evidence before they would authorize payment.

> I forward a number of claims of citizens and Indians for damages stated by them to have been sustained, principally for Horse stealing, in which the citizens as well as the Cherokees have a share. It is very difficult to ascertain facts in these cases. The difficulty arises from the inaccuracy or want of testimony; the want of testimony arises from the impossibility of obtaining it in the places where the stealing is perpetrated [it] being nearly all done in a wide wilderness principally in the Indian country. This lays the white people under great distress to make legal proof of their losses. And the Indians suffer from the same cause, and in addition to that their testimony is not allowed to be valid in a legal sense.[60]

The shortcomings of horse stealing as a way of life were obvious, and it was never respectable. Still, what was respectable anymore? What options for a viable lifestyle with a hopeful future were there? Having lost faith in their own prowess, the Cherokees saw little they could depend upon in the white man's program. It might be said that the Cherokees had nowhere to go but up at the turn of the century. In fact, the miracle is that they did not, as did so many other Indian nations, disintegrate entirely. To their own surprise, as well as to that of many of their closest observers, they discovered resources within themselves and their culture they had not realized were there.

The crisis that finally enabled them to regain a sense of their own dignity and self-respect was the effort made in the years 1806 to 1809 to persuade them to move west of the Mississippi. Their internal frictions reached a peak in 1807 when Doublehead, the "progressive" leader of the Lower Towns, was assassinated. The fact that he had been caught accepting bribes from the federal government, hidden in secret clauses of the treaties of 1805 and 1806, was only partly to blame. The deeper issue was lack of consideration for the feelings of a large proportion of the tribe, particularly the conservative elements in the Valley Towns, who wished to find a middle ground between total assimilation and the old ways. In the press of the emergency that arose when Meigs, disillusioned by the murder of his favorite chief, tried to coerce the tribe into total removal to the West, a new group of leaders emerged.

Their first task was to reunite the various regions of the tribe in a concerted effort to hold on to what remained of their ancestral land. Their second task was to create a new instrument of political control—an elected executive body empowered to act on the nation's behalf when the council of chiefs was not in session. Although about one thousand Cherokees departed for Arkansas in 1810 in the wake of the crisis, the remaining 12,000 Cherokees acquired a new sense of solidarity and purpose. Henceforth the Cherokees knew that to be a Cherokee meant to live in the land of their forefathers, to put the unity and prosperity of the "nation" before the aggrandizement of individual sections or chiefs. With the new confidence gained from their successful resistance to disunion and removal, the Cherokees were ready to begin the more difficult task of restructuring their social order. This political revitalization culminated between 1817 and 1828 in a new form of government and a firm conviction that they must retain their own distinct ethnic identity. By their own effort, the Cherokees evolved a policy that avoided both of the white man's unpalatable alternatives. They would not assimilate, and neither would they be moved. They would remain an independent, quasi-sovereign nation. By acting on these fundamental principles the Cherokee people were reborn, like the phoenix, from the ashes of defeat and confusion.[61]

NOTES

1. The standard histories of the Cherokee Nation are Henry T. Malone, *Cherokees of the Old South: A People in Transition* (Athens: University of Georgia Press, 1956); Charles C. Royce, "The Cherokee Nation of Indians: A Narrative of Their Official Relations with the Colonial and Federal Governments," U.S. Bureau of American Ethnology, *Fifth Annual Report* (Washington DC, 1887); James Mooney, "Myths of the Cherokee," U.S. Bureau of American Ethnology, *Nineteenth Annual Report*, pt. 1 (Washington DC, 1900); Grace S. Woodward, *The Cherokees* (Norman: University of Oklahoma Press, 1963); Marion L. Starkey, *The Cherokee Nation* (New York: Knopf, 1946).

2. See Leonard Bloom, "The Acculturation of the Eastern Cherokees," *North Carolina Historical Review* 19:4 (October 1942): 323–58; Fred Gearing, *Priests and Warriors: Social Structures of Cherokee Politics in the Eighteenth Century*, American Anthropological Association, Memoir no. 93 (Menasha WI, 1962); William H. Gilbert, Jr., "The Eastern Cherokees," Bureau of American Ethnology, *Bulletin 133*, Anthropological Paper no. 23 (1943) 169–413; John Philip Reid, *A Law of Blood: The Primitive Law of the Cherokee Nation* (New York: New York University Press, 1970).

3. Royce, "Cherokee Nation," 218.

4. For the inability, and often the unwillingness, of the federal government to uphold its treaty guarantees against white intruders in these years, see ch. 7 in Francis P. Prucha, *American Indian Policy in the Formative Years* (Cambridge: Harvard University Press, 1962) 139–87.

5. For the political factionalism within the Cherokee Nation in these years, see John P. Brown, *Old Frontiers: The Story of the Cherokee Indians from Earliest Times to the Date of Their Removal to the West, 1838* (Kingsport, TN: Southern Publishers, 1938) 148–453; and Mooney, "Myths of the Cherokee," 82–87. For clan revenge, or "the blood law," see Reid, *Law of Blood*. According to this custom, the closest male relative of a murdered man was personally responsible for avenging his death by taking the life of the murderer or a close relative of the murderer.

6. Royce, "Cherokee Nation," provides detailed descriptions and maps of these cessions.

7. In 1804 and 1807 the tribe faced general starvation, which only timely gifts of food from the federal agent alleviated. However, in both cases he exacted a price in land cessions for his generosity.

8. Walter Lowrie, ed., *American State Papers: Indian Affairs* (Washington, 1832) 1:631; hereafter cited as ASP (IA). As late as 1821 young Cherokees still were torn by the urge to establish themselves as warriors. One such youth left a missionary school that year: "He said he wished to leave his country and go [west] to war against the Osage." Papers of the American Board of Commissioners for Foreign Missions, Houghton Library, Harvard University, 18.3.1, 2, Brainerd Journal, 15 November 1821; hereafter cited as ABCFM Papers.

9. Richard Peters, *The Case of the Cherokee Nation Against the State of Georgia* (Philadelphia, 1831) 253.

10. ASP (IA), 1:267.

11. Microfilm Records of the Cherokee Indian Agency in Tennessee, 1801–1835 (M-208), Roll 6, Records of the Bureau of Indian Affairs (RG 75), National Archives, [December?] 1814. These records consist mostly of letters from the federal agent in the Cherokee Nation to the secretary of war. The microfilm has no frame numbers, nor are the records paginated. The documents are given in chronological order. This undated document is placed between documents dated November 1814 and January 1815. Hereafter documents from this archive will be cited as M-208 with date.

12. ABCFM Papers, Brainerd Journal, 25 December 1818.

13. For the Moravian missionaries, see Edmund Schwarze, *History of the Moravian Missions among the Southern Indian Tribes of the United States* (Bethlehem, PA: Times Publishing Co., 1923); for the first Presbyterian schools, see Dorothy C. Bass, "Gideon Blackburn's Mission to the Cherokees," *Journal of Presbyterian History* 52 (Fall 1973): 203–226.

14. *Cherokee Phoenix*, 21 January 1829. I have used the microfilm at the American Antiquarian Society, Worcester, MA.

15. Thomas Jefferson, *Notes on Virginia*, in Adrienne Koch and William Peden, eds., *The Life and Selected Writings of Thomas Jefferson* (New York: Modern Library, 1944) 211.

16. Brown, *Old Frontiers*, 18–19. See also Reid, *Law of Blood*, 37–47, 67–70, 114–16, 119–21, 128–29, 187–88.

17. M-208, Return J. Meigs's "Journal of Occurrences," August 1802.

18. Ibid., 13 February 1805.

19. ASP (IA), 1:676.

20. M-208, 3 January 1808.

21. For the uneven distribution of government technical assistance and the complaints of the Upper and Lower Towns, see Mooney, "Myths of the Cherokee," 82–83.

22. According to a census taken by Meigs in 1808–1809, the Valley Towns contained 3,648 out of 12,395 Cherokees, 5 out of 583 black slaves, 72 out of 341 whites in the nation as a whole. M-208, 17 October 1808. By 1828 the Cherokees had developed a black code within their nation in order to protect their own status. See W. G. McLoughlin, "Red Indians, Black Slavery and White Racism: America's Slaveholding Indians," *American Quarterly* 26 (October 1974): 367–85.

23. Secretary of War Lewis Cass quoted in the *Cherokee Phoenix*, 14 January 1832.

24. Secretary of War William H. Crawford, ASP (IA), 2:28.

25. ABCFM Papers, Brainerd Journal, 24 January 1818.

26. M-208, 13 February 1805.

27. Ibid., 18 February 1805.

28. Ibid., undated, but filed between 25 December 1801 and 1 January 1802; ibid., 6 June 1806.

29. Ibid.

30. This estimate is far too high and probably indicates that Meigs associated primarily with a special group of Cherokees and seldom ventured into the more remote regions of the nation. See *Cherokee Phoenix*, 1 January 1831, for an estimate that "less than one-fourth" of the Cherokees were of mixed ancestry. An analysis of the federal census of the Cherokees in 1835 reveals that the figure was less than 23 percent.

31. M-208, 27 July 1805.

32. Rachel Eaton, *John Ross and the Cherokee Indians* (Muscogee, OK: Star Printery, Inc., 1921) 3.

33. John Howard Payne Papers, Newberry Library (Chicago), 2:23.

34. M-208, 10 March, 1 May 1807. Meigs noted of this crime, "It was an act perpetrated in a barbarous manner not in defence of life but in a rage of passion excited by the pride of the Indian to be opposed by a Negro, which even Indians effect to look down on with contempt." Ibid., 22 February, 20 April 1810. Meigs's phrase, "even Indians," speaks volumes on this issue.

35. Ibid., 19 March 1812.

36. Ibid., 10 June 1802.

37. Ibid., 26 July 1802.

38. Ibid.

39. Ibid., 7 April 1801.

40. Ibid., 6 April 1812.

41. Ibid., 21 July 1811.

42. Henry Timberlake, *Memoirs,* ed. Samuel C. Williams (Marietta, GA: Continental Book Company, 1948) 79.

43. M-208, 11 February 1813.

44. Microfilm, Letters Sent by the Secretary of War Relating to Indian Affairs, 1800–1824 (M-15), Records of the Bureau of Indian Affairs (RG 75), National Archives, 18 May 1802; hereafter cited as M-15.

45. M-15, 30 May 1803; 7 January 1804.

46. Ibid., 6 July 1820.

47. M-208, 22 February 1810.

48. Ibid., 3 August 1817.

49. Treaty of 26 June 1794, cited in Richard Peters, *The Case of the Cherokee Indians* (Philadelphia, 1831) 254.

50. For an example of illicit slave trading among the Cherokees, see ABCFM Papers, Barinerd Journal, 10 October 1819. A white man was purchasing Osage and other captive Indian children within the Cherokee Nation and claiming they were "Mulattos"; he sold them as black slaves to whites outside the nation. "This man," said the missionaries, "had endeavored to persuade another to join in this business, stating that there were a number of [Indian] captives in the Cherokee Nation which he thought he could obtain at a low price."

51. M-208, 13 February 1805.

52. My analysis here owes something to the chapter entitled "Crime As a Way of Life" in Daniel Bell, *The End of Ideology* (New York: Free Press, 1961).

53. M-208, 19 December 1807.

54. ASP (IA), 1:438.

55. Ibid., 265 (5 May 1792).

56. M-208, 19 December 1807.

57. Ibid.

58. Cited in Prucha, *American Indian Policy,* 204.

59. ASP (IA), 1:281 (13 September 1792).

60. M-208, 19 December 1807.

61. For a discussion of the first removal crises of 1806–1809 and the revitalization that emerged from it, see W. G. McLoughlin, "Thomas Jefferson and the Beginning of Cherokee Nationalism, 1806–1809," *William and Mary Quarterly,* 3rd ser., 32 (October 1975): 547–80.

THE STAFF OF LEADERSHIP: INDIAN AUTHORITY IN THE MISSIONS OF ALTA CALIFORNIA

22

Steven W. Hackel

Spain's territorial interests in the Western Hemisphere concentrated on the Caribbean basin and the adjoining territory, stretching from Florida across an arc that ran through Mexico, Central America, and northern South America. But the Spanish also wanted to extend their empire along the Pacific coast of North America. When men from Spain sailed northward up the Pacific coast in the first half of the sixteenth century, they renamed it Alta California and tried to control it by using two familiar tools of European empire-builders—soldiers and missionaries—that had proven so effective in Spain's conquest of the lands they claimed near the Atlantic.

But in Alta California, as Steven W. Hackel demonstrates here, the Spanish lacked the resources to station large numbers of either soldiers or missionaries among the natives. As a result, Spain's colonists had to rely on Indian allies to advance their goals. That meant the sharing of power between missionaries, who had garnered a reputation among some of the indigenous peoples as ruthless advocates for the progress of the Gospel, and Indian converts, whose authority increased over time. The story in Alta California bears comparison with Amy Turner Bushnell's chronicle of Spanish Florida a century before, and with the relations between missionaries and converts elsewhere in North America.

The issues Hackel describes remain very much alive today. Given the current controversy over the possible canonization of the Franciscan missionary Fray Junípero Serra, the man the Catholic Church believes brought Christianity to California, relations between California's native peoples and Spanish colonizers have been the subject of close scrutiny and intense debate. Whatever the outcome of the canonization process, the history of Alta California has now become central to the larger story of Indian-European relations in North America.

THE STAFF OF LEADERSHIP:
INDIAN AUTHORITY IN THE MISSIONS
OF ALTA CALIFORNIA

Steven W. Hackel

IN 1769, SPAIN SET OUT to defend the Pacific Coast against settlement by other European powers by developing a series of colonial outposts that eventually stretched from San Diego to San Francisco. In this region, known to Europeans as Alta California, Spain depended on religious missions more than military fortifications or civilian towns to solidify its control. During the second half of the eighteenth century, missions had declined in importance in the rest of northern New Spain. In 1767, the crown expelled the Jesuits from Spain and its colonies and gradually converted most surviving missions in Arizona, New Mexico, and Texas to parishes overseen by secular priests.[1] But in Alta California, Franciscan missions steadily increased in number and power as the most important centers of interaction between Indians and Spaniards. By 1821, when Spanish rule gave way to Mexican independence, roughly 70,000 Indians had been baptized in the region's twenty missions. Even after more than five decades of demographic disaster brought on by the ravages of disease, mission Indians still outnumbered Spanish settlers and soldiers 71,750 to 3,400; missions outnumbered military garrisons by a ratio of five to one and civilian settlements by six to one.[2]

The Franciscans' strategies to convert and control Indians in Alta California have sparked an intense debate that has recently involved the general public as well as scholars. Public interest has focused on the canonization of Fray Junípero Serra, founding father of the California missions, and more generally on Indian-Spanish relations in those missions.[3] Promoters of the Spanish colonial past portray the Franciscans as saving childlike Indians from savagism; detractors depict the missions as brutal labor camps, committed to cultural genocide.[4] Although participants in this dispute have generated a considerable number of articles and books, the involvement of Indian leaders in the running of the California missions remains largely unexplored.[5] Neither side has sufficiently examined the extent to which the missions

SOURCE: *William and Mary Quarterly*, 3d Ser. 54 (1997), 347–76.

depended on the persistence of Indian leadership, nor has either explored how Indian authority was created and legitimated within the missions.

Most Alta California missions counted between 500 and 1,000 Indian residents, two missionaries, and a military guard of four or five soldiers. Because their numbers were few and their resources limited, Spaniards looked to Indian leaders to help organize and regulate the missions' life and work. To this end, they instituted and directed annual elections in which the mission community chose its own officials, thereby enabling Spanish religious and military authorities to rule Indians through Indians. This system, though hierarchical in form, was flexible in operation. Indian officials not only served the needs of Spanish overlords, but they also protected the interests of the Indian community and, in some cases, ultimately rebelled against the Spanish order.

Recent studies of Indian communities in colonial America have noted the importance of Indian leaders and the challenges of their position. Colonists frequently tried to advance their objectives by co-opting Indian leaders, on whom they attempted to impose European forms of leadership. This practice involved a risk, for Indian leaders could subvert as well as implement colonial objectives. They, too, had much to gain though even more to lose in these encounters, for by participating in European systems of governance, they could foster or hinder their own autonomy as well as that of their communities. Indians, therefore, responded in a variety of ways to imposed forms of governance, and Europeans accommodated those forms to the communities they sought to control. These responses and accommodations are crucial to the ethnohistory of all of colonial America from the sixteenth century through the nineteenth, from New France to New England to New Spain.[6]

After giving an overview of the Indians of Alta California and the colonial strategies of the Spaniards who settled among them, this article analyzes the system of elections and the responsibilities of Indian officials in the missions and identifies patterns of Indian leadership among the men who served as officials. These patterns, which are most visible at Mission San Carlos Borromeo on the Monterey peninsula, reveal a complex interplay of Indian and Spanish priorities. At first, the Spanish system of indirect rule relied on Indians who held power in their own communities before the missions were founded. Later, annual elections promoted new Indian leaders, from whose ranks came men who instigated rebellions against the Franciscans in the 1820s and reorganized Indian communities after the missions collapsed in the 1830s. Thus the Spaniards' use of and dependence on Indian officials reveal a noteworthy paradox of the colonial history of the Americas: indirect rule not only reshaped Indian lives, but it also provided Indians with the means and the personnel to retain control over some aspects of their communities, in some areas long after the collapse of colonial rule.

IN CALIFORNIA, SPANIARDS encountered the most linguistically diverse and densely settled native population in all North America. Estimating that 310,000 Indians lived within the boundaries of the present state on the eve of Spanish colonization, scholars have classified these Indians into six culture areas and at least ninety distinct languages.[7] Spanish settlement was concentrated in the coastal region between San

Diego and San Francisco, where Indians probably numbered around 60,000 in 1769.[8] As settlement spread north from San Diego, it most directly and immediately affected the Tipai and Ipai around San Diego, the Luiseño to their immediate north, the Gabrielino of Los Angeles, the Chumash of the Santa Barbara region, the Yokuts of the Central Valley, the Salinan, Esselen, and Costanoan of the central coast, and the Miwok, Wappo, and Pomo of the San Francisco Bay area. These classifications simplify a complex mosaic, for Indians encompassed by them lived in semisedentary settlements of 100 to 1,000 people, and language and culture often varied from village to village. Trade, marriage, and ritual connected these communities, but most villages steadfastly maintained autonomy and protected their areas against encroachment.[9]

Despite this great linguistic and cultural diversity, Indians in Alta California pursued a common subsistence strategy. They were hunter-gatherers who used burning, irrigation, and pruning to maximize food sources.[10] Women collected and processed the acorns, seeds, roots, and berries that constituted the mainstay of the diet; men fished and hunted game, birds, and sea mammals. Crafts were also divided by sex: women wove baskets, clothes, and household articles; men made tools and weapons.[11]

Social organization in precontact California is poorly understood, but recent studies suggest that villages—the principal unit of organization—were stratified into a ruling elite, commoners, and an underclass. The elite was treated with respect, awe, and caution by commoners, who had no rank, and the underclass, who had no formal ties to an intact lineage. Social status was ascribed and authority was distributed hierarchically: elite males inherited political, religious, and economic power through their fathers' lines. Access to power and control of ritual knowledge distinguished the elite, who also wore the finest clothes, inhabited the largest houses, and avoided manual labor. The community owned the village land, but the elite determined its use. At the top of the village hierarchy stood a chief, who oversaw the production, allocation, and trade of the community's food and material goods.[12] This was the complex and stratified Indian world Spain sought to control after 1769.

IN CALIFORNIA, SOLDIERS and friars drew on policies, developed during the Reconquest of the Iberian peninsula and refined through two and a half centuries of colonization in New Spain, that promoted the incorporation of frontier peoples and regions into the expanding Spanish realm. In the Reconquest, the *municipio* (township) emerged as the principal vehicle through which new territories were settled and secured, and in the New World it became the primary form of local political organization.[13] In areas settled by Spain, formal attachment to a municipality was not an option but a legal requirement and one of the preconditions for a productive and civilized life. As early as 1501, Ferdinand and Isabella instructed Nicolás de Ovando, the first royal governor of Hispaniola, to ensure that none of that island's Christian inhabitants "lives outside the communities that are to be made on the said island."[14] Within a few years, the monarchs extended a similar requirement to Indians: in 1503, they ordered Ovando to gather the Indians into towns in order to facilitate their economic integration and religious instruction.[15] This policy of *congregación* became a basic strategy for community organization and social control in virtually all of New Spain, especially after Old World diseases had decimated native populations.[16]

To eighteenth-century Spaniards, the California Indians' small huts and scattered villages were a sure indication of a savage and undisciplined existence. Like their predecessors elsewhere in New Spain, the Franciscans took as their first goal the resettlement of Indians into compact villages. In Alta California, as in Baja California and Sonora, where Indian settlements were dispersed, missionaries combined coercion and incentives to create new, large, Indian communities.[17] Furthermore, disease reduced the Indian population, undercut the native economy, and prompted Indians to relocate to the missions. As a result, Indians from different villages, who had had only occasional contact in trade or war, began to live, work, and pray together.

Officials in New Spain used the Castilian *cabildo* (town council) as a model for the political organization of these new Indian communities as well as of their own. In Spain, most towns were governed by a council composed of six to twelve *regidores* (councilmen). Regidores usually represented the economic interests of the most important families, and they served long tenures, sometimes for life. Two *alcaldes* (judges) served ex officio on the town council, but unlike regidores, who were their social superiors, they rotated off the cabildo after a single year in office.[18] A *corregidor*, a crown-appointed outsider who represented both the town and the central government, presided over the cabildo. True to this model, most Spanish towns in the Americas were administered by a cabildo composed of four to eight regidores, two elected alcaldes, and various minor officials, all governing in concert with an *adelantado* or a governor.[19] These New World cabildos, whose members were usually *encomenderos* or Spaniards with aristocratic pretensions, had authority over the basics of urban life: they drafted ordinances, punished wrongdoing, and regulated the local economy.[20]

As conquered peoples, Indians rarely served on Spanish cabildos, but they retained a measure of control over their communities through annually elected cabildos of their own.[21] Known collectively as the "Republic of Indians," these councils by the late seventeenth century were regulated by the *Recopilación de leyes de los reynos de las Indias*, which prescribed the frequency of elections and the number of officials. Most Indian cabildos in New Spain were composed of a governor, several regidores and alcaldes, and various lesser officials, in numbers proportional to the population of the settlement.[22]

In establishing Indian cabildos in New Spain, Spaniards accommodated and to a certain extent institutionalized Indian forms of social and political organization.[23] In central Mexico, newly appointed Indian governors continued the roles of preconquest dynastic rulers: they had judicial and financial responsibilities and oversaw the use of land.[24] These governors, who were assigned to assist in the collection of tribute, marshal military support for the Spaniards, and promote the spread of Catholicism, retained or increased their sizable landholdings and the economic advantages they derived from them.[25] Although their participation in the collection of taxes and in the exploitative *encomienda* (royal grant of Indian tribute and labor) and *repartimiento* (forced labor draft) led to frequent disputes between them and their communities, Indian governors could limit the Spaniards' demands through litigation.[26]

The responsibilities of Indian alcaldes and regidores in central Mexico also blended Indian leadership responsibilities with Castilian political forms. These officials collected tribute and organized labor, handled local land deals, oversaw the apprehension of criminals, supported the local church, and, through litigation, tried to protect the interests of the community.[27]

In addition to the governor, alcaldes, and regidores, most Indian cabildos had a religious official known as a *fiscal*. Because there were so few missionaries in New Spain, *fiscales* frequently held wide-ranging responsibilities. Elected or appointed annually, they managed local church finances, rang bells for mass, and gathered parishioners for religious celebrations. At a minimum, fiscales were "church constables" who punished villagers for violating Catholic teachings, but usually they were full members of the cabildo; most had previously served as regidores or alcaldes.[28] All together, the officials of the cabildo formed an elite that controlled many of the most important aspects of Indian community life in New Spain.[29]

As the seventeenth century drew to a close, Spanish settlement in northern New Spain took different forms than in central Mexico. *Presidios* (military garrisons) and missions became the primary means for extending Spanish control into the region and for protecting the silver mines and the roads linking them to central Mexico.[30] In Nueva Galicia, Nueva Vizcaya, Baja California, and Sonora, many factors limited the full elaboration of Indian cabildos: the loose organization of Indian settlements, the resistance of many Indians to Spanish intrusion, the waning of the encomienda and repartimiento, and the priorities of the Jesuit and Franciscan missionaries who oversaw the appointment and election of Indian officials.[31] In these northern areas, although Indian officials rarely sat on full-blown cabildos, they nevertheless held a wide range of offices. Most of the Indian communities in these regions were based on a mission, and many of these offices were tied to the mission church. Thus, as Spaniards advanced into the far reaches of northern New Spain during the eighteenth century, they adapted the cabildo as a model for the political organization of new communities.[32]

In December 1778, after a decade of Franciscan activity in Alta California and the founding of eight missions, Felipe de Neve, military and civil governor of California, ordered the Franciscans to allow the Indians in the oldest missions to elect their own alcaldes and regidores. Neve based his order on historical precedent and his interpretation of the *Recopilación*. Missions San Diego (1769) and San Carlos Borromeo (1770) were to proceed with the election of two alcaldes and two regidores; smaller, more recently founded missions, such as San Antonio (1771), San Gabriel (1771), and San Luis Obispo (1772), were to elect one alcalde and one regidor.[33] On election, each official was to report to the nearest military garrison, where the commander would install him in office in the name of the king. The presidial commander would then give the official the certificate he needed to exercise his powers; alcaldes also received a large wooden staff of leadership that symbolized their authority.[34]

Despite the acceptance of Indian officials in missions elsewhere in New Spain, the Franciscans in Alta California bitterly opposed the elections. The ensuing conflict between Neve and the friars emerged not from Franciscan objections to indirect rule

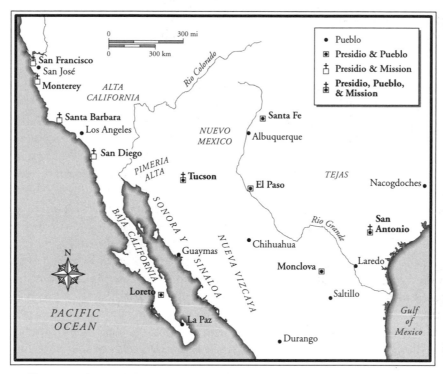

Figure I: Selected Spanish Settlements in Northern New Spain, ca. 1785.

but from suspicions between secular and religious officials in New Spain that deepened during the late eighteenth century. Although Roman Catholicism was the official religion of Spain, church and state officials held opposing views about the origin of civil authority, and each claimed ultimate jurisdiction over Indians. Royal jurists increasingly insisted that the king was the vicar of Christ and that the power to oversee the church and instruct Indians therefore resided, first and foremost, with the king and his representatives. Clerics and canon lawyers maintained that the king was a vicar of the pope and that the church was therefore the principal protector and instructor of Indians.[35] These disputes intensified under the Bourbon ascendancy. They became urgent after Spain's defeat in the Seven Years' War, when Charles III (1759–1788) and his ministers set out to bolster royal authority by curtailing the powers of the Catholic church and strengthening the economy of New Spain.[36]

True to the spirit of the Bourbon reforms, the first military and civil administrators of Alta California brought to their posts an official hostility to religious orders in general and missions in particular, which they saw as impediments to the transformation of Indians into useful subjects of the king. In 1767, just two years before the Franciscans founded the first mission in Alta California, Charles III expelled the Jesuits from New Spain because he feared they would use their wealth and independence to obstruct his secular reforms. Gaspar de Portolá, who commanded the first overland expedition to Alta California, oversaw the Jesuits' removal from Baja California, and Neve himself directed their expulsion from the mining center of Zacatecas.[37] At the same time, it was the crown's need to conserve troops and limit expenditures, not an enthusiasm for missionary orders, that led royal emissary José de Galvez to enlist the mendicant Franciscan order to pacify the Indians of Alta California.[38]

As governor of Alta California, Neve implemented the national policy of assimilating Indians into the conquerors' political system. In Neve's words: "With the elections and the appointment of a new Republic, the will of His Majesty will be fulfilled in this region, and under our direction, in the course of time, He will obtain in these Indians useful vassals for our religion and state."[39] Neve and his successors believed that extending to Indians the rudiments of Spanish municipal government would teach them a civics lesson that was at least equal in importance to the Franciscans' catechism.

The governor's inclusive political vision was challenged by the Franciscans' restrictive religious agenda. The friars wanted absolute control over the missions and the Indians who lived in them, and they believed that Indians so recently subjugated to the church and the crown could not possibly be ready for a measure of self-government, no matter how elementary its form. Moreover, they did not want the Indians to understand that the Spanish governor had civil and judicial authority over Indians, and the Franciscans feared that Indian officials would use their status to pursue their own goals. The Franciscans formally based their opposition to Indian elections on a legal technicality. The *Recopilación* specified that in each Indian town and *reducción* Indians were to elect officials and that *curas* (local priests) should supervise these elections.[40] The Franciscans argued that they themselves were apostolic missionaries, not parish priests; therefore, the *Recopilación* did not apply, and the governor's order had no foundation in law.[41]

At San Diego, where in 1775 the Tipai and Ipai had signaled their rejection of Spanish authority by destroying the mission and killing one Franciscan and two Spaniards, the governor's insistence in 1779 on elections in the rebuilt mission prompted the Franciscans to threaten resignation. Fray Junípero Serra called on the governor to suspend the elections in all the designated missions.[42] The conflict came to a climax just before mass on Palm Sunday in 1779 when Governor Neve and Father Serra exchanged bitter words. Later that evening, overcome with agitation and unable to rest, Serra cried out: "¿Qué es esto Señor?" (What is the meaning of it, Lord?) Serra was calmed by a voice from within that repeated one of Christ's admonitions to the apostles: "Be prudent as serpents and simple as doves."[43] Reassured, Serra decided to go along with the governor's orders but only in ways that would not "cause the least change among the Indians or in the mode of governing" that the Franciscans had established.[44] Serra believed that, with God's help, he could join the simplicity of the dove with the cunning of the serpent and thus outmaneuver the governor and prevent the elections from decreasing Franciscan authority.[45] After the early 1780s, elections of Indian officials usually occurred annually in the largest and oldest missions.[46]

As Serra intended, the Franciscans quickly gained a large degree of control over the elections. Even though Neve sought to extend the crown's power into the missions, the Franciscans convinced him that only with their guidance would Indians and Spaniards profit from the elections. At several of the missions, according to Serra, Indian officials had committed crimes or behaved arrogantly, as if they were "gentlemen."[47] By January 1780, when the second annual elections were to take place, several of the officials had abandoned their missions, while others were too ill to vote. Consistent with Spanish law, Neve specified that only former Indian officials could vote, but he increased the missionaries' role in the elections telling them to supply "direction" when necessary.[48] The Franciscans usually supplied direction by controlling the nomination of candidates, as Pedro Fages, Neve's successor as governor, described:

> It has been established that each mission at the completion of [its first] five years must elect one or two alcaldes and the same number of regidores according to the number of individuals in the mission who have been reduced. They are to make these appointments successively, at the beginning of the year, with the assistance and intervention

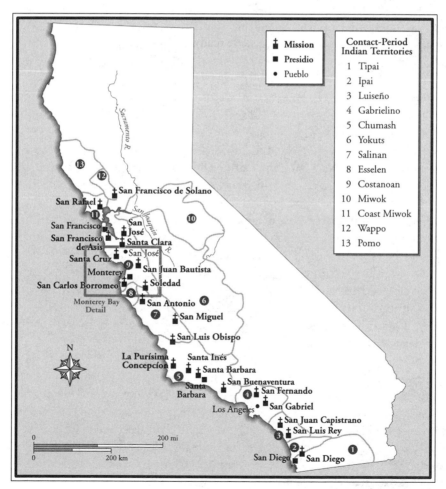

Figure II: Contact-Period Indian Territories with Spanish Settlements in Alta California.

of the respective missionaries, who propose three of the least unqualified. A plurality of votes decides the elected, [whose names] are submitted to the governor, who approves or disapproves them according to his criteria, in the name of His Majesty.[49]

By narrowing the field of candidates, the Franciscans guaranteed the election of men whom they expected to facilitate their control of the mission.[50]

In addition to securing for the missionaries a large measure of control over the elections, Serra tried to prevent Indian officials from learning that the military constituted a powerful secular counterpart to Franciscan authority. Serra instructed his trusted subordinate at San Diego, Fray Fermín Francisco de Lasuén, to speak to the presidio officer whose responsibility it was to confirm the Indians in office: "Ask him to carry out this function so that, without failing in the slightest degree in his duty toward his superior officer, the Indians may not be given a less exalted opinion of the fathers than they have had until now." Furthermore, Serra preferred that the Indian officials remain ignorant of the responsibilities with which the military charged them. "The document that is used in conferring these offices on them," Serra advised Lasuén, "may be as powerful as they wish, provided Your Reverences are the only ones to receive it and read it."[51] Even after these precautions, the Franciscans resisted sending newly elected Indians to the presidios for installation. An inquiry in the mid-1700s by Governor Diego de Borica revealed that none of the current presidio commanders had ever been called on to give Indians their oaths of office.[52]

The Indian cabildos elected in the California missions—like those in the missions of Sonora, Texas, and New Mexico—had fewer officials, smaller responsibilities, and less autonomy than those in the Indian *pueblos* and parishes of central Mexico at the same time. Rarely did a California mission have more than two alcaldes and two regidores.[53] Nor was an Indian governor appointed. Throughout the missions of northern New Spain, the duties of ecclesiastical and civil Indian officials overlapped, but in Alta California, perhaps to a greater extent than elsewhere in the Spanish borderlands, Indian alcaldes and regidores served as assistants to the missionaries, much like the fiscales of central Mexico.[54]

The subordination of Indian officials to the Franciscans was noted in 1787 by Governor Fages: "Although these authorities are granted some powers, they are necessarily dependent on the missionaries, without whose direction they would not be able to exercise them."[55] Franciscans treated Indian officials with the same heavy-handed paternalism that characterized all their interactions with Indians. Officials were subject to corporal punishment at Franciscan hands,[56] and they were not permitted to bring charges against the missionaries.[57] This disability set them apart from their counterparts in central Mexico, who frequently used legal channels to claim that their curates manipulated elections, misappropriated communal funds, and imposed excessive labor demands. In New Spain, to be left without the right to seek protection or redress through the law rendered one virtually defenseless.[58]

Under Franciscan supervision, Indian officials in California nevertheless had wide-ranging authority over other mission Indians. According to the *Recopilación,* they were charged with ensuring that Indians attended mass and remained sober.[59] They were to "keep guard" around the mission village at night and to "lead the people to prayer and to work."[60] Pablo Tac, a Luiseño who in 1832 at age ten was taken from California to Europe by a Franciscan, was one of a handful of California Indians who provided a description of the responsibilities of the Indian officials. According to the narrative Tac wrote while studying Latin in Rome, one of the alcaldes' main functions was to speak for the Franciscans: "In the afternoon, the alcaldes gather at the house of the missionary. They bring the news of that day, and if the missionary tells them something that all the people of the country ought to know, they return to the villages . . . [and] each one of the alcaldes wherever he goes cries out what the missionary has told them, in his language, and all the country hears it." Given the alcaldes' roles in conveying Franciscan directives to the missions' Indians, Tac's statement that Indian officials "knew how to speak Spanish more than the others" comes as no surprise.[61]

The Franciscans, emphasizing religious indoctrination, used catechisms to ready Indians for baptism and confessional manuals to prepare them for penance and communion.[62] Whether Indian officials helped translate these handbooks into local languages is not clear, but the records show that they were among the few Indians who participated in the sacraments of baptism and marriage as godparents and witnesses. On these occasions, the Franciscans relied on Indian officials to translate Catholic rites into terms that were comprehensible to their people. We do not know the content of these unrecorded translations, but in trying to explain Catholic rituals, officials may well have invoked concepts that gave the rituals an Indian meaning.

Never content simply to instruct Indians, the Franciscans tried to control their lives, especially their sexual behavior. To that end, most missions had single-sex dormitories for the unmarried, and Indian officials were charged with keeping unmarried men and women from having illicit contact. In 1797, Mission Santa Cruz even had one alcalde for men and another for women.[63] In this area of responsibility, many alcaldes showed more regard for the desires of other Indians than for the demands of the Franciscans. In 1821, Modesto, an alcalde at Mission San Juan Bautista, took advantage of the illness of one of the friars and "delivered" the single women to the men. He was quickly suspended from office and replaced by Francisco Sevilla, a former alcalde who had "taken good care of the single women."[64]

Franciscans also attempted to remake the Indians' daily routines, primarily through a rigid labor regime; here, too, Indian officials often played a crucial role. Tac recounted how alcaldes circulated through the villages telling people when and where to report for work: "Tomorrow the sowing begins and so the laborers go to the chicken yard and assemble there."[65] When their calls went unheeded, officials punished those who they or the Franciscans believed were shirking. In 1797, Claudio, an Indian baptized at Mission San Francisco who later absconded, declared that one of the reasons he had run away was that the alcalde Valeriano "made him go to work" when he was sick.[66] Homobono, who also fled, declared that Valeriano "hit him with a heavy cane for having gone to look for mussels at the beach," an outing that most likely took him away from his work at the mission.[67] Not all Indian officials could be counted on to enforce the Franciscans' labor regime. In 1814, the *padres* at Mission San Francisco lamented that, when they asked the alcaldes to supervise work in and around the mission, "not infrequently the alcaldes and the men spend their time in play and remain away [from the mission] for another day despite the fact that their task is an urgent one."[68]

Franciscans also looked to Indian officials to administer a share of the corporal punishment they considered necessary for the Indians' souls. Foreign visitors and Anglo-American immigrants emphasized that Indians "did a great deal of chastisement, both by and without [Franciscan] orders."[69] Frederick Beechey, an English sea captain who visited Mission San Francisco in 1826, claimed that officials used goads to keep fellow Indians kneeling during mass, for "goads were better adapted to this purpose than the whips, as they would reach a long way, and inflict a sharp puncture without making a noise."[70] Hugo Reid, a Scot who married an Indian from Mission San Gabriel, later wrote that alcaldes carried "a wand to denote their authority, and what was more terrible, an immense scourge of raw hide, about ten feet in length, plaited to the thickness of an ordinary man's wrist!"[71] Although these may well be exaggerations motivated by religious and national differences, Indian complaints substantiate the basic claim of alcalde violence in the mission. However severe, corporal punishments by Indian officials did not take the place of beatings dealt directly by the Franciscans.[72] Viewing themselves as the spiritual fathers of the Indians, Franciscans maintained that it was their responsibility to chastise them; they flogged Indians for repeatedly running away, for practicing native religious beliefs, and for performing a host of other acts considered disrespectful or sinful.[73] When Indians remained incorrigible after several floggings, the friars sent them to the presidio for more beatings and hard labor.

In addition to being the intelligible voice and strong arm of the Franciscans, Indian officials were meant to be the military's eyes and ears at the missions.[74] Military officials expected Indian alcaldes to investigate and report crimes that occurred at the missions. When a man at Mission San Juan Capistrano killed his wife, it was Bruno, the mission alcalde, who heard the murderer's first admission of guilt and carried the news to Spanish officials.[75] Indian officials, however, rarely cooperated as readily as Bruno; in fact, alcaldes exposed very few of the crimes committed at the missions. In 1808, after several Indians at Mission San José brawled and fled the mission, an alcalde failed to notify the Spanish authorities, a dereliction of duty that led the governor to brand him a criminal accomplice.[76] More often than not, when Indian officials were called on to explain murders or robberies at their missions, their testimony proved unremarkable, merely echoing accounts offered by others.

Some actions of Indian officials, such as administering punishment, may have had no precedent in pre-mission village leadership, but many of their duties and responsibilities resembled those of earlier native leaders. Village leaders oversaw the production of the community's food while remaining exempt from basic manual labor; similarly, alcaldes participated in the productive life of the mission as coordinators, not laborers. Village captains made crucial decisions concerning the distribution of food[77]; alcaldes, too, decided how to allocate the mission's food resources. In

1786, for example, Franciscans at Mission Santa Clara discussed the distribution of the mission's harvest with the Indian leaders:

> We called together the principal [Indian] leaders at the mission and we said to them: . . . The soldiers are suffering much from hunger. They have no corn, no wheat, no beans. They are asking us to sell them some of these things. . . . If we do sell, there will not be enough on hand to support you until the time of the wheat harvest. If you wish to go away for some weeks to gather nuts, it will be possible to sell them some corn, and there will be that much extra to spend on clothes. You may consult with your own people if you wish.
>
> In less than an hour they returned to say that they would choose life in the open, for the pinole was already getting ripe.[78]

Indian village captains reportedly led their people in battle, a responsibility subsequently held by alcaldes when the Franciscans and presidio commanders experimented with using armed parties of Indian auxiliaries to defend the missions from foreign attack.[79]

The alcaldes' perquisites of office resembled the advantages that had distinguished village captains from the rest of the Indian community. The elite had constituted a self-perpetuating oligarchy; similarly, in the early years of the elections, only Indian officials cast votes for their successors. Village captains, like Indian officials, were supported by the labor of the community.[80] Both sets of leaders wore distinctive clothing and lived in special houses.[81] And according to Julio César, an Indian baptized at Mission San Luis Rey, alcaldes were among the few Indians allowed to ride horseback, a privileged act in Spanish California.[82] Despite these advantages, Indian officials—like village captains—enjoyed only a slight material advantage over their people, and that advantage was never secure, dependent as all Indians were on a fragile mission economy.[83]

As intermediaries between cultures, Indian officials were often caught between the conflicting demands of the Indian community and the Franciscans. Indians such as Homobono and Claudio at San Francisco—and surely others who do not appear in the historical record—resisted the labor regime the alcaldes reinforced and so resented the alcaldes' use of their authority that they left the missions. Conversely, officials' conformity to Indian expectations often invited Franciscan condemnation. Baltazar, one of the first alcaldes at San Carlos Borromeo, ran afoul of Serra when he fathered a child by his wife's sister. Serra's god demanded that his people be monogamous, whereas Indians expected their leaders to be polygamous.[84] The Indian community probably saw Baltazar's moral polygyny as an emblem of his status, the Franciscans considered it proof of his depravity. They hounded him out of the mission, branded him a deserter, and tried to sever his connection to his people. Serra then accused Baltazar of "sending messages to the people here, meeting personally with those who leave here with permission, and thereby trying to swell the numbers of his band from the mountains by new desertions of the natives of this mission."[85]

Resistance by some alcaldes, such as Modesto and Baltazar, to Franciscan notions of marriage and sexuality and acquiescence by others, such as Francisco Sevilla and Valeriano, to their directives suggest the ambiguities of the alcalde's role and rule.

Even though their behavior at times appeared unpredictable—even unacceptable—to Indians or Spaniards, Indian officials occupied a privileged space in the Spanish system as interpreters, mediators, and enforcers of the new colonial order. The influence of Indian officials within the Indian community, however, depended not only on the authority Spaniards invested in them but also on the legitimacy these men brought to their leadership positions. Based on kinship and lineage networks, this legitimacy, in turn, helps explain the ability of Spanish officials to orchestrate social, religious, economic, and political change within native communities and the ability of native officials on occasion to keep such initiatives at bay.

THE HISTORICAL RECORD speaks far more directly about what Indian officials did than about who they were—an imbalance that is mirrored in the scholarship.[86] Fortunately, records created by colonial administrators allow investigation of the place of Indian leaders in the complex web of kinship and lineage that defined the Indian community. Franciscans notified presidio commanders of election results and occasionally mentioned Indian officials in baptismal, marriage, and burial records. By combining these reports—fragmentary as they are—with information on family relations, village affiliations, and vital statistics contained in sacramental registers, we can sketch a composite portrait of the mission staff of leadership.[87]

Mission San Carlos Borromeo presents the most complete materials for a case study. Its sacramental registers are intact and thorough, and more reports of its annual elections have survived than for any other California mission.[88] Established in June 1770 as the second mission in Alta California and the first on the central coast, San Carlos Borromeo served as the early residence of the father president, who set policy for the region. Located about three miles from the Monterey presidio, the headquarters of the region's governor, Mission San Carlos was overseen by Franciscans until its secularization by the Mexican government in 1834. The record keeping of the Franciscans and the efficiency of the microcomputer enable one to identify and suitable within the native community forty-six alcaldes and regidores who served ar San Carlos Borromeo from 1779 to 1831, probably about half the officials during those five decades.[89] References by Franciscans at San Carlos Borromeo to fiscales cease at roughly the same time that elections for alcaldes and regidores begin. The Franciscans may have continued to appoint fiscales, but in all likelihood they relied on alcaldes and regidores instead.

Typically diverse, the Indian community at the mission comprised Indians from the Costanoan and Esselen linguistic families who came from at least ten different villages.[90] At the time the mission was founded, the population of the Monterey region seems to have numbered around 2,800.[91] In almost every year, because disease was endemic, the Franciscans recorded more burials than births; only the baptisms of Indians from the surrounding area allowed the mission's population to reach a peak of around 875 in the mid-1700s. The mission population subsequently declined, and after 1808, when the friars recorded the baptisms of the last Indians they recruited from the surrounding area, went into free fall. Disease continued to take a heavy toll, and by 1825, the mission had only about 300 Indians.[92]

At San Carlos Borromeo, Indian officials were always baptized men who were married or widowed.[93] They were usually older and had been baptized earlier than other men from their villages. Thirteen out of fourteen, for example, who served during the period 1779–98 fit this pattern. Of those who served in 1792, Hilario José was one of the first adult Esselen men baptized, Atanasio José was older and had been in the mission longer than most Cosranoan men, and Sancio Francisco and Nicomedes were older than most of the men from their communities.

During the mission's early recruiting years, Indian officials were likely to have been village captains or their close associates. For example, the sacramental registers identify Sancio Francisco and Abrahan—officials in the 1790s—as former village leaders. The baptismal record of Nicomedes, also an official in the 1790s, describes him as the "principal confidant" of the village captain Aristeo José.[94] Later, the mission community tended to produce its own leadership. After the early 1790s, fewer captains came to the mission; those who did were not elected to leadership positions.[95] As the mission population matured, it developed a cadre of men who spoke Spanish and were familiar with the Franciscan regime—qualifications that supplanted previous experience as village captains.

In native California, political leadership customarily descended from father to son.[96] This practice carried over to San Carlos Borromeo, although it was disrupted by persistently high mortality.[97] Of the thirty-seven baptized sons of village captains identified in the mission's records, only eight lived to their mid-thirties. Four of these gained positions of responsibility, three as officials, one as an interpreter.[98] The high death rate among the young made it very hard for elite families to maintain a direct line of influence. Yet the son of a village leader who lived to adulthood had a far better chance of becoming a mission official than others his age.[99] Officials who did not have blood ties to former village captains were frequently related to other leading Indians: two were the sons of officials, three pairs were brothers, ten pairs were brothers-in-law, and eleven officials had close ties to mission interpreters. In addition, many alcaldes were related by marriage to soldiers. For example, Atanasio José, an alcalde for many years, had a daughter whose first and second husbands were soldiers at the Monterey presidio. Other officials were related to privileged Indians from Baja California who worked closely with the Franciscans during the first years of the mission. Extended leadership families such as these suggest that in the face of high death rates, marriage provided a means for surviving members of powerful Indian families to maintain leadership status in the mission.

Spanish laws regulating cabildos promoted turnover in office-holding, but at San Carlos Borromeo, as elsewhere in New Spain, these laws proved ineffective, because they conflicted with the native practice of long-term rule and the Spanish desire to support cooperative local leaders. A common strategy to assure continuity of leadership was to rotate alcaldes and regidores in office each year. At Mission San Carlos, Oresio Antonio was regidor in 1810, 1812, and 1814 and alcalde in 1811, 1813, and 1815. Other officials sat out a year or two and then returned to office. As the rotational system suggests, differences between the responsibilities of alcaldes and of regidores faded over

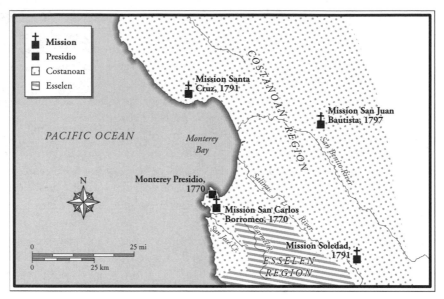

Figure III: Monterey Bay Area. Contact-Period Indian Territories with Spanish Settlements.

time. Important and cooperative Indians, provided they could stay alive, were thus never far from office; some served continuously for up to six years, and others rotated in and out over more than fifteen years.

Indian officials reflected the ethnic and linguistic diversity of the mission community, as the mission's two language families and four largest village groups could each frequently claim one of the officials.[100] After 1776, when Esselen villagers first came to the mission, San Carlos was composed of both Costanoan- and Esselen-speakers, the former enjoying numerical superiority over the latter throughout the mission's life. The Franciscans carefully noted the village affiliation of all Indians at baptism and monitored the changing composition of the population.[101] If late-eighteenth-century guidelines for the Franciscan missionaries at Mission Nuestra Señora de la Purísima Concepción in San Antonio, Texas, are typical of Franciscan electoral management in northern New Spain—and there is no reason to suppose otherwise—the Franciscans at San Carlos Borromeo worked hard to ensure that officials were drawn from the mission's largest groups. The San Antonio instructions, probably written in 1787 or 1788 by Fray José Garcia, urged the missionaries to "remind" voters that the positions of governor and alcalde alternated annually between the most populous groups at the mission, the Pajalache and the Tacame.[102] This correlation between the ethnic and linguistic composition of officials and that of the mission population reflected the needs of Spaniards and Indians alike. Franciscans and governors would have found it difficult to incorporate and control the Indians without assistance from native leaders who could effectively communicate with the mission's most populous groups, and powerful Indian groups might have rebelled had they been excluded from positions of authority.

Not until 1810, when twenty-six-year-old Teopisto José became regidor did a mission-born Indian serve as an official at San Carlos Borromeo. The policy of drawing the officials from the mission's different village and linguistic groups helps to explain why so few—only seven—were born in the mission. Indian officials were usually in their late twenties or early thirties when first elected. Thus Indians born in the 1770s at the mission could not have served until the mid-1790s, and yet they did not dominate the leadership positions when they reached maturity. Rather, the representation of different village groups, some of which did not come to the mission until the mid-1780s, took precedence over the selection of the individuals who, having spent their entire lives in the mission, might have been the most acculturated to Spanish ways and loyal to Franciscan wishes.[103] Even after 1810, Indians born at the mission filled only one quarter of the leadership positions; those baptized before age ten took only slightly more than half.

BEGINNING IN 1810, repercussions from the Mexican independence movement shook the hybrid system of indirect and representative rule in the missions of Alta California. Economic and political support for frontier missions evaporated during the Mexican struggle, and, after Mexico won independence in 1821, the new federal government attempted to expel Spanish missionaries, whose loyalty it doubted, and challenged the missions as anachronistic relics of Spanish rule and impediments to economic growth.[104] Municipal electoral reforms that were instituted elsewhere in Mexico after 1810 did not directly affect the missions.[105] While politicians at the national level debated the form that the new government would take, Indians contested political authority in the missions, as they, too, tried to clarify who had the right to rule.

During the 1820s, soldiers and settlers increasingly relied on the missions for food and Indian laborers. The missions themselves continued to be unhealthy, and labor demands on Indians increased, just as Franciscan authority was weakening. At several missions, these circumstances prompted Indian officials to reject the colonial order altogether and lead their people out of the missions. Had the officials been given the right to bring charges against the missionaries, they might have used that legal leverage to improve conditions in the disintegrating missions. Had they been in a better position to profit personally from the missions' economic system, they might have been more loyal. But in Alta California at this time, many Indian officials found little to gain by preserving the Franciscans' collapsing regime.

Lacking both an institutional means to reform the system from within and a significant personal stake in its survival, Indian officials at several missions turned their authority against the Spanish system. In 1824, Andrés, an alcalde at Mission Santa Barbara, joined forces with Indians at Missions Santa Inés and La Purísima to lead the largest of the Indian uprisings in Mexican California.[106] In 1827, Narciso and two other officials persuaded 400 Indians to flee San José[107]; another alcalde, Estanislao, joined the resistance the following year[108]; and a fifth San José official, Victor, was later implicated and punished.[109] These insurgencies dealt hard blows to the missions even though soldiers eventually put them down. Such rebellions did not merely demonstrate the dissatisfaction of Indians with the Franciscan regime. Taken collectively, they laid bare the dependence of the Spanish colonial system on Indian authority, for they showed how Indian officials frequently held the fate of the missions in their hands.

At San Carlos Borromeo during the 1820s, worsening economic conditions and declining Franciscan control did not lead to overt rebellion; instead, they prompted a scramble among Indians for authority in the crumbling mission. No longer a source of conflict solely between Franciscans and soldiers, political control of the mission was openly negotiated and disputed among the Indians, some of whom held power while others wanted it. As disease, disaffection, and flight greatly reduced the pool of Indians most likely by lineage to assume the staff of leadership, Indian elections began to create rather than merely reinforce Indian political authority, and the elections themselves became vulnerable to contestation. When the Franciscan-brokered electoral system failed, one group of Costanoan Indians came to control the vast majority of leadership positions.[110] Their political dominance in the decade 1822–31 finally provoked open dispute and formal appeals for the intervention of Mexican secular authorities.

The time, day, and place of the contested election of 1831 show how far Indians at San Carlos Borromeo had transformed and made their own a practice that Spaniards had originally considered an emblem of Spanish civility. Held on Sunday after mass under the watchful eyes of the Franciscans, Indian elections in the 1780s and 1790s had been thoroughly infused with Catholic meaning and Franciscan authority.[111] As time passed, however, elections combined Indian culture and Spanish procedures. By 1831, the annual election was no longer fixed to the Catholic schedule of worship; rather, it occurred on Saturday evening, a time when Indians gathered for their own diversions and discussions. Furthermore, elections did not take place in or near the church but in the ritual space of an Indian *temescal,* or sweatbath, a place sheltered from Franciscan oversight.[112] In addition to the return to an Indian ceremonial site, this election also reveals continuities in the way mission Indians recognized and achieved leadership early and late in the mission period, for, in conformity with an earlier pattern, two of the Indians elected, Domicio and Romano, were sons of a village captain.

Although this election of Indian officials linked to earlier authority systems demonstrates a continuity with pre-mission times, the dispute afterward signals that some Indians at the mission had grown accustomed to the representative system that the Franciscans had overseen. In January 1831, four Indians asked that the recent election be invalidated because it had not occurred at the proper time and place and because the winners did not represent the different village groups in the mission. The Indians' letter to Antonio Buelna, magistrate at the Monterey presidio, stated their principal objections to the recently elected officials: "Domicio is the half-brother of Romano, and the first cousin of Francisco. Francisco is the brother-in-law of Agricio, and furthermore, Agricio is a distant relative of Domicio; they are one people." The protesters proposed a return to the system of drawing officials from the mission's different groups, arguing that "it be made a condition that each direction or tribe will elect only one [official]."[113] Their awareness of the winners' shared family ties and their assertion of diversity in the mission underscore the extent to which mission Indians continued to derive their identities from their places of origin decades after their ancestral villages were incorporated into the mission. Furthermore, the protectors implicitly accepted the annual elections as a means of generating and legitimating Indian authority: their letter denounced the procedures of one election, not the practice of electing officials annually.

DURING THE 1830S, national and provincial political leaders transferred control of the missions to secular administrators and parceled out the bulk of mission lands and resources to local soldiers and settlers.[114] Some former missions continued as secular communities; most fell in ruins after the exodus of Indians to their ancestral homelands or the emerging pueblos. In all of these places—former missions, Mexican towns, and regions beyond state control—vestiges of the Indian-Spanish political system survived: Indian officials continued to lead their communities in the face of growing economic, political, and demographic challenges.[115]

Two Indian officials, José Jesús of Mission San José, a recently baptized Miwok, and Romano of San Carlos Borromeo, baptized three decades earlier, took divergent paths after the missions were secularized; José Jesús cut his ties to Mexican California while Romano became more entrenched in its political system. Their experiences suggest that former mission officials were among the few Indians who had the skills to negotiate two cultures during this period of accelerating change. José Jesús returned to the Central Valley, where he led a group of Indians who stole livestock from Mexican ranchers. In 1845, he was briefly engaged by John Sutter—whose fame in the Gold Rush still awaited him—to catch horse thieves. Two years later, Sutter enlisted him again to form an Indian brigade for the California Battalion in action against Mexican resistance to the United States regime. In 1848, to prove his friendship to the new government, José Jesús offered the San José magistrate Indian laborers whom he and his men had captured in the surrounding hills. Never far removed from important events, during the Gold Rush José Jesús also supplied Indian laborers to Charles Weber, the founder of Stockton.[116]

Like José Jesús, Romano participated in many of the central transformations of California. Born the son of a village captain and baptized as an infant in 1799, he served as an official at San Carlos Borromeo in 1830 and 1831, the year of the disputed election. Romano lived through epidemics at the mission and made an effective adjustment to life in Mexican California. In 1835, a year after the secularization of Mission San Carlos, he served as alcalde for the Indian community living at the site of the former mission. And in 1844, the Monterey municipal government appointed him *Juez de Campo* for this community, called San Carlos by the 1840s.[117] Romano's duties as *juez* (judge) are unknown, but his appointment demonstrates a continuity of leadership from pre-mission times. Few Indians in Alta California had the linguistic and cultural skills, much less the good fortune, to survive such remarkable changes. Fewer still have had their stories told. But the experiences of Indians like José Jesús and Romano testify to the ability and creativity of California Indians who did adjust to life in a rapidly changing world.

TO MOST INDIANS in Alta California, Spaniards brought disease, cultural dislocation, and an early grave; to some, they also provided political opportunity. The prominence of individuals like Baltazar, Andrés, José Jesús, and Romano and the coherence of the groups they led suggest that the political system the Spaniards relied on to control the missions—and the Indians' ability to shape that system to their needs—fostered the preservation and creation of Indian authority. Indians who held legitimate authority among their people frequently served as officials, and the composition of the Indian cabildos reflected the divisions of village groups in the missions. When officials did not reflect the community, disgruntled or excluded Indians sought redress from Spanish authorities. For the most part, Indian officials cooperated with the Spanish, but a personal crisis or the declining welfare of their communities could incite them to reject the colonial system and replace Spanish authority with their own. When Indian officials contradicted or challenged Spanish authorities, they courted dismissal. Still, it was never in the interest of Spaniards to replace uncooperative officials with Indians whose legitimacy was not recognized by their own people. Nor was it in their interest to level the distinctions of rank among Indians. To have done so would have provoked opposition from the Indians who could most effectively assist in controlling the missions.[118]

Doubtless, there were Indian officials in the missions of Alta California whose malleability rather than their kinship or lineage recommended them to the Franciscans. But for the most part the alcalde system depended on the extent to which native villages, leadership, and traditions were incorporated into the missions. The authority of Indian officials in colonial California originated from more than brute force, Franciscan missionaries, or the Spanish state. It was carried over from native villages, legitimated and re-created in annual mission elections, and ultimately strengthened by the extent to which the staff of Indian leadership remained embedded in a network of shifting family relations that defined Indian communities throughout the colonial period.

NOTES

1. David J. Weber, "The Spanish-Mexican Rim," in *The Oxford History of the American West,* ed. Clyde A. Milner II, Carol A. O'Connor, and Martha A. Sandweiss (New York, 1994), 65; Weber, *The Mexican Frontier, 1821–1846: The American Southwest under Mexico* (Albuquerque, 1982), 43–60.

2. Population estimates are for 1820. Peter Gerhard, *The North Frontier of New Spain* (Princeton, 1993; orig. pub. 1982), 309.

3. The debate over the canonization of Father Serra has been summarized cogently by James A. Sandos, "Junípero Serra's Canonization and the Historical Record," *American Historical Review,* 93 (1988), 1253–69.

4. Notable examples of the pro-Franciscan interpretation are Zephyrin Engelhardt, *The Missions and Missionaries of California.* 4 vols. (San Francisco, 1908–16); Maynard J. Geiger, *The Life and Times of Fray Junipero Serra, O.F.M.,* 2 vols. (Washington, D.C., 1959); Francis F. Guest, "An Inquiry into the Role of the Discipline in California Mission Life," *Southern California Quarterly,* 71 (1989), 1–68; and Guest, "Cultural Perspectives on California Mission Life," ibid., 65 (1983), 1–65. Critics include Rupert Costo and Jeannette Henry Costo, eds. *The Missions of California: A Legacy of Genocide* ([San Francisco], 1987); Sherburne F. Cook, *The Conflict between the California Indian and White Civilization* (Berkeley, 1976), Robert F. Heizer, "Impact of Colonization on the Native California Societies," *Journal of San Diego History,* 24 (Winter 1978), 121–39; Edward D. Castillo, "The Impact of Euro-American Exploration and Settlement," in Heizer, ed., *California,* vol. 8 of William C. Sturtevant, gen. ed., *Handbook of North American Indians* (Washington, D.C., 1978), 99–127; Robert H. Jackson, *Indian Population Decline: The Missions of Northwestern New Spain, 1687–1840* (Albuquerque, 1994); and Jackson and Castillo, *Indians, Franciscans, and Spanish Colonization: The Impact of the Mission System on California Indians* (Albuquerque, 1995).

5. Scholars have maintained that the Indians who served as officials derived their authority solely from the Spaniards, not from their own people, and acted as overseers, not community representatives. George Harwood Phillips, "The Alcaldes: Indian Leadership in the Spanish Missions of California," in *The Struggle for Political Autonomy: Papers and Comments from the Second Newberry Library Conference on Themes in American History,* Occasional Papers in Curriculum Series, no. 11 (Chicago, 1989), 83–89; Castillo, "The Other Side of the 'Christian Curtain': California Indians and the Missionaries," *The Californian. The Magazine of California History,* 10 (Sept.–Oct. 1992), 8–17; Robert L. Hoover, "Spanish-Native Interaction and Acculturation in the Alta California Missions," in David Hurst Thomas, ed., *Columbian Consequences,* vol. I: *Archaeological and Historical Perspectives on the Spanish Borderlands West,* (Washington, D.C., 1989), 397.

6. An extensive literature discusses the intersection of Indian and Spanish structures of authority in Mesoamerican communities. An important early work is Pedro Carrasco, "The Civil-Religious Hierarchy in Mesoamerican Communities: Pre-Spanish Background and Colonial Development," *American Anthropologist,* 63 (1961), 483–97. Charles Gibson argued that the institutionalization of the Spanish municipal system in Indian towns led to a displacement of Indian leadership lineages, and by the late colonial period Indian town councils "functioned principally to collect tribute and to dispense minor punishments," in *The Aztecs under Spanish Rule: A History of the Indians of the Valley of Mexico, 1519–1810* (Stanford, 1964), quotation on 191, and see esp. 166–93; Gibson, "Rotation of Alcaldes in the Indian Cabildo of Mexico City," *Hispanic American Historical Review,* 33 (1953), 212–23.

Recent literature emphasizes the persistence of Indian sociopolitical structures in Indian towns throughout the colonial period; Robert Haskett, *Indigenous Rulers: An Ethnohistory of Town Government in Colonial Cuernavaca* (Albuquerque, 1991), "Indian Town Government in Colonial Cuernavaca: Persistence, Adaptation, and Change," *HAHR,* 67 (1987), 203–231, and "Living in Two Worlds: Cultural Continuity and Change among Cuernavaca's Colonial Indigenous Ruling Elite," *Ethnohistory,* 35 (1988), 34–59; James Lockhart, *The Nahuas after the Conquest: A Social and Cultural History of the Indians of Central Mexico, Sixteenth through Eighteenth Centuries* (Stanford, 1992), 28–58; William B. Taylor, *Landlord and Peasant in Colonial Oaxaca* (Stanford, 1972), 35–66; John K. Chance, *Conquest of the Sierra: Spaniards and Indians in Colonial Oaxaca* (Norman, Okla., 1989), 123–50; Ronald Spores, *The Mixtecs in Ancient and Colonial Times* (Norman, Okla., 1984), 165–86. On indirect rule in the Yucatan see Nancy Farriss, *Maya Society under Colonial Rule: The Collective Enterprise of Survival* (Princeton, 1984), esp. 86–114, 231–37.

Some of the most interesting discussions of indirect rule in the Spanish empire focus on Peru: Steve J. Stern, "The Rise and Fall of Indian-White Alliances: A Regional View of 'Conquest' History," *HAHR* 61 (1981), 461–91, and *Peru's Indian Peoples and the Challenge of Spanish Conquest: Huamanga to 1640* (Madison, 1982); and Karen Spalding, "Social Climbers: Changing Patterns of Mobility among the Indians of Colonial Peru," *HAHR,* 50 (1970), 645–64, "*Kurakas* and Commerce: A Chapter in the Evolution of Andean Society," ibid., 53 (1973), 581–99, and *Huarochiri: An Andean Society under Inca and Spanish Rule* (Stanford, 1984). For Florida see Amy Turner Bushnell, "Ruling 'the Republic of Indians' in Seventeenth-Century Florida," in *Powhatan's Mantle: Indians in the Colonial Southeast,* ed. Peter H. Wood, Gregory A. Waselkov, and M. Thomas Hatley (Lincoln, 1989), 134–50, and John H. Hann, *Apalachee: The Land Between the Rivers* (Gainesville, 1988), 102.

For the persistence of native leaders in mission communities of the northeast see Jean O'Brien, "Community Dynamics in the Indian-English Town of Natick, Massachusetts, 1650–1790" (Ph.D. diss., University of Chicago, 1990), 12–13, 40–41, 62–63; Susan L. MacCulloch, "A Tripartite Political System among Christian Indians of Early Massachusetts," *Kroeber Anthropological Society Papers,* no. 34 (1966), 63–73; Elise M. Brenner, "To Pray or to Be Prey, That Is the Question: Strategies for Cultural Autonomy of Massachusetts Praying Town Indians," *Ethnohistory,* 27 (1980), 135–52, esp. 143–44. For assertions that the Puritan missions constituted an attack on Indian leadership see Francis Jennings, *The Invasion of America: Indians, Colonialism, and the Cant of Conquest* (Chapel Hill, 1975), 228–53. On Indian leaders and Jesuit missions consult Daniel K. Richter, *The Ordeal of the Longhouse: The Peoples of the Iroquois League in the Era of European Colonization* (Chapel Hill, 1992), 112, 118, and "Iroquois versus Iroquois: Missions and Christianity in Village Politics, 1642–1686," *Ethnohistory,* 32 (1985) 1–16.

7. Cook, *The Population of the California Indians, 1769–1970* (Berkeley, 1976), 43. The speculative methodologies that Cook and others have used to estimate precontact native populations are the subject of John D. Daniels, "The Indian Population of North America in 1492," *WMQ,* 3d Ser., 49 (1992), 298–320. On

Indian languages in California see Michael J. Moratto, *California Archaeology* (New York, 1984), 530–74, and William F. Shipley, "Native Languages of California," in Heizer, ed., *California*, 80–90.

8. Cook, *Population of the California Indians*, 20–43; Gerhard, *North Frontier of New Spain*, 309.

9. Heizer and Albert B. Elsasser, *The Natural World of the California Indians* (Berkeley, 1980); Julia G. Costello and David Hornbeck, "Alta California: An Overview," in Thomas, ed., *Archaeological and Historical Perspectives on the Spanish Borderlands West*, 304–308; James T. Davis, "Trade Routes and Economic Exchange among the Indians of California," *Reports of the University of California Archaeological Survey*, no. 54 (Berkeley, 1961).

10. For a collection of articles that discusses how California Indians modified their environment to increase food yields see Thomas C. Blackburn and Kat Anderson, eds., *Before the Wilderness: Environmental Management by Native Californians* (Menlo Park, Calif, 1993).

11. Edith Wallace, "Sexual Status and Role Differences," in Heizer, ed., *California*, 683–84; Nora Christensen Willougbly, "Division of Labor among the Indians of California," *Reports of the University of California Archaeological Survey*. no. 60 (Berkeley, 1963), reprinted in *Ethnology of the Alta California Indians*, vol. I: *Precontact*, ed. Lowell John Bean and Sylvia Brakke Vane (New York, 1991), 427–99.

12. Bean, "Social Organization," in Heizer, ed., *California*, 673–82; Bean, "Power and Its Applications in Native California," in *Native Californians: A Theoretical Retrospective*, ed. Bean and Blackburn (Ramona, Calif., 1976), 407–420. Jeanne E. Arnold provides a theoretical discussion of the rise of cultural complexity in the precontact Chumash, in "Complex Hunter-Gatherer-Fishers of Prehistoric California: Chiefs, Specialists, and Maritime Adaptations of the Channel Islands," *American Antiquity*, 57 (1992), 60–84.

13. Lyle N. McAlister, *Spain and Portugal in the New World, 1492–1700* (Minneapolis, 1984), 133–52; Mario Góngora, *Studies in the Colonial History of Spanish America*, trans. Richard Southern (Cambridge, 1975), 98–107; John E. Kicza, "Patterns in Early Spanish Overseas Expansion," *WMQ*, 3d Ser., 49 (1992), 233. For an introduction to the literature of Spanish municipal planning in North America see Dora P. Crouch, Daniel J. Garr, and Axel I. Mundigo, *Spanish City Planning in North America* (Cambridge, Mass., 1982), and Garr, ed., *Hispanic Urban Planning in North America* (New York, 1991).

14. "Royal Instructions to Ovando" (1501), in Gibson, ed., *The Spanish Tradition in America* (New York, 1968), 55–57, quotation on 56.

15. Robert Ricard, *The Spiritual Conquest of Mexico: An Essay on the Apostolate and the Evangelizing Methods of the Mendicant Orders in New Spain: 1523–1572*, trans. Lesley Byrd Simpson (Berkeley, 1966), 136.

16. McAlister, *Spain and Portugal in the New World*, 170–73; Ricard, *Spiritual Conquest of Mexico*, trans Simpson, 136–37. For Spanish attempts to relocate Indians in Florida into sedentary settlements see Bushnell, "The Sacramental Imperative: Catholic Ritual and Indian Sedentism in the Provinces of Florida," in *Columbian Consequences*. vol 2: *Archaeological and Historical Perspectives on the Spanish Borderlands East* (Washington, D.C., 1990), ed. Thomas, 475–90. The English and French also wanted Indians to settle into compact towns, but their attempts were neither as far-reaching nor as effective. On French and English policies toward Indians see James Axtell, *The Invasion Within: The Contest of Cultures in Colonial North America* (New York, 1985), 43–70, 131–78.

17. The congregation of Alta California Indians into missions is discussed in Jackson, *Indian Population Decline*, 37–41. In some areas of northern New Spain, like New Mexico, most Indians lived in compact communities before the Spaniards' arrival; Edward H. Spicer, *Cycles of Conquest: The Impact of Spain, Mexico, and the United States on the Indians of the Southwest, 1533–1960* (Tucson, 1962), 288.

18. Lockhart, *Nahuas after the Conquest*, 36; J. H. Elliott, *Imperial Spain, 1469–1716* (New York, 1990; orig. pub. 1963), 93–97.

19. An adelantado was a royal deputy. The title was granted by the Spanish crown to the conquerors and founders of new colonies.

20. McAlister, *Spain and Portugal in the New World*, 135; Góngora, *Studies in the Colonial History of Spanish America*, 100–102; C. H. Haring, *The Spanish Empire in America* (New York, 1963; orig. pub. 1947), 147–65. An encomendero held a royal grant of the tribute and, occasionally, the labor of a specified number of Indians. In return, he was to provide military service to the crown and spiritual guidance for his allotted Indians.

21. Góngora, *Studies in the Colonial History of Spanish America*, 110, 116–19; McAlister, *Spain and Portugal in the New World*, 395–96; Bushnell, "Ruling 'the Republic of Indians,'" 137–39.

22. Book 6, title 3, law 15, *Recopilación de leyes de los reynos de las Indias*, 4 vols. (Madrid, 1681). For an English translation of this law see "The Indian cause in the Spanish Laws of the Indies," *American West Center*

The Staff of Leadership • 499

Occasional Paper, no. 16 (Salt Lake City, 1980), 115. The Republic of Indians was, ideally, to be segregated from Spanish society, yet its religious and political institutions would be modeled after Spain's.

23. See note 6.

24. Among the responsibilities of the Indian governors were protecting the community from excessive demands, collecting rents, keeping the community treasury, confirming elections in subject cities, allocating land, hearing minor cases "concerning debts, petty theft, assault, and the local market," and apprehending criminals; Haskett, *Indigenous Rulers*, 99–102.

25. Taylor, *Landlord and Peasant*, 39.

26. Indian governors initiated or threatened court cases over "land usurpation boundary conflicts, water-rights struggles, and rental disputes," according to Haskett, *Indigenous Rulers*, 101. For legal channels open to Indians in New Spain see Woodrow Borah, *Justice by Insurance: The General Indian Court of Colonial Mexico and the Legal Aides of the Half-Real* (Berkeley, 1983).

27. Haskett, *Indigenous Rulers*, 104–07.

28. Ibid., 114–16; Chance, *Conquest of the Sierra*, 154.

29. Haskett, *Indigenous Rulers*, 95–123.

30. J. H. Parry, *The Audiencia of New Galicia in the Sixteenth Century: A Study in Spanish Colonial Government* (Cambridge, 1948); Philip Wayne Powell, *Soldiers, Indians, and Silver: The Northward Advance of New Spain, 1550–1600* (Berkeley, 1952).

31. On the persistence and decline of encomienda and repartimiento in northern New Spain see José Cuello, "The Persistence of Indian Slavery and Encomienda in the Northeast of Colonial Mexico, 1577–1723," *Journal of Social History*, 21 (1988), 683–700, and Susan M. Deeds, "Rural Work in Nueva Vizcaya: Forms of Labor Coercion on the Periphery," *HAHR* 69 (1989), 425–49.

32. Indian officials in these regions donned the following titles: *gobernador, teniente de gobernador, capitán, sargento, alférez, alcalde, regidor, fiscal, alguacil, topil, sacristán,* and *cantor*. An overview of Spanish attempts to introduce a Spanish governmental system among the Indians of Sonora and New Mexico is provided by Spicer, *Cycles of Conquest*, 289–91, 303–304, 328, 388–95. Indian officials in Nueva Vizcaya are discussed in Deeds, "Indigenous Responses to Mission Settlement in Nueva Vizcaya," in *The New Latin American Mission History*, ed. Erick Langer and Robert H. Jackson (Lincoln, 1995), 82–83, 88–89, and William B. Griffen, *Indian Assimilation in the Franciscan Area of Nueva Vizcaya* (Tucson, 1979), 45. On Sonora see John L. Kessell, *Friars, Soldiers, and Reformers: Hispanic Arizona and the Sonora Mission Frontier, 1767–1856* (Tucson, 1976), 71–72, Evelyn Hu DeHart, *Missionaries, Miners, and Indians: Spanish Contact with the Yaqui Nation of Northwestern New Spain, 1533–1820* (Tucson, 1981), 32–36, and Cynthia Radding, "Ethnicity and the Emerging Peasant Class of Northwestern New Spain, 1760–1840" (Ph.D. diss., University of California at San Diego, 1990), 53, 80, 105–106, 139, 450–55. Ramón A. Gutiérrez discusses how Indians in New Mexico understood their town officials, in *When Jesus Came, the Corn Mothers Went Away: Marriage, Sexuality, and Power in New Mexico, 1500–1846* (Stanford, 1991), 156–61. The role of Indian officials in the missions of Texas is discussed in Mardith Keithly Schuetz, "The Indians of the San Antonio Missions, 1718–1821" (Ph.D. diss., University of Texas at Austin, 1980), 254–67.

33. The only record of Neve's original order is Fray Fermín Francisco de Lasuén's response, Jan. 25, 1779, in *Writings of Fermín Francisco de Lasuén*, ed. and trans. Finbar Kenneally, 2 vols. (Washington, D.C., 1965), 1:75–77. Neve notified Teodoro de Croix, commander general of the interior provinces of his directive, Feb. 24, 1779 (copy certified in Monterey, Nov. 15, 1796), ramo Californias, tomo 65, expediente 7, fol. 303r, Archivo General de la Nación (AGN) Mexico City, Mexico. De Croix sent his approval, July 28, 1779, ibid., fol. 304r. The most recently established missions at San Francisco (1776), San Juan Capistrano (1776), and Santa Clara (1777) were exempt from the governor's orders.

34. This process is described in Lasuén to Neve, Jan. 25, 1779, in *Writings of Lasuén*, ed. Kenneally, 1:74. Regidores apparently did not carry a staff; Serra to Lasuén, [Mar. 29], 1779, *Writings of Junípero Serra*, 4 vols., ed. Antonine Tibesar (Washington, D.C., 1955–66), 3:295. All quotations of Serra are my translations from the Spanish text in Tibesar. All other translations, with the exception of the letters by Lasuén, are mine.

35. Gutiérrez, "Church and State: Spanish," in Jacob Ernest Cooke, ed., *Encyclopedia of the North American Colonies* (New York, 1993), 3:520–28.

36. For Bourbon policies toward the church and the military see Farriss, *Crown and Clergy in Colonial Mexico, 1759–1821: The Crisis of Ecclesiastical Privilege* (London, 1968), and Christon I. Archer, *The Army in Bourbon Mexico, 1760–1810* (Albuquerque, 1977).

37. Magnus Morner, ed., *The Expulsion of the Jesuits from Latin America* (New York, 1965); Weber, *The Spanish Frontier in North America* (New Haven, 1992), 242; Edwin A. Beilharz, *Felipe de Neve, First Governor of California* (San Francisco, 1971), 9–13.

38. Weber, *Spanish Frontier in North America*, 242.

39. Neve to Serra, quoted in Serra to Neve, Jan. 7, 1780, *Writings of Serra*, ed. Tibesar, 3:410–11.

40. Book 6, title 3, law 15, *Recopilación*. A reducción was a community in which Indians were taught the rudiments of Spanish religion and political organization. A useful discussion of the different terms used by Spaniards to describe mission settlements is found in Bushnell, *Situado and Sabana: Spain's Support System for the Presidio and Mission Provinces of Florida* (Athens, Ga., 1994), 20–23.

41. Lasuén to Neve, Jan. 25, 1779, *Writings of Lasuén*, ed. Kenneally, 1:75–77.

42. Serra to Lasuén [Mar. 29], 1779, *Writings of Serra*, ed. Tibesar, 3:292–95.

43. Matt. 10:16. Serra to Lasuén [Mar. 29], 1779, *Writings of Serra*, ed. Tibesar, 3:294–95.

44. Serra to Lasuén [Mar. 29], 1779, *Writings of Serra*, ed. Tibesar, 3:294–95.

45. Genesis 2:4; Serra to Lasuén [Mar. 29], 1779, *Writings of Serra*, ed. Tibesan 3:296–97.

46. Mission San Diego was an exception; local village captains were recognized outright as alcaldes. By Jan. 1783, Gov. Pedro Fages had ordered the Franciscans at Missions San Francisco, San Juan Capistrano, and Santa Clara to oversee Indian elections. The Franciscans' grumbling continued until 1797, when Viceroy Miguel de la Grua Talamanca y Branciforte upheld the governor's position; Nov. 15, 1797, AGN Californias 65:7, fols. 323v–330v.

47. Serra to Lasuén Aug. 16, 1779, *Writings of Serra*, ed. Tibesar, 3:364–67.

48. Serra to Neve, Jan. 7, 1780, ibid., 408–409. The restriction of the franchise to a select few was consistent with practices in Spain and its colonies; Haskett, *Indigenous Rulers*, 29–30.

49. Fages, General Report on the Missions, [1787], paragraph 32, Archives of California, C-A 52:144, Bancroft Library, Berkeley, Calif.

50. A limitation on the number of candidates eligible for election was not unique to California missions, nor did it apply only to Indians. In San José (Alta California's first Spanish *pueblo*) during the early 1780s, the settlers' elections were restricted after the settlers had elected men who proved unwilling or unable to control the community. The governor appointed a *comisionado* (military deputy) and an alcalde to supervise the town. Later, the outgoing alcalde submitted three names to the comisionado; if he approved, the three cast lots. The winner was named alcalde and the other two regidores. As in the missions, these appointments had to be approved by the governor, who occasionally rejected them and appointed new officials; Guest, "Municipal Government in Spanish California," *California Historical Society Quarterly*, 46 (1967), 307–335, esp. 312–13, and "Municipal Institutions in Spanish California, 1769–1821" (Ph.D. diss., University of Southern California, 1961), 202, 227–29.

51. Serra to Lasuén [Mar. 29], 1779, *Writings of Serra*. ed. Tibesar, 3:296–97.

52. Correspondence between Borica and commanders of presidios of San Francisco, Monterey, Santa Barbara, and San Diego, Mar. 2–30, 1796, AGN Californias 65:7, fols. 307r–314v.

53. Mission San Luis Rey may have had 7 alcaldes. See the narrative of Pablo Tac, in *Native American Perspectives on the Hispanic Colonization of Alta California*, ed. Castillo (New York, 1991), 35–58, esp. 51. This volume includes other native accounts of life in colonial California. For politics in Mission San Luis Rey see Florence Connolly Shipek, "A Strategy for Change: The Luiseño of Southern California" (Ph.D. diss., University of Hawaii, 1977), 145–54.

54. Conversely, in New Mexico at roughly the same time, Indian officials came under the authority of the civilian government, not the clerics. Gutiérrez, *When Jesus Came, the Corn Mothers Went Away*, 158–59. For Indian officials in 18th-century central Mexico see William B. Taylor, *Magistrates of the Sacred: Priests and Parishioners in Eighteenth-Century Mexico* (Stanford, 1996), esp. 345–691.

55. Fages, General Report on the Missions, [1787], paragraph 33.

56. For Serra's argument that the Franciscans had flogged and would flog Indian officials see Serra to Neve, Jan. 7, 1780, *Writings of Serra*, ed. Tibesar: 3: 407–17, and Serra to Lasuén Apr. 25, 26, 1780, ibid., 4:3–11.

57. Fages, General Report on the Missions, [1787], paragraph 33.

58. In California, like most of the frontier of northern New Spain, in the absence of standing courts, the provincial governor assumed most judicial responsibilities. The legal system of New Mexico and Texas is

clearly delineated in Charles R. Cutter, *The Legal Culture of Northern New Spain, 1700–1810* (Albuquerque, 1995). In New Mexico, the *protector de Indios* played a crucial role in assisting Indians with judicial matters; Cutter, *The Protector de Indios in Colonial New Mexico, 1659–1821* (Albuquerque, 1986).

59. Book 6, title 3, law 16, *Recopilación*.

60. Serra to Neve, Jan. 7, 1780, *Writings of Serra*, ed. Tibesar, 3:406–407.

61. Tac, in *Native American Perspectives on . . . Alta California*, ed. Castillo, 51.

62. On Franciscan religious instruction of Indians see Ricard, *Spiritual Conquest of Mexico,* trans. Simmons, 101–102; Lino Gómez Canedo, *Evangelización y conquista: Experiencia francisana en hispanamérica*, 2d ed. (Mexico City, 1988), 148–62, 169–72; Charles W. Polzer, "Roman Catholicism: The Spanish Borderlands," in *Encyclopedia of the North American Colonies.* ed. Cooke, 3:537–40; Weber. *Spanish Frontier in North America*, 106–111; and Bushnell, *Situado and Sabana,* 95–103.

63. Fray Manuel Fernandez to Borica, Dec. 12, 1797, Alexander S. Taylor Collection, no. 120, Henry E. Huntington Library, San Marino, Calif.; see also Juan Bautisra Alvarado, "Historia de California (1876)," 5 vols., vol. I, C-D 1:85–86, Bancroft Library.

64. Fray Estevan Tapis to Gov. Pablo Vicente de Solá, Feb. 24, 1821, Taylor Coll., No. 1200.

65. Tac, in *Native American Perspectives on . . . Alta California*, ed. Castillo, 51.

66. Claudio, quoted from "Testimony of Runaway Christian Indians Taken by Lieutenant José Arguello, San Francisco, August 12, 1797," in Randall Milliken, *A Time of Little Choice: The Disintegration of Tribal Culture in the San Francisco Bay Area, 1769–1810* (Menlo Park, Calif, 1995), 300.

67. Homobono, quoted ibid., 301.

68. Ramón Abella and Juan Sainz de Lucio, Nov. 11, 1814, quoted in Geiger, ed. and trans., *As the Padres Saw Them: California Indian Life and Customs as Reported by the Franciscan Missionaries, 1813–1815* (Santa Barbara, 1976), 128.

69. Hugo Reid, [Letter No. 19], "New Era in Mission Affairs," in Susanna Bryant Dakin, *A Scotch Paisano in Old Los Angeles: Hugo Reid's Life in California, 1852–1852, Derived from His Correspondence* (Berkeley, 1978; orig. pub. 1939), 273. For a discussion of Anglo-American and foreign views of the Indians and Franciscans in early California see James J. Rawls, *Indians of California: The Changing Image* (Norman, Okla., 1984).

70. Castillo, "Other Side of the 'Christian Curtain,'" 13.

71. Reid, quoted in Dakin, *A Scotch Paisano in Old Los Angeles*, 272–73. Reid, who died in 1852, married Bartolomea in 1837.

72. An extensive literature debates the Franciscans' use of physical punishment in the missions of California. The classic condemnation is Cook, "The Indian versus the Spanish Mission," *Ibero-Americana,* 21 (1943), 1–194, republished in his *Conflict between the California Indian and White Civilization.* For an opposing view see Guest, "An Examination of the Thesis of S. F. Cook on the Forced Conversion of Indians in the California Missions," *SCQ,* 61 (1979), 1–77; Guest, "Cultural Perspectives on California Mission Life"; Guest, "Inquiry into the Role of the Discipline in California Mission Life"; and Guest, "The California Missions Were Far from Faultless," *SCQ,* 76 (1994), 255–307. Guest does not deny that the Franciscans beat the Indians; rather, he argues that the corporal punishment was rarely worse than a parental spanking.

73. As Serra declared in 1780, "that spiritual fathers should punish their Indian children with whippings appears to be as old as the conquest of these kingdoms; so general, in fact, that the saints do not seem to be any exception to the rule." Serra to Neve, Jan. 7, 1780, *Writings of Serra*, ed. Tibesar, 3: 412–13. Serra took inspiration from Saint Francis Solano, who worked for two decades among the Indians of Peru and Paraguay. Solano, according to Serra, did not hesitate to have Indians whipped when they did not follow his commands. Thirty-five years later, Fray José Francisco de Paula Señán, the fourth president of the California missions, echoed this belief: "The missionary father attends to the correction and suitable chastisement and he applies the punishment like a natural father on his sons." Señán, Aug. 11, 1815, quoted in Geiger. ed and trans., *As the Padres Saw Them,* 114.

74. For a description of some of the constabulary duties of the Indian officials, as outlined by a former governor of California, see Alvarado, "Historia de California," C-D 1:85–86.

75. Pedro Poyorena to Antonio Grajera, Mar. 5, 1797, Mission San Juan Capistrano, AGN Californias 65:8, fol. 336r-v.

76. Gov. José Joaquin de Arrillaga to the commander of the San Francisco presidio, May 12, 1808, Archives of California, C-A a6:503.

77. Bean, "Social Organization," 678.

78. Tomás de la Peña, quoted in Lasuén to Fages, Apr. 7, 1786, *Writings of Lasuén*, ed. Kenneally, 1:105.

79. Mariano Payeras, 1821, Taylor Coll., no. 1257.

80. Bean, "Social Organization," 678.

81. Ibid.; Serra to Lasuén, [Mar. 29], 1779, *Writings of Serra*, ed. Tibesar, 3:295.

82. César, "Recollections of My Youth at the San Luis Rey Mission," trans. Nellie Van de Grift Sánchez. First published in *Touring Topics*, 22 (1930), 42–43, reprinted in *Native American Perspectives on . . . Alta California*, ed. Castillo, 13–15.

83. Lasuén worried that the missions would not have enough food to support officials who would be entitled to special portions of grain but whose manual labor would be lost to the mission; Lasuén to Neve, Jan. 25, 1779, *Writings of Lasuén*, ed. Kenneally, 1:76–77. The most thorough discussion of the mission economy is Robert Archibald, *The Economic Aspects of the California Missions* (Washington, D.C., 1978). See also Steven W. Hackel, "Land, Labor, and Production: The Colonial Economy of Spanish and Mexican California," *California History* 76 (1977), 111–46.

84. Bean, "Social Organization," 677.

85. Serra to Neve, Jan. 7, 1780, *Writings of Serra*, ed. Tibesar, 3:408–409.

86. Scholars have portrayed the Indian officials as little more than blind enforcers of the Franciscans' commands. They have interpreted the role of Indian officials with little knowledge of who the officials were or how they fit into their native communities. In such work, the identities of individual Indian officials become insignificant because the mission is described as a polarized "plural institution" composed of two antagonistic groups: Indians and Spaniards. See, for example, Phillips, "Indians and the Breakdown of the Spanish Mission System in California" *Ethnohistory*, 21 (1974), 291–302, and Heizer, "Impact of Colonization on the Native California Societies," 130. These issues are explored in Hackel, "Indian-Spanish Relations in Alta California: Mission San Carlos Borromeo, 1770–1833" (Ph.D. diss., Cornell University, 1994).

87. Sacramental registers contain information relevant to the life histories of individual Indians not elsewhere available, but cross-cultural misunderstandings, clerical errors, illegible handwriting and inconsistent record keeping present challenges for the historian. These difficulties are discussed in John R. Johnson, "Mission Registers as Anthropological Questionnaires: Understanding Limitations of the Data," *American Indian Culture and Research Journal*, 12 (1988), 9–30, and Cook and Borah, "Mission Registers as Sources of Vital Statistics: Eight Missions of Northern California," in *Essays in Population History: Mexico and California*, vol. 3, ed. Cook and Borah (Berkeley, 1979), 177–311.

88. On the destruction of a significant portion of the historical documents relating to Spanish California see Henry Putney Beers, *Spanish and Mexican Records of the American Southwest* (Tucson, 1979), 224. The sacramental registers of Mission San Carlos are available on microfilm from the Family History Library, Church of Jesus Christ of the Latter-Day Saints. See Mission San Carlos Borromeo Baptisms, 1770–1855, Film 0913159; Mission San Carlos Borromeo Burials, 1770–1915, Film 0913162; Mission San Carlos Borromeo Marriages, 1772–1908, Film 0913161.

89. I uncovered the names of more than 46 officials but identified only 46 in the sacramental registers. During the period 1779–1831, there were a total of 212 leadership spots (53 years $\times$ 4 = 212). Of these 212 spots, the identified 46 officials filled at least 99.

90. The number of villages represented at Mission San Carlos is a matter of debate as are the exact boundaries of the Costanoan- and Esselen-speaking groups. For discussions of the settlement areas of the Indians baptized at the mission see Milliken, "Ethnohistory of the Rumsen," in *Papers in Northern California Anthropology*, no. 2, ed. Stephen A. Dietz, Northern California Anthropological Group (April 1987); Milliken, "Ethnographic Context," in "Archaeological Investigations at Elkhorn Slough: CA-MNT-229, A Middle Period Site on the Central California Coast," ed. Dietz, William Hildebrandt, and Terry Jones, ibid., no. 3, Northern California Anthropological Group (March 1988), 57–94; Richard Levy, "Costanoan," in Heizer, ed., *California*, 485–86; Milliken, "Ethnogeography and Ethnohistory of the Big Sur District, California State Park System during the 1770–1810 Time Period," Anthropology Dept., Univ. of California, Berkeley (March 1990); Gary Breschini and Trudy Haversat, "An Overview of the Esselen Indians of Central Monterey County," June 20, 1993, Archaeological Consulting, Salinas, Calif; Cook, "The Esselen: Territory, Villages, and Population," *Monterey County Archaeological Society Quarterly*, 3 (January 1974), 6–7; and Thomas Roy Hester, "Esselen," in Heizer, ed., *California*, 496–97.

91. All population figures for precontact California are speculative. This tabulation relies on estimated population totals from Milliken, "Ethnohistory of the Rumsen," 47–52, "Ethnogeography and Ethnohistory of the Big Sur District," 74–76, and "Ethnographic Context," 64–66.

92. "Appendix B, Spiritual Results, Indians," Engelhardt, *Mission San Carlos Borromeo (Carmelo): The Father of the Missions,* ed. Felix Pudlowski (Ramona, Calif, 1973; orig. pub. 1934), 243; Jackson, *Indian Population Decline,* 89–90.

93. The Franciscans did not recognize women as political leaders. General studies suggest that political leadership in California before the conquest was nearly the exclusive domain of males: Levy, "Costanoan," 487; Bean, "Social Organization," 678; Wallace, "Sexual Status and Role Differences," 687; Joseph G. Jorgensen, *Western Indians: Comparative Environments, Languages, and Cultures of 172 Western American Indian Tribes* (San Francisco, 1980), 223–24.

94. Mission San Carlos Baptism 1074, Mar. 19, 1785, entered by Fray Matias de Santa Catalina Noriega.

95. Three latecomers, Joaquín Chato Torres, Agustín Pasay, and Cornelio, lived for a long time at the mission but are not identified as officials. Possibly, they served as officials during one of the years for which the election results are lost or incomplete (20–25 percent of the total years of the alcalde system). But their absences as witnesses from the register suggest that they were never part of the mission leadership hierarchy. Nearly all Indian officials at Mission San Carlos seem to have served as marriage witnesses sometime before their election as officials, but not all marriage witnesses went on to serve as officials. To the extent that there was a ladder of leadership at the mission, serving as a marriage witness seems to have been an important rung. While these village captains may not have had the necessary qualifications for election, they may have retained a measure of influence among their own village groups. It is these captains, perhaps, to whom Fray Juan Amorós referred in 1814 when he stated the Indians at the mission "show more respect and submission to their chiefs than to the alcaldes who have been placed over them for their advancement as citizens"; Amorós, Feb. 3, 1814, quoted in Geiger, ed. and trans., *As the Padres Saw Them,* 126–27.

96. See studies cited in note 93 above.

97. An extensive body of literature documents Indian mortality in the missions of Alta California. See Cook and Borah, "Mission Registers as Sources of Vital Statistics," 177–311, and Jackson, *Indian Population Decline.*

98. Marcos Chaulis had two sons, Romano and Domicio, who were officials. Nestor, son of the captain Abrahan (who also was an official), was a regidor. Misael José, son of village captain Felipe Jesús, was an interpreter at the mission.

99. Indians selected as alcaldes were not the only individuals of leadership age in their respective ethnic-linguistic groups. The size of the pool of potential Indian officials differed from group to group. In most years, there were 10–30 additional men of leadership age (25–50) who could have served as Indian officials had age been the only qualification. For the year 1792, Hilario was among 21 Excelen villagers, Nicomedes was one of 5 Sargentaruc, Sancio Francisco was one of 11 Kalendaruc-Locuyusta, and Atanasio José was one of 12 Tucurnut villagers and one of 27 Indians from the 5 Rumsen villages who were the right age. If one considers the whole mission population, in 1792 there were 112 men ages 25–50.

100. In Texas, at Mission San Francisco Solano, a similar situation prevailed: each major group was represented by a fiscal. Until the mid-1740s at neighboring Missions San Antonio de Valero and Nuestra Señora de la Purísima Concepción, each major ethnic group was probably represented by an alcalde; Schuetz, "Indians of the San Antonio Missions, 1718–1821," 266–65. For examples of the ethnic distribution of Indian officials in the towns of colonial Mexico see Haskett, *Indigenous Rulers,* 22, and Chance, *Conquest of the Sierra,* 134–35.

101. In 1789, "to facilitate and make more expedient the government of the mission," the Franciscans considered Mission San Carlos to be composed of two "Nations," each of which spoke a different language; Report by Fathers Pasqual Martinez de Arenaza and José Senan entitled "Informe de esta Misión de San Carlos según el estado en que se hallaba el día último de Diciembre, 1789," quoted, in Milliken, "Ethnohistory of the Rumsen," 31. Original is in the AGN, Archivo Históricode Hacienda (AHH), Colección de Documentos para la Historia de México (DPHM), Serie 11, Tomo 2 (2), and available on microfilm ar the Bancroft Library.

102. Benedict Leutenegger, trans., *Guidelines for a Texas Mission: Instructions for the Missionary of Mission Concepción San Antonio, ca. 1760* (San Antonio, 1990; orig. pub. 1976), paragraph 18, republished in *Archaeology of the Spanish Missions of Texas,* ed. Anne A. Fox (New York, 1991), 18. The Pajalache Indians are also known as the Pajalat; T. N. Campbell, "Coahuiltecans and Their Neighbors," in Alfonso Ortiz, ed., *Southwest,* vol. 10 of Sturtevant, gen. ed.. *Handbook of North American Indians* (Washington, D.C., 1993), 343–58.

103. By 1805, the Franciscans at Mission San Carlos could count more than 18 mission-born men who were at least age 25. Mission San Carlos, especially during its first decade, had one of the highest birth rates of any mission in Alta California; Jackson, *Indian Population Decline,* 83–108.

104. Weber, *Mexican Frontier,* 43–68.

105. For municipal, electoral reform during the revolutionary period see Roger L. Cunniff, "Mexican Municipal Electoral Reform, 1810–1822," in *Mexico and the Spanish Cortes, 1810–1822: Eight Essays,* ed. Nettie Lee Benson (Austin, 1966), 59–86. Most Indian communities during this period were subsumed into larger political units, and the Indian cabildo was displaced by a municipal government, which was usually dominated by non-Indians. In many areas, these changes spelled the end of Indian political autonomy; Farriss, *Maya Society under Colonial Rule,* 375–79; Haskett, *Indigenous Rulers,* 197; Cheryl English Martin, *Rural Society in Colonial Morelos* (Albuquerque, 1985), 196–97.

106. There is an extensive literature on the Chumash uprising. See, for example, Sandos, *"Levantamiento!* The 1824 Chumash Uprising Reconsidered," *SCQ,* 67 (1985), 109–133; Sandos, "Christianization among the Chumash: An Ethnohistoric Perspective," *American Indian Quarterly,* 15 (Winter 1991), 65–89; and Phillips, *Indians and Intruders in Central California, 1769–1849* (Norman, Okla., 1993), 65–69.

107. Ignacio Martínez to Gov. José Marla Echeandia, May 21, 1827, Taylor Coll., no. 1936.

108. Jack Holterman, "The Revolt of Estanislao," *Indian Historian,* 3 (Winter 1970), 43–54, 66.

109. Echeandía, Feb. 7, 1829, Archives of California, C-A 18:442–43.

110. During the period 1822–31, 19 of 23 known leadership positions went to Costanoan Indians. In the mission, Costanoan-speaking Indians outnumbered Esselen-speaking Indians roughly 2 to 1 by 1821.

111. José Joaquín de Arrillaga to Borica, Apr. 28, 1796, AGN California 65:8. fols. 307r–308v.

112. Letters signed with the marks of Antonio, Landelíno, Gaudín, and Martín to Buelna, Jan. 18, 1831, Archives of Monterey, C-A 150, 1:266–68, Bancroft Library. The letter is in the hand of José Joaquin Gómez, customs officer for Monterey.

113. Ibid.

114. Weber, *Mexican Frontier,* 60–68, takes a wide-ranging look at the secularization of the missions in California. A useful summary of the historical antecedents to the mission secularization in California is Gerald J. Geary, *Secularization of the California Missions (1810–1846)* (Washington, D.C., 1934). C. Alan Hutchinson provides a thorough analysis of the local proponents of secularization in *Frontier Settlement in Mexican California: The Híjar-Padrés Colony and Its Origins, 1769–1835* (New Haven, 1969). Hutchinson examines the Mexican government's role in secularization in "The Mexican Government and the Mission Indians of Upper California, 1821–1835," *The Americas,* 21 (1965), 335–62. Hubert Howe Bancroft summarized the main events of secularization in his monumental *History of California,* 7 vols. (San Francisco, 1884–90), 3:301–355. Castillo has examined one Indian's narrative of the years after secularization, in "An Indian Account of the Decline and Collapse of Mexico's Hegemony over the Missionized Indians of California," *Amer. Indian Q,* 13 (1989), 391–408. See also Manuel P. Servín, "The Secularization of the California Missions: A Reappraisal," *SCQ,* 47 (1965), 133–49.

115. For an examination of mission communities after secularization see Daniel J. Garr, "Planning, Politics, and Plunder: The Missions and Indian Pueblos of Hispanic California," *SCQ,* 54 (1972), 291–312. Phillips argues that the Indians left the missions en masse after secularization, in "Indians and the Breakdown of the Spanish Mission System in California," 291–302. Compare Clement W. Meighan, "Indians and California Missions," *SCQ,* 69 (1987), 187–201. See Lisbeth Haas, *Conquests and Historical Identities in California. 1769–1936* (Berkeley, 1995), 39–41, and Phillips, *Chiefs and Challengers: Indian Resistance and Cooperation in Southern California* (Berkeley, 1975), for discussions of southern California Indian leaders during and after mission secularization.

116. Albert L. Hurtado, *Indian Survival on the California Frontier* (New Haven, 1988), 52, 81–82, 99, 112.

117. Testimony of Romano, in "Criminal contra el Indio José," Apr. 1835, Archives of Monterey, C-A 150, 2:69–70; "Libro de Actas," Jan. 3, 1844–Mar. 9, 1844, Monterey Collection, box 3, file MR 255, Monterey Ayuntamiento, Huntington Library.

118. Farriss, *Maya Society under Colonial Rule,* 237.

James A. Sandos

When Spanish authorities decided in the sixteenth century to give missionaries a prominent role in the administration of New Spain, they assumed that Native Americans would quickly convert to Christianity. Yet even as late as the early nineteenth century, many Indians in Alta California still refused to accept either the legitimacy of the missionaries' authority or the power of the clerics' faith. In some areas, as Steven Hackel has argued, the Spanish recognized that they had to share power with Indians. When the colonizers refused to do so, trouble erupted.

James A. Sandos chronicles one notable episode of that trouble. Focusing on the Chumash Indians, and paying close attention to how they understood their world and their relations with colonists, Sandos considers an 1824 rebellion in which some Chumash fought the Spanish while others fled. This moment of decision, rooted in smoldering resentment of previous Spanish mistreatment, exploded when a comet crossed the skies, signaling, natives believed, the dawn of a new age.

Like Ruth Herndon and Ella Sekatau, Sandos imaginately combines written documents and oral histories gathered from native informants. His in-depth analysis of these sources reveals the difficulties that Indians and Spaniards had in coping with the other's faith. As it did among the nativists Gregory Dowd studied in the Ohio country, religion played a crucial role. The conflict was an unexpected spiritual contest fought between peoples, each convinced that they, and they alone, had the answers to the mysteries of this world, and the next.

LEVANTAMIENTO!: THE 1824 CHUMASH UPRISING RECONSIDERED

James A. Sandos

TRADITIONAL INTERPRETATIONS of the largest uprising of California Indians during the Mission Era (1769–1834) hold that it was a fairly brief, unsuccessful, military revolt against the exploitation of the Mexican government.[1] The outpouring of material on Chumash culture over the past fifteen years, most of it based on the publication of the previously unavailable field notes of ethnographer John P. Harrington, forces a reconsideration of the uprising from a Chumash perspective.[2] Moreover, the discovery and publication of confessional aids (*confesionarios*) composed by the Franciscans in the Chumash area along with responses to questionnaires (*interrogatorios*) and other pertinent documents permit a reassessment of the uprising from a clerical viewpoint. Taken together, these sources reveal an uprising markedly different from conventional wisdom. Chumash selected both secular and religious targets, and in addition to their celebrated fight at Mission La Purísima Concepcion, they manifested at least three distinguishable patterns of flight from the Euro-Indian environment. One of these flights culminated in the successful creation of a new culture by the Chumash in the interior.

CHUMASH ETHNOGRAPHY

As a departure point, consider Harrington's contribution to Chumash studies. As an ethnographer laboring on his own and later employed by the Smithsonian Institution, Harrington worked with Chumash informants from 1912–28, and afterward, he returned episodically to collecting information on these Indians until his death in 1961. Secretive and not given to publishing his scholarship, his most significant publications have been posthumous. In the areas of material culture,[3] economic activity,[4] folklore,[5] cosmology,[6] and ritual ceremony,[7] Harrington's information has provided an astonishing range of hitherto unknown insights into Chumash life. From this new information an approximation can be attempted of a Chumash society in which Christianity sought to effect change.

SOURCE: *Southern California Quarterly* LXVII (1985), 109–33.

The overlap and interweaving of political and religious power defined the parameters of village life. Hereditary chieftainship resided in the *wot*, who in turn was assisted by a *paxa* or ceremonial leader and two messengers known as *ksen*. The paxa held a doubly important post, for he constituted a link with and sometimes the leadership of the religious *?antap* cult. In major villages at least a dozen *?antap* operated performing ceremonies and rituals locally and traveling to disparate villages to participate in ceremonies there. The *?antap* cult helped to integrate Chumash society across geographical boundaries, and membership in the cult enhanced a person's status.[8]

Within the village the paxa usually initiated the adolescents into the use of *datura* (*Datura meteloides*), a plant with hallucinogenic properties. Since the effective dose was slightly less than the lethal, knowledge of the drug's effects and how to administer it became specialized skills in Chumash society. Individuals who developed such skills, whether members of the *?antap* cult or not, were highly valued and were known in Spanish as *toloacheros*, those who administered toloache, the Spanish word for datura.[9] Toloacheros assumed importance because adult Chumash of both sexes routinely ingested the drug. Taking datura enabled an Indian to contact his or her supernatural guardian, to reinforce that bond with the dream helper who would enable the petitioner to obtain either a specific goal or a general increase in supernatural powers. Individuals of all stations used it, including shamen and curers, the latter administering it occasionally to their patients. Chumash used datura for individual rather than collective reasons, and people consumed it routinely in the village rather than at a special site. Datura suffused all of Chumash society. It stood at the center of Chumash life, fully integrated into mythology, used in religion, medicine, and personal spiritual growth. The chewing of *pespibata* (*Nicotiana attenuata*), a native tobacco known for its potent effects, frequently accompanied the taking of datura and was generally associated with the hallucinogen. Franciscan missionaries were alert to the use of pespibata or toloache by their charges.

Chumash personal conduct, involving a degree of sexual activity shocking to European standards, posed a behavioral challenge to the Spanish priests. By Chumash standards sexual liaisons could be accepted between the unmarried, between the married if the person desired was the spouse of a sibling's or sibling's equivalent (brother or sister-in-law), and between men through the acknowledgement of *joyas*, or transvestites. In this society marriage proved a fragile institution that could be readily set aside. Since the padres considered the husband-wife relationship the center of European society, they seem never to have understood the centrality of the sibling relationship to Chumash culture. To the Chumash the relationship between siblings, either same sex or opposite, proved so strong that nothing, not even sexual jealousy, could be allowed to harm it. In trying to ferret out kinship patterns between sexual partners, then, the Franciscans probably employed the terms "grandfather" (*abuelito*) and "uncle" (*tio*) in misleading ways.

In a society with both a high degree of sexual activity and ritual it was inevitable that the Chumash would engage in activities offensive to Christian doctrine. Three of these practices merit our consideration. Chumash women believed that if they did not kill their first-born child then they would never have another. Such belief led to abortion or infanticide.[10] The Chumash propitiated spirits and deities by making offerings within the village in an enclosure dominated by painted poles topped with feathers. Outside the village they scattered seeds and sometimes feathers in certain areas to acknowledge the existence and largess of a particular god.[11] Finally, the Chumash engaged in certain dance rituals which the clergy found repulsive. The Coyote Dance, a favored ritual usually performed away from the priest's eyes, involved a single man with his body painted and wearing a loin cloth, dancing and singing before an assembled crowd. As an informant remembered:

> During the last part of . . . the song which Coyote sang, he was trying to persuade someone to come over to lick his penis. But by the time of the last verse of the song, he had lost all hope and so did it himself . . . When he finished he squatted down and defecated amid the people.[12]

Another dance between Coyote and the Devil, including defecation, was performed at Mission Santa Barbara and involved Chumash dancers from several missions.[13] Here the observer must wonder whether the Chumash used the dance to resist Christianity by incorporating the Euro-Christian Devil into their Coyote ritual, enabling them thereby to engage in behavior that the priests considered repugnant.

CHRISTIANIZATION EFFORTS

Christianization efforts by Franciscans in the Chumash area began with the founding of Mission San Luis Obispo in 1772. A decade elapsed before the friars could establish another, San Buenaventura in 1782, and then within five years they began Santa Barbara (1786) and La Purísima Concepción (1787). Not until 1804, just twenty years prior to the insurrection, did work on Santa Ynéz begin.[14] The last three missions established in the area witnessed the Chumash uprising.

The California missions, deriving from the mission experience in Mexico, operated on the principle of immersion. Converts were to be located in or adjacent to the mission compound in order to contribute their labor to the survival of the institution and to learn in every facet of daily life the meaning of being Christian. Priests tried diligently to extirpate indigenous cult activity and to inculcate the values of a Roman Catholic and Spanish society. From the wearing of European-styled clothing deemed appropriate for Indians, to farming, herding, riding horses, making adobe bricks, singing in the choir, learning catechism, receiving the sacraments, and the sequestering of unmarried women, the padres sought to meet all Indian needs and to infuse all Indian life with a new socioreligious order through the mission environment.[15]

To accomplish these tasks the Franciscans had important advantages in the Chumash area. They regarded these Indians highly and assigned priests of a somewhat better quality than those found elsewhere in the system. In terms of rectitude of personal conduct, thoughtful pursuit of conversion among their charges, and mission administration, these priests distinguished themselves amongst their peers.[16] Moreover, the ratio of priests to Mission Indians stood at an impressively high level: at La Purísima 1:760 in 1804, at Santa Ynéz: 1:285 in 1806, and at Santa Barbara and San Buenaventura 1:510 and 1:788 respectively.[17] When these ratios are compared to the 1:800 that obtained in colonial Mexico,[18] the apparent advantage enjoyed by the missionaries in Alta California seems quite favorable.

Yet four long-standing difficulties negated the evangelical advantage and challenged the Franciscans to their limits. From the standpoint of the crown, Spanish missionary efforts in Alta California constituted the foundation of successful settlement, an effective hedge against the encroachment of foreign intrusion. Missionary work would prepare Indians to take their place as lower-class citizens in Spanish society. The crown envisioned a ten-year period from religious mission to secularized township or pueblo. In practice the ten-year plan failed as all missions remained religious congregations until a Mexican government ordered secularization in 1834.[19] Thus a tension arose between priests seeking the spiritual welfare of the Indians in their missions and the Spanish colonists who sought Indian labor.

A second difficulty, related to the first, arose from language. In 1795 the Spanish crown reaffirmed its traditional policy by again decreeing that native languages in the empire should be suppressed and that all instruction should be given in Spanish so that Indians might more quickly learn it.[20] This crown-mandated practice conflicted with a church-imposed requirement to teach Indians in their own languages.[21] In the Santa Barbara region six different dialects of Chumash prevailed and the priests had difficulty in communicating with neophytes in any but their native tongues. In the often cited *preguntas y respuestas* (questions and answers) to the famous *interrogatorio* (questionnaire) of 1811 posed to the priests at each of the missions,[22] the replies from the Chumash illustrate the point of contention. To the query whether or not the Indians knew Spanish the responses came:

> Some understand and speak Spanish. (Santa Ynéz) . . . The reason why they do not know it [Spanish] is their frequent communication and intercourse with their relatives and country men, both Christian and heathen. (Santa Barbara)[23]

The more instruction the priests gave in Spanish, the greater the risk of not reaching their charges; the more they worked to master the local dialects, the greater the separation of Indian from Spanish society.

The language issue, as the reply from Santa Barbara observed, related directly to culture. Christian conversion occurred in a milieu of struggle with Chumash culture, a struggle between family members and between converts at the missions and the gentiles in the villages removed from them. To succeed in this struggle against the old ways, the missionary needed the aid of sound "instruction, time, and apostolic patience."[24]

Fray José Señán, president of the missions at the time of the *interrogatorio*, described the spiritual status of the Indians in his charge in terms which typified all Chumash missions:

The son counts eighteen years as a Christian but the father is an obstinate savage still enamored of his brutal liberty and perpetual idleness. The granddaughter is a Christian but the grandmother is a pagan. Two brothers may be Christian but the sister stays in the mountains. A neophyte twenty years a Christian marries a woman but recently baptized. Such is the situation.[25]

Reports from other friars among the Chumash bore the president out. Fray Ramón Olbés at Santa Barbara wrote:

Every effort is being made to make them forget the ancient beliefs of paganism and this is done with even greater energy with regard to those who have become Christian at an advanced age despite the fact that there still exist among them those who induce them to carry on certain pagan practices and who are reputed to have the characteristics of the pagan state.[26]

At Santa Ynéz the old men and women still persisted in their "pagan superstitions." Before being baptized they had openly fixed feathers to a pole at places they designated sacred. They "cast seeds and beads" to insure their harvests. Since baptism ". . . these feathered poles have disappeared. If such an object however, is found in the country or open fields the devotees are careful to do in secret what they formerly conducted in a public manner."[27]

Native cultural patterns persisted inside the mission partly because of the long-standing need for the institution to be self-sufficient. Indian labor built the churches, *conventos*,[28] *monjerios*,[29] kitchens, shops, corrals, mills, water systems, tanning vats, soldiers' quarters—in short—all edifices. Indian labor sowed seed, then harvested, milled or ground, and cooked it. Indian labor tended flocks and herds, then sheared or butchered the stock, rendered tallow and tanned hides. Without Indian labor the mission could not survive; without Indian souls to save, the mission could not exist.

The struggle to achieve autarchy meant that the priests both made concessions to the neophytes to keep them attached and encouraged gentiles to enter the mission. With a fugitivism rate among converts of 10 percent throughout the system and with the highest posted at Santa Barbara of 15 percent,[30] the priests made such concessions as allowing Indians to visit their native villages, which permitted the Christianized to retain contact with their gentile families and friends. To offset losses occasioned by fugitivism and death, priests encouraged converts to invite others to explore the Christian life. Thus newcomers, undoubtedly including *ʔantap* cult members, entered the mission compound unrestricted. These people could and did retain old cult ritual and encouraged traditional Chumash behavior.

Even strategies to build mission populations in the Chumash area with Christianized Indians worked in favor of the *ʔantap* cult. By late 1804 too few Indians had been baptized at mission Santa Ynéz to sustain it, so the padres sent neophytes from the two closest missions. Within two years 132 Chumash had come from Santa Barbara and 145 from La Purísima.[31] Such practices provided the cover whereby shamen and members of the *ʔantap* could maintain contact, cult continuity, and influence.

An analogous situation existed among the island Chumash. Those seeking baptism went to the mainland, where they accepted the sacrament at their mission of choice. Their names have been recorded at all but San Luis Obispo. The new converts could elect either to remain at their baptismal mission or return to the island.[32] Many stayed on the mainland, and some of those shared their knowledge of how to construct the *tomol,* the Chumash seagoing canoe. In this way the village social structure and *ʔantap* cult could be preserved and reinforced on the mainland.[33]

CONFESIONARIOS

Lest this newfound appreciation of the vitality of the indigenous Chumash culture mislead the reader, it must be noted that new evidence brings new insight as well to the missionary attempt to uproot that culture. Confessional aids (*confesionarios*), bilingual guides in the native dialect and Spanish to aid the priest in confessing the sins of his charges, had been composed and used at nearly every mission. As a priest at La Purísima wrote the president of the missions in 1810:

> I believe I have written to your Reverence in these past years, that with the help of interpreters I have compiled a large catechism with the acts of Faith, Hope, and Charity, and another with what is necessary for salvation, a complete *confesionario,* and other little things, all in the language of the natives.[34]

Putting doctrine into native tongues in the form of a catechism bespoke what Europeans wanted Indians to learn. A *confesionario,* properly crafted, could tell the European how well the Indian practiced what he had learned or if he had learned it at all. A *confesionario,* more than any other single document, should indicate how deeply the priests could probe local society. But these documents were as private as they were ubiquitous. Only two *confesionarios* yet have been found, but they are singular. Composed approximately twenty years apart, both sought to elicit detailed information from Chumash confessants. More remarkable still, both reflect the intellectual odyssey of a single mind engaging in ongoing evangelization. These extraordinary documents, especially when considered within the sacramental framework of Penance and Easter Duty, provide new clues to the motives behind the Chumash revolt.

Inspiration for the Alta California *confesionarios* came from two principal sources: the decrees of the Provincial Councils of Lima in the sixteenth century and the practical experience of earlier missionaries in converting Indians in Mexico. As earlier alluded, missionaries had been exhorted by the church to evangelize in local Indian dialects. The Second Provincial Council of Lima, 1567, forbade the hearing of confession through an interpreter. In 1583 the Third Provincial Council went further and adjured priests to preach their sermons and to conduct all religious instruction in the language of those to be converted.[35] Hence, a conscientious confessor needed a phrase book to facilitate exhortation and confession.

The form of the phrase book evolved from European examples of how to confess a penitent and from Mexican aboriginal experience. The most common formula for confession involved talking the subject through the Ten Commandments. Traditionally, then, sins of idolatry would be confessed under the First Commandment, sexual transgressions under the Sixth and Ninth. In confessing Aztecs and others, early missionaries learned of the local importance Indians could attach to such things as dreams and the cry of the owl. They also learned to ask the familial relationship of sexual partners.[36]

In Alta California the first *confesionario* to have survived came from Mission Santa Barbara. In December 1798, Fray Juan Cortés wrote a guide in Spanish and Barbareño to aid in teaching and confessing the Indians. His *confesionario* followed the pattern of questioning by Commandment. Under the First, Cortés formulated questions to discover whether the confessed had scattered seeds in the field, believed in dreams, believed in the power of one who claimed to cure by the use of water or the acorn, believed in the owl?[37] Truthful responses to such questions could help determine *?antap* cult activity.

Questions regarding sexual activity reveal an awareness of the range of Chumash-tolerated sexual behavior. "Fornication, adultery, masturbation, sodomy, incest, and intercourse with animals are among the practices that appear in the Cortes *confesionario*."[38] Those questions came in response to examination for violations of the Sixth and Ninth Commandments. Queries about infanticide, abortion, and coitus interruptus came under the Fifth Commandment.

That Cortés, a priest new both to Alta California and to Mission Santa Barbara, could devise such a canny series of questions suggests that he had the assistance of a veteran counselor. That counselor appears to have been the remarkable Fray José Señán, a priest who served twice as president of the missions and who dedicated thirty-five years of his life to service in the Alta California missions.[39] Señán undoubtedly advised the younger Cortés to question his charges about ritual practices associated with the *?antap* cult and to inquire extensively about sexual practices. Señán, stationed at San Buenaventura, compiled information over the years to help himself in the same duties.

Within eight years of the Cortés *confesionario* a circular order arrived in Alta California imposing new duties regarding confession. On the first day of Lent missionaries were to give all neophytes special instructions about their annual confession and henceforth the priests at each mission would record on a "separate account" all who received the Sacraments of Penance or the Eucharist.[40] Annual Lenten confession, an ancient Roman Catholic tradition reaffirmed by the Council of Trent (1545–53),[41] constituted an indispensable part of the spiritual life of the faithful. Confession, the revealing of sins to a priest, especially the grave mortal sins, had to precede taking the Eucharist and the reception of both sacraments was required annually during the forty-day period before Easter known as Lent. Given the frequently staggering workload of the priests, it seemed unreasonable to require them to confess their charges more than once a year.

Over time, Fray Señán had observed and questioned the Indians in his area and he composed his own *confesionario* sometime between 1815 and 1819.[42] In it he went further than Cortés in questioning confessants and his deeper knowledge of the Chumash, gained over the intervening twenty years, clearly informed his queries. In keeping with convention, he patterned his guide to confess sins against the Ten Commandments. He exceeded the queries about scattering seeds, belief in dreams, and other matters he must have suggested to Cortés by asking pointedly about shamen and curers. He had learned the Chumash names for medicine man and good healer, even though he had contempt for them and could interpose the more contemptuous Chumash name if he so chose.[43] Under the Fifth Commandment he went beyond questions about abortion, infanticide, and birth control to ask if the confessant had ever become intoxicated on pespibata. In these two series of questions Señán revealed that he had learned to probe and to disturb Chumash religious life in the *?antap* cult, village life affected by shamen and curers, and personal life touching upon *datura* usage.

But in the realm of sexual conduct Señán rose to the role of ethnographer, asking questions that would have been the envy of Harrington. Not only did he ask the earlier questions about homosexual, heterosexual, sodomite, and animal sex, he asked marital status, blood relationship, and fictive kinship both direct and indirect of the sexual partners. In these questions confessing sins against the Sixth and Ninth Commandments, Señán probed and must have begun to disturb the Chumash sibling relationship. This virtually ideal ethnographer's questionnaire had not been crafted to gather information per se but to modify behavior. Eliciting answers to these questions gave the priest an ongoing view of the survivability of the culture undergoing the stress of conversion.

Organizing questions according to a European sense of order did not necessarily correspond to Indian experience. Hence, questions pertaining to religious practices, confessed under the First Commandment, imply a distinction between religious and social activities that the Chumash probably did not make, or at least did not make in the same way. Consequently, a cursory glance at the *confesionarios* of Señán and Cortés gives the impression that sexual irregularities more than religious backsliding absorbed the attention of the priests. That impression, undoubtedly caused by the practice of confessing sexual sins under the Sixth and Ninth Commandments combined, has led to the unfounded conclusion that religious backsliding was not a serious problem[44] or, conversely, that Chumash religion and culture had been virtually exterminated during the mission period. The significant revelation of the *confesionarios* is that Chumash culture remained vital but came under increasing Franciscan scrutiny and attack, especially after 1820. Over time, Señán and others must have come to realize that Chumash social behavior, particularly its sexual expression, undergirded the old society. The Lenten season, beginning on Ash Wednesday and ending on Easter Sunday, became an annual Franciscan probe of the indigenous culture, an annual inquisition that could only have intensified as years passed and Chumash converts began to change their behavior.

CULTURAL SURVIVAL STRUGGLE

Historical records provide only shadowy glimpses of the survival struggle of Chumash culture. In 1801, in the midst of a series of attacks of pneumonia and pleurisy which had struck the neophytes at Santa Barbara, an Indian woman who had used a native curer experienced a datura-induced vision. In it she encountered the Chumash earth goddess *Chupu*, who told her that all baptized Indians would die and only those would be spared who canceled their baptism by hand-washing with a water known as "tears of the sun." News of the vision spread, and Chumash from the islands to the interior came to see this woman and to propitiate Chupu. Three days elapsed before the priests discovered the movement and, by means unknown, but probably including public repudiation of the dream, they stopped it. Both the speed with which the movement spread and its secrecy alarmed the local priests.[46]

Both before and after the uprising, as one informant remembered, the Indians of Santa Barbara would:

> . . . secretly build little temples of sticks and brush, on which they hung bits of rag, cloth and other paraphernalia depositing on the inside tobacco [*pespibata*] and other articles used by them as presents to the unseen spirits. This was an occasion of great wrath to the padres who never failed to chastize the idolators *when detected.*[47]

The persistence of Chumash culture in the face of Christianization makes it nearly impossible, then, to accept the opinion of a priest at La Purísima in 1810 that worship of Chupu had been extirpated there.[48] Rotating Indians among the missions actually facilitated and reinforced cult survival.

Even as the friars deepened their probe of Indian daily life, external political events caused the Spanish to arm and organize the Indians militarily, making the uprising possible. In 1818 Hippolyte Bouchard, a privateer from Buenos Aires, threatened to invade the Alta California coast. He ultimately did so, but without serious effect. In response to his menacing behavior, enterprising priests in the Chumash area mobilized their neophytes to fight. No one undertook the task with greater vigor or effect than Fray Antonio Ripoll at Mission Santa Barbara. He organized and trained 180 Indians divided into an infantry composed of 100 archers, reinforced by fifty more carrying "chopping knives" and a cavalry of thirty lancers. Ripoll let them choose their corporals and sergeants, but he had the commanding officer at the presidio select the company commander. He called his force the "*Compañía de Urbanos Realistas de Santa Bárbara.*"[49] At La Purísima Fray Mariano Payeras organized a similar defense force of undetermined size and wrote feelingly to Governor Pablo Vicente de Solá, "It would cause me joy if you could see the preparation and enthusiasm of these Indians."[50]

These military preparations, envisioned by the priests as defensive, served as sound educational instruction for the Indians in the organization and tactics of European warfare. In their precontact state the Chumash hunted and occasionally fought in small bands. In response to Bouchard's threat they learned to mass and drill in larger units. Since the Chumash valued craftsmen and organized them into guilds in the missions, the guild for bow-maker, for example, must have become prominent after 1818.[51] Military organization superimposed upon mission organization provided new networks for preserving the old social structure and taught a new sense of power and the awareness of large group, collective action. Formal military training, added to the learning which could be obtained from watching the padres fire their mission cannons on significant feast days,[52] all permitted the Chumash to learn effective ways of resisting Spanish power militarily. This training coincided with the tightening of the European cultural noose through the confessional after 1820. In 1824 the largest uprising in mission history began on February 21, the day before Sexagesima Sunday and eleven days before Ash Wednesday, the beginning of Lent. The Chumash deferred another cycle of interrogation that year.

LEVANTAMIENTO!: FIGHT

Ostensibly, the sufficient cause of the uprising came from the flogging of a Purísima neophyte at Mission Santa Ynéz by order of the corporal of the guard, Valentin Cota.[53] The neophyte had come to visit a relative being held prisoner. In revenge Indians from both missions attacked the soldiers with bows and arrows at Santa Ynéz on Saturday afternoon February 21. In the skirmish the Indians lost two men, set a building afire, and continued to besiege the guard and a priest until a reinforcement of soldiers arrived the next day. Military augmentation forced the Indians to retreat to La Purísima.

At La Purísima Indians had risen the same afternoon and besieged the soldiers, who took refuge with their families and the two padres in a storeroom. Having exhausted their ammunition by the next day, the soldiers, through the priests, sought and secured a safe passage to Santa Ynéz. One priest who remained behind with the Indians was treated gently, but his undoubted blandishments to desist were ignored. The Indians dug themselves in for a siege by erecting "palisade fortifications" and cutting weapon slits in the adobe walls of the church and nearby buildings. They wheeled the ceremonial cannons into place to command a field of fire in front of the mission church and prepared to resist the expected Mexican counterattack. They had to wait a month.

The revolt had begun with deliberate, coordinated acts of violence at both Santa Ynéz and La Purísima. Revenge for the flogging may have been the only "legitimate" reason that the Europeans could discern for the attack, but it seems clear from the unfolding of events that the Indian conspirators envisioned a movement more of liberation than of vengeance. One of the major foci of the campaign would be the military engagement at La Purísima, an opportunity to display how well they had learned their military lessons. But they also sought to incorporate more Indians, both mission and non-mission, into their plans.

After attacking and burning at Santa Ynéz, the Indians sent a messenger to Santa Barbara to seek out, inform, and elicit the aid of the Chumash alcalde, Andrés.[54] A similar message was also sent to the alcalde at San Buenaventura, but that Indian turned the courier over immediately to the guard, who incarcerated him. Nothing further eventuated at San Buenaventura. But at Santa Barbara Andrés had other plans. Instead of seeking the guard, he went to Padre Antonio Ripoll, the man who had organized, equipped, and trained the Indian *Compañía de Urbanos Realista*. Andrés claimed that Ynézeños and Purismeños threatened him with death if he did not join them and he asked Ripoll to have the mission guard removed. Ripoll called together two other trusted neophytes who understood Spanish well, and he told them all not to fear. He then left the mission for the presidio to seek the presidio commander's written order to recall the mission guard.

Upon returning to the mission, Ripoll found the Indians assembled in their kitchen fully armed with bows, arrows, and "chopping knives" or machetes. Since he kept the weapons for the Compañía locked away,[55] only Andrés could have authorized their distribution. Ripoll seemingly ignored this fact and instead told the upset Indians that he had written orders for the guard to retire. With the Indians accompanying him, Ripoll presented the command to the guard. Indians further demanded that the soldiers leave their muskets and when two protested, they were slightly wounded by machete blows. Ripoll, acting as escort, accompanied the soldiers back to the presidio where the commander responded to the casualties by dispatching troops to the mission in a show of force.

Seeing the soldiers approach, the armed Indians "came out in force to confront the troops." The skirmish cost the soldiers four men with minor arrow wounds, and the Indians lost three dead and two wounded. For unexplained reasons the presidio force withdrew, leaving the Indians masters in the mission. The Chumash then entered the storeroom and Padre Ripoll's room where they took "everything in the shape of clothing and money," but, allegedly, nothing else. They closed and locked their quarters and the church, withdrew from the mission, and proceeded up the canyon behind the mission to a spot less than thirty miles away to await developments.

When the armed Chumash had departed, the soldiers returned to the mission environs and abused whatever old and decrepit Indians they could find. They managed to kill five Indians in their forays. Yet another detail came to the mission on Tuesday and systematically sacked both the Indians' quarters and Ripoll's room. Ripoll tried to control his sense of outrage at the soldiers' conduct and he maintained contact with the Indians in the hills through messages exchanged with Andrés by courier. Andrés convinced Ripoll that the Indians had left the mission solely as a consequence of the soldiers' mistreatment of them and that fear for their lives prevented their return. Ripoll's entreaties that the Indians return were defeated when Andrés had two Indian servants from the presidio inform the hiding Chumash that the soldiers intended to kill them all. With that news they fled farther into the interior to the *tulares* in the southern San Joaquin valley. The valued alcalde Andrés, in whom Ripoll had placed great trust, had deceived the padre. He conspired to attack the mission with a mixed force of gentiles and neophytes but, failing to secure sufficient support from nonmission Indians, Andrés took his people to the *tulares*.[56] While these Indians remained in the interior, the Mexican force, sent to punish the original insurgents, arrived at La Purísima.

Upon learning of the uprising and the Indian intention of fortifying La Purísima, the governor of Alta California ordered a force dispatched against them. A combined unit of 109 cavalry, infantry, and artillery with one four-pound cannon, all under the command of Lieutenant José María Estrada, arrived on the morning of March 16. Estrada deployed troops to prevent Indian retreat and prepared to confront the main body of defenders.[57] By then the Indian force had grown to over 400 including mission and nonmission Indians, some of the latter being Yokuts from the *tulares*.[58] When the soldiers came within range, the Indians began musket fire, followed by the discharge of the one pound ceremonial cannons, while they simultaneously let fly a volley of arrows. They could learn to load and fire the cannons by observation, but problems of range and trajectory could only be learned by the practice, which they lacked. Their cannon fire availed them nothing, while the Mexican cannon succeeded in shattering part of the adobe walls. Seeing themselves thwarted in an escape attempt, the Indians asked a priest to intercede. Fray Antonio Rodríguez, who had remained with the Indians from the beginning, negotiated their surrender. The Indians suffered sixteen dead and a large number wounded; the soldiers sustained three wounded, one of them fatally. The Mexicans tried and executed seven Indians for murder, condemned to ten years presidio labor and perpetual exile four leaders of the resistance, and sentenced eight more to eight years each of presidio labor. The attempt to test their newfound military prowess against their European teachers had failed, as had their attempt to coordinate a pan-Indian military resistance. The fight at La Purísima has been the basis for interpreting the uprising as a blow struck primarily against Mexican authority in Alta California.[59] What the Indians would have done had they prevailed cannot be known. But if the behavior of some of the Santa Barbara neophytes is indicative, then return to Chumash culture, with modifications, was an important goal. Evidence for this plan first emerged in the *tulares*.

Levantamiento!: Flight

Several Indians observed Chumash behavior under Andrés while they were all in the tulares. Five Indians representing four missions responded to questions about that conduct before an officer of the Santa Barbara presidio on June 1.[60] They all agreed that the neophytes did not pray. Four of them reported that gambling both in old Indian ways and with Hispanic playing cards, using money to wager, constituted the principal means of passing time both night and day. In matters of sexual mores these witnesses were particularly revealing. The Indian, his mission, and his observation follow:

> Zenen (Senen), La Purísima: that the married and single men lived all mixed up and did what they wished with all women, regardless of their marital [Christian] status.

Pelagio. San Fernando: That the married and single men, Christians and heathen, were living intermingled and were doing whatever they wished.

Alberto, San Gabriel: that when the Christians got to the valley they exchanged their women with those of the heathen without distinction of married or unmarried for they were all mixed up with one another.

Leopoldo, Santa Barbara: that the Christians exchanged their women with the heathen and vice versa, likewise the unmarried girls were all interchanged.

Fernando Huililiaset, Santa Barbara: that also he noticed the married couples consorting with one another, but no one knew who was married and who was not for they were all mixed up.[61]

The observations produced by this inquiry reveal the priests' concerns about prayer, idleness, and sexual activity of the neophytes away from their supervision. But from a Chumash standpoint, they partially reveal an attempt to reestablish a modified culture. The apparent abandoning of Christian prayer, the alteration of their old wagering games to include cards and Mexican money in the place of walnut-shell dice and strings of sea-shells, and the resumption of open sexual access among neophytes and gentiles, consistent with a restoration of the primacy of the sibling relationship, all speak to this new life.

That this behavior pattern had been planned seems congruent with the Indian reply to Padre Ripoll when he first asked them to return. "We shall maintain ourselves with what God will provide us in the open country. Moreover, we are soldiers, stonemasons, carpenters, etc., and we will provide for ourselves by our work."[62] In short, they had learned skills in the mission which they could apply to the environment if they so chose. For a large number of Santa Barbara neophytes, building a new life based upon the best of the old and the newly learned, constituted a major goal.

A window into this cultural revitalization is provided by the only known Chumash version of the revolt, an oral tradition related to Harrington by an Ynezeño woman.[63] In the account the revolt began with an act of deception committed by an Indian sacristan or page. He told the neophytes that they were to be punished by the priests and he told the priests that they were to be shot with arrows by the Indians on Sunday and so the priests did not hold mass. The Indians previously had used pespibata, the proxy for datura, clandestinely. Medicine men, shamen undoubtedly of the *ʔantap* cult, came forward and announced that the priests could not harm those protected with their magic. Some believed that the cannons would discharge only water or that musket fire would not penetrate their flesh. Magic made it possible for two armed Indians to enter the mission guardhouse through the keyhole. Another Indian and his horse disappeared in the grip of the soldier Valentin [Cota?] and both horse and rider reappeared on a hilltop beyond the solder's reach. Chumash practiced divination in a new way by cutting a sacred string in half and placing it on the ground in the form of a cross. An older method of divination by arrows continued. The story ended with the surrender of the Indians at La Purísima and the discovery of the sacristan's deception.[64]

Revitalization of the Chumash culture and the *ʔantap* cult, combining the Christian elements that suited them, and mobilized by fighting that permitted some to make a military stand and some to flee to the interior to create the new life, all characterized the 1824 uprising.

But if the governor of Alta California would not countenance a Chumash military stand at La Purísima, neither would he accept their flight to the *tulares*. After a first expedition had to turn back because of harsh weather, having accomplished nothing more than the killing of an unarmed, bound Indian prisoner, another larger force departed Santa Barbara for the interior on June 2.[65] Fray Vicente de Sarría, president of the missions and, at his direction, Padre Ripoll, both accompanied the column commanded by Captain Pablo de la Portilla. The Mexican force met with another in the interior, and together they numbered some 130 troops and two four-pound cannons. Portilla also brought a pardon from the governor. On June 10 the troops encountered runaway Indians commanded by a man called Jaime, who came out to confer with Portilla. With the assistance of Padres Sarría and Ripoll, the two negotiated a surrender, but on June 11 many of the Indians fled deeper into the *tulares* upon hearing a rumor that the military force would chastise them and the pardon was false. Jaime succeeded in reestablishing trust, and the neophytes who wished to return to the mission came over to the soldiers. Two days later the assembled group celebrated the feast of the Holy Trinity with Sunday Mass. Afterwards several of the neophytes informed the expedition commander that he needed to appoint new alcaldes since the authority of the old ones had expired during their absence from the mission. Captain Portilla then appointed three new alcaldes none of whom was the Andrés so valued by Ripoll.[66] During their stay in the *tulares* some of the Chumash lost faith in Andrés and set him aside when the soldiers appeared.

After appointing new Indian alcaldes, Portilla sent them out with a few soldiers to bring back more of the runaways. They met with mixed success. The main column began its return to Santa Barbara, while still leaving search parties out to bring back stragglers. The feast of Corpus Christi fell on the Thursday following Trinity Sunday and it found the major force still enroute. The Indians constructed an arbor in the wilderness and sang the Christian songs of praise and thanksgiving while Sarría and Ripoll celebrated the mass.[67] Those Chumash who wanted to return to the mission had acquiesced. Participation in two sung masses in the *tulares* in four days and acceptance of new alcaldes signified their renewed submission to the mission. But many others, perhaps nearly half the original mission population,[68] remained fugitive, pursuing the new life. Another group of approximately fifty neophytes, who had fled to Santa Cruz Island the night of February 22 in the two Santa Barbara mission canoes, could not sustain their flight. Scarcity of food probably caused them to begin to return to the mainland sometime after May 5,[69] and by June 28 only ten remained.[70] Some of those who returned quietly submitted to the mission while others did not.[71]

When the soldiers, padres, and contrite neophytes returned from the tulares to Santa Barbara on June 21, 1824, the Mexicans concluded their account of the revolt. From the Chumash perspective it was not yet finished. A group of neophytes, perhaps including Andrés, traveled deeper into the interior, well beyond the tulares, into a region of the Yokuts in what is now northeastern Kern County, and they settled in the vicinity of a mountain pass. They were discovered living there some ten years later by a North American trapping party. Zenas Leonard, a member of the trapping party led by Joseph Reddeford Walker whose name that pass now bears, left a brief but explicit account of those Indians.

Having spoken at length to the former mission Indians of Santa Barbara, he wrote that they:

> rebelled against the authority of the country; robbed the Church of all its golden images and candlesticks, and one of the priests of several thousand dollars in gold and silver, when they retreated to the spot we found them—being at least five or six hundred miles distant from the nearest Spanish settlement.[72]

Church images remained in the control of the chiefs according to Leonard, but in all likelihood the shamen of the ʔantap cult used them along with traditional Chumash artifacts to sustain their spiritual power and the life of the village.

These Chumash, at the time of Leonard's contact seven or eight hundred strong, had adopted some European-taught agricultural practices such as the planting and harvesting of corn, pumpkins, melons, and other foodstuffs. They also rode and bartered horses. Their spiritual and material culture represented a mixing of Spanish and Chumash in a place remote enough to permit it to grow.

They did not survive to be counted in the enumeration of 1850. A serious epidemic of malaria unleashed in the interior of California from 1830 to 1833, probably had been introduced to the Sacramento and San Joaquin valleys by fur trapping expeditions from the Great Plains. The Walker party was such an expedition, and it traversed those valleys in 1833. A debilitating illness to whites, malaria proved fatal to Indians. A careful student of the epidemic estimated that it reduced California Indian population by 75 percent from 1833 to 1846.[73] According to Leonard, the Walker expedition contacted the interior Chumash in April 1834 and spent one night among them. The next day Walker hired two Indians to guide them over the pass. Perhaps this visit introduced malaria to these Chumash and finally ended their resistance to the mission.

CONCLUSIONS

To Mexican authorities the most obvious lesson learned from the uprising was not to allow the Indians access to weapons. Accordingly, the president of the missions complied with the governor's request and dispatched a circular to all missions on July 22, 1824. Upon receipt of the order the priests at each mission were to surrender to the nearest presidio "all firearms, lances, and chopping knives."[74] The Indians had been disarmed. Padre Ripoll's trust and confidence in his neophytes to defend the mission had been betrayed. In the aftermath of violence that confidence had been irrevocably set aside by higher order. Ripoll returned to his tasks discouraged and sick at heart but not defeated.[75]

For the priests and the Indians who returned, there came a rededication to faith and to mission life. A separation of the old culture from the new one being created at the mission came to take hold and to grow. The old ways of the shamen and the *ʔantap* cult, as well as the primacy of the sibling bond, truly faded from the Christian environment after the revolt.[76] Instead of the principal friction point, the Lenten season became the principal focus of bonding between Indian and priest in the mission. Many years after the missions had been secularized and fallen into ruin, and eighty years after the uprising, a priest came to Santa Ynéz to minister to whatever slight congregation there might be. The Christmas season passed with few in attendance at mass. He expected nothing more for Easter. But just before Holy Week a sixty-seven-year-old Indian man presented himself and offered to act as server. Beginning with Holy Thursday Indians, in numbers previously unknown to the priest, began coming to the church for services. He heard confessions long into the night. By Easter Sunday Indians had gathered from the mountains, from across the mountains, from Lompoc and from part of Santa Barbara and they filled the church for mass.[77] The astonished priest had not expected such a celebration of Easter at the site of the 1824 uprising.

Why the Chumash chose 1824 to initiate their movement is a matter of speculation. It is known that a large comet became visible in the sky over southern California in December 1823 and persisted well into March 1824. After the first of the year it developed what appeared to be two tails. Comets held special significance for Chumash, for they believed that such fire in the sky foretold a new beginning, a sudden change. Such symbolism assumed greater meaning since it first appeared in December, the month the Chumash believed marked their own birth as a people.[78] Moreover, the year before, in December 1822, Fray Señán, whose confessional questions caused the Chumash much spiritual agony, became ill. He slowly declined and died in late summer 1823.[79] Taken together, these two powerful signs may have provided the impetus to rise at that time.

The revolt cannot be seen simply as an Indian protest against the abuses of the Mexican soldiers. Certainly those abuses contributed to resentment. But the uprising provided the Chumash a military umbrella under which individual Indians could choose to fight, as did those who came to La Purísima, or to flee, as did those who took canoes to Santa Cruz Island or those who followed Andrés into the tulares and even out to Walker Pass. Those who fled sought to create a new culture based on a fusion of Chumash and Christian religious symbols and relying on European agricultural and ranching skills. A Chumash cave painting in the San Emigdiano mountains has been found to contain a blue pigment of European origin, leading one archaeologist to date it from the 1824 revolt and flight.[80] The importance of the Christian artifacts to the Chumash deep in the interior helps to explain the kindliness with which they treated the priests during the uprising. To the Indians the priests were powerful, possibly in a shamanistic sense implying helper as well. Padre Rodríguez at La Purísima stayed with them there and aided, when it became necessary, in their surrender. At Santa Barbara they entreated the aged Padre Antonio Jayme to join them in flight but he declined.[81] Captain Portilla knew he needed the aid of the priests to bring in the Indians, and Sarria and Ripoll succeeded in bringing back those who wished to return. The Chumash chose military targets to fight and religious targets to assist them in their quest for a new beginning.

The combination of rich ethnographic information from Harrington recently made available, combined with the detailed insights yielded by the confesionarios, provides a unique dual perspective on the complex 1824 Levantamiento! This study suggests that a search of mission, Mexican and Spanish, archives for additional confesionarios may prove fruitful for further research. Examples of confessional aids from other areas, such as Salinan or Coastanoan, or from the same Indian groups such as Gabrileno or Luiseno, might enhance our understanding of the Franciscan efforts to Christianize California's aboriginal inhabitants. An any rate, it should be clear from this reexamination of the 1824 uprising that, in the Chumash area at least, missionization conquered native culture only among those who genuinely converted.

NOTES

1. Hubert H. Bancroft, *History of California* (San Francisco: The History Company Publishers, 1886–90), II: 527–38. Zephyrin Engelhardt, O.F.M., *The Missions and Missionaries of California*, Vol. III: *Upper California*, Part II: *General History* (4 vols., San Francisco: The James H. Barry Company, 1913), 194–212.

2. The most recent attempt at reassessing the 1824 revolt came before the Harrington material became generally available. E. Gary Stickel and Adrienne E. Cooper, "The Chumash Revolt of 1824: A Case of Archaeological Application of Feedback Theory," *University of California Archaeological Survey Annual Report*, Vol. XI (Berkeley, 1969), 5–21.

3. Travis Hudson and Thomas C. Blackburn, *The Material Culture of the Chumash Interaction Sphere*, V Vols. projected, III published, Vol. I: *Food Procurement and Transportation*, Vol. II: *Food Preparation and Shelter*, Vol. III: *Clothing, Ornamentation, and Grooming*, Ballena Press Anthropological Papers #25, 27, 28 (Los Altos and Santa Barbara, Calif.: Ballena Press/Santa Barbara Museum of Natural History, 1979, 1981, 1985).

4. Chester King, "Chumash Inter-Village Economic Exchange," *The Indian Historian*, IV (Spring 1971), 30–43.

5. Thomas C. Blackburn, *December's Child: A Book of Chumash Oral Narratives Collected by J. P. Harrington* (Berkeley: University of California Press, 1975).

6. Travis Hudson and Ernest Underhay, *Crystals in the Sky: An Intellectual Odyssey Involving Chumash Astronomy, Cosmotology and Rock Art*, in *Ballena Press Anthropological Papers*, number 10 (Scorro, N.M., and Santa Barbara, Calif.: Ballena Press/Santa Barbara Museum of Natural History, 1978). See also Number 8 in the series of by Jane MacLaren Walsh, *John Peabody Harrington: The Man and His California Indian Fieldnotes* (1976).

7. Travis Hudson, Thomas Blackburn, Rosario Curletti, and Janice Timebrook, eds., *The Eye of the Flute: Chumash Traditional History and Ritual as Told by Fernando Librado "Kitsepawit" to John P. Harrington* (2nd ed.: Banning and Santa Barbara, Calif.: Malki Museum Press/Santa Barbara Museum of Natural History, 1981). Richard B. Applegate also drew upon Harrington's materials for his important article, "The Datura Cult Among the Chumash," *The Journal of California Anthropology*, II (Summer 1975), 7–17.

8. The picture of Chumash village life is drawn, *inter alia*, from, Blackburn, *December's Child*, 8–88: Applegate, "The Datura Cult Among the Chumash," 7–17; King, "Chumash Inter-Village Economic Exchange," 34–35; Campbell Grant, "Eastern Coastal Chumash," in *The Handbook of North American Indians*, VIII: *California*, Robert F. Heizer, ed. (Washington, D.C., Smithsonian Institution, 1978), 509–519 (hereafter cited as *HBNAI*, VIII); R. F. Heizer, ed., *California Indian Linguistic Records: The Mission Indian Vocabularies of H. W. Henshaw*, in *Anthropological Records*, XV (Berkeley: University of California Press, 1955), 152, n. 23.

9. Although the Spanish word is masculine, it is used in the plural as an inclusive term that can and did describe women.

10. Lesley Byrd Simpson, trans. and ed., *Journal of José Longinos Martínez: Notes and Observations of the Naturalist of the Botanical Expedition in Old and New California and the South Coast, 1791–1792* (2nd ed.: San Francisco: John Howell Books, 1961), 56.

11. Grant, "The Eastern Chumash," 513.

12. Hudson et al., *The Eye of the Flute,* 86.

13. Ibid., 88–90.

14. Bruce W. Barton, *The Tree at the Center of the World: A Story of the California Missions* (Santa Barbara: Ross Erickson, 1980), 78–259.

15. Edith Buckland Webb, *Indian Life at the Old Missions* (Lincoln: University of Nebraska Press, 1982; reprint of 1952 ed.), passim; Woodrow W. Borah, "The California Mission," *Ethnic Conflict in California History,* ed. by Charles Wollenberg (Los Angeles: Toinnon-Brown, Inc., 1970), 3–16.

16. My assessment is based upon reading Maynard Geiger, O.F.M., *Franciscan Missionaries in Hispanic California, 1764–1848: A Biographical Dictionary* (San Marino, Calif.: Huntington Library, 1969). Spanish high regard for the Chumash was noted by A. L. Kroeber in 1925 as cited in Heizer, *California Indian Linguistic Records,* 149.

17. Ratios are based upon two priests per mission against (a) the peak population of mission Indians at La Purísima and Santa Ynéz from Roberta S. Greenwood, "Obispeño and Purisímeño Chumash," *HBNAI,* VIII: 52; Grant, "Eastern Coastal Chumash," ibid., 518; and (b) mean annual population 1783–1834 at Santa Barbara and San Buenaventura from a calculation based upon Sherburne F. Cook, *The Conflict Between the California Indian and White Civilization* (Berkeley: University of California Press, 1976), 37, Table 2.

18. Antonine Tibesar, O.F.M., "The Shortage of Priests in Latin America: A Historical Eva-luation of Werner Promper's *Priesternot in Latinamerika,*" *The Americas,* XXII (April 1966), 413.

19. Governor Diego de Borica to Pedro de Alberni, Monterey, August 3, 1796, cited in Francis F. Guest, O.F.M., "An Examination of the Thesis of S.F. Cook on the Forced Conversion of Indians in the California Missions," *Southern California Quarterly,* LXI (Spring 1979), 16.

20. Cook, *The Conflict Between the California Indian and White Civilization,* 143, n. 10; Barton, *The Tree at the Center of the Earth,* 260.

21. Webb, *Indian Life at the Old Missions,* 48.

22. The *interrogatorio* did not reach California until late summer 1813. The first reply came from Santa Barbara, December 31, 1813, and the last from the president of the missions, resident at San Buenaventura, August 11, 1815. Within the Chumash area the replies from La Purisima have been lost. In the opinion of the translator of these *preguntas y respuestas,* Maynard Geiger, O.F.M., the president of the missions never sent the completed interragatorio back. Geiger's search in the archives of Spain and Mexico failed to discover any copies suggesting that the material in the archive at Santa Barbara constitutes the original. It has all been published. Maynard Geiger, O.F.M., and Clement W. Meighan, eds., *As the Padres Saw Them: California Indian Life and Customs as Reported by the Franciscan Missionaries, 1813–1815.* (Santa Barbara: Santa Barbara Mission Archive Library, 1976).

23. Cook. *The Conflict Between the California Indian and White Civilization,* 143–44.

24. Fray José Señán cited in Geiger and Meighan, *As the Padres Saw Them,* 48.

25. Ibid., 61.

26. Ibid., 48.

27. Ibid.

28. Private quarters of the priests adjoining the church. Kurt Bauer, *Architecture of the California Missions* (Berkeley: University of California Press, 1958), 40.

29. Rooms where the unmarried women were kept under lock at night. Webb, *Indian Life at the Old Missions,* 27–29.

30. Cook, *The Conflict Between the California Indian and White Civilization,* 61 and Table 4.

31. Grant, "Eastern Coastal Chumash," *HBNAI,* VII, 518.

32. Campbell Grant, "Island Chumash," Ibid., 526.

33. See, for example, the case of José Sudón, cited in Dee Travis Hudson, "Chumash Canoes of Mission Santa Barbara: The Revolt of 1824," *The Journal of California Anthropology,* III (Winter 1976), 5–15.

34. Fray Mariano Payeras to Fray Estevan Tapis cited in Webb, *Indian Life at the Old Missions,* 48.

35. Zephyrin Engelhardt, O.F.M., *The Missions and Missionaries of California,* III: 608–611.

36. See, for example, Marcos de Saavedra, *Confesionario breve, activo y pasivo, en lengua mexicana . . .* (n.p., n.d., Reimpreso en México, 1746); Alonso de Molina, *Confesionario major en la lengua mexicana y castellana*

(1569, Mexico: Melchoir Ocharte, 1599); Juan Bautista, *Confesionario en lengua mexiciana y castellana con muchas advertencias muy necesarias para los confesores* (N.P., 1599), all in the Bancroft Library (hereafter cited as BL).

37. Harry Kelsey, ed., *The Doctorina and Confesionario of Juan Cortes* (Altadena, Calif.: Howling Coyote Press, 1979), 100, 120.

38. Ibid., 9.

39. Geiger, *Franciscan Missionaries in Hispanic California*, 235–39. Kelsey, *The Doctrina and Confesionario of Juan Cortés*, 11.

40. Englehardt, *The Missions and Missionaries of California* (2nd ed., rev.; Santa Barbara: Santa Barbara Mission, 1930), II: 646–47, 651.

41. H. J. Schroeder, O.P., trans., *Canons and Decrees of the Council of Trent* (St. Louis and London: B. Herder Book Company, 1941), 94. *The Catholic Encyclopedia* (New York: The Encyclopedia Press, Inc., 1908), IV: 426 and IX: 18 indicate that the practice antedated both the Councils of Trent and the 4th Lateran (1215), each of which affirmed the custom.

42. Madison S. Beeler, ed., *The Ventureno Confesionario of José Señán, O.F. M.*, in *University of Californian Publications in Linguistics*, no. 47 (Berkeley and Los Angles: University of California Press, 1967), 4.

43. Ibid., 27 and passim.

44. Kelsey, *The Doctrina and Confesionario of Juan Cortés*, 9, writes, "The *confesionario* seems not to place much importance on these practices [pagan religion], perhaps because backsliding was not a great problem at Santa Barbara."

45. For example, Campbell Grant, "Chumash: Introduction," *HBNAI*, VIII: 507.

46. Fray Estevan Tapis to José Joaquín Arrillaga, Governor of Alta California, March, 1, 1805, cited in Robert F. Heizer, "A California Messianic Movement of 1801 Among the Chumash," *American Anthropologist*, XLIII (January–March 1941), 128–29; Hudson and Underhay, *Crystals in the Sky*, 21–22, 72.

47. Arthur Woodward, "An Early Account of the Chumash," *The Masterkey*, VIII (July 1934), 118–23, quotation on 122, my emphasis.

48. A. L. Kroeber, *Handbook of the Indians of California*, 567, cited in Heizer, "A California Messianic Movement of 1801 Among the Chumash," 128, *n.* 3.

49. Zephyrin Engelhardt, O.F.M., *Santa Barbara Mission* (San Francisco: James H. Barry Company, 1923), 118–20; Maynard Geiger, O.F.M., *Mission Santa Barbara, 1782–1965* (Santa Barbara: Kimberly Litho, 1965), 80–84.

50. As translated and cited by Francis F. Guest, O.F.M., "Cultural Perspectives on California Mission Life," *Southern California Quarterly*, LXV (Spring 1983), 44–45.

51. Hudson and Blackburn, *The Material Culture of the Chumash Interaction Sphere*, I: 26.

52. Juan B. Alvarado, *History of California* (1876), trans. by Earl R. Hewitt, 44, BL.

53. The account is drawn from Bancroft, *History of California*, II: 527–38, and corrected by Engelhardt, *The Missions and Missionaries of California*, III: 194–212. Additional notes augment, clarify, or correct these texts.

54. Either Andrés Corsino Guilahuich or André Uichaja. See Maynard Geiger, O.F.M., ed. and trans., "Fray Antonio Ripoll's Description of the Chumash Revolt at Santa Barbara in 1824," *Southern California Quarterly*, LII (December 1970), 360, *n.* 21. This is the best single account of the uprising at Santa Barbara, but is incomplete. Unless otherwise cited all references to Ripoll's activity are from this source.

55. Engelhardt, *Mission Santa Barbara*, 120.

56. Testimony of Indian Alberto from San Gabriel mission, translated and cited by S.F. Cook, *Expeditions to the Interior of California: Central Valley, 1820–1840*, in *Anthropological Records*, vol. 20 (Berkeley: University of California Press, 1962), 153.

57. Englehardt, *Missions and Missionaries of California*, III: 203–204; Bancroft, *History of California*, II: 531–32.

58. Fray Juan Cabot to Governor Luis Antonio Argüello, February 28, 1824, in Cook, *Expeditions to the Interior of California*, 152.

59. For example, Alvarado, *History of California*, 43; Antonio María Osio, *Historia de la California 1815–1848*, n.d., Mss, copy made for Hubert Howe Bancroft, 1878, passim; José de Jesús Vallejo, *Reminiscencias Historicas de California*, dictated to Enrique Cerruti for Hubert Howe Bancroft, 1874, p. 82ff., all in BL.

60. Interrogatoria, Santa Barbara, June 1, 1824, in Cook, *Expeditions to the Interior of California*, 153–54.

61. Ibid.

62. Geiger, "Fray Antonio Ripoll's Description of the Chumash Revolt at Santa Barbara in 1824," 352.

63. Thomas Blackburn, "The Chumash Revolt of 1824: A Native Account," *The Journal of California Anthropology,* II (Winter 1975), 223–27.

64. Hudson and Underhay, *Crystals in the Sky,* 22.

65. The account is based upon Pablo de la Portilla, "Report of the expedition to the tulares in pursuit of the rebel mission Indians," June 27, 1824, in Cook, *Expeditions to the Interior of California,* 154–56; Bancroft, *History of California,* II: 533–36; Engelhardt, *Missions and Missionaries of California,* III: 205–207.

66. Portilla gives as the name of the alcalde Andrés Seugmatose, Cook, *Expeditions to the Interior of California,* 155, neither of the names for Andrés posited by Geiger in *note 54 supra.*

67. José Rafael Gonzales, "Experiences [*sic*] de un soldado de California," Cook, *Expeditions to the Interior of California,* 157.

68. Pablo de la Portilla to Luís Antonia Argüello, June 27, 1824, in ibid., 156–57. See also Cook, *The Conflict Between the California Indian and White Civilization,* 60, Table 3.

69. Geiger, "Fray Antonio Ripoll's Description of the Chumash Revolt at Santa Barbara in 1824," 357.

70. Pablo de la Portilla to Luís Antonio Argüello, June 28, 1824, in Cook, *Expeditions to the Interior of California,* 157.

71. Hudson, "Chumash Canoes of Mission Santa Barbara: The Revolt of 1824," 13–14.

72. John C. Ewers, ed., *Adventures of Zenas Leonard Fur Trader* (Norman: University of Oklahoma Press, 1959), ix, 121–23 , quotation at 122.

73. S. F. Cook, *The Epidemic of 1830–1833 in California and Oregon,* in *University of California Publications in American Archaeology and Ethnology,* vol. XLIII (Berkeley: University of California Press, 1955), 303–326.

74. Circular from Vicente de Sarría, July 22, 1824, Archivo De Arzobispado de San Francisco, Tomo IV, parte 2, copy in BL.

75. Engelhardt, *The Missions and Missionaries of California,* III: 205–206; Geiger, *Franciscan Missionaries in Hispanic California,* 207–208.

76. Hudson and Underhay, *Crystals in the Sky,* 22.

77. Mamie Gulet Abbot, *Santa Ines Hermosa: The Journal of the Padre's Niece* (2nd ed.; Montecito, Calif.: Sunwise Press, 1951), 72–79.

78. Gerónimo Boscana, *Chinigchinich,* a revised and annotated version of Alfred Robinson's trans., annotations by John P. Harrington (Banning, Calif.: Malki Museum Press, 1978), 89; 226, *n.* 246; Hudson and Underhay, *Crystals in the Sky,* 99–100, 128, Table 2.

79. Fray Marcos Antonio de Vitoria to Prelate Fray Agustín Garijo, August 24, 1823, in *The Letters of José Señán, O.F.M.: Mission San Buenaventura, 1796–1823,* Paul D. Nathan, trans., and Lesley Byrd Simpson, ed. (San Francisco: John Howell Books, 1962), 171.

80. "Post Modernism, CA. 1824," *California,* X (July 1985), 76–77.

81. Geiger, "Fray Antonio Ripoll's Description of the Chumash Revolt at Santa Barbara in 1824," 350.

24

Theda Perdue

The U.S. government's campaign in the 1830s to move Indians in the East to a region beyond the Mississippi River then known as "Indian Territory" (located mostly in modern-day Kansas and Oklahoma) remains one of the darkest chapters in American history. Lands occupied by the native peoples of the southeast had not only been owned by the Cherokees, Choctaws, Creeks, Chickasaws, and Seminoles since ancient times; those lands had also been recognized by treaties between native leaders and the United States, agreements that possessed a status equal in law to the United States Constitution itself. Now, forced, often fraudulent new agreements, with a guise of legality and diplomacy, terminated native ownership of this vast region. Moreover, one of those agreements, the 1835 "treaty" of New Echota, led to the "trail of tears," in which disease, hunger, and exposure killed perhaps one-third of the Cherokees. This period of removal, which the historian John Farragher has recently likened to a campaign of "ethnic cleansing," forever changed the racial composition of eastern North America.

The changes wrought by Removal obviously had a deep impact on the native peoples who made, and survived, the migration. But, as Theda Perdue notes here (echoing William McLoughlin's essay on Cherokee anomie), changes in gender relations among the Cherokees had begun before that fateful, tragic era. Those changes suggest the far-reaching alterations in native communities in the years following the American Revolution, changes that continued to shape relationships between Indian men and women well beyond the 1840s.

Perdue's essay suggests that the gender frontier found in earlier times persisted in early nineteenth-century America. Her treatment of the shifting set of ideas about gender among the Cherokees can be compared to gender-related issues among the Indians of Illinois, discussed by Raymond Hauser, and the St. Lawrence Valley, described by Natalie Zemon Davis.

CHEROKEE WOMEN AND THE TRAIL OF TEARS

Theda Perdue

ONE HUNDRED AND FIFTY YEARS AGO, in 1839, the United States forced the Cherokee Nation west of the Mississippi River to what later would become the state of Oklahoma. The Cherokees primarily occupied territory in the Southeast that included north Georgia, northeastern Alabama, southeastern Tennessee, and southwestern North Carolina. In the three decades preceding removal, they experienced a cultural transformation. Relinquishing ancient beliefs and customs, the leaders of the Nation sought to make their people culturally indistinguishable from their white neighbors in the hope that through assimilation they could retain their ancestral homeland. White land hunger and racism proved too powerful, however, and the states in which the Cherokees lived, particularly Georgia, demanded that the federal government extinguish the Indians' title and eject them from the chartered boundaries of the states. The election of Andrew Jackson in 1828 strengthened the states' cause.

While President Jackson promoted the policy of removing eastern Indians to the west, he did not originate the idea. Thomas Jefferson first suggested that removal beyond the evils of "civilization" would benefit the Indians and provide a justification for his purchase of Louisiana. In 1808–10 and again in 1817–19, members of the Cherokee Nation migrated to the west as the Cherokee land base shrank. But the major impetus for total removal came in 1830 when Congress, at the urging of President Jackson, passed the Indian Removal Act, which authorized the President to negotiate cessions of Indian land in the east and transportation of native peoples west of the Mississippi. Although other Indian Nations such as the Choctaws signed removal treaties right away, the Cherokees refused. The Nations's leaders retained legal counsel and took its case against repressive state legislation to the United States Supreme Court (*Cherokee Nation v. Georgia*, 5 Peters 1). The Cherokee Nation won, however, on the grounds that the Cherokees constituted a "domestic dependent" nation—not a foreign state under the U.S. Constitution. The state's failure to respond to the decision and the federal government's refusal to enforce it prompted an unauthorized Cherokee faction to

SOURCE: *Journal of Women's History* 1:1 (1989), 14–30.

negotiate removal. In December 1835, these disaffected men signed the Treaty of New Echota by which they exchanged the Cherokee Nation's territory in the southeast for land in the west. The United States Senate ratified the treaty, and in the summer of 1838, soldiers began to round up Cherokees for deportation. Ultimately, the Cherokees were permitted to delay until fall and to manage their own removal, but this leniency did little to ameliorate the experience the Cherokees called the "trail of tears." The weather was unusually harsh that winter; cold, disease, hunger, and exhaustion claimed the lives of at least 4,000 of the 15,000 people who traveled the thousand miles to the west.[1]

The details of Cherokee removal have been recounted many times by scholars and popular writers. The focus of these accounts has tended to be political: they have dealt primarily with the United States' removal policy, the negotiation of removal treaties, and the political factionalism that the removal issue created within Cherokee society. In other words, the role of men in this event has dominated historical analysis. Yet women also were involved. In the sesquicentennial year of the Cherokees' arrival in the West and on the occasion of the inaugural issue of the *Journal of Women's History*, it seems appropriate to reexamine the "trail of tears" using gender as a category of analysis. In particular, what role did women play in removal? How did they regard the policy? Did their views differ from those of men? How did the removal affect women? What were their experiences along the "trail of tears"? How did they go about reestablishing their lives in their new homes in the West? How does this kind of analysis amplify or alter our understanding of the event?

THE TREATY OF NEW ECHOTA by which the Cherokee Nation relinquished its territory in the Southeast was signed by men.[2] Women were present at the rump council that negotiated the treaty, but they did not participate in the proceedings. They may have met in their own council—precedents for women's councils exist—but if they did, no record remains. Instead, they probably cooked meals and cared for children while their husbands discussed treaty terms with the United States commissioner. The failure of women to join in the negotiation and signing of the Treaty of New Echota does not necessarily mean that women were not interested in the disposition of tribal land, but it does indicate that the role of women had changed dramatically in the preceding century.

Traditionally, women had a voice in Cherokee government.[3] They spoke freely in council, and the War Woman (or Beloved Woman) decided the fate of captives. As late as 1787, a Cherokee woman wrote Benjamin Franklin that she had delivered an address to her people urging them to maintain peace with the new American nation. She had filled the peace pipe for the warriors, and she enclosed some of the same tobacco for the United States Congress in order to unite symbolically her people and his in peace. She continued:

> I am in hopes that if you Rightly consider that woman is the mother of All—and the Woman does not pull Children out of Trees or Stumps nor out of old Logs, but out of their Bodies, so that they ought to mind what a woman says.[4]

The political influence of women, therefore, rested at least in part on their maternal biological role in procreation and their maternal role in Cherokee society, which assumed particular importance in the Cherokee's matrilineal kinship system. In this way of reckoning kin, children belonged to the clan of their mother and their only relatives were those who could be traced through her.[5]

The Cherokees were not only matrilineal, they also were matrilocal. That is, a man lived with his wife in a house that belonged to her, or perhaps more accurately, to her family. According to the naturalist William Bartram, "Marriage gives no right to the husband over the property of his wife; and when they part she keeps the children and property belonging to them."[6] The "property" that women kept included agricultural produce—corn, squash, beans, sunflowers, and pumpkins—stored in the household's crib. Produce belonged to women because they were the principal farmers. This economic role was ritualized at the Green Corn Ceremony every summer when an old woman presented the new corn crop. Furthermore, eighteenth-century travelers and traders normally purchased corn from women instead of men, and in the 1750s the garrison at Fort Loudoun, in present-day eastern Tennessee, actually employed a female purchasing agent to procure corn.[7] Similarly, the fields belonged to the women who tended them, or rather to the women's lineages. Bartram observed that "their fields are divided by proper marks and their harvest is gathered separately."[8] While the Cherokees technically held land in common and anyone could use unoccupied land, improved fields belonged to specific matrilineal households.

Perhaps this explains why women signed early deeds conveying land titles to the Proprietors of Carolina. Agents who made these transactions offered little explanation for the signatures of women on these documents. In the early twentieth century, a historian speculated that they represented a "renunciation of dower," but it may have been that the women were simply parting with what was recognized as theirs, or they may have been representing their lineages in the negotiations.[9]

As late as 1785, women still played some role in the negotiation of land transactions. Nancy Ward, the Beloved Woman of Chota, spoke to the treaty conference held at Hopewell, South Carolina, to clarify and extend land cessions stemming from Cherokee support of the British in the American Revolution. She addressed the assembly as the "mother of warriors" and promoted a peaceful resolution to land disputes between the Cherokees and the United States. Under the terms of the Treaty of Hopewell, the Cherokees ceded large tracts of land south of the Cumberland River in Tennessee and Kentucky and west of the Blue Ridge Mountains in North Carolina. Nancy Ward and the other Cherokee delegates to the conference agreed to the cession not because they believed it to be just but because the United States dictated the terms of the treaty.[10]

The conference at Hopewell was the last treaty negotiation in which women played an official role, and Nancy Ward's participation in that conference was somewhat anachronistic. In the eighteenth century, the English as well as other Europeans had dealt politically and commercially with men since men were the hunters and warriors in Cherokee society and Europeans were interested primarily in military alliances and deerskins. As relations with the English grew increasingly important to tribal welfare, women became less significant in the Cherokee economy and government. Conditions in the Cherokee Nation following the American Revolution accelerated the trend. In their defeat, the Cherokees had to cope with the destruction of villages, fields, corn cribs, and orchards that had occurred during the war and the cession of hunting grounds that accompanied the peace. In desperation, they turned to the United States government, which proposed to convert the Cherokees into replicas of white pioneer farmers in the anticipation that they would then cede additional territory (presumably hunting grounds they no longer needed).[11] While the government's so-called civilization program brought some economic relief, it also helped produce a transformation of gender roles and social organization. The society envisioned for the Cherokees, one which government agents and Protestant missionaries zealously tried to implement, was one in which a man farmed and headed a household composed only of his wife and children. The men who gained power in eighteenth-century Cherokee society—hunters, warriors, and descendants of traders—took immediate advantage of this program in order to maintain their status in the face of a declining deerskin trade and pacification, and then diverted their energy, ambition, and aggression into economic channels. As agriculture became more commercially viable, these men began to farm or to acquire African slaves to cultivate their fields for them. They also began to dominate Cherokee society, and by example and legislation, they altered fundamental relationships.[12]

In 1808, a Council of headmen (there is no evidence of women participating) from Cherokee towns established a national police force to safeguard a person's holdings during life and "to give protection to children as heirs to their father's property, and to the widow's share," thereby changing inheritance patterns and officially recognizing the patriarchal family as the norm. Two years later, a council representing all seven matrilineal clans, but once again apparently including no women, abolished the practice of blood vengeance. This action ended one of the major functions of clans and shifted the responsibility for punishing wrongdoers to the national police force and tribal courts. Matrilineal kinship clearly did not have a place in the new Cherokee order.[13]

We have no record of women objecting to such legislation. In fact, we know very little about most Cherokee women because written documents reflect the attitudes and concerns of a male Indian elite or of government agents and missionaries. The only women about whom we know very much are those who conformed to expectations. Nancy Ward, the Beloved Woman who favored peace with the United States, appears in the historical records while other less cooperative Beloved Women are merely unnamed, shadowy figures. Women such as Catherine Brown, a model of Christian virtue, gained the admiration of missionaries, and we have a memoir of Brown's life; other women who removed their children from mission schools incurred the missionaries' wrath, and they merit only brief mention in mission diaries. The comments of government agents usually focused on those native women who demonstrated considerable industry by raising cotton and producing cloth (in this case, Indian men suffered by comparison), not those who grew corn in the matrilineage's fields.[14] In addition to being biased and reflecting only one segment of the female population, the information from these sources is second-hand; rarely did Indian women, particularly traditionalists, speak for themselves.

The one subject on which women did speak on two occasions was land. In 1817 the United States sought a large cession of Cherokee territory and removal of those who lived on the land in question. A group of Indian women met in their own council, and thirteen of them signed a message which was delivered to the National Council. They advised the Council:

> The Cherokee ladys now being present at the meeting of the Chiefs and warriors in council have thought it their duties as mothers to address their beloved Chiefs and warriors now assembled.
>
> Our beloved children and head men of the Cherokee nation we address you warriors in council[. W]e have raised all of you on the land which we now have, which God gave us to inhabit and raise provisions[. W]e know that our country has once been extensive but by repeated sales has become circumscribed to a small tract and never have thought it our duty to interfere in the disposition of it till now, if a father or mother was to sell all their lands which they had to depend on[,] which their children had to raise their living on[,] which would be bad indeed and to be removed to another country[. W]e do not wish to go to an unknown country which we have understood some of our children wish to go over the Mississippi but this act of our children would be like destroying your mothers. Your mother and sisters ask and beg of you not to part with any more of our lands.[15]

The next year, the National Council met again to discuss the possibility of allotting Cherokee land to individuals, an action the United States government encouraged as a preliminary step to removal. Once again, Cherokee women reacted:

> We have heard with painful feelings that the bounds of the land we now possess are to be drawn into very narrow limits. The land was given to us by the Great Spirit above as our common right, to raise our children upon, & to make support for our rising generations. We therefore humbly petition our beloved children, the head men and warriors, to hold out to the last in support of our common rights, as the Cherokee nation have been the first settlers of this land; we therefore claim the right of the soil. . . . We therefore unanimously join in our meeting to hold our country in common as hitherto.[16]

Common ownership of land meant in theory that the United States government had to obtain cessions from recognized, elected Cherokee officials who represented the wishes of the people. Many whites favored allotment because private citizens then could obtain individually owned tracts of land through purchase, fraud, or seizure. Most Cherokees recognized this danger and objected to allotment for that reason. The women, however, had an additional incentive for opposing allotment. Under the laws of the states in which the Cherokees lived and of which they would become citizens if land were allotted, married women had few property rights. A married woman's property, even property she held prior to her marriage, belonged legally to her husband.[17] Cherokee women and matrilineal households would have ceased to be property owners.

The implications for women became apparent in the 1830s, when Georgia claimed its law was in effect in the Cherokee country. Conflicts over property arose because of uncertainty over which legal system prevailed. For example, a white man, James Vaught, married the Cherokee Catherine Gunter. She inherited several slaves from her father, and Vaught sold two of them to General Isaac Wellborn. His wife had not consented to the sale and so she reclaimed her property and took them with her when the family moved west. General Wellborn tried to seize the slaves just as they were about to embark, but a soldier, apparently recognizing her claim under Cherokee law, prevented him from doing so. After removal, the General appealed to Principal Chief John Ross for aid in recovering the slaves, but Ross refused. He informed Wellborn: "By the laws of the Cherokee Nation, the property of husband and wife remain separate and apart and neither of these can sell or dispose of the property of the other." Had the Cherokees accepted allotment and come under Georgia law, Wellborn would have won.[18]

The effects of the women's protests in 1817 and 1818 are difficult to determine. In 1817 the Cherokees ceded tracts of land in Georgia, Alabama, and Tennessee, and in 1819 they made an even larger cession. Nevertheless, they rejected individual allotments and strengthened restrictions on alienation of improvements. Furthermore, the Cherokee Nation gave notice that they would negotiate no additional cessions— a resolution so strongly supported that the United States ultimately had to turn to a small unauthorized faction in order to obtain the minority treaty of 1835.[19]

The political organization that existed in the Cherokee Nation in 1817–18 had made it possible for women to voice their opinion. Traditionally, Cherokee towns were politically independent of one another, and each town governed itself through a council in which all adults could speak. In the eighteenth century, however, the Cherokees began centralizing their government in order to restrain bellicose warriors whose raids jeopardized the entire nation and to negotiate as a single unit with whites. Nevertheless, town councils remained important, and representatives of traditional towns formed the early National Council. This National Council resembled the town councils in that anyone could address the body. Although legislation passed in 1817 created an Executive Committee, power still rested with the Council that reviewed all Committee acts.[20]

The protests of the women to the National Council in 1817 and 1818 were, however, the last time women presented a collective position to the Cherokee governing body. Structural changes in Cherokee government more narrowly defined participation in the National Council. In 1820 the Council provided that representatives be chosen from eight districts rather than from traditional towns, and in 1823 the Committee acquired a right of review over acts of the Council. The more formalized political organization made it less likely that a group could make its views known to the national government.[21]

As the Cherokee government became more centralized, political and economic power rested increasingly in the hands of a few elite men who adopted the planter lifestyle of the white antebellum South. A significant part of the ideological basis for this lifestyle was the cult of domesticity in which the ideal woman confined herself to home and hearth while men contended with the corrupt world of government and business.[22] The elite adopted the tenets of the cult of domesticity, particularly after 1817 when the number of Protestant missionaries, major proponents of this feminine ideal, increased significantly and their influence on Cherokee society broadened.

The extent to which a man's wife and daughters conformed to the idea quickly came to be one measure of his status. In 1818 Charles Hicks, who later served as Principal Chief, described the most prominent men in the Nation as "those who have for the last 10 or 20 years been pursuing agriculture & kept their women & children at home & in comfortable circumstances." Eight years later, John Ridge, one of the first generation of Cherokees to have been educated from childhood in mission schools, discussed a Cherokee law which protected the property rights of a married woman and observed that "in many respects she has exclusive & distinct control over her own, particularly among the less civilized." The more "civilized" presumably left such matters to men. Then Ridge described suitable activities for women: "They sew, they weave, they spin, they cook our meals and act well the duties assigned them by Nature as mothers." Proper women did not enter business or politics.[23]

Despite the attitudes of men such as Hicks and Ridge, women did in fact continue as heads of households and as businesswomen. In 1828 the *Cherokee Phoenix* published the obituary of Oo-dah-less who had accumulated a sizeable estate through agriculture and commerce. She was "the support of a large family," and she bequeathed her property "to an only daughter and three grandchildren." Oo-dah-less was not unique. At least one-third of the heads of household listed on the removal roll of 1835 were women. Most of these were not as prosperous as Oo-dah-less, but some were even more successful economically. Nineteen owned slaves (190 men were slaveholders), and two held over twenty slaves and operated substantial farms.[24]

Nevertheless, these women had ceased to have a direct voice in Cherokee government. In 1826 the Council called a constitutional convention to draw up a governing document for the Nation. According to legislation which provided for election of delegates to the convention, "No person but a free male citizen who is full grown shall be entitled to vote." The convention met and drafted a constitution patterned after that of the United States. Not surprisingly, the constitution that male Cherokees ratified in 1827 restricted the franchise to "free male citizens" and stipulated that "no person shall be eligible to a seat in the General Council, but a free Cherokee male, who shall have attained the age of twenty-five." Unlike the United States Constitution, the Cherokee document clearly excluded women, perhaps as a precaution against women who might assert their traditional right to participate in politics instead of remaining in the domestic sphere.[25]

The exclusion of women from politics certainly did not produce the removal crisis, but it did mean that a group traditionally opposed to land cession could no longer be heard on the issue. How women would have voted is also unclear. Certainly by 1835, many Cherokee women, particularly those educated in mission schools, believed that men were better suited to deal with political issues than women, and a number of women voluntarily enrolled their households to go west before the forcible removal of 1838–39. Even if women had united in active opposition to removal, it is unlikely that the United States and aggressive state governments would have paid any more attention to them than they did to the elected officials of the nation who opposed removal or the 15,000 Cherokees, including women (and perhaps children), who petitioned the U.S. Senate to reject the Treaty of New Echota. While Cherokee legislation may have made women powerless, federal authority rendered the whole Nation impotent.

In 1828 Georgia had extended state law over the Cherokee Nation, and white intruders who invaded its territory. Georgia law prohibited Indians, both men and women, from testifying in court against white assailants, and so they simply had to endure attacks on person and property. Delegates from the Nation complained to Secretary of War John H. Eaton about the lawless behavior of white intruders:

> Too many there are who think it an act of trifling consequence to oust an Indian family from the quiet enjoyment of all the comforts of their own firesides, and to drive off before their faces the stock that gave nourishment to the children and support to the aged, and appropriate it to the satisfaction to avarice.[26]

Elias Boudinot, editor of the bilingual *Cherokee Phoenix,* even accused the government of encouraging the intruders in order to force the Indians off their lands, and he published the following account:

> A few days since two of these white men came to a Cherokee house, for the purpose, they pretended, of buying provisions. There was no person about the house but one old woman of whom they inquired for some corn, beans &c. The woman told them she had nothing to sell. They then went off in the direction of the field belonging to this Cherokee family. They had not gone but a few minutes when the woman of the house saw a heavy smoke rising from that direction. She immediately hastened to the field and found the villains had set the woods on fire but a few rods from the fences, which she found already in a full blaze. There being a very heavy wind that day, the fire spread so fast, that her efforts to extinguish it proved utterly useless. The entire fence was therefore consumed in a short time. It is said that during her efforts to save the fence the men who had done the mischief were within sight, and were laughing heartily at her!

The Georgia Guard, established by the state to enforce its law in the Cherokee country, offered no protection and, in fact, contributed to the lawlessness. The *Phoenix* printed the following notice under the title "Cherokee Women, Beware":

> It is said that the Georgia Guard have received orders, from the Governor we suppose, to inflict corporeal punishment on such females as shall hereafter be guilty of insulting them. We presume they are to be the judges of what constitutes *insult.*[27]

Despite harassment from intruders and the Guard, most Cherokees had no intention of going west, and in the spring of 1838 they began to plant their crops as usual. Then U.S. soldiers arrived, began to round up the Cherokees, and imprisoned them in stockades in preparation for deportation. In 1932 Rebecca Neugin, who was nearly one hundred years old, shared her childhood memory and family tradition about removal with historian Grant Foreman:

> When the soldier came to our house my father wanted to fight, but my mother told him that the soldiers would kill him if he did and we surrendered without a fight. They drove us out of our house to join other prisoners in a stockade. After they took us away, my mother begged them to let her go back and get some bedding. So they let her go back and she brought what bedding and a few cooking utensils she could carry and had to leave behind all of our other household possessions.[28]

Rebecca Neugin's family was relatively fortunate. In the process of capture, families were sometimes separated and sufficient food and clothing were often left behind. Over fifty years after removal, John G. Burnett, a soldier who served as an interpreter, reminisced:

> Men working in the fields were arrested and driven to stockades. Women were dragged from their homes by soldiers whose language they could not understand. Children were often separated from their parents and driven into the stockades with the sky for a blanket and the earth for a pillow.

Burnett recalled how one family was forced to leave the body of a child who had just died and how a distraught mother collapsed of heart failure as soldiers evicted her and her three children from their homes.[29] After their capture, many Cherokees had to march miles over rugged mountain terrain to the stockades. Captain L. B. Webster wrote his wife about moving eight hundred Cherokees from North Carolina to the central depot in Tennessee: "We were eight days in making the journey (80 miles), and it was pitiful to behold the women & children, who suffered exceedingly—as they were all obliged to walk, with the exception of the sick."[30]

Originally the government planned to deport all the Cherokees in the summer of 1838, but the mortality rate of the three parties that departed that summer led the commanding officer, General Winfield Scott, to agree to delay the major removal until fall. In the interval, the Cherokees remained in the stockades where conditions were abysmal. Women in particular, often became individual victims of their captors. The missionary Daniel Butrick recorded the following episode in his journal:

> The poor Cherokees are not only exposed to temporal evils, but also to every species of moral desolation. The other day a gentleman informed me that he saw six soldiers about two Cherokee women. The women stood by a tree, and the soldiers with a bottle of liquor were endeavoring to entice them to drink, though the women, as yet were resisting them. He made this known to the commanding officer but we presume no notice was taken of it, as it was reported that those soldiers had those

women with them the whole night afterwards. A young married woman, a member of the Methodist society was at the camp with her friends, though her husband was not there at the time. The soldiers, it is said, caught her, dragged her about, and at length, either through fear, or otherwise, induced her to drink; and then seduced her away, so that she is now an outcast even among her own relatives. How many of the poor captive women are thus debauched, through terror and seduction, that eye which never sleeps, alone can determine.[31]

When removal finally got underway in October, the Cherokees were in a debilitated and demoralized state. A white minister who saw them as they prepared to embark noted: "The women did not appear to as good advantage as did the men. All, young and old, wore blankets which almost hid them from view."[32] The Cherokees had received permission to manage their own removal, and they divided the people into thirteen detachments of approximately one thousand each. While some had wagons, most walked. Neugin rode in a wagon with other children and some elderly women, but her older brother, mother, and father "walked all the way."[33] One observer reported that "even aged females, apparently nearly ready to drop in the grave, were traveling with heavy burdens attached to the back." Proper conveyance did not spare well-to-do Cherokees the agony of removal, the same observer noted:

> One lady passed on in her hack in company with her husband, apparently with as much refinement and equipage as any of the mothers of New England; and she was a mother too and her youngest child, about three years old, was sick in her arms, and all she could do was to make it comfortable as circumstances would permit. . . . She could only carry her dying child in her arms a few miles farther, and then she must stop in a stranger-land and consign her much loved babe to the cold ground, and that without pomp and ceremony, and pass on with the multitude.[34]

This woman was not alone. Journals of the removal are largely a litany of the burial of children, some born "untimely."[35]

Many women gave birth alongside the trail: at least sixty-nine newborns arrived in the West.[36] The Cherokees' military escort was often less than sympathetic. Daniel Butrick wrote in his journal that troops frequently forced women in labor to continue until they collapsed and delivered "in the midst of the company of soldiers." One man even stabbed an expectant mother with a bayonet.[37] Obviously, many pregnant women did not survive such treatment. The oral tradition of a family from southern Illinois, through which the Cherokees passed, for example, includes an account of an adopted Cherokee infant whose mother died in childbirth near the family's pioneer cabin. While this story may be apocryphal, the circumstances of Cherokee removal make such traditions believable.[38]

The stress and tension produced by the removal crisis probably accounts for a postremoval increase in domestic violence of which women usually were the victims. Missionaries reported that men, helpless to prevent seizure of their property and assaults on themselves and their families, vented their frustrations by beating wives and children. Some women were treated so badly by their husbands that they left them, and this dislocation contributed to the chaos in the Cherokee Nation in the late 1830s.[39]

Removal divided the Cherokee Nation in a fundamental way, and the Civil War magnified that division. Because most signers of the removal treaty were highly acculturated, many traditionalists resisted more strongly the white man's way of life and distrusted more openly those Cherokees who imitated whites. This split between "conservatives," those who sought to preserve the old ways, and "progressives," those committed to change, extended to women. We know far more, of course, about "progressive" Cherokee women who left letters and diaries which in some ways are quite similar to those of upper-class women in the antebellum South. In letters, they recounted local news such as "they had Elick Cockrel up for steeling horses" and "they have Charles Reese in chains about burning Harnages house" and discussed economic concerns: "I find I cannot get any corn in this neighborhood, so of course I shall be greatly pressed in providing provision for my family." Nevertheless, family life was the focus of most letters: "Major is well and tries hard to stand alone he will walk soon. I would write more but the baby is crying."[40]

Occasionally we even catch a glimpse of conservative women who seem to have retained at least some of their original authority over domestic matters. Red Bird Smith, who led a revitalization movement at the end of the nineteenth century, had considerable difficulty with his first mother-in-law. She "influenced" her adopted daughter to marry Smith through witchcraft and, as head of the household, meddled rather seriously in the couple's lives. Interestingly, however, the Kee-Too-Wah society that Red Bird Smith headed had little room for women. Although the society had political objectives, women enjoyed no greater participation in this "conservative" organization than they did in the "progressive" republican government of the Cherokee Nation.[41]

Following removal, the emphasis of legislation involving women was on protection rather than participation. In some ways, this legislation did offer women greater opportunities than the law codes of the states. In 1845 the editor of the *Cherokee Advocate* expressed pride that "in this respect the Cherokees have been considerably in advance of many of their white brethren, the rights of their women having been amply secured almost ever since they had written laws." The Nation also established the Cherokee Female Seminary to provide higher education for women, but like the education women received before removal, students studied only those subjects considered to be appropriate for their sex.[42]

Removal, therefore, changed little in terms of the status of Cherokee women. They had lost political power before the crisis of the 1830s, and events which followed relocation merely confirmed new roles and divisions. Cherokee women originally had been subsistence-level farmers and mothers, and the importance of these roles in traditional society had made it possible for them to exercise political power. Women, however, lacked the economic resources and military might on which political power in the Anglo-American system rested. When the Cherokees adopted the Anglo-American concept of power in the eighteenth and nineteenth centuries, men became dominant.

But in the 1830s the chickens came home to roost. Men, who had welcomed the Anglo-American basis for power, now found themselves without power. Nevertheless, they did not question the changes they had fostered. Therefore, the tragedy of the trail of tears lies not only in the suffering and death which the Cherokees experienced but also in the failure of many Cherokees to look critically at the political system which they had adopted—a political system dominated by wealthy, highly acculturated men and supported by an ideology that made women (as well as others defined as "weak" or "inferior") subordinate. In the removal crisis of the 1830s, men learned an important lesson about power; it was a lesson women had learned well before the "trail of tears."

NOTES

1. The standard account of Cherokee removal is Grant Foreman, *Indian Removal: The Emigration of the Five Civilized Tribes of Indians* (Norman, Okla., 1932), 229–312. Also see Ronald N. Satz, *American Indian Policy in the Jacksonian Era* (Lincoln, Neb., 1975); Dale Van Every, *Disinherited: The Lost Birthright of the American Indian* (New York, 1966); William G. McLoughlin, "Thomas Jefferson and the Beginning of Cherokee Nationalism, 1806 to 1809," *William and Mary Quarterly*, 3d ser., 32 (1975): 547–80; Thurman Wilkins, *Cherokee Tragedy: The Story of the Ridge Family and the Decimation of a People* (New York, 1970); Gary E. Moulton, *John Ross: Cherokee Chief* (Athens, Geo., 1978); Russell Thornton, "Cherokee Population Losses during the Trail of Tears: A New Perspective and a New Estimate," *Ethnohistory* 31 (1984): 289–300. Other works on the topic include Gloria Jahoda, *The Trail of Tears* (New York, 1975); Samuel Carter, *Cherokee Sunset: A Nation Betrayed* (Garden City, N.Y., 1976); John Ehle, *The Trail of Tears: The Rise and Fall of the Cherokee Nation* (New York, 1988). A good collection of primary documents can be found in the *Journal of Cherokee Studies* 3 (1978). For the context in which the removal policy developed, see Francis Paul Prucha, *American Indian Policy in the Formative Years: The Indian Trade and Intercourse Arts, 1790–7834* (Cambridge, Mass., 1962). Not all Cherokees went west; see John R. Finger, *The Eastern Band of Cherokees, 1879–1900* (Knoxville, Tenn., 1984).

2. Charles J. Kappler, ed., *Indian Affairs: Laws and Treaties*, 5 vols. (Washington, 1904–1941), 2: 439–49.

3. While some similarities to the role of women among the Iroquois exist, the differences are significant. Both had matrilineal kinship systems and practiced the same fundamentally sexual division of labor, but the Cherokees had no clan mothers who selected headmen, an important position among the Iroquois of the Five Nations. The Cherokees were an Iroquoian people, but linguists believe that they separated from the northern Iroquois thousands of years ago. Certainly, the Cherokees had been in the Southeast long enough to be a part of the southeastern cultural complex described by Charles Hudson in *The Southeastern Indians* (Knoxville, Tenn., 1976). Yet where women were concerned, the Cherokees differed from other southeastern peoples. James Adair, an eighteenth-century trader, gave the following analysis: "The Cherokees are an exception to all civilized or savage nations in having no laws against adultery; they have been a considerable while under a petticoat-government, and allow their women full liberty to plant their brows with horns as oft as they please, without fear of punishment" (James Adair, *Adair's History of the American Indian*, ed. Samuel Cole Williams [Johnson City, Tenn., 1930], 152–53). Indeed, Adair was correct that Cherokee women enjoyed considerable sexual autonomy. Furthermore, they seem to have exercised more political power than other eighteenth-century native women in the Southeast. Earlier sources, however, describe "queens" who ruled southeastern peoples other than the Cherokee. See Edward Gaylord Bourne, ed., *Narratives of the Career of Hernando de Soto* (2 vols.) (New York, 1922), 1: 65–72. Consequently, the unusual role of women in Cherokee society cannot be attributed definitively to either Iroquoian or southeastern antecedents.

4. Samuel Hazard, ed., *Pennsylvania Archives 1787*, 12 vols., (Philadelphia, 1852–56), 11: 181–82. See also Theda Perdue, "The Traditional Status of Cherokee Women," *Furman Studies* (1980): 19–25.

5. The best study of the aboriginal Cherokee kinship system is John Phillip Reid, *A Law of Blood: The Primitive Law of the Cherokee Nation* (New York, 1970). Also see William H. Gilbert, *The Eastern Cherokees* (Washington, 1943) and Alexander Spoehr, *Changing Kinship Systems: A Study in the Acculturation of the Creeks, Cherokee, and Choctaw* (Chicago, 1947).

6. William Bartram, "Observations on the Creek and Cherokee Indians, 1789," *Transactions of the American Ethnological Society* 3, pt. 1 (1954): 66.

7. William L. McDowell, ed., *Documents Relating to Indian Affairs, 1754–1765* (Columbia, S.C., 1970), 303; Henry Timberlake, *Lieut. Henry Timberlake's Memoirs, 1756–1765*, ed. Samuel Cole Williams (Johnson City, Tenn., 1927), 89–90; Benjamin Hawkins, *Letters of Benjamin Hawkins, 1796–1806*, vol. 9 of *Georgia Historical Society Collections* (Savannah, Geo., 1916), 110; Adair, *Adair's History*, 105–117.

8. William Bartram, *The Travels of William Bartram*, ed. Mark Van Doren (New York, 1940), 90.

9. Alexander S. Salley, ed., *Narratives of Early Carolina, 1650–1708* (New York, 1911), 90.

10. *American State Papers*, Class 2: *Indian Affairs*, 2 vols. (Washington, 1832), 1:41. For Nancy Ward, see Ben Harris McClary, "Nancy Ward: Last Beloved Woman of the Cherokees," *Tennessee Historical Quarterly* 21 (1962): 336–52; Theda Perdue, "Nancy Ward (1738?–1822)," in G. J. Barker-Benfield and Catherine Clinton, eds., *Portraits of American Women* (New York, 1991), 83–100.

11. Prucha, *American Indian*, 213–49; Bernard W. Sheehan, *Seeds of Extinction: Jeffersonian Philanthropy and the American Indian* (Chapel Hill, N.C., 1973); Robert F. Berkhofer, Jr., *Salvation and the Savage: An Analysis of Protestant Missions and American Indian Response* (Lexington, Ken., 1965).

12. William G. McLoughlin, *Cherokee Renascence in the New Republic* (Princeton, 1986); William G. McLoughlin, *Cherokees and Missionaries, 1789–1839* (New Haven, Conn., 1984); Henry T. Malone, *Cherokees of the Old South: A People in Transition* (Athens, Geo., 1956); Theda Perdue, *Slavery and the Evolution of Cherokee Society, 7540–1866* (Knoxville, Tenn., 1979).

13. *Laws of the Cherokee Nation: Adopted by the Council at Various Times, Printed for the Benefit of the Nation* (Tahlequah, Cherokee Nation, 1852), 3–4.

14. Rufus Anderson, *Memoir of Catherine Brown, A Christian Indian of the Cherokee Nation* (Philadelphia, 1832); Hawkins, 20.

15. Presidential Papers Microfilm: Andrew Jackson (Washington, 1961), Series 1, Reel 22; also mentioned in *Journal of Cyrus Kingsbury*, 13 February 1817, Papers of the American Board of Commissioners for Foreign Missions, Houghton Library, Harvard University, Cambridge, Mass. (hereafter cited as American Board Papers).

16. Brainerd Journal, 30 June 1818, American Board Papers.

17. For women's property rights in the United States, see Mary Beard, *Woman as a Force in History: A Study in Traditions and Realities* (New York, 1946); Marylynn Salmon, "Women and Property in South Carolina: The Evidence from Marriage Settlements, 1730–1830," *William and Mary Quarterly*, 3d ser., 39 (1982): 655–85; Marylynn Salmon, "Equality or Submersion? *Feme Covert* Status in Early Pennsylvania," in *Women of America*, ed. Carol Berkin and Mary Beth Norton (Boston, 1979); Marylynn Salmon, "'Life Liberty and Dower': The Legal Status of Women after the Revolution," in *Women, War, and Revolution*, ed. Carol Berkin and Clara Lovett (New York, 1980); Norma Basch, "Invisible Women: The Legal Fiction of Marital Unity in Nineteenth-Century America," *Feminist Studies* 5 (1979): 346–66; Norma Basch, *In the Eyes of the Law: Women, Marriage, and Property in Nineteenth-Century New York* (Ithaca, N.Y., 1982); Albie Sachs and Joan Hoff-Wilson, *Sexism and the Law: A Study of Male Beliefs and Legal Bias in Britain and the United States* (New York, 1979); Suzanne Lebsock, *The Free Women of Petersburg: Status and Culture in a Southern Town, 1784–1860* (New York, 1984).

18. Louis Wyeth to R. Chapman and C. C. Clay, 16 May 1838, Memorial of Isaac Wellborn to Martin Van Buren, n.d., Writ of the Morgan County (Alabama) Court, 9 June 1838 (Letters Received by the Office of Indian Affairs, 1824–1881, RG 75, National Archives, Washington); Joel R. Poinsett to Mathew Arbuckle, 17 Dec. 1838, John Ross to Joel R. Poinsett, 18 July 1839 (John Ross Papers, Thomas Gilcrease Institute, Tulsa, Okla.).

19. Charles C. Royce, *Indian Land Cessions in the United States* (Washington, 1900), 684–85, 696–97.

20. V. Richard Persico, Jr., "Early Nineteenth-Century Cherokee Political Organization," in *The Cherokee Indian Nation: A Troubled History*, ed. Duane H. King (Knoxville, Tenn., 1979), 92–109.

21. *Laws of the Cherokee Nation*, 14–18, 31–32.

22. The classic article is Barbara Welter, "The Cult of True Womanhood, 1820–1860," *American Quarterly* 18 (1966): 151–74. Also see Glenda Matthews, *"Just a Housewife": The Rise and Fall of Domesticity in America* (New York, 1987). In *The Plantation Mistress: Woman's World in the Old South* (New York, 1982), Catherine Clinton points out that southern women, particularly from the planter class, did not exactly fit the model for northern women. Yet Cherokee women may have conformed more closely to that model than many other

southern women because of the influence of northern missionaries. See Theda Perdue, "Southern Indians and the Cult of True Womanhood," in *The Web of Southern Social Relations: Essays on Family Life, Education and Women,* ed. Walter J. Frazer, Jr., R. Frank Saunders, Jr., and Jon L. Wakelyn, Jr. (Athens, Ga. 1985), 35–51. Also see Anne Firor Scott, *The Southern Lady: From Pedestal to Politics, 1830–1930* (Chicago, 1970), 3–21; Mary E. Young, "Women, Civilization, and the Indian Question," in *Clio Was a Woman: Studies in the History of American Women,* ed. Mabel E. Deutrich and Virginia C. Purdy (Washington, 1980).

23. Ard Hoyt, Moody Hall, William Chamberlain, and D. S. Butrick to Samuel Worcester, 25 July 1818 (American Board Papers); John Ridge to Albert Gallatin, 27 February 1826 (John Howard Payne Papers, Newberry Library, Chicago, III. [hereafter cited as Payne Papers]).

24. Cherokee Phoenix, 2 July 1828; Census of 1835 (Henderson Roll), RG 75, Office of Indian Affairs, National Archives, Washington; R. Halliburton, Jr., *Red over Black: Black Slavery among the Cherokee Indians* (Westport, Conn., 1977), 181–92. Robert Bushyhead, a native Cherokee speaker from Cherokee, North Carolina, identified the gender of names on the Henderson Roll.

25. *Laws of the Cherokee Nation,* 79, 120–21.

26. George Lowrey, Lewis Ross, William Hicks, R. Taylor, Joseph Vann, and W. S. Shorey to John H. Eaton, 11 February 1830, Letters received, Office of Indian Affairs, 1824–1881, National Archives, Washington.

27. *Cherokee Phoenix,* 26 March 1831, 16 July 1831.

28. Foreman, *Indian Removal,* 302–303.

29. John G. Burnett, "The Cherokee Removal through the Eyes of a Private Soldier," *Journal of Cherokee Studies* 3 (1978): 183.

30. Capt L. B. Webster, "Letters from a Lonely Soldier," *Journal of Cherokee Studies* 3 (1978): 154.

31. Journal of Daniel S. Butrick, n.d. (Payne Papers. There is another Butrick journal in the American Board Papers. The one in the Payne Papers is as much a commentary as a personal narrative).

32. J. D. Anthony, *Life and Times of Rev. J. D. Anthony* (Atlanta, 1896).

33. Foreman, *Indian Removal,* 302–303.

34. "A Native of Maine, Traveling in the Western Country," *New York Observer,* 26 January 1839.

35. A good example is B. B. Cannon, "An Overland Journey to the West (October–December 1837)," *Journal of Cherokee Studies* 3 (1978): 166–73.

36. "Emigration Detachments," *Journal of Cherokee Studies* 3 (1978): 186–87.

37. Butrick Journal (Payne Papers).

38. Story related by unidentified member of an audience at Warren Wilson College, Black Mountain, N.C., January 1983.

39. Butrick Journal, 30 April 1839, 2 May 1839 (American Board Papers).

40. Edward Everett Dale and Gaston Litton, eds., *Cherokee Cavaliers: Forty Years of Cherokee History as Told in the Correspondence of the Ridge-Watie-Boudinot Family* (Norman, Okla., 1939), 20–21, 37–38, 45–46. For comparison, see Scott, *Southern Lady,* and Clinton, *Plantation Mistress.*

41. *Indian Pioneer History,* 113 vols. (Oklahoma Historical Society, Oklahoma City), 9: 490–91; Robert K. Thomas, "The Redbird Smith Movement," in *Symposium on Cherokee and Iroquois Culture,* ed. William N. Fenton and John Gulick (Washington, 1961).

42. *Cherokee Advocate,* 27 February 1845; Rudi Halliburton, Jr., "Northeastern Seminary Hall," *Chronicles of Oklahoma* 51 (1973–74): 391–98; *Indian Pioneer History* 1: 394.

THE WINNING OF THE WEST:
THE EXPANSION OF THE WESTERN SIOUX IN
THE EIGHTEENTH AND NINETEENTH CENTURIES

25

Richard White

According to many of the essays collected here, Indians invariably suffered when European colonists arrived and, too often natives who survived the French, English, and Spanish rule had to cope with the expansionist policies of a new imperial power: the United States of America. In a sense, for Indians the "colonial period" of American history continues even today.

Richard White demonstrates here that the western Sioux of the Great Plains, like the Iroquois, Catawbas, and other eastern Indian nations, found ways to counter colonization. To be sure, the Sioux had to change their lives as a result of contact with whites; epidemic diseases raced across the continent, and the expansion of the United States in the nineteenth century had a devastating impact on the buffalo herds central to the Sioux economy. Rather than succumbing, however, the Sioux defended themselves and actually expanded the territory under their control. As a result, some of the enemies of the Sioux, such as the Pawnees, Crows, and Arikaras, elected to side with the United States against the Sioux, a strategic choice that made the most sense given the threat that the Sioux posed to these other western nations.

White's tale is more than an unexpected footnote in the history of Indian-white relations, however. By demonstrating how the Sioux managed to survive in the generations following contact with whites, he reveals that Indians' experiences, like those of non-Indians, were not always predictable. More important, he gives to the Sioux, and by extension to other native nations, what historians strive to give to all subjects of their inquiry: an honest depiction of a complicated, ever-changing series of events in which all peoples are actors on the historical stage.

THE WINNING OF THE WEST:
THE EXPANSION OF THE WESTERN
SIOUX IN THE EIGHTEENTH AND
NINETEENTH CENTURIES

Richard White

THE MOUNTED WARRIOR of the Great Plains has proved to be the most enduring stereotype of the American Indian, but like most stereotypes this one conceals more than it reveals. Both popularizers and scholars have been fascinated with the individual warrior to the neglect of plains warfare itself. Harry Turney-High, in his classic *Primitive Warfare,* provided the most cogent justification of this neglect. The plains tribes, he contended, were so loosely organized that they remained below the "military horizon"; there really was no warfare on the plains, only battles that were little more than "a mildly dangerous game" fought for largely individual reasons. In much of the literature, intertribal warfare has remained just this: an individual enterprise fought for individualistic reasons—glory, revenge, prestige, and booty. Robert Lowie's statement on warfare, in what is still the standard work on the Plains Indians, can be taken as typical of much anthropological thought: "The objective was never to acquire new lands. Revenge, horse lifting, and lust for glory were the chief motives. . . ."[1]

There is, however, a second group of anthropologists, W. W. Newcomb, Oscar Lewis, Frank Secoy, and more recently Symmes Oliver, who have found this explanation of intertribal warfare unconvincing. These scholars, making much more thorough use of historical sources than is common among anthropologists, have examined warfare in light of economic and technological change. They have presented intertribal warfare as dynamic, changing over time; wars were not interminable contests with traditional enemies, but real struggles in which defeat was often catastrophic. Tribes fought largely for the potential economic and social benefits to be derived from furs, slaves, better hunting grounds, and horses. According to these scholars, plains tribes went to war because their survival as a people depended on securing and defending essential resources.[2]

SOURCE: *Journal of American History* 65:2 (1978), 319–43.

Historians have by and large neglected this social and economic interpretation of plains warfare and have been content to borrow uncritically from the individualistic school. Western historians usually present intertribal warfare as a chaotic series of raids and counter-raids; an almost irrelevant prelude to the real story: Indian resistance to white invasion. This exaggerated focus on the heroic resistance of certain plains tribes to white incursions has recently prompted John Ewers, an ethnologist, to stress that Indians on the plains had fought each other long before whites came and that intertribal warfare remained very significant into the late nineteenth century.[3]

The neglect by historians of intertribal warfare and the reasons behind it has fundamentally distorted the historical position of the Plains Indians. As Ewers has noted, the heroic resistance approach to plains history reduces these tribes who did not offer organized armed resistance to the white American invaders, and who indeed often aided them against other tribes, to the position of either foolish dupes of the whites or of traitors to their race. Why tribes such as the Pawnee, Mandan, Hidatsa, Oto, Missouri, Crow, and Omaha never took up arms against white Americans has never been subject to much historical scrutiny. The failure of Indians to unite has been much easier to deplore than to examine.[4]

The history of the northern and central American Great Plains in the eighteenth and nineteenth centuries is far more complicated than the tragic retreat of the Indians in the face of an inexorable white advance. From the perspective of most northern and central plains tribes the crucial invasion of the plains during this period was not necessarily that of the whites at all. These tribes had few illusions about American whites and the danger they presented, but the Sioux remained their most feared enemy.

The Teton and Yanktonai Sioux appeared on the edges of the Great Plains early in the eighteenth century. Although unmounted, they were already culturally differentiated from their woodland brothers, the Santee Sioux. The western Sioux were never united under any central government and never developed any concerted policy of conquest. By the mid-nineteenth century the Plains Sioux comprised three broad divisions, the Tetons, Yanktons, and Yanktonais, with the Tetons subdivided into seven component tribes—the Oglala, Brulé, Hunkpapa, Miniconjou, Sans Arc, Two Kettles, and Sihaspas; the last five tribes having evolved from an earlier Sioux group, the Saones. Although linked by common language, culture, interest, and intermarriage, these tribes operated independently. At no time did all the western Sioux tribes unite against any enemy, but alliances of several tribes against a common foe were not unusual. Only rarely did any Teton tribe join an alien tribe in an attack on another group of Sioux.[5]

Between approximately 1685 and 1876 the western Sioux conquered and controlled an area from the Minnesota River in Minnesota, west to the head of the Yellowstone, and south from the Yellowstone to the drainage of the upper Republican River. This advance westward took place in three identifiable stages: initially a movement during the late seventeenth and early eighteenth centuries onto the prairies east of the Missouri, then a conquest of the middle Missouri River region during the late eighteenth and nineteenth centuries, and, finally, a sweep west and south from the Missouri during the early and mid-nineteenth century. Each of these stages possessed its own impetus and rationale. Taken together they comprised a sustained movement by the Sioux that resulted in the dispossession or subjugation of numerous tribes and made the Sioux a major Indian power on the Great Plains during the nineteenth century.

The Teton tribes who first appeared on the prairies of Minnesota in the eighteenth century were well-armed and formidable. They had acquired guns from the French, ending the Cree-Assiniboine monopoly of firearms that had enabled those tribes to push the Tetons and Yanktonais south from the headwaters of the Mississippi. To the east of the Tetons, the Ojibwas were growing in power, but the brunt of their attacks would be borne by the Santee Sioux who acted as a buffer against powerful eastern tribes. Thus, neither the Ojibwas nor the Crees drove the Sioux out onto the prairies. Instead, the potential profits of the region's abundant beaver and the ready food supply provided by the buffalo herds lured them into the open lands.[6]

Initially the profits of the beaver trade exerted a more powerful attraction than the subsistence gained from buffalo hunting. The fur trade brought to the Sioux European goods and the guns that not only enabled them to repulse the Crees and their Assiniboine allies, but also to dispossess the tribes who held the western hunting and trapping grounds they desired. During the late seventeenth and early and mid-eighteenth centuries, the Tetons and Yanktonais pushed the Omahas, Otos, Cheyennes, Missouris, and Iowas to the south and west and occupied their lands.[7]

The western Sioux became the dominant trappers and traders of the prairies. Until the early years of the nineteenth century the Tetons, Yanktonais, and, later, the Yanktons, regularly gathered at the great trade fairs held with the Santee. First at the Blue Earth River and later at the Yanktonai villages on the Cheyenne and James Rivers, the western tribes traded their own catch of furs, plus those acquired from tribes further west, for European goods that the Santees had obtained. As late as 1796 Jean Baptiste Truteau described the Sioux as primarily trappers and traders who also hunted buffalo:

> The Sioux tribes are those who hunt most for the beaver and other good peltries of the Upper Missouri. They scour all the rivers and streams without fearing anyone. They carry away every springtime . . . a great number of them, which they exchange for merchandise with the other Sioux situated on the St. Peter's [Minnesota] and Des Moines Rivers. . . .[8]

The Sioux pushed westward, however, involving them in a cultural and economic dilemma to which they responded unevenly. The fur trade provided them with guns and trade goods, but they depended on buffalo hunting for their food supply and most of their other necessities. According to the winter counts, pictographic records kept by the Sioux, western Dakotas were trading for horses by 1707 and had almost certainly acquired some animals even earlier. But, surprisingly, the Sioux assimilation of the horse into existing cultural patterns occurred only gradually. The winter counts do not record a mounted war party until 1757–58, and it was unsuccessful. But with the acquisition of the horse, buffalo hunting undoubtedly became easier and more lucrative.[9]

For years the two systems of hunting existed in an uneasy balance: during the summer the Sioux followed the buffalo; in the winters they trapped beaver; and with spring the bands traveled to the trade fairs. But by the late eighteenth century it had become obvious that the Teton bands to the west were devoting more and more time to the acquisition of horses and to the hunting of buffalo, while the Yanktons and Yanktonais still concentrated on beaver trapping. As late as 1803, the Yanktonais abandoned good buffalo hunting grounds along the Missouri to move to the headwaters of the Minnesota River where there were few buffalo but abundant beaver.[10]

This cultural evolution took place east of the Missouri River. By 1770 the advantage the gun had given the Sioux over the tribes further west had largely disappeared and the balance of tribal power on the eastern Great Plains seemed stable. The Sioux dominated the Missouri River drainage below the Arikara villages on the Great Bend, but these villages, along with those of the Mandans and Hidatsas further up the Missouri, blocked further advance. These horticultural peoples with their large populations, numerous horses, and fortified towns easily resisted incursions by the less numerous and poorly mounted Sioux. Further to the south the Omahas, under their great chief Blackbird, had acquired guns and halted the Sioux advance down the Missouri. The Sioux, of course, were not totally confined. Some bands regularly raided the Arikaras for horses, and the Tetons, either independently or in alliance with the Arikaras, moved across the Missouri to hunt or raid the Mandans and Hidatsas. But the Sioux were only interlopers in this territory; their power was limited.[11]

The deterioration of this balance of power and the beginning of the second stage of Sioux expansion resulted from a combination of internal and external developments. During the last quarter of the eighteenth century, Sioux hunters depleted the buffalo and beaver populations east of the Missouri. This, by itself, would have forced the Tetons and Yanktonais either to expand their hunting grounds or to alter their economy. The initial response of the Oglalas at least appears to have been not conquest, but rather imitation of the horticultural economy of the village tribes. The prosperity of these villagers—with their abundant supplies of corn, beans, squash, and their lucrative trade in hides, meat, and horses with the buffalo nomads to the west—seems to have exerted a real attraction for the Sioux. For a time the Oglalas actually settled with the Arikaras and adopted their horticultural and buffalo-hunting economy. But the arrival of European traders aborted this evolution of the Sioux into sedentary horticultural villagers.[12]

In the late eighteenth century French and Spanish traders moved up the Missouri River creating a new source of European trade goods for the villagers and for the nomadic tribes beyond. These white traders not only seriously undercut the Sioux role as middlemen, but they also set out to capture the trade of the Sioux. In the eyes of the Missouri traders, the Sioux, through their trade fairs, drew off the fur trade of the plains and Rockies from its natural route down the Missouri and diverted it into English Canada. For the French and Spanish, therefore, successful commerce on the Missouri necessarily meant the destruction of old Sioux trading patterns. The commerce they eventually succeeded in capturing, however, was not the old trade in beaver pelts, but a new trade in buffalo robes and pemmican. As products of the buffalo hunts became convertible into European trade goods, the Tetons found less and less reason to devote time to beaver trapping. By 1804 the major Teton trade items were buffalo robes and hides, and the need for horses and hunting grounds had replaced trapping grounds as the major motives for war.[13]

But far more significant in stimulating Sioux expansion than any deliberate action traders took was the accidental, if inevitable, result of their presence: the arrival of European epidemic diseases The Sioux, because they lived in small wandering groups, were far less vulnerable to these epidemics than the populous agricultural villages. The Brulé winter counts record smallpox in 1779–80, 1780–81, and 1801–1802 (the epidemics are dated slightly differently in other winter counts), but their losses were slight when compared to those of the Arikaras, Hidatsas, and Mandans. In 1795 Truteau reported that the Arikaras had been reduced from "32 populous villages" to two and from 4,000 warriors to 500—a loss of population, which, in turn, caused severe social and economic disruption. The smallpox reached the Mandan and Hidatsa villages in 1781, inflicting losses proportionate to those of the Arikaras. On the lower Missouri during the opening years of the nineteenth century, the smallpox reduced the Omahas from 700 to 300 warriors and killed Blackbird, their famous and powerful chief. These losses broke their power and their control of the Missouri below the Sioux.[14]

The epidemics not only weakened the powerful tribes that had previously held the Sioux in check, but they also ended any attempts of the Oglalas to become horticultural villagers themselves. During the late eighteenth century the Sioux pushed the Arikaras steadily up the Missouri where they joined with their old enemies, the Mandans and Hidatsas, now also under great pressure from the Sioux. By the 1790s pre-epidemic horse raids had given way to war parties of up to 2,000 men that had succeeded in pushing the Mandans out of the Heart River country into the Knife River district of their Hidatsa allies. Although not always successful, Sioux attacks could be overwhelming, as when, in the early 1790s, the Sioux captured and destroyed an entire Mandan village near Deer Creek. The alliance of the Mandans and Hidatsa with the Arikaras was short-lived, however, and by 1800 the Arikaras had moved back downstream. According to white traders, their return made them little more than serfs of the Sioux who cut them off from the buffalo, cheated them, robbed them, and, as the Sioux said, made them fulfill the economic role of women.[15]

This intertribal warfare was no game, no mere pattern of revenge killings against ancient enemies. Enemies of the Sioux, faced with disastrous losses, repeatedly sought peace. In 1803, for example, the Omahas and Poncas attempted to end their warfare with the Brulés. The largest Brulé band under Black Bull agreed, but simultaneously the Partisan, a leader of another Brulé band and supposedly envious of Black Bull's growing influence, led a horse raid against the Poncas. When the Poncas retaliated by stealing nine Sioux horses, they attacked the wrong Brulé village, Black Bull's, not the Partisan's, and the fragile peace was broken. In 1804 the Brulés, under Black Bull, fell upon a Ponca village killing half of its inhabitants, and in September of that year they destroyed an Omaha village of forty lodges, killing seventy-five men. In desperation the Omahas and Poncas abandoned their permanent villages and crops, which made them vulnerable to both the smallpox and the nomadic Sioux. For a time they became horse nomads, not from desire, but from necessity. But even this strategy weakened them, diminishing their access to the guns the traders brought up the Missouri. By 1809 some white observers predicted that the once powerful Omahas would disappear entirely. Their difficulties vividly demonstrated the near impossibility of securing peace with the loosely organized Sioux.[16]

Thus by 1803–1804, when the arrival of Merriwether Lewis and William Clark announced the new American presence on the Missouri, the Sioux had reduced the old borders and balance of power on the river to shambles. The Mandans, Hidatsas, Arikaras, and Omahas possessed only the shadow of their former strength. The Sioux now dominated the upper Missouri nearly to the Yellowstone River. Furthermore, the Sioux had crossed the Missouri, fighting and hunting in the area bordering the Mandan-Hidatsa villages. An Oglala party under Standing Bull had reached the Black Hills in 1775–76, and by the turn of the century the Oglalas were contesting the plains country between the Missouri and those mountains with the Kiowas, Arapahos, Crows, and Cheyennes.[17]

Lewis and Clark immediately recognized the Sioux as the dominant power on the Missouri, the one tribe that could seriously threaten American commerce on that river. Because of their trade fairs (in decline, but still viable) the Sioux could disrupt white trade without fear of economic retaliation. They could always obtain needed European goods at the spring fairs further east. Lewis and Clark vilified the Sioux, but their very abuse revealed their high estimation of Sioux power.

> These are the vilest miscreants of the savage race, and must ever remain the pirates of the Missouri, until such measures are pursued by our government as will make them feel a dependence on its will for their supply of merchandise. Unless these people are reduced to order by coercive measures I am ready to pronounce that the citizens of the United States can never enjoy but partially the advantages which the Missouri presents.[18]

American invective, however, was much stronger than American power in the area and was totally incapable of subjugating the Sioux. In 1807 the Sioux and their Arikara dependents first obtained tribute from a trading party under Manuel Lisa, and then drove a government party under Nathaniel Pryor, sent to escort the Mandan chief Shahaka to his village, back downstream. "I suppose a severe punishment of the Aricaras indispensible, taking for it our time and convenience," Thomas Jefferson wrote to Lewis the next year. And another year passed before Lewis decided to send a force of 250 soldiers, trappers, and traders with 300 Indian auxiliaries against the Arikaras. The party he actually dispatched in the summer of 1809, however, consisted of only 150 men, and when Pierre Chouteau, who commanded it, attempted to recruit his 300 auxiliaries among the Tetons, the very bands who had attacked

Pryor, he found them more interested in looting the expedition than joining it. According to Chouteau, the Sioux warned him that "one tribe ought not countenance an attempt to destroy another, and if I still persisted in that resolution myself and my party might be destroyed before we reached the Ricaras." They advised Chouteau to pardon the Arikaras and distribute presents, and the supposedly punitive expedition eventually did exactly that.[19]

White Americans obviously represented an important new element in the inter-tribal politics of the upper Missouri; but as the Chouteau and Pryor expeditions had demonstrated, they hardly dominated the region. And, despite their initial conflicts, the Sioux found the Americans to be useful, if dangerous, allies during their third period of expansion. For over three decades after the Chouteau expedition, the ambitions of the Sioux and the Americans proved generally complementary, and as late at 1838 Joshua Pilcher, the American agent for the upper Missouri, would write that "no Indians ever mainfested a greater degree of friendship for the whites in general, or more respect for our Government, than the Sioux."[20]

The conquests of the western Sioux during the nineteenth century were politically united in only the loosest sense. The various Sioux tribes expanded for similar demographic, economic, and social reasons, however, and these underlying causes give a unity to the various wars of the Sioux.

Unlike every other tribe on the Great Plains during the nineteenth century, the Sioux appear to have increased in numbers. They were not immune to the epidemics that decimated the other tribes, but most of the Tetons and Yanktonais successfully avoided the disastrous results of the great epidemics, especially the epidemic of 1837 that probably halved the Indian population of the plains. Through historical accident the very conquests of the Sioux protected them from disease. This occurred in two opposite ways. The advance of Oglalas and Brulés to the southwest simply put them out of reach of the main epidemic corridor along the Missouri. Furthermore, Pilcher, the Indian agent on the Missouri, succeeded in giving them advance warning of the danger in 1837, and, unlike the Blackfeet and other nomadic tribes that suffered heavily from the epidemic, they did not come in to trade. The Tetons were infected, and individual tribes lost heavily, but the losses of the Sioux as a whole were comparatively slight. The Yanktons, Yanktonais, and portions of the Saone Tetons, however, dominated the Missouri trade route, but paradoxically this probably helped to save them. In 1832 the Office of Indian Affairs sent doctors up the river to vaccinate the Indians. Many of the Sioux refused to cooperate, but well over a thousand people, mostly Yanktonais, received vaccinations. Only enough money was appropriated to send the doctors as far upriver as the Sioux; so the Mandans and Hidatsas further upriver remained unvaccinated. As a result, when smallpox came, the Yanktonais were partially protected while their enemies in the villages once again died miserably in great numbers. The renewed American efforts at mass vaccination that followed the epidemic came too late for the Mandans, but in the 1840s thousands more Sioux were given immunity from smallpox.[21]

The combination of freedom from disease, a high birth rate (in 1875 estimated as capable of doubling the population every twenty years), and continued migration from the Sioux tribes further east, produced a steadily growing population for the western Sioux. Although the various censuses taken by the whites were often little more than rough estimates, the western Sioux appear to have increased from a very low estimate of 5,000 people in 1804 to approximately 25,000 in the 1850s. This population increase, itself partly a result of the new abundance the Sioux derived from the buffalo herds, in turn, fueled an increased need for buffalo. The Sioux used the animals not only to feed their expanding population, but also to trade for necessary European goods. Since pemmican, buffalo robes, hides, and tongues had replaced beaver pelts as the main Indian trade item on the Missouri, the Sioux needed secure and profitable hunting grounds during a period when the buffalo were steadily moving west and north in response to hunting pressure on the Missouri.[22]

Increased Indian hunting for trade contributed to the pressure on the buffalo herds, but the great bulk of the destruction was the direct work of white hunters and traders. The number of buffalo robes annually shipped down the Missouri increased from an average of 2,600 between 1815 and 1830 to 40,000 to 50,000 in 1833, a figure that did not include the numbers slaughtered by whites for pleasure. In 1848 Father Pierre-Jean De Smet reported the annual figure shipped downriver to St. Louis to be 25,000 tongues and 110,000 robes.[23]

Despite what the most thorough student of the subject has seen as the Indians' own prudent use of the buffalo, the various tribes competed for an increasingly scarce resource. By the late 1820s the buffalo had disappeared from the Missouri below the Omaha villages, and the border tribes were already in desperate condition from lack of game. The Indians quickly realized the danger further up the Missouri, and upper Missouri tribes voiced complaints about white hunters as early as 1833. By the 1840s observations on the diminishing number of buffalo and increased Indian competition had become commonplace. Between 1833 and 1844 buffalo could be found in large numbers on the headwaters of the Little Cheyenne, but by the mid-1840s they were receding rapidly toward the mountains. The Sioux to a great extent simply had to follow, or move north and south, to find new hunting grounds. Their survival and prosperity depended on their success.[24]

But buffalo hunting demanded more than territory; it also required horses, and in the 1820s, the Sioux were hardly noted for either the abundance or the quality of their herds. Raids and harsh winters on the plains frequently depleted Sioux horse herds, and the Sioux had to replenish them by raiding or trading farther to the south. In this sense the economy of the Sioux depended on warfare to secure the horses needed for the hunt. As Oscar Lewis has pointed out in connection with the Blackfeet, war and horse raiding became important economic activities for the Plains Indians.[25]

The Yanktonais, Yanktons, and Saone Tetons had a third incentive for expansion. Power over the sedentary villagers secured them what Tabeau had called their serfs. Under Sioux domination these villages could be raided or traded with as the occasion demanded, their corn and beans serving as sources of supplementary food supplies when the buffalo failed. A favorite tactic of the Sioux was to restrict, as far as possible, the access of these tribes to both European goods and the hunting grounds, thus forcing the village peoples to rely on the Sioux for trade goods, meat, and robes. To escape this exploitation, the villagers, in alliance with the nomadic tribes who traded with them, waged a nearly constant, if often desultory, war.[26]

It is in this context of increasing population, increasing demand for buffalos and horses, the declining and retreating bison populations, and attempted domination of the sedentary villagers that the final phase of Sioux expansion during the nineteenth century took place. And, as the Omahas had found out, the loose structural organization of the western Sioux worked to make the impetus of their advance even more irresistible. Accommodation with one band or tribe often only served to increase inroads from others. There was no way for a tribe to deal with the whole Sioux nation.

On the Missouri the Sioux had long feared the logical alliance of all the village tribes against them, and they worked actively to prevent it. After 1810, the Arikaras sporadically attempted to break away from Sioux domination by allying themselves with the Mandans and Hidatsas. In response, the Sioux blockaded the villages, cutting them off from the buffalo and stopping the white traders who came up the Missouri from supplying them. The Mandan-Arikara alliance, in turn, sent out war parties to keep the river open. But these alliances inevitably fell apart from internal strains, and the old pattern of oscillating periods of trade and warfare was renewed.[27]

But if the Sioux feared an alliance of the sedentary village tribes, these tribes had an even greater fear of a Sioux-American partnership on the Missouri. The Arikaras, by attacking and defeating an American fur trading party under William Ashley in 1823, precipitated exactly the combination from which they had most to fear. When 1,500 Sioux warriors appeared before their village that year, they were accompanied by United States troops under Colonel Henry Leavenworth. This joint expedition took the Arikara village and sacked it, but the Sioux were disgusted with the performance of their American auxiliaries. They blamed American cautiousness for allowing the Arikaras to escape further upstream. Although they remained friendly to the United States, the whole affair gave them a low estimation of the ability of white soldiers that would last for years. They finished the removal of the Arikaras themselves, forcing them by 1832 to abandon both their sedentary villages and the Missouri River and to move south to live first with, and then just above, the Skidi Pawnees. The Yanktonais, 450 lodges strong, moved in from the Minnesota River to take over the old Arikara territory.[28]

With the departure of the Arikaras, the Mandans and Hidatsas alone remained to contest Sioux domination of the Missouri. In 1836 the Yanktonais, nearly starving after a season of poor hunts, began petty raids on the Mandans and Hidatsas. In retaliation, a Mandan-Hidatsa war party destroyed a Yanktonai village of forty-five lodges, killing more than 150 people and taking fifty prisoners. The Sioux counterattacks cost the Mandans dearly. During the next year they lost over sixty warriors, but what was worse, when the smallpox hit in 1837, the villagers could not disperse for fear of the hostile Yanktonais who still occupied the plains around the villages. The Mandans were very nearly destroyed; the Hidatsas, who attempted a quarantine, lost over half their people, and even the luckless Arikaras returned in time to be ravaged by the epidemic. The villages that survived continued to suffer from Yanktonai attacks and could use the plains hunting grounds only on sufferance of the Sioux.[29]

The Oglala-Brulé advance onto the buffalo plains southwest of the Missouri was contemporaneous with the push up the Missouri and much more significant. Here horse raids and occasional hunts by the Sioux gave way to a concerted attempt to wrest the plains between the Black Hills and the Missouri from the Arapahos, Crows, Kiowas, and Cheyennes. By 1825, the Oglalas, advancing up the drainage of the Teton River, and the Brulés, moving up the drainage of the White River, had dispossessed the Kiowas and driven them south, pushed the Crows west to Powder River, and formed with the Cheyennes and Arapahos an alliance which would dominate the north and central plains for the next half century.[30]

Historians have attributed the movement of the Sioux beyond the Black Hills into the Platte drainage to manipulations of the Rocky Mountain Fur Company, which sought to capture the Sioux trade from the American Fur Company. But, in fact, traders followed the Sioux; the Sioux did not follow the traders. William Sublette of the Rocky Mountain Fur Company did not lure the Sioux to the Platte. He merely took advantage of their obvious advance toward it. He was the first to realize that by the 1830s Brulé and Oglala hunting grounds lay closer to the Platte than to the Missouri, and he took advantage of the situation to get their trade. The arrival of the Sioux on the Platte was not sudden; it had been preceded by the usual period of horse raids. Nor did it break some long accepted balance of power. Their push beyond the Black Hills was merely another phase in the long Sioux advance from the edge of the Great Plains.[31]

What probably lured the Sioux toward the Platte was an ecological phenomenon that did not require the total depletion of game in the area they already held and that was not peculiar to the plains. Borders dividing contending tribes were never firm; between the established hunting territory of each people lay an indeterminate zone, variously described as war grounds or neutral grounds. In this area only war parties dared to venture; it was too dangerous for any band to travel into these regions to hunt. Because little pressure was put on the animal populations of these contested areas by hunters, they provided a refuge for the hard-pressed herds of adjacent tribal hunting grounds. Since buffalo migrations were unpredictable, a sudden loss of game in a large part of one tribe's territory could prompt an invasion of these neutral grounds. Thus, throughout the nineteenth century, there usually lay at the edges of the Sioux-controlled lands, a lucrative area that held an understandable attraction for them. In the contest for these rich disputed areas lay the key not only to many of the Sioux wars, but also to many other aboriginal wars on the continent.[32]

These areas were, of course, never static. They shifted as tribes were able to wrest total control of them from other contending peoples, and so often created, in turn, a new disputed area beyond. Between 1830 and 1860, travelers on the plains described various neutral or war grounds ranging from the Sand Hills north of the Loup River in Nebraska down to the Pawnee Fork of the Arkansas. But for the Sioux four areas stand out: the region below Fort Laramie between the forks of the Platte in dispute during the 1830s; the Medicine Bow-Laramie plains country above Fort Laramie, fought over in the 1840s; the Yellowstone drainage of the Powder, Rosebud, and Big Horn rivers initially held by the Crows but reduced to a neutral ground in the 1840s and 1850s; and portions of the Republican River country contested from the 1840s to the 1870s. Two things stand out in travelers' accounts of these areas: they were disputed by two or more tribes and they were rich in game.[33]

Francis Parkman vividly described and completely misinterpreted an episode in the Sioux conquest of one of these areas, the Medicine Bow Valley, in 1846. He attributed the mustering of the large expedition that went, according to his account, against the Shoshones, and according to others against the Crows, to a desire for revenge for the loss of a son of Whirlwind, an important Sioux chief, during a horse raid on the Shoshones. But in Parkman's account, Whirlwind, who supposedly organized the expedition, decided not to accompany it, and the Oglalas and Saones who went ended up fighting neither the Crows nor the Shoshones. What they did, however, is significant. They moved into disputed Medicine Bow country west of Fort Laramie, land that all of these tribes contested.

The Sioux entered the area warily, took great precautions to avoid, not seek out, Crow and Shoshone war parties, and were much relieved to escape unscathed after a successful hunt. Parkman was disgusted, but the Sioux were immensely pleased with the whole affair. They had achieved the main goal of their warfare, the invasion and safe hunting of disputed buffalo grounds without any cost to themselves. White Shield, the slain man's brother, made another, apparently token, attempt to organize a war party to avenge his loss, but he never departed. The whole episode—from the whites' confusion over what tribe was the target of the expedition, to their misinterpretation of Indian motives, to Parkman's failure to see why the eventual outcome pleased the Sioux—reveals why, in so many accounts, the logic of Indian warfare is lost and wars are reduced to outbursts of random bloodletting. For the Sioux, the disputed area and its buffalo, more than the Shoshones or Crows, were the targets of the expedition; revenge was subordinate to the hunt. Their ability to hunt in safety, without striking a blow, comprised a strategic victory that more than satisfied them. To Parkman, intent on observing savage warriors lusting for blood revenge, all this was unfathomable.[34]

Not all expeditions ended so peacefully, however. Bloodier probes preceded the summer expedition of 1846, and others followed it. When the Sioux arrived in strength on the Platte in the mid-1830s, their raiding parties were already familiar to peoples from the Pawnee south to the Arkansas and the Santa Fe Trail. As early as the 1820s, their allies, the Cheyennes and Arapahos, had unsuccessfully contested hunting grounds with the Skidi Pawnees. But by 1835, these tribes had agreed to make peace.[35]

The arrival of the Oglalas and Brulés at the Laramie River presented both the Pawnees and the Crows with more powerful rivals. The Crows were by now old enemies of the Tetons. Initially as allies of the Mandans and Hidatsas, and later as contestants for the hunting grounds of the plains, they had fought the Sioux for at least fifty years. By the 1840s, however, the once formidable Crows were a much weakened people. As late as the 1830s they had possessed more horses than any other tribe on the upper Missouri and estimates of their armed strength had ranged from 1,000 to 2,500 mounted men, but the years that followed brought them little but disaster. Smallpox and cholera reduced their numbers from 800 to 460 lodges, and rival groups pressed into their remaining hunting grounds. The Blackfeet attacked them from the north while the Saones, Oglalas, and Brulés closed in on the east and south. Threatened and desperate, the Crows sought aid west of the Rockies and increasingly allied themselves with the Shoshones and Flatheads.[36]

The Pawnees, the last powerful horticultural tribe left on the plains, did not have a long tradition of warfare with the Sioux. The four Pawnee tribes—the Republicans, Skidis, Tapages, and Grands—lived in permanent earth-lodge villages on the Platte and Loup rivers, but twice a year they went on extended hunts in an area that stretched from between the forks of the Platte in the north to the Republican, Kansas, and Arkansas rivers in the south. Sioux horse raids had originally worried them very little, but, after the wars with Arapahos and Cheyennes, the growing proximity of the Sioux and their advantage in firearms had begun to concern the Pawnees enough to ask Americans to act as intermediaries in establishing peace. In the 1830s they remained, in the words of their white agent, along with the Sioux, one of the "two master tribes in the Upper Indian Country . . . who govern nearly all the smaller ones."[37]

Under Bull Bear the Oglalas spearheaded the conquest of the Platte River hunting grounds of the Skidi Pawnees. By 1838, the Pawnee agent reported that the Skidis, fearing the Sioux would soon dominate the entire buffalo country, were contesting "every inch of ground," and, he added, "they are right for the day is not far off when the Sioux will possess the whole buffalo region, unless they are checked." In 1838, smallpox struck both the Oglalas and the Pawnees, but, as happened further north, the populous horticultural villages of the Pawnees suffered far more than the nomadic Sioux bands. The next year the intertribal struggle culminated in a pitched battle that cost the Pawnees between eighty and one hundred warriors and led to the de facto surrender of the Platte hunting grounds by the Skidis.[38]

The murder of the Bull Bear in 1841 during a factional quarrel prompted a split in the Oglalas. One band, the Kiyuskas, Bull Bear's old supporters, continued to push into the Pawnee lands along the Platte and Smoky Hill Rivers, while the other faction, the Bad Faces, moved west and north often joining with the Saone bands who were pushing out from the Missouri in attacks on the Crows. During these advances the Utes and Shoshones would be added to the ranks of Teton enemies, and further north the Yanktonais and Hunkpapas pushed into Canada, fighting the Metis, Plains Crees, and Assiniboines.[39]

The Oregon, California, and Utah migrations of the 1840s made the Platte River Valley an American road across the plains. Like the traders on the Missouri before them, these migrants drove away game and created a new avenue for epidemic diseases, culminating in the cholera epidemic of 1849–50. For the first time, the whites presented a significant threat to Sioux interests, and this conflict bore as fruit the first signs of overt Teton hostility since Chouteau's and Pryor's expeditions. But on the whole whites suffered little from the initial Teton reaction to the Oregon trail. The Crows and Pawnees bore the consequences of the decline of the Platte hunting grounds.[40]

The Brulé and Kiyuska Oglalas attacked the Pawnee on the South Platte and the Republican. The Tetons did not restrict their attacks to the buffalo grounds; along with the Yanktons and Yanktonais from the Missouri, they attacked the Pawnees in their villages and disrupted the whole Pawnee economy. While small war parties stole horses and killed women working in the fields, large expeditions with as many as 700 men attacked the villages themselves. This dual assault threatened to reduce the Pawnees to starvation, greatly weakening their ability to resist.[41]

The Sioux struck one of their most devastating blows in 1843, destroying a new village the Pawnees had built on the Loup at the urging of the whites. They killed sixty-seven people and forced the Pawnees back to the Platte, where they were threatened with retribution by whites for their failure to remove as agreed. The Pawnees vainly cited American obligations under the treaty of 1833 to help defend them from attacks by other tribes; and they also repeatedly sought peace. Neither availed. Unlike the Otos, Omahas, and Poncas, who eventually gave up all attempts to hunt on the western plains, the Pawnees persisted in their semiannual expeditions. The tribal census taken in 1859 reveals the price the Pawnees paid. When Zebulon Pike had visited the Pawnees in 1806 he found a roughly equivalent number of men and women in each village. In his partial census, he gave a population of 1,973 men and 2,170 women, exclusive of children. In 1859, agent William Dennison listed 820 men and 1,505 women; largely because of war, women now outnumbered men by nearly two to one.[42]

The final blow came in 1873, three years before the Battle of the Little Bighorn, when the Sioux surprised a Pawnee hunting party on the Republican River, killing about 100 people. The Pawnees, now virtually prisoners in their reservation villages, gave in. They abandoned their Nebraska homeland and, over the protests of their agents, moved to Indian Territory. White settlers may have rejoiced at their removal, but it was the Sioux who had driven the Pawnees from Nebraska.[43]

The experience of the Crows was much the same. Attacked along a front that ran from the Yellowstone to the Laramie Plains, they were never routed, but their power declined steadily. The Sioux drove them from the Laramie Plains and then during the 1850s and 1860s pushed them farther and farther up the Yellowstone. In the mid-1850s, Edwin Denig, a trapper familiar with the plains, predicted their total destruction, and by 1862 they had apparently been driven from the plains and into the mountains. They, too, would join the Americans against the Sioux.[44]

In a very real sense the Americans, because of their destruction of game along the Missouri and Platte, had stimulated this warfare for years, but their first significant intervention in intertribal politics since the Leavenworth expedition came with the celebrated Laramie Peace Conference of 1851. Although scholars have recognized the importance of both intertribal warfare and the decline of the buffalo in prompting this conference, they have, probably because they accepted without question the individualistic interpretation of Indian wars, neglected the Indian political situation at the time of the treaty. They have failed to appreciate the predominance of the Sioux-Cheyenne-Arapaho alliance on the northern and central plains.[45]

By 1851, American Indian officials had recognized that white travel and trade on the Great Plains had reduced the number of buffalo and helped precipitate intertribal wars. They proposed to restore peace by compensating the Indians for the loss of game. Their motives for this were hardly selfless, since intertribal wars endangered American travelers and commerce. Once they had established peace and drawn firm boundaries between the tribes, they could hold a tribe responsible for any depredations committed within its allotted area. Furthermore, by granting compensation for the destruction of game, the government gave itself an entrée into tribal politics: by allowing or withholding payments, they could directly influence the conduct of the Indians.[46]

Although American negotiators certainly did not seek tribal unity in 1851, it is ethnocentric history to contend that the Fort Laramie treaty allowed the Americans to "divide and conquer." Fundamentally divided at the time of the treaty, the plains tribes continued so afterward. The treaty itself was irrelevant; both the boundaries it created and its prohibition of intertribal warfare were ignored from the beginning by the only tribal participants who finally mattered, the Sioux.[47]

Indeed the whole conference can be interpreted as a major triumph for the Tetons. In a sense, the Fort Laramie Treaty marked the height of Sioux political power. Of the 10,000 Indians who attended the conference, the great majority of them were Sioux, Cheyennes, and Arapahos. Sioux threats kept the Pawnees and all but small groups of Crows, Arikaras, Hidatsas, and Assiniboines from coming to Fort Laramie. The Shoshones came, but the Cheyennes attacked their party and part turned back. With the Sioux and their allies so thoroughly dominating the conference, the treaty itself amounted to both a recognition of Sioux power and an attempt to curb it. But when American negotiators tried to restrict the Sioux to an area north of the Platte, Black Hawk, an Oglala, protested that they held the lands to the south by the same right the Americans held their lands, the right of conquest: "These lands once belonged to the Kiowas and the Crows, but we whipped those nations out of them, and in this we did what the white men do when they want the lands of the Indians." The Americans conceded, granting the Sioux hunting rights, which, in Indian eyes, confirmed title. The Sioux gladly accepted American presents and their tacit recognition of Sioux conquests, but, as their actions proved, they never saw the treaty as a prohibition of future gains. After an American war with the Sioux and another attempt to stop intertribal warfare in 1855, Bear's Rib, a Hunkpapa chief, explained to Lieutenant G. K. Warren that the Tetons found it difficult to take the American prohibition of warfare seriously when the Americans themselves left these conferences only to engage in wars with other Indians or with the Mormons.[48]

After the treaty, the lines of conflict on the plains were clearly drawn. The two major powers in the area, the Sioux and the Americans, had both advanced steadily and with relatively little mutual conflict. Following the treaty they became avowed and recognized rivals. Within four years of the treaty, the first American war with the Tetons would break out; and by the mid-1850s, American officers frankly saw further war as inevitable. The Sioux, in turn, recognized the American threat to their interests, and the tribes, in a rare display of concerted action, agreed as a matter of policy to prohibit all land cessions and to close their remaining productive hunting grounds to American intrusions. These attempts consistently led to war with the Americans. After a century of conquest the Sioux had very definite conceptions of the boundaries of their tribal territory. Recent historians and some earlier anthropologists contended that Indians never fought for territory, but if this is so, it is hard to explain the documented outrage of the Saones, Oglalas, and Brulés at the cession of land along the Missouri by the Yanktons in 1858. The Tetons had moved from this land decades before and had been replaced by the Yanktons, but from the Teton point of view the whole western Sioux nation still held title to the territory and the Yanktons had no authority to sell it. Fearing that acceptance of annuities would connote recognition of the sale, the Saone tribes refused them, and the cession provoked a crisis on the western plains and hardened Teton ranks against the Americans.[49]

The warfare between the northern plains tribes and the United States that followed the Fort Laramie Treaty of 1851 was not the armed resistance of a people driven to the wall by American expansion. In reality these wars arose from the clash of two expanding powers—the United States, and the Sioux and their allies. If, from a distance, it appears that the vast preponderance of strength rested with the whites, it should be remembered that the ability of the United States to bring this power to bear was limited. The series of defeats the Sioux inflicted on American troops during these years reveals how real the power of the Tetons was.

Even as they fought the Americans, the Sioux continued to expand their domination of plains hunting grounds, as they had to in order to survive. Logically enough, the tribes the Sioux threatened—the Crows, Pawnees, and Arikaras especially—sided with the Americans, providing them with soldiers and scouts. For white historians to cast these people as mere dupes or traitors is too simplistic. They fought for their tribal interests and loyalties as did the Sioux.

It is ironic that historians, far more than anthropologists, have been guilty of viewing intertribal history as essentially ahistoric and static, of refusing to examine critically the conditions that prompted Indian actions. In too much Indian history, tribes fight only "ancient" enemies, as if each group were doled out an allotted number of adversaries at creation with whom they battled mindlessly through eternity. Historians have been too easily mystified by intertribal warfare, too willing to see it as the result of some ingrained cultural pugnacity. This is not to argue that the plains tribes did not offer individual warriors incentives of wealth and prestige that encouraged warfare, but, as Newcomb pointed out, the real question is why the tribe placed such a premium on encouraging warriors. This is essentially a historical question. Without an understanding of tribal and intertribal histories, and an appreciation that, like all history, they are dynamic, not static, the actions of Indians when they come into conflict with whites can be easily and fatally distorted.[50]

NOTES

1. W. W. Newcomb, Jr., "A Re-examination of the Causes of Plains Warfare," *American Anthropologist*, 52 (July–Sept. 1950), 317–30; Harry Holbert Turney-High, *Primitive Warfare: Its Practice and Concepts* (Columbus, 1971), 104, 134, 147, 169–70; Robert Lowie, *Indians of the Plains* (New York, 1963), 114.

2. Oscar Lewis, *The Effects of White Contact Upon Blackfoot Culture with Special Reference to the Role of the Fur Trade* (New York, 1942), 53–59; Frank Raymond Secoy, *Changing Military Patterns on the Great Plains (17th Century through Early 19th Century)* (New York, 1953); Symmes C. Oliver, *Ecology and Cultural Continuity as Contributing Factors in the Social Organization of the Plains Indians* (Berkeley, 1962), 13, 52, 59.

3. John C. Ewers, "Intertribal Warfare As the Precursor of Indian-White Warfare on the Northern Great Plains," *Western Historical Quarterly*, VI (Oct. 1975), 397–410.

4. Ibid., 409–10.

5. John C. Ewers, *Teton Dakota, Ethnology and History* (Berkeley, 1937), 63–64; Lowie, *Indians of the Plains*, 11. These divisions of the Tetons will be called tribes instead of bands since they were subdivided into smaller units to which the term band is more applicable.

6. Secoy, *Changing Military Patterns on the Great Plains*, 42, 66–67; Lawrence J. Burpee, ed., *Journal and Letters of Pierre Gaultier De Varennes De La Verendrye and His Sons* (Toronto, 1927), 135–39, 210–12, 262, 380; James Howard, "Yanktonai Ethnohistory and the John K. Bear Winter Count," *Plains Anthropologist, Memoirs 11*, 21 (Aug. 1976), 21. For a differing view see George Hyde, *Red Cloud's Folk* (Norman, 1937), 3–8.

7. Secoy, *Changing Military Patterns on the Great Plains*, 75; Mildred Mott Wedel, "LeSueur and the Dakota Sioux," *Aspects of Upper Great Lake Anthropology: Papers in Honor of Lloyd A. Wilford* (St. Paul, 1974), 165–67.

8. Abraham Nasatir, ed., *Before Lewis and Clark: Documents Illustrating the History of the Missouri* (2 vols., St. Louis, 1952), II, 382; George Hyde, *Spotted Tail's Folk: A History of the Brulé Sioux* (Norman, 1961), 14–15; Annie Heloise Abel, ed., *Tabeau's Narrative of Loisel's Expedition to the Upper Missouri* (Norman, 1939), 120–23; Donald Jackson, ed., *Letters of the Lewis and Clark Expedition with Related Documents* (Urbana, 1962), 536; Victor Collot, *A Journey in North America* (Florence, 1924), I, 294; Howard, "Yanktonai Ethnohistory," 6–7. "Trade fair" is a white term; to the Sioux these gatherings took place for religious and social reasons as well as economic.

9. Howard, "Yanktonai Ethnohistory," 25; Garrick Mallery, *Picture-Writing of the American Indians* (Washington, 1893), 298, 304.

10. Abel, *Tabeau's Narrative of Loisel's Expedition*, 84–85. Tabeau says Yanktons, but from the location he is obviously referring to the Yanktonais; Collot, *Journey in North America*, I, 294; Secoy, *Changing Military Patterns on the Great Plains*, 67.

11. Mallery, *Picture-Writing of the American Indians*, 301–308; Burpee, *Journal and Letters of La Verendrye*, 313, 321, 333; "Journal of Jean Baptiste Trudeau [sic]," *Missouri Historical Society Collections*, 4 (1912–13), 28; Abel, *Tabeau's Narrative of Loisel's Expedition*, 123; R. G. Thwaites, ed., *Original Journals of the Lewis and Clark Expedition* (8 vols., New York, 1905), I, 220; Nasatir, *Before Lewis and Clark*, I, 282–89; Secoy, *Changing Military Patterns on the Great Plains*, 72–74.

12. Nasatir, *Before Lewis and Clark*, I, 268–69; ibid., II, 378–79, 382; Preston Holder, *The Hoe and the Horse on the Plains* (Lincoln, 1970). For later attempts of the Sans Arcs (1815–17) and the Yanktonais (1850s) to become sedentary villagers see Mallery, *Picture-Writing of the American Indians*, 316–17; House Exec. Docs., 34 Cong., 1 Sess. (16 vols., Washington, 1856), IX, no. 65, pp. 5–6; Howard, "Yanktonai Ethnohistory," 7–8; Abel, *Tabeau's Narrative of Loisel's Expedition*, 104.

13. Abel, *Tabeau's Narrative of Loisel's Expedition*, 123, 168, 169; Collot, *Journey in North America*, I, 294.

14. Mallery, *Picture-Writing of the American Indians*, 308–33; Garrick Mallery, *Pictographs of the North American Indian: A Preliminary Paper* (Washington, 1886), 103; Abel, *Tabeau's Narrative of Loisel's Expedition*, 123, 168–69; Nasatir, *Before Lewis and Clark*, I, 299; Frank Stewart, "Mandan and Hidatsa Villages in the Eighteenth and Nineteenth Centuries," *Plains Anthropologist*, 19 (Nov. 1974), 287; Elliot Coues, ed., *Manuscript Journals of Alexander Henry and David Thompson* (3 vols., Minneapolis, 1897), I, 345–48; Thwaites, *Original Journals of the Lewis and Clark Expedition*, VI, 88, 106, 107; Jackson, *Letters of the Lewis and Clark Expedition*, 524.

15. Collot, *Journey in North America*, I, 284; Nasatir, *Before Lewis and Clark*, I, 268–69; ibid., II, 378–79; Abraham P. Nasatir, trans. and ed., "Spanish Explorations of the Upper Missouri," *Mississippi Valley Historical Review*, XIV (June 1927), 59. Reuben Gold Thwaites, ed., *Early Western Travels 1748–1846* (32 vols., Cleveland,

1904–1907), Vol. XXIII: *Part II of Maximilian, Prince of Wied's Travels in the Interior of North America 1832–1834*, 230–32; Coues, *Manuscript Journals of Henry and Thompson*, I, 330–33; Thwaites, *Original Journals of the Lewis and Clark Expedition*, I, 220; V, 347–48; VI, 89; Abel, *Tabeau's Narrative of Loisel's Expedition*, 169–71; Stewart, "Mandan and Hidatsa Villages," 292–93. Why this seemingly natural alliance of village peoples failed to hold until the mid-nineteenth century has never been adequately explained.

16. Abel, *Tabeau's Narrative of Loisel's Expedition*, 165, 99–101, 110; Thwaites, *Original Journals of the Lewis and Clark Expedition*, I, 168, VI, 88; Donald Jackson, ed., "Journey to the Mandans, 1809: The Lost Narrative of Dr. Thomas," *Bulletin of the Missouri Historical Society*, 20 (April 1964), 186. That warfare at this period was a serious and costly endeavor provoked by real economic needs does not mean that precontact warfare did not conform to the game model. Other evidence, however, suggests it may not have fit the game model either. See Secoy, *Changing Military Patterns on the Great Plains*, 34; Lewis, *Effects of White Contact Upon Blackfoot Culture*, 49–51.

17. Jackson, *Letters of the Lewis and Clark Expedition*, 166, 228; Thwaites, *Original Journals of the Lewis and Clark Expedition*, VI, 96, 98, 100, 103; Mallery, *Pictographs of the North American Indian*, 130, 132–33. The Yanktons and Yanktonais were above the Little Sioux River, the Oglalas were between Cheyenne River and the Teton River. The Brulés were near the Great Bend and on the White River drainage. The Miniconjous hunted near the Cheyenne River while the other Saones were below the Arikaras.

Some scholars date Sioux expansion onto the Great Plains west of the Missouri much earlier than the nineteenth century, but thus far the evidence simply does not seem adequate to sustain this position. The recently published John K. Bear winter count has a Yanktonai war party near the Big Horn Mountains in 1725, but this seems unlikely for several reasons. The Yanktonais historically moved out onto the Great Plains behind the Tetons, yet the earliest winter count record of the Tetons in the plains beyond the immediate Missouri River region is that of the Oglala party that reached the Black Hills in 1775. Furthermore the Big Horn area was never Yanktonai territory in any sense, making it even more unlikely that they would penetrate it so early. The Yanktonais remained a Missouri River tribe. Lastly, the John K. Bear winter count refers at least once to an event (the Pawnee defeat of the Spanish in 1720, recorded for 1732) that does not even concern the Sioux. The Big Horn entry could be a similar reference to an event they did not participate in. Howard, "Yanktonai Ethnohistory," 29.

18. Thwaites, *Original Journals of the Lewis and Clark Expedition*, VI, 98.

19. Elliot Coues, ed., "Letters of William Clark and Nathaniel Pryor," *Annals of Iowa*, I (Jan. 1895), 615–19; Clarence Carter, *The Territorial Papers of the United States: Vol. 14: The Territory of Louisiana-Missouri, 1806–1814* (Washington, 1949), 222, 345, 348–50; Louise Barry, *The Beginning of the West: Annals of the Kansas Gateway to the American West, 1540–1854* (Topeka, 1972), 61.

20. Senate Exec. Docs., 25 Cong., 3 Sess. (5 vols., Washington, 1839), I, no. 1., 499.

21. Mallery, *Pictographs of the North American Indian*, 108; Mallery, *Picture Writing of the American Indians*, 317. This paper deals largely with external influences on the Sioux, not with the internal political and social changes that took place within the Confederacy during this period. This is an important study in its own right. Dr. M. Martin, Vaccination Report, Nov. 28, 1832, and Martin to Lewis Cass, Nov. 27, 1832, St. Louis Superintendency, Letters Received, Records of the Office of Indian Affairs, RG 75 (National Archives); Thwaites, *Part II of Maximilian*, 359; J. Pilcher to Wm. Clark, Feb. 27, 1838, July 3, 1838, and Sept. 12, 1838, Upper Missouri Superintendency, Letters Received, Records of the Office of Indian Affairs. The winter counts differ. The Sans Arc, Yanktonais, Miniconjou, and Oglala counts in Garrick Mallery do not mention the epidemic. Mallery, *Pictographs of the North American Indian*, 117. The counts in James Howard do, with four saying few died and one saying many died. James Howard, "Dakota Winter Counts as a Source of Plains History," Bureau of American Ethnology *Bulletin* 173 (1960), 374. Edwin Denig notes that the Hunkpapa, one of the tribes included in the divergent account in Howard, did suffer heavily in 1838. Edwin Thompson Denig, *Five Indian Tribes of the Upper Missouri*, John C. Ewers, ed. (Norman, 1961), 28.

22. The following censuses fall into a definite pattern: 15,000–17,000 in the 1820s, 11,000–30,000 in the 1830s, and about 25,000 for the 1840s and 1850s. The variation in the 1830s probably resulted from the exclusion of the Brulés and Oglalas by some writers after these tribes left Missouri for the Platte. Thwaites, *Original Journals of the Lewis and Clark Expedition*, VI, 96–98; Jackson, *Letters of the Lewis and Clark Expedition*, 536; House Exec. Docs., 19 Cong., 1 Sess. (10 vols., Washington, 1826), VI, no. 117, pp. 8–10; Estimate of the Current Expenses for the Upper Missouri Agency, Sept. 1828, St. Louis Superintendency, Letters Received, Records of the Office of Indian Affairs; Remarks, J. L. Bean, 1st quarter, 1831, Upper Missouri Superintendency, Letters

Received, Records of the Office of Indian Affairs; Pilcher to Clark, July 18, 1835, Oct. 1835, and Sept. 1837, ibid.; Denig, *Five Indian Tribes*, 22, 29, D. D. Mitchell to H. Crawford, St. Louis Superintendency, Letters Received, Records of the Office of Indian Affairs; Senate Exec. Docs., 34 Cong., 1 Sess. (20 vols., Washington, 1856), XIII, no. 76, pp. 15–16; Reuben Gold Thwaites, ed., *Early Western Travels 1748–1846* (32 vols., Cleveland, 1904–1907), vol. XXII: *Part I of Maximilian, Prince of Wied's Travels in the Interior of North America, 1832–1834*, 304–05; F. V. Hayden, *Contributions to the Ethnography and Philology of the Indian Tribes of the Missouri Valley* (Philadelphia, 1862), 371; Hyde, *Red Cloud's Folk*, 29–30; Senate Exec. Docs., 22 Cong., 1 Sess. (3 vols., Washington, 1832), II, no. 90, p. 47; Tho. Harvey to Wm. Medill, Feb. 4, 1847, St. Louis Superintendency, Letters Received, Records of the Office of Indian Affairs.

23. Senate Exec. Docs., 22 Cong., 1 Sess., II, No. 90, pp. 52–53, Thwaites, *Part I of Maximilian*, XXII, 380–81; Hiram Martin Chittenden and Alfred Talbot Richardson, eds., *Life, Letters and Travels of Father Pierre-Jean De Smet, S.J., 1801–1873* (4 vols., New York, 1905), II, 635. Also see Lewis, *Effects of White Contact Upon Blackfoot Culture*, 28.

24. Buffalo herds did not, as was once believed, migrate hundreds of miles each spring and fall. The herds migrated within a restricted range. See Frank Gilbert Roe, *The North American Buffalo: A Critical Study of the Species in its Wild State* (Toronto, 1951), 116–18, 505–506; Paul Wilhelm, Duke of Wuerttemberg, "First Journey to North America in the Years 1822 to 1824," *South Dakota Historical Collections*, 19 (1938), 369; Senate Exec. Docs., 22 Cong., 1 Sess., II, no. 1, pp. 52–53; J. Dougherty to Thom. McKenney, Sept. 14, 1827, Upper Missouri Superintendency, Letters Received, Records of the Office of Indian Affairs, Speech of Big Elk, June 24, 1828, ibid.; Dougherty to Clark, July 16, 1835, ibid.; J. Sanford to Clark, Aug. 17, 1833, St. Louis Superintendency, Letters Received, Records of the Office of Indian Affairs, Mitchell to O. Brown, Oct. 13, 1849, ibid.; Denig, *Five Indian Tribes*, 22–29.

25. Wilhelm, "First Journey to North America," 406; F. G. Roe, *The Indian and the Horse* (Norman, 1955), 302; Lewis, *Effects of White Contact Upon Blackfoot Culture*, 54; John C. Ewers, *The Horse in Blackfoot Culture With Comparative Material From Other Western Tribes* (Washington, 1955), 174.

26. Abel, *Tabeau's Narrative of Loisel's Expedition*, 130–35, 151; Reuben Gold Thwaites, ed., *Early Western Travels, 1748–1846* (32 vols., Cleveland, 1904–1907), Vol. V: *Bradbury's Travels in the Interior of North America, 1809–1811*, 103, 173; John C. Luttig, *Journal of a Fur-Trading Expedition on the Upper Missouri, 1812–1813*, Stella M. Drumm, ed. (St. Louis, 1920), 104; Denig, *Five Indian Tribes*, 56–57; Coues, *Manuscript Journals of Henry and Thompson*, I, 336.

27. Abel, *Tabeau's Narrative of Loisel's Expedition*, 130; *Bradbury's Travels*, 103, 108, 113; Reuben Gold Thwaites, ed., *Early Western Travels, 1748–1846* (32 vols., Cleveland, 1904–1907), Vol. VI: *Brackenridge's Journal up the Missouri, 1811*, 98–99; Luttig, *Journal of a Fur-Trading Expedition*, 68–69, 76, 79, 82, 104, 108, 115, 127.

28. Wilhelm, "First Journey to North America," 405; Denig, *Five Indian Tribes*, 56–57; Annie Heloise Abel, *Chardon's Journal at Fort Clark, 1834–39* (Pierre, S.D., 1932), 205, 311–12; Dougherty to Clark, Nov. 12, 1834, Upper Missouri Superintendency, Letters Received, Records of the Office of Indian Affairs; Pilcher to Clark, July 18, 1835, ibid.; Sanford to Clark July 17, 1832, St. Louis Superintendency, Letters Received, Records of the Office of Indian Affairs.

29. Mitchell to Wm. N. Fulkerson, June 10, 1836, and Fulkerson to Clark, Oct. 1, 1835, Oct. 1, 1837, Upper Missouri Superintendency, Letters Received, Records of the Office of Indian Affairs; Abel, *Chardon's Journal*; Senate Exec. Docs., 25 Cong., 2 Sess. (6 vols., Washington, 1838), I, no. 1, p. 557; House Exec. Docs., 37 Cong., 3 Sess. (12 vols., Washington, 1863), I, no. 1, p. 194.

30. House Exec. Docs., 19 Cong., 1 Sess., VI, no. 117, p. 9. The Kiowa resisted as late as 1814–1815. It should be emphasized that the Oglala and Brulé formed the alliance with the Cheyenne; the Yanktonais apparently did not make peace with them until much later. Mallery, *Picture-Writing of the American Indians*, 316, 281; Secoy, *Changing Military Patterns on the Great Plains*, 75. Nor does it appear that the Oglala-Cheyenne alliance was without its disruptions. Mallery, *Pictographs of the North American Indian*, 139. Why these tribes allied with the Sioux at all is not clear.

31. The development of this myth may be followed in Hiram Chittenden, *The American Fur Trade of the Far West* (3 vols., New York, 1902), I, 305; Bernard De Voto, *Across the Wide Missouri* (Boston, 1947), 224; Hyde, *Red Cloud's Folk*, 43–46; Robert A. Trennert, Jr., *Alternative to Extinction: Federal Indian Policy and the Beginnings of the Reservation System, 1846–51* (Philadelphia, 1975), 161. Only Bernard De Voto questioned the evidence, and even he finally accepted it. The main evidence cited is a letter from Lucien Fontenelle to Pierre Chouteau saying

William Sublette had built a fort on the Platte to capture the Sioux trade. But, as Joshua Pilcher pointed out, the Sioux for years had been going as far south as the Arkansas to raid, and winter counts record battles on the Platte in 1832–1833. Pilcher to G. Harris, Jan.23, 1837, Upper Missouri Superintendency, Letters Received, Records of the Office of Indian Affairs; Mallery, *Picture-Writing of the American Indians,* 319. Another letter indicates that the Rocky Mountain Fur Company was trying to win the trade of the Oglalas already present on the Platte. Wm. Laidlaw to Pratte and Chouteau, Oct. 26, 1835, Ayer Ms. 486, Ayer Collection, Newberry Library (Chicago).

32. For insights into this phenomenon and the general formulation of it, see an excellent article by Harold Hickerson, "The Virginia Deer and Intertribal Buffer Zones in the Upper Mississippi Valley," Anthony Leeds and Andrew P. Vayda, eds., *Man, Culture and Animals: The Role of Animals in Human Ecological Adjustments* (Washington, 1965), 43–66.

33. Rufus B. Sage, *Scenes in the Rocky Mountains* (Philadelphia, 1846), 125; Francis Parkman, *The Oregon Trail* (Madison, 1969), 197; *American State Papers, Military Affairs,* 24 Cong., 1 Sess. (7 vols., Washington, 1837), VI, no. 654, p. 138; Senate Exec. Docs., 35 Cong., 1 Sess. (16 vols., Washington, 1858), II, no. 11, p. 461; Senate Exec. Docs., 34 Cong., 1 Sess., XIII, no. 76, p. 9, Chittenden and Richardson, *Life, Letters and Travels of De Smet,* II, 657, 665, Reuben Gold Thwaites, ed., *Early Western Travels, 1748–1846* (32 vols., Cleveland, 1904–1907), Vol. XXIX: *De Smet's Oregon Missions and Travel over the Rocky Mountains, 1845–1846,* 365; House Exec. Docs., 36 Cong., 1 Sess. (12 vols., Washington, 1855–60), II, no. 78, p. 24.

34. Parkman, *Oregon Trail,* 121–22, 135, 137, 140, 197, 206, 214–24; Dale Morgan, ed., *Overland in 1846: Diaries and Letters of the California-Oregon Trail* (2 vols., Georgetown, Cal., 1963), II, 573; I, 214.

35. Thwaites, *Part I of Maximilian,* 304–305; Reuben Gold Thwaites, ed., *Early Western Travels, 1748–1846* (32 vols., Cleveland, 1904–1907), Vol. XIX: *Part I of Gregg's Commerce of the Prairies,* 321; *American State Papers, Military Affairs,* 24 Cong., 1 Sess., VI, no. 654, pp. 143, 133.

36. Hayden, *Contributions to the Ethnology and Philology of the Indian Tribes,* 394; Denig, *Five Indian Tribes,* 142, 144–45, 166, 185–86, 353; Thwaites, *Part I of Maximilian,* 351.

37. Dougherty to Clark, Nov. 29, 1832, Nov. 12, 1834, Upper Missouri Superintendency, Letters Received, Records of the Office of Indian Affairs; Dougherty to C. H. Harris, June 27, 1837, Council Bluffs, Letters Received, ibid. The best account of the Pawnees is Gene Weltfish, *The Lost Universe* (New York, 1965). A badly biased and far less useful history is George E. Hyde, *Pawnee Indians* (Denver, 1951).

38. Senate Exec. Docs., 25 Cong., 3 Sess., I, no. 1, 504; Mallery, *Picture-Writing of the American Indians,* 320–21; "Letters Concerning the Presbyterian Mission in the Pawnee Country Near Bellvue, Neb., 1831–1849," *Collections of the Kansas State Historical Society, 1915–1918,* XIV (1918), 630–31; Hyde, *Red Cloud's Folk,* 46–47.

39. Denig, *Five Indian Tribes,* 22–23, 25, 29; James C. Olson, *Red Cloud and the Sioux Problem* (Lincoln, 1965), 20–21; House Exec. Docs., 34 Cong., 1 Sess., XIII, no. 65, pp. 5–6; J. Hewitt, ed., *Journal of Rudolph Friederich Kurz* (Washington, 1937), 191–92.

40. Trennert, *Alternative to Extinction,* 160–92; Denig, *Five Indian Tribes,* 16–18.

41. "Letters Concerning the Presbyterian Mission," 659, 664, 730; Harvey to L. H. Crawford, July 25, 1845, Harvey to Medill, Oct. 17, 1847, Nov. 22, 1847, and H. Wharton to G. Manypenny, Dec. 1851, Council Bluffs, Letters Received, Records of the Office of Indian Affairs; (John Dunbar, "The Pawnee Indians: Their Habits and Customs," *Magazine of American History,* V (Nov. 1880), 341–42.

42. "Letters Concerning the Presbyterian Mission," 659, 730. Daniel Miller to Mitchell, Dec. 23 and 24, 1843, Harvey to Medill, Oct. 17, 1847, Council Bluffs, Letters Received, Records of the Office of Indian Affairs; "The Expedition of Major Clifton Wharton in 1844," *Collections of the Kansas State Historical Society, 1923–1925,* XVI (1925), 284–85, Donald Jackson, *The Journals of Zebulon Montgomery Pike* (2 vols, Norman, 1966) II, 41; Wm. Dennison to A. M. Robinson, July 16, 1859, Otoe Agency, Letters Received, Records of the Office of Indian Affairs; Wm. Albin to W. Dole, Oct. 1, 1864, Pawnee Agency, Letters Received, Records of the Office of Indian Affairs.

43. John W. Williams to Wm. Burgess, Aug. 12, 1873, Letter of Pawnee Chiefs to E. P. Smith, Aug. 21, 1874, Speeches in Council with Quakers, N. D. [circa Aug. 1874], and Petition of Pawnee Chief and Head Men, Oct. 8, 1874, Pawnee Agency, Letters Received, Records of the Office of Indian Affairs. For warfare in alliance with white Americans, see George Bird Grinnell, *Two Great Scouts and their Pawnee Battalion* (Cleveland, 1928).

44. Denig, *Five Indian Tribes,* 19, 204; House Exec. Docs., 34 Cong., I Sess. (16 vols., Washington, 1856), IX, no. 65, pp. 10, 14; Stanley Vestal, *New Sources of Indian History, 1850–1891* (Norman, 1934), 167–72; House Exec. Docs. 37 Cong., 3 Sess., I, no. 1, p. 193.

45. American expeditions on the Great Plains from Lewis and Clark to Colonel Dodge made attempts at establishing intertribal peace, but none of these efforts was on the same scale as the Laramie Conference. For the two most thorough treatments of policy during this period, see Trennert, *Alternative to Extinction,* 178–97; James C. Malin, *Indian Policy and Westward Expansion* (Lawrence, Kansas, 1921), 72–75.

46. Mitchell to Brown, Oct. 13, 1849, and Mitchell to Brown, March 9, 1851, St. Louis Superintendency, Letters Received, Records of the Office of Indian Affairs; Senate Exec. Docs., 31 Cong., 1 Sess. (2 vols., Washington, 1850), 1, no. 70.

47. Trennert, *Alternative to Extinction,* 191, 188–92.

48. Percival G. Lowe, *Five Years a Dragoon and Other Adventures on the Great Plains* (Kansas City, 1906), 78–81; Chittenden and Richardson, *Life, Letters and Travels of De Smet,* II, 679–80, 687; Capt. H. M. Wharton to Capt. M. Sevill, June 6, 1852, Council Bluffs, Letters Received, Records of the Office of Indian Affairs; Trennert, *Alternative to Extinction,* 188–90; Senate Exec. Docs., 35 Cong., 2 Sess. (18 vols., Washington, 1859), II, no. 1, 630–31; St. Louis *Missouri Republican,* Oct. 29. 1851, and Nov. 9. 1851.

49. Letter of G. K. Warren to George Jones, "Relative to his explorations of Nebraska, Jan. 21, 1858," printed copy, Graff Collection, Newberry Library (Chicago); House Exec. Docs., 34 Cong., 1 Sess., XIII, no. 65, pp. 4–5, 10–11; Denig, *Five Indian Tribes,* 30, 32–33; W. H. Wessels to Adj. Gen., July 7, 1858, Central Superintendency, Letters Sent, Records of the Office of Indians Affairs; Trennert, *Alternative to Extinction,* 13–15; Wilcomb E. Washburn, *The Indian in America* (New York, 1975), 64–65; Lowie, *Indians of the Plains,* 114; Senate Exec. Docs., 35 Cong., 2 Sess., 11, no. 1, 630–33, 668–70.

50. Out of what must only be habit Wilcomb E. Washburn described the Sioux as confronting their "Ancient enemies," the Snakes (Shoshones), at Ft. Laramie in 1851 at a time when the Sioux advance had only recently prompted warfare between these previously widely separated peoples. Washburn, *Indian in America,* 192; Newcomb, "A Re-examination of the Causes of Plains Warfare."

Further Reading

Anderson, Karen. *Chain Her By One Foot: The Subjugation of Women in Seventeenth-Century New France.* New York: Routledge, 1991.

Anderson, Virginia DeJohn. "King Philip's Herds: The Problem of Livestock in Early New England." *William and Mary Quarterly,* 3d Ser. 51 (1994): 601–624.

Axtell, James. *After Columbus: Essays in the Ethnohistory of Colonial North America.* New York: Oxford University Press, 1988.

_____. *Beyond 1492: Encounters in Colonial North America.* New York: Oxford University Press, 1992.

_____. *The European and the Indian: Essays in the Ethnohistory of Colonial North America.* New York: Oxford University Press, 1981.

_____. *The Indians' New South: Cultural Change in the Colonial Southeast.* Baton Rouge: Louisiana State University Press, 1997.

_____. *The Invasion Within: The Contest of Cultures in Colonial North America.* New York: Oxford University Press, 1985.

Baker, Emerson W. "'A Scratch with a Bear's Paw': Anglo-Indian Land Deeds in Early Maine." *Ethnohistory* 36 (1989): 235–56.

Black-Rogers, Mary. "Varieties of 'Starving': Semantics and Survival in the Subarctic Fur Trade, 1750–1850." *Ethnohistory* 33 (1986): 353–83.

Bragdon, Kathleen J. *Native People of Southern New England, 1500–1650.* Norman, Okla.: University of Oklahoma Press, 1996.

Braund, Kathryn E. Holland. *Deerskins and Duffels: The Creek Indian Trade with Anglo-America, 1685–1815.* Lincoln, Neb.: University of Nebraska Press, 1993.

Bushnell, Amy. *Situado and Sabana: Spain's Support System for the Presidio and Mission Provinces of Florida.* Athens, Ga.: University of Georgia Press, 1994.

Calloway, Colin G. *The American Revolution in Indian Country: Crisis and Diversity in North American Indian Communities.* New York: Cambridge University Press, 1995.

_____. *Crown and Calumet: British-Indian Relations, 1783–1815.* Norman, Okla.: University of Oklahoma Press, 1987.

_____, ed. *After King Philip's War: Presence and Persistence in Indian New England.* Hanover, N. H.: University Press of New England, 1997.

_____. *New Worlds for All: Indians, Europeans, and the Remaking of Early America.* Baltimore: The Johns Hopkins University Press, 1997.

_____. *The Western Abenakis of Vermont, 1600–1800: War, Migration, and the Survival of an Indian People.* Norman, Okla.: University of Oklahoma Press, 1990.

Carson, James Taylor. "Horses and the Economy and Culture of the Choctaw Indians, 1690–1840." *Ethnohistory* 42 (1995): 495–513.

Cave, Alfred A. "The Failure of the Shawnee Prophet's Witch-Hunt." *Ethnohistory* 42 (1995): 445–75.

Cayton, Andrew R. L., and Fredrika J. Teute, eds. *Contact Points: American Frontiers from the Mohawk Valley to the Mississippi, 1750–1830.* Chapel Hill, N.C.: University of North Carolina Press, 1998.

Ceci, Lynn. "Watchers of the Pleiades: Ethnoastronomy Among Native Cultivators in Northeastern North America." *Ethnohistory* 25 (1978): 301–317.

Cronon, William. *Changes in the Land: Indians, Colonists, and the Ecology of New England.* New York: Hill and Wang, 1983.

Crosby, Alfred W. *The Columbian Exchange: Biological and Cultural Consequences of 1492.* Westport, Conn.: Greenwood Publishing Company, 1972.

_____. *Ecological Imperialism: The Biological Expansion of Europe, 900–1900.* New York: Cambridge University Press, 1986.

Delâge, Denys. *Bitter Feast: Amerindians and Europeans in Northeastern North America, 1600–1664.* Trans. by Jane Brierley. Vancouver: University of British Columbia Press, 1993.

Demos, John. *The Unredeemed Captive: A Family Story from Early America.* New York: Alfred A. Knopf, 1994.

Dennis, Matthew. *Cultivating a Landscape of Peace: Iroquois-European Encounters in Seventeenth-Century America.* Ithaca: Cornell University Press, 1993.

Devens, Carol. *Countering Colonization: Native American Women and Great Lakes Missions, 1630–1900.* Berkeley: University of California Press, 1992.

Dickason, Olive Patricia. *The Myth of the Savage: And the Beginnings of French Colonialism in the Americas.* Edmonton, Alberta, Canada: University of Alberta Press, 1984.

Dowd, Gregory Evans. "The Panic of 1751: The Significance of Rumors on the South Carolina-Cherokee Frontier." *William and Mary Quarterly*, 3d Ser. 53 (1996): 527–60.

_____. *A Spirited Resistance: The North American Indian Struggle for Unity, 1745–1815.* Baltimore: The Johns Hopkins University Press, 1992.

Dunaway, Wilma A. "Rethinking Cherokee Acculturation: Women's Resistance to Agrarian Capitalism and Cultural Change, 1800–1838." *American Indian Culture and Research Journal* 21 (1997): 155–92.

Fenton, William N. *The Great Law and the Longhouse: A Political History of the Iroquois Confederacy.* Norman, Okla.: University of Oklahoma Press, 1998.

Flores, Dan. "Bison Ecology and Bison Diplomacy: The Southern Plains from 1800 to 1850." *Journal of American History* 78 (1991): 465–85.

Fogelson, Raymond D. "Who Were the Ani-Kutani: An Excursion into Cherokee Historical Thought." *Ethnohistory* 31 (1984): 255–63.

Frazier, Patrick. *The Mohicans of Stockbridge.* Lincoln: University of Nebraska Press, 1992.

Galloway, Patricia. *Choctaw Genesis, 1500–1700.* Lincoln: University of Nebraska Press, 1995.

Ghere, David. "Mistranslations and Misinformation: Diplomacy on the Maine Frontier, 1725 to 1775." *American Indian Culture and Research Journal* 8 (1984): 3–26.

Gilman, Carolyn. *Where Two Worlds Meet: The Great Lakes Fur Trade.* St. Paul, Minn.: Minnesota Historical Society, 1982.

Gleach, Frederic W. *Powhatan's World and Colonial Virginia: A Conflict of Cultures.* Lincoln, Neb.: University of Nebraska Press, 1997.

Grumet, Robert S., ed. *Northeastern Indian Lives, 1632–1816.* Amherst, Mass.: University of Massachusetts Press, 1996.

Gutiérrez, Ramón A. *When Jesus Came, The Corn Mothers Went Away: Marriage, Sexuality, and Power in New Mexico, 1500–1846.* Stanford, Calif.: Stanford University Press, 1991.

Hall, Thomas D. *Social Change in the Southwest, 1350–1800.* Lawrence, Kan.: University Press of Kansas, 1989.

Harris, Cole. "Voices of Disaster: Smallpox around the Strait of Georgia in 1782." *Ethnohistory* 41 (1994): 591–626.

Hatley, M. Thomas. *The Dividing Paths: Cherokees and South Carolinians Through the Era of Revolution.* New York: Oxford University Press, 1993.

Hill, Sarah H. *Weaving New Worlds: Southeastern Cherokee Women and Their Basketry.* Chapel Hill, N.C.: University of North Carolina Press, 1997.

Hinderaker, Eric. *Elusive Empires: Constructing Colonialism in the Ohio Valley, 1673–1800.* New York: Cambridge University Press, 1997.

_____. "The 'Four Indian Kings' and the Imaginative Construction of the First British Empire." *William and Mary Quarterly,* 3d Ser. 53 (1996): 487–526.

Hirsch, Adam J. "The Collision of Military Cultures in Seventeenth Century New England." *Journal of American History* 74 (1988): 1187–1212.

Hudson, Charles. *Knights of Spain, Warriors of the Sun: Hernando de Soto and the South's Ancient Chiefdoms.* Athens, Ga.: University of Georgia Press, 1997.

Jaenen, Cornelius J. *Friend and Foe: Aspects of French-Amerindian Cultural Contact in the Sixteenth and Seventeenth Centuries.* New York: Columbia University Press, 1976.

Jennings, Francis. *The Ambiguous Iroquois Empire: The Covenant Chain Confederation of Iroquois and Allied Tribes with English Colonies from Its Beginnings to the Lancaster Treaty of 1744.* New York: W. W. Norton, 1984.

_____. *Empire of Fortune: Crowns, Colonies, and Tribes in the Seven Years War in America.* New York: W. W. Norton, 1988.

_____. *The Invasion of America: Indians, Colonialism, and the Cant of Conquest.* Chapel Hill, N.C.: University of North Carolina Press, 1975.

Karr, Ronald Dale. "'Why Should You Be So Furious': The Violence of the Pequot War." *Journal of American History* 85 (1998): 876–909.

Krech, Shepard III, ed. *Indians, Animals, and the Fur Trade: A Critique of* Keepers of the Game. Athens, Ga.: University of Georgia Press, 1981.

Kupperman, Karen Ordahl. *Settling with the Indians: The Meeting of English and Indian Cultures in America, 1580–1640.* Totowa, N.J.: Rowman and Littlefield, 1980.

Lepore, Jill. "Dead Men Tell No Tales: John Sassamon and the Fatal Consequences of Literacy." *American Quarterly* 46 (1994): 479–512.

_____. *The Name of War: King Philip's War and the Origins of American Identity.* New York: Alfred A. Knopf, 1998.

Malone, Patrick M. *The Skulking Way of War: Technology and Tactics Among the New England Indians.* Lanham, Md.: Madison Books, 1991.

Mancall, Peter C. *Deadly Medicine: Indians and Alcohol in Early America.* Ithaca, N.Y.: Cornell University Press, 1995.

_____. "Men, Women, and Alcohol in Indian Villages in the Great Lakes Region in the Early Republic." *Journal of the Early Republic* 15 (1995): 425–48.

_____. *Valley of Opportunity: Economic Culture Along the Upper Susquehanna, 1700–1800.* Ithaca: Cornell University Press, 1991.

Mandell, Daniel. Behind the Frontier: Indians in Eighteenth-Century Eastern Massachusetts. Lincoln, Neb.: University of Nebraska Press, 1996.

Martin, Calvin. "The Four Lives of a Micmac Copper Pot." *Ethnohistory* 22 (1975): 111–33.

_____. *Keepers of the Game: Indian-Animal Relationships and the Fur Trade.* Berkeley, Cal.: University of California Press, 1978.

_____, ed. *The American Indian and the Problem of History.* New York: Oxford University Press, 1987.

Martin, Joel W. *Sacred Revolt: The Muskogees' Struggle for a New World.* Boston: Beacon Press, 1991.

McConnell, Michael N. *A Country Between: The Upper Ohio Valley and Its Peoples, 1724–1774.* Lincoln, Neb.: University of Nebraska Press, 1992.

McLoughlin, William G. *Cherokees and Missionaries, 1789–1839.* New Haven: Yale University Press, 1984.

_____. *Cherokee Renascence in the New Republic.* Princeton: Princeton University Press, 1986.

Merchant, Carolyn. *Ecological Revolutions: Nature, Gender, and Science in New England.* Chapel Hill, N.C.: University of North Carolina Press, 1989.

Merrell, James H. "'The Customes of Our Countrey': Indians and Colonists in Early America." In Bernard Bailyn and Philip D. Morgan, eds. *Strangers within the Realm: Cultural Margins of the First British Empire.* Chapel Hill, N.C.: University of North Carolina Press, 1991.

_____. "Declarations of Independence: Indian-White Relations in the New Nation." In Jack P. Greene, ed. *The American Revolution: Its Character and Limits.* New York: New York University Press, 1987.

_____. *The Indians' New World: Catawbas and their Neighbors from European Contact Through the Era of Removal.* Chapel Hill, N.C.: University of North Carolina Press, 1989.

_____. *Into the American Woods: Negotiators on the Pennsylvania Frontier.* New York: W. W. Norton, 1999.

Merritt, Jane T. "Dreaming of the Savior's Blood: Moravians and the Indian Great Awakening in Pennsylvania." *William and Mary Quarterly,* 3d Ser. 54 (1997): 723–46.

Miller, Jay. "The 1806 Purge Among the Indiana Delaware: Sorcery, Gender, Boundaries, and Legitimacy." *Ethnohistory* 41 (1994): 245–66.

Naeher, Robert James. "Dialogue in the Wilderness: John Eliot and the Indian Exploration of Puritanism as a Source of Meaning, Comfort, and Ethnic Survival." *New England Quarterly* 62 (1989): 346–68.

O'Brien, Jean M. *Dispossession by Degrees: Indian Land and Identity in Natick, Massachusetts, 1650–1790.* New York: Cambridge University Press, 1997.

Perdue, Theda. *Cherokee Women: Gender and Culture Change, 1700–1835.* Lincoln, Neb.: University of Nebraska Press, 1998.

_____. *Slavery and the Evolution of Cherokee Society, 1540–1866.* Knoxville: University of Tennessee Press, 1979.

Peterson, Jacqueline. "Ethnogenesis: The Settlement and Growth of a 'New People' in the Great Lakes Region, 1702–1815." *American Indian Culture and Research Journal* 6 (1982): 23–64.

Quitt, Martin H. "Trade and Acculturation at Jamestown, 1607–1609: The Limits of Understanding." *William and Mary Quarterly,* 3d Ser. 52 (1995): 227–58.

Ramenovsky, Ann. *Vectors of Death: The Archaeology of European Contact.* Albuquerque: University of New Mexico Press, 1987.

Richter, Daniel K. *Ordeal of the Longhouse: The Peoples of the Iroquois League in the Era of European Colonization.* Chapel Hill, N.C.: University of North Carolina Press, 1992.

_____, and James H. Merrell, eds. *Beyond the Covenant Chain: The Iroquois and Their Neighbors in Indian North America, 1600–1800.* Syracuse, N.Y.: Syracuse University Press, 1987.

Ronda, James P. "The Sillery Experiment: A Jesuit-Indian Village in New France, 1637–1663." *American Indian Culture and Research Journal* 3 (1979): 1–18.

_____. "'We are Well as We Are': An Indian Critique of Seventeenth-Century Christian Missions." *William and Mary Quarterly,* 3d Ser. 34 (1977): 66–82.

Rountree, Helen C. *Pocahontas's People: The Powhatan Indians of Virginia Through Four Centuries.* Norman, Okla.: University of Oklahoma Press, 1990.

_____. *The Powhatan Indians of Virginia: Their Traditional Culture.* Norman, Okla.: University of Oklahoma Press, 1989.

Salisbury, Neal. *Manitou and Providence: Indians, Europeans, and the Making of New England, 1500–1643.* New York: Oxford University Press, 1982.

Sayre, Gordon M. *Les Sauvages Americains: Representations of Native Americans in French and English Colonial Literature.* Chapel Hill, N.C.: University of North Carolina Press, 1997.

Shaffer, Lynda Norene. *Native Americans Before 1492: The Moundbuilding Centers of the Eastern Woodlands.* Armonk, N.Y.: M. E. Sharpe, 1992.

Shoemaker, Nancy. "How Indians Got to Be Red." *American Historical Review* 102 (1997): 625–44.

_____, ed. *Negotiators of Change: Historical Perspectives on Native American Women.* New York: Routledge, 1995.

Silver, Timothy. *A New Face on the Countryside: Indians, Colonists, and Slaves in the South Atlantic Forests, 1500–1800.* New York: Cambridge University Press, 1990.

Starna, William A. "The Biological Encounter: Disease and the Ideological Domain." *American Indian Quarterly* 16 (1992): 511–19.

Steele, Ian K. *Warpaths: Invasions of North America.* New York: Oxford University Press, 1994.

Szasz, Margaret Connell, ed. *Between Indian and White Worlds: The Cultural Broker.* Norman, Okla.: University of Oklahoma Press, 1994.

_____. *Indian Education in the American Colonies, 1607–1783.* Albuquerque: University of New Mexico Press, 1988.

Thornton, Russell. *American Indian Holocaust and Survival: A Population History Since 1492.* Norman, Okla.: University of Oklahoma Press, 1987.

_____. *Cherokees: A Population History.* Lincoln, Neb.: University of Nebraska Press, 1990.

Trigger, Bruce G. *The Children of Aataentsic: A History of the Huron People to 1660.* Montreal: McGill-Queen's University Press, 1976.

Turgeon, Laurier, "French Fishers, Fur Traders, and Amerindians During the Sixteenth Century: History and Archaeology." *William and Mary Quarterly,* 3d Ser. 55 (1998): 585–610.

Usner, Daniel H., Jr. *Indians, Settlers, and Slaves in a Frontier Exchange Economy: The Lower Mississippi Valley before 1783.* Chapel Hill, N.C.: University of North Carolina Press, 1992.

Van Lonkhuyzen, Harold W. "A Reappraisal of the Praying Indians: Acculturation, Conversion, and Identity at Natick, Massachusetts, 1646–1730." *New England Quarterly* 63 (1990): 396–428.

Vaughan, Alden T. *New England Frontier: Puritans and Indians, 1620–1675.* 3d ed. Norman, Okla.: University of Oklahoma Press, 1995.

Verano, John W., and Douglas H. Ubelaker, eds. *Disease and Demography in the Americas.* Washington, D.C.: Smithsonian Institution Press, 1992.

Wallace, Anthony F. C. *The Death and Rebirth of the Seneca.* New York: Alfred A. Knopf, 1969.

_____. *The Long, Bitter Trail: Andrew Jackson and the Indians.* New York: Hill and Wang, 1993.

Weber, David J. *The Spanish Frontier in North America.* New Haven: Yale University Press, 1992.

White, Bruce. "Encounters with Spirits: Ojibwa and Dakota Theories About the French and their Merchandise." *Ethnohistory* 41 (1994): 369–405.

White, Richard. *The Middle Ground: Indians, Empires, and Republics in the Great Lakes Region, 1650–1815.* New York: Cambridge University Press, 1991.

_____. *The Roots of Dependency: Subsistence, Environment, and Social Change Among the Choctaws, Pawnees, and Navajos.* Lincoln, Neb.: University of Nebraska Press, 1983.

Wogan, Peter. "Perceptions of European Literacy in Early Contact Situations." *Ethnohistory* 41 (1994): 407–429.

Wood, Peter H., Gregory A. Waselkov, and M. Thomas Hatley, eds. *Powhatan's Mantle: Indians in the Colonial Southeast.* Lincoln, Neb.: University of Nebraska Press, 1989.

Wright, J. Leitch, Jr. *The Only Land They Knew: American Indians in the Old South.* Lincoln, Neb.: University of Nebraska Press, 1999 [orig. pub. 1981].

Young, Mary. "The Cherokee Nation: Mirror of the Republic." *American Quarterly* 33 (1981): 502–24.

Notes on Contributors

James Axtell is professor of history at the College of William and Mary. His books include *The Invasion Within: The Contest of Cultures in Colonial North America; Beyond 1492: Encounters in Colonial North America,* and *The Indians' New South: Cultural Change in the Colonial Southeast.*

Amy Turner Bushnell, associate professor of history at the College of Charleston, is the author of *Warrior Nations: Liberty, Death, and Manhood in Indian America.*

Alfred W. Crosby is professor of history at the University of Texas, Austin. His books include *Ecological Imperialism: The Biological Expansion of Europe, 900–1900; The Measure of Reality: Quantification and Western Society, 1250–1600,* and *The Columbian Exchange: Biological and Cultural Consequences of 1492.*

Natalie Zemon Davis is professor emerita of history at Princeton University and the University of Toronto. She is the author of *The Return of Martin Guerre* and *Women on the Margins: Three Seventeenth-Century Lives,* among many other works.

Gregory Evans Dowd, associate professor of history at Notre Dame University, is the author of *A Spirited Resistance: The North American Indian Struggle for Unity, 1745–1815.*

Steven W. Hackel is an assistant professor of history at Oregon State University. He is completing a book on Indian-Spanish relations in colonial California, 1769–1835.

George R. Hamell, senior exhibits planner at the New York State Museum in Albany, New York, has written extensively on Iroquois history and culture.

M. Thomas Hatley is executive director of the Catskill Center in Arkville, New York, and the author of *The Dividing Paths: Cherokees and South Carolinians through the Era of Revolution.*

Raymond Hauser teaches history at Waubonsee Community College in Sugar Grove, Illinois.

Ruth Wallis Herndon teaches history at the University of Toledo and has recently completed a book manuscript, *Unwelcome Americans: Voices of the Transient Poor in Eighteenth-Century Rhode Island.*

Cornelius J. Jaenen teaches history at the University of Ottawa and is the author of *Friend and Foe: Aspects of French-Amerindian Cultural Contact in the 16th and 17th Centuries.*

Rebecca Kugel, assistant professor of history at the University of California at Riverside, is the author of *To Be the Main Leaders of Our People: A History of Minnesota Ojibwe Politics, 1825–1898.*

Peter C. Mancall (editor) is professor of history at the University of Kansas and author of *Deadly Medicine: Indians and Alcohol in Early America* and *Valley of Opportunity: Economic Culture along the Upper Susquehanna, 1700–1800.*

William G. McLoughlin taught history at Brown University. His many books include *Cherokee Renascence in the New Republic; Cherokees and Missionaries, 1789–1839;* and *After the Trail of Tears: The Cherokees' Struggle for Sovereignty, 1839–1880.*

James H. Merrell (editor) is professor of history at Vassar College and the author of *The Indians' New World: Catawbas and their Neighbors from European Contact through the Era of Removal* and *Into the American Woods: Negotiators on the Pennsylvania Frontier.*

Christopher L. Miller teaches history at Pan-American University, and is the author of *Prophetic Worlds: Indians and Whites on the Columbia Plateau.*

Theda Perdue is professor of history at the University of North Carolina. Her publications include *Slavery and the Evolution of Cherokee Society, 1540–1865* and *Cherokee Women: Gender and Culture Change, 1700–1835.*

Daniel K. Richter is professor of history at the University of Pennsylvania and the author of *The Ordeal of the Longhouse: The Peoples of the Iroquois League in the Era of European Colonization.*

James P. Ronda teaches history at the University of Tulsa. His many books include *Lewis and Clark Among the Indians* and *Astoria and Empire.*

Neal Salisbury, professor of history at Smith College, is the author of *Manitou and Providence: Indians, Europeans, and the Making of New England, 1500–1643.*

James A Sandos is professor of history at University of Redlands and author of *The Hunt for Willie Boy: Indian-hating and Popular Culture.*

Ella Wilcox Sekatau is a member of the Narragansett Indian tribe and a recognized ethnohistorian, tribal genealogist, medicine woman, and teacher. She has been a consultant to many publications and is currently working with the Narragansett Indian Tribal Historical Preservation Office.

Timothy J. Shannon is assistant professor of history at Gettysburg College and the author of *Indians and Colonists at the Crossroads of Empire: The Albany Congress of 1754.*

Helen Hornbeck Tanner is on the staff of The Newberry Library in Chicago and is the editor of the *Atlas of Great Lakes Indian History.*

Daniel H. Usner, Jr. is a professor of history at Cornell University and the author of *Indians, Settlers, and Slaves in a Frontier Exchange Economy: The Lower Mississippi Valley before 1783.*

Daniel Vickers teaches history at the University of California at San Diego and is the author of *Farmers and Fishermen: Two Centuries of Work in Essex County, Massachusetts, 1630–1850.*

Richard White is professor of history at Stanford University and the author of *The Middle Ground: Indians, Empires, and Republics in the Great Lakes Region, 1650–1815,* and *"It's Your Misfortune and None of My Own": A History of the American West,* among other works.

Permissions Acknowledgments

James Axtell, "The White Indians of Colonial America," *William and Mary Quarterly*, 3d Ser. 32 (1975): 55–88. Reprinted from *William and Mary Quarterly* by permission of the Omohundro Institute of Early American History and Culture.

Amy Turner Bushnell, "Ruling 'the Republic of Indians' in Seventeenth-Century Florida." Reprinted from Peter H. Wood, Gregory A. Waselkov, and M. Thomas Hatley, eds., *Powhatan's Mantle: Indians in the Colonial Southeast* by permission of the University of Nebraska Press. Copyright © 1989 by the University of Nebraska Press.

Alfred W. Crosby, "Ecological Imperialism: The Overseas Migration of Western Europeans as a Biological Phenomenon." Reprinted from Alfred W. Crosby, *Germs, Seeds, and Animals: Studies in Ecological History*, M.E. Sharpe, 1994, by permission of the author.

Natalie Zemon Davis, "Iroquois Women, European Women." Reprinted from Margo Hendricks and Patricia Parker, eds., *Women, "Race," and Writing in the Early Modern Period*, Routledge, 1994, by permission of the author. Copyright © 1994 by Natalie Zemon Davis.

Gregory Evans Dowd, "Thinking and Believing: Nativism and Unity in the Ages of Pontiac and Tecumseh," *American Indian Quarterly* XVI (1992): 309–35. Reprinted from *American Indian Quarterly* by permission of the University of Nebraska Press. Copyright © 1992 by the University of Nebraska Press.

Steven W. Hackel, "The Staff of Leadership: Indian Authority in the Missions of Alta California," *William and Mary Quarterly*, 3d Ser. 54 (1997): 347–76. Reprinted from *William and Mary Quarterly* by permission of the Omohundro Institute of Early American History and Culture.

M. Thomas Hatley, "The Three Lives of Keowee: Loss and Recovery in Eighteenth-Century Cherokee Villages." Reprinted from Peter H. Wood, Gregory A. Waselkov, and M. Thomas Hatley, eds., *Powhatan's Mantle: Indians in the Colonial Southeast* by permission of the University of Nebraska Press. Copyright © 1989 by the University of Nebraska Press.

Raymond Hauser, "The *Berdache* and the Illinois Indian Tribe during the Last Half of the Seventeenth Century," *Ethnohistory* 37:1 (Winter 1990): 45–65. Copyright © 1994 by American Society for Ethnohistory. Reprinted by permission of Duke University Press.

Ruth Wallis Herndon and Ella Wilcox Sekatau, "The Right to a Name: The Narragansett People and Rhode Island Officials in the Revolutionary Era," *Ethnohistory* 44:4 (Fall 1997): 433–62. Copyright © 1997 by American Society for Ethnohistory. Reprinted by permission of Duke University Press.

Cornelius Jaenen, "Amerindian Views of French Culture in the Seventeenth Century," *Canadian Historical Review* 55 (1974): 261–91. Reprinted from *Canadian Historical Review* by permission of the University of Toronto Press, Incorporated.

Index